Lecture Notes in Computer Science 3824

Commenced Publication in 1973
Founding and Former Series Editors:
Gerhard Goos, Juris Hartmanis, and Jan van Leeuwen

AF819836

Laurence T. Yang   Makoto Amamiya
Zhen Liu   Minyi Guo
Franz J. Rammig (Eds.)

Embedded and Ubiquitous Computing – EUC 2005

International Conference EUC 2005
Nagasaki, Japan, December 6-9, 2005
Proceedings

Springer

Volume Editors

Laurence T. Yang
St. Francis Xavier University, Department of Computer Science
Antigonish, NS, B2G 2W5, Canada
E-mail: lyang@stfx.ca

Makoto Amamiya
Kyushu University, Faculty of Information Science and Electrical Engineering
Department of Intelligent Systems
6-1 Kasuga-Koen, Kasuga, Fukuoka 816-8580, Japan
E-mail: amamiya@al.is.kyushu-u.ac.jp

Zhen Liu
Nagasaki Instiute of Applied Science, Graduate School of Engineering
536 aba-machi, Nagasaki 851-0193, Japan
E-mail: liuzhen@cc.nias.ac.jp

Minyi Guo
University of Aizu, Department of Computer Software
Aizu-Wakamatsu City, Fukushima 965-8580, Japan
E-mail: minyi@u-aizu.ac.jp

Franz J. Rammig
University of Paderborn, Heinz Nixdorf Institute
33102 Paderborn, Germany
E-mail: franz@uni-paderborn.de

Library of Congress Control Number: 2005936806

CR Subject Classification (1998): C.2, C.3, D.4, D.2, H.4, H.3, H.5, K.4

ISSN 0302-9743
ISBN-10 3-540-30807-5 Springer Berlin Heidelberg New York
ISBN-13 978-3-540-30807-2 Springer Berlin Heidelberg New York

Springer is a part of Springer Science+Business Media

springeronline.com

Printed in Germany

Typesetting: Camera-ready by author, data conversion by Scientific Publishing Services, Chennai, India
Printed on acid-free paper SPIN: 11596356 06/3142 5 4 3 2 1 0

Preface

Welcome to the proceedings of the 2005 IFIP International Conference on Embedded and Ubiquitous Computing (EUC 2005), which was held in Nagasaki, Japan, December 6–9, 2005.

Embedded and ubiquitous computing is emerging rapidly as an exciting new paradigm to provide computing and communication services all the time, everywhere. Its systems are now pervading every aspect of life to the point that they are hidden inside various appliances or can be worn unobtrusively as part of clothing and jewelry. This emergence is a natural outcome of research and technological advances in embedded systems, pervasive computing and communications, wireless networks, mobile computing, distributed computing and agent technologies, etc. Its tremendous impact on academics, industry, government, and daily life can be compared to that of electric motors over the past century, in fact it but promises to revolutionize life much more profoundly than elevators, electric motors or even personal computers.

The EUC 2005 conference provided a forum for engineers and scientists in academia, industry, and government to address profound issues including technical challenges, safety, and social, legal, political, and economic issues, and to present and discuss their ideas, results, work in progress, and experience on all aspects of embedded and ubiquitous computing.

There was a very large number of paper submissions (376), not only from Europe, but also from Asia and the Pacific, and North and South America. All submissions were reviewed by at least three Program or Technical Committee members or external reviewers. It was extremely difficult to select the presentations for the conference because there were so many excellent and interesting submissions. In order to allocate as many papers as possible and keep the high quality of the conference, we finally decided to accept 114 papers for oral presentations. We believe that all of these papers and topics not only provided novel ideas, new results, work in progress, and state-of-the-art techniques in this field, but also stimulated future research activities in the area of embedded and ubiquitous computing.

The exciting program for this conference was the result of the hard and excellent work of many others, such as Program Vice-chairs, external reviewers, Program and Technical Committee members, all working under a very tight schedule. We were also grateful to the members of the Organizing Committee for supporting us in handling many organizational tasks, and to the keynote speakers for accepting to come to the conference with enthusiasm. Last but not least, we hope you enjoy the conference proceedings.

October 2005

Laurence T. Yang, Mokoto Amamiya
Zhen Liu, Minyi Guo and Franz J. Rammig
EUC 2005 Program and General Chairs

Executive Committee (continued)

	Ryuzo Takiyama, Nagasaki Institute of Applied Science, Japan
	Xiaopeng Wei, Dalian University, China
	Laurence T. Yang (Chair), St. Francis Xavier University, Canada
Panel Chairs:	Jianhua Ma, Hosei University, Japan
	Pao-Ann Hsiung, National Chung Cheng University, Taiwan
Workshop Chairs:	Makoto Takizawa, Tokyo Denki University, Japan
	Seongsoo Hong, Seoul National University, Korea
Industrial Liaison:	Shih-Wei Liao, Intel, USA
	Zhaohui Wu, Zhejiang University, China
Publicity Chairs:	Hui Wang, University of Aizu, Japan
	Andrea Acquaviva, University of Urbino, Italy
Demo and Exhibition:	Tomoya Enokido, Rissho University, Japan
Tutorial Chairs:	Beniamino Di Martino, Second University of Naples, Italy
	Chung-Ta King, National TsingHua University, Taiwan
Web Masters:	Shinichi Kamohara, Nagasaki Institute of Applied Science, Japan
	Noriyuki Kitashima, Nagasaki Institute of Applied Science, Japan
Publication Committee:	Haibo Yu (Chair), Kyushu University, Japan
	Tony Li Xu, St. Francis Xavier University, Canada
Local Organizing Chairs:	Kenichi Ito, Siebold University of Nagasaki, Japan
	Brian Burke-Gaffney, Nagasaki Institute of Applied Science, Japan
NIAS Executive	Ryuzo Takiyama (Chair), Susumu Yoshimura (Vice-chair)
Committee:	Yoshito Tanaka, Junichi Ikematsu, Brian Burke-Gaffey
	Makoto Shimojima, Noriyuki Kitajima, Teruyuki Kaneko
	Shinichi Kamohara, Takahiro Fusayasu, Kouji Kiyoyama
	Shinichiro Hirasawa, Saori Matsuo

Program/Technical Committee

Ben A. Abderazek	University of Electro-Communications, Japan
Jose Albaladejo	Polytechnical University of Valencia, Spain

Program/Technical Committee (continued)

Luis Almeida	University of Aveiro, Portugal
Giuseppe Anastasi	University of Pisa, Italy
Aldo Baccigalupi	University of Naples “Federico II”, Italy
Juergen Becker	University of Karlsruhe, Germany
Davide Bertozzi	Università di Ferrara, Italy
Enrico Bini	Scuola Superiore Sant’Anna, Italy
Rajkumar Buyya	Melbourne University, Australia
Jean Carle	University of Lille, France
Sun Chan	ASTRI, Hong Kong, China
Chih-Yung Chang	Tamkang University, Taiwan
Naehyuck Chang	Seoul National University, Korea
Han-Chieh Chao	National Dong Hwa University, Taiwan
Jiann-Liang Chen	National Dong Hwa University, Taiwan
Yuh-Shyan Chen	National Chung Cheng University, Taiwan
Tzung-Shi Chen	National University of Tainan, Taiwan
Guihai Chen	Nanjing University, China
Jorge Juan Chico	Universidad de Sevilla, Spain
Li-Der Chou	National Central University, Taiwan
Sajal K. Das	University of Texas at Arlington, USA
Alex Dean	North Carolina State University, USA
Lawrence Y. Deng	St. John’s and Mary’s Institute of Technology, Taiwan
Giuseppe De Marco	Fukuoka Institute of Technology, Japan
Bjorn De Sutter	Ghent University, Belgium
Carlos Dominguez	Polytechnical University of Valencia, Spain
Chi-Ren Dow	Feng Chia University, Taiwan
Arjan Durresi	Lousiana State University, USA
Paal E. Engelstad	University of Oslo, Norway
Tomoya Enokido	Rissho University, Japan
Raffaele C. Esposito	University of Sannio, Italy
Jih-Ming Fu	Cheng-Hsiu University of Technology, Taiwan
Marisol Garcia Valls	Universidad Carlos III de Madrid, Spain
Luis J. Garcia Villalba	Complutense University of Madrid, Spain
Rung-Hung Gau	National Sun Yat-sen University, Taiwan
Antonio Gentile	University of Palermo, Italy
Luis Gomes	Universidade Nova de Lisboa, Portugal
Hani Hagras	University of Essex, UK
Takahiro Hara	Osaka University, Japan
Houcine Hassan	Polytechnical University of Valencia, Spain
Naohiro Hayashibara	Tokyo Denki University, Japan
Pin-Han Ho	University of Waterloo, Canada
Pao-Ann Hsiung	National Chung Cheng University, Taiwan

Program/Technical Committee (continued)

Chung-hsing Hsu	Los Alamos National Laboratory, USA
Yueh-Min Huang	National Cheng Kung University, Taiwan
Chung-Ming Huang	National Cheng Kung University, Taiwan
Jason C. Hung	Kung Wu Institute of Technology, Taiwan
Hoh Peter In	Korea University, Korea
Pedro Isaias	Portuguese Open University, Portugal
Kenichi Ito	Siebold University of Nagasaki, Japan
Rong-Hong Jan	National Chiao Tung University, Taiwan
Qun Jin	Waseda University, Japan
Mahmut Kandemir	Pennsylvania State University, USA
Jien Kato	Nagoya University, Japan
Daeyoung Kim	Information and Communications University, Korea
Akio Koyama	Yamagata University, Japan
Christian Landrault	LIRMM, France
Trong-Yen Lee	National Taipei University of Technology, Taiwan
Yannick Le Moullec	Aalborg University, Denmark
Regis Leveugle	INPG/CSI, France
Xiaoming Li	Peking University, China
Yiming Li	National Chiao Tung University, Taiwan
Zhiyuan Li	Purdue University, USA
Minglu Li	Shanghai Jiaotong University, China
Wen-Hwa Liao	Tatung University, Taiwan
Shih-wei Liao	INTEL, USA
Man Lin	St. Francis Xavier University, Canada
Youn-Long Lin	National Tsing Hua University, Taiwan
Alex Zhaoyu Liu	University of North Carolina at Charlotte, USA
Lucia Lo Bello	University of Catania, Itlay
Renato Lo Cigno	University of Trento, Italy
Jianhua Ma	Hosei University, Japan
Petri Mahonen	Aachen University, Germany
Juan-Miguel Martinez	Polytechnical University of Valencia, Spain
Pedro M. Ruiz Martinez	University of Murcia, Spain
Geyong Min	University of Bradford, UK
Marius Minea	Politehnica University of Timisoara, Romania
Daniel Mosse	University of Pittsburgh, USA
Takuo Nakashima	Kyushu Tokai University, Japan
Amiya Nayak	University of Ottawa, Canada
Joseph Ng	Hong Kong Baptist University, Hong Kong
Sala Nicoletta	University of Italian Switzerland, Switzerland
Gianluca Palermo	Politecnico di Milano, Italy

Program/Technical Committee (continued)

Vassilis Paliouras	University of Patras, Greece
Raju Pandey	University of California at Davis, USA
Preeti Panta	Indian Institute of Technology, India
Massimo Poncino	Politecnico di Torino, Italy
Isabelle Puaut	University of Rennes, France
Sanjay Rajopadhye	Colorado State University, USA
Maurizio Rebaudengo	Politecnico di Torino, Italy
Xiangshi Ren	Kochi University of Technology, Japan
Achim Rettberg	University of Paderborn, Germany
Bikash Sabata	IET Inc., USA
Takamichi Saito	Meiji University, Japan
Biplab K. Sarker	University of New Brunswick, Canada
Fumiaki Sato	Shizuoka University, Japan
Klaus Schneider	University of Kaiserslautern, Germany
Berhard Scholz	University of Sydney, Australia
Win-Bin See	Aerospace Industrial Development, Taiwan
Jaume Segura	University of Illes Balears, Spain
Weisong Shi	Wayne State University, USA
Timothy K. Shih	Tamkang University, Taiwan
Kuei-Ping Shih	Tamkang University, Taiwan
Dimitrios Soudris	Democritus University of Thrace, Greece
Robert Steele	University of Technology Sydney, Australia
Takuo Suganuma	Tohoku University, Japan
Kaoru Sugita	Fukuoka Institute of Technology, Japan
Walid Taha	Rice University, USA
David Taniar	Monash University, Australia
Tsutomu Terada	Osaka University, Japan
Eduardo Tovar	Instituto Politecnico do Porto, Portugal
Yu-Chee Tseng	National Chiao Tung University, Taiwan
Hung-ying Tyan	National Sun Yat-sen University, Taiwan
Tom Vander Aa	IMEC, Belgium
Luminita Vasiu	University of Westminster, UK
Diego Vazquez	Centro Nacional de Microelectronica, Spain
Jari Veijalainen	University of Jyvaskyla, Finland
Salvatore Venticinque	Second University of Naples, Italy
Arnaud Virazel	LIRMM, France
Salvatore Vitabile	University of Palermo, Italy
Natalija Vlajic	York University, Canada
Guojun Wang	Central South University, China
Cho-Li Wang	The University of Hong Kong, China
Frank Zhigang Wang	Cranfield University, UK
Hengshan Wang	University of Shanghai for Science and Technology, China

Embedded Software

Real-Time Systems

Power-Aware Computing

H/S Co-design and Systems-on-Chip

Testing and Verification

Reconfigurable Computing

Multimedia, HCI and Pervasive Computing

Network Protocol, Security and Fault-Tolerance

Middleware and P2P Computing

Parallel Embedded Systems: Optimizations and Challenges*

Edwin H.-M. Sha

University of Texas at Dallas,
Richardson, Texas 75083, USA
edsha@utdallas.edu

With the advance of system level integration and system-on-chip, the high-tech industry is now moving toward multiple-core parallel embedded systems using hardware/software co-design approach. To design and optimize an embedded system and its software is technically hard because of the strict requirements of an embedded system in timing, code size, memory, low power, security, etc. while optimizing a parallel embedded system makes research even more challenging. The research in embedded systems needs integrated efforts in many areas such as algorithms, computer architectures, compilers, parallel/distributed processing, real-time systems, etc.

This talk will first use an example to illustrate how to find the best parallel algorithm and architecture for this example application, and the technical challenges on design of parallel embedded systems. Because loops are usually the most critical parts to be optimized in DSP or any computation-intensive applications, the talk will then present our results in various types of optimizations for loops in timing, code-size, memory, power consumption, heterogeneous systems, etc. Many of our techniques give the best known results available in literatures. This talk will show that using our multi-dimensional retiming technique, any uniform nested loops can be transformed such that all the computations in the new loop body can be executed simultaneously. This is the best possible result and can be applied to many applications executed on VLIW or other types of parallel systems.

* This work is partially supported by TI University Program, NSF EIA-0103709, Texas ARP 009741-0028-2001, NSF CCF-0309461, NSF IIS-0513669, Microsoft, USA.

L.T. Yang et al. (Eds.): EUC 2005, LNCS 3824, p. 2, 2005.

Progress of Ubiquitous Information Services and Keeping Their Security by Biometrics Authentication

Kazuo Asakawa

Fujitsu Laboratories, Ltd.,
4-1-1 Kamikodanaka, Nakahara-ku,
Kawasaki 211-8588, Japan
asakawa@labs.fujitsu.com

With progress of both fixed and mobile networks, various ubiquitous information services have been brought up to apply in actual business scene. In fact, it becomes possible to receive and send information in various access points not only in offices but also in cars through sophisticated ubiquitous terminals such as PDA, cellular phone, mobile PC and so on. Moreover, the spread of RFID-tag application to household commodities will accelerate the popularization of ubiquitous services. Every ubiquitous terminal will have RFID reader/writer on board in near future. By using the ubiquitous information service environment, variety of services such as e-government, e-bank, e-commerce, Intelligent Transport Systems service that usually require customized services for each customer has already been provided. However, high-tech crimes such as skimming and phishing are increasing day by day inversely increment of its convenience. Such high-tech crimes were happened in worldwide actually. It is impossible to keep security by 4 or more digits PIN code any longer. Biometrics authentication is promising to protect against high-tech crimes in the present situation. I will give an overview of current ubiquitous information services, focusing on some of actual services in keeping security by biometrics authentication.

L.T. Yang et al. (Eds.): EUC 2005, LNCS 3824, p. 3, 2005.

Implementing and Evaluating Color-Aware Instruction Set for Low-Memory, Embedded Video Processing in Data Parallel Architectures*

Jongmyon Kim[1], D. Scott Wills[2], and Linda M. Wills[2]

[1] Chip Solution Center, Samsung Advanced Institute of Technology,
San 14-1, Nongseo-ri, Kiheung-eup, Kyungki-do, 449-712, South Korea
jongmyon.kim@samsung.com
[2] School of Electrical and Computer Engineering,
Georgia Institute of Technology, Atlanta, Georgia 30332-0250
{scott.wills, linda.wills}@ece.gatech.edu

Abstract. Future embedded imaging applications will be more demanding processing performance while requiring the same low cost and low energy consumption. This paper presents and evaluates a color-aware instruction set extension (CAX) for single instruction, multiple data (SIMD) processor arrays to meet the computational requirements and cost goals. CAX supports parallel operations on two-packed 16-bit (6:5:5) YCbCr data in a 32-bit datapath processor, providing greater concurrency and efficiency for color image and video processing. Unlike typical multimedia extensions (e.g., MMX, VIS, and MDMX), CAX harnesses parallelism within the human perceptual color space rather than depending solely on generic subword parallelism. Moreover, the ability to reduce data format size reduces system cost. The reduction in data bandwidth also simplifies system design. Experimental results on a representative SIMD array architecture show that CAX achieves a speedup ranging from 5.2× to 8.8× (an average of 6.3×) over the baseline SIMD array performance. This is in contrast to MDMX (a representative MIPS multimedia extension), which achieves a speedup ranging from 3× to 5× (an average of 3.7×) over the same baseline SIMD array. CAX also outperforms MDMX in both area efficiency (a 52% increase versus a 13% increase) and energy efficiency (a 50% increase versus an 11% increase), resulting in better component utilization and sustainable battery life. Furthermore, CAX improves the performance and efficiency with a mere 3% increase in the system area and a 5% increase in the system power, while MDMX requires a 14% increase in the system area and a 16% increase in the system power. These results demonstrate that CAX is a suitable candidate for application-specific embedded multimedia systems.

1 Introduction

As multimedia revolutionizes our society, its applications are becoming some of the most dominant computing workloads. Color image and video processing in particular

* This work was performed by authors at the Georgia Institute of Technology (Atlanta, GA).

L.T. Yang et al. (Eds.): EUC 2005, LNCS 3824, pp. 4 – 16, 2005.

has garnered considerable interest over the past few years since color features are valuable in sensing the environment, recognizing objects, and conveying crucial information [10]. These applications, however, demand tremendous computational and I/O throughput. Moreover, increasing user demand for multimedia-over-wireless capabilities on embedded systems places additional constraints on power, size, and weight.

Single instruction, multiple data (SIMD) architectures have demonstrated the potential to meet the computational requirements and cost goals by employing thousands of inexpensive processing elements (PEs) and distributing and co-locating PEs with the data I/O to minimize storage and data communication requirements. The SIMD Pixel (SIMPil) processor [2, 4], for example, is a low memory, monolithically integrated SIMD architecture that efficiently exploits massive data parallelism inherent in imaging applications. It reduces data movement through a processing-in-place technique in which image data are directly transported into the PEs and stored there. Two-dimensional SIMD arrays, including SIMPil, are well suited for many imaging tasks that require processing of pixel data with respect to either nearest-neighbor or other 2-D patterns exhibiting locality or regularity. However, they are less amenable to vector (multichannel) processing in which each pixel computation is performed simultaneously on 3-D YCbCr (luminance-chrominance) channels [1], which are widely used in the image and video processing community. More specifically, since the 3-D vector computation is performed within innermost loops, its performance does not scale with larger PE arrays.

This paper presents a color-aware instruction set extension (CAX) for such SIMD arrays as a solution to this performance limitation by supporting two-packed 16-bit (6:5:5) YCbCr data in a 32-bit register, while processing these color data in parallel. (CAX was introduced previously for superscalar processors [7], but this paper is investigating its use in SIMD image processing architectures.) The YCbCr space allows coding schemes that exploit the properties of human vision by truncating some

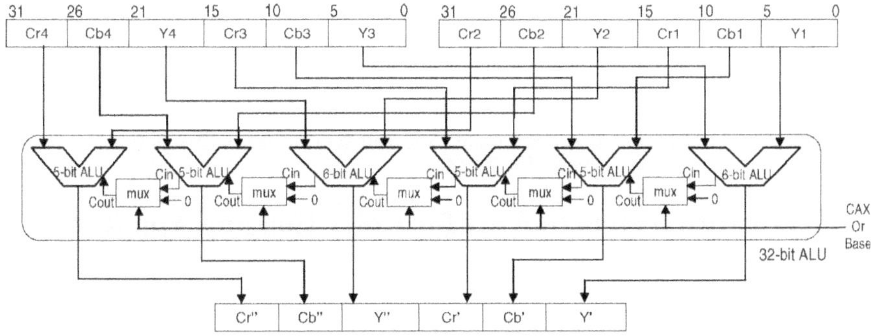

Fig. 1. An example of a partitioned ALU functional unit that exploits color subword parallelism

of the less important data in every color pixel and allocating fewer bits to the high-frequency chrominance components that are perceptually less significant. Thus, it provides satisfactory image quality in a compact 16-bit color representation that consists of a six-bit luminance (Y) and two five-bit chrominance (Cr and Cb)

the output result to the largest or smallest value for the given data type when an overflow occurs. Saturating arithmetic is particularly useful in pixel-related operations, for example, to prevent a black pixel from becoming white if an overflow occurs. The parallel average instruction, which is useful for blending algorithms, takes two packed data types as input, adds corresponding data quantities, and divides each result by two while placing the result in the corresponding data location. The rounding is performed to ensure precision over repeated average instructions.

2.2 Parallel Compare Instructions

Parallel compare instructions include `CMPEQ_CRCBY`, `CMPNE_CRCBY`, `CMPGE_CRCBY`, `CMPGT_CRCBY`, `CMPLE_CRCBY`, `CMPLT_CRCBY`, `CMOV_CRCBY` (conditional move), `MIN_CRCBY`, and `MAX_CRCBY`. These instructions compare pairs of sub-elements (e.g., Y, Cb, and Cr) in the two source registers. Depending on the instructions, the results are varied for each sub-element comparison. The first seven instructions are useful for a condition query performed on the incoming data such as chroma-keying [9]. The last two instructions, `MIN_CRCBY` and `MAX_CRCBY`, are especially useful for median filtering, which compare pairs of sub-elements in the two source registers while outputting the minimum and maximum values to the target register.

2.3 Parallel Permute Instructions

Permute instructions include `MIX_CRCBY` and `ROTATE_CRCBY`. These instructions are used to rearrange the order of quantities in the packed data type. The mix instruction mixes the sub-elements of the two source registers into the operands of the target register, and the rotate instruction rotates the sub-elements to the right by an immediate value. These instructions are useful for performing a vector pixel transposition or a matrix transposition [13].

2.4 Special-Purpose Instructions

Special-purpose CAX instructions include `ADACC_CRCBY` (absolute-differences-accumulate), `MACC_CRCBY` (multiply-accumulate), `RAC` (read accumulator), and `ZACC` (zero accumulator), which provide the most computational benefits of all the CAX instructions. The `ADACC_CRCBY` instruction, for example, is frequently used in a number of algorithms for motion estimation. The `MACC_CRCBY` instruction is useful in DSP algorithms that involve computing a vector dot-product, such as digital filters and convolutions. The last two instructions `RAC` and `ZACC` are related to the managing of the CAX accumulator.

3 Methodology

This section describes modeled architectures and a methodology infrastructure for the evaluation of the CAX instruction set.

3.1 Modeled Architectures

The SIMD Pixel (SIMPil) processor is used as the baseline SIMD image processing architecture for this study. Fig. 3 shows the microarchitecture of the SIMD array, along with its interconnection network. When data are distributed, the processing elements (PEs) execute a set of instructions in a lockstep fashion. With 4×4 pixel sensor sub-arrays, each PE is associated with a specific portion (4×4 pixels or 16 pixel-per-processing-element) of an image frame, allowing streaming pixel data to be retrieved and processed locally. Each PE has a reduced instruction set computer (RISC) datapath with the following minimum characteristics:

- Small amount of local storage (128 32-bit words),
- Three-ported general-purpose registers (16 32-bit words),
- ALU – computes basic arithmetic and logic operations,
- Barrel shifter – performs multi-bit logic/arithmetic shift operations,
- MACC – multiplies 32-bit values and accumulates into a 64-bit accumulator,
- Sleep – activates or deactivates a PE based on local information,
- Pixel unit – samples pixel data from the local image sensor array,
- ADC unit – converts light intensities into digital values,
- RGB2YCC and YCC2RGB unit– converts RGB to/from YCbCr, and
- Nearest neighbor communications through a NEWS (north-east-west-south) network and serial I/O unit.

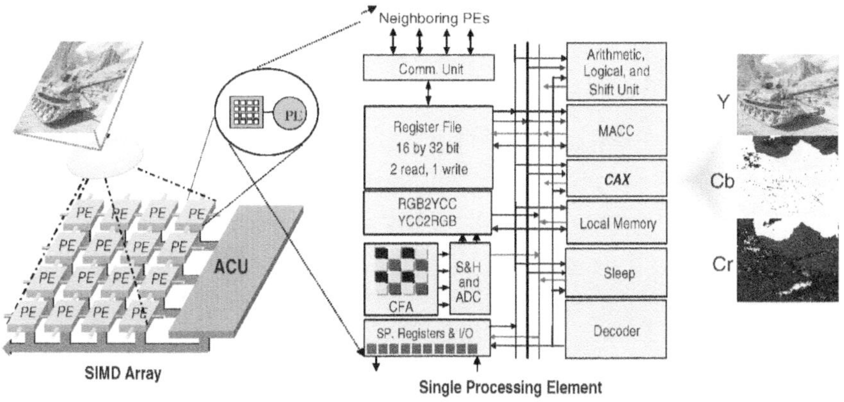

Fig. 3. Block diagram of a SIMD array and a processing element

To improve the performance of vector processing of color image sequences, CAX instructions are included in the instruction set architecture (ISA) of the SIMPil array. For a performance comparison, MDMX-type instructions are also included in the SIMPil ISA. Table 1 summarizes the parameters of the modeled architectures. An overall simulation infrastructure is presented next.

Table 1. Modeled architecture parameters

Parameter	Value
System Size	44×38 (1,584 PEs)
Image Sensor per PE (vertor pixel per PE ratio)	4×4 (16 VPPE)
VLSI Technology	100 nm
Clock Frequency	80 MHz
Interconnection Network	Mesh
intALU/intMUL/Barrel Shifter/intMACC/Comm	1 / 1 / 1 / 1 / 1
MDMX/CAX: intALU/intMACC	1 / 1
Local Memory Size (baseline/MDMX/CAX)	128 32-bit/ 128 32-bit/ 64 32-bit word

3.2 Methodology Infrastructure

Fig. 4 shows a methodology infrastructure that is divided into three levels: application, architecture, and technology.

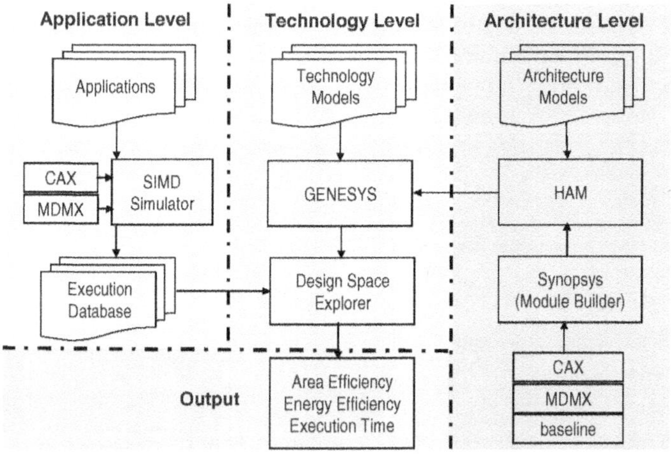

Fig. 4. A methodology infrastructure for exploring the design space of three modeled architectures: baseline SIMPil, MDMX-SIMPil, and CAX-SIMPil

At the application level, an instruction-level SIMD simulator, called SIMPilSim, has been used to profile execution statistics, such as cycle count, dynamic instruction frequency, and PE utilization, for the three different versions of the programs: (1) baseline ISA without subword parallelism (SIMPil), (2) baseline plus MDMX ISA (MDMX-SIMPil), and (3) baseline plus CAX ISA (CAX-SIMPil). The benchmark suite includes five imaging applications (see more details at [5]): a chroma-keying program (CHROMA), color edge detection using a vector Sobel operator (VSobel), the vector median filter (VMF), vector quantization (VQ), and the full-search vector block-matching algorithm of motion estimation (FSVBMA) within the MPEG standard.

At the architecture level, the heterogeneous architectural modeling (HAM) of functional units for SIMD arrays, proposed by Chai *et al.* [3], has been used to calculate the design parameters of modeled architectures. For the design parameters of the MDMX and CAX functional units (FUs), Verilog models for the baseline, MDMX, and CAX FUs were implemented and synthesized with the Synopsys design compiler (DC) using a 0.18-micron standard cell library. The reported area specifications of the MDMX and CAX FUs were then normalized to the baseline FU, and the normalized numbers were applied to the HAM tool for determining the design parameters of MDMX- and CAX-SIMPil. The design parameters are then passed to the technology level.

At the technology level, the Generic System Simulator (GENESYS) developed at Georgia Tech [8] has been used to calculate technology parameters (e.g., latency, area, power, and clock frequency) for each configuration. Finally, the databases (e.g., cycle times, instruction latencies, instruction counts, area, and power of the functional units) obtained from the application, architecture, and technology levels are combined to determine execution times, area efficiency, and energy efficiency for each case. The next section presents the system area and power of the modeled architectures.

4 System Area and Power Evaluation Using Technology Modeling

Fig. 5 shows the system area and power of MDMX-SIMPil and CAX-SIMPil, normalized to the baseline SIMPil. Experimental results indicate that MDMX requires a 14% increase in the entire system area and a 16% increase in the peak system power. However, CAX only requires a 3% increase in the system area and a 5% increase in the system area and power because of the reduced pixel word storage (local memory). These system area and power results are combined with application simulations for determining processing performance, area efficiency, and energy efficiency for each case, which is presented next.

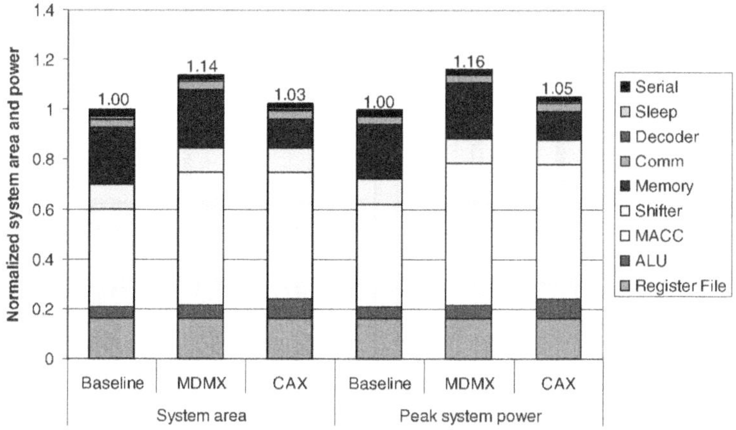

Fig. 5. System area and power of CAX-SIMPil and MDMX-SIMPil, normalized to the baseline SIMPil

50% increase with CAX, but only an 11% increase with MDMX. This is because CAX achieves higher sustained throughputs with a smaller increase in the system power. Increasing energy efficiency improves sustainable battery life for given system capabilities.

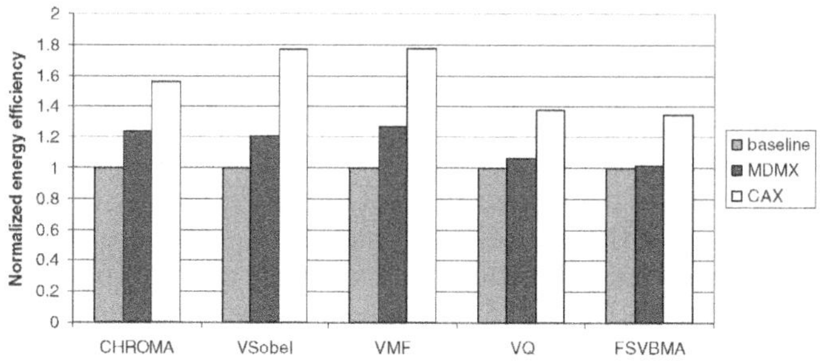

Fig. 8. Energy efficiency for the SIMPil system with CAX and MDMX, normalized to the baseline version

5.3 Area Evaluation Results

Fig. 9 shows area efficiency, the task throughput achieved per unit of area, for the SIMPil system with MDMX and CAX, normalized to the baseline version. As with energy efficiency, CAX outperforms MDMX for all the programs in the area efficiency, indicating a 52% increase with CAX, but only a 13% increase with MDMX. This is because CAX achieves higher sustained throughput with smaller area overhead. Increasing area efficiency improves component utilization for given system capabilities.

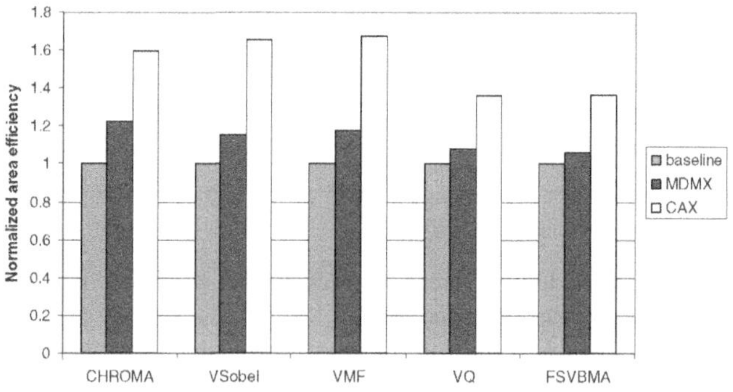

Fig. 9. Area efficiency for the SIMPil system with CAX and MDMX, normalized to the baseline version

6 Conclusions

As emerging portable multimedia applications demand more and more tremendous computational throughput with limited area and power, the need for high efficiency, high throughput embedded processing is becoming an important challenge in computer architecture. In this regard, this paper has addressed application-, architecture-, and technology-level issues in an existing processing system to efficiently support vector processing of color image sequences. In particular, this paper has focused on the color-aware instruction set (CAX) for memory- and performance-hungry embedded applications in a representative SIMD image processing architecture. Unlike typical multimedia extensions, CAX harnesses parallelism within the human perceptual color space (e.g., YCbCr). Rather than depending solely on generic subword parallelism, CAX supports parallel operations on two-packed 16-bit YCbCr data in a 32-bit datapath processor, providing greater concurrency and efficiency for color image and video processing. The key findings are as follows:

- CAX achieves a speedup ranging from 5.2× to 8.8× (an average of 6.3×) over the baseline SIMD array performance without subword parallelism. This is in contrast to MDMX, which achieves a speedup ranging from only 3× to 5× (an average of 3.7×) over the same baseline SIMD array.
- CAX reduces energy consumption from 80% to 89%, but MDMX reduces energy consumption from only 60% to 79% over the baseline version.
- Moreover, CAX benefits from reduced pixel word storage in addition to greater concurrency. As a result, CAX outperforms MDMX for all the programs in area efficiency and energy efficiency. The area efficiency increases from 36% to 68% (an average of 52%) with CAX, but only 6% to 22% (an average of 13%) with MDMX. The energy efficiency increases from 35% to 77% (an average of 50%) with CAX, but only 2% to 24% (an average of 11%) with MDMX. Increasing area and energy efficiencies yield greater component utilization and sustainable battery life, respectively, for given system capabilities.
- Furthermore, CAX improves the performance and efficiency with a mere 3% increase in the silicon area and a 5% increase in the system power, while MDMX requires a 14% increase in the silicon area and a 16% increase in the system power.

In the future, a heuristic compiler support will be explored that extracts both data-level parallelism and color subword parallelism from high level language programs to overcome tedious hand optimization and/or special programming libraries.

References

1. V. Bhaskaran and K. Konstantinides, Image and Video Compression Standards: Algorithms and Architectures, Kluwer Academic Publishers (1997)
2. H. H. Cat, A. Gentile, J. C. Eble, M. Lee, O. Verdier, Y. J. Joo, D. S. Wills, M. Brooke, N. M. Jokerst, A. S. Brown, and R. Leavitt, SIMPil: An OE integrated SIMD architecture for focal plane processing applications, in Proc. Massively Parallel Processing Using Optical Interconnection (MPPOI-96), pp. 44-52 (1996)

SIMD operation unit [11]. In order to reduce the number of packing operations, the processor should support various types of packed data. However, since the code space allowed for the DSP-enhancements is limited as mentioned above, we focus on accelerating the MAC operations which are apparently the most popular operations in the DSP applications. We implement two types of MAC operations shown in Fig. 1: the parallel SIMD type and the sum-of-products type. The parallel SIMD type of MAC operation, shown in Fig. 1(a), is much more efficient than any other types of operations for processing the arrays of structured data such as RGBA formatted pixel data. On the other hand, the sum-of-products type of MAC operation, shown in Fig. 1(b), is efficient for processing general data arrays.

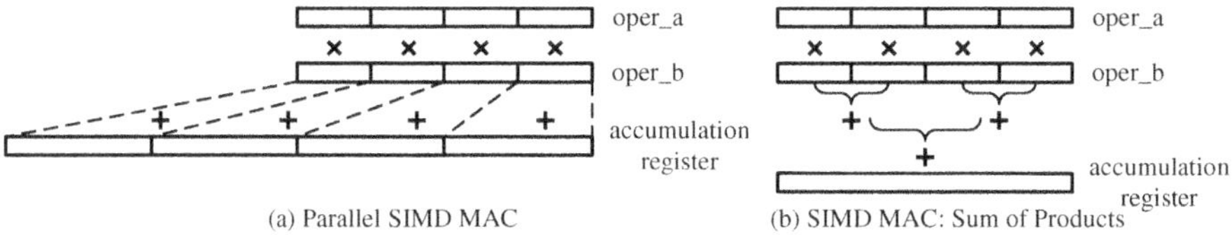

Fig. 1. Two types of the SIMD MAC operations supported in the proposed DSP-enhanced processor

We also adopt the instructions for the saturation arithmetic which is often used in DSP applications. Unlike the wrap-around arithmetic, the saturation arithmetic uses the maximum or the minimum value when it detects an overflow or an underflow.

In the signal processing, the fixed-point arithmetic is commonly used because it is much cheaper and faster than the floating-point arithmetic. During the multiplication of two 32-bit fixed-point numbers, the results are stored in the 64-bit multiplication result register (MR). Since the position of radix point in a fixed-point number can be changed during multiplications, we need to select a part of the 64-bit multiplication result to make a 32-bit fixed-point number. For that purpose, *base* would require a sequence of five instructions looking like the one in the first box shown below. We propose to use an instruction with the mnemonic `mrs` (*multiplication result selection*), as shown below.

```
mfmh   %Rx             # move MR(H) to GPR(Rx)
mfml   %Ry             # move MR(L) to GPR(Ry)
asl    DP, %Rx         # DP-bit shift left Rx
lsr    (32-DP), %Ry    # (32-DP)-bit shift right Ry
or     %Rx, %Ry        # Ry = Rx | Ry
```

↓

```
mrs    DP, %Ry
```

3.2 Accelerating Address Generation

DSP applications usually perform a set of computations repeatedly for streaming data that have almost uniform data patterns. In this section, we introduce a loop-efficient hardware address generator that can accelerate the memory-addressing processes. We intend to use this address generator for accelerating DSP applications, including the memory-copy operations, with low cost.

The proposed address generator has a capability of handling the auto-increment addressing mode which is usually used for various applications including the memory-copy operations. As DSP operations use a loop for computing processes to handle streaming data, the proposed address generation unit is equipped with a comparator to detect the end-offset for loop. The address generator is also intended for supporting other special memory-addressing modes, such as the wrap-around incremental addressing mode for a virtual circular buffer and the bit-reversal addressing mode for transform kernels. We only support the post-modifying scheme because it is more popularly used [12].

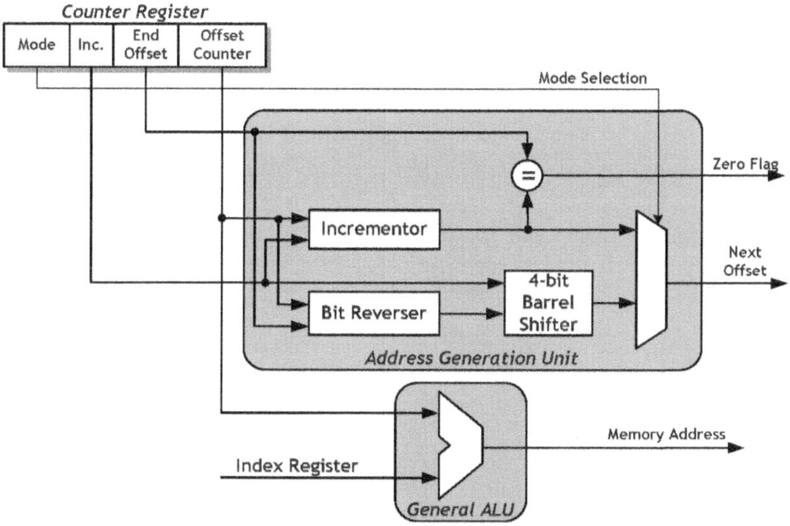

Fig. 2. Proposed address generation unit

Since the hardware complexity is important, the proposed address generator only produces the small sized offset instead of the entire addresses. Fig. 2 shows the block diagram of the proposed address generator and the counter register. The control register is used to control the address generator and holds a control word regarding generation pattern, offset counter, end offset for looping, and incremental offset. Since we use a post-modifying scheme, the ALU uses the previously generated offset counter to make a memory address, while the incrementor uses it to generate the next offset. The generated offset is written back to the offset counter field in the counter register.

3.3 Register Extension

Almost DSP routines use many coefficients and temporary values simultaneously. However, most embedded microprocessors do not have enough registers to hold those values. A general approach for resolving this problem of shortage of registers is to spill the contents of registers into the memory. However, media data often take the form of data streams, in which case they are temporarily stored in the memory, continuously read into the processor, and used only a few times. Therefore, media applications running on an embedded processor often suffer from significant performance losses due to the frequent register spilling processes.

We propose a register extension scheme that increases the effective number of registers by adopting the idea of shadow register to hold temporary values in the registers. The idea of shadow register has been used in various aspects, such as the context switching latency [13]. We find that this idea is also very useful for embedded processors which have limited code spaces, such as the EISC processors, since it is hard for them to allocate additional bits for register indexing [9].

For the register extension scheme, we divide the register file into two parts: one part consists of a set of smaller register files, *register pages*, and another part consists of eight registers to be shared among register pages. Each register page consists of eight registers. We use three bits in the status register to select active register page. Thus we can use up to seventy two registers, eight shared registers and eight register pages with eight registers, in the proposed processor when whole register pages are implemented. The use of register pages decreases memory traffic due to memory spilling.

4 Evaluations

The designed DSP-enhanced microprocessor has been modeled in Verilog HDL as a synthesizable RTL model. We synthesize the model using the Samsung STD130 $0.18\mu m$ CMOS standard cell library [14] and the Synopsys DesignCompiler. The critical path delay is estimated by using the Synopsys PrimeTime under the worst-case operating condition (1.65V supply voltage and 125 °C junction temperature.) The results are summarized in Table 1. As shown in Table 1, the critical path delay is almost the same even through some units are added to accelerate DSP applications. The enhancements we add cost about 10270 equivalent gates, most of which are used for the shadow register file and the SIMD MAC unit. The others cost less than 1000 gates per each unit.

In order to evaluate the performance of the proposed architecture, we use DSP kernels used commonly in many DSP applications: IMDCT (inverse modified discrete cosine transform), FFT (fast Fourier transform), DCT (discrete cosine transform), and FIR (finite impulse response) filter. The IMDCT routine is used for reducing aliases in high fidelity audio coding applications including MP3, and AAC. The DCT is commonly used in the image compression. The FFT and FIR

Table 1. Cost and power performance of the enhancements

	Area [equi. gates]	Critial Path Delay [ns]
Base processor	56852	6.25
Proposed processor	67122	6.19

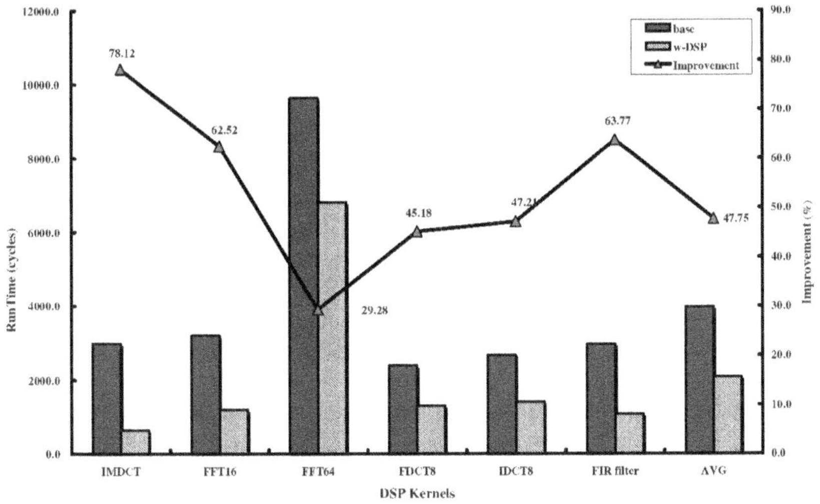

Fig. 3. Performance gain for popular DSP kernels

filter are the most common DSP functions in many DSP applications. We use the verilog-HDL model with the perfect memory model during the performance evaluation.

The results of the experiments are summarized in Fig. 3. The proposed DSP architecture reduces the average execution time of the DSP kernels considered by 47.8%. For IMDCT, the use of the `mac` and `mrs` results in the reductions of the computation time. Furthermore, the use of the register extension scheme reduces the number of memory accesses by 9%. For FFT kernels, the performance improvement is mainly due to the parallel SIMD MAC operations. However, we observe a limited performance enhancement for the 64-point FFT, since it takes too much time to process the data packing and the memory accesses for spilling temporary values. For DCT and FIR filter, the instruction for sum of products is used efficiently and results in the performance gain. Moreover, the register extension scheme reduces memory operations in the FIR filter application. In our experiments, the coefficients for an 8-TAP FIR filter are loaded just once during the processing.

We also experiment with real DSP applications such as MP3 decoding program which uses MAD (MPEG audio decoding) library, ADPCM (Adaptive

Acknowledgements

The authors wish to acknowledge the CAD tool support of IDEC (IC Design Education Center), Korea and the financial support of Advanced Digital Chips Inc., Korea. The authors would also like to thank the anonymous reviewers for their valuable comments.

References

1. Francis, H.: ARM DSP-Enhanced Instructions White Paper, http://arm.com/pdfs/ARM-DSP.pdf
2. MIPS Tech. Inc.: Architecture Set Extension, http://www.mips.com/content/Documentation/MIPSDocumentation/ProcessorArchitecture/doclibrary
3. Cho, K.Y.: A Study on Extendable Instruction Set Computer 32 bit Microprocessor, J. Inst. of Electronics Engineers of Korea, **36-D(55)** (1999) 11–20
4. Lee, H., Beckett, P., Appelbe, B.: High-Performance Extendable Instruction Set Computing, Proc. of 6th ACSAC-2001 (2001) 89–94
5. Kim, H.-G., Jung, D.-Y., Jung, H.-S., Choi, Y.-M., Han, J.-S., Min, B.-G., Oh, H.-C.: AE32000B: A Fully Synthesizable 32-bit Embedded Microprocessor Core, ETRI Journal **25(5)** (2003) 337–344
6. Lee, C., Potkonjak, M., Mangione-Smith. H.: MediaBench: A Tool for Evaluating and Synthesizing Multimedia and Communications Systems, MICRO-30(1997) 330–335
7. ARM Ltd.: The Thumb Architecture Extension, http://www.arm.com/products/CPUs/archi-thumb.html
8. Kissell, K.D.: MIPS16: High-density MIPS for the Embedded Market, Technical Report, Silicon Graphics MIPS Group (1997).
9. Park, G.-C., Ahn, S.-S., Kim, H.-G., Oh, H.-C.: Supports for Processing Media Data in Embedded Processors, Poster Presentation, HiPC2004 (2004).
10. Cho,K.Y., Lim, J.Y., Lee, G.T., Oh, H.-C., Kim, H.-G., Min, B.G., Lee, H.: Extended Instruction Word Folding Apparatus, U.S. Patent No.6,631,459, (2003)
11. Talla, D., John, L.K., Buger, D.: Bottlenecks in Multimedia Processing with SIMD Style Extensions and Architectural Enhancements, IEEE Tras. of Comp. **52(8)** (2003) 1015–1011
12. Hennessy, J.L, Patterson, D.A.: Computer Architecture; A Quantitative Approach 3rd Ed., Morgan Kaufmann Publishers (2003)
13. Jayaraj, J., Rajendran, P.L., Thirumoolam, T.: Shadow Register File Architecture: A Mechanism to Reduce Context Switch Latency, HPCA-8 (2002) Poster Presentation
14. Samsung Electronics: STD130 0.18um 1.8V CMOS Standard Cell Library for Pure Logic Products Data Book, Samsung Electronics (2001)
15. Advanced Digital Chips Inc.: GMX1000: A High Performance Multimedia Processor User Manual, Advanced Digital Chips Inc. (2005)

An Intelligent Sensor for Fingerprint Recognition

Salvatore Vitabile[2,3], Vincenzo Conti[1],
Giuseppe Lentini[1], and Filippo Sorbello[1,3]

[1] Dipartimento di Ingegneria Informatica, Universita' di Palermo,
Viale delle Scienze, Edificio 6, 90128, Palermo, Italy
{conti, sorbello}@unipa.it, lentini@csai.unipa.it

[2] Dipartimento di Biotecnologie Mediche e Medicina Legale, Universita' di Palermo,
via del Vespro, 90127, Palermo, Italy
vitabile@unipa.it

[3] Istituto di CAlcolo e Reti ad alte prestazioni, Italian National Research Council,
Viale delle Scienze, Edificio 11, 90128, Palermo, Italy

Abstract. In this paper an intelligent sensor for fingerprint recognition is proposed. The sensor has the objective to overcome some limits of the fingerprint recognition software systems, as elaboration time and security issues related to fingerprint transmission between sensor and processing unit. Intelligent sensor has been prototyped using the Hamster Secugen sensor for image acquisition and the Celoxica RC1000 board, employing a Xilinx VirtexE2000 FPGA, for image processing and analysis. Resources used, elaboration time as well the recognition rates in both verification and identification modes are reported in the paper. To the best of our knowledge, this is the first implementation for a full hardware implemented fingerprint recognition system.

1 Introduction

Biometric based systems for personal identification are always an open research issue. In literature many approaches have been proposed to develop fingerprint recognition systems. Generally, they are characterized by three main steps: image acquisition, 'biometric signature' extraction, matching between the acquired biological signature and the stored one.

Fingerprint minutiae extraction task is a very critical and complex step, so, different dedicated software algorithms have been proposed in literature [1], [2], [4], [5], [6], [7], [8], [9].

In this paper an intelligent hardware sensor for fingerprint recognition is proposed. Sensor prototype has been developed using the Celoxica RC1000 board [12]. The board employs a 2M gates Xilinx VirtexE FPGA [13]. The sensor implements ad hoc image processing algorithms selected evaluating both their performance when implemented in fixed point arithmetic and their requested hardware resources.

L.T. Yang et al. (Eds.): EUC 2005, LNCS 3824, pp. 27–36, 2005.

The proposed intelligent sensor is composed by a *Sensor Acquisition Module* (SAM) and a *Sensor Processing Module* (SPM). The first one is based on Hamster Secugen sensor [19] for fingerprint image acquisition. The second one is an FPGA based prototype implementing the whole fingerprint recognition chain. Modules have been installed on a standard workstation and their communication exploits standard PCI bus.

The proposed system has been tested using 384 fingerprints belonging to 96 different people, and the F.A.R. (False Acceptation Rate) and the F.R.R (False Rejection Rate) have been used to verify its performance. Experimental trials shows that an interesting working point could be reached by the system with a F.A.R. of about 1% with the related F.R.R. of 8%.

The proposed system can be employed as an automatic fingerprint discriminator, too. The system has been evaluated with an identification test where each fingerprint has been compared with each database item in order to find a similarity index. The obtained results show that the processed image is in the subset composed by the 5 most similar fingerprints with a percentage of 84%.

The paper is organized as follow. Some related works are briefly described in section 2, whilst in section 3 some guidelines for algorithms profiling in terms of execution time and FPGA resources are presented. The proposed system as well as each processing phase are described in section 4. In section 5, both system elaboration times and recognition rates are presented. Finally, in section 6 the conclusion of this work is reported.

2 Related Works

In literature many approaches have been proposed and many software systems have been implemented to develop fingerprint based recognition system [1], [2], [5], [6], [8]. Generally, these systems exploit filters and image enhancement algorithms [21], classification algorithms and matching techniques and they are developed with standard high level programming languages on general purpose computers.

In [10] an hardware fingerprint recognition system is presented. However, in the system the fingerprint matching phase has not been developed. The rest of the fingerprint processing tasks were implemented in a FPGA device with a clock frequency of 27,65 Mhz, and a processing time of 589,46 ms.

3 The Hardware Design Guidelines

FPGA devices are widely used for rapid system prototyping. However, an efficient image processing algorithms implementation on FPGA requires an algorithms profiling phase before their implementation. Fingerprint processing algorithms have been analyzed and evaluated in order to optimize FPGA used resources, system elaboration time and result accuracy.

With the respect the FPGA requested resources, each image processing algorithm must be evaluated through the number of loop, the presence of recursion, the number of divisions, square roots operators, and powers different from 2, the presence and the dimension of typical high level language structures as "union", "array", and "circular lists" [3]. Further analysis on image processing algorithms concerns their inclination for parallel and/or pipeline implementation.

The above points are very critical for an high efficient system implementation and they concern each phase of the identification system. The Quantitative Index, *QI*, to individualize the *a priori* performance of the fingerprint processing algorithms for the embedded solution is now introduced:

$$QI = X + 0.6 * Y + 0.3 * Z + 0.05 * W \qquad (1)$$

where X is the number of the loops in the algorithm, Y is the number of recursion and dynamic structures in the algorithm, Z is the number of division and square root operators and powers different from 2 in the algorithm, and W is the number of union and array data structure in the algorithm.

For each phase of the fingerprint processing tasks, several algorithms have been profiled, modified and re-profiled in order to optimize system performance with respect to the hardware resources, processing time and recognition rate.

4 The Intelligent Sensor

As pointed out before, most of the proposed solutions are developed with standard high level programming languages on general purpose computers. In this paper the authors present an intelligent sensor that is able to acquire a fingerprint image, process it and select the corresponding database item for person identification. The sensor is composed by a *Sensor Acquisition Module* (SAM) and a *Sensor Processing Module* (SPM). The first one is based on Hamster Secugen sensor [19] for fingerprint image acquisition. The second one is a FPGA based prototype implementing the whole fingerprint recognition chain.

With more details the SPM is based on five sequential phases: the normalization phase; the binarization phase; the thinning phase; the minutiae extraction phase and the matching phase. In Figure 1 the SAM, the SPM and their relative connections with the Host buses are depicted. The SAM, based on Hamster Secugen sensor [19], acquires a fingerprint image. Successively the SAM transfers the acquired image to the SPM using both the host expansion bus and the host PCI bus. The SPM prototype has been developed on the RC1000 Celoxica board [12] equipped with a 2M gates Xilinx VirtexE FPGA [13]. SPM communications use only the host PCI bus and its clock has been set to 90/4 MHz in order to guarantee the correct data exchange between FPGA and board RAM. The RAM is used to store the fingerprint database, i.e. fingerprint image coding.

Exploiting the high data parallelism of the application, different algorithms have been parallelized. In addition, fingerprint processing phases have been pipelined in order to increase execution time as well as the final throughput. In what follows, the FPGA implementation of the five sequential phases for fingerprint recognition will be described.

time but too many resources are requested for their implementation. Sequential thinning algorithms show bad elaboration performances. This limit is overcome by the parallel thinning algorithms.

Following the proposed guidelines, the MB2 algorithm [20] and the Zhang-Suen algorithm [16] were profiled. The first algorithm uses the recursive operation, with an high resources consumption. The second algorithm is based on moving kernels without any recursion. In addition, the algorithm can be parallelized since for a faster execution.

In the FPGA implementation, the binary image was split in four sub-images (we exploit the RC1000 memory banks). Sub-images thinning based on moving kernels was pipelined as shown for the binarization phase.

4.4 Fingerprint Minutiae Extraction on FPGA

The minutiae, i.e. ridge endings and ridge bifurcations, are usually detected in the thinned fingerprint image [11]. Due to the presence of either original noise or preprocessing caused noise, the thinned image contains a large number of false minutiae.

Among the profiled algorithms, the Tico and Kuosmanen one [17] extracts every true minutia in one step without any noise reduction step. The same authors in [18] present a new version of their algorithm to remove the false minutiae caused by broken ridges into a 9x9 window.

The Tico and Kuosmanen algorithm works on adjacent matrixes of pixels so it was immediately pipelined in the related FPGA implementation. Algorithm performance were improved adding the false minutiae elimination in the boundary of the image. However, the new version of the Tico and Kuosmanen algorithm leaves an high number of false minutiae caused by broken ridges. Using the direction of every ridge-ending, the number of the erased false minutiae increases significantly.

4.5 Fingerprint Matching on FPGA

Several matching algorithms proposed in literature have been profiled. Algorithms based on pattern matching give the best performance due their possibility of parallel implementation. With more details, the algorithms proposed in [1], [2], were adapted for their efficient digitalization.

A fingerprint minutiae descriptor is used to implement the pattern matching. With more details, a list of both minutiae spatial coordinates and minutiae direction are used as descriptor to codify the fingerprint image. The algorithm receives as input two descriptors extracted from the enrolled fingerprint image and from the on-line processed image. As result, the algorithm gives a matching score with the similarity degree of the two fingerprints. A threshold is applied to the above matching score to decide if the processed fingerprints belong to the same person.

5 Experimental Results

5.1 Hardware and Software Environments

The proposed intelligent sensor is composed by a *Sensor Acquisition Module* and a *Sensor Processing Module*. The first one is based on Hamster Secugen sensor [19] for fingerprint image acquisition. The second one is an FPGA based prototype implementing the whole fingerprint recognition chain. Modules have been installed on a standard workstation and their communication exploits standard PCI bus. Sensor prototype has been developed using the Celoxica RC1000 board [12]. The board employs a 2M gates Xilinx VirtexE FPGA [13]. FPGA programming has been performed using both Celoxica DK2 [12] and Xilinx ISE [13] development environments. Algorithms have been described using the an algorithmic-like hardware programming language: the Handel-C language [12].

5.2 Elaboration Time

The board work frequency is limited by the work frequency of the RAM memory banks (see Figure 1). Celoxica RC1000 board manual suggests 25 MHz as maximum work frequency for board memory. We have performed several reading/writing data tests with the board memory banks. A clock frequency of 90/4 MHz, with 90 MHz the main board frequency, has assured proper and correct memory operations.

In the Table 1 some information about the implemented pipelined steps are illustrated in detail. With more details, the processed pixels mask dimension, the latency and running clock cycles, the real board work frequency and the obtained execution time are reported for each of the 5 processing steps.

Table 1. Processed mask dimension, latency and running clock cycles, real board work frequency and obtained execution time for each of the 5 processing steps

Processing Steps	Latency Clock Cycles	Running Clock Cycles	Working Freq.(MHz)	Execution Time(ms)
Normalization	8	6	20.9	12.5
Binarization	60	10	20.9	18.6
Thinning	83	73	21.1	39.8
Minutiae Detection	95	13	20.6	24.3
Matching	23	21	20.5	6.75

5.3 Resources Analysis

As pointed out before, both Celoxica DK2 [12] and Xilinx ISE [13] development environments have been used for FPGA programming. Algorithms have been described using the Handel-C language [12]. The Map Report tool inside the Xilinx ISE [13] development environment gives an output with the FPGA resources used by the fingerprint elaboration chain. Table 2 summaries the used resources for the 2M gates Xilinx VirtexE FPGA [13].

Table 2. FPGA resources used by the fingerprint elaboration chain

Resources Type	FPGA Total Resources	Used Resources	Used Resources (%)
GCLK	4	2	50
GCLKIOB	4	1	25
IOB	404	273	67
SLICE	19200	16178	84
LUT	38400	27027	70
BLOCKRAM	160	6	3

5.4 Recognition Rates

In the registration phase, a sequence of 4 fingerprints of the same finger was acquired in different days. So for each person 4 biological signatures or descriptors were extracted and stored in the 4 board memory banks.

In the matching phase, the on-line extracted biological signature is compared with the registered signatures for a typical verification. With more details, the proposed sensor has been evaluated in both verification tasks (a username is used to select the database item and perform a 1-¿1 match) and identification tasks (no username is used so 1-¿all matches must be performed in order to select the highest matching score candidate).

Due the sensor design features, four security levels could be chosen on the basis of the matched biological signature number: the *basic security level*, if the on-line extracted biological signature matches one of the four stored signatures; *normal security level*, if the on-line extracted biological signature matches two of the four stored signatures; *high security level*, if the on-line extracted biological signature matches three of the four stored signatures; *very high security level*, if the on-line extracted biological signature matches each of the stored signatures. Exploiting both Celoxica RC1000 memory banks and the *par* feature of the Handel-C language, the four fingerprint matches are parallel executed. Experimental trials have demonstrated that the *normal security level* is the best trade-off between security and performance.

Intelligent sensor recognition performance were evaluated using the following indexes: F.A.R. (False Acception Rate) and the F.R.R (False Rejection Rate). Experimental tests were executed on a sample of 384 fingerprints taken by the Secugen sensor [19] belonging to 96 different individuals.

The first set of experiments was conducted to evaluate the performance of the proposed intelligent sensor in verification mode. So with a matching score of 95%, intelligent sensor performance are summarizes by FAR=1,07% and FRR=8,33%. In Figure 3 are plotted FAR and FRR vs the matching score for the normal security level. With the second set of experiments we address the problem of individual identification in large fingerprint database. Experiments aim with a database subset selection, composed by only 5 fingerprints, that always contains the processed fingerprint. In the best case, a recognition rate of 84% with a maching score of 93% is obtained, i.e. the processed fingerprint is among the 5 selected ones.

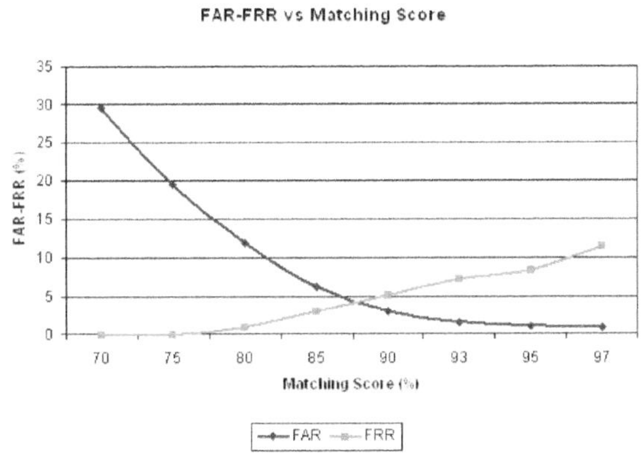

Fig. 3. FAR and FRR vs the matching score for the normal security level

6 Conclusion

In this paper an hardware intelligent sensor for fingerprint recognition is proposed. The sensor has been tested with 384 fingerprints belonging to 96 different people. Sensor performance have been evaluated with F.A.R. and F.R.R indexes in both verification and identification modes. In the verification mode, a F.A.R. of about 1% and a F.R.R. of about 8% are obtained. The sensor has been used as fingerprint discriminator, too. Each processed fingerprint is among the set of 5 similar fingerprints with recognition rate of 84%. The obtained experimental results are comparable with the full software recognition systems. In Bonato at al. [10] an incomplete hardware implemented recognition system (the matching process was not implemented) was proposed. System elaboration time was about 590 ms, while the proposed sensor elaboration time is about 102 ms, considering the full fingerprint matching process.

References

1. V. Conti, G. Pilato, S. Vitabile, F. Sorbello, *A Robust System for Fingerprints Identification*, Knowledge-Based Intelligent Information Engineering System and Allied Technologies, Crema September 2002, pp. 1162-1166
2. V. Conti, G. Pilato, S. Vitabile, F. Sorbello, *Verification of Ink-on-paper Fingerprints by Using Image Processing Techniques and a New Matching Operator*, AI*IA September 2002, pp. 594-601
3. S. Vitabile, A. Gentile, S.M. Siniscalchi, F. Sorbello, *Efficient Rapid Prototyping of Image and Video Processing Algorithms*, Proc. of EUROMICRO Symposium on Digital System Design - Architectures, Methods and Tools, Rennes 2004, pp. 452-457, IEEE Computer Society Press.
4. Jain A., *A Multichannel Approach to FingerPrints Classification*, IEEE Transaction on Pattern Analysis and Machine Intelligence, Vol.21, n.4, 1999, pp. 348-358

Issue 1: How to analyze register-usage in a program to find out unused registers?
Issue 2: How to control register voltages by different working modes?
Issue 3: How to limit energy and performance penalty?

The rest of this paper is organized as follows. Section 2 introduces and discusses related works, such as the dynamic voltage scaling technology and the low-power register file design. Section 3 proposes hardware/software co-design approach to exploit register-usage in a program for register energy saving. Section 4 discusses evaluation environment and evaluation results, including the metrics of register file energy consumption, processor energy consumption, performance penalty and energy-delay product. Section 5 gives conclusion and future works.

2 Related Works

In this section, we discuss the development of the dynamic voltage scaling (DVS) technique, which is a well-known approach in reducing hardware energy consumption. Then we discuss some previous research about low-power register file design.

2.1 Dynamic Voltage Scaling Technique

The dynamic voltage scaling (DVS) technique is widely used to reduce power consumption or leakage energy for hardware components. The main idea of the DVS technique is to dynamically control supply voltages to a hardware by its working modes, including the active mode, the drowsy mode and the destroy mode, based on the access behaviors.

Most previous researches about the DVS technique focus on hardware solutions by utilizing hardware monitor to dynamically control the supply voltages. However, pure hardware solution has its drawbacks. For example, it may increase more hardware area due to the need of extra logic to control voltage scaling. In addition, the hardware solution does not precisely analyze overall program execution behavior, e.g., register usage; as a result, it cannot get much energy saving.

Due to these reasons, in recent years, the trend of the DVS technique has focused on coupling with the hardware/software co-design principle. This kind of approaches uses software analysis to get sufficient information from user programs, and then uses these information to help hardware components to switch among different working modes to get energy saving.

2.2 Hardware/Software Co-design for Register File

In [1], authors used the hardware/software co-design approach with the DVS technique to reduce register file energy. They analyze loop sections in a program to find unused registers, and then inserted power-controlling instructions in the loops to turn unused registers into drowsy mode. The advantages of this approach are easy analysis and simple implementation, because it focuses only on the loop sections. Also, it can reduce power-controlling instruction annotations, which may be the potential performance penalty. However, this approach, which did not consider other non-loop sections in a program, may possibly get little energy saving for the whole program.

3 Hardware/Software Co-design Approach

In this study, we propose a novel hardware/software co-design approach to exploit register usage for register-file energy saving. The proposed approach can be partitioned into the hardware part and the software part.

In the hardware part, we propose a voltage-scaling mechanism that contains two major components: the connected power-state-register design and the voltage-scaling control logic. The connected power-state-register is to record the power states (i.e., working modes) for multiple registers. The voltage-scaling control logic is to control different supply voltages to registers by individual working modes.

In the software part, we propose a power-controlling code annotation method that has two major components, including the power-controlling instruction design and the power-controlling code generation. The power-controlling instruction is to write a value into a power-state-register to change the working modes for multiple registers. The power-controlling code generation is to analyze the register-usage in a program and annotate power-controlling instructions into the program, based on a proposed voltage-scaling strategy, to determine the register working modes.

3.1 The Hardware Part: Voltage-Scaling Mechanism

Fig. 1 shows the voltage-scaling mechanism. When a power-controlling instruction writes a new value into a connected power-state-register, the voltage-scaling control logic will switch the supply voltages to corresponding registers.

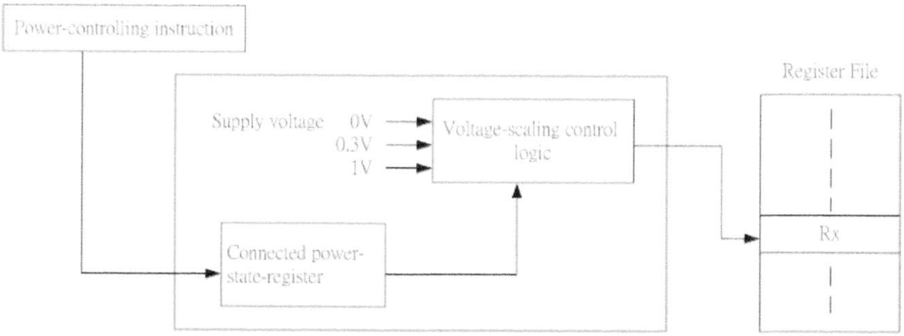

Fig. 1. Voltage-scaling mechanism

3.1.1 Connected Power-State-Register Design

The design goal of the proposed power-state-register is to reduce power-controlling instruction annotations for saving potential performance penalty. In conventional design, each register is controlled by an individual 1- or 2-bit power-state-register, causing that multiple sequential power-state-register updates require multiple sequential power-controlling instruction annotations. Therefore we "connected" those individual power-state-registers into a single multi-bit register, called the connected power-state-register, for merging multiple sequential updates into just one annotation. The number of the connected power-state-registers for a register file can be determined by $\lceil 2n/m \rceil$, where n is the total register number to be controlled, and m is the default length of a connected power-state-register.

3.1.2 Voltage-Scaling Control Logic

The design goal of the voltage-scaling control logic is to control different supply voltages by different working modes, including the active mode (1Volt), the drowsy mode (0.3Volt), and the destroy mode (0Volt). In [1], authors proposed a control logic by applying the "switch" characteristic of transistors to turning on/off the supply voltages for each register. In this paper, we use the same control logic, but the power-state-register is replaced by the proposed connected power-state-register, as shown in Fig. 1.

3.2 The Software Part: Power-Controlling Code Annotation

3.2.1 Power-Controlling Instruction Design

The power-controlling instruction writes a value into the connected power-state-register to control working modes for multiple registers. Through the connected power-state-register design, each value-update (i.e., instruction annotation) requires only few ISA modifications. We can directly use the instructions, e.g., ADD or SUB, to change the value of a connected-power-state-register at the time that the working modes of some registers should change. These instructions will be annotated in the program execution code to control the working modes for each register.

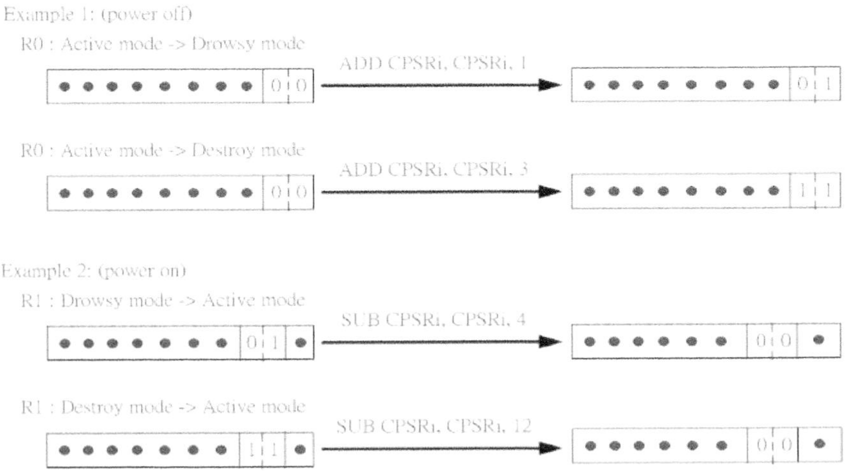

Fig. 2. Two examples of changing the working modes by ADD or SUB instructions

Fig. 2 shows two examples to change the working modes of registers R0 and R1 through ADD and SUB instructions, respectively. In example 1, if we want to change the working mode of R0 from the active mode to the drowsy mode, we can update the value of the connected power-state-register (CPSRi) by annotating the instruction "ADD CPSRi, CPSRi, 1". This is because the bit-0 and bit-1 of the CPSRi control the supply voltages to R0, and state "01" represents 0.3-Volt drowsy mode. Similarly, we can annotate the instruction "ADD CPSRi, CPSRi, 3" to represent the change of working mode from the active mode (00) to the destroy mode (11). Example 2, on the other hand, shows how to change the working mode of R1 (i.e., bit-2 and bit-3) from the drowsy mode (01), or from the destroy mode (11) to the active mode (00).

3.2.2 Power-Controlling Code Generation

To precisely predict register-usages in a program, we take the trace file for analysis. The reason to do so is that we can exactly measure how the power-controlling code affects power consumption and performance penalty during program execution. First, the program is partitioned into sections for register-usage analysis. In [1] authors take the loop body as analyzed sections (we call it the Loop-based approach for convenience). In this paper, we propose another two more straightforward partitioning approaches, i.e., partition the program by fixed interval (called the FI-based approach), and by basic blocks (called the BB-based approach), for sections not limited to loops. Though these three approaches (FI-, BB-, and Loop-based) are employed for simple analysis and easy implementation, they cannot precisely reflect register-usage. A more "making-sense" option would be the approach that partitions the program by register-live-ranges (we call it the RLR approach).

Fig. 3 shows the register-live-range graph for a piece of instruction sequences in program basicmath of benchmark MiBench [3]. (In Fig. 3, we draw the live-ranges by solid lines, as well as the access point of register contents by small circles.) From the register-live-range graph, we found that the distribution of live-ranges is not so uniform; there did exist "sparse" and "dense" sections. The sparse section, in fact, represents the section that has more chances we can get energy saving from it, due to large amounts of unused registers. On the other hand, the dense section represents the section that the register pressure is heavy, and it is not worth to annotate extra power-controlling instructions to enlarge either energy or performance penalties. Therefore, in the RLR approach, only sparse sections will be taken for register-usage analysis. The partitions of the sparse sections and the dense sections can be performed by setting a scanning line across the register-live-ranges. When the scanning line scans along each instruction, if intersection numbers is less than a threshold (IT), we call it in a sparse section, and vice versa. After scanning the whole program, we get the sparse and dense sections alternatively appeared in the register-live-range graph.

In a sparse section, there are two types of ranges can be considered for energy saving. The first type, called the type-I range as shown in Fig. 3, means that the corresponding register is temporarily unused, and we may change it to the drowsy mode (the data will be kept for later use). The other type, called the type-II range, means that the value in the corresponding register is no longer to be used, and we can change it to the destroy mode. For both types of ranges, we will apply the same energy cost function to judge whether it is worth to insert power-controlling instructions.

C. Performance Penalty

Fig. 6 shows the performance penalty for the four approaches. In Fig. 6, on average, the loop-based approach outperforms the other approaches by 17% ~ 23%. This is because the loop-based approach only considers the loop-sections in a program; hence, it results in the fewest power-controlling code annotations. On the other hand, the RLR approach performs better than the FI and BB -based approaches. This is because it focuses only on the sparse sections instead of the whole program. Hence, for the RLR approach, the number of power-controlling-code annotations can be limited.

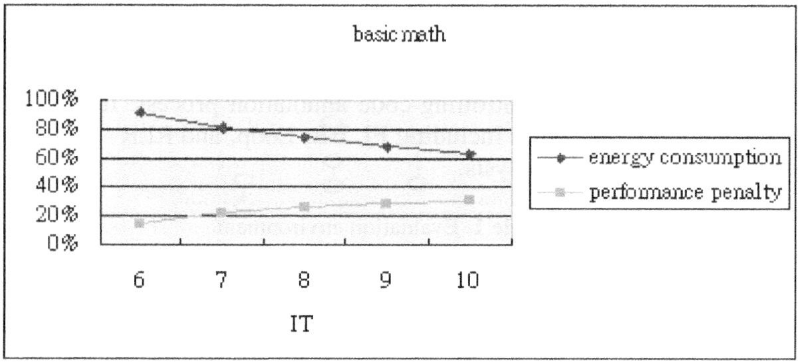

Fig. 4. Effect of IT in the RLR approach for basicmath of MiBench

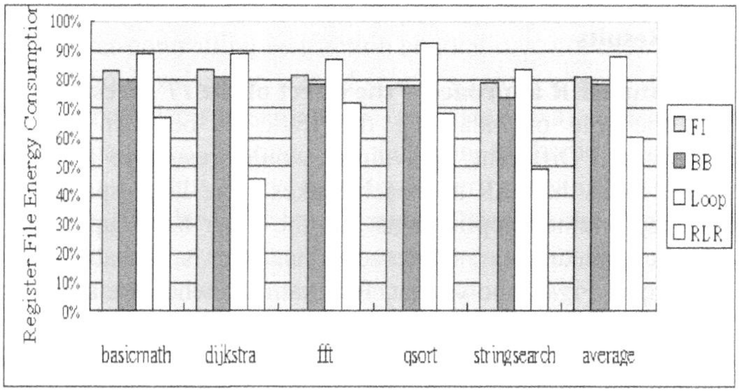

Fig. 5. Register-file energy-consumption for the four approaches

D. Energy-Delay Product

The energy-delay product is a widely-used metric to balance benefits in energy saving with any potential degradation in performance [2]. Fig. 7 shows the energy-delay products for the four approaches, and each approach is normalized to the FI approach. In Fig. 7, we find that the RLR approach would be a good choice among the others when the value of *IT* equals to 8. (It outperforms the other approaches by 21% - 67%.) This shows that the RLR approach gets a great balance between energy saving and performance penalty.

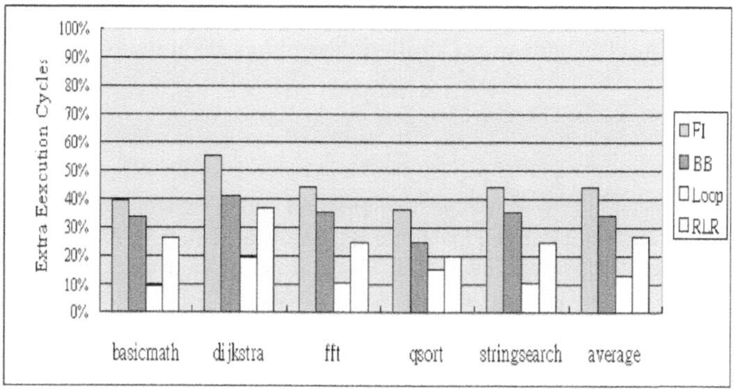

Fig. 6. Performance penalty for the four approaches

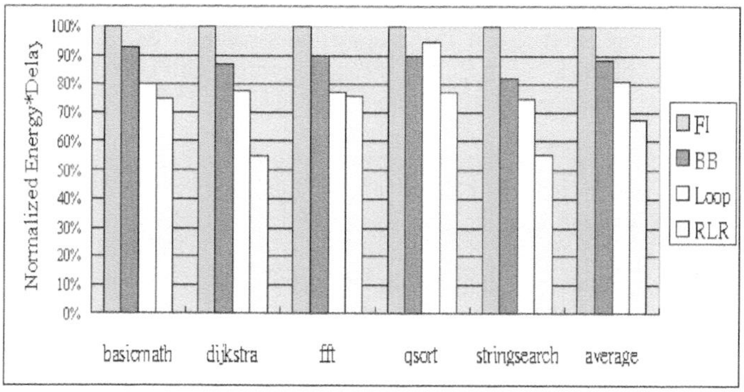

Fig. 7. Normalized energy-delay product for the four approaches

5 Conclusion

In this paper, we propose a hardware/software co-design approach for register-file energy saving. On the hardware part, we propose a voltage-scaling mechanism, including the connected power-state-register design and the voltage-scaling control logic. On the software part, we proposed a power-controlling code annotation mechanism, including the power-controlling instruction design and the power-controlling code generation. We partition the programs into sections to analyze register-usage. Simulation results show that the RLR-based approach outperforms the other partitioning approaches in terms of the energy, and energy-delay product. In addition, by varying the *IT* threshold in the RLR-based approach, the trade-off between energy saving and performance penalty can be well balanced.

There are some future works in this paper. For example, energy and performance penalty due to power-controlling code annotations could be reduced further by hardware supports. We know that a "power-on" instruction is annotated before a register tends to be read or updated. In fact, we can catch this register-usage information in early pipeline stages, e.g., ID stage, without compiler notification. By forwarding a signal from the ID stage to a voltage-scaling control logic, we can power up a register on time for later use. Detailed design has been under development.

References

1. J. L. Ayala,et al.: Power-Aware Compilation for Register File Energy Reduction. International Journal of Parallel Programming, Vol. 31, No. 6 (2003)
2. W.Zhang, et al.: Reducing Instruction Cache Energy Consumption Using a Compiler-based Strategy. ACM Transactions on Architecture and Code Optimization, Vol.1, No. 1 (2004)
3. M. R. Guthaus, et al.: MiBench: A free, commercially representative embedded benchmark suite. IEEE International Workshop on WWC-4, (2001) 3 – 14
4. D. Brooks, et al.: Wattch: A Framework for Architectural-Level Power Analysis and Optimizations. Proceedings of the 27th International Symposium on Computer Architecture (2000) 83 – 94
5. J. L. Ayala, et al.: Reducing Register File Energy Consumption using Compiler Support. Spanlish Ministry of Science and Technology under contract TIC 2000-0583-C02-02.
6. J. L. Ayala, et al.: Power-aware Register Renaming in High-Performance Processors using Compiler Support. Spanlish Ministry of Science and Technology under contract TIC 2003-0708.
7. J. L. Ayala, et al.: Energy-Efficient Register Renaming in High-Performance Processors. Spanlish Ministry of Science and Technology under contract TIC 2000-0583-C02-02.
8. J. Abella :On Reducing Register Pressure and Energy in Multiple-Banked Register Files. Proceedings of 21st International Conference on Computer Design (2003) 14 – 20
9. www.simplescalar.com/docs/simple_tutorial_v4.pdf
10. Http://www.arm.com/documentation/Software_Development_Tools/index.html

Hardware Concurrent Garbage Collection for Short-Lived Objects in Mobile Java Devices

Chi Hang Yau, Yi Yu Tan, Anthony S. Fong, and Wing Shing Yu

Department of Electronic Engineering, City University of Hong Kong,
Tat Chee Avenue, Hong Kong
Anthony.Fong@cityu.edu.hk

Abstract. jHISC is an object-oriented processor for embedded system aiming at accelerating Java execution by hardware approach. Garbage collection is one of the critical tasks in a Java Virtual Machine. In this paper, we have conduct a study of dynamic object allocation and garbage collection behavior of Java program based on SPECjvm 98 benchmark suite and MIDP applications for mobile phones. Life, size, and reference count distribution of Java objects are measured. We found most Java objects die very young, small in size and have small number reference counts. Reference counting object cache with hardware write barrier and object allocator is proposed to provide the hardware concurrent garbage collection for small size objects in jHISC. Hardware support on write barrier greatly reduces the overhead to perform the reference count update. The reference counting collector reclaims the memory occupied by object immediately after the object become garbage. The hardware allocator provides a constant time object allocation. From the investigation, over half of Java objects can be garbage collected by the object cache that makes it unnecessary for these objects to copy to the main memory.

1 Introduction

Java is a widely used programming technology for developing applications on different kinds of mobile devices. Fast product development, portability and secure environment are the advantages that Java offers for the mobile devices. Connected Limited Device Configuration (CLDC) and Mobile Information Device Profile (MIDP) provide the core application functionality required by mobile applications, in the form of a standardized Java runtime environment and a rich set of Java APIs. Sun Microsystems announce that there are over 250 million handsets already in people's hands which support Java, over 200 different Java handset models (globally) and around 77 network operators' deploying Java based Web services in worldwide.

Java KVM is the traditional JVM on mobile devices, simple mark-sweep algorithms are used to collect garbage objects. The mark-sweep collector traverses the heap from the root to determine the reachability, and then sweep the heap by collect the reclaimed memory into a freelist. The major weakness of the classic mark-sweep GC method is that all other threads within JVM have to be suspended while the garbage collector is running. The suspension time is directly proportional to the number of objects on the heap.

L.T. Yang et al. (Eds.): EUC 2005, LNCS 3824, pp. 47 – 56, 2005.

In the MIDP study, we focus on the object life. We have modified the source code of the KVM to trigger garbage collector before every object allocation. The garbage collection scheme used on KVM is the simple Mark-Sweep algorithm. It is a Stop-the-World algorithm. Only garbage collector thread is active during garbage collection in progress, and other threads are suspended [5]. Object allocation is not allowed during garbage collection in progress. After the garbage collection is completed, no newly created object is in the object that makes sure all the memory used by the garbage objects are freed and available immediately for further object allocation.

Table 2. Accumulative Distribution of Object Size on Java MIDP applications

Applications	Percentage of objects which the size is smaller than <= 48 bytes
WebViewer	87.01%
WormGame	91.00%
PhotoAlbum	91.28%
AudioDemo	92.75%
Overall	90.51%

3.1 Size Distribution

The object size is the first category we are concerned. On KVM runtime environment, each object has an object header which is 2 words (a word is 32-bit) in size. The minimum size of an object in KVM is 8 bytes. Each data inside Java object would use a word to store, regardless if it is an integer or a character. In our study, we found that most object sizes are small. Over 90% of objects are equal to or smaller than 48 bytes (12 words).

3.2 Age Distribution

The relative age of an object we defined is the number of objects allocated between the object allocation and de-allocation events. According to the example of figure 2, there are two object allocation events between the allocation and de-allocation of object A. Based on the definition, the relative age of object A is 3. Applying the same rule on object C, the life of object C is zero.

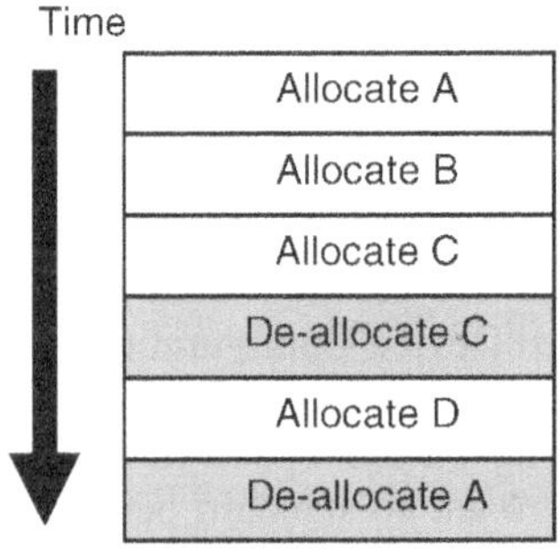

Fig. 2. Definition of relative age for Java objects

We found that more than half of the Java objects (~50%) have relative ages of 0, and over 90% of objects have relative ages less than 16. We can make a conclusion that the life span of a typical object in embedded Java environment is short. Half of the Java objects can be garbage collected immediately before an object allocation event.

Table 3. Accumulative Distribution of Object AGE on Java MIDP applications

Applications	AGE = 0	AGE <=15
WebViewer	30.92%	83.54%
WormGame	55.80%	92.41%
PhotoAlbum	62.95%	95.59%
AudioDemo	58.15%	92.81%
Overall	51.95%	91.09%

3.3 Reference-Count Distribution

Jikes RVM (Research Virtual Machine) is used to study the reference-count of Java objects. It is designed to execute Java programs that are typically used in research on fundamental virtual machine design issues [9].

Our experiment is mainly targeted on the reference-counting collector. We are interested in the reasonable maximum reference-count of java objects. Through the experiment of running JVM SPEC 98 [17] in RVM, the reference-count of each object is obtained. We have modified the object header of the RVM in order to record the maximum reference-count of the object. The maximum value of the maximum reference-count is set to 255. If it is overflow, the reference-count will be reset to zero, and the object is subject to garbage collection.

According to the measurement, the average value of the maximum references is small (<= 2). There are over 99% of objects of which the maximum reference-count is less than or equal to two. Therefore, four bits for reference-count for each object are sufficient to cover 99% of Java objects.

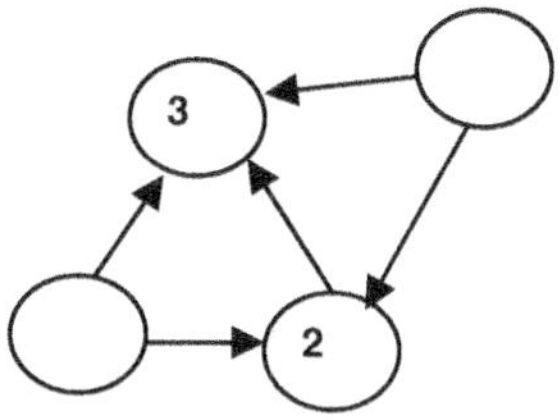

Fig. 3. Definition of reference count for Java objects

4 jHISC Architecture

In Java bytecode specification, there are several instructions defined to perform the tasks of the object-oriented features such as invokevirtual and putstatic. The ratio of the object-oriented bytecodes (including access constant pool instruction and method call instructions) on SPEC JVM 98 benchmark is 31.87% [17]. Object-oriented instructions are added into jHISC instructions set in order to accelerate the object-manipulation operations by hardware support.

In jHISC architecture, three-address register-to register instruction form is used. jHISC processor have a register engine which contains 32 general registers of32 bits wide. Beside the 32-bit data, each register contains a 4-bit type field to describe the type of the data inside the register. During the process of the method invocations caused by ivk instruction, a method frame is allocated in the register. The method frame acts as the stack frame in Java virtual machine which is the method code working space. The register engine can be used to translate all the stack operations, which defined in Java bytecode, into 3 addressing jHISC instructions to accelerate the execution of Java applications.

5 Garbage Collection for Young Object

Generational garbage collection is used. The whole object heap is divided into two generation spaces. They are young space and mature space. All the new objects will be allocated in young space. Objects will be promoted into mature space after it is still alive in the young space for a period of time. In order to support real-time application, concurrent garbage collection will be used in both generation spaces. On this paper, we are focusing on the young space.

5.1 Reference Counting Object Cache

The main design concern of the memory management in young space is to provide fast object allocation. According to the research about the java object size and life, we have found that in most Java programs the vast majority of objects (often >95%) are very short-lived (i.e. are used as temporary data structures), small in size (90% objects =< 48 bytes). The object allocation occurs frequently.

The purpose of the scheme is to hold objects with their respective reference-counts in the cache to speedup the algorithm. The reference-count is modified directly in the cache to avoid accessing the main memory. For each instruction which will copy, delete or set a reference between two objects, it will check if the objects are held on the cache or not. If all the objects involved by this instruction are on the cache, the reference-count of these objects will be modified concurrently while the instruction is executing.

When the reference-count becomes zero, this implies that the object is not referenced by other objects and the running program cannot reach it. The cache line occupied by this object can then be reclaimed by the collector. When the reference-count of an object stays on cache overflow, it will be promoted to the mature space. Its reference-count field will be invalidated and it will be ignored by the reference-counting collector. Beside newly allocated instance objects, objects residing in the main

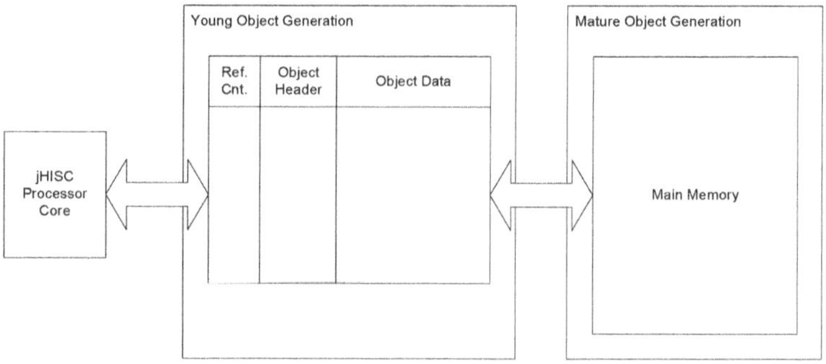

Fig. 4. Overview of jHISC Garbage Collection scheme

memory are allowed to be brought into the cache. In these cases, their reference-counts are set to all "1"s and they will not be collected by the reference-counting collector.

There is a 3-bit reference-count field to store the reference-count. Zero represents that the object is garbage and all '1's represents overflow. There is an M-bit to represent that the object has references form the mature space's object.

One of the main drawbacks of reference-counting is its computational expense. Therefore, we only maintain reference-count of an object in the cache. After an object is moved out from the cache, it will not be collected by the reference-counting collector and the reference-count on the cache will be invalidated. It reduces the computational expense for adjusting the reference-count in main memory.

5.2 Object Allocation for Small Size Objects

Object creation takes place in the object-cache directly instead on the main memory. As the lifetimes of small-size object in Java are short and there are spatial localities in the memory allocation and deallocation patterns in Java, hardware object allocator is proposed to do the small block sizes memory allocations and deallocations. Many of objects will die in the cache, without ever being written to the main memory.

A separated object allocation bit vector and a decision tree are used to allocate an object in hardware level [6] [7]. Buddy System is used to find the appropriate contiguous free bits in a bit vector. This allocation scheme supports the objects sizes of power of two. In our instance object cache, each object will occupy a whole cache line. The young object space is divided into slots of same size. Design of the binary tree can be further simplified. The object allocator determines if there is an available slot or not. If so, the allocator locates the address.

Objects of data size smaller or equal to a cache line, are allocated in the cache directly by the hardware object allocator. For objects of size greater than a cache line, the allocation request will be transferred to the operating system. These objects will be allocated in the mature object space. A free list is maintained by the memory manager of the operating system. Suitable free space will be searched to adapt the allocation request.

10. H.Azatchi and E. Petrank. Integration generations with advanced reference counting garbage collectors. In International Conference on Compiler Construction, Warsaw, Poland, Apr. 2003.
11. D. F. Bacon and V. T. Rajan. Concurrent cycle collection in reference counted systems. In J. L. Kuden Knudsen, editor, Proceedings of 15th European Conference on Object-Oriented Programming Languages, New Orleans, Louisiana, January 15-17, 2003, volume 38(1) of ACM SIGPLAN Notices. ACM Press, Jan. 2003.
12. L. Peter Deutsch and Daniel G. Bobrow. An efficient incremental automatic garbage collector. Communications of the ACM, 19(9):522-526, September 1976.
13. Geoergo E.Collins. A method for overlapping and erasure of lists. Communications of the ACM, 3(12):655-657, December 1960.
14. Adele Goldberg and D. Robson. Smalltalk-80: The Language and its Implementation. Addison-Weslev, 1983.
15. Larry Wall and Randal L. Scheartz. Programming Perl, O'Reilly and Associates, Inc., 1991.
16. Sun claims it's winning developer space, http://www.theinquirer.net, May, 2004
17. Young-Min Lee, Byung-Chul Tak, Hye-Seon Maeng, and Shin-Dug Kim. Real-Time Java Machine for Information Appliances. IEEE Transactions, volume 46, issue 4, p.949-957. 2000.
18. SPEC JVM98. http://www.specbench.org/osg/jvm98/

An Effective Instruction Cache Prefetch Policy by Exploiting Cache History Information*

Soong Hyun Shin, Cheol Hong Kim, and Chu Shik Jhon

Department of Electrical Engineering and Computer Science,
Seoul National University, Shilim-dong, Kwanak-gu, Seoul, Korea
{shordan, kimch, csjhon}@panda.snu.ac.kr

Abstract. The hit ratio of the first level cache is one of the most important factors in determining the performance of embedded computer systems. Prefetching from lower level memory structure is one of the techniques for improving the hit ratio of the first level cache. This paper proposes an effective prefetch scheme for the first level instruction cache by exploiting cache history information. The proposed scheme utilizes two factors to improve the prefetch efficiency: the disparity of block size between memory hierarchies and continuous same page hits. According to our simulations, the proposed prefetching scheme improves the performance by up to 6.3%.

Keywords: Computer architecture, embedded processor, instruction cache, cache prefetching.

1 Introduction

Minimizing the average data access time is crucial in designing embedded computer systems. As the gap between processor cycle speed and memory access time grows, access time to lower level memory structure has increased dramatically. Accordingly, first level cache plays one of the most important roles in determining the performance of computer systems.

Many researchers have examined how to improve the hit ratio of the first level cache. Prefetching from lower level memory structure is one of the techniques to improve the hit ratio of the first level cache. Prefetching can be implemented by software or hardware. Software-based prefetching needs compiler supports to insert prefetch instructions selectively by analyzing the program. However, it is very difficult to predict the block to be prefetched precisely at compile time, resulting in passing up many prefetching opportunities. Contrary to the software-based prefetching, hardware-based prefetching can use run-time information to predict the block to be prefetched. However, hardware-based prefetching schemes require additional hardware overhead. In this paper, we propose a hardware-based prefetching scheme to improve the hit ratio of the first level instruction cache (iL1) with little hardware overhead.

* This work was supported by Brain Korea 21.

L.T. Yang et al. (Eds.): EUC 2005, LNCS 3824, pp. 57–66, 2005.

The hardware-based prefetching schemes are classified into sequential prefetching schemes and non-sequential prefetching schemes. Smith proposed sequential prefetching scheme for the first time[1]. OBL (One Block Lookahead) scheme[1] initiates prefetching only for the sequential block. There are three ways in prefetching by OBL scheme: always-prefetch, prefetch-on-miss and tagged-prefetch. The always-prefetch scheme prefetches the next block on each reference, so it increases the number of cache lookups significantly. The prefetch-on-miss scheme simply prefetches the next block only when one block is required due to a cache miss. The tagged-prefetch scheme is a modified version of the prefetch-on-miss scheme. It associates a tag bit with every memory block, and the tag bit is used to avoid prefetching same block again. Dahlgren et al. proposed an adaptive sequential prefetching scheme, varying the prefetch degree (the number of blocks to prefetch) dynamically[2]. In this scheme, the proportion of useful prefetches to total prefetches is periodically calculated. The prefetch degree is controlled according to the proportion. Jouppi suggested a FIFO stream buffer, which contains prefetched blocks before they are brought into the cache, to avoid cache pollution due to prefetching[3]. Each block in the buffer is brought into the cache if it is referenced, then a new block is pushed into the FIFO stream buffer. The cache pollution is avoided by using this buffer. However, if a cache miss occurs and the requested block is not located in the head entry of the buffer, the buffer is flushed and new sequences of blocks are fetched to the buffer, resulting in no use of prefetched blocks. The fetch directed instruction prefetching scheme[4] proposed by Reinman et al., one of the non-sequential prefetch schemes, utilizes the branch predictor for predicting program stream. In this scheme, the prefetch unit prefetches blocks according to the predicted program stream. Similar to the fetch directed instruction prefetching scheme, the execution history guided instruction prefetching scheme[5] proposed by Zhang et al. utilizes execution history. It is done by correlating execution history with cache miss history. Batcher et al. proposed the cluster miss prediction scheme for embedded cpu instruction caches[6]. The scheme is for real-time networking applications, so they profiles the characters of the dedicated application traces.

In most prefetch schemes, there are two types of references to the lower level memory structure; actual lookup and prefetch lookup. The actual lookup, caused by a cache miss in the first level cache, services normal memory reference. The prefetch lookup is caused by a predicted memory reference. If the prefetch prediction is incorrect, the prefetch lookup is turned out to be unsuccessful. These unsuccessful prefetch lookups increase the contention to the lower level memory structure without any contribution to the hit ratio of the first level cache.

For the iL1, utilizing sequential prefetch is more effective than non-sequential prefetch[7], but sequential prefetches increase the traffic to the lower level memory structure significantly. To reduce the traffic, we propose a prefetch scheme which doesn't request the prefetch lookup to the lower level memory structure separately, but requests the missed block and the next block simultaneously when a cache miss occurs. It is done by simply doubling the block fetch size. Moreover, the proposed scheme improves the prefetch accuracy by tracing the memory page access pattern of executed instruction sequence.

The rest of this paper is organized as follows. Section 2 describes the motivation of this paper. Section 3 presents the proposed prefetching scheme. Section 4 describes our evaluation methodology and shows detailed simulation results. Section 5 concludes this paper.

2 Motivation

It is commonly regarded that the program control flows sequentially. Generally, branch instructions occupy only 0 – 30% of total instructions[8][9]. Therefore, most instructions are expected to be accessed sequentially in the iL1. We try to exploit benefits from this characteristic of the program. Fig.1 shows the probability according to the relative distance between continuously referenced cache blocks in the iL1, obtained from our simulations using SimpleScalar[10]. We simulated 22 benchmarks from SPEC CPU2000[9]. The relative distance in the graph denotes the distance between continuously referenced cache blocks in the iL1. For example, in case that $n+1$th instruction is referenced after nth instruction in the iL1, the relative distance is one if the $n+1$th instruction is within the next block to the block containing nth instruction. In this graph, we excluded the probability of accessing same cache block (the relative distance is zero). The probability (the nth and the $n+1$th instruction are within the same block in the iL1) is meaningless with respect to prefetching, because the needed block is already located in the iL1. As shown in Fig.1, the probability that the relative distance is one is over 70%. From this result, we realized that the next block is referenced in the iL1 with very high probability after one cache block is referenced. Therefore, the hit ratio of the iL1 is expected to increase if the next block is prefetched from lower level memory structure when one block is requested due to iL1 cache miss. However, prefetching every next cache block is very expensive, because it may increase the bus contention significantly.

To find the way to maximize the prefetch efficiency, we also observed the relative distance between continuously referenced blocks in case that two blocks

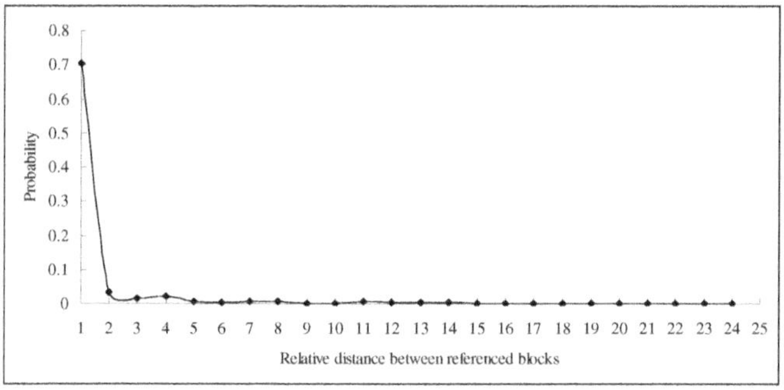

Fig. 1. The probability according to the relative distance between instructions executed. (Instruction cache block size=32B, Memory page size=4KB).

As described, the CSPA scheme requests the missed block and the next block simultaneously when a cache miss occurs and two conditions(as described above) are satisfied. It is done by simply doubling the block fetch size. To make it possible, we assume that the *fetch size* signal(Fig.3(b)) controls whether the L2 returns one sub-block or two sub-blocks.

It is easily noticed whether missed block is the last sub-block of the L2 cache block. The block offset of the L2 cache is divided into two fields: the lower field is a part overlapped by the block offset of the iL1, the upper field is the other part that indicates the sub-block in the L2 cache. Fig.5 shows an example. Memory address is divided into a tag, an index, and a block offset (Fig.5(a)). Fig.5(b) and Fig.5(c) depict the block offset masks of iL1 and L2, respectively. In this example, the iL1 cache block size is 32 bytes and the L2 cache block size is 256

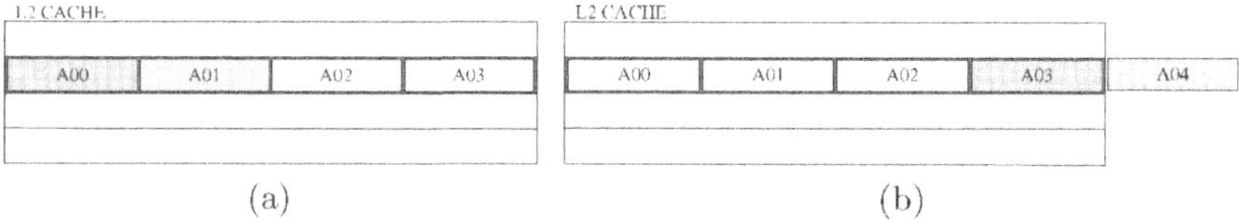

Fig. 4. Examples of allocation of a missed block and a prefetched block

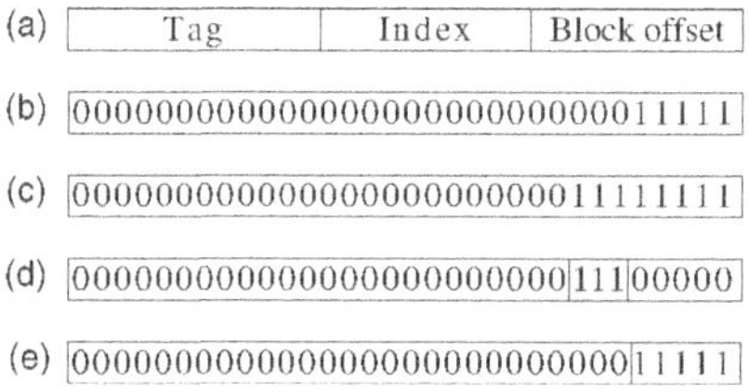

Fig. 5. Example of block offset masks and a last sub-block mask

bytes, that is, the bit widths of block offset are 5 and 8, respectively. The lower field of L2 block offset mask, shown in the Fig.5(e), is not used in the L2. L2 cache is searched by the upper field (Fig.5(d)) to find the sub-block which is requested by the first level cache. If the higher field is filled with '1', the requested block is the last sub-block of the L2 cache block. As shown in the Fig.5(d), if we apply XOR to the block offset of the iL1 and L2, the result is the $last\ sub-block\ mask$, indicated the upper field.

Consequently, through this operation, if the missed block is not the last sub-block, the *double block enable*(Fig.3(b)) is set. If all two enable signals, the *fetch enable* and the *double block enable*, are set, *fetch size* is set and the prefetch unit requests two blocks from the L2 cache(Fig.3(b)).

4 Performance Evaluation

4.1 Simulation Model

In order to determine the performance of the proposed prefetching scheme, we simulatated various benchmarks using SimpleScalar simulator[10]. Simulated applications are selected from SPEC2000 suite[9]. Simulated system parameters are shown in Table 1.

Table 1. System Parameters

System Parameter	Value
Processor	2-way superscalar processor
Level 1 instruction cache	16KB, 4way, 32bytes cache line, 1cycle latency
Level 1 data cache	16KB, 4way, 32bytes cache line, 1cycle latency, write-back
Level 2 cache	unified, 256KB, 8way, 256bytes cache line, 8cycle latency
Memory latency	32cycle latency + 1 cycles/8bytes

4.2 Simulation Results

At first, we simulated to determine the threshold value for the CSPH. Fig.6 shows the iL1 cache miss ratio and normalized execution time for various threshold values. The execution time is normalized to no-prefetch scheme. In the graph, 'CSPA-n' means that the threshold value is n. As shown in Fig.6, the CSPA-1, CSPA-2, and CSPA-4, show better performance than the others. We choose '4' for the threshold value among 1, 2, and 4 because the total number of prefetched instructions in the CSPA-4 scheme is less than the others. If the threshold value is too high, the performance degrades. As shown in Fig.6, as the threshold value increases, the iL1 miss ratio and the execution time increase. It is because, the successful prefetch ratio increases slightly as the threshold value increases, but

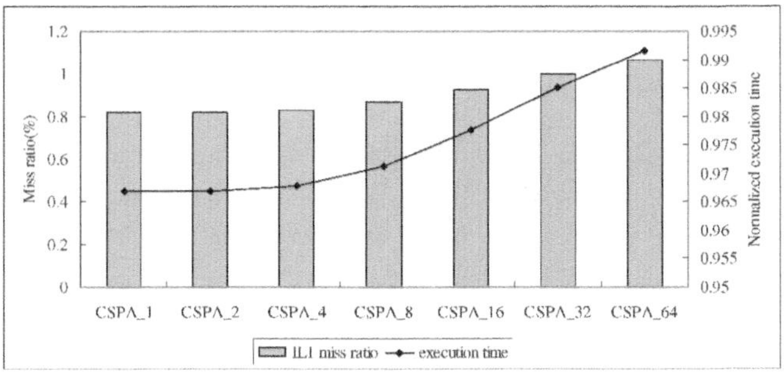

Fig. 6. Level 1 instruction cache miss ratio and normalized execution time. The execution time is normalized to no-prefetch scheme.

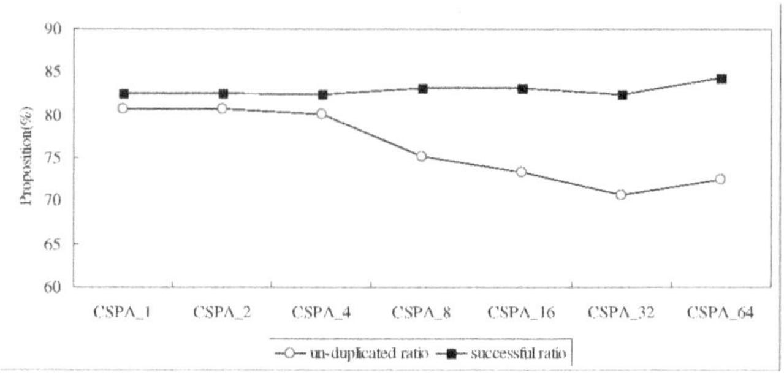

Fig. 7. The un-duplicated ratio and the successful ratio of prefetch for various prefetch configurations

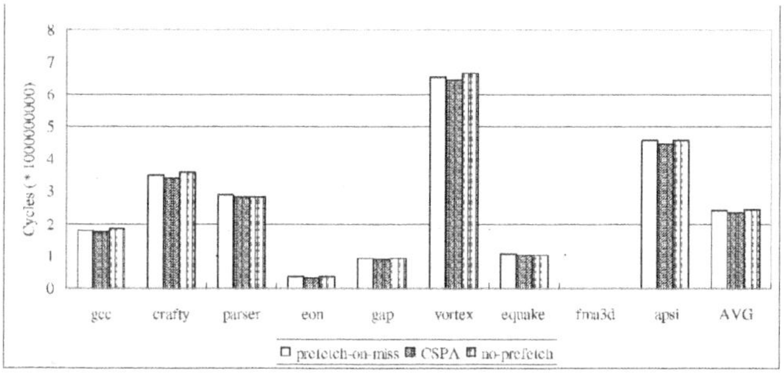

Fig. 8. The execution time for SPEC2000 benchmarks

the un-duplicated ratio decreases conspicuously as shown in Fig.7. The successful prefetch ratio is the proportion that prefetched block is used in the iL1 before it is evicted from the iL1, and the duplicated prefetch ratio is the proportion that prefetched block is useless because the block is already located in the iL1. It is because while the CSPH increases (instructions within the same page are referenced continuously), the probability increases that the prefetched blocks are already referenced. Besides we found the probability of accessing the next block is 84% when executed instructions are within the same page, as shown in the Fig.2, and the successful prefetch ratio of the CSPA is 82 – 84%. It means that the CSPA utilizes the sequential characteristic of benchmarks so effectively to maximize the prefetch efficiency and the successful prefetch ratio doesn't increase any more.

We compare the CSPA with the no-prefetch scheme and the prefetch-on-miss scheme, because the CSPA needs hardware overhead comparable to that of these two schemes, and other schemes like[4], [5], and [6] uses tables to keep informations which are heavier than the hardware cost of CSPA. In the iL1, the sequential prefetch scheme outperforms the non-sequential scheme[7] and hardware cost of sequential prefetch is less than that of non-sequential prefetch.

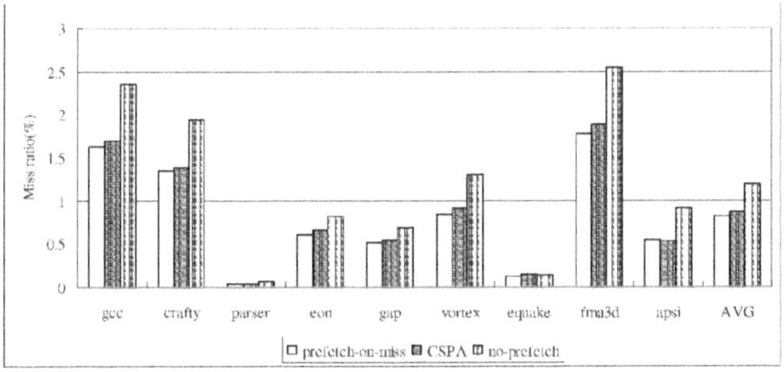

Fig. 9. The miss ratio for SPEC2000 benchmarks

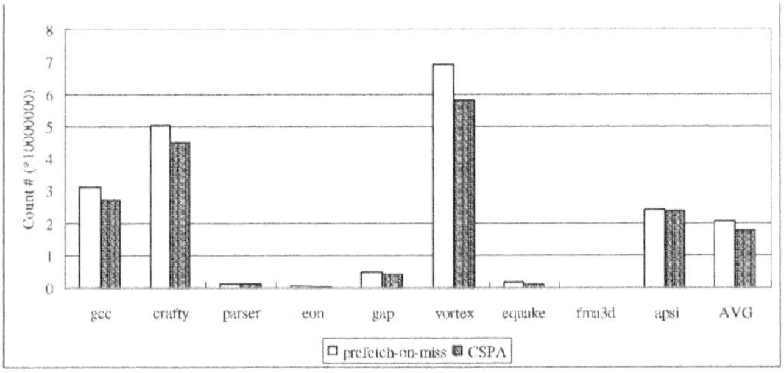

Fig. 10. The total number of prefetch for SPEC2000 benchmarks

Fig.8 and Fig.9 show the execution time and the miss ratio in the iL1. As shown in Fig.8, the performance of the CSPA is superior to other schemes. The CSPA outperforms the no-prefetch by 3.3% on the average and especially in the benchmarks, crafty and equake, the performances increase 5.3% and 6.3%,respectively. The CSPA also outperforms the prefetch-on-miss by 2.4% on the average. The miss ratio of the no-prefetch is 1.14% and that of the CSPA is 0.82%. The CSPA reduces miss ratio by 0.3%. Though the miss ratio of the prefetch-on-miss is less than that of the CSPA, the execution time of the CSPA is better. It is because the prefetch-on-miss performs prefetches 14% more than the CSPA, as shown in Fig.10. It is shown well in the benchmarks, gcc, crafty and vortex. As compared with the prefetch-on-miss scheme, the miss ratio of the CSPA is higher by 0.1% and the execution time is less by 2%. The reason of this conflicting result is that the CSPA reduces the total number of prefetch by 15.6%.

5 Conclusions

We have proposed the prefetch on continuous same page access scheme, which utilizes the disparity of block size between iL1 and the lower level memory structure and continuous same page hits. The simulation shows that the CSPA scheme

IPs in SoC. Such on-chip interconnection networks provide a high-performance chip-level communication infrastructure with regularity and modularity. Fig. 1 shows the communication infrastructure of NoC with a 2D-mesh tile-based architecture [2], [3], [4], [5].

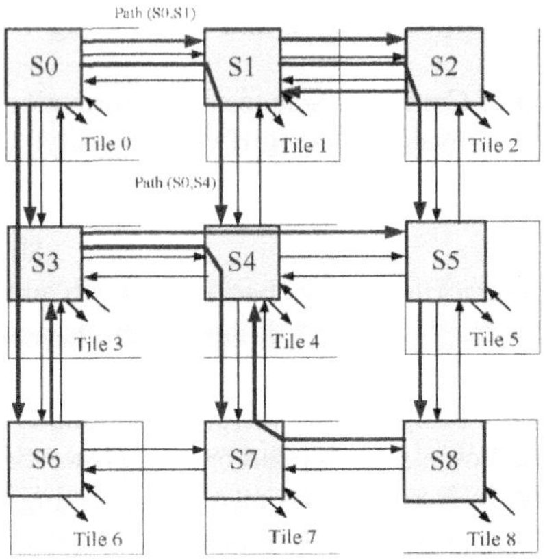

Fig. 1. The communication infrastructure of NoC with a 2D-mesh tile-based architecture. The dotted lines indicate some of the circuit paths provided by the circuit-switched network.

The major component in the communication infrastructure of NoC is the routing switch. In Fig. 1, each switch connects up to four neighboring switches and an associated local tile. The switch forwards packets from an input port to the destined output port according to the routing result of the network. In many applications such as multimedia, mobile component, telecommunication and consumer electronics, the characteristics of the communication traffic between IPs can be diversified. The switch needs to efficiently utilize the limited bandwidth of the links to deliver communication data between IPs and satisfies the different requirements of IPs. However, VLSI design is very cost-sensitive, and the required communication quality-of-service (QoS) must be achieved at a reasonable cost.

The circuit-switched network is suitable for NoC architectures since the transmission latency and throughput can be guaranteed. Furthermore, the complexity of the switch architecture in the circuit-switched network is low since its main function is to connect the incoming links to the outgoing links. The drawback of circuit-switched networks is locking resources for the duration of the data transfer. However, this can be alleviated by using virtual channel networks.

In this paper, we address a pre-scheduled circuit-switched network. Such network is suitable for the on-chip network. We also design and implement three efficient switches for such on-chip network. Compared with the design proposed in [9], our first design provides a lower cost. Furthermore, for decreasing the cost and latency, we design other two switch architectures. Our design provides high performance at a reasonable cost.

The next section describes the architecture of the circuit-switched network briefly. In Section 3, we present the design of our switches. Section 4 shows the implementation results. Finally, concluding remarks are given in Section 5.

2 Circuit-Switched Networks for SoC

When a sender wants to deliver data to a receiver in a circuit-switched network, the communication path between the sender and the receiver is established firstly. If there are lots of communication paths in the network at the same time, a link may be shared by multiple paths. Fig. 1 has shown such a network for example. In this diagram, the dotted lines represent the communication paths. The two paths *path(S0,S1)* and *path(S0,S4)* share the link between *Tile0* and *Tile1*. Time-division multiplexing (TDM) technique can solve the problems of sharing links. In TDM, a frame is divided into a fixed number of time slots. When a communication circuit is established across a TDM link, the network allocates a certain number of time slots in each frame of this circuit for the sole use of data transmission.

Before transmitting data, traditional computer networks use the routing probe to establish communication circuits. The routing probe progresses toward the destination to reserve a certain number of time slots for a communication circuit as it is transmitted through intermediate switches. When the probe reaches the destination, the communication circuit has been set up and an acknowledgement is transmitted back to the source. The circuit is released as the data has been transmitted. Fig. 2 shows the time-space diagram of a circuit-switched message. In such architecture, switches need to allocate the valid time slots for the circuit setup. If the network is congested, the setup time t_{setup} might be unacceptable. The traditional computer networks use this approach to achieve guaranteed service, since the communication paths in the cyberspace are too diverse to predict.

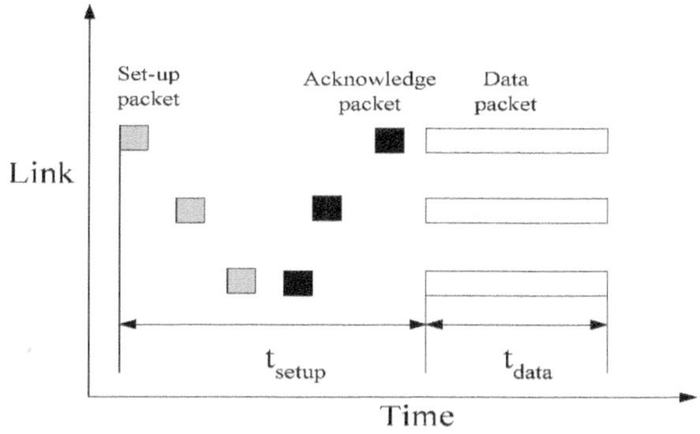

Fig. 2. The time-space diagram of a circuit-switched message

In NoC design, the requirements of communication between IPs are estimated before they are assigned to the tiles. The pre-established circuit-switched network is appropriate for NoC. In many methodologies of NoC approaches [4], [6], [7], [10], a mapping algorithm is needed to map IPs onto the tiles in the NoC architecture. The mapping algorithm must consider the communication delays and bandwidths between the tiles while it maps the IPs onto the tiles. Thus, after all IPs have been mapped, the communication paths among the tiles of the NoC are potentially existent. Switches can use a table in the switch to store the routing information. Therefore, before transmitting data, switches do not have to set up a communication circuit.

There have been several recent studies on NoC architectures [2], [3], [4], [5], [8], [9], [11], [12], [13], [14], [15], [16], [17]. In [12], the proposed architecture differs from others in that they use the Butterfly Fat Tree architecture as the backbone of NoC. They also design a switch with wormhole routing for their NoC architecture. In [9], a guaranteed-throughput switch is presented. Their switch supports unicast and multicast with pre-scheduling. The input buffers and output buffers in this switch use several frame buffers implemented with random access memory. The cost of their design is too high to be useful in the on-chip network.

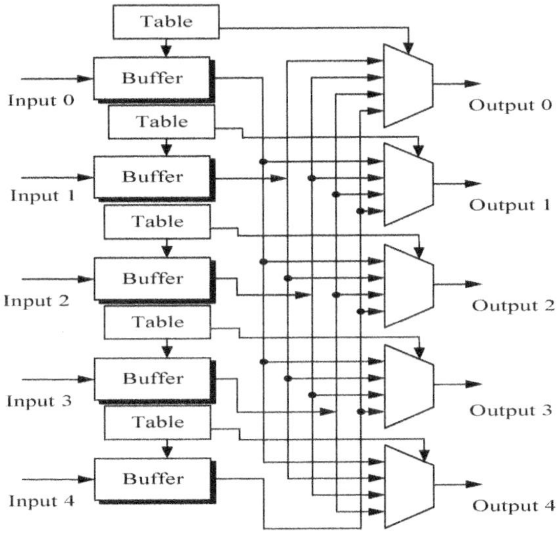

Fig. 3. The diagram of input buffering architecture

Switches connect to up to five links, as *S4* in Fig. 1. An arriving flit may be stored in the buffer firstly. The output port of the switch selects a flit from the buffer and injects it into the network according to the routing table. In the buffering strategy, we distinguish *output buffering* and *input buffering* by the location of buffers inside the switch [13]. An input buffering architecture is shown in Fig. 3. In this architecture, the buffers are at the inputs of the switch. This architecture needs a routing table to determine at which times which buffers are connected to which output ports with contention freedom. In this switch, flits from the input ports are buffered awaiting transmission by the output ports. The size of a frame buffer, FB, in the switch is:

$$FB = BW \times N \times S \quad (1)$$

where BW is the link bandwidth, N is the number of time slots, and S is the interval of the time slot. With a link bandwidth of 1Gbps, the number of time slots of 16, and the interval of the time slot of 2μs, the size of the FB is more than 33Kb. The sizes of the buffer in previously proposed architectures are over than two frames [9], [13].

Since NoC architecture design is cost-sensitive, the buffer size must be decreased as much as possible. We hence propose the switch architecture with only a frame buffer at every input.

We show the diagram of this architecture with one input and its associated output port in Fig. 4. We omit the global signals such as *clocks*, *reset* and some stimulating signals in this diagram for simplicity. In this architecture, each input has a frame buffer (FB) and two *input slot address tables*, ISATa and ISATb. The FB is used to store the input frame data, while the ISATs are used to store the addresses of the input data in the FBs. Each output port has a private *input time slot table* (ITST), and the ITST has two fields, *input port* (IP), *input time slot* (ITS). Furthermore, each input port has a private *output port table* (OPT). The OPT and the ITST determine at which times which buffers are connected to their output port respectively.

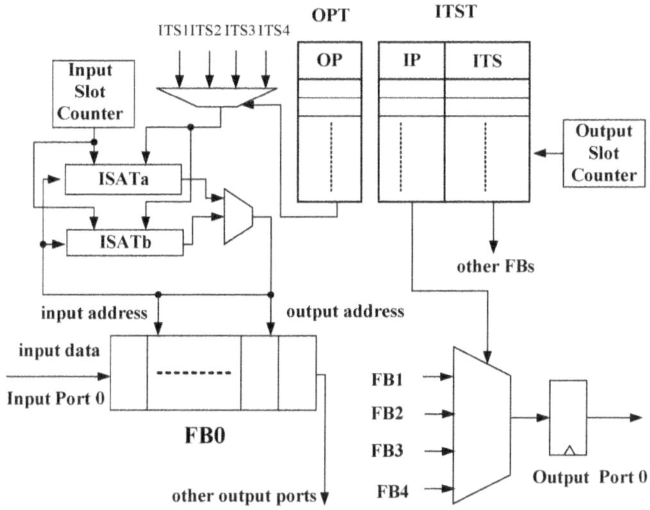

Fig. 4. The switch architecture with a frame buffer at each input

Latency is defined as the duration of a packet being transported from the sender to the receiver. The major factors of the latency are the latency of the switch and latency of the link, denoted by L_s and L_l. The latency for sending one bit of data from tile $tile_i$ to tile $tile_j$ can be analytically calculated as:

$$L_{bit}^{tile_i,tile_j} = \sum_{i \le n_{hops}} L_{S_i} + (n_{hops} - 1) \times L_l \tag{2}$$

where n_{hops} is the number of switches the bit passes on its way from tile $tile_i$ to tile $tile_j$. If the latencies of all switches in NoC are equal, the equation (5) becomes:

$$L_{bit}^{tile_i,tile_j} = n_{hops} \times L_s + (n_{hops} - 1) \times L_l \tag{3}$$

4 Implementation

We have implemented the designs described in the above. We use pipelining technique to improve the performance. This architecture has three pipeline stages. The number of the time slots in a frame is 16. The data bus of the input port is 128 bits. We need one clock cycle for a packet crossing a link. Thus, the packet size is 128 bits. The table setup circuit is responsible for setting up the OPT and ITST and forwards the setup message to the next switch. Before initializing the system, the data for the setup table must be pre-scheduled and generated by a software scheduler. The scheduler could be part of the EDA tools for the NoC platform. On the other hand, we can also embed the scheduler into the chip and run be a processor core. Such design can dynamically schedule the circuits in NoC. Our design can support both scheduling methods.

Table 1 illustrates the chip area of three designs. Each is a 5 × 5 switch with a clock rate of at least 1 GHz supporting 16 time slots. The link width of the first and the third architectures is 128 bits while the second is 32 bits. The size of the buffer at each input of the switch for the first and the second architectures is a frame while the third is half a frame. In the experiment results, the third architecture reduces the cost significantly.

Table 1. Chip areas of three designs

Switch Architecture	Chip Area
128 bits with one frame buffer at each input	1.48mm^2
32 bits with one frame buffer at each input	0.4mm^2
128 bits with half a frame buffer at each input	0.26mm^2

Table 2. The comparison between our design and others

Design	Link Width	Freq.	A. Bandwidth	Area	Technology
Ours	128	1GHz	640Gb/s	0.26mm^2	0.18μm
[8]	32	185MHz	29.6Gb/s	3.5 mm^2	0.25μm
[13]	32	500MHz	80Gb/s	0.175mm^2	0.13μm

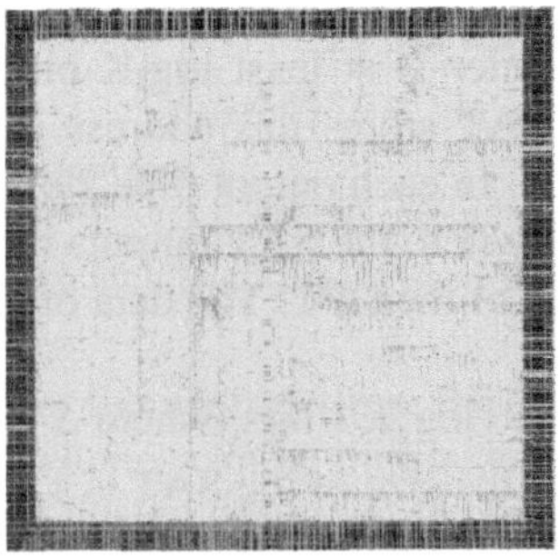

Fig. 7. The layout of the design of 128 bits with one frame buffer at each input

We have used TSMC 0.18μm technology to implement our designs. The layout of the first design in the table is shown in Fig. 7. Our chip has an aggregate bandwidth of 5 × 1 GHz × 128 bits = 640 Gbit/s. Table 2 shows the comparison between our design and others. In [8], a switch for multiprocessor with latency insensitive NoC is proposed. In [13], their switch also provides both circuit-switched and packet-switched transmissions. To reduce area, they have implemented a dedicated FIFO architecture with full-custom design. However, our design achieves higher throughput with less advanced technology.

5 Conclusions

In this paper, we propose the pre-scheduling circuit-switched network for the on-chip network in embedded system design. Such network does not set up communication paths before transmitting data. Thus, it provides guaranteed transmission throughputs and latencies. We have designed three efficient switch architectures to support this network. In these architectures, we show the trade-offs between hardware complexity and efficiency. We have used TSMC 0.18μm technology to implement our designs. The layout of one of the designs has an area of 0.26 mm^2 and offers 640 Gbit/s aggregate throughputs.

References

1. Semiconductor Industry Association, *International Technology Roadmap for Semiconductors*, World Semiconductor Council, 1999.
2. L. Benini, G. De Micheli, "Networks on Chips: A New SoC Paradigm," *IEEE Computer*, vol. 35, pp. 70 -78, Jan. 2002.
3. W. J. Dally and B. Towels, "Route packets, not wires: On-Chip Interconnection Networks," *Proceedings of 38th Design Automation Conference*, pp 684-689, June 2001.
4. S. Kumar, A. Jantsch, J.-P. Soininen, M. Forsell, M. Millberg, J. Oberg, K. Tiensyrja, A. Hemani, "A Network on Chip Architecture and Design Methodology, " *Proceedings of the IEEE Computer Society Annual Symposium on VLSI, 2002 (ISVLSI.02)* , pp 105-112, April 2002.
5. A. Hemani, A. Jantsch, S. Kumar, A. Postula, J. Oberg, M. Millberg, and D. Lindqvist, "Network on Chip: An Architecture for Billion Transistor Era," *Proceedings of IEEE NorChip Conference*, pp. 166-173, Nov. 2000.
6. J. Hu and R. Marculescu, "Exploiting the Routing Flexibility for Energy/Performance Aware Mapping of Regular NoC Architectures," *Proceedings of Design Automation and Test in Europe Conference and Exhibition*, pp. 688-693, March 2003 .
7. T. Lei and S. Kumar, "A Two-step Genetic Algorithm for Mapping Task Graphs to a Network on Chip Architecture," *Proceedings of Euromicro Symposium on Digital System Design: Architectures, Methods and Tools, Turkey,* Sept. 2003.
8. L.-Y. Lin, C.-Y. Wang, P.-J. Huang, C.-C. Chou, J.-Y. Jou, "Communication-driven Task Binding for Multiprocessor with Latency Insensitive Network-on-Chip," *Proceedings of Asia and South Pacific. Design Automation Conference 2005.*
9. J. Liu, L.-R. Zheng and H. Tenhunen, "A Guaranteed-Throughput Switch for Network-on-Chip," *Proceedings of International Symposium on System-on-Chip,* Nov. 2003.

10. S. Murali and G. D. Micheli, "Bandwidth-Constrained Mapping of Cores onto NoC Architectures," *Proceedings of Design Automation and Test in Europe Conference and Exhibition*, pp. 869-901, Feb. 2004.
11. J. Nurmi, I. Saastamoinen, and D. Siguenza-Tortosa, "Interconnect IP Node for Future System-on-Chip Designs," *Proceedings of 1st IEEE International Workshop on Electronic Design, Test and Applications (DELTA '02)*, Jan. 2002.
12. P. P. Pande, C. Grecu, A. Ivanov, R. Saleh,"Design of a Switch for Network on Chip Applications," *Proceedings of IEEE International Symposium on Circuits and Systems (ISCAS)*, Jan. 2003.
13. E. Rijpkema, K. G. W. Goossens, A. Radulescu, J. Dielissen, J. Van Meerbergen, P. Wielage, and E. Waterlander, "Trade Offs in the Design of a Router with Both Guaranteed and Best-Effort Services for Networks on Chip," *Proceedings of Design Automation and Test in Europe Conference and Exhibition*, March 2003.
14. M. Sgroi, M. Sheets, A. Mihal, K. Keutzer, S. Malik, and J. Rabaey, and A. Sangiovanni-Vencentelli, "Addressing the System-on-a-Chip Interconnect Woes through Communication-Based Design," *Proceedings of 38th Conference on Design automation*, June 2001.
15. S. Sathe, D. Wiklund, D. Liu, "Design of a Switching Node (Router) for On-chip Networks," *Proceedings of the 6th International Conference on ASIC (ASICON 2003)*, Oct. 2003.
16. D. Wiklund and D. Liu, "SoCBUS: Switched Network on Chip for Hard Real Time Embedded Systems," *Proceedings of International Parallel and Distributed Processing Symposium,* April 2003.
17. D. Wingard, "MicroNetwork-Based Integration for SOCs," *Proceedings of 38th Design Automation Conference*, June 2001.

An Efficient Dynamic Switching Mechanism (DSM) for Hybrid Processor Architecture

Akanda Md. Musfiquzzaman, Ben A. Abderazek, Sotaro Kawata, and Masahiro Sowa

Graduate School of Information Systems,
The University of Electro-Communications,
1-5-1 Chofugaoka, Chofu-shi, 182-8585 Tokyo, Japan
akanda@sowa.is.uec.ac.jp

Abstract. Increasing the processor resources usability and boosting processor compatibility and capability to support multi-executions models in a single core are highly needed nowadays to benefit from the recent developments in electronics technology. This work introduces the concept of a dynamic switching mechanism (DSM), which supports multi-instruction set execution models in a single and simple processor core. This is achieved dynamically by execution $mode-switching$ scheme and a $sources-results$ locations computing unit for a novel queue execution model and a well-known stack based execution model. The queue execution model is based on queue computation that uses queue-registers, a circular queue data structure, for operands and results manipulations and assigns queue words according to a single assignment rule. We present the DSM mechanism and we describe its hardware complexity and preliminary evaluation results. We also describe the DSM target architecture.

Index Words: Hybrid processor, compatibility, design, dynamic switching mechanism, FaRM computing algorithm.

1 Introduction

Generally, the motivation for the design of a new architecture arose from the technological development, which changed gradually the architecture parameters traditionally used in the computer industry. With this growing changes, the computer architect is faced with answering the question what functionality has to be put on a single chip, giving them an extra performance edge. Nowadays, as we enter into an era of constant demand for faster and compatible processors as well as different Internet and network appliances using different processor architectures, it becomes extremely complicated and costly to develop a separate processor for every execution model that satisfy this demand. Internet applications, which are generally *stackbased* need high execution speed or high performance as defined by the literature. However, recently the term "high performance" is questioned again by many processor designers and computer users. Some consider that high performance means high execution speed or low execution time of some given

L.T. Yang et al. (Eds.): EUC 2005, LNCS 3824, pp. 77–86, 2005.

Hence, the FCU calculates the sources and destination for corresponding instructions.

In FSM, implicitly referenced operands are retrieved from the head of the operand stack and results are returned back onto the head of the stack. For example consider a *sub* instruction. In SEM model, the *sub* instruction pops two operands from the top of the stack (TOS), computes the difference and pushes the results back onto the top of the stack. In QEM mode, the *sub* instruction removes two operands from the front of the Queue (FOQ), computes their difference, and puts the results at the rear of the Queue (ROQ) indicated by the RQP. In the former case, the result of the operation is available at the TOS. In the later case, the result is behind any other operand in the Queue. This will have an enormous potential to effectively exploit pipelined ALU with a simple hardware, which, due to their hardware structure, normal SEM obviously cannot guaranty.

For better understanding of the novel QEM, we show in Fig. 1 a sample example that calculates a simple mathematical expression $x = (a + b)/(c * d)$. In the above example, the QEM instruction sequences were generated using the level order scan algorithm (LOST) published in our earlier work[2]. That is, in order to get instruction sequence that can be correctly executed in FQM, the data flow graph for the given expressing should be traversed from the deep level to the top level and from left to right. In Fig. 1(c) the queue contents (later reffered as shared storage unit) at each cycle are shown. As illustrated in Fig. 1(a) and Fig. 1(b),the first four instructions are independent. Hence , they are processed in parallel (q-satel). The second level in the data flow graph also has two independent instructions (+ and *). These two instructions are also executed in parallel (q-state2). At the third level, only *div* instruction is generated and is separately executed (q-state3). The result is finally stored into the PROG/DATA memory (not shown in the figure).

3 DSM Mechanism Overview

The DSM mechanism is implemented in a so-named hybrid processor architecture (FARM)[1]. Before we describe the DSM mechanism and its functional description, we first give a brief architectural overview about the FARM core that adopts the DSM mechanism. The target processor is based on Consume-produce Order Queue Computational Model(FQC) and Stack computational model(FSC)[1]. The processor has six pipeline stages and is based on 16-bit instruction set architecture. It supports two execution modes: Queue mode (FQM) and Stack mode (FSM). The basic block diagram of FaRM is given in Fig. 2. The FARM core consists of the following units: (1) Instruction Fetch unit (FU), (2) Decode Unit (DU), (3) FaRM Computation unit (FCU), (4) Issue Unit (IU), (5) Execution Unit (EXE) and (6) Shared Storage Unit (SSU). The basic block diagram of FaRMqs is given in Fig. 2.

Instruction Fetch: The fetch unit fetches 4*16-bits instructions/cycle from the program memory and inserts them into the fetch buffer.

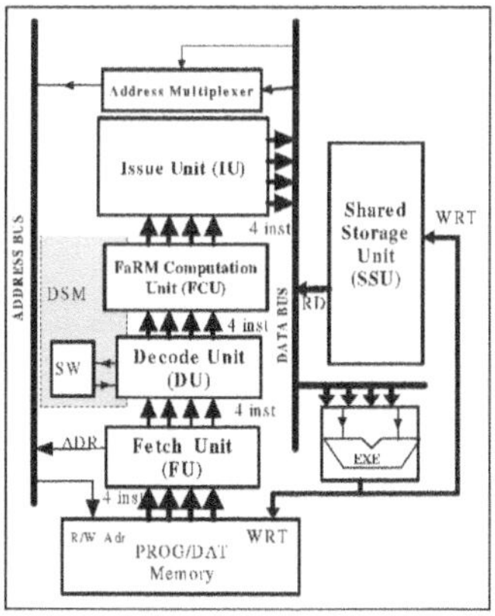

Fig. 2. Hybrid FARM system architecture

Instruction Decode: Decodes the instruction opcode and operands. The DU has four decode circuits (DC) and one Mode Selector Register (MS) that is set to zero or one according the type of instruction being decoded.
FaRM Computing Unit: The FaRM Computation unit gathers information mainly from the decode unit and uses them to compute the instruction sources and destination locations for FQM and FSM models.
Issue stage: The Issue stage issues ready instructions to the execution unit. Memory and registers dependency are checked by this unit/stage. This unit also checks the sources availability for each instruction.
Execution Unit: The EXE executes issued instructions and sends the results to the SSU or the data memory. The EXE consists of: (1) Arithmetic logical unit (ALU), (2) Shift unit, (3) Set register unit, (4) Load/Store unit, (5) Move and Compare unit and (7) Branch unit.
Write back Unit: The write back unit writes the result back to the PROG/DATA memory or the shared storage unit (SSU). The SSU is a 32*256 registers and is shared by both FQM and FSM execution models. In FQM, the SSU behaves as a conventional register file-like. However, in FSM, the system organizes the SSU access as a last-in-first-out.

4 DSM Architectural Details

As we earlier mentioned, the DSM system consists of a switching circuitry (SW) and a dynamic computation unit (FCU). It is implemented in a hybrid processor architecture. The FCU unit calculates $on-the-fly$ the sources and destinations for instructions in both FQM and FSM executions modes. A block diagram of the DSM mechanism is illustrated in Fig. 3. The DSM detects the instruction mode by decoding the operand of the *switch* instruction. After the mode detection, it inserts a $mode-bit$ for all instructions between the current and the next *switch* instruction. Hence, the same operation can be used for both modes. This will

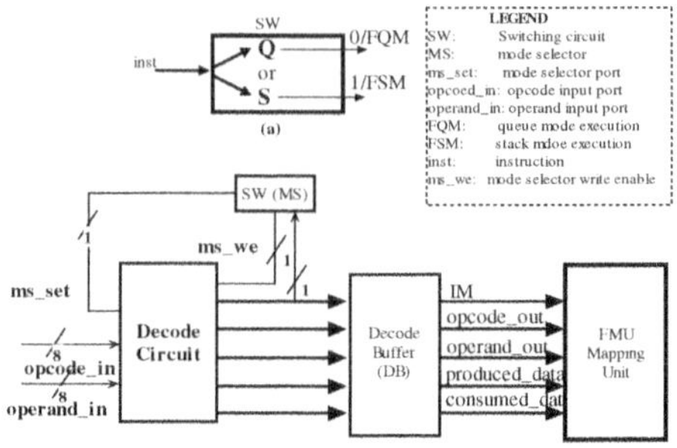

Fig. 3. DSM Basic Block Diagram

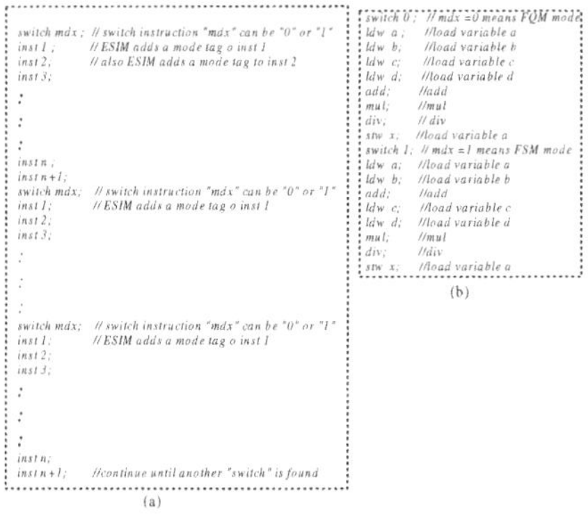

Fig. 4. FARM programming Models:(a) Programming Model, (b) Example of FQM and FSM assembly program

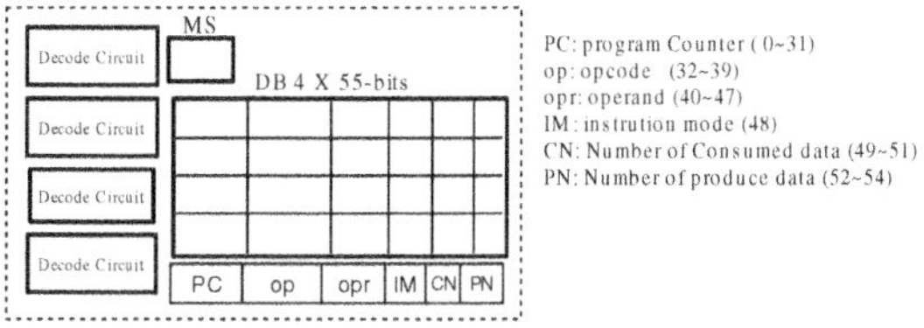

Fig. 5. DSM hardware components

increase the resources usability and the overall system performance (discussed later).

Dynamic switching example: In Fig. 4, we show the FARM programming model and an assembly program example. The first instruction at a given program should be always a "switch" instruction. This instruction will guide the decode unit to dynamically *reprogram* itself according to the *switch* instruction's operand value (*zero* for FQM mode and *one* for FSM mode). Instructions that follow *switch* instruction continue, then, execution in the FSM or FQM

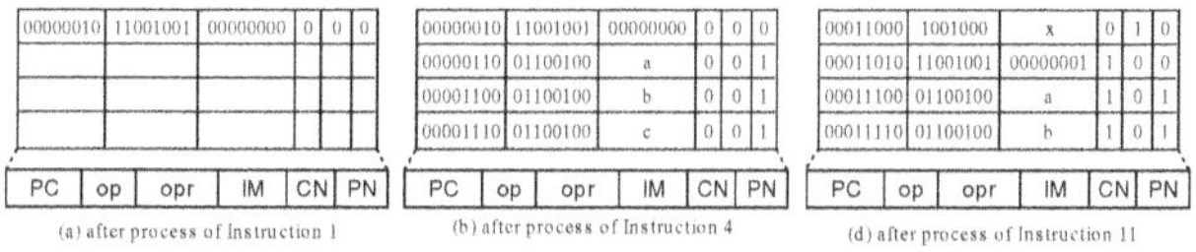

Fig. 6. Various DSM states over hybrid execution modes

until another *switch* instruction is found (refer to Fig. 4). The DSM (major hardware components) mechanism are illustrated in Fig. 5. This figure shows the initial state of the decode buffer (DB)and mode switch (MS) register before switch instruction is decoded. Fig. 6 shows the contents of the DB at different states for different instructions.

4.1 Dynamic Computation Algorithm

Dynamic Computation Algorithm (DCA) has two mapping algorithms: (1) FARM Queue Computing and (2) FARM Stack Computing.

FQM sources and destination computing: In order to have a correct execution, each instruction needs to know the values of the QH (Queue Head) and the QT (Queue Tail). The above values are easy to know in serial Queue execution model, since the QH is always used to fetch instruction from the operand queue (OPQ) and the QT is always used to store the result of the computation in to the tail of the OPQ. However, in the parallel execution scheme the above pointers are not explicitly determined. This is due to the fact that previous instructions are simultaneously executed and may not be completed in order. Fig. 7(a) shows the block diagram of queue computing circuits (FQC). The FQC is based on the Produce-consume order Queue Computation Mechanism.

The QH calculation for an instruction I(n+1) is given by:

$$QH(n+1) = QH(n) + (consumed\_data) \tag{1}$$

Where, Consumed Data is the number of fetched operands of an instruction.

The QT calculation of an instruction I(n+1) is calculated by:

$$QT(n+1) = QTP(n) + (produced\_data) \tag{2}$$

Where, Produced Data is the number of the results generated by an instruction

FSM sources and destination computing: FARM Stack Mechanism (FSM) is based on the pure stack Mechanism. For mapping the source and destination FSM used only one register named *Top*. Fig. 7(b) shows the block diagram of FaRM Stack (FSM) mechanism. The *Top* pointer calculation for an instruction (n±1)is given bellow:

$$TOP(n \pm 1) = TOP(n) - consumed\_data + produced\_data \tag{3}$$

Here, we use ± because top pointer does not only increase but also decrease. For *load* instruction *Top* pointer will increase and for *store* instruction *Top* will

We designed the hardware of the DSM and verify its functionality and overall complexity. From the design and evaluation results, we proved that the DSM mechanism can be used without enormous additional hardware when compared with conventional queue processor core (about 9.72% for DU and 3.77% for FMU extra hardware when compared with Queue processor core). We also conclude that the overall performance of the hybrid FARM architecture, which is still in its infancy, is acceptable. Hence, the DSM system increases the resources usability and the overall performance of the FARM processor.

Our future work is to evaluate the whole system with real benchmark programs and estimate the real complexity of the whole system.

References

1. M. M. Akanda , B. A. Abderazek , T. Yoshinaga, M. Sowa, "FaRMqs: Hybrid Processor Architecture in Verilog HDL" IPSJ, 67th Conf., March 2 3, 2005. for Parallel Execution in Parallel Queue Processor", IPSJ, 66th Conf., March 9 11, 2004, pp.1-69 1-70.
2. B. A. Abderazek, Kirilka Nikolova, and M. Sowa: "FARM-Queue Mode: On a Practical Queue Execution Model", Proceedings of the Int. Conf. on Circuits and Systems, Computers and Communications, Tokushima, Japan, pp.939-944, July 2001
3. M. Sowa, B. A. Abderazek, S. Shigeta, K. Nikolova, and T. Yoshinaga, " Proposal and Design of a Parallel Queue Processor Architecture (PQP) ", 14th IASTED Int. Conf. on Parallel and Distributed Computing and System, Cambridge, USA, pp. 554-560, Nov. 2002.
4. N. VijayKrishnan, "Issues in the Design of JAVA Processor Architecture". PhD dissertation, University of South Florida, Tampa, FL-33620. December 1998.
5. R. Radhakrishnan, N. Vijaykrishnan, L. John and A. Sivasubramanium, "Architectural issues in java runtime systems," Tech. Rep. TR-990719, 1999.
6. Sowa Laboratory, www.sowa.is.uec.ac.jp

Design of Face Recognition Door Manager System Based on DSP

Dongbing Pu[1,2], Changrui Du[1], Zhezhou Yu[1], and Chunguang Zhou[1,*]

[1] Department of Computer Science, Jilin University, Changchun, 130012, China
[2] College of Computer, Northeast Normal University, Changchun, 130024, China
Jilin University, Changchun, 130012, China
cgzhou@jlu.edu.cn

Abstract. This paper focuses on the design of hardware framework with DSP based on embedded face recognition door manager system including the detailed technology of circuit design among the image sensor, DSP, the door manager controller, FLASH, SDRAM, RJ45 port, timer and reset. At the same time, both the programs and algorithms are discussed in the paper. The program on face recognition has been tested on the designed board; it runs all right with fixed light condition. Not only the size and cost of the board are small, but also it is fast and highly reliable.

1 Introduction

The Digital Signal Processor (DSP) is a kind of specialized microprocessor designed for realization of digital signal processing quickly in the real time, which adopts the Harvard structure. [1] It has some good characteristics such as the convenient interface, the good stability, the high accuracy, the good reusability and convenient integration etc. [2] Along with a fast development of DSP, its function is more and more stronger, the function price ratio rises continuously, the method of development has been improved continuously, so it also quickly becomes the core component of numerous electronic products. It is extensively applied to many fields such as the correspondence electronics, signal processing, automatic control, radar, military, aviation, medical treatment, home appliances, electric power and electronics etc. On the other hand, the traditional methods of identification such as passwords, certificates, IC card etc, which often cause the falsification, theft and crack as they can be separated from the owner. They couldn't fully be satisfied with the modern social economic activities and social safety. Therefore, the personal identification system based on the human body biologic characteristic gradually becomes very well known to the society. But the traditional face recognition system are achieved depending on large-scale integrated circuits same as microcomputers, both drivers of peripherals and image capturing depended on the hardware and operating system in a computer, which result in some disadvantages such

* Corresponding author.

L.T. Yang et al. (Eds.): EUC 2005, LNCS 3824, pp. 87 – 97, 2005.

as the slow image processing, low reliability, poor function in real time etc. [3] Applying DSP and the image sensor to the body identification system with door manager system can achieve such advantages as quick speed, low cost and considerable reliability. This paper focuses on the design of hardware framework in a small face recognition door manager system, which based on DSP and image sensor. Such problems as the peripherals, interface design and the program of face recognition also have been discussed elaborately in the paper.

2 System Architecture Design

The architecture of the system is shown in Figure 1. BlackfinADSP-532 is the core of the hardware. On the other hand, the peripheral chips primarily consist of asynchronous FLASH, SDRAM, the image sensor, the door manager controller, network chip, clock, power, resets, and JTAG.

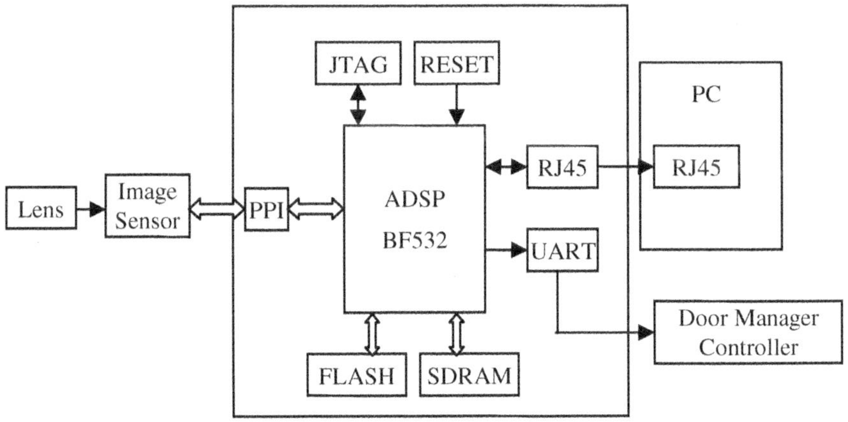

Fig. 1. Architecture of system

Firstly the system is initialized and boots along with electrifying, then it loads programs and data from FLASH to SDRAM. The data mainly includes the face detection and location template, mean face matrix, eigenface template and match template etc. When someone wants to pass the door, he or she gives an interrupt signal to the system by pressing the interrupt key. The image sensor captures the image via PPI interface under DSP controlling. Then the captured image is transmitted to the off-chip SDRAM. A feature value of person face will be achieved here when programs complete to process the image information. Since programs bring about a great deal of temporary data when obtain the feature value of person face, whereas the on-chip RAM for DSP is not enough to hold them. Thus an extended off-chip SDRAM of 4M*16-bit is added to the system. Those tasks including face detection and location, feature extraction is mainly processed in the extended SDRAM. The following task is matching the extracted feature value with data stored in the database of face feature, and calculating the threshold value of similar degree. Eventually DSP sends message to the door manager controller through the UART interface according to the similar degree threshold value. The door manager controller can send message to open the door or play warning sound. Meanwhile, the log of recognition will be stored in server-named PC through RJ45 interface. These log information can be available for management. The JTAG of the system is used for emulating, debugging on-line and updating the information of person's face feature periodically.

3 Interface Design

3.1 Image Sensor Interface Design

In order to increase the speed of image capturing, the system adapts HDCS1020 image sensor. It can capture the image of CIF (352*288) up to 30f/s with A/D conversion itself. [4] And it can joint the data bus of DSP directly without any conflict.

Because programs of system process black/white image, so the data bus D0-D7 of image sensor connects with the PPI pins of DSP. DSP's GPIO pin can imitate the I2C protocol to control the image sensor.[5] Figure 2 shows the way of connection between DSP and the image sensor.

The control signals sent by DSP include two parts: address codes and control signals. Address codes are used to select the image sensor, and control signals perform the initialization and image capture. Control signals include beginning signal, response signal and ending signal. Beginning signal shows that SCL is high Data begin to be transmitted when SDA jumping from high to low. The image sensor sends response signal to DSP when it has already received 8-bit data. DSP sends signals to the image sensor and waits until response signals from the image sensor arriving to decide whether continue signal from it. When SCL is high and SDA jumps from low to high, DSP sends the end signal. Figure 3 shows the scheduling of I2C bus protocol. [6]

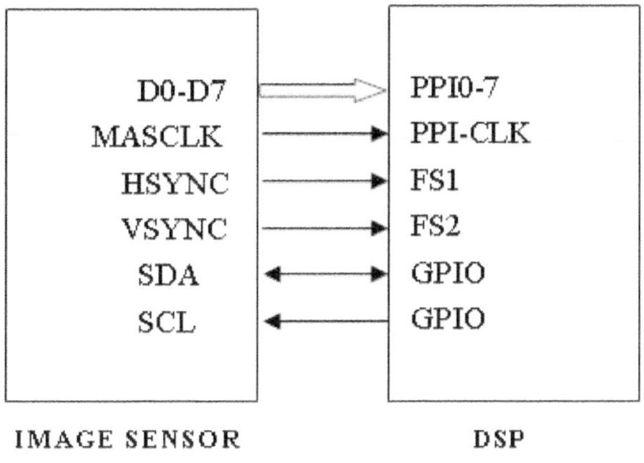

Fig. 2. Connection between image sensor and DSP

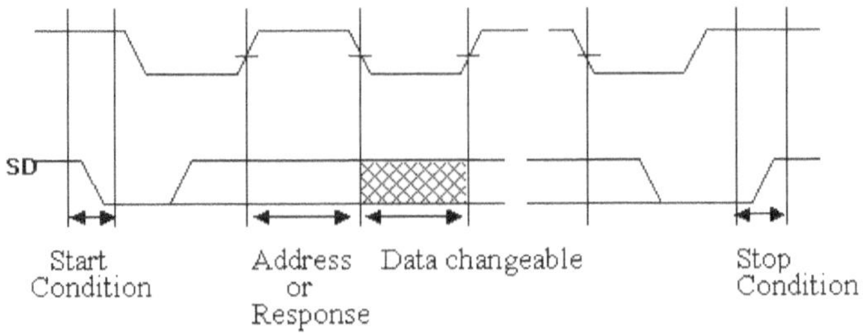

Fig. 3. Scheduling of I^2C bus protocol

3.2 FLASH Design

DSP uses a 16-bit EMIF loading model. In this model, pins of BOOTM [1:0] are set to 01. The boot kernel in the on-chip Boot Rom loads the programs and data from FLASH to SDRAM, and then the system begins to run. [7-8] The address corresponds to the BANKO space of DSP, so we connect $\overline{CE}$ of FLASH to $\overline{AMSO}$ of DSP. As the programs and data are enormous, we added an extended 4BANK*512K*16-bit of FLASH to the system. $\overline{AMSO\text{-}3}$ pins of DSP respectively connect to $\overline{CE}$ pin of four FLASH chips. A[19..1] are address lines of DSP, they are connected corresponding to A[18..0] of FLASH which is shown in figure 4. 4MB spaces of FLASH can be enough to hold system program, data and face feature templates of about 1000 persons.

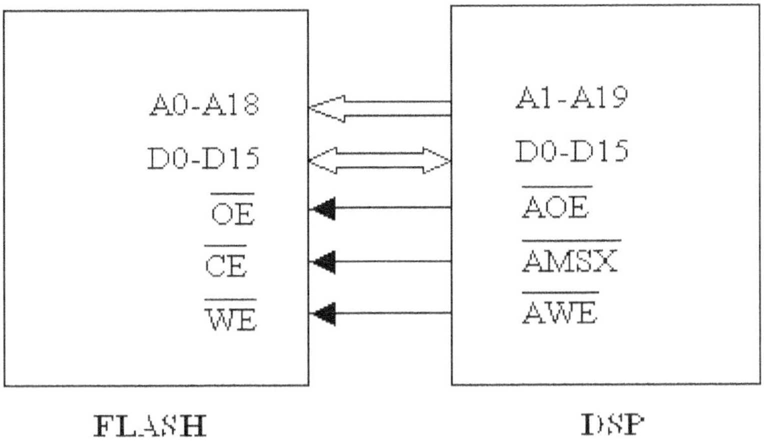

Fig. 4. Connection between FLASH and DSP

3.3 SDRAM Design

In order to provide a bigger space for programs and data of the algorithm, an extended 4M*16-bit of SDRAM is added to the system. As the row and line address are reusable for Blackfin, its connection way is greatly different from DSP 54X series of TI. The connection way for boundary/row and column address is shown in figure 5. The row selecting $\overline{\text{SRAS}}$, column selecting $\overline{\text{SCAS}}$ and writable signal $\overline{\text{SWE}}$ of DSP are directly connected to the corresponding pin of SDRAM. A1-10, A12 and A18-19 address bus of DSP are respectively connected to A1-10, A11 and BA0-BA1 of SDRAM; SA10 and SDQM0-1 of DSP are connected to A10, DQML and DQMH of SDRAM respectively.[9]

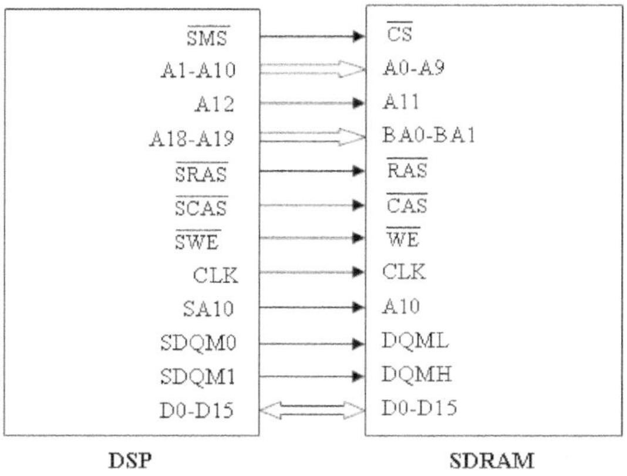

Fig. 5. Connection between DSP and SDRAM

3.4 Corresponding Interface Design Between DSP and PC

The LAN91C111 network chip is built in the hardware of our system. It is 3.3v MII (media independent interface) integrated the MAC+PHY on-chip and 128 pins QFP package. [10] The LAN91C111 integrates the IEEE802.3 Physical Layer (PHY) and Media Access Control (MAC) into the same silicon. The data path connection between the MAC and the internal PHY is provided by the internal MII. The LAN91C111 also supports the EXT-PHY mode for use of an external PHY. It provides a flexible slave

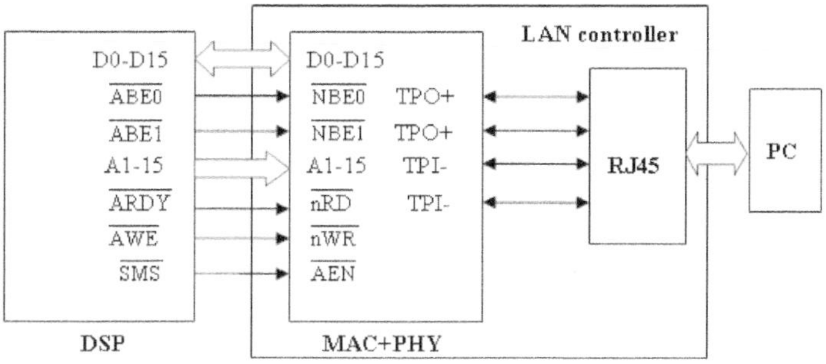

Fig. 6. Connection between DSP and LAN controller

interface for easy connectivity with industry standard buses. The Bus Interface Unit (BIU) can handle synchronous as well as asynchronous transfer, with different signals being used for each one. The total internal memory FIFO buffer size is 8k bytes. These properties are satisfied to the system request. The TJ45 adopt HFJ11-2450s chip. The system bus is 16-bit. So the $\overline{\text{ABE0-1}}$ pins of DSP connect to the $\overline{\text{NBE0-1}}$ pins of network chip. $\overline{\text{NBE2-3}}$ connects to high impedances. The hardware connection is shown in figure 6.

3.5 Other Peripheral Circuit Design

In order to provide real-time debugging for program in DSP, we connect JTAG with the emulator in our system. Furthermore, it also can be used to burn data and programs to FLASH. The periodical update task of face feature information is also completed by JTAG. [11-13] The UART interface is the equipment between DSP and the door manager controller, which can send message to open door or play warning sound.

The power equipment of system is TPS70302PWP. It can supply double adjustable voltage. One is 3.3V for peripheral circuits; the other is 1.2V for the kernel of DSP. To avoid destroying DSP by error of incorrect electrifying sequence, the system supplies electricity with peripheral circuits at first, and then DSP. The automatic and manual reset signal outputted by the power source do logical ‘AND’ operation before they are connected to DSP and peripheral circuits so as to reset system automatically or manually when the supplied voltage of system is too low. To prevent from the disturbance of high frequency caused by the high clock frequency of peripheral circuit, which can reduce the stability of system, peripheral clock circuit supplies 20MHz clock for DSP to match its kernel clock by PLL of DSP. [7]

4 Software Design

Firstly, the system will be initialized as soon as it is power on. Whenever someone passes the door, he or she can press the specified key to send interruption signal system. The system will mask the external interruption when it received the signal, and then it sends instructions to the image sensor to capture an image. The image sensor will notify DSP through interruption that the capture operation ends when it has completed to capture an image. Then the system starts to process the image and recognize. Finally it gives the recognition result and opens the door in so far as right or gives a warning message (the speaker is beeping) for wrong. Figure 7 shows the main flowchart of our system.

During the system initialization, DSP reads data from pm, mean, facetpl, eyetp1, and then store them in the variable of Pm, Mean, Facet, Eyet respectively for the following feature extraction to use. The data of captured image are stored in the fdata variable. The image sensor can capture the image without any software; it is different from the existing system in which the captured image should be converted through A/D before processing. The captured image of face will be performed unitary operation on size and

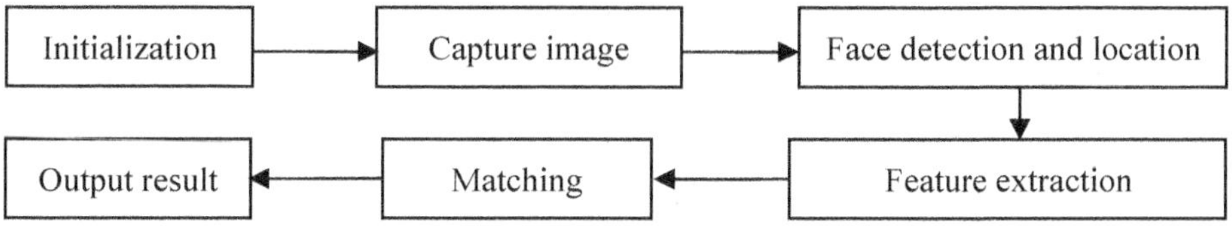

Fig. 7. System main flowchart

gray degree. The following step is to judge whether there is a face existed in the picture and give the accurate location if a face existed. Program locates such parts of the face as head, face, and eyes pupils. The flow chart is shown in figure 8.The method of detection and location in our system is based on the traditional template matching, and it is used for those images, which are static and gray, captured under simple background and even shine. The result will be better if the image is positive face picture.[14-15]The method of traditional template matching is to calculate the Euclidean distance between the captured image matrix and the face template(or eye template).

After the location, the feature extraction is beginning. Firstly the data of face location subtract the data of even face stored in Mean, and then an array can be generated, the array is projected at the feature face matrix pm to extract the feature value. The method of feature extraction and selection in our system is PCA (Principal Component Analysis). [15-17]

Then program matches the extracted feature value with those templates that have been trained and stored. The algorithm for matching is NNA (Nearest Neighbor Algorithm). [18-19] In addition, the face and eye templates for detection and location, the feature face template for extracting the feature value and the match template for matching are all trained and generated in PC beforehand and burned to the FLASH of our system. The match template is composed of the face feature value so that FLASH can accommodate more people's feature value in the limited space.

The maximum count of studying & training samples is 5 to 8 for every person. These samples have been appended in out system by generating image so as to improve the rate of recognition.[20]The sample is generated and append by a series of transformation. The main transformations are mirror transformations; rotate transformations of the picture and the changing of gray information of bottom for an image.

The most important aspect in the whole system is to select the threshold value of similar degree. The similar degree of our system is measured by cosine angle of two eigenvectors.[21] The threshold value determines the safety and efficiency of our system. If the threshold value is too high, those people who have the right to pass the door can't pass it; on the contrary, if the threshold value is too low, the reliability of system is reduced, as a result, those people who have not the right to pass the door can pass it. There are two factors to judge whether the similar degree threshold value is good or not. One is the mistake-passing rate; another is the mistake-refusing rate on the threshold value. Generally, both of factors are restricted mutually. If the mistake-passing rate were low, the mistake-refusing rate would be high. If the mistake-refusing rate were low, the mistake-

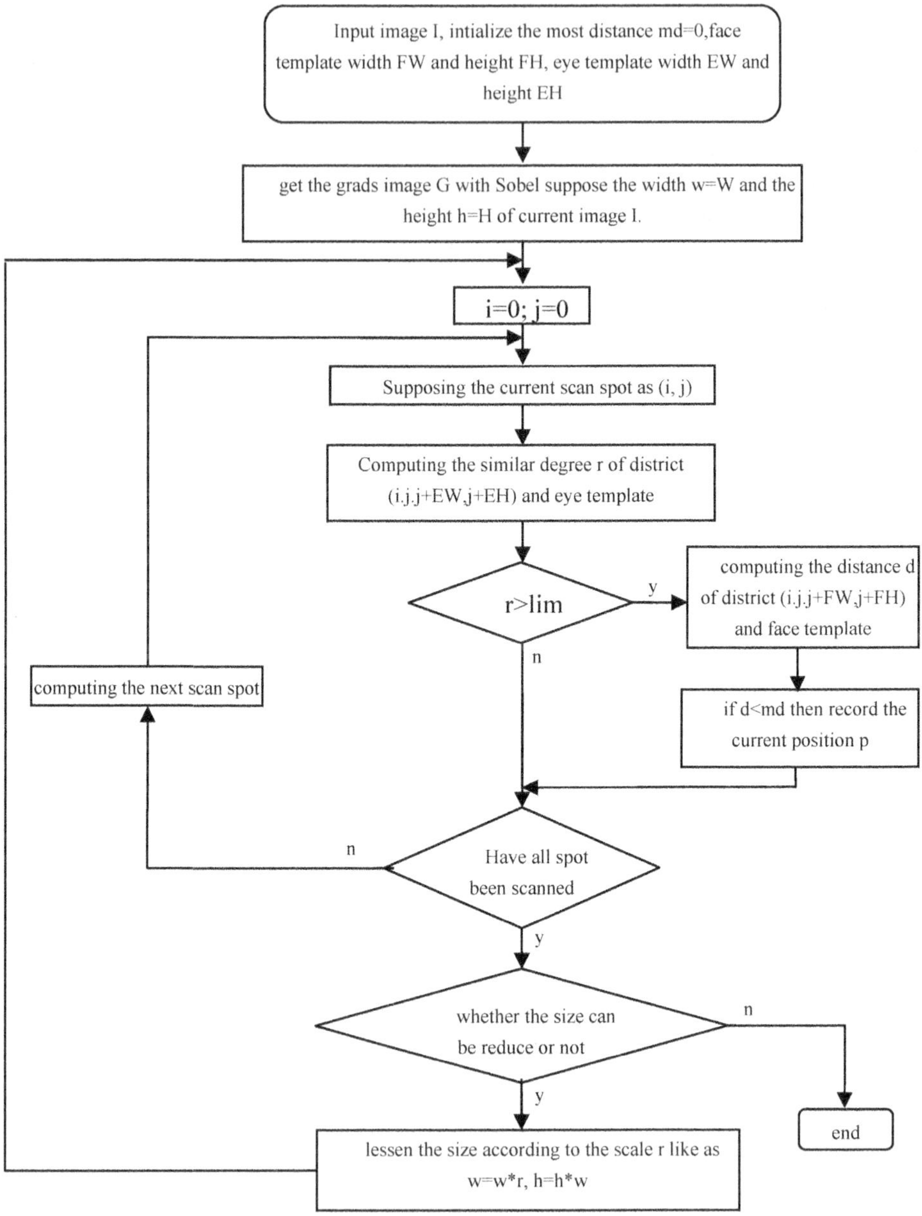

Fig. 8. Flowchart of detection and location

passing rate would be accordingly high. The curve in Figure 9 shows the variation of the mistake-passing rate and the mistake-refusing rate following the variation of the similar degree threshold value.

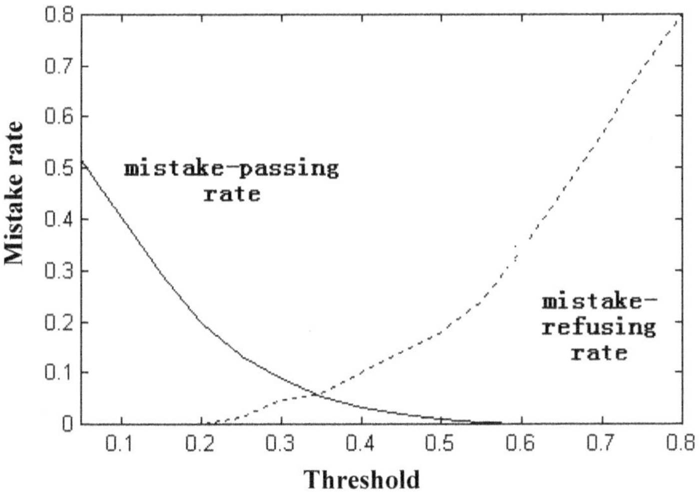

Fig. 9. Variation of the mistake-passing rate and the mistake-refusing rate following the variation of the similar degree threshold value

Figure 10 shows the results of our system.

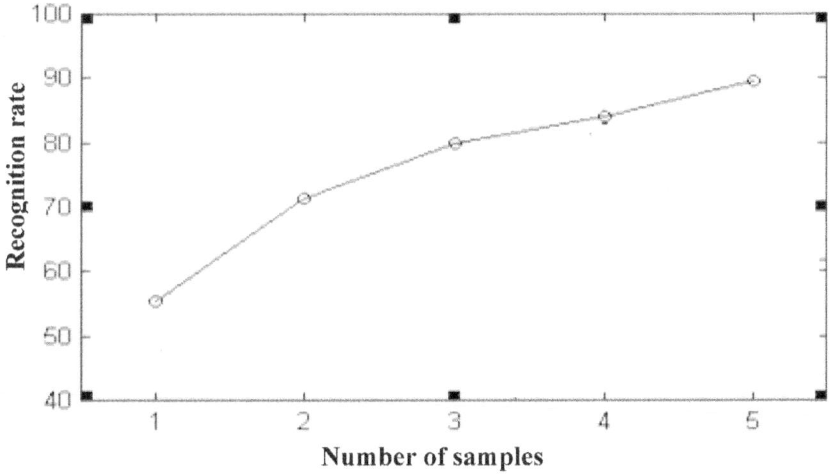

Fig. 10. Result of Recognition in system

5 Conclusion

In this paper, we have designed a hardware framework, which based on the face recognition of door manager requirement. DSP is the kernel of the door manager system and face recognition algorithm has been applied in it. We have implemented the hardware interface circuit design of the system and the algorithm testing. The result is good under the still light. In the same time, the system integrates image sensor, DSP, FLASH, network chip and other peripheral equipments on a single board. Not only it is smaller in size, lower in cost, but also it can work faster and more reliably. In a word, it will be applied in many fields in the future.

Acknowledgement

This work was supported by the National Natural Science Foundation of China under Grant No.60433020, and the Key Science-Technology Project of the National Education Ministry of China under Grant No.02092.the Key Laboratory for Symbol Computation and Knowledge Engineering of the National Education Ministry of China.(93K-17).

References

1. Wang, C.M., Sun, H.B., (2004), System Design and Development Instance for DSP of TMS320C5000, Publishing House of Electronic Industry.
2. Zhang, X.W., Chen, L., (2003), Principle and Development Application of DSP, Publishing House of Electronic Industry.
3. Yu, M, Zhen, H., (Vol.19.No.6, 2003), Face Recognition System Based on DSP, Microcomputer Information Press, P: 55.
4. HDCS-1020/2020 CMOS Image Sensors Datasheet.
5. ADSP_BF531_2_3_a datasheet.
6. Zheng, J.F., (No.7, 2004), VHDL Design and Implement of I2C Bus Design of Electronic Application Press.
7. DSP Principle and System Design of Blackfin, P120-122.
8. ADSP-BF533 Blackfin Processor Hardware Reference, P197.
9. MT48LC4M16A2TG DATASHEET.
10. SMSC The LAN91C11 DATASHEET.
11. Xiao, Y.N., Yi, J., Song, Y.S., (No.4, 2004), DSP Boot under Emulator Environment for TMS320C6000, Overseas Electronic Component Press, P33.
12. Ding, J., Wei, F., Li, G.Y., (No.8, 2003), Research of FLASH Building in DSP for System Program and Boot Loading Method Collaterally, Electronic Technology Application Press, P78.
13. Visual DSP++4.0 User's Guide Datasheet.
14. Surendra Ranganath, Krishnamurthy Arun, (Vol.30.No.10, 1997), Face Recognition Using Transform Features And Neural Network, Pattern Recognition Press, P1615-1622.
15. Shao, Q., Zhang, XG., (2000), Pattern Recognition, Publishing house of Tsinghua University, P223-227.
16. Alex(Sandy) Pentland, Tanzeem Choudhury, (No.2, 2000), Face Recognition for Smart Environments, IEEE Computer, P50-55.

17. Ian Craw, Takashi Kato, Shigeru akamatsu, (Vol.21.No.8, 1999), How Should We Represent Faces for Automatic Recognition, IEEE Transaction on Pattern Analysis and Machine Intellignece.
18. Mark J.L.Orr, (No.8, 1996), Introduction to Radial Basis Function Nerworks.
19. Abhijit S.Pandya Robert B.Macy, Pattern Recognition and Implement in Neural Network, Publishing House of Electronic Industry.
20. Terence Sim, Rahul Sukthandar, Matthew Mullin, Shumeet Baluja, (2000), Memory-based Face Recognition for Visitor Identification, Proceedings of the Fourth IEEE International Conference on Automatic Face and Gesture Recognition.
21. Zhou, C.G., Cui, Z., Zhang, Y., Duan, J., (Vol.23, No.12, 2002), Visiting and Controlling System Based on Face Recognition, Microcomputer System Press.

AlchemistJ: A Framework for Self-adaptive Software*

Dongsun Kim and Sooyong Park

Department of Computer Science and Interdisciplinary
Program of Integrated Biotechnology, Sogang University,
Shinsu-Dong, Mapo-Gu, Seoul, 121-742, Republic of Korea
{darkrsw, sypark}@sogang.ac.kr

Abstract. The major goal of self-adaptive software is to provide a mechanism that allows a software system to dynamically change its architectural configuration during run-time to cope with requirement changes and unexpected conditions. Software which needs to handle dynamically changing internal and external environment is one of the areas in which self-adaptive software may do an important role in improving the reliability and performance of software systems. There are three main capabilities that are necessary to support self-adaptive software: the ability to monitor and recognize internal/external situations that affect behavior of the software system; the ability to determine when and what to reconfigure in the software system to handle the situations; and the ability to dynamically change the software architecture during run-time to make the reconfiguration effective. In this paper, we describe a software framework to support such capabilities to realize self-adaptive software and its experiment results.

1 Introduction

Intelligent software systems embedded in dynamic devices such as intelligent service robots should provide various capabilities in various environment continuously. This requirement makes the internal operations in software systems more complex. Due to the complexity, unpredictable errors and changes of situation often occurs at run-time[10]. Those unpredictable errors and changes of situations disturb maintaining proper performances of a system at run-time. In addition, it is a major factor which makes stable and persistent services of a system impossible.

In particular, the embedded software, which needed in more dynamic and complex changes of environment, faces the following problems:

1. *Various unexpected situations* that cannot be handled by pre-programmed actions

* This research was performed for the Intelligent Robotics Development Program, one of the 21st Century Frontier R&D Programs funded by the Ministry of Commerce, Industry and Energy of Korea.

L.T. Yang et al. (Eds.): EUC 2005, LNCS 3824, pp. 98–109, 2005.

2. *Changing user requirements* that are encountered after deploying the embedded software
3. *Faults and errors* (in embedded hardware and software) that make some parts of embedded software unusable or malfunctioned
4. *Frequent replacement and reconfiguration* of hardware components, which may cause some inconsistency problems in software that depends on the hardware components

To overcome the problems above, the embedded software need to have the ability to maintain and improve its own capabilities. The embedded software should maintain three capabilities even in complex and exceptional situation of external environment, which are changing dynamically. The followings are three capabilities to maintain and improve its own functionalities:

1. *Interfaces* for implementing recognition of environment
2. *Decision making and learning* for the adaptive behavior by using reinforcement learning
3. *Dynamic reconfiguration* by using role- and port- based software architecture

Three capabilities above cannot directly overcome all situations such as unexpected problems, changes of user's requirements, disorders in hardware and software, and inconsistency in a system. However, the capabilities offer flexibility and opportunity for software to adapt itself against environmental changes. Self-adaptive software attaches new operations, modifies the current operations, and removes unnecessary operations in order to overcome problems. In this paper, we propose a framework for self-adaptive software called 'AlchemistJ'.

We explain the framework proposed in this research in detail in section 2, and then show a case study using Robocode in section 3. We comment on other significant work in Section 4 before drawing conclusions and proposing future research in section 5.

2 Approach

2.1 Overall Architecture

AlchemistJ consists of the Monitor package('env'), the Decision maker & Learner package('learner') and the Reconfigurator package('recon'). The Monitor package contains interfaces to support observation of situations and rewards of environment. Each situation is a vector of factors which can affect behavior of the software system. Each reward is a real-numbered value that evaluates behavior of the software system. The Decision maker & Learner package contains components to support decision making and learning of software. This makes decisions based on situations and rewards given by a monitor. The Reconfigurator package provides components to maintain software architecture of the systems and reconfigure the architecture based on adaptation decisions from the Decision Maker. AlchemistJ assumes software is designed by using role- and port-based software architecture and reconfigures software architecture at run-time.

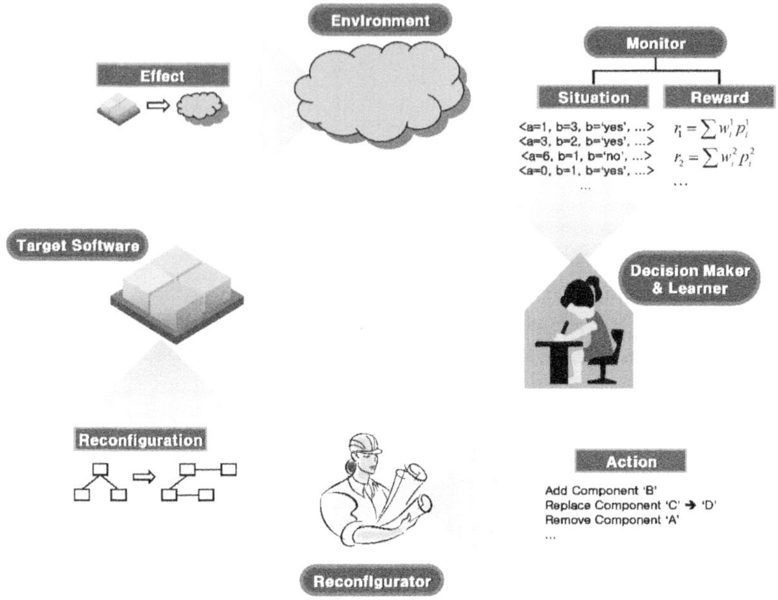

Fig. 1. The Process of AlchemistJ

Reconfigurations leads to changes of behavior of the software system. The changed behavior affects its environment. This affection changes situations of its environment because of not only the changed behavior but also other factors(for example, human factors, randomness, etc). The software system observes a new situation and reward by using the Monitor. The Learner updates its knowledge using the observed situation and reward. The software system repeats this iterations at run-time to adapt its operations and to accumulate experience.

Fig. 1 shows the process of AlchemistJ explained above.

2.2 The Monitor

The Monitor package defines basic interfaces for observation of environment and a process for passing situations and rewards to the Decision Maker and Learner. This package has three interfaces, 'IState', 'IReward' and 'IEnvironment'.

'IState' defines how to implement situation information. 'IState' has two methods as follows:

1. `public String getStateCode()`
2. `public void setStateCode(String code)`

'getStateCode()' returns the unique situation code which is a string of characters. 'setStateCode()' replaces the unique situation code with a given situation code. Developers should implement a monitor instance which is appropriate for a target domain to observe environment and implement a class to contain situation information using 'IState'. Each object of the class contains a situation of environment. Each situation is mapped to the unique situation code. 'IReward' defines how to express reward information. 'IReward' has one method as follows:

1. `public double getReward()`

'getReward()' returns a real-numbered reward value. This value is determined by a predefined equation. This equation should be defined by developers. AlchemistJ basically assumes software maximize rewards. If a developer is eager to minimize rewards, the Monitor should be implemented to multiply rewards by '-1'.

'IEnvironment' defines connections of the Monitor, the Decision maker & Learner and the Reconfigurator. 'IEnvironment' provides four methods:

1. `public IState getState()`
2. `public boolean giveAction(IAction action)`
3. `public IReward getReward()`
4. `public ActionSet getAdmissibleActionSet(IState s)`

Developers should implement a component in compliance with 'IEnvironment'. 'getState()' returns the current situation of environment. The current situation is a object of the class which implements 'IState'. 'giveAction()' gives an adaptation decision made by the Decision Maker to the Reconfigurator. The Reconfigurator reorganizes components of the software system and composes them into a new architecture. 'getReward()' returns rewards which are observed from environment. Each reward is a instance of the class which implements 'IReward'. 'getAdmisibleActionSet()' returns a set of possible adaptation actions. These actions describe architecture-based adaptation actions such as component replacement, component attachment and topology changes. The Decision Maker determines one of the adaptation actions as the current adaptation decision.

2.3 The Decision Maker and Learner

AlchemistJ applies reinforcement learning to the Decision Making & Learning. Reinforcement learning is a mathematical formulation of interaction between an agent and its environment[13]. There are lots of specific algorithms that carry out reinforcement learning. AlchemistJ offers Q-learning implementation which is one of the specific algorithms of reinforcement learning[14][15]. Q-learning assumes a modeless environment. In other words, software cannot know deterministic model of state transitions.

The Decision Maker receives the current situation as input data from the Monitor. Then, the Decision Maker chooses an action to be applied. After applying the action to the system, The Learner receives the next situation and the immediate reward from the Monitor and updates Q-values, $Q(s,a)$. This updating is carried out by equation (1):

$$\begin{aligned} &Q(s_t,a_t) \leftarrow (1-\alpha)Q(s_t,a_t) + \alpha[r_{t+1} + \gamma \max_a Q(s_{t+1},a)], \\ &where \quad 0<\alpha<1, \quad 0<\gamma<1 \end{aligned} \tag{1}$$

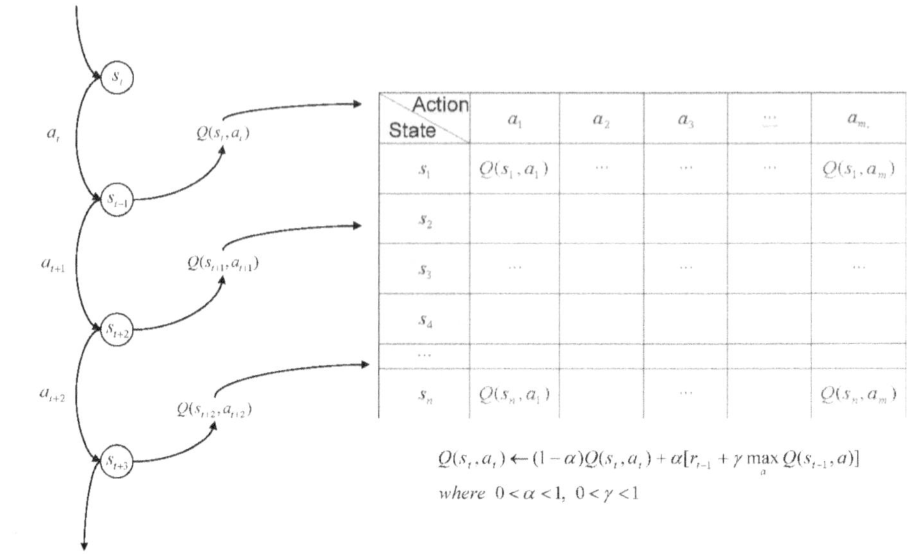

Fig. 2. Q-learning accumulates experiences of the software system by updating Q-values

In equation (1), $Q(s_t, a_t)$ indicates the Q-value for the situation s_t and the taken action a_t where t is time. The term $(1 - \alpha)Q(s_t, a_t)$ represents knowledge that the software system experienced and the term $\alpha[r_{t+1} + \gamma \max_a Q(s_{t+1}, a)]$ represents the current experience where r_{t+1} is an immediate reward from monitor and γ is a discount factor[13]. The value α controls weights of two terms.

Fig. 2 depicts a conceptual process of Q-learning in the Decision Maker & the Learner. In each state the Decision Maker takes an action and moves to the next state. In every transition, the Learner records rewards which is evaluated by the monitor.

'learner' package implements the Decision Maker & Learner. 'AbstractLearner' contains general functionalities for decision making & learning. This is connected with the Monitor which implements 'IEnvironment' interface. 'AbstractLearner' receives situation and reward information from the Monitor through 'IEnvironment' interface and makes decisions and learns its environment using the information. Basically, AlchemistJ offers 'QLearner' as an implementation of 'AbstractLearner'. If developers want to design a new decision maker & learner, they should implement a class that inherits 'AbstractLearner' and connect it with the Monitor.

2.4 Role- and Port-Based Software Architecture

To make self-adaptation possible, the software system should contain flexible components. These components should be reorganized into architecture to op-

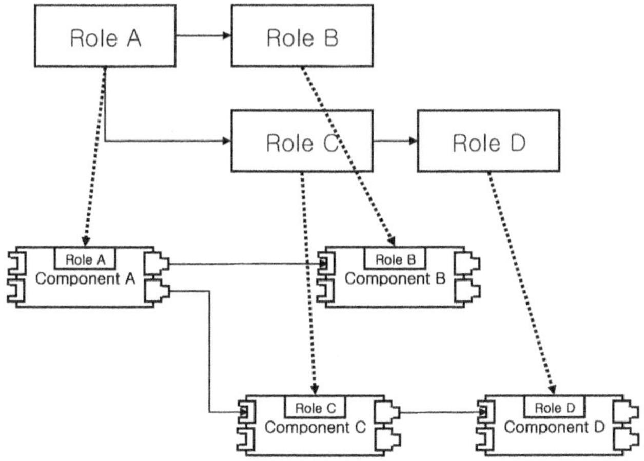

Fig. 3. Correspondence between roles and components

erate its functionalities. For this reason, self-adaptive software development requires predefined component & architecture design principle.

AlchemistJ provides role- and port-based architecture[9][6][3] as a design principle. Assuming software is designed by role- and port-based architecture design method, AlchemistJ reconfigures target software architecture. To construct role- and port-based architecture, developers must decompose software into roles. Each role describes abstract functionalities of each independent part of software. Roles do not express concrete capabilities or strategies. In other words, they should not define 'how to do', but 'what to do'. A role can be connected to make use of another role. After defining roles, they should be composed into a role-model. This role-model is a basis of software architecture.

A role-model describes relationship among roles. The Reconfigurator of AlchemistJ makes it possible to change a role-model at run-time. A role can be attached in and removed from the role-model. Each role should correspond to a component. This component should play the corresponding role. Each component consists of component body, role description, required ports, provided ports. The component body contains executable code that the component executes. The role description indicates a role that the component plays. One component can play only one role. The required ports describes other components(actually provided ports) that the component needs. The Provided ports describe what the component can do. One provided port should be connected with only one required port. Fig. 3 shows a sample of correspondence between roles and components.

2.5 Reconfigurator

AlchemistJ supports reconfiguration of roles and components at run-time. Role reconfiguration consists of role attachment, role removal and changes of topology.

Component reconfiguration comprises component attachment because of role attachment, component removal because of role removal, changes of a component topology because of changes of role topology and component replacement. These capabilities are implemented in 'recon' package.

'Reconfigurator' maintains the role-model and components in software architecture and reorganizes components into a new architecture. Components maintained by 'Reconfigurator' should comply role- and port-based architecture. To do this, 'recon' package offers five interfaces. 'IPort' contains basic methods for ports. 'IPortRequired' and 'IPortProvided' which inherit 'IPort' describe required ports and provided ports respectively. All components should implements 'IComponent' interface which provides basic operations of components. 'IRole' contains basic operations to describe a role. Every component has an object implementing 'IRole'. 'recon' package basically provides 'SimpleRole' as an implementation of 'IRole'.

3 Experiment

3.1 Introduction to Robocode

Robocode is a platform which includes the environment for game development and a simulator and is developed by IBM. The game simulator in Robocode provides a rectangular field for a battle. In the field, robots participating battle away each other in order to destroy the opposing robot. In order to simplify the implementation, this paper supposes that only two robots can participate in a battle.

3.2 Implementation of a Robot Using AlchemistJ

We have implemented the robot's capability to recognize environment according to interfaces provided by 'env' package in the framework. As mentioned in Section 2.2, 'env' package provides three kinds of interfaces. First, 'RobotState' class implements 'IState' interface. 'RobotState' class contains the number of hit by bullets and the number of hit by wall. This class converts and encodes the current situation into the unique situation code. 'RobotReward' class implements 'IReward' interface. An equation for rewards is set up as follows.

$$r_t = 0.3 \cdot \triangle E_S + (-1) \cdot 0.7 \cdot \triangle E_E \quad (2)$$

In equation (2), r_t, the reward value in time t, is calculated by summation of two terms, $\triangle E_S$ and $\triangle E_E$. $\triangle E_S$ is the difference of the robot's energy between time $t-1$ and t. $\triangle E_E$ is the difference of the enemy's energy between time $t-1$ and t. Weights of two terms are 0.3 and 0.7 respectively. Since the energy of the enemy should be minimized, we multiplied $\triangle E_E$ by (-1).

3.3 Construction of Software Architecture

We design a robot in compliance with Role- and port-based software architecture proposed in section 2.4. Fig. 4 shows the roles of the robot and the relationship among them.

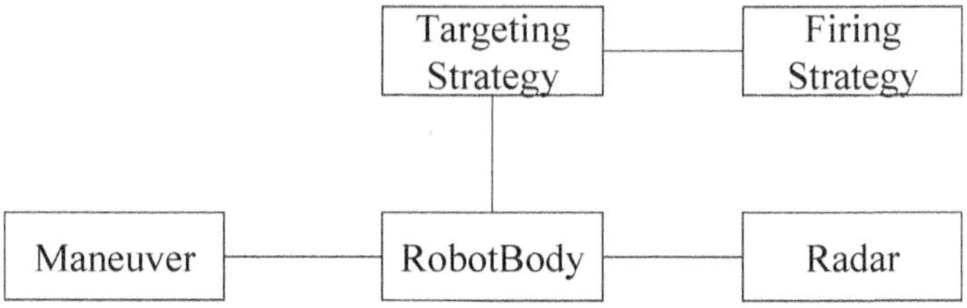

Fig. 4. The Role-model of the Robot

Table 1. The component list of robot architecture

Component name	Role of component	Required ports	Provided ports
NewRobot	RobotBody	RadarPort, ManeuverPort, TargetPort	N/A
Radar	Radar	N/A	RadarPortP
LinearManeuver	Maneuver	N/A	ManeuverPortP
CircularManeuver	Maneuver	N/A	ManeuverPortP
AdvancedTargeting	Targeting Strategy	FiringPort	TargetPortP
RammingTargeting	Targeting Strategy	FiringPort	TargetPortP
LinearTargeting	Targeting Strategy	FiringPort	TargetPortP
Firing	Firing Strategy	N/A	FiringPortP

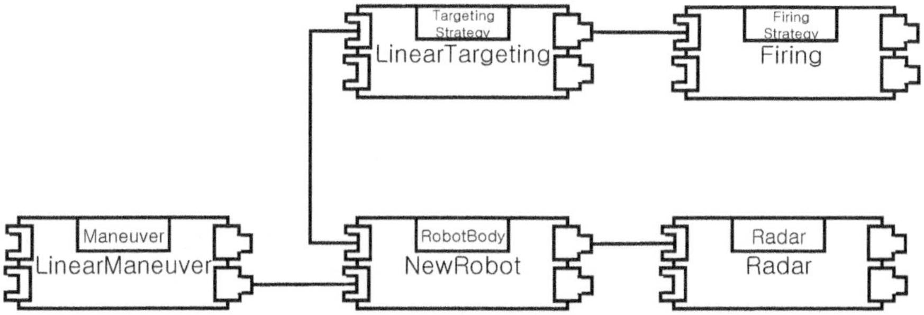

Fig. 5. The Initial Architecture of the Robot

The robot has five roles. 'Maneuver' is responsible for how to move. 'Radar' determines how to find an enemy robot by using a radar, and 'Targeting Strategy' determines how to target the enemy robot. 'Firing Strategy' determines how to fire at the enemy robot. 'RobotBody' has a role to relay over to the other 4 roles. In this experiment, 'Maneuver' and 'Targeting Strategy' are the target of adaptation.

Based on the components shown in table 1, the robot is constituted. Fig. 5 shows the structure of the components assigned roles of the robot in the initial state. The 'LinearManeuver' component works a role as 'Maneuver' and the 'LinearTargeting' does as 'Targeting Strategy' in the initial state of the robot.

3.4 The Result from An Experiment

We have performed two experiments in order to verify effectiveness of adaptation of the robot implemented by AlchemistJ. The first experiment is a battle our robot which has no adaptation capabilities(Robot X) and an enemy robot from outside. We design our robot without adaptation capabilities but this robot has 'CircularManeuver' component which plays 'Maneuver' role and 'Advanced-Targeting' component which plays 'Targeting Strategy'. 'CircularManeuver' component outperforms 'LinearManeuver', and 'AdvancedTargeting' component outperforms 'RammingTargeting' and 'LinearTargeting'. The enemy of this robot is 'Antigravity Robot' which is one of the best robots. Fig. 6 shows that 'Antigravity Robot' has a predominant winning average against a robot without adaptation capabilities. On the basis of this experiment, we designed the next experiment.

The second experiment is a battle between our robot with adaptation capabilities(Robot A) and 'Antigravity Robot'. 'Robot A' can reconfigure its architecture using components which plays 'Maneuver' role and 'Targeting Strategy' role such as 'LinearManeuver' and 'RammingTargeting'. Fig. 7 shows the result from the battle between two robots.

The result from the battle between 'Robot A' and 'Antigravity Robot' shows that 'Robot A' has a 60~70% winning average against 'Antigravity Robot'. It means that the dynamic reconfiguration with diverse 'Maneuver' and 'Targeting Strategy' components gives better performance than the maintenance with only one moving component and one targeting component even though those outperform other components.

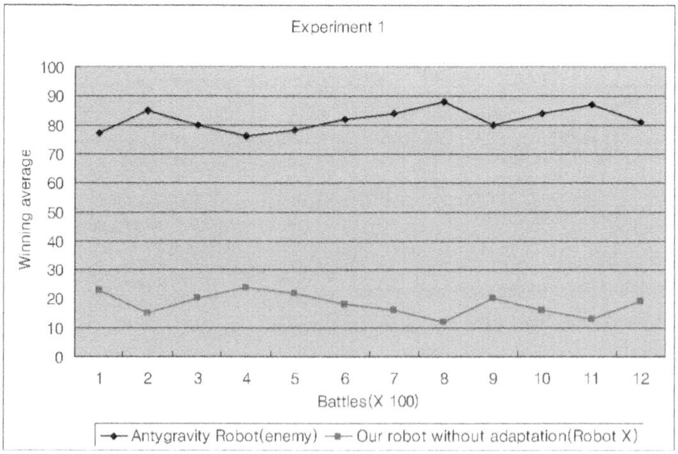

Fig. 6. The Result of the First Experiment

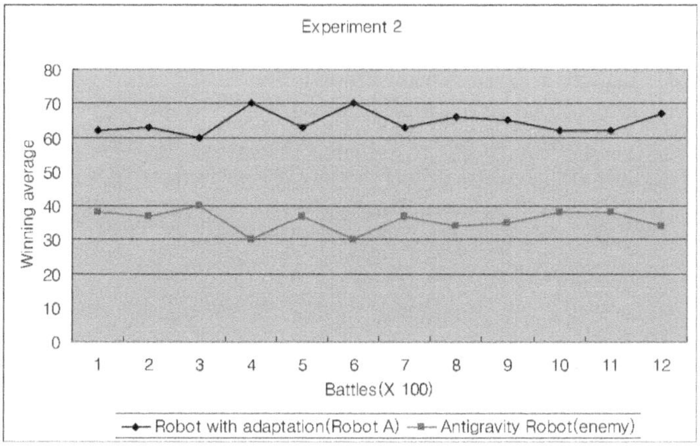

Fig. 7. The Result of the Second Experiment

Our approach has the exact difference from a sequence of `if-then-else` statements. A sequence of `if-then-else` statements is hard-coded in source code. Each `if-then-else` statement consists of a condition and an action. To modify a condition or an action, a programmer must rewrite the source code, compile it, shutdown the software system to be modified, re-link the compiled component, and re-execute again. However, AlchemistJ provides the characteristics to reduce the burden of a programmer. Of course, the programmer can make a situation(condition)-behavior(action) lookup table and propose a mechanism for updating the table dynamically, but the mechanism is already another version of AlchemistJ.

4 Related Work

The researches of Richard N. Taylor(University of California, Irvine)[12][11][2], David Garlan(Carnegie Mellon University)[4][1][5], Jamie Hillman(Lancaster University)[8][7] provide the capability of dynamic reconfiguration. The capabilities of dynamic reconfiguration proposed in each framework are different, but they have similarity in terms of changing software structure in the architecture level. All of the three frameworks cannot provide decision making and learning of the adaptive behavior. Even though they mention its necessity, they cannot suggest what technology and theory to use and to implement in practice. Except Garlan's research[5], they do not provide a implementation, but conceptually mention only the necessity of it.

We proposed the AlchemistJ framework integrating three capabilities. AlchemistJ is implemented by Java, and comprises three packages to support recognition of environment by defining interfaces for the monitor, decision making and learning by Q-learning implementation, and dynamic reconfiguration using role- and port-based software architecture.

5 Conclusions

Self-adaptive software recognizes environments, and determines the adaptation behavior according to the situations it recognized. In addition, it can change its own architecture in order to perform the adaptation behavior.

We proposed AlchemistJ as a software framework to support developing self-adaptive software. This framework proposed in this paper supports the followings.

1. It prescribes interfaces to support the implementation for recognition of its environment.
2. It employs reinforcement learning to the framework in order to support decision making and learning of the adaptive behavior.
3. It prescribes role- and port-based software architecture and reconfiguration principle in order to support dynamic reconfiguration at run-time.

In order to verify operations of the framework, we have implemented an instance of self-adaptive robot software with Robocode, and examined the ability of adaptation of software from two experiments.

Further study is the development of visualization tools and measurement tools to improve the efficiency of the framework. Also we need to develop a repository for framework to maintain components. In AlchemistJ, we implemented a simple and local repository which can only gives a component corresponding a simple message. The more advanced repository should manage components with more specific description and give components via online connection.

References

1. R. J. Allen, R. Douence, and D. Garlan. Specifying dynamism in software architectures. In *Proceedings of the Workshop on Foundations of Component-Based Software Engineering*, 1997.
2. E. M. Dashofy, A. van der Hoek, and R. N. Taylor. Towards architecture-based self-healing systems. In *Proceedings of the First Workshop on Self-Healing Systems*, 2002.
3. K. R. Dixon, T. Q. Pham, and P. K. Khosla. Port-based adaptable agent architecture. In *First International Workshop, IWSAS 2000*, 2000.
4. D. Garlan, S.-W. Cheng, A. C. Huang, B. Schmerl, and P. Steenkiste. Rainbow: Architecture-based self-adaptation with reusable infrastructure. *IEEE Computer*, 37(10):46–54, October 2004.
5. D. Garlan, B. Schmerl, and J. Chang. Using gauges for architecture-based monitoring and adaptation. In *the Working Conference on Complex and Dynamic Systems Architecture*, 2001.
6. M. M. Gorlick and R. R. Razouk. Using weaves for software construction and analysis. In *Proceedings of the 13th International Conference on Software Engineering*, 1991.
7. J. Hillman and I. Warren. Meta-adaptation in autonomic systems. In *10th IEEE International Workshop on Future Trends of Distributed Computing Systems*, 2004.

8. J. Hillman and I. Warren. An open framework for dynamic reconfiguration. In *26th International Conference on Software Engineering*, 2004.
9. T.-H. Kim and Y.-G. Shin. Role-based decomposition for improving concurrency in distributed object-oriented software development environments. In *23rd International Computer Software and Applications Conference*, 1999.
10. R. Laddaga. Active software. In H. S. Pual Robertson and R. Laddaga, editors, *First International Workshop on Self-Adaptive Software(IWSAS 2000)*, volume 1936 of *Lecture Notes in Computer Science*, pages 11–26. Springer, 2000.
11. P. Oreizy. Issues in the runtime modification of software architectures. Technical report, Department of Information and Computer Science, University of California, Irvine, 1996.
12. P. Oreizy, M. M. Gorlick, R. N. Taylor, D. Heimbingner, G. Johnson, N. Medvidovid, A. Quilici, D. S. Rosenblum, and A. L. Wolf. An architecture-based approach to self-adaptive software. *IEEE Intelligent Systems*, 14(3):54–62, May 1999.
13. R. S. Sutton and A. G. Barto. *Reinforcement Learning: An Introduction.* Cambridge, Massachusetts, The MIT Press, 1998.
14. C. J. C. H. Watkins. *Learning from Delayed Rewards.* PhD thesis, Cambridge University, 1989.
15. C. J. C. H. Watkins and P. Dayan. Technical note: Q-learning. *Machine Learning*, 8(3-4):279 – 292, May 1992.

Design and Implementation of Accounting System for Information Appliances

Midori Sugaya[1], Shuichi Oikawa[2], and Tatsuo Nakajima[1]

[1] Department of Computer Science, Waseda University
[2] Department of Computer Science, University of Tsukuba
{doly, tatsuo}@dcl.info.waseda.ac.jp, shui@cs.tsukuba.ac.jp

Abstract. This paper presents the design and implementation of Accounting System that is a resource monitoring and restriction system. The system improves the reliability and security of a system. Accounting System is a generic to offer various services, such as security improvement, overload control, class-based accounting, and resource reservation that require CPU resource control.

1 Introduction

Information appliances [5] are important elements to realize the ubiquitous computing vision [3]. Nowadays, most consumer electronics appliances have computing capability in order to retrieve data from sensors, to process the data, and to control devices. The recent emergence of information appliances requires more advanced features, such as networking and GUI. Those features dramatically complicate the appliances, software systems and increase their code sizes.

Networked systems need to be prepared for security attacks through the Internet. Since we expect users to be system administrators of applications, their software systems must be more robust than personal computers. Software bugs can also cause the monopolization of CPU resources. Real-time operating systems may be vulnerable to bugs of real-time programs that easily consume the whole CPU resources. For example, a problem can happen when multimedia applications process continuous media streams. Those multimedia applications have strict timing constrains, and are given the real-time priority in general. Therefore, once they process the streams, they can easily monopolize the whole CPU resources. In such a situation, the GUI process that is usually executed on the time-sharing scheduler cannot consume necessary CPU capacity, so that a user cannot control the multimedia applications through the GUI buttons. Another example is an overload condition. If an overload condition occurs, the response time of the system becomes worse.

General embedded operating systems have not yet provided a resource protection mechanism that aims to protect the CPU resources from such monopolizations and overload situations. Therefore, it is necessary to offer a generic mechanism to restrict the use of CPU resources to develop reliable information

L.T. Yang et al. (Eds.): EUC 2005, LNCS 3824, pp. 110–120, 2005.

appliances. In this paper, we propose Accounting System, a general-purpose resource monitoring and restriction system that prevents the excessive use of the CPU capacity of a process or a group of processes.

The following two points are our design principles.

- *Simple design* to be applied to various services. Accounting System focuses on providing a simple and generic model and interface. Therefore, the system should be able to be easily applied to various kinds of services.
- *Accurate resource management* by using a fine-grain resolution timer. Future information appliances require to support a fine-grained rate based execution that can be realized by the accurate resource management, for offering better response time and more stable execution.

Information appliances have become very complex. Most of them nowadays contain web browsers, Java Virtual Machines, and many other applications. Implementing these applications in a robust way needs a more powerful operating system. Linux is an open-source operating system, and supports various CPU architectures. Those features are very suitable for information appliances. Therefore, many industries consider adopting Linux for their products. While the use of Linux is increasing, it does not restrict the resource consumption for their processes. We assume Accounting System can solve this problem, and implement it in the Linux kernel.

The remaining of the paper is structured as follows. Section 2 describes the design and model of Accounting System. Section 3 presents the architecture and implementation. Section 4 shows the services that can be implemented by Accounting System, such as the secure resource protection, class-based accounting, and overload monitoring. Section 5 presents the evaluation results. Finally, in Section 6, we conclude the paper.

2 Accounting System Model

Accounting System and Accounting Object: Accounting System is a system to offer the functions that monitor and restrict the execution time of a process or a group of processes. We have developed it as a part of the kernel services. Accounting System provides an abstraction to manipulate the CPU capacity of each process named *accounting object*. An accounting object represents a capacity of the CPU resource on a single processor. The CPU time of each process bound to an accounting object is accumulated in it. Through an accounting object, a user can control the allocation of CPU resources for each accounting object. When a user binds a process to an accounting object through the system call, the process is given the restricted execution time specified by its accounting object.

Time Management Model: To realize the restriction, an accounting object has two parameters C and T, where T represents a period that is a constant period to control the object, and C is the maximum time to be able to execute processes within T. The process bound to the accounting object cannot consume the CPU time more than C within T. When processes consume the entire CPU time within each period T, the process is blocked until the next period comes.

3 Implementation

3.1 Callback Hooks

In Accounting System, callback hooks are introduced into the process management system in the host kernel for the purpose of catching events about processes. Those hooks catch the relevant events, and deliver those events to Accounting System. On our design principle, Accounting System should be independent of the host kernel, and the only minimum points in the host kernel should be modified. Accounting System assumes that the four callback hooks as described next are inserted in the host kernel.

- *schedule_hook:* It catches scheduling events on context switching among processes. The hook delivers the scheduling events to Accounting System that changes the state of an accounting object.
- *fork_hook:* It catches events when a new process is created. These events are required to start the accounting for the newly created processes. If a parent process has already been bound to an accounting object, its child processes inherited the same accounting object.
- *exit_hook:* It catches events on process termination. The events notify the timing to unbind the termination of a process from its accounting object.
- *kernel_callback_hook:* It catches events when a system call returns from the kernel mode to the user mode. Accounting System checks the state of an accounting object for the blocking of the process to execute the system call.

3.2 Timer Management System

The management of timers has an important role of Accounting System. In Accounting System, there are two types of timers, a replenishment timer and an enforcement timer. A replenishment timer is a periodic timer for each accounting object that is constantly expired. An enforcement timer keeps to watch on the elapsed time of the currently executing process. They are implemented by using kernel software timers. In the following paragraph, we describe the details of them.

- *Replenishment timer:* It manages the periodic time of an accounting object. Each accounting object has its own replenishment timer. When an accounting object is created, the timer is also created. In the replenishment timer, first the expiration time is set by adding the periodic time to the current time. If the elapsed time reaches the expiration time, the registered timer handler is executed to set the next expiration time. These replenishments are recursively done by the replenishment timer until it is destroyed.

- *Enforcement timer:* It watches the elapsed time of the currently executing process. The timer accumulates the execution time of the process, until it reaches to the maximum execution time of the accounting object. At that time, the registered timer handler is invoked to change the state of the accounting object. By using schedule_hook, the enforce timer catches the events about context switching among processes, and stops and starts its timer to monitor the CPU usage of processes.

3.3 Account Object Management Operations

To manage accounting objects, the system provides the accounting object management function. It introduces the following accounting object's basic operations. To receive the accounting object services, an application firstly invokes the *create* operation to allocate the accounting object in the kernel memory. Each created accounting object has a unique object ID. To bind a process to the specified accounting object with the object ID, the application invokes the *bind* operation. When the application no longer requires the accounting services, it invokes the *destroy* operation to terminate the accounting object service and to free the object memory in the kernel space. The *set* operation changes the parameters of an accounting object. The *get* operation obtains the parameter in an accounting object.

3.4 State Management

There are three states to represent an accounting object's status. *null* status represents the status that an accounting object is created, but no process is bound to the accounting object. *running* status represents the accounting object is running, and the status also represents that available time are left within the period time. *depleted* status represents the status that no more available time is left within the period time. The *depleted* status also represents that the accumulated execution time of a process is reached to the maximum execution time specified in the accounting object.

The state of an accounting object is changed by events. At first, when a process binds to a specific accounting object, the state becomes *running.* If the sum of the execution time of the bound processes equals to the maximum execution time of the accounting object, the object changes its state to *depleted.* Accounting System here to take action to stop their execution or deliver the notice to the bound process which is on the excessive use of the CPU capacity. The actions are classified into *block* and *signal.* If it is *block*, the system puts the processes to the wait queue. When the next expiration time comes, the replenish timer checks the wait queue, and if it finds the processes in the wait queue, sets the *running* state to the accounting object, and wakes up the processes. When a process uses excessive CPU capacity, a signal is delivered to the process. Using the state transition mechanism, Accounting System restricts the CPU usage of the processes accurately.

3.5 High Resolution Timer

For Accounting System, the high-precision clock and timestamp counter are essential to maintain the fidelity of its accuracy. To provide less than 10ms resolution for monitoring, there are some approaches. The most straightforward way is to make the clock interrupt frequency higher than 100Hz in order to issue more interrupts. This allows the kernel to provide a precise timing and to increase the system responsiveness. However, shorter intervals require CPU to spend a longer time in the kernel mode. Therefore, user programs run slower because of the system overhead to handle interrupts. Our system solves the problem by using the high resolution timer [2]. The high-resolution timer in Intel x86, is implemented by using the one shot mode of the APIC clock timer chip. Therefore, the extra timer interrupt overhead will never happen. The high-resolution timer allows us to specify microsecond granularity parameters in accounting objects.

4 Services Using Accounting System

4.1 Secure Resource Protection

Accounting System protects the CPU resource from downloaded programs that behave maliciously. We assume that there is a manager process that starts processes to execute downloaded programs. The manager process is bound to an accounting object, of which C and T are 50ms and 100ms, respectively. When the manager process receives a request to execute a downloaded application, it creates a new process. The process is automatically bound to the accounting object to which the manager process is bound. Therefore, the newly created process cannot consume more than 50% of CPU capacity, and it cannot monopolize the CPU resource.

Binding Multiple processes: Accounting System provides the *bind* operation that binds a process to the accounting object. We also provide some useful interfaces to bind multiple processes to an accounting object. For example, if a malicious program consecutively invokes the *fork* system call, the whole system resources may be consumed. We implement the following two methods. The one is to inherit an accounting object when creating a child process. The other is to bind an accounting object using group ID. The former function is realized by using a hook within the *fork* system call. If a parent process is bound to an accounting object, the child process who is forked from the parent inherits the same accounting object. Thus, the same restriction as its parent is applied. The latter uses UNIX group process ID. The system binds the group of processes to a specific accounting object. It is safer than binding all processes to the same accounting object respectively. For example, when several commands connected by pipes are started, they can be easily bound to the same accounting object by using group ID.

Access Control: Each accounting object has an owner attribute for controlling the access to a specific accounting object. The owner attribute of the accounting object is assigned by a process that creates it. For the consideration of the security, our system allows them to be manipulated only by their owners except the privileged user. In resources reservation systems such as Linux/RK [4], there is no support of access control. Therefore, these previous system cannot be used for protecting the CPU resource from malicious programs.

Kernel Interface: The following is the kernel interface offerd by Account System.

- *account_create(&object_id,&object_attr)* It creates a new accounting object. When created, the object is not bound to any processes. A privileged or owner application program sets the parameters, such as C, T, in the object_attr memebers.
- *account_destroy(&object_id)* It destroys the accounting object specified by object_id. This deletes the associated timers, and frees the memory of the accounting object in the kernel address space.
- *account_bind/unbind_pid(object_id, pid_t)* It binds/unbinds the specified accounting object through object_id to a process whose process ID is pid. An accounting object can be bound to multiple processes. If the process is terminated, the process is automatically unbound from the accounting object.
- *account_get/set(object_id, &object_attr)* It retrieves/changes the parameters of the specified accounting object.

4.2 Class-Based Accounting

In this section, we propose a class-based accounting as the one of the services that uses Accounting System. A class is defined here as a group of processes that belong to a specific scheduling class, such as the real-time scheduling class. The class-based accounting is realized by binding the processes belonging to the same scheduling class.

A problem of process starvation: When a user forgets to bind a real-time process to an accounting object, the real-time process may monopolize the entire CPU resource. Even if most real-time processes are restricted, the only one real-time process can consume the rest of all the CPU resources; thus, all other time-sharing processes are starved. To avoid such a situation, the system designer should estimate the total maximum utilization of the accounting objects, which bind to the all real-time processes. We called the approach class-based accounting.

Class-based Accounting: The class-based accounting is realized by binding processes in the specific scheduling class to an accounting object. A class contains all processes that are scheduled by the same scheduling policy. The system allocates the CPU resources proportionally to each scheduling class. The total proportions of the classes are set to 100%. For example, a user can allocate 40%

of the CPU capacity for the real-time scheduling class, and the remaining 60% of the CPU capacity for the time-sharing scheduling class. The system assumes to have two classes that are necessary to allocate the absolute rate of the CPU capacity.

The processes bound to each class cannot excessively use the maximum utilization of the CPU resources that are set in each scheduling class. Since the real-time process cannot use more than the assigned capacity, the time-sharing process can use the remaining capacity without process starvation.

Implementation: The current class-based accounting allocates the CPU capacity for the real-time and time-sharing scheduling class. The accounting object for each scheduling class is created at the boot time. When it is created, all processes that belong to the same scheduling class are bound to the same accounting object. In order to set the parameter easily, class-based accounting adopts weight as its interface parameters. The weight is the parameter that represents a proportion and can easily be specified like (2,3). If weight (2,3) given, the real-time class and the time-sharing class are allocated 40% and 60% CPU capacity respectively. In class-based accounting, the accounting object of each scheduling class should use the same period time. Also, a user needs to set the resolution time that is a period for the accounting objects. For example, if the resolution is 100ms and the class proportion is 40%, the class is received 40ms within the 100ms period.

Kernel Interface: We design the kernel interface for class-based accounting as described as following.

- *weight_set (wt_ts, wt_rt, res)* Sets the weight and resolution to the accounting object for respective scheduling classes. When the class accounting object is started, it monitors the execution time of the bound processes.

4.3 Overload Monitoring

Conceiving the overload situation: For general-purpose operating systems, controlling overload situations is very important to offer services in a stable way. In such critical situations, the computational requests from the process will exceed the time that is available in the system. As for time-sharing processes, the average response time is increasing. We propose the monitoring function that keeps to watch the total utilization of the CPU. If the overload condition happens, the overload monitoring system issues a signal to notify to the registered administrator process. If there is a notification for the administrator process, some recovery procedures can be taken to stabilize the system.

Design and Implementation: The overload monitoring can also be realized by Accounting System. In this system, an accounting object bound to the idle process is used to monitor the total utilization of the system resources. The idle process is executed when there is no runnable process. If the system becomes busy, the idle process consumes a very little CPU capacity. Through monitoring the CPU usage of the idle processes, the system can detect the overload situation. Our system allows an application to receive a signal when the CPU usage of the idle process becomes lower than the specified CPU. The service is available when a system designer creates an overload accounting object, and sets the parameters to it. There is the only one overload accounting object in a system. A system designer should explicitly set the C and T parameter to the overload accounting object. Suppose the designer sets C and T to 75ms and 100ms respectively, it monitors the CPU capacity not to exceed 75%. If the designer would like to check the overload condition every minute, C and T should be set to 45sec and 60sec respectively. If the total usage of CPU utilization exceeds 75%, an overload notification signal is delivered to a specific process. A system designer also should set a process as a receiver of the signal. The signal number can be freely decided by a user. In consideration of the security, only a privileged user can create and destroy the overload accounting object.

Kernel Interface: The overload monitoring offers the kernel interface as described as follows.

- *overload_create (&object_attr, pid)* The function binds an idle process to the overload accounting object. The user sets an administrator process ID that accepts a signal from the system and a signal number that is used to deliver the signal to the administrator process when an overload condition occurs.
- *overload_destroy(void)* It destroys the overload accounting object.

4.4 Resource Reservation

An application running on our system can request the reservation of a certain amount of CPU resources. The OS-enforced resource reservation can be introduced similar to CPU capacity reserves [1] [4], which provide the framework for managing the processor capacity. Accounting System can implement the framework easily by adding a mechanism for the admission control as a user-level service.

5 Evaluation

We have evaluated Accounting System by running several benchmarks. The evaluation uses a standard PC that has Celeron 300MHz CPU and 512MB of RAM, and the results were measured using the built-in high-resolution timestamp counter.

5.1 Accuracy of Accounting System

This section evaluates the accuracy of Accounting System. To evaluate the effectiveness of high-resolution timer support, we use the benchmark program that executes the infinite-loop. We create two accounting objects that set 20ms and

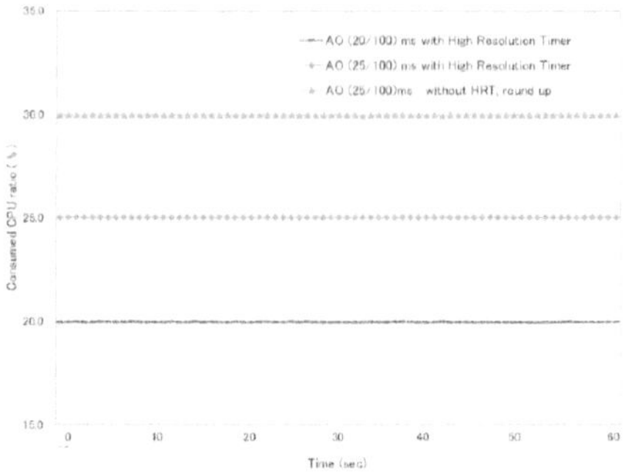

Fig. 1. With/Without High Resolution Timer Support

25ms of CPU time every 100ms, and bind the program to each accounting object. Figure 1 shows the result of the consumed CPU ratio with/without the support of a high-resolution timer. In this figure, the bottom two lines are the results of the high-resolution timer support. It shows that each 20% and 25% resource restriction is correctly limited. In the contrast, without the high-resolution timer support, the program bound to the accounting object whose execution time is 25ms executes 30ms within 100ms. These are apparently due to the fact that Linux updates its internal timer-clock at the 10ms intervals. Even if a user sets a parameter whose resolution is less than 10ms, it is impossible to ensure the resolution. The results shows that the effectiveness of the accurate resource accounting.

5.2 Effectiveness of CPU Protection

This section evaluates the effectiveness of the CPU resource protection in Accounting System. First, we show the effect of the security attacks, then, show the result of the class-based accounting.

Attacks to create multiple processes: Figure 2 shows the consumed CPU ratio of multiple processes bound to an accounting object. To evaluate the effectiveness for protecting from attacks to create multiple processes, we run an evil

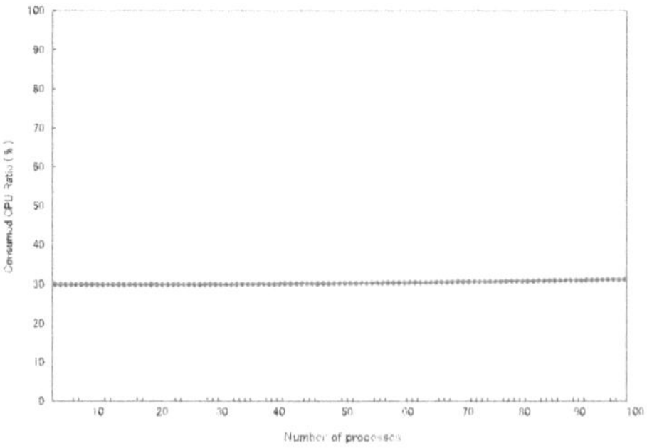

Fig. 2. The Numbers of Process and Accounting Object Ratio

program that invokes fork() consecutively and produces a lot of child processes that execute their infinite-loops. The response time becomes very bad by this malicious program because these processes consume the whole CPU resource. In the evaluation, if the first process is bound to the 30% restricted accounting object, the forked processes cannot use more than 30% of the CPU capacity, even if the numbers of processes are increasing. The result shows the effectiveness of Accounting System as shown in Figure 2. The loss of the accuracy appears as the numbers of created process is increased. In the current implementation, a process that executes a system call is blocked after the system call is returned, when the execution time of the accounting object is expired. If there are multiple processes that are bound to the same accounting object, and they execute system calls, the system calls can be executed before blocking themselves. This is a reason to exceed the specified execution time when the number of process bound to the same accounting object is increased.

Class-based Accounting: Figure 3 and Figure 4 show the results of the evaluation of class-based accounting. To evaluate the effectiveness of the class-based accounting, the benchmark runs a real-time process to execute an infinite loop with/without the class-based accounting. Figure 3 shows the result when the class-based accounting is not used. The result shows that all CPU resources are consumed by the real-time process. Then, we evaluate the class-based accounting in which each class is set the weight (4,1) where 80% and 20% CPU capacity are allocated for real-time processes and time-sharing processes respectively. The Xserver (X Window System display server) process runs on the time-sharing scheduler. On Xserver, some game programs are running. Figure 4 shows the result that the real-time processes can not exceed 80% CPU resources, where the Xserver process can use 20% CPU resource at a maximum.

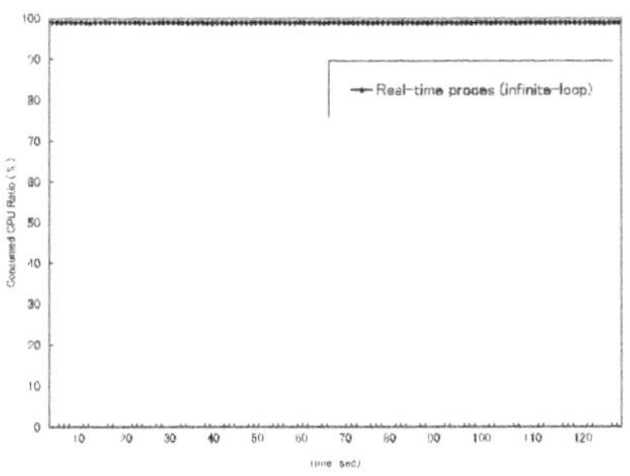

Fig. 3. Without Class-Based Accounting

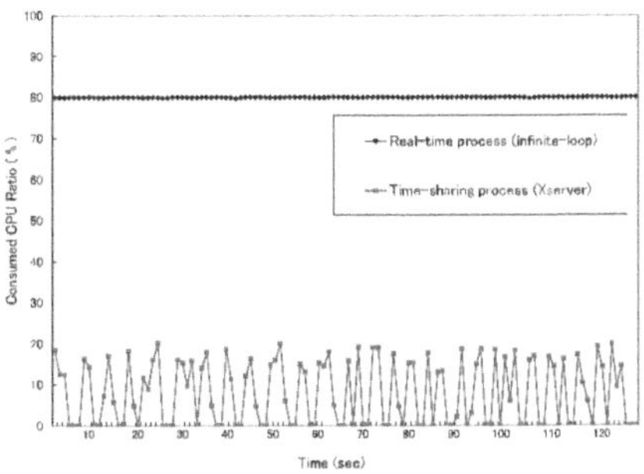

Fig. 4. With Class-Based Accounting

6 Conclusion

In this paper, we have proposed Accounting System. This system provides the generic accounting model that can be applied various services that are used to increase the system security and reliability. It also supports a fine-grained resource accounting with the high-resolution timer. This makes the system more stable because the application can obtain the necessary rate precisely even in the microsecond resolution. The performance evaluation results have showed that the system effectively protects the malicious use of CPU resources.

References

1. Clifford W. Mercer, Stefan Savage, and Hideyuki Tokuda.: Processor capacity reserves: Operating system support for multimedia applications. In Proceedings of the IEEE Internation Conference on Multimedia Computing and Systems, pages 90–99, May 1994.
2. High Resolution Timer, http://high-res-timers.sourceforge.net/
3. Mark Weiser.: The Computer for the 21st Centriy, Scientific American, Vol 265, No.3, 1991.
4. Shuichi Oikawa and Ragunathan Rajkumar.: Portable RK: A portable resource kernel for guaranteed and enforced timing behavior. In Proc. IEEE RTAS, 1999.
5. W. P. Sharpe, S. P. Stenton.: Information Appliances, The Human-Computer Interaction Handbook : Fundamentals, Evolving Technologies and Emerging Applications - Human Factors and Ergonomics, Chapter37, Lawrence Erlbaum Assoc Inc Published 2002.

Loop Distribution and Fusion with Timing and Code Size Optimization for Embedded DSPs*

Meilin Liu[1], Qingfeng Zhuge[1], Zili Shao[2], Chun Xue[1], Meikang Qiu[1], and Edwin H.-M. Sha[1]

[1] University of Texas at Dallas,
Richardson, Texas 75083, USA
{mxl024100, qfzhuge, cxx016000, mxq012100, edsha}@utdallas.edu
[2] Hong Kong Polytechnic University,
Hung Hom, Kowloon, Hong Kong
cszlshao@comp.polyu.edu.hk

Abstract. Loop distribution and loop fusion are two effective loop transformation techniques to optimize the execution of the programs in DSP applications. In this paper, we propose a new technique combining loop distribution with direct loop fusion, which will improve the timing performance without jeopardizing the code size. We first develop the loop distribution theorems that state the legality conditions of loop distribution for multi-level nested loops. We show that if the summation of the edge weights of the dependence cycle satisfies a certain condition, then the statements involved in the dependence cycle can be distributed; otherwise, they should be put in the same loop after loop distribution. Then, we propose the technique of maximum loop distribution with direct loop fusion. The experimental results show that the execution time of the transformed loops by our technique is reduced 21.0% on average compared to the original loops and the code size of the transformed loops is reduced 7.0% on average compared to the original loops.

Keywords: Loop Fusion, Loop Distribution, Embedded DSP, Code Size, Scheduling.

1 Introduction

Timing performance and code size are two major concerns for embedded systems with very limited on-chip memory resources [9]. Since loops are prevalent in multimedia processing, digital signal processing, etc., loop transformations such as loop fusion, loop distribution are needed to optimize the execution of the loops in embedded DSP applications [8, 1, 2, 3, 5].

Loop distribution separates independent statements inside a single loop (or loop nest) into multiple loops (or loop nests) [8, 1, 3, 2, 5]. Loop distribution

* This work is partially supported by TI University Program, NSF EIA-0103709, Texas ARP 009741-0028-2001, NSF CCF-0309461, NSF IIS-0513669, Microsoft, USA.

L.T. Yang et al. (Eds.): EUC 2005, LNCS 3824, pp. 121–130, 2005.

can be used to break up a large loop that doesn't fit into the cache [2, 3, 8, 1]. It can also improve memory locality by fissioning a loop that refers to many different arrays into several loops, each of which refers to only a few arrays. Loop distribution can also enable other loop optimization techniques such as loop fusion, loop interchanging and loop permutation [8, 1, 3, 5].

Loop fusion, on the other hand, groups multiple loops to increase the instruction level parallelism, and correspondingly reduces execution time. There are a lot of previous works using loop fusion to optimize the execution of loops [2, 3, 8, 1, 4, 5, 7]. But sometimes loop shifting or retiming is needed to enable loop fusion, which will cause the code size expansion because of the generation of the prologue and epilogue. The maximum loop fusion technique (Max_LF) proposed in [4] can maximize the opportunities of loop fusion, but it cannot be applied in the cases where strict memory constraint applies.

A combination of loop distribution and loop fusion can find an optimization solution with both reduced execution time and restricted code size if the loop properties are fully understood. Therefore, it is very important to revisit and formalize the loop distribution and loop fusion theorems on graph models, and find an effective way to combine these two oppositely directed optimization techniques. In this paper, we propose a technique of *maximum loop distribution with direct fusion* (MLD_DF), which performs *maximum loop distribution*, followed by *direct loop fusion*. The technique significantly improves the timing performance compared to the original loops without jeopardizing the code size.

Loop distribution is an important part of our technique of maximum loop distribution with direct fusion (MLD_DF). But loop distribution is not simple. All the data dependences have to be preserved when breaking one single loop into multiple small loops. The authors of [2, 3, 5] stated that loop distribution preserves dependences if all statements involved in a data dependence cycle in the original loop are placed in the same loop. We show that dependence cycle is a restriction for loop distribution for one-level loops only. For multi-level nested loops, dependence cycle is not always a restriction for loop distribution. If the summation of the edge weights of the dependence cycle satisfies a certain condition, then the statements involved in the dependence cycle can be distributed.

In this paper, we propose general loop distribution theorems for multi-level loops to state the legality conditions of loop distribution based on the understanding of loop properties on graph models. Then, we show how to conduct maximum loop distribution for N-level loops based on the loop distribution theorems. We then propose the technique of maximum loop distribution with direct fusion (MLD_DF). The experimental results showed that the execution time of the transformed loops by our MLD_DF technique can be improved 21.0% on average compared to the original loops when there are eight functional units.

The rest of the paper is organized as follows: We introduce the basic concepts and principles related to our technique in Section 2. In Section 3, we propose the loop distribution theorems to guide loop distribution. We propose the technique of maximum loop distribution with direct fusion (MLD_DF) in Section 4. Section 5 presents the experimental results. Section 6 concludes the paper.

2 Basic Concepts

In this section, we provide an overview of the basic concepts and principles related to our technique.

2.1 Data Flow Graph

We use a multi-dimensional data flow graph($MDFG$) to model the body of one nested loop. A MDFG $G = (V, E, \boldsymbol{d}, t)$ is a node-weighted and edge-weighted directed graph, where V is the set of computation nodes, $E \subseteq V \times V$ is the set of edges representing dependences, $\boldsymbol{d}$ is a function from E to Z^n, representing the multi-dimensional delays between two nodes, where n is the number of dimensions, and t is a function from V to positive integers, representing the computation time of each node.

```
for i=0, N
    for j=0, M
        D[i,j]=B[i-1,j+1]*C[i-1,j-1];
        A[i,j]=D[i,j]*0.5;
        B[i,j]=A[i,j]+1;
        C[i,j]=A[i,j]+2;
    endfor
endfor
```

(a)

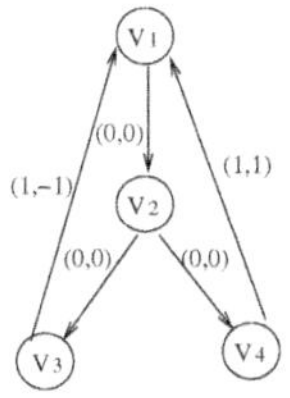

(b)

```
for i=0, N
    for j=0, M
        D[i,j]=B[i-1,j+1]*C[i-1,j-1];
    endfor
    for j=0, M
        A[i,j]=D[i,j]*0.5;
    endfor
    for j=0, M
        B[i,j]=A[i,j]+1;
    endfor
    for j=0, M
        C[i,j]=A[i,j]+2;
    endfor
endfor
```

(c)

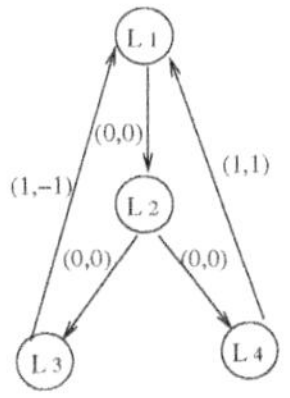

(d)

Fig. 1. (a) A loop extracted from a Wave Digital Filter. (b) The corresponding Data Flow Graph. (c) The distributed loop. (d) The loop dependence graph of the distributed loop.

The execution of each node in V exactly once represents an iteration, i.e., the execution of one instance of the loop body. Iterations are identified by a vector $\boldsymbol{i}$, equivalent to a multi-dimensional index. Inter-iteration dependences are represented by vector-weighted edges. For any iteration $\boldsymbol{j}$, an edge e from u to v with delay vector $\boldsymbol{d}(e)$ means that the computation of node v at iteration $\boldsymbol{j}$ requires the data produced by node u at iteration $\boldsymbol{j} - \boldsymbol{d}(e)$. An edge with delay $(0, \cdots, 0)$ represents a data dependence within the same iteration. A legal MDFG must have no zero-delay cycle, i.e., the summation of the edge weights along any cycle can not be $(0, \cdots, 0)$.

The program shown in Fig. 1(a) is extracted from a wave digital filter and its corresponding data flow graph is shown in Fig. 1(b).

2.2 Loop Dependence Graph

Loop dependence graph (LDG) is a higher-level graph model compared to the data flow graph [4]. It is used to model the data dependences between multiple loops. A multi-dimensional loop dependence graph (MLDG) $G = (V, E, \delta, o)$

```
for i=0, N
  for j=0,M
    A[i,j]=C[i-2,j+1];                 (L1)
  endfor
  for j=0, M
    B[i,j]=A[i,j+1]+A[i,j]+C[i-1,j];   (L2)
  endfor
  for j=0, M
    C[i,j]=B[i,j]+A[i,j+2]+A[i,j+1];   (L3)
  endfor
endfor
```

(a)

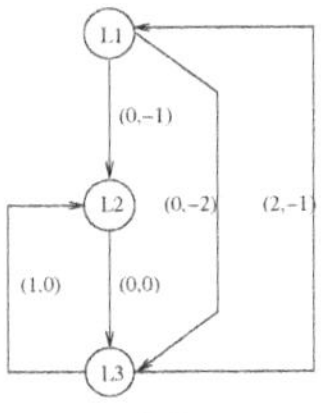

(b)

Fig. 2. A loop and its corresponding LDG

is a node-labeled and edge-weighted directed graph, where V is a set of nodes representing the loops. $E \subseteq V \times V$ is a set of edges representing data dependences between the loops. δ is a function from E to Z^n, representing the minimum data dependence vector between the computations of two loops. o is a function from V to positive integers, representing the order of the execution sequence. All the comparisons between two data dependence vectors are based on the lexicographic order in this paper.

The loop dependence graph of the loop in Fig. 2(a) is shown in Fig. 2(b). There are three nodes $V = \{L1, L2, L3\}$ in the loop dependence graph that represent the three innermost loops in the program. The loop dependence edges are $E = \{e_1 : L1 \to L2,\ e_2 : L1 \to L3,\ e_3 : L2 \to L3,\ e_4 : L3 \to L2,\ e_5 : L3 \to L1\}$. The data dependence vectors are $\{(0,-1),(0,0)\}$ between nodes $L1$ and $L2$, $\{(0,-2),(0,-1)\}$ between nodes $L1$ and $L3$, $\{(0,0)\}$ between nodes $L2$ and $L3$, $\{(1,0)\}$ between nodes $L3$ and $L2$, and $\{(2,-1)\}$ between nodes $L3$ and $L1$. According to our MLDG definition, $\delta(e_1) = (0,-1)$, $\delta(e_2) = (0,-2)$, $\delta(e_3) = (0,0)$, $\delta(e_4) = (1,0)$, $\delta(e_5) = (2,-1)$.

In a loop dependence graph, a fusion-preventing dependence is represented by an edge e with edge weight $\delta(e) < (0,0,\cdots,0)$. The fusion-preventing dependence edges for the LDG shown in Fig. 2(b) are e_1 and e_2.

A backward edge in the loop dependence graph is defined as an edge from a node labeled with a larger number to a node labeled with a smaller number. For example, in the loop dependence graph shown in Fig. 2(b), node $L1$ represents the first inner loop of the loop shown in Fig. 2(a), which is labeled with 1 according to the execution sequence. Node $L3$ represents the third inner loop of the loop shown in Fig. 2(a), which is labeled with 3. According to the definition, in the loop dependence graph shown in Fig. 2(b), the backward edges include the edge from node $L3$ to $L1$, and the edge from $L3$ to $L2$.

3 Theorems of Loop Distribution

In the process of loop distribution, we must maintain all the data dependences to ensure that we won't change the semantics of the original program. To guarantee the correctness of loop distribution, we propose several theorems to guide loop distribution. In this paper, we only consider the loops with uniform data dependences. A lot of DSP applications fit in this category. In the following, the general theorems for the N-level nested loops is proposed.

Theorem 1. *Given a N-level perfect nested loop and its corresponding data flow graph, after loop distribution, if the shared outer loop level is J, $J \leq N-1$, then the backward edge e in the LDG $G = (V, E, \delta, o)$ of the distributed loop must satisfy that $(\delta_1(e), \cdots, \delta_J(e)) \geq (0, \cdots, 1)$.*

If we distribute the loop on the $(J+1)$-th loop level, then the distributed loop has J-level shared outer loop. A backward edge e in a LDG represents loop-carried data dependence. The first J elements in an edge weight vector $(\delta_1(e), \cdots, \delta_J(e))$ represent the dependence distance of the shared outer loop. If $(\delta_1(e), \cdots, \delta_J(e))$ of a backward edge e in the LDG of the distributed loop is a non-positive value, then true data dependences are changed to anti-data dependences by loop distribution. Thus, loop distribution becomes illegal. Obviously, the code shown in Fig.3(b) computes differently from the code shown in Fig.3(a). $A[i,j]$ is dependent on $B[i,j-1]$, which is a true data dependence in the original program as shown in Fig.3(a). If we directly distribute the loop shown in Fig.3(a), then this true data dependence becomes an anti-data dependence in the distributed loop as shown in Fig. 3(b). Therefore, any legal LDG of an N-level nested loop (distributed loop) must have a positive value on the first J elements of the weight vectors of the backward edges.

```
for  i=0, N
    for  j=0, M
        A[i,j]=B[i,j-1]*2;
        B[i,j]=A[i,j]+5;
    endfor
endfor
```

(a)

```
for  i=0, N
    for  j=0, M
        A[i,j]=B[i,j-1]*2;
    endfor
    for  j=0, M
        B[i,j]=A[i,j]+5;
    endfor
endfor
```

(b)

Fig. 3. An illustration example

Fig. 1(c) shows the distributed loop of the original program shown in Fig. 1(a). Because the backward edges $e_1 : L3 \rightarrow L1$ and $e_2 : L4 \rightarrow L1$ in the LDG shown in Fig. 1(d) have the edge weight (1,-1) and weight (1,1) respectively, i.e., the backward edges e_1 and e_2 both have positive value on the first element, the correct execution of the original loop is able to be preserved in the distributed loop.

When there are dependence cycles existing in the data flow graph of a loop, it's important to know whether the computations involved in a dependence cycle can be distributed or not. In the following, we show that the nodes in the dependence cycles of the LDG of a N-level nested loop can be *completely distributed* when the necessary condition in Theorem 2 is satisfied. A loop is completely distributed when each loop unit after distribution only has one array assignment statement.

Theorem 2. *Given a N-level perfect nested loop and its corresponding data flow graph $G = (V, E, \mathbf{d}, t)$,*

1. *if there is no dependence cycle in the data flow graph G,*
2. *or if for any dependence cycle $c = \{v_1 \rightarrow v_2 \rightarrow \cdots \rightarrow v_n \rightarrow v_1\}$ in G, the summation $\mathbf{d}(c)$ of the edge weights of cycle c satisfies that $(\mathbf{d}_1(c), \cdots, \mathbf{d}_J(c)) \geq (0, \cdots, 1), J \leq N - 1$,*

then the loop can be completely distributed on the $(J + 1)$-th level loop until the N-th level.

Due to the space limit, we do not give a formal proof here. It directly follows from Theorem 1, since all the data dependences in the LDG of the distributed loop come from the data dependences of the original loop. Theorem 2 also shows that if we can distribute the loop at the J-th ($J < N$) loop level for a N-level loop, we can distribute this N-level loop at the innermost loop level.

For example, there is one cycle in the data flow graph of the 3-level loop shown in Fig. 4(a). The summation of the edge weights of the dependence cycle c in the corresponding data flow graph has the property that $d_1(c) = 1$. According to theorem 2, we can distribute the loop at the second loop level. The distributed loop is shown in Fig. 4(b). There is one-level shared outer loop in the distributed loop. Also we can distribute the innermost loop of this 3-level loop, and the distributed loop is shown in Fig. 4(c).

```
for i=0, N
  for j=0, M
    for k=0, S
      A[i,j,k]=C[i-1,j,k]+7;
      B[i,j,k]=A[i,j,k]*3;
      C[i,j,k]=B[i,j,k]+5;
    endfor
  endfor
endfor
```

(a)

```
for i=0, N
  for j=0, M
    for k=0, S
      A[i,j,k]=C[i-1,j,k]+7;
    endfor
  endfor
  for j=0, M
    for k=0, S
      B[i,j,k]=A[i,j,k]*3;
    endfor
  endfor
  for j=0, M
    for k=0, S
      C[i,j,k]=B[i,j,k]+5;
    endfor
  endfor
endfor
```

(b)

```
for i=0, N
  for j=0, M
    for k=0, S
      A[i,j,k]=C[i-1,j,k]+7;
    endfor
    for k=0, S
      B[i,j,k]=A[i,j,k]*3;
    endfor
    for k=0, S
      C[i,j,k]=B[i,j,k]+5;
    endfor
  endfor
endfor
```

(c)

Fig. 4. (a)A 3-level nested loop. (b) The distributed loop with 1-level outer shared loop. (c) The distributed loop with 2-level outer shared loop.

Theorem 3 identifies the dependence cycle in the data flow graph that prevents the statements involved in the dependence cycle from distribution.

Theorem 3. *Given a N-level nested loop and its corresponding data flow graph $G = (V, E, \mathbf{d}, t)$, for any dependence cycle $c = \{v_1 \rightarrow v_2 \rightarrow \cdots \rightarrow v_n \rightarrow v_1\}$ in G, such that the summation of the edge weights $\mathbf{d}(c)$ satisfies that $(\mathbf{d}_1(c), \cdots, \mathbf{d}_J(c)) = (0, \cdots, 0)$, the statements involved in dependence cycle c must be placed in the same loop after the loop is distributed on the $(J + 1)$-th loop level.*

If we distribute the statements in a dependence cycle c with $(\boldsymbol{d}_1(c), \cdots, \boldsymbol{d}_J(c)) = (0, \cdots, 0)$, then there will be a dependence cycle c with $(\boldsymbol{d}_1(c), \cdots, \boldsymbol{d}_J(c)) = (0, \cdots, 0)$ in the correspondent LDG of the distributed loop. For a legal program, all the edges e involved in a dependence cycle c in the LDG must have the property $(\boldsymbol{d}_1(c), \cdots, \boldsymbol{d}_J(c)) \geq (0, \cdots, 0)$. So the backward edge e' in the cycle c must have $(\boldsymbol{d}_1(e'), \cdots, \boldsymbol{d}_J(e')) = (0, \cdots, 0)$, which is contradictory to Theorem 1. When the first J elements of the summation of the edge weights of a cycle are all zeros, it indicates that all the statements in the cycle have to be computed within one loop. In other words, all the statements involved in a dependence cycle c with $(\boldsymbol{d}_1(c), \cdots, \boldsymbol{d}_J(c)) = (0, \cdots, 0)$ must be put into one loop after the loop is distributed on the $(J+1)$-th loop level.

4 Loop Distribution and Loop Fusion

In this section, we first use an example to show how to conduct maximum loop distribution for N-level nested loops based on the loop distribution theorems proposed in Section 3. Then, we propose the technique of maximum loop distribution with direct fusion (MLD_DF).

4.1 Maximum Loop Distribution

To conduct maximum loop distribution for a multi-level loop on the innermost loop level, we first remove the edges e with weight $(\boldsymbol{d}_1(e), \cdots, \boldsymbol{d}_{N-1}(e)) \geq (0, \cdots, 1)$ from the LDG of the given loop. Thus, if the summation $\boldsymbol{d}(c)$ of the edge weights of a cycle c in the LDG satisfies that $(\boldsymbol{d}_1(c), \cdots, \boldsymbol{d}_{N-1}(e)) \geq (0, \cdots, 1)$, then cycle c is broken. Then, we merge each cycle c with $(\boldsymbol{d}_1(c), \cdots, \boldsymbol{d}_{N-1}(c)) = (0, \cdots, 0)$ into one node. This is used to guarantee that the statements involved in the dependency cycle whose summation of the edge weights satisfies that $(\boldsymbol{d}_1(c), \cdots, \boldsymbol{d}_{N-1}(c)) = (0, \cdots, 0)$ will be put into the same loop after loop distribution. Then, we can reorder the nodes by the topological order to ensure that the edge weight $\delta(e)$ of a backward edge e in the LDG of the distributed loop has positive value on its first $N-1$ elements, i.e., $(\delta_1(e), \cdots, \delta_{N-1}(e)) \geq (0, \cdots, 1)$. Every node in the transformed graph corresponds to a loop unit in the distributed loop.

```
for i=0, N
  for j=0, M
    for k=0, S
      A[i,j,k]=D[i,j,k-2];
      B[i,j,k]=A[i-1,j,k];
      C[i,j,k]=B[i,j,k]+D[i,j,k-1];
      D[i,j,k]=C[i,j,k]+7;
    endfor
  endfor
endfor
```

(a)

```
for i=0, N
  for j=0, M
    for k=0, S
      B[i,j,k]=A[i-1,j,k];
    endfor
    for k=0, S
      C[i,j,k]=B[i,j,k]+D[i,j,k-1];
      D[i,j,k]=C[i,j,k]+7;
    endfor
    for k=0, S
      A[i,j,k]=D[i,j,k-2];
    endfor
  endfor
endfor
```

(b)

Fig. 5. (a)An example loop. (b) The distributed loop.

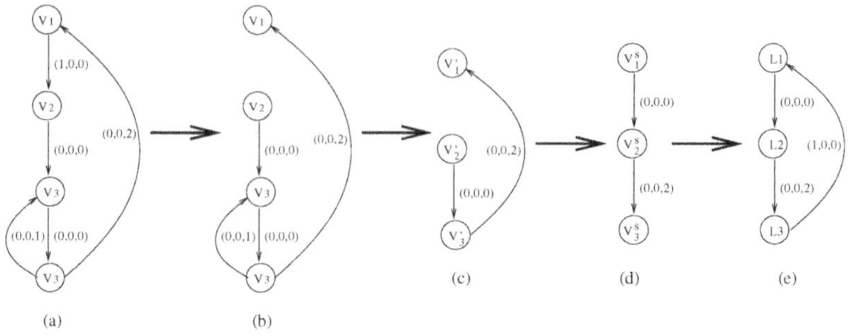

Fig. 6. The graph transformation process of the maximum loop distribution algorithm

We use a 3-level nested loop as shown in Fig. 5(a) to show the graph transformation process of maximum loop distribution for N-level nested loops. There are two cycles c_1, c_2 in its corresponding data flow graph as shown in Fig. 6(a). The summation of the edge weights of the first cycle $c_1 = \{V_1 \to V_2 \to V_3 \to V_4 \to V_1\}$ satisfies that $\boldsymbol{d}(c_1) = (1, 0, 2)$, so cycle c_1 will be broken after the edges e with $(\boldsymbol{d}_1(e), \boldsymbol{d}_2(e)) \geq (0, 1)$ are removed. The summation of the edge weights of the second cycle $c_2 = \{V_3 \to V_4 \to V_3\}$ has the property that $\boldsymbol{d}(c_2) = (0, 0, 1)$, so cycle c_2 will be merged into one node according to the basic idea of maximum loop distribution since $(\boldsymbol{d}_1(c), \boldsymbol{d}_2(c)) = (0, 0)$. Thus, we get a DAG G'. Then, we perform topological sort on graph G' and obtain the node-reordered graph G^s shown in Fig. 6(d). Each node in the graph G^s corresponds to one loop unit in the distributed loop. According to the sorted nodes, we can generate the code of the distributed loop as shown in Fig. 5(b). Then we can get the LDG of the distributed loop as shown in Fig. 6(e). Fig. 6 shows the graph transformation process.

4.2 Maximum Loop Distribution with Direct Loop Fusion

Direct loop fusion is to fuse two or more loops into one loop when there are no fusion-preventing dependences between these loops. Our direct loop fusion technique is based on the loop dependence graph, and it is mapped to the graph partitioning technique [3, 5]. To apply direct loop fusion, we partition the loop nodes in the LDG into several partitions so that loop nodes connected by a fusion-preventing dependence edge are partitioned into different partitions. Thus, we guarantee that there is no fusion-preventing dependence existing between the nodes inside one partition and all the loop nodes inside one partition can be directly fused.

The technique of maximum loop distribution with direct fusion (MLD_DF) is to perform maximum loop distribution followed with direct loop fusion, such that the timing performance of the loops is increased without the increase of the code size. We first apply maximum loop distribution on a given loop. After we perform maximum loop distribution, we partition the loop nodes in the LDG of the distributed loop such that there is no fusion-preventing dependences existing between the nodes inside one partition and all the loop nodes inside one partition can be directly fused [3]. Then, direct loop fusion is applied.

5 Experiments

This section presents the experimental results of our technique. We simulate a DSP processor with eight functional units. We compare the code sizes and the execution time of the original loops with those of the fused loops produced by the technique of maximum loop distribution with direct fusion (MLD_DF). The execution time is defined to be the schedule length times the total iterations. The schedule length is the number of time units to finish one iteration of the loop body. For the sequentially executed loops, the execution time is the summation of the execution time of each individual loop. The standard list scheduling algorithm is used in our experiments.

LDG1, LDG2, and LDG3 refer to the examples presented in Figure 2, 8, and 17 in [6]. LDG4 and LDG5 refer to the examples shown in Figure 2(a) and Figure 6(a) in [4]. Each node of an LDG is a DSP benchmark. The DSP benchmarks include WDF (Wave Digital filter), IIR (Infinite Impulse Response filter), DPCM (Differential Pulse-Code Modulation device), and 2D (Two Dimensional filter). We estimate the code size in memory by the number of instructions.

In Table 1, the column "*Original*" contains three fields: the number of loop nodes (#Node), the code size (Size), and the execution time (Time). The Column "*MLD_DF*" contains five fields: the number of loop nodes (#Node), the code size (Size), the execution time (Time), the improvement of the execution time (Time Impro.), and the reduction of the code size (Size Red.). The Column "*Original*" shows the number of the loop units, the code size and the execution time of the original loop. The Column "*MLD_DF*" shows the number of the loop units, the code size, the execution time, the improvement of the execution time of the fused loop by the MLD_DF technique and the reduction of the code size of the fused loop by the MLD_DF technique. Here, N is the total number of the iterations for the outermost loop, and M is the total number of the iterations for the innermost loop.

Although the maximum loop fusion technique (Max_LF) proposed in [4] can always achieve a shorter execution time than the technique of maximum loop dis-

Table 1. The code size and the execution time of the original loops and the transformed loops by the MLD_DF technique

	Original			MLD_DF				
Program	**#Node**	**Size**	**Time**	**#Node**	**Size**	**Time**	**Time Impro.**	**Size Red.**
LDG1	4	15	9*N*M	4	15	9*N*M	0%	0%
LDG2	7	84	36*N*M	2	74	26*N*M	27.8%	11.9%
LDG3	7	102	38*N*M	3	94	29*N*M	23.7%	7.8%
LDG4	3	36	23*N*M	2	34	17*N*M	26.1%	5.6%
LDG5	4	42	29*N*M	2	38	21*N*M	27.6%	9.5%
Improvement	-			-			21.0%	7.0%

tribution with direct fusion (MLD_DF), it increases the code size. In many cases, this technique cannot be applied because of the memory constraint. Compared to the Max_LF technique, the MLD_DF technique takes advantage of both loop distribution and loop fusion, so it reduces the original execution time and also avoids the code-size expansion. The experimental results showed that the timing performance of the fused loop by our MLD_DF technique can be improved 21.0% on average compared to the original loops, and the code size is reduced 7.0% on average compared to the original loops.

6 Conclusion

The maximum loop fusion technique (Max_LF) proposed in [4] can maximize the opportunities of loop fusion, but it also increases code size. In this paper, we developed the technique of combining loop distribution and loop fusion to achieve a shorter execution time with a reduction of the code size. The experimental results showed that the timing performance of the transformed loops by our MLD_DF technique can be improved significantly compared to the original loops, and the code size of the transformed loops is also reduced compared to the original loops.

References

1. R. Allen and K. Kennedy. *Optimizing Compilers for Modern Architectures: A Dependence-based Approach.* Morgan Kaufmann, 2001.
2. K. Kennedy and K. S. Mckinley. Loop distribution with arbitrary control flow. In *Proc. of the 1990 conference on Supercomputing*, pages 407 – 416, Nov. 1990.
3. K. Kennedy and K. S. Mckinley. Maximizing loop parallelism and improving data locality via loop fusion and distribution. In *Languages and Compilers for Parallel Computing, Lecture Notes in Computer Science, Number 768*, pages 301–320, 1993.
4. M. Liu, Q. Zhuge, Z. Shao, and E. H.-M. Sha. General loop fusion technique for nested loops considering timing and code size. In *Proc. ACM/IEEE International Conference on Compilers, Architectures, and Synthesis for Embedded Systems (CASES 2004)*, pages 190–201, Sep. 2004.
5. K. S. McKinley, S. Carr, and C.-W. Tseng. Improving data locality with loop transformations. *ACM Transactions on Programming Languages and Systems (TOPLAS)*, 18(4):424 – 453, July 1996.
6. E. H.-M. Sha, T. W. O'Neil, and N. L. Passos. Efficient polynomial-time nested loop fusion with full parallelism. *International Journal of Computers and Their Applications*, 10(1):9–24, Mar. 2003.
7. S. Verdoolaege, M. Bruynooghe, and F. Catthoor. Multi-dimensional incremental loop fusion for data locality. In *Proc. of the Application-Specific Systems, Architectures, and Processors*, pages 14–24, 2003.
8. M. Wolfe. *High Performance Compilers for Parallel Computing.* Addison-Wesley Publishing Company, Inc., 1996.
9. Q. Zhuge, B. Xiao, and E.-M. Sha. Code size reduction technique and implementation for software-pipelined DSP applications. *ACM Transactions on Embedded Computing Systems(TECS)*, 2(4):590–613, Nov. 2003.

Ensuring Real-Time Performance Guarantees in Dynamically Reconfigurable Embedded Systems*

Aleksandra Tešanović[1], Mehdi Amirijoo[1], Daniel Nilsson[1], Henrik Norin[1], and Jörgen Hansson[1,2]

[1] Linköping University, Department of Computer Science, Linköping, Sweden
{alete, meham, jorha}@ida.liu.se
[2] Software Engineering Institute, Carnegie Mellon University, Pittsburgh, PA, USA
hansson@sei.cmu.edu

Abstract. In this paper we present a quality of service (QoS) adaptive framework for dynamic reconfiguration of component-based real-time systems. Our framework is light-weighted enabling reconfiguration in resource constrained embedded environments. Furthermore, it is possible to reconfigure both components and aspects of a system, hence, enabling finer tuning of a real-time system. Real-time QoS guarantees are maintained in the system and under reconfiguration by employing feedback-based scheduling methods.

1 Introduction

A large majority of computational activities in modern society are performed within embedded and real-time systems. For a real-time system, it is essential that results produced by the system are both produced correctly and in a timely manner. To ensure timeliness, tasks[1] in a real-time system are associated with deadlines, and a number of real-time scheduling techniques have been developed ensuring that tasks meet their respective deadlines (see [1]).

Successful deployment of real-time and embedded systems strongly depends on low development costs, a short time to market, and a high degree of reconfigurability. One way to meet these requirements is to adopt the component-based software development (CBSD) paradigm for real-time systems. This way systems are developed out of pre-defined software components to fit a specific real-time application. Component-based real-time system approaches, e.g., [2, 3, 4], do not provide efficient support for crosscutting features such as concurrency control or scheduling algorithms that typically crosscut the structure of the overall system. Aspect-oriented software development (AOSD) [5] has emerged as a new principle for software development that provides an efficient way of modularizing crosscutting concerns in software systems in "modules", called aspects. Using

* This work is supported by the Swedish Foundation for Strategic Research (SSF), the Swedish National Graduate School in Computer Science (CUGS), and the Center for Industrial Information Technology (CENIIT) under contract 01.07.

[1] Real-time systems are typically constructed out of concurrent programs called tasks.

L.T. Yang et al. (Eds.): EUC 2005, LNCS 3824, pp. 131–141, 2005.

AOSD, systems can be built to contain only the required functionality, while other functional and non-functional crosscutting features encapsulated into aspects can be added to the system in a process called aspect weaving.

In an effort to integrate the two software engineering techniques, namely AOSD and CBSD, into real-time system development we have developed an approach to aspectual component-based real-time system development, ACCORD [6]. Given some system requirements ACCORD enables efficient system configuration from components and aspects from a library.

Most real-time component-based software systems, including our earlier work on ACCORD, are pre-compiled. This implies that the resulting running system is monolithic and not dynamically reconfigurable. Consequently, when updating or maintaining these systems, they need to be shut down for recompilation. However, reconfiguring a system on-line is desirable for embedded real-time systems that require continuous hardware and software upgrades in response to technological advancements, environmental change, or alteration of system goals during system operation [7, 3]. For example, small embedded real-time sensor-based control systems must be designed and developed such that software resources, e.g., controllers and device drivers, change on the fly. Hence, a reconfiguration mechanism, enabling adding removing, and exchanging components on-line, is needed to ensure that the software is updated without interrupting the execution of the system.

However, dynamic reconfiguration of a real-time system changes the temporal behavior of the system. For example, exchanging a component for a new version could result in a task execution time that is higher than the execution time obtained when using the existing component in the system. This in turn influences the real-time performance of the system negatively. Hence, the dynamic reconfiguration mechanism should be capable of ensuring that the system satisfies real-time performance guarantees, in terms of quality of service (QoS).

In this paper we present a QoS-adaptive framework for dynamic reconfiguration of real-time systems. The QoS-adaptive framework is an extension of the previous work on ACCORD to support exchange of components and aspects during run-time while preserving real-time performance guarantees. The main benefits introduced by this framework are as follows.

- The framework enables dynamic reconfiguration of real-time systems in embedded environments. We have identified a list of requirements that dynamically reconfigurable real-time and embedded systems need to satisfy, and we show that our framework fulfills these requirements.
- The framework is novel in that it supports dynamic reconfiguration in two dimensions: reconfiguration of components and reconfiguration of aspects. Dynamic reconfiguration of both components and aspects provides higher reusability and flexibility of a real-time system.
- The framework ensures that QoS guarantees are maintained even under reconfiguration. By employing feedback control structure we ensure that a real-time system adapts to the changes in the temporal behavior of components which occur during dynamic reconfiguration.

The paper is organized as follows. We formulate the problem in section 2. Our QoS-adaptive framework for dynamic reconfiguration is presented in section 3. The paper finishes with main conclusions in section 4.

2 Problem Formulation

In this section we identify a number of requirements that the reconfiguration framework needs to fulfill to ensure dynamic reconfigurability in a real-time system and discuss to what degree these requirements are fulfilled by existing approaches.

R1 A reconfiguration framework of a real-time system should be light-weight, implying that in normal operation of the system this framework must not introduce any significant overhead in the task execution and memory consumption of the system. This is to ensure that the system is usable in an embedded and real-time environment with sparse recourses in terms of CPU and memory.

R2 There should not be a restriction on the number of components that could be exchanged or added/removed from the system since reconfiguration may affect the entire system.

R3 Reconfiguration may be requested at any time, and the system has no a priori knowledge of the possible components that are to be reconfigured in the system.

R4 Reconfiguration must be carried out efficiently in terms of the granularity of exchangeable parts, implying that flexibility for fine-tuning of an embedded real-time application should be ensured. One should be able to exchange both functionality that is encapsulated into components and real-time algorithms that typically crosscut several components.

Accurate temporal characteristics of software components that are being added, removed, or exchanged in the system are not always available. Moreover, if temporal characteristics are available, the problem of determining exact temporal characteristics of software on a target platform is known to be difficult due to, e.g., cache and branch prediction [8]. Therefore, we need to ensure that, when reconfiguring the real-time system, the reconfiguration does not affect the performance of the system negatively. That is, a real-time system under reconfiguration should consider the varying temporal behavior of the software components being reconfigured and adapt accordingly. The adaptation should be such that specified performance requirements expressed in terms of a desired QoS, bounded worst-case QoS, and timely adaptation are satisfied. Hence, the following additional requirements on dynamically reconfigurable system arise.

R5 The system user must be able to specify the desired system QoS during steady state, i.e., the state in which no reconfiguration is applied.

R6 In the face of a transient state during which reconfiguration is applied, the worst-case system QoS and temporal adaptation must comply with the specified requirements. More specifically, the QoS must satisfy worst-case system QoS requirements and the QoS must converge towards and reach the desired QoS within a certain specified time interval (also known as settling time).

The majority of approaches enabling development of configurable real-time systems is concerned with configuration of a real-time system in the design and compilation phase and does not provide flexibility by dynamically reconfiguring the system [9, 4, 3]. Existing approaches [10, 11, 2] enabling dynamic reconfiguration do not fulfill all of the identified requirements. The approach presented in [11] does not satisfy requirement R1, and is not suitable for embedded environments. Approaches that do comply with R1, e.g., [10, 2], do not provide flexible way of reconfiguration, e.g., system reconfiguration is done by pre-compiling possible configurations into the monolithic system, violating requirement R3 [2]. The named approaches to dynamic real-time reconfiguration do not provide means for exchanging algorithms and other crosscutting concerns in the system, and, therefore, are not fulfilling requirement R4. There has been work on maintaining performance guarantees under reconfiguration of real-time systems, addressing requirements R5 and R6, but this has been done assuming that the worst-case temporal behavior of components is known prior to the reconfiguration and/or that the reconfiguration is done off-line [12, 11].

3 Approach

In this section we present our QoS-adaptive framework for dynamic reconfiguration of real-time systems that fulfills identified requirements R1-R6. We first review main characteristic of the ACCORD approach, as they were presented in our previous work. Then we present extensions to the approach that enable dynamic reconfiguration of a real-time system and discuss how QoS guarantees are maintained under reconfiguration.

3.1 ACCORD

ACCORD [6] prescribes that real-time systems should first be decomposed into a set of components followed by decomposition into a set of aspects. Aspects are properties of a system affecting its performance or semantics, and crosscutting the functionality of a system.

ACCORD provides a real-time component model, denoted RTCOM, to support reconfigurability [6]. RTCOM components are "grey" as they are encapsulated in interfaces, while changes to their behavior can be performed in a controlled way by aspect weaving. The process of weaving is typically done off-line and it generates the modified source code of a component as specified by aspects. An aspect consist of pointcuts, describing places in the code of components where aspect should be woven, and advices, defining code that is to be woven.

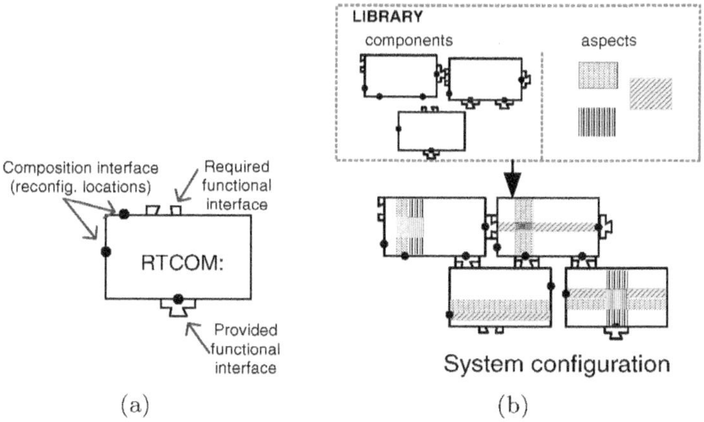

Fig. 1. (a) Reconfigurable real-time component model (RTCOM), and (b) ACCORD system configuration

Each RTCOM component has two types of functional interfaces: provided and required (see figure 1(a)). Provided interfaces reflect a set of operations that a component provides to other components, while required interfaces reflect a set of operations that the component requires from other components. Composition interfaces define reconfiguration locations in the component code. Reconfiguration locations define the points in the component code where additional modification of components can be done by aspect weaving. These points can be used by the component user (or component developer) to reconfigure a component for a specific application. Reconfiguration locations are also used for analysis purposes.

Figure 1(b) illustrates the way a system is configured and deployed in the underlying environment. Here, the composition and configuration of the system via aspects and components is done at compile time. The final system deployed in the environment is monolithic and cannot be reconfigured on-line.

3.2 Enabling Dynamic Reconfiguration

To enable dynamic reconfiguration we extend the original ACCORD approach in two ways. Firstly, we extend the RTCOM component model to ensure preservation of component and aspect states during reconfiguration. Secondly, we introduce a middleware layer, denoted ACCORD component framework, which handles communication among components and aspects.

Note that, in the context of ensuring real-time performance, an exchange of a component encompasses all the dimensions of the dynamic reconfiguration as it includes also a removal of the old version of a component and the addition of a new version. Therefore, in the following, we focus primarily on explaining the component exchange[2] part of the dynamic reconfiguration.

[2] A component exchange in the literature is also referred to as a live update of a system.

Extensions to RTCOM. To be able to preserve the internal state of components and aspects under reconfiguration, RTCOM is extended as follows. The provided interface of a component is extended with two mandatory operations, `export` and `import`. The `export` operation enables a component under reconfiguration to export its state, i.e., to store its state outside its data space (in the ACCORD component framework). The `import` operation ensures that the exported state of a component, which is to be replaced, is correctly imported into a new version of the component.

Enabling aspect exchange implies changing the way aspects are implemented within RTCOM. To conform to the dynamic aspect reconfiguration, a feature not supported by current aspect languages, and still enable general use of our framework with any of the aspect and/or component languages, we augment aspects with provided and required interfaces. These interfaces play an important role in communication and reconfiguration as we describe later in this section. Observe also that having interfaces defined for each aspect provides better encapsulation of aspect functionality and still preserves the crosscutting nature of an aspect.

System composition out of components and aspects now consists of the following steps (see figure 2(a)). First, aspects are woven off-line into components they affect. Then, using information stored in interfaces of components and aspects, these are translated into run-time entities (shared objects) recognized by the component framework. These run-time entities are then deployed onto the component framework. Conceptually, this means that weaving and run-time entity generation are done on a separate computer, and the obtained run-time entities are uploaded in the system running on another computer. Having components and aspects mapped into run-time entities that communicate via the component framework enables easy reconfiguration of both components and aspects, satisfying requirement R4.

ACCORD Component Framework. The ACCORD component framework is a middleware layer between a run-time environment and the components, which handles communication among components and aspects using jump tables (inspired by [10]). The jump table contains the list of pointers to provided and required interfaces of components and aspects. When exchanging a component or an aspect, the jump table entries for the functional interface of a component or an aspect are re-pointed to the new version of the component/aspect. As mentioned, during reconfiguration the component framework temporarily stores component and aspect internal states, using the `export` and `import` operations.

The component framework provides a user interface for reconfiguration. This reconfiguration user interface consists of operations that enable adding, removing, or exchanging components (see figure 3). During the system lifetime, reconfiguration can be requested at any time using these operations, thus, fulfilling requirement R3.

Before allowing reconfiguration to take place, the component framework always makes sure that the system can undergo reconfiguration without interrupting the task execution (line 2 in figures 3(a-c)). Tasks, which rely on operations

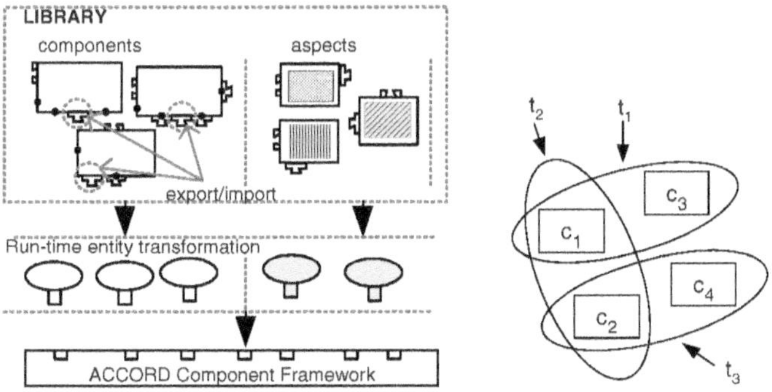

(a) (b)

Fig. 2. (a) ACCORD system configuration revisited, and (b) an example of the relation between tasks and components

of components that are to be reconfigured, have to be completed before the reconfiguration is carried out. This is exemplified in figure 2(b), where there are four components denoted by $c_1, \ldots, c_4$, and three tasks denoted by $t_1, \ldots, t_3$. Task t_1 uses operations of component c_1 and c_3, while t_2 uses c_1 and c_2. Both t_1 and t_2 have to complete executing before c_1 can be exchanged. However, only t_1 needs to be completed before c_3 can be exchanged. Once the system can undergo reconfiguration, the actual exchange of components is initiated.

For example, the exchange of an old version of a component c, denoted c^1, with a new version, c^2, is carried out after the system is prepared for exchange, by first removing the component from the system (line 3 in 3(a)). The removal is carried out by exporting the state of (an old version) of a component into the framework (lines 3-5 in figure 3(a)). Then the jump table is re-pointed to the functional interfaces of the new version, c^2, of the component (line 4 in figure 3(b)). Finally, the new component is added to the system (line 5 in figure 3(a)). The operation `add` restores states in the new version of the component using the `import` operation (line 4 in figure 3(c)). The role of the `statePresent` variable in `remove` and `add` operations is to ensure that the state of a component is restored only if it is needed. Described reconfiguration mechanism is hidden in the component framework and it enables fast and light-weight reconfiguration, satisfying requirement R1.

```
1 exchange(c¹,c²){
2   makeSystemReady();
3   remove(c¹);
4   redirect(c¹,c²);
5   add(c²);
6 }
```

(a) exchange

```
1 remove(c){
2   makeSystemReady();
3   if (c.hasState(){
4     state=c.export();
5     statePresent=true;
6   }
7 }
```

(b) remove

```
1 add(c){
2   makeSystemReady();
3   if (statePresent){
4     c.import(state);
5     statePresent=false;
6   }
7 }
```

(c) add

Fig. 3. Reconfiguration of a component

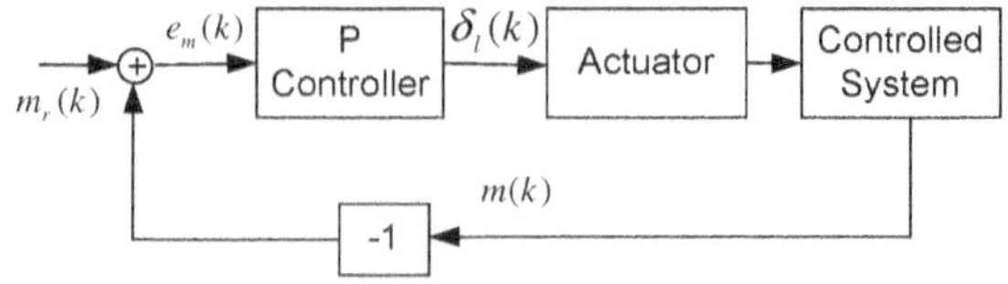

Fig. 4. Feedback control structure

The reconfiguration of any number of components can be done by a user, which can either be the system user (human) or an application (requirement R2). The component framework is aware of the version of a component, via the version number of a component, in the current configuration. When a new version is compiled into the run-time directory (the component is loaded in the memory by the framework), this is detected during application self-inspection and the component is exchanged with another version using the `exchange` operation of the component framework (see figure 3(a)). If an arbitrary number of components needs to be exchanged this can be done by invoking `exchange` operation for each of the components. This also implies that components with dependencies can be exchanged safely, in a sequence of appropriate `exchange` calls, since the tasks using these components will be completed before the exchange takes place.

When wanting to exchange one of the algorithms that crosscut the overall system, the reconfiguration can be done by exchanging aspects. Exchange is done by first weaving the desired new aspect into affected components off-line, and then employing the reconfiguration of affected components as described above[3]. Note that it is not possible to exchange aspects if they are not encapsulated into interfaces and translated into corresponding real-time entities. Although the dynamic reconfiguration of aspects is done via component exchange, the benefits of aspect-orientation are still fully retained as changes to the code that crosscut many components are still done in an automated, efficient, and modular way via aspect weaving.

3.3 Enabling QoS Adaptiveness

Recall requirements R5 and R6, stating that the system administrator must be able to specify desired system QoS and transient state system QoS in terms of worst-case QoS and how fast the QoS should converge toward the desired QoS. To fulfill R5 and R6 and, therefore, provide QoS guarantees under system reconfiguration we employ feedback control [14]. Applying feedback to control the QoS of computer systems is referred to as feedback control scheduling (FCS), and this technique has been introduced as a promising foundation for QoS control of complex real-time systems [13, 14, 15].

The desired nominal system QoS is expressed in terms of a reference QoS, which gives the level of QoS that the system must provide when it is in the steady

[3] An aspect exchange can be, from the dynamic reconfiguration perspective, regarded as exchange of a number of components with new (woven) versions.

state, i.e., when no reconfiguration is currently taking place and any effects of previous reconfiguration have passed. When a reconfiguration is taking place the system alternates to the transient state, which is characterized by fluctuations in QoS. The desired transient state QoS is usually expressed in terms of the maximum overshoot and the settling time [14]. The maximum overshoot M_p is the worst-case system QoS in a transient system state (under reconfiguration) and it is given in percentage. Hence, the maximum performance degradation of the system under reconfiguration is bounded by M_p. The settling time T_s is the time for the transient overshoot to decay and reach the steady state QoS. Hence, the settling time is a measure of system adaptability, i.e., how fast the system converges toward the desired QoS in the face of reconfiguration.

Typically, one is interested in controlling the performance of real-time systems using the metric deadline miss ratio [15], which gives the ratio of tasks that have missed their deadlines. We have employed a feedback-based QoS management method, referred to as FC-M [15], in the ACCORD dynamic reconfiguration framework. Using FC-M deadline miss ratio is controlled by modifying the admitted load. We say that a task is terminated when it has completed or missed its deadline. Let $missedTasks(k)$ be the number of tasks that have missed their deadline and $terminatedTasks(k)$ be the number of terminated admitted tasks in the time interval $[(k-1)T, kT]$. The deadline miss ratio, $m(k) = \frac{missedTasks(k)}{terminatedTasks(k)}$, denotes the ratio of tasks that have missed their deadlines.

In figure 4, the performance error, $e_m(k) = m_r(k) - m(k)$, is computed to quantize the difference between the desired deadline miss ratio, given by the reference $m_r(k)$, and the measured deadline miss ratio $m(k)$. The change to the load $\delta_l(k)$, which we denote as the manipulated variable, is derived using a P controller, hence, $\delta_l(k) = K_P e_m(k)$, where K_P is a tunable variable. The load target $l(k)$ is the integration of $\delta_l(k)$, i.e., $l(k+1) = l(k) + \delta_l(k)$. Admission control is then used to carry out the change in load, where a task is admitted into the system if the sum of the load of the task (that is waiting to be admitted) and the load of the already admitted tasks is less than the load target $l(k)$.

Consider the following example where the deadline miss ratio reference is set to 0.1 and the load threshold at the 10th sampling instant is set to 0.9, i.e., $m_r = 0.1$ and $l(10) = 0.9$. A component exchange during the previous sampling interval has resulted in an increase in the execution time of the tasks, and consequently the deadline miss ratio has increased to $m(10) = 0.2$. Clearly, the component exchange has degraded the performance of the system. Therefore, we need to reduce the deadline miss ratio to the reference value $m_r = 0.1$. This is done by taking the measured value of the deadline miss ratio from the system and computing the performance error $e_m(10) = m_r(10) - m(10) = (0.1 - 0.2) = -0.1$ and then computing the change in load, i.e., $\delta_l(10) = -0.1K_P$; following the steps in the feedback structure from figure 4. The load threshold during the next sampling interval is changed to $l(11) = l(10) + \delta_l(10) = 0.9 - 0.1K_P$. The admitted load is reduced as a result of a decrease in the load threshold and, consequently, the deadline miss ratio for the 11th sampling instant is reduced.

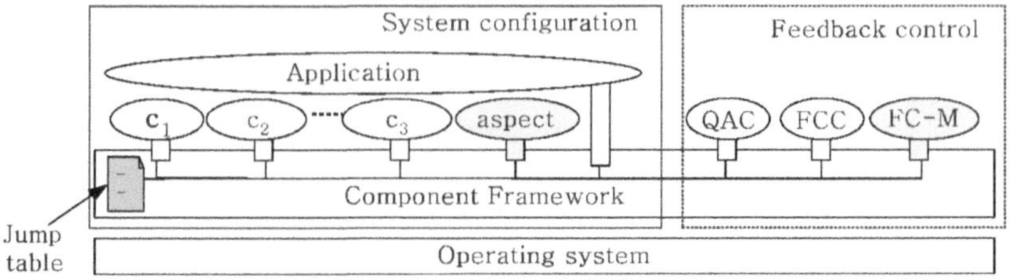

Fig. 5. ACCORD system configuration revisited

QoS management related components and aspects are implemented according to the extended RTCOM model and deployed into the ACCORD component framework. The structure of the dynamically reconfigurable system that guarantees QoS is depicted in figure 5. QoS guarantees are now satisfied in the framework by having an actuator component (AC) that implements changes in the manipulated variable and the feedback control component (FCC), which implements the control loop by measuring the controlled variable and computing the manipulated variable. The FC-M QoS algorithm is implemented as an aspect, crosscutting AC and FCC. For more details on how feedback loop can be designed using aspects and components and configured statically, as well as what types of possible QoS algorithms are supported, we refer interested readers to [16].

4 Summary

The majority of the component-based real-time systems focuses on static reconfiguration of a real-time system. However, real-time systems that are tightly coupled with their environment cannot be halted for reconfiguration to take place as their continuous operation is of paramount importance. Even if a reconfiguration takes place, affecting the temporal behavior of the system, the QoS provided by these systems must remain unaltered.

We have addressed this problem by presenting a QoS-adaptive framework for dynamic reconfiguration of real-time systems. Our framework is founded on aspectual component-based real-time system development, an approach that combines component-based and aspect-oriented software development with real-time system development. Hence, the framework supports reconfiguration in terms of components and aspects, which increases the granularity of exchangeable parts. The framework also ensures that real-time performance guarantees are maintained even when the system undergoes dynamic reconfiguration. Using the QoS-adaptive framework for dynamic reconfiguration results in efficient development and software upgrading of real-time systems, conforming to strict QoS requirements that are applied to performance-critical real-time systems.

References

1. Buttazzo, G.C.: Hard Real-Time Computing Systems. Kluwer (1997)
2. van Ommering, R.: Building product populations with software components. In: Proceedings of the 24th ACM International Conference on Software Engineering (2002) 255–265
3. Stewart, D.B., Volpe, R., Khosla, P.K.: Design of dynamically reconfigurable real-time software using port-based objects. IEEE Transactions on Software Engineering **23** (1997)
4. Sandstrm, K., Fredriksson, J., kerholm, M.: Introducing a component technology for safety critical embedded realtime systems. In: Proceedings of the International Symposium on Component-based Software Engineering, Springer-Verlag (2004)
5. Kiczales, G., Lamping, J., Mendhekar, A., Maeda, C., Lopes, C., Loingtier, J.M., Irwin, J.: Aspect-oriented programming. In: Proceedings of the ECOOP. Volume 1241 of Lecture Notes in Computer Science., Springer-Verlag (1997) 220–242
6. Tešanović, A., Nyström, D., Hansson, J., Norström, C.: Aspects and components in real-time system development: Towards reconfigurable and reusable software. Journal of Embedded Computing **1** (2004)
7. Cerpa, A., Estrin, D.: ASCENT: Adaptive Self-Configuring sEnsor Networks Topologies. IEEE Transactions on Mobile Computing **3** (2004) 272–285
8. Engblom, J.: Analysis of the execution time unpredictability caused by dynamic branch prediction. In: Proceedings of the IEEE Real-Time and Embedded Technology and Applications Symposium (RTAS). (2003) 152–159
9. Isovic, D., Lindgren, M., Crnkovic, I.: System development with real-time components. In: Proceedings of ECOOP Workshop - Pervasive Component-Based Systems (2000)
10. ITEA project: (ROBOCOP deliverable 1.5) ROBOCOP ITEA project.
11. Hissam, S., Moreno, G., Stafford, J., Wallnau, K.: Enabling predictable assembly. The Journal of Systems and Software **65** (2003) 185–198
12. Daz, M., Garrido, D., Llopis, L.M., Rus, F., Troya, J.M.: Integrating real-time analysis in a component model for embedded systems. In: Proceedings of the 30th IEEE Euromicro conference (2004)
13. Amirijoo, M., Hansson, J., Gunnarsson, S., Son, S.H.: Enhancing feedback control scheduling performance by on-line quantification and suppression of measurement disturbance. In: Proceedings of the IEEE Real-Time and Embedded Technology and Applications Symposium (RTAS). (2005)
14. Hellerstein, J.L., Diao, Y., Parekh, S., Tilbury, D.M.: Feedback Control of Computing Systems. Wiley-IEEE Press (2004)
15. Lu, C., Stankovic, J.A., Tao, G., Son, S.H.: Feedback control real-time scheduling: Framework, modeling and algorithms. Real-time Systems **23** (2002)
16. Tešanović, A., Amirijoo, M., Björk, M., Hansson, J.: Empowering configurable QoS management in real-time systems. In: Proceedings of the Fourth ACM SIG International Conference on Aspect-Oriented Software Development (2005)

ANTS: An Evolvable Network of Tiny Sensors*

Daeyoung Kim[1], Tomás Sánchez López[1], Seongeun Yoo[1], Jongwoo Sung[1], Jaeeon Kim[1], Youngsoo Kim[1], and Yoonmee Doh[2]

[1] Information and Communications University (ICU), 119 Munji-Dong, Yuseong-Gu, 305-714, Korea
{tomas, kimd, seeyoo, jwsung, jekim, pineland}@icu.ac.kr
[2] Electronic and Telecommunications Research Institute (ETRI), 161 Gajeong-dong, Yuseong-gu, 305-700, Korea
ydoh@etri.re.kr

Abstract. As a promising technology that enables ubiquitous computing and leads IT industries of next generation, sensor networks (SN) are foreseen to expand and populate the globe in such a way as the present Internet does. In this scenario, new challenges appear with such massive deployment, as the constant interaction of nodes and networks will transform them in dynamic entities that will need to evolve with their environment. In this paper, we discuss the future of sensor networks defining the concept of evolvability and its application. We also describe ANTS, a complete new architecture for wireless sensor networks, as our implementation to solve the challenges imposed by this evolvable future.

Keywords: Sensor Networks, Evolvability, Operating Systems, Middleware, Localization, Synchronization, Security, Network Protocols

1 Introduction

Small devices with integrated sensor capabilities are gaining credit by industries and institutions all over the planet. From the work started by some visionaries several years ago, research in the field leads old skeptics and new believers into a dream of potential applications for present and future. However, the track towards SN's future has several challenges to overcome. In this near future, when sensor nodes will be embedded in everyday's life, vehicles, food, clothes and any other kind of movable products will travel around interacting with each other and stationary networks creating and destroying communication bridges which will remain transparent to regular users. Living in this close tomorrow, we will witness the expansion of the ubiquitous computing, not only with the presence of sensor devices everywhere, but also with its global interconnection. Sensor networks will be born, will grow and will reconfigure autonomously, getting upgrades from the network, adapting to changes while learning from their environment and their fellow networks. But to get to this future, we have to think about the present and how this omnipresence of sensor devices should be managed by adaptability and autonomy capabilities. Here is where the concept of evolvability and the need for evolvable architectural design comes into play.

* This research has been partially supported by ITRC project of Korea Ministry of Information and Communication.

L.T. Yang et al. (Eds.): EUC 2005, LNCS 3824, pp. 142 – 151, 2005.

WSN applications are numerous, such as habitat [1] and health monitoring [11], environment control and actuation [2] or even parent control [6]. Some architectures have been developed as a base for this applications [3]. However, although some efforts have been done in the development of evolvability capabilities, the results are either far away from the desirable functionalities or are not applicable to the constrained WSN devices. In this paper we introduce ANTS: An evolvable Network of Tiny Sensors. ANTS is a new architecture for the development of sensor networks which functionalities are built applying the concept of evolvability. ANTS not only develops system functionalities (Section 3) but also implements application level and middleware solutions such as context aware and UPnP (Universal Plug and Play) frameworks [10].

The rest of the paper is organized as follows: Section 0 describes generally the concept of evolvability and its characteristics. Section 0 presents our specific architecture, discussing one by one all its functionalities. Finally Section 0 depicts ANTS test-beds while Section 0 concludes the paper with a summary of the introduced concepts.

2 Evolvability in Sensor Networks

According to what has been introduced in the previous section, we could call evolvability to the capability to adapt to changes, some induced by the users according to the evolution of their needs, others provoked uncontrollably by the network nature itself and the surroundings. Evolvability support for WSN implies a series of requirements that will following be introduced. A summary also can be found in Table 1.

Indeed, the ability to adapt to changes is a key characteristic for evolvable systems (i.e. WSN), but as we will describe afterwards, a deeper view requires further considerations. Anyway, as a fundamental attribute for our analysis, we will characterize *adaptability* as the capability of a system to change or be changed to fit changed circumstances. But can a system be adaptable if it doesn't consider its interaction with other systems? For this reason we also include the definition of *interoperability*, as the ability of two or more systems or components to exchange information and to use the information that has been exchanged.

If we concentrate on the system design, we find that systems aiming to provide adaptability features must be flexible in its implementation, as monolithic approaches would require a complete redesign for any minimal change. Modular architectures, however, supply the needed looseness to address the problems of flexibility, providing well defined modules for different functionalities. We call *modularity* to the characteristic of those systems which are based in a set of interchangeable components rather than a monolithic approach. In order to guarantee a feasible modularity we also define *scalability* as the characteristic of those systems that can adapt, at any time and with the minimum cost, to a set of necessities that can be changing. Note that this definition might include configuration issues, in the sense that the highest the ease of the system to be configured to adapt to the changes, the highest its scalability. Examples of scalability and modularity applied to the SN are the support for sensor node addition or removal and the creation of modular software and hardware components.

3.2 ANTS Operating System

ANTS Operating System (ANTS EOS) [8] is the core of our architecture and coordinates the structural design to provide evolvability services. ANTS EOS is a multi-threaded operating system offering two kind of threads (shared-stack and self-stack) that contribute to enhance the capabilities needed for a sensor network OS. These capabilities include, amongst others, a strong concurrency model, small footprint, low power consumption, robust operation and collaborative and distributed processing. ANTS EOS also includes other advanced features , such as a flexible Hardware Abstraction Layer (i.e. to accommodate different hardware nodes), a POSIX-like API set and an efficient message handling engine valid for both local and remote communication. Fig. 3 presents the ANTS EOS architecture.

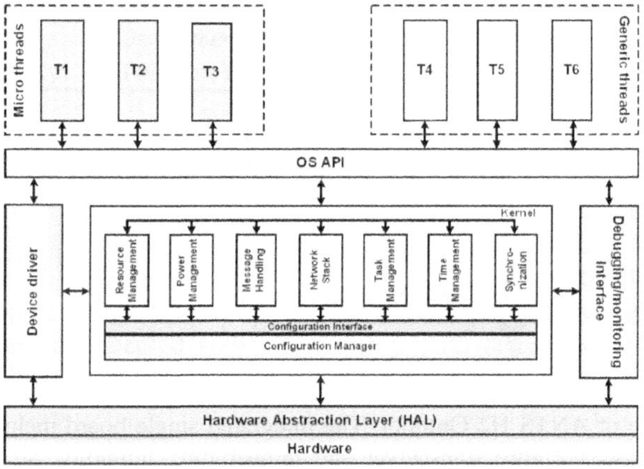

Fig. 3. ANTS EOS Architecture

The base of ANTS EOS evolvability is a modular design (implementing *modularity*) comprised of well defined modules that make use of a provided interface for upgrading processes. Capable of offering both kernel and user level upgrades, we foresee a dependable OS architecture, enforced by middleware, monitoring activities and dynamic updates able to take place remotely and without endangering the kernel or any other system functionalities (implementing *upgradability* and *dependability*).

3.3 Network Architecture

ANTS builds a two-tier, two-dimensional network architecture (NA) for optimum node communication, whose different capable nodes and different purpose network levels assure the efficiency needed for such restricted systems as sensor networks are.

On one hand, the two-tier NA is composed by two kinds of sensor nodes distinguishable by their hardware capabilities and, hence, by their potential functionalities. Together with the standard sensor network devices (micro nodes), ANTS includes more complex and powerful devices whose special resources (i.e. GPS, high bandwidth radio) make them suitable for specific functionalities such as localization anchors, synchronization cluster heads or interoperable gateways (macro nodes). This approach offers the desired *scalability* and *interoperability* needs described previously.

On the other hand, the need for specific sensor application services builds a two-dimensional NA in which the transport domain is complemented with an additional context (application) domain for exclusive context-aware services. This way, ANTS defines the existence of an overlay network on top of the transports sensor network, which using explicit network protocols (i.e. location aimed routing protocols, [Section 0]) can offer concrete services (i.e. Context-Awareness) out of the limitations imposed by the standard transport layer (see Fig. 4 for an example on the ANTS Network Architecture).

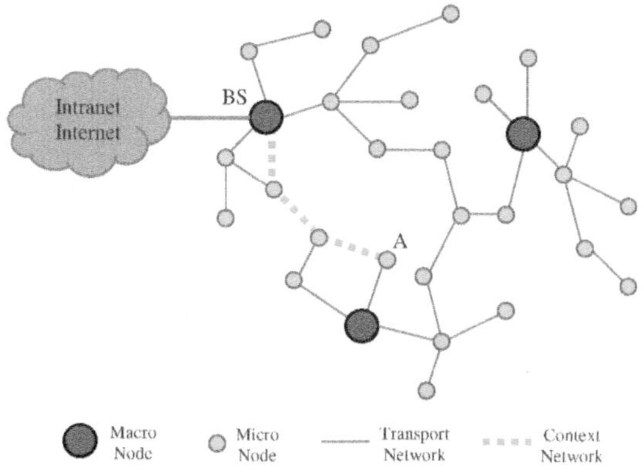

Fig. 4. ANTS Network Architecture example

Table 2. Summary of System Evolvability requirements

Protocol Name	Main characteristics
PAD [4] (Power Aware Data-centric)	-Enhanced MEPG (Minimum Energy Path Graph) -Able to provide mobility and self-healing -Hop count and power consumption as metrics -Minimizes packet delivery by being fully triggered -Supports adding or removing of nodes
PAC [9] (Power Aware Chain)	-Chain-based routing scheme -Calculates transm. costs from receiving signal strength. -Power-aware leader node election & better net. lifetime
PPVR [13] (Power-aware Position Vector Routing)	-Greedy approach to minimize flooding overhead -On-demand route discovery -Effectively avoids out-of-range communication areas -High successful rate of packet delivery.
SUMMA [7] (Sub-network Mobility support with Multi-channel Assignment)	-Temporal packet routing to mobile attached sub-networks -Gateway election & gateway data aggregation -Robust interconnection and longer life times -Multi-channel for interference and packet collision.

3.4 Communication Protocols

ANTS develops several lightweight communication protocols that efficiently deal with delay and power consumption problems applying the evolvability concept. Table **2** shows their main characteristics. Currently we have 3 routing protocols and one mobility schema while are able to provide *scalability* (with the number of nodes) and *adaptability* & *dependability* (by supporting death of nodes and mobility).

3.5 Localization

ANTS also implements a localization algorithm which is based both on measured distances and hop information obtained by the use of position aware anchors. Para-LDL-EI (Parametric Learning-based Distance Localization with Evolution Improvement) [5] supports position information search of new nodes by taking profit of past network information and causing extremely low overhead. Para-LDL-EI provides the capability for new sensor nodes to obtain automatically its position without the need to run the localization algorithm again on live nodes. It shows excellent results in up to 50% of new deployed devices and, thus, presents promising results to support efficiently multiple generation sensor networks. The support of birth and death of nodes implements *dependability, adaptability* and *scalability.*

3.6 Time Synchronization

Maintaining accurate time information in the SN does not only provide meaningful information, but also combines the system with our real physical world, allowing, for example, savings in energy or prevention of redundant information. Local clocks of inexpensive devices such as sensor network nodes are inherently inaccurate and prone to deviations of up to several seconds per week. To maintain network requirements,

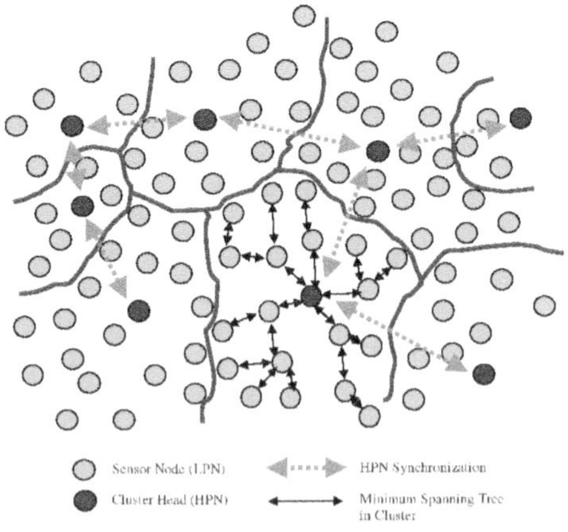

Fig. 5. Cluster-bases synchronization scheme in ANTS

periodical synchronizations of sensor nodes are required, but problems with specifying reference clocks and dealing with network time forwarding inaccuracies increasing with number of hops arise. We propose a clustering based synchronization architecture in which higher level High Precision Nodes (HPN), with accurate timing information and less frequent time synchronization needs, synchronize periodically with lower level Low Precision Nodes (LPN). Our algorithm is capable of building synchronized sensor networks from a single cluster-head reference clock, transmitting its timing information to other cluster heads and defining minimum spanning trees in cluster areas for least hop count and synchronization error. Fig. 5 shows an example of sensor field clustering, where one of the cluster is detailed with cluster-level synchronization.

3.7 Security

Existing approaches to SN security, which are mostly focused on cryptographic or multiple-path prevention schemes, have the problem that they just satisfy a part of the security requirement obviating other necessary concerns such as intrusion detection and certain key management techniques. We propose a trust evaluation based security framework for SN [12], which effective decisions on security scheme selection are based on an abstract node behavior coming from the network communication packets. Incoming packets are analyzed and their characteristics mapped to trust evaluation parameters, which will be computed locally or sent to the base station in order to build global and local trust relationships. Then the SN, considering all these trust values and relationships, will be easily able to make effective decisions in areas such as routing taking into account security concerns. This way we pretend to achieve the best combination of security level, performance, robustness, efficiency and deployment cost for SN. Fig. 6 presents a basic block diagram of the ANTS security framework.

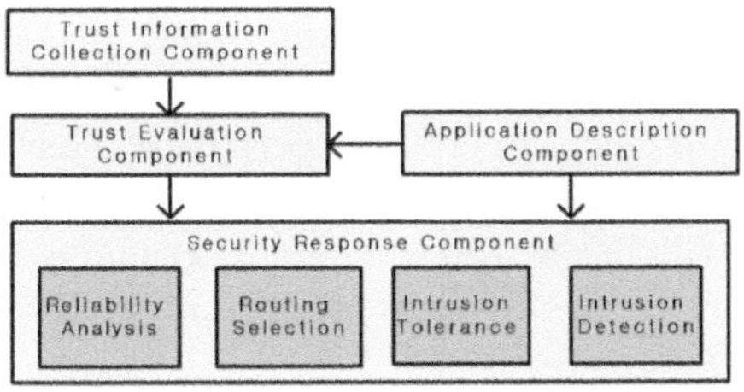

Fig. 6. ANTS Security Framework

By computing new trust values dependent on incoming packets our security framework achieves *adaptability*. Additionally, by allowing the introduction of new security values at application level, *scalability* and *modularity* are realized, while *dependability* is accomplished by supporting activity values for dead nodes.

4 ANTS Test-Beds

The ANTS team has developed two different application platforms as test-beds for our work: ANTS Smart Home and ANTS Surveillance. A graphical representation of the ANTS Surveillance test-bed is shown at Fig. 7: A helicopter deploys micro and macro sensors nodes in a target area aimed to detect the presence and movement of vehicles. The SN, aerial vehicles and other devices connect via an AODV (Ad-hoc On-demand Distance Vector) based network, forwarding the information and obtaining other services such as accurate GPS information (DGPS station).

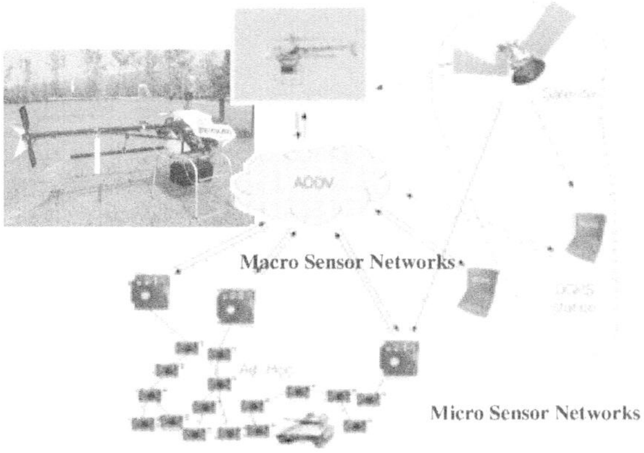

Fig. 7. ANTS Surveillance application platform

5 Conclusions

We have presented the concept of evolvability, and how the new emerging WSN technologies will need to apply it to fulfill the needs for their future prospected applications. Our particular project, ANTS, collects these ideas and builds a complete architecture distinguishable by its adaptability and flexibility, becoming the first WSN system to truly evolve with its environment and its changing needs.

Acknowledgements

We would like to thank: from ICU, *Mr. Sungjin Ahn, Mr. Bui Duy Bach, Mr. Seungki Hong, Ms. Junghyun Kim, Mr. Hyunhak Kim, Mr. Sangsoo Lee, Mr. Jihoon Park, Mr. Noseong Park, Mr. Long Minh Pham, Ms. Do Thu Thuy, Mr. Hyungjoo Song* and *Ms. Zhiying Yao*; from ITRC *Prof. Joongsoo Ma*; from Samsung *Mr. SeungRyong Park* and *Mr. K.S Chang*, and from ETRI *Dr. J.S. Jang, Dr. Jaedoo Heo* and *Mr. S. Park.*

References

1. A. Mainwaring, J. Polastre, R. Szewczyk, D. Culler and J. Anderson: Wireless Sensor Networks for Habitat Monitoring, WSNA'02, September 28, 2002, Atlanta, Georgia, USA.
2. D. Wang, E. Arens, T. Webster and M. Shi: How The Number And Placement Of Sensors Controlling Room Air Distribution Systems Affect Energy Use And Comfort, Center for Environmental Design Research, University of California, Berkeley.
3. J. Hill, R. Szewczyk, A. Woo, S. Hollar, D. Culler and K. Pister: System Architecture Directions for Networked Sensors, ASPLOS IX, November 2000, Cambridge, MA, USA
4. N. Park, D. Kim, Y. Doh, S. Lee and J. Kim: Power Aware Data-centric Routing Protocol for Sensor Networks, Submitted to SCCI'05
5. D. Bach and D. Kim: A Localization Algorithm Extension for The Evolvable Sensor Network, PDCS 2004, Cambridge, MA, USA
6. M. Srivastava, R. Muntz, M. Potkonjak: Smart Kindergarten: Sensor-based Wireless Networks for Smart Developmental Problem-solving Environments, SIGMOBILE 7/01, Italy
7. J. Park, D. Kim: SUMMA: Sub-network Mobility support using Muli-channel Assignment in wireless sensor networks, Master Thesis, School Engineering, ICU 2005
8. T. Do, D. Kim, T. Sanchez, H. Kim, S. Hong, M. Pham, K. Lee, S. Park: An Evolvable Operating System for Wireless Sensor Networks, IEHSC, Singapore, May 10-13, 2005.
9. M. Pham, D. Kim, Y. Doh, S. Yoo: Power Aware Chain Routing Protocol for Data Gathering in Sensor Networks, ISSNIP 2004, , Australia, Dec. 14-17, 2004.
10. H. Song, D. Kim: Sensor Network Management System using UPnP, KISS Fall Conference, Oct. 2004.
11. Victor Shnayder et all.: Sensor Network for medical care, Technical Report, Harvard University, 2005
12. Z. Yao, D. Kim, I. Lee, K. Kim, J. Jang: A Security Framework with Trust Management for Sensor Networks, IEEE/CREATE-NET SecQoS 2005, Greece , September 9, 2005
13. S. Lee, D. Kim, S. Ahn, N. Park, " Power-aware Position Vector Routing for Wireless Sensor Networks," To appear in USN'2005, Nagasaki, Japan, 6-9 December 2005

Design Models for Reusable and Reconfigurable State Machines

Christo Angelov, Krzysztof Sierszecki, and Nicolae Marian

Mads Clausen Institute for Product Innovation, University of Southern Denmark,
Grundtvigs Alle 150, 6400 Soenderborg, Denmark
{angelov, ksi, nicolae}@mci.sdu.dk

Abstract. The widespread use of embedded systems mandates a rigorous engineering approach towards embedded software development, i.e. model-based design of embedded software. The paper presents design models of reusable and reconfigurable state machines that have been conceived in the context of the COMDES framework and in particular - the State Logic Controller and the Hybrid State Logic Controller, whose principles of operation are presented in the paper. The latter has been instrumental in developing a reconfigurable executable component, i.e. a function block of class State Machine, which can be used to implement a broad range of embedded applications such as sequential, continuous and hybrid control systems, as well as complex systems specified with hierarchical and concurrent state machines.

1 Introduction

State machines play an important role in embedded software design and recent research has focused on the efficient software implementation of state machines in terms of various types of design patterns [2, 7] and reconfigurable software components [3, 4, 9].

The conventional implementation of state machines is based on manual encoding of an abstract model such as the state transition graph, using 'switch-case' design patterns [7]. With this approach the state transition logic is built into the code, whereby a program has to be manually developed for each particular instance of the state machine. Consequently, such a program is difficult to modify and maintain. Moreover, this approach scales up badly with complex hierarchical and concurrent state machines. Therefore, a number of other design methods have been developed, e.g. The Quantum Framework [2] and the StateTable design pattern [7]. These methods provide design patterns that are potentially reusable at the source-code level but manual coding is not completely eliminated: the programmer is always required to code certain parts of the application (e.g. manual encoding of guards leading to selection of successor state and execution of related action). There are also some other problems, such as the use of sparse state transition tables resulting in considerable memory overhead, and in some cases – run-time creation of tables, which make such methods impractical for deeply embedded applications.

L.T. Yang et al. (Eds.): EUC 2005, LNCS 3824, pp. 152 – 163, 2005.

Industrial computer systems usually adopt a different approach, whereby a software state machine is implemented by modeling the structure of its hardware counterpart, i.e. making a program that computes the state transition logic functions and executes the actions that are associated with various states. In particular, this is how sequential control programs are implemented in programmable logic controllers [9].

In both cases, conventional design methods have a major shortcoming: the resulting implementation is not reusable, because the logic of the state machine is "hardwired" in the code. Specifically, this means that a separate program has to be developed for each particular application. That might not be a problem for small state machines but it is obviously a big problem with large state machines having tens or hundreds of states. In this case the software implementation of the state machine is a time-consuming and error-prone process, and the complexity of this problem rapidly grows with the number of states and state transitions.

The above problem can be eliminated through *reusable* implementation of state machines being based on re-configurable data structures and executable components such as discrete I/O drivers, state machine drivers, function blocks, etc. [3, 4]. The resulting software construction can be viewed as a higher-level object of type 'state machine'. That object might have multiple instances depending on the contents of the encapsulated data structures (configuration tables). The latter can be configured and re-configured via a dedicated configuration tool. In this way configuration of reusable components is substituted for conventional software design, and as a result of that manual coding of state machines can be potentially eliminated.

Configuration tables may contain information representing either state machine *structure* or state machine *behaviour*. In the former case the software implementation emulates the circuit diagram of the state machine (and indirectly – the behaviour of the state machine) by computing the corresponding state variables and the associated output signals for every invocation of the control program. Industrial controllers using this technique are known as *programmable logic controllers* (*PLCs*). In the latter case the software implementation emulates the behaviour of the state machine by directly interpreting a data structure representing the state transition graph or an equivalent behavioural model, e.g. a state machine flowchart. Industrial controllers using that technique are known as *state logic controllers* (*SLCs*).

The latter approach has a number of advantages: it is easier to use as it does not require preliminary logical design of the state machine, and it is ultimately simpler to implement. Therefore, this technique has been adopted while developing a reusable and reconfigurable state machine component in the context of COMDES - a software framework for component-based design of embedded control systems [1]. The related design issues are presented in this paper, which is structured as follows: Section 2 presents design models for reconfigurable state machines, such as the State Logic Controller and its enhanced version – the Hybrid State Logic Controller. Section 3 deals with the implementation of a reconfigurable function block of class State Machine. Section 4 presents related research. A summary of the proposed software design method and its implications is given in the concluding section of the paper.

2 Design Models for Reconfigurable and Reusable State Machines

The State Logic Controller (SLC) is built around a data structure, i.e. a state transition table that contains the computer representation of the state transition graph. This data structure can be efficiently implemented as a table containing modified (multiple-output) binary decision diagrams that represent the next-state mappings Fa_1, Fa_2, ... , and so on, of various states within the state transition graph – the BDD Table (see Fig. 1 and Table 1).

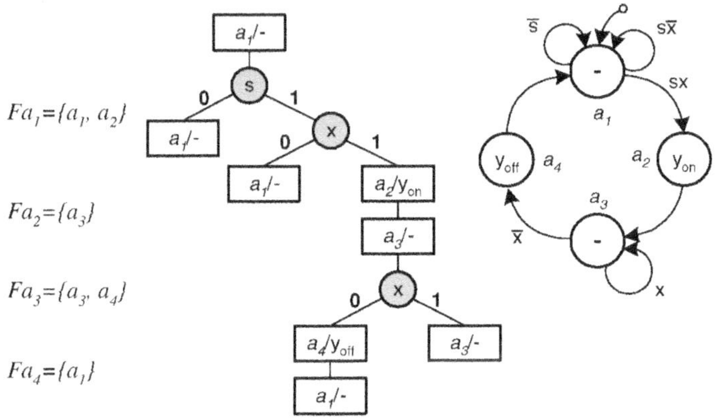

Fig. 1. Binary decision diagrams for next state mappings (Moore model)

Table 1. BDD Table of State Logic Controller for the example state machine

row	node	succTrue	succFalse	next-state mapping BDD
0	s	1	2	
1	x	3	2	Fa_1
2	a_1 / -	0	-	
3	a_2 / y_{on}	4	-	
4	a_3 / -	5	-	Fa_2
5	x	6	7	
6	a_3 / -	5	-	Fa_3
7	a_4 / y_{off}	8	-	
8	a_1 / -	0	-	Fa_4

This model is interpreted at run time, resulting in direct emulation of system behaviour: While operating, the SLC visits a number of states during successive control cycles *1, 2, 3,* ... and executes the control actions associated with the visited states. These constitute a trace *P* in the state transition graph, e.g.:

$$P_i : a^i_1(1) \rightarrow a^i_2(2) \rightarrow a^i_3(3) \rightarrow \dots , \tag{1}$$

where a^i_1 is the initial (entry) state, $a^i_2 \in Fa^i_1$, $a^i_3 \in Fa^i_2$, etc. This type of behaviour can be illustrated by an execution trace of the example state machine shown in Fig. 1:

$$a_1 \rightarrow a_1(!s) \rightarrow a_1(s!x) \rightarrow a_2(sx) \rightarrow a_3 \rightarrow a_3(x) \rightarrow a_4(!x) \rightarrow a_1 \rightarrow \dots \tag{2}$$

Such behaviour can be implemented with a standard application-independent routine - the *state machine driver* whose algorithm is given below assuming a *synchronous*, i.e. clock-driven Moore machine with binary (on/off) inputs and outputs:

```
State machine driver is: {
  // assuming knowledge of the last state visited during
  // the previous invocation
  do {
    determine current state from among the successors of the
    previous state;
      // by processing the next-state mapping BDD of that
      // state
    execute control action associated with current state
    (if non-empty);
      // read out corresponding word of control memory and
      // generate corresponding binary (on/off) signals
  } while (not(stable_state));
}
```

The binary decision diagrams of next-state mappings Fa_1, Fa_2, Fa_3, ... are usually processed one at a time, i.e. only one BDD is processed during the current cycle, which contains the successor states of the last state visited in the previous cycle. This mode of operation results in *step-wise* execution of control actions in successive time instants *1, 2, 3,* etc., which amounts to a strictly synchronous mode of operation. In practice, the above limitation can be relaxed in a number of ways, i.e. there are specific cases that introduce asynchrony, such as wait states of unspecified duration (e.g. states a_1 and a_3 in Fig. 1) and wait states of specified duration implemented with hardware or software timers. In these two cases some states may be revisited over and over again during a sequence of control cycles, which amounts to having states whose duration is a multiple of the basic clock period.

There is yet another case that introduces a different type of asynchrony, whereby a number of states may be visited in a sequence of *immediate transitions* carried out during the current control cycle. In this case the controller executes a sequence of operations (e.g. arithmetic and comparison operations) before reaching a *stable* state, where it breaks out of the sequence and exits.

The above discussion has been made assuming binary encoding of the control memory of the state machine. However, this assumption limits the presented software design to basic sequential control applications featuring binary input and output signals and predominantly synchronous mode of operation. In a more general context it might be necessary to implement additional functionality such as timers, event counters, arithmetic and comparison operators used to compute derivative condition variables, etc.

That can be accomplished by introducing lower-level software objects called *function blocks* (FBs) implementing the above functions, whereby function block

The above feature can be used to implement complex behaviours modelled by *hierarchical* and *concurrent* state machines [1]. In that case, during each invocation the program executes sequentially the constituent state machines until a *global stable state* is reached, and then breaks out until the next invocation, etc. A global stable state denotes a situation, whereby all constituent state machines have reached a stable state within the current step of execution.

Hierarchical composition of state machine function blocks provides a solution to the problems of complexity and scalability: a complex control system may be represented by a hierarchical model, whereby each constituent state machine is implemented with a different instance of that function block. An alternative approach is to decompose the object of control into functional subsystems, whereby each subsystem is assigned an individual controller modeled by a conventional (flat) state machine. In that case the overall control system may be viewed as a composition of interacting state machines that closely reflects the structure of the application [3].

3 Implementation Aspects

The algorithm given above outlines the principle of operation of the hybrid state machine driver. However, certain refinements to the algorithm need to be highlighted before discussing the actual implementation in more detail:

- The state machine driver interacts with two types of function block: function blocks that generate condition variables (*condition function blocks*) and function blocks that generate control signals (*control function blocks*). Both of them may be basic or composite function blocks (CFBs).
- The execution of condition function blocks is actually integrated with BDD processing, i.e. a FB is executed and its output signal is immediately used to make a branching decision before executing the next one, and so on, until a state node is reached,
- A condition function block might be executed only once if it generates several sequentially tested condition variables. Moreover, it is possible to test a number of such variables simultaneously via bit-patterns (mask and value) specifying the corresponding subsets of the tested variables and their values,
- The execution of condition function blocks is ultimately integrated with the execution of control function blocks, whereby BDD processing ends up with the selection of current state and the execution of a control function block associated with that state,
- It is possible to specify empty (Null) states, e.g. wait states.

It is assumed, that state transitions are complete and consistent. Completeness and consistency must be checked at configuration time, and this can be done using techniques similar to those presented in [8].

The above options have been taken into account when designing the data structures and the algorithm of the hybrid state logic controller, which are presented below. The discussion is illustrated with the example hybrid state machine given in Figs. 1 and 3.

The SLC algorithm parses a state transition table (STT), which consists of data records of the following structure:

Table 2. Description of state transition table record fields

Field Name	Field Description
type	Type of function block to be executed, index of function block type table: FBTypes[type]
function	Routine of the FB to be executed, index of function block routine: FBTypes[]→FBFunctions[function]
instance	Pointer to the FB instance execution record, argument passed to function block routine: FBTypes[]→FBFunctions[](instance)
conditionVar	Pointer to condition variable used in order to access results of function block computation
mask	AND mask imposed on condition variable
value	Value of expected masked condition variable used in order to evaluate transition guards either to True or False
successorTrue / nextState	Index pointing to successor row in case of transition guard variable evaluated to True / Index to the initial row of next state mapping in case of control action execution (state execution)
successorFalse / iTransition	Index pointing to successor row in case of transition guards evaluated to False / Flag indicating immediate transition to *nextState* in case of control action execution (state execution)

```
typedef struct {
    TFBType          type;
    TFBFunction      function;
    TFBInstance      instance;
    TConditionVar*   conditionVar;
    TConditionVar    mask;
    TConditionVar    value;
    union {
      TSTTRow        successorTrue;
      TSTTRow        nextState;
    };
    union {
      TSTTRow        successorFalse;
```

```
        TBool           immediateTransition;
      };
    } TSTTRecord;
```

The records are grouped in segments representing the next-state mappings of various states of the state machine. A brief description of record fields is given in Table 2, whereby the function block is specified by three fields: *type*, *function*, and *instance*. These are used to invoke a function of a specified type on a given instance. The evaluation of transition guards to either True or False is based on the assessment of condition variables, via the *conditionVar* pointer, masked by *mask* field, and compared to required *value*. The execution of a control FB in a state is distinguished from the computation of condition variables by assigning Null to the *conditionVar* field of the STT record. Moreover, in the case of state node, *mask* and *value* fields are not used, and the meaning of the last two fields is *nextState* and *immediateTransition*. In case of transition guards evaluation all fields are used and the meaning of the last two fields is *successorTrue* and *successorFalse*.

The implementation of the hybrid state machine driver is presented below:

```
 1  row = tableRow;
 2  do {
 3    if (row->instance != NULL)
 4      FBTypes[row->type]
 5        ->FBFunctions[row->function](row->instance);
 6
 7    if (row->conditionVar != NULL) {
 8      if ( (*row->conditionVar & row->mask)
 9                                     == row->value) {
10        row = row->successorTrue;
11      }
12      else {
13        row = row->successorFalse;
14      }
15    }
16    else {
17      tableRow = row->nextState;
18      if (row->immediateTransition == FALSE) {
19        return;
20      }
21      else {
22        row = tableRow;
23      }
24    }
25  } while(TRUE);
```

STT parsing is started from the row previously saved in the *tableRow* variable (line 1). Then, the algorithm will loop until a stable state is reached (line 2-25). In the loop, first the function block routine is executed if the *instance* is specified (line 3-5). It is possible to parse the STT without executing a function block, e.g. an empty state, or a transition guard evaluation based on condition variables computed earlier (see example below). If the *conditionVar* field is not Null, evaluation of a guard variable takes place, and a successor row is chosen (line 7-15). When the *conditionVar* field is Null, the control function block associated with state has been just executed, and a state has been reached (line 16-24). If the *immediateTransition* field is equal to False a stable state has been reached and the SLC leaves the loop (line 18-20), otherwise it continues looping (line 21-23).

The presented design pattern will be illustrated with the example state machine shown in Fig. 1 and Fig. 3. Table 3 shows the encoding of the state transition table for that example, where grey rows represent condition nodes and white rows - state nodes of the BDD shown on Fig. 1.

Table 3. State transition table of example state machine

row	cond. var. / state	type	function	instance	condVar / state	mask	value	succTrue / nextState	succFalse / iTrans	next-state mapping
0	s	-	-	Null	&inpDriver.s	1	1	1	2	
1	x	TCFB	fBD	&composite	&composite.x	1	1	3	2	Fa_1
2	a_1	-	-	Null	Null	-	-	0	False	Fa_4
3	a_2	TBCtrl	main	&bCtrl1	Null	-	-	4	True	
4	a_3	-	-	Null	Null	-	-	5	False	Fa_2
5	x	TCFB	fBD	&composite	&composite.x	1	1	4	6	Fa_3
6	a_4	TBCtrl	main	&bCtrl2	Null	-	-	2	True	

It can be seen from the table that state nodes are differentiated by means of Null *condVar* pointers. This is because state nodes are associated with control function blocks, e.g. a_2 and a_4, or may represent empty states having a Null *instance* (e.g. a_1). Condition nodes are associated with condition function blocks, whose output location is accessed by means of a *condVar* pointer, and the corresponding output bit(s) are tested using the specified *mask* and *value* fields. A condition node may have a Null *instance* if the corresponding function block has been previously executed (e.g. the input driver FB generating signal s).

Rows are usually grouped in contiguous segments representing the next-state mappings (i.e. subsets of successor states) for the corresponding states of the state machine. However, the table can be eventually minimized taking into account that some of those mappings may be subsets of other next-state mappings. Here, $Fa_2 \subset Fa_3$, *and* $Fa_4 \subset Fa_1$, which is reflected in the composition of the example state transition table (see also Fig. 1).

When invoked, the state machine driver processes the table segment corresponding to the next-state mapping of the previous state (e.g. Fa_1) in order to select the current state (a_1 or a_2), execute the associated control function block and exits (if no immediate transition has been specified). During the next invocation the driver processes the segment containing the successors of the previously chosen state (e.g. Fa_2), and so on. However, in case of immediate transitions, the driver may process two or more segments in succession before a stable state is reached and the program is exited (e.g. state a_2 which is immediately followed by the stable state a_3, and likewise a_4, which is immediately followed by the stable state a_1).

4 Related Research

The increasing complexity of embedded applications has stimulated the investigation of hybrid models, e.g. mode-automata implemented in LUSTRE [5] and the hybrid models combining state machine and data flow domains in the Ptolemy II framework [6], which are similar to the hybrid state machine presented in the paper (Fig. 2). However, the above models are not implemented as reusable and reconfigurable components.

The importance of reconfigurable components, and in particular - reconfigurable state machines has been recognized, and there are already several research projects and industrial developments illustrating this approach, e.g. StateWORKS [3]. The latter employs 'virtual' finite state machines (VFSMs), which use state transition tables that are interpreted at run time by a standard routine called the VFSM executor. The system uses a non-hierarchical event-driven state machine model with a combined Moore/Mealy semantics. Consequently, an application is conceived as a hierarchy of flat state machines, which can be (re)configured by generating the necessary state transition tables. A similar approach has been developed for open machine control systems [4], where reconfigurable state machine components are once again implemented by means of state transition tables interpreted at run time by a state machine driver. This architecture uses a purely event-driven Mealy model (i.e. no guards are specified in the state transition table) and it supports hierarchical state machines in a Statecharts-like fashion.

However, these two systems do not support function blocks as defined in IEC 61131-3 and similar industrial standards [9]. Instead, the StateWORKS environment uses the concept of virtual inputs/outputs provided by a virtual I/O processor (also denoted as real-time data base). The latter consists of objects that are instances of predefined or user-supplied object classes. Likewise, the open machine control architecture employs user-supplied functions invoked from within the state machine driver in order to execute output actions. Another difference is in the data structures used to implement the state transition tables. These are relatively complex in both cases, resulting in processing and memory overhead, which can be substantially reduced by using BDD-based data structures, as suggested in this paper.

The presented function block model (Fig. 2) bears certain resemblance to function blocks defined in standard IEC 61499, which also incorporates an execution control state machine. However, that state machine is "hardwired" in the function block, i.e. it uses predefined sets of inputs and outputs and its configuration cannot be changed without reprogramming.

5 Conclusion

The paper has presented design models of reconfigurable state machines that have been conceived in the context of the COMDES framework, and in particular - the state logic controller and the extended (hybrid) state logic controller, whose principles of operation are presented in the paper. The latter has been used to develop a generic reusable component, i.e. a function block of class State Machine, which can be used to implement a broad range of embedded applications, such as sequential, continuous and hybrid control systems.

The main idea of the proposed method is to provide a universal *executable* component that can be reconfigured *without any re-programming*. This is accomplished by updating the supporting data structure, i.e. a state transition table, whereas the executable code remains unchanged and may be stored in permanent memory. The state transition table consists of multiple-output binary decision diagrams (BDDs) that represent the next-state mappings of various states and the associated control actions. This solution has important implications:

- BDDs allow for compact encoding of state transition tables resulting in considerable memory savings in comparison with other design methods,
- BDDs allow for extremely fast processing of state transition tables via guided execution/testing of condition function blocks while evaluating a single guard specifying a transition to a successor state, thus avoiding the need to compute multiple guards in order to determine the successor state,
- This has also safety implications as long as BDD processing always results in the selection of a successor state, whereas other methods are prone to software errors that may result from incomplete and inconsistent specification of state transitions.

The presented function block design method has been validated in a number of real-time control experiments and most notably – a modal control system for a DC motor (speed and direction control) and a sequential control system for a complex plant specified in the Production Cell case study [5]. A configuration and analysis tool supporting the method is now under development.

References

1. Angelov, C., Sierszecki, K.: A Software Framework for Component-Based Embedded Applications. Proc. of the Asia-Pacific Software Engineering Conference APSEC'2004, Busan, Korea (2004)
2. Samek, M.: Practical Statecharts in C/C++: Quantum Programming for Embedded Systems. CMP Books (2002)
3. Wagner, F., Wolstenholme, P.: Modeling and Building Reliable, Re-usable Software. Proc. of the 10th IEEE International Conference and Workshop on the Engineering of Computer-Based Systems, Huntsville, USA (2003)
4. Wang, S., Shin, K. G.: Constructing Reconfigurable Software for Machine Control Systems. IEEE Trans. on Robotics and Automation, vol. 18, No 4, August (2002), 475-486
5. Maraninchi, F., Remond, Y.: Applying Formal Methods to Industrial Cases: the Language Approach (The Production-Cell and Mode-Automata). Proc. of the 5th International Workshop on Formal Methods for Industrial Critical Systems, Berlin (2000)
6. Lee, E.: Embedded Software – an Agenda for Research. UCB ERL Memorandum M99/63, University of California at Berkeley, USA (1999)
7. Douglass, B., P.: Real-Time UML: Developing Efficient Objects for Embedded Systems. Addison Wesley (1998)
8. Heimdahl, M. P. E., Leveson, N.G.: Completeness and Consistency Analysis of State-Based Requirements. IEEE Transactions on Software Engineering, TSE 22(6), (1996), 363-377
9. John, K-H., Tiegelkamp, M.: IEC61131-3: Programming Industrial Automation Systems. Springer (2001)

Optimizing Nested Loops with Iterational and Instructional Retiming*

Chun Xue[1], Zili Shao[2], MeiLin Liu[1], Mei Kang Qiu[1], and Edwin H.-M. Sha[1]

[1] University of Texas at Dallas,
Richardson, Texas 75083, USA
{cxx016000, mxl024000, mxq012100, edsha}@utdallas.edu
[2] Hong Kong Polytechnic University,
Hung Hom, Kowloon, Hong Kong
cszlshao@comp.polyu.edu.hk

Abstract. Embedded systems have strict timing and code size requirements. Retiming is one of the most important optimization techniques to improve the execution time of loops by increasing the parallelism among successive loop iterations. Traditionally, retiming has been applied at instruction level to reduce cycle period for single loops. While multi-dimensional (MD) retiming can explore the outer loop parallelism, it introduces large overheads in loop index generation and code size due to loop transformation. In this paper, we propose a novel approach, that combines iterational retiming with instructional retiming to satisfy any given timing constraint by achieving full parallelism for iterations in a partition with minimal code size. The experimental results show that combining iterational retiming and instructional retiming, we can achieve 37% code size reduction comparing to applying iteration retiming alone.

1 Introduction

Constant advance in gate capacity and reduction in chip feature size made it possible to implement system-on-chip (SoC) that allows parallel embedded systems. Parallel embedded systems, typically with VLIW or multi-core architecture, are becoming more widely used in computation-intensive applications. A large group of such applications are multi-dimensional problems, i.e., problems involving more than one dimension, such as computer vision, high-definition television, medical imaging, and remote sensing. There are usually stringent requirements in timing performance and code size for these applications. How to design parallel embedded systems that conforms timing performance requirements while minimizing code size is an interesting research topic. This paper combines iterational retiming with instructional retiming, to achieve given timing requirements for nested loops with minimal code size overhead.

There has been a lot of research on program transformations to enhance parallelism for loops. Many forms of program transformations have been proposed,

* This work is partially supported by TI University Program, NSF EIA-0103709, Texas ARP 009741-0028-2001, and NSF CCR-0309461, NSF IIS-0513669, Microsoft, USA.

L.T. Yang et al. (Eds.): EUC 2005, LNCS 3824, pp. 164–173, 2005.

a catalog of which can be found in a survey by Bacon, Graham, and Sharp [3]. Numerous techniques have been proposed for one-dimensional loops [1] [4] [5] [8]. Renfors and Neuvo have proved that there is a lower bound of iteration period for one-dimensional loops [10]. Optimal scheduling for one-dimensional loops could reach this lower bound[5], but can not do better than this lower bound. In this paper, we show that there is no lower bound of iteration period for multi-dimensional loops. Using our proposed technique, we can achieve any given timing requirement.

A lot of works also have been done for nested loops to increase parallelism. Majority of these works are based on wavefront transformation [2][7], which achieves higher level of parallelism for nested loops by changing the execution sequence of the nested loops. This sequence of execution is commonly associated with a schedule vector s, also called an ordering vector, which affects the order in which the iterations are performed. The iterations are executed along hyperplanes defined by s. When the execution of a hyperplane reaches the boundaries of the iteration space, it advances to the next hyperplane according to the direction of s. All the iterations on the same hyperplane can be executed in parallel.

Iterational retiming first partitions the iteration space into basic partitions, and then retiming is performed at iteration level so that all the iterations in each partition can be executed in parallel. In this way, we achieve higher level of parallelism while maintaining simple loop bounds and loop indexes with minimal overhead. Two main techniques are applied in iterational retiming, namely loop partitioning and retiming. Various techniques have been proposed for loop partitioning [6] [11]. most of the loop partitioning algorithm are targeting better data locality. In our algorithm, partition is used to increase parallelism. Retiming [8] [9] has been widely applied to increase instruction level parallelism. We apply the retiming technique to iterations instead of instructions, and we show that full-parallelism for iterations in each partition can always be achieved by iterational retiming. Experimental results show that our proposed technique can always reach the given timing requirement. While iterational retiming can always satisfy the timing requirement, it is best to be combined with instructional retiming. We show that when instructional retiming is combined with iterational retiming, code size is reduced 37% in average, while achieving the same given timing performance constraint.

The remainder of this paper is organized as follows. Section 2 introduces basic concepts and definitions. The algorithm for instructional timing is presented in Section 3. The algorithm for iterational retiming is proposed in Section 4. Section 5 proposes the algorithm that combines iterational retiming and instructional retiming. Experimental results and concluding remarks are provided in Section 6 and 7, respectively.

2 Basic Concepts and Definitions

In this section, we introduce some basic concepts which will be used in the later sections. First, we introduce the model and notions that we use to analyze nested loops. Second, loop partitioning technique is introduced. In this paper, our technique is presented with two dimensional notations. It can be easily extended to multi-dimensions.

2.1 Modeling Nested Loops

Multi-dimensional Data Flow Graph is used to model nested loops and is defined as follows. A *Multi-dimensional Data Flow Graph (MDFG)* $G = \langle V, E, d, t \rangle$ is a node-weighted and edge-weighted directed graph, where V is the set of computation nodes, $E \subseteq V * V$ is the set of dependence edges, d is a function and d(e) is the multi-dimensional delays for each edge $e \in E$ which is also known as dependence vector, and t is the computation time of each node. We use d(e) = (d.x, d.y) as a general formulation of any delay shown in a two-dimensional DFG (2DFG). An example is shown in Figure 1.

```
for i=0 to n  do
   for j=0 to m do
      A[i,j] = B[i,j-1] + B[i-1,j];
      B[i,j] = A[i,j] + A[i-1,j+1];
   end for
end for
```

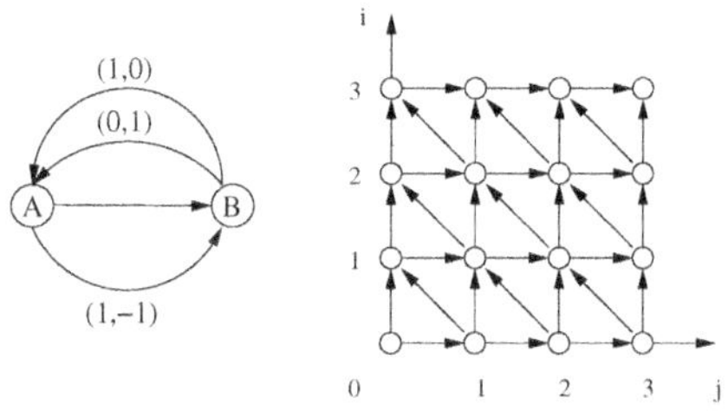

Fig. 1. A nested loop, its MDFG and its iteration space

An **iteration** is the execution of each node in V exactly once. The computation time of the longest path without delay is called the *iteration period.* For example, the iteration period of the MDFG in Figure 1 is 2 from the longest path, which is from node A to B. If a node v at iteration j, depends on a node u at iteration i, then there is an edge e from u to v, such that d(e) = j - i. An edge with delay (0,0) represents a data dependence within the same iteration. A legal MDFG must not have zero-delay cycles. Iterations are represented as integral points in a Cartesian space, called *iteration space* , where the coordinates are defined by the loop control indexes.

A **schedule vector s** is the normal vector for a set of parallel equitemporal hyperplanes that define a sequence of execution of an iteration space. By default, a given nested loop is executed in a row-wise fashion, where the schedule vector $s = (1, 0)$.

Retiming [8] can be used to optimize the cycle period of a DFG by evenly distributing the delays in it. Given a MDFG $G = \langle V, E, d, t \rangle$, retiming r of G is a function from V to integers. For a node $u \in V$, the value of $r(u)$ is the number of delays drawn from each of its incoming edges of node u and pushed to all of its outgoing edges. Let $G_r = \langle V, E_r, d_r, t\rangle$ denote the retimed graph of G with retiming r, then $d_r(e) = d(e) + r(u) - r(v)$ for every edge $e(u \to v) \in E_r$ in G_r.

2.2 Partitioning the Iteration Space

Instead of executing the entire iteration space in the order of rows and columns, we can first partition it and then execute the partitions one by one. The two boundaries of a partition are called the *partition vectors*. We will denote them by P_x and P_y. Due to the dependencies in the MDFG, partition vectors need to be carefully chosen to ensure there is no two-way dependency so that the partition is a legal partition.

Iteration Flow Graph is used to model nested loop partitions and is defined as follows. An *Iteration Flow Graph (IFG)* $G_i = \langle V_i, E_i, d_i, t_i\rangle$ is a node-weighted and edge-weighted directed graph, where V_i is the set of iterations in a partition. The number of nodes $|V_i|$ in an IFG G_i is equal to the number of nodes in a partition. $E_i \subseteq V_i * V_i$ is the set of iteration dependence edges. d_i is a function and $d_i(e)$ is the multi-dimensional delays for each edge $e \in E_i$. t_i is the computation time for each iteration. An iteration flow graph $G_i = \langle V_i, E_i, d_i, t_i\rangle$ is *realizable* if the represented partition is legal.

3 The Instructional Retiming for Nested Loops

We propose an algorithm to do maximum instructional retiming while maintaining the original execution sequence in this section.

The instructional retiming we are applying in this setting is unique. We are retiming along one dimension of a multi-dimensional loop. This is because we wish to maintain either row-wise or column-wise execution after the retiming. The problem is equivalent to removing all the (i,j)-delays, where both i and j are none zero values, and producing a retiming such that all the edges are non-zero-delay edges if possible. If there is at least one (i,j)-delay, we can always find a retiming solution because the cycle becomes a DAG after removing (i,j)-delay edge. If there is no (i,j)-delay, then no retiming solution exists because the total delay of a cycle is a constant according to retiming property. In this case, the total delay of the cycle is always (0,k). According to retiming theory, DAG can always be retimed such that any edge has at least one delay. In the other words, a cycle with any (i,j) delay, $i > 0$, can be fully parallelized using schedule vector $s = (1, 0)$. Thus, we can directly apply one-dimensional retiming to minimize the cycle period after removing the (i,j)-delay edges. Detail of our instructional retiming algorithm is shown in 3.1.

4 Iterational Retiming

In this section, we propose a new loop transformation technique, iterational retiming. First the basic concepts and the theorems related to iterational retiming are discussed. Then the procedures and algorithms to transform the loops are presented in the second section.

Algorithm 3.1 INSTRUCTIONAL-RETIME Algorithm

Require: MDFG $G = \langle V, E, \mathbf{d}, t\rangle$, schedule vector' $\mathbf{s}$.
Ensure: Retiming function $\mathbf{r}(v)$, retimed MDFG $G_r = \langle V, E, \mathbf{d}_r, t\rangle$, minimum cycle period $\mathbf{c}$.

```
/* Check the legality of s. */
if d(e) · s < 0 then
   Report: s is unfeasible.
   Break.
end if
/* For the feasible clock-period test algorithm */
Compute D(u, v) and T(u, v) for any two nodes u and v on G'.
Sort the elements in the range of T(u, v).
for all Elements in the range of T(u, v) do
   Binary search to find the minimum achievable cycle period c.
   /* Determine if cycle period c is feasible */
   r ← (0, 1); s ← (1, 0);
   /* Remove the edges that are not parallel to r. */
   E' ⟵ E − {e | d(e) ∦ r, ∀e ∈ E}
   d'(e) ⟵ d(e)/r, ∀e ∈ E'
   /* The feasible clock-period test algorithm */
   Compute D(u, v) and T(u, v) for any two nodes u and v on G'.
   Construct the constraint graph according to the legality and feasible conditions of
   retiming with the desired cycle period c.
   Use the shortest path algorithm to find a solution.
   if There exists a retiming r' of G' such that Φ(G'_r') ≤ c then
      /* Update the retimed graph */
      r(v) ⟵ r'(v) · r(v), ∀v ∈ V
      c feasible; Use retiming r to retime the MDFG G.
   else
      Error: Unfeasible cycle period.
   end if
end for
```

4.1 Definitions and Theorems

Iterational retiming is carried out in the following steps. Given a MDFG, first the directions of legal partition vectors will be decided. Second, partition size will be determined to meet the input timing constraint. Third, iterational retiming will be applied to create the retimed partition.

Among all the delay vectors in a MDFG, two extreme vectors, the clockwise (CW) and the counterclockwise (CCW), are the most important vectors for deciding the directions of the legal partition vectors. Legal partition vector cannot lie between CW and CCW. In other words, they can only be outside of CW and CCW or be aligned with CW or CCW. For the basic partition in our algorithm, we choose P_x to be aligned with x-axis, and P_y to be aligned with CCW. This is a legal choice of partition vectors because the y elements of the delay vectors of the input MDFG are always positive or zero, which allows the default row-wise execution of nested loops. For convenience, we use P_{x0} and P_{y0} to denote the base partition vectors. The actual partition vectors are then denoted by $P_x = f_x P_{x0}$ and $P_y = f_y P_{y0}$, where f_x and f_y are called partition factors, which are related to the size of the partition.

After basic partition is identified via P_x, and P_y, an IFG $G_i = \langle V_i, E_i, d_i, t_i \rangle$ can be constructed. An *iterational retiming* r is a function from V_i to Z^n that redistributes the iterations in a partition. A new IFG $G_{i,r}$ is created, such that the number of iterations included in the partition is still the same. The retiming vector r(u) of an iteration $u \in G_i$ represents the offset between the original partition containing u, and the one after iterational retiming. When all the edges $e \in E_i$ have non-zero delays, all the nodes $v \in V_i$ can be executed in parallel, which means all the iterations in a partition can be executed in parallel. We call such a partition a *retimed partition.* Properties, algorithms and supporting theorems for iterational retiming are presented below. We will first show how to choose f_x so that retimed partition can be achieved.

Given a MDFG G, let min_k be the minimum k of all the (0, k) delays in G. Let f_x be the size of partition in the x dimension. Given an Iteration Flow Graph (IFG) after we partition the iteration space with f_x and f_y, we want to make sure that the IFG can be retimed to be fully parallel using basic retiming $r = (0, 1)$. There are two types of cycles in an IFG, one with delay $d(c) = (0, y)$ and the other with delay $d(c) \geq (1, -\infty)$. The cycles with delays $d(c) \geq (1, -\infty)$ can be easily retimed to be fully parallel by using $r = (0, 1)$. But for cycles with delays $d(c) = (0, y)$, y must be $\geq$ n(c), where n(c) denotes the number of nodes in cycle c, in order to distribute (0, 1) delay to each edge in cycle c. To simplify notations, we just focus on the $(0, k)$ cycles and delays, so when we say $d(c) \geq n(c)$, it means that $d(c) = (0, y)$, $y \geq n(c)$.

Property 1. Given f_x, an edge with d(e) = (0, b) in DFG will become f_x edges in IFG from iteration node i (here we use i to denote (0, i)), $0 \leq i < f_x$, to node (i+b) mod f_x with delay = (i +b) div f_x.

Theorem 1. *If $f_x > min_k$, in the resulting Iteration Flow Graph (IFG), there exists a cycle c where $d(c) < n(c)$ and $n(c)$ denotes the number of nodes in cycle c.*

Theorem 2. *If $f_x \leq min_k$, for each cycle c in IFG, d(c) must be $\geq n(c)$.*

As a result of the above theorems, we know that let $f_x \leq min_k$, and $r = (0, 1)$ as the retiming function, a basic partition can be retimed into retimed partition. After the iterational retiming transformation, the new program can still keep row-wise execution, which is an advantage over the loop transformation techniques that need to do wavefront execution and need to have extra instructions to calculate loop bounds and loop indexes.

4.2 The Iterational Retiming Technique

In this section, the iterational retiming algorithm is presented and explained. The complexity of the algorithm is given at the end of this section.

Algorithm 4.1 ITERATIONAL-RETIME

Require: MDFG $G = \langle V, E, d, t \rangle$, timing requirement T
Ensure: A retimed partition that meets timing requirement

/* Step 1. Based on the input MDFG, find a basic partition that is legal and have enough number of iterations to meet the timing requirement T; */
$c \leftarrow$ cycle period of MDFG ;
$P_{x0} \leftarrow (0,1)$; /* 1.1 find P_{x0} */
$P_{y0} \leftarrow$ CCW vector of all delays; /* 1.2 find P_{y0}*/
f_x = { k | $(0, k)$ is smallest $(0, x)$ delays }; /* 1.3 find f_x*/
$f_y = \left\lceil \frac{c}{T \cdot f_x} \right\rceil$; /* 1.4 find f_y*/
$P_x = f_x \cdot P_{x0}$; /* 1.5 find P_y and P_y*/
$P_y = f_y \cdot P_{y0}$;
obtain basic partition with P_x, P_y;
/* Step 2. Call iterational retiming to transform the basic partition into a retimed partition; */
/* use r=(0,1) repeatedly to achieve full parallelism. */
Step 2.1 Apply r=(0,1) to any node that has all incoming edges with non-zero delays and at least one zero-delay outgoing edge.
Step 2.2 Since the resulting IFG is still realizable, if there are zero delay edges, go back to step 2.1.

The requirement for f_x is discussed in detail in section 4.1. We want f_x to be as large as possible. The larger f_x is, the smaller the prolog and epilog will be. Since $f_x \leq min_k$, so we pick $f_x = min_k$. Once f_x is identified, we can find f_y with the given timing requirement T and the original cycle period c. Since we need to meet the timing constraint T,

$$\Rightarrow T \geq \frac{c}{f_x \cdot f_y}$$
$$\Rightarrow f_y \geq \frac{c}{T \cdot f_x}$$
$$\Rightarrow f_y = \left\lceil \frac{c}{T \cdot f_x} \right\rceil$$

Let G_i be a realizable IFG, the iterational retiming algorithm transforms G_i to $G_{i,r}$, in at most $|V|$ iterations, such that $G_{i,r}$ is fully parallel.

For algorithm 4.1, in step 1, it takes $O(|V|)$ to find the cycle period, $O(|E|)$ to find P_{y0}, and $O(|E|)$ to find f_x. So it takes $O(|V| + |E|)$ to execute step 1. In step 2, it takes at most $|V|$ iterations, and each iteration takes at most $O(|E|)$ time. So it takes $O(|V||E|)$ to execute step 2. As a result, algorithm 4.1 takes $O(|V||E|)$ to complete.

5 Combining Iterational and Instructional Retiming

The COMBINE-RETIME algorithm is presented in this section. It combines instructional retiming with iterational retiming to optimize nested loops for both timing performance and code size.

Algorithm 5.1 COMBINE-RETIME

Require: MDFG $G = \langle V, E, d, t \rangle$, timing requirement T
Ensure: A retimed MDFG that meets timing requirement with smallest overheads

```
/* Step 1. apply instructional retiming */
if apply INSTRUCTIONAL-RETIME algorithm with s = (0,1) can satisfy T then
  return s = (0,1);
else if apply INSTRUCTIONAL-RETIME algorithm with s = (1,0) can satisfy T
then
  return s = (1,0);
else
  if s = (1,0) is legal and INSTRUCTIONAL-RETIME with s = (1,0) give a
  smaller cycle period then
    apply loop index interchange;
  end if
  /* Step 2. apply iterational retiming reach timing requirement T */
  call ITERATIONAL-RETIME algorithm;
end if
```

The COMBINE-RETIME algorithm first applies the INSTRUCTIONAL-RETIME algorithm in one dimension to minimize the cycle period. Row-wise execution sequence, i.e. schedule vector $s = (0, 1)$ is first attempted. Then column-wise execution sequence is attempted if schedule vector $s = (1, 0)$ is legal. When both instructional retiming failed to meet the required timing constraint T, ITERATIONAL-RETIME algorithm is called to perform iterational retiming. When column-wise execution sequence is legal and it gives a smaller cycle period after iterational retiming, loop index interchange is applied before performing iteration retiming. Applying instructional retiming reduces iteration period before iterational retiming is applied. Smaller partition size is needed in iterational retiming process, hence code size is reduced given the same timing performance requirement.

6 Experiments

In this section, we conduct experiments based on a set of DSP benchmarks with two dimensional loops: WDF (Wave Digital Filter), IIR (the Infinite Impulse Response Filter), 2D (the Two Dimensional filter), Floyd (Floyd-Steinberg algorithm), and DPCM (Differential Pulse-Code Modulation device).

Table 1 shows the code size comparison between applying iterational retiming alone and applying both iterational retiming and instructional retiming transformation, while achieving the same timing performance. In this table, code size is measure in the number of iterations included in each partition, which equals $f_x \times f_y$. Column "ITER-RE" represents the code size by applying iterational retiming alone. Column "COM-RE" represents the code size by applying both instructional retiming and iterational retiming. From this table, we can see that by applying instructional retiming before iterational retiming, we can reduce code size in an average of 37%.

Table 1. Comparison of code size between iterational retiming only and combined retiming

Bench.	**Code Size (Iterations)**					
Iteration Period = 1						
Bench.	f_x	f_y	**ITER-RE.**	f_x	f_y	**COM-RE.**
IIR	1	5	5	1	2	**2**
WDF	6	1	6	1	1	**1**
FLOYD	1	10	10	1	8	**8**
DPCM	1	5	5	1	2	**2**
2D(1)	1	9	9	1	1	**1**
2D(2)	1	4	4	1	4	**4**
MDFG1	1	7	7	1	7	**7**
MDFG2	1	10	10	1	10	**10**
Iteration Period = 1/2						
Bench.	f_x	f_y	**ITER-RE.**	f_x	f_y	**COM-RE.**
IIR	1	10	10	1	4	**4**
WDF	12	1	12	2	1	**2**
FLOYD	1	20	20	1	16	**16**
DPCM	1	10	10	1	4	**4**
2D(1)	1	18	18	1	2	**2**
2D(2)	1	8	8	1	8	**8**
MDFG1	1	14	14	1	14	**14**
MDFG2	1	20	20	1	20	**20**
Iteration Period = 1/4						
Bench.	f_x	f_y	**ITER-RE.**	f_x	f_y	**COM-RE.**
IIR	1	20	20	1	8	**8**
WDF	24	1	24	4	1	**4**
FLOYD	1	40	40	1	32	**32**
DPCM	1	20	20	1	8	**8**
2D(1)	1	36	36	1	4	**4**
2D(2)	1	16	16	1	16	**16**
MDFG1	1	28	28	1	28	**28**
MDFG2	1	40	40	1	40	**40**
Avg. Iter.			16.3			10.2
Avg Impv			**37%**			

From our experiment results, we can clearly see that combining iterational retiming with instructional retiming can reduce code size significantly while achieving the same timing performance constraints.

7 Conclusion

In this paper, we propose a new loop transformation approach that combines iterational retiming with instructional retiming to optimize both timing performance and code size. We believe iterational retiming is a promising technique and can be applied to different fields for nested loop optimization. Combining instructional retiming and iterational retiming, we can achieve timing performance requirement for nested loops with minimal code size.

References

1. A. Aiken and A. Nicolau. Optimal loop parallelization. *ACM Conference on Programming Language Design and Implementation*, pages 308–317, 1988.
2. A. Aiken and A. Nicolau. *Fine-Grain Parallelization and the Wavefront Method.* MIT Press, 1990.
3. D. Bacon, S. Graham, and O. Sharp. Compiler transformations for high-performance computing. *Computing Srveys*, pages 345–420, 1994.
4. L.-F. Chao, A. S. LaPaugh, and E. H.-M. Sha. Rotation scheduling: A loop pipelining algorithm. *IEEE Trans. on Computer-Aided Design*, 16(3):229–239, March 1997.
5. L.-F. Chao and E.-M. Sha. Rate-optimal static scheduling for dsp data-flow programs. *IEEE Third Great lakes Symposium on VLSI*, pages 80–84, March 1993.
6. F. Chen and E.-M. Sha. Loop scheduling and partitions for hiding memory latencies. *International Symposium on System Synthesis*, 1999.
7. L. Lamport. The parallel execution of do loops. *Communications of the ACM SIG-PLAN*, 17:82–93, FEB. 1991.
8. C. E. Leiserson and J. B. Saxe. Retiming synchronous circuitry. *Algorithmica*, 6:5–35, 1991.
9. N. Passos and E. Sha. Full parallelism of uniform nested loops by multi-dimensional retiming. *Internal conference on Parallel Processing*, 2:130–133, Aug. 1994.
10. M. Renfors and Y. Neuvo. The maximum sampling rate of digital filters under hardware speed constraints. *IEEE Transactions on Cirtuits and Systems*, pages 196–202, March 1981.
11. Z. Wang, Q. Zhuge, and E.-M. Sha. Scheduling and partitioning for multiple loop nests. *International Symposium on System Synthesis*, pages 183–188, October 2001.

Realtime H.264 Encoding System Using Fast Motion Estimation and Mode Decision

Byeong-Doo Choi, Min-Cheol Hwang, Jun-Ki Cho,
Jin-Sam Kim, Jin-Hyung Kim, and Sung-Jea Ko

Department of Electronics Engineering, Korea University,
5-1 Anam-Dong, Sungbuk-ku, Seoul 136-701, Korea
sjko@dali.korea.ac.kr

Abstract. H.264 provides various useful features such as improved coding efficiency and error robustness. These features enable mobile device to adopt H.264/AVC standard to achieve effective video communications. However, the encoder complexity is greatly increased mainly due to motion estimation (ME) and mode decision. We implemented a realtime H.264 encoding system based on DSP and FPGA chip using the propose scheme to jointly optimize inter mode selection and ME using the multi-resolution analysis. In our paper, we focus on reducing the complexity while maintaining the visual quality output. Experimental results show that the proposed algorithm is over 3 times faster than the existing method while maintaining the coding efficiency and the implemented system. The implemented H.264 encoder meets the common requirement of the real-time video coding [30 frames/sec].

Keywords: H.264, inter mode decision, motion estimation, MRME, mobile video communication.

1 Introduction

Recent advances in wireless communication technology have introduced various mobile services such as multimedia message services, video on demand, and mobile video communications. Especially, there are increasing demands on mobile video communications with prevailing of the mobile devices equipped with camera module. To realize this service, video sequences have to be compressed with high coding efficiency and error robustness. The H.264/AVC is the state-of-the-art video compression standard recently developed by the ITU-T/ISO/IEC Joint Video [1].

The H.264/AVC provides various useful features such as improved coding efficiency, error robust data partitioning, and network friendliness with the network abstraction layer (NAL). These features enable mobile devices to adopt H.264/AVC standard to achieve effective video communications [2]. H.264 supports multiple reference frames and various block sizes for ME. It uses tree-structured hierarchical macroblock (MB) partitions. There are 7 different block sizes (16x16, 16x8, 8x16, 8x8, 4x8 and 4x4 blocks) that are used in a macroblock.

L.T. Yang et al. (Eds.): EUC 2005, LNCS 3824, pp. 174–183, 2005.

The current H.264 reference software is based on a rate- distortion optimization framework for both ME and mode decision.

Among all modules in the H.264 encoder, ME and mode decision require a heavy computation of H.264 encoder, especially when rate distortion optimization is used. ME has to be performed for every MB coding mode to find the best matching block. For mode decision searches, all possible combinations of coding modes are considered to obtain the MB with the minimum cost. Moreover, since these operations are performed in multiple reference frames, the computational load significantly increases at the encoder.

The computational burden can be reduced by applying fast ME methods, such as the three step search [3], the four step search [4], the diamond search [5], and the hexagon search [6]. Recently, the UMHexagonS has been adopted for fast ME in H.264 encoder reference software (JM 84) [7]. To optimize the mode decision process, the H.264 software adopts the full mode decision algorithm (FMD) [8] inducing an exhaustive computation. For fast mode decision, the early termination technique [9] reduces the number of potential prediction modes. In [10], a classification method is proposed to reduce the average number of block types while maintaining the coding performance.

In this paper, we propose new fast ME and inter mode decision techniques using the multi-resolution analysis for the H.264/AVC encoder. For fast ME, the proposed method is based on the multi-frame/multi-resolution ME using Hexagon searching. For the fast decision of inter coding mode, we introduce a down-top merge method. The proposed method splits all MBs into 4x4 sub-MBs and merges the sub-MBs when they are classified as the same class by using a new hypothesis-and-test based method.

The organization of the paper is as follows. The proposed fast ME method is introduced in Section II. In Section III, the proposed fast inter mode decision method is given. Finally, the implemented H.264 embedded system and the simulation results are shown in Section IV and the conclusions are described in Section V.

2 The Proposed Motion Estimation Method

The multi-resolution ME (MRME) technique is an alternative ME method to the conventional block-matching algorithm. In the conventional MRME, MVs are estimated at the lowest resolution and the estimated MV is scaled appropriately to be used as an initial bias and refined for remained sub-bands on wavelet transform. However, adopting the MRME for the H.264 requires wavelet transform as well as the integer transform, which results in additional computations.

To solve this problem, we propose a modified fast integer transform that can obtain wavelet coefficients by factorizing integer transform into two steps properly. Fig. 1 shows the modified implementation of a 4x4 fast integer transform. Unlike Malvar's fast integer transform approach [11], its first step is equal to the Haar wavelet transform. The first step of the modified fast integer transform

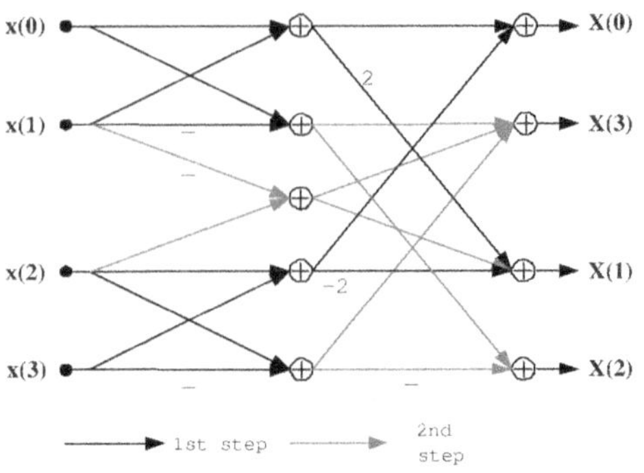

Fig. 1. Modified implementation of fast integer transform

decomposes a whole image into three layers. The coefficients in multi-layers are utilized in the proposed ME and mode decision methods.

With the modified fast integer transform, we propose a fast ME algorithm using MRME, Hexagon Searching, and Multi-frame reference. The proposed method exploits the cross correlation among multi-frames and layers of wavelet transform to reduce the computational complexity. It can achieve a smaller number of search points over other fast methods and can maintain similar or even smaller distortion error.

Fig. 2 shows the proposed searching patterns; the small square (SS), the uneven multi-hexagon-grid (UMHG), and the extended hexagon (EH). The SS and UMHG searching patterns are applied to find the coarse MV at layer 2. The EH is used to refine the MV at lower layers.

Fig. 3 shows the concept of the proposed MFMRME-HS method consisting of four steps. The detailed procedure is followed:

1. Search the MV in the object region with small motion by using the SS searching pattern at layer 2 of the reference frame (t-1) shown in Fig. 4. If the minimum sum of absolute difference (SAD) is smaller than an initial threshold, go to Step 3 to perform MV refinement at lower layers. Otherwise, go to Step 2 to keep searching the MV at layer 2. The MV obtained from Step 1 becomes the initial search center for the next step.
2. Find the MV by using the UMHG pattern at layer 2 of the reference frame (t-1) shown in Fig. 4. The MV obtained from Step 2 becomes the search center for the next step, and its corresponding minimum SAD becomes the threshold for the fast reference frame selection (FRFS) in Step 4.
3. Use the EH to refine the MV obtained from Steps 1 and 2 around the search center at lower layers. The MV refined in this step becomes a candidate of the best MV.
4. Step 2 and 3 are iterated at all the remained reference frames. For the FRFS, if the minimum SAD at layer 2 is over a threshold, MV refinement (Step 3) is not performed for its corresponding reference frame. As a result, this FRFS

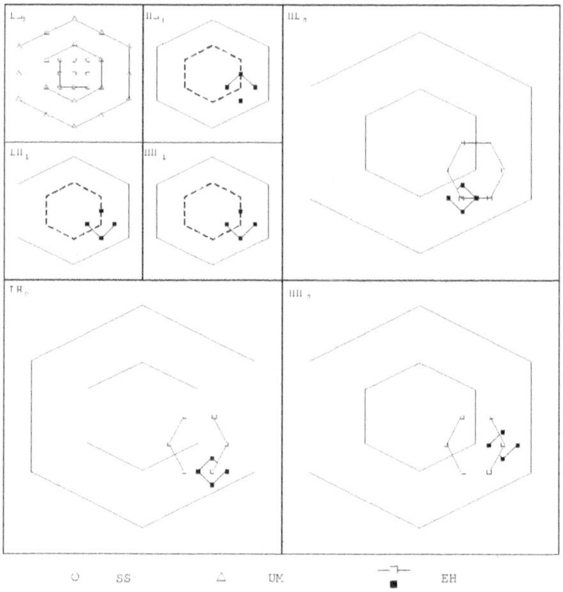

Fig. 2. Search pattern for multi-resolution

improves the performance of the proposed MFMRME-HS. Finally, select the best MV with the minimum SAD among all candidate MVs obtained from Step 3.

The proposed MFMRME-HS algorithm utilizes the correlation between multi-frames and sub-bands of wavelet transform to reduce the time complexity of ME.

3 The Proposed Fast Inter Mode Selection Method

In this section, we propose a down-top merge method for fast inter mode decision. Fig. 4 shows the proposed down-top merge method. The proposed method splits all 16x16 MBs into 4x4 sub-MBs and determines the class of each 4x4 sub-MBs by using both MVs in the LL band and the edge information. The 4x4 sub-MBs with the same class can be merged into three ways such as modes 4, 5, or 6 shown in Fig. 5, and 8x8 sub-MBs merged as mode 4 can be further grouped into one of the three block modes; modes 1, 2, and 3. After inter mode decision, ME is performed using MFMRME-HS only for the selected mode.

In order to classify 4x4 sub-MBs, we propose a new classification method based on statistical hypothesis testing. A region tends to be homogeneous if the textures in the region have very similar spatial property. Since blocks in the homogeneous region of the image can have similar MVs, they are not further split into smaller blocks. An effective way of determining the homogeneous region is

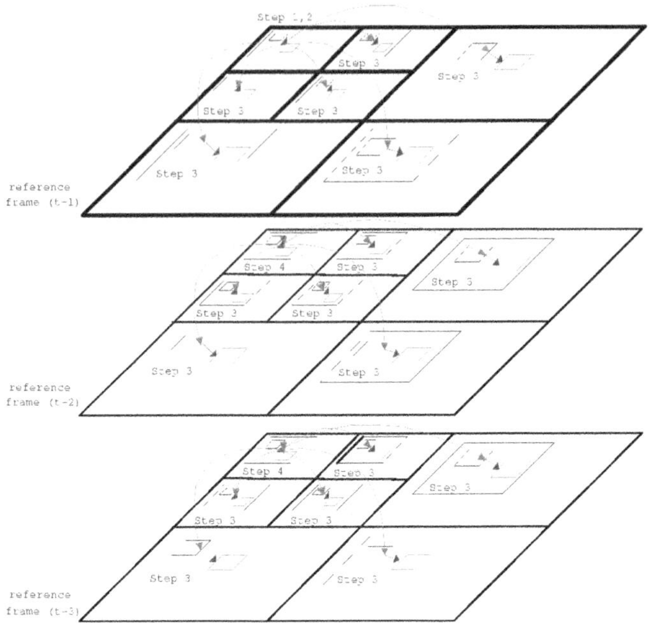

Fig. 3. Multi-frames/multi-resolution motion estimation scheme

to use the edge information, since sub-MBs in a homogeneous region have similar edge patterns.

In the proposed method, the vertical, horizontal, and diagonal edges in each sub-band of wavelet transform are used to determine the homogeneous region. The test of homogeneity hypothesis is as follows: Let $X = \{ x_0, x_1, x_2, x_3, x_4 \}$ be the feature vectors for hypothesis testing where x_0 is the absolute of motion vector in the LL band, x_1 is the average of pixel intensities in the LL band, x_2 is the sum of the amplitude of the horizontal edge in the LH band, x_3 is the sum of the amplitude of the vertical edge in the HL band, and x_4 is the sum of the amplitude of the diagonal edge in the HH band. Assume that the elements of the feature vector are independent each other. Since wavelet transform is an orthogonal transform, the amplitude of each edge is independent. Moreover, it is assumed that the distributions for the elements of the feature vector are Laplacian given by

$$f(x) = \frac{\lambda}{2} e^{-\lambda |x-\mu|} \tag{1}$$

This model is the most popular statistical model for coefficients in frequency domain and MVs [12] $\sim$ [14]. When the above assumptions are adopted, the proposed classifier can be approximated to the minimum distance classifier from

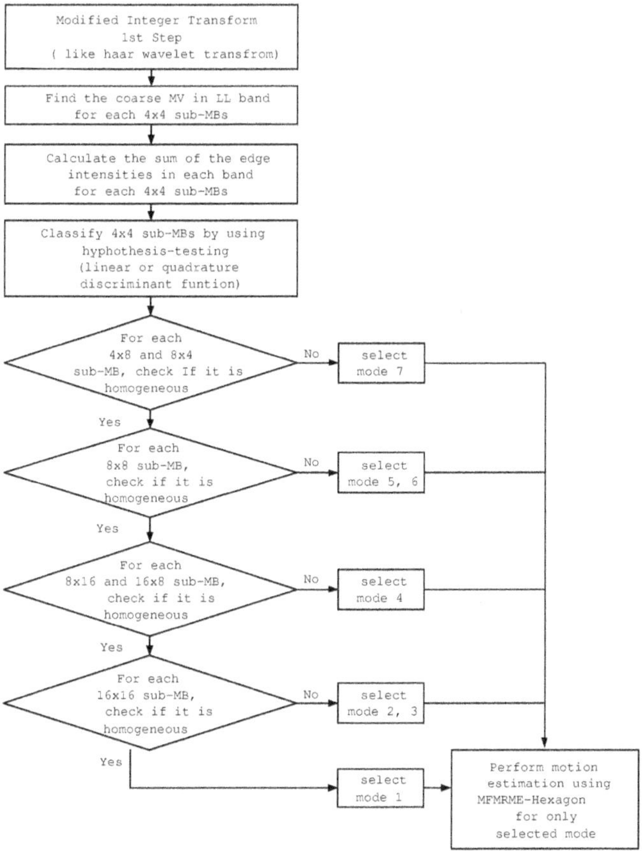

Fig. 4. Flow chart of fast inter mode decision by classifying sub-MBs

Bayes decision rule. The approximated discriminant functions for Laplacian distribution is given by

$$g_i(x) = \sum_{j=0}^{n-1} \lambda |x_j - \mu_{ij}| \tag{2}$$

where i is the index of classes and j is the index of the feature vector. We can classify each 4x4 sub-MB by calculating $g_i(x)$ for all classes and obtaining the minimum $g_i(x)$. Unlike conventional methods, the proposed inter mode decision method does not require ME and rate distortion optimization for every inter modes. However, the minimum distance classifier with a small computation is needed. Therefore, the proposed down-top merge method achieves fast inter mode decision.

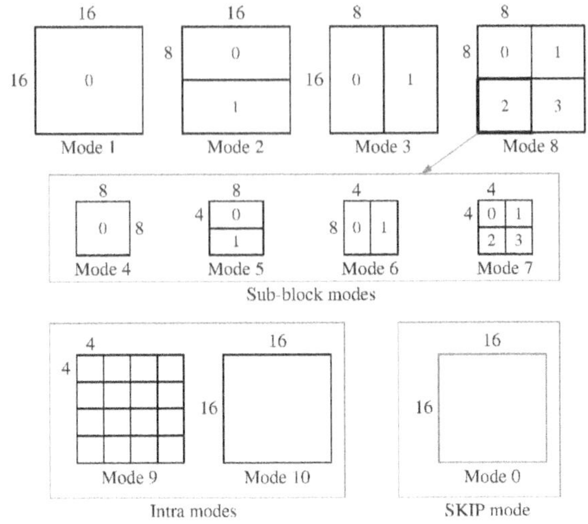

Fig. 5. Block modes of H.264/AVC

4 Experimental Results

To demonstrate the performance of the proposed system, we implemented the H.264 system which includes a 32-bit DSP processor and a FPGA, as shown in Fig. 6. The implemented H.264 encoder system targets a cost effective and high performance micro controller solution for system on chip. This system is under development with ALTERA Stratix (25,660 LEs) and TMS320C6416 (600 Mhz, 4800 MIPS, 128kb cache). Simulations have been conducted using JM 84 and the computational complexity is measured by the number of DSP clock cycles.

Fig. 7 shows the processing time of ME for multiple references. The proposed method is faster than UMHexagonS approach over 3 times since the redundant process among reference frames is reduced.

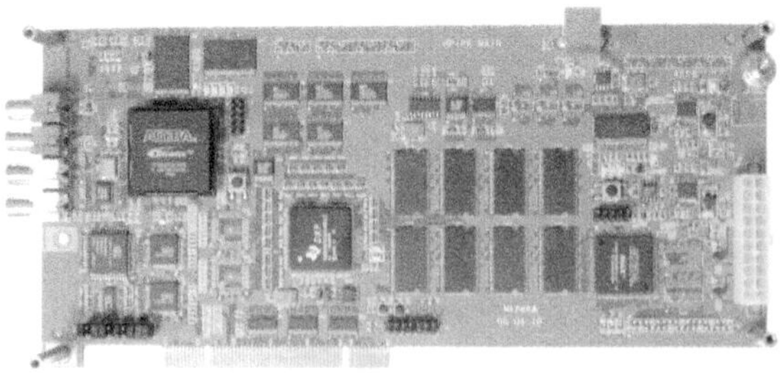

Fig. 6. The implemented H.264 system using DSP and FPGA

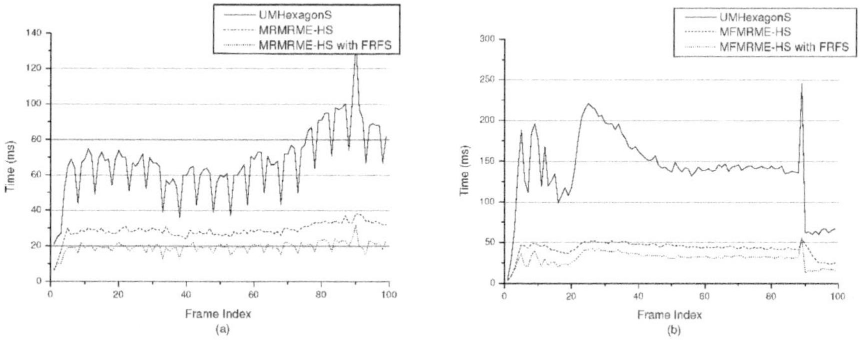

Fig. 7. Comparison of processing times. (a) "News", (b) "Table tennis".

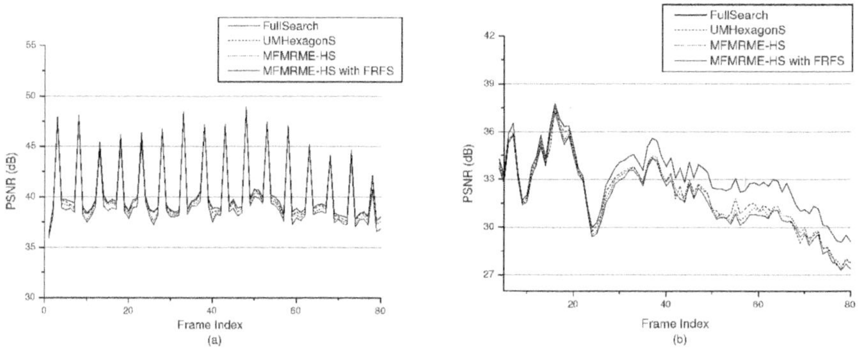

Fig. 8. Comparison of PSNR's. (a) "News", (b) "Table tennis".

Fig. 9. Simulation results of inter mode selection. (a)FMD, (b)The proposed method.

Table 1. Test Condition Video Sequence Comparison (QP=28)

Sequence	GOP Structure	Change of PSNR(dB)	Processing Time Saving(%)
News	IPPP	-0.04	67.75
Table Tennis	IPPP	-0.02	55.25

Table 2. Test Condition Video Sequence Comparison (QP=32)

Sequence	GOP Structure	Change of PSNR(dB)	Processing Time Saving(%)
News	IPPP	-0.05	67.50
Table Tennis	IPPP	-0.03	47.75

Fig. 8 shows the change of peak-to-peak signal-to-noise ratio (PSNR) and bitrate of reconstructed images for H.264 encoder reference software with the full search, UMHexagonS search, and the proposed MFMRME-HS algorithm. The PSNR curves obtained by these methods are almost the same. As far as the processing time is concerned, the proposed method is quite efficient.

Fig. 9(a) and (b) shows simulation results of the inter mode decision with FMD and the proposed method. The modes selected by the proposed methods are close to those obtained by FMD. A group of experiments were carried out on the test sequence with 2 quantization parameters, QP = 28, 32. Table 1 and 2 show the results according to quantization parameters. The experimental results show that the proposed method reduces the encoding time by 60% on average. The PSNR loss is negligible with the highest loss at 0.05 dB.

5 Conclusions

In this paper, we have proposed a new scheme to jointly optimize inter mode selection and motion estimation using the multi-resolution analysis and show the implemented H.264 embedded system. Experimental results show the proposed MFMRME-HS method is over 3 times faster than the existing ME method while maintaining the visual quality. Moreover, the proposed mode decision method has reduced the encoding time by 60% on average. The PSNR loss is negligible with the highest loss at 0.05 dB. Experimental results indicate that the proposed fast motion estimation and inter-prediction method enable the H.264/AVC coder to be effectively adopted for the mobile video communication.

References

[1] Wiegand, T., Sullivan, G.J.: Overview of the H.264/AVC video coding standard. IEEE Trans. Circuits Syst. Video Technol. 13 (2003) 560-576 Netravali, A.N., Haskell, B.G. : Digital Pictures, 2nd ed., Plenum Press (1995) 613-651

[2] ITU-T recommendation, H.264/ISO/IEC 14496-10 AVC : Draft ITU-T recommendation and final draft international standard of joint video specification. Joint Video Team (JVT) of ISO/IEC MPEG and ITU-T VCEG, JVT-G050. (2003)

[3] Li, R., Zeng, B., Liou, M.L.: A new three-step search algorithm for block motion estimation. IEEE Trans. Circuits Syst. Video Technol. 4 (1994) 438-443

[4] Po, L.M., Ma, W.C.: A novel four-step search algorithm for fast block motion estimation. IEEE Trans. Circuits Syst. Video Technol. 6 (1996) 313-317

[5] Tham, J.Y., Ranganath, S., Ranganath, M., Kassim, A.A.: A novel unrestricted center-biased diamond search algorithm for block motion estimation. IEEE Trans. Circuits Syst. Video Technol. 8 (1998) 369-377

[6] Zhu, C., Lin, X., Chau, L.: Hexagon-based search pattern for fast block motion estimation. IEEE Trans. Circuit Syst. Video Technol. 12 (2002) 349-355

[7] Chen, Z., He, Y.: Fast Integer and Fractional Pel Motion estimation. Joint Video Team (JVT) of ISO/IEC MPEG and ITU-T VCEG, JVT-F017 (2002)

[8] Sullivan, G., Wiegand, T., Lim, K.P.: Joint model reference encoding methods and decoding concealment methods. Joint Video Team (JVT) of ISO/IEC MPEG and ITU-T VCEG, JVT-J049 (2003)

[9] Yin, P., Tourapis, H.C., Tourapis, A.M., Boyce, J.: Fast mode decision and motion estimation for JVT/H.264. Proc. IEEE Int. Conf. Image Processing, Barcelona, Spain. 3 (2003) 14-17

[10] Lim, K.P., Wu, S., Wu, D.J., Rahardja, S., Lin, X., Pan, F., Li, Z.G.: Fast inter mode selection. Joint Video Team (JVT) of ISO/IEC MPEG and ITU-T VCEG, JVT-I020 (2003)

[11] Malvar, H.S., Hallapuro, A., Karczewicz, M., Kerofsky, L.: Low-complexity transform and quantization in H.264/AVC. IEEE Trans. Circuits Syst. Video Technol. 13 (2003) 598-603

[12] Chiang, T., Zhang, Y.Q.: A new rate control scheme using quadrature distortion mode. IEEE Trans. Circuit Syst. Video Technol. 7 (1997) 246-250

[13] Jayant, N., Noll,P.: Digital coding of waveforms. Englewood Cliffs, NJ: Prentice Hall (1984)

[14] Cheung, C.H., Po, L.M.: A novel cross-diamond search algorithm for fast block motion estimation. IEEE Trans. Circuit Syst. Video Technol. 12 (2002) 1168-1177

Polyhedra-Based Approach for Incremental Validation of Real-Time Systems

David Doose and Zoubir Mammeri

IRIT - Paul Sabatier University - Toulouse, France

Abstract. Real-time embedded systems can be used in hightly important or even vital tasks (avionic and medical systems, etc.), thus having strict temporal constraints that need to be validated. Existing solutions use temporal logic, automata or scheduling techniques. However, scheduling techniques are often pessimistic and require an almost complete knowledge of the system, and formal methods can be ill-fitted to manipulate some of the concepts involved in real-time systems.

In this article, we propose a method that gives to the designer the advantages of formal methods and some simplicity in manipulating real-time systems notions. This method is able to model and validate all the classical features of real-time systems, without any pessimism, while guaranteeing the terminaison of the validation process. Moreover, its formalism enables to study systems of which we have only a partial knowledge, and thus to validate or invalidate a system still under design. This latest point is very important, since it greatly decreases the cost of design backtracks.

1 Introduction

Validation is a mandatory step in critical real-time systems design, and can be important even for non-critical ones. There are many ways to check the temporal behavior of a real-time systems: we can use formal methods based upon logic (LTL, CTL, etc.) or automata [3,2,1] (Petri nets, linear hybrid automata, etc.), or we can use scheduling techniques [7] (RMA method, etc.). Methods based on logic give precise results and have a great expressive power. They can model very specific features, but involve a strenuous designing process. Indeed, they are not initially fitted to the particular case of real-time system validation, and such notions as tasks or resources sharing do not exist in Petri nets or linear hybrid automata. Scheduling techniques have two main advantages. Firstly, they are of course completely fitted to real-time systems. Secondly, they usually have a very low complexity. However, they often are pessimistic, they require an almost complete knowledge of system parameters (tasks periods, priorities, precedences, etc.), and they give quite limited results, confined mostly to the possible schedulability of the system.

Our goal is to combine formal methods and scheduling techniques by devising a method fitted for scheduling analysis while preserving the expressivity and precision of formal methods such as linear hybrid automata. The study of linear

L.T. Yang et al. (Eds.): EUC 2005, LNCS 3824, pp. 184–193, 2005.

hybrid automata solvers [10,11,12] led us to the use of polyhedral domains, that enable a powerful modeling and checking. This way, we devised the only method (as far as we know) that brings together the following features:

- It can model and study classical features of real-time systems (tasks, resources sharing, precedence, atomic task executions, etc.).
- It guarantees the ending of the validation process (decidability), contrary to linear hybrid automata [13,9].
- It is non-pessimistic.
- It gives precise results on the behavior of the system: we can deduce the response times of tasks, preemptions between tasks, etc., and of course the schedulability of the system.
- It enables to validate/invalidate systems under partial knowledge. Moreover, any parameter constraint (value or linear equation on parameter value) is taken into account by the model.

The ability to check a system schedulability during its design ("under partial knowledge") can lead to important savings by avoiding backtracks. Besides, the non-pessimism implies that we can avoid system over-sizing. Lastly, since the method core works by computing all the different possible behaviors of a system, we can highlight the fact that it is similar to the use of an exhaustive set of simulations, while being far less time-consuming.

The paper is structured as follows: in section two, we introduce the notion of polyhedra and the PV-domains. In section three, we describe our method. In section four, we propose an example comparing the proposed method and a simple schedulability analysis. Finaly, we conclude in section five.

2 Notion of Polyhedra

2.1 Polyhedron

The model we propose allows to take into account any constraint based on linear inequalities. It uses polyhedra [19,14,15] to represent the parameters and the properties of the real-time system under construction.

Definition 1. *A* ***polyhedron*** *P is the intersection of a finite family of closed linear half-spaces of the form $\{x|ax \geq c\}$ where a is a non-zero row vector and c is a scalar constant.*

Double representation: A polyhedron has a dual representation: an implicit representation and a parametric representation. Indeed, a polyhedron P can be represented with a set of linear inequalities which represent its constraints. Its *implicit definition* is the following one: $P = \{x \mid Ax = b,\ Cx \geq d\}$ in which A and C are matrices and x, b and d are vectors. The *parametric representation* of the polyhedron is the following one: $P = \{x \mid L\lambda + R\mu + V\nu,\ \mu,\ \nu \geq 0,\ \sum \nu = 1\}$ In which the polyhedron is composed of several lines (columns of the matrix L), a convex combination of vertices (columns of the matrix V), and a combination of external rays (columns of the matrix R). Algorithms exist to compute the second representation from the first one, and reciprocally. Both representations are useful. Indeed, the implicit representation is more intuitive, so we use it to represent the different constraints of the system and the results of the validation. However, the parametric representation is more efficient to compute the operations on polyhedral domains. Thus, we will use algorithms based on the dual representation, which computes both representations simultaneously.

Polyhedral domain: We mainly use two operations on polyhedra: *intersection* and *union* of polyhedra. Contrary to the intersection, the result of a polyhedra union may not be a convex polyhedron. That is why the notion of polyhedral domain is needed.

Definition 2. *A polyhedral* **domain** *of dimension n is defined as $\mathcal{D} : \{i | i \subset \mathcal{Z}^n,\ i \subset \mathcal{P}\} = \mathcal{Z}^n \bigcap \mathcal{P}$ where $\mathcal{P}$ is a union of polyhedra of dimension n.*

2.2 PV-Domain

We introduce a new notion that aims to create a link between the variables corresponding to the system parameters and their polyhedral representation. A **PV-domain** (Polyhedral representation of Variables) is composed of a list of variables ($\mathcal{V}$) and a polyhedral domain ($\mathcal{S}$). The variables can either be a value or a dimension of the polyhedral domain.

PV-domain operations: Adding a variable consists in adding a space dimension at the end of the polyhedral domain and adding a variable to the variables list $\mathcal{V}$ (noted: $\mathcal{D}^{'} = \mathcal{D} \oplus \{v\}$).

Removing a variable consists in removing the variable from the list and removing the corresponding dimension in the polyhedral domain $\mathcal{D}$ ($\mathcal{D}^{'} = \mathcal{D} \ominus \{v\}$).

Reducing the PV-domain consists in modifying each variable of the list representing a dimension which has a unique value in the polyhedral domain ($\forall_{v \in \mathcal{V}} \forall_{p \in \mathcal{S}}$, $\{v = a\} \subset p$) by removing the corresponding dimension in the polyhedral domain and transforming the variable representing a dimension into a variable representing the value a ($\mathcal{D}^{'} = \odot(\mathcal{D})$).

The intersection (resp. union) of the PV-domain $\mathcal{D} = (\mathcal{V}, \mathcal{S})$ and $\mathcal{D}^{'}$ is noted $\sqcap$ (resp. $\sqcup$) and defined as follows: $\mathcal{D} \sqcap \mathcal{D}^{'} = \left(\mathcal{V}, \mathcal{S} \cap \mathcal{S}^{'}\right)$ (resp. $\sqcup$).

Efficiency: The complexity and thus the computation time of intersections (resp. unions) of polyhedra depends (exponentially) on their space dimension. That is why the main objective is to reduce as much as possible the space dimension of the system model. The real efficiency of the space reduction made by the PV-domain reduction operator can be shown by simulations. The simulations on figure 1 are run on one polyhedron with ten unknown dimensions and from 20 to 500 space dimensions. In each case (i.e. for each total number of dimensions), we run 500 intersections (resp. unions) with and without using the space dimension reduction. The computation time of the unions is due to the polyhedra power-set

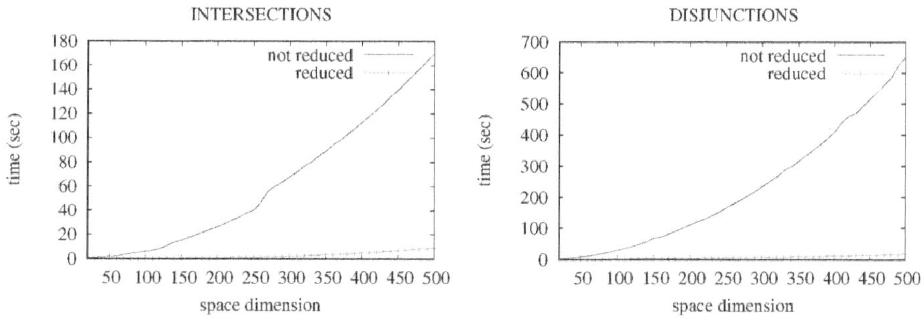

Fig. 1. PV-domain operations computation time

[5,16] operations used for the representation of the disjunctions. We can see here how efficient the dimension reduction can be, but it is important to notice that the dimension reduction is not an invertible operation.

3 The Proposed Method

System parameters: Each task instance i has four *descriptive parameters*: its period (T_i), its release time (R_i), its execution time (C_i) and its absolute deadline (D_i); and two *behavioral parameters*: the time when the task instance begins its execution (b_i), and the moment when it ends its execution (e_i). The *hidden parameters* (see below) are mandatory to represent some information specific to the system. From a geometric point of view, each descriptive, behavioral or hidden parameter corresponds to a variable of the PV-domain. Last, *static parameters* are useful to take into account some specific properties of the system. The main difference between static parameters and the others is that their values are always known.

Interactions and Behavior: In the proposed model, only two interactions are needed to represent tasks instances and their evolution. Indeed, an instance can either **preempt** or **delay** another instance. The behavior of tasks instances is defined by the interactions which can either exist between the instances. In the paper we will compute *possible behaviors*. A behavior is possible for a group of instances (see below) if all the interactions characterizing this group can occur on the instances of the group, with the respect of all the constraints of the system.

Group: A group of tasks instances is characterized by:

- a list of instances with interactions (noted *interactions*);
- the first instance in interaction of the group (*first*);
- a list of context instances (noted *contexts*);

- a PV-domain representing the properties of the previous groups (i.e. the constraints of the systems before the creation of the group noted *pre_constraints*);
- a PV-domain representing the properties of the groups (*part_system*).

Each instance of the *interactions list* is at least in interaction with another instance of the list. The first instance in interaction and the number of instances of each task are useful to determine the beginning and the end of the group. The list of context instances is made of instances which, under the same constraints, are not in interaction with any instance of the list of the instances in interaction.

3.1 Method Overview

Analysis of real-time systems with the proposed method has two main parts. The first part consists in taking into account the knowlegde of the system by: adding the tasks of the system, modifying the static parameters, adding the tasks constraints and adding the invariants. The second part consists in analysing the behaviors of the system by determining all the groups of interactions and analysing the schedulability of each group. At the end of the validation process the method provides the list of the situations in which the system is schedulable, and the list of the situations in which the system is not schedulable.

3.2 Static Steps

The first step consists in simply adding the tasks of the system in order to determine the number of tasks.

In this first step no information about the tasks are taken into account. The second step consists in setting the static parameters of the system. Thus, we determine whether the tasks are periodic, atomic, ... We also determine the scheduler category (EDF or fixed priority). At the end of this step, the static parameters of the system and the number of tasks are known, thus we can create the first polyhedral representation of the system.

In the third static step, the designer takes into account the system information by adding constraints to the domain representing the system as previously described. For example, if the worst execution time of task τ_1 is $20\,ms$, the system is equal to $system \cap (C_1 \leq 20)$. At the end of this step, the domain representing the system contains all the information about the tasks.

In the last static step, the invariants of the system concerning the tasks are taken into account by adding the corresponding constraints. If the previously added information of the system does not respect these invariants, then the domain is empty, and the validation ends. The domain representing the system is: $system = \odot(information \cap (\forall_{\tau_i} (R_i \geq 0) \cap (C_i > 0t) \cap (D_i \geq 0)))$

3.3 Determining Groups

The principle is to determine all the possible groups of instances as shown by the following algorithm:

```
groups: stack of Group ;
groups.push(Group(system)) ;
while groups.not_empty() do
    Group g = groupes.pop() ;
    if g.complete() then
        if (not g.cycle) and g.validation then
            groups.push(g.next()) ;
    else
        for each instance τi do
            if g.can_interact_with(τi) then
                goups.push((new Group()).add_interaction(τi)) ;
            if g.can_be_context_of(τi) then
                goups.push((new Group()).add_context(τi)) ;
```

The function *can_add_interaction* (resp. *can_be_context*) determines whether or not the instance τ_i can interact (resp. can be a context instance) in the group g. This is determined by verifying the non-emptyness of the following PV-domain representing the addition of the instance: *part_system* $\cap (r_{i,j} \geq r_{first}) \cap (r_{i,j} < r_{first} + c_{tot})$ (resp. *part_system*$\cap (r_{i,j} \geq r_{first} + c_{tot})$) while r_{first} represents the release time of the first instance of the group (i.e. the beginning of the group), $r_{i,j}$ the release time of the instance j of the task i and c_{tot} represents the length of the group.

The function *cycle* aims to determine if the the group g is in a behavioral cycle with another group that has already been computed. The notion of cycle is important because it guarantees the end of the validation process. A group G is in behavioral cycle with the group G' if the instance in interaction can correspond (verifyed with the function *mapping*) and if the constraints of the system are the same but at another moment. The function *validation* determines if the group of instances is schedulable or not. This function is described in the following subsection.

3.4 Group Schedulability

In this subsection, we detail the validation of a group. The tasks instances are not linked to the corresponding tasks, thus the instances parameters are noted with lowercase letters with a single index representing the instance number.

General information and invariants: The invariants are mandatory to maintain the correctness of the model. They are added like any information about the system. The following invariants are useful in the proposed method: $\forall \tau_i$, $(b_i \geq r_i)$ $\cap$ $(e_i \geq b_i + c_i)$

Scheduler information: In practice, two schedulers are used: fixed priority and EDF. In this paper, a lower priority value means a greater priority.

Determining priorities: In order to represent a fixed priority scheduler, the priority of a task instance just has to be equal to the priority of the corresponding task. If the priority of one or more tasks is not known, it is important to add the following information to the system: $\forall_{i,j,k}\, P_{i,j} = P_{i,k}$; because without this equation, two task instances of the same task can have different priorities. If the scheduler of the system is EDF, then the priority of each task instance is equal to the absolute deadline: $\forall_i\, p_i = d_i$.

Determinism: A scheduler is said to be deterministic if for every situation for every system with the same parameters, the same task instance is executed. The previously defined properties and hypotheses of the system and the method do not induce that the scheduler is deterministic; because two instances can have the same priority. However, the following property must be guaranteed:

Property 1. If several task instances that need the processor at the same time have the same priority which is the smallest of the system, then the scheduler must choose one and only one instance to execute.

Property 2. Once this choice done, the scheduler must not change it until the next system's change.

These two properties aim to prevent two task instances from being executed at the same time. To represent a possible non-deterministic scheduler, we introduce another parameter, the hidden parameter Π_i. This parameter acts as a hidden secondary priority, known by the scheduler only. Consequently, a task instance (i) has a higher priority than another (j) if and only if: $prio(i, j) = (p_i < p_j) \cup ((p_i = p_j) \cap (\Pi_i < \Pi_j))$. In order to verify the previous properties, the following constraint is added to the system: $\forall_{i,j}\, such\, as\, i \neq j,\ (p_i = p_j) \cap (\Pi_i \neq \Pi_j)$. The non-determinism of the scheduler comes from the fact that the hidden parameter Π_i is not given a fixed value.

Task instances behaviors: The notion of time is introduced with parameters which represent a moment when a particular action happens and thus a behavior. The complete behavior of a task instance is described with the following equation: $instance\, behavior_i = (\bigcup (possible\, b_i)) \cap (\bigcup (possible\, e_i))$.

The execution beginning of a task instance (b_j) can be *delayed* by another task instance (τ_i) with a higher priority: $delay(i, j) = prio(i, j) \cap (b_i \leq r_j) \cap (e_i > r_j)$. It is important to notice that only the task instance with the latest end of execution really delays the task instance. If the task instance i delays the task instance j, then the task instance j begins its execution when the task instance i ends: $b_j = e_i$.

The execution end of a task instance depends on the moment the task instance begins its execution and on the interactions with other task instances during its execution. In this case the interactions are *preemptions*. The end of an instance execution: $e_j = b_j + c_j + \sum_{i\, preempt\, j} c_i$. The task instance i preempts the task instance j if: $preempt(i, j) = prio(i, j) \cap (b_i > b_j) \cap (b_i < e_j)$.

Verifying properties: The result of the behavioral step represent all the possible behaviors of the system. The question consists in asking what is possible in the system behaviors by adding the correspond constraint. Thus, the PV-domain $\mathcal{D}$ representing the system is schedulable if: $\forall_{\tau_i} \mathcal{D} \cap (e_i > d_i) = \emptyset$

Specific characteristics

Atomic task instances: A task instance that cannot be preempted is said to be atomic. Thus, we introduced the static parameter $atomic(i)$ (and $not\, atomic(i)$) to indicate whether a task instance can be preempted. This induces a modification of the previously defined interactions by adding $\cup$ (resp. $\cap$) $atomic(i)$ to the equation $delay(i,j)$ (resp. $preempt(i,j)$).

Resource sharing: Sharing resources [18,6] is a complex problem in real-time systems and several algorithms exist to solve it, thus we won't study it in detail. But we want to show how easy it is for this method to handle this problem by considering mutexes. The static parameter $Res(i,r)$ indicates that the task instance i needs the shared resource r. The function $Resource(i,j)$ represents that the task instance i and the task instance j need a common shared resource. This function is defined as follows: $Resouce(i,j) = \exists r, Res(i,r)\, and\, Res(j,r)$. Thus, the equations of the interactions are modified:

$$delay(i,j) = (prio(i,j) \cup atomic(i) \cup Resource(i,j)) \cap (b_i \leq r_j) \cap (e_i > r_j)$$
$$preempt(i,j) = prio(i,j) \cap \neg atomic(j) \cap \neg Resource(i,j) \cap (b_i > b_j) \cap (b_i < e_j)$$

4 Example

In this section we present a simple example in which the system is made of three aperiodic tasks. The priorities of the tasks are known: $P_0 = 1$, $P_1 = 2$ an $P_2 = 3$. The deadlines are also known: $D_0 = 6$, $D_1 = 6$ et $D_2 = 20$. The release time are partially known: $R_0 = 0$, $R_1 = 3$ and R_2 is unknown. The execution times of τ_0 and τ_2 are partially known: $2 \leq C_0 \leq 5$ and $C_2 = 2$. The execution time of τ_1 depends on the execution of the other tasks. Indeed, $C_1 = 3$ if τ_1 begins its execution before the end of τ_0; $C_1 = 4$ if τ_1 begins its execution before the end of τ_2 and after τ_0; and $C_1 = 5$ if τ_1 begins its execution after τ_0 and τ_2.

To validate this system with a scheduling technique we proceed as follows: first, we determines the worst case values of the system parameters. Thus $C_0 = 5$, $C_1 = 5$ and $C_2 = 2$. This approximation induces the pessimism of this method. That is why we show that the system is not schedulable. Indeed, a simple execution trace highlights that the second task misses its deadline (figure 2).

The main advantage of our method is it can represents the specific constraint of the execution of the second task. Thus, the following equation represent this information: $((C_1 = 3) \cap (b_1 < e_0)) \cup ((C_1 = 4) \cap (b_1 \geq e_0) \cap (b_1 < e_2)) \cup ((C_1 = 5) \cap (b_1 \geq e_0) \cap (b_1 \geq e_2))$. Then, the behavioral step is done. In the result representing the possible behaviors of the system we can highlight the invariants

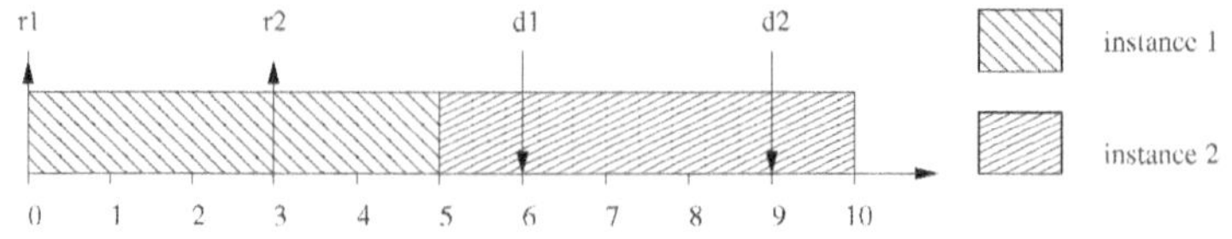

Fig. 2. Example

of the system behavior: $b_0 = 0$, $C_1 = 4$, $e_0 = C_0$. It shows that the first task is neither delayed nor preempted and also that the execution time of the second task is $C_1 = 4$. That means the second task begins its execution after the first one and before the third one, in all the possible situations. Thus, the worst value for this parameter ($C_1 = 5$) determined with the scheduling technique is impossible. The proposed method is not pessimistic; that is why we can prove that the system is schedulable with this method but not with a schedulability analysis.

With this simple example we show that it is possible to validate a real time system in which some parameters are exactly known, some are partially known, some are unknown and some parameters are defined with specific constraints. We also highlight that the proposed method is not pessimistic, contrary to a simple scheduling analysis.

5 Conclusions

We propose a new non-pessimistic method to analyse real-time systems. This method can be used to represent systems with specific behaviors and complex relationships between their parameters, because any information that can be represented with a linear inequality can be taken into account. A major advantage of this method is that can be used to analyse study a system at any design step. Indeed, this method can be used with partial knowledge and thus it is well adapted to reduce costs. To complete this work, we intend to focus on two points: taking into account new system characteristics, and implementing a complete software. Indeed, several system behaviors have to be represented in our method (dependable and/or non-preemptive tasks, resources sharing, partitioning [8,20,17,4]), which implies some modifications of the previously defined equations. We also plan to include specific components such as bounded buffers.

References

1. R. Alur, C. Courcoubetis, N. Halbwachs, T. A. Henzinger, P.-H. Ho, X. Nicollin, A. Olivero, J. Sifakis, and S. Yovine. The algorithmic analysis of hybrid systems. *Theoretical Computer Science*, 138(1):3–34, 1995.
2. Rajeev Alur, Costas Courcoubetis, Thomas A. Henzinger, and Pei-Hsin Ho. Hybrid automata: An algorithmic approach to the specification and verification of hybrid systems. In *Hybrid Systems*, pages 209–229, 1992.

3. Rajeev Alur and David L. Dill. A theory of timed automata. *Theoretical Computer Science*, 126(2):183–235, 1994.
4. B. Andersson and J. Jonsson. Fixed-priority preemptive multiprocessor scheduling: To partition or not to partition. In *Proceedings of the Int'l Conf. on Real-Time Computing and Applications*, pages 337–346, Cheju Island, Korea, December 2000. IEEE Computer Society Press.
5. R. Bagnara. A hierarchy of constraint systems for data-flow analysis of constraint logic-based languages. In *Science of Computer Programming*, pages 30(1–2):119–155, 1998.
6. T. P. Baker. A stack-based resource allocation policy for realtime. In *Real-Time Systems Symposium*, pages 191–200. IEEE Computer Society Press, 1990.
7. L. P. Briand and D. M. Roy. *Meeting Deadlines in Hard Real-Time Systems: The Rate Monotonic Approach.* IEEE Computer Society, 1999.
8. Airlines Electronic Engineering Committee. Arinc specification 653, January 1997.
9. N. Halbwachs, Y-E. Proy, and P. Raymond. Verification of linear hybrid systems by means of convex approximations. In *Static Analysis Symposium*, pages 223–237, 1994.
10. T. A. Henzinger, P-H. Ho, and H. Wong-Toi. Hytech: The next generation. In *IEEE Real-Time Systems Symposium*, pages 56–65, 1995.
11. T. A. Henzinger, P-H. Ho, and H. Wong-Toi. A user guide to hytech. In *Tools and Algorithms for Construction and Analysis of Systems*, pages 41–71, 1995.
12. T. A. Henzinger, P-H. Ho, and H. Wong-Toi. HYTECH: A model checker for hybrid systems. *International Journal on Software Tools for Technology Transfer*, 1(1–2):110–122, 1997.
13. Thomas A. Henzinger, Peter W. Kopke, Anuj Puri, and Pravin Varaiya. What's decidable about hybrid automata? In *Proceedings of the 27th Annual Symposium on Theory of Computing*, pages 373–382, 1995.
14. Doran K.Wilde. A library for doing polyhedral operations. Technical Report 2157, December 1993.
15. Sanjay Rajopadhye Patrice Quinton and Tanguy Risset. On manipulating z-polyhedra. Technical Report 1016, Jully 1996.
16. P. M. Hill R. Bagnara and E. Zaffanella. Widening operators for powerset domains. In *Quaderno 349, Dipartimento di Matematica, Universit di Parma, Italy*, 2004.
17. J. Rushby. Partitioning in avionics architectures: Requirements, mechanisms, and assurance. Technical report, Menlo Park USA, March 1999.
18. L. Sha, R. Rajkumar, and J.P. Lehoczky. Priority inheritance protocols: An approach to real-time synchronization. *IEEE Transactions on Computers*, 39:1175–1185, September 1990.
19. H. Le Verge. A note on cherniakova's algorithm. Technical Report RR-1662, April 1992.
20. B. L. Di Vito. A formal model of partitionning for integrated modular avionics. Technical report, August 1998.

Checkpointing for the Reliability of Real-Time Systems with On-Line Fault Detection*

Sang-Moon Ryu and Dong-Jo Park

Korea Advanced Institute of Science and Technology,
373-1 Guseong-dong, Yuseong-gu, Daejeon 305-701, Republic of Korea
smryu@kaist.ac.kr, djpark@ee.kaist.ac.kr

Abstract. The checkpointing problem in real-time systems equipped with on-line fault detection mechanisms is dealt with from a reliability point of view. The reliability analysis is performed with the assumption that transient faults occur in accordance with a Poisson process and are detected immediately by the detection mechanisms. And the best equidistant checkpointing strategy that maximizes the reliability of the system against transient faults is derived.

1 Introduction

Transient faults in semiconductor devices are becoming more significant because of increased density, low supply voltage, fast switching signals and so on [1]. Checkpointing is a well known technique to overcome transient faults in computer systems. It means periodically saving the state of a task in a safe storage place. When the manifestation of a transient fault is detected, the state of the affected task will be restored to the state stored at the latest checkpoint. This process is called rollback-recovery. The specific points at which checkpointing is performed are called checkpoints and the length of the time between two successive checkpoints is said to be a checkpoint interval.

Many papers dealt with the problems of checkpointing in real-time systems from various points of view [2,3,4,5,6]. In this paper, the reliability problem of equidistant checkpointing, which relies on the use of a constant checkpoint interval, in a single task real-time system under transient faults is explored. The transient faults are assumed to occur according to a Poisson process and be detected by on-line detection mechanisms [7,14,15,16] with no latency. The reliability of the system with equidistant checkpointing is analyzed and the best checkpointing strategy is derived, which achieves the maximum probability of successful task completion with given parameters such as task execution time, available slack time, checkpointing and recovery overheads.

The following assumptions were made in this work, which were used in other literature:

- Transient faults occur according to a Poisson process with rate λ, which is common in many papers dealing with transient faults [2,3,4,5,8,10,11,12,13].

* This work was supported by SaTReC of KAIST.

L.T. Yang et al. (Eds.): EUC 2005, LNCS 3824, pp. 194–202, 2005.

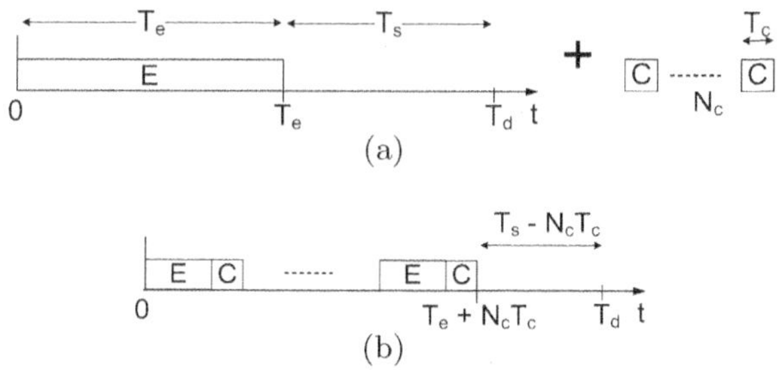

Fig. 1. The task (a) before inserting checkpoints (b) after inserting checkpoints

- The effect of a transient fault disappears during the corresponding recovery operation.
- The manifestation of transient faults is perfectly detected by the detection mechanisms [3,4,5,10]. If necessary, the fault detection coverage [14] may be taken into account after the reliability model is obtained.
- Checkpointing is possible anywhere in the task with a constant checkpoint interval [5]. In practice, it might be difficult to accomplish. But the result of analysis with equidistant checkpointing can give an insight into how checkpoints should be inserted to improve the reliability of a system.
- Checkpointing and recovery overheads are same and remain constant [5].

2 Reliability Analysis

If N_c checkpoints are inserted uniformly into the task whose worst case execution time, relative deadline, slack time, and checkpointing/recovery overhead are T_e, T_d, T_s, and T_c, respectively, as shown in Fig. 1(a), the task is divided into N_c subsections creating N_c time-slots as illustrated in Fig. 1(b). Each time-slot is composed of a part of normal execution and a checkpointing operation, and its length is $\frac{T_e}{N_c} + T_c$. Due to the checkpointing overheads, the available slack time of the task is reduced from T_s to $T_s - N_cT_c$.

With on-line fault detection mechanisms, the recovery process can be performed immediately after a fault occurrence as shown in Fig. 2. To tolerate transient faults that may occur during either checkpointing or recovery operation, at least two secure storage places should be provided and used for checkpointing alternately. The storage place where the earlier state was saved should be used for the current checkpointing operation and the other one where the more recent state was saved should be reserved for a recovery operation in case of a fault occurrence during the current checkpointing operation.

Transient faults can be classified into two types: One type is those which may occur during normal task execution or during checkpointing operations (fault type 'E' and 'C' in Fig. 2), and the other type is those which may occur during recovery operations (fault type 'R' in Fig. 2). Transient faults of the former type

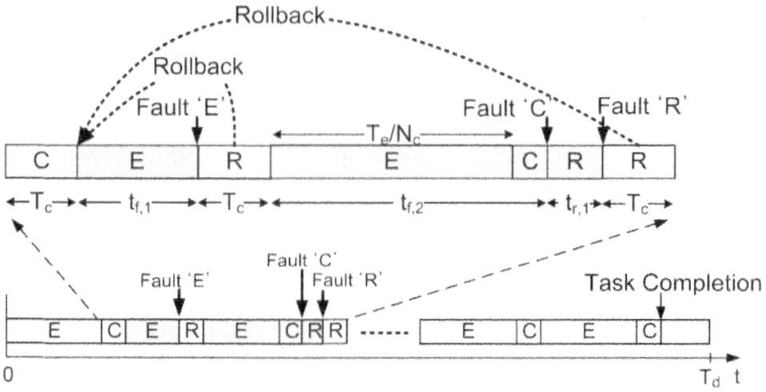

Fig. 2. Checkpointing with on-line fault detection

will be counted to N_f and transient faults of the latter type will be counted to N_r. Then the sum of N_f and N_r is the total number of transient faults that may occur in $[0,\ T_d]$. As shown in Fig. 2, let the time elapsed since the last checkpointing when a fault occurs during normal execution or checkpointing operations be denoted by $t_{f,i}$, $i = 1, 2, \cdots, N_f$, and the time elapsed since the beginning of a recovery operation when a fault occurs during the recovery operation be denoted by $t_{r,l}$, $l = 1, 2, \cdots, N_r$ and define T_t as $\frac{T_e}{N_c} + T_c$. Then the time intervals $t_{f,i}$ and $t_{r,l}$ can be thought of as independent identically distributed (i.i.d.) random variables with exponential distributions on intervals $[0,\ T_t]$ and $[0,\ T_c]$, respectively.

Now we derive the probability of task completion in the presence of transient faults. Since theoretically the number of faults of type 'E' or 'C' in interval $[0,\ T_d]$ ranges from 0 to ∞, N_f ranges from 0 to ∞ as well. A fault of type 'R' can be brought about only after a fault of type 'E' or 'C' occurs. Therefore N_r can range from 0 to N_f. The probability, $P(N_c)$, that the task completes its execution in the presence of transient faults is

$$P(N_c) = Pr\{\text{success with no fault}\} + \sum_{N_f=1}^{\infty} \sum_{N_r=0}^{N_f} Pr\{\text{success with } N_f \text{ and } N_r \text{ faults}\} .$$

Since we assumed that faults occur in accordance with a Poisson process, the probability of successful task completion with no fault is

$$Pr\{\text{success with no fault}\} = e^{-\lambda(T_e + N_c T_c)} . \tag{1}$$

The probability of successful task completion with N_f and N_r faults is the product of three probabilities: the probability that no fault occurs in N_c time-slots for task completion, the probability that N_f and N_r faults occur before the task completes its execution, and the probability that the time lost by these faults is small enough for the task to meet its deadline.

$$
\begin{aligned}
Pr\{\text{success with } N_f \text{ and } N_r \text{ faults}\} = {} & Pr\{\text{no fault in } N_c \text{ time-slots}\} \\
& \cdot Pr\{\text{lost time by } N_f \text{ and } N_r \text{ faults is small}\} \\
& \cdot Pr\{N_f \text{ and } N_r \text{ faults occur}\}\,. \qquad (2)
\end{aligned}
$$

The first probability in the right side of (2) is the same as the probability in (1). In the following, we derive the second and the third probabilities in the right side of (2).

In order for the task to meet its deadline, N_c checkpointing operations, N_f recovery operations should be done within the slack time T_s in spite of the loss in time caused by the faults. If we define T_{ns} as $T_s - N_c T_c - N_f T_c$ and S_{fr} as $\sum_{i=1}^{N_f} t_{f,i} + \sum_{l=1}^{N_r} t_{r,l}$, the probability that the lost time by these faults is small enough for the task to meet its deadline can be expressed as

$$Pr\{\text{lost time by } N_f \text{ and } N_r \text{ faults is small}\} = P(S_{fr} \le T_{ns})\,. \qquad (3)$$

In order to get the probability in (3), we have to find out the probability density function (pdf) of S_{fr}. It is already known that the sum of exponential random variables has the Erlang distribution [17]. If T_i's, $i = 1, 2, \cdots, n$, denote i.i.d. exponential random variables, and S_n denotes the sum of these exponential random variables, i.e., $S_n = T_1 + T_2 + \cdots + T_n$, the corresponding pdf's are, respectively,

$$f_{T_i}(x) = \lambda e^{-\lambda x}, \; x \ge 0 \qquad (4)$$

and

$$f_{S_n}(x) = \frac{(\lambda x)^{n-1}}{(n-1)!} \lambda e^{-\lambda x}, \; x \ge 0\,. \qquad (5)$$

From the definition of the characteristic function of a random variable [17], the characteristic functions of T_i and S_n are, respectively,

$$\Phi_{T_i}(\omega) = \frac{\lambda}{\lambda - j\omega} \qquad (6)$$

and

$$\Phi_{S_n}(\omega) = \left(\frac{\lambda}{\lambda - j\omega}\right)^n\,. \qquad (7)$$

The characteristic function of S_{fr} can be derived from those of $t_{f,i}$ and $t_{r,l}$. Since the time intervals $t_{f,i}$ and $t_{r,l}$ are random variables with exponential distribution on intervals $[0,\ T_t]$ and $[0,\ T_c]$, their pdf's are, respectively,

$$f_{t_{f,i}}(x) = \begin{cases} \frac{\lambda e^{-\lambda x}}{1-e^{-\lambda T_t}}, & \text{when } 0 < x < T_t \\ 0, & \text{otherwise} \end{cases}$$

and

$$f_{t_{r,l}}(x) = \begin{cases} \frac{\lambda e^{-\lambda x}}{1-e^{-\lambda T_c}}, & \text{when } 0 < x < T_c \\ 0, & \text{otherwise}\,. \end{cases}$$

Then the characteristic functions of $t_{f,i}$ and $t_{r,l}$ are, respectively,

$$\Phi_{t_{f,i}}(\omega) = \frac{\lambda}{\lambda - j\omega} \frac{1 - e^{-\lambda T_t} e^{jT_t\omega}}{1 - e^{-\lambda T_t}}$$

and

$$\Phi_{t_{r,l}}(\omega) = \frac{\lambda}{\lambda - j\omega} \frac{1 - e^{-\lambda T_c} e^{jT_c\omega}}{1 - e^{-\lambda T_c}} .$$

Since the characteristic function of the sum of two random variables is the product of the characteristic functions of these random variables, the characteristic function of S_{fr} is

$$\Phi_{S_{fr}}(\omega) = \left(\Phi_{t_f}(\omega)\right)^{N_f} \left(\Phi_{t_r}(\omega)\right)^{N_r} ,$$

which is

$$\begin{aligned}
\Phi_{S_{fr}}(\omega) &= \left(\frac{\lambda}{\lambda - j\omega}\right)^{N_f+N_r} \frac{1}{(1-e^{-\lambda T_t})^{N_f}} \frac{1}{(1-e^{-\lambda T_c})^{N_r}} \\
&\quad \cdot \sum_{i=0}^{N_f} \binom{N_f}{i} \left(-e^{-\lambda T_t}\right)^i e^{jT_t\omega i} \cdot \sum_{l=0}^{N_r} \binom{N_r}{l} \left(-e^{-\lambda T_c}\right)^l e^{jT_c\omega l} \\
&= \left(\frac{\lambda}{\lambda - j\omega}\right)^{N_f+N_r} \frac{1}{(1-e^{-\lambda T_t})^{N_f}(1-e^{-\lambda T_c})^{N_r}} \\
&\quad \cdot \sum_{i=0}^{N_f} \left[\binom{N_f}{i} \left(-e^{-\lambda T_t}\right)^i \sum_{l=0}^{N_r} \binom{N_r}{l} \left(-e^{-\lambda T_c}\right)^l e^{j(iT_t+lT_c)\omega}\right] .
\end{aligned}$$

Then the pdf of S_{fr} can be derived by using the relationship among (4), (5), (6) and (7) as

$$\begin{aligned}
f_{S_{fr}}(x) &= \frac{1}{(1-e^{-\lambda T_t})^{N_f}(1-e^{-\lambda T_c})^{N_r}} \\
&\quad \cdot \sum_{i=0}^{N_f} \left[\binom{N_f}{i} \left(-e^{-\lambda T_t}\right)^i \sum_{l=0}^{N_r} \binom{N_r}{l} \left(-e^{-\lambda T_c}\right)^l f(x - iT_t - lT_c)\right] ,
\end{aligned}$$

where

$$f(x) = \frac{(\lambda x)^{N_f+N_r-1}}{(N_f+N_r-1)!} \lambda e^{-\lambda x}, \ x \geq 0 .$$

Now that the pdf of S_{fr} is obtained, the probability in (3) can be calculated.

Finally, the third probability in the right side of (2) is derived, which can be decomposed as

$$\begin{aligned}
Pr\{N_f \text{ and } N_r \text{ faults occur}\} &= Pr\{N_f \text{ faults occur}\} \\
&\quad \cdot Pr\{N_r \text{ faults occur} \mid N_f \text{ faults occur}\} .
\end{aligned}$$

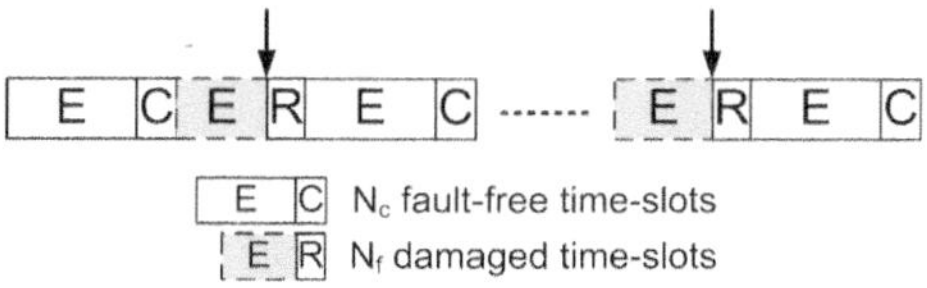

Fig. 3. Possible cases for N_f faults

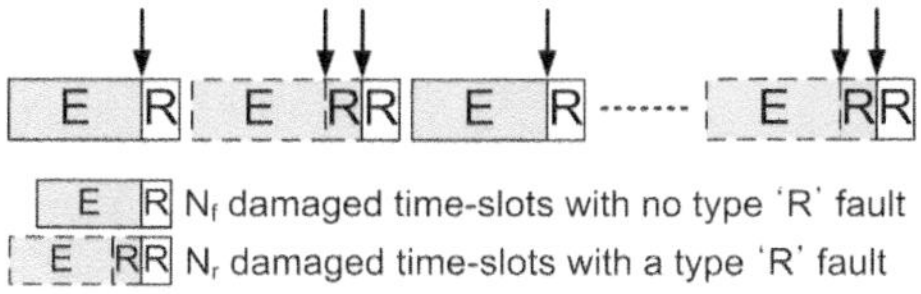

Fig. 4. Possible cases for N_r faults

The probability that a fault occurs and damages a time-slot of length T_t is $1 - e^{-\lambda T_t}$. Among N_c fault-free time-slots, the N_f faults of type 'E' or 'C' can occur in $\binom{N_c+N_f-1}{N_f}$ ways as illustrated in Fig. 3. Therefore the probability that N_f faults occur before the task completion is

$$Pr\{N_f \text{ faults occur}\} = \binom{N_c + N_f - 1}{N_f} \left(1 - e^{-\lambda T_t}\right)^{N_f} .$$

The N_f faults of type 'E' or 'C' would bring about N_f times of recovery operations. Among the N_f recovery operations, N_r operations are damaged by the N_r faults of type 'R'. The probability that N_r recovery operations are damaged is $(1 - e^{-\lambda T_c})^{N_r}$, and the probability that $N_f - N_r$ recovery operations are performed normally is $e^{-\lambda(N_f - N_r)T_c}$. Since the N_r faults may occur among the N_f damaged time-slots in $\binom{N_f}{N_r}$ ways as shown in Fig. 4, the probability that N_r faults of type 'R' occur given that the N_f faults of type 'E' or 'C' have occurred is

$$Pr\{N_r \text{ faults occur} \mid N_f \text{ faults occur}\} = \binom{N_f}{N_r} \left(1 - e^{-\lambda T_c}\right)^{N_r} e^{-\lambda(N_f - N_r)T_c} .$$

Consequently the probability, $P(N_c)$, that the task completes its execution even in the presence of transient faults is

$$P(N_c) = e^{-\lambda(T_e + N_c T_c)} \left(1 + \sum_{N_f=1}^{\infty} \sum_{N_r=0}^{N_f} P_{fr}(N_c, N_f, N_r)\right) ,$$

where

$$P_{fr}(N_c, N_f, N_r) = \binom{N_c + N_f - 1}{N_f} \binom{N_f}{N_r} e^{-\lambda(N_f - N_r)T_c}$$

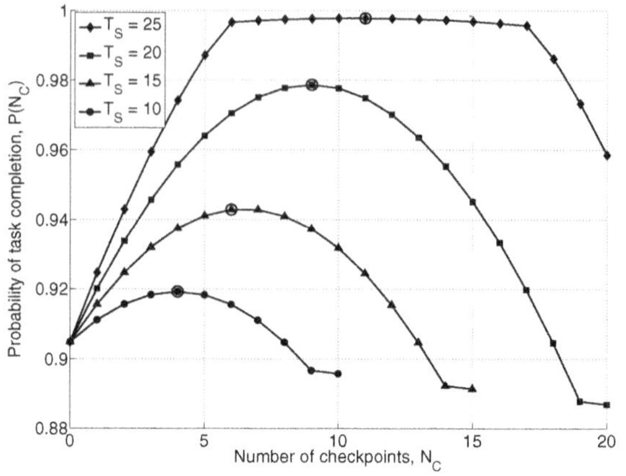

Fig. 5. $P(N_c)$ when $\lambda = 0.001$, $T_e = 100$ and $T_c = 1$

$$\cdot \sum_{i=0}^{N_f} \left[\binom{N_f}{i} \left(- e^{-\lambda T_t} \right)^i \sum_{l=0}^{N_r} \binom{N_r}{l} \left(-e^{-\lambda T_c} \right)^l \int_0^{T_{ns}} f(x - iT_t - lT_c)\, dx \right]$$

and

$$f(x) = \frac{(\lambda x)^{N_f + N_r - 1}}{(N_f + N_r - 1)!} \lambda e^{-\lambda x}, \; x \geq 0 \, .$$

3 Numerical Examples

Figures 5 and 6 show the graphs of $P(N_c)$ with different values of T_s and λ, respectively. In theses figures, only the terms up to $N_f = 5$ were calculated for each value of $P(N_c)$. The probability of task completion in $[0,\ T_d]$ increases as the available slack time increases. And excessive checkpointing can result in adverse effect. This is because transient faults may occur during checkpointing operations, and more checkpoints than necessary may expose the task to more transient faults and cause the net slack time to decrease leading to the lack of extra time for recovery operations in case of fault occurrences.

4 Best Checkpointing Strategy

From Figs. 5 and 6, it is apparent that there exists the best number of checkpoints which maximizes the probability of successful task completion for the given parameters, such as execution time, checkpointing overhead and available slack time. In practice, the value of λT_d is much smaller than 1. Therefore the value of $P(N_c)$ is mainly dominated by the term resulting from $N_f = 1$ and $N_r = 0$, and can be approximated as

$$P(N_c) \approx e^{-\lambda(T_e + T_c N_c)} \left[1 + N_c \left(1 - e^{-\lambda(T_s - T_c - T_c N_c)} \right) e^{-\lambda T_c} \right] .$$

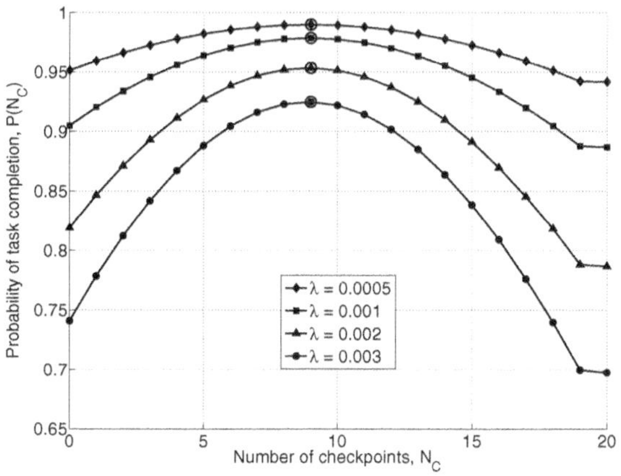

Fig. 6. $P(N_c)$ when $T_e = 100$, $T_c = 1$ and $T_s = 20$

Since it is reasonable that the total checkpointing overhead, $N_c T_c$, is less than the execution time of the task, we have $e^{-\lambda T_c N_c} \approx 1 - \lambda T_c N_c + \frac{1}{2}(\lambda T_c N_c)^2$. And the probability $P(N_c)$ can be approximated once more as

$$P(N_c) \approx e^{-\lambda T_e} \left[1 + (b - a - bc)N_c + (\frac{a^2}{2} - ab)N_c^2 + \frac{a^2 b}{2} N_c^3 \right] , \tag{8}$$

where $a = \lambda T_c$, $b = e^{-\lambda T_c}$ and $c = e^{-\lambda(T_s - T_c))}$.

Then, by temporarily assuming N_c to be continuous and by solving the equation which results from taking the derivative of the right side of (8) with respect to N_c and letting it be zero, we can obtain two candidates for the value of N_c that maximizes $P(N_c)$:

$$\left\lfloor \frac{(2b - a) - \sqrt{(2b - a)^2 - 6b(b - a - bc)}}{3ab} \right\rfloor$$

and

$$\left\lceil \frac{(2b - a) - \sqrt{(2b - a)^2 - 6b(b - a - bc)}}{3ab} \right\rceil .$$

The best number of checkpoints is one of the above candidates which leads to the larger value of $P(N_c)$. In Figs. 5 and 6, the points corresponding to the best number of checkpoints for each case are marked by a circle.

5 Conclusion

In this paper, we considered the best equidistant checkpointing strategy for real-time systems from a reliability point of view with the assumption that transient faults are detected with no latency by on-line detection mechanisms. The reliability analysis shows that the reliability of the system can be improved as much as expected by providing the required slack time with the tasks of the system, and the best number of checkpoints hardly depends on the occurrence rate of transient faults.

References

1. E. Dupont, M. Nicolaidis and P. Rohr, "Embedded Robustness IPs for Transient-Error-Free ICs," IEEE Design & Test of Computers, vol. 19, pp. 56–70, May–Jun. 2002.
2. K. G. Shin, T.-H. Lin and Y.-H. Lee, "Optimal Checkpointing of Real-Time Tasks," IEEE Trans. Computers, vol. C-36, no. 11, pp. 1328–1341, Nov. 1987.
3. S. Punnekkat, A. Burns and R. Davis, "Analysis of Checkpointing for Real-Time Systems," Real-Time Systems, vol. 20, no. 1, pp. 83–102, Jan. 2001.
4. Y. Zhang and K. Chakrabarty, "Energy-Aware Adaptive Checkpointing in Embedded Real-Time Systems," Proc. Design, Automation and Test in Europe Conference and Exhibition, pp. 918–923, Messe Munich, Germany, 2003.
5. S. W. Kwak, B. K. Kim and B. J. Choi, "An Optimal Checkpointing-Strategy for Real-Time Control Systems under Transient Faults," IEEE Trans. Reliability, vol. 50, no. 3, pp. 293–301, Sep. 2001.
6. A. Ranganathan and S. J. Upadhyaya, "Simulation Analysis of a Dynamic Checkpointing Strategy for Real-Time Systems," Proc. 27th Annual Simulation Symp., pp. 181–187, Apr. 1994.
7. D. P. Siewiorek, Reliable Computer Systems: Design and Evaluation, A K Peters, 1998.
8. A. Duda, "The Effects of Checkpointing on Program Execution Time," Information Processing Letters, vol. 16, pp. 221–229, Jun. 1983.
9. P. L'ecuyer and J. Malenfant, "Computing Optimal Checkpointing Strategies for Rollback and Recovery Systems," IEEE Trans. Computers, vol. 37, no. 4, pp. 491–496, Apr. 1988.
10. V. Grassi, L. Donatiello and S. Tucci, "On the Optimal Checkpointing of Critical Tasks and Transaction-Oriented Systems," IEEE Trans. Software Engineering, vol. 18, no. 1, pp. 72–77, Jan. 1992.
11. A. Ziv and J. Bruck, "An On-Line Algorithm for Checkpoint Placement," IEEE Trans. Computers, vol. 46, no. 9, pp. 976–985, Sep. 1997.
12. R. Geist, R. Reynolds and J. Westall, "Selection of a Checkpoint Interval in a Critical-Task Environment," IEEE Trans. Reliability, vol. 37, no. 4, pp. 395–400, Nov. 1988.
13. A. M. Saleh and J. H. Patel, "Transient-Fault Analysis for Retry Techniques," IEEE Trans. Reliability, vol. 37, no. 3, pp. 323–330, Aug. 1988.
14. B. W. Johnson, Design and Analysis of Fault-Tolerant Digital Systems, Addison-Wesley, 1989.
15. J. Sosnowski, "Transient Fault Tolerance in Digital Systems," IEEE Micro, vol. 14, no. 1, pp. 24–35, Feb. 1994.
16. M. Pflanz and H. T. Vierhaus, "Online Check and Recovery Techniques for Dependable Embedded Processors," IEEE Mirco, vol. 21, no. 5, pp. 24–40, Sep.–Oct. 2001.
17. A. Leon-Garcia, Probability and Random Processes for Electrical Engineering, Addison Wesley, 1994.

Parallelizing Serializable Transactions Within Distributed Real-Time Database Systems

Subhash Bhalla and Masaki Hasegawa

The University of Aizu, Aizu-Wakamatsu,
Fukushima PO 965-8580, Japan
{bhalla, d8041201}@u-aizu.ac.jp

Abstract. A real-time database system supports a mix of transactions. These include the real-time transactions that require completion by a given deadline. At the support side, existing concurrency control procedures introduce delays due to non-availability of data resources. The present study makes an effort to introduce a higher level of parallelism for execution of real-time transactions. It considers simple extensions within a transaction processing system. These permit a real-time transaction to avoid delays due to ordinary transactions. These also eliminate elements of other unpredictable delays, due to deadlocks or simple waiting for data resources. Thus, the investigated procedures can perform critical functions in parallel to process time-critical transactions. In effect, it is a model of transaction execution that permits execution of real-time transactions without interference from other executing transactions, and by reducing other probabilistic delays.

1 Introduction

The use of real-time database systems is growing in many application areas such as, industrial process control systems, multi-media systems and many critical data access applications. In such a system, a critical transaction (computational task) is characterized by its computation time and a completion deadline. These systems are characterized by stringent deadlines, and high reliability requirements. Many approaches for implementation of Real-Time systems are being studied [9], [1], [4]. In most cases, the designers tend to extend the available approaches for concurrency control for the new environments. However, we propose to eliminate the elements that cause delays and consider introduction of parallelism based on alternative procedures.

Our research is aimed at isolation of real-time transactions (RTTs). Such transactions are proposed to be executed in parallel with no interference from other transactions. Earlier research efforts within concurrency control also try to isolate transaction classes. For example, isolation of read-only transactions [1], [7], multi-class queries [8], and class for restricting admission [1]. Briefly, our goal is -

1. Isolate a RTT and permit it to execute freely in parallel; and
2. Execute two conflicting RTTs with better completion guarantee for both transactions.

L.T. Yang et al. (Eds.): EUC 2005, LNCS 3824, pp. 203–213, 2005.

For our purpose, we examine the process of data allocation. The characteristics of the 2 Phase Locking based Concurrency Control scheme has been studied. The rest of this paper is organized in the following manner. Section 2. describes the problem with background. Section 3 proposes a validation based selective concurrency control mechanisms that can eliminate delays for the RTTs and reduce interference among other transactions. Section 4 presents a system model of transaction execution. Section 5 examines a criterion for serializability based on the notions of local access graphs (LAGs). Section 6 presents an algorithm for constructing the LAGs. The proof of correctness has been studied in section 7. Section 8 presents a study of performance evaluation. Finally, conclusions and summary are presented in section 9.

2 Nature of Delays

The present study aims at exploring,

- **Transaction Classification**
  - possibility of executing RTTs (time-critical transactions) with no interference from ordinary transactions;
- **Conflicts Among Remaining RTTs**
  - possibility of switching precedence in favor of a more urgent transaction; and
  - eliminate computational losses due to deadlocks, aborts, repeated rollbacks, and excessive overheads associated with access of frequently sought data items.

2.1 Real-Time System Environment

A requirement often imposed on transaction processing systems is that the schedule formed by the transactions, be Serializable [1]. A common method of enforcing serializability is based on two-phase locking. In a real-time environment, preceding ordinary transactions render a substantial portion of database inaccessible to an arriving real-time transaction. The RTDBS environment has the following type of transactions :

1. Real-Time Transactions (RTTs);
   These transactions are characterized by a known computation time estimate (Ct), and a execution time deadline (Dt), as -

$$Ct \ + delays \ll Dt$$

2. Status queries : the read only transactions; and
3. Ordinary Transactions (OTs) : the non-critical transactions that have no execution deadline associated with them.

The prominent delays on account of scheduled transactions are -

1. **Preceding Ordinary Transactions** - The transaction T4 fails to get data items requested (with exclusive access). Also, the transaction T6 fails to get data items requested (with shared access). Thus, an incoming RTT may need to wait until the executing transactions, release the data item [1].
2. **Delays and Conflicts Among RTTs** - The problem is further aggravated in case of RTTs that do not have predeclared read-set and write-set items. These seek locks for data items as these proceed with the computation. Consider a transaction T that reads data item x and writes on data item y. After a delay of d1 units, on receiving a lock for data item x, it computes the update values and seeks an exclusive lock for data item y, which becomes available after a delay of d2 units of time. Hence, the worst time estimate for computation time T is given by :

$$Ct + (d1 + d2) \ll Dt$$

3. **Deadlocks Among RTTs** The situation is further complicated by the occurrence of deadlocks, that can introduce more delays.

Thus, RTTs can have worst case estimates depending on the number of transactions executing in the system and the number of items sought by the transactions. This possibility can lead to a failure of an RTT.

3 The Proposed Model

3.1 Interference from Ordinary Transactions

In many of cases, a large component of the data resources are held by the scheduled (executing) ordinary transactions. The existing approaches are primitive in nature. These make a transaction manager (TM) dependent on multiple data managers (DMs) for priority based executions and aborts [1].

A conceptual model of transaction processing is shown in Figure 2. As per the idea, only the RTTs are permitted to lock data items. The ordinary transactions can execute by performing an additional validation based check [1], [3] [2]. It ensures that, there is no overlap among items in the RTT lock table, and the items read by ordinary transactions. In case of an overlap, the ordinary transactions roll-back. The resulting transaction processing system can perform all RTTs by ignoring existence of ordinary transactions.

For sake of implementation, in case of conflict between a RTT and an OT, the locks granted to ordinary transactions are ignored. The ordinary transaction is informed about possibility of failure during validation. The transaction commitment by the data manager is denied success, in case of a failure (of validation). Such an implementation reduces the data conflicts. These remain to exist among the few executing RTTs.

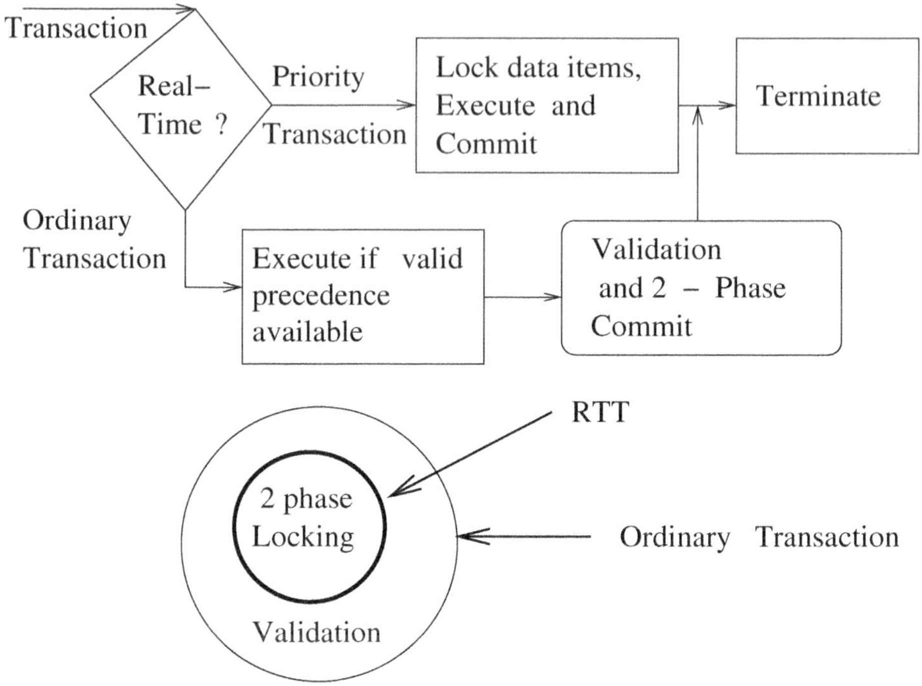

Fig. 1. Execution of real-time transactions in isolation (Brute-force Method)

3.2 Delays and Conflicts Among RTTs

In case of blocking, transactions begin to prepare Transaction-Wait-For graphs (TWFGs). Alternatively, probe messages are sent in order to detect the cause of blocking [1]. Consider an example, a frequently sought after item 'X'. Transactions T4, T3, T5, and T1 arrive in the same order. Other than T4, the three transactions detect that they need to wait for T4. Depending on there relative priority of execution, T3 may abort T4. Subsequently, T3 is aborted by T1, due to a higher priority. Similar aborts in the case of multiple frequently sought data items (**hot-spots** [1]), can cause delays due to deadlocks and frequent aborts. The proposed technique transforms the lock table at the DM level into a local access graph. It aligns the incoming transactions as T4 - T1, T3, T5 (if T4 is completing 2nd phase of '2-phase commit'), or as, T1 - T3, T4, T5.

3.3 Delays Due Dead-Locks

A distributed deadlock occurs when a transaction waits for locks held by another transaction, which in turn, is waiting (directly or indirectly) for locks held by the first transaction. The presence of any deadlock introduces delays and degrades the database performance [5].

4 The System Model

Based on the models of 2 phase locking and real-time computational environment [6], a set of assumptions are organized. It is assumed that a 2 phase locking discipline is followed. In the following section, a scheme to execute transactions in accordance with a precedence order is described.

4.1 Definitions for Real-Time Database System

The distributed database system (DDBS) consists of a set of data items (say set 'D'). The DDBS is assumed to be based on a collection of (fixed) servers that are occasionally accessed by real-time hosts. A data item is the smallest accessible unit of data. It may be a file, a record, an array, or an object. Each data item is stored at a site (one only). However, this assumption does not restrict the algorithm in any way and can be relaxed in a generalized case. Transactions are identified as $T_i, T_j, \ldots$; and sites are represented by $S_k, S_l\ \ldots$; where, $i, j, k, l\ \ldots$ are integer values. The data items are stored at database sites connected by a computer network.

Each site supports a transaction manager (TM) and a data manager (DM). The TM supervises the execution of the transactions. The DMs manage individual databases. The network is assumed to detect failures, as and when these occur. When a site fails, it simply stops running and other sites detect this fact. The communication medium is assumed to provide the facility of message transfer between sites. A site always hands over a message to the communication medium, which delivers it to the destination site in finite time. For any pair of sites S_i and S_j , the communication medium always delivers the messages to S_j in the same order in which they were handed to the medium by S_i.

4.2 The Transaction Model

We define a transaction as a set of atomic operations on data items. The system contains a mixture of real-time transactions and ordinary transactions. We assume that the ordinary transactions can be aborted, in case of a data conflict with the real-time transactions. An operation is either a read (returns the value of the data item), or a write (updates the item with a specified new value). For sake of simplicity, we assume that every transaction can read and write on any data item at most once. For any T_i and data item X, $r_i[X]$ denotes a read executed by T_i on X. Similarly, $w_i[X]$ denotes a write executed by T_i on X. The notation o_i denotes an operation of transaction T_i (i.e., either r_i or w_i). We let OS_i denote the set of all operations in T_i (i.e., $OS_i = \cup_j O_{ij}$). Where the notation, $O_{ij}[X]$ or O_{ij} denotes j-th operation o_i of transaction T_i on a data item X.

We denote by N_i the termination condition for T_i, where $N_i \in \{abort, commit\}$. In general, a transaction does not have to be a totally ordered sequence. When two operations are not ordered relative to each other, these can be executed in any order. However a read and a write on the same element, must be ordered.

Definition 1 : Two operations $o_i[X]$ and $o_j[X]$ conflict with each other, if they operate on data item (X) and at least one of them is a Write.

Definition 2 : A transaction T_i is a partial order $T_i = \{\sum_i, \ll_i\}$, where

1. $\sum_i = OS_i \cup \{N_i\}$.
2. For any two operations $O_{ij}, O_{ik} \in OS_i$, if $O_{ij} = r(X)$ and $O_{ik} = w(X)$ for any data item X, then either $O_{ij} \ll_i O_{ik}$ or $O_{ik} \ll_i O_{ij}$.
3. $\forall\, O_{ij} \in OS_i$, $O_{ij} \ll_i N_i$.

The items to be locked by the transaction for the purpose of read and write steps are termed as read-set (RS) and write-set (WS), respectively. The union of the read-set and the write-set of a T_i constitutes locking variables (LV_i). Our definition of a transaction conflict is the same as the commonly accepted notion [1]. Hence, $LV_i \cap LV_j = \phi$, implies that no conflict exists between T_i, T_j.

A transaction asks for an exclusive lock, if it reads and writes on a data item. Non-compatible locks are granted after completion of the preceding transaction. However, the compatible locks are granted in parallel. Local computation starts after the lock grants have been received. After the computation, the write phase is initiated. Updated data items are sent to the data sites and are stored in a temporary memory. It is assumed that, the 'two-phase commit' protocol [1] is employed to guarantee the atomicity of transactions that involve multiple sites. The real-time transactions are accorded priority and are always committed by local DMs, in preference over local computations.

Let $T = T_1, \ldots, T_n$ be a set of active transactions in a DDBS. The notion of correctness of transaction execution is that of serializability [1]. Hence, a transaction number (TN) assigned to a transaction for its identity has a 5 element value, as (site-id,local-clock,type,priority,global-identity).

5 Ordering of Transactions in a Distributed System

In the proposed approach, the transactions are ordered by constructing local access graphs (LAGs) for access requests. In this section, we define a LAG.

Definition 3 : A directed graph G consists of a set of vertices $V = V_1, V_2, \ldots$, a set of edges $E = E_1, E_2, \ldots$, and a mapping function Ψ that maps every edge on to some ordered pair of vertices $< V_i, V_j >$. A pair is ordered, if $< V_i, V_j >$ is different from $< V_j, V_i >$. A vertex is represented by a point, and an edge is represented by a line segment between V_i and V_j with an arrow directed from V_i to V_j.

Insertion of an edge $< V_i, V_j >$ into the graph G =(V,E) results in graph G' =(V',E'), where $V' = V \cup \{V_i, V_j\}$ and $E' = E \cup \{< V_i, V_j >\}$. The union of two graphs $G_1 = (V_1, E_1)$ and $G_2 = (V_2, E_2)$ is another graph G_3 (written as $G_3 = G_1 \cup G_2$), whose vertex set is $V_3 = V_1 \cup V_2$ and the edge set is $E_3 = E_1 \cup E_3$.

Let, there be a partial ordering relation $\ll_T$ defined over T (the collection of executing transactions $T_1, \ldots, T_n$), to indicate a precedence order among transactions, based on criteria of serializability.

Definition 4 : An access graph of T_i (AG_i) is a graph $AG_i(V, E)$, where $V \subseteq T$, and $E = \{< T_j, T_i > | LV_j \cap LV_i \neq \phi \text{ and } T_j \ll_T T_i\}$.

Example 2 : Consider the transactions RT_a, RT_b, RT_c, RT_d and RT_e as shown below. Let X,Y,Z be data items. Also,

- $RT_a = r_a(X)r_a(Y)w_a(X)w_a(Y).$
- $RT_b = r_b(X)r_b(Y)r_b(Z)w_b(X)w_b(Y)w_b(Z).$
- $RT_c = r_c(Z)w_c(Z).$
- $RT_d = r_d(X)r_d(Z)w_d(X)w_d(Z).$
- $RT_e = r_e(Y)r_e(Z)w_e(Y)w_e(Z).$

Consider a situation, where X,Y and Z are located at one site. The execution of above transactions' operations can follow any one of the sequences in accordance with the criteria of serializability [1]. For each execution (equivalent to a serial execution), the AGs of transactions are different. If we consider the arrival pattern of transactions in the order RT_b, RT_c, RT_d and RT_e, RT_a, then, the corresponding AGs of above transactions are shown in Figure 4. Noting that the real-time transaction priority is highest for RT_a, and lowest for RT_e. In this, $RT_i \longrightarrow^x RT_j$ indicates, RT_j is waiting for data item X which will be released after completion of RT_i.

Definition 5 : A local access graph (LAG) of T_i at S_k, is a graph $LAG_{ik}(V, E)$, where, $V \subseteq T$, and $E = \{< T_j, T_i > | LV_{jk} \cap LV_{ik} \neq \phi \text{ and } T_j \ll_T T_i\}$. In this expression, T_j has previously visited site S_k, and LV_{ik} denotes the part of LV_i, resident at S_k.

When a locking request LR_i (for RT_i) is sent to S_j, a LAG_{ij} is constructed at S_j.

$.RT_a$ z: free	$RT_a \longrightarrow^{x,y} RT_b$	$RT_b \longrightarrow^{z} RT_c$	$RT_a \longrightarrow^{x} RT_d$ $RT_b \longrightarrow^{x,z} RT_d$ $RT_c \longrightarrow^{z} RT_d$	$RT_a \longrightarrow^{y} RT_e$ $RT_b \longrightarrow^{y,z} RT_e$ $RT_c \longrightarrow^{z} RT_e$ $RT_d \longrightarrow^{z} RT_e$
1. AG_a	2. AG_b	3. AG_c	4. AG_d	5. AG_e

Fig. 2. Access Graphs (AGs) of transactions

Observation 1: Let LV_i be stored at sites $S_1, \ldots, S_m$. And, LAG_{ij} be the LAG of T_i at S_j. Then,

$$AG_i = \cup_{j=1}^{m} LAG_{ij}$$

6 An Algorithm to Construct LAG

In this section, we describe some of the terms used in the algorithm. The algorithm is presented in the following section.

6.1 Terms Used to Describe the Algorithm

- Home site ($\mathbf{SH_i}$):
  The site of origin of T_i is referred to as the home site.
- Transaction number ($\mathbf{TN_i}$):
  A unique number (TN_i), is assigned to the transaction T_i on its arrival at the home site. In this paper, both notations TN_i and T_i are used interchangeably and represent individual transactions. A real-time transaction is allotted a distinct identity indicating its type and priority.
- Locking variables ($\mathbf{LV_i/LV_{ik}}$):
  The items read or to be written by a T_i, constitute the LV_i. The locking variables at S_k constitute LV_{ik}.
- Lock request ($\mathbf{LR_{ik}}$):
  It consists of TN_i and LV_{ik}. It is prepared by SH_i on arrival of T_i, and is sent to each concerned site S_k.
- **Odd edge, Even edge** :
  As per access ordering based on dataflow graphs, an edge $< T_j, T_i >$, such that $TN_j > TN_i$, is called as odd edge. It is treated as a negative priority edge as it needs to be interchanged (verified), upon its occurance.

  The even edges are also called priority edges. A real-time transaction always forms a priority edge (or even edge) with other transactions, due to its real-time priority.
- Access grant status ($\mathbf{AGS_{ik}}$):
  It has values 0 or 1. After granting of all the requested locks of data items at S_k to LR_{ik}, the AGS_{ik} is changed to 1 at site S_k. Otherwise, AGS_{ik} is 0 for waiting transactions.
- Active list:
  The Active list is maintained by each S_k. The Active list of S_k is divided into two tables: active list of lock requests at S_k ($\mathbf{ALT_k}$), and active list of LAGs at S_k ($\mathbf{ALG_k}$). These tables are:
  - $ALT_k = \{(LV_i, AGS_{ik}) \mid T_i$ requested data items at S_k }.
  - ALGk = { LAG_{ik} — T_i requested data items at S_k }.

  A transaction T_i is inserted into the ALT_{ik}, after initializing AGS_{ik}. On getting the access grants for LV_{ik}, AGS_{ik} is changed to 1. As a next step, these access grants are sent to SH_i.
- Data table ($\mathbf{DT_i}$):
  This table is maintained at the SH_i for each T_i. The DT_i contains the lock grants (with values) of T_i. Whenever S_k receives any lock grant from another site, it stores it in a corresponding DT_i.

- Status of a transaction ($\mathbf{ST_i}$):
  For a T_i, ST_i is maintained at the SH_i. It has values 0 or 1. Initially, ST_i is 0. After receiving all commitment messages in phase 1 of '2-phase commit', ST_i is changed to 1. After this, the final phase of commitment of T_i begins.
- Conflict-set of LAG ($\mathbf{LAG_{ik}.conflict - set}$):
  Set of transactions in LAG_{ik} which are in conflict with T_i. That is, $LAG_{ik}.conflict - set \;=\; \{vertex - set[LAG_{ik}] \;-\; [T_i]\}$.

6.2 Informal Description of the Algorithm

If a transaction needs to access data items, its LR_{ik} are sent to each (concerned) site S_k. The LAG_{ik} is updated at these sites. At any site S_k, if LAG_{ik} contains odd edge $< T_j, T_i >$, then it is an indication of possible blocking or delay. It is proposed that the real-time transactions exchange the precedence with the lock holding transaction, to generate a normal precedence (even edge). In all cases, the odd edge is nullified by exchange of precedence to revoke the grant. This is called the confirmation of the edge.

An **edge is confirmed** by checking the existing AGS_{jk} **locally**, or by sending an "abort the edge" message to the SH_j. That is, if the AGS_{jk} is 0, then an even edge $< T_i, T_j >$ is inserted into the LAG_{jk} and odd edge $< T_j, T_i >$ is deleted from LAG_{ik}. Otherwise, at the SH_j, if T_j is under execution, then a **reverse** grant message is sent to SH_j, and the odd edge $< T_j, T_i >$ is substituted at the LAG_{ik}. The executing transaction T_j performs a partial roll-back.

If T_i is a **real-time transaction**, but the local site is participating in a '2-phase commit' for T_j, the SH_j is sent a message $'T_j.STATE'$. In response, its home site terminates T_j, or communicates the updated values, within a time-out period. Else, the site is treated as a failed site.

If T_i is an **ordinary transaction**, but the local site is executing the 2nd phase of 2 phase locking for T_j, the SH_j is sent a message $'T_j.STATE'$. In response, its home site completes T_j, and communicates the updated values (within a larger time frame). Thus, a time-critical transaction is permitted to execute a revoke grant (if necessary) for the conflicting item, in order to cancel an odd edge.

7 Proof of Correctness

Theorem 1: Let H be the history over T. And there are 'm' sites in the system. Then the execution produced by the algorithm is Serializable.

Proof: In the algorithm, the conflicts are ordered through the LAGs. So, if $G_L = \cup LAG_{ik}$, where i=1 to n, and k= 1 to m, then, we prove the following.
(i) $G_L = SG(H)$.
(ii) G_L is acyclic.
(i) For any two transactions T_i and T_j, if these have a conflict between them, then - either $< T_i, T_j > \in LAG_{jk}$ or $< T_j, T_i > \in LAG_{ik}$ at some S_k. So, the edge set of G_L contains all conflicting pairs. So, $G_L = SG(H)$.

(ii) The algorithm follows two phase locking principle. That is, the data manager does not releases any lock until it acquires all required locks. Then, G_L is acyclic [1].

Theorem 2: Let $T = \{T_1, T_2, \ldots, T_n\}$ be the set of conflicting transactions in the system. The above algorithm results in a deadlock free environment.

Proof: Every deadlock cycle results in the formation of at least one odd edge in some LAG_{ik} at some S_k. Suppose, T_i forms an odd edge $< T_k, T_i > \in LAG_{ip}$ at some S_p. In this case, in accordance with the proposed algorithm, if T_k has not started completion of transaction commitment, the odd edge is removed, and corresponding even edge is inserted in the respective LAG, which breaks the deadlock cycle. Otherwise, if T_k has started completion and broadcast of committed values, then also the cycle will be broken.

Theorem 3: Let $T = \{T_1, T_2, \ldots, T_n\}$ be the set of conflicting transactions in the system. The above algorithm results in a priority inversion free environment.

If all transactions access data items in accordance with the precedence order assigned to them, no priority inversion occurs. Priority inversion results from formation of an odd edge in some LAG_{ik} at some S_k. As shown above, odd edges are eliminated, as these occur.

8 Summary and Conclusions

In the distributed locking based approaches, if transactions from different sites, are in serializability conflict, then some of the submitted transactions are rejected. Transaction rejects and delays are two of the main problems that concern real-time transaction processing activity. In this study, a procedure has been identified that shows a possibility of execution of critical transactions under serializability conditions. A higher level of concurrency is achieved, as a result of removal of excessive blocking, and roll-backs for critical transactions.

References

1. P.A.Bernstein, V.hadzilacos and N.Goodman, "Two Phase Locking", Chapter 3, *Concurrency control and recovery in database systems*, Addison-Wesley,1987.
2. Bhalla, S. and S.E. Madnick, "Asynchronous Backup and Initialization of a Database Server for Replicated Database Systems", The Journal of Supercomputing, Vol. 27, No. 1, pp. 69-89, Kluwer Academic Publishers, January 2004.
3. Reddy, P.K., and S. Bhalla, "Asynchronous Operations in Distributed Concurrency Control", IEEE Transactions on Knowledge and Data Engineering, Vol. 15, No. 3 May-June 2003, pp. 721-733.
4. Bhalla, S., "The Performance of an Efficient Distributed Synchronization and Recovery Algorithm", The Journal of Supercomputing, Kluwer Academic Publishers, vol. 19, no. 2, June 2001, pp. 199-220.

5. A.N.Choudhary, " Cost of distributed deadlock detection: A performance study", *Proceedings of the Sixth International Conference on Data Engineering*, pp.174-181, February 1990.
6. Korth H.F., E. Levy, and A. Silberschatz, "Compensating Transactions: a New Recovery Paradigm," in *Proc. 16th Intl. Conf. Very Large Databases*, Brisbane, Australia, 1990, pp. 95-106.
7. Lam Kwok-wa, S.H. Son, V.C.S. Lee, and Sheung-Lun Hung, "Using Separate Algorithms to Process Read-Only Transactions in Real-Time Systems", *Proceedings of IEEE Real Time Systems Symposium*, Dec. 1998, pp. 50-59.
8. Pang, H., M.J. Carey, and M. Linvy, "Multiclass Query Scheduling in Real-time Database Systems", *IEEE Transactions on Knowledge and Data Engineering*, Vol. 7, No. 4, August 1995.
9. Ramamritham K., "Real-Time Databases", *Distributed and Parallel Databases*, Kluwer Academic Publishers, Boston, USA, Vol. 1, No. 1, 1993.

Timing Analysis of Distributed End-to-End Task Graphs with Model-Checking

Zonghua Gu

Department of Computer Science,
Hong Kong University of Science and Technology

Abstract. Real-time embedded systems must satisfy system-level timing constraints between external sensor inputs and actuator outputs. Real-time scheduling theory can be used to verify that the system is schedulable, that is, no deadlines are missed, but that alone is not enough. Given that the system is schedulable, how to verify that it satisfies system-level end-to-end timing constraints, such as freshness, correlation and separation? To address this question, we adopt the approach of formal modeling and model-checking. Specifically, we use Timed Automata and the model-checker UPPAAL for verification purposes. We have developed generic modeling templates for a class of distributed task systems that can be used as input the the model-checker in order to verify system-level end-to-end timing constraints. We use an application example of distributed real-time control system to illustrate the utility of our approach.

1 Introduction

Real-time embedded systems must satisfy system-level timing constraints between external sensor inputs and actuator outputs. Gerber *et al* [1] identified three classes of *system-level end-to-end timing constraints*:

- *Freshness constraints* bound the maximum time it takes for the data to flow through the system. For example, the time interval between reading input data d from the sensor and writing output data calculated using d to the actuator can not exceed 10ms.
- *Correlation constraints* bound the maximum time-skew between several inputs used to produce an output. For example, if input data d_1 and d_2 are used to produce output data d_3, then d_1 and d_2 must be sampled within 2ms of each other. Generally it is desirable to minimize the data correlation from distributed sensors in order for the controller to have a realistic and consistent view of the physical environment.
- *Separation constraints* bound the maximum jitter between consecutive values on a single output channel.

Given a set of such timing constraints, as well as timing attributes of the tasks composing the system, we would like to verify that the system satisfies

L.T. Yang et al. (Eds.): EUC 2005, LNCS 3824, pp. 214–223, 2005.

these constraints. Real-time scheduling theory can be used to prove that the system is schedulable, that is, no deadlines are missed, but that alone is not enough. A schedulable system may still violate system-level freshness, correlation and separation constraints. In this paper, we address this question: *Given that the system is schedulable, how to verify that it satisfies system-level end-to-end timing constraints, such as freshness, correlation and separation?*

The growing complexity of modern real-time embedded systems makes it imperative to apply formal analysis techniques at early stages of system development. In this paper, we adopt the approach of formal modeling and model-checking, which is a promising technique for analysis of finite state systems by exhaustive exploration of the system state space. Specifically, we use *Timed Automata* (TA) and the model-checker UPPAAL [2] for this purpose. Our main contribution in this paper is developing modeling techniques for a class of distributed task systems that are used as input the the model-checker UPPAAL to verify system-level end-to-end timing constraints. We make the assumption that the system is already schedulable before applying model-checking. Without this assumption, we would have a much larger state space due to deadline misses, an error condition that should never arise in a production system, without gaining any additional insight into the system's normal operation.

Some authors have developed modeling formalisms and analysis techniques for real-time scheduling analysis. For example, ACSR [3] is a resource-aware real-time process algebra for specification and formal verification of distributed real-time systems. Its main features include the ability to specify resources and their usage by system components, and prioritized execution that allows to express different preemptive and non-preemptive scheduling policies. Similarly, TIMES [4] is based on Timed Automata, and can be used for modelling, schedulability analysis and synthesis of optimal schedules for a set of tasks that are triggered periodically by timers, or sporadically by external interrupts. These approaches have the benefit of being able to deal with more general task models than real-time scheduling theory, which is typically restricted to periodic task models, and has to make pessimistic assumptions when dealing with sporadic or aperiodic tasks. However, modeling real-time scheduling inevitably introduces a much larger state space caused by interleaving of task executions on a shared processor, and has a negative impact on the scalability of model-checking, which is already the most important limiting factor for its industry adoption. In contrast, we adopt an approach of separation of concerns. We do not consider real-time scheduling issues caused by interference among tasks sharing a processor. We either assume a distributed system, where each task has its own dedicated processor, or a system with shared processors, but the timing attributes of tasks already take into account interference caused by multiple tasks sharing one processor, i.e., we use *worst-case response time* instead of *worst-case execution time* as a task's timing attribute. By using real-time scheduling theory to verify the schedulability assumption, and model-checking to verify system-level timing properties, we can achieve much better scalability than using model-checking to check for both schedulability and system-level timing properties.

This paper is structured as follows. In Section 2, we present our system modeling techniques. In Section 3, we use an application example to illustrate the complexity involved in timing analysis of distributed end-to-end task systems, and apply our modeling and model-checking approach to its timing analysis. In Section 4, we discuss related work, and in Section 5, we draw some conclusions.

2 System Modeling with TA

A *Timed Automaton* (TA) is a standard finite-state automaton extended with a finite collection of real-valued clocks, which proceed at the same rate and measure the amount of time that has elapsed since they were last reset. The model-checker UPPAAL [2] adds a few extensions to the standard definition of TA, such as integer variables, CCS-style [5] synchronous communication, urgent channels, etc. For space limitations, we do not provide a detailed description of TA and UPPAAL.

We define the system under analysis with an Asynchronous Task Graph [1], which is a *Directed Acyclic Graph* (DAG), where vertices denote tasks, which have input and output data ports. Directed edges denote dataflow communication between tasks. Tasks execute asynchronously and communicate with each other through shared buffers of size 1. Reading and writing are both non-blocking, i.e., writing a data token to a shared buffer overwrites the previous data token contained in it. Reading and writing are both assumed to be instantaneous, hence we do not require the use of mutual exclusion mechanisms such as mutex or semaphore. Forks and joins in the task graph are of type *AND*. That is, when a task executes, it reads in one data token from each of its input ports in an instantaneous, atomic action at the start of its execution, and then writes out one data token to each of its output ports in another instantaneous, atomic action at the end of its execution.

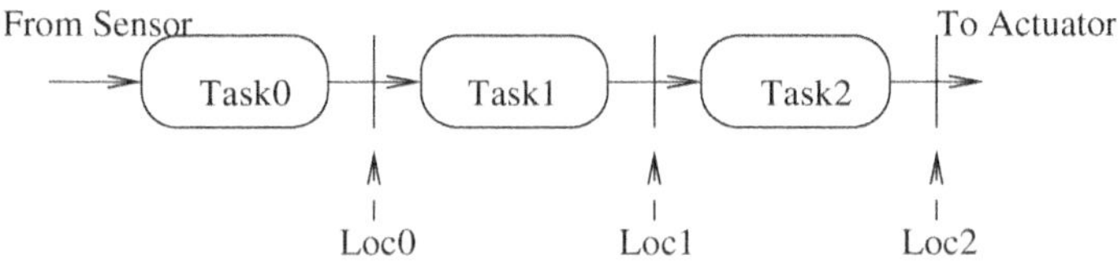

Fig. 1. An end-to-end task graph consisting of a linear chain of sub-tasks, with *atomic, non-interleaving* task execution

Consider a linear chain of sub-tasks in an end-to-end task graph from external stimulus from the environment to eventual output to the environment, as in Figure 1. The taskset is $\{T_0, T_1, \ldots, T_{N-1}\}$, where T_{i-1} is the immediate predecessor of T_i, where $i = 1, \ldots, N-1$. Since tasks communicate through shared buffers, the system events that we are concerned with are the read/write events of the shared buffers. Suppose that we know the execution time intervals of each

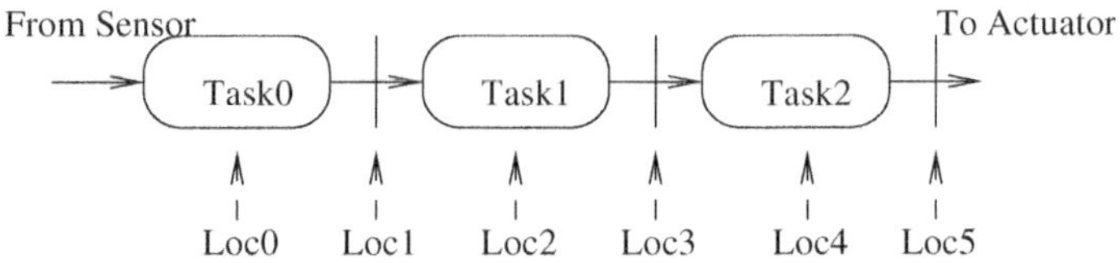

Fig. 2. An end-to-end task graph consisting of a linear chain of sub-tasks, with *non-atomic, interleaving* task execution

task block, and we want to model this task chain with timed automata. This is straightforward if the execution is single-rate, and there is no pipelining, i.e., each invocation of the task chain executes from start to finish before the next invocation. However, the situation becomes more complicated if *pipelined* and *multi-rate executions* are allowed. The execution is pipelined if it is possible for new inputs to come in from the environment before the previous output has been produced. The execution is multi-rate if it is possible for each task's execution rate to be different from each other. Think of each piece of data read in from a sensor task as a data token. In the case of pipelined and multi-rate execution, multiple data tokens read in by the same sensor task in different execution periods may coexist in the system at the same time.

For illustration purposes, imagine that we attach a real-time clock that is reset to 0 with each data token coming in from the head of the pipeline, and mark this particular clock as being in use. Every time a data token goes through the entire pipeline and falls off the end of the task chain, we pick up the clock on that token, read off the value as the end-to-end delay suffered by that token, and mark the clock on that token as free and can be reused for a new token in the future. When the pipeline stalls at a task i, and the data token in the location before task i gets overwritten, We can also mark the clock of that data token as free. We can view a fresh data token read in from the environment as birth of that token, and token falling out of the end of the pipeline, or overwritten in the middle of the pipeline, as death of that token. A clock not currently in use is attached to each newborn token, and is marked in use. Upon death of a data token, either because it has gone through the entire pipeline, or it was over-written (killed prematurely) in the middle of the pipeline, we mark its clock as free and available for future use. It is important to note that when attaching a clock to a newborn token t_{new}, that clock must not be already in use by some other token t_{old} currently in the pipeline, for otherwise we will lose track of the time stamp of t_{old}.

If task execution is atomic and non-interleaving, then we need to keep track of clocks at the the inter-task buffer locations, as shown in Figure 1. Atomicity means that no other task can perform read or write operations in between a task's start and end. However, if task execution is non-atomic and interleaving, which means that it is possible for other tasks to perform read or write operations in between a task's start and end, then we need to keep track of clocks at both the inter-task buffer locations and the task bodies between its start and end, as shown in Figure 2. In other words, we can view a task that executes non-atomically as two tasks, one read task and one write task, which execute atomically, and view the task body between its read and write operations as another data buffer.

Atomic execution is the case where tasks run on a single processor with non-preemptive scheduling, which effectively serializes the task execution. Non-atomic execution is the case where tasks run on a single processor with preemptive scheduling (pseudo concurrency), or where tasks run on a multi-processor platform (true concurrency).

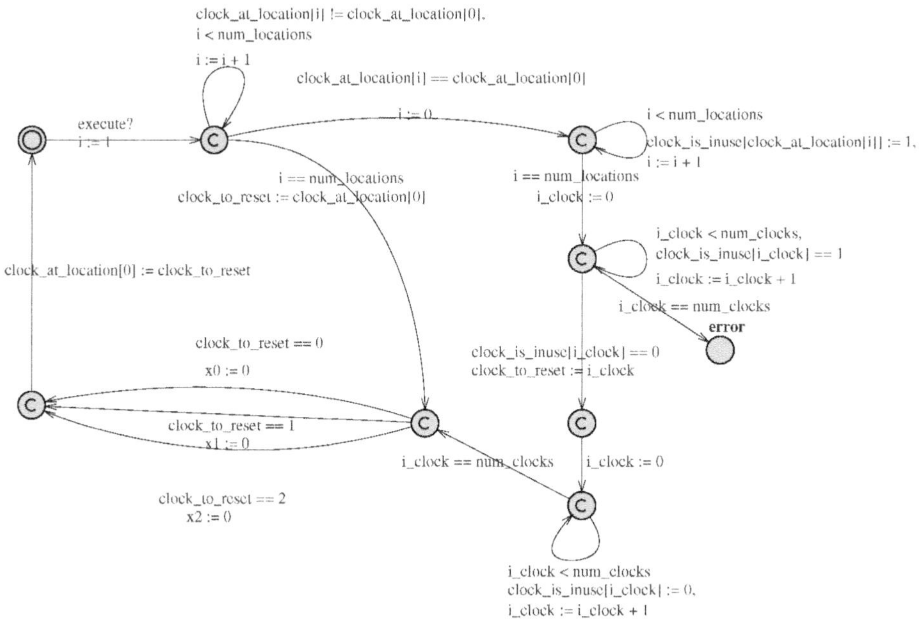

Fig. 3. TA template for tracking the timestamps of $location_0$

The discussion above applies to a linear chain of tasks, but it can be easily extended to deal with a more general task graph with AND style synchronization. When a data token flows to an AND fork in the task graph, the token and its clock are replicated and sent along each of the forked paths. When several data tokens converge at an AND join in the task graph, all the tokens should be carrying the same clock that was replicated at the previous fork to ensure data consistency. Note that this behavior is not necessarily guaranteed. A certain branch of the AND fork may have a pipeline stall, so that the AND join point may see different clocks from different incoming paths. This should be detected and flagged as a runtime error.

To instantiate these concepts within the modeling tool UPPAAL, Figure 3 shows a generic TA template for modeling the output buffer of the head of the

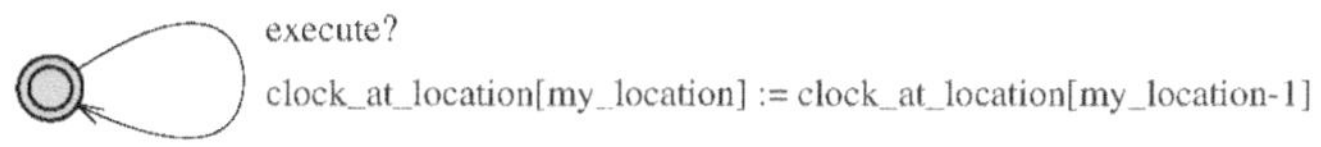

Fig. 4. TA template for tracking the timestamps of locations other than $location_0$

task chain ($location_0$), and Figure 4 shows a generic TA template for modeling of buffers at locations other than $location_0$. The latter template is simple: the task simply copies the clock value at its input port to its output port. The task at the head of the chain needs to read in a fresh data token from the environment and attach to it a clock that is not currently in use. With these model templates, we can easily model larger systems by instantiating the model with different parameters.

3 An Application Example

Consider the system in Figure 5, where two distributed sensors read data from the external environment and feed them into the controller, which processes the sensor data and compute signals to the actuator. The network connections between sensors and controllers are modeled as separate tasks. We assume this is a distributed system, where each task has its own dedicated processor, so we do not need to address real-time scheduling issues caused by multiple tasks sharing one processor. We can view the system as being composed of 2 linear task-chains: Path A is from Sensor A to Network A to Controller, and Path B is from Sensor B to Network B to Controller. Task execution is non-atomic, hence each task chain corresponds to Figure 2. All tasks read input at startup and write output at finish. The table in Figure 5 shows the task timing parameters.

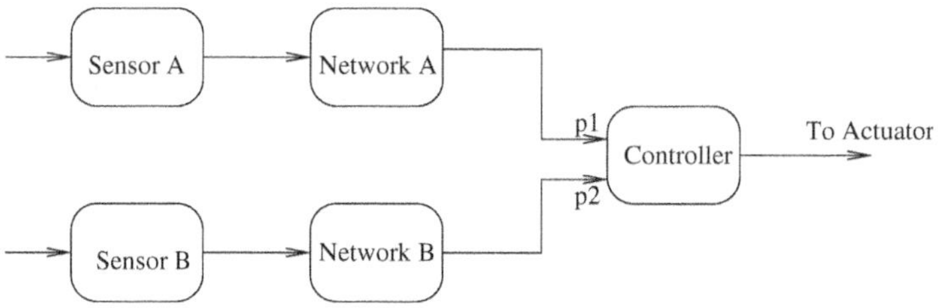

Task ID	Period	Offset	BCET	WCET
SensorA	10	0	1	3
SensorB	10	1	3	4
Controller	10	7	2	2
NetworkA	–	1	2	–
NetworkB	–	2	5	–

Fig. 5. A system consisting of two distributed sensors and one central controller

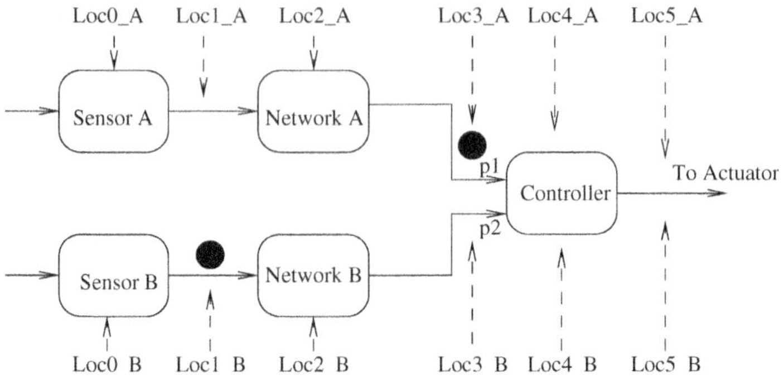

Fig. 6. Each black dot denotes one data token. The figure shows that the input data token read by Sensor A has gone through Network A and reached the input port $p1$ of the Controller, while the input data token read by Sensor B has not gone through Network B yet.

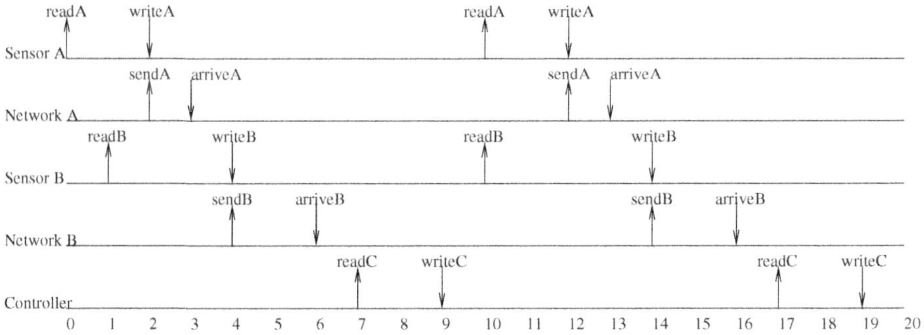

Fig. 7. One possible execution trace for the taskset specified in Figure 5

We have two system-level end-to-end timing constraints:

- *Freshness constraint*: the time interval between reading input data from either Sensor A or Sensor B to writing output data by the Controller must be less than 10ms;
- *Correlation constraint*: if input data d_1 read by Sensor A and input data d_2 read by Sensor B are used to produce output data d_3, then d_1 and d_2 must be sampled within 2ms of each other.

Figure 6 shows a snapshot during system execution. Figure 7 shows one possible execution trace for two consecutive execution periods. Sensor A reads input at time 0 and writes output at time 2ms. Network A is triggered by the completion event of Sensor A, and takes 1 time unit to deliver the message to input port $p1$ of the Controller. Similarly, Sensor B reads input at time 1ms and writes output at time 4ms. Network B is triggered by the completion event of Sensor

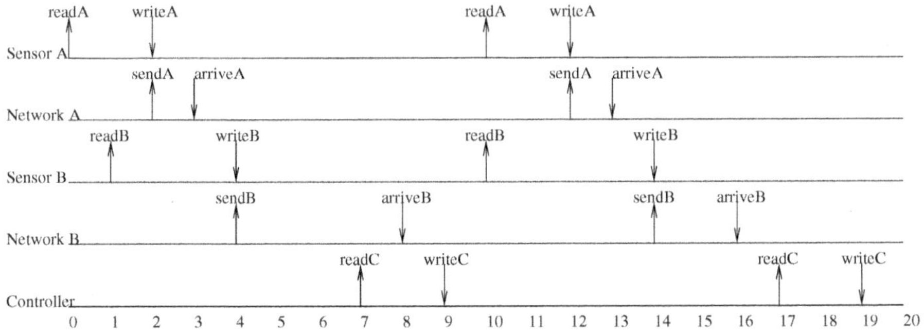

Fig. 8. Another possible execution trace for the taskset specified in Figure 5

B, and takes 2ms to deliver the message to input port $p2$ of the Controller. The Controller reads its input at time 7ms, and writes its output to the actuator at time 9ms. The next period is a repeat of the first. Therefore, the end-to-end delay of data tokens from Sensor A to the external actuator is 9ms, and from Sensor B to the external actuator is 8ms, both within the freshness constraint of 10ms. The correlation between data tokens at the 2 controller input ports is 1ms, i.e., the data token at $p1$ is sampled from Sensor A 1ms earlier than the data token at $p2$ from Sensor B. So the correlation constraint is also satisfied.

However, if Network B causes a slightly longer time delay of 4ms instead of 2ms, but still within the specification of [2,4]ms, then we have a different data token propagation scenario, as shown in Figure 8. Now the end-to-end delay for Sensor B's data token is 18ms, while the delay for Sensor A's data token remains at 9ms. So the freshness constraint is violated for Sensor B's data token. At the time of data reading of the Controller at time 17ms, the token at $p1$ from Sensor A is 7ms old, while the token at $p2$ from Sensor B is 16ms old. So there is a 9ms age difference between the two data tokens read by the Controller. This violates the correlation constraint, which states that the two input data tokens must be sampled within 2ms of each other. Intuitively, the data token read by Sensor A at time 0 was consumed by the Controller at time 7ms before the arrival of data token read by Sensor B at time 1ms, due to the long time delay caused by Network B. Therefore, the data token read by Sensor B at time 1ms is paired up with the data token read by Sensor A at time 10ms in the next execution cycle. This caused the large age difference between the data tokens consumed by the Controller at time 17ms.

As this example indicates, a small additional delay at Network B can cause a relatively large difference for the end-to-end delay and input correlation. Therefore, it is important to analyze the system timing behavior carefully. For realistic systems with larger sizes, it is tedious and error-prone to perform the analysis by hand, therefore, it is desirable to apply automated techniques such as model-checking to discover timing anomalies by exhaustive state space exploration.

We have used UPPAAL to prove the following properties:

- The maximum end-to-end delay for sensor A data is 9ms.
- The maximum end-to-end delay for sensor B data is 18ms.
- the maximum age difference between the data tokens at the two input ports of the Controller is 9ms.

If we change the task parameters, so that Network B task causes a deterministic delay of 2ms instead of an interval of [2,4]ms, we can verify that the maximum age difference reduces to 1ms, and the maximum end-to-end delay of Sensor B data reduces to 8ms. This corresponds to avoiding the execution scenario in Figure 8.

4 Related Work

Wall *et al* [6] designed a TA model for end-to-end task graphs. However, the size of their model grows exponentially with the number of tasks, while the size of our model grows only linearly. We can model larger systems easily by instantiating the proposed modeling templates with different parameters. In general, to keep track of clocks at N buffer locations, the automaton in their approach consists of $N * N$ locations and $N * N * N$ edges. Furthermore, they only considered atomic task executions (non-preemptive scheduling on a single processor), and they used a task execution trace to drive the Time Stamp Tracker automaton. We take into account non-atomic task executions, and accurately model task execution dynamics, which enables exploration of the full system state space with model-checking.

Haveman *et al* [7] manually analyzed a task model that consists of 2 sensors and 1 monitor that merges the 2 sensor readings. They considered a general multi-rate execution scenario, where each task may execute at arbitrary periods that are not necessarily harmonically related, and derived equations for calculating various end-to-end timing properties. We can map their task model into the TA modeling framework discussed in this paper, and analyze it through model-checking, thus obviating the need for tedious and error-prone manual analysis.

There are other techniques and tools for model-checking for timed automata, e.g., Kronos [8], which provides slightly different definitions of timed automata. For example, UPPAAL's definition of TA adopts CCS-style [5] pair-wise synchronization between two automata, while Kronos' definition uses globally-shared synchronization among all automata in the system. Our choice of the model-checker UPPAAL was motivated by several factors, including modeling convenience (pair-wise synchronization turns out to be convenient for our particular problem) and ease of use (UPPAAL provides a graphical user interface, while the other tools only provide textual interfaces). However, the main concepts of our approach are not restricted to any particular tool, but are generally applicable to other formalisms and model-checkers.

5 Conclusions

In this paper, we have explored application of model-checking to timing analysis of distributed end-to-end task graphs. We have developed generic modeling templates for a class of distributed task systems that can be used as input to the the model-checker UPPAAL in order to verify system-level end-to-end timing constraints. We have used a two-sensor-one-controller system to illustrate the complexity involved in end-to-end timing analysis, and applied our techniques to modeling and analysis of this system. Our approach is applicable to any real-time system that satisfies the assumptions stated in Section 2, i.e., tasks executing asynchronously and communicating through shared buffers.

References

1. R. Gerber, S. Hong, and M. Saksena, "Guaranteeing end-to-end timing constraints by calibrating intermediate processes," in *Proc. IEEE Real-Time Systems Symposium*, December 1994, pp. 209–213.
2. J. Bengtsson, K. G. Larsen, F. Larsson, P. Pettersson, and W. Yi, "UPPAAL - a tool suite for automatic verification of real-time systems," in *Proc. Workshop on Verification and Control of Hybrid Systems*, October 1995, pp. 232–243.
3. H. Ben-Abdallah, D. Clarke, I. Lee, and O. Sokolsky, "Paragon: A paradigm for the specification, verification, and testing of real-time systems," in *Proc. IEEE Aerospace Conference*, Feb 1997, pp. 469–488.
4. T. Amnell, E. Fersman, L. Mokrushin, P. Pettersson, and W. Yi, "Times: a tool for schedulability analysis and code generation of real-time systems," in *Proc. International Workshop on Formal Modeling and Analysis of Timed Systems*, Sept. 2003.
5. R. Milner, *A Calculus of Communicating Systems, LNCS 92*. Springer-Verlag, 1980.
6. A. Wall, K. Sandstrom, J. Maki-Turja, C. Norstrom, and W. Yi, "Verifying temporal constraints on data in multi-rate transactions using timed automata," in *Proc. IEEE International Conference on Real-Time Computing Systems and Applications*, December 2000, pp. 263–270.
7. J. Haveman, "Transaction decomposition: refinement of timing constraints," in *Proc. South Pacific Conference on Formal Methods*, 1997.
8. S. Yovine, "Kronos: A verification tool for real-time systems," *Software Tools for Technology Transfer*, vol. 1, pp. 123–133, 1997.

Voronoi-Based Improved Algorithm for Connected Coverage Problem in Wireless Sensor Networks

Jie Jiang, Zhen Song, Heying Zhang, and Wenhua Dou

School of Computer,
National University of Defense Technology,
410073, Changsha, China
jiangjie@nudt.edu.cn

Abstract. In this paper, we consider the connected coverage problem and aim to construct a minimal connected cover set that is sufficient for a given query in wireless sensor networks. We propose a centralized, Voronoi tessellation (CVT) based algorithm to select the minimum number of active sensor nodes needed to cover the target region completely. The constructed sensor set proves to be connected when sensor node's communication range is at least twice of its sensing range. For other situations where the CVT algorithm alone cannot guarantee the network connectivity, we design a Steiner minimum tree (SMT) based algorithm to ensure the network connectivity. Theoretical analysis and simulation results show that our algorithm outperforms the greedy algorithm in terms of both the time complexity and the needed number of sensor nodes that must be kept active to respond to a given query.

1 Introduction

Because of advances in micro-sensors, wireless networking and embedded processing, wireless sensor networks (WSN) are becoming increasingly available for commercial and military applications, such as environmental monitoring, biological attack detection, and battlefield surveillance, etc [1, 2].

Minimizing energy consumption to prolong the network lifetime is a major design objective for wireless sensor networks since tiny sensor devices usually operate on limited battery power due to low cost and small size. Many research efforts have been made to improve the energy efficiency of wireless sensor networks [3, 4, 5, 6, 7].

In this paper we aim to improve the energy efficiency of wireless sensor network by constructing an energy-efficient network topology. The motivation of our work is the spatial query execution in sensor networks. In the process of spatial query, the sink node needs to gather sensor data within a specific target region in order to obtain the status of the monitored target region. An energy efficient way to respond to the query is to activate only a subset of sensor nodes to monitor the field and send back report data. The active node subset must satisfy two requirements: (1) coverage requirement. Each point in the monitored region must

L.T. Yang et al. (Eds.): EUC 2005, LNCS 3824, pp. 224–233, 2005.

be covered by at least one sensor in this subset. (2) connectivity requirement. The communication network induced by active nodes must be connected.

For a given target region, the problem of finding a minimal subset of sensor nodes which meets the above two requirements at the same time is NP-hard. We propose a centralized Voronoi tessellation (CVT) based heuristic algorithm to compute the near optimal set of sensor nodes needed to cover the target region completely. In case of sensor's communication range is at least twice of its sensing range, the constructed sensor set is connected. In other cases where the CVT algorithm alone cannot guarantee the network connectivity, we design a Steiner minimum tree (SMT) based algorithm to ensure the communication connectivity. The proposed algorithm outperforms the greedy algorithm[9] in terms of both time complexity and the size of active sensor set.

2 Problem Statement

We consider static sensor networks in the 2D plane $\mathbb{R}^2$ and use binary sensing model to model sensor node's sensing capability. In this model, the coverage area of a sensor node s_i is a circle centered at s_i with radius R_s (sensing radius). The circular sensing/coverage area is called s_i's *sensing disk* and denoted by $S_i = \{p \in \mathbb{R}^2 | d(p, s_i) \leq R_s\}$, where d is the Euclidean distance metric. Each senor node has a limited communication range. $N(i) = \{s_j | d(s_j, s_i) \leq R_c, j \neq i\}$ denotes s_i's communication neighbor sets, where R_c is sensor node's wireless communication radius.

Definition 1. *(Connected cover set) A set of sensors S is a cover set for a region R if each point in R is covered at least by one sensor in S. If the communication graph induced by the cover set S is connected, set S is called a connected cover set (CCS) for R.*

For a given sensor network S deployed in a target region R, our goal is to calculate the minimum set of active senor nodes that can both cover the region R completely and form a connected communication network. This problem has been proved to be NP-hard and a greedy algorithm has been proposed in [9]. In this paper, we propose a new, novel algorithm based on Voronoi diagram.

3 Voronoi-Based Heuristic Algorithm

The minimal connected cover set is constructed in two steps. First, we construct the minimal cover set based on the Voronoi tessellation of the target region. When $R_c \geq 2R_s$, the constructed cover set proves to be connected. When $R_c < 2R_s$, we design a Steiner minimum tree (SMT) based algorithm to find the additional sensors needed to make the communication graph induced by the cover set connected. Not loosing generality, we assume that the target region is bounded and convex.

3.1 CVT Algorithm

The minimal cover set can be obtained by turning off the maximal number of redundant sensors. A sensor is redundant if its sensing coverage is completely subsumed by other sensors. Turning off a redundant sensor will not leave sensing hole in the target region.

Definition 2. *(Sensing hole) A sensing hole is a subarea of the target region R where points are not covered by any sensor.*

According to definition 1 and 2, a target region R is completely covered by a sensor network is equal to there is no sensing hole in R. The sensing hole is detected by utilizing the Voronoi tessellation [10] of R. Given a finite set of sensor nodes $S = \{s_1, \ldots, s_n\}$, the Voronoi region V_i associated with node s_i is defined by $V_i = \{p \in \mathbb{R}^2 | d(p, s_i) \leq d(p, s_j), j \neq i\}$, where d denotes the Euclidean distance. In general, the Voronoi polygon associated with node s_i is unbounded if s_i is on the boundary of the convex hull of S [10]. But when R is bounded, the unbounded Voronoi polygons of sensors on the boundary of the convex hull of S will be bounded by the boundary of R.

Definition 3. *(Bounded Voronoi tessellation) A Voronoi tessellation with all Voronoi polygons bounded is called a bounded Voronoi tessellation.*

Let $BVT(S, R)$ denote the bounded Voronoi tessellation of the bounded region R when taking S as the generator set, $BVC_i(S, R)$ denote the bounded Voronoi polygon associated with sensor s_i, $BVV_i(S, R)$ denote the set of vertices of $BVC_i(S, R)$ and $BVN_i(S, R)$ denote s_i's Voronoi neighbors in $BVT(S, R)$. Since the Voronoi polygon is convex [10] and R is also convex, all the Voronoi polygons in the bounded Voronoi tessellation are convex.

Theorem 1. *Consider a sensor network deployed in a bounded, convex region R. R is completely covered by S if and only if for each sensor $s_i \in S$, all the vertices of $BVC_i(S, R)$ are within s_i's sensing disk S_i.*

Proof. (Sufficient condition) For any sensor $s_i \in S$, if all the vertices of $BVC_i(S, R)$ are within S_i, then $BVC_i(S, R) \subseteq S_i$. Since $R = \bigcup_{s_i \in S} BVC_i(S, R)$, we have $R = \bigcup_{s_i \in S} BVC_i(S, R) \subseteq \bigcup_{s_i \in S} S_i$. Therefore S is a cover set for R.

(Necessary condition) If S is a cover set for R, each point in R is covered at least by one sensor in S. According to the definition of Voronoi tessellation, each point must be covered by its Voronoi generator. ∎

Theorem 1 gives a method to judge whether a sensor node is redundant. Sensor node s_i is redundant if $S \backslash s_i$ is still a cover set for R ($S \backslash s_i$ represents the set of remaining sensors after removing s_i from S). That is, for any sensor $s_j \in S \backslash s_i$, all the elements of BVV_j in $BVT(S \backslash s_i, R)$ are within S_j. Furthermore, we observe that only $BVC_j(S \backslash s_i, R), j \in BVN_i(S, R)$ may be different from $BVC_j(S, R)$. Other sensors' bounded Voronoi polygons will not change after excluding sensor

s_i from S because their Voronoi neighbors don't change. We conclude the above discussion as follows.

Coverage Redundancy Condition: Given a bounded convex region R and a sensor network consisting of a set of sensors S, sensor s_i is redundant if and only if for any sensor $s_j \in BVN_i(S,R)$, all the elements of BVV_j in $BVT(S \backslash s_i, R)$ are covered by S_j.

In order to judge whether a sensor node is coverage redundant, the above condition needs to compute the Voronoi tessellation among all remaining $n-1$ sensor nodes. Therefore it will need n times computation of such Voronoi tessellation of the target region R so as to judge the redundant status of each of the n sensor nodes. The time complexity of Voronoi tessellation with n generators is about $O(nlogn)$ in the worst case. So the total time complexity is about $O(n^2logn)$ and it is computation expensive. To reduce the computation cost, we propose the following optimization method.

Suppose we are checking whether sensor node s_i is coverage redundant. And $BVN_i(S,R)$ is s_i's Voronoi neighbor set. For any sensor node $s_j \in BVN_i(S,R)$, s_j's possible Voronoi neighbor set $BVN_j(S \backslash s_i, R)$ must be a subset of the union of $BVN_j(S,R)$ and $BVN_i(S,R)$ because of the nearest proximity characteristic of Voronoi tessellation, i.e., $BVN_j(S \backslash s_i, R) \subseteq (BVN_j(S,R) \backslash s_i) \cup BVN_i(S,R)$. This implies that $BVC_j(S \backslash s_i, R) = BVC_j(U_j, R)$, where $U_j = BVN_j(S,R) \backslash s_i \cup BVN_i(S,R)$. Therefore, it is sufficient to compute the Voronoi tessellation of R taking U_j as the generator set while determining whether s_i is coverage redundant. Using this optimization, the time complexity can be reduced to $O(nklogk)$, where $k = \max(\|U_j\|) \ll n$.

We propose the optimized coverage redundant condition as follows.

Optimized Coverage Redundancy Condition: Given a bounded convex target region R and a sensor network consisting of a set of sensors S, sensor s_i is redundant if and only if for any sensor $s_j \in BVN_i(S,R)$, all the elements of $BVV_j(U_j,R)$ are covered by s_j, where $U_j = BVN_j(S,R) \backslash s_i \cup BVN_i(S,R)$.

After all redundant sensors have been identified, we further classify redundant sensors into two sub-categories: independently and dependently redundant sensor.

Definition 4. *(Independently/Dependently redundant sensor) An independently redundant sensor is a redundant sensor whose Voronoi neighbors are all non-redundant. A dependently redundant sensor is a redundant sensor whose Voronoi neighbors include at least one redundant sensor.*

Non-redundant sensors must be kept active and independently redundant sensors are safe to be turned off. If two dependently redundant sensors, which are Voronoi neighbors each other, are turned off simultaneously, an area between them may be left uncovered, thus a sensing hole will occur. So the problem of calculating the minimal set of the active sensors is equivalent to determining the maximal set of the dependently redundant sensors that can be turned off simultaneously. In our solution, we use Redundant Dependency Graph to resolve the dependency relationship.

Definition 5. *(RDG graph) A Redundant Dependency Graph, $RDG = (V_r, E_r)$, is an undirected graph, where V_r is the set of all dependently redundant sensors and $\forall v_{ri}, v_{rj} \in V_r, (v_{ri}, v_{rj}) \in E_r$ if and only if v_{ri} and v_{rj} are Voronoi neighbors.*

The problem of determining the maximal set of dependently redundant sensors that can be deactivated simultaneously is equal to the problem of calculating the maximal independent set (MIS) of the RDG graph. In this paper, we adapt the greedy algorithm in [11] to calculate the MIS of the RDG graph.

When CVT algorithm terminates, all independently redundant sensors and all dependently redundant sensors selected into the MIS of the RDG graph form a Safe Set (SS), which includes all sensors that can be deactivated safely at the same time. And all other sensors form the final cover set for the target region and must be kept active to respond a specific query.

The pseudocode of the CVT algorithm is presented in Algorithm 1. The input of the CVT algorithm are the initial set of sensors $IS = \{s_1, \ldots, s_n\}$ and the target region R. Its output is a cover set (CS) for R. In the description, IRS denotes Independently Redundant sensor Set, DRS denotes Dependently Redundant sensor Set, SS denotes Safe sensor Set, S denotes temporary sensor Set and MIS denotes Maximal Independent Set.

Algorithm 1 CVT Algorithm

$SS = CS = \emptyset, S = IS$
if $R \not\subset \bigcup_{s_i \in S} S_i$ **then**
    Return $CS = \emptyset$
end if
while $S \neq \emptyset$ **do**
    $IRS = DRS = MIS = \emptyset$
    Identify all redundant sensor nodes in S
    for each redundant sensor $s_i \in S$ **do**
        if s_i is independently redundant **then**
            $IRS = IRS \bigcup \{s_i\}$
        else
            $DRS = DRS \bigcup \{s_i\}$
        end if
    end for
    if $DRS \neq \emptyset$ **then**
        Compute MIS of the RDG graph
        $SS = SS \bigcup IRS \bigcup MIS$
        $S = IS - SS$
    else
        $SS = SS \bigcup IRS$
        Break out the **while** loop
    end if
end while
$CS = IS - SS$

The approximation performance of the CVT algorithm is determined by the greedy algorithm for the MIS problem. It has been shown that in any graph with N vertices, M edges and average degree δ, the greedy algorithm can take at most $O(M)$ steps to find an independent set of size at least $N/(\delta+1)$[11].

In the following, we analyze the time complexity of the CVT algorithm.

Lemma 1. *The maximum possible number of Voronoi vertices in a two dimensional Voronoi tessellation is* $2n-5$*, and the maximum possible number of Voronoi edges is* $3n-6$*, where* n *is the number of generators [10].*

Lemma 2. *The average number of Voronoi edges per Voronoi polygon does not exceed 6 [10].*

Lemma 3. *Any algorithm for constructing Voronoi tessellation requires at least* $O(nlogn)$ *time in the worst case, where* n *is the number of generators [10].*

Theorem 2. *The worst-case time complexity of the CVT algorithm is less than* $O(mnk\log k)$*, where* k *is the maximum possible number of Voronoi neighbor of each sensor,* n *is the total number of sensors initially deployed in the network,* m *is the maximum iterative times of the* **While** *loop of the CVT algorithm and* $m \leq \log_{7/6} n$*.*

Proof. Step $2 \sim 4$ can be completed in $O(n\log n)$. In the **While** loop, step 7 can be done in $O(nk\log k)$ using the optimized coverage redundancy condition, where k is the maximum number of Voronoi neighbors. Step $8 \sim 14$ need $O(n)$ to classify redundant sensors. Step 16 needs $O(l)$ to calculate the MIS of RDG graph, where l is the edge number of RDG and $l \leq 3n-6$. Therefore one pass of the **While** loop can be done at most in $O(nk\log k)$ in the worst case. Suppose the total iterative number of **While** loop is m. According to the approximation ratio of the greedy algorithm for the MIS problem, we can get $m \leq \log_{7/6} n$. The total time complexity of the CVT algorithm is dominated by step $5 \sim 23$ and thus is less than $O(mnk\log k)$. ■

3.2 SMT Based Connection Algorithm

It has been shown that the complete coverage of a convex region implies connectivity of the communication network induced by all active sensor nodes if $R_c \geq 2R_s$ [12]. Therefore the cover set constructed by the CVT algorithm is connected if $R_c \geq 2R_s$. But when $R_c < 2R_s$, the communication connectivity of the cover set can't be ensured. In this subsection, we propose a Steiner Minimum tree (SMT) based connection algorithm to make the cover set connected if necessary.

Definition 6. *(Primary/Assistant sensor) A sensor in the cover set is called a primary sensor. Otherwise it is an assistant sensor.*

Definition 7. *(Connected component) A connected component in the cover set is a connected subgraph of* G_c *whose vertices only involve primary sensors, where* G_c *is the communication graph induced by all initially deployed sensors.*

Suppose that sensors in the cover set constructed by the CVT algorithm form m separated connected components in G_c as shown in Fig.1. The connected component consists of only primary sensors (denoted by solid circular dots). These components are connected through assistant sensors (denoted by hollow circular dots). We abstract each connected component as one virtual vertex and use v_i to represent $comp_i$. Then we attach to v_i all edges in G_c that connect one primary sensor in $comp_i$ and another assistant sensor. After this conversion, we get an abstract communication graph $G_c{}'$ (see Fig.2).

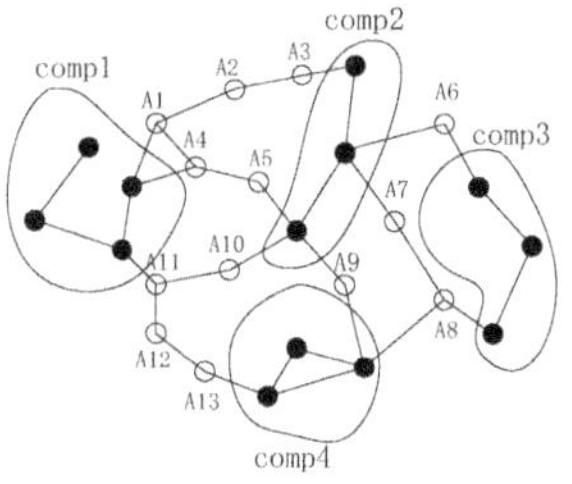

Fig. 1. Connected Components in G_c

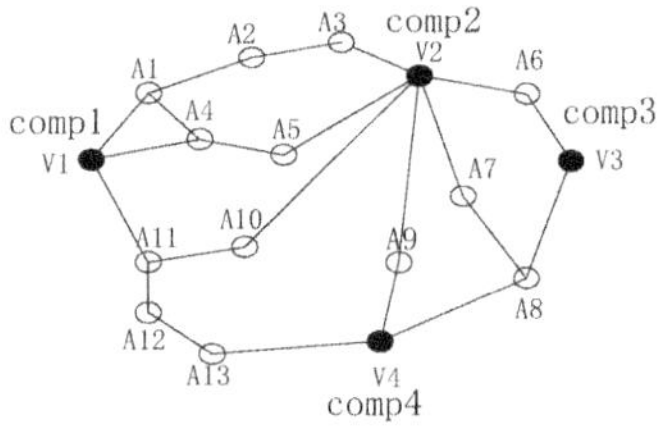

Fig. 2. Abstract Communication Graph $G_c{}'$

If we assign weight 1 to each edge in $G_c{}'$, selecting the minimal number of additional sensors needed to connect the components in G_c is equivalent to solving the Steiner Minimum Tree problem in the 1-weighted graph $G_c{}'$, where the virtual vertices representing components are considered as "terminals" and the needed assistant sensors are those "Steiner points" that are needed to construct the Steiner Minimum Tree to connect all the terminals. We present the SMT-based connection algorithm in Algorithm 2.

Algorithm 2 SMT-based Connection Algorithm

1: Create the 1-weighted abstract communication graph $G_c{}'$ as described
2: Calculate the Steiner Minimum Tree (SMT) to connect all virtual vertices in $G_c{}'$.
3: Return all the assistant sensors corresponding to the Steiner points in the computed SMT.

4 Performance Evaluation

To evaluate the performance of the proposed algorithms, we have constructed a simulator in C programming language under Linux operating system. The target region is a square of size 400×400. The default sensing radius is 30. We change the communication radius to evaluate the performance under different ratio of R_c to R_s. To ensure the target region is completely covered by the initial sensor network and the initial network is connected when all sensors are active, we first divide the region into grid cells with dimension of 40 and deploy one sensor at the center of each grid cell. In this deployment, the minimal communication range that can ensure network connectivity is 40. When the sensing range is 30, each sensor can only cover the grid where it is located. So we can expect the minimal size of the cover set is about 100 when the sensing range is 30. Besides the 100 fixed sensors, we also randomly deploy lots of sensors in the region.

4.1 Comparison with Greedy Algorithm

The greedy algorithm in [9] is also a centralized algorithm. This algorithm firstly needs to divide the target region into many subelements, where points in the same subelement are covered by the same set of sensors.

As stated in [9], the maximum number of subelements on a 2-demensional plane with n circles is $n(n+1)$. When there are totally K sample points needed to be examined, the preprocessing of generating subelements takes $O(Kn^3)$ [6]. The number of sample points is related to the size of the region and the grid cell. And the size of the grid cell is closely related to the coverage accuracy. Larger cell size can result in smaller K, thus less time is needed, but the coverage performance becomes worse. In application that requires every point is covered at least by one sensor, the size of the grid cell must be small enough. On the other hand, the region monitored by sensor networks is usually vast. Therefore the number of sample points is usually several orders of magnitude of the number of the sensors in the network, i.e., $K \gg n$. Therefore the time complexity of the greedy algorithm is much larger than that of CVT algorithm.

The comparison of the size of the connected cover set constructed by the greedy algorithm and our proposed algorithms is illustrated in Fig.3. It is clear that both the CVT and CVT+SMT algorithms generate much smaller CCS than the greedy algorithm when $R_s = 30$ and $R_c = 60, 40$ respectively. While the algorithm in [9] is globally greedy, our proposed algorithm can definitely identify all non-redundant sensors that must be kept active, all independently

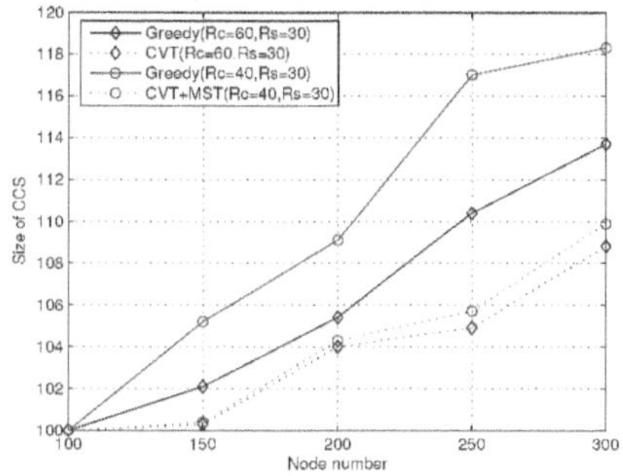

Fig. 3. Size of CCS

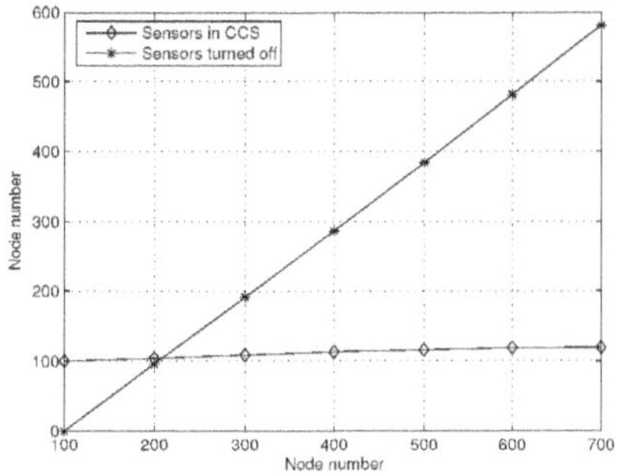

Fig. 4. Size of CCS and number of off-duty nodes vs. node density ($R_s = 30, R_c = 60$)

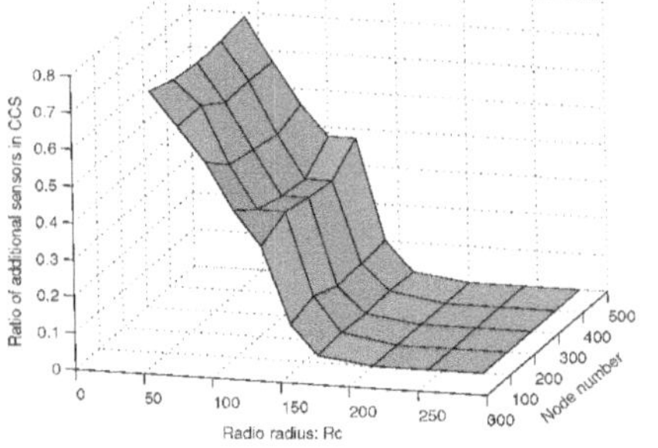

Fig. 5. Ratio of additional sensor in final CCS

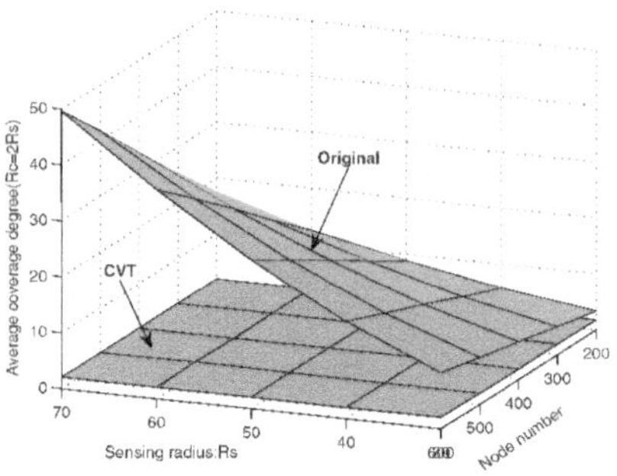

Fig. 6. Average coverage degree vs. node density

redundant sensors that can be safely turned off, and only apply the greedy algorithm to determine the maximal number of dependently redundant sensors that can be turned off simultaneously.

In summary, our proposed algorithm outperforms the greedy algorithm in terms of both the time complexity and the size of the final connected cover set (i.e., the number of sensors that must be kept active).

4.2 Simulation Results

Fig.4 shows how the size of CCS and the number of the sensors turned off vary when the number of deployed sensors changes from 100 to 700. Initially, when there are only 100 fixed sensors in the region, all sensors must be active to provide the coverage and connectivity. We observe that the size of CCS constructed by the CVT algorithm almost keeps constant and is very close to the expected number of active sensors, i.e., 100 when $R_c \geq 2R_s$. Note these 100 sensors are not the same as the 100 fixed sensor nodes.

When $R_c < 2R_s$, more additional sensors are needed to maintain the communication connectivity. Fig.5 shows the ratio of additional sensor nodes calculated by the SMT connection algorithm in the final CCS under different node density and sensing radius.

The average coverage degree can reflect the sensing redundancy of the network. To calculate the sensing degree, we divide the region into 1×1 unit cells and assume an event occurs at the center of each cell. The coverage degree is defined as the number of sensors that can detect the event. As illustrated in Fig.6, although the original sensing degree varies from 3 to 50, our proposed CVT algorithm can result in about 2 degree when $R_c = 2R_s$.

5 Conclusions

In this paper, we have designed centralized algorithms to construct a minimal connected cover set for wireless sensor networks. The basic idea is to calculate the cover set firstly and then make it connected if needed. We propose a centralized, Voronoi tessellation (CVT) based algorithm to calculate the near optimal cover set for the target region. The constructed cover set is connected if $R_c \geq 2R_s$. In case of $R_c < 2R_s$ where the cover set constructed by the CVT algorithm is not connected, we design a Steiner minimum tree (SMT) based algorithm to compute the minimal set of additional sensors needed to make the cover set connected. Theoretical analysis and simulation results show that our proposed algorithm outperforms the greedy algorithm.

References

1. I. F. Akyildiz, W. Su, Y. Sankarasubramaniam and E. Cayirci, Computer Networks (Elsevier). Vol.38 (4). March. 2002.
2. J. Elson and D. Estrin, Wireless Sensor Networks(Kluwer), 3-20 2004
3. S. Slijepcevic and M. Potkonjak. Power Efficient Organization of Wireless Sensor Networks. in Proc. of IEEE ICC'01, Helsinki, Finland, 2001.
4. F. Ye, G. Zhong, S. Lu, and L. Zhang. Peas: A Robust Energy Conserving Protocol for Long-Lived Sensor Networks. in Proc. of ICDCS, 2003.
5. D. Tian and N. D. Georganas. A Coverage-Preserving Node Scheduling Scheme for Large Wireless Sensor Networks. in Proc. of WSNA'02, Atlanta, Georgia, USA, 2002.
6. H. Chen, H. Wu, and N. Tzeng. Grid-Based Approach for Working Node Selection in Wireless Sensor Networks. in Proc. of IEEE International Conference on Communications (ICC), Paris, France, 2004.
7. B. Carbunar, A. Grama, J. Vitek and O. Carbunar, *Proceedings of the 1st IEEE Communications Society Conference on Sensor and Ad Hoc Communications and Networks (SECON)*, 377-386 (2004).
8. T. Yan, T. He, and J. Stankovic. Differentiated Surveillance Service for Sensor Networks. in Proc. of SenSys'03, Los Angels, CA, USA, 2003.
9. H. Gupta, S. R. Das, and Q. Gu. Connected Sensor Cover: Self-Organization of Sensor Networks for Efficient Query Execution. in Proc. of MobiHoc'03, Annapolis, Maryland, USA, 2003.
10. A. Okabe, B. Boots, K. Sugihara, and S. N. Chiu. Spatial Tessellations: Concepts and Applications of Voronoi Diagram. John Wiley & Sons, New York, 1999.
11. D. S. Hochbaum. Approximation Algorithms for Np-Hard Problems. PWS Publishing Company, 1995.
12. H. Zhang and J. C. Hou. Maintaining Sensing Coverage and Connectivity in Large Sensor Networks. Proceedings of NSF International Workshop on Theoretical and Algorihtmic Aspects of Sensors, Ad Hoc Wireless, and Peer-to-Peer Networks, 2004.

Near Optimal and Energy-Efficient Scheduling for Hard Real-Time Embedded Systems*

Amjad Mohsen and Richard Hofmann

Department of Communication Systems and Computer Networks,
University of Erlangen, Martensstr. 3, 91058 Erlangen, Germany
Amjad.muhsen@infromatik.uni-erlangen.de, rhofmann@cs.fau.de

Abstract. In this paper, we present a new energy-aware scheduling scheme for real-time applications using architectures that employ voltage scaling technologies. Both dynamic voltage scaling (DVS) and dynamic threshold voltage scaling (DVTHS) can benefit from this scheduling scheme. The start time of each task is adapted to enhance the efficiency of voltage scaling schemes while still satisfying the required time feasibility. The introduced scheduling scheme is able to escape local minima and it can generate near-optimal schedules in terms of energy reduction. The scheduling paradigm is integrated into our automated and multiobjective system-level co-synthesis tool that performs system optimization. We report in this paper up to about 30% higher energy reduction compared to only performance-aware scheduling.

1 Introduction

The complexity of real-time embedded systems is increasing rapidly with a non-stopping demand for higher performance. Especially for mobile systems, power consumption is a real challenge since these systems depend on a battery that can supply energy only for limited time. The steady move towards deep submicron technologies will make power rather dominate all other design constraints. Therefore, new methodologies and automated tools are required to handle design tradeoffs at all abstraction levels in order to sharply reduce the consumed energy. Without such methodologies that deal with all requirements and tradeoffs concurrently, designed systems will continue to dissipate unnecessary energy that can be saved by using more efficient and energy-aware design tools.

A prominent approach which remarkably reduces total power/energy consumption is dynamic voltage scaling (DVS). DVS was proposed in order to trade performance for power without loosing the peak performance of the system [1]. Reducing the supply voltage by a factor of two in DVS-enabled systems reduces the consumed (dynamic) energy by a factor of four. As technologies continue to scale down, the leakage power will account to about 50% of the total consumed power or even more. Applying DVS alone can achieve only linear reduction in the leakage power. An efficient scheme which can limit the leakage power is adaptive body biasing (ABB).

* We are grateful indeed that DAAD (German Academic Exchange Service) supports this research since 2002.

L.T. Yang et al. (Eds.): EUC 2005, LNCS 3824, pp. 234 – 244, 2005.

In this scheme, the threshold voltage is modified based on demand according to the state of the system and its workload [2]. This scheme can cause exponential reduction in leakage power.

Applying voltage scaling schemes to exploit slack intervals in the system can reduce the total power/energy dissipated in digital systems. However, the availability of enough slack intervals and their distribution, which are directly influenced by the time schedule of the tasks, are crucial efficiency issues for voltage scaling schemes. Additionally, it is essential to consider power profiles of the tasks in distributed embedded systems when deriving the schedule [4]. Therefore, additional power/energy reduction can be achieved when the time schedule is planned with these issues in mind. The time schedule should be modified to enable tasks which are major consumers of energy to exploit longer slack intervals when applying voltage scaling.

This paper is organized as follows: The next section surveys some energy-aware related approaches. Section 3 reviews our energy-aware co-synthesis approach. Section 4 introduces basic concepts in voltage scaling schemes. In section 5, we present the proposed time scheduling algorithm. The obtained experimental results are presented and analyzed in section 6. We conclude this paper in section 7.

2 Related Work

Many approaches were proposed to solve the scheduling problem while considering energy issues. Gruian and Kuchcinski introduced a task scheduling heuristic based on list-scheduling [3]. The scheme dynamically calculated priorities of the tasks and tried to choose the best supply voltage levels (assuming DVS-enabled architectures) that minimize the consumed energy. The presented priority function was aware of energy aspect but might fail when the deadline was tight. To compensate for this drawback, a priority function tuning mechanism was used.

A static voltage scheduling problem was proposed and formulated as an integer linear programming (ILP) problem in [4]. The tasks were assumed to have different average switching capacitance per cycle to consider processing elements' power profiles. It was shown that considering the power profile when scaling the voltage could be a source of additional power reductions. Some other studies also reached a similar conclusion [5], [6]. However, these studies were done for single processor systems and did not show the effect of scheduling in the time domain on the performance of the voltage scheduler.

Grajcar suggested a genetic list scheduling algorithm without tackling the power problem [7]. In this approach, each individual represented an encoded schedule and the individuals of a population are ranked based on their fitness. A similar approach was used by Schmitz et al. in [8] to achieve energy–efficient scheduling when using DVS-enabled architectures. Priorities of the tasks were encoded into priority strings which are iteratively optimized by an evolutionary algorithm. The list scheduler then determines the start execution time based on the optimized priorities. The authors suggested the genetic list-based scheduling algorithm inside a global mapping optimization loop which was based on genetic algorithms.

Part of the proposed approaches may fail under stringent delay constraints. Others did not concretely tackle factors which have significant influence on total reduced energy such as continuous slack availability and distribution. We propose in this paper a near-optimum energy-aware scheduling scheme which modifies the time schedule iteratively in order to maximize the achieved energy reduction assuming that voltage scaling enabled architectures are used. The lengths of slack intervals available in the time schedule as well as their distribution are *improved* to achieve higher energy reduction. Different from previous approaches, our scheme has the ability to escape local minima. The scheduling algorithm is integrated inside our own automated genetic-based co-synthesis tool.

3 Overview of System-Level Co-synthesis

System-level synthesis is considered here as mapping a behavioural description onto a structural specification. Functional objects have the granularity of algorithms, tasks, procedures, etc, while structural objects are processors, ASICs, buses, etc. In order to automate the synthesis process, system specification is captured into a system model.

3.1 System Model

The system is described here using two graphs: a task graph (*TG*), and an architecture graph (*AG*). Both graphs are automatically generated from SDL/MSC specification. The *TG* is a directed acyclic graph $F_p(\Psi,\Omega)$, where Ψ represents the set of vertices in the graph $(\psi_i \in \Psi)$ and Ω is the set of directed edges representing precedence constraints and data dependencies $(\omega_i \in \Omega)$. Hard real-time constraint(s) T_i is/are forced on a node or a set of nodes as well as an absolute time constraint T_T. The *AG* is $F_A(\Theta,\Re)$, where Θ stands for the set of available architectures $(\theta_i \in \Theta)$ and $(\rho_i \in \Re)$ represents possible connections between hardware components. For each component $(\theta_i \in \Theta)$, a finite set of resource types (S) is defined. For each resource type ($s_i \in S$) there is a set of associated ratios (R_s) that specify power-, delay-, and cost-scaling when using this type.

3.2 Optimization Approach

System-level synthesis requires optimizing three basic sub-problems: First, allocation (α) which selects a set of hardware components for implementation purposes. Second, mapping (β) which determines which single hardware resource is used to execute each task. Based on the allocation and mapping, the schedule of tasks is then optimized to achieve time feasibility and to maximize energy saving when applying voltage scaling. In our approach, a voltage schedule specifies the voltage levels required to execute each task. Therefore, the schedule (sc) includes a time and a voltage schedule. The time schedule is optimized to achieve time feasibility and to maximize simultaneously energy reduction when applying voltage scaling.

The synthesis process is considered in our approach as a multiobjective optimization problem which can be stated as: *minimize the function* $f(\alpha,\beta,sc) = (f_1(\alpha,\beta,sc), f_2(\alpha,\beta,sc), f_3(\alpha,\beta,sc))$ while all design constraints are satisfied. This formulation considers three objectives: performance (f_1), power (f_2), and cost (f_3). The proposed synthesis methodology applies evolutionary algorithms (EAs) to optimize the allocation/binding (global optimization) based on the objective vectors (f_1, f_2, f_3). The schedule is optimized for each individual separately as an integrated part of the global optimization loop. EAs are suitable for such optimization problems since they work in parallel on a population of individuals. Each individual encodes a potential implementation. Also, EAs work well on problems with large search spaces.

The EA consists of an optimization loop inside which the principles of reproduction, crossover and mutation are applied on the population's individuals. The purpose is to find iteratively better population based on a set of design objectives. Each individual is evaluated and assigned a fitness value based on the objective vector and fittest individuals are allowed to mate. Fitness values reflect the superiority of each individual in terms of *all* objectives. Computing fitness and performing selection are carried out by the widely used evolutionary optimizer, SPEA2 which is integrated to our synthesis tool. SPEA2 is an up-to-date optimizer which offers several merits over normal evolutionary approaches [9]. The optimization loop terminates when the pre-specified condition(s) is/are satisfied. A set of implementation alternatives which spans the Pareto-optimal front are produced. Each implementation alternative includes an allocation, a mapping, and a time- and voltage-schedule. The designer selects one of these design alternatives based on market requirements.

4 Voltage Scaling

Because of its quadratic relationship to power, voltage reduction has the most drastic means of reducing total consumed power/energy. DVS increases the energy efficiency of a device by dynamically adapting its speed and voltage as needed. However, in heterogeneous systems, the variation in the power profiles of the tasks when executed on different components influences the amount of energy reduction that can be achieved when scaling the voltage. This can be seen in the equation below:

$$E'(\psi_i) = \left(\frac{V_{level}^2}{V_{supply}^2} \right) E(\psi_i) \Big|_{V = V_{supply}} \tag{1}$$

In the above equation, $E'(\psi_i)$ refers to the energy consumed by task ψ_i after scaling the operating voltage to V_{level} ($V_{level} \leq V_{supply}$). $E(\psi_i)$ stands for the energy consumed by this task at nominal voltage (V_{supply}) based on a certain mapping. Therefore, the higher the consumed power and the lower the adopted voltage level to execute a task the more energy reduction is achieved.

Voltage scaling schemes can also be applied to limit the amount of consumed leakage power in digital circuits. Dynamic threshold voltage (V_{th}) scaling (DVTHS) is a candidate scheme which dynamically adapts V_{th} by means of varying the body bias voltage (V_{bs}) in order to save leakage power. The relationship between V_{bs} and the consumed static power (P_{static}) is given below:

$$P_{static} = V_{dd} K_3 e^{K_4 V_{dd}} e^{K_5 V_{bs}} + |V_{bs}| I_j \tag{2}$$

In this equation, V_{dd} is the supply voltage, K_3, K_4, K_5, are constant fitting parameters which are technology dependent, and I_j is the current due to junction leakage [2].

Voltage scaling is an efficient method to reduce the total consumed power/energy. Nevertheless, scaling the voltage has negative influence on circuit delay which can be formulated as follows [2]:

$$D = \frac{K_6 L_d V_{dd}}{((1+K_1)V_{dd} + K_2 V_{bs} V_{bs} - V_{th1})^{\alpha}} \tag{3}$$

In this equation, K_1, K_2, K_6, and V_{th1} are circuit dependent constants. L_d is the logic depth and α is the logic depth which is technology dependent ($1.4 \leq \alpha \leq 2$). Hence, voltage scaling mechanisms can only be applied if degradation in performance can be tolerated. Key efficiency factors for voltage scaling schemes are the availability of enough continuous slack intervals and the way in which these intervals are exploited. The proposed scheduling scheme which is presented in the next section handles these issues efficiently. It constructs a time schedule which considers future needs of voltage scaling schemes. Without any loss of generality, we examined the proposed algorithms by applying DVS only.

5 Energy-Efficient Time Scheduling

Scheduling in our case can be defined as determining the start time and the required voltage level(s) needed to execute each task. Precedence constraints and data dependencies must be fulfilled. Hence, the problem can be seen here as a two dimensional (2-D) optimization problem. The start time of each task ψ_i, $\tau_i(t)$, and the voltage level(s) $V(\tau) = \{v_1, v_2, \ldots, v_n\}$ should be optimized to maximize the power/energy reduction. In our approach, the time schedule is determined first with an *eye on energy*. Based on the derived time schedule, the voltage schedule is determined based on a global view of all tasks. So, the objective is to optimize the start execution time of each task such that more energy reduction can be achieved when applying voltage scaling schemes. In this section, the time scheduling is presented whereas the proposed voltage scheduling algorithm can be found in [10].

As mentioned previously, the available slack intervals and their distribution among the tasks are basic efficiency factors for voltage scaling schemes. Considering power profiles of different processing elements when executing different tasks makes the influence of slack distribution more crucial. Therefore, the time schedule has to be adapted such that tasks which are major consumers of energy exploit longer slack intervals. Moreover, tasks which consume more energy should have higher priority to scale their operating voltage when deriving the voltage schedule. The proposed scheduling algorithm considers all these issues as explained below.

5.1 Scheduling Algorithm

The proposed time scheduling algorithm considers *future* needs of voltage scaling schemes in order to maximize energy reduction. The algorithm has an iterative nature and it is based on the paradigm originally proposed by Kernighan and Lin (KL) for graph partitioning problem (min-cut partitioning) [11]. Based on ASAP and ALAP schedules, and the mobility value of each task, initial priorities are computed for all tasks. A list-based scheduler is then used to generate an initial feasible schedule. According to ASAP and ALAP, a task can be scheduled earlier or later as long as no data dependency or delay constraint will be violated. For example, task ψ_8 can be scheduled between 12 and 22 in Fig. 3.

```
Input: Fp(Ψ,Ω), FA(Θ, ℜ), Mapping
Output: Time Schedule: UpToDate_sched

REPEAT
   Unlock all tasks;
   Work_sched = UpToDate_sched;
   C = 0;
   WHILE There is a movable task
      C = C + 1;
       Power_gain[C]  = - ∞ ;
      FOR each task(i) ∈ {movable tasks}
         FOR each scheduling step in the ready list (step_j,r)
            Temp_sched = MOVE_TASK(Work_sched, task(i), step_j,r);
            Temp_gain = POWER(Work_sched) – POWER(Temp_sched);
            IF Temp_gain > Power_gain[C];
                 Power_gain [C] =  Temp_gain;
                 Sequence [C] = task(i);
                 Sched_step[C] = step_j,r;
            ENDIF
          ENDFOR
      ENDFOR
      Lock (moved tasks)
      Work_sched=MOVE_TASK(Work_sched, Sequence [C], Sched_step[C]);
      ENDWHILE
      Select a sequence q based on Power_gain[];
      IF maximum cumulative power reduction (Po_R)> 0
         Update the UpToDate_sched with the sequence;
      ENDIF
UNTIL Po_R < 0;
```

Fig. 1. Energy-aware time scheduling algorithm

The proposed scheduling algorithm iteratively selects a task and a scheduling step based on the ready list of an allocated hardware such that no delay constraint will be violated. The scheduling step that maximizes the energy reduction (when applying voltage scaling) is fixed for this task and the task itself is locked and disallowed to move later unless all tasks are locked. One task is moved at a time and each move leads to a new schedule. The new (*temporal*) schedule is repeatedly evaluated after scaling the voltage. After a set of m such moves, a subsequence of $q \leq m$ that maximizes the total energy reduction can be reached. The schedule is then changed to include these q moves. The process is repeated and all tasks are unlocked until no further improvement in terms of energy could be achieved. This scheduling approach has been chosen because KL is known to find good solutions in small CPU time and it has been successfully applied for long time in various placement and routing applications. At the same time, this methodology allows *bad* solutions to arise and then chooses the set of moves that leads to the maximum energy reduction.

The entire scheduling algorithm is shown in details in Fig. 1. In this algorithm, Work_sched and Temp_sched are temporary schedules whereas UpToDate_sched represents the maintained up-to-date schedule. Power_gain[] stores the power gain for each iteration. The function MOVE_TASK(Work_sched, task(i), $step_{j,r}$) returns a new schedule after modifying Work_sched by scheduling task(i) into $step_{j,r}$; j represents a scheduling step and r stands for the selected ready list. The *function* POWER() takes a schedule and computes its power/energy consumption. The two arrays Sequence[] and Sched_step[] maintain the sequence of moved tasks and the corresponding scheduling steps, respectively.

The iterative nature of the algorithm might appear to be a disadvantage. When all possible moves for each task are considered the time complexity will be $O(n)$, where n is the total number of tasks and moves. At the same time, implementing DVS requires substantial algorithms to determine the required operating voltage and the corresponding speed/frequency. These algorithms affect the performance of the device and increase the overall consumed energy. In our approach, we emphasize that scheduling processes are off-line processes that optimize start time and voltage level(s) required to execute each task during the design phase. The planned voltage levels and the time schedule are stored in a table form for run-time use. As a result, the additional energy consumption related to the scheduling process is omitted and the run-time performance overhead due to this additional process is reduced to a minimum. However, voltage switching cost in terms of energy is still considered during run-time.

5.2 Illustration Example

To demonstrate the influence of the proposed energy-ware time schedule consider the task graph presented in Fig. 2. Tasks' mapping and other supporting information regarding worst case execution time (WCET) and power consumption are found in the table shown on the right hand side in the same figure. Fig. 3 shows an initial time schedule based on the information presented in Fig. 2. The time schedule is derived using a list-based scheduling algorithm and it is presented here as a Gantt chart.

Columns 3 and 4 in the table shown in Fig. 1 give the WCET and the average power consumption for each task according to the given mapping, respectively. The start time for each task according to "as soon as possible" (ASAP) and "as late as possible" (ALAP) scheduling algorithms are given in columns 5 and 6, respectively. The mobility which is defined in column 7 of the same table is defined as the difference between ALAP and ASAP. The priority of each task is calculated based on the mobility. Based on the table shown in the above figure, it can be seen that tasks which have major energy reduction effects (high power profiles), such as tasks ψ_6, ψ_8, and ψ_9, have low priority. This means that they are scheduled in time after other higher priority tasks. As it can be seen in Fig. 3, task ψ_6 has no slack at all while tasks ψ_8 and ψ_9 have both 6 slack slots assuming that the deadline is 26. No other task can make any benefit from voltage scaling schemes.

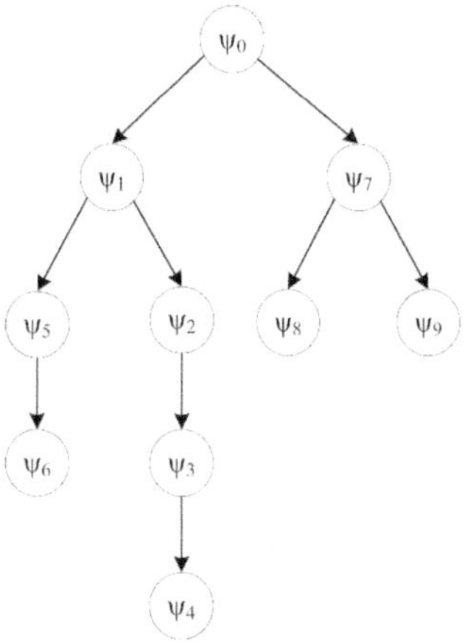

Task	Mapping	WCET	Power	ASAP	ALAP	Mobility
ψ_0	HW1	2	10	0	9	9
ψ_1	HW1	5	15	2	11	9
ψ_2	HW2	4	10	7	16	9
ψ_3	HW2	2	5	11	20	9
ψ_4	HW2	4	10	13	22	9
ψ_5	HW2	4	10	7	17	10
ψ_6	HW1	5	25	11	21	10
ψ_7	HW1	5	15	2	17	15
ψ_8	HW0	4	50	7	22	15
ψ_9	HW0	4	50	7	22	15

Fig. 2. Task graph and mapping example

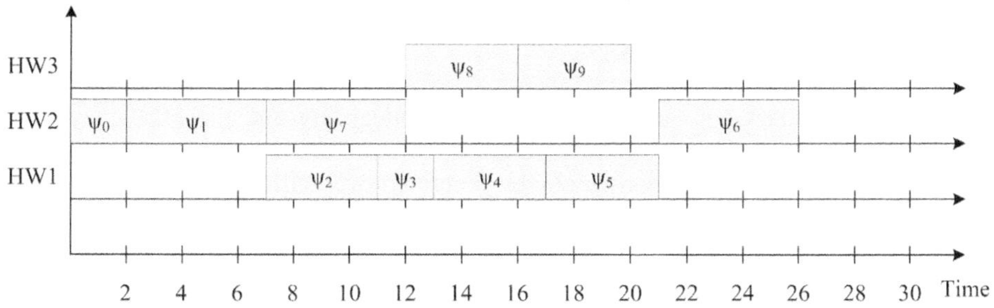

Fig. 3. Initial schedule

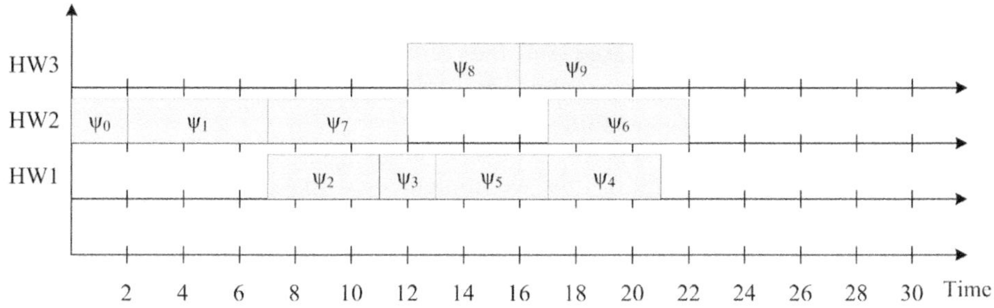

Fig. 4. Modified schedule

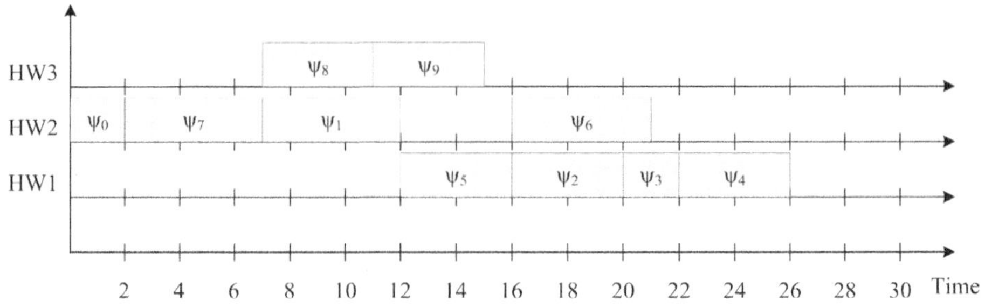

Fig. 5. An energy-efficient time schedule

Consider now the time schedule in Fig. 4 where task ψ_5 is scheduled before task ψ_4, independent on their priorities. As it can be seen in the figure, additional 4 slack slots are now available for task ψ_6 which causes higher energy reduction when applying voltage scaling. A more efficient time schedule from the energy point of view is shown in Fig. 5. In this figure, 9 time slots are now available to tasks ψ_8 and ψ_9. Task ψ_6 has now 5 time slots which can be exploited when applying voltage scaling. In this schedule ψ_7, for example, is scheduled before ψ_1 although the later has higher priority.

6 Experimental Results

A set of benchmarks are used to prove the applicability and the efficiency of our approach in reducing the total consumed energy. The benchmarks include a set of 20 publicly available benchmarks which are generated originally by using "Task Graphs For Free" TGFF [12] and obtained from [8].

Our 2-D scheduling methodology has been integrated to our automated co-synthesis tool which is presented previously. For comparison purposes, another energy-efficient time scheduling algorithm was also implemented and integrated to our tool. This later time scheduling algorithm is called evolutionary list-based scheduling algorithm (ELSA). This algorithm is also based on a list scheduling algorithm. Priorities of tasks are optimized using an up-to-date evolutionary algorithm. An optimization objective is increasing the energy reduction when applying voltage scaling. Based on the *optimized* priorities, the list schedule determines the start execution time for each task. An energy-ware scheduling algorithm similar to ELSA was proposed in [8].

In order to enable fair comparison, the 2-D and ELSA schemes were tested under the same conditions. To achieve this, we implemented ELSA and integrated it to our global optimization tool. At the same time, the same voltage scheduling algorithm was applied in all experiments. To further demonstrate the influence of energy-aware scheduling, another separate experiment was conducted. In this experiment, a traditional list scheduling algorithm was implemented to optimize the time scheduling without considering energy. We call this scheme the 1-D scheduling. Results of this experiment are shown in columns 2 and 6 of Table 1. Columns 3 and 7 present the energy reduction achieved when applying ELSA whereas energy reductions obtained when applying the 2-D scheme are shown in columns 4 and 8 for all the included benchmarks. Obtained energy reductions are reported here in percentage.

Table 1. Energy reduction in % obtained when using 1-D, ELSA, and 2-D scheduling

Benchmark	1-D	ELSA	2-D	Benchmark	1-D	ELSA	2-D
tgff1	68.1	82.6	83.5	tgff11	24.3	30.1	33.6
tgff2	36.4	43.9	49.1	tgff12	62.6	74.6	76.0
tgff3	64.6	70.8	75.9	tgff13	60.9	72.0	73.2
tgff4	82.6	88.0	90.1	tgff14	10.0	26.4	27.6
tgff5	60.1	61.1	61.1	tgff15	14.1	27.4	27.9
tgff6	83.5	87.8	90.1	tgff16	27.4	37.9	39.1
tgff7	30.2	43.3	45.0	tgff17	40.0	58.8	63.1
tgff8	76.6	76.7	77.0	tgff18	31.0	43.5	43.6
tgff9	37.3	38.1	45.0	tgff19	47.0	58.3	76.7
tgff10	19.6	31.7	33.7	tgff20	78.5	84.1	86.6

The above presented results show that all benchmarks made benefit of the 2-D scheduling scheme, but in varying degrees. The maximum energy reduction (90.1%) is obtained for tgff4 and tgff6. The presented results indicate that the 2-D scheduling scheme can perform at least as good as the ELSA algorithm. Additional energy reduction of up to 18.4% could be achieved by the 2-D scheduling over ELSA. This can be related to fact that the 2-D scheduling scheme can escape local minima. It accepts unacceptable moves for the tasks as long as these belong to a scheduling sequence that maximizes the overall energy reduction. The results obtained when applying the 2-D scheme shows that up to about 30% higher energy reduction can be achieved over 1-D scheduling (TGFF19). ELSA can only achieve up to about 19% higher energy reduction compared to the 1-D scheduling scheme (tgff17).

7 Summary and Conclusion

This paper presented a new two-dimensional (2-D) scheduling scheme that is able to remarkably increase energy reduction obtained when applying voltage scaling. This scheduling scheme has the tendency to reach near-optimal schedules in terms of energy when applying voltage scaling. This is achieved by adopting the set of task-moves that lead to a maximum *cumulative* energy reduction which enables the algorithm to escape local minima. Experimental results indicate that up to about 30% energy reduction could be achieved.

A basic conclusion that can be drawn based on the experimental results is that it is essential to consider energy-related issues when optimizing the time schedule. Time feasibility should firstly be guaranteed but at the same time the schedule should be adapted based on certain optimization criterion to increase its energy-efficiency.

References

1. Pering, T., Burd, T., Broderson, R.: Dynamic Voltage Scaling and the Design of a Low-Power Microprocessor System. In *Power Driven Micro-Architectures Workshop*, attached to ISCA'98, Barcelona, Spain, June, (1998).
2. Martin, S., Flautner, K., Mudge, T., Blaauw, D.: Combined Dynamic Voltage Scaling and Adaptive Body Biasing for Lower Power Microprocessors under Dynamic Workloads. In *Proceedings of the International Conference on Computer-Aided Design*, ICCAD'02, (2002) 721-725.
3. Gruian, F., Kuchcinski, K., LEnS: Task Scheduling for Low-Energy Systems Using Variable Supply Voltage Processors. In *Proceedings of Asia and South Pacific Design Automation Conference*, ASP-DAC, January (2001) 449-455.
4. Ishihara T., Yasuura, H.: Voltage Scheduling Problem for Dynamically Variable Voltage Processors. In *Proceedings of the International Symposium on Low Power Electronics and Design*, ISLPED, (1998) 197-202.
5. Okuma, T., Ishihara, T., Yasuura, H.: Real-Time Task Scheduling for a Variable Voltage Processor. In *Proceedings of the 12th International Symposium on System Synthesis*, ISSS, (1999) 24-29.
6. Manzak A., Chakrabarti, C.: Variable Voltage Task Scheduling for Minimizing Energy or Minimizing Power. In *Proceedings of the International Conference on Acoustics, Speech, and Signal Processing*, November (2000) 3239-3242.
7. Grajcar, M.: Genetic List Scheduling Algorithm for Scheduling and Allocation on a Loosely Coupled Heterogeneous Multiprocessor System. In *Proceedings of the 36th ACM/IEEE Conference on Design Automation*, (1999) 280-285.
8. Schmitz, M., Al-hashimi, B., Eles, P.: Energy-Efficient Mapping and Scheduling for DVS Enabled Distributed Embedded Systems. In *Proceedings of Design, Automation and Test in Europe Conference and Exhibition, DATE,* March, (2002) 514-521.
9. Zitzler, E., Laumanns, M., Thiele, L.: SPEA2: Improving the Strength Pareto Evolutionary Algorithm for Multiobjective Optimization. In *Proceedings of Evolutionary Methods for Design, Optimization, and Control, CIMNE,* Barcelona, Spain, (2002) 95-100.
10. Mohsen, A., Hofmann R.: Efficient Voltage Scheduling and Energy-aware Co-synthesis for Real-time Embedded Systems. Tenth Asia-Pacific Computer Systems Architecture Conference, Singapore, October 24-26, 2005.
11. Kernighan K., Lin, S.: An Efficient Heuristic Procedure for Partitioning Graph. *Bell System Technical Journal*, vol. 49, no. 2, (1970) 291-307.
12. Dick, R., Rhodes, D., Wolf, W.: TGFF: Tasks Graphs for Free. In *Proceedings of International Workshop on Hardware/Software Codesign*, March, (1998).

Performance Evaluation of Power-Aware Communication Network Devices

Hiroyuki Okamura and Tadashi Dohi

Department of Information Engineering,
Graduate School of Engineering,
Hiroshima University, Higashi-Hiroshima, 739–8527, Japan
{okamu, dohi}@rel.hiroshima-u.ac.jp

Abstract. In this paper, we focus on power-aware network devices, and propose a stochastic model to evaluate their performance quantitatively. More precisely, applying the Markovian additive process (MAP) to the arrival stream for network devices, we develop a stochastic dynamic power management (DPM) model with shutdown policy. Two performance measures for power-saving and processing; steady-state power consumption and throughput, are derived analytically for the DPM model. In numerical examples, we investigate the performance of the power-aware communication device with shutdown in terms of power-saving and processing.

1 Introduction

Energy consumption is a critical issue for ubiquitous computing such that a huge number of computer systems are embedded everywhere. Since most ubiquitous systems have to process the tasks imposed with the limited amount of power supplied by battery packs, both technologies on power reduction and power saving are important to design the ubiquitous systems with embedded, portable and wearable architecture. Thus the power management to reduce energy consumption has received considerable attention for recent years.

Generally speaking, since computer systems, including ubiquitous systems, consist of a number of electric components and devices, the main issues on power management are to reduce energy consumption in each component such as IC chip, microprocessor, CPU, disk drive, display *etc.* To save energy consumption for a lot of devices, the software-based power management technique seems to be more effective than the hardware-based power reduction from the view points of cost and flexibility. In fact, note that the devices installed in most systems are capable to reconfiguration by software control. The simplest but effective idea for saving electricity is to stop the electricity supply for the devices when they become idle. In other words, when the devices terminate their own tasks, the controller of software-based power management, *i.e.* a power manager (PM), should shut down the devices immediately. Such a software-based power management is often called *dynamic power management* (DPM). DPM is a control scheme that reconfigures components dynamically to serve the tasks imposed

L.T. Yang et al. (Eds.): EUC 2005, LNCS 3824, pp. 245–254, 2005.

with a minimum number of active components [1, 3]. In DPM, two approaches on reduction of power consumption are available: *shutdown* and *variable-voltage*. The shutdown approach is the simplest way for the power reduction, and is to shut down a device when it has been idle for long time. On the other hand, the variable-voltage approach is to reduce the supply voltage for processors. That is, adjusting system speed at the minimum level necessary to processing the tasks leads to drastically reducing energy consumption.

Benini *et al.* [1] discuss the system-level DPM. In their modeling, the system can be mainly classified into three states: active, idle and sleep. In this framework, by taking account of trade-off relationship between processing performance and energy consumption, PM can control the system under the DPM. For instance, when applying the shutdown and the variable-voltage, we can carry out the performance evaluation under these basic DPM models. In particular, Benini *et al.* [3] describe that the control with fixed shutdown timing takes an advantage of the implementation, but in the fixed shutdown policy, the inadequate (shorter or longer) timing of shutdown, may cause a failure for reducing energy consumption. That is, it implies that there is an optimal control policy to save energy consumption effectively in DPM. Srivastava *et al.* [12] propose predictive shutdown policies to improve the fixed shutdown timing by making decisions as soon as the device becomes idle, based on the successive observations for active and idle states. The shutdown policy by Hwang and Wu [5] uses the weighted sum of the last idle period and the last prediction as the upcoming prediction of the idle period, and improves ones in [12]. Unlike these models, the stochastic DPM models are considered in [2, 4, 10]. Qiu and Pedram [10] and Benini *et al.* [2] study DPM models with shutdown by applying the Markov decision processes. In their models, the workload is modeled by a simple two-state Markov chain, and the problem is formulated as choosing the optimal strategies on each state. Chung *et al.* [4] point out that the policy optimization in [2, 10] is based on a priori knowledge of the system and its workload statistics, but that the workload is generally much harder to characterize in advance. Since workloads should be often non-stationary in general, they consider a DPM model for non-stationary service requests. Similar shutdown approaches can be applied to the hard disk power management on personal computers. Sandoh *et al.* [11] develop a simple renewal reward model and derive the optimal timing at which the hard disk device should go to the sleep state. Lu and De Micheli [6] and Lu *et al.* [7] present the computation algorithms for controlling the power states of a hard disk device. On the other hand, as the DPM models based on stochastic processes, Okamura *et al.* [8, 9] develop some shutdown models based on the renewal structure and queueing theory to represent the number of arrival requests, *i.e.* arrival stream of requests, more strictly. In their works, under the circumstance that the arrival process of requests is according to the Poisson process, it is optimal to shut down the device just after each task is terminated, or not to shut the device at all, depending on the arrival rate.

This paper focuses on power-aware communication network devices such as a wireless LAN. In such devices, the problem on power reduction is critical, because the energy consumption of network devices cannot be ignored for the total consuming electricity for mobile system. After developing a stochastic DPM model for the network device and the mobile communication environment, we derive analytically some performance measures on both power-saving and processing. As mentioned before, if the arrival stream is given by the Poisson process, it is proved that the optimal shutdown timing becomes zero or infinity. However, in the practical communication network, the arrival stream for devices might not obey a simple Poisson process, because there is the correlation of requests. This implies that there are the states of high and low arrival rates in the communication network. Thus it is worth noting to consider the modeling with the correlation of requests. For the modeling with correlation, the Markov modulated Poisson process (MMPP) is often used. The MMPP is the stochastic process in which the arrival rate changes according to a continuous-time Markov chain (CTMC), and is one of the simplest stochastic processes to represent correlation of accesses. Since the Markovian additive process (MAP) includes the MMPP as a special case and allows the arrival rate to change at the occurrence of an arrival, it can model the more complex correlation of accesses.

2 Model Description

2.1 Modeling of Arrival Stream

First we model an arrival stream of requests in the underlying network device. Suppose that an arrival stream for the underlying device has a number of internal states which are called phases, and that the transition of phases occurs according to a CTMC. Let $\{J(t); t \geq 0\}$ be the CTMC which indicates the phase at time t, and the corresponding infinitesimal generator is given by

$$\boldsymbol{M} = \begin{pmatrix} -\sum_j \mu_{1,j} & \mu_{1,2} & \cdots & \mu_{1,m} \\ \mu_{2,1} & -\sum_j \mu_{2,j} & \cdots & \mu_{2,m} \\ \vdots & \vdots & \ddots & \vdots \\ \mu_{m,1} & \mu_{m,2} & \cdots & -\sum_j \mu_{m,j} \end{pmatrix}. \tag{1}$$

For sake of simplification, the number of phases, m (≥ 1), is to be finite. The arrival rate of requests depends on the phase, and is governed by a CTMC of phases. That is, from the Markovian property, the arrival rate can be determined only by the current phase. Define the following matrix whose element indicates the arrival rate of request on the corresponding phase:

$$\boldsymbol{D} = \begin{pmatrix} \lambda_{1,1} & \lambda_{1,2} & \cdots & \lambda_{1,m} \\ \lambda_{2,1} & \lambda_{2,2} & \cdots & \lambda_{2,m} \\ \vdots & \vdots & \ddots & \vdots \\ \lambda_{m,1} & \lambda_{m,2} & \cdots & \lambda_{m,m} \end{pmatrix}. \tag{2}$$

The diagonal elements of the matrix $\boldsymbol{D}$ indicate the occurrence rates of requests corresponding to each phase. This rate does not include the occurrence rate of phase transition, *i.e.* the corresponding event is that one request occurs but the phase does not change. On the other hand, non-diagonal elements represent the rates of the simultaneous events that a request occurs and the phase changes.

Let $\{N(t); t \geq 0\}$ denote the cumulative number of requests before time t and $\boldsymbol{P}(t)$ be the matrix whose (i,j)-element is given by

$$p_{i,j}(t) = \Pr\{N(t) = n, J(t) = j \mid N(0) = 0, J(0) = i\} \quad i,j = 1,2,\ldots,m. \quad (3)$$

From the matrix-based Markovian analysis, we obtain the following differential-difference equations:

$$\frac{d}{dt}\boldsymbol{P}_0(t) = \boldsymbol{P}_0(t)\boldsymbol{C}, \quad (4)$$

$$\frac{d}{dt}\boldsymbol{P}_k(t) = \boldsymbol{P}_k(t)\boldsymbol{C} + \boldsymbol{P}_{k-1}(t)\boldsymbol{D}, \quad k = 1,2,\ldots \quad (5)$$

and

$$\boldsymbol{C} = \boldsymbol{M} - \mathrm{diag}(\boldsymbol{De}), \quad (6)$$

where $\boldsymbol{e}$ is the column vector whose elements are 1 and $\mathrm{diag}(\boldsymbol{a})$ gives a matrix with the elements of $\boldsymbol{a}$ on the leading diagonal. Then the stochastic process $N(t)$ is called the Markovian additive process (MAP) with parameters $\boldsymbol{C}$ and $\boldsymbol{D}$.

For example, letting $\boldsymbol{C} = -\lambda$ and $\boldsymbol{D} = \lambda$, the corresponding MAP is reduced to the homogeneous Poisson process with the arrival rate λ. Also, we can represent the switched Poisson process (SPP), interrupted Poisson process (IPP) and the Markov modulated Poisson process (MMPP) with the same framework. Further the MAP models an arrival stream in the practical situation. Actually, if we set the parameters as,

$$\boldsymbol{C} = \begin{pmatrix} 0 & 0 \\ \mu & -(\lambda_a + \mu) \end{pmatrix}, \quad \boldsymbol{D} = \begin{pmatrix} 0 & \lambda_s \\ 0 & \lambda_a \end{pmatrix}, \quad (7)$$

then the associated MAP can represent the situation where a communicative session starts and terminates at the rates λ_s and μ, respectively, and the requests arrive at the underlying network device with the rate λ_a while the session is alive.

An advantage of the MAP is to represent convolutional of arrival streams easily. Let $\boldsymbol{C}_k$ and $\boldsymbol{D}_k$, $k = 1,\ldots,K$ denote the parameters of MAPs representing the arrival streams by respective peripheral devices. Then the total number of requests for the underlying devices is given by the convolutional of these MAPs with the parameters

$$\boldsymbol{C} = \boldsymbol{C}_1 \oplus \cdots \oplus \boldsymbol{C}_K, \quad \boldsymbol{D} = \boldsymbol{D}_1 \oplus \cdots \oplus \boldsymbol{D}_K, \quad (8)$$

where $\oplus$ is the Kronecker sum.

2.2 Modeling of the Network Device

Consider a network device which has the three energy consumption states: active, idle and inactive (sleep). The total number of requests from other devices follows

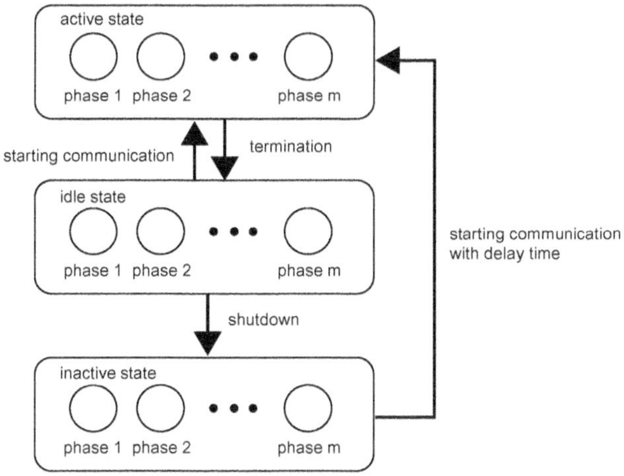

Fig. 1. Configuration of state transition in DPM model

the MAP with parameters $\boldsymbol{M}$ and $\boldsymbol{D}$. To simplify the discussion, the arrival stream has m (> 0) different states of phases. When a request arrives at the underlying network device, the device communicates with the corresponding device. The time required to communicate the other is given by a random variable S having the probability distribution function $F(t)$. During the communication, the other succeeding requests are completely refused. After the communication is terminated, the device waits for next request in the idle state. If no access occurs for a limited time period t_0, PM shuts down the device to save the electricity, *i.e.* the state of device becomes inactive. In the inactive state, when a request occurs, the device starts to communicate with the other device, where it takes a random time delay D to set up for the communication, having the probability distribution function $H(t)$. On energy consumption, it is assumed that the amounts of energy consumption per unit time in active, idle and inactive states are given by P_1 ($>$ 0), P_2 ($0 < P_2 < P_1$) and 0, respectively. Figure 1 shows the state transition diagram of DPM model.

3 Performance Measures

Here two kinds of performance measures will be considered in terms of power saving and processing: (i) Steady-state power consumption and (ii) Throughput. To derive these performance measures, we apply the hidden Markovian method. Define the time period between two successive terminations of communication as one cycle. Taking account of the state transition of phase at each termination, the temporal behavior of phase transition is described by a discrete-time Markov chain (DTMC). Let $\boldsymbol{G}_0(t_0)$ denote the transition probability matrix for phases at time instance of communicative termination, provided that the shutdown time is given by t_0. From the matrix-based Markovian analysis [13], the transition probability matrix is given by

$$\begin{aligned}\boldsymbol{G}_0(t_0) &= \int_0^{t_0} \exp(\boldsymbol{C}t)dt\boldsymbol{D}\boldsymbol{F} + \int_{t_0}^{\infty} \exp(\boldsymbol{C}t)dt\boldsymbol{D}\boldsymbol{H}\boldsymbol{F} \\ &= \{\boldsymbol{I} - \exp(\boldsymbol{C}t_0)\}(-\boldsymbol{C})^{-1}\boldsymbol{D}\boldsymbol{F} + \exp(\boldsymbol{C}t_0)(-\boldsymbol{C})^{-1}\boldsymbol{D}\boldsymbol{H}\boldsymbol{F} \\ &= (-\boldsymbol{C})^{-1}\boldsymbol{D}\boldsymbol{F} - \exp(\boldsymbol{C}t_0)(-\boldsymbol{C})^{-1}\boldsymbol{D}\{\boldsymbol{I} - \boldsymbol{H}\}\boldsymbol{F}. \end{aligned} \tag{9}$$

In this equation, the matrices $\boldsymbol{H}$ and $\boldsymbol{F}$ denote the transition probability matrices for the delay time and the communication time, respectively, where

$$\boldsymbol{H} = \int_0^{\infty} \exp(\boldsymbol{Q}t)dH(t), \quad \boldsymbol{F} = \int_0^{\infty} \exp(\boldsymbol{Q}t)dF(t), \tag{10}$$

and $\boldsymbol{Q} = \boldsymbol{C} + \boldsymbol{D}$. Let us define the steady-state probabilities for phases on the hidden Markov chain, provided that the shutdown timing is t_0 as

$$\boldsymbol{\pi}(t_0) = [\pi_1(t_0), \pi_2(t_0), \ldots, \pi_m(t_0)]. \tag{11}$$

Then it is evident that

$$\boldsymbol{\pi}(t_0) = \boldsymbol{\pi}(t_0)\boldsymbol{G}_0(t_0), \quad \boldsymbol{\pi}(t_0)\boldsymbol{e} = 1. \tag{12}$$

In fact, the computation in Eq. (12) can be reduced into the problem on eigenvalue and eigenvectors for matrices.

(i) Steady-state power consumption
First, we consider the expected time length of one cycle. Since the expected time length depends on the state of phase at the beginning of cycle, *i.e.*, the termination of communication, the expected time length of one cycle is represented by a column vector. When the shutdown timing is given by t_0, the expected time length of one cycle becomes

$$\begin{aligned}\boldsymbol{\tau}(t_0) &= \int_0^{t_0} \{t + \mathrm{E}[S]\} \exp(\boldsymbol{C}t)\boldsymbol{D}\boldsymbol{e}dt \\ &\quad + \int_{t_0}^{\infty} \{t + \mathrm{E}[D] + \mathrm{E}[S]\} \exp(\boldsymbol{C}t)\boldsymbol{D}\boldsymbol{e}dt \\ &= (-\boldsymbol{C})^{-2}\boldsymbol{D}\boldsymbol{e} + \mathrm{E}[S]\boldsymbol{D}\boldsymbol{e} + \mathrm{E}[D]\exp(\boldsymbol{C}t_0)(-\boldsymbol{C})^{-1}\boldsymbol{D}\boldsymbol{e}. \end{aligned} \tag{13}$$

Similarly, the expected power consumption during one cycle also depends on the state of phases at the beginning of cycle, and is given by

$$\begin{aligned}\boldsymbol{\xi}(t_0) &= \int_0^{t_0} \{P_1 t + P_2\mathrm{E}[S]\} \exp(\boldsymbol{C}t)\boldsymbol{D}\boldsymbol{e}dt \\ &\quad + \int_{t_0}^{\infty} \{P_1 t_0 + P_2(\mathrm{E}[D] + \mathrm{E}[S])\} \exp(\boldsymbol{C}t)\boldsymbol{D}\boldsymbol{e}dt \end{aligned}$$

$$= P_1(-\boldsymbol{C})^{-2}\boldsymbol{De} + P_2\mathrm{E}[S](-\boldsymbol{C})^{-1}\boldsymbol{De}$$
$$+ \{P_2\mathrm{E}[D]\boldsymbol{I} - P_1(-\boldsymbol{C})^{-1}\}\exp(\boldsymbol{C}t_0)(-\boldsymbol{C})^{-1}\boldsymbol{De}. \quad (14)$$

From the renewal reward argument on the Markov renewal process [14], the steady-state power consumption is given by

$$C_{ss}(t_0) = \lim_{t\to\infty}\frac{\mathrm{E}[\text{the amount of consuming electricity during } [0,t)]}{t}$$
$$= \frac{\boldsymbol{\pi}(t_0)\boldsymbol{\xi}(t_0)}{\boldsymbol{\pi}(t_0)\boldsymbol{\tau}(t_0)}. \quad (15)$$

(ii) Throughput
The throughput for the network device is defined as

$$T_{ss}(t_0) = \lim_{t\to\infty}\frac{\mathrm{E}[\text{the number of achieved tasks during } [0,t)]}{t}. \quad (16)$$

Similar to the steady-state power consumption, since the network device always processes only one task requested during one cycle, the throughput can be derived as

$$T_{ss}(t_0) = \frac{1}{\boldsymbol{\pi}(t_0)\boldsymbol{\tau}(t_0)}. \quad (17)$$

4 Performance Evaluation

In this section, we investigate the effectiveness of shutdown policy on the network device under the performance measures. In particular, we consider the following four kinds of arrival streams:

Case 1: Poisson process with the parameters:

$$\boldsymbol{C} = -\lambda, \quad \boldsymbol{D} = \lambda. \quad (18)$$

Case 2: IPP with 2-phases

$$\boldsymbol{C} = \begin{pmatrix} -\mu_1 & \mu_1 \\ \mu_2 & -(\mu_2+\lambda) \end{pmatrix}, \quad \boldsymbol{D} = \begin{pmatrix} 0 & 0 \\ 0 & \lambda \end{pmatrix}. \quad (19)$$

Case 3: IPP with 2-phases and the first arrival causes succeeding requests

$$\boldsymbol{C} = \begin{pmatrix} -\mu_1 & 0 \\ \mu_2 & -(\mu_2+\lambda) \end{pmatrix}, \quad \boldsymbol{D} = \begin{pmatrix} 0 & \mu_1 \\ 0 & \lambda \end{pmatrix}. \quad (20)$$

Case 4: Convolutional of two IPPs in Case 3

$$\boldsymbol{C} = \begin{pmatrix} -2\mu_1 & 0 & 0 & 0 \\ \mu_2 & -(\mu_1+\mu_2+\lambda) & 0 & 0 \\ \mu_2 & 0 & -(\mu_1+\mu_2+\lambda) & 0 \\ 0 & \mu_2 & \mu_2 & -2(\mu_2+\lambda) \end{pmatrix}, \quad (21)$$

$$\boldsymbol{D} = \begin{pmatrix} 0 & \mu_1 & \mu_1 & 0 \\ 0 & \lambda & 0 & \mu_1 \\ 0 & 0 & \lambda & \mu_1 \\ 0 & 0 & 0 & 2\lambda \end{pmatrix}. \tag{22}$$

As shown in Section 3, the arrival stream in Case 3 represents the situation where a communicative session starts and terminates at the rates μ_1 and μ_2, respectively, and where the requests occur at the rate λ while the session is alive. In Case 4, we consider the convolutional of such two arrival streams. Also, it is assumed that both communication time and delay time obey the Gamma distributions with respective shape and scale parameters; (m_s, η_s) and (m_d, η_d), *i.e.*,

$$F(t) = \int_0^t \frac{\eta_s^{m_s} u^{m_s-1} e^{-\eta_s u}}{\Gamma(m_s)} du, \quad H(t) = \int_0^t \frac{\eta_d^{m_d} u^{m_d-1} e^{-\eta_d u}}{\Gamma(m_d)} du. \tag{23}$$

Under these assumptions, the mean times of communication and delay are given by

$$\mathrm{E}[S] = \frac{m_s}{\eta_s}, \quad \mathrm{E}[D] = \frac{m_d}{\eta_d}. \tag{24}$$

If PM does not perform the shutdown, then the traffic intensity is given by

$$\rho = \boldsymbol{\pi}_0 \boldsymbol{D} \boldsymbol{e} \mathrm{E}[S]. \tag{25}$$

Note that this is not an actual traffic intensity, because the additional arrivals are canceled while the network device communicates with one device, but is a appropriate measure to evaluate the busyness of network device. In this paper, we set the above traffic intensity as $\rho = 0.3, 0.5$ by adjusting the parameter λ in each case.

The basic parameters are set as follows.

$\rho = 0.3, 0.5,$ $\mu_1 = 0.05,$ $\mu_2 = 0.05,$ $m_s = 2.0,$ $\mathrm{E}[S] = 1.0,$
$m_d = 2.0,$ $\mathrm{E}[D] = 1.0,$ $P_1 = 1.0,$ $P_2 = 10.0$

Figure 2 shows the behavior of steady-state power consumption and throughput. Especially, we illustrate the dependence of each measure on varying shutdown timing. From Fig. 2, except for Case 1, *i.e.*, Poisson arrival stream case, there is a unique optimal shutdown timing which minimizes the steady-state power consumption. Also, the minimum expected power consumptions in Case 2 and Case 3 are lower than those in the other cases, so that the effectiveness of power-saving in Case 2 and Case 3 is relatively higher. Next, we focus on the throughput. In this result, the processing performance of network device becomes higher as the shutdown timing is longer. Although the traffic intensities are fixed as 0.3 in all the cases, the throughput in Case 1 is better than the other cases. In other words, the evaluation of performance is considerably optimistic. This is because the Poisson arrival stream has no correlation of arrivals. Figure 3 shows the results in the case of $\rho = 0.5$. For these results, we can make similar observations to the case of $\rho = 0.3$. Thus the optimal shutdown timing strongly

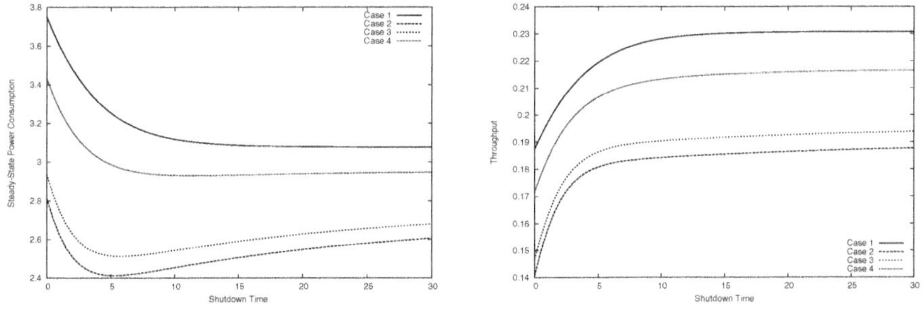

Fig. 2. Performance measures ($\rho = 0.3$)

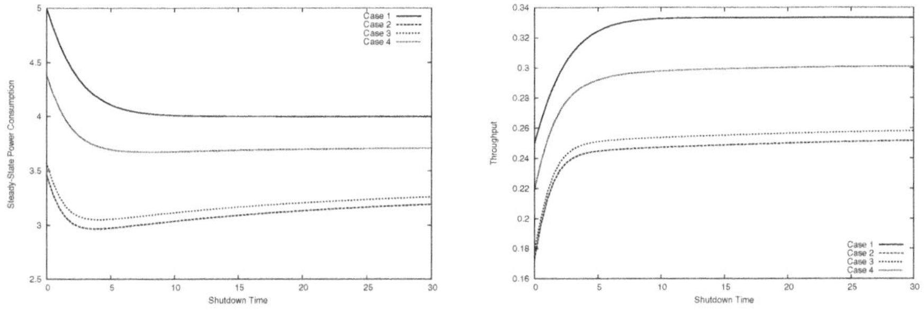

Fig. 3. Performance measures ($\rho = 0.5$)

depends on the correlation of arrivals, rather than the quantities of network traffic. In the situation where the arrival streams are IPPs, the optimal shutdown timing leads to higher power-saving performance in the network device.

5 Conclusion

In this paper, we have considered the power-saving for network devices. Applying the MAP to the arrival stream, we have proposed the DPM model with shutdown policy. Furthermore, based on the DPM model, two performance measures for power-saving and processing have been delivered from the renewal reward theory. In the numerical examples, for four kinds of arrival streams, we have examined the difference on the steady-state power consumption and throughput. As a result, the power-saving performance strongly depends on the correlation of arrival requests. In future, we will develop the DPM model for the network device with communication buffer and the computation algorithm for the optimal shutdown timing.

References

1. L. Benini and G. De Micheli, *Dynamic Power Management: Design Techniques and CAD Tools*, Kluwer Academic Publishers, New York, 1997.
2. L. Benini, A. Bogliolo, G. A. Paloologo, and G. De Micheli, Policy optimization for dynamic power management, *IEEE Trans. on Computer-Aided Design of Circuits Systems*, vol. 18, no. 6, pp. 813–833, 1999.
3. L. Benini and G. De Micheli, System-level power optimization: techniques and tools, *ACM Trans. on Design Automation of Electronic Systems*, vol. 5, no. 2, pp. 115–192, 2000.
4. E. Chung, L. Benini, A. Bogliolo, and G. De Micheli, Dynamic power management for non-stationary service requests, *Proc. 1999 Design Automation and Test in Europe*, pp. 77–81, IEEE Computer Society Press, Los Alamitos, 1999.
5. C. Hwang and A. C. Wu, Predictive system shutdown method for energy saving of event-driven computation, *ACM Trans. on Design Automation of Electronic Systems*, vol. 5, no. 2, pp. 226–241, 2000.
6. Y. Lu and G. De Micheli, Adoptive hard disk power management on personal computers, *Proc. 9th Great Lakes Symp. on VLSI*, pp. 50–53, IEEE Computer Society Press, Los Alamitos, 1999.
7. Y. Lu, T. Šimunić, and G. De Micheli, Software controlled power management, *Proc. 7th Int'l Workshop on Hardware/Software Codesign*, pp. 157–161, ACM Press, New York, 1999.
8. H. Okamura, T. Dohi, and S. Osaki. The phase type approximation for the optimal auto-sleep scheduling. *Mathematical and Computer Modelling*, vol. 38, nos. 11/13, pp. 1391–1398, 2003.
9. H. Okamura, T. Dohi, and S. Osaki. A structural approximation method to generate the optimal auto-sleep schedule for a computer system. *Computers and Mathematics with Applications*, vol. 46, no. 7, pp. 1103–1110, 2003.
10. Q. Qiu and M. Pedram, Dynamic power management based on continuous-time Markov decision processes, *Proc. 36th Design Automation Conference*, pp. 555–561, IEEE Computer Society Press, Los Alamitos, 1999.
11. H. Sandoh, H. Hirakoshi, and H. Kawai, An optimal time to sleep for an auto-sleep system, *Computers & Operations Research*, vol. 23, pp. 221–227, 1996.
12. M. Srivastava, A. Chandrakasan, and B. Brodersen, Predictive system shutdown and other architectural techniques for energy efficient programmable computation, *IEEE Trans. on Very Large Scale Integrated Systems*, vol. 4, no. 1, pp. 42–55, 1996.
13. M. F. Neuts, *Matrix-Geometric Solutions in Stochastic Models: An Algorithmic Approach*, Johns Hopkins University Press, Baltimore, 1981.
14. D. R. Cox, *Renewal theory*, John Wiley & Sons Inc., London, 1962.

An Energy Aware, Cluster-Based Routing Algorithm for Wireless Sensor Networks*

Jyh-Huei Chang** and Rong-Hong Jan

Department of Computer and Information Science,
National Chiao Tung University, Hsinchu, 30050, Taiwan
jhchang@cis.nctu.edu.tw

Abstract. Cluster-based routing protocol has special advantages to enhance scalability and efficiency of the routing protocol. The technique to network clustering that maximizes the network lifetime is an important topic of research in wireless sensor networks. In this paper, we present an energy aware cluster-based routing algorithm (ECRA) for the wireless sensor networks such that the network lifetime can be maximized. ECRA randomly selects some nodes as cluster-heads to construct Voronoi diagram and rotates the intra-cluster nodes to distribute the energy load to all sensors in the network. The simulations show that ECRA algorithm outperforms than direct communication, static clustering and LEACH. The system lifetime of ECRA is approximately 2 times than LEACH. This is because the ECRA rotates intra-cluster-heads to balance the load to all nodes in the sensor networks.

1 Introduction

The technologies of micro-electro-mechanical systems (MEMS) have quickly progressed. These MEMS technologies combine with the wireless communication make it possible to deploy low-cost and low-power sensor network. Many civil and military applications of wireless sensor network such as environmental monitors, informational gathers, battlefields monitors and detecting ambient conditions such as sound, temperature or light. The sensor device has limited energy and transmitting range. Thus, finding the best use for this limited resources is an important and key research topic in wireless sensor network.

Many studies have focused on saving energy in different ways such as reducing the power spent on the modulation circuits[1], or managing the power usage on the MAC layer of sensor nodes [2, 3]. However, these schemes cared of the individual device that is not enough in wireless sensor networks. Since sensor nodes have limited transmitting ranges so that only a few nodes can communicate directly with the sink node. In most cases, the sensor nodes gather sensing

* This research was supported in part by the National Science Council, Taiwan, ROC, under grant NSC 94-2219-E-009-005 and NSC94-2752-E-009-005-PAE and in part by the Intel.

** Corresponding Author. Fax: 886-3-5721490

L.T. Yang et al. (Eds.): EUC 2005, LNCS 3824, pp. 255–266, 2005.

data which must be forwarded by other node to the sink node. These relaying operations consume too much energy such that the relay nodes will rapidly expend much of their energy. Therefore, developing an energy-aware and load-balanced routing algorithms to maximize the network lifetime has become an important research issue in wireless sensor network.

A large number of routing protocols for wireless sensor networks have been proposed. In the fixed path schemes [4, 5], sensor nodes which are in a fixed path will consume much energy and get exhausted rapidly. This is because they provide relaying service. Flooding scheme consumes too much energy for relaying duplicate packets. Source routing schemes [6, 7] improved the drawback of flooding scheme. However, they can not operate well when the number of hops between source and sink is large. Regarding energy-aware, multi-path routing schemes [8, 9, 10] have the advantage sharing the energy between all sensor in the wireless networks. Nevertheless, the disadvantage of multi-path routing schemes [8, 9] is that the sensor nodes only keep a local view of energy usage and the nodes in the network can not have even traffic dispatch.

There are many studies focus on cluster-based energy-efficient routing protocol for wireless sensor networks [11-19]. The Low Energy Adaptive Clustering Hierarchy (LEACH) [11, 12] randomly selects some nodes as cluster-heads and rotates the cluster-head to distribute the load to all sensors in the wireless sensor networks. It's performance is better than direct communication and static clustering routing protocols. However, the issues of LEACH are as follows: First, if the coverage of cluster-head is too small area, then some cluster-heads will not have any member in its cluster. Second, LEACH has a long latency for the base station to receive the data from the cluster-heads. A chain-based enhanced protocol over LEACH was proposed [13]. It allows nodes need only communicate with their closest neighbors and take turns in communicating with the sink. This routing scheme can increases the operating lifetime of each node and reduces bandwidth consumed. However, this scheme assumes that each node maintains a full database about the position of all other nodes, but the method is not outlined. In [14, 15, 16], a family of adaptive protocols that address the classic flooding using negotiation and resource adaptation was presented. Nevertheless, the high degree nodes of this scheme consume more energy and reduce network lifetime. The above cluster-based schemes require global cluster-heads rotation. This cluster-heads re-election increases many processing and communications overhead. Thus, this paper presents a energy-aware routing scheme to reduce the overhead of cluster-heads rotation for cluster-based wireless sensor networks.

Figure 1 shows an example of wireless sensor network with cluster-based routing scheme. In Figure 1, each cluster has one cluster-head. The non-cluster-head nodes transmit its sensing data to cluster-head which forwards the aggregated data to the sink node. The use of cluster leverages the benefits of small transmit distance for most nodes. The cluster-head acts as a fusion point to aggregate the sensing data such that the amount of data that is actually transmitted to the sink node is reduced [11, 12]. Thus, network clustering can contribute to system

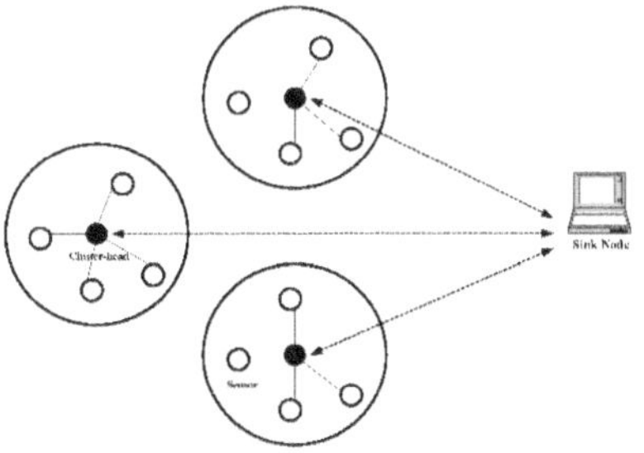

Fig. 1. Wireless sensor network organized in clusters

lifetime and energy efficiency. Cluster-based routing protocol has special advantages to enhance scalability and efficiency of the routing protocol such as reduces the routing complexity [20], reduces the complexity of location management [21], and improves the power control procedure [22]. This technique to network clustering that maximize the network lifetime is an important topic of research in wireless sensor networks. In this paper, we present an energy aware cluster-based routing algorithm (ECRA) for the wireless sensor network such that the network lifetime can be maximized. The ECRA algorithm includes three phases: clustering, data transmission and intra-cluster-head rotation. In our work, we assume that the sensors are location aware. The ECRA algorithm randomly selects some nodes as cluster-heads to construct Voronoi diagram and rotates the intra-cluster nodes to distribute the energy load to all sensors in the network. These are the differences from LEACH. Our motivation is to balance the load to all sensors and avoid too many cluster-heads focusing on the small area. Simulation results show that the system lifetime of ECRA is approximately 2 times than LEACH. ECRA achieves as much as a factor of 9 reduction in the energy dissipation compared with direct communication. This is, ECRA gives better performance than other schemes in system lifetime and energy dissipation. This means that ECRA scheme shares the load evenly to all sensor nodes in the wireless sensor network and it can achieve a better lifetime.

The remainder of this paper is organized as follows. In section 2, we describe energy-based localization. Section 3 illustrates the details of ECRA algorithm. The simulation results and performance analysis are shown in section 4. Finally, the conclusions are given in section 5.

2 The Energy Model of ECRA

In our work, the energy model is the same as in [11]. In this energy model, the electronics energy E_{elec} =50 nJ/bit to operate the transmitter or receiver circuit. The transmitter amplifier $\epsilon_{amp} = 100$ $pJ/bit/m^2$. Equations (1) and (2) are used to calculate the transmission energy, denoted as $E_{Tx}(k,d)$, spend for a k bits message over a distance d.

$$E_{Tx}(k,d) = E_{Tx\_elec}(k) + E_{Tx\_amp}(k,d) \tag{1}$$

$$= E_{elec} * k + \epsilon_{amp} * k * d^2 \quad (2)$$

and to receive this message, the energy expends:

$$E_{Rx}(k) = E_{Rx\_elec}(k) = k * E_{elec} \quad (3)$$

Where E_{Tx_elec} is the energy dissipation of transmitter electronics and E_{Rx_elec} is energy dissipation of receiver electronics. E_{Tx_amp} is the energy of transmitter amplifier. Assume that $E_{Tx\_elec} = E_{Rx\_elec} = E_{elec}$. From equation (3), receiving data is also a high overhead procedure. Thus, the number of transmission and receiving operations must be minimized to reduce the energy dissipation. We also assume that the radio channel is symmetric such that the energy required to transmit a message from node i to node j is the same as the energy required to transmit a message from node j to node i for a given signal to noise ratio.

3 The Details of ECRA

The ECRA algorithm includes the following three phases: clustering, data transmission and intra-cluster-head rotation. The details of the algorithm are given as follows.

Phase 1: Clustering

Initially, the base station randomly selects 5 percentage[1] of total sensor nodes as the cluster heads and informs these nodes that they will become cluster-heads. The set of cluster-heads is denoted as S_c. CH_i represents the cluster-head of cluster i. The set of nodes is denoted as S_n. N_{ij} represents node j of cluster i (It is shown in Figure 2). In this wireless sensor networks, the locations of the sensors are static such that the intersection area can be determined by Voronoi diagram.

We define the Voronoi diagram as follows [23, 24]. Assume that $P = \{p_1, p_2, ..., p_n\}$ stands for the set of points in the n-dimensional space. Their location vectors of p_i and p_j is denoted as l_i and l_j. $l_i \neq l_j, \forall i \neq j$. The region that is given by $S(p_i) = \{l \mid \| l - l_i \| \leq \| l - l_j \|, \forall i \neq j\}$ that is called the Voronoi region. $V(P) = \bigcup_{1 \leq i \leq N} S(p_i)$ is called the Voronoi diagram. The half-space is bounded by the hyperplane that is perpendicular bisector of a segment. $S(p_i)$ is the intersection area of these half-space. Therefore, the Voronoi region can defined as follow. $S(p_i) = \bigcap_{1 \leq j \leq N, j \neq i} h(p_i, p_j)$. Where, $h(p_i, p_j)$ stands for the half-space containing p_i. In our ECRA scheme, the Voronoi diagram is applied for network clustering. The base station constructs Voronoi diagram to cover the sensing field and selects a sensor node as cluster-head for each Voronoi cell. The base station also informs each cluster-head which nodes are its members. The cluster-head broadcasts an advertisement message to their members. After each node known which cluster it belongs, then it informs the cluster-head that it will be a member of the cluster using a CSMA MAC protocol. During this time, all cluster-heads must keep in active.

---

[1] This parameter has minimal normalized total energy dissipation [11].

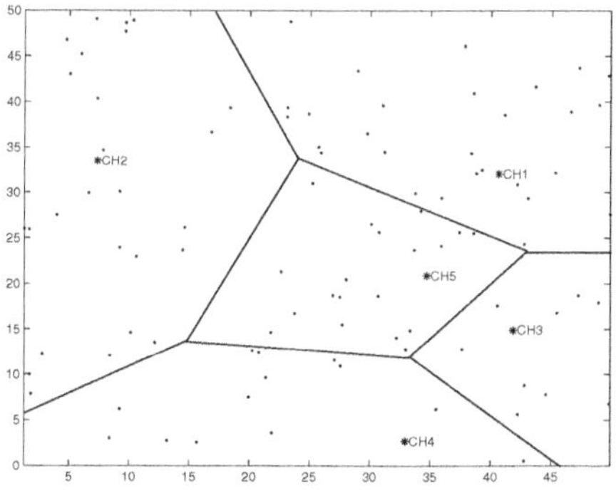

Fig. 2. Voronoi diagram of the 100-node random sensor network

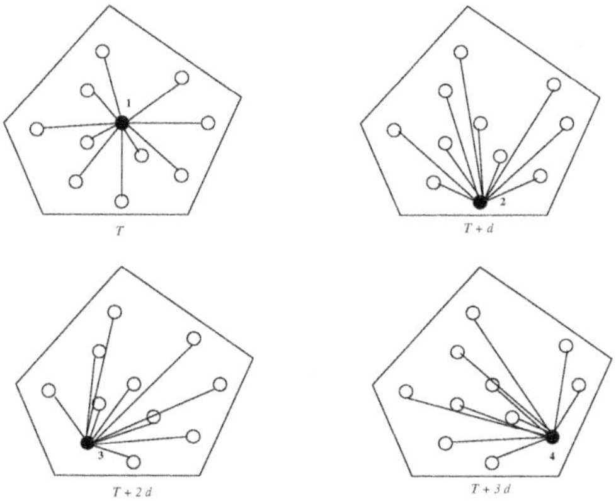

Fig. 3. An example of intra-cluster-head rotation. Where T is the current round and $T + d$ is the next round, and so on.

Phase 2: Data transmission

When the clusters are created such that the data transmission can begin. The nodes use single hop to communicate with their cluster-heads, and the cluster-heads also use single hop to communicate with the base station. Each node has M bits messages to transmit. The non-cluster-head node can turned-off until its allocated transmission time to minimize the energy dissipation. When all data from the nodes has been received, the cluster-head aggregates the total data into a single message to reduce the amount of information that transmitted to the base station.

Phase 3: Intra-cluster-head rotation

When a round is end, then rotate the cluster-head within the same cluster based on a parameter called O_{ij} which considers the distance from node j in cluster i to base station and the residual energy of each node. The distance from node j in cluster i to base station is denoted as d_{ij}.

Table 1. The pseudo code of ECRA algorithm

```
begin Clustering
  Randomly select cluster-heads
   for (every S_c)
     Construct Voronio diagram
   end for
end Clustering
begin Data transmission
while ( data size < M )
      for ( every S_c )
         for ( every N_ij )
           Transmit data
         end for
      end for
end while
end Data transmission
begin Intra-cluster-head rotation
while ( data size = M )
      for ( every S_c )
         for ( every N_ij )
            Calculate O_ij
            CH_i,new = N_ij
            j = j + 1
         end for
      end for
end while
end Intra-cluster-head rotation
```

$$d_{ij} = \sqrt{(X_{ij} - X_{bs})^2 + (Y_{ij} - Y_{bs})^2} \tag{4}$$

$$E_{new} = E_{old} - E_{expend} \tag{5}$$

$$O_{ij} = \frac{E_{new}}{d_{ij}} \tag{6}$$

Where the position of node j in cluster i is at (X_{ij}, Y_{ij}) and the position of base station is at (X_{bs}, Y_{bs}). In equation (5), E_{old} is the residual energy of each node at current round and E_{new} is the residual energy of each node at next round. E_{expend} is the energy expend of each node in the current round. From equation (6), O_{ij} is a function of d_{ij} and E_{new}. The node with the maximal value of O_{ij} will become a cluster-head at the next round (It is shown in Figure 3). When all data are received in current round. The base station informs the cluster-head of current round that the other node will become the new cluster-head $CH_{i,new}$ at next round. The base station has the location of each node andit can calculate the value of O_{ij}. When the current round is end, the cluster-head will rotate to the other node that informed by the base station. Then, the new cluster-head begins to advertise using the same method as phase 1. The pseudo code of ECRA algorithm is shown in Table 1.

4 Simulation Results

4.1 Performance Metrics and Environment Setup

This section presents the performance analysis of the ECRA algorithm. The metrics for performance are given as follows.

1) The lifetime for first node to die (FND): FND is defined as the time that the first node run out of energy. The non-cluster-head nodes transmit their sensing data to cluster-head. The cluster-heads returned their aggregated data to the sink periodically. We use the number of *rounds* to represent the network lifetime of FND. A round is defined as all nodes in the wireless network that finish returning their gathered data to the sink. The time interval between two rounds is assumed to be large enough for last node to return its sensing data.
2) The lifetime for last node to die (LND): LND is defined as the time that last node run out of energy and the network crashed. We also use the number of *rounds* to represent the network lifetime of LND.
3) The total energy dissipation: This value is defined as the energy dissipation for all nodes that finish returning their gathered data.

Four different sizes of deploying regions were simulated. There are $50 \times 50\ m^2$, $100 \times 100\ m^2$, $150 \times 150\ m^2$ and $200 \times 200\ m^2$. In each region, 100 nodes was deployed by uniform distribution. Assume that the energy model is the same as in [11]. The electronics energy E_{elec} =50 nJ/bit. $\epsilon_{amp} = 100\ pJ/bit/m^2$. The energy of data aggregation is 5 nJ/bit/message. There is a 100 - node random network with 5 percentage cluster heads. The sink node was located at the position (x = 25, y = -100). Each sensor has 2000 bits data packet to the base station during each round. We evaluate three performance metrics of ECRA and compare with other schemes.

4.2 Numerical Results

Comparisons of the three performance metrics were made for four schemes: the direct communication (DC), static clustering (SC), LEACH and ECRA. These performance metrics includes the FND, LND and total energy dissipation in the system that will illustrate as follows.

1) The lifetime of FND under different initial energy

Figure 4 shows that the lifetime of ECRA in FND is approximately 1.8 times than LEACH, 13 times than direct communication and 29 times than static

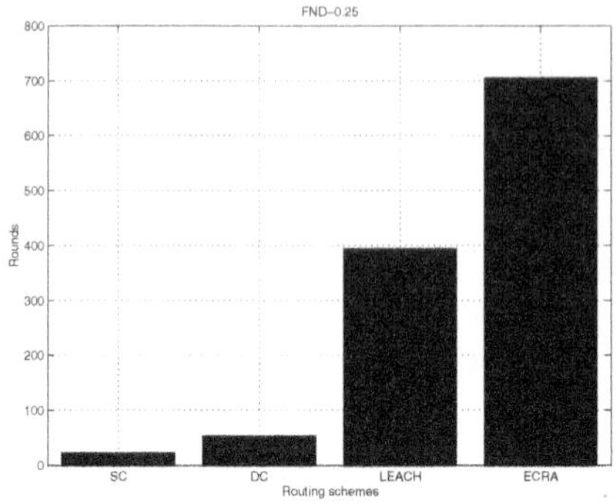

Fig. 4. The lifetime of first node died (FND) under different methods. The initial energy of each sensor is 0.25.

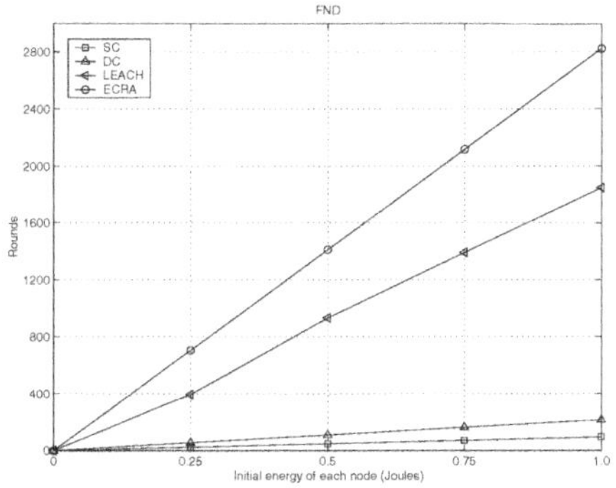

Fig. 5. The lifetime of first node died (FND) using different amounts of initial energy for the sensors

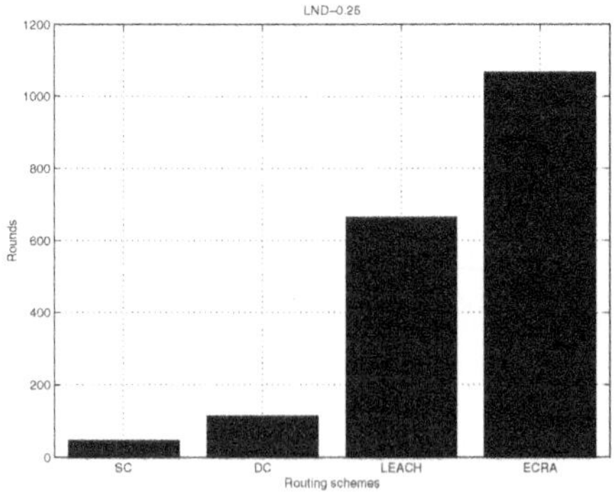

Fig. 6. The lifetime of last node died (LND) under different methods. The initial energy of each sensor is 0.25.

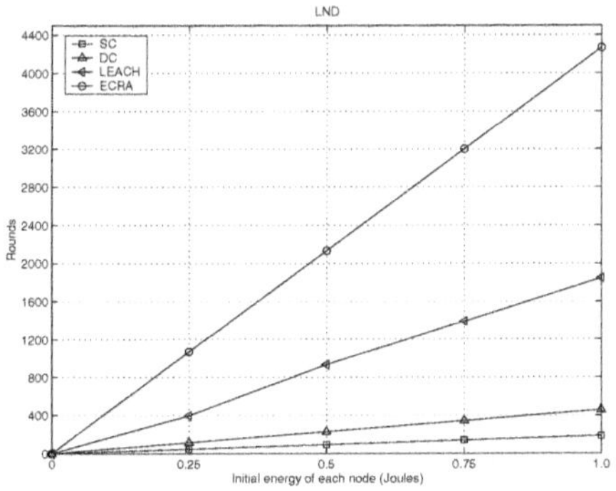

Fig. 7. The lifetime of last node died (LND) using different amounts of initial energy for the sensors

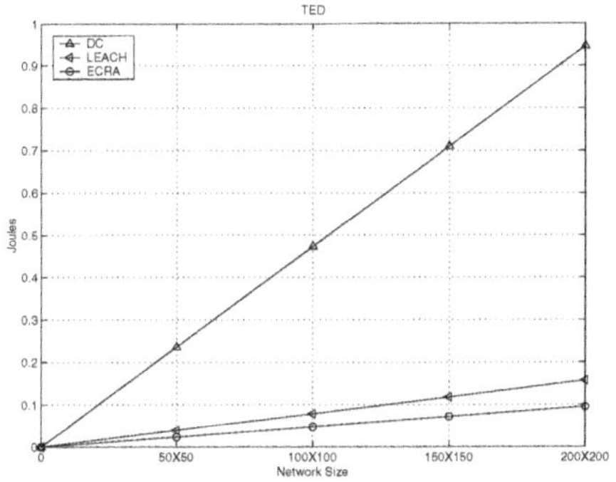

Fig. 8. Total energy dissipation (TED) using direct communication, LEACH and ECRA. The messages are 2000 bits.

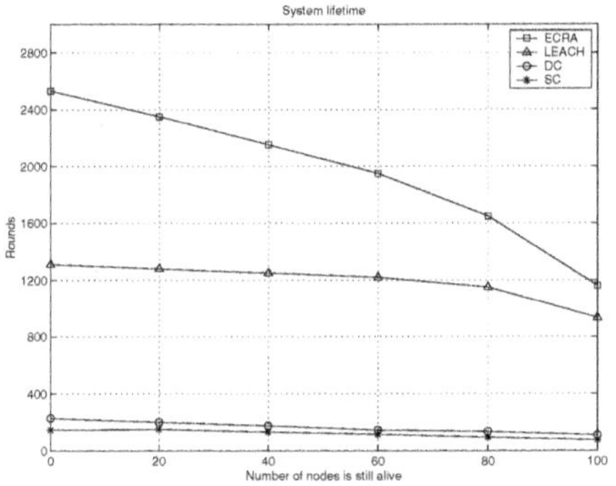

Fig. 9. System lifetime using direct communication, static clustering, LEACH and ECRA with 0.5 J / node

clustering if the initial energy of each sensor is 0.25 J. Figure 5 shows that the lifetime of FND under different methods with different initial energy of each node. Overall, the lifetime of FND is increasing when the initial energy of each sensor is greater. This figure shows that the lifetime of FND in ECRA is approximately up to 2 times than LEACH, over 13 times than direct communication and static clustering. That is, ECRA gives better performance than DC, SC, and LEACH in the lifetime of FND.

2) The lifetime of LND under different initial energy

Figure 6 shows that the lifetime of ECRA in LND is approximately 1.7 times than LEACH, 10 times than direct communication and 23 times than static clustering if the initial energy of each sensor is 0.25 J. Figure 7 shows that the lifetime of LND under different methods with different initial energy of each node. Overall, the lifetime of LND is increasing when the initial energy of each sensor becomes large. This figure shows that the lifetime of LND in ECRA is approximately up to 2 times than LEACH, over 18 times than direct communication and static clustering. The results show, ECRA gives better performance than DC, SC, and LEACH in the lifetime of LND. From Figure 5 and Figure 7, note that a scheme shares the load evenly to all sensor nodes in the network, it can achieve a better lifetime.

3) Total energy dissipation under different network diameter

Figure 8 shows that ECRA achieves as much as a factor of 9 reduction in the energy dissipation compared with direct communication. This means that the use of cluster leverages the benefits of small transmit distance for most nodes and distributes the energy among the sensor nodes in the network can reduce total energy dissipation.

Figure 9 shows that the system lifetime is decreasing when the the number of rounds is greater. From this figure shows that the system lifetime of ECRA is approximately 2 times than LEACH. According to above analysis, our ECRA algorithm has better performance than other schemes in system lifetime and energy dissipation. These simulation results show that ECRA has the advantages of load-balancing and energy-saving.

5 Conclusions

Cluster-based routing protocol has special advantages to enhance scalability and efficiency of the routing protocol. This paper presents an energy aware cluster-based routing algorithm for wireless sensor networks. Compared with direct communication, static clustering and LEACH, our ECRA scheme can achieve longer lifetime. This is because the ECRA rotates intra-cluster-heads to balance the load to all nodes in the sensor networks. The numerical results show that ECRA gives better performance in load-balancing and energy-saving than other schemes. We are confident that ECRA is an efficient and useful algorithm for further wireless ad hoc sensor networks.

References

[1] C. Chien, I. Elgorriaga, and C. McConaghy: Low-Power Direct-Sequence Spread-Spectrum Modem Architecture for Distributed Wireless Sensor Networks. Proceedings of the 6th ACM International Symposium on Low Power Electronics and Design (ISLPED'03). (2003) 251-254

[2] A. Sinha and A. Chandrakasan: Dynamic Power Management in Wireless Sensor Networks. IEEE Design and Test of Computers. (2001) 62-74

[3] Y. Wei, J. Heideman, and D. Estrin: An Energy-Efficient MAC Protocol for Wireless Sensor Networks. Proceedings of 21th Annual Joint Conference of the IEEE Computer and Communications Societies. (2002) 1567-1576

[4] J. Moy: OSPF Version 2. RFC 2178. Internet Engineering Task Fource (1997)

[5] J. Moy: OSPF : Anatomy of An Internet Routing Protocol, Addison-Wesley (1998)

[6] A. Boukerche, X. Cheng, and J. Linus: Energy-Aware Data-Centric Routing in Microsensor Networks. Proceedings of the 6th ACM International Workshop on Modeling Analysis and Simulation of Wireless and Mobile Systems. (2003) 459-468

[7] R. C. Shah and J. M. Rabaey: Energy Aware Routing for Low Energy Ad Hoc Sensor Networks. Proceedings of Wireless Communications and Networking Conference. (2001)

[8] X. Hong, M. Gerla, R. Bagrodia, J. K. Taek, P. Estabrook and P. Guangy: The Mars Sensor Network: Efficient, Power Aware Communications. Proceedings of Military Communications Conferences (MILCOM'01). (2001) 418-422

[9] X. Hong, M. Gerla, W. Hanbiao, and L. Clare: Load Balanced, Energy-Aware Communications for Mars Semsor Networks. Proceedings of IEEE Aerospae Conference. (2002) 1109-1115

[10] K. Sohrabi, J. Pottie: Protocols for Self-Organization of a wireless Sensor Network. IEEE Personal Communications. (2000) 16-27

[11] W. R. Heinzelman, A. Chandrakasan, and H. Balakrishnan: Energy-Efficient Communication Protocol for Wireless Microsensor Networks. Proceedings of HICSS. (2000) 1-10

[12] W. R. Heinzelman, A. Chandrakasan, and H. Balakrishnan: An Application-Specific Protocol Architecture for Wireless Microsensor Networks. IEEE Transactions on Wireless Communications. (2002)

[13] S. Lindsey and C. Raghavendra: PEGASIS: Power-Efficient Gathering in Sensor Information Systems. IEEE Aerospace Conference Procedings. (2002) 1125-1130

[14] W. R. Heinzelman, J. Kulik, and H. Balakrishnan: Adaptive Protocols for Information Dissemination in Wireless Sensor Networks. Proceedings of the ACM MobiCom'99. (1999) 174-185

[15] J. Kulik, W. R. Heinzelman, and H. Balakrishnan: Negotiation-based Protocols for Disseminating Information in Wireless Sensor Networks. Wirelwss Networks. (2002) 521-534

[16] C. Chiasserini, I. Chlamtac, P. Monti, and A. Nucci: An Energy-Efficient Method for Nodes Assignment in Cluster-Based Ad Hoc Networks. ACM Wireless Networks. (2004) 223-231

[17] S. Bandyopadhyay and E. J. Coyle: An Energy Efficient Hierarchical Clustering Algorithm for Wireless Sensor Networks. IEEE INFOCOM. (2003) 1713-1723

[18] M. Younis, M. Youssef, and K. Arisha: Energy-Aware Routing in Cluster-based Sensor Networks. Proceedings of the 10th IEEE International Symposium. (2002) 129 -136

[19] V. Mhatre and C. Rosenberg: Homogeneous vs Homogeneous Clustered Sensor Networks: A Comparative Study. IEEE International Conference on Communications (ICC'04). (2004)
[20] A. Iwata, C.-C. Chiang, G. Pei, M. Gerla and T.-W. Chen: Scalable Routing Strategies for Ad Hoc Wireless Networks. IEEE JSAC. (1999) 1369-1379
[21] W. Chen, N. Jain, and S. Singh: ANMP: Ad Hoc Network Management Protocol. IEEE JSAC. (1999) 1506-1531
[22] T. Kwon and M. Gerla: Clustering with Power Control. Proceedings of Military Communications Conferences (MILCOM'99). (1999) 1424-1428
[23] K. Mulmuley: Computational Geometry, Prentice Hall (1994)
[24] F. Aurenhammer: Voronoi Diagrams - A Survey of A Fundamental Geometric Data Structure. ACM Computing Surveys 23. (1991) 345-405

Energy-Constrained Prefetching Optimization in Embedded Applications*

Juan Chen, Yong Dong, Hui-zhan Yi, and Xue-jun Yang

School of Computer, National University of Defense Technology,
Changsha 410073, China
juanchen@nudt.edu.cn, luckpeople@163.com
huizhanyi@nudt.edu.cn

Abstract. In energy-constrained settings, most low-power compiler optimization techniques take the approach of minimizing the energy consumption while meeting no performance loss. However, it is possible that the available *energy budget* is not sufficient to meet the optimal performance objective. To limit energy consumption within a given energy budget, energy-constrained optimization approach is more significant. In this paper, we present an energy-constrained prefetching optimization approach through which memory or CPU stalls (caused by too early or too late prefetching) can be reduced so that energy budget is met. Optimal performance objective is achieved under a given energy budget. We evaluate the effectiveness of our energy-constrained prefetching optimization approach through simulations.

Keywords: software prefetching, energy-constrained, DVS, embedded applications.

1 Introduction

With the development of wireless, portable and embedded devices, power-aware systems have moved to the forefront of computer research in recent years, among which **Dynamic Voltage Scaling (DVS)** is major low-power techniques [1][2][3][4][5].

Many low-power techniques focus on minimizing the energy consumption with performance constraints. In this paper, we look at the problem from the other perspective: we consider optimized application with energy constraint (limitation). We assume that a limited energy budget (E_{budget}) is provided and it is usually less than the energy bound (E_{bound}) for the optimal performance objective. Such a situation is significant when the computing device depends on the battery power supply, such as military, space, and disaster recovery missions, etc. In this paper, we are concerned

* This work was supported by the National High Technology Development 863 Program of China under Grant No. 2002AA1Z2101 and No. 2004AA1Z2210.

L.T. Yang et al. (Eds.): EUC 2005, LNCS 3824, pp. 267 – 280, 2005.

with energy-constrained prefetching optimization. With our approach, applications optimized with prefetching reach the optimal performance within the available energy budget. Clearly, the compiler can make use of well-known power-aware scheduling techniques (such as DVS) for energy savings. In scarce-energy settings where $E_{budget} < E_{bound}$, we have a serious problem: we have to sacrifice some prefetching optimization performance.

Software prefetching improves performance by effectively hiding memory access latency through overlapping memory access with computation [6]. However, software prefetching does not always implement perfect data prefetching because it requires prefetch instructions are inserted at the right places. Prefetching too early or too late may yield memory or CPU stalls. By reducing memory frequency or CPU frequency or both, we not only can reduce these stalls but also can limit energy consumption within a given energy budget.

There usually exist two imperfect prefetch optimization cases: **CPU-bound case** and **memory-bound case**. In CPU-bound case, prefetching operation is too early or memory access latency is too short so that the prefetched data is provided before actually being used. Although memory access latency is completely hidden, prefetching too early makes memory access completes ahead of the actual data access. We refer to this time interval as *memory stalls*. The second case is memory-bound case, where memory access dominates the whole time and CPU stalls cannot be avoided due to prefetching too late or too long memory access latency. Figure 1 illustrates the behavior of prefetching.

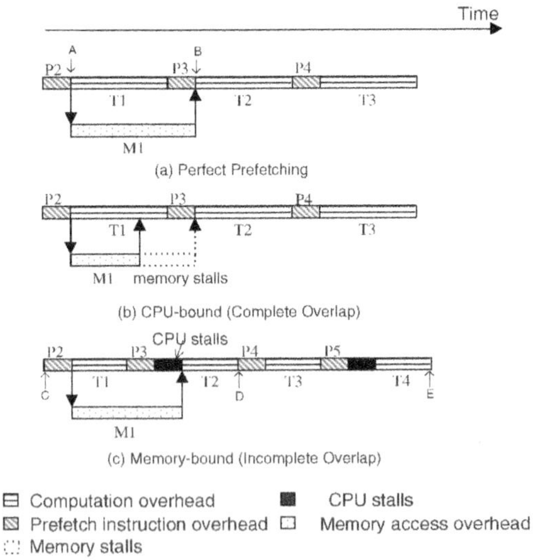

Fig. 1. Prefetching Optimization. P2, P3, P4, P5 represent prefetch instrution overhead for the second, third, fourth and fifth iteration, respectively. M1 represents memory access overhead caused by prefetching. T1, T2, T3 and T4 represent computation overhead in the first, second, third and fourth iteration. Note: here iteration denotes the outmost iteration.

With DVS, we utilize CPU stalls and memory stalls to reduce memory frequency or CPU frequency or both so as to meet scarce energy budget. In CPU-bound case, the major method is to adjust memory frequency to eliminate memory stalls combined with small CPU frequency scaling. In memory-bound case, the major approach is to reduce CPU frequency to eliminate CPU stalls combined with small memory frequency scaling. Furthermore, it is necessary to adjust both of their frequencies instead of one of them for the optimal performance under energy constraint.

In this research effort, we introduce the notion *time* to characterize the performance benefits—*time* denotes the program execution time with software prefetching optimization. Optimal performance objective is minimizing *time*.

When energy is scarce, DVS capability (DVS for memory and CPU) guarantees that maximum performance objective will be met while staying within a given energy budget.

We simulate the impact of different parameters on our optimization. Experimental results show our approach is effective in implementing energy-constrained performance optimization.

The remainder of this paper is organized as follows. Section 2 reviews the related works. In section 3, we formulate an energy-constrained software prefetching problem to an optimization problem. Section 4 gives compilation strategy. Section 5 provides experimental results and analysis. Section 6 gives the conclusions.

2 Related Works

There are a lot of literatures on software prefetching techniques [6][7][8]. Todd [6] provided a comprehensive analysis on software prefetching. Ricardo Bianchini et al. [9] presented analytical models of the performance benefits of multithreading and prefetching. Our work built the energy model of prefetching.

DVS for CPU has been widely researched [1][2][3][4][10][11]. Furthermore, currently power-aware memory has been concerned by some researches besides DVS of CPU [5][12]. Pouwelse [12] alluded to the problem that the high cost of memory may dominate the overall power consumption of a system so that effective DVS of the CPU delivers marginal benefit. Xiaobo Fan et al. [5] exploited a positive synergistic effect between DVS and power-aware memories that can be transferred into lower power states. They believe that the best frequency/voltage for minimizing power consumption should be obtained by including memory power in the decision (The energy savings from DVS alone with standard memory are only 39% compared with energy savings of 89% by consistent method).

We exploited memory stalls and CPU stalls existing in imperfect prefetching and utilized them to reduce CPU or memory frequency/voltage for energy savings.

3 Energy-Constrained Prefetching Optimization

The prototypical loop that we optimize with prefetching looks like:

```
for ( i = 0 ; i < N ; i ++)  Compute ( i ) ;
```

After software prefetching optimization, the above loop is changed into:

```
// iteration 0, prefetch b blocks
prefetch ( 0, b );
for ( i = 0 ; i < N - step ; i += step ) {
    // prefetch b blocks for iterations i+step to i+2*step-1
    prefetch  ( i + step , b);
    // compute iterations i to i + step - 1
    for ( j = 0 ; j < step ; j ++ )  Compute ( i * step + j );
}
for ( j = 0 ; j < step ; j++ )  Compute ( i * step + j ) ;
```

In the above prefetching loop, several prefetch instructions are inserted. The major parameters involved in modeling the energy behavior of the above prefetching loop are the number of the cache blocks prefetched for each prefetching instruction, b; the number of prefetching instructions per iteration, N_b; the energy overhead of each prefetched cache block, E_b; the time overhead of each prefetched cache block, C_p; the total latency of cache misses per iteration, C_m; and the computation between two consecutive prefetch instructions, C_c. Table 1 summarizes these parameters.

Prefetching allows greater flexibility when trying to overlap memory access and computation, since the compiler or user can schedule the prefetches according to the memory access latency and the amount of work per iteration of each loop in the program. This intelligent scheduling of prefetches adjusts b and the iteration *step* size appropriately as the above code segment shows.

The optimal number of blocks to prefetch at a time depends on the available cache space; blocks prefetched into the cache may be replaced before being used. Another limitation is the number of prefetched blocks that can fit in a prefetch/transaction buffer. With these constraints, the amount of useful work that can be overlapped with memory access may be insufficient to hide memory latency completely. To analyze this problem, we simplify it as Figure 1 shows.

Figure 1 illustrates the behavior of the prefetching loop. The execution alternates between prefetch instruction and computation intervals. Each prefetch accessing cache blocks are to be used one computation block ahead. While it is possible to have loops that prefetch more than one computation block ahead, we can always transform such loops into an equivalent loop that prefetches a single computation block ahead.

In Figure 1(a), **P2** denotes prefetch instruction operation, where calculates the data address to be prefetched (b, N_b, E_b are involved). **M1** executes memory access operations caused by prefetch instruction (C_m, f_m are involved). **T2** accesses the prefetched data at point **B** (C_c, f_c are involved). Figure 1(a) shows perfect prefetching behavior. Memory accesses caused by prefetch are fully overlapped with computation, where no CPU stall or memory stall exists. If prefetech instructions cannot be inserted at the right places, two kinds of imperfect prefetchings occur as shown in Figure 1(b) and Figure 1(c). In terms of CPU-bound or memory-bound case, we adjust memory frequency f_m and CPU frequency f_c to meet energy budget.

Our energy-constrained prefetching optimization problem is stated as follows: given a loop L optimized with software prefetching and a DVS-enabled CPU and memory system, find the optimal CPU frequency f_c and memory frequency f_m, then the performance objective (time) is minimized while meeting a given energy budget.

3.1 Energy Constraint

The total energy consumption E_{total} consists of three parts: E_p, E_c, and E_m. That is,

$$E_{total} = E_p + E_c + E_m$$

where E_p represents the energy consumption of prefetching instructions. We assume the number of prefetched cache block per iteration is B, which is the product of b and N_b. Thus the energy consumed per loop iteration is $E_b \cdot b \cdot N_b$ and the energy consumption of the prefetching instructions E_p for N loop iterations is:

$$E_p = E_b \cdot b \cdot N_b \cdot N$$

E_c represents the energy consumption of CPU computation. Due to continuously variable CPU frequency, $P_c(f_c)$ is denoted the CPU power dissipation for CPU frequency of f_c. $\frac{C_c}{f_c}$ represents CPU computation time. Then CPU energy consumption during N loop iterations is:

$$E_c = P_c(f_c) \cdot \frac{C_c}{f_c} \cdot N$$

E_m represents memory energy consumption. Due to continuously variable memory frequency, $P_m(f_m)$ represents the memory power dissipation for memory frequency of f_m. $\frac{C_m}{f_m}$ represents memory access time. Then the memory access energy consumption for N iterations is:

$$E_m = P_m(f_m) \cdot \frac{C_m}{f_m} \cdot N$$

Thus E_{total} can be represented by:

$$E_{total} = E_b \cdot b \cdot N_b \cdot N + P_c(f_c) \cdot \frac{C_c}{f_c} \cdot N + P_m(f_m) \cdot \frac{C_m}{f_m} \cdot N$$

Given an energy budget E_{budget}, the following energy constraint must be satisfied:

$$E_b \cdot b \cdot N_b \cdot N + P_c(f_c) \cdot \frac{C_c}{f_c} \cdot N + P_m(f_m) \cdot \frac{C_m}{f_m} \cdot N \le E_{budget} \quad (1)$$

Power characteristics of CMOS is $P = \alpha C V^2 f$ and the relationship between supply voltage V and frequency f is $f \propto \frac{(V - V_{th})^\beta}{V}$, where V denotes supply voltage, f denotes clock frequency, P denotes power dissipation, α represents the activity factor, C represents the capacitance, V_{th} represents threshold voltage, and β is a proportional factor between 1 and 2. It is reasonable to assume frequency f is linearly proportion with voltage V so that we can get formula (2).

$$P = \alpha \cdot C \cdot f^3 \tag{2}$$

According to formula (2), we can achieve $P_c(f_c) = \alpha_1 \cdot C_1 \cdot f_c^3$ and $P_m(f_m) = \alpha_2 \cdot C_2 \cdot f_m^3$. So formula (1) is transformed to formula (3).

$$E_b \cdot b \cdot N_b \cdot N + k_1 \cdot f_c^2 \cdot C_c \cdot N + k_2 \cdot f_m^2 \cdot C_m \cdot N \le E_{budget} \tag{3}$$

where k_1 represents $\alpha_1 \cdot C_1$ and k_2 represents $\alpha_2 \cdot C_2$.

3.2 Optimal Performance Objective

In the previous section, we have defined performance objective—*time*. To calculate this value, two cases need to be considered. In CPU-bound case (Figure 1(b)), the total execution time of prefetching loop is calculated by prefetching instruction and CPU computation as follows.

$$T_{total} = N \cdot \left(\frac{b \cdot N_b \cdot C_p}{f_c} + \frac{C_c}{f_c}\right) \quad cond1$$

In memory-bound case, CPU stall occurs every other prefetching operation as Figure 1(c) shows. The time interval from **C** to **D** and the time interval from **D** to **E** are the same. We can conclude that the total execution cycles are *N/2* times as many as the execution cycles during **C** to **D**. Since the execution cycles during **C** to **D** are $\left(\frac{b \cdot N_b \cdot C_p}{f_c} + \frac{C_m}{f_m} + \frac{C_c}{f_c}\right)$, the total execution time is[1]

---

[1] Here we assume $N \bmod 2 = 0$. If $N \bmod 2 = 1$, $T_{total} = \frac{N+1}{2} \cdot \left(\frac{b \cdot N_b \cdot C_p}{f_c} + \frac{C_m}{f_m} + \frac{C_c}{f_c}\right) - \frac{C_m}{f_m}$. When N is large enough, this little difference caused by N can be ignored.

$$T_{total} = \frac{N}{2} \cdot (\frac{b \cdot N_b \cdot C_p}{f_c} + \frac{C_m}{f_m} + \frac{C_c}{f_c}) \quad cond2$$

where *cond1* and *cond2* represent CPU-bound case and memory-bound case, respectively. That is,

$$cond1 \quad represents \quad \frac{C_m}{f_m^0} \le \frac{b \cdot N_b \cdot C_p}{f_c^0} + \frac{C_c}{f_c^0}$$

$$cond2 \quad represents \quad \frac{C_m}{f_m^0} > \frac{b \cdot N_b \cdot C_p}{f_c^0} + \frac{C_c}{f_c^0}$$

where f_c^0 and f_m^0 represent initial CPU and memory frequencies, respectively.

The optimal performance objective is:

$$\min T_{total} = \begin{cases} \min(N \cdot (\frac{b \cdot N_b \cdot C_p}{f_c} + \frac{C_c}{f_c})) & cond1 \\ \min(\frac{N}{2} \cdot (\frac{b \cdot N_b \cdot C_p}{f_c} + \frac{C_m}{f_m} + \frac{C_c}{f_c})) & cond2 \end{cases} \quad (4)$$

3.3 Energy-Constrained Optimization Problem

Based on previous analysis, when CPU-bound case, energy-constrained optimization problem is represented as follows.

CPU-bound case		memory-bound case	
$\min(N \cdot (\frac{b \cdot N_b \cdot C_p}{f_c} + \frac{C_c}{f_c}))$	(5)	$\min(\frac{N}{2} \cdot (\frac{b \cdot N_b \cdot C_p}{f_c} + \frac{C_m}{f_m} + \frac{C_c}{f_c}))$	(10)
$E_b \cdot b \cdot N_b \cdot N + k_1 \cdot f_c^2 \cdot C_c \cdot N + k_2 \cdot f_m^2 \cdot C_m \cdot N \le E_{budget}$	(6)	$E_b \cdot b \cdot N_b \cdot N + k_1 \cdot f_c^2 \cdot C_c \cdot N + k_2 \cdot f_m^2 \cdot C_m \cdot N \le E_{budget}$	(11)
$C_m / f_m - (b \cdot N_b \cdot C_p + C_c) / f_c \le 0$	(7)	$C_m / f_m - (b \cdot N_b \cdot C_p + C_c) / f_c > 0$	(12)
$f_c^{'} \le f_c \le f_c^{''}$	(8)	$f_c^{'} \le f_c \le f_c^{''}$	(13)
$f_m^{'} \le f_m \le f_m^{''}$	(9)	$f_m^{'} \le f_m \le f_m^{''}$	(14)

Here formula (7) and (12) guarantee CPU-bound case is still CPU-bound during frequency scaling and memory-bound case is still memory-bound. Inequality (8)-(9) and inequality (13)-(14) define the ranges of CPU and memory frequency scaling. The detailed meaning of each parameter and variable can be found in Table 1.

4 Compilation Strategy

Our energy optimization approach is profile-driven. The prototype implementation consists of four phases. It starts by instrumenting the original program at selected program locations (instrumentation phase). The instrumented code is then simulated, drawing out some profiled data, such as C_c, C_m (profiling phase). Once the profiling is done, all the parameters of this optimization problem are determined. The next work is to obtain the optimal CPU and memory frequencies through solving the above optimization problem (solution phase). Finally, the frequency-setting calls are inserted at the appropriate situations so that the selected region is executed at the appropriate frequency and the rest of the program is executed at the highest frequency (code generation phase). In the future work, we will extend our approach to deal with other program segments besides regular loop segments. The whole compilation framework is shown in Figure 2.

In the next experiments, we will analyze the impact of parameters on our optimization approach and then choose a set of array-dominated applications to validate our optimization approach.

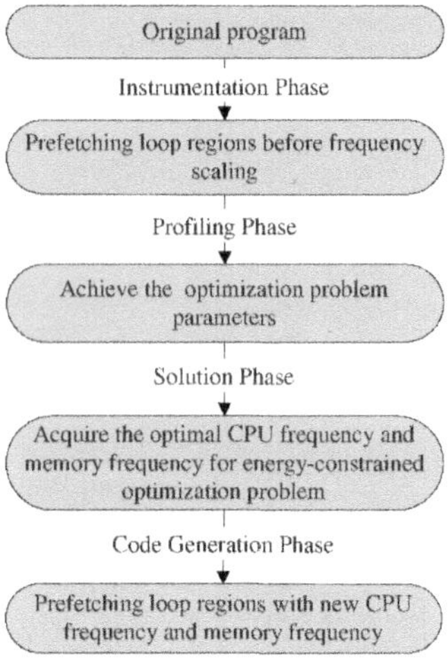

Fig. 2. Compilation Framework

Table 1. System parameters and program parameters for our optimal problemsolution

System Parameter	Meaning	Value
E_b	Energy consumption by a cache block prefetched	10 pJ
b	The number of cache block prefetched by a prefetching instruction	4
C_p	A prefetched cache block computation time	1 cycles
k_1	The coefficient for $P_c = k_1 \cdot f_c^3$	7.72e-27
k_2	The coefficient for $P_m = k_2 \cdot f_m^3$	1.09e-24
f_c^0	Initial CPU frequency	1000 MHz
f_m^0	Initial memory frequency	133 MHz
$f_c^{'}$	The lower bound of continous CPU frequency	433 MHz
$f_c^{''}$	The upper bound of continuous CPU frequency	1000 MHz
$f_m^{'}$	The lower bound of continuous memory frequency	83 MHz
$f_m^{''}$	The upper bound of continuous memory frequency	133 MHz
Program Parmeter	**Meaning**	**Value**
N	Prefetching loop iteration counts	Program specified
C_c	Computation time in once iteration (cycles)	Profiled
C_m	Memory access time in once iteration (cycles)	Profiled
N_b	The number of prefetching instructions in one iteration	Optimization specified
E_{budget}	Energy budget	specified

5 Experiments

5.1 Simulation Platform

In our simulation, CPU and memory both are DVS-enabled. We build a simple energy model for this DVS-enabled CPU and memory in terms of formula (2). That is,

$$P_c = (7.72e-27) \cdot f_c^3 \tag{15}$$

$$P_m = (1.09e-24) \cdot f_m^3 \tag{16}$$

The above formula (15) and (16) also refer to Transmeta's Crusoe TM5900 processor parameters [13]. The summary of power specifications for TM5900 CPU and

DDR can be found in [15]. All the parameters and profiled data for this optimal problem are shown in Table 1.

We use SimpleScalar tool set [14] to profile some necessary parameters such as C_c and C_m. Modified SimpleScalar tool set models a 1 GHz 4-way issue dynamically-scheduled processor. This simulator models all aspects of the processor including the instruction fetch unit, the branch predictor, register renaming, the functional unit pipelines, and the reorder buffer. This modified SimpleScalar tool set enables software prefetching through adding a prefetch instruction to the ISA of the processor model. In addition, our simulator also models the memory system in detail. A split 8-Kbyte direct-mapped L1 cache with 32-byte cache blocks, and a unified 256-Kbyte 4-way set-associative L2 cache with 64-byte cache blocks are assumed. Such cache configuration can meet our input data sets.

5.2 Parameters Analysis

5.2.1 The Impact of E_{budget} on Optimization

We only consider scarce-energy settings, where $E_{budget} < E_{bound}$. To describe the degree of energy scarcity, we define α as the ratio of energy budget to energy bound.

$$E_{budget} = \alpha \cdot E_{bound}$$

As α increases, energy budget is more approach to energy bound so that performance is more approach to the optimal value as Figure 3(a) and Figure 4(a) show, where blue solid lines represent execution time under different α values and black dot lines represent the optimal performance when energy bound is reached.

For CPU-bound case (Figure 3(a)), when $\alpha = 91.1\%$, performance has reached the optimal value instead of $\alpha = 100\%$. In contrast, for memory-bound case (Figure 4(a)), performance doesn't achieve the optimal level until $\alpha = 100\%$. This shows that in CPU-bound case, the optimal performance can be reached at less energy budget (less than energy bound). While in memory-bound case, the optimal performance must be reached with energy bound. In other words, in CPU-bound case, some energy can be saved without performance loss. While in memory-bound case, energy saving must cause performance loss.

Figure 3(b)-(c) and Figure 4(b)-(c) show CPU and memory frequency variances under the same conditions. In CPU-bound case (Figure 3(b)-(c)), when $\alpha > 91.1\%$ CPU frequency keeps at 1GHz while memory frequency is climbing and it reaches the highest point until $\alpha = 100\%$. Due to objective (5), the performance value in CPU-bound is determined by CPU frequency. Therefore, when CPU frequency reaches the highest value, performance reaches the optimal value. After that, memory frequency increase consumes unnecessary energy, which explains why some energy savings can be obtained without performance loss in CPU-bound case.

In contrast, in memory-bound case, performance is determined by both CPU frequency and memory frequency in terms of objective (10). Only when both of them reach the highest values, the performance reaches the optimal.

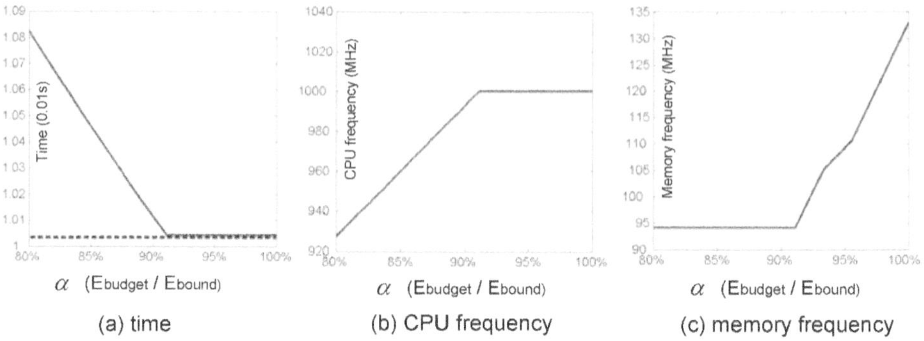

Fig. 3. The impact of Ebudget on the optimization results when CPU-bound case. Cc=1000, Cm=90.

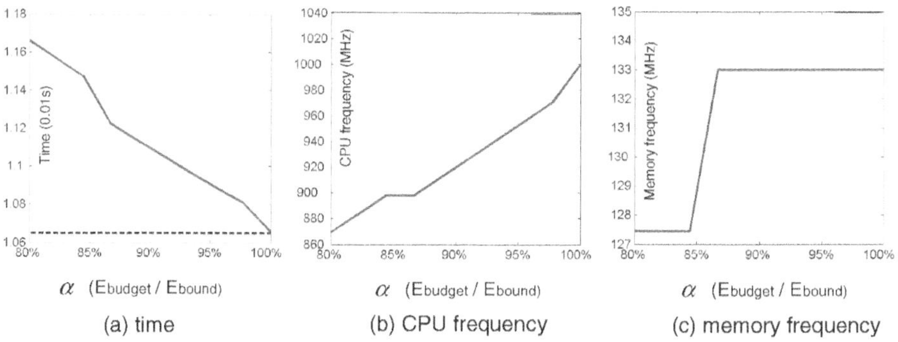

Fig. 4. The impact of Ebudget on the optimization results when memory-bound case. Cc=1000, Cm=150.

5.2.2 The Impact of C_c and C_m on Optimization

We also simulated the changes of time as C_c and C_m vary shown in Figure 5, where $\alpha = 90\%$. From point **Ai** to **Bi** (i=1, 2, 3, 4), the varying trends occur an exception. That is because the cases before **Ai** belong to memory-bound while the cases after **Bi** belong to CPU-bound and the calculation formulas for these two cases are different.

Figure 6 and Figure 7 give the optimal CPU and memory frequency settings as C_c and C_m vary. From these two graphs, the optimal CPU frequency value is non-decreasing as C_c increases while the optimal memory frequency value is non-increasing as C_c increases under a fixed C_m value. The C_c value and C_m value at points **Ai** and **Bi** (i=1, 2, 3, 4) are the same with those in Figure 5. Therefore, we can contrast Figure 6 and Figure 7 with Figure 5. Here $\alpha = 90\%$.

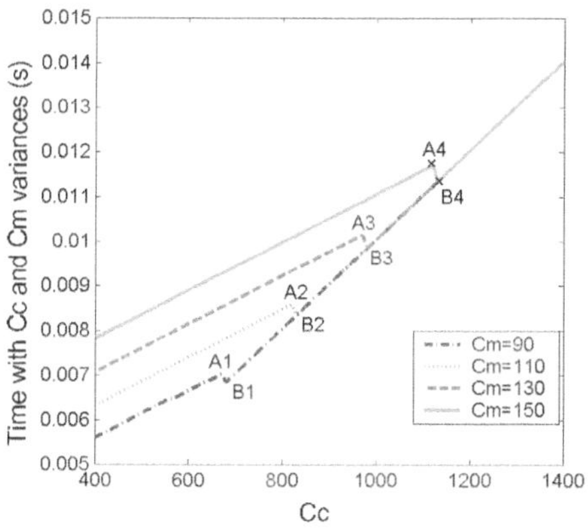

Fig. 5. Time variances with Cc and Cm variances

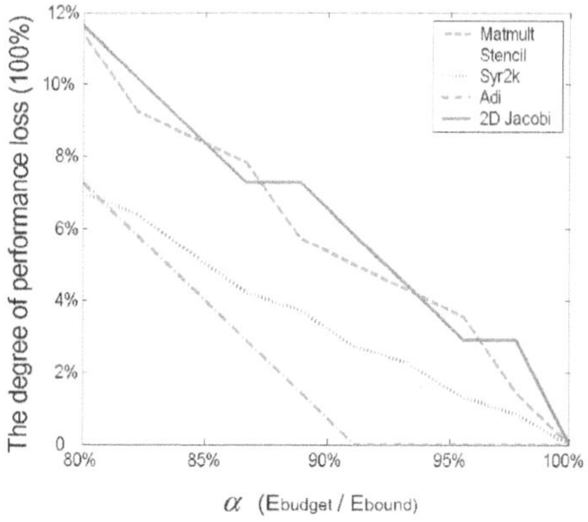

Fig. 8. The degree of performance loss for eachbenchmark

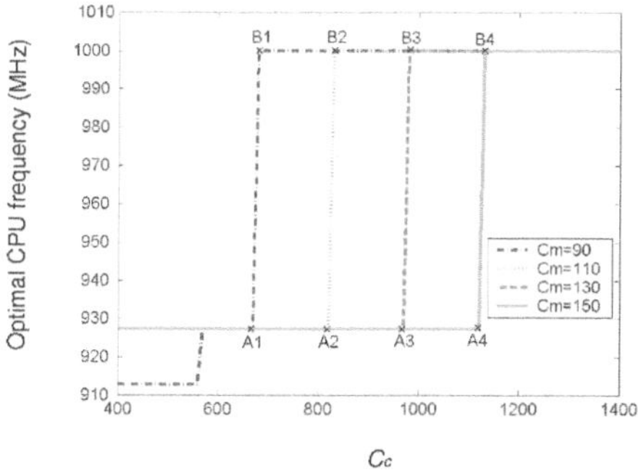

Fig. 6. Optimal CPU frequency variances with *Cc* and*Cm* variances

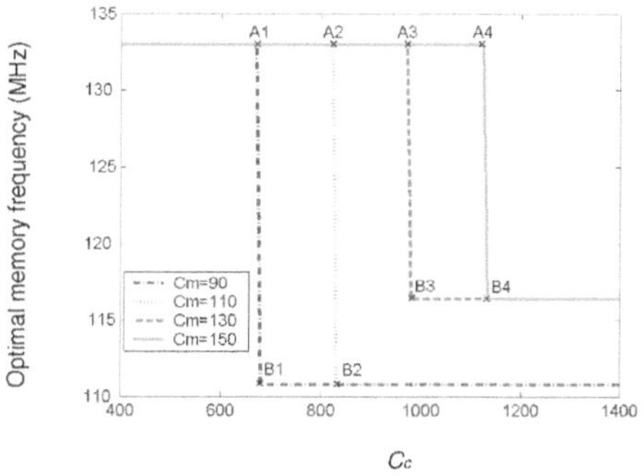

Fig. 7. Optimal memory frequency variances with *Cc*and *Cm* variances

5.3 Experimental Results

After the detailed parameters analysis, we choose a set of array-dominated applications to test the effectiveness of our energy optimization approach. They include Matmult, Stencil, Adi, 2D Jacobi and Syr2k. These benchmarks descriptions are given in Table 2.

Assume the time under energy constraint is *Time* and the time without energy constraint is *InitialTime*, the degree of performance loss can be calculated by formula (17).

$$Performance\ Loss\ (100\%) = \frac{\frac{1}{InitialTime} - \frac{1}{Time}}{\frac{1}{InitialTime}} \times 100\% \tag{17}$$

Table 2. The description of benchmarks

Benchmarks	description	The number of Array	Size
Matmult	matrices product	3	1024*1024
Adi	the core base benchmark of Livermore	6	1024*1024*3
2D Jacobi	2D Jacobi relaxation	2	1024*1024
Stencil	a stencil computing program for five dots	2	1024*1024
Syr2k	Rank-2K update computation program for solving zonal symmetry matrix from BLAS	3	1024*1024

Table 3. Optimal CPU and memory frequency settings and performance loss for each benchmark with variable

memory-bound benchmarks	α	CPU Fre. (MHz)	Memory Fre.(MHz)	Perf. Loss
Matmult	82.2%	898	122	9.3%
	86.7%	927	122	7.8%
	91.1%	942	127	5.0%
	95.6%	971	127	3.6%
	100%	1000	133	0
Stencil	82.2%	782	133	6.3%
	86.7%	840	133	4.4%
	91.1%	898	133	2.7%
	95.6%	942	133	1.5%
	100%	1000	133	0
Syr2k	82.2%	811	133	6.4%
	86.7%	869	133	4.2%
	91.1%	913	133	2.7%
	95.6%	956	133	1.3%
	100%	1000	133	0

memory-bound benchmarks	α	CPU Fre. (MHz)	Memory Fre.(MHz)	Perf. Loss
Adi	82.2%	942	88.6	5.8%
	86.7%	971	88.6	2.9%
	91.1%	1000	88.6	0
	95.6%	1000	111	0
	100%	1000	133	0
2D Jacobi	82.2%	898	122	10.2%
	86.7%	927	122	7.3%
	91.1%	942	127	5.8%
	95.6%	971	127	2.9%
	100%	1000	133	0

As α value varies, the performance loss for each benchmark is shown in Figure 8. Table 3 gives the detailed experimental data for the optimal CPU and memory frequency setting and performance loss percentage. In these five benchmarks, Matmult, Stencil and Syr2k belong to memory-bound cases and Adi and 2D Jacobi belong to CPU-bound cases. Experimental results validate our conclusions from the following aspects:

- Benchmark Adi reaches the optimal performance with 91.1% of energy bound, which validates that in CPU-bound case, the optimal performance can be reached under less energy budget (less than energy bound).
- For each benchmark belonging to memory-bound case, the optimal performance is only achieved with energy bound.
- The optimal CPU and memory frequency variances conform to Figure 3(b)-(c) and Figure 4(b)-(c).

6 Conclusions

Energy consumption is more and more important for battery-powered embedded systems due to the need for longer battery life and portability. Compiler-directed optimization techniques are more and more concerned. In our article, we provide an energy-constrained prefetching optimization approach, which obtains the optimal performance with energy constraint through adjusting CPU and memory frequencies. For CPU-bound case and memory-bound case, frequency scaling shows the different characteristics. It is necessary to adjust both of CPU and memory frequencies for the optimization problem. We analyze the impact of several parameters on our energy-constrained optimization problem and draw some conclusions. Finally, experimental results validate the effectiveness of our approach.

Reference

1. Gang Qu. What is the Limit of Energy Saving by Dynamic Voltage Scaling? In ICCAD. page 560-563. 2001.
2. H. Saputra, M. Kandemir, N. Vijaykrishnan, M. J. Irwin, J. S. Hu, C-H. Hsu, U. Kremer. Energy-Conscious Compilation Based on Voltage Scaling. In LCTES'02-SCOPES'02, June 19-21, 2002, Berlin, Germany.
3. Fen Xie, Margaret Martonosi and Sharad Malik. Compile-Time Dynamic Voltage Scaling Settings: Opportunities and Limits. In PLDI'03, June 9-11, 2003, San Diego, California, USA.
4. Woo-Cheol Kwon and Taewhan Kim. Optimal Voltage Allocation Techniques for Dynamically Variable Voltage Processors. In DAC'03, June 2-6, 2003, Anaheim, California, USA.
5. Xiaobo Fan, Carla S. Ellis and Alvin R. Lebeck. The Synergy between Power-aware Memory Systems and Processor Voltage Scaling. In *Proceedings of the Workshop on Power-Aware Computer Systems (PACS'03)*, Dec 2003.
6. Todd C. Mowry. Tolerating Latency Through Software-Controlled Data Prefetching. Ph.D. thesis, Stanford University, Computer System Laboratory, March 1994.
7. Shimin Chen, Phillip B. Gibbons and Todd C. Mowry. Improving Index Performance through Prefetching. In *Proceedings of the 2001 SIGMOD International Conference on Management of Data*. Page 235-246. May 2001.
8. Abdel-Hameed Badawy, Aneesh Aggarwal, Donald Yeung, and Chau-Wen Tseng. The Efficacy of Software Prefetching and Locality Optimizations on Future Memory Systems. Journal of Instruction-Level Parallelism. June 2004.
9. Ricardo Bianchini and Beng-Hong Lim. Evaluating the Performance of Multithreading and Prefetching in Multiprocessors. Journal of Parallel and Distributed Computing (JPDC), special issue on Multithreading for Multiprocessors, August 1996.
10. C. Hsu, U. Kremer, and M. Hsiao. Compiler-Directed Dynamic Voltage/Frequency Scheduling for Energy Reduction in Microprocessors. In *International Symp. On Low Power Electronics and Design (ISLPED)*, pages 275-278, August 2001.
11. Chung-Hsing Hsu. Compiler-Directed Dynamic Voltage and Frequency Scaling for CPU Power and Energy Reduction. Ph. D. Dissertation. New Brunswick, New Jersey. October 2003.
12. J. Pouwelse, K. Langendoen, and H. Sips. Dynamic Voltage Scaling on a Low-Power Microprocessor. In *the Seventh Annual International Conference on Mobile Computing and Networking 2001*, pages 251-259, 2001.
13. Crusoe Processor Model TM5700/TM5900 Data Book.http://www.transmeta.com/crusoe_docs/tm5900_databook_040204.pdf

14. D. Burger and T. M. Austin. The SimpleScalar Tool Set, Version 2.0. CS TR 1342, University of Wisconsin-Madison, June 1997.
15. Juan Chen, Yong Dong, Xue-jun Yang. Energy Optimization for Software Prefetching in Embedded Applications. *In the proceedings of Asia and South Pacific International Conference on Embedded SoCs (ASPICES 2005).* July 5-8, 2005, Bangalore, India.

An Energy Reduction Scheduling Mechanism for a High-Performance SoC Architecture

Slo-Li Chu

Department of Information and Computer Engineering,
Chung Yuan Christian University, Chung-Li, Taiwan, R.O.C.
slchu@cycu.edu.tw

Abstract. Continuous improvements in semiconductor technology are supporting new classes of System-on-a-Chip (SoC) architectures that combine extensive processing logic with high-density memory. Such architectures are generally called Processor-in-Memory (PIM) or Intelligent Memory (I-RAM) and can support high-performance computing by reducing the performance gap between the processor and the memory. The PIM architecture combines various processors in a single chip. These processors are characterized by their computation, memory-access and power consumption capabilities. Therefore, a novel parallelizing system, SAGE II, has been developed to identify their capabilities and dispatch the most appropriate jobs to them in order to exploit the advantages of PIM architectures. However, the SAGE II system only can deal with performance issues but power consumption is gradually becoming an important issue of current computing systems. This paper provides a new low-power transformation mechanism, called Energy-Oriented Power Reduction Scheduling (EOPRS), to extend the capability of SAGE II system. It can reduce the power consumption for the Processor-in-Memory system without losing execution performance. The detailed EOPRS transformation technique is presented later. The experimental results of several benchmarks are also discussed.

Keywords: EOPRS, SAGE II, SoC, Processor-in-Memory, Power Reduction.

1 Introduction

In current high-performance computer architectures, processors run many times faster than the computer's main memory. This performance gap is often referred to as the Memory Wall [2]. This gap can be reduced using the System-on-a-Chip (SoC) strategy, which integrates the processor(s) and memory on a single chip. Accordingly, many researchers have considered integrating computing logic and high density DRAM on a single die [3, 5, 8, 10] as so-called Processor-in-Memory (PIM) or Intelligent RAM (IRAM). This class of architectures constitutes a hierarchical hybrid multiprocessor environment that involves host (main) and memory processors. The host processor (P.Host) is more powerful but have a deep cache hierarchy and higher latency when accessing memory. In contrast, memory processors (P.Mem) are typically less powerful but have a lower latency in memory access. With respect to energy consumption, host processor consumes more energy than memory processors when computing and accessing memory. These capability differences make parallelization and energy reduction more difficult.

L.T. Yang et al. (Eds.): EUC 2005, LNCS 3824, pp. 281 – 290, 2005.

The main problems addressed are how to dispatch appropriate tasks to these various processors according to their characteristics, to reduce their execution time, energy consumption, or both, and how to partition the original program so that it can be executed on these heterogeneous processor mixtures. Accordingly, an automatic source-to-source parallelizing and optimizing system, SAGE II (Statement- Analysis-Grouping- Evaluation II) is designed and implemented. The main difference between SAGE II and other parallelizing systems is that it uses statement rather than iteration as the basic unit of analysis. By integrating statement splitting, weight evaluation and several scheduling mechanisms, SAGE II can automatically analyze Fortran source program; partition it into statements; generate a Weight Partition Dependence Graph (WPG), determine the weight of each block in the WPG, and schedule these blocks to improve the performance by dispatching the most suitable blocks for execution on host and memory processors. To extend the capability of reducing power consumption of software running on the SoC architecture, this study presents a novel scheduling technique, called Energy-Oriented Power Reduction Scheduling (EOPRS), for to reduce the energy consumed for the one-P.Host and one-P.Mem configuration without losing performance. The remainder of this paper is organized as follows: Section 2 introduces the related work. Section 3 describes the PIM architecture we adopt. Section 4 describes SAGE II system. Section 5 provides the EOPRS mechanism. The experimental results are shown in Section 6. Finally, conclusion is given in Section 7.

2 Related Work

Since energy limited the growth of the mobile computers and embedded computing devices, it is very important to reduce the consumption of energy and increase battery lifetimes. Therefore the analysis and optimization of the energy consumed by all components become important not only for battery-powered personal devices, but also for large computing systems.

Current work on energy saving using software can be classified into two categories. In one, special architecture is required to support the software. For example, an additional mini cache between the I-Cache and the CPU core called the "L-Cache" or "I-Filter" can be used [1, 5, 6]. Such mini cache buffers only the reused instructions within loops. It consumes less energy than I-Cache and so eliminates the fetching of unnecessary instructions fetching, reduce signal switching activity and dissipated energy. It requires compilers to cooperate to the rearrange original codes to ensure that it fits the L-Cache. However, it also has the disadvantage of requiring a special architecture.

Another category of work considers instruction-level scheduling mechanisms to reduce energy consumption [4, 7, 9, 12]. If a previously executed instruction differs from the present instruction, the control circuit must activate different hardware functional units. Switching consumes energy, so appropriately reordering instructions in a program reduce the energy consumption. This method need to measure the inter-instruction effects and establishes an energy transition cost table, before performing instruction-level scheduling according to the cost of switching. However, such a method has two disadvantages. First, the source program must be written in a low-level language such that the scheduler cannot understand all of the behavior of this program, limiting the application of high-level transformation techniques, such as tiling. Second, the cost of switching instructions is only around 2% ~ 10% of the base cost of the instructions; therefore the energy reduction is not significant.

3 The Processor-in-Memory Architecture

Figure 1 depicts the organization of the PIM architecture evaluated in this study. It contains an off-the-shelf processor, P.Host, and a PIM chip. The PIM chip integrates one memory processor, P.Mem, with 64 Mbytes of DRAM. This architecture is derived from FlexRAM [5]. The tiny memory processors (P.Array) in the original FlexRAM are omitted to reduce the complexity of analysis. The techniques presented in this paper involve a one P.Host and one P.Mem configuration, and can be extended to support multiple P.Mems.

Table 1. Major parameters of the PIM architecture

P.Host	P.Mem	Bus & Memory
Working Freq: 800 MHz	Working Freq: 400 MHz	Bus Freq: 100 MHz
Dynamic issue Width: 6	Static issue Width: 2	P.Host Mem RT: 262. 5 ns
Integer unit num: 6	Integer unit num: 2	P.Mem Mem RT: 50. 5 ns
Floating unit num: 4	Floating unit num: 2	Bus Width: 16 B
FLC_Type: WT	FLC_Type: WT	Mem_Data_Transfer: 16
FLC_Size: 32 KB	FLC_Size: 16 KB	Mem_Row_Width: 4K
FLC_Line: 64 B	FLC_Line: 32 B	
FLC_Replace policy: LRU	FLC_Replace policy: LRU	
SLC_Type: WB	SLC: N/A	
SLC_Size: 256 KB		
SLC_Line: 64 B		
Replace policy: LRU		
Branch penalty: 4	Branch penalty: 2	
P.Host_Mem_Delay: 88	P.Mem_Mem_Delay: 17	

** FLC stands for the first level cache, SLC for the second level cache, BR for branch, RT for round-trip latency from the processor to the memory, and RB for row buffer.*

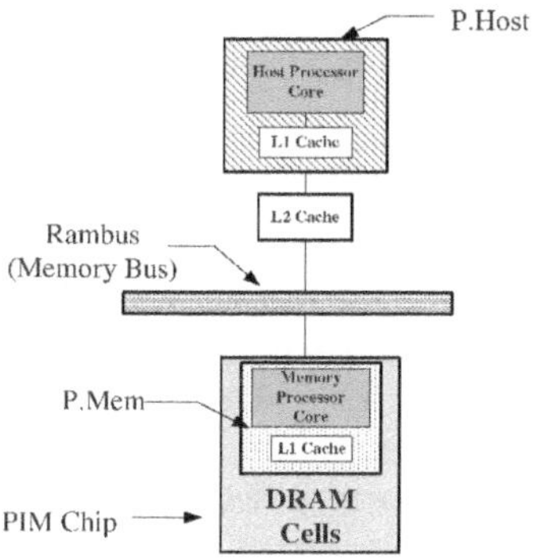

Fig. 1. Organization of the PIM architecture

Table 2. Power consumption parameters of the PIM architecture

	P.Host		P.Mem	
Integer Unit	ALU	194.46	ALU	97.23
	Shift	194.46	Shift	97.23
	Mult/div	210.45	Mult/div	105.23
	Branch	194.46	Branch	97.23
Load/Store Unit	Load	194.46	Load	97.23
	Store	194.46	Store	97.23
Floating point Unit	Add/Sub	210.45	Add/Sub	105.23
	Mult	210.45	Mult	105.23
	Div	210.45	Div	105.23
Clock energy	957		26.24	

Table 1 and Table 2 list the main architectural parameters of the PIM architecture. P.Host is a six-issue superscalar processor that allows out-of-order execution and runs at 800MHz, while P.Mem is a two-issue superscalar processor with in-order capability and runs at 400MHz. There is a two-level cache in P.Host and a one-level cache in P.Mem. P.Mem has lower memory access latency than P.Host since the former is integrated with DRAM. Thus, computation-bound codes are more suitable for running on the P.Host, while memory-bound codes are preferably running on the P.Mem to increase efficiency.

The PIM chip is designed to replace regular DRAMs in current computer systems, and must therefore conform to a memory standard that involves additional power and ground signals to support on-chip processing. One such standard is Rambus, so the PIM chip is designed with a Rambus-compatible interface.

4 The SAGE II System

Most current parallelizing compilers focus on transforming loops to execute iterations concurrently, in a so-called iteration-based approach. This approach is suited to homogeneous and tightly coupled multi-processor systems. However, it has an obvious disadvantage for heterogeneous multi-processor platforms because iterations have similar behavior but the capabilities of heterogeneous processors are diverse. Therefore, a different approach is adopted here, using the statements in a loop as a basic analysis unit, called statement-based approach, to develop the SAGE system.

SAGE II (Statement-Analysis-Grouping-Evaluation II) is an automatic parallelizing compiler, which partitions and schedules an original program to exploit the specialties of the host and the memory processor. At first, the source program is split into blocks of statements according to dependence relations. Then, the Weighted Partition Dependence Graph (WPG) is generated, and the weight of each block is evaluated. Finally, the blocks are dispatched to either the host or the memory processors, according to which processor is more suitable for executing the block. The major difference between SAGE II and other parallelizing systems is that it uses a statement rather than an iteration as the basic unit of analysis. This approach can fully exploit the characteristics of statements in a program and dispatch the most suitable tasks to the host and the memory processors.

Table 3 presents a simple example to demonstrate the advantages of statement-based parallelization. The program is fully parallelizable and can be partitioned into statements or iterations. The table lists the assumed statement weights for the P.Host and P.Mem. Table 4 shows five parallelization cases and their execution times. The first two involve executing the program solely on P.Host and P.Mem, respectively. Case 3 parallelizes the program using conventional parallelizing compilers, such as SUIF [2] or Polaris [2] to identify the parallelizable loops and dispatch them for execution on P.Host and P.Mem. This approach only achieves good speedup for processors with homogeneous capabilities (including memory access latency, computing power, and so on). In case 4, the iterations are dispatched to the processors according to the processors' capabilities, but the compiler does not consider the discrepancies among processors in executing statements. Case 5 uses the statement-based analysis approach (i.e., optimized by SAGE

II). This approach outperforms all the others since it dispatches statements to P.Host and P.Mem by accounting for the characteristics of statements and the capabilities of processors, motivating the development of the SAGE II system for asymmetric multiprocessor environments. The compiling sequence of the SAGE II is shown in Figure 2. The major stages are described later.

Table 3. A fully parallelizable program

Program	*Weight for *PH*	*Weight for *PM*
DO I = 1 to N		
S1: A= A mod B	3	6
S2: C= D[I]+E	5	1
S3: F= G[I]+H[I]	6	2
ENDDO		

**PH* stands for host processor and *PM* for memory processor.

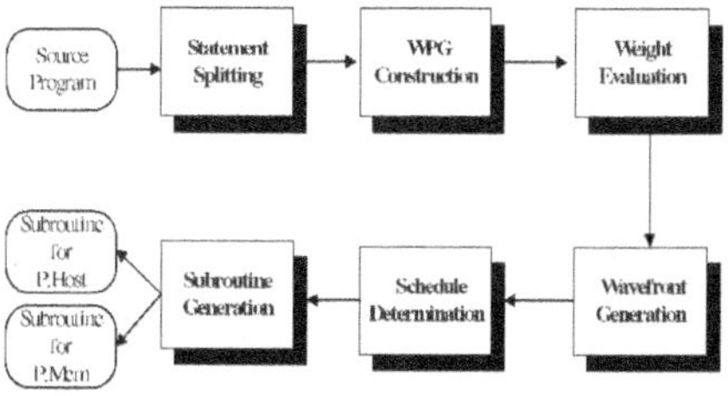

Fig. 2. The sequence of compiling stages in SAGE II

Table 4. Five parallelizing cases and their execution times

	Description	*Execution Time*
1	Host processor operates solely	Latency = [PH(S1)+PH(S2)+PH(S3)]*# of iterations = (3+5+6)N = 14 N
2	Memory processor operates solely	Latency =[PM(S1)+PM(S2)+PM(S3)]* # of iterations = (6+1+2)N = 9 N
3	Host and memory processors cooperate in symmetric workload	Latency = max((3+5+6)* 0.5N, (6+2+1)* 0.5 N) = 7 N
4	Host and memory processors cooperate in asymmetric workload by parallelizing the *iteration* space of the loop	The workload is dispatched based on the capability ratio of PH and PM obtained from Case 1 and Case2, i.e., PH: PM = 9:14. Hence, latency=14* (9/(9+14))N= 5.48 N
5	Host and memory processors cooperate in asymmetric workload by SAGE optimization	Latency = max (PH(S1) * N, PM(S2,S3)*N) = 3 N (Here S1 is more suitable for P.Host, but S2 and S3 are more suitable for P.Mem.)

4.1 Statement Splitting and WPG Construction [2]

Statement Splitting splits the dependence graph by Node Partitioning as introduced in [2]. WPG Construction constructs the Weighted Partition Dependence Graph (WPG), to be used in the subsequent stages of Weight Evaluation, Wavefront Generation and Schedule Determination.

The definitions relevant to Statement Splitting are introduced in the literature [2]. It is ignored for the page limitation but still listed the Statement Splitting algorithm (Algorithm 1) to partition the loops:

Algorithm 1. (Statement Splitting Algorithm)

Given a loop L = (i_1, i_2, ... i_n) (s_1, s_2, ... s_d)

Step 1: Construct dependence Graph G by analyzing subscript expressions and index pattern.

Step 2: Establish a node partition Π on G as defined in Definition 2. If there are large blocks caused by control dependence relations, convert control dependence into data dependence first [2], and then partition the dependence graph.

Step 3: On the partition Π, establish a weighted partition dependence graph WPG(B,E) defined in Definition 3.

4.2 Weight Evaluation

Two approaches to evaluating weight can be taken. One is to predict the execution time of programs by profiling the dominant parts [2]. The other considers the operations in a statement and estimates the program execution time by looking up an operation weight table [2]. The former method called code profiling may be more accurate, but the predicted result cannot be reused; the latter called code analysis can determine statements for suitable processors but the estimated program execution time is not sufficiently accurate. Hence, the Self-Patch Weight Evaluation scheme was designed to combine the benefits of both approaches. It integrates these two approaches together by analyzing code and searching weight table first to estimate the weight of a block. If the block contains unknown operations, the patch (profiling) mechanism is then activated to evaluate the weights of unknown operations. The obtained operation weights are added into the weight table for next look-up. For a detailed description of this scheme, please refer to [2]

5 Energy-Oriented Power Reduction Scheduling Mechanism

5.1 Algorithm Description

This paper has proposed an automatic source-to-source parallelizing compiler, SAGE II (Statement- Analysis- Grouping- Evaluation), which integrates statement splitting, weight evaluation, scheduling and optimizing mechanisms. However, the best execution schedule in terms of performance is not usually the same as the best execution schedule in terms of energy. This section focuses on reducing the energy consumption of PIM architecture. For the reason mentioned in the previous descriptions, statements are adopted as the analyzing units. Each statement unit has a delay weights and an energy weight for P.Host and P.Mem, respectively, and will be assigned to the most suitable processor according to these weights. Here we introduce

---

Algorithm 2: Energy-Oriented Power Reduction Scheduling

[Input]

WPG=(P, E): the order of blocks and weights are determined.
Percent: the percent user want to constrain.

[Output]

An execution wavefront schedule $WF= \{Wf_1, Wf_2, \ldots\}$ where $Wf_i=\{PH(b_a \ldots b_b), PM(b_c \ldots b_d)\}$ in which $PH(b_a \ldots b_b)$ means that blocks $b_a \ldots b_b$ will be assigned to PHost in wavefront i, $PM(b_c \ldots b_d)$ means that blocks $b_c \ldots b_d$ will be assigned to PMem in wavefront i.

[Intermediate]

W: a working set of blocks to be visited.
max_pred_O(b_i): the maximum execution order for all b_i's predecessor blocks.
min_pred_O(b_i): the minimum execution order for all b_i's predecessor blocks.
wf_tmp: working sets of blocks for wavefront scheduling.
ph_tmp(h), pm_tmp(m): working arrays to store the blocks for wavefront scheduling.
ph_d_wei(h), pm_d_wei(m) working arrays to store the total delay weights of blocks .
ph_e_wei(h), pm_e_wei(m) working arrays to store the total energy weights of blocks .
max_wf: the maximum number of wavefront.
PHEW_origin(max_wf): the energy weight of b_i for Phost each wavefront.
Deadline(max_wf): the deadline of each wavefront.
PHDW(b_i): the delay weight of b_i for PHost.

```
    PMDW(bi): the delay weight of bi for PMem.
    PHEW(bi): the energy weight of bi for PHost.
    PMEW(bi): the energy weight of bi for PMem.
[Method]
for each bi ∈P do /*Initialization and weight determination for each blocks */
    Oi = 0; evaluate PHDW(bi), PMDW(bi), PHEW(bi) and PMEW(bi) by weight evaluation;
end for
W = P;
for each bi with no predecessors do /* Execution order assignment */
    Oi = 1; W = W – { bi };
end for
done = False; max_wf=0;
while done = False AND W ≠ φ do
    done = True
    for each bi ∈ W do
        if min_pred_O(bi) = 0 then done = False
        else
            Oi = max_pred_O(bi)+1; W=W-{ bi }; max_wf = max(max_wf, Oi);
        end if
    end for
end while
energy_temp = 0
for j = 1 to max_wf
    wf_tmp=ph_tmp=pm_tmp={φ};h=m=Opt_energy(j)=PHEW_origin(j)=Deadline(j)=0;
    ph_d_wei(j)=ph_e_wei(j)=pm_d_wei(j)=pm_e_wei(j)=0;
    store all of bi whose Oi = j in wf_tmp;
    for each bi∈ wf_tmp
        if PHEW(bi ) - PMEW(bi) ≤0
            h = h + 1; Store bi in ph_tmp (h);
            ph_d_wei(j)=ph_d_wei(j)+PHDW(bi ); ph_e_wei(j)=ph_e_wei(j)+PHEW(bi );
        else
            m = m + 1; Store bi in pm_tmp (m);
            pm_d_wei(j)=pm_d_wei(j)+PMDW(bi ); pm_e_wei(j)=pm_e_wei(j +PMEW(bi );
        end if
        PHEW_origin(j)=PHEW_origin(j)+PHEW(bi );
        Opt_energy(j) = Opt_energy(j) + Min(PHEW(bi ), PMEW(bi ));
        Sort ph_tmp (h) in decreasing order by PHDW(bi );
        Sort pm_tmp (m) in decreasing order by PMDW(bi);
    end for
    Deadline(j)=Opt_energy(j)+(PHEW_origin(j)–Opt_energy(j))*(1–Percent);
    Deadline(j)=Deadline(j)+energy_temp; p = q = 0; done = FALSE;
    if ph_d_wei(j) ≥ pm_d_wei(j)
        for p =1 to h
            ph_e_wei(j) = ph_e_wei(j) – PHEW ( ph_tmp(p))
            pm_e_wei(j) = pm_e_wei(j) + PMEW ( ph_tmp(p))
            ph_d_wei(j) = ph_d_wei(j) – PHDW ( ph_tmp(p))
            pm_d_wei(j) = pm_d_wei(j) + PMDW ( ph_tmp(p))
            if ph_e_wei(j) + pm_e_wei(j) ≤ Deadline(j)
                ph_tmp = ph_tmp – {ph_tmp(p)}; pm_tmp = pm_tmp + {ph_tmp(p)};
            else
                pm_d_wei(j) = pm_d_wei(j) – PMDW ( ph_tmp(p))
                ph_d_wei(j) = ph_d_wei(j) + PHDW ( ph_tmp(p))
                pm_e_wei(j) = pm_e_wei(j) – PMEW ( ph_tmp(p))
                ph_e_wei(j) = ph_e_wei(j) + PHEW ( ph_tmp(p))
            end if
        end for
    else
        for q =1 to m
            ph_e_wei(j) = ph_e_wei(j) + PHEW ( pm_tmp(q))
            pm_e_wei(j) = pm_e_wei(j) – PMEW ( pm_tmp(q))
            ph_d_wei(j) = ph_d_wei(j) + PHDW ( pm_tmp(q))
            pm_d_wei(j) = pm_d_wei(j) – PMDW ( pm_tmp(q))
            if ph_e_wei(j) + pm_e_wei(j) ≤ Deadline(j)
                pm_tmp = pm_tmp – {pm_tmp(q)}
                ph_tmp = ph_tmp + {pm_tmp(q)}
            else
                ph_d_wei(j) = ph_d_wei(j) – PHDW ( pm_tmp(q))
```

```
            ph_e_wei(j) = ph_e_wei(j) – PHEW ( pm_tmp(q))
            pm_d_wei(j) = pm_d_wei(j) + PMDW ( pm_tmp(q))
            pm_e_wei(j) = pm_e_wei(j) + PMEW ( pm_tmp(q))
         end if
      end for
   end if
   energy_temp=Deadline(j)–( ph_e_wei(j)+pm_e_wei(j)); Wfj ={ph_tmp, pm_tmp };
end for
```

the Energy-Oriented Power Reduction Scheduling, EOPRS, which allows the user to specify the energy limit. If the energy limit is met, the scheduler will use the performance-oriented principle to schedule the blocks. For simplicity, this paper considers only the system with a single P.Host and single P.Mem. The rest of this section presents the mechanisms in detail. Section 6 presents the experimental results.

This EOPRS approach enables the user to adjust the energy reduction ratio to get more speedup. In this approach, the energy weights and delay weights of each block in the WPG are determined first. Then the execution order for each block is determined according to their dependence relations. The blocks that can be executed simultaneously are assigned to a wavefront. Then the scheduler dispatches blocks in a single wavefront according to their energy weights, minimizing the energy consumption. According to the energy specified by the user, the maximum energy acceptable consumption, called the "deadline" is determined herein. The deadline is given by minimum energy consumption + (original energy consumption - minimum energy consumption) * (1 - energy reduced limit %). Then, the mechanism can automatically adjust schedule sequence to obtain the maximum potential speedup, such that the energy consumption is less than the maximum acceptable. The details mechanism of this approach is presented in Algorithm 2.

6 Experimental Results

This experiment focuses on the one-P.Host and one-P.Mem configuration of PIM architecture to evaluate the energy reduction scheduling mechanism mentioned in Section 5. The energy consumption parameters of this PIM architecture can be found in the Table 2.

The evaluated applications include five programs - swim from SPEC95, cgemm from BLAS3, ft and cg from the serial version of NAS, and mdg from Perfect Benchmark. Table 5 shows the results of the experiment. "Std-" denotes that the applications are executed on P.Host alone; "Opt-" denotes that the applications are transformed by the one-P.Host and one-P.Mem performance scheduling mechanism mentioned in literature [2] for execution on one P.Host and one P.Mem simultaneously; "Ene-" denotes that the applications are transformed by "Energy-Oriented Energy Reduction Scheduling" as mentioned in Section 5 with the energy reduced ratio set to 70%.

In Table 5, swim, cg, and cgemm exhibit good speedup "Opt-" case because they all can be partitioned into many blocks for scheduling to P.Host and P.Mem, according to the characteristics of blocks and processors. Also, they can achieve a good energy reduction ratio; ft can obtain good speedup "opt-" case but some performance in "Ene-" case is lost because its block sizes are very different.

Table 5. Experimental results of five benchmarks

benchmark	form	Execution cycles	Speedup	Energy consumption (joule)	Energy Reduce Ratio
swim	Std-	228289321	1.00	43.49	0
	Opt-	116669760	1.96	35.29	18.85%
	Ene-	262401518	0.87	28.18	35.20%
cg	Std-	91111840	1.00	19.58	0
	Opt-	51230772	1.78	14.73	24.77%
	Ene-	67993910	1.34	12.66	35.34%
cgemm	Std-	257528272	1.00	50.26	0
	Opt-	147769271	1.74	38.63	23.14%
	Ene-	238641808	1.07	33.02	34.30%
ft	Std-	544099032	1.00	111.9	0
	Opt-	368981380	1.47	86.59	22.62%
	Ene-	549370943	0.99	74.41	33.50%
mdg	Std-	174506369	1.00	65.5	0
	Opt-	160335813	1.08	63.95	2.37%
	Ene-	385931357	0.45	41.68	36.37%

Scheduling these blocks is difficult when the power reduction ratio is set to 70%. In contrast, mdg is intrinsically sequential. It can only be partitioned into several large blocks, preventing the generation of load-balance schedules, so the speedup of "Opt-" case is only 1.08. The EOPRS can further reduce the energy but the speedup is decreased to 0.45. Thus, the user can select different scheduling approaches according to their requirements.

7 Conclusions

In this paper, we presented a new program transformation technology, Energy-Oriented Power Reduction Scheduling, EOPRS. Integrated with SAGE II system, EOPRS reduces the energy consumption on the PIM System. This approach allows the user to set the speedup limit. If the speedup limit is met, then the scheduler will use the energy reduction principle to schedule the blocks. Results of the experiments demonstrate the capabilities of the extended SAGE II system. In the experiment, the energy consumption was reduced by up to 36.37%. The author believe that the techniques proposed here can be extended to run on DIVA, EXECUBE, FlexRAM, and other high-performance SoC architectures by slightly modifying the code generator of the SAGE system.

Acknowledgement

This work is supported in part by the National Science Council of Republic of China, Taiwan under Grant 94-2213-E-033-032-

References

[1] Bajwa, R. S., et al.: Instruction Buffering to Reduce Power in Processors for Signal Processing. IEEE Transactions on Very Large Scale Integration (VLSI) Systems, Vol.5(4). IEEE, (1997) 417-424.
[2] Chu, S. L., Huang, T. C.: SAGE: A Comprehensive Parallelizing Framework for Processor-in-Memory Architectures. Journal of Systems Architecture. Vol. 50 (1). Elsevier Science, (2004) 1-15.
[3] M. Hall, et al,: Mapping Irregular Applications to DIVA, a PIM-Based Data-Intensive Architecture. Proc. of 1999 Conference on Supercomputing. ACM, (1999).
[4] Horowitz, M., Indermaur, T., Gonzalez, R.: Low-Power Digital Design. Proc. of Symposium on Low Power Electronics. 8-11, (1994).
[5] Kang, Y., et al.: FlexRAM: Toward an Advanced Intelligent Memory System. Proc. of International Conference on Computer Design. (1999).
[6] Kin, J., et al.: The filter cache: an energy efficient memory structure. Proc. of Thirtieth Annual IEEE/ACM International Symposium on Microarchitecture. (1997) 184-193.
[7] Lee, L. H., Moyer, B., Arends, J.: Instruction Fetch Energy Reduction Using Loop Caches for Embedded Applications with Small Tight Loops. Proc. of 1999 International Symposium on Low Power Electronics and Design. (1999) 267-269.
[8] Oskin, M., Chong, F. T., Sherwood, T.: Active Page: A Computation Model for Intelligent Memory Computer Architecture. Proc. 25th Annual International Symposium on Computer Architecture. (1998) 192 –203.
[9] Parikh, A.., et al.: Energy-Aware Instruction Scheduling. Proc. of 7th International Conference on High Performance Computing-HiPC (2000) 335-344.
[10] Patterson, D., et al.: A Case for Intelligent DRAM. IEEE Micro, IEEE (1997) 33-44.
[11] Press,W. H., et al., Numerical Recipes in Fortran 77. Cambridge University Press (1992).
[12] Raghunathan, A., Jha, N. K., Dey, S.: High-Level Power Analysis and Optimization. Kluwer Academic Publishers, (1998).
[13] Tiwari, V., Malik, S., Wolfe, A.: Power Analysis of Embedded Software: a First Step Towards Software Power Minimization. IEEE Transactions on Very Large Scale Integration (VLSI) Systems, Vol. 2 (4). IEEE (1994) 437-445.

A New Buffer Planning Algorithm Based on Room Resizing*

Hongjie Bai, Sheqin Dong, Xianlong Hong, and Song Chen

Department of Computer Science and Technology,
Tsinghua University, Beijing, China
bhj04@mails.tsinghua.edu.cn, dongsq@mail.tsinghua.edu.cn

Abstract. This paper studies the buffer planning problem for interconnect centric floorplanning. Dead-spaces not held by blocks are the available location for buffer insertion. To make best use of these spaces for buffer requirements, we have to move blocks so that blocks' room size is adjusted and dead-spaces could be redistributed. In this paper, we introduce a new algorithm to move blocks not only within its room, but also in the space currently held by other blocks by pushing away these blocks if necessary without violating the topological and the total area. After applying this method of redistributing dead-spaces, the number of nets satisfying delay constraint can be optimized.

1 Introduction

As the VLSI circuits are scaled into nanometer dimensions, interconnect plays a dominant role in the performance and cost. To ensure the timing closure of design, interconnects must be considered as early as possible. Buffer insertion is among most effective ways to reduce interconnect delay which breaks long interconnects into shorter ones so that overall delay can be reduced. However, most buffer insertion algorithms were designed for post-layout interconnect optimization. Obviously it is not suitable if we have no global planning for tens of thousands of nets that need buffers to be inserted. Also, buffers take up silicon resources, so it is necessary to plan buffer as early as possible in the design of VLSI.

1.1 Previous Work

[3] introduced the concept of feasible region which employs Elmore delay model to generate buffer blocks. [5] extends it by adding independence to feasible region and also tries to relieve routing congestion. [6] proposed an optimal algorithm which assumes only one buffer per net. [7] use multi-commodity flow-based approach which allocates buffers to pre-existing buffer blocks. [8] proposes

* This paper is supported by National Nature Science Foundation of China (NSFC): 60473126, NSFC 60121120706 and National Natural Science Foundation of USA (NSF) CCR-0096383, Hi-Tech Research & Development (863) Program of China 2004AA1Z1050

L.T. Yang et al. (Eds.): EUC 2005, LNCS 3824, pp. 291–299, 2005.

a routability driven floorplanning. Most of these methods try to allocate buffers into dead spaces, however none of these methods take concern of using dead spaces effectively enough so that many dead spaces are left unused while still many buffers have no space to insert. [2] introduces a dead space redistribution-based method to make better use of dead space for buffer insertion. However, there exists a drawback that it can only move blocks within its room. Figure 1(a) is an example. With the algorithm introduced in [2], block C can't be moved horizontally so that some buffer requirements can't be satisfied. However, if E could move right a little to lend some space to C, all buffers can be successfully inserted as shown in Fig. 1(b) .

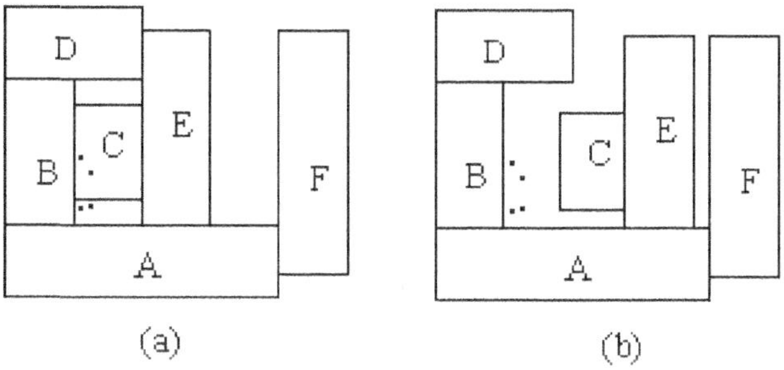

Fig. 1. Buffers can't be placed in (a) if C only moves within its room, but can be successfully placed in (b) if we enlarge C's room

1.2 Our Contribution

Except for moving blocks within their rooms, the rooms' size could be adjusted without changing the blocks' relative positions and buffer planning could be improved greatly. In that case, if we wish to find the optimal solution to insert buffers, we have to try moving blocks which may even push other blocks. So our algorithm is concentrated on moving blocks as much as possible in order to provide dead-spaces for buffer, at the same time, the dead-spaces of the total placement are managed systematically. This new method will be very effective for IP based SOC planning. For instance, for design reuse where topological relations among blocks could not be changed, this method can make blocks move in a range as much as possible to optimize buffer planning.

The rest of the paper is organized as follows, section 2 gives a problem definition and a brief overview to the background including Feasible Region and Corner Block List. Section 3 discusses our algorithm. Section 4 and section 5 give the experimental result and conclusion.

2 Preliminary

2.1 Problem Formulation

Given an initial placement and the nets with timing constraint, for the nets that does not satisfy timing closure, we determine the buffer number needed for each net and the definite buffer locations. Since buffer requires silicon resources, it can only be located in dead-spaces which are not held by blocks. To best satisfy buffer requirements, blocks have to be moved to make more nets meet timing closure while the total area and topology remain unchanged.

2.2 Corner Block List (CBL)

Corner block list (CBL) is a topological representation introduced in [1]. CBL uses three lists S,L,T to represent a floorplan. Each member in S represents a block, L and T are lists of 0 and 1. While applying a CBL to a floorplan, we assign the blocks in S one by one to the up-right corner. The corresponding number in L denotes the direction. 0 makes the new block come from the top direction and 1 makes the new block come from the right direction. The segments lying on the left and bottom boundary of the corner block compose a T-junction which defines the orientation of the corner block. The number of consecutive 1 in T means the number of T-Junctions the new block will cover. The insertion process of a block is shown in Fig. 2. Details can be found in [1] .

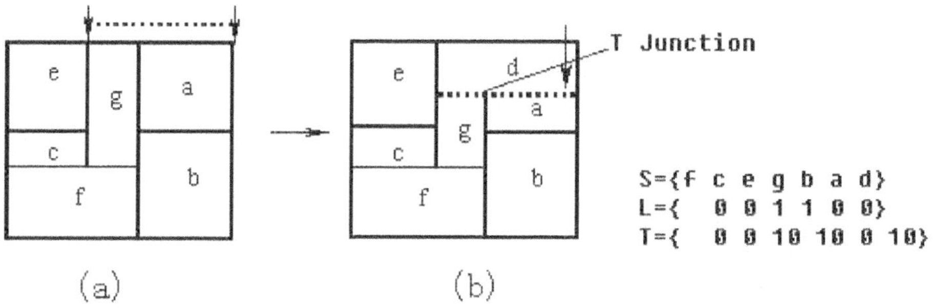

Fig. 2. From CBL to packing, insert corner block d to the corner and it covers one T junction so that it covers g and a

3 Room Resizing

Our algorithm is composed of four steps: (1)Determine maximum move space of each block, (2)try moving some block within its maximum move space, (3)applying traditional buffer insertion algorithm and (4) repeating 1,2,3 to search for an optimized solution. We will explain in details in the following subsections.

3.1 Determine Dead Spaces and Associate Them with Blocks

Dead space is defined to be space not held by blocks. During process of CBL packing, after placing the corner block from the top direction(L=0), all its covered blocks' top dead-spaces can be determined. Similarly, placing blocks from the right direction(L=1) will determine its covered blocks' right dead space. The blocks on right boundary and top boundary are not covered by blocks and their dead spaces are settled with help of top boundary and right boundary. An example is shown in Fig. 3. In Fig. 3(a), corner block covers A so that X is A's top dead space. In Fig. 3(b), corner block covers D, C and A so that Y is A's right dead space and Z is C's Right dead space.

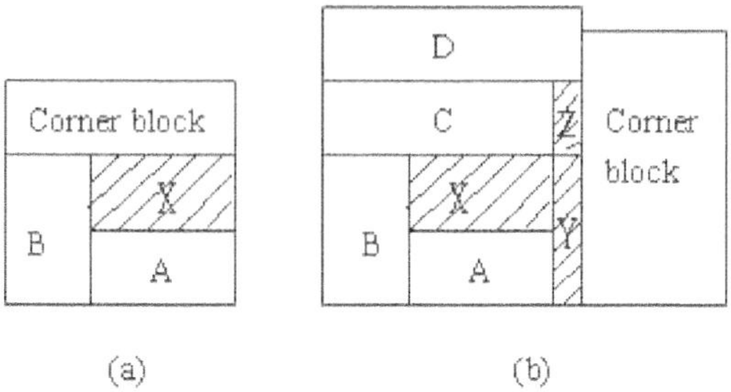

Fig. 3. While placing a corner block, its covered blocks' dead spaces could be determined

After the process of CBL packing, we not only determine all the dead-spaces, but also cut dead-spaces into rectangles naturally. At the same time, each dead-space is associated with a block and none of them intersect with each other. A block together with its dead spaces is defined to be this block's room. Since CBL is left-bottom packed, dead-spaces of a block are either on the top or on the right or both initially. Only moving blocks or redistributing dead-spaces can make a dead-space be on the left or bottom of its associated block. A more detailed description can be found in [4].

3.2 Vertical and Horizontal Constraint Graph

Building constraint graph during CBL Packing is a necessary step for our algorithm because constraint graph is a most efficient way to determine blocks' relative position. Firstly, we build a start vertex S and an ending vertex T. During CBL packing process, if the corner block covers from the top direction, we draw an edge from covered blocks to the corner block in vertical constraint graph, at the same time, we draw edges to the corner block from the blocks which lie left to the left-most covered block. If there are no blocks that lie left to left-most covered block which means the left-most covered block is on the left boundary, we draw an edge from S to the corner block. New blocks coming from right direction could be done similarly. In the end, we draw an edge from each block on top/right border to T. Considering edge-cost, we define it to be the dead space height/width between two neighboring blocks. An example is shown in Fig. 4, A comes from top and covers B and C, so we draw C->A and B->A in vertical graph in Fig. 4(a). C is the left-most covered-by-A block. E and F are Left to C, so we draw E->A and F->A in horizontal graph in Fig. 4(b). The only non-zero-cost edges are C->B, B->T.

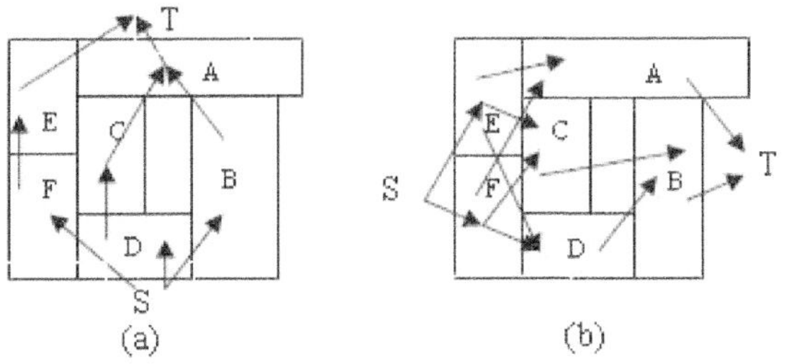

Fig. 4. Vertical(a) and horizontal(b) graph for a packing generated through a CBL

3.3 Maximum-Allowable Move Space (MAMS)

Since each block can be moved in four direction, up, down, left, right, so we keep a note of how much distance a block can be moved in one direction while the total area and topology remain unchanged.

Definition 1. *A block's maximum allowable move space on the right direction (MAMSR) is the maximum distance a block can be moved right, during which the other blocks that block the way may have to be pushed, but the total area and topology remain unchanged.*

The MAMSU, MAMSD, MAMSL, MAMSR which corresponds to the maximum-allowable move space on up/down/left/right direction can be defined similarly. An example is shown in Fig. 5. MAMSR of B is 4 because B can be moved right for distance 4 which pushes C, D and E, the total area and topology is unchanged. Placement after this move is shown in Fig. 5(b). After we move B, MAMSR of B is decreased to 0. Take D for another example, in Fig. 5(a), MAMSR of D is 7, after pushed by B, in Fig. 5(b), MAMSR of D is decreased to 3, but MAMSL of D is increased to 4 from 0.

Initially after CBL packing, each block's MAMSL and MAMSD is zero since we are packing them to left-bottom and none of them can be moved left ordown.

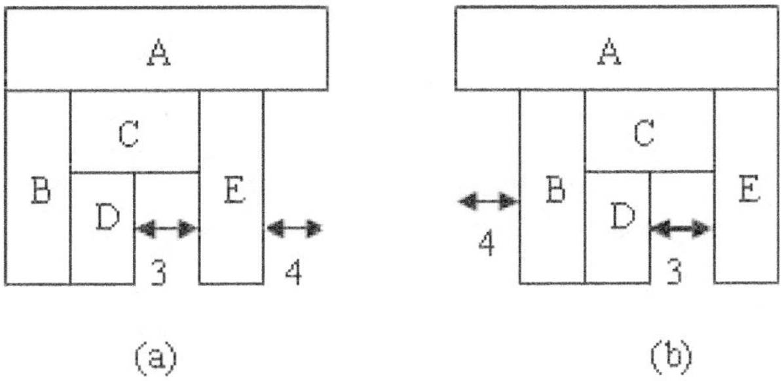

Fig. 5. An example for explaining MAMSR and MAMSL

MAMSR and MAMSU have to be calculated through constraint graph, a formula is shown below to determine MAMSR of block A.

$$MAMSR[A] = Min\,\{MAMSR[B] + edge\_cost(A, B)\} \quad \text{with} \quad (A, B) \in E_h \tag{1}$$

$(A, B) \in E_h$ means that edge A->B is on the horizontal graph. This is a recursive algorithm to determine each block's MAMSR starting from blocks on the right border to left. Take Fig. 5(a) for example: MAMSR[E]= 4, MAMSR[A]=0,

MAMSR[C]=MAMSR[E]+ edge_cost(C,E)=4,
MAMSR[D]=MAMSR[E]+edge_cost(D,E)=7,
MAMSR[B]=MIN(MAMSR[C],MAMSR[D])= 4.

3.4 Room Resizing

After collecting information from the above algorithms, we have got enough knowledge for our next step, resizing room. Of course, we move blocks to achieve these. Before a block move, we must determine if this move is valid.

Definition 2. *A block move is a valid move if that, after moving this block which may push other blocks, the total area and topology could remain unchanged.*

Theorem 1. *A move is a valid move if and only if the distance is less than MAMS of the corresponding direction of that block.*

Proof. Take a right directed move for example without loss of generality, firstly, MAMSR is the cumulative distance a block can be moved right due to the dead spaces that lie on the right. If the distance exceeds this value, the blocks rightmost may be pushed out of the right boundary which causes the area to be enlarged; on the opposite, if there are enough cumulated dead spaces on the right to handle this move, the total area could remain unchanged. After we move the block right, MAMSR is decreased by that distance and MAMSL is increased by that distance. For example in Fig. 5(a), move B right 3 and Move D right 6 are both valid move, however Move B right 8 or Move C right 5 are both invalid moves. Moving any block left will be invalid because all blocks' MAMSL is zero.

Since dead spaces are the only spaces for buffer sites, the ultimate objective of our block moving and room resizing is to redistribute dead spaces to make it more suitable for buffer requirements. Room resizing and dead space updating algorithm is shown as follows which takes moving right as an example.

```
MoveRight (block A, distance i)
  If(A's right dead space is less than i)
    Foreach block B that lies right to A
      If( i >edge_cost(A,B))
         MoveRight(B, i-edge_cost(A,B));
      End if
      Allocate B's left dead-space
         to its left blocks(including A);
```

```
8.        End for.
9.      End if.
10.     Decrease width of A's right dead space by i;
11.     Increase width of A's left dead space by i;
12.     Update coordinates of block A;
13.     Update edge cost in horizontal graph;
```

This algorithm is also recursive that if a block wishes to move right, its right dead space width must be greater than the distance it wishes to move. If this is the fact, then moving will be easy and algorithm starts from step 10; if not, we have to push blocks that lie right and this will give this block larger room and enough right dead-space. We note that in step 7, giving left dead space to its left blocks will cause all its left blocks' right space to be broadened including "A" so that "A" will have enough right dead space for move and step 10 is able to go on.

3.5 Searching for Optimal Solution Using Simulated Annealing

Our final searching algorithm is based on Simulated Annealing (SA) to make each move effective for satisfying timing constraint. We start with an initial packing which is generated through simulated annealing(this is the first phase traditional simulated annealing which specialized on minimizing area and total wire length and it is quite different from the simulated annealing step in our algorithm). Based on this packing, we start to try moving blocks to optimize timing performance. We randomly find a block not on critical path, randomly select a direction it can be moved, and move it at a random distance which does not exceed corresponding MAMS. Then we update dead spaces and update the nets affected by the blocks having been moved. To analyze whether this move is an optimized move, we apply traditional buffer insertion algorithm on this packing. [3] displays details for the buffer-insertion algorithm which firstly calculate the number of buffers each net requires, get feasible region for each buffer and intersect buffer's feasible region with dead spaces. If the intersection is empty, the buffer will fail to be inserted. Only nets with no buffer need or with all buffers successfully placed is taken as timing-constraint-satisfied. So the effectiveness of each move is evaluated by whether it could make more nets meet timing constraint. With the random move of each blocks, the final result through simulated annealing process could minimize the number of nets which violate timing closure. The SA algorithm is shown below.

```
1.    Find an initial packing which satisfies basic requirement
         such as area and wire length;
2.    Draw constraint graph and determine each blocks MAMS
         and dead-spaces;
3.    While(Temperature>min_temperature)
4.       Randomly select a block not on critical path and a
           direction whose corresponding MAMS is greater than zero;
```

```
    Move that block on that direction at a random distance
      less than MAMS;
    Update MAMS, dead-spaces and nets information;
    Apply buffer allocation algorithm;
    If optimized accept it; else accept with a probability;
    Decrease temperature;
  End while
```

4 Experimental Result

The buffer planning and optimization algorithm have been implemented on SUN Ultra-SPARC and benchmarks are MCNC and CSTC(generated by duplicating ami33 and ami49 blocks and nets) benchmarks. The values for parameters are based on a 0.18m technology in the NTRS97 roadmap[11]. Since we are concentrating on two-pin nets, we decompose each net to two-pin nets using minimum-spanning tree. Because these benchmarks have no timing information and are not fit for direct buffer evaluation, we compute optimal delay Topt under optimal buffer insertion [10] (the minimized delay if we insert enough buffers on optimized locations) and assign a constraint delay 1.05 and 1.20 times Topt to the net. We choose this delay assign method so that each net's timing is possible to be satisfied and some buffers are often necessary to achieve this . Since the timing closures are randomly generated, it is not easy to compare it directly with result shown in [2]. However, we have implemented all these algorithms to make comparison in Table 1. The first column "No blocks moved" displays results after applying buffer allocation algorithm on the initial packing after CBL without optimization. The second column "DS redis. within room" displays results on packing generated by algorithm introduced in [2] which moves block within its room. The third column displays results on packing generated by our algorithm which redistributes dead-space based on room resizing. "Met/Total" is the number of nets satisfying timing constraint compared to the total number of nets, "Time" is the time consumed by each algorithm and "Improved" is the improving percent of our algorithm compared to the other algorithms. From the table below, we could see that our algorithm has an average improvement of 3.3% compared to algorithm without optimization and has an improvement of 1.58% compared to algorithm introduced in [2].

Table 1. Experimental Results

	No blocks moved		DS redis. within room		Our algorithm		Improved
	Met/Total	Time	Met/Total	Time	Met/Total	Time	Perc%
AMI33	340/363	<1s	348/363	6s	353/363	19s	3.8%/1.4%
AMI49	443/545	<1s	454/545	15s	463/545	72s	4.5%/2%
CSTC132	1313/1434	1s	1329/1434	52s	1351/1434	120s	2.9%/1.6%
CSTC199	1898/2111	1s	1913/2111	64s	1938/2111	160s	2%/1.3%
Average							3.3%/1.58%

5 Conclusion

In this paper, on the base of dead space redistribution buffer-insertion algorithm introduced in [2], we extend it by resizing rooms to improve number of nets that satisfy timing closure without violating topology and total area. Our algorithm provides steps for determining a block's maximum allowable move space and organize the dead spaces systematically so that buffer planning could be improved gradually with simulated annealing. Experimental results show that our algorithm is efficient for resolving the problem of buffer planning. Additionally, our algorithm is fit for IP based SOC planning since it often requires improving timing performance without violating topology. However, because a move may cause many blocks to move and room resizing and dead space update is more complicate, a faster moving solution and faster buffer evaluation method is in great need, which will be our future work.

References

1. X.L. Hong, S. Dong, G. Huang, et al: Corner block list representation and its application to floorplan optimization. IEEE Trans. on Circuits and Systems II: Express Briefs, Vol. 51, No. 5 , 2004, pp.228 - 233.
2. S. Chen, X.L. Hong, S.Q. Dong, Y.C. Ma: A buffer planning algorithm based on dead space redistributio. ASP-DAC, 2003.
3. J. Cong, T. Kong, and D. Z. Pan: Buffer block planning for interconnect-driven floorplanning. IEEE/ACM ICCAD, 1999.
4. Y.C. Ma, X.L.Hong, S.Q. Dong, S. Chen, Y.C. Cai: An Integrated Floorplanning with an Efficient Buffer Planning Algorithm. ISPD, 2003.
5. P. Sarkar, C. K. Koh: Routability-driven repeater block planning for interconnect-centric floorplanning. ISPD, 2000.
6. X. Tang and D.F. Wong: Planning buffer locations by network flows. Intl. Symp. Physical Design, 2000, pp. 180-185.
7. F. F. Dragan, A. B. Kahng, et al: Provably good global buffering by multiterminal multicommodity flow approximation. ASP-DAC, 2001.
8. C. W. Sham, F. Y. Young: Routability driven floorplanner with buffer block planning. ISPD, 2002.
9. F. Ragiq, M. C. Jeske, H. H. Yang, N. Sherwani: Integrated floorplanning with buffer/channel insertion for bus-based microprocessor designs. ISPD, 2002.
10. C. J. Alpert and A. Devgan: Wire segmenting for improved buffer insertion. Proc. Design Automation Conf, pp. 588C593, June 1997.
11. Semiconductor Industry Association, National Technology Roadmap for Semiconductors, 1997.

Analyzing the Performance of Mesh and Fat-Tree Topologies for Network on Chip Design

Vu-Duc Ngo, Huy-Nam Nguyen, and Hae-Wook Choi

System VLSI Lab Laboratory, SITI Research Center, School of Engineering
Information and Communications University (ICU),
Yusong P.O. Box 77, Taejon 305-714, Korea
{duc75, huynam, hwchoi}@icu.ac.kr

Abstract. The demand of integration of many heterogeneous semiconductor intellectual property (IP) blocks has been introducing a new chip design paradigm so called on chip network. This paradigm promisingly offers a packet switched network among IPs to reduce the main problems in the very deep sub micron technologies that arise from non-scalable global wire delay, failure to achieve global synchronization, errors due to the signal integrity, non-scalable bus based functional interconnection, etc. This paper introduces interconnected or switched network topologies and also analyze their performances in terms of communication protocol related to the issues such as routing strategy, buffer size, routing algorithm , etc. The above mentioned evaluations are done by utilizing the tool that has been widely used in the research domain of computer network design, so called NS-2.

1 Introduction

The continuation of scaling down of transistor size is leading to the fact that a large number of IPs can be integrated on a single chip. This integration, according to [1], gives rise to new challenges. The most prominent issue allied with the mass integration design comes up with non-scalable global wire delay [2]. Though sub-micron technology creates the good chance to reduce the gate delays, global wire delays significantly increase or remain constant by including repeaters. This matter also leads to the high consumption of silicon area and power. The other critical concerns related to forthcoming technology and current NOC design methodology are global synchronization and non-scalable bus based functional interconnection (especially when the number of integrated IPs is numerous). To overcome the above mentioned problems, we can propose the use of switching based topologies that have been extensively used for computer network to integrate IPs. Another word, the on-chip topology resembles the interconnect architecture of high performance parallel computing systems [3]. By using this design approach, the communications between IPs can be the packet based. We also realize that the needs of global wire can be omitted. The wires are now used only as the connections between switches. Also, we do not any longer worry about global synchronization due to decoupling of the processing

L.T. Yang et al. (Eds.): EUC 2005, LNCS 3824, pp. 300–310, 2005.

nodes. To get over the induced noise caused by unreliable physical channels, the packet based error control mechanisms can be applied. The two promising on chip network topologies have been mostly proposing are Mesh and Fat-Tree, respectively. The comparison of performance evaluation of the two topologies with respected to physical constraints was made by Petrini and et al. [4]. The comparison showed clearly that the Fat-Tree topology proposed firstly by Leiserson [5], with several merits such as:

- *Scalability; Reliability; Regular and simple topology; High throughput; Good performance,*

has superior performance to that of the Mesh topology. To verify these above mentioned merits in terms of on chip network topology design approach, we need to carry out the high level simulation Fat-Tree topology in the scenario of on chip network implementation. However, the high level simulation of on chip network is still in its infancy. Choosing simulation tool and defining the physical constraints for it are now at the beginning stage. There is no gate level simulation tool, which is known as the best method to evaluate the physical behavior of SOC design, can be developed to adapt to on chip network design and verification. To conquer this limitation we choose network simulation tool to simulate the on chip network with respect to high level approach. Among network simulation tools, NS2 [6] emerges to be the best solution to simulate the high level of on chip network architecture. The NS2 is widely used in the research for design and evaluation of computer network domain. We take the advantage of NS2 in terms of communication protocol (OSI protocol) to simulate and verify the performance of our proposed interconnection architecture for on chip network's application, including topologies selection, the design of router, and routing schemes, as well as queuing schemes. In [7] and [8], the authors proposed the Mesh and Fat-Tree architectures for on chip network topology design, respectively. However, the performances of these architectures are not yet mentioned in terms of high level of topology evaluation. In this paper, we report several experiment results of general NoC and H.264 video decoder design based on the simulation of on chip network using NS2 for Mesh and Fat-Tree architectures with the relevant routing and queuing schemes. By using these simulation results with certain comparisons, we propose to use Fat-Tree as on chip network interconnection topology. Our paper is organized as follows: The interconnection architectures and routing schemes are introduced and compared in section II. The NS2 and its mapping to on chip network is conducted in section III. The simulation results and their comparisons are analyzed in section IV. Finally the conclusion and future work will be given in section V.

2 Interconnection Architectures and Routing Schemes

2.1 Interconnection Architecture

Mesh architecture: The $k-ary\ d-dimensional$ Mesh architecture is built by its dimension d and radix k. This follows that the total number of switches

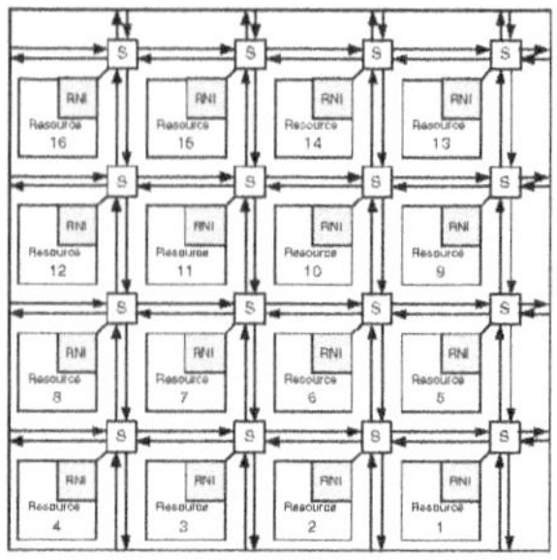

Fig. 1. 4-ary 2-dimensional Mesh topology

is k^d. The k^d switches are organized in an $d - dimensional$ grid such that there are k switches located in each dimension and wrap-around connections. Since the number of IPs that can be connected to one switch is $d - 1$, it follows that the total number of mounted IPs is clearly calculated by

$$N_{Mesh} = k^d(d - 1). \tag{1}$$

We denote b as the unidirectional bandwidth, the total bandwidth of the network is obtain by

$$B_{Mesh} = 2k^d b. \tag{2}$$

Moreover, this architecture offers a simple connection scheme. Therefore, the Shortest Path routing is mostly applied on it. Also the number of the mounted IPs is relatively high compared to the total bandwidth. So that the performance of Mesh architecture is not high.

The Fig.1 shows an example of $4 - ary\ 2 - dimensional$ Mesh architecture. We can see in this figure the number of switches and the number of the mounted IPs are both equal 16.

Fat-Tree architecture: The Fat-Tree is an indirect interconnection network based on a complete binary tree, which was proposed by Leiserson [5]. There is a significant difference from the traditional tree in computer science, Fat-Tree copies image from real tree that it gets as thicker as it approaches the root. A set of processors are located at the leaves of the Fat-Tree and each edge of

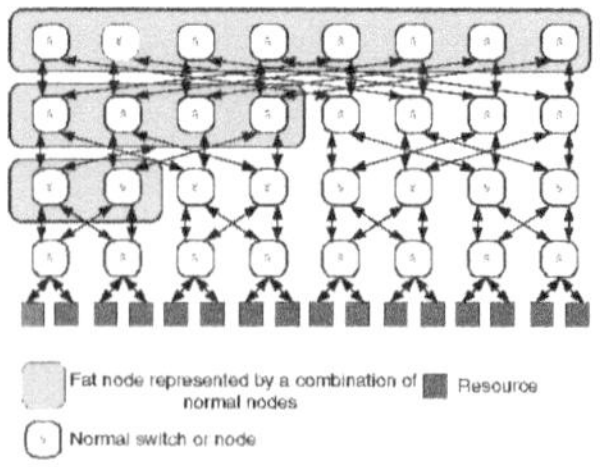

Fig. 2. 4-ary 2-dimensional Fat-Tree topology

the underlying tree corresponds to a bi-directional channel between parent and child. The bandwidth of the Fat-Tree increases as it goes closer to the root. This feature makes Fat-Tree to be sufficiently applicable with advanced routing algorithm as the Distance Vector instead of Shortest Path. Furthermore, since the depth of the tree is calculated by the dimensional metric plus 1, it follows that the size or the number of IPs that can be mounted on one certain Fat-Tree topology depends on the depth of the tree. As the depth of the tree increases, the number of IPs as well as the total capacity of the network gets bigger. These two significant characteristics lead Fat-Tree having better performance in comparison with Mesh architecture. More analytically, we introduce some calculations in $k - ary\ d - dimensional$ Fat-Tree architecture, which is shown in Fig.2 (case of $k = 4$, $d = 2$).

As can be seen in the Fig.2 the fat nodes are the switches that are located in the higher degrees of the tree and they can be considered as the combination of $2^{(t_d-1)}$ single nodes, where t_d presents the node's degree on the tree. The number of mounted IPs $N_{Fat-Tree}$ and the number of switches $S_{Fat-Tree}$ are straightforwardly calculated as follows:

$$N_{Fat-Tree} = k^d, \tag{3}$$

$$S_{Fat-Tree} = k^{d-1}d, \tag{4}$$

respectively. Therefore with the unidirectional bandwidth defined by b, the total bandwidth is presented by

$$B_{Fat-Tree} = 2k^d db. \tag{5}$$

We carry out the comparison of this above total bandwidth with the case of the $k - ary\ d - dimensional$ Mesh's total bandwidth, which is shown in (1). With $d \geq 2$, the total bandwidth of the $k - ary\ d - dimensional$ Fat-Tree architecture is equal d times of the total bandwidth of $k - ary\ d - dimensional$ Mesh architecture. Since more available total bandwidth is offered, it follows that the more propagation delay can be decreased. This fact is very good factor to consider Fat-Tree as a appropriate candidate for on chip network topology. However, the designers have to accept the higher network cost or complexity.

2.2 Routing Schemes

Shortest Path: The distributed Shortest Path routing scheme [12] is an iterative procedure to find out the routing table which contains the shortest paths from all the nodes of the network to each common destination which also belongs to the network. Let one of the common nodes be defined as x. In order to keep track of the shortest paths, we label each non-destination node i with a pair (η, d_i^x) where d_i^x represents the current iteration for the shortest distance from the node to x and η is the number of next nodes along the currently computed shortest path. The iterative algorithm is presented as the following 4 steps:

- Initialization: Set the initial value for the destination node x:

$$d_x^x = 0, \tag{6}$$

and label all other non-destination nodes $(\bullet, +\infty)$.
- Updating: Update d_i^x for each non-destination node i by checking the current value of d_j^x for each neighbor node j and carrying out the operation:

$$d_i^x \leftarrow \min_j [d_j^x + l(i,j)], \tag{7}$$

where $l(i,j)$ denotes the length of the link from node i to node j.
- Node j's label is completely updated by replacing the metric η by the number of the neighbor nodes which minimize the (7).
- Step 2 is repeated at each node until no further changes occur.

This above algorithm is terminated with the output of routing table. By this table the data packet with a destination node identifier in its header can reach it's desired destination node with a certain route that contains specifically preferred neighbors assigned by predetermined routing table. This fact significantly affects network performance due to its static characteristic. We will discuss this issue in the IV section. However, this routing algorithm is still widely applied over others for implementation within operational networks due to its simplicity.

Distance Vector: In this context we reintroduce the Distance Vector routing algorithm [12] that was proposed relying on Distributed Bellman-Ford algorithm. In this algorithm, each node i maintains a set of distances d_{ij}^x where j varies over the neighbors of i. Moreover, node i treats its neighbor k as the next intermediate node that the data packet visits before reaching the given destination x if:

$$d_{ik}^x = \min_j \{d_{ij}^x\}. \tag{8}$$

The succession of next intermediate nodes selected in this above method leads to x along the shortest path. To keep track of the distance estimation up-to-date, each node monitors the length metrics of its available outgoing links. It periodically broadcasts its current estimate of the shortest distance to every other node inside the network to each of its neighbors . By checking out the available outgoing links, this algorithm outperforms to that of Shortest Path algorithm. The comparisons will be performed by simulation in section IV.

3 NS2 and Its on Chip Network Mapping

The network simulator, NS2, with its capabilities of describing network topologies, network protocols, routing algorithms, packet scheduling schemes, as well as traffic generation methods, has been broadly used in the field of computer network design and simulation. Referring to the article [9], the authors used NS2 to simulate the Mesh architecture with dimension of 5x5 for on chip network topology. However, only the simplest cases of routing algorithm, routing strategy, queuing algorithm, transmission protocol are defined as simulation constraints. In this paper, we not only carry out the simulations for $2-dimensional$ Mesh architecture with the advanced issues of those mentioned constraints but also for $2-dimensional$ Fat-Tree architecture to make a comparison and choose a good candidate for on chip network topology.

For both of Mesh and Fat-Tree topologies, one IP, called resource, is always connected to one switch, called router. The interface between IP and switch is called Resource Network Interface (RNI). The functions of RNI cover 4 upper layers of the internet 5 layers model. The physical layer is functioned by the linkages between resources and routers (Rs2Rt) or between routers and routers (Rt2Rt). In NS2 environment the transmission protocol can be defined as UDP or TCP. The exponential traffic generator model is applied. The routing strategies can be: Shortest path, Dynamic or Distance Vector (DV), according to the choice of two architectures (Mesh or Fat-Tree). Since IPs (resources) of on chip network platform can be CPU, RAM, DSP, FPGA, USB, etc, the demand of communication loads originated from each IP are different. This leads us use the fair queuing scheme like Stochastic Fairness Queuing (SFQ) instead of DropTail introduced in [9]. The uses of FQ and SFQ for our mentioned architectures achieve overperformance to that of the DropTail in terms of drop probability, delay, as well as throughput. The Table. 1 shows the summary of mapped NS2 constraints for our experiments on the two mentioned architectures.

4 Simulation Results and Discussion

In this paper, we firstly simulate several cases with different constraints of routing and queuing algorithms as well as buffer sizes for the 4x4 Mesh and $4-ary$ $2-dimensional$ Fat-Tree architectures. In detail, we simulate these two architectures with Shortest Path and Distance Vector routing algorithms, also we attach the congestion control or Queuing algorithms such as DropTail, RED (Random Early Detection), DRR (Deficit Round Robin), and SFQ (Stochastic Fairness Queuing)to the switches of both architectures. Finally, we compare the simulation results of all simulated cases to choose the best combination of embedded routing and queuing algorithms for each topology. We also compare the

Table 1. Application of On chip network constraints to NS2

On chip network model	Applied NS2 constraints
Connections	Rs2Rt and Rt2Rs
Transmission protocols	UDP and TCP
Packet size	8 bytes
Buffer size	8, 16, 32 (packets)
Queuing schemes	DropTail, DRR, RED, SFQ
Routing schemes	Shortest Path, Distance Vector
Traffic generator	Exponential
Bisection bandwidth (Max)	8 Gbits (expected)

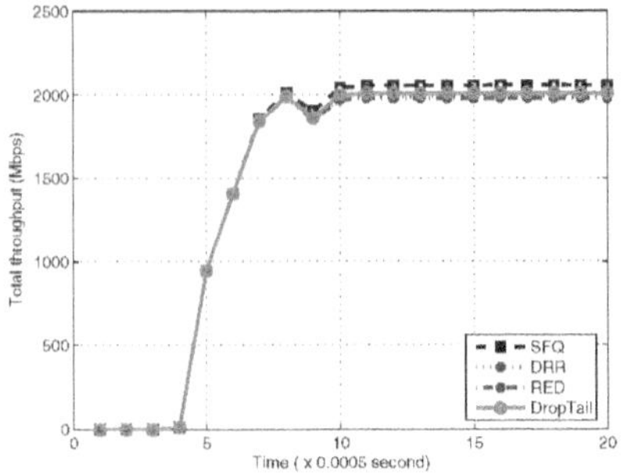

Fig. 3. Throughput of Mesh (Shortest Path) vs. Queuing Schemes

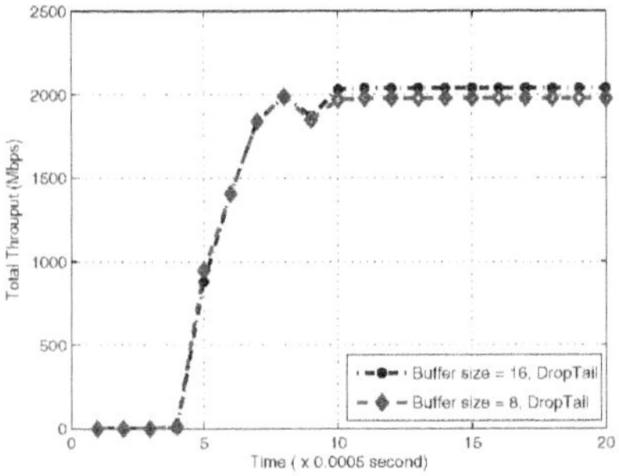

Fig. 4. Throughput of Mesh (Shortest Path) vs. Buffer sizes

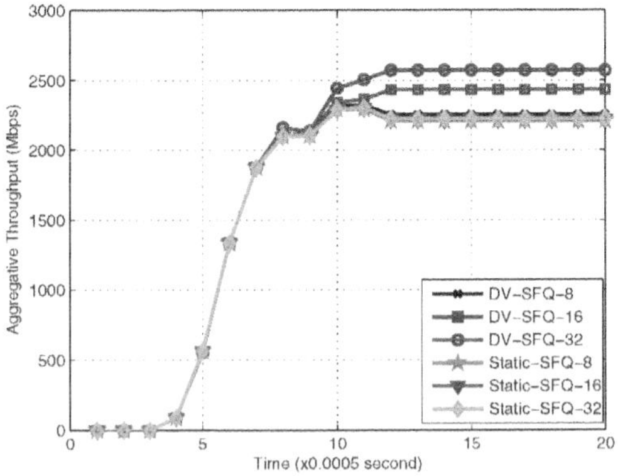

Fig. 5. Throughput of Fat-Tree (SFQ queuing schemes) vs. Buffer sizes and routing schemes

performances offer by two architectures in the cases of using the similar options of routing, queuing, as well as the buffer sizes. We already defined the on chip network model and it mapped constraints onto NS2 simulator in the Table. 1. Due to the limitation of the computer capability, we just limited the data rate

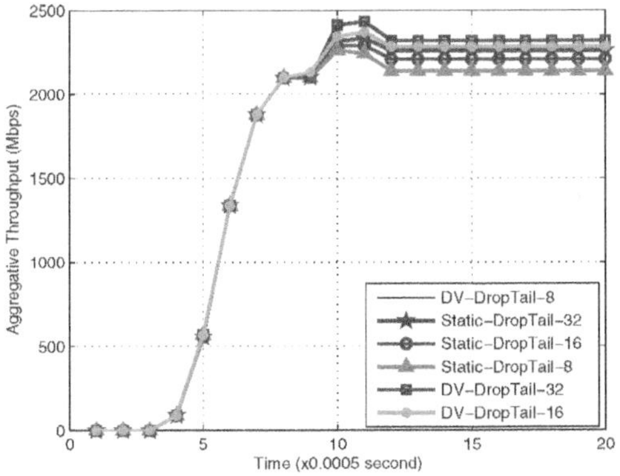

Fig. 6. Throughput of Fat-Tree (DropTial queuing schemes) vs. Buffer sizes and routing schemes

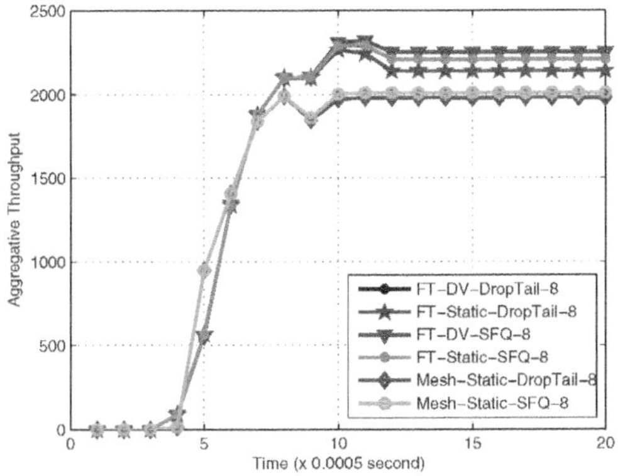

Fig. 7. Throughput Comparison of Fat-Tree (FT) and Mesh topologies

of each resource up to 200Mbps. The resources are activated to generate data packets randomly. The Fig. 3 and Fig. 4 depict the aggregative throughput of 4x4 Mesh topology vs. different options of applied queuing schemes and buffer sizes, respectively. As can be seen in the Fig. 3, with the same buffer size as well as routing scheme (Shortest Path), the use of SFQ queuing scheme offers us the best performance with respect to total throughput on 4x4 Mesh topology. The Fig.4 shows that the bigger buffer size is applied, the higher throughput is achieved. The throughputs of Fat-Tree topology with queuing schemes of SFQ and DropTail are depicted in Fig. 5 and 6, respectively. We realize that by applying Distance Vector routing algorithm to Fat-Tree topology, with its own merits as pointed out in previous sections, the system throughput can be increasingly achieved. In the last figure, Fig. 7, we compare Fat-Tree and Mesh topologies with the same buffer size of 8 packets in terms of system throughput related to different choices of routing and queuing schemes. We can see that the Fat-Tree topology with the embedded routing algorithm of Distance Vector and queu-

From/To	DB	MC	FR_MEM	ITIQ	LENT	VOM	Processor	REC	MVMVD	IPRED	IS
DB			7114								
MC	4475		345								
FR_MEM	2650	10652			63	4802		40			
ITIQ		5949						642			
LENT				6592			408		496		
VOM											
Processor	326	322		186	232	12		7	922	59	12
REC	321	13	27							145	
MVMVD							828				
IPRED								321			
IS			63								

Fig. 8. IPs and their connections (in kbps) of H.264 video decoder

ing algorithm of SFQ gains highest throughput. In the stable period, this design achieves approximately 250Mbps higher to that of Mesh topology using Shortest Path and DropTail schemes [9].

More specifically, we implement the H.264 video decoder on those mentioned NoC architectures. The IPs and their connections represented by the directional data rates are defined by the table in Fig. 8. There are 11 IPs that are allocated onto 11 corresponding switches. To maximize the throughput transactions among the IPs, we adopt the Branch and Bound technique presented in [13] for the cost function of data rates. The results of optimum mapping shows that the IPs which are connected by the connections of high data rates should be allocated next to each others. This mapping reduces the drop packets that is very high rate if we allocate the mentioned IPs far away since huge number of packets from the original IP need to go through a lot of intermediate switches before reach the destination. In order to make this argument clearly, two mapping schemes of IPs onto the 4x4 Mesh architecture are simulated as depicted in Fig. 9. As seen in this figure, the throughputs of IPs of random mapping is shown by Fig. 9a are almost similar to that of the throughputs of IPs of the optimum mapping shown by Fig. 9b, but the corresponding bisectional bandwidth required for random case of 30Mbps is much more higher to that of 15Mbps for the optimum case. These two simulations are done with SFQ queuing scheme and DV routing scheme. The last experiment is carried out to show the superior performance of using Fat-Tree compared to Mesh architecture. As seen in Fig. 10, with bisectional bandwidth of 20Mbps, not only the system requirement of throughput is met but also the throughputs of IPs are almost similar to the case of random mapping of Mesh architecture with the bisectional bandwidth of 30Mbps.

In conclusion, we propose to use Fat-Tree topology with embedded Distance Vector routing and SFQ queuing schemes as on chip network switching core topology.

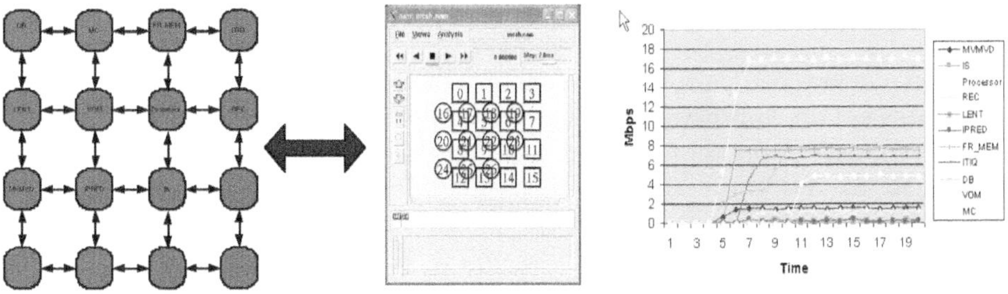

(a). Bisectional bandwidth of 30Mbps, SFQ, DV

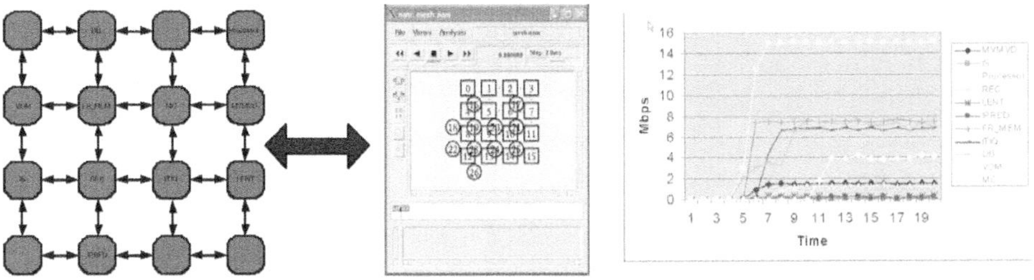

(b). Bisectional bandwidth of 15Mbps, SFQ, DV

Fig. 9. IPs allocation schemes their throughputs (in Mbps) of H.264 video decoder with Mesh architecture: (a) random allocation, (b) optimum allocation

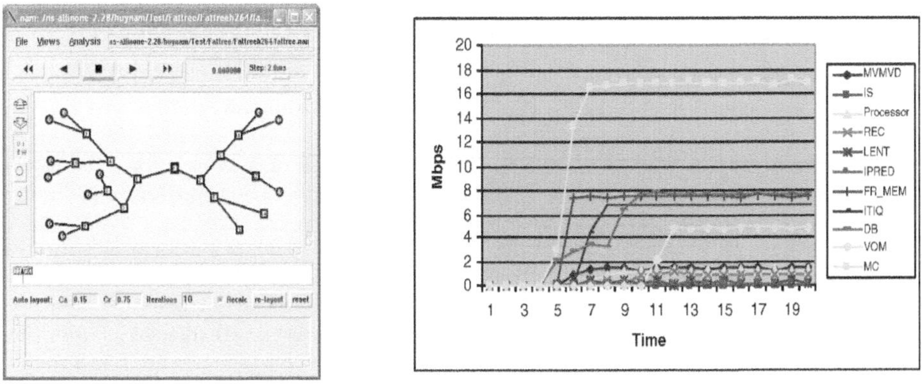

Bisectional bandwidth of 20Mbps, SFQ, DV

Fig. 10. IPs allocation scheme their throughputs (in Mbps) of H.264 video decoder with Fat-Tree architecture

5 Conclusion

In this paper, we compare the performance of Fat-Tree and Mesh architectures in the sense of on chip network design methodology. We also carry out the high level simulation of on chip network based on Mesh and Fat-Tree architectures using NS2 to verify our analysis. The simulations of the Mesh and Fat-Tree architectures are done with advanced routing algorithms and router queueing mechanisms for general NoC design as well as H.264 video decoder. Finally, by numerical and simulation results we can conclude that the Fat-Tree architecture is suitable for on chip network switching core. By utilizing Fat-Tree architecture and Distance Vector routing algorithm as well as Stochastic Fairness Queue algorithm, we can achieve the best combination for our design in terms of choosing on chip network topology. It has superior performance to that of Mesh architecture, in which Shortest Path routing algorithm is applied, with respected the system throughput.

References

1. L. Benini and G. DeMicheli,"Networks On Chips: A new SoC paradigm," IEEE computer, Jan, 2002.
2. M. A. Horowitz et al.,"The future of wires," Proceeding of IEEE, Vol. 89, Issue. 4 , pp. 490-504, Apr 2001
3. P. Guerrier, A. Grenier,"A generic architecture for on-chip packet-switched interconnectio,"Design automation and test in Europe conference, pp. 250-256, Aug 2000.
4. F. Petrini and M. Vanneschi, "Network performance under Physical Constrain," Proceedings of International Conference on Parallel Processing, pp.34 - 43, Aug 1997.
5. C. E. Leiserson,"Fat Trees: Universal networks for hardware efficient supercomputing," IEEE Transactions on Computer, C-34, pp. 892-90,1 Oct 1985.
6. Ns2: www.isi.edu/nsnam/ns/.
7. H. Kariniemi, J. Nurmi, "New adaptive routing algorithm for extended generalized fat trees on-chip," Proceedings of International Symposium on System-on-Chip, pp. 113 - 118, Nov 2003.
8. P. P. Pande, C. Grecu, A. Ivanov, R. Saleh, "Design of a switch for network on chip applications," Proceedings of the 2003 International Symposium on Circuits and Systems, pp. V-217 - V-220 vol. 5, May 2003.
9. Yi-Ran Sun, S. Kumar, A. Jantsch, "Simulation and Evaluation for a Network on Chip Architecture Using Ns-2," Proceeding of 20th IEEE Norchip Conference, Nov 2002.
10. D. Berozzi, L. Benini and G. DeMicheli,"Low-Power Error Resilient Encoding for On-chip Data Buses," DATE-International Conference on Design and Test Europe, Jun 2002.
11. J. Muttersbach et al., "Globally-asynchronous locally synchronous architectures to simplify the design of on-chip systems," Proc. 12th Annual IEEE International ASIC/SoC Conference, pp. 317-321, Sep 1999.
12. D. Bertsekas and R. Gallager, "Data Networks," Chapter 5., Second Edition, Prentice-Hall, Inc., 1992.
13. S.Murali and G.De Micheli, Bandwidth-Constrained Mapping of Cores pnto NoC Architectures, , DATE, International Conference on Design and Test Europe, 2004, pp. 896-901.

Hierarchical Graph: A New Cost Effective Architecture for Network on Chip

Alireza Vahdatpour[1], Ahmadreza Tavakoli[2], and Mohammad Hossein Falaki[1]

[1] Computer Engineering Department,
Sharif University of Technology
{vahdatpour, falaki}@ce.sharif.edu
[2] Electrical Engineering Department,
Sharif University of Technology
artavakoli@ee.sharif.edu

Abstract. We purposed a new Network on Chip (NoC) architecture called Hierarchical Graph. The most interesting feature of this novel architecture is its simple implementation process. Furthermore, the flexible structure of this topology makes it suitable for use in application specified chips. To benchmark the suggested architecture with existing ones, basic models of physical implementation have been extracted and simulated using NS-2. The results compared with the common used architecture Mesh show that HG has better performance, especially in local traffics and high loads.

1 Introduction

As predicted in [1], we will enter the *Ultra Large Scale Integration* (ULSI) design world with 45nm technology in 2010. Integration of multibillion transistors will be possible and device delays will get smaller. The dominant issue in design would be the interconnection between transistors.

The closer we get to large chip integration, the more we need smart design plans. Currently one of the most accepted plans is *System on a Chip* (SoC). In SoC methodology a number of IP-cores (FPGAs, mixed signal blocks, processors, memory blocks etc.) are placed together on a single chip, with proper systematic interconnections. Today the most common method of interconnection is BUS. While the number and complexity of cores are increasing in *Ultra Deep Submicron*, interconnections become more challenging.

Computer networks have been successful in handling the problems of managing large number of resources. This has led to a new paradigm in the design of SoC systems, called *Network on Chip* [2] which is compatible with *Globally Asynchronous Locally Synchronous* (GALS) design method. NoC design uses protocols similar to OSI reference model of networking [3], as the interconnection facility between IP cores. Currently, the most common network architectures for NoC systems are Mesh and Fat-Tree [4].

In this paper we have introduced a new architecture for NoC systems named *Hierarchical Graph* (HG). Some related work is addressed in the next section and

L.T. Yang et al. (Eds.): EUC 2005, LNCS 3824, pp. 311–320, 2005.

then various aspects of the proposed architecture are introduced in section 3. In section 4 some physical properties of the implementation of HG are discussed and then the performance of the new architecture is compared with Mesh through the simulation. Finally the results of simulations are presented in section 5.

2 Related Work

There are many research groups working on SoC systems from architectural point of view. In [4] Shashi Kumar et al. introduced a new methodology for designing mesh architecture for NoC. Lacking specific tools for evaluating networks on chip, the performance of Mesh and Fat-Tree were compared using Network Simulator (NS-2) in [5] and [6]. Some useful strategies were introduced by Daniel Wiklund et al. in [7] for benchmarking on chip networks.

3 Architecture

Hierarchical Graph (HG) network topology is designed specially for NoC systems to be compatible with Ultra Deep Submicron fabrication technologies.

Fat-Tree as a network topology has good performance, but its irregular and intensive interconnection lines make it impractical to be implemented on a chip. Although the throughput of HG is not as good as Fat-Tree, it can be implemented with a single metal layer because of its simple interconnection rules. Decreased ratio of switch per resource and simpler switch implementations decreases the implementation cost.

As the name suggests, HG consists of a hierarchical structure of plain graphs (see Fig.1(a)). In each level, there is a graph of interconnected switches, some of which named *Border Switches* are responsible for connecting the graph of this

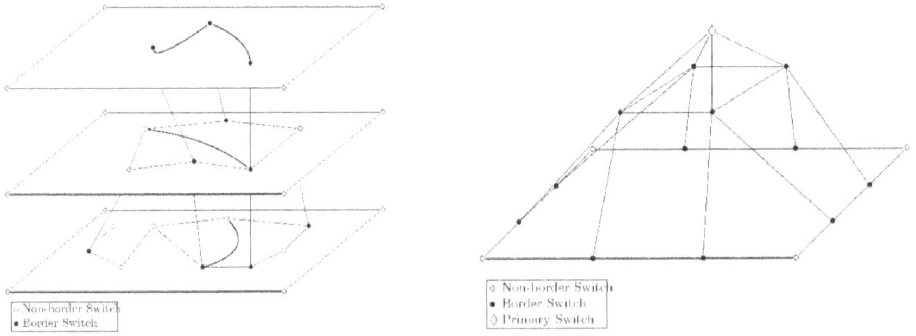

(a) General Hierarchical structure of HG

(b) Structure of proposed Square HG(SHG.)

Fig. 1.

level to the upper level graph. To facilitate physical implementation of interconnections, the graph in each level can have a regular shape e.g. square, which leads to *Square Hierarchical Graph* (SHG). The main focus in this paper is on SHG. The number and position of the border switches are flexible parameters of this architecture. A good choice of border switches in a SHG network would avoid diagonal links as shown in Fig.2(a). In the highest hierarchy, there is always a single powerful switch called *primary switch.* In HG the cores can be placed in different levels of the hierarchy according to their specific communication needs. For example the cores with higher traffic requirements such as central processing units or shared memories can be placed in higher levels to reduce latency and increase the overall performance of the chip.

To analyze performance parameters of HG we used a specific version of SHG. For N^2 general cores, such a SHG network uses $(N-1)^2$ switches with strict connection lines to make a symmetric graph with maximum performance and minimum latency. When N is odd, the central core is substituted with a high performance switch named primary to make the graph more symmetric. The network in Fig.1(b) which is a version of the SHG just mentioned consists of 17 switches, one powerful switch in the highest level, 4 ones in the second level and 12 switches in the third level. Four of the switches in the lowest level are not border switches and the rest are all border switches.

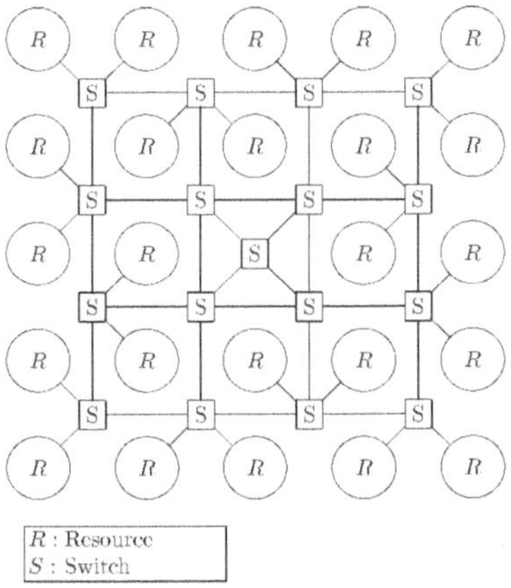

(a) Overview of SHG architecture

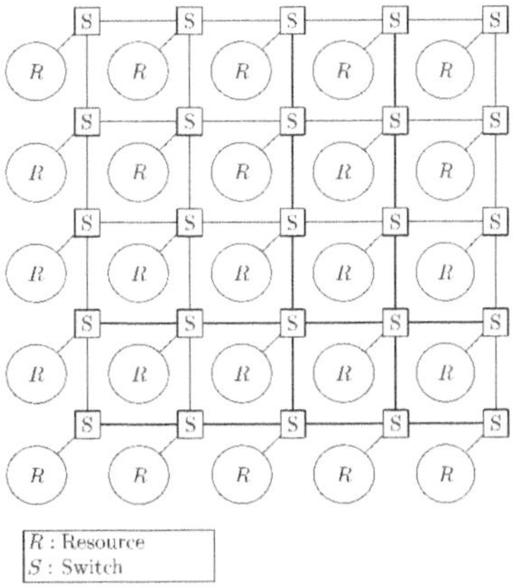

(b) Overview of Mesh architecture

Fig. 2.

Simulations in section 4 demonstrate that, this type of SHG outperforms Mesh in many benchmarks while its number of switches is less than the equivalent Mesh (see Fig.2(b)). It is predicted that the complexity of switches in NoC systems would increase dramatically as the need for implementation of heavy weighted routing algorithms, large queues and queue management disciplines increases. Thus the fewer number of switches would reduce the chip area and overall cost. According to [8], switches with less than five inputs and output virtual channels have simple implementation. So HG switches are not more complex in comparison to common switches used in Mesh.

4 Simulation

Simulations were used to compare the new architecture with existing ones from the performance point of view. Our intention was to prove the suggested architecture has no or little performance penalty while reduces costs. Among the two other architectures , Mesh and Fat-Tree, only Mesh is compared to HG. This is because of the implementation issues of Fat-Tree, discussed in 4.1. In the section 5 the results are compared and different aspects of performance issues of the new architecture are discussed.

Simulations were done using two different traffic models: random traffic and local intensive traffic. In each simulation scenario we used a Mesh of 25 cores which requires 25 switches and a SHG with 24 cores in which 17 switches are involved. The two measured performance indicators were "drop probability" and "overall packet delay". Drop probability is the ratio of the number of dropped packets to the total number of generated packets. For the overall packet delay, end to end delay of all delivered packets was measured and averaged.

The underlying transmission protocol used was UDP. UDP offers no congestion control and reliability. While these two issues are not covered well in NoC researches, TCP is not a good choice because of its high overhead, non predictable delay and other implementation issues. The use of an application specific congestion control can increase the overall performance. There should also be methods to detect and recover delivery failures either in application layer or network layer. These issues are still open to research. Since we are just interested in the architectural performance evaluation, we can safely use UDP for all architectures.

The two traffic models discussed before differ in the choice of sender-receiver pairs. In the random traffic model, each node sends data to another random node. Since each node has no more than one traffic sink and source, this is equivalent to a uniform distribution of sink and source pairs among the cores. While this traffic model can indicate some performance features of any architecture, in practice the locality of traffic is important. For the local traffic model we chose source and sink pairs in a way that 75% of traffic is local. The rest 25% was distributed randomly among the remaining nodes.

The traffic source behavior is also of special importance, while the particular traffic behavior can greatly depend on the specific application, exponential traffic seems most suitable for the simulation purpose. All simulations were also repeated with randomized Constant Bit Rate (CBR) to cover a wider range of traffic behaviors in real applications.

4.1 Modeling Simulation Parameters

For simulation of any network architecture for NoC, we need system level modeling of different chip implementation parameters such as switch delays, link maximum bandwidth and delay of links.

Our modeling parameters are based on the ITRS 2004 data for 45 nm technology predicted to come to market in 2010 [1]. For modeling purposes we will use the top level global interconnection parameters. As predicted in [1], these interconnections will have RC delay about $143ps/mm$ to $189ps/mm$ (the exact amount of delay depends on scattering effects). Also the intrinsic delay of each NMOS is considered to be about $0.39ps$ to $0.98ps$, (the exact amount of delay depends on performance and power efficiency of the device). With these delay values for NMOS the delay of a NAND gate would be about $9.88ps$ to $24.8ps$. The number of maximum parallel lines that can be used to increase bandwidth of a link is also important. This depends on global links wiring pitch size which is predicted to be about $205nm$.

In Fig.2(a) there are 24 cores, one primary switch and 16 ordinary switches. If we assume the cores and primary switch to be about $2.5 \times 2.5mm^2$ and the ordinary switches about $0.5 \times 0.5mm^2$, in a chip area of $1.5 \times 1.5cm^2$, the length of the links between ordinary switches would be $2.5mm$ and the length of the links between cores or primary switch and ordinary switches is $0.1mm$. The overall length of the links is smaller than $10cm$, so using the given pitch size there could be more than 5000 parallel lines in each link. For simplification of modeling only 1024 parallel lines have been used. Using $\sim 200ps/mm$ delay for links, delay of a link between two switches will be about $500ps$ and the links from a switch to a core would have about $20ps$ delay. The switch implementation is based on [8]. The delay of this switch could be modeled with 5 series of NAND gates estimated about $50ps$. The delay of each *Resource Network Interface* (RNI) is about half of the delay of an ordinary switch and thus about $25ps$.

For a signal transmitted from a RNI and received by a switch, the overall delay consists of RNI delay, link delay and half of a switch delay which is totally about $70ps$. This means $550ps$ switch to switch delay. For calculating switch to link bandwidth, $550ns$ delay is considered leading to $2GHz$ bandwidth for each line. So 1024 parallel lines bundled in a link would have $2048GHz$. Using this method the bandwidth of the link between a switch and a core is $51.2GHz$.

In Mesh topology (Fig.2(b)) core to switch links and switch to switch links are the same as in SHG. Also RNI and Switches have approximately the same structure as in SHG. So the same model as SHG is used for Mesh.

In Fat-Tree the connections cannot be implemented on a single metal layer and its long link distances in real chips make the bandwidth of links very poor in comparison to the two other topologies, Mesh and HG.

4.2 Simulation Experiment

All simulations were done using the publicly available Network Simulator (NS-2) [9]. Both a traffic sink and a traffic generator were attached to each node. In other words each node could both send and receive data which is near to what is expected in real applications. Since the selected Mesh network had one core more then SHG, the central core of Mesh was not involved in simulations.

To reduce high variations in random traffic model we had to repeat each simulation and use the average result.

Since NS-2 is designed for computer networks, the bandwidth and delays proposed for a NoC system are not suitable for simulation. We scaled down all the estimated quantities by dividing all bandwidth values by a factor of 10240 and multiply delay values by a factor of 10240, so all simulation results are in terms of scaled quantities.

5 Results

As mentioned before the results of simulations are average packet delay and drop ratio for Mesh and SHG, using two traffic models and two traffic source behaviors. The results are presented here according to the traffic model. In the following graphs delay and drop probability are shown versus traffic load generated by a single traffic source.

5.1 Random Traffic Model

Although the random traffic model is not what is expected to happen in real applications it can provide a good measure for comparing the two architectures.

The use of random CBR traffic generators in the random traffic model for SHG and Mesh resulted in Fig.3 and Fig.4. The graph in Fig.3 shows average packet delivery delay versus traffic load of any traffic source and the graph in Fig.4 depicts packet drop ratio vs. traffic load. While in SHG, packet drop begins near $85Mb/s$ for a source, in Mesh packet drop begins from $90Mb/s$. No NoC

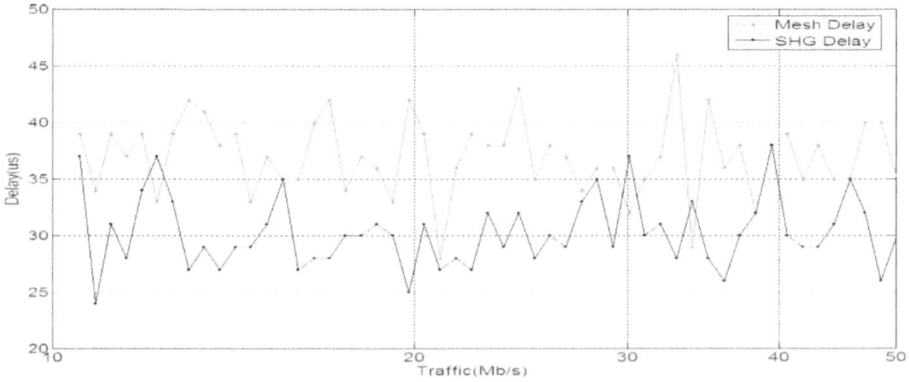

Fig. 3. Packet delay vs. traffic load of a random CBR source in a random traffic network (random traffic model)

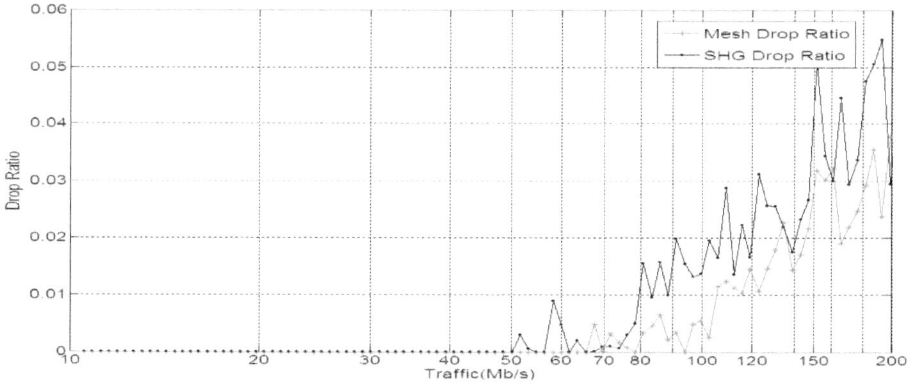

Fig. 4. Drop probability vs. traffic load of a random CBR source in a random traffic network (random traffic model)

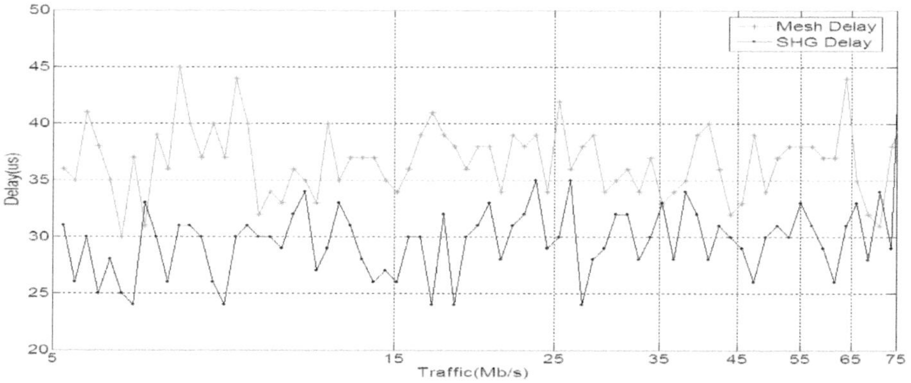

Fig. 5. Packet delay vs. traffic load of an exponential source in a random traffic network (random traffic model)

system can be used in traffic loads near these values but for comparison purposes we continued the simulations beyond these points.

Fig.3 shows that the overall packet delay in SHG is less than Mesh by a constant factor. On the other hand packet drop ratio is less in Mesh.

The exponential traffic source simulations lead to similar results in Fig.5 and Fig.6.

The exponential traffic source is expected to be more realistic as a traffic source. As the graphs show, the results for this type of traffic source have very little difference from the outcome of random CBR traffic source simulations.

The results of random traffic model indicate that SHG performs better when considering overall packet delay. On the other hand SHG is defeated by Mesh when considering drop. The point where considerable packet drop begins is the same in both topologies and after that the drop rate is higher for SHG. After the

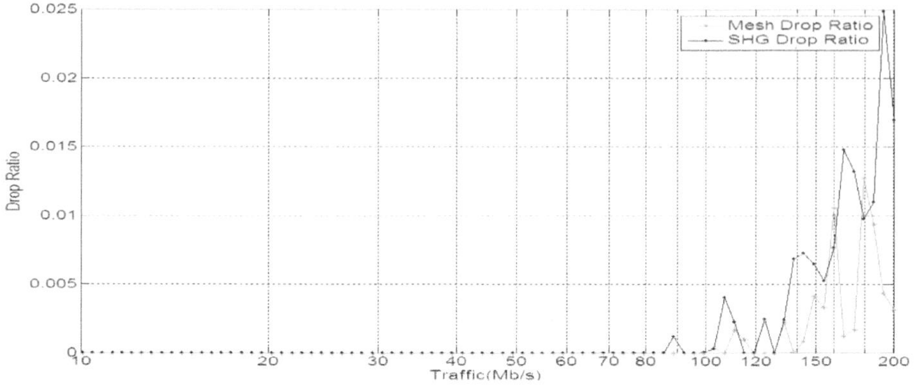

Fig. 6. Drop probability vs. traffic load of an exponential source in a random traffic network (random traffic model)

packet drop starts the network is considered unusable. Thus the most important section of all simulations is where the network is working without any drop.

5.2 Local Traffic Model

The local traffic model resembles real applications to a greater extent than random traffic. Thus the results of this section are of more interest and importance. Besides the more interesting nature of local traffic model, the absence of random variations makes the graphs more readable especially for the exponential simulation.

Fig.7 shows the results of simulating random CBR sources in SHG and Mesh in a local traffic model.

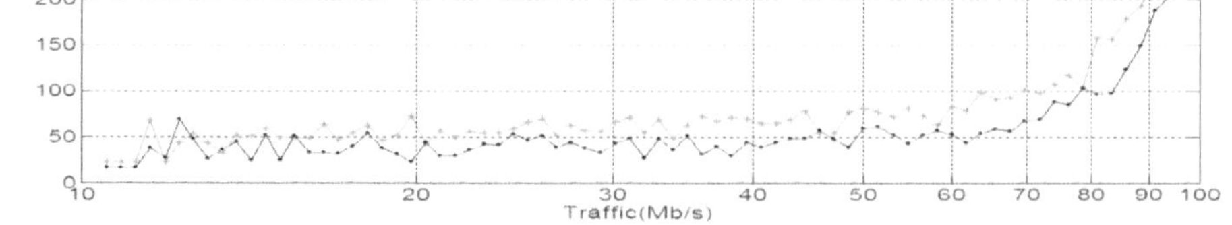

Fig. 7. Packet delay vs. traffic load of a random CBR source in a local traffic network (local traffic model)

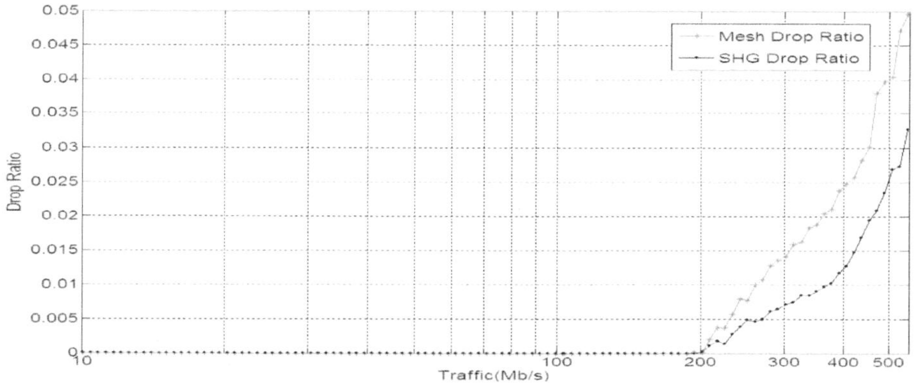

Fig. 8. Drop ratio vs. traffic load of exponential sources in a local traffic network (local traffic model)

Unlike the random traffic model, SHG shows better results for drop ratio in local traffic simulations. The reason is that in SHG there exist neighbor nodes with only one switch between but in Mesh the minimum number of switches between two resources is two. In other words SHG shows better locality than Mesh. Exactly the same reason stands for the bigger gap in delay of SHG and Mesh in higher loads.

In Fig.8 the drop ratio of SHG is much less than Mesh and the difference becomes more as the traffic load increases.

Fig.9 shows the delay of delivered packets for a local traffic model using exponential traffic sources.

These graphs shows that in lower traffic loads SHG performs better by a constant factor, and as the load increases the difference becomes more.

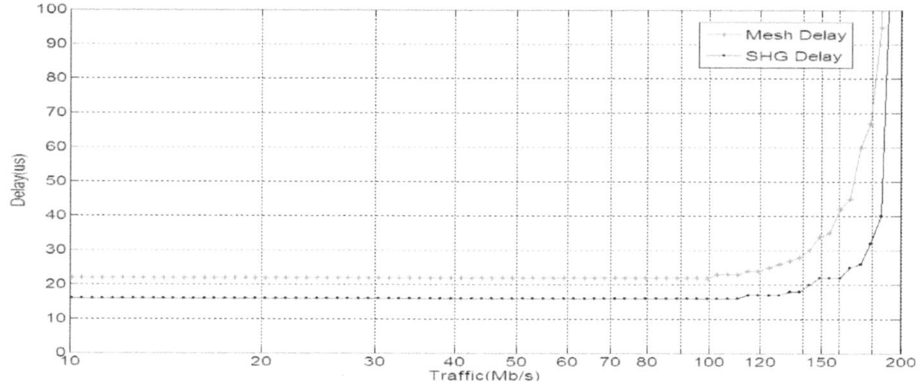

Fig. 9. Packet delay vs. traffic load of exponential sources in a local traffic network (random traffic model.)

6 Conclusion

This paper introduced HG as a flexible topology, specially designed for on chip networks. The flexibility of HG makes it suitable for various applications of SoC. HG provides a network infrastructure that can be easily altered to suite different applications. As an example SHG was introduced and benchmarked with a common used architecture (Mesh). The simulations proved that while SHG is easier to implement it outperforms Mesh in many aspects.

7 Future Work

The performance of HG depends on the appropriate choice of different topological parameters and many other factors such as switch buffer size, bandwidth and etc. The best approach is to find suitable values for these parameters for specific applications. These problems can be addressed in future work.

Furthermore, there are uncovered issues such as congestion and reliability control protocols, routing protocols and many other issues that are common among a very wide range of applications.

References

1. ITRS. International technology roadmap for semiconductors - 2004 edition, http://public.itrs.net/
2. L. Benini and G. De Micheli, Networks on Chip: A New SoC paradigm, IEEE Computer, January 2002(Vol. 35, No. 1), pp. 70-78.
3. JD Day, H Zimmermann, "The OSI reference model", Proceedings IEEE, 1334-1340, December 1983.
4. Shashi Kumar, et al., "A Network on Chip Architecture and Design Methodology", IEEE Computer Society Annual Symposium on VLSI, Pittsburgh, Pennsylvania, USA, April 2002.
5. Yi-Ran Sun, Shashi Kumar, Axel Jantsch, "Simulation and Evaluation for a Network on Chip Architecture Using Ns-2", Proceedings of 20th NORCHIP conference, Copenhagen, November 2002.
6. Vu-Duc Ngo and Hae-Wook Choi "On Chip Network: Topology design and evaluation using NS2".
7. Daniel Wiklund, Sumant Sathe, and Dake Liu, "Network on chip simulations for benchmarking", Proceedings of the International workshop on SoC for real-time applications, Banff, Canada, July 2004.
8. Nikolay Kavaldjiev, Gerard J. M. Smit, Pierre G. Jansen "A Virtual Channel Router for On-chip Networks", Proceedings of IEEE International SOC Conference, Santa ClaraSep, California, 2004
9. The network simulator - NS-2, http://www.isi.edu/nsnam/ns/

RISC/DSP Dual Core Wireless SoC Processor Focused on Multimedia Applications

Hyo-Joong Suh[1] and Jeongmin Kim[2]

[1] School of Computer Science and Information Engineering,
The Catholic University of Korea,
San 43-1 Yeoggog 2 Dong, Wonmi Gu, Bucheon, Gyeonggido, 420-743 Korea
hjsuh@catholic.ac.kr
[2] GCT Semiconductor, Inc.,
2121 Ringwood Avenue San Jose CA 95131

Abstract. The key technology of the mobile multimedia application is System-On-Chip processor that integrates the major function unit with low power consumption using a small battery. The wireless communication is practical technology, which makes comfortable communications between devices, such as IEEE 802.11a/b/g and Bluetooth. By the modern streaming technology with compression, like mpeg, the wireless communication triggers high quality media service without wires.

The wireless communication spend a quite large portion of energy of mobile device if data flows continuously, hence a delicate energy control may needed to fulfill a saving of the limited energy. Due to these issues, integrating the wireless function units into the high performance embedded processor supports a seamless control of power consumption of wireless part, and the communication data flows are sealed in the SoC chip, which reduces inter-chip communiaction energy between a main processor and a wireless media access controller.

We focused the high performance wireless multimedia applications are suffered by the energy consumption, so we alleviated the power issue by integrating of IEEE 802.11a/b/g media access controller, modem, ADC/DAC, high performance DSP, and RISC core in a silicon.

We present a wireless capable SoC processor, GDM5104, that integrated the multiple wireless media access controller as well as CCK/ OFDM/ GFSK modem and ADC/DAC also. Furthermore, the processor integrates RISC and DSP independent cores with appropriate caches, and rich peripherals that sufficient to implement mobile multimedia applications, hence the processor exhibits wireless connectivity with low power consumption. The processor is fabricated in a 0.18um standard CMOS technology, and operates at 133MHz RISC, and 100MHz DSP, which provides full capability of wireless multimedia processing.

1 Introduction

The progress of sub-micron technology allows an integration of various function units on a single system-on-chip (SoC), and appearances of some sophisticated

L.T. Yang et al. (Eds.): EUC 2005, LNCS 3824, pp. 321–330, 2005.

Fig. 1. GDM5104 embedded processor(256 pin, 169 pin fpBGA package)

multimedia processing algorithms induce a lot of multimedia applications that come onto the market. In terms of mobile applications, power energy is provided by primary or secondary batteries, which capacity is quite small to process a complex computation. Several energy saving methods are studied that include frequency control [1], voltage control [2], power control of peripheral block[3], and some power management techniques are implemented on the off-the-shelf embedded processors such as PXA270 by Intel[4].

Portability of a mobile application can be maximized if it communicates using wireless protocol. IEEE 802.11a/b/g [5] wireless standards are one of the rapidly imported technologies that applied on the mobile systems, however the wireless communications consume a lot of energy than wire communication standards such as USB and IEEE 1394. Hence the wireless mobile application is suffered by a shortage of energy, thus operation time is insufficient to play some multimedia titles.

Another issue arises from digital multimedia processing that consumes a lot of processor performance. Many multimedia processing algorithms are inefficient if it operates on the common reduced instruction set computer (RISC) style microprocessor, and if the multimedia algorithm processed on the RISC processor, it consumes lots of energy than a special unit for processing of the algorithm. By the viewpoint of energy consumption and performance, digital signal processing (DSP) processor is suitable to process a most multimedia algorithms, while the RISC processor performs better a general portion of the application code like user interface and TCP/IP protocol [6]. One example of the voice over wireless LAN that utilizes the wireless technology on mobile handset using voice over internet protocol. In this case, DSP processor supports to process speech vocoder, line/acoustic echo cancellation, DTMF, and CPT also. Parallel with the DSP processor, RISC processor supports the operating system, TCP/UDP/IP, RTP, device control, and other user interface parts.

By integrating of IEEE802.11a/b/g, RISC processor, DSP processor, USB2.0, NAND flash, IEEE802.3 MII interface, ATA, Bluetooth [7], and other peripherals on a chip, GDM5104, which presents a capability of powerful and energy-efficient operation in case of wireless mobile applications.

Next section presents the detailed processor internals of chip and low power features. Section 3 describes operating system, software environment, and debug interface of the processor, and Section 4 shows early-stage performance evaluation. Finally, concluding remarks appear in Section 5.

2 GDM5104 Embedded Processor

The GDM5104 is a successor of GDM5302 [8], and these processors are wireless multimedia chips, which are under development. The advanced points of GDM5104 compared to the prior processor are independent structure of RISC and DSP dual processor cores and integration of wireless MAC/modem. Core of the prior GDM5302 processor was RISC/DSP hybrid structure that the core operates DSP mode or RISC mode exclusively, while the successor, GDM5104, has independent cores with independent caches respectively.

Figure 2 shows the dual cores and connected peripherals that exhibit lots of wireless and wire connectivity standards. Internal memory bus (IMB) is the high bandwidth internal bus that connects two cores and high-speed SDRAM, USB2.0, and DMA unit. Peripherals, DMA, and processor cores are connected via AMBA open standard bus [9] with enhanced features. There are two AHB buses of internal and external and APB bus for register access of peripherals. Each peripheral has two AHB bus masters for both AHB buses and one APB slave that will be used to access internal registers or command mapped coprocessor memory. XMEM (X-memory) and YMEM (Y-memory) are AHB slaves to internal AHB, and external memories are AHB slaves to external AHB. Therefore, internal AHB bus is used for the access between internal memories and AHB masters, and external AHB bus is used for the access between external memory and AHB masters. The enhanced features are multi-clock supporting and multiple byte write operations which provides independent bandwidth control on each block to control an energy consumption of each block.

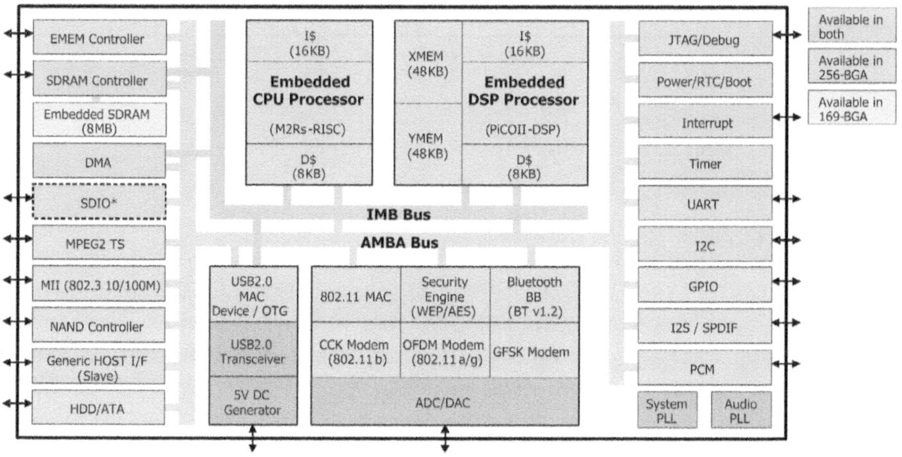

Fig. 2. Internal blocks of GDM5104 processor

2.1 Internal Bus Architecture

Detailed bus architecture of the processor is shown in Figure 3. The memory access priorities of each masters are decided as round robin in AHB arbiter. Since external memory is only connected to external AHB bus, its access priority is dependent on the AHB arbiter. However, internal memory such as XMEM and YMEM is not only connected to internal AHB bus, but also connected to internal CPU and DMA directly. Memory accesses from internal AHB bus have highest priority than the lower priority accesses from processors and DMA requests. AHB and APB bus operates at 88 or 80 MHz fixed frequency while each block is connected to bus through interface logics that can operate by ratios of 44 or 40 MHz reference clock. Speed of function blocks are tuned by the requirement of the bandwidth, thus they operate using multiple or fixed frequency by application requirements.

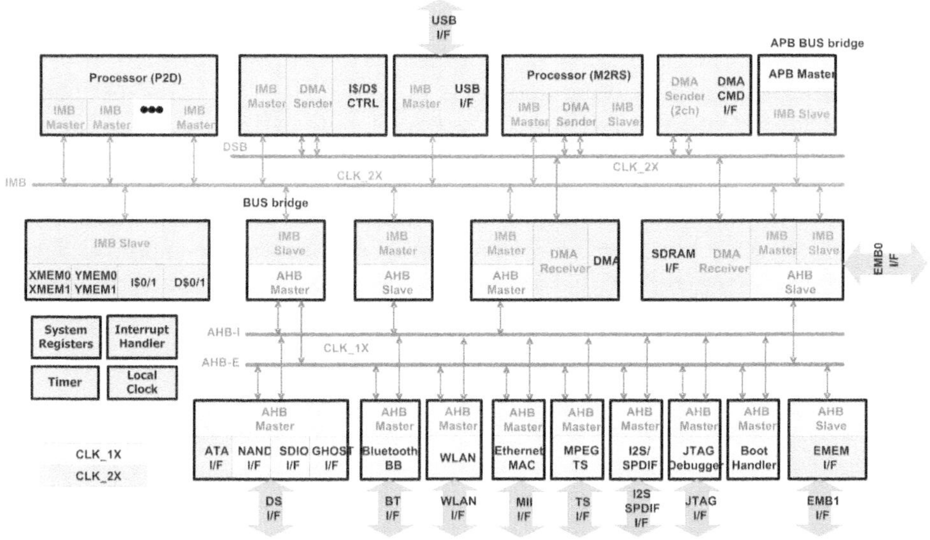

Fig. 3. System bus and operation clock of each block

2.2 DSP Core

The architecture of the PiCOII-DSP (P2D) core is RISC/DSP hybrid structure that has the capable of processing of DSP instructions as well as RISC instructions also. The P2D was the main core of its precedence processor, GDM5302. Like other conventional RISC, P2D adopts fixed length instructions format for simple decoding, 32 general purpose registers, and load-store architecture. Furthermore, P2D supports additional features to support DSP application effectively, P2D adopts an extra datapath for MAC-base operations used in the conventional DSP. In addition to MAC-based datapath, P2D includes several

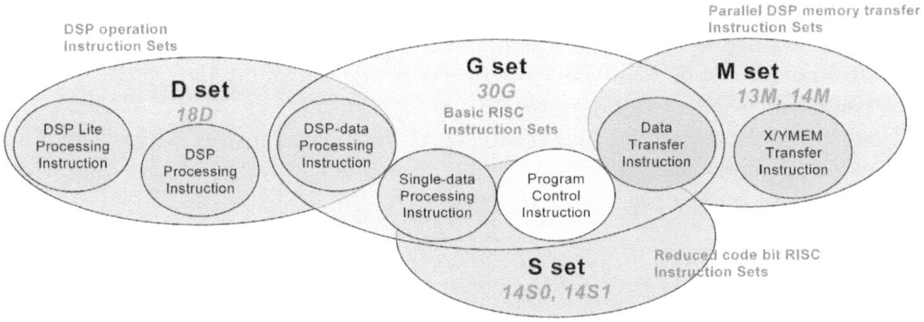

Fig. 4. Instruction sets classification of the P2D core

DSP operations such as saturation, scaling and round operations [10] in the instruction sets. Also, it supports Single Instruction Multiple Data (SIMD) features, which results in high performance in 16-bit speech applications [11]. The shift amount field of the special DSP mode registers automatically scales the source or destination registers. In addition to the data cache, P2D employs the parallel memory access operations of the internal data memories such as XMEM or YMEM. Thus P2D provides high memory bandwidth requirements in real-time multimedia applications. For XMEM or YMEM accesses, P2D supports memory accesses with special registers for address calculation. With the special address mode registers, P2D supports various addressing modes used in the conventional DSPs such as circular and bit-reverse addressing, which are used in many DSP applications. The features of P2D can be summarized as follows.

- RISC and DSP operation, single G set issue, dual S set issues, dual M set issues, both D set and M set operation simultaneously
- 32bit fixed instruction set
- Five stage pipeline : FE - DE - E0 - E1 - E2
- Interrupt disable during instruction execution within delayed slot
- 4read-2write register file
- 16bit/32bit DSP operation with one 48bit accumulator and 4 address registers
- 24bit x 24bit signed multiplication
- SIMD operations
- 1 delay slot for decode stage branch and execution stage branch and link
- 2 delay slot for execution stage branch
- 1 delay slot for load operation

P2D core has RISC and DSP instruction sets by its hybrid architecture, the instructions can be classified by four sets. Figure 4 describes detail of instruction sets and classifications.

G set Basic RISC instruction set that including integer scalar and DSP data processing with single memory transfer and control handling. Encoded as 30bit width.

S set Compact encoded width which provides a subset of G instruction set with reduced opcode and register field. Encoded as 14bit width.

D set Fixed 16bit or 32bit DSP operation including accumulation. Encoded as 18bit width with extending register field.

M set Specialized for internal scratch-pad memory transfers with several addressing mode and address registers. Encoded as with 13 or 14bit width dependent on the size of register field.

2.3 RISC Core

To optimize power consumption without sacrificing a performance that needed to operate a stream data manipulation with general network protocol and/or user interface processing, MiCROII-RISC (M2R) core is the embedded processor that used in mobile system that requires high-performance general operations along with the signal processing by the P2D. Instruction of the M2R core is the same as *G set* which is subset of the P2D instructions. It also has basic DSP data processing capability that accelerate simple computation in the protocol and display of user interface processing. The features of M2R can be summarized as follows.

- RISC with single 30G set issue
- 32bit fixed instruction set
- Six stage pipeline : FE - PD - DE - E0 - E1 - E2
- Interrupt disable during instruction execution within delayed slot
- 3read-1write register file
- 2 delay slot for decode stage branch and execution stage branch and link
- 3 delay slot for execution stage branch
- 2 delay slot for load operation

Each processor core adopts a programmable dynamic clock control that balances power consumption by the complexities of protocol tracking, user interface, and DSP processing. Clock speed of each core can be programmed in a real-time in order to match a requirement of target application. Each core also provides four states to control an energy, active state, sleep state, deep sleep state and power-off state. In active state, processor can change the processor clock between normal operation clock, a half of one, and a third of one. When a program execute *idle* instruction in the active state, processor pull down the processor clock without affecting the I/O device operation. Under the sleep state, whole system clock includes processor and I/O device disabled except real time clock (RTC). Wake-up will be occurred by the RTC time-out or external trigger signal since on-chip phase locked loop (PLL) is still working in order to fast response. An extreme power saving is possible if the processor enters to the Deep sleep state, which the whole clock stopped including PLL. Wake-up from the Deep sleep states takes more latency because it requires PLL boot-up time.

Each core has independent caches to reduce memory access latency. 16 Kbytes instruction and 8 Kbytes data caches on each RISC and DSP cores, and furthermore, the DSP core have scratch-pad memory such as 48 Kbytes XMEM and 48

Kbytes YMEM [12]. On-chip data cache can be configured as copy-through or copy-back mode dependent on the section indicator of address field. In cooperate with data cache, total 96 Kbytes internal scratch-pad memory is integrated enough to support hardware FIFO for each peripheral, which results in cost-effective and low power consumption systems. Whole memories can be byte and word accessible to save a valuable internal space as general-purpose data memory. Boot-up code of the processor can be placed in diverse devices such as NOR type flash, NAND type flash, and serial EEPROM, which reduce a total cost of system by minimizing a number of memory devices.

2.4 Wireless Connectivity

The GDM5104 medium access controller implements the IEEE 802.11 MAC sublayer using dedicated hardware and embedded firmware. MAC hardware implements real-time functions including data pump at transmit mode, validation check and filtering at receive mode, access protocol management, and DMA transferring of data between baseband and internal shared memory. Also, the most time critical frame such as ACK, CTS or response to CF-poll can be executed by MAC hardware itself. The embedded processor handles both Lower MAC and Upper MAC altogether as well as upper layer networking protocol such as TCP/IP. The lower MAC software handles the control of MAC hardware directly and its related lower layer of MAC protocols. It also handles the WEP hardware engine for encryption and decryption. The upper MAC software handles the BSS management, power state control, Beacon generation, data queue management, and host interface. The embedded processor runs low-layer firmware that manages the flow of command/data and upper-layer firmware to/from the application including the scan and join operations, and maintains transmit and receive queues, as well as a WEP key and engine control. Of course, the embedded CPU can control the time critical frame in the manual mode.

2.5 Peripheral Interface

The GDM5104 provides various peripheral interfaces such as off-chip memory interface, host interface, PCI/mini-PCI/CardBus, ATAPI, USB, UART, PCM, I2S, SPDIF, JTAG, Flash Memory/Card, and up-to 100-general purpose programmable I/O(GPIO) interfaces. The GDM5104 has two systems bus called IMB and AMBA. The IMB bus is specialized for high-speed communication between high bandwidth devices such as CPU, USB2.0, on-chip memory, and external SDRAM. Operation clock of the IMB bus is the same as processor clock to reduce the latency for high bandwidth data. Through the superior high performance bus, the embedded processor provides a sufficient bandwidth to execute the application that requires the large size of code and high throughput data movement. For the general peripheral data communication, each block is connected to AMBA AHB and APB bus also, which the AHB provides higher speed than the APB.

Table 1. Chain tools

tool	description
vincent-elf-gcc	Vincent C compiler
vincent-elf-g++	Vincent C compiler
vincent-elf-as	Vincent assembler
vincent-elf-ld	Vincent linker
vincent-elf-ar	Vincent librarian
vincent-gdb	Vincent source-level debugger
vincent-binutils	Vincent binutils
elf2flt	used to create a flat format output executable binary file
genromfs	used to create a file image for flash from a directory

3 Software Environment

3.1 Operating Systems and Tool Chain

Linux is one of the prominent operating system in the embedded world. Open source kernel and rich application can be migrated into the embedded application easily, and its powerful network protocols and applications are providing the network accessibility in the embedded system. We select the uClinux operating system on the GDM5104, which is one of the variations of Linux for embedded systems. For applications that require preemptive kernel, eCos[13] on GDM5104 is under development also. Vincent Software Development Toolkits (VSDT) is a development package that includes the basic tool chain and programming software to support the RISC and DSP processors. Sparc-Solaris, x86-Linux, and x86-cygwin platforms are supported to develop applications using VSDT.

3.2 Debug Support

The P2D and M2R cores have on-chip hardware debugger to support run-time debugging, and the on-chip debugger cooperates with external off-chip debuggers, GCoH and GNU debugger. JTAG, IPC, and PCI interfaces can be used as a communication channel between on-chip and off-chip debuggers. Figure 5 shows the debugging environment operates on run-time. Off-chip debugger controls on-chip debugger through the debug command register (DEBUG_CMD). Five types of commands are supported by DEBUG_CMD: SET, RUN, INTERRUPT GENERATION, RESOURCE ACCESS, and BIST commands. Special bit fields are prepared in the cores that generate internal exception for the purpose of hardware debugging only. By the value of each bit, the corresponding exception will be generated internally.

By control of the external off-chip debugger, the processor cores can be configured as one of the three processor modes, which are normal run, debug wait, and debug run. Under normal run mode, the on-chip debugger only provides limited commands related with memory and non-conflict resources with processor

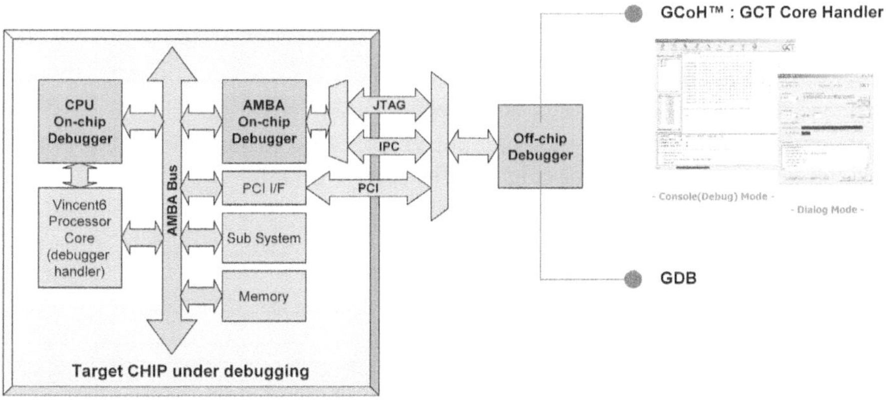

Fig. 5. On-chip and off-chip debug interface

core. Debug wait mode provides holding of execution that cooperated with the off-chip debugger. Under debug wait mode, the pipeline of the processor core is stopped but other sub-systems, such as peripheral devices, are working except timer. The timer can stop or work according to the specific configuration. Under the debug run mode, processor executes operations but the execution will be stopped at the preset counts of instructions or predefined breakpoint position by the configuration. The boot-up state of processor mode is defined by external chip interface signals, and off-chip debugger can change each mode anytime.

4 Performance Evaluation

By the M2R and P2D dual core architecture, it offers unique advantages in performance and power consumption for wireless multimedia systems. The M2R is well suited for handling protocol, user interface code, OS, and applications. The P2D, on the other hand, is better suited for the real-time signal processing applications commonly used in multimedia codec. In this paper, we present several audio codec performances using P2D core as shown in Table 2. In terms of optimization, quality of the source code is in early-stage to conclude the performance of P2D, so we expect the performance will be improved by the profiling of the code, further detailed performance will be released within near future.

Table 2. Performance of audio processing codecs using P2D (Mcycles/sec)

AMR		G.729AB		G.723.1 (6.3Kbps)		G.169
encoder	decoder	encoder	decoder	encoder	decoder	
25.5	4.4	21.5	3.9	29.9	2.3	15.7

5 Conclusion

Advent of the low power embedded processor pushes the digital appliances to an outdoors. The wireless technology enlarges a capability of the mobile application by its excellence of connectivity compared to wire communications. One of the most laborious obstacles is saving of the energy of mobile applications that operate using primary or secondary batteries. For the low power consumption and high computation/data-rate applications with the wireless connectivity, we integrate the high performance RISC and DSP cores with most wireless standards, IEEE802.11a/b/g and Bluetooth, on single silicon. By the seamless control of function units with high performance buses, every complicated application that require various peripheral operations, complex computations, and high-speed wireless communications can be offered using minimal power.

References

1. G. Semeraro and G. Magklis, R. Balasubramonian, D. Albonesi and S., Dwarkadas and M. Scott: Dynamic frequency and voltage control for a multiple clock domain microarchitecture Intl. Symp. on Microarchitecture (MICRO) (2002) 356–367
2. A. Iyer, D. Marculescu: Power efficiency of voltage scaling in multiple clock Proc. Intl. Conf. CAD (2002) 379–386
3. E. Macii, M. Pedram and F. Somenzi: High-Level Power Modeling, Estimation and Optimization Proc. DAC (1997) 504–511
4. Intel PXA27x Processor Family Developer's Manual (2004)
5. Brian P. Crow, Indra Widjaja, Jeon Geun Kim, Prescott T. Sakai: IEEE 802.11 Wireless Local Area Networks IEEE Commun. Mag. Vol.35 N.9 (1997) 116–126.
6. K. Brandenburg: MP3 and AAC Explained K. Brandenburg. MP3 and AAC Explained 17th Intl. Conf. High Quality Audio Coding (1999)
7. J. C. Haartsen: The Bluetooth radio system IEEE Pers. Commun. Mag. (2000) 28–36
8. H-J. Suh, H.J. Lim, J. Kim: GDM5302: Wireless Integration of a Mobile Multimedia Processor 2005 Intl. Conf. Embedded Systems and Applications (2005) 182–187
9. AMBA Specification rev 2.0 ARM (1999)
10. K. Wires, M. Schulte and J. Stine: Variable-Correction Truncated Floating Point Multipliers 34th Intl. Asilomar Conf. Signals, Circuits and Systems (2000)1344–1348
11. S. Kanthak, K. Schutz and N. Ney: Using SIMD Instructions for Fast Likelihood Calculation in LVCSR Proc. of the IEEE Int. Conf. on Acoustics, Speech and Signal Processing (2000)
12. M. Kandemir and A. Choudhary: Compiler-directed scratch pad memory hierarchy design and management 39th ACM/IEEE Design Automation Conf. (2002) 690–695
13. eCos User Guide Red Hat, Inc., eCosCentric Ltd. (2003) available on http://ecos.sourceware.org/docs-latest/

An Accurate Architectural Simulator for ARM1136

Hyo-Joong Suh[1] and Sung Woo Chung[2,*]

[1] School of Computer Science and Information Engineering,
The Catholic University of Korea,
San 43-1 Yeoggog 2 Dong, Wonmi Gu, Bucheon, Gyeonggido, 420-743 Korea
hjsuh@catholic.ac.kr
http://esca.catholic.ac.kr

[2] Department of Computer Science,
University of Virginia,
Charlottesville VA 22901 USA
schung@cs.virginia.edu

Abstract. Cycle-accurate simulators are basic tools to evaluate performance improvements of computer architecture. Before confirming of the architecture improvements using cycle-accurate simulation, the simulator itself should be validated. However, off-the-shelf processors have been continuously improved, though the cycle-accurate simulators were not reflected the improved features. Simulation results show that the difference between the IPC (Instruction Per Cycle) of the modified model for ARM1136 (Sim-ARM1136) and the IPC of the original model for ARM7 (Sim-Outorder) is 19%, on average, which is large enough to mislead the impact of architecture improvements.

1 Introduction

Every architect try to improve the performance of microprocessors to achieve a high speed, low power consumption, and large bandwidth, by examining a real silicon takes a lot of resources, cost and time. Practically, however, we can not explore all architectural alternatives on the silicon, and most researchers, especially in academia, do not analyze the impact of their idea in the silicon level. Instead, they disbranch useless alternatives using architecture simulators [1][2][3][4][5]. According to detail of the simulation level, the architecture simulators can be classified into two classes : instruction-accurate and cycle-accurate. Instruction accurate simulators aim at instruction level performance evaluation, which does not includes the detailed cycle information, and the correctness is limited within the instruction level. Compared to the instruction accurate simulators, cycle accurate simulators are focused on the lower level that requires the performance evaluation as well as correctness check.

About a year ago, we had been trying to deploy an existing processor simulator for architecture explorations. However, insufficient degree of details made

* Corresponding Author.

L.T. Yang et al. (Eds.): EUC 2005, LNCS 3824, pp. 331–339, 2005.

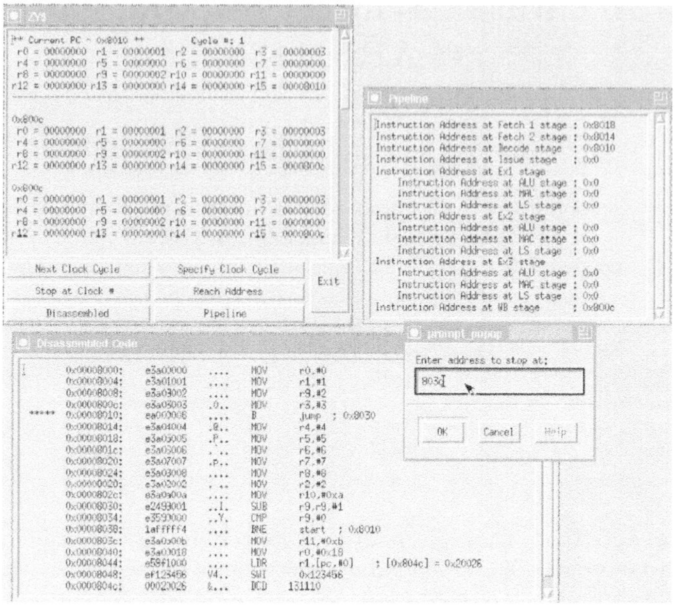

Fig. 1. Sim-ARM1136 GUI

us hesitate to utilize the existing simulators as they are. We worried about the abstraction errors that may draw wrong conclusions when evaluating new techniques [6].

Cycle-accurate simulators are powerful tools to evaluate a performance sensitive architecture alteration with time and cost efficiency, while these tools must be validated against the processor architecture. Usually, cycle-accurate simulators tend to trade-off between exactness and simulation speed, and moreover, many improved features are added on off-the-shelf microprocessors, which weaken a rationale of outdated cycle-accurate simulator as an architecture evaluation tool. For example, the cycle-accurate simulator (called *Sim-Outorder*) from Simplescalar-ARM [5] was shown to be cycle-accurate by comparing the ARM 7 [7] silicon [8]. However, ARM 1136 [9] has a lot of different features from ARM 7 : number of pipeline stages, organization of execution units, write buffers, and so on. Nevertheless, many researchers use existing simulators not even modifying pipeline structure and functions in each pipeline, when they evaluate their embedded processor designs. In this paper, we will discuss the inaccuracy that arises from the use of an existing cycle-accurate simulator without modifications, and compare with modified simulator that reflects many architecture updates.

To discuss this issue, we modified Sim-Outorder from Simplescalar[10] to reflect the off-the-shelf processor (ARM1136) [9] features. The modified model is called *Sim-ARM1136* in this paper. We selected Sim-Outorder from Simplescalar to compare with, because it is known as one of the most popular cycle-accurate simulators for the computer architecture research. To validate Sim-ARM1136,

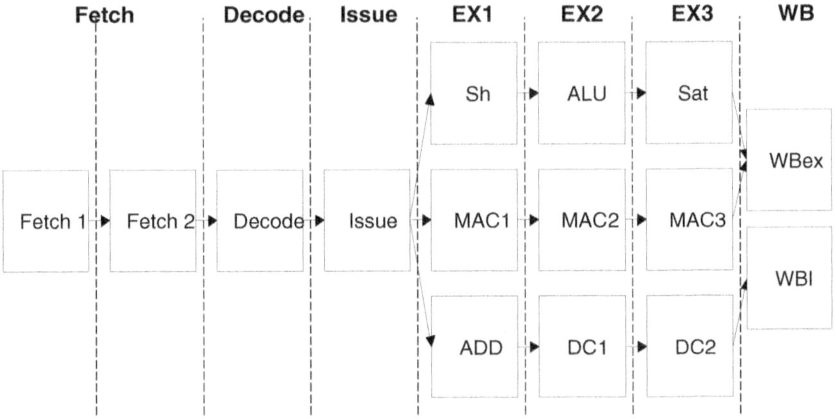

Fig. 2. Overall Pipeline Structure of Sim-ARM1136

we compare Sim-ARM1136 outputs with the RTL (register transfer level) simulation results of ARM1136. For convenience of operation, graphic interface was prepared on Sim-ARM1136, shown in Figure 1, and the user interface provided cycle-by-cycle validation against ARM1136 RTL by running some test programs.

In the next section, we describe Sim-ARM1136, focusing on the difference from Sim-Outorder. Section 3 describes the methodology that we used in this study. Section 4 shows the simulation results, and Section 5 concludes this paper.

2 Sim-ARM1136 Enhancements

In this section, we briefly describe Sim-ARM1136 enhancements compare with Sim-Outorder based on Simplescalar. Following features are the enhancement of Sim-ARM1136, and ARM1136 naturally.

– Pipeline stage modification

Sim-Outorder has 6-stage pipeline : fetch, decode, issue, execution, writeback, and commit. While Sim-ARM1136 is composed of 8-stage pipeline : fetch1, fetch2, decode, issue, execution1, execution2, execution3, and writeback as shown in Figure 2. Fetch and branch prediction consumes two cycles, resulting in two fetch stages, and execution is divided into three cycles.

In Sim-Outorder, one execution stage plays a role of multiple execution stages by setting latency and allowing multiple instructions in an execution unit. However, this structure can not support data forwarding in the execution stage. In Sim-ARM1136, we explicitly divide one execution stage into three execution stages for three kinds of execution units : Integer pipeline, MAC (Multiply and Accumulate) pipeline, and LS (Load/Store) pipeline.

Integer pipeline consists of Shift, ALU, and Saturation. If an instruction includes an operand to be shifted, the operand is shifted in the Shift stage. The

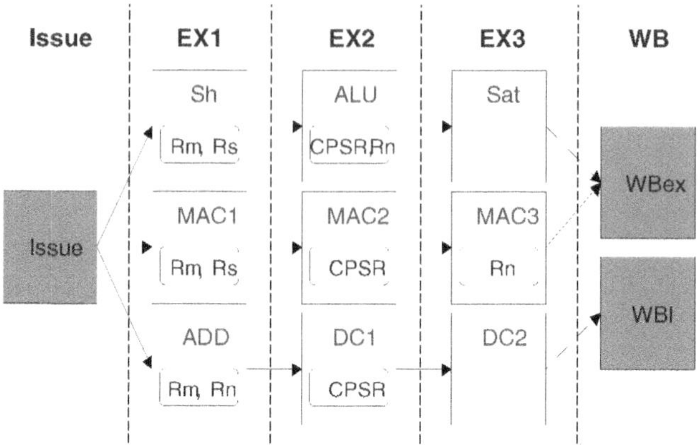

Fig. 3. Necessary Resolution of Data Dependency

ALU stage calculates the operands and the Saturation stage saturates the output from the ALU stage, if necessary. MAC pipeline consists of MAC1, MAC2, and MAC3. In the MAC1 stage and the MAC2 stage, operands are multiplied. In the MAC3 stage, the output from the previous stage is accumulated. The LS pipeline has ADD, DC1, and DC2. In the ADD stage, load/store address is calculated. If a shift operation is required to calculate the address in a load/store instruction, the shift operation in the Shift stage of the Integer pipeline should precede load/store instruction. In other words, if a shift operation is necessary for a load/store, the load/store instruction is implicitly split into two instructions. One goes through the Integer pipeline and the other goes through the LS pipeline. The data cache is accessed in the DC1 and DC2 stages.

The commit stage is merged into the writeback stage. We also modify the branch misprediction resolution mechanism to be appropriate for the modified pipeline structure.

– Interlock and data forwarding

In Sim-Outorder, instructions are issued after all data dependencies are resolved, while in Sim-ARM1136, instructions are issued regardless of data dependencies. In Sim-ARM1136, data dependencies are checked in every execution stage. If the required data dependency is not resolved, the instruction can not proceed until complete the resolution of the data dependency. Figure 3 shows the resolution of dependencies to proceed to the next stage. The dependency by the CPSR (Current Program Status Register) is also checked to match the condition code flags.

– Hit under miss

When Sim-Outorder is set to run in in-order, multiple data cache misses can go out to fetch data from memory by absence of second level cache in ARM1136. In case of a cache miss occurs, subsequent data cache access can fetch data only if there is a free entry in load store queue. In Sim-ARM1136, only one data cache miss can fetch data from memory. If there is more than one cache misses, pipeline stalled until there remains only one cache miss.

– Memory interface

In modern processors, there is a write buffer between a first level cache and memory, whose purpose is to decouple stores from the pipeline. In Sim-Outorder, the entry of the write buffer is not limited. To reflect ARM1136 features, Sim-ARM1136 has an 8-entry write buffer, which may affect performance much. CWF (Critical Word First) is also modeled in Sim-ARM1136.

We also implemented 64-bit wide internal bus between the pipeline and the first level cache, which support two-word transfer at a time in case of LDM (LoaD Multiple) or STM (STore Multiple) operations.

– Static branch prediction

In Sim-Outorder, there are only dynamic branch predictions, while in Sim-ARM1136, static branch prediction as well as dynamic branch prediction is modeled also. ARM1136 uses bimodal prediction for dynamic branch prediction, and forward taken/backward untaken for static branch prediction. In the first fetch stage, dynamic prediction is performed and BTAC (Branch Target Address Cache) is accessed that is similar to BTB (Branch Target Buffer). In the second fetch stage, static prediction is performed if a miss occurs in the BTAC.

– Other miscellaneous enhancements

In the cache model of Sim-Outorder, there is no option for turn off the write allocation policy, while in ARM1136, a cache line for a read operation should be allocated in the cache.

MAC pipeline can not process MAC instruction for every cycle. At least one cycle stall is required between adjacent MAC instructions, and if the former MAC instruction is 64-bit operation, two cycle stalls is required. Data dependency and forwarding of the MAC instructions were implemented also, but we think the model of MAC instructions need to be detailed in Sim-ARM1136.

3 Methodology

We built the many enhancement of ARM1136 in Sim-ARM1136 as described, we discuss a validation process of Sim-ARM1136 and compare the accuracy of Sim-ARM1136 to that of Sim-Outorder in this section.

1). Simple test programs are made to verify the latencies and enhanced features in ARM1136 TRM[9] with Sim-ARM1136. These program includes the validation of ALU execution, MAC execution, interlock forwarding, hit under miss, and branch prediction/recovery.
2). Execution of Dhrystone (1-iteration) using ARM1136 RTL, Sim-ARM1136 and Sim-Outorder.
3). We assume the enhanced features of simulator are evaluated and stabilized if it provides similar improvement/degradation across

Table 1. Processor Parameters

Parameter	Value
Issue Policy	In-order
Branch Predictor	Bimodal, 128-entry
BTB (Branch Target Buffer)	128-entry
Instruction Cache	16KB, 32B line size, 4-way set associative
Data Cache	16KB, 32B line size, 4-way set associative
Cache Latency	1 cycle
Memory Latency	8 (first chunk), 12 (second), 16 (third), 20 (fourth)

other validated environments. In order to validation the stability of the simulators, we repeat procedure 2) by turning off the branch predictor. Turning off the branch predictor in ARM1136 RTL simulation can be done, by changing a status register value.

4). Procedure 2) and 3) are repeatedly done on Dhrystone (100-iteration)

5). Six applications are selected from the EEMBC benchmark suite, and compare the applications on ARM1136 RTL and Sim-ARM1136 with 1-iteration.

6). We compare the IPC of Sim-ARM1136 to that of Sim-Outorder on all the applications with default number of iterations by running the EEMBC benchmark suite. We could not run the applications on ARM1136 RTL, due to the running default iterations in the RTL simulation requires excessively long time.

Other processor parameters are complying with the ARM1136 features that detailed in Table 1. Please note that Sim-Outorder only accepts ARM7 binaries. For an appropriate comparison, we use ARM7 binaries compiled by the RVCT (RealView Compilation Tools) [12] as an input for all three simulators (RTL simulation, Sim-Outorder, and Sim-ARM1136).

4 Simulation Results

4.1 IPC Comparison: ARM1136 vs. Sim-Outorder vs. Sim-ARM1136 (Dhrystone)

When running Dhrystone 1-iteration, the IPC (Instruction Per Cycle) from the ARM1136 RTL simulation is 0.19 as shown in Figure 4. In this case, the IPC from Sim-Outorder and that from Sim-ARM1136 is 0.22 and 0.20, respectively. All the results are similar. When simulating without the branch predictor, the relative performance loss in Sim-ARM1136 is as close as that in ARM1136. However, the performance loss in Sim-Outorder is as much as 24%. Different from Sim-ARM1136, Sim-Outorder can issue multiple outstanding data cache miss requests to memory. However, without the branch predictor, the effect of multiple outstanding data miss requests decreases.

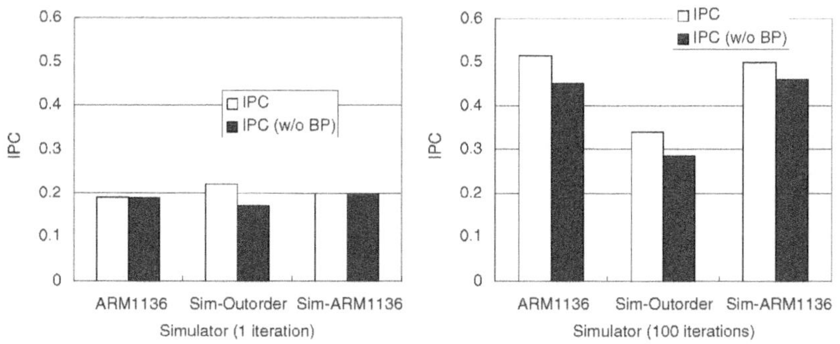

Fig. 4. IPC Comparison (Dhrystone)

Table 2. IPC Comparison between ARM1136 and Sim-ARM1136 (EEMBC, 1-iteration)

Applications	IPC (ARM1136)	IPC (Sim-Outorder)	Difference (%)	IPC (Sim-ARM1136)	Difference (%)
autcor00	0.57	0.73	-28.07	0.62	-8.77
bitmnp01	0.71	0.75	-5.63	0.71	0.86
bitmnp816	0.60	0.63	-5.00	0.55	8.33
memacc816	0.32	0.35	-9.38	0.35	-9.38
pntrch816	0.53	0.48	9.43	0.51	3.77
rspeed816	0.19	0.22	-15.79	0.25	-31.58
Mean	0.48	0.60	12.22	0.58	10.45

When running Dhrystone 100-iteration, the results from ARM1136 and Sim-ARM1136 shows less than 3% difference. Sim-Outorder has 36% lower IPC, compared to the ARM1136. There are two reasons for that. First, running more iterations reduce data cache miss rate, leading to decrease of the multiple data cache miss effect. Second, data dependency prevents instructions from being issued in Sim-Outorder, where only dependency-resolved instructions can be issued.

4.2 IPC Comparison: ARM1136 vs. Sim-Outorder vs. Sim-ARM1136 (EEMBC, 1-Teration)

Table 2 shows the accuracy of Sim-Outorder and Sim-ARM1136 to that of Sim-Outorder by running EEMBC benchmark suite [11]. The average difference is 12.22% and 10.45% in Sim-Outorder and in Sim-ARM1136, respectively. Main source of differences may be caused by not modeled features (more detailed MAC pipeline, return address stack, branch folding and so on).

Since the first iteration incurs much more data cache misses that account for large portion of execution time, the IPC of Sim-Outorder is very close to that of Sim-ARM1136. In the next Subsection, we show the difference between Sim-ARM1136 and Sim-Outorder by running the default number of iterations of all applications in the EEMBC benchmark suite.

4.3 IPC Comparison: Sim-ARM1136 vs. Sim-Outorder (EEMBC, Default-Iteration)

As shown in Figure 5, the simulation results show that Sim-Outorder has higher IPC than Sim-ARM1136 in most applications. These results are reverse, compared to the results in Section 4.1. The reason is that EEMBC benchmark suite incurs much more data cache misses than Dhrystone, which results in performance gain from multiple outstanding cache misses in Sim-Outorder. Though Sim-ARM1136 allows the instructions whose data dependencies are not resolved, this effect is compensated by hit under miss feature (explained in Section 2) that allows only one outstanding data cache miss. The average IPCs for Sim-ARM1136 and for Sim-Outorder are 0.55 and 0.63, respectively. The average difference is as much as 19.0%. Moreover, the increased IPC in Sim-Outorder is not proportional among the applications. Therefore, the amount of performance improvement or degradation by researcher's new idea would be different between in Sim-ARM1136 and in Sim-Outorder.

Though Sim-ARM1136 shows lower IPC in most applications, Sim-ARM1136 shows higher IPC in some applications that are expected to have a lot of data forwarding and utilize the 64-bit wide internal bus. Especially, in puwmod816

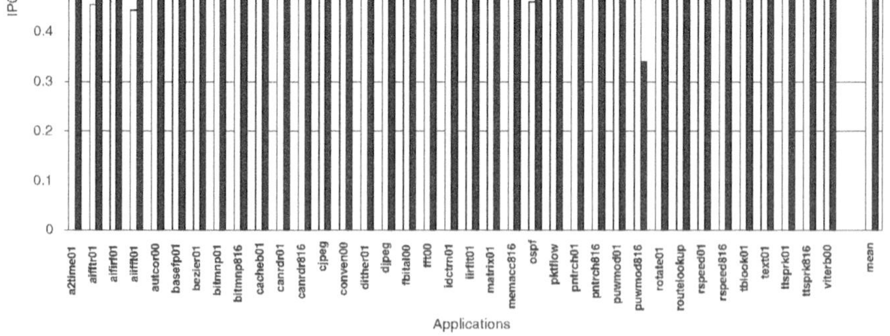

Fig. 5. IPC Comparison between Sim-ARM1136 and Sim-Outorder (EEMBC,default-iteration)

that has much more LDM/STM, the IPC difference is as much as 38%. Since LD/ST generates two operations (shift operation for address calculation and practical LD/ST), it seriously increases data dependencies. In this case, data dependency can be resolved by data forwarding, resulting in relative performance gain in Sim-ARM1136.

5 Conclusions

Simulators are essential tools for most researchers to analyze their valuable idea without costly silicon implementation. However, state-of-the art embedded processors have many architectural improvements than the simple simulators. By the absence of improved features of embedded processors on simulators, if researchers put ideas in the simulators without reflecting of the improvements, simulation results can be distorted by impacts of added features. Thus, this might unintentionally conclude valuable idea as useless.

In this paper, we validated Sim-ARM1136, which simulates the processor parameters of ARM1136 as well as the extended features. We also presented the difference between Sim-ARM1136 and Sim-Outorder where only processor parameters are changed without modifying pipeline features. The simulation results show the difference that might mislead to incorrect performance evaluation. Now, Sim-ARM1136 is adopted by Samsung electronics to evaluate of high-performance embedded processors.

References

1. V. Pai, P. Ranganathan, and S. Adve: RSim: A Simulator for Shared Memory Multiprocessor and Uniprocessor Systems that Exploit ILP In Proceedings of the 3rd Workshop on Computer Architecture Education (1997)
2. M. Rosenblum, S. Herrod, E. Witchel, and A. Gupta: Complete Computer Simulation : The SimOS Approach In IEEE Parallel and Distributed Technology (1995)
3. D.M. Tullsen, S.J. Eggers, and H.M. Levy: Simultaneous Multithreading: Maximizing On-Chip Parallelism In 22nd Annual International Symposium on Computer Architecture, June (1995)
4. Virtutech: Simics Simulator. available at http://www.virtutech.com.
5. Simplescalar LLC: Simplescalar 3.0 available at http://www.simplescalar.com.
6. Bryan Black and Jhon Paul Shen: Calibration of Microprocessor Performance Models Computer, 31 (5):41-49, May (1998)
7. ARM Corp.: ARM 7 Technical Reference Manual available at http://www.arm.com.
8. Simplescalar LLC: Simplescalar Tutorial available at http://www.simplescalar.com.
9. ARM Corp.: ARM 1136 Technical Reference Manual available at http://www.arm.com
10. Simplescalar LLC: Pre-release of Simplescalar 4.0, (2004)
11. The Embedded Microprocessor Benchmark Consortium: EEMBC Benchmark Suite available at http://www.eembc.org.
12. ARM Corp.: RealView Compilation Tools available at http://www.arm.com.

Modular Design Structure and High-Level Prototyping for Novel Embedded Processor Core

Ben A. Abderazek, Sotaro Kawata, Tsutomu Yoshinaga, and Masahiro Sowa

Graduate School of Information Systems,
The University of Electro-Communications,
1-5-1 Chofugaoka, Chofu-shi, 182-8585 Tokyo, Japan
ben@is.uec.ac.jp

Abstract. In this research work, we present a high-level prototyping of a new processor core based on Queue architecture as starting point for application-specific processor design exploration. Using modular design structure with control logic implemented as a set of communicating state machines, we show hardware emulation and optimizations results of a parallel queue proecssor architecture (QueueCore). We also show how to to fully exploit the capabilities of the designed QueueCore, while maintaining a common source base. From the evaluation results, we show that the QueueCore prototype fits on a single conventional FPGA device, thereby obviating the need to perform multi-chip partitioning which results in a loss of resource efficiency.

1 Introduction

In our previous work, we have researched about queue computing infrastructure as a starting point for cooperative design space exploration for general and embedded applications[1, 2]. The choice of this architecture was based on a number of factors, such as its suitability for embedded applications.

A parallel Queue processor architecture[2] exploits instruction-level parallelism without considerable effort and need for heavy run time data dependence analysis, resulting in a simple hardware organization when compared with conventional superscalar processors. These features allow the inclusion of a large number of functional units into a single chip, increasing parallelism exploitation.

The key idea of the Queue processor is the manupilation scheme of instruction operands and result. The Queue computing scheme adopted in this work stores intermediate results into a so called queue-registers (QREG). In this model, a given instruction implicitly reads its first operand from the head of the QREG, its second operand from a location explicitly addressed with an integer offset from the first operand location and stores the computed result into the tail of the QREG. An important feature of this scheme is that write after read false data dependency does not occur[1]. Furthermore, since there is no explicit referencing to the QREG, it is easy to add extra storage locations to the QREG when needed.

Since the operands and result addresses of a given static-instruction (compiler generated) are implicitly *computed* during run-time, an efficient and fast

L.T. Yang et al. (Eds.): EUC 2005, LNCS 3824, pp. 340–349, 2005.

hardware mechanism is imperatively needed for parallel execution. The proposed architecture, which is named QueueCore, implements a so named queue computation mechanism that calculates operands and result addresses for each instruction. The mechanism used for calculating these addresses will be described in the coming section. An important aspect of developing any new architecture is verification which usually requires complicated and lengthly software simulation of an emulated model. An event-based or cycle level simulation becomes increasingly inadequate to verify a significant execution trace for a given problem. These software-based simulation approaches are not capable of predicting all micro-architectural issues related to final physical design[3]. To this end, we consider prototyping-based emulation that substitutes real time hardware emulation for slow simulator-based execution. Prototyping-based design itself is not a new idea as several designers already adopted this method. However, what is important for us is to investigate how to describe the novel QueueCore architecture to achieve good synthesis results for FPGA implementation with sufficient performance to support realistic evaluation.

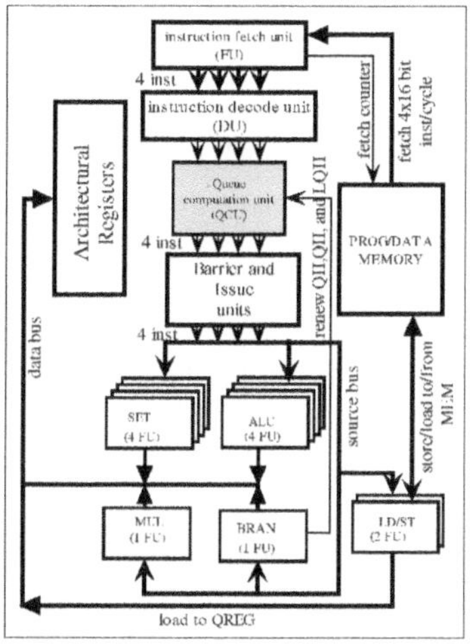

Fig. 1. QueueCore architecture block diagram. During RTL description, the core is broken into small and manageable modules using modular approach structure for easy verification, debugging and modification.

Using a hardware description language, we have created the Synthesizable model of the QueueCore for the integer subset of parallel Queue processor (PQP) architecture[1, 2]. A prototype implementation is produced by synthesizing the high-level model for the Stratix FPGA device[4, 6]. As results, we were able to evaluate relative circuit area and speed metrics for design alternatives.

2 QueueCore Architecture

The QueueCore block diagram is shown in Fig. 1. The system has six pipeline stages:

(1) *Fetch (FU)*: at each cycle the fetch counter is sent to PROG/DATA memory and eight bytes (four instructions) are fetched then inserted into the fetch buffer (FB).
(2) *Decode (DU)*: this unit reads eight bytes from the FB every cycle, decodes them, then inserts decoded information into the decode buffer. This stage also calculates the number of consumed (CNBR) and produced (PNBR) data for each instruction. The CNBR and PNBR are used by the next pipeline stage (queue computing stage) to calculate the sources and destination locations for each instruction.
(3) *Queue computation (QCU)*: calculates the first operand (*source*1) and destination addresses for each instruction. The mechanism used for calculating the *source*1 address in given in Fig. 2. The QCU unit keeps track on the current value of the QH and QT pointers. Four instructions arrive to the QCU unit each cycle. For the first instruction, the number of the consumed operands (CNBR) (8-bit field) is added to the current QH value (QH0) to find the address of the first operand (QHN) and the number of produced results (PNBR) (8-bit filed) is added to the current QT value (QT0) to find the result address (QT1) of the first instruction. The other three instruction's first operand and result addresses are calculated similarly as indicated in the lower part of Fig. 2. Notice that the calculation is performed sequentially.
(4) *Barrier:* inserts barrier flag for dependency resolutions.
(5) *Issue:* four instructions are issued for execution each cycle. In this stage, the

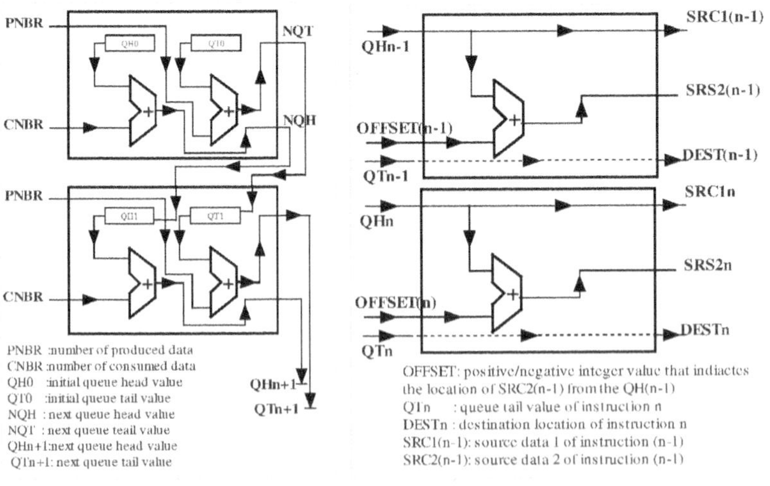

Fig. 2. Address calculation mechanism for *source*1, *destination* (left part of the figure), and source two calculation mechanism (right part of the figure)

second operand (*source2*) of a given instruction is first calculated by adding the address *source1* to the displacement that comes with the instruction. The second operand address calculation could be earlier calculated in the QCU stage. However, for timing balance consideration, the *source2* is calculated in the IS stage. The hardware mechanism used for calculating the second operand (*source2*) address is shown in the right part of Fig. 2.
An instruction is ready to be issued if its data operands and its corresponding functional unit are available.
6) *Execution (EXE)*: the QueueCore's execution unit computes the effective address for loads and stores, and executes ALU instructions. During the EXE stage, the machine also determines whether a conditional branch is taken and, if so, updates the program counter and send the QH and QT of branch instruction to the QCU unit.

3 QueueCore Implementation

To the best of our knowledge, this is the first hardware design of a Queue processor architecture. Therefore, there are no related works in the literature that give design issues or methodology related to hardware Queue processor.

To make the QueueCore design easy to debug, modify and adaptable, we decided to use a high-level description, which was also used by other system designers. We have developed the QueueCore system in Verilog HDL.

3.1 QueueCore System Pipeline Control

In many conventional processors, the control unit is centralized and controls all central processing core functions. This scheme introduces pipeline stalls, bubbles, etc. However, especially for pipelined architecture, this control unit is one of the most complex part of the design, even for processors with fixed functionality.

In this design, we have decided to break up the unstructured control unit to small, manageable units. Each unit is described in a separate HDL module. That is, instead of a centralized control unit, the control unit is integrated with the pipeline data path. Thus, each pipeline stage is mainly controlled by its own, simple control unit as illustrated in Fig. 3. In this scheme, each distributed state machine corresponds to exactly one pipeline stage, and this stage is controlled exclusively by its corresponding state machine. Overall flow control of the processor is implemented by cooperation of the control units in each stage based on communicating state machines. Each pipeline stage is connected to its immediate neighbours, and indicates whether it is able to supply or accept new instructions. Communication with adjacent pipeline stages is performed using two asynchronous signals, *AVAILABLE* and *PROCEED*. When a stage has finished processing, it asserts the *AVAILABLE* signal to indicate that data is available to the next pipeline stage. The next stage will, then, indicate whether it can proceed these data by using the *PROCEED* signal.

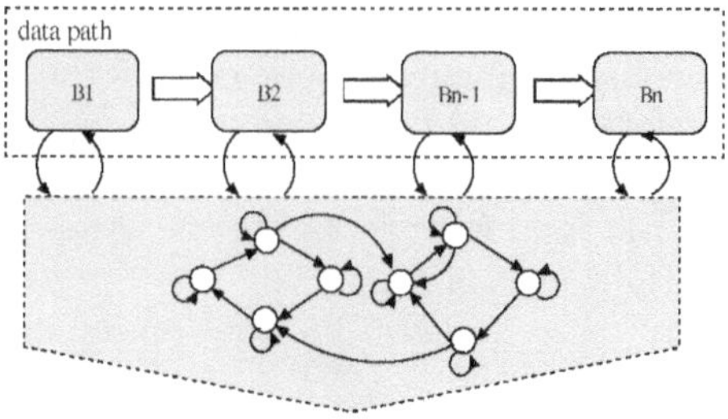

(a)

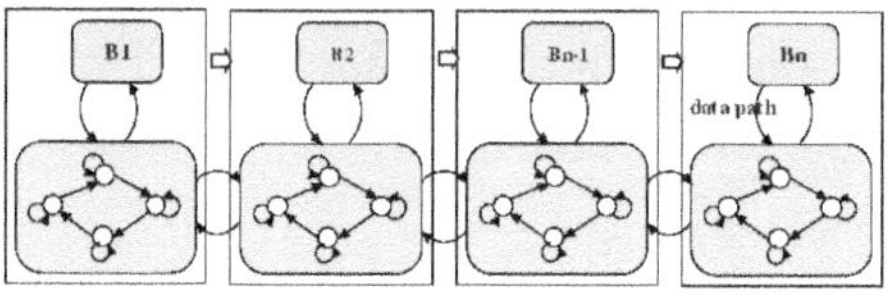

(b)

Fig. 3. Control unit: (a) In conventional Processor design, (2) in PQP processor design

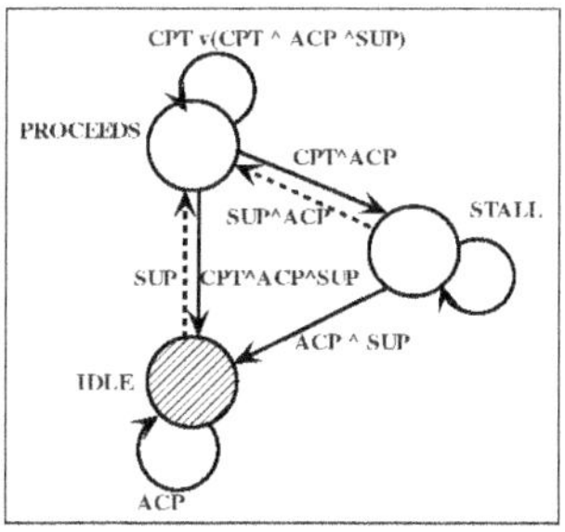

Fig. 4. Finite state machine transition for QueueCore pipeline synchronization. The following conditions are evaluated: next stage can accept data (ACP), previous pipeline stage can supply data (SUP), last cycle of computation (CPT).

Since all field necessary to find what actions are to be taken next are available in the pipeline stage(for example operation status ready bits and synchronization signals from adjacently stages), computing the next stage is simple. The state transition of a pipeline stage in the QueueCore is illustrated in Fig. 4. This basic state machine is extended to cover the operational requirements of each stage, by dividing the *PROCEED* state into substates as needed. An example is the implementation of the Queue computation stage, where *PROCEED* is divided into substates for reading initial addresses values, calculating next addresses values, and addresses fixup (when needed).

4 QueueCore Validation

Validation loosely refers in this paper to the process of determining that the designed processor is correct. It is performed at multiple abstraction levels by integrating several approaches performed in three phases and based on the same HDL that describe the processor core: (1)Functional verfication,(2)Rapid Prototyping, and (3)Gate Level Simulation. The QueueCore graphical validation tool (GVT) display the validated output ports when the source clock changes. A summary of the memory, QREG, the genral purpose registers (GPR) status and the instructions processing counters can be monitored with the GVT tool.

5 FPGA Synthesis of the QueueCore

In order to estimate the impact of the description style on the target FPGA efficiency, we have explored logic synthesis for FPGAs. The idea of this experiment was to optimize critical design parts for speed or resource optimizations. The optimizations of the Verilog HDL models for FPGAs can be arranged into two distinctive approaches: (1) Coding style and (2) Usage of special-purpose Devices on FPGA. In this work, our experiments and the results described are based on the Altera Stratix architecture [4]. We selected Stratix FPGA device because it has a good tradeoffs between routability and logic capacity. In addition it has an internal embedded memory that eliminates the need for external memory module and offers up to 10 Mbits of embedded memory through the TriMatrix TM memory feature. We also used Altera Quartus II professional edition [6] for simulation, placement and routing. Simulations were also performed with Cadence Verilog-XL tool [5]. The quality of the final QueueCore hardware and the resource usage of the target FPGA device depend very much on the description style used at a higher level. To account for this, the high-level HDL description has to be adapted to guide the synthesis tool to choose the appropriate implementation method for functionality. The coding style also affects the design of finite-state automata/machine (FSM) that are common is the QueueCore. A poor choice of codes will result in a state machine that uses too much logic, or is too slow, or both. Many advanced techniques have been developed for choosing an optimal state assignment. Typical such approaches use the minimum number of state bits or assume a two-level logic [7].

Fig. 5 compares the encoding tradeoffs for a simple FSM for the Altera STRATIX-EP1S FPGA and Structured ASIC library using three encoding techniques: *gray* code encoding, *binary* encoding, and *onehot* encoding of states.

When ASICs models are the target process, fully encoded representation such as binary or gray code encoding of states lead to space efficient design, wheres the one-hot encoding scheme consumes more resources. This is different for FPGA devices with a large number of flip-flops, where a decoded representation reduces decoding logic at the cost of typically underutilized flip-flops.

Since the resource distribution of the *onehot* encoded FSM maps well to the resource distribution of the target architecture, it is a very compact representation.

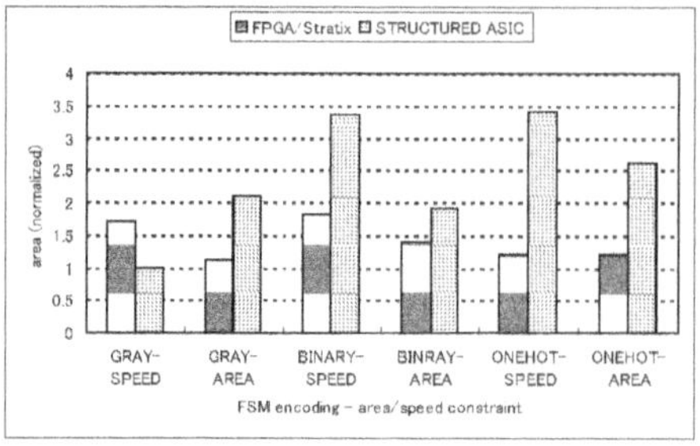

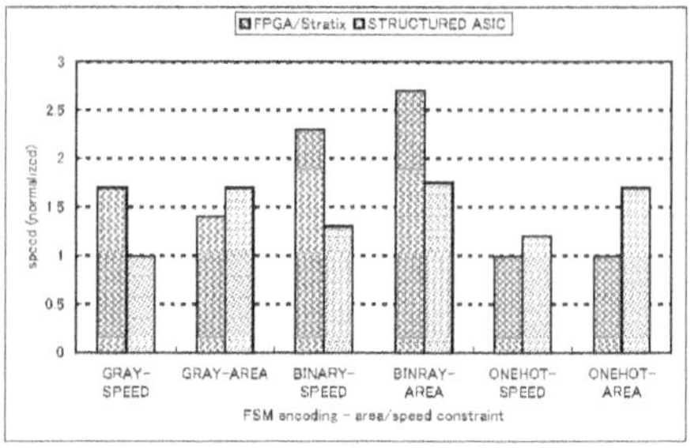

Fig. 5. Resource usage and timing for state machine synthesis using different encoding schemes

6 Modeling Style with Special FPGAs Circuits and Storage Structure

To compare different modeling styles and their implementation in hardware, we have considered the design for an adder module with several different algorithm:

DEDA uses of dedicated logic,
LGCA use only logic element,
DFTA use of default implementation

To compare these design styles, we have compiled these adders with and without target-specific module generators. Resource usage and timing of these implementations of a 32 bit adder are shown in Figures 6. The *DFTA* implementation was slightly better than *LGCA* and *DRDA* version, because the synthesis tool contains a powerfully library of module generators. Implementations not based on the fast arithmetic functionality of the FPGA have almost similar resource usage which is much higher than the technology-specific version, and their performance is slower by a factor of 1.1 to 1.4. Fig. 7 compares two different target

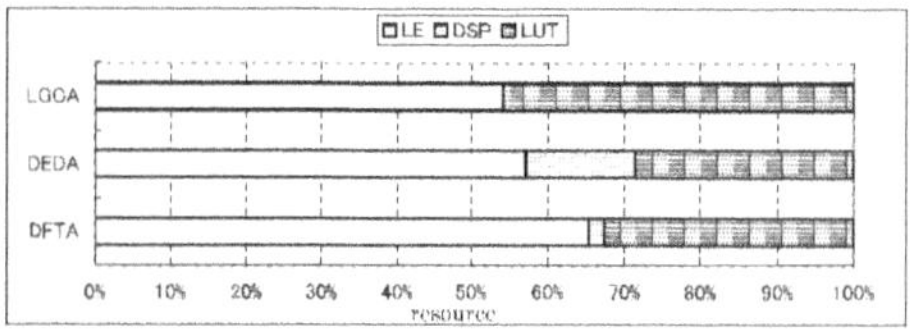

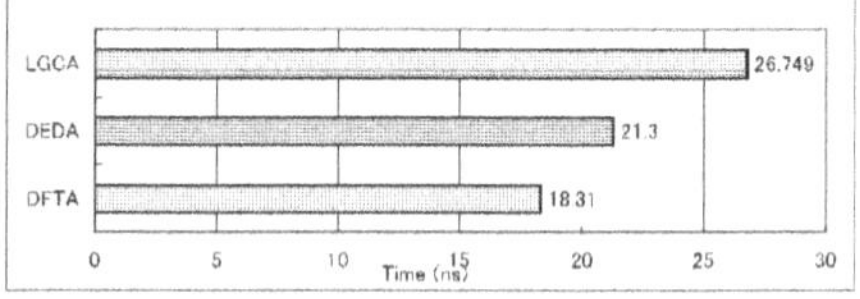

Fig. 6. Resource usage and timing for 32 bit adder

implantation for 256x33 QREG for various optimizations. Depending on the target implementations device, either logic elements (LEs) or total combinational functions (TC) are generated as storage elements. Implementations based on HardCopy device, which generates TCF functions give almost similar complexity

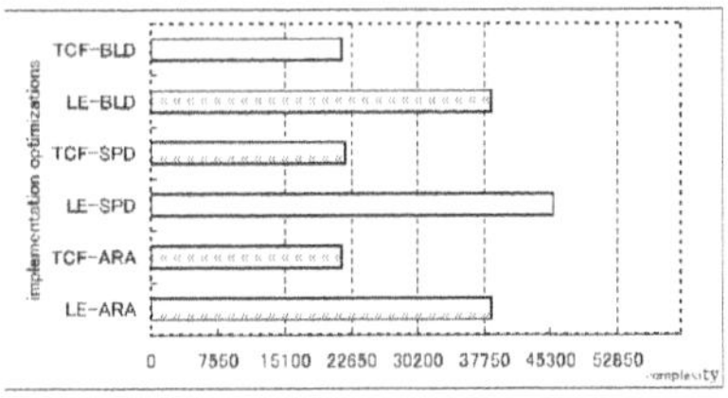

Fig. 7. Resource usage and timing for 256*33 bit QREG unit for different coding and optimization strategies

for the three used optimizations – area(ARA), speed (SPD) and balanced(BLD). For FPGA implementation, the complexity for SPD optimization is about 17% and 18% higher than that for ARA and BLD optimizations respectively.

7 Results and Discussions

Table 1 summarizes the synthesis results of QueueCore for FPGA Stratix and HardCopy devices. The complexity of each processor module as well as the whole processor core are given as the number of logic elements(LEs) for the Stratix FPGA device and as the TCF cell count for the HardCopy device (Stuructured ASIC). The design was optimised for BLD optimization guided by a properly implemented constraint table. Figure 9 shows the floorplan of the placed and routed QueueCore processor. The pipeline stages have been placed from the top right to the lower left corner of the target Stratix EP1S device. From the above experiment, we found that the processor consumes about 80.4% of the total logical elements of the target device.

Figure 8 shows the achievable throughput which can be obtained from this design on different execution platforms. For the hardware platforms, we show the processor frequency. For comparison purposes, the Verilog HDL simulator per-

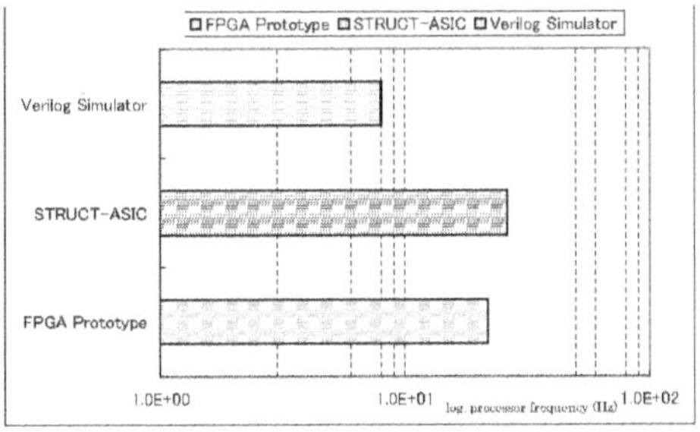

Fig. 8. Achievable frequency is the instruction throughput for hardware implementations of the QueueCore processor. Simulation speeds have been converted to a nominal frequency rating to facilitate comparison.

Table 1. Queue processor design results: modules complexity as LE (logic elements) and TCF (total combinational functions) when synthesised for FPGA (with Stratix device) and Structured ASIC (HardCopy II) families

Descriptions	Modules	LE	TCF
instruction fetch unit	IF	633	414
instruction decode unit	ID	2573	1564
queue compute unit	QCU	1949	1304
barrier queue unit	BQU	9450	4348
issue unit	IS	15476	7065
execution unit	EXE	15868	7241
queue-registers unit	QREG	38543	21590
memory access	MEM	5158	3936
control unit	CTR	171	152
Queue processor core	QueueCore	89821	47614

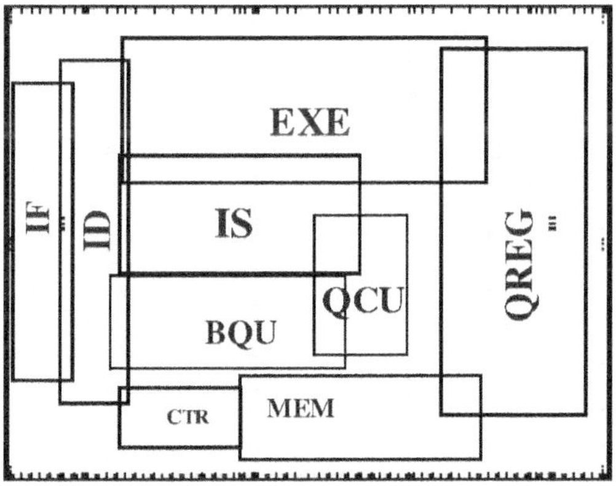

Fig. 9. Floorplan of the placed and routed processor core. The modules of the processor show considerable overlap as logic is mapped according to interconnect requirements.

formance has been converted to an artificial frequency rating by dividing the simulator throughput by a cycle count of 1 CPI. This chart shows the benefits which can be derived from direct hardware execution using a prototype when compared to processor simulation. The data used for this simulation are based on event-driven functional Verilog HDL simulation.

8 Concluding Remarks

A Queue (QueueCore) procerssor for Stratix FPGA was created using modular design structure in high-level prototyping system. The architecture is flexible, with library files controlling key definitions needed by various components. Recompilation can be done to make desired changes to pipeline information,

QREG size, memory size and various other architectural features. Each architectural components has been tested through extensive simulation, as well as actual implementation in the Stratix FPGA device.

We also described what constraints contribute to efficient FPGA implementation. This has been demonstrated by target processor core as a single high-density FPGA.

Evaluation results reveal that queue processor achieves a speed of about 22.5 and 25.5 MHZ for QREG16 (QREG size is 32*16 entries) and QREG264 (QREG size is 32*264 entries) respectively. We also found that the processor consumes about 80.4% of the total logical elements of the Stratix device. As a result, it fits on a single Stratix device with an internal embedded memory that eliminates the need for external memory module, thereby obviating the need to perform multi-chip partitioning which results in a loss of resource efficiency. Only, few clearly identified such as the Barrier and the QREG units need to be specially optimised at the HDL source level to achieve efficient resources usage.

References

1. M. Sowa , Ben A. Abderazek, T. Yoshinaga, "Parallel Queue Processor Architecture Based on Produced Order Computation Model", Int. Journal of Supercomputing, HPC, Vol. 32,No. 3, pp. 217-229, June 2005.
2. B. A. Abderazek, M. Arsenji, S. Shigeta, T. Yoshinaga, M. Sowa, Queue Processor for Novel Queue Computing Paradigm Based on Produced Order Scheme, Proc. of HPC, IEEE CS, 0-7695-2138-X/04, pp. 169-177, July 2004
3. M. Sheliga, and E. H. sha,Hardware/Software Co-design With the HMS Framework," Journal of VLSI Signal Processing Systems, Vol. 13, No. 1,pp. 37-56, 1996.
4. D. Lewis et al, The Stratix Logic and Routing Architecture, Proc FPGA-02, pp 12-20, 2002
5. Cadence Design Systems:http://www.cadence.com/
6. Altera Design Software: http://www.altera.com/
7. A.E.A Almaini, et al.: State Assignment of Finite State Machines using a Genetic Algorithm, IEE Proc. on Computers and Digital Techniques, pp. 279-286. 1995.

Pipelined Bidirectional Bus Architecture for Embedded Multimedia SoCs*

Gang-Hoon Seo, Won-Yong Jung, Seongsoo Lee, and Jae-Kyung Wee

School of Electronics Engineering, Soongsil University, 156-743, Korea
wjk@ssu.ac.kr

Abstract. This paper proposes novel high-performance bus architecture for memory-intensive embedded multimedia SoCs. It has a pipelined bidirectional bus for high speed and small area. It has two separate bus called system bus and memory bus, where memory-intensive IPs are connected to memory bus so not to degrade system bus performance. To avoid starvation of low-priority masters, the proposed bus exploits probability-based arbitration policy where the arbitration probability of each master is determined in proportion to its execution time. To increase transmission bandwidth, it also exploits bus partitioning where several masters often access their slaves concurrently without multilayer structure. The proposed bus is designed, implemented, verified, and evaluated in hardware level. Simulation results show that the proposed bus improves effective bandwidth by 2.8~3.6 times and communication latency by 3.1~4.7 times when compared to AMBA bus.

1 Introduction

Recently, advances of integrated circuit technology have enabled development of complex embedded systems into systems-on-chip (SoC) [1], where pre-designed IP cores are stitched together through various communication links. Design of high performance global communication architecture has become a key to successful embedded SoC designs. On-chip buses [2]-[6] are often used for on-chip communication between internal IP cores.

On-chip buses are classified into standard buses [2]-[5] and wrapper-based buses [6]. Standard on-chip buses specify its own protocol over wiring connections between IP cores. Any IP cores complying that protocol can be reused in other embedded SoCs using same bus type. However, interface logic should be redesigned when different bus type is used. Wrapper-based approaches use IP core interface protocol independent of physical bus protocol, and they use hardware wrappers to handle core-to-core communication. Hence, IP cores complying with the interface protocol can be integrated into embedded SoC, even if their physical bus types are different. However, complex wrapper architecture is required to reduce access latency. In practical applications, wrapper-based buses such as virtual component interface (VCI) and open core protocol (OCP) are widely used.

* This work was supported by grant No. R01-2005-000-10540-0 from the Basic Research Program of the Korea Science and Engineering Foundation.

L.T. Yang et al. (Eds.): EUC 2005, LNCS 3824, pp. 350 – 359, 2005.

Recently, embedded multimedia systems are often designed into SoCs based on IP cores. Most multimedia applications store large amount of picture data in the external memory. Therefore effective on-chip bus architecture is required to handle large memory access. In this paper, novel wrapper-based on-chip bus architecture is proposed for embedded multimedia SoCs. It has a separate memory bus so that it can handle large memory bandwidth and frequent memory access. It has a pipelined architecture to support multitasking on a single layer bus, i.e. in some cases several masters can access several slaves simultaneously. It has a probability-based arbitration policy to avoid starvation of low-priority masters.

2 Problems of Conventional Bus Architectures

AMBA bus [2] is one of the most popular on-chip bus architecture in IP-based embedded SoCs. It consists of AHB bus and APB bus, where the former is designed for high-performance operation and the latter is designed for low-performance external devices. AMBA bus shows good performance in on-chip IPs. However, it suffers from the following problems when applied to multimedia applications such as MPEG.

AMBA bus shows serious performance degradation in external memory with long or variable latency time. For example, MPEG system often requires external SDRAM memory to store large picture data. Therefore, SDRAM is connected with AHB bus due to huge memory access. However, SDRAM is accessed so frequently in the multimedia applications, and it has long latency time from the master's request. In AMBA bus, other IPs cannot use the bus when one IP already occupies it. Therefore, the IP accessing SDRAM occupies AHB bus during most of the operation time, and other IPs hardly share AHB bus. This seriously reduces the efficiency of AMBA bus. To overcome this problem, AMBA bus provides multilayer scheme to support multi-masters-to-single-slave connection. However, as the number of masters increases, bus area becomes large and wiring scheme becomes complicated. Furthermore, in the multilayer scheme, complex arbiter hardware is required because AMBA bus has only one arbiter that decides the priority of multi-masters.

Sonics bus [4] makes arbitration based on time schedule (TDMA). When SDRAM is connected to Sonics bus, SDRAM interface can directly require a master to read or write in order to prevent delaying due to long latency time of SDRAM. Sonics bus is easier to optimize than AMBA bus, and IP reuse is also easier because it supports OCP. However, very complicated SDRAM interface is required to increase bus efficiency, and the very detailed design information of IPs is also required.

SAMBA bus [7] is a synchronous bi-directional bus with multitasking. It shows better bus bandwidth over AMBA. It also reduces performance degradation due to long arbitration latency. However, it shows long latency time to read data from external memory, and it is not suitable for multimedia applications.

In segment bus [8], the response of slow slaves may cause severe performance degradation because it remains idle while the master is waiting for the response. Split transactions of segment bus are used to avoid such performance degradation. However, in split transactions, the bus access right of the master is released after the slave obtains the communication request. The slave has to initiate a new bus transaction to transfer the response. Therefore, split transactions lead to an increase in arbitration complexity. Also, it can not assure the compatibility of the developed IPs with the conventional chip architectures.

3 Proposed Bus Architecture

3.1 Overview

In this paper, we propose a hierarchical bus structure for multimedia applications. Fig. 1 illustrates the proposed bus architecture. It exploits probability-based arbitration policy to avoid starvation of low-priority masters, which is described in the next section. It consists of two separate buses, i.e. system bus (SBUS) and memory bus (MBUS). SBUS is a bi-directional bus with pipelined architecture to support multitasking. MBUS is a multi-masters-to-single-slave single layer bus, and it has an efficient communication protocol with external SDRAM memory. External SDRAM memory and IPs with large memory access is connected to MBUS. When an IP directly accesses SDRAM via MBUS, other IPs can communicate with each other via SBUS, and it significantly reduces the performance degradation from memory access. SBUS and MBUS communicate with each other via memory bus bridge (MBridge).

The proposed bus architecture has three types of arbiters. Local arbiter (LArbiter) is attached to each master in SBUS. It performs arbitration based on TDMA. The priority is calculated from the pre-design analysis of each master. Central arbiter (CArbiter) performs channel control of SBUS. It grants approval of each master according to the channel status when local arbiter requests channel access. Control signals of LArbiters and CArbiter have short latency time, since they are separate from command transfer signals, address transfer signals, and data transfer signals. LArbiters and CArbiter are not integrated in order that additional masters can be easily inserted. MBUS arbiter (MArbiter) controls MBUS when a master in MBUS accesses external SDRAM memory. When a master in SBUS accesses SDRAM, it communicates with MBridge via SBUS, and then MBridge accesses SDRAM via MBUS. MBridge acts as a slave in SBUS and a master in MBUS.

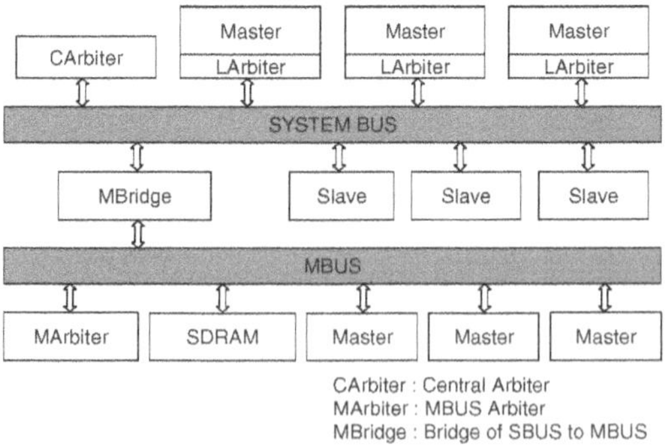

Fig. 1. Proposed bus architecture

3.2 Probability-Based Arbitration Policy

AMBA bus exploits priority-based arbitration policy. Each master has its own fixed priority, and a master with higher priority is selected among waiting masters. Unfortunately, in AMBA bus, masters with lower priority sometimes fall into starvation. For example, assume that (1) there are four masters M_i (i=1..4) where lower i has higher priority, (2) their execution times are 30ms, 30ms, 20ms, and 20ms, respectively, and (3) they send next bus requests at 30ms after they finish current execution. As shown in Fig. 2 (a), when M_1, M_2, M_3, and M_4 send bus requests simultaneously at t=0ms, M_1 occupies the bus at t=0ms and M_2 occupies it at t=30ms. At t=60ms, M_1 sends next request and it occupies the bus again. At t=90ms, M_2 sends next request and it occupies the bus again. In this way, M_3 and M_4 can hardly access the bus and they fall into starvation, unless M_1 and M_2 stop sending their requests.

To avoid this problem, the proposed bus architecture exploits probability-based arbitration policy, where the arbitration probability of each master is determined in proportion to its execution time. In the previous example, M_1, M_2, M_3, and M_4 get the bus at t=0ms with the probability of 3/10, 3/10, 2/10, and 2/10, respectively, as illustrated in Fig. 2 (b). Assume that M_1 and M_2 are determined to get the bus at t=0ms and t=30ms, respectively. At t=60ms, M_1, M_3 and M_4 wait for bus arbitration, and M_3 and M_4 still have chance to get the bus with the probability of 2/7 and 2/7,

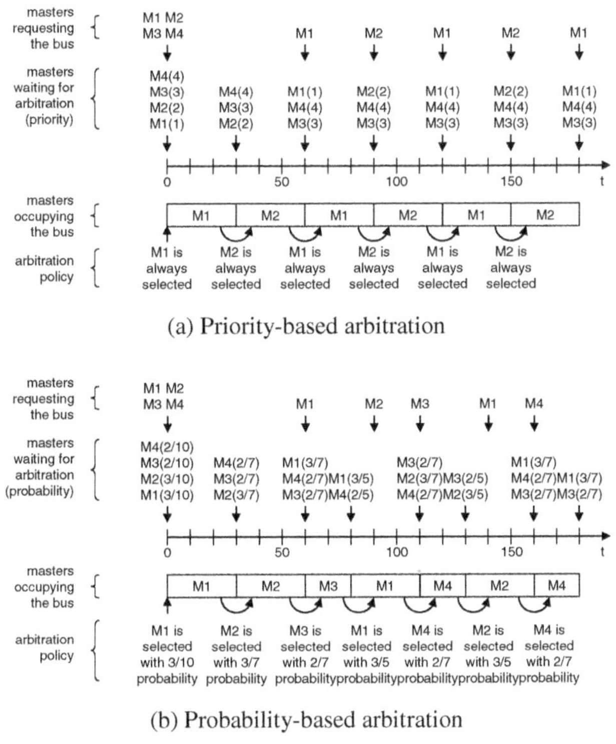

Fig. 2. Probability-based arbitration policy

respectively. Assume that M_3 and M_1 are determined to get the bus at t=60ms and t=80ms, respectively. At t=110ms, M_2, M_3 and M_4 wait for bus arbitration, and M_4 still have chance to get the bus with the probability of 2/7. Thus, starvation hardly occurs. The probability-based arbitration is implemented by simple logic gates with negligible hardware overhead.

3.3 Bus Partitioning for Concurrent Multiple Master-to-Slave Communications

In AMBA bus, several masters and slaves are connected to a common bus. Consequently, when a master accesses a slave, other masters cannot access other slaves even if each master tries to access different slave, as shown in Fig. 3 (a).

In the proposed bus architecture, we propose bus partitioning as illustrated in Fig. 3 (b). The proposed bus is partitioned into N partitions, where N is the number of masters. Each partition is connected via N-1 partition switches. When a switch is off, partitions in the left and right of the switch act as two separate buses. Therefore, more than two masters can access their slaves concurrently. In Fig. 3 (b), there are 4 masters (master1, master2, master3, and master4) and 4 slaves (slave1, slave2, slave3, and slave4). The bus is divided into 4 partitions (P1, P2, P3, and P4), and they are connected via 3 partition switches (W1, W2, and W3). When master1, master2, and

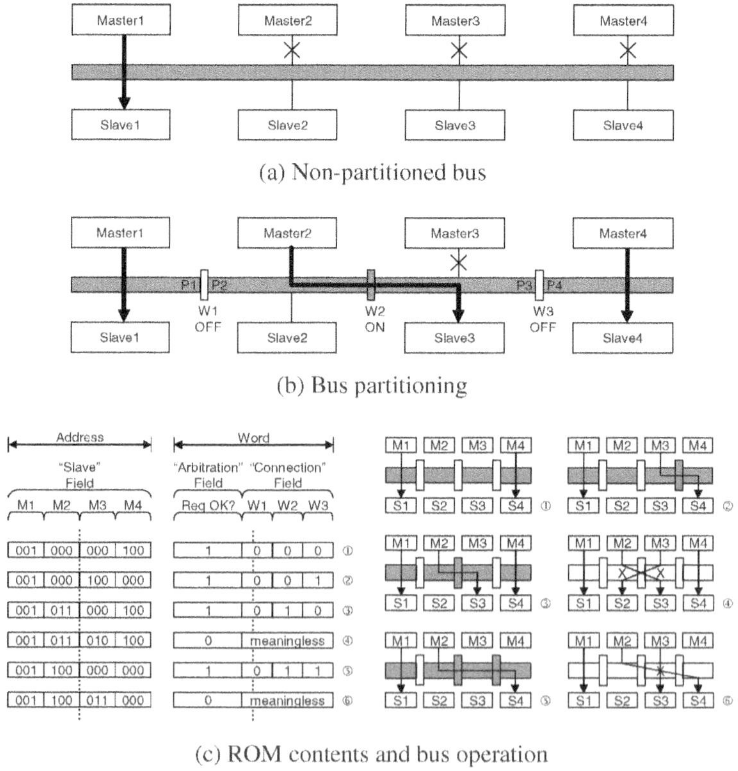

Fig. 3. Bus partitioning for concurrent multiple master-to-slave communications

master4 try to access slave1, slave3, and slave4, respectively, the bus arbiter opens W1 and W3, and it closes W2. Thus, the bus acts as three separate buses (P1, P2+P3, and P4), and three masters access three slaves concurrently (master1→slave1, master2→slave3, and master3→slave4).

Proposed bus arbitration is performed as follows. Assume the followings: (1) there are M masters denoting master$i$ (i=1..M) and S slaves denoting slave$i$ (i=1..S), (2) the bus is divided into max(M, S) partitions denoting Pi (i=1..max(M, S)) and they are connected via max(M, S) – 1 switches denoting Wi (i=1..max(M, S) – 1), (3) c connections denoting $C_i(m_i, s_i)$ (i=1..c, $c<M$) are made currently, where $C_i(m_i, s_i)$ indicates that masterm_i is connected to slaves_i. When masterm_k tries to access slavem_k, it can get bus arbitration when Eqn. (1) is satisfied. Otherwise, masterm_k should wait for bus arbitration until Eqn. (1) is satisfied.

$$(m_k > m_i \text{ and } s_k > s_i) \text{ or } (m_k < m_i \text{ and } s_k < s_i) \text{ for all connections } C_i\ (i=1..c,\ c<M) \quad (1)$$

When masterm_k gets bus arbitration, the bus arbiter opens W*left* and W*right*, and it closes W*mid*, where *left*, *right*, and *mid* are given as Eqn. (2)-(4).

$$left = \min(m_k, s_k) \quad (2)$$

$$right = \max(m_k, s_k) \quad (3)$$

$$mid = (left + 1) .. (right - 1) \quad (4)$$

Practically, the proposed bus arbitration is implemented by simple ROM as illustrated in Fig. 3 (c). ROM address is $\{M \times \log_2(S+1)\}$ bits and ROM word is max(M, S) bits, where M and S are the number of masters and slaves, respectively. 'Slave' field indicates the slave ID in connection, and 0 means that the corresponding master accesses no slave currently. 'Arbitration' field indicates whether the requested access is possible or not. 0 means that such request is impossible and the requested master should wait for next chance. 'Switch' field indicates the partition switch status, and 0 means that the corresponding partition switch is off. When there are 4 masters and 4 slaves, ROM size is only 12bit address × 4 bit word, which is quite small. Even when there are 16 masters and 16 slaves, ROM size is only 80bit address × 16 bit word, which is quite tolerable.

3.4 Bus Architecture

Fig. 4 shows the SBUS architecture for command signals, address signals, and data signals. When a master transmits a request, LArbiter sends a 'Request' signal to CArbiter. After CArbiter checks channel status, it sends 'Done' and 'Accept' signals to the master. Simultaneously, channel gate signals of CArbiter control channel gates with pipelined architecture. Dashed block in Fig. 4 is a transmission control unit for command signals, address signals, and data signals. It consists of multiplexers, flip-flops, and tri-state buffers. It exploits bidirectional transmission for wiring efficiency. Pipelined structure with flip-flops is also employed for performance improvement and accurate data transmission. Masters in SBUS communicate with SDRAM via

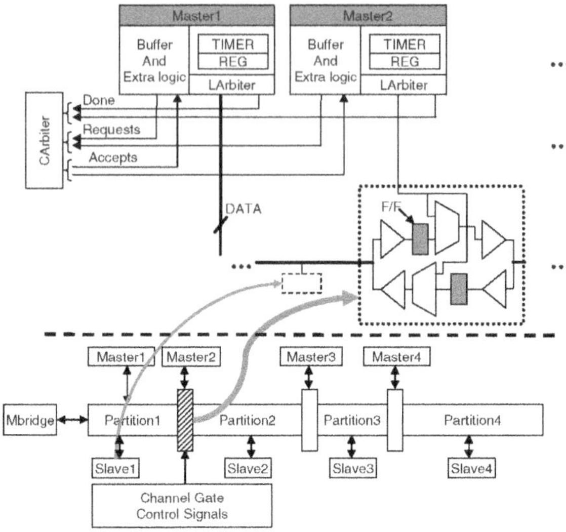

Fig. 4. SBUS architecture

MBridge and access latency time is different for each master. Leftmost master in SBUS has minimum latency time, so the master accessing SDRAM most frequently should be assigned to partition1. Therefore, when designing SBUS, masters should be assigned according to the descending order of SDRAM access frequency.

When LArbiter of a master sends 'request' signal to CArbiter, CArbiter looks up its internal ROM. When its 'arbitration' field is 1, CArbiter sends channel gate control signals to open or close partition switches. Partition switch is tri-state buffers in Fig. 4, and CArbiter directly controls it to reduce latency time. At the same time, it sends 'accept' signal to the master. Then, the master begins data transmission.

3.5 Bus Operation

There are two modes in SBUS bus protocols, i.e. request mode and response mode. Request mode is used when a master sends data to a slave, and response mode is used when a slave sends data to a master. These two modes have symmetrical structures with command bus, address bus, and data bus. SBUS has four direct control signals. DCS1 is 'request' signals from LArbiter to CArbiter. DCS2 is 'accept' signals from CArbiter to master. DCS3 is 'done' signals from slave to CArbiter. DCS4 is channel control gate signals (CGCS) from CArbiter to partition switch. Bit width of DCS1, DCS2, DCS3, and DCS4 are M bits, M bits, S bits, and $4P$ bits, respectively, where M, S, P are the number of masters, slaves, and partitions, respectively.

Fig. 5 illustrates data flow of concurrent multiple master-to-slave communications when master1 sends data to slave2 and master3 sends data to slave4. When master1 tries to send data to slave3, master1 sends 'request' signal to CArbiter (①). CArbiter checks if such arbitration is possible, and sends 'accept' signals to master1 (②). At the same time, CArbiter sends CGCS to open or close partition switches (②). In this case, partition gates W1, W2, and W3 are on, off, and off, respectively. After that,

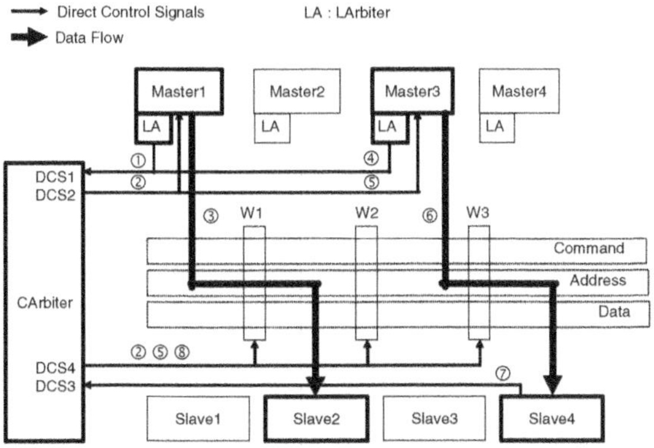

Fig. 5. Data flow of concurrent multiple master-to-slave communications

data is transmitted from master1 to slave2 (③).When master3 tries to send data to slave4, master3 sends 'request' signal to CArbiter (④). CArbiter checks if such arbitration is possible, and sends 'accept' signals to master3 (⑤). At the same time, CArbiter updates CGCS to open or close partition switches (⑤). In this case, partition gates W1, W2, and W3 are on, off, and on, respectively. After that, data is transmitted from master3 to slave4 (⑥). When the transmission from master3 to slave4 finishes, slave4 sends 'done' signal to CArbiter (⑦). Then CArbiter updates CGCS to open or close partition switches (⑧). In this case, partition gates W1, W2, and W3 are on, off, and off, respectively.

4 Simulation Results

To evaluate the performance of the proposed bus architecture, we designed both AMBA bus and the proposed bus, and implemented them with Verilog HDL. They were verified and simulated on hardware level, and their performances were evaluated for comparison. We used SDRAM as external memory.

The number of masters, slaves, and partition are assumed as 3, 4, and 4, respectively. We assumed that the workload of master1, master2, master3, and master4 are 40%, 30%, 20%, and 10%, respectively. We used three test patterns, i.e. uniform traffic pattern, non-uniform traffic pattern, and random traffic pattern. In the uniform traffic pattern, each master accesses 4 slaves equally. Master1 equally accesses slave1, slave2, slave3, and slave4 in 25%. Master2, master3, and master4 access slaves in a same way. In the non-uniform traffic pattern, each master accesses adjacent slave more frequently than other slaves. Master1 accesses slave1 in 85% and it equallyaccesses slave2, slave3, and slave4 in 5%. Master2 accesses slave2 in 85% and it equally accesses slave1, slave3, and slave4 in 5%. Master3 and master4 access slaves in a same way. In the random traffic pattern, each master accesses 4 slave randomly. Bit width of data bus and address bus is 32 bits. TDMA is exploited as priority scheme. In multimedia applications, large amount of picture data is sequentially accessed in frame memory, so the transmission is modeled as burst mode with 16 increments. Inter-communication interval is 3, 6, and 9. We used two performance measures to evaluate the proposed bus architecture. Normalized effective bandwidth is defined as the normalized value of (amount of transmitted data) / (elapsed bus cycles) with AMBA bus. Average communication latency is the average of latency cycles from bus request to bus accept.

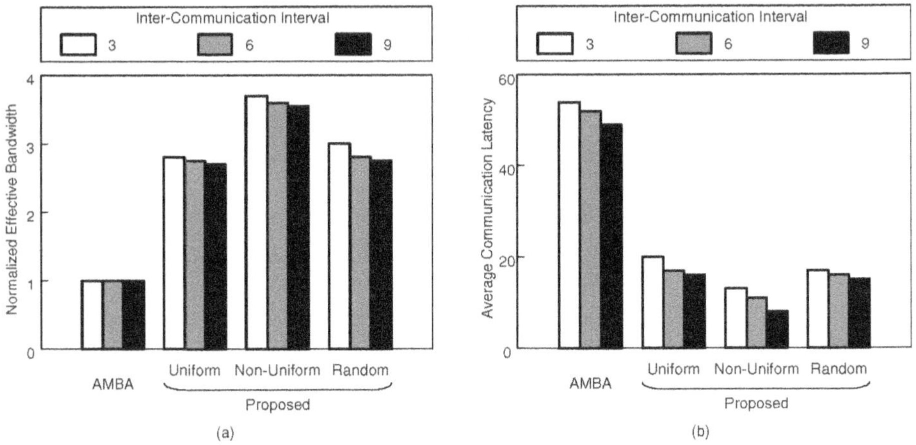

Fig. 6. Simulation results (a) Normalized effective bandwidth (b) Average communication latency

Fig. 6 shows the simulation results. Both AMBA bus and the proposed bus are designed in Verilog HDL and synthesized on Synopsys CAD tools supported by IC Design Education Center. The bus operation is simulated in Synopsys CAD tools, not in C++. Therefore, the simulation results consider all hardware effects including gate delay, bus line delay, buffer operation, and pipelining. Note that the simulation results of AMBA bus are identical regardless of traffic patterns. In AMBA bus, only one master can access a slave at a time and there is no difference in bus performance which slave a master accesses. We performed 320 bursts from every 4 masters to every 4 slaves, and the amount of transmitted data is 320 (burst number) × 32 bits (bandwidth) × 16 (16 increments burst) × 4 (masters) × 4 (slaves) = 327,680 bytes. In this case, AMBA bus takes about 20,000 cycles. On the contrary, the proposed bus takes about 7,250 cycles in the uniform traffic pattern. Consequently, the proposed bus achieves 2.8 times speed-up in the uniform traffic pattern. Similarly, it achieves 3.6 and 2.8 times speed-up in the non-uniform traffic pattern and random traffic pattern, respectively. As for average communication latency, the proposed bus achieves 3.1, 4.7, and 3.3 times speed-up in the uniform traffic pattern, non-uniform traffic pattern, and random traffic pattern, respectively. In the simulation results, the proposed bus shows best performance improvement in the non-uniform traffic pattern. This is due to the fact that the bus partitioning shows better performance when a master accesses its adjacent slaves more frequently than other slaves.

5 Conclusion

This paper proposes novel bus architecture for embedded multimedia SoCs. It consists of two separate buses called system bus (SBUS) and memory bus (MBUS) for effective memory access. It effectively handles huge memory bandwidth and frequent memory access of multimedia applications, since most memory-intensive IPs are connected to MBUS and they hardly disturb SBUS operations. The proposed bus architecture exploits probability-based arbitration policy, and masters with low priority hardly fall into starvation. It exploits bus partitioning to enable concurrent multiple master-to-slave communications to increase transmission bandwidth. It exploits pipelined bidirectional architecture to achieve high performance. It supports VCI and OCP to reuse IPs easily. The proposed bus architecture is designed, implemented, verified, and evaluated in hardware level. From the simulation results, it shows 2.8~3.6 times speed-up in effective bandwidth and 3.1~4.7 times speed-up in communication latency. Especially, it shows significant performance improvement when each master accesses its adjacent slave than other slave, which is typical in embedded multimedia SoCs.

References

1. Keating, M., Bricaud, P.: Reuse Methodology Manual for System-on-a-Chip Designs, Kluwer Academic Publishers (1998).
2. ARM: AMBA Specification Overview, http://www.arm.com/ Pro+Peripherals/AMBA.
3. IBM: CoreConnect Bus Architecture, http://www.chips.ibm.com/products/coreconnect/ docs/ cron_wp.pdf.
4. Sonics: Sonics μNetwork Technical Overview, http: http//:www.sonicsinc.com/Documents/ Overview.pdf.
5. OCP International Partnership: Open Core Protocol Specification, http://www.ocpip.org.
6. Anjo, K., Okamura, A., Motomura, M.: Wrapper-Based Bus Implementation Techniques for Performance Improvement and Cost Reduction, IEEE Journal of Solid-State Circuits **35** (2004) 804-817.
7. Lu, R., Koh, C.-K.: SAMBA-bus: A High Performance Bus Architecture for System-on-Chips, Proceedings of International Conference on Computer-Aided Design (2003) 8-12.
8. Plosila, J., Seceleanu, T., Liljeberg, P.: Implementation of a Self-Timed Segmented Bus, IEEE Design and Test of Computers **20** (2003) 44-45.

On Tools for Modeling High-Performance Embedded Systems

Anilkumar Nambiar and Vipin Chaudhary

Department of Computer Science, Wayne State University
{anambiar, vipin}@wayne.edu

Abstract. Most of the new embedded systems require high performance processors at low power. To cater to these needs, most semiconductor companies are designing multi-core processors, also known as chip-multiprocessors, while some are developing multi-chip boards with existing multi-core processors. Developing applications on these powerful architectures require specialized tools to obtain the optimum performance. Most applications running on these processors not only require high processing power, but also have tight resource constraints. For both, chip-multiprocessors and multi-chip boards, one faces some common problems while developing applications for them. To meet this end, we have developed tools to model high-performance embedded applications on these complex high-end systems. We have integrated these tools in the modeling framework of MILAN, and have modeled a real application, Mpeg-2 Audio Video Decoder. For validation we have used Cradle Technologies MDSP multi-core chip as the target processor.

1 Introduction

Chip Multiprocessors are being widely used to develop System-on-Chip (SOC) solutions for high-end embedded systems. An SOC consists of processors (RISC/DSP), internal memory, external memory, device controllers, timers, etc. SOC architecture for a low/medium scale device would not require more than a couple of processors. On the other hand, high-end embedded systems, such as HDTV, bio-medical applications, high capacity printers and copiers would require multiple cores of RISC/DSP or a combination of both, to fulfill the high performance requirement. Most of these applications can be parallelized over multiple low power processors to obtain the desired performance.

Most of the multi-core chips available consist of not more than 8 cores on a single chip [1]. For a high-end application this might not be suitable. ASIC-based solutions are not suitable either, as these solutions take longer time to market and have high cost per unit. There are few companies developing multi-core chips with 30-60 cores in one chip [2] [3]. While other companies, in order to achieve the high performance requirements for these high-end applications, develop multi-chip boards, with each board housing 2-4 chips, where each chip has 4-8 processors [4][5][6]. This gives enough computational power for the high-end systems.

As the number of processors increase, the bandwidth requirement for the application over the shared global bus increases. In order to sustain such high

L.T. Yang et al. (Eds.): EUC 2005, LNCS 3824, pp. 360 – 370, 2005.

requirements, these systems have a hierarchical architecture consisting of clusters. Each cluster is made up of RISC and/or DSP processors with some shared internal memory to be used as a scratch pad. In addition, it has semaphores, timers and interrupts. Any access to the resource within the cluster takes less time as compared to any access to resources in the other cluster or global resources since the request has to be served through shared global bus. The desirable implementation on this system would be to reduce access outside the cluster in order to improve performance. The programmer can also benefit from the nature of most of the high-end applications, where the computation to communication ratio is high.

Due to similarity in architecture, these high processor-count chip-multiprocessors and multi-chip board solutions face some common problems for developing applications. Though these systems provide high computational power, they require specialized tools to harness their raw power. One requires tools to design and map resource constraint applications on these high performance systems, tools to simulate the system at various granularity levels and provide feedback through profiling statistics, which can be incorporated back into the design to optimize the application. As most of the high-end system would be heterogeneous, the tools must provide mechanisms or interfaces for seamless integration of different simulators for different types of processors in the underlying system.

There are lots of tools for modeling SOC systems. Some of them are Ptolemy[7], Polis [8], Chinook [9], SystemC [10] and MILAN [11]. We tried to use these tools for modeling systems on such clustered/hierarchical architecture and found that they were not suitable in their existing setup. Modification needs to be done to incorporate the type of architecture we were using. Most of these tools are complex and proved cumbersome to integrate the simulators for this architecture. MILAN is relatively easy to understand and provides simple interface to integrate any new simulator. It also provides Design Space Exploration capability to obtain a near optimum design solution for the system under consideration.

For validation, we have considered Cradle Technologies' MDSP architecture [12]. This architecture uses a combination of low performance RISC and DSP processors, with each chip consisting of 36 to 60 processors. This architecture provides a very high raw computational power in the range of 10-15 GMACs. We have developed an interpreter for MILAN to model applications for MDSP. In addition, we have developed and incorporated a new heuristic for mapping applications on clustered architecture. In this paper, we have presented modeling of a complex application Mpeg-2 Audio Video Decoder (MAVD) using MILAN on the MDSP chip.

The paper is organized as follows. Section 2 gives the problem definition, section 3 discusses the Model Interpreter, section 4 discusses the MAVD modeling, section 5 discusses the related work in this area and section 6 has the concluding remarks.

2 Problem Definition

The MDSP is a heterogeneous multi-core chip developed by Cradle Technologies. The chip has a hierarchical architecture, with clusters within a chip. Each cluster or Quad consists of 4 RISC processors or PEs, 8 DSP co-processors or DSEs, 64 Kbytes of data memory, 4 channel DMA engines and other resources such as semaphores, and timers. Each chip may have varying number of clusters from 1 to 5. If one wants to design an MPEG-2 Audio Video Decoder (MAVD) system using the MDSP chip, one needs to decide on the resource requirements for each task. A typical MAVD system will consists of following tasks: Audio Decoder, Video Decoder, Audio Renderer, Video Renderer, TS Parser, System Controller, TS Feeder Simulator. The memory and processor requirement provided by Cradle Technologies is given in the Fig. 1.

Program and its Resources	Audio Deco-der	Audio Rend-erer	Video Deco-der	Video Rend-erer	TS Parser	System Cont-roller	TS Feeder Simulato	ISR Simu-lator	Timer Simu-lator
Compu-tation	1 PE 1 DSE (1 data DSE)	1 PE 1 DSE	6 PE 12 DSE	1 PE 2 DSE	1 PE 1 DSE	1 PE	1 PE	1 DSE	1 DSE
Private Local Memory	0x22D0	0xDD0	0xD68	0xBF8	0xED8	0x2F0	0x78	-	-
Shared Local Memory	-	-	0x9C0	-	0x8	-	-	-	-

Fig. 1. MAVD System Resource Requirement Table

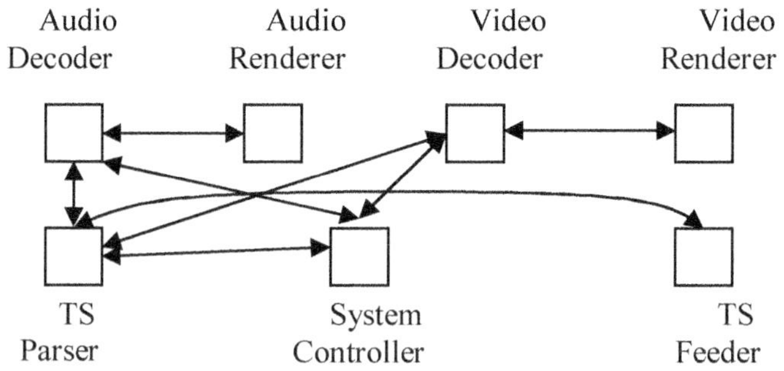

Fig. 2. MAVD System Communication Graph

While designing such a complex system, the extent of communication between different modules might not be obvious. One would like to select a design, which would minimize the execution time. Most of the time the system tasks are developed independently and needs to be integrated. During integration, one would like to map the system on the chip, which would reduce the communication time, which in turn would minimize the execution time. MILAN provides excellent design space exploration functionality, whereby one can consider different designs, simulate those at high level or low level using the appropriate architecture simulators and then choose a good solution. In our case, since we are only considering one chip, the simulation becomes simple.

MILAN incorporates an optimal mapping algorithm for linear array of tasks [13]. But it requires the tasks to be executed in linear order, whereas in our case, the tasks are executed concurrently on different processors. Hence it cannot be used for our problem domain. In order to support MDSP chip in MILAN, one needs to provide:

a. MILAN interpreter to interpret system models and generate output for MDSP simulator, and associated tools.
b. A new mapping heuristic to map applications on MDSP processor.

3 Model Interpreter

MILAN uses GME or Generic Modeling Environment [14] to synthesize a domain specific modeling interface for modeling the system. GME provides interfaces to specify different modeling paradigm for different domains. Modeling paradigm is a set of building blocks and composition rules using which, the designer models the system. MILAN is an example of such a modeling paradigm.

While modeling any system, the designer will perform two main activities:

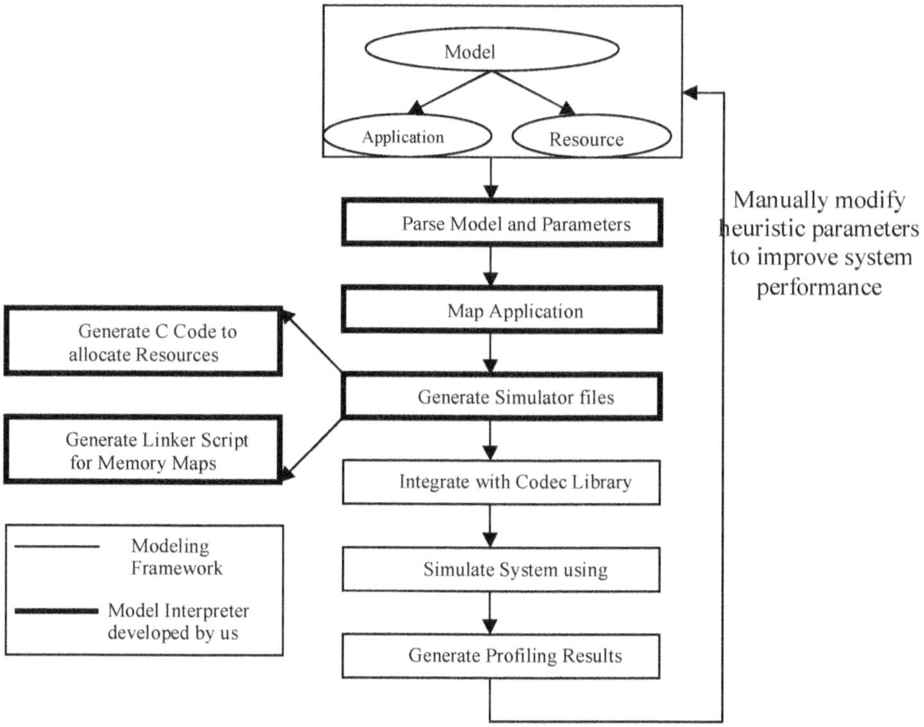

Fig. 3. System Modeling

1. Application Modeling, where the designer defines application modules or tasks and inter-task communication between different modules using task-graph.
2. Resource modeling, where the designer models the underlying architecture. In this the designer defines various architecture parameters such as frequency, power consumption, cache size etc. for the architecture under consideration.

In application modeling, we found no provision to specify shared memory communication between multiple modules. In the existing setup in order to represent shared memory communication one would have to show it by connecting different modules using communication channels. This might complicate the design with lots of connections between modules involved in communication. In order to represent shared memory communication, we added a new feature to the paradigm to represent shared memory communication.

MILAN provides various model interpreters to interpret the model and generate output for different simulators. In order to generate the output for MDSP simulator, we developed our own interpreter. This interpreter takes the model and applies our proposed heuristic to generate a good mapping scheme and then generate code to allocate resources and launch the specific threads of various tasks on the processors. This divides the interpreter into three main components, the Model Parser, the Mapping Heuristic and the Code Generator.

3.1 Model Parser

The Model parser is a COM object, which is invoked from the GME as an interpreter. This parser performs a top-down parsing of the components defined in the GME and forms the input to the Mapping heuristics. It forms the list of tasks T defined, based on primitive components. It also forms the resource requirement matrix and communication matrix. The priority for each task is obtained from the attributes of the task. The processor requirement for each task is obtained from the resource reference provided by the user in the Mapping Aspect window. These inputs are provided to the Mapping heuristic module to provide a good mapping scheme.

3.2 Mapping Heuristic

MILAN provides a mapping algorithm to map linear array of tasks onto single and multiple device. It requires the tasks to be in linear order where, given a set of tasks T = $\{t_1, t_2, \ldots . t_n\}$, t_{i+1} executes only after t_i, $1 \leq i \leq n$. The mapping problem in our case is different than the one discussed.

Suppose we want to map the MAVD system on the MDSP processor by integrating different tasks, which were developed independently. In this case some of the tasks are independent, while others have inter-task communication. The first requirement would be to allocate all the processors for a given task in the same cluster, as most of the tasks will have more intra-task communication than inter-task communication. In addition to intra-task communication, the tasks will communicate with the allocated resources to varying degree. The resources in this case are memory, and co-processor. If there were more communication between co-processor and processor than inter-task communication, it would be better to allocate the co-processor from the same cluster in which the task is running, and then try to see if the two tasks involved in communication can be allocated to the same cluster.

We have developed Improved First Fit Decreasing [15], which improves over the existing First Fit Decreasing (FFD) algorithm [16]. Since we use a priority queue, if there are *m* clusters then this will require $O(nlogn*m)$ time, where *n* is the number of tasks to be mapped. So, in worst case it would be $O(n^2logn)$, where the number of tasks is equal to the number of clusters in the chip.

3.3 Code Generation Module

The code generation module generates C code to allocate processors and launch programs on the processors. To compile a multi-task program on MDSP, one needs a loader script also known as *LD* script to determine the code sections and the memory requirement for the executable. This *LD* script is used by the GNU *ld* program to generate the executable. The script specifies the tasks running with information about the local and DRAM data memory used by each task. In addition it also specifies the code sections for each task.

For any program running on MDSP, the main thread is started on QUAD 0, PE 0. This thread will start the other threads on the other processors. The task, which is mapped to QUAD 0, PE 0 forms the main thread. This thread will launch one thread from each of the other tasks on the mapped processors. Those threads in turn will start threads from its task. The launching is similar to a tree structure and its shown in the following figure.

The code in table 1 is from the main task launched on QUAD 0 PE 0.

During application modeling one specifies the buffer length to be used in the communication between different modules. This buffer length is used to allocate the shared memory structure. A shared memory structure consists of the following fields, Memory ID, Semaphore, Thread Count, Buffer Size, and Buffer Pointer.

Based on the tasks involved in communication the buffer will be allocated in local memory or shared DRAM. If all the tasks involved in communication are in the same cluster, then the shared memory is allocated in the local memory of the cluster. This would reduce the communication latency as the local memory access takes far less amount of time than DRAM. But, this is based on the availability of the local memory.

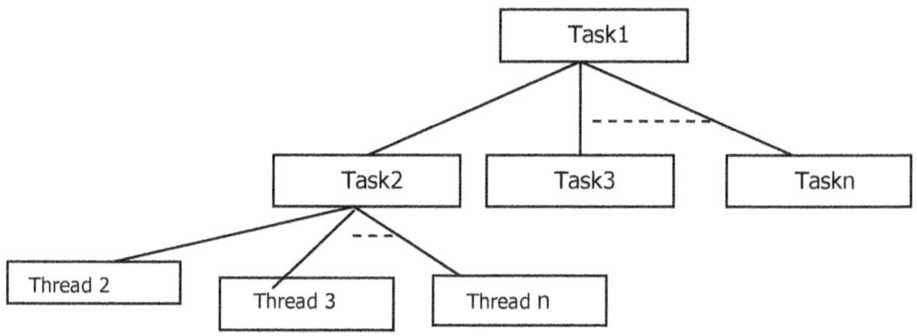

Fig. 4. Task Startup Tree

If the tasks involved in communication are in different cluster, then the buffer is allocated in the Shared DRAM. Some communication buffers require to be guarded by a semaphore. Again, based on the tasks involved in communication, the semaphores are allocated from the local or global pool. The thread count indicates the number of threads involved in communication. The buffer can be freed when the thread count goes to zero.

For shared memory communication one has to generate structures to be used with the shared memory library. We developed this library, and it has a similar structure to that of the windows shared memory library API. The shared memory library structures are generated in common header files. Once this code is generated, the user can integrate it with the core Intellectual Property modules developed. In the case of MAVD, the audio and video library forms the IP libraries.

This code is compiled and linked using the LD script generated to produce the executable. This executable is run on the hardware or the simulator to verify the results.

Table 1. Code generated by the Mapping tool for one of the synthetic test application

```
#define MAX_PROCS 20          /*total processors on the chip*/
void main()
{
        int procArray[MAX_PROCS] = {0,0,0,5,6,6,6,6,2,2,2,5,3,3,3,7,1,1,4,4}; /* application number
        loaded on proc */
        int my_peid;
        my_peid = (_QUAD_INDEX * 4) + _PE_INDEX;
        if(my_peid == 0)
        {
                StartPrograms(procArray);          /* start 1  instance of each task*/
                start_other_pes(0, 2, procArray); /* other instances of this task */
        }       my_peid = get_PE_number();  /* get my PE ID*/
        /*Perform useful computation*/
        terminate_program(my_peid, (Load_Table *)load_table_address, FREE_PL | FREE_PD); /*
        terminate the task*/
}
StartPrograms(int *procArray)
{
        int i;
        for(i = 1; i < MAX_PROCS; i++) /* for all the tasks*/
        {
                if(procArray[i] != -1)
                {
                        if(procArray[i-1] != procArray[i]) /* start only one instance of this task*/
                                start_program_on_proc(procArray[i], i, 0);
                }
        }
}
```

4 MAVD Modeling

The two main types of modeling in MILAN are Application Modeling and Resource Modeling. During application modeling, one builds the dataflow model in the dataflow aspect window. There are three main types of dataflow classes; Primitive,

Compound, and Alternate. Compounds are composite dataflow nodes. They contain dataflow graphs themselves. For example, in MAVD, the Audio Decoder is a composite model. It will contain the PE component and the DSE component, which forms the primitive model. Alternates are similar to composite models, but they represent alternative implementation. Suppose a component can be executed on PE and on DSE then one would specify it as an alternate. During mapping one can select the processor based on the availability. For system instantiation only one alternate is selected. Figure 5 shows the MAVD model created in GME using MILAN paradigm. On the right hand window the folder structure is shown. MAVD is the root composite folder with different modules in it. These folders in the root folder are composite module and form root for the module. The communication between different modules are bi-directional and is shown using connection between in-port and out-port of the specific modules.

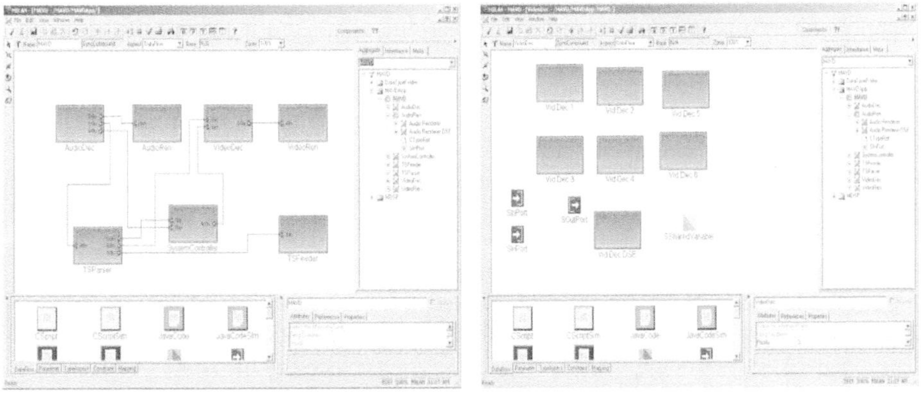

Fig. 5. Modeling MAVD using GME

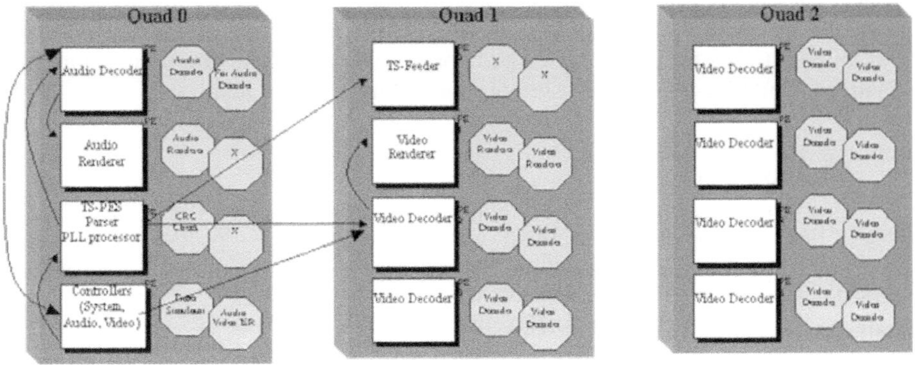

Fig. 6. MAVD Solution for MDSP Chip

For each of the composite module there are primitive or composite modules within these modules. Figure 6 shows the Video Decoder Module. There are 6 Video Decoder threads running on 6 PEs and 12 Video Decoder threads running on 12 DSEs. The 6 PE threads are shown as 6 primitive components, while the 12 DSE threads are enclosed within a composite component, which has 12 primitive components. This makes design easy to understand.

In dataflow model there are two ways of showing shared memory communication. One way is to show it through connection between all the modules. This becomes complicated with too many connections. The other way is add a new primitive called SharedMemory in the window, which will show the shared memory communication between all the modules shown in the current window. We have defined a new Atom [13] called SSharedVariable in the MILAN paradigm.

Once a primitive component is defined, it needs to be mapped onto one type of processor. But before we map onto processor, we need to model these processors. This is done using the Resource Modeling paradigm in MILAN. MILAN provides support for resource modeling to model various architecture capabilities that can be exploited to perform design space exploration and drive a set of widely used energy and latency simulators from a single model. The Resource Modeling provides support for modeling of various architectural components such as CPU, BUS, Memory, IO. One can even specify the type of cache used in the architecture. For each component one can specify what is the throughput, energy estimate, latency estimate and various other parameters. To specify that the current primitive module is going to run on a particular processor, one has to provide a reference to the processor in the primitive module in the mapping aspect.

Figure 6 shows the final mappin. In the MAVD system, the Video Decoder and Video Renderer has more communication, so they are placed within the same cluster. Similarly, Audio Decoder and Audio Renderer are placed in the same cluster. There is more communication between TS-PES Parser task and Audio Decoder task, so they have to be placed in the same cluster. Similarly, the System Controller has more communication with Audio Decoder due to higher rater of Audio ISR than Video ISR and needs to be placed in the same cluster.

We compared the mapping obtained by our algorithm and the mapping done manually by experienced system designers from Cradle over the span of two years and found it to be same. The design had gone through multiple iterations before it was finalized, while we obtained it using our tool within the first iteration.

5 Related Work

One of the most popular hardware/software co-design tools is Ptolemy. It provides an environment for design, modeling, and simulation of concurrent heterogeneous embedded systems. Though Ptolemy provides different models of computation, the main problem with it is, it does not provide mechanisms for integration of external simulators.

Writing simulators of complex multiprocessor systems for the modeling environment is not a trivial task. Instead, one can use the existing simulators provided with these processors and use them in the modeling environment. This is precisely what MILAN offers. Easy integration of existing simulators, ease in modification of the paradigm to suit the underlying architecture.

There are other co-design or modeling projects for embedded system. Some of them are Polis [8], which uses finite state machine model for hardware/software co-design, Chinook [8], which focuses on IP composition, communication synthesis and rapid evaluation. In Chinook, one has to provide behavioral description of the application, target description and mapping function in order to synthesize the system. But none of these tools could suffice our need of simulator integration. The mechanism for mapping application onto the architecture was not present in Chinook. Instead, the user has to provide the allocation function. Though Polis provides mapping mechanism, it was not for clustered architecture like the one we are considering.

MILAN incorporates an optimal mapping algorithm for linear array of tasks [13]. But it requires the tasks to be executed in linear order, whereas in our case, the tasks are executed concurrently on different processors. Hence it cannot be used for our problem domain. There has been lot of research in scheduling theory for various types of problems [17] [18][19][20]. The solutions from these researches could not be directly applied to the problem under consideration.

6 Conclusions

In this paper we have presented tools to model complex high-performance embedded systems. We have validated our techniques by modeling a complex application using a multi-core processor. The same techniques can be used to model complex applications on multi-chip boards.

The tools still require man-in-loop process to provide feedback to the modeling environment after simulation, based on the profiling results. The future direction of the research would be to automate this process, so that given a system, the tools would optimize the design automatically without much human intervention.

References

1. Arm Corporation, www.arm.com
2. Cradle Technologies, www.cradle.com
3. Azul Systems, www.azulsystems.com
4. Kestral Multiprocessor, http://www.soe.ucsc.edu/research/kestrel/
5. Orion Multisystems, www.orionmulti.com
6. ClearSpeed, www.clearspeed.com
7. Davis J. et al. , Overview of the Ptolemy project, ERL Technical Report CB/ERL No. M99/37, Dept EECS, University of California Berkeley, July 1999
8. Balarin F. et. al. : Hardware-Software Co-Design of embedded Systems: The POLIS Approach, *Kluwer Academic Publisher* 1997
9. Chou P. et. al.: IPChinook: An integrated IP-based design framework for Distributed Embedded Systems, *DAC* 1999
10. SystemC user Guide, http://www.systemc.org

11. "MILAN: A Model Based Integrated Simulation Framework for Design of Embedded Systems", Agrawal A., Bakshi A., Davis J., Eames B., Ledeczi A., Mohanty S., Mathur V., Neema S., Nordstrom G., Prasanna V., Raghavendra, C., Singh M. *Workshop on Languages, Compilers, and Tools for Embedded Systems (LCTES 2001),* Snowbird, Utah, June 2001
12. "3400 Hardware Architecture Reference", Cradle Technologies, www.cradle.com.
13. Milan Manual, http://milan.usc.edu
14. Ledeczi A., et.al., The Generic Modeling Environment, *Workshop on Intelligent Signal Processing* , Budapest, Hungary, May 17, 2001
15. A. Nambiar and V. Chaudhary, "Mapping Resource Constrained Applications on Chip Multiprocessors", *Proceedings of the 2005 International Conference on Embedded Systems & Applications (ESA'05),* Las Vegas, Nevada, June 2005.
16. E. G. Coffman, M. R. Garey, D. S. Johnson "Approximation algorithm for Bin Packing: A Survey, Appears in Approximation Algorithms for NP-Hard Problems", D. Hochbaum(ed) PWS Publishing(1996)
17. V. Chaudhary and J. K. Aggarwal, ``A generalized scheme for mapping parallel algorithms'', in *IEEE Trans. on Parallel and Distributed Systems,* Mar '93, pp. 328 - 346.
18. D. G. Feitelson and L. Rudolph, "Distributed hierarchical control for parallel processing." *Computer 23(5), pp. 65-77 , May 1990*
19. Dror G. Feitelson, "Packing Schemes for Gang Scheduling", *Job Scheduling Strategies for Parallel Processing -- Proceedings of the IPPS'96 Workshop* (1996)
20. Y.-K. Kwok, I. Ahmad. "Dynamic critical-path scheduling: An effective technique for allocating task graphs to multiprocessors." *IEEE Trans. on Parallel and Distributed Systems, vol.7, pages 506--521,* March 1996

A Hardware/Software Co-design and Co-verification on a Novel Embedded Object-Oriented Processor

Chi Hang Yau, Yi Yu Tan, Pak Lun Mok, Wing Shing Yu, and Anthony S. Fong

Department of Electronic Engineering, City University of Hong Kong,
Tat Chee Avenue, Hong Kong
Anthony.Fong@cityu.edu.hk

Abstract. In the past, programming language are procedural, the design concept is based on the module and scope which are difficult to manage, but nowadays, the programming trend is Object-Oriented Programming (OOP), where objects are the key elements to build up application and the communications between different objects are through method invocation. A novel object-oriented processor offers an opportunity to enhance the system security, performance and provides a more effective way to manipulate OOP instead of using a software Virtual Machine. jHISC is a novel object-oriented processor which provides a natural way to map the concept of OOP into architectural level through the hardware object data structure. Our solution is to design secure hardware object data structures on a novel processor with Just-In-Time compilation for Java which then makes it possible to implement complex OO related bytecodes at hardware level and access some fields of object in parallel to improve the execution speed. It mainly targets J2ME and implements about 93% bytecodes and 83% OO related bytecodes in hardware directly.

1 Introduction

Computer hardware becomes quite mature, however, software trend is moving to Object-Oriented Programming (OOP) with advantages on reusable design and better security. In traditional systems, processor architecture like Complex Instruction Set Computer (CISC) or Reduced Instruction Set Computer (RISC) does not support object manipulation directly on hardware. To support object technology in nowadays system, there are mainly three categories, which are compiling objects into native (Fig. 1), developing software-based object virtual machine (Fig. 1) and developing an object-oriented processor (Fig. 2).

For the first approach, since traditional computer system does not support object-oriented programming, applications written in object-oriented programming languages like C++ are compiled into native instructions for execution. Application processes will be created and executed in their own spaces, and they are invisible from each other through the use of virtual memory system. Through the specific compiler, objects will be translated into subroutines, which are machine readable for direct execution. Compilation approach can fully optimize the generated codes, but object-oriented features, such as dynamicity behavior, will be removed. Modification of a single class requires the whole application to be re-compiled.

L.T. Yang et al. (Eds.): EUC 2005, LNCS 3824, pp. 371 – 380, 2005.

In the second approach, an object virtual machine application is built on top of the traditional operating system. From the view of operating system, the application is just a usual process like other applications. Protection of different processes is the same as in compilation approach and objects are manipulated on this software virtual machine. The advantages of this method are that without the modification of hardware platform and current system, object technology can be supported through software emulation. But the two layers of software, virtual machine and operating system, also introduce much overhead to the overall computing system and increase the memory footprint of the system.

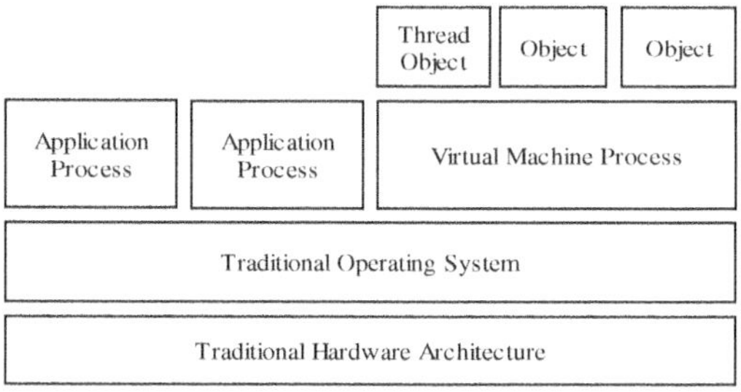

Fig. 1. System Architecture of Compilation Approach and Virtual Machine Approach

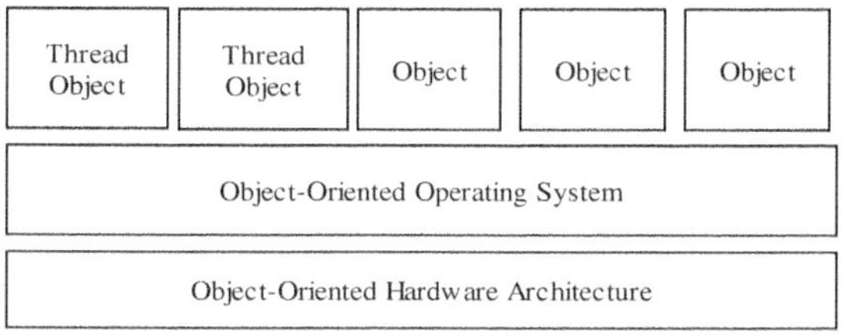

Fig. 2. System Architecture of Object-Oriented Hardware Approach

In our solution, we will use the third approach where the objects are directly manipulated on an object-oriented processor, and an object-oriented operating system will be built to assist hardware in managing the heap (Fig 2). In this approach, protection of objects is governed by the object-oriented operating system with the protection features offered by the object-oriented processor. This approach can manipulate objects directly and the efficiency of the computing system is increased because no page table updating is required during context switching.

In the following sections, we will firstly discuss our secure hardware object architecture on section 2, their overall security features on section 3. Moreover, we will show the hardware/software co-verification methodology which verifies the Java compatibility on our novel architecture, through the Just-In-time compilation on Java bytecode and demonstrate some co-verification results on section 4. Finally, a conclusion will be presented on Section 5.

2 jHISC v3 Architecture with Object Representation

In Java, objects are created with some class templates, which provide information of the object instance, such as methods, fields, etc. Object instances of the same class share the same method codes, but each instance maintains its own copy of instance variables.

There are different kinds of objects in an object-oriented system. An object can have three contexts which are the instance context, the class context, and the method context. In jHISC v3, it maps the three contexts to architecture. The information about objects in different contexts is stored in different data structures which are defined by the architecture for object representation. Generally, all the objects share the same extendable object data structure. Array and thread objects, which require additional support by hardware, are represented differently.

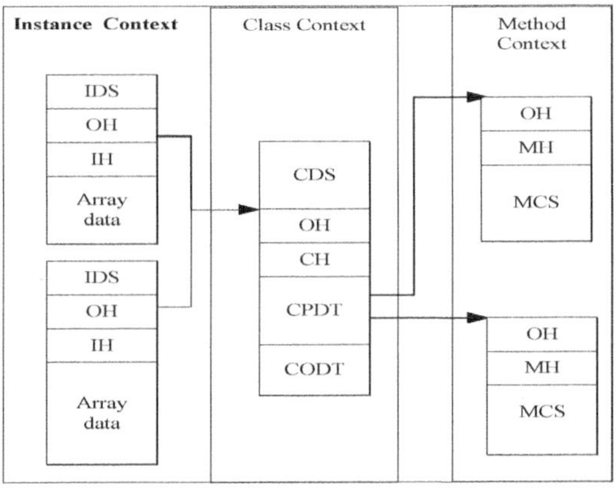

Fig. 3. Object Data Structure relationship

Three headers are defined. They are object, class, and method headers. These headers store information for describing the object, class, and method itself. A header may associate with other data structures for describing different aspects of the context.

Descriptor tables store descriptors. Each descriptor contains information about an element within the class. Two kinds of descriptor table are defined. They are Class Operand Descriptor Table (CODT), and Class Property Descriptor Table (CPDT).

Data spaces provide spaces for the storage of data. There are three types of data space. They are the Class Data Space (CDS), the Instance Data Space (IDS) and the Local Variable Frame (LVF). Unlike CDS and IDS, LVF are dynamically created inside the register file upon method invocation and destroyed upon method revocation.

Inside the method context, Method Code Space (MCS) is defined to store the instructions. Fig 3 shows the relationships between different data structures. On the following of this section, we will show each of our hardware data structure in details.

2.1 Descriptor Format

jHISC uses a 32-bit operand descriptors to describe properties own by a class or resources accessed by the class. Descriptor is a data structure which stores the information about a variable, reference or any data structures. In jHISC v3, a single descriptor format is defined, which combined both fields in Class Operand Descriptor (COD) and Class Property Descriptor (CPD). The descriptor length is 32-bit, with five fields defined according to the specification of Java virtual machine. These fields are, Address Field, Access Modifier, Type Field, Static Flag, Read Only Flag, and Resolved Flag.

2.2 Instruction Set

jHISC is a RISC based core with some object-oriented features enhancement processor. Its Instruction length is 32-bit and supports up to three operands. Each instruction uses 8-bit opcode for defining instruction operation and references data in current LVF with 7 bits, addressing up to 128 registers. In addition, jHISC provides object-oriented manipulation instructions to handle the object-oriented related processing.

In traditional computers, memory-register data transfer instructions allow program to access memory directly which may result in security problems. In jHISC, all data are encapsulated into objects, and each object associates with a pair of memory boundaries (see Section 3). A program needs to pass the bound control checks before it accesses the data and out-of-bound accesses are prohibited. Two instructions "gifld" and "pifld" are introduced in our architecture to perform data transfer operations between memory and register with rigid memory access checking.

There are totally seven groups of instruction defined in jHISC v3, they are: logical instructions, arithmetic instructions, branching instructions, array Instructions, Object-Oriented (OO) instructions and data manipulation instructions. Excluding the float-point and 64-bit operation instructions, jHISC implements 93% bytecodes and 83% OO related bytecodes in hardware directly (Table 1). The rests are executed through software traps, such as "new", "newarray".

Table 1. The bytecodes supported by jHISC

Number of bytecodes	226
Number of bytecodes excluding the float-point and 64-bit operations	140
Number of bytecodes supported by the hardware directly	130
Number of bytecodes done by the software traps	10
Number of bytecodes for OO operations	40
Number of OO bytecodes supported by the hardware directly	33
Percentage of bytecodes supported by the hardware directly	93%
Percentage OO bytecodes supported by the hardware directly	83%

3 Security Features

Nowadays computing systems are multi-tasked. Multiple applications are executed on the same machine simultaneously. As more parties are involved in a computing system, it raises some concern of information privacy between different applications.

For object-oriented hardware approach, different objects share the same addressing space. Protection features for object access should be provided by the processor and used by the operating system in order to guarantee security between objects. Unlike traditional processor architecture, object-oriented processor has built-in protection logics to ensure security, in order to minimize execution errors.

Operations in a processor can be roughly categorized into two groups. The first group performs real calculation and data movement. They are used for generating the results of execution. Another group provides the support for control flow. Such operations include branching, subroutine calling and returning. They let a sequential execution machine to change the order of instruction execution according to the flow of program.

The switch of control from one domain to another provides some possible back holes for hacking programs and viruses. In order to secure the system from damages, checking routines are introduced directly to the architecture. In jHISC v3, the secure control transfer mechanism is based on object-oriented programming and the concept of object-oriented programming features like data encapsulation, messaging, etc, is used to restrict access of information from intrusion.

3.1 Strong Type and Structural Memory Access

jHISC v3 is a strong typed system based on the definition of objects. Every data is associated with a type field, which indicates the data type. Data are encapsulated inside an object. All data types are specified upon compilation and they cannot be changed at run-time.

Direct memory accessing operations is prohibited in the jHISC v3 system. Instead of using direct memory accessing operations like load/store, jHISC v3 provides indirect memory accessing operations such as oo.getfield, oo.putfield, array.load and array.store.

3.2 Local Variable Frame and Object Data Structure Out of Bound Checking

Local variables are maintained inside Register Stack Engine (RSE). The RSE contains embedded logics for checking the out of boundary access of local variables. Any out of boundary access to local variables would cause the system a protection violation. This feature removes the potential bugs on the software or corrupted executable programs.

Pair of registers is maintained in the processor for object data structure access. A base register is used to locate the address of the object data and a size register records its size for out of boundary checking. Logics are embedded to do this kind of checking every time the data is accessed through the object-oriented instructions. Since every object has only bounded access to other objects, the sharing of address spaces in object-oriented hardware approach could be achieved with this protection features.

3.3 Intra-method and Inter-method Control Transfer

Intra-method control transfer instructions are defined for conditional statements in programming languages, such as if-then-else, while-loop, for-loop, etc. In jHISC v3, these instructions are based on branching instructions with an additional checking to avoid branching outside of the current method space. A pair of register is used to store the base address and size of current running method. The branch target is an offset to the base address (Fig. 4). The avoidance of branching outside the current method space enables all objects running in the same addressing space.

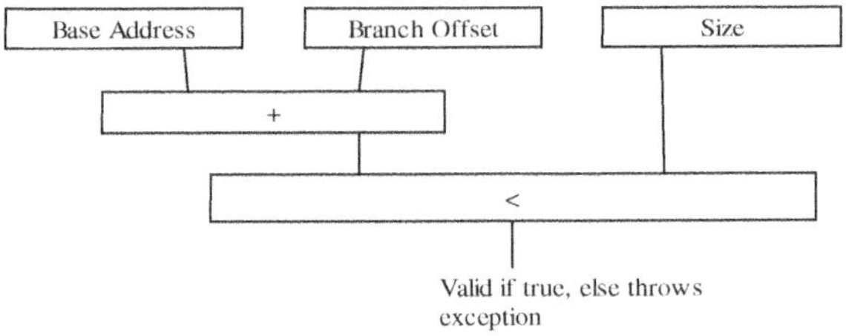

Fig. 4. Branch target checking in jHISC v3

Inter-method control transfer instructions include method invocation and method revocation. Method invocation is a procedure to call a method, while method revocation is a procedure to return from a method. They provide functionality for messaging between objects. Each method in jHISC v3 is defined to have only single entry point of calling. This feature prohibits the code bypassing in the same addressing space (Fig 5).

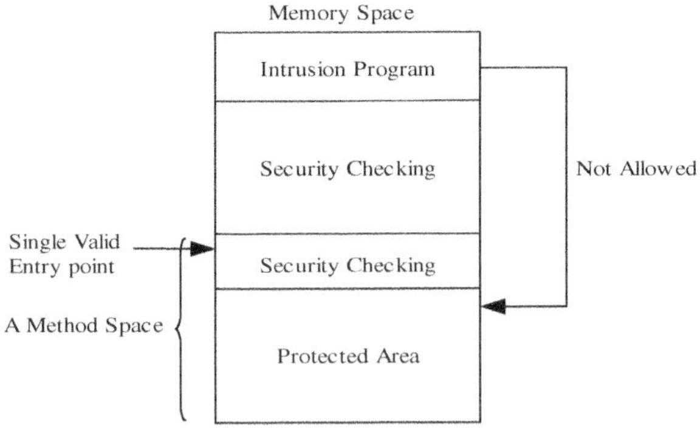

Fig. 5. Single entry point of Method in jHISC v3

4 Co-verification Methodology and Result

The jHISC V3 with 4KB instruction cache and 8KB data cache has already been implemented on a Xilinx Virtex XCV800 FPGA to verify our concept. During implementation, the caches are generated by Xilinx CORE Generator and the whole system costs about 600K equivalent gates in FPGA.

In order to test the compatibility of running Java programs on our architecture, we built a software verification platform to compile all the JVM instructions into jHISC instructions and verify the functionality of the secure architecture through the Just-In-Time compilation of bytecode stream and run it on the FPGA. With the software testing implementation of Just-in-time compilation for jHISC, compatibility of Java program can be assured and tested. With some I/O display operations that have been implemented, the bytecode can be compiled and loaded into the FPGA board through the PCI interface and the required results can be dumped back for display. The linker has also been built to link and demonstrate the executable results that were obtained in our architecture. As shown in Fig. 6, the executable memory map is loaded into the FPGA board through the linker by calling the DimeJavaAPI.

All implemented instructions are tested to verify whether they are operated correctly. The related results are shown on Table 2. Besides, assembly program are written to infringe the system and test whether the jHISC core can detect such infringement and throws an exception to the system. The results are shown on Table 3.

Finally, some testing Java programs are compiled through our JIT compilation and loaded into the system for execution. With the verification of all the data structures and resolutions which are built through the compiler with GUI display (Fig. 7), the compiled code are successfully run in the jHISC core and the results are dumped back through the linker to the Console (see Fig. 8). Table 4 shows results of testing on some simple Java program.

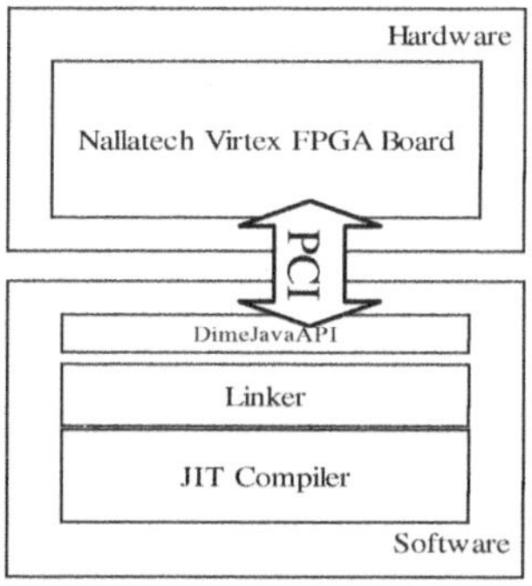

Fig. 6. The Flow of the Co-verification Methodology

Table 2. Result of Instruction Verification

Instruction Group	Result
Logical Instructions	passed
Arithmetic Instructions	passed
Branching Instructions	passed
Array Instructions	passed
Object-Oriented Instructions	passed
Data Manipulation Instructions	passed

Table 3. Result of Protection Features Verification

Tests	Result
Index a register that is out of current LVF	Causes Exception
Modification of a reference type register	Causes Exception
Operation on two different typed (Float and Int) register	Causes Exception
Branch outside the current MCS	Causes Exception
Access an element index that is larger than the array size	Causes Exception
Invoke a non reference type CPD	Causes Exception
Invoke with an index that is larger than CPDTS	Causes Exception
Invoke a non-static method in a static method	Causes Exception
The address of CPB is larger than CDSS	Causes Exception
Invoke a non-method typed object	Causes Exception
Allocate registers (In + Local + out) larger than 32	Causes Exception
Incompatible argument size for invoked method	Causes Exception
Invoke with an index that is larger than CODTS	Causes Exception
Invoke with a non property type COD	Causes Exception
Invoke an unresolved method	Causes Exception
Invoke with a class reference that is not class typed	Causes Exception
Revoke with IVKTYPE = 00b	Causes Exception
Access non-static field in static method	Causes Exception
Access a static field that out of CDS	Causes Exception
Access a field that is out of IDS	Causes Exception
Modify a read only field	Causes Exception
Access an unresolved field	Causes Exception

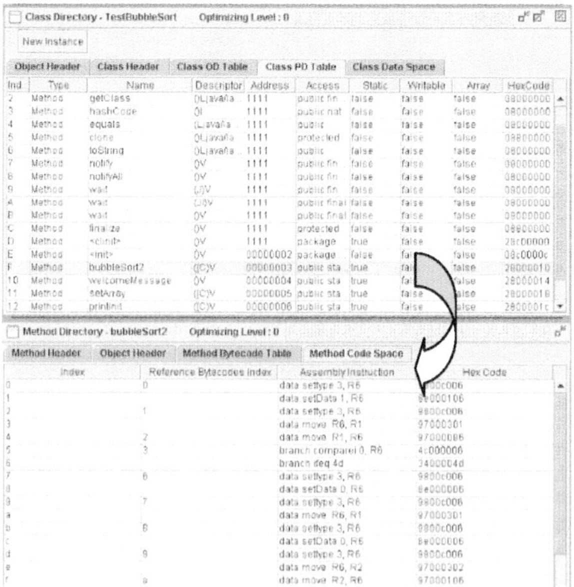

Fig. 7. Class and Method Directory Frame (GUI) displaying information of Class and Method Context which are built from a bubble sort class program and verified through our JIT compiler

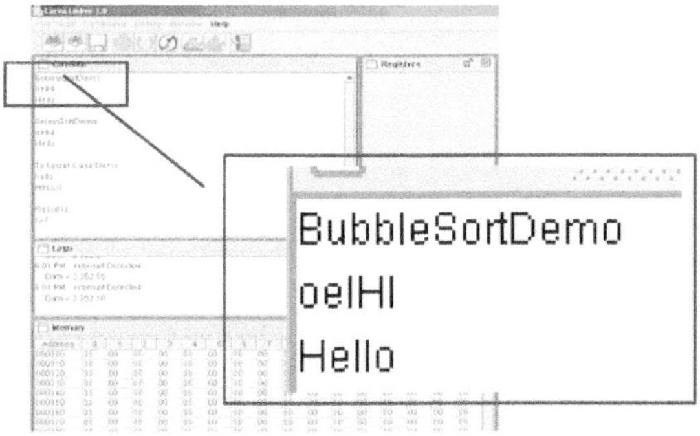

Fig. 8. Executing results of some Java programs

Table 4. Results of testing on some Java programs

Tests	Result
Helloworld – display a 'helloworld' text	Correct
Interactive sorting programs – input a sequence of numbers and sorted the numbers with different sorting	Correct
Perform some arithmetic calculation	Correct
Program to convert all input lower case characters to upper case	Correct
Min/Max – input a sequence of numbers and the minimum and maximum value are displayed	Correct
Message Program – an interactive program that can let user to store message, remove message and read message	Correct

5 Conclusion

In this paper, we have discussed the secure hardware data structure on jHISC, which has been built with FPGA technology, and a software platform to co-verify the compatibility, through Just-In-Time compilation, on some Java class files. Through this hardware/software co-design, some resolution burdens in JVM have been compensated through our novel architecture. Besides, comparing with the traditional system where the security and boundary checking of methods are controlled by software, our approach in putting the security and boundary checking jobs into hardware would move the burden of security checking into some pipeline stages and greatly improve the overall system security and throughput of the processor. Moreover, a secure method invocation can safeguard any error or bad reference produced by erroneous programming. Furthermore, our co-verification process verifies the functionalities of the instructions set, exception handling of our hardware protection features and the execution of some Java program examples. Eventually, Java can be run as a native language in the jHISC architecture and all Object-Oriented and Java's protection features are penetrated from software to hardware in order to increase the overall system security and performance.

Acknowledgements

The work described in this paper was partially supported by a grant from City University of Hong Kong (Strategic Research Grant Project No. 7001548).

References

1. Andrew S. Tanenbaum. Structured Computer Organization, Forth Edition. Prentice Hall, 1999.
2. Fong, A., S., "HISC: A High-level Instruction Set Computer". In 7th European Simulation Symposium, pages 406-410. The Society for Computer Simulation, Oct 1995.
3. Mok Pak Lun, Richard Li, Anthony Fong. "Method manipulation in an object oriented processor". ACM SIGARCH Computer Architecture News archive. Volume 31, Issue 4, September 2003.
4. Bill Venners. Inside the Java 2 Virtual Machine. Mc Graw Hill 1999.
5. Tim Lindholm, Frank Yellin The Java(TM) Virtual Machine Specification (2nd Edition). Addison-Wesley Pub Co; 2nd edition,1999
6. Austin Kim, Yang Qian and J. M. Chang, " Designing a Memory System Using a Static Loader For Embedded Java Architectures" , The Second International Workshop on Compiler and Architecture Support for Embedded Systems (CASES'99) , Washington, D.C., October 1-3, 1999
7. Chang, L.-C., Ton, L.-R., Kao, M.-F., Chung, C.-P., "Stack operations folding in Java processors", Computers and Digital Techniques, IEE Proceedings- Volume 145, Issue 5, Sept. 1998, pp. 333 – 340
8. Kim, A.; Chang, M, "Advanced POC Model-Based Java Instruction Folding Mechanism", Euromicro Conference, 2000. Proceedings of the 26th Volume 1, 5-7 Sept. 2000, pp. 332 - 338 vol.1
9. Sun Microsystems, Inc. The Java HotSpot performance engine architecture.
10. M. W. El-Kharashi, "Java Microprocessors: Computer Architecture Implications", IEEE Pacific Rim Conference on Communications, Computers and Signal Processing, Vol. 1, August, 1997, pp. 277-280.
11. D. Mulchandani, "Java for Embedded Systems", IEEE Internet Computing, June, 1998, pp. 30-39.

Timed Weak Simulation Verification and Its Application to Stepwise Refinement of Real-Time Software

Satoshi Yamane

Graduate School of Natural Science, Kanazawa University,
Kanazawa City, Japan, ZIP/CODE 920-1192
syamane@is.t.kanazawa-u.ac.jp

Abstract. Real-time software runs over real-time operating systems, and guaranteeing qualities are difficult. In this paper, we propose timed weak simulation relation verification and apply it to a refinement design method of real-time software. Moreover, we apply our proposed method to general real-time software scheduled by fixed-priority preemptive policy.

1 Introduction

As real-time software is reactive and concurrent, and its timing conditions are strict, it is difficult to design real-time software [1]. It is important to specify and verify real-time software. In this paper, we propose timed weak simulation relation verification method based on timed automata [2], and apply it to stepwise refinement of real-time software over fixed priority preemptive schedulers [3]. In general, real-time software is designed by dividing it into tasks [1] In this case, it is difficult to design real-time software by the following points: (1)Real-time software consists of many tasks, which concurrently behave. Moreover, tasks interact with external environments. In this situation, it is useful to distinguish between internal events and external events in the sense of process algebra [4]. (2)In real-time software, stepwise refinement is useful, and it is important to automatically verify whether the concrete specification refines the abstract specification.

From the above results, we propose the followings: (1)We use nondeterministic timed automata, which have internal and external events. We construct real-time software by parallel composition of nondeterministic timed automata. (2)We verify whether the concrete specification refines the abstract specification based on a timed weak simulation.

In general, refinement relations such as language inclusion, timed bisimulation and timed strong simulation are useful as follows: (1)We can easily and naturally verify fairness and regularity as acceptance conditions by language inclusion. But if we specify verification properties using nondeterministic timed automata, language inclusion problems are undecidable [2]. On the other hand, R. Alur proposed an event-clock automata, which is a determinizable of timed

L.T. Yang et al. (Eds.): EUC 2005, LNCS 3824, pp. 381–394, 2005.

automaton [5,6]. But an event-clock automaton is a subclass of a timed automaton, and accepts a finite timed word (though a general timed automaton accepts an infinite timed word). As the determinization of an event-clock automaton causes an exponential blow-up in the number of locations, the verification cost increases. Moreover, we can not verify some deadlock using language inclusion [4,7]. (2)Timed bisimulation relation is useful for verifying a kind of invariant holding between the more concrete specification and the more abstract specification [8]. On the other hand, timed strong simulation relation is useful for verifying stepwise refinement [9]. But when we stepwise develop specifications, we may add exception procedures to the concrete specification, which are not contained in the abstract specification. Both timed bisimulation relation and timed strong simulation relation are not adequate for this reason.

From the above result, we use timed weak simulation relation in order to verify whether the concrete specification refines the abstract specification.

We survey related works as follows: (1)In 1992, Cerans has shown that timed strong and weak bisimulation equivalence problem for timed automata are decidable [8]. But he has not developed bisimulation algorithms. (2)In 1996, Tasiran and his colleagues have developed the verification algorithm of timed strong simulation relation [9]. But they have not developed a timed weak simulation relation. (3)In 1999, Braberman and his colleagues have developed reachability analysis method of preemptive scheduling using timed automata [10]. But they have not developed refinement verification method.

In this paper, we define a timed weak simulation relation, and propose the verification algorithm of timed weak simulation relation. Moreover we apply our proposed method to general real-time software scheduled by fixed-priority preemptive policy. As it is difficult to treat internal behaviors, timed weak simulation verification methods of timed automata have never been developed before now. Timed weak simulation verification is our original work. The paper is organized as follows: In section 2, we define specification method. In section 3, we define timed weak simulation relation verification method and apply it to stepwise refinement of real-time software. In section 4, we present design supprt system and some example. Finally, in section 5, we present conclusions.

2 Specification of Real-Time Software

In this paper, we specify tasks using nondeterministic timed automata with internal and external events, and construct real-time software by parallel composition of tasks.

2.1 Syntax and Semantics of Timed Automata

First we define clock as follows:

Definition 1 (Clock and clock interpretation).
Given a finite set of variables $X = \{x_1, \ldots, x_n\}$, a valuation is a function $v : X \rightarrow \mathbb{R}^{+0}$, which assigns a nonnegative real value to each clock variable. We

define V^X *as the set* $[X \rightarrow \mathbb{R}^{+0}]$. $\mathbf{0}$ *denotes the valuation that assigns the value 0 to each* $x \in X$. *For* $\lambda \subseteq X$, $v[\lambda := 0]$ *denotes the valuation that assigns the value 0 to each* $x \in \lambda$ *and agrees with* v *for all clocks in* $X \setminus \lambda$. *Moreover, for every* $t \in \mathbb{R}^+$, $v + t$ *denotes the clock valuation for which all clocks* $x \in X$ *take the value* $v(x) + t$.

■

Definition 2 (Clock constraints).
For a set X *of clock variables, the set* Ψ^X *of clock constraints* ψ *is inductively defined by* $\psi ::= x \sim c \mid \psi_1 \wedge \psi_2$, *where* $\sim \in \{\leq, =, \geq\}$, $c \in \mathbb{N}$. *We write* $v \models \psi$ *if the valuation* v *satisfies the formula* ψ. *For each clock* $x \in X$, $c_x(\Psi^X)$ *denotes the maximal clock constant in* Ψ^X.

■

Definition 3 (Syntax of timed automata).
A timed automaton $\mathbf{G}$ *is a tuple* $\langle S, \bar{s}, \Sigma, X, inv, E\rangle$, *where*

(1) S *is the finite set of locations.*
(2) $\bar{s} \in S$ *is an initial location.*
(3) $\Sigma = EXT \cup INT$ *is the finite set of events, where* EXT *is the finite set of external events,* INT *is the finite set of internal events.*
(4) X *is the finite set of real-valued variables, called clocks.*
(5) $inv : S \rightarrow \Psi^X$ *is the invariant function that assigns* Ψ^X *to each location* $s \in S$.
(6) E *is the finite set of edges. Each edge* e *is a tuple* $\langle s, \sigma, \psi, \lambda, s'\rangle = e \in E$ *consisting of the source location* s, *the target location* s', *clock constraint* $\psi \in \Psi^X$, *the set* λ *of clocks to be reset,* $\sigma \in \Sigma$ *is an event, where* $\lambda = \emptyset$ *if* $\sigma \in INT$.

■

Next we formally define semantics of timed automata.

Definition 4 (Semantics of timed automata).
A state of $\mathbf{G}$ *is a pair* $\langle s, v\rangle$ *containing the location* $s \in S$ *and the valuation* $v \models inv(s)$. *The set of all states is denoted* Ω. *The initial state is a pair* $\langle \bar{s}, \mathbf{0}\rangle$. *For each state* $\langle s, v\rangle$, *the transition is defined as follows:*

1. *Discrete transitions:*
$$\frac{\langle s, \sigma, \psi, \lambda, s'\rangle \in E,\ v \models \psi,\ v[\lambda := 0] \models inv(s')}{\langle s, v\rangle \xrightarrow{\sigma} \langle s', v'\rangle}\ ,\ \text{where } v' = v[\lambda := 0].$$
2. *Timed transitions:*
$$\frac{\delta \in \mathbb{R}^+\ \forall \delta' \leq \delta.\ v + \delta' \models inv(s) \text{ implies } \langle s, v + \delta\rangle}{\langle s, v\rangle \xrightarrow{\delta} \langle s, v'\rangle}\ ,\ \text{where } v' = v + \delta.$$

A run of timed automaton is an infinite sequence as follows:

$$\langle \bar{s}, \mathbf{0}\rangle \xrightarrow{\ell_1} \langle s_1, v_1\rangle \xrightarrow{\ell_2} \langle s_2, v_2\rangle \xrightarrow{\ell_3} \cdots,$$

where $\langle \bar{s}, \mathbf{0}\rangle$ *is an initial state,* $\langle s_i, v_i\rangle \in \Omega$ *is a state,* $\ell_i \in (\Sigma \cup \mathbb{R}^+)$ *is a label.*

■

In this paper, we assume that timed automaton is *nonZeno*. It is easy to verify whether a timed automaton is *nonZeno* or not using HYTECH [11].

2.2 Parallel Composition of Timed Automata

In this paper, we construct real-time software by parallel composition of tasks. We define parallel composition of timed automata as follows:

(1) If the external event of a task is equal to the external event of environments, the task is synchronized with environments by the same external event.
(2) As internal events of tasks are unobservable from environments, internal events of tasks and events of environments are disjoint.

Definition 5 (Parallel composition).
Let be two timed automata $\mathbf{G_1} = \langle S_1, \bar{s}_1, \Sigma_1, X_1, inv_1, E_1\rangle$ *and* $\mathbf{G_2} = \langle S_2, \bar{s}_2, \Sigma_2, X_2, inv_2, E_2\rangle$. *The parallel composition of* $\mathbf{G_1}$ *and* $\mathbf{G_2}$ *is the timed automaton* $\mathbf{G} = \langle S, \bar{s}, \Sigma, X, inv, E\rangle$, *where* $\Sigma_1 = EXT_1 \cup INT_1$, $\Sigma_2 = EXT_2 \cup INT_2$. *Here* $INT_1 \cap \Sigma_2 = \Sigma_1 \cap INT_2 = \emptyset$.

(1) $S \subseteq S_1 \times S_2$.
(2) $\bar{s} = (\bar{s}_1, \bar{s}_2)$.
(3) $\Sigma = EXT \cup INT$, *where* $EXT = EXT_1 \cup EXT_2$, $INT = INT_1 \cup INT_2$.
(4) $X = X^A \cup X^B$.
(5) $inv((s_1, s_2)) = inv_1(s_1) \wedge inv_2(s_2)$.
(6) $\langle s, \sigma, \psi, \lambda, s'\rangle \in E$, *where for* $\langle s_1, \sigma, \psi_1, \lambda_1, s'_1\rangle \in E_1$ *and* $\langle s_2, \sigma, \psi_2, \lambda_2, s'_2\rangle \in E_2$, *each element is as follows:*
  (a) When $\sigma \in \Sigma_1 \cap \Sigma_2$, $s = (s_1, s_2), \psi = \psi_1 \wedge \psi_2, \lambda = \lambda_1 \cup \lambda_2, s' = (s'_1, s'_2)$.
  (b) When $\sigma \in \Sigma_1$ *and* $\sigma \notin \Sigma_2$, $s = (s_1, s_2), \psi = \psi_1, \lambda = \lambda_1, s' = (s'_1, s_2)$.
  (c) When $\sigma \in \Sigma_2$ *and* $\sigma \notin \Sigma_1$, $s = (s_1, s_2), \psi = \psi_2, \lambda = \lambda_2, s' = (s_1, s'_2)$.

■

2.3 Specification Method

We decide parameters such as priorities and timing constraints by V. Braberman's method [10], which is based on WCRT(Worst Case Response Time) [12].

First we define Worst-Case Response Time as follows:

Definition 6 (Worst-Case Response Time).
If every task j, $j < i$, *has higher priority than task* i, *the worst-case response time* R_i *of task* i *is given as recursive equation* ($i = 1, \ldots, n$). *The* $(k+1)th$ *worst-case response time* $Ri^{(k+1)}$ *for task* i *is as follows* ($k \geq 0$) :

$$R_i^{(k+1)} = \sum_{j=1}^{i-1} (\lceil \frac{R_i^{(k)}}{T_j} \rceil \times C_j) + C_i,$$

where period T_i, *execution time* C_i, *deadline* D_i *of a periodic task* i. *We can compute* $R_i = lim_{k \to \infty} R_i^{(k)}$ *as* $Ri^{(0)} = C_i$.

■

Using R_i, we can check whether real-time software is schedulable or not as follows:

Real-time software is schedulable if the following condition is satisfied:
For $\forall i$, $R_i \leq D_i$(i=1,..,n) holds true.[12]

Next we specify real-time software using timed automata.

In general, it is not possible to exactly specify preemptive scheduling using timed automata. Therefore, R. Alur and T.A. Henzinger have specified preemptive scheduling using hybrid automata [13]. In this paper, we approximately specify timing constraints by $c_{min} \leq x \leq c_{max}$ using timed automata, where we set c_{min} using timing constraints of edges, and set c_{max} using worst-case response time. Therefore, we can realize the automatic verification of timed weak simulation relation. If we specify real-time software of preemptive scheduling using hybrid automata, it is not possible to automatically verify timed weak simulation [14].

3 Refinement Design Method

It is important to design real-time software by stepwise refinement as real-time software is a complex system. In this case, it is important to verify whether the concrete specification is satisfied by the abstract one or not. First we define a timed weak simulation. Next we define the verification method of a timed weak simulation. Finally we explain the stepwise refinement design method of real-time software.

3.1 A Timed Weak Simulation

First we define observable transitions as follows:

Definition 7 (Observable transitions).
For each state $\langle s, v\rangle \in \Omega$ of timed automaton $\mathbf{G} = \langle S, \bar{s}, \Sigma, X, inv, E\rangle$, observable transitions are defined as follows:

Here Let $\stackrel{\epsilon}{\Longrightarrow}$ if and only if $(\stackrel{\tau}{\rightarrow})^*$, where $\Sigma = EXT \cup INT$, $\tau \in INT$.

(1) For an external event $\sigma \in EXT$,

Define $\langle s, v\rangle \stackrel{\sigma}{\Longrightarrow} \langle s', v'\rangle$ as $\langle s, v\rangle \stackrel{\epsilon}{\Longrightarrow}\stackrel{\sigma}{\rightarrow}\stackrel{\epsilon}{\Longrightarrow} \langle s', v'\rangle$.

(2) For delay $\delta_1, \dots \delta_k, \delta \in \mathbb{R}^+$,

Define $\langle s, v\rangle \stackrel{\delta}{\Longrightarrow} \langle s', v'\rangle$ as $\langle s, v\rangle \stackrel{\epsilon}{\Longrightarrow}\stackrel{\delta_1}{\rightarrow} \cdots \stackrel{\epsilon}{\Longrightarrow}\stackrel{\delta_k}{\rightarrow}\stackrel{\epsilon}{\Longrightarrow} \langle s', v'\rangle$ $(k \geq 0)$.

In this case, a state $\langle s, v\rangle$ is called stable from environments, and we denote **wait**$(\langle s, v\rangle)$, *where $\delta = \delta_1 + \cdots + \delta_k$*

■

Definition 8 (Timed weak simulation).
Let $\mathbf{G_1} = \langle S_1, \bar{s}_1, \Sigma_1, X_1, inv_1, E_1\rangle$ and $\mathbf{G_2} = \langle S_2, \bar{s}_2, \Sigma_2, X_2, inv_2, E_2\rangle$ be two timed automata. A timed weak simulation relation from $\mathbf{G_1}$ to $\mathbf{G_2}$ is a binary relation $Sim \subseteq \Omega_1 \times \Omega_2$ if the following three conditions are satisfied. Moreover we denote $\mathbf{G_1} \preceq \mathbf{G_2}$ if there exists a timed weak simulation relation, where

Ω_1 is the set of $\langle s_1, v_1\rangle$, Ω_2 is the set of $\langle s_2, v_2\rangle$, $\Sigma_1 = EXT_1 \cup INT_1$, $\Sigma_2 = EXT_2 \cup INT_2$, $s_1, s_1' \in S_1$, $v_1, v_1' \in V^{X_1}$, $s_2, s_2' \in S_2$, $v_2, v_2' \in V^{X_2}$.

(1) External event condition:
$EXT_1 \subseteq EXT_2$.

(2) Simulation condition:
For every $(\langle s_1, v_1\rangle, \langle s_2, v_2\rangle) \in Sim$ and for every $\theta \in (EXT_1 \cup \mathbb{R}^+)$,
if $\langle s_1, v_1\rangle \stackrel{\theta}{\Longrightarrow} \langle s_1', v_1'\rangle$ then there exists $\langle s_2', v_2'\rangle$ such that $\langle s_2, v_2\rangle \stackrel{\theta}{\Longrightarrow} \langle s_2', v_2'\rangle$ and $(\langle s_1', v_1'\rangle, \langle s_2', v_2'\rangle) \in Sim$.

(3) Initial condition:
$(\langle \bar{s}_1, \mathbf{0}\rangle, \langle \bar{s}_2, \mathbf{0}\rangle) \in Sim$.

■

3.2 Verification Method of a Timed Weak Simulation

We achieve a timed weak simulation by converting this check to a finite check on the finitely many equivalence classes, which is called a region weak simulation relation. First we define a region graph, and next define a region weak simulation, and the conversion technique. Finally we show the verification algorithm of a timed weak simulation.

Region graph. Since the number of states is infinite, we cannot possibly build a finite automaton. But if two states with the same location agree on the integral parts of all clock values, and also the ordering of the fractional parts of all clock values, then the runs starting from the two states are very similar. From the above facts, we can construct region graphs, which are finite quotient structures by equivalence relations [2].

First we define equivalence relations of clock values.

Definition 9 (Equivalence relations of clock values).
Let V^X be the set of clock values, and Ψ^X be the set of clock constraints. For any $t \in \mathbb{R}^{+0}$, $\lfloor t \rfloor$ denotes the integral part of t, and $fract(t)$ denotes the fractional part of t. For $v, v' \in V^X$, v and v' are equivalent iff the following three conditions are satisfied. We denote $v \cong v'$.

(1) For clock $x \in X$, $\lfloor v(x) \rfloor$ and $\lfloor v'(x) \rfloor$ are the same, or both $v(x)$ and $v'(x)$ are greater than $c_x(\Psi^X)$.

(2) For all $x, y \in X$ with $v(x) \le c_x(\Psi^X)$ and $v(y) \le c_y(\Psi^X)$, $fract(v(x)) \le fract(v(y))$ iff $fract(v'(x)) \le fract(v'(y))$.

(3) For $x \in X$ with $v(x) \le c_x(\Psi^X)$, $fract(v(x)) = 0$ iff $fract(v'(x)) = 0$.

■

We use $[v]$ to denote the clock region to which v belongs.

Next we define the successor of equivalence classes.

Definition 10 (Successor of equivalence classes).
Let α and β be distinct clock equivalence classes of V^X and Ψ^X. For each $v \in \alpha$ and any $\delta \in \mathbb{R}^+$, we define the successor of equivalence classes:

(1) We denote $\beta = \mathbf{succ_0}(\alpha)$ *iff there exists* δ *such that* $\alpha = \beta$ *and* $\delta \in \beta$.
(2) We denote $\beta = \mathbf{succ_1}(\alpha)$ *iff there exists* $\delta' \le \delta$ *such that* $\alpha \ne \beta$ *and* $v + \delta' \in \alpha \cup \beta$ *and* $v + \delta \in \beta$.

■

Region is denoted by $\langle s, [v] \rangle$, or, $\langle s, \alpha \rangle$.
Next we define region graph of timed automaton as follows:

Definition 11 (Region graph).
For a timed automaton $\mathbf{G} = \langle S, \bar{s}, \Sigma, X, inv, E \rangle$, *the corresponding region graph* $\mathbf{R}(\mathbf{G}) = \langle Q, \bar{q}, L, N \rangle$ *consists of four tuples:*

(1) the finite set of states Q.
(2) the initial state $\bar{q} \in Q$, *where* $\bar{q} = \langle \bar{s}, [\mathbf{0}] \rangle$.
(3) the finite set of labels $L = \Sigma \cup SUCC$, *where* $SUCC$ *is the set of labels, which represent successor relations of equivalence classes.*
(4) a set of transition relations $N \subseteq Q \times L \times Q$.
For any $\langle s, \alpha \rangle$, *a set of transition relations are defined as follows:*
  (a) If there exists $\langle s, v \rangle \xrightarrow{\sigma} \langle s', v' \rangle$ *such that* $v' \in \beta$ *for each* $v \in \alpha$, *it is possible to transit to* $\langle s', \beta \rangle$ *by an event, and we denote* $\langle s, \alpha \rangle \xrightarrow{\sigma} \langle s', \beta \rangle$.
  (b) If there exists $\langle s, v \rangle \xrightarrow{\delta} \langle s, v' \rangle$ *such that* $\beta = \mathbf{succ_i}(\alpha)$ *and* $v' \in \beta$ *for each* $v \in \alpha$, *it is possible to transit to* $\langle s, \beta \rangle$ *by a time delay, and we denote* $\langle s, \alpha \rangle \xrightarrow{succ_i} \langle s, \beta \rangle$ $(i = 0, 1)$, *where* $succ_i \in SUCC$.

■

Region Weak Simulation Relation. We will show that the problem of checking the existence of a timed weak simulation relation is decidable. We achieve this by converting this check to a finite check on the finitely many equivalence classes of an equivalence relation (what we call region weak simulation relation) defined on parallel composition of timed automata. We define a region weak simulation relation on parallel composition of timed automata from the following reasons:

(1) We can construct all the pairs of $(\langle s_1, v_1 \rangle, \langle s_2, v_2 \rangle) \in Sim$ as $\langle (s_1, s_2), v_{12} \rangle$ of parallel compostion of timed automata, where s_1 and v_1 are the node and clock value of timed automaton 1, s_2 and v_2 are the node and clock value of timed automaton 2, v_{12} is the clock values of parallel composition of timed automaton 1 and 2. Therefore a set of state pairs Sim, which represent region weak simulation relation, is a subset of a set of states of product automaton (parallel composition of timed automata) $\Omega_{\mathbf{G_1} \| \mathbf{G_2}}$. Namely, $Sim \subseteq \Omega_{\mathbf{G_1} \| \mathbf{G_2}}$.
(2) As it is easy to trace the relation between v_1 and v_2, we trace it by v_{12} of product automaton.
(3) If one timed automaton has $\langle s_1, v_1 \rangle \xrightarrow{\delta} \langle s_1, v_1' \rangle$ and another timed automaton has $\langle s_2, v_2 \rangle \xrightarrow{\delta} \langle s_2, v_2' \rangle$, product automaton has $\langle (s_1, s_2), v_{12} \rangle \xrightarrow{\delta} \langle (s_1, s_2), v_{12}' \rangle$. Therefore we easily represent two timed automata by product timed automaton.

Definition 12 ($\mathbf{R}(\mathbf{G_1} \parallel \mathbf{G_2})$).
We construct product timed automaton $\mathbf{G_1} \parallel \mathbf{G_2}$ from $\mathbf{G_1}$ and $\mathbf{G_2}$ by parallel composition, where $EXT_1 \subseteq EXT_2$. We define the region of region graph $\mathbf{R}(\mathbf{G_1} \parallel \mathbf{G_2})$ as $\langle (s_1, s_2), \alpha \rangle$, where $s_1 \in S_1$, $s_2 \in S_2$, α is the equivalence class of $V^{X_1 \cup X_2}$ and $\Psi^{X_1 \cup X_2}$. Let $Q_{\mathbf{G_1} \parallel \mathbf{G_2}}$ be the set of equivalence classes on $\mathbf{G_1} \parallel \mathbf{G_2}$, where $\langle (s_1, s_2), \alpha \rangle \in Q_{\mathbf{G_1} \parallel \mathbf{G_2}}$. With $\mathbf{R}(\langle s_1, v_1 \rangle, \langle s_2, v_2 \rangle)$, denote the equivalence class $\langle (s_1, s_2), \alpha \rangle$ that the state $(\langle s_1, v_1 \rangle, \langle s_2, v_2 \rangle) \in \Omega_{\mathbf{G_1} \parallel \mathbf{G_2}}$ belongs to.

For any region $\langle (s_1, s_2), \alpha \rangle$, observable transitions are as follows:

(1) For an external event $\sigma \in EXT$,
Define $\langle (s_1, s_2), \alpha \rangle \stackrel{\sigma}{\Longrightarrow} \langle (s_1', s_2'), \beta \rangle$ as $\langle (s_1, s_2), \alpha \rangle \stackrel{\epsilon}{\Longrightarrow} \stackrel{\sigma}{\rightarrow} \stackrel{\epsilon}{\Longrightarrow} \langle (s_1', s_2'), \beta \rangle$.

(2) For $succ_i \in SUCC$,
Define $\langle (s_1, s_2), \alpha \rangle \stackrel{succ_i}{\Longrightarrow} \langle (s_1', s_2'), \beta \rangle$ $(i = 0, 1)$ as $\langle (s_1, s_2), \alpha \rangle \stackrel{\epsilon}{\Longrightarrow} \stackrel{succ_i}{\rightarrow} \stackrel{\epsilon}{\Longrightarrow} \langle (s_1', s_2'), \beta \rangle$.

■

Next we define a region weak simulation relation on region graph $\mathbf{R}(\mathbf{G_1} \parallel \mathbf{G_2})$.

Definition 13 (Region weak simulation relation).
We say that $\chi \subseteq Q_{\mathbf{G_1} \parallel \mathbf{G_2}}$ is a region weak simulation from $\mathbf{G_1}$ to $\mathbf{G_2}$ iff for each $\mathbf{R}(\langle s_1, v_1 \rangle, \langle s_2, v_2 \rangle) \in \chi$, the following three conditions are satisfied.

(1) For every $\sigma \in EXT$, if $\langle s_1, v_1 \rangle \stackrel{\sigma}{\Longrightarrow} \langle s_1', v_1' \rangle$, $\langle s_2, v_2 \rangle \stackrel{\sigma}{\Longrightarrow} \langle s_2', v_2' \rangle$ and $\mathbf{R}(\langle s_1, v_1 \rangle, \langle s_2, v_2 \rangle) \stackrel{\sigma}{\Longrightarrow} \mathbf{R}(\langle s_1', v_1' \rangle, \langle s_2', v_2' \rangle)$ such that $\mathbf{R}(\langle s_1', v_1' \rangle, \langle s_2', v_2' \rangle) \in \chi$.

(2) If $\mathbf{wait}(\langle s_1, v_1 \rangle)$, for any $succ_i \in SUCC$, $\mathbf{R}(\langle s_1, v_1 \rangle, \langle s_2, v_2 \rangle) \stackrel{succ_i}{\Longrightarrow} \mathbf{R}(\langle s_1', v_1' \rangle, \langle s_2', v_2' \rangle)$ such that $\mathbf{R}(\langle s_1', v_1' \rangle, \langle s_2', v_2' \rangle) \in \chi$ $(i = 0, 1)$.

(3) $\mathbf{R}(\langle \bar{s}_1, \mathbf{0} \rangle, \langle \bar{s}_2, \mathbf{0} \rangle) \in \chi$.

■

Theorem 1 (Timed weak simulation and region weak simulation).
For $\mathbf{R}(\langle s_1, v_1 \rangle, \langle s_2, v_2 \rangle) \in \chi$, let $\mathbf{R}_\chi = \{(\langle s_1, v_1 \rangle, \langle s_2, v_2 \rangle) | \mathbf{R}(\langle s_1, v_1 \rangle, \langle s_2, v_2 \rangle) \in \chi\}$. $\mathbf{R}_\chi$ is a weak timed simulation relation from $\mathbf{G_1}$ to $\mathbf{G_2}$ iff χ is a region weak simulation relation from $\mathbf{G_1}$ to $\mathbf{G_2}$.

Proof 1. *We prove it by dividing it into two cases.*

(I) To prove that if $\mathbf{R}_\chi$ is a weak timed simulation relation from $\mathbf{G_1}$ to $\mathbf{G_2}$, χ is a region weak simulation relation from $\mathbf{G_1}$ to $\mathbf{G_2}$:
Assuming that $\mathbf{R}_\chi$ is a weak timed simulation relation from $\mathbf{G_1}$ to $\mathbf{G_2}$. From the definition, we can directly prove χ is a region weak simulation relation from $\mathbf{G_1}$ to $\mathbf{G_2}$.

(II) To prove that if χ is a region weak simulation relation from $\mathbf{G_1}$ to $\mathbf{G_2}$, $\mathbf{R}_\chi$ is a weak timed simulation relation from $\mathbf{G_1}$ to $\mathbf{G_2}$:
Assuming that χ is a region weak simulation relation from $\mathbf{G_1}$ to $\mathbf{G_2}$. For some $\theta \in (EXT \cup \mathbb{R}^+)$, $(\langle s_1, v_1 \rangle, \langle s_2, v_2 \rangle) \in \mathbf{R}_\chi$ and

$\langle s_1, v_1\rangle \stackrel{\theta}{\Longrightarrow} \langle s_1', v_1'\rangle$.

We need to show that there exists $\langle s_2', v_2'\rangle$ *such that*

$$\langle s_2, v_2\rangle \stackrel{\theta}{\Longrightarrow} \langle s_2', v_2'\rangle \text{ and } (\langle s_1', v_1'\rangle, \langle s_2', v_2'\rangle) \in \mathbf{R}_\chi.$$

(1) When θ *is* $\sigma \in EXT$*:*
From the definition of $\mathbf{R}(\mathbf{G_1} \parallel \mathbf{G_2})$*, there exists* $\langle s_2', v_2'\rangle$ *such that*
$\langle s_2, v_2\rangle \stackrel{\sigma}{\Longrightarrow} \langle s_2', v_2'\rangle$ *and* $(\langle s_1', v_1'\rangle, \langle s_2', v_2'\rangle) \in \mathbf{R}_\chi$.

(2) When θ *is* $\delta \in \mathbb{R}^+$*:*
Let be $\mathbf{R}(\langle s_1, v_1\rangle, \langle s_2, v_2\rangle) = \langle (s_1, s_2), [v]\rangle$ *and* $\mathbf{R}(\langle s_1', v_1'\rangle, \langle s_2', v_2'\rangle) = \langle (s_1', s_2'), [v']\rangle$.
First we define equivalence classes $\alpha_0, \ldots, \alpha_{k+1}$ *corresponding to* v *as follows:*

$$\begin{cases} \alpha_0 = [v] \\ \alpha_{i+1} = \mathbf{succ_1}(\alpha_i) \ (0 \le i \le k) \end{cases}$$

Next we define real values $\delta_1, \ldots, \delta_k, \delta'$ *and clock values* $v^{(0)}, \ldots, v^{(k)}$ *corresponding to* α_i *as follows:*

$$\begin{cases} v^{(0)} = v \\ v^{(i+1)} = v^{(i)} + \delta_{i+1} \in \alpha_{i+1} \ (0 \le i < k) \\ v' = v^{(i)} + \delta' \in \alpha_i \cup \alpha_{i+1} \quad (i = k) \end{cases}$$

As there exists k *such that* $\delta = \delta_1 + \cdots + \delta_k + \delta'$*, there are two cases*$(k \ge 0)$.

(a) $k = 0$*:*
In this case, as $v' \in \alpha_0 \cup \alpha_1$ *by* $\delta = \delta'$*, the transition is as follows:*
$\langle s_1, s_2, \alpha_0\rangle \stackrel{succ_i}{\Longrightarrow} \langle s_1', s_2', \alpha_i\rangle$
Therefore clearly, there exists $\langle s_2', v_2'\rangle$ *such that*
$\langle s_2, v_2\rangle \stackrel{\delta}{\Longrightarrow} \langle s_2', v_2'\rangle$ *and* $(\langle s_1', v_1'\rangle, \langle s_2', v_2'\rangle) \in \mathbf{R}_\chi$ $(i = 0, 1)$.

(b) $k > 0$*:*
We consider the following regions as $\langle s_1^{(i)}, s_2^{(i)}, v_i\rangle \stackrel{\delta_{i+1}}{\Longrightarrow} \langle s_1^{(i+1)}, s_2^{(i+1)}, v_{i+1}\rangle$ *of* $\mathbf{G_1} \parallel \mathbf{G_2}$ $(0 \le i \le k)$.
(i) $\langle s_1^{(0)}, s_2^{(0)}, \alpha_0\rangle = \langle s_1, s_2, [v]\rangle$.
(ii) $\langle s_1^{(i)}, s_2^{(i)}, \alpha_i\rangle \stackrel{succ_1}{\Longrightarrow} \langle s_1^{(i+1)}, s_2^{(i+1)}, \alpha_{i+1}\rangle$.
(iii) $\langle s_1^{(i)}, s_2^{(i)}, \alpha_i\rangle \in \chi$.
$\langle s_1^{(k)}, s_2^{(k)}, \alpha_k\rangle \in \chi$ *is inductively derived from* $\langle s_1, s_2, [v]\rangle$*. As* $v' \in \alpha_k \cup \alpha_{k+1}$ *by* $\delta = \delta_1 + \cdots + \delta_k + \delta'$*, we get the following transition:*
$\langle s_1^{(k)}, s_2^{(k)}, \alpha_k\rangle \stackrel{succ_j}{\Longrightarrow} \langle s_1', s_2', \alpha_{k+j}\rangle$.
Therefore clearly there exists $\langle s_2', v_2'\rangle$ *such that*
$\langle s_2, v_2\rangle \stackrel{\delta}{\Longrightarrow} \langle s_2', v_2'\rangle$ *and* $(\langle s_1', v_1'\rangle, \langle s_2', v_2'\rangle) \in \mathbf{R}_\chi$ $(j = 0, 1)$.

■

Verification algorithm of a timed weak simulation. We define the verification algorithm of a timed weak simulation as follows:

Definition 14 (Verification algorithm of a timed weak simulation). *For the concrete specification* $\mathbf{G_L}$ *and the abstract specification* $\mathbf{G_H}$*, we construct* $\mathbf{G_L} \parallel \mathbf{G_H}$*, and the region graph* $\mathbf{R}(\mathbf{G_L} \parallel \mathbf{G_H})$*. In this case, we define the verification algorithm in order to verify whether there exists a timed weak simulation from* $\mathbf{G_L}$ *to* $\mathbf{G_H}$*. Basically first we define* $\chi^{(0)}$*, and inductively compute* $\chi^{(k+1)}$ *from* $\chi^{(k)}$*. First if* $EXT_1 \not\subseteq EXT_2$*, there does not exists a timed weak simulation relation. If* $EXT_1 \subseteq EXT_2$*, we compute the followings:*

(1) First we compute the relation $\chi^{(0)} = Q_{\mathbf{G_L} \parallel \mathbf{G_H}}$*, and initialize* k *by* $k := 0$*.*

(2) Next we inductively compute $\chi^{(k+1)}$ *from* $\chi^{(k)}$ *by repeating the following procedures* $(k \geq 0)$*.*

(a) $\chi^{(k+1)} = \emptyset$*.*

(b) If $\mathbf{R}(\langle s_1, v_1 \rangle, \langle s_2, v_2 \rangle) \in \chi^{(k)}$*, we set* $\chi^{(k+1)} = \chi^{(k+1)} \cup \{\mathbf{R}(\langle s_1, v_1 \rangle, \langle s_2, v_2 \rangle)\}$ *when the two following conditions are satisfied.*

(i) For every $\sigma \in EXT$*, if there exists* $\langle s_1', v_1' \rangle$ *such that*

$$\langle s_1, v_1 \rangle \stackrel{\sigma}{\Longrightarrow} \langle s_1', v_1' \rangle,\ \langle s_2, v_2 \rangle \stackrel{\sigma}{\Longrightarrow} \langle s_2', v_2' \rangle,$$

$\mathbf{R}(\langle s_1, v_1 \rangle, \langle s_2, v_2 \rangle) \stackrel{\sigma}{\Longrightarrow} \mathbf{R}(\langle s_1', v_1' \rangle, \langle s_2', v_2' \rangle)$*, and*
$\mathbf{R}(\langle s_1', v_1' \rangle, \langle s_2', v_2' \rangle) \in \chi^{(k)}$*.*

(ii) If $\mathbf{wait}(\langle s_1, v_1 \rangle)$*, for every* $succ_i \in SUCC$*,*
$\mathbf{R}(\langle s_1, v_1 \rangle, \langle s_2, v_2 \rangle) \stackrel{succ_i}{\Longrightarrow} \mathbf{R}(\langle s_1', v_1' \rangle, \langle s_2', v_2' \rangle)$
and $\mathbf{R}(\langle s_1', v_1' \rangle, \langle s_2', v_2' \rangle) \in \chi^{(k)}$ $(i = 0, 1)$*.*

(c) If $\chi^{(k+1)} = \chi^{(k)}$*, go to (3). If* $\chi^{(k+1)} \neq \chi^{(k)}$*, set* $k := k + 1$*, and return (2)(a).*

(3) If $\chi^{(k+1)}$ *includes* $\mathbf{R}(\langle \bar{s}_1, \mathbf{0} \rangle, \langle \bar{s}_2, \mathbf{0} \rangle)$*, we decide* χ *is a timed weak simulation relation. If not so, we decide* χ *is not a timed weak simulation relation.*

■

As this algorithm can be formalized as the greatest fixpoint computation, the algorithm terminates.

3.3 Stepwise Refinement Design Method

We represent both the abstract specification and the concrete one by nondeterministic timed automata, and verify the consistencies between them by a timed weak simulation relation.

Definition 15 (Stepwise refinement design method).
The stepwise refinement design method of real-time software consists of the following procedures.

(1) First we decide task priorities and parameters by WCRT, and specify $\mathbf{TASK}_\mathbf{i}^{(0)}$ *by timed automata* $(i = 1, \ldots, n)$*, where* n *is a number of tasks and* (0) *is the level of refinement.*

(2) Next we refine $\mathbf{TASK_i^{(k)}}$ *into* $\mathbf{TASK_i^{(k+1)}}$*, and specify* $\mathbf{TASK_i^{(k+1)}}$ *by timed automata* ($k \geq 0$)*.*

(3) Finally, we construct $\mathbf{SOFT^{(k)}} = \mathbf{TASK_1^{(k)}} \parallel \cdots \parallel \mathbf{TASK_n^{(k)}}$ *and* $\mathbf{SOFT^{(k+1)}} = \mathbf{TASK_1^{(k+1)}} \parallel \cdots \parallel \mathbf{TASK_n^{(k+1)}}$*. We revise* $\mathbf{SOFT^{(k+1)}}$ *until there exists a timed weak simulation relation from* $\mathbf{SOFT^{(k+1)}}$ *to* $\mathbf{SOFT^{(k)}}$*.*

(4) We repeat the above step (1)-(3), and specify the final one.

■

4 Example of Refinement Design

We show our proposed method effective by a plant system. We have implemented our proposed method as design support system. The design support system is implemented by C++ language(7000 lines) on Sun Blade1000(CPU UltraSPARC-III 900MHz, Main memory 1GB). The plant system is an embedded real-time system, and behaves by fixed priority preemptive scheduling. The plant system samples data from *Sensor*, and controls *Valve*, and outputs information on *Display*. If *Sensor* is in bad condition, this information is announced to administrator by *Lamp*. Even if *Sensor* is in bad condition, the plant system continue to behave by control data. The real-time software of the plant system consists of two periodic tasks such as *SAMPLER* and *MANAGER*. The two tasks communicate with each other by *QUEUE*. In this paper, we think the plant system is implemented by rate monotonic scheduling. Therefore this rate monotonic scheduling algorithm assigns priorities to tasks based on their periods: the shorter the period, the higher the priority. Moreover, we assume $D_i = T_i$ ($i = 1, 2$). We compute WCRT(Worst Case Response Time) [12]. From the results, we can determine two tasks are schedulable. The parameters are shown as follows: *SAMPLER* has parameters such as $T_i = 20$, $C_i = 6$, $B_i = 1$, $R_i = 7$. *MANAGER* has parameters such as $T_i = 30$, $C_i = 10$, $B_i = 0$, $R_i = 16$.

4.1 Specification of the Plant System

We design the plant system, and specify it by timed automata. External events are classified into three types such as system call($start_i$, end_i, *push_queue*, *pop_queue*), task control($dispatch_i$) and API(APplication Interface)(*read_sensor*, *write_lamp*, *write_display*, *write_valve*). Next we show the shared resource **QUEUE** in Figure 1.

Next we design the abstract specifications $\mathbf{SAMPLER^{(0)}}$ and $\mathbf{MANAGER^{(0)}}$, and specify them by timed automata, and show them in Figure 2 and 3. In abstract specification, we specify only external events and abstract behaviors. For example, we specify $\mathbf{SAMPLER^{(0)}}$ by nondeterministically behaving *write_lamp*. Finally we design the concrete specifications $\mathbf{SAMPLER^{(1)}}$ and $\mathbf{MANAGER^{(1)}}$, and show them in Figure 4 and 5. We refine the abstract specification into the concrete one by adding internal behaviors, transforming nondeterministic behaviors into deterministic behaviors and specifying detailed timing constraints. For example, **SAMPLER**$^{(1)}$ executes *read_sensor* once or twice, and if it fails, **SAMPLER**$^{(1)}$ executes *make_alternate_data*. As the deviation of control data is larger the processing of *write_valve* takes longer time, in **MANAGER**$^{(1)}$, *deviation_Small* takes 1, *deviation_Medium* takes 2 and *deviation_Large* takes 3.

4.2 Verification Experiment

We verify whether **SOFT**$^{(1)} \preceq$ **SOFT**$^{(0)}$ holds true or not using our design support system, where the abstract specification is defined as **SOFT**$^{(0)}$ =

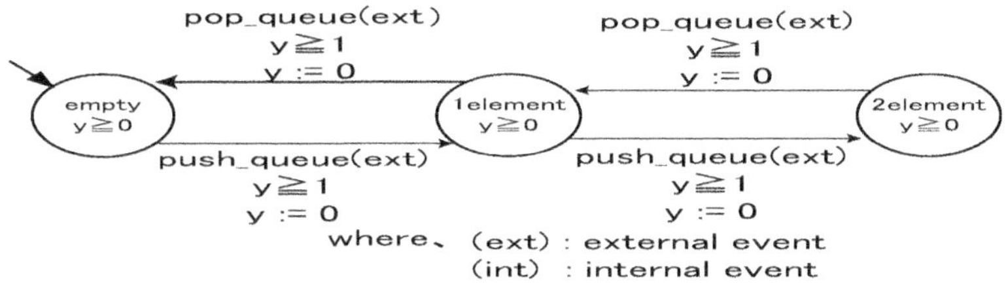

Fig. 1. Specification of the shared resource **QUEUE**

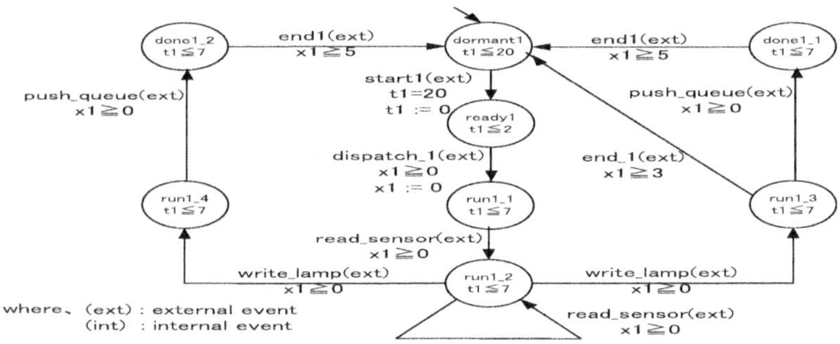

Fig. 2. Specification of the periodic task **SAMPLER**$^{(0)}$

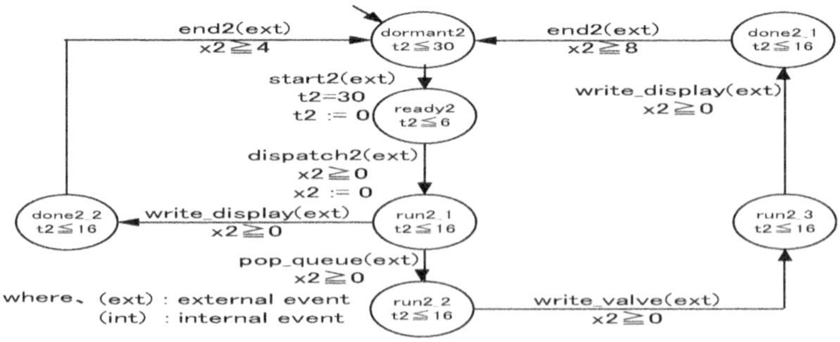

Fig. 3. Specification of the periodic task **MANAGER**$^{(0)}$

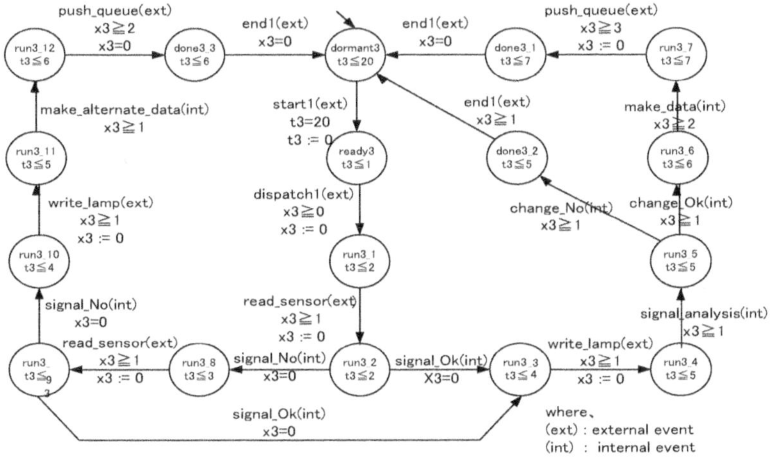

Fig. 4. Specification of the periodic task $\mathbf{SAMPLER}^{(1)}$

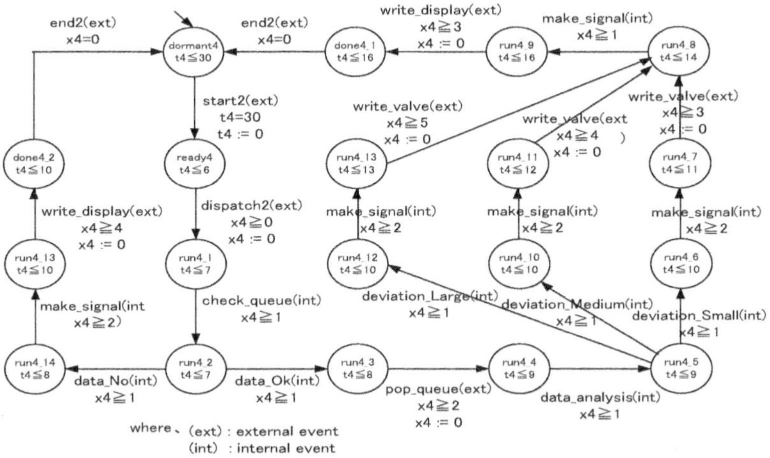

Fig. 5. Specification of the periodic task $\mathbf{MANAGER}^{(1)}$

$\mathbf{SAMPLER}^{(0)} \parallel \mathbf{MANAGER}^{(0)} \parallel \mathbf{QUEUE}$, the concrete specification is defined as $\mathbf{SOFT}^{(1)} = \mathbf{SAMPLER}^{(1)} \parallel \mathbf{MANAGER}^{(1)} \parallel \mathbf{QUEUE}$. We measured required memory=325744kB and execution time=62.30min using ps command. In region graph $\mathbf{R}(\mathbf{SOFT}^{(1)} \parallel \mathbf{SOFT}^{(0)})$, the number of the equivalence classes is 62367, the number of regions of $Q_{\mathbf{SOFT}^{(1)} \parallel \mathbf{SOFT}^{(0)}}$ is 1645498 and the number of members of region weak simulation χ is 1408290. The members of the set χ, which are contained in the region weak simulation relation. As an initial region is contained in χ, $\mathbf{SOFT}^{(1)} \preceq \mathbf{SOFT}^{(0)}$ is satisfied. Namely, there exists a timed weak simulation from the concrete specification to the abstract one. Though the verification cost is large, we can specify both the abstract and the concrete specifications of real-time software using timed automata, and automatically verify whether there exists a timed weak simulation from the concrete specification to the abstract one.

5 Conclusion

In this paper, we have proposed the following stepwise refinement design methodology of real-time software : First as we extend general timed automata by distinguishing between internal and external events, this timed automata are suitable for stepwise specifying and designing real-time software. Next we automatically verify whether there exists a timed weak simulation relation from the concrete specification to the abstract one. To the best of our knowledge, a timed weak simulation verification methods of timed automata have never been developed before now.

References

1. J.W.S. Liu. : Real-Time System, Prentice-Hall (2000).
2. R. Alur, D.L. Dill. : A theory of timed automatoa, Theoretical Computer Science, Vol. 126, pp.183-235 (1994).
3. Giorgio C. Buttazzo. : Hard Real-Time Computing Systems, Kluwer Academic Publishers (1987).
4. R. Milner. : Operational and Algebraic Semantics of Concurrent Processes. Handbook of Theoretical Computer Science, MIT Press, pp. 1201-1242 (1990).
5. R. Alur, L. Fix, T.A. Henzinger. : Event-Clock Automata: A Determinizable Class of Timed Automata, in Proc. of CAV'94, LNCS 818, pp.1-13 (1994).
6. C. Dima. : Removing slient transitions from event-clock automata, in Proc. of CITTI 2000, pp 75-81 (2000).
7. A. Pnueli. : Linear and Branching Structures in the Semantics and Logics of Reactive Systems. ICALP 1985, volume 194 of LNCS, pp. 15-32 (1985).
8. K. Cerans. : Decidability of bisimulation equivalences for parallel timer processes. LNCS 663, pp.269-300, Springer Verlag (1992).
9. S.Tasiran, R.Alur, R.P.Kurshan, and R.K.Brayton. : Verifying Abstractions of Timed Systems. LNCS 1119, pp.546-562, Springer Verlag (1996).
10. V.Braberman, M.Felder. : Verification of Real-Time Designs: Combining Scheduling Theory with Automatic Formal Verification, LNCS 1687, pp.494-510(1999)
11. T. Henzinger, X. Nicollin, J. Sifakis, S. Yovine. : Symbolic model checking for real-time systems, Information and Computation 111, pp.193–244(1994).
12. M.Joseph. : Real-Time System Specification, Verification and Analysis. Prentice Hall (1996).
13. R. Alur, T.A. Henzinger, P.-H. Ho. : Automatic symbolic verification of embedded systems. IEEE Trans. on Software Engineering 22(3), pp.181-201(1996).
14. T.A. Henzinger, P.W. Kopke, A. Puri, and P. Varaiya. : What's decidable about hybrid automata? Journal of Computer and System Sciences 57, pp.94–124(1998).

Checking Component-Based Embedded Software Designs for Scenario-Based Timing Specifications*

Jun Hu, Xiaofeng Yu, Yan Zhang, Tian Zhang, Xuandong Li, and Guoliang Zheng

State Key Laboratory of Novel Software Technology,
Department of Computer Science and Technology,
Nanjing University, Nanjing, Jiangsu,
P.R. China 210093
hujun@seg.nju.edu.cn

Abstract. In this paper, for real-time embedded software we consider the problem of checking component-based designs for scenario-based timing specifications. By adding time intervals on the actions, we extend the interface automata for modelling real-time systems. The component-based designs are modelled by real-time interface automaton networks, which includes a set of real-time interface automata synchronized by shared actions, and the scenario-based timing specifications are specified by UML sequence diagrams with a set of boolean expressions. Based on analyzing the compatible integer state space of a real-time interface automaton network and its compatible reachability graph, we develop an algorithm to check the consistency between real-time component-based designs and the scenario-based timing specifications.

Keywords: embedded software designs, real-time systems, model checking, interface automata, UML sequence diagrams.

1 Introduction

For most embedded systems, the system correctness not only depends on functionality but also timeliness. And in recent years, a prevalent trend in the embedded computing area is that systems are more and more dominated by software. The software determines the functionality and quality of systems, hence presents lots of challenges to current software techniques. Using component-based design methodology in embedded software domain have been considered as an effective way for handling complexity, increasing system quality. One of the major goals in developing such systems is the validation that whether the component-based designs satisfy the specified timing specifications.

* Supported by the National Natural Science Foundation of China (No.60425204, No.60233020, and No.60273036), the National Grand Fundamental Research 973 Program of China (No.2002CB312001), and by Jiangsu Province Research Foundation (No.BK2004080).

L.T. Yang et al. (Eds.): EUC 2005, LNCS 3824, pp. 395–404, 2005.

In this paper, for real-time embedded software we consider the problem of checking the consistency of component-based designs for scenario-based timing specifications. Firstly the scenario-based timing specifications are specified by UML sequence diagrams[1] with a set of timming constraints. Then the interface automata[2] are used as a formal model to describe the dynamic behavior of software components, which is suitable for component-based verification. By introducing time intervals into interface automata, we make an extension for modelling real-time systems. And the component-based designs are modelled by real-time interface automaton networks, which includes a set of real-time interface automata synchronized by shared actions. Through analyzing the compatible integer state space of a real-time interface automaton network and its compatible reachability graph, finally we develop an algorithm for the timing behavior consistency checking problem.

2 UML Sequence Diagrams with Timing Constraints

In component-based system designs, the UML sequence diagrams can be used to describe the component interactions. It focus on the temporal order of the message flow. And sending a message, receiving a message, creating or deleting a component instance are all considered as events. According to [3], the semantics of each sequence diagram can be treated as a visual order sequence, which shows a partially ordered set of events displayed in the notation. Therefore, we can formalize the timing sequence diagrams and its behavior as follows:

Definition 1. A timing sequence diagram is a tuple $D = (C, E, M, F, W, S)$ where

- C is a finite set of components;
- E is a finite set of events;
- M is a finite set of messages. For any message $g \in M$, let $g!$ and $g?$ represent the sending and the receiving for g respectively. For any $e \in E$, it is corresponding to the sending or receiving for a message g, denoted by $\phi(e) = g!$ or $\phi(e) = g?$;
- $F : E \mapsto C$ is labelling function which maps each event $e \in E$ to a component $F(e) \in C$;
- W is a finite set whose elements are of the form (e, e') where e and e' are in E and $e \neq e'$, which represents a visual order displayed in D;
- S is a set of boolean expressions on event names, which represents the timing constraints enforced on D. □

Without loss of generality, let any timing constraint expression be of the form $c_0(t_{e_0} - t_{e_0'}) + c_1(t_{e_1} - t_{e_1'}) + \ldots + c_n(t_{e_n} - t_{e_n'}) \sim b$, where t_{e_0}, $t_{e_0'}$, t_{e_1}, $t_{e_1'}$, $\ldots$, t_{e_n}, $t_{e_n'}$ present the time of the event occurrence respectively and c_0, c_1, $\ldots$, c_n, b are real numbers $(b \neq \infty)$, $\sim \in \{\leq, <\}$.

Definition 2. For any $D = (C, E, M, F, W, S)$, an event sequence $e_0\hat{}e_1\hat{}\ldots\hat{}e_m$ is a *trace* of D iff the following conditions hold:

- all events in E occur in the sequence, and each event occurs only once, i.e. $\{e_0, e_1, \ldots, e_m\} = E$ and $e_i \neq e_j$ for any i, j $(i \neq j,\ 0 \leq i, j \leq m)$; and
- $e_0, e_1, \ldots, e_m$ satisfy the visual order defined by W, i.e. for any e_i and e_j, if $(e_i, e_j) \in W$, then $0 \leq i < j \leq m$. □

We use *timed event sequences*, with the form of $(e_0, \tau_0)\hat{}(e_1, \tau_1)\hat{}\ldots\hat{}(e_m, \tau_m)$, to represent the behavior of real-time systems, in which each event e_i occurs with a relative time stamp τ_i. It means that e_0 takes place τ_0 time units after the system starts, then e_1 takes place τ_1 time units after e_0 takes place, so on and so forth, at last e_m takes place τ_m time units after e_{m-1} takes place.

Definition 3. A timed event sequence $\sigma = (e_0, \tau_0)\hat{}(e_1, \tau_1)\hat{}\ldots\hat{}(e_m, \tau_m)$ is a behavior of a timing sequence diagram $D = (C, E, M, F, W, S)$ iff $e_0\hat{}e_1\hat{}\ldots\hat{}e_m$ is a trace of D, and $\tau_0, \tau_1, \ldots, \tau_m$ satisfy the timing constraints described by S, i.e. for any boolean expression $\sum_{i=0}^{n} c_i(t_{f_i} - t_{f_i'}) \sim b$ in S, there is $\sum_{i=0}^{n} c_i \Delta_i \sim b$ where for each i $(0 \leq i \leq n)$, if $f_i = e_j$ and $f_i' = e_k$, then $\Delta_i = \sum_{u=k+1}^{j} \tau_u$ $(j > k)$or $\Delta_i = -\sum_{u=j+1}^{k} \tau_u$ $(j < k)$. □

3 Real-Time Interface Automata and Component-Based Designs

3.1 Real-Time Interface Automata

Interface automaton[2] is a light-weight formal language to describe the temporal aspects of software component interfaces. Specifically, it's designed to capture effectively both input assumptions and output guarantees about the order of the interactions between component and its environment. To further describe real-time properties, we need to extend the interface automata with timeliness. In the following, a *real-time interface automaton (RIA)* model is introduced, in which for any transition there is a time interval constraint.

Definition 4. A *RIA* is a tuple $P = (V_P,\ v_P^{Init},\ A_P,\ I_P, \Gamma_P)$ where:

- V_P is a finite set of states, each state $v \in V_P$;
- $v_P^{Init} \in V_P$ is the initial state;
- A_P is the set of all actions, which includes A_P^I, A_P^O and A_P^H, the mutually disjoint set of input, output and internal actions respectively.
- I_P is a finite set of time intervals; each interval has the form of $[x, y]$ where x, y are nonnegative integer numbers ($x \leq y$, y may be ∞);
- $\Gamma_P \subseteq V_P \times A_P \times I_P \times V_P$ is a set of transitions. □

An action $a \in A_P$ is *enabled* at state $v \in V_P$ if there is a transition $(v, a, [x, y], v') \in \Gamma_P$. An interface automaton is *non-input-enabled*; that is, it's not require that $A_P^I(v) = A_P^I$ for all states $v \in V_P$.

We use a *timed state sequence* of the form $v_0 \stackrel{a_0,\tau_0}{\longrightarrow} v_1 \stackrel{a_1,\tau_1}{\longrightarrow} \ldots \stackrel{a_{m-1},\tau_{m-1}}{\longrightarrow} v_m \stackrel{a_m,\tau_m}{\longrightarrow} v_{m+1}$ to describe a behavior of a *RIA*, which means that the system is starting at state v_0, after τ_i time units changing to v_1 through the transition ignited by the action a_0 and staying there for τ_1 time units, and so on. As the same we have mentioned before, each $\tau_i(0 \leq m)$ is a nonnegative integer number representing the relative time stamp.

Definition 5. For a real-time interface automaton $P = (V_P, v_P^{Init}, A_P, I_P, \Gamma_P)$, a timed state sequence $v_0 \xrightarrow{a_0,\tau_0} v_1 \xrightarrow{a_1,\tau_1} \ldots \xrightarrow{a_{n-1},\tau_{n-1}} v_n \xrightarrow{a_n,\tau_n} v_{n+1}$ is a behavior of P iff $v_0 = v_P^{Init}$, and for each $i(0 \leq i \leq n)$, there is $(v_i, a_i, [x_i, y_i], v_{i+1}) \in \Gamma_P$, $x_i \leq \tau_i \leq y_i$. □

3.2 Real-Time Interface Automaton Networks

We use *real-time interface automaton networks (RIAN)* to model the component-based designs for a real-time embedded software. It consists of a set of real-time interface automaton which represent the dynamic behaviors of software components. Since an input action of one interface automaton may concide with an output action of the other one, these two interface automata will synchronize on such shared actions, asynchronously interleaving on other actions. Those synchronized actions between any two interface automata (P_i, P_j) are denoted by *shared*$(P_i, P_j) = A_{P_i} \cap A_{P_j} = (A_{P_i}^O \cap A_{P_j}^I) \cup (A_{P_i}^I \cap A_{P_j}^O)$. More details about the composition of interface automata can be refereed to [2].

For solving the verification problem, we give the formalism of a *RIAN* as follows, including the states , actions and transitions.

Definition 6. Let $N = (K, Z)$ be a *RIAN* where $K = \{P_1, P_2, \ldots, P_n\}$, each $P_i = (V_{P_i}, v_{P_i}^{Init}, A_{P_i}, I_{P_i}, \Gamma_{P_i})$, and $Z = \{\mathit{shared}(P_i, P_j) \mid 1 \leq i, j \leq n, i \neq j\}$ is a set of all shared actions. The states and actions are defined as below:

- an *untimed state* $\overline{v}$ of N is in $V_{P_1} \times V_{P_2} \times \ldots \times V_{P_n}$, that is, $\overline{v} = (v_1, v_2, \ldots, v_n)(v_i \in V_{P_i}, 1 \leq i \leq n)$. The *initial untimed state* of N is $\overline{v}_N^{Init} = (v_{P_1}^{Init}, v_{P_2}^{Init}, \ldots, v_{P_n}^{Init})$;
- a *state* u of N is a pair $u = (\overline{v}, c)$ where $\overline{v} = (v_1, v_2, \ldots, v_n)$ is an untimed state of N and $c : \{v_i | 1 \leq i \leq n\} \mapsto \{R^+\} \cup \{0\}$ is called the *clock function* which maps each v_i to a nonnegative real number that indicates for the P_i how long the system has been staying at v_i. The *initial state* of N is $u_N^{Init} = (\overline{v}_N^{Init}, c^{Init})$ where $\overline{v}_N^{Init}$ is the initial untimed state of N and $c^{Init}(v_{P_i}^{Init}) = 0$ for any $i(1 \leq i \leq n)$. The set of states of N is denoted by U_N;
- the set of actions of N is $A_N = A_N^I \cup A_N^O \cup A_N^H$, where the set of input actions is $A_N^I = \left(\bigcup_{1 \leq i \leq n} A_{P_i}^I\right) / Z$, the set of output actions is $A_N^O = \left(\bigcup_{1 \leq i \leq n} A_{P_i}^O\right) / Z$, and the set of internal actions is $A_N^H = \left(\bigcup_{1 \leq i \leq n} A_{P_i}^H\right) \cup Z$.
- the set of time intervals of N is $I_N = \bigcup_{1 \leq i \leq n} I_{P_i}$. □

Definition 7. Let $N = (K, Z)$ be a *RIAN* where $K = \{P_1, P_2, \ldots, P_n\}$ and $P_i = (V_{P_i}, v_{P_i}^{Init}, A_{P_i}, I_{P_i}, \Gamma_{P_i})(1 \leq i \leq n)$, and $u = (\overline{v}, c)$ and $u' = (\overline{v}', c')$ be its states where $\overline{v} = (v_1, v_2, \ldots, v_n)$ and $\overline{v}' = (v_1', v_2', \ldots, v_n')$. Then the system can change from the state u to u' by an transition within a delay d(denoted by $u \xrightarrow{a,d} u'$), if one of the following conditions holds:

- for an action $a \notin Z$, there is a transition $(v_k, a, [x_k, y_k], v'_k) \in \Gamma_{P_k}$ $(1 \le k \le n)$ satisfying $x_k \le c(v_k) + d \le y_k$ and $c'(v'_k) = 0$. At the same time $v_i = v'_i$ and $c'(v_i) = c(v_i) + d$ for any i $(i \ne k, 1 \le i \le n)$; or
- for an action $a \in$ *shared*$(P_i, P_j)(1 \le i, j \le n, i \ne j)$, there are transitions $(v_i, a!, [x_i, y_i], v'_i) \in \Gamma_{P_i}$ ($a!$ denote a is an output action) and $(v_j, a?, [x_j, y_j], v'_j) \in \Gamma_{P_j}$ ($a?$ denote a is an input action) satisfying $x_i \le c(v_i) + d \le y_i$, $x_j \le c(v_j) + d \le y_j$, $c'(v'_i) = 0$ and $c'(v'_j) = 0$. At the same time, $v_k = v'_k$ and $c'(v_k) = c(v_k) + d$ for any $k(k \ne i, j, 1 \le k \le n)$.

Then a behavior of N is a timed state sequence: $u_0 \xrightarrow{a_0,d_0} u_1 \xrightarrow{a_1,d_1} \ldots \xrightarrow{a_{n-1},d_{n-1}} u_n \xrightarrow{a_n,d_n} u_{n+1}$ where u_0 is the initial state of N. □

4 Checking Real-Time Component-Based Designs for Scenario-Based Specifications

Now, for a real-time embedded software the component-based designs are modelled by a real-time interface automaton network, and the scenario-based timing specifications are specified by the sequence diagrams with timing constraints. The problem we concern is to check if the real-time interface automata interact according to the scernio specified by the timing sequence diagrams.

Firstly, we need to give the relation between a behavior of the *RIAN* and a trace of the timing sequence diagram. Let $N = (K, Z)$ be a *RIAN*, and $\varrho = u_0 \xrightarrow{a_0,d_0} u_1 \xrightarrow{a_1,d_1} \ldots \xrightarrow{a_{n-1},d_{n-1}} u_n \xrightarrow{a_n,d_n} u_{n+1}$ be a behavior of N. Then the corresponding timed action sequence of ϱ is $(a_0, d_0)\hat{}(a_1, d_1)\hat{}\ldots\hat{}(a_n, d_n)$, and those timed internal action (a_i, d_i) (which satisfies $a_i \in Z$) can be replaced by a pair of timed input and output actions $(a_i!, d_i)\hat{}(a_i?, 0)$, as a result we can get an timed action sequence which only contains input and output actions. In fact, each input(resp. output) action a can be considered as an input(resp. output) event e, thus a corresponding timed event sequence, with a form of $(e_0, \tau_0)\hat{}(e_1, \tau_1)\hat{}\ldots\hat{}(e_r, \tau_r)(r \ge n)$, is obtained which is called the *trail* of ϱ. On the other hand, notice that any message appeared in a sequence diagram actually should be one of the shared actions in N, and each event such as sending message or receiving message should be one of the output or input actions of the corresponding component's *RIA*. However, in the formal definition of the sequence diagram $D = (C, E', M, F, W, S)$ an event $e' \in E'$ just represents an event name and the event content is denoted by $\phi(e')$. Thus if we want to compare the events between the trail of ϱ and the trace of D, it need to compare e with $\phi(e')$.

Let ϱ be a behavior of N, σ be the trail of ϱ, and σ_1 be a subsequence of σ of the form $(e_0, \tau_0)\hat{}(e_1, \tau_1)\hat{}\ldots\hat{}(e_m, \tau_m)$. For a trace of D with the form of $f_0\hat{}f_1\hat{}\ldots\hat{}f_n$, if there are $e_{k_0}, e_{k_1}, \ldots, e_{k_n}$ satisfying that (1) $0 = k_0 < k_1 < \ldots < k_n = m$, (2)$\phi(f_i) = e_{k_i}$ for any i $(0 \le i \le n)$, and (3)for any i $(0 \le i \le n)$, for any $j \ne k_p$ $(0 \le j \le m, 0 \le p \le n)$, $\phi(f'_i) \ne e_j$, then the subsequence σ_1 is considered as a *projection* of σ over D. In fact, σ_1 shows that an scenario described by D *occurs* exactly in behavior ϱ of N. Based on above discussion, we give the formal description of the timing consistency verification problem as below:

Definition 8. Let N be a *RIAN*, and $D = (C, E, M, F, W, S)$ be a timing sequence diagram. N *satisfies* D iff the following conditions hold:

- the scenario described by D occurs in a behavior of N; and
- for any behavior of N, the projection of its trail over D, which have a form of $(e_k, \tau_k)\hat{}(e_{k+1}, \tau_{k+1})\hat{}\dots\hat{}(e_r, \tau_r)$, satisfies the timing constraints of D, i.e. for any boolean expression $\sum_{i=0}^{n} c_i(t_{f_i} - t_{f_i'}) \sim b$ in S, there is $\sum_{i=0}^{n} c_i\Delta_i \sim b$, where for each i $(0 \le i \le n)$ if $\phi(f_i) = e_g$ and $\phi(f_i') = e_h(k \le g, h \le r)$, then $\Delta_i = \sum_{u=h+1}^{g} \tau_u$ $(g > h)$or $\Delta_i = -\sum_{u=g+1}^{h} \tau_u$ $(g < h)$. □

It's clearly that the state space of *RIAN* is infinite, so the key point is to find a way for verification in a finite manner.

4.1 Constructing an Integer Reachability Graph

We introduce the *integer behavior* as follows. Let $\varrho = u_0 \xrightarrow{a_0,d_0} u_1 \xrightarrow{a_1,d_1} \dots \xrightarrow{a_{n-1},d_{n-1}} u_n \xrightarrow{a_n,d_n} u_{n+1}$ is a behavior of a *RIAN*. If d_i is an integer for any i $(0 \le i \le n)$, the ϱ is called an *integer behavior* . It follows that any state $((v_1, v_2, \dots, v_m), c)$ occurring in an integer behavior satisfies $c(v_j)$ is an integer for any j $(1 \le j \le m)$, which is called *integer state.*

Theorem 1. Let N be a *RIAN*, and $D = (C, E, M, F, W, S)$ be a timing sequence diagram. N satisfies D iff the scenario described by D occurs in an integer behavior of N, and for any integer behavior of N, the projection of its trail over D satisfies the timing constraints of D. □

Then, for above checking problem, we only need to consider the integer behaviors of the *RIAN*.

To deal with the infinite case in some time intervals, we represent a *time bound* of N by $K = \max\{X_{max}, Y_{max}\}$, where $X_{max} = \max\{x_i | [x_i, \infty) \in I_N (0 \le i \le |I_N|)\}$ and $Y_{max} = \max\{y_i | [x_i, y_i] \in I_N (x_i \le y_i, y_i \ne \infty), 0 \le i \le |I_N|\}$. Then let $u = (\overline{v}, c)$ and $u' = (\overline{v}', c')$ be the integer states of N where $\overline{v} = (v_1, v_2, \dots, v_n)$ and $\overline{v}' = (v_1', v_2', \dots, v_n')$. and define a time-zone relation R_t over U_N as below:

$$R_t = \left\{ < u, u' > \middle| \begin{array}{l} \overline{v} = \overline{v}' \text{ and for each } v_i (1 \le i \le n), \text{ either} \\ c(v_i) = c'(v_i) \text{ or } c(v_i) > K \wedge c'(v_i) > K \end{array} \right\}.$$

R_t is an equivalent relation over U_N, and the number of the equivalent class is finite. We use $[u]$ to represent the equivalent class, that is,$[u] = \{u' | uR_tu'\}$, and denote by $[N]$ the finite space which comprise of the equivalent classes under R_t.

Theorem 2. Let N be a *RIAN*, and u_1 and u_2 are the integer states such that $u_1 R_t u_2$. Then there is an integer state u_1' such that $u_1 \xrightarrow{a,d} u_1'$ iff there is an integer state u_2' such that $u_2 \xrightarrow{a,d} u_2'$ and $u_1' R_t u_2'$. □

It shows that the set of integer behaviors of $[N]$ are consistent with those of N.

Based on the time-zone equivalent relation, we can construct a reachability graph $G = \{V_G, L_G\}$ for a *RIAN* N as follows, where V_G is a set of nodes and L_G is a set of edges:

1. for the initial state u_N^{Init} of N, $[u_N^{Init}]$ is in the set V_G, which is called the *initial node*;
2. let $[u]$ be in the set V_G, and K be the time bound of N. For an event a, for an integer d $(0 \leq d \leq K+1)$, if $u \xrightarrow{a,d} u'$ then $[u']$ is in V_G, and the edge $[u] \xrightarrow{a,d} [u']$ is in the set L_G. When $a \in A_N^I$ (resp. A_N^O, A_N^H), the edge $[u] \xrightarrow{a,d} [u']$ is called input (resp. output, internal) edge. We use L_G^I,L_G^O and L_G^H to represent the set of input, output and internal edges respectively.

Let $\rho = l_0\hat{\ }l_1\hat{\ }\ldots\hat{\ }l_n(l_i : [u_i] \xrightarrow{a,d} [u_{i+1}] \in L_G, 0 \leq i \leq n)$ be a path of G which is an edge sequence starting from the initial node. From its corresponding timed action sequence $(a_0, d_0)\hat{\ }(a_1, d_1)\hat{\ }\ldots\hat{\ }(a_{n-1}, d_{n-1})$, we can replace those (a_i, d_i) satisfying that a_i is a shared action with a pair of input and output actions $(a_i!, d_i)\hat{\ }(a_i?, 0)$, as the same way mentioned before. Then we can also get a timed event sequence, with a form of $(e_0, \tau_0)\hat{\ }(e_1, \tau_1)\hat{\ }\ldots\hat{\ }(e_s, \tau_s)(s \geq n-1)$, which is called the *trail* of path ρ. Any edge sequence $l_i\hat{\ }l_{i+1}\hat{\ }\ldots\hat{\ }l_{i+k}$ $(0 \leq i \leq n-1-k)$is called a *subpath* of ρ. We denote the trail of a subpath $l_i\hat{\ }l_{i+1}\hat{\ }\ldots\hat{\ }l_j$ by $\sigma(l_i, l_j)(i \leq j)$, the tail of path ρ by σ_ρ or $\sigma(l_0, l_n)$. Thus each label on the edges either contains an input(output) event or a pair of input and output events. It denotes by $\psi(l_k)$ the event pair corresponding to l_k.

4.2 Eliminating the Illegal States

Since the interface automaton is *non-input-enabled*, there will be some *illegal states* during the composition of two interface automata. The illegal state represents that one automaton in *RIAN* may produce an output event that is an input event of another automaton, but is not accepted by the latter one on that state. The formal definition is given below:

Definition 9. Let $N = (K, Z)$ be a *RIAN* where $K = \{P_1, P_2, \ldots, P_n\}$ and $P_i = (V_{P_i}, v_{P_i}^{Init}, A_{P_i}, I_{P_i}, \Gamma_{P_i})(1 \leq i \leq n)$,the set of illegal states is shown as:

$$illegal(N) = \left\{ ((v_1, v_2, .., v_n), c) \in N \;\middle|\; \begin{array}{l} \exists (v_i, v_j)(i \neq j, 1 \leq i, j \leq n), \\ \exists a \in shared(P_i, P_j), \\ \left(\begin{array}{c} a \in A_{P_i}^O(v_i) \wedge a \notin A_{P_j}^I(v_j) \\ \vee \\ a \in A_{P_j}^O(v_j) \wedge a \notin A_{P_i}^I(v_i) \end{array} \right) \end{array} \right\} \square$$

Based on the theorem 2 and the above definition, the following claim can be established: if u is an integer state satisfying $u \in illegal(N)$, then all the integer states in the time-zone equivalent class $[u]$ are illegal. In this case, $[u]$ is called an *illegal time-zone equivalent class*. And we use $illegal(G)$ to represent those nodes of reachability graph G which corresponds to the set of illegal time-zone equivalent classes of $[N]$.

Theorem 4. Let N be a *RIAN*, and G be its integer reachability graph. For a timing sequence diagram D, N satisfies D iff:

- there is a projection path in $com(G)$;
- any projection path in $com(G)$ satisfies D; and
- there is not any flaw projection path for D in $com(G)$. □

Based on the above theorem, we can develop an algorithm for the verification problem, which is depicted in Fig.1. The algorithm consists of two phases which are implemented by depth first search. The first search is to get all simple flat loops for D which are used for checking if there is a flaw point in a projection path. The second one is to find out all the projection paths in $com(G)$ and to check them for D. Since there is only a finite number of projection paths in $com(G)$ and the algorithm is based on depth first search method, the complexity of the algorithm is proportional to number and length of projection paths in $com(G)$.

5 Conclusion

Based on the solution in this paper, we are developing a prototype tool. For future work, we will do more case studies in practical use, and consider the resource and energy analysis in the embedded real-time software systems.

References

1. G. Booch, J. Rumbaugh and I. Jacobson. *The Unified Modeling Language User Guide*, Addison-Wesley, 1999.
2. L. de Alfaro and T. A. Henzinger. Interface Automata. In *Proc. of ESEC/FSE 01*, Austria, 2001
3. Doron A. Peled. *Software Reliability Methods.* pp300-305, Springer, 2001.
4. J. Seemann, J. WvG. Extension of UML Sequence Diagrams for Real-Time Systems. In *Proc. International UML Workshop*, LNCS 1618, pp240-252, 1998.
5. Rajeev Alur and Mihalis Yannakakis. Model Checking of Message Sequence Charts. In *Proc. the 10th International Conference on Concurrency Theory*, LNCS 1664, pp114-129, 1999.
6. Thomas Firley, Michaela Huhn, Karsten Diethers, et al. Timed Sequence Diagrams and Tool-Based Analysis - A Case Study. In *Proc. of the Second International Conference on UML (UML99)*, LNCS 1732, pp.645-660, 1999.
7. L. de Alfaro, T. A. Henzinger, and M. Stoelinga. Timed Interfaces. In *Proc. of EMSOFT 2002*, LNCS 2491,pp108-122, 2002.
8. Alexandre David, M. Oliver, and Wang Yi. Formal Verification of UML Statecharts with Real-Time Extensions. In: *FASE2002*, LNCS 2306, 2002, pp.218-232.
9. Hu Jun, Yu Xiaofeng, Zhang Yan, et al. Scenario-Based Verification for Component-Based Embedded Software Designs. In *Proc. of ICPP 2005 Workshops*,pp.240-247,June 2005, IEEE Computer Society Press.

Dependable Polygon-Processing Algorithms for Safety-Critical Embedded Systems

Jens Brandt and Klaus Schneider

University of Kaiserslautern,
Reactive Systems Group, Department of Computer Science,
P.O. Box 3049, 67653 Kaiserslautern, Germany
http://rsg.informatik.uni-kl.de

Abstract. Algorithms that process geometric objects become more and more important for many safety-critical embedded systems, e.g. for motion planning or collision detection, where correctness is indispensable. The main challenge to demonstrating correctness is the consistent handling of degenerate cases like collinear line segments. In this paper, we therefore propose the use of an interactive theorem prover to develop dependable geometry algorithms for safety-critical embedded systems. Our solution is based on the use of a three-valued logic to make degenerate cases explicit. Using the theorem prover, we are not only able to prove the correctness of the obtained algorithms, but also to directly derive a software library of provably correct geometry algorithms for safety-critical applications.

1 Introduction

Applications like motion planning in robotics or collision detection of autonomous vehicles have to observe and to control the positions of certain objects in a particular environment. To this end, it is often sufficient to model the environment as a two-dimensional plane and the objects can be approximated as polygons on that plane. For this reason, fundamental algorithms of computational geometry [7] like polygon clipping or computing convex hulls can be used to develop embedded systems for these applications. As these embedded systems work in safety-critical domains, where even human live could be endangered, it is mandatory to guarantee their correctness. For this reason, it is necessary to built up specification languages and verification formalisms that allow the designers of such systems to reason about their correctness.

Geometric problems appear to be easy, since they can be visualised in a natural and intuitive way. However, at a second glance, even simple definitions turn out to be more complicated than expected: For example, what is the intersection point of two lines, if both lines are identical? For this reason, most algorithms work under certain preconditions like 'all points are pairwise distinct' or 'no three points are collinear'.

In order to guarantee that all possible cases are consistently handled and that the used algorithms work as expected, we recommend the use of interactive theorem provers to reason about required definitions and algorithms. However, establishing consistent definitions for geometric primitives that can be universally used for all algorithms and even degenerate inputs turns out to be a great challenge [8]. For example,

L.T. Yang et al. (Eds.): EUC 2005, LNCS 3824, pp. 405–417, 2005.

to define whether a point on the edge of a polygon belongs to the interior or not, yields essential problems when this definition is used in one or the other algorithm. These problems impose inherent difficulties to develop a software library for safety-critical embedded systems to process geometric data.

In our opinion, the best solution is to make degenerate cases explicit, which requires the introduction of a third truth value for geometric primitives that normally are either true or false. We therefore extended the interactive theorem prover HOL [10] by a theory on two-dimensional analytic geometry [3] that is based on a three-valued logic. We formalised geometric objects, geometric primitives, and finally entire algorithms, so that we are able to reason about the correctness of geometric computations. As a first experiment, we successfully verified the Cohen-Sutherland clipping algorithm [9].

Though reasoning about geometric problems has a long tradition, our work deviates from existing work in several ways. In particular, Wu's work [21, 6] on translating geometric propositions to algebraic forms, i.e. equations between polynomials is well-known. However, this approach is limited to the automated solution of particular instances of geometric problems, while we have to argue about the problems (and their algorithmic solutions) themselves. The work closest to ours is [15], where also an interactive theorem prover is used to formally reason about geometric problems. However, in contrast to our work, they used two-valued logic to formalise geometric primitives. To circumvent problems of degenerate cases, they modified definitions or used techniques like perturbation which, however, turned out to be problematic in practise [5].

In this paper, we therefore propose to use three-valued logic for the implementation of algorithms that process geometric data. Three-valued logic has proved to be an adequate tool in many areas of computer science [4, 20, 13, 2, 18, 16, 1, 19]. We show that three-valued logic is well suited to define geometric primitives so that degenerate cases are consistently and concisely handled. To guarantee the correctness of the derived algorithms, we employ the interactive theorem prover HOL [10] to set up a library on two-dimensional, linear objects like lines, segments, and polygons [3]. Based on this library for the theorem prover, we derive a dependable software library that provides algorithms for geometric problems that have to be solved in upcoming embedded systems.

The paper is organised as follows: In Section 2, the specification and verification of polygon processing algorithms is described. Section 3 illustrates our formalisation approach by the verification of the Cohen-Sutherland algorithm for line clipping. Section 4 sketches the implementation of a software library for algorithms of computational geometry based on our three-valued formalisations. Finally, Section 5 draws some preliminary conclusions.

An extended version of this paper, the proof code, additional material, as well as detailed descriptions of all theories and examples described in this paper are available on our website.

2 Specification

In this section, we describe our three-valued formalisation of analytic geometry. We first consider degenerate cases and three-valued logic (Section 2.1) and then more complex geometric objects and primitives (Section 2.2).

2.1 Degenerate Cases and Three-Valued Logic

Most algorithms of computational geometry are designed for the 'general case', thus excluding so-called degenerate cases: Depending on the algorithm, several preconditions are assumed, e.g. that no points coincide, that given lines are not parallel, or that no three lines intersect in a common point [8, 14]. Handling degenerate cases is a well-known problem in computational geometry.

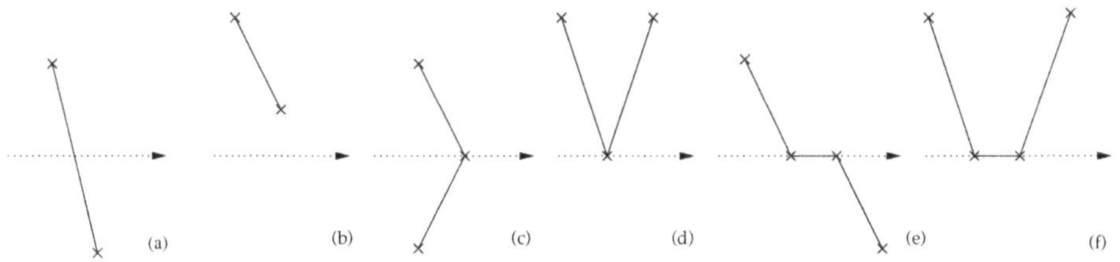

Fig. 1. Winding number algorithm

As an example, consider the winding number algorithm: It calculates the winding number of a point p relative to a polygon P, i.e. how often the directed sequence of connected line segments of P turns around p (see [11] for a precise definition). To this end, it counts the intersections of an arbitrary ray starting in p with edges of the polygon P. If the intersected edge runs from the bottom to the top, it is counted positively - in the opposite direction negatively. Figure 1 shows the possible cases, where the ray is drawn with a dotted line and some edges of polygon P are drawn with straight lines: (a) and (b) show simple cases without problems, while (c) to (f) show degenerate cases, i.e. a vertex or an edge of the polygon is on the ray. Depending on the position of the adjoining edges of the polygon, the situation must be counted as an intersection or not. In the presented examples, cases (c) and (e) have to be defined as intersections, whereas cases (d) and (f) should not be intersections.

The explicit treatment of degeneracies requires substantial effort. In particular, to decide whether all cases have been considered is often unclear and nontrivial. Simple solutions like perturbation or other techniques have shown not to be as applicable as desired [5], so that degeneracies still form an impediment for the development of dependable algorithms: On the one hand, the enormous number of different degenerate cases does not allow an explict treatment, and on the other hand, consistent definitions of geometric primitives that implicitly handle all degenerate cases for all algorithms in an adequate way are not available, and probably do not exist: For example, consider the problem to determine whether a point is inside or outside a polygon. Assume that the points on the edge are considered to be outside the polygon (i.e. polygons are 'open' point sets). If we calculate the difference of two polygons as a set difference, the result is possibly a polygon that contains points on its edge.

For this reason, we propose the use of three-valued logic to handle degeneracies. Three-valued logic has already proven to be useful in many areas, e.g. for the analysis of asynchronous circuits [13, 4, 20], for program analysis [16, 2, 17, 18], for the analysis

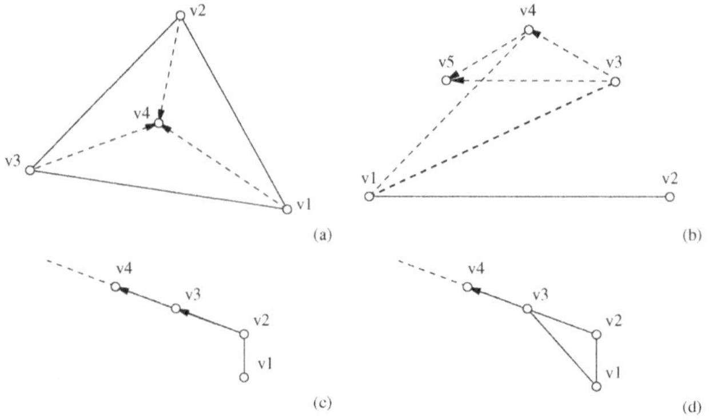

Fig. 4. Properties of the left-turn primitive

Degeneracies with respect to a such a primitive P are inputs $\boldsymbol{x}$ that cause the characteristic function to become zero $\chi_P(\boldsymbol{x}) = 0$. Following the approach presented in Section 2.1, the result U is returned in these cases. To define the primitives, we use the three-valued relation $\prec$ of the previous section. Since all primitives of the previous section compare their result with zero, we additionally introduce a relation pos :

$$\texttt{rat\_pos} \vdash_{\text{def}} \mathsf{pos}\ r = 0 \prec r$$

With its help, the primitive *left* and *below* can be defined as follows:

$$\texttt{left} \vdash_{\text{def}} \mathsf{left}(v, w) = \mathsf{pos}\ (\mathsf{x}_w - \mathsf{x}_v)$$
$$\texttt{below} \vdash_{\text{def}} \mathsf{below}(v, w) = \mathsf{pos}\ (\mathsf{y}_w - \mathsf{y}_v)$$

The primitives make use of the three-valued relation $\prec$, and thus, they have similar properties: The following theorems prove some sort of reflexivity, antisymmetry, and transitivity laws.

$$\texttt{LEFT\_REF} \vdash \mathsf{left}(v, v) = \mathsf{U}$$
$$\texttt{LEFT\_ASYM} \vdash \mathsf{left}(v, w) = \ddot{\neg}\mathsf{left}(w, v)$$
$$\texttt{LEFT\_TRANS} \vdash \mathsf{left}(u, v)\ \ddot{*}\ \mathsf{left}(v, w) \twoheadrightarrow \mathsf{left}(u, w)$$

LEFT_TRANS makes use of the connectives $\ddot{*}$ and $\twoheadrightarrow$, which usually appear together in a proposition. They allow a succinct description of the following cases:

- If $\mathsf{left}(u, v) = \mathsf{T}$ and $\mathsf{left}(v, w) = \mathsf{T}$, then $\mathsf{left}(u, w) = \mathsf{T}$.
- If $\mathsf{left}(u, v) = \mathsf{T}$ and $\mathsf{left}(v, w) = \mathsf{U}$ or vice versa, then $\mathsf{left}(u, w) = \mathsf{T}$).
- If $\mathsf{left}(u, v) = \mathsf{U}$ and $\mathsf{left}(v, w) = \mathsf{U}$, then $\mathsf{left}(u, w) = \mathsf{U}$.
- If $\mathsf{left}(u, v) = \mathsf{F}$ or $\mathsf{left}(v, w) = \mathsf{F}$, then nothing is said about $\mathsf{left}(u, w)$.

The orientation primitives can be analogously defined:

$$\texttt{lturn} \vdash_{\text{def}} \mathsf{lturn}(u, v, w) = \mathsf{pos}\ ((v - u) \times (w - v))$$
$$\texttt{rturn} \vdash_{\text{def}} \mathsf{rturn}(u, v, w) = \mathsf{lturn}(w, v, u)$$

Again, various properties can be proven for the orientation primitive:

$$\texttt{LTURN\_REF} \vdash \mathsf{lturn}(v_1, v_1, v_2) = \mathsf{U}$$
$$\texttt{LTURN\_SYM} \vdash \mathsf{lturn}(v_1, v_2, v_3) = \mathsf{lturn}(v_2, v_3, v_1)$$
$$\texttt{LTURN\_ASYM} \vdash \mathsf{lturn}(v_1, v_2, v_3) = \ddot{\neg}\mathsf{lturn}(v_2, v_1, v_3)$$
$$\texttt{LTURN\_TRIAN} \vdash$$
$$\mathsf{lturn}(v_1, v_2, v_4) \ddot{*} \mathsf{lturn}(v_2, v_3, v_4) \ddot{*} \mathsf{lturn}(v_3, v_1, v_4) \twoheadrightarrow \mathsf{lturn}(v_1, v_2, v_3)$$
$$\texttt{LTURN\_TRANS} \vdash (\mathsf{lturn}(v_1, v_2, v_3) \ddot{\wedge} \mathsf{lturn}(v_1, v_2, v_4) \ddot{\wedge} \mathsf{lturn}(v_1, v_2, v_5) \geq \mathsf{U})$$
$$\Rightarrow \mathsf{lturn}(v_1, v_3, v_4) \ddot{*} \mathsf{lturn}(v_1, v_4, v_5) \twoheadrightarrow \mathsf{lturn}(v_1, v_3, v_5)$$
$$\texttt{LTURN\_MOD1} \vdash (\mathsf{onRay}(\overrightarrow{(v_2, v_3)}, v_4) = \mathsf{T}) \Rightarrow \mathsf{lturn}(v_1, v_2, v_3) = \mathsf{lturn}(v_1, v_2, v_4)$$
$$\texttt{LTURN\_MOD2} \vdash (\mathsf{onRay}(\overrightarrow{(v_4, v_3)}, v_2) = \mathsf{T}) \Rightarrow \mathsf{lturn}(v_1, v_2, v_4) = \mathsf{lturn}(v_1, v_3, v_4)$$

These theorems are three-valued reformulations of the ones that can be found in [15]. The first three theorems (LTURN_REF, LTURN_SYM and LTURN_ASYM) state that a sequence in which a point appears at least twice is a degenerate case. Moreover, a sequence can be rotated without changing the orientation, and two points can be interchanged with negating the orientation of the sequence. LTURN_TRIAN describes the situation depicted in Figure 4 (a): If a point is on the positive side of three pairwise connected segments, they form a triangle with positive orientation. LTURN_TRANS proves the transitivity of the left-turn primitive under the condition that the three points v_3, v_4 and v_5 lie on the positive side of a segment from v_1 to v_2 (see Figure 4 (b)). The last two theorems (Figure 4 (c) and (d)) are used in [15] to handle degenerate cases. Actually, they are not needed in our approach, since LTURN_TRIAN already covers these cases. This illustrates the advantages of our approach: We always address general and degenerate cases at the same time, which makes the description succinct and readable. The same holds for later implementations that are made with three-valued data types.

3 Cohen-Sutherland Line Clipping

3.1 Formalisation of the Algorithm in HOL

A frequent operation in many graphic applications is the line clipping to an upright rectangular window. To this end, the Cohen-Sutherland algorithm divides the plane into nine regions: Each of the edges of the clip window defines an infinite line that divides the plane into inside and outside half-spaces (see Figure 5 (a)). The resulting regions can be described using a four bit *outcode*. The four bits of this code denote whether this region is situated *above*, *below*, *left* and *right* of the window, respectively

With the help of this outcode, necessary conditions can be formulated to check whether the line segment is inside or outside the window: The line segment is inside the window iff no bit of the outcodes of the endpoints is set. If a common bit is set in the outcodes of the endpoints, then both endpoints are outside the same side of the window. Thus, the entire line segment is outside the window. In most cases, a line segment will have been either accepted of rejected by these conditions.

In all other cases, the line segment is split into two pieces at an appropriate clipping edge. Assume that the considered end point (x_1, y_1) is above the window (see Figure 5 (b)). Removing the portion of the line that is above the window results in a new line segment with the old endpoint (x_2, y_2) and the new endpoint (x'_1, y'_1). Since the new

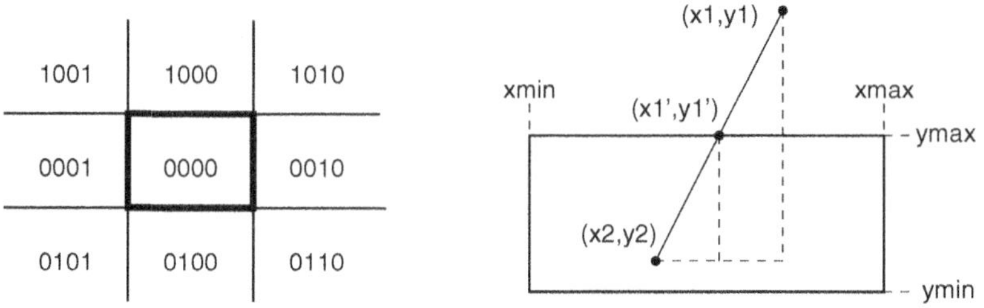

Fig. 5. Cohen-Sutherland Algorithm: (a) *Outcodes*, (b) Computing the intersection

endpoint is on the top border of the window, we have $y_1' = y_{\max}$. The other coordinate x_1' can be computed as follows:

$$x_1' = x_1 + (x_2 - x_1) \cdot \frac{y_{\max} - y_1}{y_2 - y_1}.$$

Once the line segment is identified, the outcode of the new endpoint is computed. After this, the algorithm is restarted with the new values.

In order to formalise the algorithm in HOL, we start with the definition of the outcodes. To this end, we use the primitives $\mathsf{lole}(w)$ and $\mathsf{upri}(w)$, which denote the lower left and the upper right corner of the window w:

$\texttt{outcode} \vdash_{\text{def}} \mathsf{code}(w,v) = (\mathsf{below}(v,\mathsf{lole}(w)) = \mathsf{T},\ \mathsf{above}(v,\mathsf{upri}(w)) = \mathsf{T},$
$\quad \mathsf{left}(v,\mathsf{lole}(w)) = \mathsf{T},\ \mathsf{right}(v,\mathsf{upri}(w)) = \mathsf{T})$
$\texttt{INSIDE} \vdash_{\text{def}} \mathsf{INSIDE}(c_1) = (c_1 = (\mathsf{F},\mathsf{F},\mathsf{F},\mathsf{F}))$
$\texttt{BOTTOM} \vdash_{\text{def}} \mathsf{BOTTOM}(c_1) = c_1[0]$
$\texttt{TOP} \vdash_{\text{def}} \mathsf{TOP}(c_1) = c_1[1]$
$\texttt{LEFT} \vdash_{\text{def}} \mathsf{LEFT}(c_1) = c_1[2]$
$\texttt{RIGHT} \vdash_{\text{def}} \mathsf{RIGHT}(c_1) = c_1[3]$
$\texttt{ACCEPT} \vdash_{\text{def}} \mathsf{ACCEPT}(c_1,c_2) =$
$\quad \neg(c_1[0] \vee c_2[0] \vee c_1[1] \vee c_2[1] \vee c_1[2] \vee c_2[2] \vee c_1[3] \vee c_2[3]\ )$
$\texttt{REJECT} \vdash_{\text{def}} \mathsf{REJECT}(c_1,c_2) =$
$\quad c_1[0] \wedge c_2[0] \vee c_1[1] \wedge c_2[1] \vee c_1[2] \wedge c_2[2] \vee c_1[3] \wedge c_2[3]$

The actual algorithm is taken from [9], where the loop is replaced by a recursive call. Moreover, as the algorithm does not return an edge in all cases, an *option type* is used for the result, returning NONE if the line is rejected, and $\mathsf{SOME}(e)$ if the edge e is accepted.

$\texttt{csa\_clip} \vdash_{\text{def}} \mathsf{csaClip}(w,(v_{\text{b}},v_{\text{e}})) =$
$\quad \mathbf{if}\ \mathsf{ACCEPT}(\mathsf{code}(w,v_{\text{b}}),\mathsf{code}(w,v_{\text{e}}))\ \mathbf{then}$
$\quad\quad \mathsf{SOME}((v_{\text{b}},v_{\text{e}}))$
$\quad \mathbf{else\ if}\ \mathsf{REJECT}(\mathsf{code}(w,v_{\text{b}}),\mathsf{code}(w,v_{\text{e}}))\ \mathbf{then}$
$\quad\quad \mathsf{NONE}$
$\quad \mathbf{else\ if}\ \mathsf{INSIDE}(\mathsf{code}(w,v_{\text{b}}))\ \mathbf{then}$
$\quad\quad \mathsf{csaClip}(w,(v_{\text{e}},v_{\text{b}}))$
$\quad \mathbf{else}$
$\quad\quad \mathsf{csaClip}(w,\mathsf{shortenedLine}(w,(v_{\text{b}},v_{\text{e}})))$

shortened_line $\vdash_{\text{def}}$ $\mathsf{shortenedLine}(w, (v_b, v_e)) =$

let

$x_{\min} = \mathsf{x}_{\mathsf{lole}(w)}$ **and** $y_{\min} = \mathsf{y}_{\mathsf{lole}(w)}$ **and**

$x_{\max} = \mathsf{x}_{\mathsf{upri}(w)}$ **and** $y_{\max} = \mathsf{y}_{\mathsf{upri}(w)}$ **and**

$x_1 = \mathsf{x}_{v_b}$ **and** $y_1 = \mathsf{y}_{v_b}$ **and** $x_2 = \mathsf{x}_{vE}$ **and** $y_2 = \mathsf{y}_{v_e}$ **and**

$c_1 = \mathsf{code}(w, v_b)$

in

if $\mathsf{TOP}(c_1)$ **then**

$$\left(\left(x_1 + (x_2 - x_1) \cdot \frac{y_{\max} - y_1}{y_2 - y_1}\ ;\ y_{\max}\right), v_e\right)$$

else if $\mathsf{BOTTOM}(c_1)$ **then**

$$\left(\left(x_1 + (x_2 - x_1) \cdot \frac{y_{\min} - y_1}{y_2 - y_1}\ ;\ y_{\min}\right), v_e\right)$$

else if $\mathsf{LEFT}(c_1)$ **then**

$$\left(\left(x_{\min}\ ;\ y_1 + (y_2 - y_1) \cdot \frac{x_{\min} - x_1}{x_2 - x_1}\right), v_e\right)$$

else

$$\left(\left(x_{\max}\ ;\ y_1 + (y_2 - y_1) \cdot \frac{x_{\max} - x_1}{x_2 - x_1}\right), v_e\right)$$

3.2 Verification

As a first step of the verification, we have to set up a formal specification of the algorithm: Given a line segment (by its two endpoints v_b and v_e) and a rectangular window (given by its lower left and its upper right corners), return the line segment that is inside the window, where all points on the edge are considered to be inside. To keep the specification concise, we use the following two primitives: $\mathsf{csaInWin}(w_1, v)$ holds if the point v is inside or on the edge of window w_1, and $\mathsf{csaOnSeg}((v_b, v_e), v)$ holds if the point v is on the line segment from v_b to v_e (including the endpoints). As before, $\mathsf{lole}(w_1)$ and $\mathsf{upri}(w_1)$ denote the lower left and upper right corner of the clipping window. Note that degenerate inputs and outputs are possible, since the input and the output segments may consist of a single point.

csa_in_win $\vdash_{\text{def}}$ $\mathsf{csaInWin}(w_1, v) = \mathsf{inWin}(\mathsf{lole}(w_1), \mathsf{upri}(w_1), v) \geq \mathsf{U}$

csa_on_seg $\vdash_{\text{def}}$ $\mathsf{csaOnSeg}((v_b, v_e), v) =$

if $(v_b = v_e)$ **then** $(v_b = v)$ **else** $\mathsf{onSeg}(\overrightarrow{(v_b, v_e)}, v) \geq \mathsf{U})$

In any case, the result is a value of an option type: it is either NONE (if the line segment is outside the window) or it represents a pair of points defining the clipped line segment.

CSA_CORRECTNESS $\vdash$

let $r = \mathsf{csaClip}(w_1, (v_b, v_e))$ **in**

if $(\mathsf{IS\_NONE}(r))$ **then**

$\neg(\exists v.\ \mathsf{csaOnSeg}((v_b, v_e), v) \wedge \mathsf{csaInWin}(w_1, v))$

else

$\forall v.\ \mathsf{csaOnSeg}(\mathsf{THE}(r), v) = (\mathsf{csaOnSeg}((v_b, v_e), v) \wedge \mathsf{csaInWin}(w_1, v))$

The correctness of the above specification is proven by induction over the recursive calls of the clipping function $\mathsf{csaClip}(w_1, (v_b, v_e))$. There are two base cases: In the first case,

Provided that `e[i]` denotes the i-th of n edges of a polygon and `xRay(v)` is the ray from v to the right, the following C fragment calculates the winding number w of v.

```
w = 0;
for( i = 0 ; i < n ; i++ )
if( doIntersect( xRay(v),e[i] ) >= U )
{
    w += below( v, e[i].begin );
    w += above( v, e[i].end );
}
w = w / 2;
```

5 Conclusions

In this paper, we propose the use of three-valued logic to develop dependable algorithms for geometric applications to be used in safety-critical embedded systems. The use of a third truth value allows us to make degenerate cases explicit so that they can be appropriately handled by different algorithms. Starting from applications like motion planning and collision detection, we dealt with basic geometric objects and primitives.

The obtained software library has been formalised in the interactive theorem prover HOL. Moreover, we used HOL to formally reason about the geometric primitives in order to assure their consistent use. In particular, we are able to verify entire algorithms that are used in embedded systems in order to guarantee that required safety properties like avoidance of collisions are met.

Furthermore, since degenerate cases are succinctly described by three-valued primitives, the derived algorithms are both robust and compact, and their results are to a large extent independent of the numeric precision of the underlying microprocessors.

References

1. M. Alt, C. Ferdinand, F. Martin, and R. Wilhelm. Cache behavior prediction by abstract interpretation. In *Static Analysis Symposium (SAS)*, volume 1145 of *LNCS*, pages 52–66, Aachen, Germany, 1996. Springer.
2. G. Berry. The constructive semantics of pure Esterel. http://www-sop.inria.fr/esterel.org, July 1999.
3. J. Brandt and K. Schneider. Using three-valued logic to specify and verify algorithms of computational geometry. In *International Conference on Formal Engineering Methods (ICFEM)*, LNCS, Manchester, UK, 2005. Springer.
4. J.A. Brzozowski and C.-J.H. Seger. *Asynchronous Circuits*. Springer, 1995.
5. C. Burnikel, K. Mehlhorn, and S. Schirra. On degeneracy in geometric computations. In *Symposium on Discrete Algorithms (SODA)*, pages 16–23, Arlington, Virginia, USA, 1994. ACM.
6. S.C. Chou, X.S. Gao, and J.Z. Zhang. *Machine Proofs in Geometry*. World Scientific, Singapore, 1994.
7. M. de Berg, M. van Kreveld, M. Overmars, and O. Schwarzkopf. *Computational Geometry*. Springer, 2000.
8. H. Edelsbrunner and E.P. Mücke. Simulation of simplicity: a technique to cope with degenerate cases in geometric algorithms. *ACM Transactions on Graphics*, 9(1):66–104, 1990.

9. J.D. Foley, A. van Dam, S.K. Feiner, and J.F. Hughes. *Computer Graphics: Principles and Practice*. Addison Wesley, 2000.
10. M.J.C. Gordon and T.F. Melham. *Introduction to HOL: A Theorem Proving Environment for Higher Order Logic*. Cambridge University Press, 1993.
11. K. Hormann and A. Agathos. The point in polygon problem for arbitrary polygons. *Computational Geometry*, 20(3):131–144, 2001.
12. S.C. Kleene. *Introduction to Metamathematics*. North Holland, 1952.
13. S. Malik. Analysis of cyclic combinational circuits. In *Conference on Computer Aided Design (ICCAD)*, pages 618–625, Santa Clara, California, November 1993. IEEE Computer Society.
14. K. Mehlhorn and S. Näher. *The LEDA Platform of Combinatorial and Geometric Computing*. Cambridge University Press, 1999.
15. D. Pichardie and Y. Bertot. Formalizing convex hull algorithms. In R.J. Boulton and P.B. Jackson, editors, *Higher Order Logic Theorem Proving and its Applications (TPHOL)*, volume 2152 of *LNCS*, pages 346–361, Edinburgh, Scotland, UK, 2001. Springer.
16. T.W. Reps, M. Sagiv, and R. Wilhelm. Static program analysis via 3-valued logic. In R. Alur and D.A. Peled, editors, *Conference on Computer Aided Verification (CAV)*, volume 3114 of *LNCS*, pages 15–30, Boston, MA, USA, 2004. Springer.
17. K. Schneider, J. Brandt, T. Schuele, and T. Tuerk. Improving constructiveness in code generators. In *Synchronous Languages, Applications, and Programming (SLAP)*, Edinburgh, Scotland, UK, 2005.
18. K. Schneider, J. Brandt, T. Schuele, and T. Tuerk. Maximal causality analysis. In *Conference on Application of Concurrency to System Design (ACSD)*, pages 106–115, St. Malo, France, June 2005. IEEE Computer Society.
19. T. Schuele and K. Schneider. Three-valued logic in bounded model checking. In *Formal Methods and Models for Codesign (MEMOCODE)*, Verona, Italy, 2005. IEEE Computer Society.
20. T.R. Shiple. *Formal Analysis of Synchronous Circuits*. PhD thesis, University of California at Berkeley, 1996.
21. W.-T. Wu. On the decision problem and the mechanization of theorem proving in elementary geometry. *Scientia Sinica*, 21:157–179, 1978.

New Area Management Method Based on "Pressure" for Plastic Cell Architecture

Taichi Nagamoto, Satoshi Yano, Mitsuru Uchida,
Yuichiro Shibata, and Kiyoshi Oguri

Department of Electrical Engineering and Computer Science,
Graduate School of Science and Technology, Nagasaki University,
1-14 Bunkyo-machi, Nagasaki 852-8521, Japan
{taichi, yano, uchida}@pca.cis.nagasaki-u.ac.jp
{shibata, oguri}@cis.nagasaki-u.ac.jp

Abstract. In the present paper, we propose a novel area management method based on the concept of "pressure". Plastic Cell Architecture (PCA) is a dynamically reconfigurable architecture that was proposed paying attention to the essentials of processing and the flexibility of Von Neumann architecture. Mechanisms in which area are managed require a function similar to "malloc" in the C language. However, for dynamically reconfigurable architectures such as PCA, uniform management and parallelism are incompatible. Therefore, it is necessary for any PCA circuit to determine its own vacant areas without assistance from an administrator. We therefore introduced a new area management method that obtains the vacant areas by moving the surrounding objects by "pressure". "Pressure" is realize by adding new command set to original commands of PCA. We describe the basic structure for the new command set, and consider herein the development of three new command sets. Finally, we evaluate these command sets with respect to execution area and rate of effective use.

1 Introduction

In the age of ubiquitous computing, the von Neumann type computer effects every aspect of life and has infiltrated every corner of our society. The key to the success of the von Neumann type computer is its generality. We believe that the architecture of the hardware and the software (i.e. program) drive the generality. Any function can be realized both in program logic and wired logic. Important difference between correct program logic and wired logic is that only program logic can allow dynamical constitution with an object instance during execution of a procedure. This heap management is thought to be the source of the pliability of the CPU + MEM structure. Therefore, heap management should also be considered in the domain of wired logic.

Plastic Cell Architecture (PCA) is a new computer architecture having a high degree of parallelism that can replaces the von Neumann type architecture. PCA was designed taking flexibility in wired logic domain [1], [2]. PCA has a structure in

L.T. Yang et al. (Eds.): EUC 2005, LNCS 3824, pp. 418–427, 2005.

which LUTs (Look-Up Tables), which are small-scale truth value tables, are set into the routing network. PCA can perform "processing, transmission, and holding" of data by using the LUTs as memory or as a circuit and the routing network.

In order to use enable dynamic-reconfigurability, which is characteristic of PCA, a functions such as "malloc" and "new", from the C/C++ language, are required. PCA is not yet provided with a domain management method for using these functions because of a problem concerning placement of a new instance. For example, there exists a method of using "domain administrator" that manages areas, but management and the parallel system are incompatible. Furthermore, access to the domain administrator may increase the processing overhead, causing deadlock.

In this paper, we propose a area management method that uses the concept of "pressure". This method is based on a cell division mechanism, whereby existing cells are pushed out of the way when by the growth of a new cell. In this case, the "cell" is the new instance. This method can be performed independently in several places, so that domain administrator is not necessary. PCA achieves dynamic-reconfigurability using commands that are implemented in the built-in part (see Section 2). Therefore, this method is realized as a extension of commands in the built-in part.

In Section 2, we present the background and the related work. In Section 3, we propose a new area management scheme, and in Section 4, we describe the mechanism required to create a command set. In Section 5, three command sets are introduced, and these command sets are evaluated in Section 6. Finally, conclusions are presented in Section 7.

2 Background

2.1 PCA (Plastic Cell Architecture)

The composition of PCA is covered with LUTs that are in the routing network. In this composition, data processing, transmission, and memory can be performed directly and in parallel[1], [2].

Figure 1(a) shows the basic structure of PCA, which is referred to as the PCA cell. PCA cells are arranged in a two-dimensional mesh. Each PCA cell consists of a plastic part and a built-in part. Plastic parts are reconfigurable circuits that can perform memory and operation tasks, and built-in parts performs control and communication tasks for each of the plastic parts. Plastic parts have 8×8 basic cells. The basic cell consists of four 16-bit LUTs. An LUT has a memory of 4 bits for address input and 1 bit for data output.

Figure 1(b) shows an example of communication between objects. An aggregate of PCA cells that performs processing is referred to as an object. Objects that become elements (e.g. add, sub, conditional branch) of a process are arranged to correspond to a Data Flow Diagram. Communication between objects is performed by a built-in part. When two or more objects send messages to each other, the built-in part operates in parallel. Furthermore, an object can be dynamically created by sending a composition message to the built-in part.

operation (e.g. add, sub, conditional branch). Communication between objects is performed through the built-in parts. A new method of area management is shown below.

When object B needs a new object B', it sends a "pressure command" to the surrounding objects (Fig. 2(a)). The surrounding objects receive the pressure command and move to vacant areas. (In the figure, object E moved (Fig. 2(b)).) If the area is vacant, object B makes a new object (B'). This mechanism is realized as an extension of the command in the built-in part.

In clarifying the characteristics and the effect of area management caused by the pressure, we assumed the following in order to simplify the problems.

1. Routing lines between objects are not considered.
2. An object consists of one PCA cell.

There are numerous command sets that would allow us to realize this method. However, creating the correct command set is difficult. In this paper, we present three types of correct command sets having different characteristics. These command sets were obtained by trial and error.

4 Mechanism Required in Order to Create a Command Set

In order to create a command set, we implemented a simulator on a PC and performed trial and error repeatedly. As a result, the mechanism shown in Fig. 3 was found to be necessary. Cells are arrayed onto 2D meshes, as in PCA, to process pressure commands (Fig. 3 left). Each cell consists of a state machine to identify the condition (e.g. vacant state, circuit state, or receiving a pressure state). Cells have five input-output ports (north, south, east, west and feedback), and a switch to limit the direction of entered commands (Fig. 3 right).

Communication Path for Commands. In communication between cells, deadlock is a very important problem. The structure buffer and e-cube routing, for example, are reported to be communicative methods that do not incur deadlock. However, these method are expensive to implement on PCA hardware. When deadlock occurs, the sender must wait until a receiver becomes

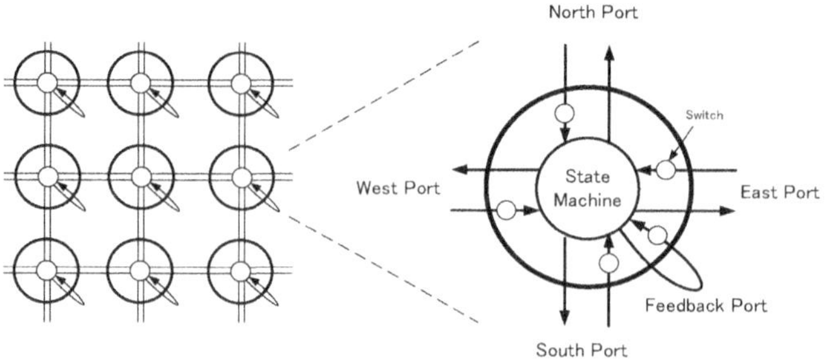

Fig. 3. Cells

available. Therefore, we adopted a communication system that does not wait for responses. The system is based on wormhole routing and can output commands without waiting for a response from the receiver side, even if a cell that receives a command is processing. Although this system prevents deadlock, the possibility exists that commands will be overwritten.

Function to Limit the Input Port. When a cell moved by pressure duplicates, a contradiction occurs if this information is not correctly communicated. Therefore, in order to transmit the information correctly, we added a function whereby the cells do not process commands from cells that are not companion cells. In other words, the cell can limit the direction from which commands are accepted.

Feedback Port. Even if a cell outputs a pressure command once, the neighborhood is not always vacant. Therefore, the cell must output the pressure command several times. As such, we added one input-output port for feedback so that the cell can operate continuously with outputting a command to itself.

5 Explanation of Command Sets

We present three kinds of command sets that were obtained by trial and error. These command sets can increase an object to 1,024 (1, 2, 4, ..., 512, 1,024) cells. The correctness of the increase is checked by an ID that is distributed to objects.

5.1 Command Set 1

Command Set 1 indicates that an object that is going to duplicate itself places pressure only on the objects that exist in the vertical and horizontal directions, as shown in the figure. Therefore, it is not possible to increase the number of cells when the cells in the vertical and horizontal directions are all objects.

For example, consider the case of the cells shown in Fig. 4(a). Suppose Cell 13 wants to make a duplicate of itself. In this case, the pressure command is first sent in the vertical and horizontal directions. Then, Cells 3, 11, 15, and 23, which are at the outermost location in these direction are pushed out outward (Fig. 4(b)). Since locations next to Cell 13 are not vacant yet, the press command is resent, and Cells 8, 12, 14, and 18 are pushed outward, leaving a vacancy next to Cell 13 (Fig. 4(c)). Since the locations next to Cell 13 are now vacant, a clone can be generated (Fig. 4(d)).

5.2 Command Set 2

This command set has the ability to apply pressure in all directions.

In Fig. 5(a), when cell No. 13 increases, it sends "main pressure commands" to the surrounding cells (Nos. 8, 14, 18 and 12). Main pressure commands are

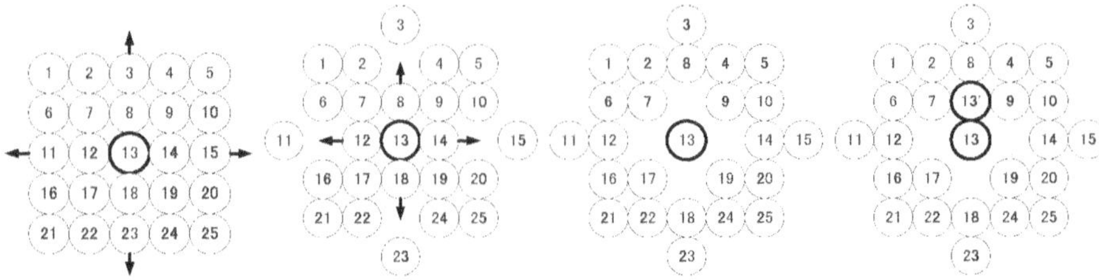

(a) Step 1 (b) Step 2 (c) Step 3 (d) Step 4

Fig. 4. Example operation in command set 1

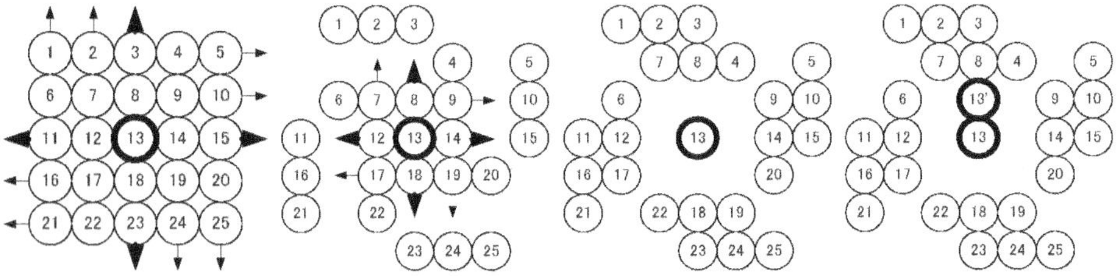

(a) Step 1 (b) Step 2 (c) Step 3 (d) Step 4

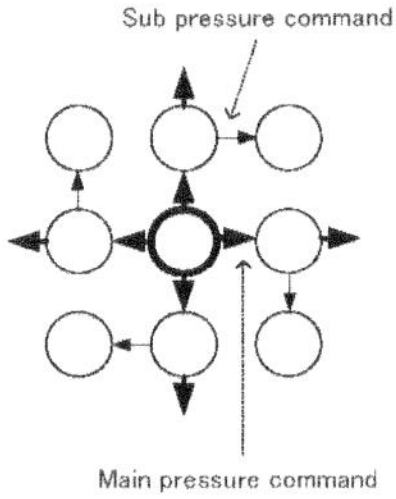

(e) Pressure command

Fig. 5. Example operation in command set 2

transmitted directly and generate a "sub-pressure command" on the way (Fig. 5(e)). Cell Nos. 3, 15, 23 and 11, which received the main pressure command, are extruded. In addition, cell Nos. 1, 2, 5, 10, 25, 24, 16 and 21 are extruded by the sub-pressure command (Fig. 5(b)). Since the cells surrounding cell No. 13 are not vacant, cell No. 13 sends main pressure commands. As a result, cell Nos. 8, 14, 18 and 12) are extruded by this command, and cell Nos. 7, 9, 19 and 17) are extruded by sub-pressure commands (Fig. 5(c)). Since the cells surrounding cell No. 13 are vacant, a copy of cell No. 13 is made (No. 13') (Fig. 5(d)).

5.3 Command Set 3

This command set has a different method of applying pressure. A cell that is going to duplicate itself moves until a vacancy is found. The movement of the cell is realized by exchanging locations with the next cell until a vacancy is found.

which LUTs (Look-Up Tables), which are small-scale truth value tables, are set into the routing network. PCA can perform "processing, transmission, and holding" of data by using the LUTs as memory or as a circuit and the routing network.

In order to use enable dynamic-reconfigurability, which is characteristic of PCA, a functions such as "malloc" and "new", from the C/C++ language, are required. PCA is not yet provided with a domain management method for using these functions because of a problem concerning placement of a new instance. For example, there exists a method of using "domain administrator" that manages areas, but management and the parallel system are incompatible. Furthermore, access to the domain administrator may increase the processing overhead, causing deadlock.

In this paper, we propose a area management method that uses the concept of "pressure". This method is based on a cell division mechanism, whereby existing cells are pushed out of the way when by the growth of a new cell. In this case, the "cell" is the new instance. This method can be performed independently in several places, so that domain administrator is not necessary. PCA achieves dynamic-reconfigurability using commands that are implemented in the built-in part (see Section 2). Therefore, this method is realized as a extension of commands in the built-in part.

In Section 2, we present the background and the related work. In Section 3, we propose a new area management scheme, and in Section 4, we describe the mechanism required to create a command set. In Section 5, three command sets are introduced, and these command sets are evaluated in Section 6. Finally, conclusions are presented in Section 7.

2 Background

2.1 PCA (Plastic Cell Architecture)

The composition of PCA is covered with LUTs that are in the routing network. In this composition, data processing, transmission, and memory can be performed directly and in parallel[1], [2].

Figure 1(a) shows the basic structure of PCA, which is referred to as the PCA cell. PCA cells are arranged in a two-dimensional mesh. Each PCA cell consists of a plastic part and a built-in part. Plastic parts are reconfigurable circuits that can perform memory and operation tasks, and built-in parts performs control and communication tasks for each of the plastic parts. Plastic parts have 8×8 basic cells. The basic cell consists of four 16-bit LUTs. An LUT has a memory of 4 bits for address input and 1 bit for data output.

Figure 1(b) shows an example of communication between objects. An aggregate of PCA cells that performs processing is referred to as an object. Objects that become elements (e.g. add, sub, conditional branch) of a process are arranged to correspond to a Data Flow Diagram. Communication between objects is performed by a built-in part. When two or more objects send messages to each other, the built-in part operates in parallel. Furthermore, an object can be dynamically created by sending a composition message to the built-in part.

operation (e.g. add, sub, conditional branch). Communication between objects is performed through the built-in parts. A new method of area management is shown below.

When object B needs a new object B', it sends a "pressure command" to the surrounding objects (Fig. 2(a)). The surrounding objects receive the pressure command and move to vacant areas. (In the figure, object E moved (Fig. 2(b)).) If the area is vacant, object B makes a new object (B'). This mechanism is realized as an extension of the command in the built-in part.

In clarifying the characteristics and the effect of area management caused by the pressure, we assumed the following in order to simplify the problems.

1. Routing lines between objects are not considered.
2. An object consists of one PCA cell.

There are numerous command sets that would allow us to realize this method. However, creating the correct command set is difficult. In this paper, we present three types of correct command sets having different characteristics. These command sets were obtained by trial and error.

4 Mechanism Required in Order to Create a Command Set

In order to create a command set, we implemented a simulator on a PC and performed trial and error repeatedly. As a result, the mechanism shown in Fig. 3 was found to be necessary. Cells are arrayed onto 2D meshes, as in PCA, to process pressure commands (Fig. 3 left). Each cell consists of a state machine to identify the condition (e.g. vacant state, circuit state, or receiving a pressure state). Cells have five input-output ports (north, south, east, west and feedback), and a switch to limit the direction of entered commands (Fig. 3 right).

Communication Path for Commands. In communication between cells, deadlock is a very important problem. The structure buffer and e-cube routing, for example, are reported to be communicative methods that do not incur deadlock. However, these method are expensive to implement on PCA hardware. When deadlock occurs, the sender must wait until a receiver becomes

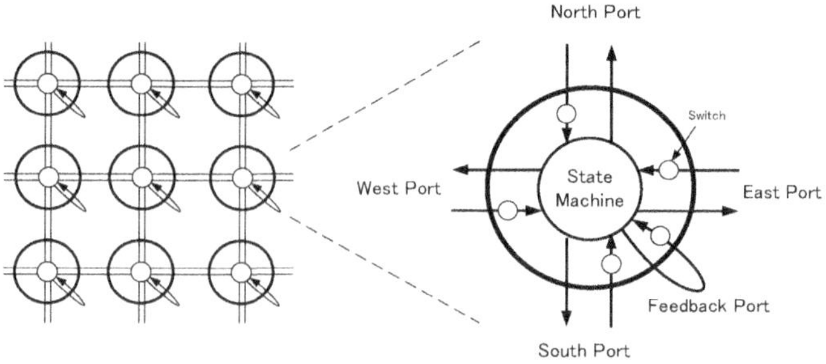

Fig. 3. Cells

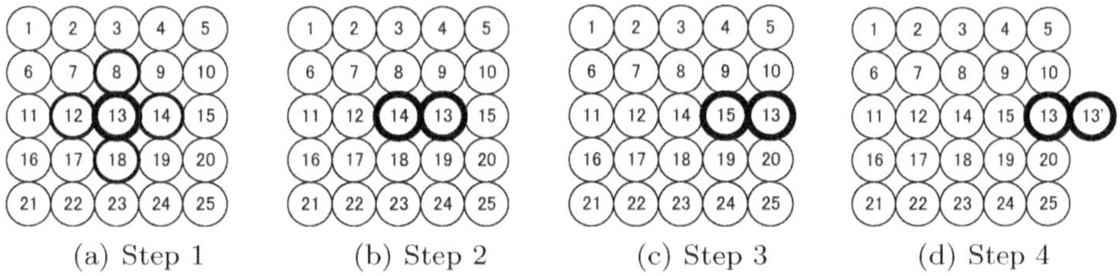

Fig. 6. Example operation in command set 3

In Fig. 6, Cell 13 gives increase demand to Cells 8, 12, 14, and 18 (Fig. 6(a)). Cell 13 exchanges locations with Cell 14, which gives the fastest acknowledgement (Fig. 6(b)). Cell 13 exchanges locations with Cell 15, in the previous direction (Fig. 6(c)). Cell 13 duplicates Cell 13' in the vacancy (Fig. 6(d)).

6 Evaluation of Command

6.1 Area of Implementation

In order to evaluate the mounting area, we compared the number of commands and the number of states among the command sets. The results are shown in Table 1.

This table shows the number of commands and the number of states for each command set. These values (number of states and number of command) are related to the mounting area. As a result, "command set 1" can be implemented in the smallest area and "command set 3" can be implemented in the largest area.

6.2 Rate of Effective Utilization

In order to evaluate the rate of effective use, we measured the rate of use at the time of increase until it became impossible for the number of cells to increase. The experiment was conducted for 12×12 cells. This is the number of cells of PCA-2 [10]. The rate of utilization was deduced from the number of objects when it becomes impossible to increase. A rate of utilization of 100% indicates that all of the cells can be used. The increase command is given randomly. The rate of utilization was obtained by averaging ten measurements.

The results are shown in Table 2. The rate of utilization for "command set 2" is 100%, indicating that all cells can be used ($12 \times 12 = 144$). Among the three

Table 1. Number of commands and number of states

Command set	Number of commands	Number of states
Command set 1	6	5
Command set 2	8	5
Command set 3	11	4

Evaluation of Space Allocation Circuits

Shinya Kyusaka[1], Hayato Higuchi[1], Taichi Nagamoto[1],
Yuichiro Shibata[2], and Kiyoshi Oguri[2]

[1] Department of Electrical Engineering and Computer Science,
Graduate School of Science and Technology, Nagasaki University,
1–14 Bunkyo-machi, Nagasaki 852-8521, Japan
{qsaka, higuchi, taichi}@pca.cis.nagasaki-u.ac.jp
[2] Department of Electrical Engineering and Computer Science,
Nagasaki University, 1–14 Bunkyo-machi, Nagasaki 852-8521, Japan
{shibata, oguri}@cis.nagasaki-u.ac.jp

Abstract. This paper describes the design and evaluation of the PCA (Plastic Cell Architecture) cell, which implements a novel space allocation method. PCA is a dynamically reconfigurable architecture which exceeds the FPGA (Field Programmable Gate Array) in flexibility and generality. Circuit dynamically reconfiguration is achieved as administrators manage the heap areas. But, because objects operate and require new space in parallel, it is difficult to manage them collectively. So, we introduced the concept of pressure, which enables space allocation. As a simulation result, we found that this new method, which relies on pressure commands, could solve the problems of object management efficiently. We designed the PCA cell with space allocation capability. Consequently, the number of gates per PCA cell is 200, and the maximum delay time per cell is 3.55 ns. Moreover, the 3×3 PCA cell processing of six space-allocation commands consumes 306.3μW.

1 Introduction

Real operations of functions are performed by hardware. To perform arbitrary function, the hardware itself must have a variable part. However, if the hardware is composed of only variable parts, it cannot be configured or given any logic. Therefore, hardware is composed of dual components – a variable part and a fixed part.

Based on this consideration, we conducted a study on a novel architecture called PCA (Plastic Cell Architecture), which is different from conventional computers in its realization of the double dual-structure. In the structure of the PCA, SRAM-type FPGAs (Field Programmable Gate Arrays) are scattered over fine-grain networks spanning all of the chip. By making the best use of this structure, it can directly perform computing, *e.g.*, memory storage, processing and information transfer in parallel. In addition, the structure and scale of the configured circuits can be adapted to the behavior of applications by transferring the configuration information of the FPGAs. A unit of configuration of circuits is called an object in the PCA. Circuits are configured separately for each object

L.T. Yang et al. (Eds.): EUC 2005, LNCS 3824, pp. 428–437, 2005.

and are added into the system on-the-fly. The objects in the system that become unused are stopped and detached. To make adding and removing objects on-the-fly easy, PCA has taken the approach of using asynchronous circuits, which have been widely recognized as a means of designing low power consumption circuits and alleviating the performance degradation caused by its global clock skew.

The most difficult problem has been space allocation in the PCA. Because objects move in parallel, it is hard to manage them collectively. Thus, the *pressure command* was proposed as a new space allocation method to solve the abovementioned problem. First, we created a simulator to evaluate the pressure concept, and then we developed three pressure command sets. Next, we decided to implement one command set and evaluate its performance. This evaluation is presented here.

The composition of this paper is as follows. In Section 2, a description of PCAs along with related work is presented as the background of this study. In Section 3, details of the mechanism of the pressure command are described. In Section 4, the pressure commands that we designed are described. In Section 5, the evaluation is described. The paper ends with a short summary in Section 6.

2 Background

2.1 Plastic Cell Architecture

PCA (Plastic Cell Architecture) [1]–[3] is a dynamically reconfigurable architecture enhanced by the flexibility and the generality of the FPGA. PCA-1, developed by NTT (Nippon Telegraph and Telephone Corporation), was the first LSI to realize this concept. This LSI is an array of PCA cells, each of which

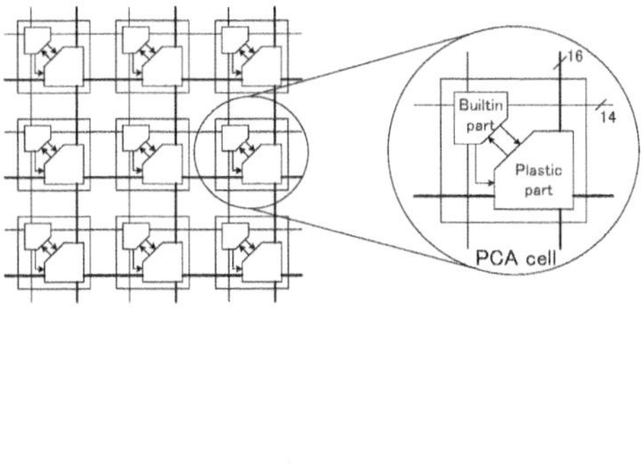

Fig. 1. Plastic Cell Architecture

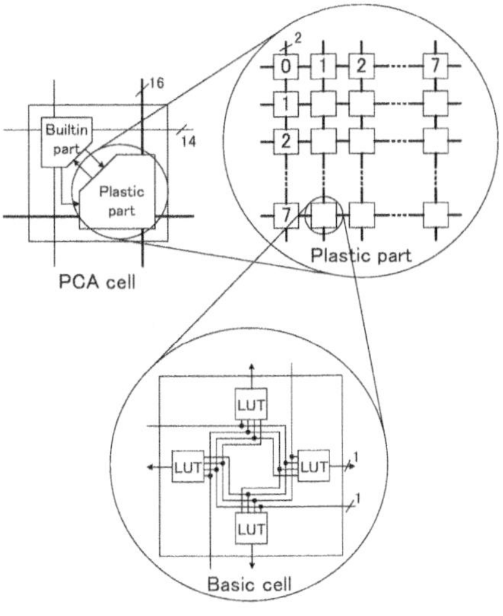

Fig. 2. Structure of plastic part

is composed of a plastic part and a built-in part (Fig. 1). The PCA cells are expected to realize the high integration of the LSI because of its homogeneous structure. Each PCA cell is connected with the adjoining cells in four directions. The plastic part works as both reconfigurable logic and local memory.

When it operates as a circuit, a circuit of arbitrary size is composed by connecting the plastic parts. When it operates as memory, the plastic part in the PCA cell is used with the unit. On the other hand, the built-in part connects the circuit and the memory in the plastic part and performs the data communication. The plastic part is composed of 8×8 two-dimensional basic cell mesh (Fig. 2). The basic cell is connected to four adjoining basic cells with 1-bit input and 1-bit output. Moreover, it has a 64-bit memory unit because it is composed of four 16-bit LUTs (look-up tables). This structure of the plastic cell that is composed of LUTs is called the Sea of LUTs.

The bit-serial PCA is an advanced PCA that adopts the asynchronous circuit system to a bit-serial data path. Asynchronous designs are clockless, so clock skews are avoided and an object can be designed with completely independent timing constraints. PCA operates by objects and messages, and the circuit structure based on local handshaking is also suited for miniaturization because it dispenses with long lines. A processing function is realized by state machines and shift registers in Bit Serial PCA. This coarse-grained composition can acquire efficiency higher than the Sea of LUTs.

2.2 Related Work

PCA-2 is being developed by NTT [4]. PCA-1 uses a $0.35-\mu$m process, but PCA-2 uses a $0.14-\mu$m process. The number of basic cells of the plastic parts are enhanced to 256, so the number of LUTs in a PCA cell are 1024. The width of the passing of data between built-in parts is enhanced to 9 bits. And the circuit composition for throughputs, such as making the detailed pipelines between modules, is changed. With such improvements, the performance has become better in the degree of integration and operation speed. PCA-Chip2, an experimental device of the PCA that uses a synchronous circuit, was developed at Kyoto University. The granularity that minimizes the amount of resources for logical synthesis was found by the method of synthesizing the benchmark circuit of MCNC to the various granularities [5]–[7].

The DRP (Dynamically Reconfigurable Processor) of NEC Electronics Corp. is a coarse-grained multi-context device [8]. The prototype chip DRP-1 was developed as the first LSI to use DRP architecture. DRP-1 has DRP cores, memory controllers, PCI controllers, and multipliers. The processing element (PE) of the DRP that is the reconfigurable element is the 8-bit arithmetic and logic unit/data management unit (ALU/DMU). The Digital Application Processor with Distributed Network Architecture (DAP/DNA), which IPFlex announced in 2002 [9], consists of parallel execution engine DNA matrices which are mounted for the exclusive use of the 32-bit RISC and 144 data processing elements. The DAP RISC core controls the processor's dynamic reconfiguration, while portions of an application that require high-speed data processing are handled by the PE Matrix, which provides flexible parallel and pipelined operation. A DNA configuration memory consists of four banks. The Xpp of PACT XPP Technologies, Inc [10] consists of 128 32-bit processing array elements (PAEs). The PAEs and corresponding I/Os are segmented into two processing array cluster (PAC) blocks. A supervising confirmation manager (SCM) governs the configuration handling to local configuration managers, which further provide the necessary connectivity and processing for an algorithm.

3 Pressure Command

3.1 Space Allocation

The domain administrator of a conventional PCA manages space allocation. It receives the demand of a new domain from some objects, and pays out some new domains. But it has the following problems.

–An administrator has to always know all objects and vacant areas, because these consume unnecessary electric power. This ruins the advantage of an asynchronous circuit.

–It is a bottleneck of processing that a lot of requests concentrate on the administrator. This disrupts the essential parallel processing of the PCA.

–The method of reducing overhead by dividing the administrator has been proposed, but this method is thought to cause various problems because communication between the administrators is difficult.

To solve the abovementioned problem, the *proliferation protocol* with the *pressure command* was proposed as a new method of space allocation. The concept is shown in Fig. 3. The communication among modules is performed through the built-in parts. Space allocation is also performed through the built-in parts with the proliferation protocol. If the module **A** needs the new module **A'**, it sends the pressure command to the surrounding modules, as shown in Fig. 3 (a).

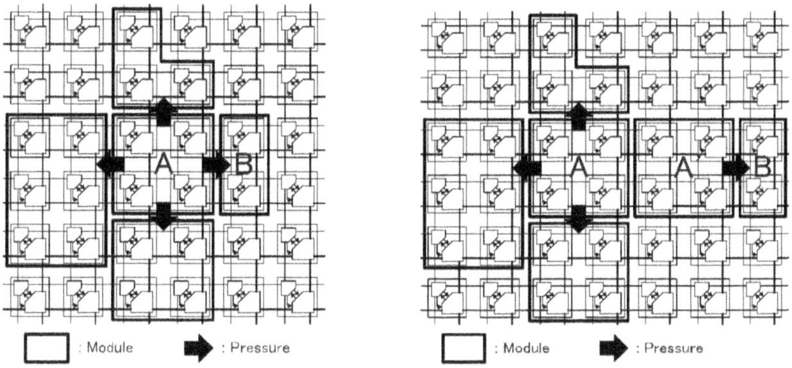

(a) module A needs a new module

(b) module A makes a new module A'

Fig. 3. Pressure command

4.1 Outline

We designed the PCA cell which implements the pressure command to evaluate the performance. Because this design focused on the justification and performance of the pressure command, the synchronous circuit system is adopted for design simplification.

4.2 Tools

SFL (Structured Function description Language), which is HDL (Hardware Description Language) developed at the NTT Research Institute for the logic composition tool PARTHENON (Parallel Architecture Refiner Theorized by NTT Original Concept), was used as HDL. SFL can make descriptions more elegantly than other languages can because it extracts the candidate for description to a single-layer synchronous circuit. 2SECONDS and PARTHENON were used as the simulator and logic composition tool for SFL, respectively. SFL2Verilog, which is one of the functions of PARTHENON, was used as a tool to change SFL into Verilog. and Design Compiler by Synopsis was used as the logic composition tool for Verilog.

4.3 Specification of PCA Cell

The PCA cell is shown in Fig. 6. The concrete functions of each part are described in the following.

–Input and output

Because the number of pressure commands is eight, as mentioned in the previous section, the input and the output need only 3 bits to express them. Moreover, there is a 3-bit register for memorizing the input command at the input ports.

–"*lock*" and "*looked*"

Because one *State Machine* can receive only one command at once, there are two 4-bit registers called *lock* and *looked* inside. These are used to control the commands.

lock is used to carry out the command processing exclusively. Each bit corresponds as follows. Namely, bit 1 (MSB) is south, bit 2 is west, bit 3 is east and bit 4 is north. Data processing can be performed where the bit is 1. (*e.g.*, If the value of *lock* is 0b1000, it means that the state machine receives only the command from the north.) The initial value of *lock* is 0b1111.

looked is used in order to memorize the direction of a command entering and going out. Each bit corresponds as in *lock*. If the corresponding value is 1 when a command enters, it shows that the command enters from that direction. If the corresponding value is 1 when a command goes out, it shows that the command goes out to that direction. (*e.g.*, If the value of *looked* is 0b0010 when a command enters, it means that the command enters from the west.) The initial value of *looked* is 0b0000.

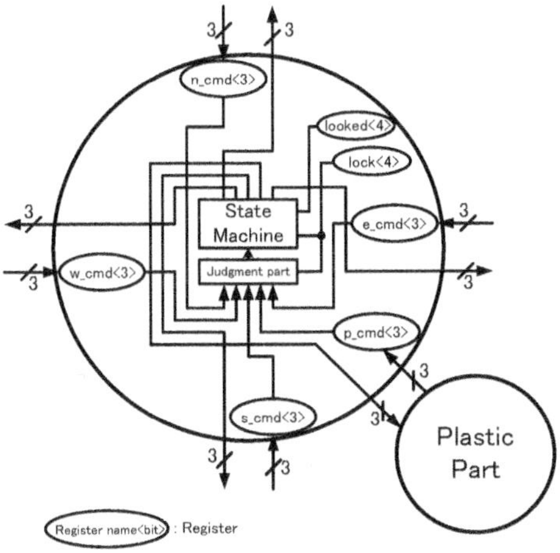

Fig. 6. PCA cell which implements the pressure command

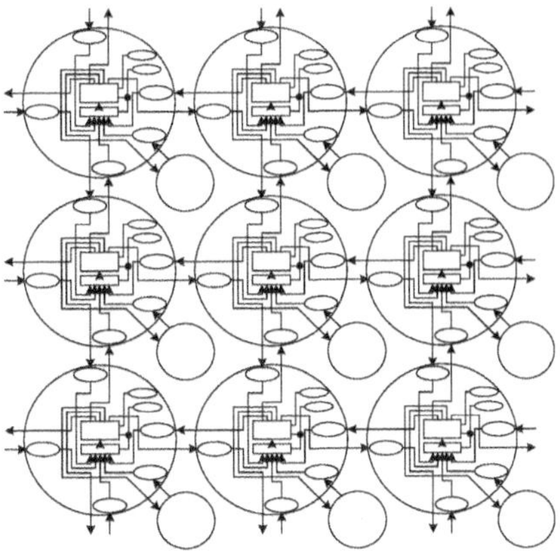

Fig. 7. 3 × 3 PCA cell

–*Judgment Part*

Input commands are sent to the portion called the *Judgment Part*. Here, the flag and *lock* of each direction investigate the commands before they enter the *Judgment Part*. If these bits are 1, the command from that direction can enter the *State Machine*. Moreover, as soon as the command goes into the *State Machine*, the bit of *looked* corresponding to the direction containing the command is set to 1, and the direction where the command was input is stored. If the following command doesn't enter from the direction that the command enters, the flag in that direction is adjusted to 0.

–*State Machine*

The *State Machine* receives input commands and determines the next command output and its direction. It can receive only one command at once. The *State Machine* has five states, and its processing is different from the command and the state described in the previous section.

5 Evaluation

We evaluated following items.

- Number of gates and maximum delay time of one PCA cell.
- Power consumption in an asynchronous circuit system of a 3 × 3 PCA cell (Fig. 7) processing six "START" commands.

We had to measure two power consumptions of the 3 × 3 PCA cell, i.e., processing six "START" commands and processing no commands, to determine the power consumption in the asynchronous circuit system. The power consumption of the 3 × 3 PCA cell processing six "START" commands consists of the power to process the actual commands and the power to make a clock signal. And

Table 1. Evaluation of one PCA cell

Number of gates of one PCA cell	200
Maximum delay time of one PCA cell	3.55 ns

Table 2. Evaluation of 3×3 PCA cell

Power consumption of 3×3 *PCA cell processing 6 commands*	16.0182 mW
Power consumption of 3×3 *PCA cell processing no commands*	15.7119 mW
Power consumption of 3×3 *PCA cell in an asynchronous circuit*	0.3063 mW (306.3 μW)

the power consumption of the 3×3 PCA cell processing no commands contains only the power to make a clock signal. Therefore, the result, which subtracts the latter from former, is the power consumption of the 3×3 PCA cell in an asynchronous circuit system which has no clock signals.

The number of gates and the maximum delay time of one PCA cell is shown in Table 1. Since the number of gates of the built-in part in PCA-1 is about 2500, the ratio of the space allocation part is about 7%. The maximum delay time of the space allocation is lightly affected because its value is 25 ns in PCA-1.

The power consumption of the 3×3 PCA cell processing the six "START" commands and processing nothing are shown Table 2. From these results, we could find the power consumption of the 3×3 PCA cell in an asynchronous circuit system. So, the power consumption of the 3×3 PCA cell per processing command is 51.0 μW.

6 Conclusion

This paper introduced command sets for the PCA. These command sets, based on the concept of pressure, were invented in order to realize a new space allocation method. After that, we implemented one command set in the PCA cell, and confirmed that it operated according to the protocol. The results of evaluating the performance of one PCA cell showed that the number of gates was 200, and the maximum delay time was 3.55 ns. Furthermore, the power consumption of the 3×3 PCA cell processing six commands in an asynchronous circuit system was 306.3 μW. Therefore, we found that the power consumption of the 3×3 PCA cell per processing command was 51.0μW. The ratio of the number of PCA cell gates (200) to the number of PCA gates of the built-in part (2500) showed that the space allocation part was only 7%. This fact indicates that it is possible to implement the space allocation part in the built-in part without large overhead.

Acknowledgment

The authors would like to express their sincere gratitude to the colleagues in their laboratory. The VLSI chip in this study was designed with PARTHENON,

Synopsys Design Compiler, Cadence and Avant! CAD tools through the chip fabrication program of the VLSI Design and Education Center (VDEC) at the University of Tokyo in collaboration with the Rohm Corporation and Toppan Printing Corporation.

References

1. K. Oguri, "New general-purpose information processing architecture PCA1 by cloth line theory", bit, January 2000, Vol. 32, No. 1, pp. 27-35 Kyoritsu Syuppan (2000).
2. K. Oguri, "New general-purpose information processing architecture PCA1 by cloth line theory", bit, March 2000, Vol. 32, No. 3, pp. 54-62 Kyoritsu Syuppan (2000).
3. K. Oguri, "New general-purpose information processing architecture PCA1 by cloth line theory", bit, July 2000, Vol. 32, No. 7, pp. 51-59 Kyoritsu Syuppan (2000).
4. H. Ito, R. Konishi, H. Nakata, A.Nagoya, "Dynamically reconfigurable method LSI PCA-2", The 1st reconfigurable system society, pp. 119-126 (2003).
5. K. Soda, "Design of LUT array type PLD and method of burying logical function", Kyoto university graduate school graduation thesis, (2000).
6. Y. Soga, N. Sugimoto, T. Izumi, T. Ogata, Y. nakamura, "Examination of granularity of PCA-chip2 based on logical mounting efficiency", The 19th PARTHENON society", pp. 15-20 (1999).
7. N. Sugimoto, A. Tomita, H. TsuTsumi, K. Sakai, K. Soda, Y. Nakamura, "Design and making for trial purposes of LUT array type PLD", VDEC LSI design forum, September (2000).
8. M. Motomura, "A Dynamically Reconfigurable Processor Architecture", Microprocessor Forum,October (2002).
9. http://www.ipflex.com
10. http://www.pactcorp.com

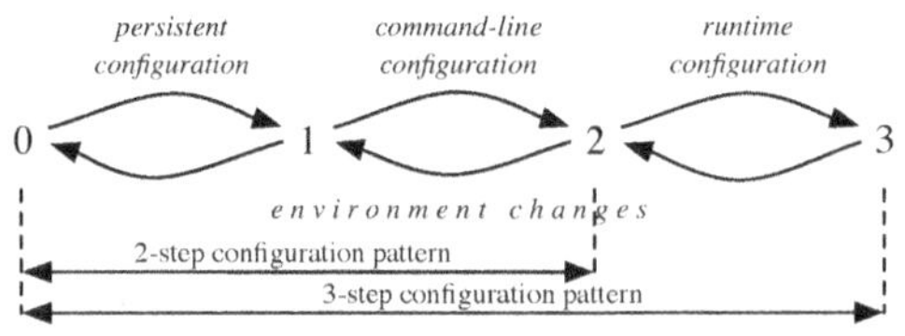

Fig. 1. Sequential configuration pattern

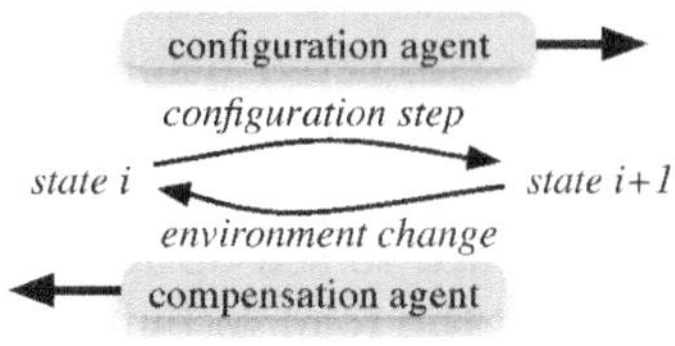

Fig. 2. Compensation agent

Nevertheless, the time at which the configuration of a specific parameter might take place is important, because it will affect the reconfiguration process. An application supporting only persistent and command-line parameters will have to be restarted for reconfiguration, whereas applications supporting runtime modification of their parameters won't need it, hence a shorter (re)configuration time, and fewer resources used. The sequential nature of the configuration patterns guarantees that minimizing configuration time amounts to minimizing the number of configuration steps as these operations are performed sequentially.

Configuration parameters provide information on the execution environment of an application, hence each configuration step leads the application closer to a state where its set-up is coherent with its environment. However, this set-up might get in an incoherent state after a change in the execution environment, thus requiring reconfiguration. The configuration state to which an application should return after an *environment change* is determined by the number of configuration steps needed to set up the modified parameters. For instance, a mailer for which the SMTP server can be given only through it's configuration file (persistent configuration) has to be restarted to cope with any environment change affecting this server, hence returning to state 0 of the process (see Figure 1). If runtime configuration had been an option, going back to state 2 would have been more efficient, avoiding restart.

Computing the shortest configuration sequence requires the knowledge of the parameters that have changed, i.e. needing reconfiguration, and the state in which their configuration is possible. To solve these issues we propose the Application Configuration Policy (ACP) and the Environment Awareness Policy (EAP), presented in the remainder of this section.

2.1 Application Configuration Policy

The Application Configuration Policy (ACP) describes the configuration operations. Each one is performed by a configuration agent that executes configuration commands, and uses a set of resources (parameters) provided by the execution environment.

Each configuration agent has a counterpart in the form of a compensation agent that can undo its actions, thus returning in a previous state (see Figure 2). The compensation agents have a roll-back effect. When the application is reconfigured, they bring it in the state from where the shortest configuration sequence (performed by configuration agents) can start.

The ACP specifies a list of parameters for which configuration agents need values as inputs. The Environment Awareness Policy defines how to get them.

2.2 Environment Awareness Policy

The Environment Awareness Policy (EAP) define how to gather up-to-date values for the configuration parameters. These parameters are resources provided by the execution environment and needed by the application, and whose modification should trigger reconfiguration, using the configuration agents specified by the ACP.

For each parameter, the EAP lists the appropriate tools that must be used to detect changes, and to fetch the most recent value. They are called sources, and for a given parameter, they are considered equivalent, as they implement different ways to obtain the same value, but have priorities defining the order in which they are inquired. For example, the parameter for an SMTP server might have three distinct sources, one relying on DHCP, the second using a service discovery protocol, the third asking input to the user.

By combining the ACP and EAP, we can detect when and how the execution environment modifies its characteristics, infer the state in which the application must return in order to be properly reconfigured, bring the application in that state by applying compensations, and finally perform the configuration. We built the configuration framework in order to address these issues.

3 Configuration Framework

The configuration framework is a generic piece of software that takes as entries an Application Configuration Policy (ACP) and the correspondent Environment Awareness Policy (EAP), and generates a conflet specific to the application. It was first developed as part of the OmniSphere project that aims at developing personalized communication spaces offering the user new applications built on-the-fly by data-flow composition from dynamically discovered services [4, 5, 6]. The conflet does not depend on the programming language of the application, and uses operating system standard facilities, such as process or file handling, implemented within configuration and compensation agents. We chose to implement the framework in Java, and to code both policies in XML.

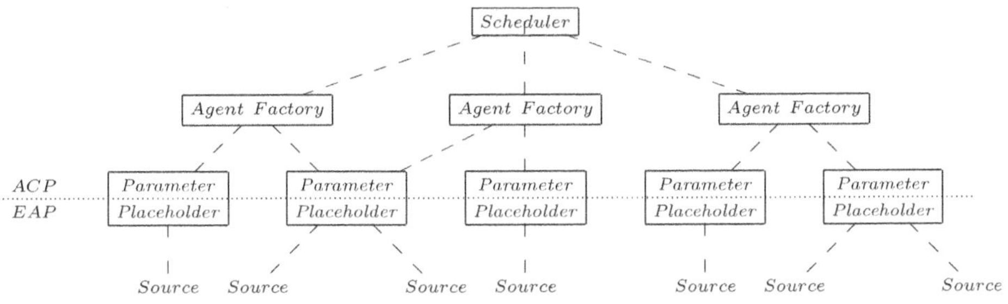

Fig. 3. Conflet architecture for a three-step configuration pattern

3.1 Conflet Architecture

A conflet has a tree-like structure. Figure 3 shows the conflet of an application that follows a three-step configuration pattern. The top element is the scheduler. It governs the execution of configuration and compensation agents. Agents are generated on-the-fly by agent factories whenever the value of one of subjacent parameters changes. Up-to-date parameter values are produced by parameter sources embedded in the environment.

The implementation of each component of the conflet depends on the application to be configured. However the basic behavior is provided through generic classes that can be specialized. The generic architecture follows the pipes-and-filters pattern, receiving event via an entry queue, performing its task, and notifying other registered components about the result of this task.

Parameter Placeholders. The sources send modifications events each time they detect a specific modification in the environment. The parameter placeholders listen for such events, analyze the conveyed modification, and decide whether to propagate it or not.

Low-Pass Filters. Allowing the components of the conflet to send notifications too often is an open door for denial-of-service attacks. Therefore, the parameter placeholders, and the agent factories implement output low-pass filters that prevent the components downstream from flooding or bursts. A filter behaves like a leaky bucket that can hold at most one item (or event). Although a typical leaky bucket would discard any item arriving when another is already in, the low-pass filter keeps the arriving item and discards the other. Each filter has a sending frequency. At each tick, the event in the bucket (which represents the last modification) is retrieved and transmitted to registered listeners. Ignoring several modifications that occur too quickly has no negative effect, as the agent factories and the scheduler (the components that receive modifications events) do not depend on the modification events history.

Agent Factories. The role of the agent factories is to gather up-to-date values from all managed parameters, and to generate agents. The factories receive modification events from parameters and, in response, generate new pairs of agents (configuration and compensation agents). An agent is initialized with the list of current parameter values, and a set, called Δ, of references to the parameters whose values have changed since the last agent passed through the factory low-pass filter.

Scheduler. Both new configuration and compensation agents are not executed immediately after creation. The exact moment of execution and their relative order is given by the conflet scheduler that has a global view of the application state. For example, a configuration agent that starts an application, cannot be executed if the application is already started. Before, the scheduler must roll-back the current configuration by executing necessary compensation agents. In the next section, we discuss the scheduling algorithm that decides the agents to be executed and their order.

3.2 Scheduling Algorithm

To manage the application state, the scheduler uses a compensation stack. Every time a configuration agent is executed, the corresponding compensation agent is pushed into the stack. When the execution environment changes and obsoletes the current configuration, one or more compensation agents are retrieved from the stack and executed before the new configuration is applied. The last-in, first-out property of the stack guarantees that the compensations are performed in reverse order. The number of compensations that should be retrieved from the stack and executed depends on the new configuration and is calculated by the scheduling algorithm.

The algorithm uses a list containing the last generated agent for each agent factory. When a new agent is provided to the scheduler, it replaces, in the list, the previous agent generated by the same agent factory. As a new agent means that the application must be reconfigured, the scheduler must then decide what compensation and configuration agents should execute. It calculates therefore the shortest configuration sequence.

First, it computes the global Δ set for all agents, as the union of Δ sets of all agents in the list:

$$\Delta = \Delta_1 \cup \Delta_2 \cup \cdots \cup \Delta_n.$$

The global Δ set contains references to all parameters whose values have changed since the last configuration, and needs to be addressed by the current one. Executing all agents surely configures them all, and hence represents a valid method of reconfiguration. However, it implies as well that the longest possible sequence of configuration agents is executed. And because different agents can configure the same parameter (that is, a parameter can appear in the Δ set of several agents), there may be a shorter sequence with the same Δ set. The scheduling algorithm then calculates m, with the following properties:

$$\Delta = \bigcup_{i=m}^{n} \Delta_i,\ m \in \{1 \dots n\},\ m \text{ is maximal}$$

Because it is maximal, m gives the minimal number of agents $(n - m + 1)$ that must be executed in order to reconfigure all parameters in the global Δ set. It also represents the number of compensation agents to be retrieved from the compensation stack and executed before. As configuration agents m to n are executed, their compensation agents are pushed into the compensation stack.

The scheduling algorithm calculates a sequence of agents, which reconfigures all parameters referenced in the global Δ set. The maximum property of m guarantees that the result is the shortest valid sequence. Additionally, because of the sequential nature of the configuration pattern, all the other valid sequences would be longer and would include the calculated sequence. Therefore, the scheduling algorithm indirectly minimizes the length and the resources used by the configuration.

to react appropriately. The ability to deal with the dynamism of the execution environment is the principal concern of service discovery protocols [7, 8, 9, 10]. Within our configuration framework such tools can be wrapped by parameter sources, and used to detect changes, such as services that are added, or removed from the network.

While service discovery protocols are considered well suited for ad-hoc environments, DHCP [11] is preferred in administered environments. DHCP allows clients to obtain configuration information from a local server manually initialized by an administrator. Akin to service discovery protocols, DHCP clients can be wrapped by parameter sources.

Self-configuration is addressed by several projects that, still, focus mainly on component-based applications. Fabry explained in 1976 how to develop a system in which modules can be changed on the fly [12]. Henceforth, lots of projects dealing with the modification of interconnections between components appeared [13, 14, 15]. Such approaches can be employed by configuration agents specific to component-based applications.

The Harmony project, proposed by Keleher et al. [16, 17], allows applications to export tuning alternatives to a higher-level system, by exposing different parameters that can be changed at runtime. Although Harmony and the conflet framework share the same vision, the former focuses on performance tuning and requires that applications are "Harmony-aware". Conversely, the conflet framework can configure applications that were not designed for automatic configuration and whose source code is not available.

5 Conclusion

In this paper, we presented a configuration framework that allows applications to be automatically (re)configured. Automatic configuration is made possible by separating the information about the configuration in two complementary classes. The first describes the application configuration policy, while the second details the external factors that influence the application. The conflet combines both: it monitors the execution environment and reacts to the modifications of external factors by reconfiguring the application accordingly. An external tool, the conflet, that is automatically generated from an XML description, manages the application's execution to adapt it to the dynamism of the execution environment.

A significant advantage of separating the configuration policies from the execution environment awareness, and externalizing them into XML, is the ability to add new detection tools without modifying the application.

References

1. Hermann, R., Husemann, D., Moser, M., Nidd, M., Rohner, C., Schade, A.: DEAPspace – Transient Ad Hoc Networking of Pervasive Devices. Computer Networks **35** (2001) 411–428
2. Tennenhouse, D.: Proactive Computing. Comm. of the ACM **43** (2000) 43–50

3. Kephart, J., Chess, D.: The Vision of Autonomic Computing. IEEE Computer Magazine **36** (2003) 41–50
4. Rousseau, F., Oprescu, J., Paun, L.S., Duda, A.: Omnisphere: a Personal Communication Environment. In: Proceedings of HICSS-36, Big Island, Hawaii (2003)
5. Oprescu, J., Rousseau, F., Paun, L.S., Duda, A.: Push Driven Service Composition in Personal Communication Environments. In: Proceedings of PWC 2003, Venice, Italy (2003)
6. Oprescu, J.: Service Discovery and Composition in Ambient Networks. PhD thesis, Institut National Polytechnique Grenoble (2004) in french.
7. Guttman, E., Perkins, C., Veizades, J., Day, M.: Service Location Protocol, Version 2. IETF RFC 2608, Network Working Group (1999)
8. Jini Community℠: Jini™ Architecture Specification (2005) `http://www.jini.org/standards`.
9. UPnP Forum: UPnP™ Device Architecture 1.0 (2003) Version 1.0.1 `http://www.upnp.org/resources/documents.asp`.
10. Cheshire, S., Krochmal, M.: DNS-Based Service Discovery. IETF draft (2004) Expires August 14, 2004.
11. Droms, R.: Dynamic Host Configuration Protocol. IETF RFC 2131, Network Working Group (1997)
12. Fabry, R.: How to design a system in which modules can be changed on the fly. In: 2nd Intl Conf. on Software Engineering. (1976)
13. Plasil, F., Balek, D., Janecek, R.: SOFA/DCUP: Architecture for Component Trading and Dynamic Updating. In: Proceedings of ICDCS 1998. (1998)
14. De Palma, N., Bellissard, L., Riveill, M.: Dynamic Reconfiguration of Agent-based Applications. In: The European Research Seminar on Advances in Distributed systems (ERSADS). (1999)
15. Batista, T., Rodriguez, N.: Dynamic Reconfiguration of Component-Based Applications. In: Intl Symp. on Software Engineering for Parallel and Distributed Systems. (2000)
16. Keleher, P., Hollingsworth, J.K., Perkovic, D.: Exploiting Application Alternatives. In: Proceedings of ICDCS 1999. (1999)
17. Ţăpuş, C., Chung, I.H., Hollingsworth, J.: Active Harmony: Towards Automated Performance Tuning. In: Proceedings of SuperComputing. (2002)

Path Concepts for a Reconfigurable Bit-Serial Synchronous Architecture*

Florian Dittmann[1], Achim Rettberg[2], and Raphael Weber[2]

[1] University Paderborn/HNI, Fuerstenallee 11, 33102 Paderborn, Germany
[2] University Paderborn/C-LAB, Fuerstenallee 11, 33102 Paderborn, Germany
{roichen, syne}@upb.de, achim@c-lab.de

Abstract. This paper develops path concepts for the execution of different algorithms on a reconfigurable architecture. New architecture concepts demand for permanent evaluation of such extensions, also including validating case studies. The recently patented synchronous bit-serial pipelined architecture, which we investigate in this paper, comprises synchronous and systematic bit-serial processing without a central controlling instance. It targets future high speed applications due to the abdication of long wires. The application specificity of the basic version of the architecture can be overcome by so called routers, achieving a reconfigurable system. This paper focuses on the difficulty to conceptualize these routers and proposes several variations for implementation. The case study, which comprises a combined version of the FDCT/IDCT algorithm, serves as an application example for the reconfigurability of the architecture. The example – implementing both algorithms in one operator network – broadens the application area of the architecture significantly.

1 Introduction

The bit-serial architecture (referred to as MACT – Mauro, Achim, Christophe and Tom), which we examine and extend in this paper, was invented in response to current problems of chip design. MACT combines ideas of asynchronous design and bit-serial processing, and represents a synchronous and pipelined architecture without central controlling instance.

Implementations of the so far presented version of the MACT architecture would be application specific [1, 2]. This limitation is only partly in line with current market conditions of the intended application area: data-stream oriented processing (e. g., image compression or filtering).

In this paper, we investigate how to realize multiple paths, and how to model and implement routers and multiplexors to enable path merging and path selection. We abstract and conceptualize graph variations capable for path selection. Strict categorization helps us to distinguish possible cases and to develop solutions for the high level synthesis of such elements. Thereby, we can fall back on

* This work was partly funded by the Deutsche Forschungsgemeinschaft (DFG) in SPP 1148.

L.T. Yang et al. (Eds.): EUC 2005, LNCS 3824, pp. 448–457, 2005.

an already realized high level synthesis for the architecture [3, 4], which automatically generates MACT implementations in VHDL out of data flow graphs. In the high level synthesis, we avoid deadlocks and establish the local control mechanism of the MACT architecture.

As an example for the effectiveness of the extended MACT architecture, we implemented parts of the MPEG-2 algorithm with the components of our architecture.

The rest of this paper is organized as follows. First, we resume related work. Next, we shortly explain the MACT architecture, summarizing the main aspects and benefits of the architecture. Then, we systematically introduce concepts for multi paths within the MACT architecture, including detailed description of the extension. Section 5 familiarizes the reader with the example: combining IDCT and FDCT. Section 7 sums up with a conclusion and gives an outlook.

2 Related Work

Adding routers to the MACT architecture means extending MACT towards a reconfigurable architecture. In the literature, we find several concepts, which can be related to the reconfigurable MACT architecture and give some basic information for our router conceptualization.

The concept of wormhole run time reconfiguration [7] relies on a distributed control scheme and therefore avoids central controllers. Wormhole run time reconfiguration is based on the stream concept. The idea is implemented in the Colt Configurable Computing Machine [8]. Our architecture relies on a similar concept. In contrast to wormhole reconfiguration, we transport only the information when and which path to select and not the whole reconfiguration stream.

So-called self-reconfiguration [9] can be seen as one step towards easing the control process, as the part of the controller tracking the processing can become obsolete. Yet, advanced concepts are needed. One idea is to locate the state machine inside the FPGA, either in a soft- or hard-core processor. Considering Xilinx's Virtex FPGAs, both is possible using MicroBlaze or a PowerPC.

In [10], we find basic work for deadlock-free routing. The authors introduce virtual channels to achieve deadlock-freeness. In principle, MACT relies on a similar concept; yet, the deadlock-freeness is realized by the local control mechanism triggered by data packets traversing the architecture. Thus, the architecture itself bears the capability to avoid deadlocks. Deadlock avoidance is a critical issue during the high level synthesis especially if routers are added to the MACT architecture (see below).

3 MACT Architecture

MACT is an architecture, that breaks with classical design paradigms. Its development came in combination with a design paradigm shift to adapt to market requirements. The architecture is based on small and distributed local control units instead of a global control instance. The communication of the components is realized by a special handshake mechanism driven by the local control units.

Tree The simple tree case comprises two alternatives as displayed in Figure 3 and Figure 4. In the first, we only find routers, which distribute incoming packets to the appropriate output, while in the latter, we combine multiple inputs to one output via multiplexors.

Fork – Join In Figure 5 a, we display the possibility of alternative paths. There, data packets arrive at the router and are forwarded to one path according to their routing information. This kind of path option can be reasonable for data stream processing, where only parts are different, e. g., encoding granularity varies.

Join – Fork In contrast to the latter characteristic, Figure 5 b shows how similar sections within a processing algorithm can be utilized using MACT with routers.

Combinations The above mentioned basic characteristics can be combined in several ways. Apart from a random combination, there may exist an ordered structure, e. g., mesh-based. While random based versions require extended generation algorithms, mesh-based structures can base on principles of systolic arrays. These concepts are out of the scope of this paper.

4.2 Path Encoding

We can encode the information for path selection into several parts of the data packet (refer to Figure 1). Thereby, we can indicate different paths using only a few bits due to logarithmic dependency.

Header We can use the header to hold the routing information, i. e., the information for the path selection. This localization is the most appropriate, as headers precede in the data packet and their content is more easily accessible.

Data If we make a path decision based on the content of the data, we introduce if-then-else to the MACT architecture. We can use this style, when specific paths are only needed, after the data has passed a threshold, etc.

Header + Data When we use both section of a data packet, we can process both by the routers. Thus, we can base the path selection not only on the header information, but also on the data content itself. Thus, individual routers forward packets depending on either the control information present in the header, the data content present in the data section, or on both.

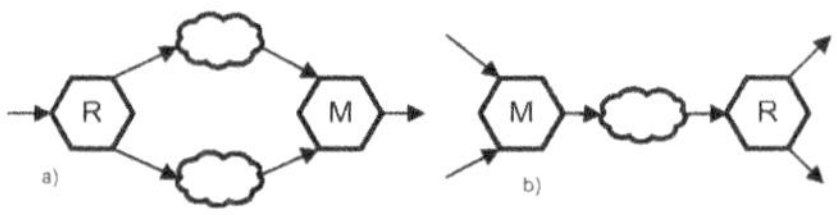

Fig. 5. a) Fork and Join, b) Join and Fork

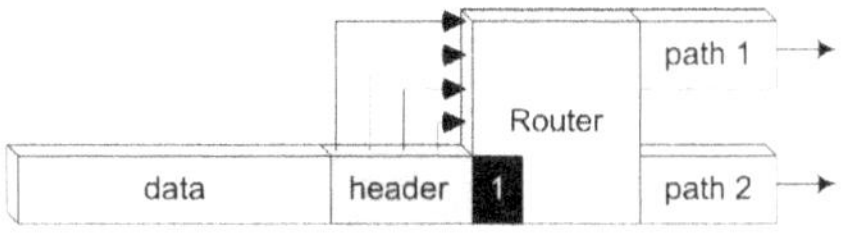

Fig. 6. Router implementation

4.3 Router Implementation

Figure 6 shows an exemplary implementation of a router. Routers tap the information of approaching data packets, when the preceding '1' of every packet arrives at the router. Within one step (clock cycle), the router processes the information and subsequently forwards the data packet to the appropriate path based on predefined table entries. Yet, the paradigms, which lie behind the routers, can follow different principles.

Basic In the basic version, the router only reads the information, selects the appropriate path for the packet and forwards the packet without modifications.

Consuming In a more advanced concept, the router can consume parts of the information of the header, i. e., the corresponding section in the header is removed. Thus, we can decrease the packet length, which can lead into less area needed and shorter wire lengths.

Additive Further, routers may extend packets by additional information. This possibility makes sense, e. g., when there exists a short common section, and packets must be distinguished directly after this section.

4.4 High Level Synthesis and Extensions

Both routers and multiplexors represent new parts of the MACT architecture and therefore must be considered by the high level synthesis. Thereby, we can mainly rely on our already developed high level synthesis.

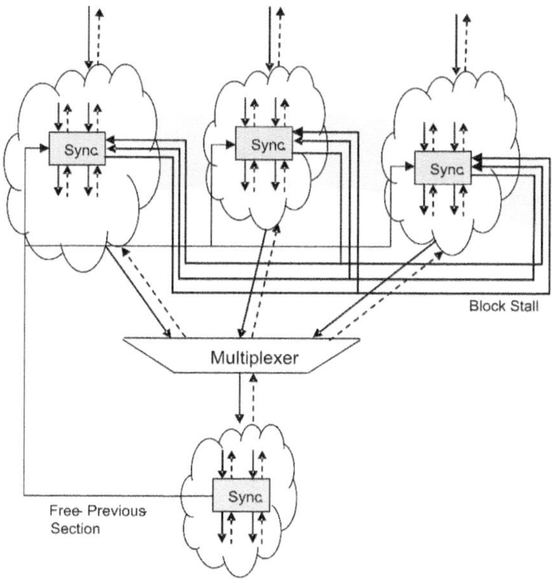

Fig. 7. Multiplexer realization

Router: As routers distribute packets to different paths only, and therefore do not affect preceding paths, they can be treated as normal operator elements by the high level synthesis. In detail, they accept new packets, when all possible succeeding paths are empty, i. e., no packet is present within the tapping range of the control signals.

Multiplexer: In contrast, multiplexer re-unit data paths, i. e., they combine more than one line. The arrival of two packets at the same or nearly same time can cause problems due to false free path information.

The deadlock free processing of the MACT architecture relies on gap and data periods (processing in waves). In order to guarantee a minimal lower bound between two data packets, we enhance multiplexors by *block stall* signals (refer to Figure 7). These signals are activated as soon as one data packet reaches the area between the last synchronizer and the multiplexer of the current path. All other similar areas of the other paths preceding the multiplexer receive a block stall signal, and thus deny arriving packets to enter this section. The packet of the one valid path can be processed without interferences.

Yet, all sections must be freed again, which is done by the *free previous section* signal, which is generated by local logic when the data packet has exited the critical section. It is received by all synchronizers preceding the multiplexer and frees all corresponding paths.

Up-to-date technologies of chip design enable to increase the router concept further. So far, all possible paths must be known at implementation time. Routers enable dynamic path selection between predefined processing paths. Reconfigurable devices (e. g. Xillinx Virtex FPGAs) possess the capability of partial run time reconfiguration. Thus, we can add additional paths of the MACT architecture including routers to our system during run-time (using partial reconfiguration), i. e., new path alternatives can be realized.

We thus achieve a specific self-controlled run time reconfiguration. Generally speaking, during run time reconfiguration, tasks are dynamically loaded into the reconfigurable processing unit on demand. The area currently reconfigured does not influence other regions in operation at the same time. In the MACT version, we additionally avoid a usually large and complex central control entity. There is no need to track the data in the operator network by a central control unit, in order to activate reconfiguration. The request for reconfiguration is generated locally.

Therefore, we modify the routers of MACT. Upon arrival of a new packet, the modified router detects the information needed (header and/or data section) and checks for the availability of the required data path. If the needed path is not resident, the router activates the run time reconfiguration.

5 Case Study

We use as a case study some tasks of MPEG-2. These are the FDCT/IDCT and some video conversion formats. The FDCT/IDCT algorithm is implemented according to the Chen/Wang [5,6] approach. The task of the FDCT is to transform

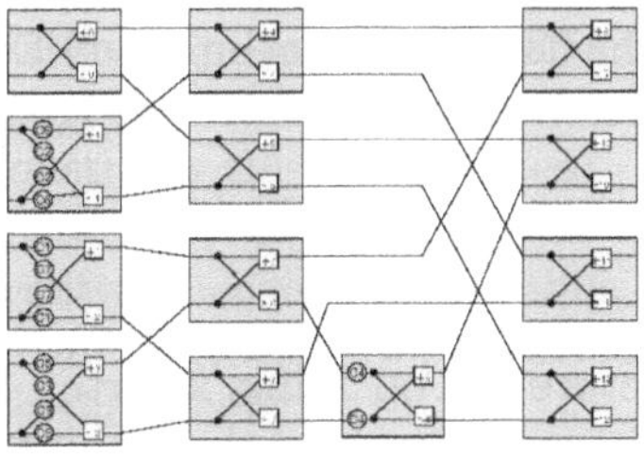

Fig. 8. Inverse Discrete Cosine Transformation

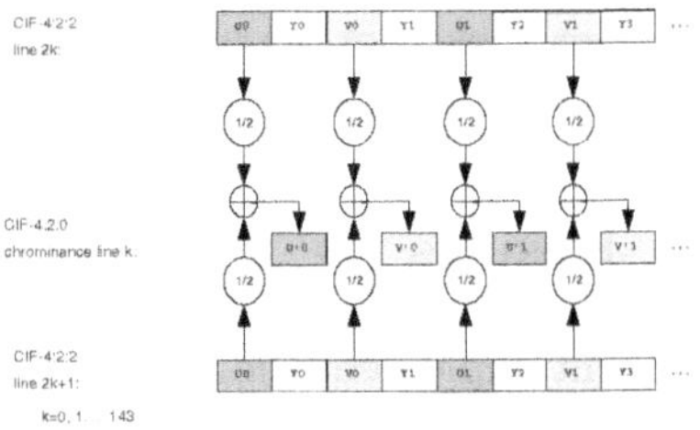

Fig. 9. CIF 4:2:2 to 4:2:0 conversion

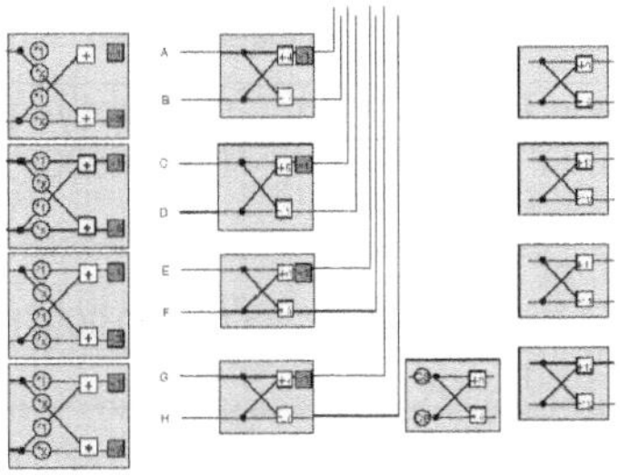

Fig. 10. CIF 4:2:2 to 4:2:0 conversion

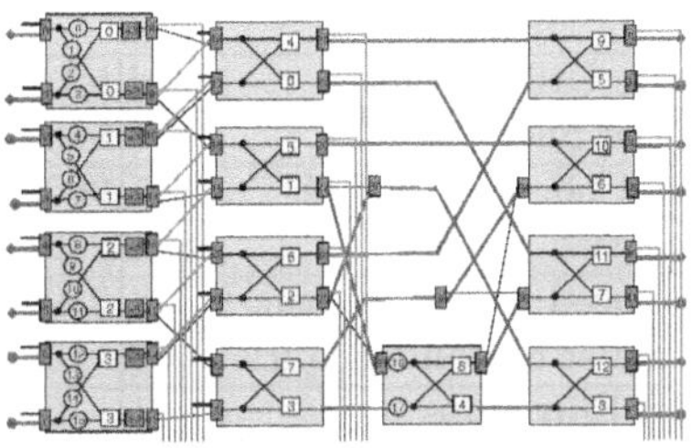

Fig. 11. Mapped Network

the luminance and chrominance data in a block-wise manner. The task of the IDCT is to re-transform the inverse quantized luminance and chrominance coefficients block-wise into the spatial domain. The input coefficients are provided as 12bit values by the control processor.

Obviously the IDCT depicted in Figure 8 is the reversed graph of the FDCT. Both consist of the same amount of operators, and both implementations use a similar operator network. Therefore, we map both graphs onto one common operator network. As a result, we get a re-configurable operator network. That means, we can use the operator network for encoding (FDCT) and decoding (IDCT) of a video image.

Lee [12] introduces an algorithm to split the N point FDCT/IDCT into two (N/2) point FDCTs/IDCTs. Therefore, to realize a 2D-FDCT/2D-IDCT we need eight instances of the FDCT/IDCT operator network. The throughput remains unchanged for the 2D-FDCT/2D-IDCT implementation.

Another algorithm is the video conversion CIF 4:2:2 to 4:2:0 (refer to Figure 9). The conversion CIF 4:2:2 to 4:2:0 is calculated by using the average value of the chrominance values. That means, previously, there are eight and after the conversion there are four values.

If we investigate the FDCT/IDCT network, part of the structure is similar to the CIF algorithm. We can use the second row to calculate the CIF conversion. Figure 10 shows the FDCT/IDCT network with the wires for the CIF algorithm. We place multiplexors before the operators, and routers at the output of the four

An FPGA-Based Parallel Accelerator for Matrix Multiplications in the Newton-Raphson Method*

Xizhen Xu[1], Sotirios G. Ziavras[1], and Tae-Gyu Chang[2]

[1] Department of Electrical and Computer Engineering,
New Jersey Institute of Technology,
Newark, NJ 07102, USA
ziavras@adm.njit.edu

[2] School of Electrical and Electronics Engineering,
Chung-Ang University,
Seoul 156-756, South Korea

Abstract. Power flow analysis plays an important role in power grid configurations, operating management and contingency analysis. The Newton-Raphson (NR) iterative method is often enlisted for solving power flow analysis problems. However, it involves computation-expensive matrix multiplications (MMs). In this paper we propose an FPGA-based Hierarchical-SIMD (H-SIMD) machine with its codesign of the Hierarchical Instruction Set Architecture (HISA) to speed up MM within each NR iteration. FPGA stands for Field-Programmable Gate Array. HISA is comprised of medium-grain and coarse-grain instructions. The H-SIMD machine also facilitates better mapping of MM onto recent multimillion-gate FPGAs. At each level, any HISA instruction is classified to be of either the communication or computation type. The former are executed by a controller while the latter are issued to lower levels in the hierarchy. Additionally, by using a memory switching scheme and the high-level HISA set to partition applications, the host-FPGA communication overheads can be hidden. Our test results show sustained high performance.

1 Introduction

It is not uncommon in power flow analysis to make a good initial guess regarding the solution, e.g., a hot or flat start[16]. Thus, the Newton-Raphson iterative method is often used in power flow problems because a good initial guess leads to desirable convergence properties. If we profile the code of the NR algorithm, we will find out that the most expensive computations are MMs. Real time solutions to power flow problems are absolutely essential in power grid configurations, operating management and contingency analysis. In this paper, an FPGA-based parallel computing architecture is proposed to speed up the MM component in the NR iterations.

* This work was supported in part by the US Department of Energy under grant DE-FG02-03CH11171.

L.T. Yang et al. (Eds.): EUC 2005, LNCS 3824, pp. 458–468, 2005.

Multimillion-gate FPGAs can form promising hardware accelerators for conventional hosts, e.g., a workstation or an embedded microprocessor[1][2][13][14][15]. The workstation-FPGA combination is popular for data-intensive applications due to high FPGA resource efficiency and flexible workstation control. However, the substantial communication and interrupt overheads between the workstation and the FPGAs is also becoming a major performance bottleneck that may prevent further exploitation of the performance benefits gained from the parallel FPGA implementation [3][14].

Specifically, the contributions of our work are: i) We explore the FPGA-based design space to accelerate MM computations in NR iterations. To this extent, a hierarchical multi-FPGA system is proposed where each FPGA works in the SIMD (Single-Instruction Multiple-Data) parallel-processing mode. Under SIMD, all processors execute the same instruction simultaneously but on different data. Due to task partitioning with different granularities at various levels, we can eliminate communication requests of the processing elements (PEs) within the H-SIMD machine if a block-based matrix multiplication algorithm is employed. ii) We employ a memory switching scheme to overlap communications with computations as much as possible at each level. The conditions to fully overlap communications with computations are investigated as well. This technique overcomes the FPGA interrupt overheads and the rather low speed of the PCI bus that connects our FPGA-based target platform to the host [7]. Thus, our proposed methodology makes it possible to synthesize a scheme that brings together the computing power of the workstation and the FPGAs seamlessly for the NR algorithm.

Many research projects have studied MM for reconfigurable systems [4][5][6]. [4] proposed scalable and modular algorithms. Yet the authors point out that the proposed algorithms still incur high configuration overhead and large-sized configuration files. [5] introduced a parallel block-based algorithm for MM with substantial results. Though their design is based on a host-FPGA architecture and pipelined operation control is employed as well, the interrupt overhead from the FPGA to the host is not taken into consideration for a workstation host. Hence, [4][5] can not be used to accelerate MM in the NR method. [6] concluded that FPGAs can achieve higher performance with less memory and bandwidth than a commodity processor.

The rest of this paper is organized as follows. Section 2 analyzes the NR iterative method, and presents the H-SIMD machine design and its memory switching scheme. Section 3 presents the HISA instruction set for NR and analyzes workload balancing for MM across H-SIMDs different layers. Section 4 shows implementation results and a comparative study with other works. Section 5 draws conclusions.

2 Multi-layered H-SIMD Machine and Newton-Raphson Method

2.1 Newton-Raphson Iterative Method

The NR method employs Taylors series expression for a function with two or more variables [16]. It replaces the Gauss-Seidel method which is characterized

```
Initialization & flat start;
X1_matrix= alpha*transpose(A);
do{
   X0_matrix = X1_matrix;
   multiply_matrix(A_matrix, X0_matrix, temp1_matrix);
   multiply_minus(2*I, temp1_matrix, temp2_matrix);
   multiply_matrix(X0_matrix, temp2_matrix, X1_matrix);
}while( ||X1_matrix - X0_matrix|| > 0.000001);
```

Fig. 1. The pseudo-code for the NR iterations

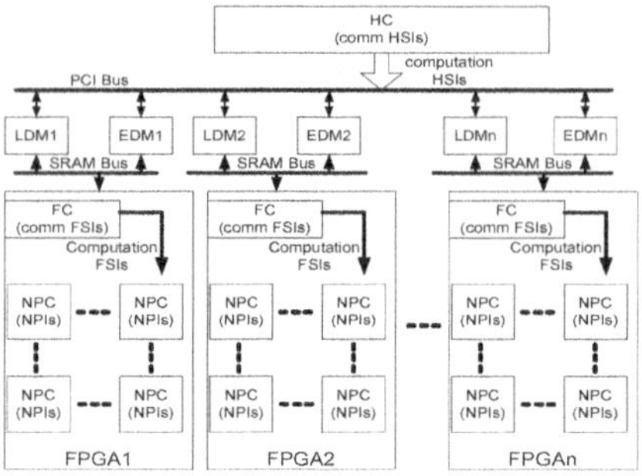

Fig. 2. H-SIMD machine architecture

by slower convergence. The nonlinear Newton-Raphson-type iteration for finding the reciprocal $1/A$ of matrix A is $X(k+1) = X(k)(2I - AX(k))$, where k is the iteration number and $X(0)$ is the initial guess for A^{-1}. The iterative technique proceeds until the sum of the absolute values of the off-diagonal elements in $AX(k)$ is less than ϵ, where ϵ is the required accuracy. The convergence rate is determined by the initial choice of $X(0)$. The process converges if and only if all eigenvalues of $I - AX(0)$ have absolute value less than one. Convergence, when it occurs, is generally quadratic. An improvement can be made so that the algorithms convergence is cubic. The pseudo-code for the NR algorithm is shown in Fig. 1. We can tell that two matrix multiplications are needed per iteration. Hence, our H-SIMD machine is designed for the acceleration of MM in the NR iterations.

2.2 H-SIMD Architecture

The H-SIMD control hierarchy is composed of three layers: the host controller (HC), the FPGA controllers (FCs) and the nano-processor controllers (NPCs), as shown in Fig. 2. The HC encounters the coarse-grain host SIMD instructions (HSIs) in the application program, which are classified into host-FPGA communication HSIs and time-consuming computation HSIs. The HC executes the communication HSIs only and issues computation HSIs to FCs. Inside each FPGA, the FC further decomposes the received computation HSIs into a sequence of medium-grain FPGA SIMD instructions (FSIs). The FC runs them in a manner similar to the HC: executing communication FSIs and issuing the computation FSIs to the nano-processor array. The NPCs finally decode the received computation FSIs into fine-grain nano-processor instructions (NPIs) and sequence their execution. Due to the difference between computation instructions and communication instructions at all levels, the H-SIMD machine configures one of the FPGAs as the master FPGA which sends an interrupt signal back to the HC once the previously executed computation HSI has been completed. Similarly, one NP within each FPGA is configured as the master NP

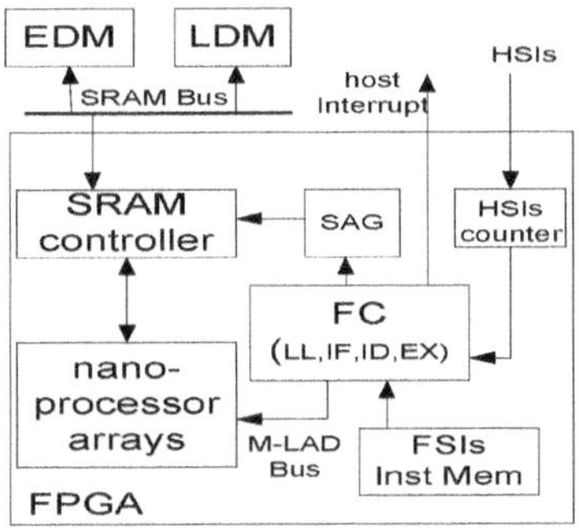

Fig. 3. HC-level memory switching scheme

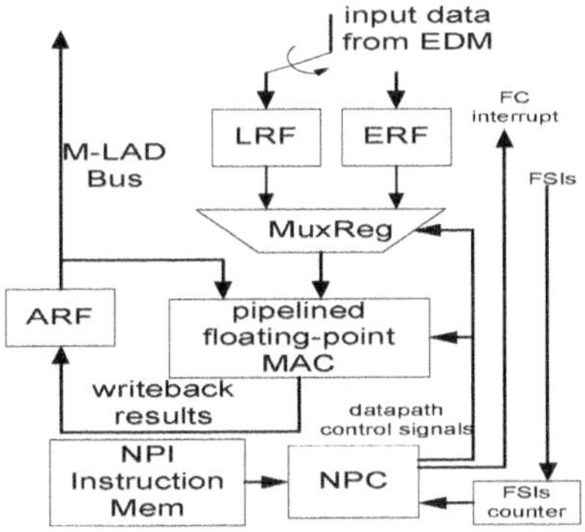

Fig. 4. Nano-processor datapath and control unit

that sends an interrupt signal back to its FC so that a new computation FSI can be executed.

The communication overhead between the host and the FPGAs is very high primarily due to the nature of the non-preemptive operating system on the workstation. Based on tests in our laboratory, the one-time interrupt latency for a Windows-XP installed workstation running the PCI bus at 133MHz is about 1.5 ms. This penalty is intolerable in high-performance computing [14]. Thus, a design objective of the H-SIMD machine is to reduce the interrupt overheads. A memory switching scheme has been applied successfully before in [5]. However, they did not specify the conditions to fully overlap communications with computations, a focus of our study. [14] studied such conditions but for another application problem.

The HC-level memory switching scheme is shown in Fig. 3. The SRAM banks on the FPGA board are organized into two functional memory units: the execution data memory (EDM) and the loaded data memory (LDM). Both are functionally interchangeable. At one time, the FCs access EDMs to fetch operands for the execution of received computation HSIs while LDMs are referenced by the host for the execution of communication HSIs. When the FCs finish their received computation HSI, they will switch between EDM and LDM to begin a new iteration. The FC is a finite-state machine responsible for the execution of the computation HSI. The FCs have access to the NP array over a modified LAD (M-LAD) bus. The LAD bus was originally developed by the Annapolis Micro Systems company for our target board and was used for on-chip memory references [7]. The M-LAD bus controller is changed from the PCI controller to the FCs. The HSI counter is used to calculate the number of finished computation HSIs. The SRAM address generator (SAG) is used to calculate the SRAM load/store addresses in EDM banks. The FC is pipelined and sequentially traverses the pipeline stages LL (Loading LRFs), IF (Instruction Fetch), ID (Instruction Decode) and EX (execution). The transition condition from EX to LL is triggered by the master NPs interrupt signal. The interrupt request/response latency is one cycle only as opposed to the tens of thousands of cycles between the host and FPGAs, thus enhancing the H-SIMDs performance.

The nano-processor array forms the customized execution units in the H-SIMD machine datapath. Each nano-processor has three large-sized register files: the load register file (LRF), the execution register file (ERF) and the accumulation register file (ARF), as shown in Fig. 4. Both the LRFs and ERFs work in a "memory" switching scheme, similarly to the LDMs and EDMs. The ERFs are used for the execution of computation FSIs while the LRFs are referenced by the communication FSIs at the same time. The computation results are accumulated in the ARFs which can be accessed by the FCs.

3 HISA and Task Partitioning for MM

3.1 HISA: Instruction Set Architecture for MM

Similar to the approach for PC clusters in [10], we suggest here that an effective instruction set architecture (ISA) be developed at each layer for each application domain. The HC is programmed by host API (Application Programming Interface) functions for the FPGA board. They can initialize the board, configure the FPGAs, reference the on-board/on-chip memory resources and handle interrupts. We present here the tailoring of HSIs for a block-based MM algorithm. More specifically, we assume the problem C=A*B, where A, B, and C are NxN square matrices. When N becomes large, block matrix multiplication is used that divides the matrix into smaller blocks to exploit data reusability. Due to limited space here, refer to [9] for more details about block-based MM.

In the H-SIMD machine, only a single FPGA or NP is employed to multiply and accumulate the results of one block of the product matrix at the HC and FC levels, respectively. Coarse-grain workloads can keep the NPs busy on MM computations, while the HC and FCs load operands into the FPGAs and NPs sequentially. This simplifies the hierarchical design of the architecture and eliminates the need for inter-FPGA and inter-NP communications. Based on the H-SIMD architecture, the HC issues N_hxN_h sub-matrix blocks for all the FPGAs to multiply. N_h is the block matrix size for the HSIs. We have three HSIs here: i)$host\_matrix\_load(i, S_{LDM}, N_h)$; ii)$host\_matrix\_store(i, S_{LDM}, N_h)$; iii)$host\_matrix\_mul\_accum(H_A, H_B, H_C, N_h)$. The first two HSIs are the communication instructions while the third one is the computation instruction.

The FC is a finite state machine in charge of executing the computation HSI. It decomposes *host_matrix_mul_accum* of size N_hxN_h into FSIs of size N_fxN_f, where N_f is the sub-block matrix size for the FSIs. Enlisted is the same block matrix multiplication algorithm as the one for the HC. The code for *host_matrix_mul_accum* is pre-programmed by FSIs and stored into the FC instruction memory. The FSIs are 32-bit instructions with mnemonics as follows: i)$FPGA\_matrix\_load(i, S_{LRF}, N_f)$; ii)$FPGA\_matrix\_store(i, S_{ARF}, N_f)$; iii)$FPGA\_matrix\_mul\_accum(F_a, F_b, F_c, N_f)$. They are in charge of the communications and computations at the FPGA level.

The NPIs are designed for the execution of the computation FSI. The code for $FPGA\_matrix\_mul\_accum$ is pre-programmed with NPIs and stored into the NPC instruction memory. There is only one NPI to be implemented: the floating-point multiply accumulation $NP\_MAC(R_a, R_b, R_c)$, where R_a, R_b, and R_c are registers for $R_c = R_a * R_b + R_c$. The NPI code for computation FSIs needs to be scheduled to avoid data hazards. They occur when operands are delayed in the addition pipeline whose latency is L_{adder}. Thus, the condition to avoid data hazards is $N_f^2 > L_{adder}$, which can be easily met.

3.2 Analysis of Task Partitioning

The bandwidth of the communication channels in the H-SIMD machine varies greatly. Basically, there are two interfaces in the H-SIMD machine: a PCI bus of bandwidth B_{pci} between the host and the FPGAs; and the SRAM bus of B_{sram} between the off-chip memory and the on-chip nano-processor array. The HSI parameter N_h is chosen in such a manner that the execution time $T_{host\_compute}$ of *host_matrix_mul_accum* is greater than $T_{host\_i/o}$ which is the sum of the execution time T_{HSI_COMM} of all the communication HSIs and the master FPGA interrupt overhead T_{fpga_int}. If so, the communication and interrupt overheads can be hidden. Let us assume that there are q FPGAs of p nano-processors each. Specifically, the following lower/upper bounds hold for matrix multiplication:

$$T_{host\_compute} > \tau * N_h^3/p$$

$$T_{host\_i/o} < T_{HSI\_COMM} * q + T_{fpga\_int} = 4 * b * N_h^2/B_{pci} * q + T_{fpga\_int}$$

where τ is the nano-processor cycle time and b is the width in bits of each I/O reference. Simulation results in Fig. 5 show that the HSI computation and I/O communication times vary with N_h, p and q for b=64 and τ=7 ns. With increases in the block size of HSIs, the computation time grows in a cubic manner and yet the I/O communication time grows only quadratically, which is exploited by the H-SIMD machine. This means that the host may load the LDMs sequentially while all the FPGAs run in parallel the issued HSI.

For FC-level N_fxN_f block MM, we tweak N_f to overlap the execution time $T_{FPGA\_compute}$ of $FPGA\_matrix\_mul\_accum$ with the sum $T_{FPGA\_i/o}$ of the execution times $T_{NP\_i/o}$ of all the communication FSIs and NP interrupt overheads T_{NP_int}. The following lower/upper bounds hold:

$$T_{FPGA\_compute} > \tau * N_f^3$$

$$T_{FPGA\_i/o} < T_{NP\_i/o} * p + T_{NP\_int} = 4 * b * N_f^2/(B_{sram} * N_{bank}) * p + T_{NP\_int}$$

N_{bank} is the number of available SRAM banks for each FPGA. This condition can be easily met [14]. More SRAM banks can provide higher aggregate bandwidth to reduce the execution times of the communication FSIs. By using the above analysis of the execution time, we explored the design space for the lower bound on N_h and N_f, respectively. On the other hand, the capacity of the on-board and on-chip memories defines the upper bounds on N_h and N_f. For each FPGA on

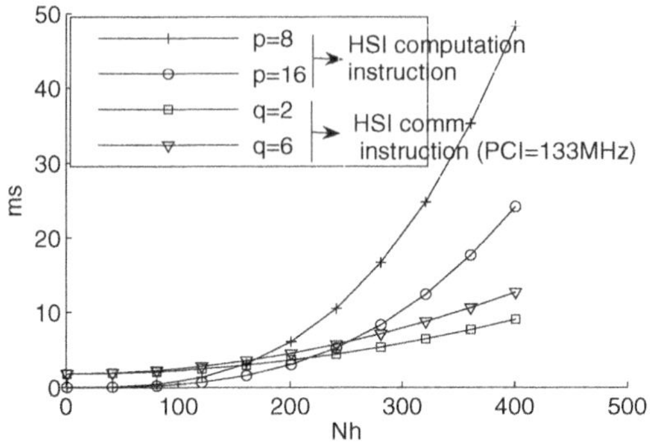

Fig. 5. Execution times of the computation and communication HSIs as a function of N_h, p and q

MM operations: $4*r*N_h^2*b < C_{sram}*N_{bank}$ and $4*r*N_f^2*b < C_{on-chip}$, where C_{sram} represents the capacity of one on-board SRAM bank; $C_{on-chip}$ represents the on-chip memory capacity of one FPGA; r stands for the redundancy of the memory systems, so r=2 for our memory switching scheme. In summary, N_h and N_f are upper-bound by $\sqrt{C_{SRAM}*N_{bank}/(8*b)}$ and $\sqrt{C_{on-chip}/(8*b)}$, respectively.

4 Implementation and Experimental Results

The H-SIMD machine was implemented on an Annapolis Wildstar II PCI board containing two Xilinx XC2V6000-5 Virtex-II FPGAs [7]. We used the Quixilica FPU [8] to build the NPs floating point MAC. In our design environment, ModelSim5.8 and ISE6.2 are enlisted as development tools. The Virtex-II FPGA can hold up to 16 NPs running at 148MHz. Broadcasts of FSIs to the nanoprocessor array are pipelined so that the critical path lies in the MAC datapath. The 1024x1024 MM operation was tested. The block size N_f of the FSIs was set to 8. The test results break down into computation HSIs, host interrupt overhead, PCI reference time, and initialization and NP interrupt overhead, as shown in Fig. 6. We can tell that the performance of the H-SIMD machine depends on the block size N_h. When N_h is set to 64, the frequent interrupt requests to the host contribute to performance penalty. When N_h is set to 128, the computation time does not increase long enough to overlap the sum of the host interrupt overhead and the PCI sequential reference overheads. If N_h is set to 512, there is long enough computation time to overlap the host interrupt. However, the memory switching scheme between the EDMs and LDMs does not work effectively because of the limited capacity of the SRAM banks, which results in penalties from both host interrupts and PCI references. If N_h is set to 256, the H-SIMD pipeline is balanced along the hierarchy such that the total execution time is very close to the peak performance $T_{peak} = N^3 * \tau/(p*q)$, where all the nanoprocessors work in parallel. We can sustain 9.1 GFLOPS, which is 95% of the

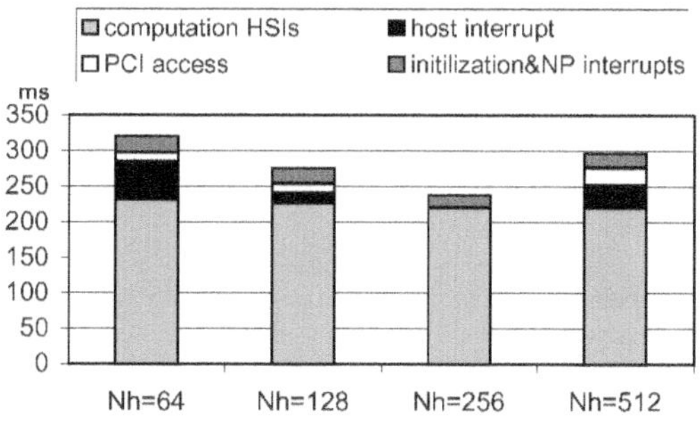

Fig. 6. 1024x1024 MM execution time as a function of N_h

peak performance. The execution overhead on the H-SIMD machine comes from the LDM and LRF initializations and the nano-processor interrupt to the FCs.

For arbitrary sizes of square matrices, a padding technique is employed to align the sizes to multiples of N_f because *FPGA_matrix_mul_accum* works on N_fxN_f matrices. N_f is set to 8 during the test. Let A and B be square matrices of size NxN. If N is not a multiple of eight, then both the A and B input matrices are padded up to the nearest multiples of eight by the ceiling function. Table 1 presents the test results for different cases. For matrices of size less than 512, the H-SIMD machine is not fully exploited and does not sustain high performance. For a large matrix ($N > 512$), the H-SIMD machine with two FPGAs can achieve about 8.9 GFLOPS on the average.

Table 2 compares the performance of our H-SIMD machine with that of previous work on FPGA-based floating-point matrix multiplications [4][5]. Their designs were implemented on Virtex II Pro125 containing 55,616 Xilinx slices as opposed to our Virtex II 6000 FPGA that contains 33,792 slices. We scaled up the H-SIMD size to match the resources in the Virtex II Pro125. After ISE place and route, 26 NPs can fit into one Virtex II Pro125 running at 180MHz and hence achieve the peak performance of 9.36GFLOPS per FPGA. The H-SIMD running frequency can be further increased if optimized MACs are enlisted. [4][5] presented a systolic algorithm to achieve 8.3 GFLOPS and 15.6 GFLOPS on a single XC2VP125 FPGA. However, the H-SIMD machine can be used as a computing accelerator for the workstation when the NR algorithm is implemented. In con-

Table 1. Execution times of MM for various test cases

Matrix size	H-SIMD machine(ms)	GFLOPS
200	7	2.28
400	18	7.111
600	50	8.683
1024	238	9.023
2048	1900	9.042
4000	14100	9.078

Table 2. Performance comparisons between H-SIMD and other works for a Virtex II Pro125 FPGA

	H-SIMD	[4]	[5]
Frequency	180	200	200
Number of PEs	26	24	39
GFLOPS	9.36	8.3	15.6
Hide interrupt overhead	Yes	No	No
Size of configuration files (MB/100 cases)	5	500	500

Table 3. Cost-performance comparison of the H-SIMD machine and the Xeon processor

System	Transistors (millions)	Execution time T(ms)	VLSI Cost	Speedup
2.8GHz	286	3.9	1	1
H-SIMD (2 FPGAs)	700	1.9	0.58	2.05

trast, the systolic approach does not fit into this computing paradigm because of the FPGA configuration overheads and the large size of configuration files.

The H-SIMD performance also compares favorably to that of state-of-the-art general purpose processors. The Intel Math Kernel Library (Intel MKL) contains the BLAS implementation that has been highly optimized for Intel processors. For double-precision general-purpose matrix multiplication (DGEMM), a 2.8 GHz Xeon with 512 KB L2 cache achieves 4.5 GFLOPS [11]. The time-consuming computations in the NR algorithm correspond to MMs. Thus, the H-SIMD machine can speed up the NR method by a factor of 1.9. A cost-performance analysis of the H-SIMD machine and a Xeon processor is in order now. The ten million system gates in the Virtex II FPGA consume about 400 million transistors. The H-SIMD machine built on the Annapolis board contains two Virtex II FPGAs. Thus, our current implementation of the H-SIMD machine employs roughly 700 million transistors. On the other hand, a 2.8GHz Xeon processor is comprised of about 286 million transistors [12]. For 2048x2048 MM on IEEE-754 double-precision numbers, it takes 3.9s on a Xeon processor as opposed to 1.9s on H-SIMD. According to a widely used VLSI complexity model, the cost C of implementing an algorithm is defined as $C = A * T^2$, where A is the chip area and T is the execution time. The chip area is directly proportional to the number of transistors, so we substitute in the cost equation the latter for the former. The VLSI cost and speedup results in Table 3 are normalized with respect to the Xeon processor. The H-SIMD machine can speedup the MM by a factor of two with only about half the VLSI cost.

5 Conclusions

In this paper, we analyzed the NR iteration algorithm for power flow problems and designed an FPGA-based MM accelerator for the host workstation. The proposed multi-layered H-SIMD machine paired with an appropriate multi-layered HISA software approach is effective for the host-FPGA architecture and can be synthetically used to speed up MM in NR iterations. To yield high performance, task partitioning is carried out at different granularity levels for the host, the FPGAs and the nano-processors. If the parameters of the H-SIMD machine are chosen properly, the memory switching scheme is able to fully overlap communications with computations. In our current implementation of matrix multiplication, a complete set of HISA for this application was developed. Its good performance was demonstrated. More recently introduced FPGAs, e.g, XC2VP125, could improve performance even further.

References

1. M. J. Wirthlin, B. L. Hutchings and K. L. Gilson: The Nano Processor: a Low Resource Reconfigurable Processor. Proc. IEEE FPGAs Custom Comput. (March 1994) 22-30
2. X. Wang and S. G. Ziavras: Performance Optimization of an FPGA-Based Configurable Multiprocessor for Matrix Operations. IEEE Intern. Conf. Field-Programmable Tech., Tokyo, (Dec. 2003)
3. P. H. W. Leong, C. W. Sham, W. C. Wong, H. Y. Wong, W. S. Yuen and M. P. Leong: A Bitstream Reconfigurable FPGA Implementation of the WSAT Algorithm. IEEE Trans. VLSI Syst., Vol. 9, No. 1, (Feb. 2001)
4. L. Zhuo and V. K. Prasanna: Scalable and Modular Algorithms for Floating-Point Matrix Multiplication on FPGAs. 18th Intern. Parallel Distr. Proc. Symp., (April 2004)
5. Y. Dou, S. Vassiliadis, G. K. Kuzmanov and G. N. Gaydadjiev: 64-bit Floating-Point FPGA Matrix Multiplication. 2005 ACM/SIGDA 13th Intern. Symp. FPGAs, (Feb. 2005)
6. K. D. Underwood and K. S. Hemmert: Closing the Gap: CPU and FPGA Trends in Sustainable Floating-Point BLAS Performance. IEEE Symp. Field-Progr. Custom Comput. Mach., (April 2004)
7. Wildstar II Hardware Reference Manual, Annapolis Microsystems, Inc, Annapolis, MD, (2004)
8. Quixilica Floating Point FPGA Cores Datasheet, QinetiQ Ltd, (2004)
9. R. Schreiber: Numerical Algorithms for Modern Parallel Computer Architectures. Springer-Verlag, New York, NY, (1988), 197–208
10. D. Jin and S. Ziavras: A Super-Programming Approach for Mining Association Rules in Parallel on PC Clusters. IEEE Trans. on Parallel Distr. Systems, Vol. 15, No. 9, (Sept. 2004)
11. Performance Benchmarks for Intel Math Kernel Library, Intel Corporation White Paper, (2003)
12. http://www.intel.com/pressroom/kits/quickreffam.htm#Xeon
13. X. Wang and S.G. Ziavras: Parallel LU Factorization of Sparse Matrices on FPGA-Based Configurable Computing Engines. Concurrency and Computation: Practice and Experience, Vol. 16, No. 4, (April 2004) pp.319–343

14. X. Xu and S.G. Ziavras: A Hierarchically-Controlled SIMD Machine for 2D DCT on FPGAs. IEEE International Systems-On-Chip Conference, Washington, D.C., (Sept. 2005)
15. X. Wang and S.G. Ziavras: Parallel Direct Solution of Linear Equations on FPGA-Based Machines. Workshop on Parallel and Distributed Real-Time Systems (in conjunction with the 17th Annual IEEE International Parallel and Distributed Processing Symposium), Nice, France, (April 2003)
16. W. F. Tinney and C. E. Hart: Power Flow Solution by Newton's Method. IEEE Trans. AS, PAS-86, No. 11, (1967) 1449–1460

A Run-Time Partitioning Algorithm for RTOS on Reconfigurable Hardware*

Marcelo Götz[1], Achim Rettberg[2], and Carlos Eduardo Pereira[3]

[1] Heinz Nixdorf Institute,
University of Paderborn, Germany
mgoetz@uni-paderborn.de
[2] C-LAB,
University of Paderborn, Germany
achim@c-lab.de
[3] Departamento de Engenharia Eletrica,
UFRGS - Universidade Federal do Rio Grande do Sul - Brazil
cpereira@eletro.ufrgs.br

Abstract. In today's system design, reconfigurable computing plays more and more an important role. By the extension of reconfigurable devices like FPGAs with one or more CPUs new challenges in system design should be solved. These new hybrid FPGAs (e.g. Virtex-II Pro^{TM}), provides a hardcore general-purpose processor (GPP) embedded into a field of programmable gate arrays. Furthermore, they offer partial reconfiguration. Therefore, those hybrid FPGAs are very attractive for implementation of run-time reconfigurable embedded systems. However, most of the efforts in this field were made in order to apply these capabilities at application level, leaving to the Operating System (OS) the provision of the necessary mechanisms to support these applications. In this paper, an approach for run-time reconfigurable Operating System, which takes advantage of the new hybrid FPGAs to reconfigure itself based on online estimation of application demands, is presented. Especially run-time assignment and reconfiguration of OS services over hybrid architecture are discussed. The proposed model uses a 0-1 Integer programming strategy for assigning OS components over hybrid architecture, as well as an alternative heuristic algorithm for it. Furthermore, the evaluation of the reconfiguration costs are presented and discussed.

1 Introduction

Nowadays, the usage of Field Programmable Gate Array (FPGA) in the field of Reconfigurable Computing (RC) has become widely used. In particular the capability of a FPGA to be run-time reprogrammed makes its use for reconfigurable systems very attractive Even more attractive is the emerging hybrid

* This work was developed in the course of the Special Research Initiative 614 - Self-optimizing Concepts and Structures in Mechanical Engineering - University of Paderborn, and was published on its behalf and funded by the Deutsche Forschungsgemeinschaft.

L.T. Yang et al. (Eds.): EUC 2005, LNCS 3824, pp. 469–478, 2005.

FPGAs, which has a hardcore or softcore general purpose processor (GPP) surrounded by a large field of reprogrammable logic. These new components open several interesting possibilities to design reconfigurable architectures for Systems on Chip (SoC). [1].

One of the challenges of our research is to provide support for run-time reconfigurable architectures, which may be used for self-optimizing systems. In dynamic environments, where application requirements may dynamically change, the concept of reconfigurable operating systems appears, which is emerging as new research field.

Differently from the normal approach where the design of such operating system (OS) is done offline, the proposed approach suggests the use of new partial reconfigurable architectures in order to support the development of a hardware/software reconfigurable operating system [2]. In this proposed architecture, the Real-Time Operating System (RTOS) is capable to adapt itself to current application requirements, tailoring the RTOS components for this purpose. Therefore, the system continuously analyze the requirements and reconfigure the RTOS components at the hybrid architecture optimizing the use of system resources. Hence, the system is capable to decide on-the-fly which RTOS components are needed and also to which execution environment (CPU or FPGA) they will be assigned.

The paper focuses on an online partitioning algorithm for a real-time operating system services, which tries to minimize the whole resource utilization and to reduce the reconfiguration costs.

The remaining of the paper is organized as follows: Section 2 presents a brief state-of-the-art analysis regarding hardware implementation of OS services their flexibilities. Then, section 3 shortly presents the architecture used. Section 4 presents the system formulation using 0-1 Integer Programming (BIP) and the reconfiguration costs evaluation. An analysis of the run-time execution of this evaluations, with an heuristic algorithm for the components assignment problem are presented in section 5. Section 6 presents some evaluation results using MATLAB to compare the proposed heuristic algorithm with the original one presented in [3]. Finally, some conclusions and future work are shown in section 7.

2 Related Work

The idea of implementing OS services in hardware is not new. Several works in the literature, [4],[5],[6],[7] and [8]. show that hardware implementation may significantly improve performance and determinism of RTOS functionalities. The overhead imposed by the operating system, which is carefully considered in embedded systems design due to usual lack of resources, is considerably decreased by having RTOS services implemented in hardware. However, up to now all approaches have been based on implementations that are static in nature, that means, they do not change during run-time even when application requirements may significantly change.

In the field of reconfigurable computing, reconfiguration aspects have been concentrated at application level (see [9], [10] and [11]). At the OS level the research are limited to provide run-time support for those applications (see [6], [12] and [13]).

In the approach presented in this paper we expand the usage of those concepts and the hardware support to the OS level. Additionally, based on the state-of-the-art analysis, for a self-optimized reconfigurable RTOS none such similar approach has been proposed yet.

3 Basic Architecture

Our target architecture is composed of one CPU, configurable logic elements (FPGA), memory and a bus connecting the components. Most of these elements are provided in a single CHIP, such as the Virtex II Pro^{TM}, from Xilinx company. The RTOS services that are able to be reconfigured are stored on an external SDRAM chip in two different implementations: as software object and as FPGA configuration bitstream.

Abstractly, the system can be seen as presented in Figure 1. The target RTOS provide services to the application as a set of hardware and software components. These components may, during run-time, be reallocated (reconfigured) over the hybrid architecture in order to better use the available resources and still meet the application requirements.

Our system concept has a similar approach than a microkernel RTOS, as it is being the concept adopted by most RTOSs. Thus, just absolutely essential core operating system functions are provided by the kernel (which are fixed and can not be reconfigured). The other functionalities (services) are provided by components attached at the kernel. However, these components are reallocated during run-time in order to meet the application requirements and the resource usage constraints.

The usage of microkernel also incorporates the nature advantage of flexibility and extensibility (among others) of it, which is very desired in our case in order to better perform the reconfigurability aspects. Nevertheless, it has the disadvantage to slow down the performance due to the increased necessity of messages changes by the components. Therefore, the Communication Layer presented in Figure 1 performs a efficient communication infrastructure in order to reduce this effect and to offer a transparent set of services to the application (independent of the allocation of the components). The details of the architecture is in its development phase will not be treated in the scope of this paper.

4 Problem Definition

The problem of assigning RTOS components over the two execution environments can be seen as a typical assignment problem. Therefore, we decided to model the problem using Binary Integer Programming (BIP) [14]. A set of available services is represented as $S = \{s_{i,j}\}$, where every service i has its implemen-

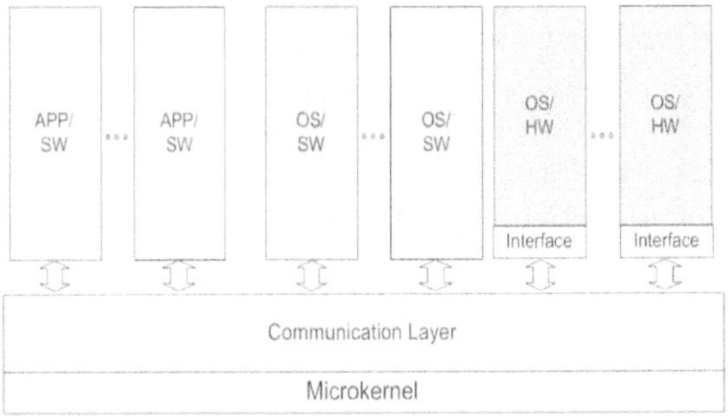

Fig. 1. Proposed microkernel based architecture

tation for CPU ($j = 1$) or FPGA ($j = 2$). Every component has an estimated cost $c_{i,j}$, which represents the percentage of resource from the execution environment used by this component. On the FPGA it represents the circuit area needed by the component and at CPU it represents the processor used by it. Note that these costs are not static, since the application demands are considered to be dynamic. This topic will be addressed later on in subsection 4.2.

4.1 OS Service Assignment

The assignment of a component to either CPU or FPGA is represented by the variable $x_{i,j}$. We say that $x_{i,j} = 1$ if the component i is assigned to the execution environment j, and $x_{i,j} = 0$ otherwise. As some of the components may not necessary be needed by the current application, they should neither be assigned to the CPU ($j = 1$) nor to the FPGA ($j = 2$). Therefore, to proper represent this situation we consider that this component should stay at memory pool ($j = 3$). As we are focusing on the resource utilization optimization between CPU and FPGA we define that a component i placed on the memory pool ($j = 3$) does not consume any resource ($c_{i,3} = 0$). The definition of a third assignment place for an OS component is more useful for reconfiguration costs estimation, that will be seen in section 4.2.

The resources are limited, which derive two constraints for our BIP formulation: the maximum FPGA area available (A_{max}) and the maximum CPU workload (U_{max}) reserved for the operating system. Thus, the total FPGA area (A) and total CPU workload (U) used by the hardware components and the software components, respectively can not exceed their maximums. These constraints are represented by

$$U = \sum_{i=1}^{n} x_{i,1}c_{i,1} \leq U_{max}, \qquad A = \sum_{i=1}^{n} x_{i,2}c_{i,2} \leq A_{max}$$

We also consider that a component i can be assigned just to one of the execution environment: $\sum_{j=1}^{3} x_{i,j} = 1$ for every $i = 1, ..., n$.

To avoid that one of the execution environment would have its usage near to the maximum, we specify a constraint to keep a balanced resource utilization (B) between the two execution environments: $B = |w_1 U - w_2 A| \leq \delta$. Where δ is the maximum allowed unbalanced resource utilization between CPU and FPGA. The weights w_1 and w_2 are used to proper compare the resource utilization between two different execution environments. If the resource used from an execution environment are not near to its maximum, it will have the capability to absorb some variation of the application demands. This characteristic are useful for real-time system in order to avoid the application to miss its deadlines due to workload transients. Note that this approach cannot guarantee hard real time constraints. However, for soft real-time systems it can be considered valid.

The objective function used to minimize the whole resource utilization is defined as

$$min\{\sum_{j=1}^{3}\sum_{i=1}^{n} c_{i,j}x_{i,j}\}$$

The solution of this BIP are the assignment variables $x_{i,j}$, which we define as being a specific system configuration: $\Gamma = \{x_{i,j}\}$.

4.2 Reconfiguration Costs

As is has been said in the section 4, the application requirements are considered to change over system life time. These modifications are represented by changes of the component costs $c_{i,j}$. This leads to the fact that a certain system configuration Γ may no longer be valid after application changes. Therefore, a continuously evaluation of the components partitioning is necessary. Whenever the systems reaches a unbalanced situation ($|w_1 U - w_2 A| > \delta$), the RTOS components should be reallocated in order to bring the system again in the desired configuration. In this situation, not just the new assignment problem need to be solved (Γ') again, but also the costs (time) necessary to reconfigure the system from Γ to Γ' need to be evaluated. This evaluation is necessary since we are dealing with real-time systems. Thus, we have a limited time available for reconfiguration activities.

The reconfiguration cost of every component represents the time necessary to migrate a component from one execution environment to the other one. Therefore, we need to specify for every possible migration of a component its correspondent cost. As it was shown in section 4.1, our model assumes three different environments ($j = \{1, 2, 3\}$). The definition of the environment $j = 3$ (memory pool) is necessary to proper represent the case where a new OS service arrives in the system. This happens when the application requires a service that is neither at CPU nor at FPGA available, but it is stored at the memory pool. The same is valid for a service that leaves the system (it is not more needed by the application). So, we define for a component i a 3×3 size migration costs matrix R_i. Let $R_i = \{r^i_{j,j'}\}$, where j and j' are the current and new execution environment of component i.

swapped and locked according to some rules. If, at least, one of the components from the pair keeps its position in relation to the current system configuration, the pair swap is allowed. In addition, the component that preservers its position (or both) are locked (no longer a candidate to be swaped). However, if both components of the pair change their positions in relation to the current system configuration, no swap occurs. Moreover, just one component (which provides the smaller reconfiguration cost) is locked. This lock is necessary, otherwise the algorithm would not terminate. This process is then repeated until all pairs have been locked or no improvement can be obtained by any interchange. By applying those rules, the algorithms tries to reduce the numbers of components needed to be reconfigured. Also note that the algorithm does not terminate if the δ constraint is fulfilled. This enforce the search for more components (pairs) that could be kept in its current allocation solution.

The algorithm terminates by returning the new assignment solution X that provides a better (or at least an equal) balancing B than the solution provided by the first one. In addition, the number of components being reconfigured is reduced. The complexity of the balancing improvement algorithm is (worst case) $O(m^3)$, where m is the maximum number of pairs. This is due to the fact that we have one *for* loop (1 to m) where in each loop interaction the combination of all components assigned to the CPU with all components assigned to the FPGA are tested (m^2). The algorithm for balancing improvement is shown in Algorithm 1.

6 Experimental Results

For system evaluation of the run-time assignment problem, we made some simulations using MATLAB tool. The results achieved by the original balance improvement algorithm (published in [3]) and the improved one (presented in this paper) were compared. We generated a number of 100 different systems having randomly costs: $1\% \leq c_{i,1} \leq 15\%$ and $5\% \leq c_{i,2} \leq 25\%$; and fixed size: $n = 20$ components. The maximum FPGA resource was defined to be 100% ($A_{max} = 100$), as well as for the CPU ($U_{max} = 100$). The components assignment were calculated for every system using the 0-1 Integer Programming (optimal solution) and the heuristic algorithm (first and second one). The absolute difference cost ($|w_1U - w_2A|$) and the number of components being reconfigured achieved each version of the balancing improvement algorithm were compared for different values of δ (the resource usage balancing restriction): $(0.5, 1, 2, 3, 4, 5, 10, 20, 30, 40, 50 \; and \; 60)$. The current system configuration considered was the previous random system generated.

The Figure 2 shows the results of the balance improvement achieved by the original algorithm (Heuristic-2a) and the optimized one (Heuristic-2b). The improvement made in both case were satisfactory. Note that the results achieved by Heuristic-2b, concerning the balance, are quite under the constraint δ. This is due to the fact that the Heuristic-2a algorithm still search for more pairs to be swapped, even with the δ constraint being fulfilled, in order to reduce the number of reconfigurations. This effect can be seen in Figure 3.

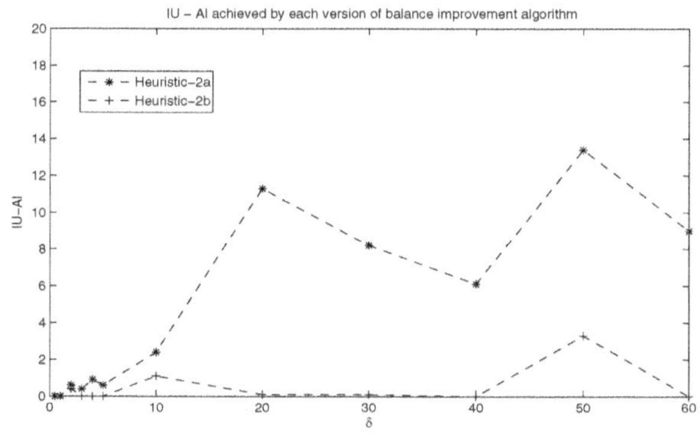

Fig. 2. Unbalance average for different δ constraints

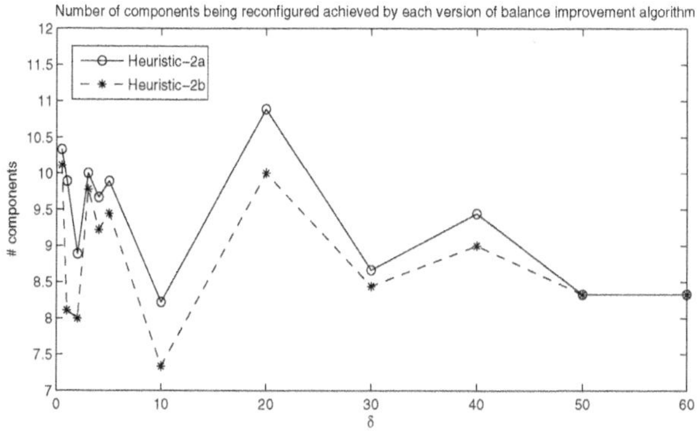

Fig. 3. Number of components being reconfigured for different δ constraints

7 Conclusions and Future Work

In this paper we have presented our investigation towards a run-time reconfigurable RTOS running over a hybrid platform, focusing in the OS service assignment and system reconfiguration. Looking at the related work, we are quite convinced that this is a novel approach for a self-optimized RTOS.

A shortly presentation of the concept of our architecture was also presented. The 0-1 Integer Programming model of the system and the reconfiguration cost evaluation have been presented. Additionally, considerations of a run-time execution of this technics, in order to support real-time applications have been discussed.

As a future work, the investigation of a proper OS components assignment algorithm which takes into consideration the application time constraints and the integration of the communication costs among the components are going to be made. Moreover, the schedule of the components reconfiguration using technics of RTOS Scheduling, necessary to guarantee the application time requirements are going to be integrated.

References

1. Andrews, D., Niehaus, D., Ashenden, P.: Programming models for hybrid cpu/fpga chips. Computer - Inovative Thecnology for Computer Professionals (2004) 118–120 IEEE Computer Society.
2. Götz, M.: Dynamic hardware-software codesign of a reconfigurable real-time operating system. In: Proc. of ReConFig04, Mexican Society of Computer Science, SMCC (2004)
3. Götz, M., Rettberg, A., Pereira, C.E.: Towards run-time partitioning of a real time operating system for reconfigurable systems on chip. In: Proceedings of International Embedded Systems Symposium 2005, Manaus, Brazil (2005)
4. Lee, J., III, V.J.M., Ingstrm, K., Daleby, A., Klevin, T., Lindh, L.: A comparison of the rtu hardware rtos with a hardware/software rtos. In: ASP-DAC2003, (Asia and South Pacific Design Automation Conference). (2003) 6 Japan.
5. Kuacharoen, P., Shalan, M., Mooney, V.: A configurable hardware scheduler for real-time systems. In: Proc. of ERSA. (2003)
6. Kohout, P., Ganesh, B., Jacob, B.: Hardware support for real-time operating systems. In: International Symposium on Systems Synthesis, Proceedings of the 1st IEEE/ACM/IFIP International conference on HW/SW codesign and system synthesis (2003)
7. Lee, J., Ryu, K., III, V.J.M.: A framework for automatic generation of configuration files for a custom hardware/software rtos. In: Proc. of ERSA. (2002)
8. Lindh, L., Stanischewski, F.: Fastchart - a fast time deterministic cpu and hardware based real-time-kernel. In: EUROMICRO'91. (1991) 12–19 Paris, France.
9. Harkin, J., McGinnity, T.M., Maguire, L.P.: Modeling and optimizing run-time reconfiguration using evolutionary computation. Trans. on Embe.Comp.Sys. (2004)
10. Quinn, H., King, L.A.S., Leeser, M., Meleis, W.: Runtime assignment of reconfigurable hardware components for image processing pipelines. In: FCCM. (2003)
11. Mignolet, J.Y., Nollet, V., Coene, P., Verkest, D., Vernalde, S., Lauwereins, R.: Infrastructure for design and management of relocatable tasks in a heterogeneous reconfigurable system-on-chip. In: DATE. (2003)
12. Wigley, G., Kearney, D.: The development of an operating system for reconfigurable computing. In: FCCM. (2001)
13. Walder, H., Platzner, M.: A runtime environment for reconfigurable hardware operating systems. In: FPL. (2004)
14. Wolsey, L.A.: Integer Programming. Wiley-Interscience (1998)
15. Eles, P., Kuchcinski, K., Peng, Z.: 4. In: System Synthesis with VHDL: A Transformational Approach. Kluwer Academic Publishers (1998)

UML-Based Design Flow and Partitioning Methodology for Dynamically Reconfigurable Computing Systems

Chih-Hao Tseng and Pao-Ann Hsiung

Department of Computer Science and Information Engineering,
National Chung-Cheng University, Chiayi, Taiwan, R.O.C.
hpa@computer.org

Abstract. Dynamically reconfigurable computing systems (DRCS) provides an intermediate tradeoff between flexibility and performance of computing systems design. Unfortunately, designing DRCS has a highly complex and formidable task. The lack of tools and design flows discourage designers from adopting the reconfigurable computing technology. A UML-based design flow for DRCS is proposed in this article. The proposed design flow is targeted at the execution speedup of functional algorithms in DRCS and at the reduction of the complexity and time-consuming efforts in designing DRCS. In particular, the most notable feature of the proposed design flow is a HW-SW partitioning methodology based on the UML 2.0 sequence diagram, called *Dynamic Bitstream Partitioning on Sequence Diagram (DBPSD)*. To prove the feasibility of the proposed design flow and DBPSD partitioning methodology, an implementation example of DES (Data Encryption Standard) encryption/decryption system is presented in this article.

Keywords: UML, sequence diagram, partitioning, design flow, reconfigurable computing, FPGA, codesign.

1 Introduction

The acceleration of computing-intensive applications requires more powerful computing architectures. Continuing improvement in microprocessor has increased computing speed, however it is still slower than the speed required by the computing-intensive applications. Microprocessors provide high flexibility in executing a wide range of applications, but they suffer from limited performance. Application specific integrated circuits (ASICs) provide superior performance, but are restricted by limited set of applications. Thus, a new computing paradigm is called for. DRCS [1], [2] is a promising solution, which provides an intermediate tradeoff between flexibility and performance.

The work in this article is concerned with the development of a design flow and of related supporting tools for DRCS. The proposed design flow takes a UML-based application model and facilitates the co-synthesis and rapid prototyping of dynamically reconfigurable computing systems. The outputs of our

L.T. Yang et al. (Eds.): EUC 2005, LNCS 3824, pp. 479–488, 2005.

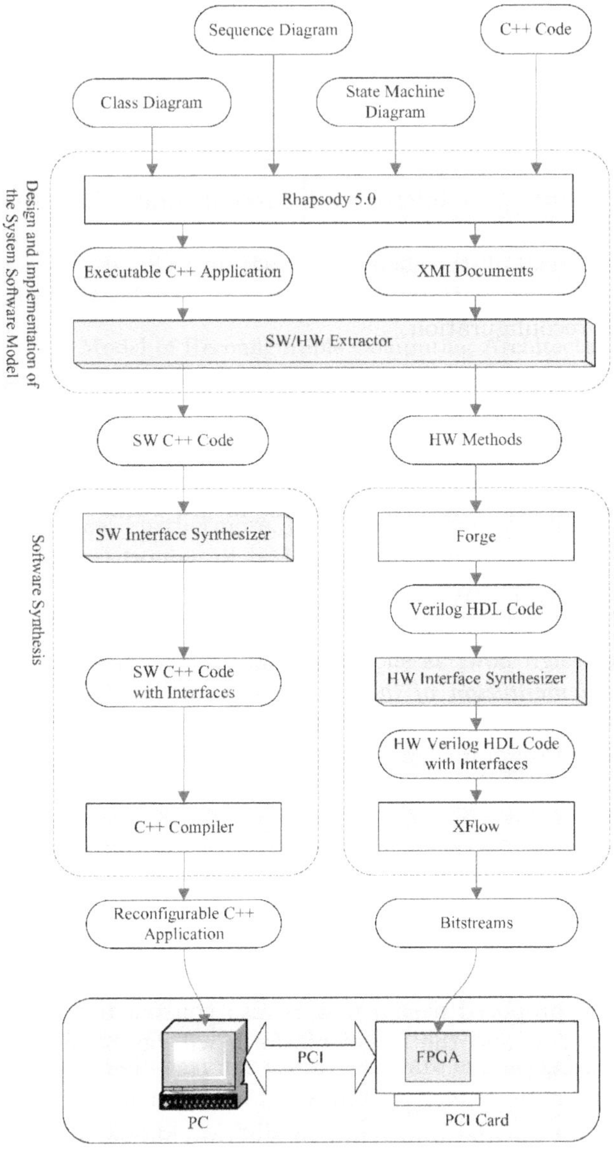

Fig. 2. Design Flow for Dynamically Reconfigurable Computing Systems

marked by user, then it extracts this portion of C++ method as HW method for post synthesis in the *Hardware Synthesis* phase. The SW C++ code is another output of SW/HW Extractor, which represents all of the C++ application code. This SW C++ code will be the input of the *Software Synthesis* phase. After the *Design and Implementation of System Software Model* phase, the design flow is split up into the *Hardware Synthesis* phase and the *Software Synthesis* phase.

The Unified Modeling Language (UML) [3] is a standard modeling language used in the software industry. In this work, we have chosen three diagrams from UML 2.0 for building the system model, namely class diagram, state machine diagram, and sequence diagram. Class diagrams are used to model the architecture of software application.

State machine diagrams describe the dynamic behavior of a class in response to external stimuli, such as event or trigger. There exists a gap between the state machine diagram and its implementation. According to [4], the state machine diagrams include many concepts such as states and transitions that are not present in most object-oriented programming languages, like Java or C++. In order to overcome this gap, we adopt Rhapsody [5] as our UML modeling tool. After drawing UML models in Rhapsody, the tool can generate Ada, C, C++, or Java code. Rhapsody provides an Object Execution Framework (OXF) [5], which enables state machine diagrams to be implemented in object-oriented programming languages.

Sequence diagrams show the interactions between classes in a scenario that is a partial system behavior of overall system specifications. In a sequence diagram, classes and objects are listed horizontally as columns, with vertical lifelines indicating the lifetime of the object over time. Messages are rendered as horizontal arrows between classes or objects and represent the communication between classes or objects.

2.2 Hardware Synthesis

The purpose of the *Hardware Synthesis* phase is to synthesize the hardware bitstreams which will be used by software applications, to perform some required computing-intensive operation. The HW Methods derived from SW/HW Extractor are the inputs of this phase. First, the Forge tool is used to transform the HW Methods into synthesizable Verilog HDL (Hardware Description Language) code. Secondly, the HW Interface Synthesizer adds PCI wrapper for the Verilog HDL code, then produces the HW Verilog HDL code with interface which enable communication from software. Finally, the XFlow tool will synthesize the HW Verilog HDL code with interface into the hardware bitstreams for execution in FPGA.

2.3 Software Synthesis

The purpose of the *Software Synthesis* phase is to build an executable C++ application, which is capable of invoking hardware methods on demand. The Software C++ code which was derived from the SW/HW Extractor is the input of this phase. Starting from this code, the Sofware Interface Synthesizer is used to synthesize code for accessing hardware methods. After that, the produced Software C++ code with interfaces is the final source code. Finally, this code is compiled by a C++ compiler to generate a ready-to-run C++ program, called Reconfigurable C++ Application. During the execution on the host processor, this Reconfigurable C++ Application can reconfigure required hardware method into FPGA for acceleration of the software execution.

2.4 Target Platform

Target platform allows system designers to verify the overall system behavior and to evaluate the overall system performance. Our target platform is a dedicated Xilinx Virtex-II FPGA (XC2V3000, 28,672 LUTs, at 40MHz) board connected to the host computer (Pentium 4 2.8GHz, 1GB RAM, Windows XP) over the PCI interface.

3 The DBPSD Partitioning Methodology

We propose a *Dynamic Bitstream Partitioning on Sequence Diagrams (DBPSD)*, which is a partitioning methodology based on the UML 2.0 sequence diagrams and includes *partitioning guidelines* to help designers make prudent partitioning decisions at the granularity of class methods. Sequence diagrams in UML 2.0 have been significantly enhanced for specifying complex control flows in one sequence diagram. As shown in the middle of Fig. 3, the most obvious changes are the three rectangular boxes, called *interaction fragments.* The five-sided box with labels such as **alt**, **opt**, or **loop** at the upper left-hand corner is the *interaction operator* of the interaction fragment.

The interaction operator gives the interaction fragment specific meaning. The **alt** operator denotes a conditional choice according to the evaluation results of

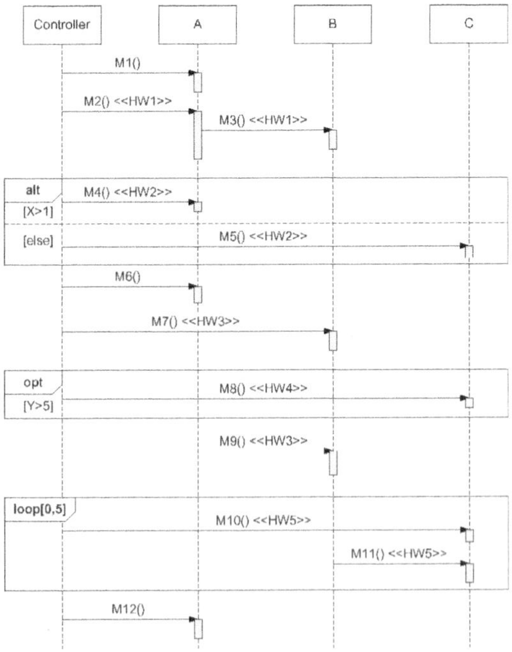

Fig. 3. The Example of the Partitioning on UML 2.0 Sequence Diagram

the guards. For example, if the guard **[x>1]** is evaluated to true, then the **M4()** method will be called, otherwise the **[else]** guard will be evaluated to true and then the **M5()** method will be called. The **opt** operator is the **if** portion of the **alt**, that is the same as the **if** construct in the C language. The **loop** operator defines that an interaction fragment shall be repeated several times.

When doing partitioning on the sequence diagrams, a designer may add a UML stereotype <<HWx>> for a method to be implemented in hardware. For example, in Fig. 3 the methods M2() and M3() are marked by the same stereotype <<HW1>>, but the method M4() is marked by another stereotype <<HW2>>. As a consequence, the methods M2() and M3() will be synthesized into the same bitstream, but the method M4() will be synthesized into another bitstream. Calling a hardware method that is synthesized into a different bitstream will require the FPGA to be reconfigured, therefore additional time overhead will be incurred.

The key performance penalties in DRCS are the FPGA reconfiguration time and the communication time between the CPU and the FPGA. These overheads are mainly dependent on the hardware restrictions. However, we can reduce the number of FPGA reconfigurations, so that reconfiguration overhead is decreased.

To reduce the number of FPGA reconfigurations, we need to take the control flow and execution order into consideration when doing partitioning on sequence diagrams. Hence, in DBPSD the following partitioning guidelines are provided:

Guideline 1: *Add the same stereotype <<HWx>> to all computing-intensive methods.* For example, M1() <<HW1>>, M2() <<HW1>>, ..., M12() <<HW1>>. If synthesis is feasible, only one bitstream is produced, thus only one reconfiguration action is needed.

Guideline 2: *Add the same stereotype <<HWx>> to all dependent methods.* For example, M3() is invoked by M2().

Guideline 3: *For the **alt** operator, add the same stereotype <<HWx>> to all the computing-intensive methods in all condition branches.* If the synthesis of the stereotyped methods is not possible, then start moving the last conditional branch to another stereotype <<HWy>> first, until synthesis is successful.

Guideline 4: *For the **opt** operator, associate all of the methods inside this interaction fragment with a stereotype different from the methods outside this interaction fragment.*

Guideline 5: *For the **loop** operator, associate the same stereotype <<HWx>> to all the computing-intensive methods inside this interaction fragment.* If the synthesis of the stereotyped methods is not possible, then start moving the less computing-intensive method to another stereotype <<HWy>> first, until synthesis is successful.

4 Implementation Example

An implementation example of DES (Data Encryption Standard) encryption system is presented to prove the feasibility of the proposed design flow and

4. I. A. Niaz and J. Tanaka, "Mapping UML statecharts to Java code," in Proceedings of the IASTED International Conference on Software Engineering (SE 2004), pages 111-116, February 2004.
5. Rhapsody case tool reference manual, I-Logix Inc, http://www.ilogix.com.
6. T. Beierlein, D. Fröhlich, and B. Steinbach, "UML-based co-design for run-time reconfigurable architectures," in Proceedings of the Forum on Specification and Design Languages (FDL03), pages 5-19, September 2003.
7. T. Beierlein, D. Fröhlich, and B. Steinbach, "Model-driven compilation of UML-models for reconfigurable architectures," in Proceedings of the Second RTAS Workshop on Model-Driven Embedded Systems (MoDES04), May 2004.
8. J. Fleischmann, K. Buchenrieder, and R. Kress, "A hardware/software prototyping environment for dynamically reconfigurable embedded systems," in Proceedings of the 6th International Workshop on Hardware/Software Codesign, pages 105-109, IEEE Computer Society, March 1998.
9. J. Fleischmann, K. Buchenrieder, and R. Kress, "Java driven codesign and prototyping of networked embedded systems," in Proceedings of the 36th ACM/IEEE Design Automation Conference (DAC99), pages 794-797, ACM Press, June 1999.
10. I. Robertson and J. Irvine, "A design flow for partially reconfigurable hardware," ACM Transactions on Embedded Computing Systems, 3(2):257-283, May 2004.

Hardware Task Scheduling and Placement in Operating Systems for Dynamically Reconfigurable SoC

Yuan-Hsiu Chen and Pao-Ann Hsiung

National Chung Cheng University, Chiayi, Taiwan–621, ROC
pahsiung@cs.ccu.edu.tw

Abstract. Existing operating systems can manage the execution of software tasks efficiently, however the manipulation of hardware tasks is very limited. In the research on the design and implementation of an embedded operating system that manages both software and hardware tasks in the same framework, two major issues are the dynamic scheduling and the dynamic placement of hardware tasks into a reconfigurable logic space in an SoC. The distinguishing criteria for good dynamic scheduling and placement methods include the total schedule length and the amount of fragmentation incurred while tasks are dynamically placed and replaced. Existing methods either do not take fragmentation into consideration or postpone the consideration of fragmentation to a later stage of space allocation. In our method, we try to reduce fragmentation during placement itself. The advantage of such an approach is that not only the reconfigurable space is utilized more efficiently, but the total schedule length is also reduced, that is, hardware tasks complete faster. Experimental results on large random tasks sets have shown that the proposed improvement is as much as 23.3% in total fragmentation and 2.0% in total schedule time.

Keywords: Operating System for Reconfigurable SoC, Hardware Scheduling, Placement, Dynamic Partial Reconfiguration.

1 Introduction

The advent of reconfigurable technologies in hardware design is making a significant impact on the design and the architectures of embedded systems and Systems-on-Chip (SoC). The hardware technologies for supporting reconfiguration are rapidly maturing, however the related software tools and design environments are relatively immature. For instance, we already have dynamic partial reconfiguration hardware such as Xilinx Virtex-II Pro FPGA; however the supporting software tools and runtime environments such as the support from embedded operating systems is still very much limited. In this work, we try to bridge this gap further by proposing scheduling and placement methods for hardware tasks in an SoC with dynamic partially reconfigurable logic.

In the design and implementation of an operating system for dynamically reconfigurable SoC, as shown in Fig. 1, hardware tasks can be dynamically scheduled and placed. For scheduling and placing hardware tasks, besides the desired efficiency, other important issues include the fragmentation of reconfigurable logic space and the total schedule time for a set of tasks. Existing methods either do not consider the issue of

L.T. Yang et al. (Eds.): EUC 2005, LNCS 3824, pp. 489–498, 2005.

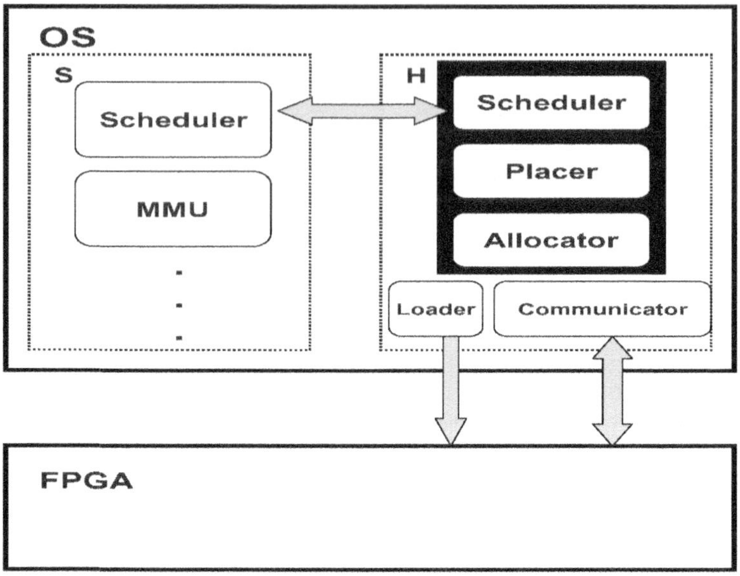

Fig. 1. Operating system for dynamically reconfigurable systems

fragmentation or postpone it to some later stage of space allocation. In this work, we will try to consider the fragmentation of reconfigurable space during scheduling and placement. The goal here is to reduce the amount of unused space that is wasted. As a result not only is the fragmentation reduced but the overall response and total schedule length of the tasks are also reduced.

FPGA is the most widely used reconfigurable logic nowadays. We will model the FPGA space and also the hardware tasks so that they can be used in the proposed scheduling and placement methods. Through experiments, we will also show how much reduction we obtained in fragmentation and in total time through a very simple task classification scheme that nearly does not incur any overhead during dynamic scheduling and placement. The techniques developed in this work will thus be very useful in the design of an operating system for dynamically reconfigurable systems.

The rest of this article is organized as follows. Section 2 presents some previous work in scheduling and placement of hardware tasks for dynamically reconfigurable systems. Section 3 describes the models for FPGA and for hardware tasks, which are used in our proposed method. Section 4 presents the two different scheduling algorithms that we used for scheduling the hardware tasks. Section 5 describes the proposed placement method for hardware tasks. Experimental results are given in Section 6. The article is concluded with future research directions in Section 7.

2 Previous Work

Scheduling hardware tasks is almost similar to scheduling software tasks. Scheduling methods can be classified into static and dynamic depending on when the scheduling is done. Static scheduling can spend more time to find an optimal schedule, but it is fixed before run-time and thus cannot be changed once a system is running, making it quite inflexible. In contrast, dynamic scheduling must make scheduling decisions quickly so that the FPGA is not kept idle for too long without executing any hardware tasks; however the schedules might not be optimal. For static scheduling, variants of list scheduling have been proposed and used in several works, which differ mainly in their assignment of task priorities. Random priority list scheduling was used in the reconfigurable environment scheduling model [3] and dynamic priority list scheduling was proposed in [4].

For dynamic scheduling, the following methods have been proposed or used. Priority-based scheduling was used in the task and context schedulers [5]. Non-preemptive methods such as First-Come First-Serve (FCFS) and Shortest-Job First (SJF) scheduling were used in the online scheduler of [7]. Preemptive methods such as Shortest-Remaining Processing Time (SRPT) and Earliest Deadline First (EDF) were used also used in [7]. Steiger et al proposed a horizon and a stuffing method for dynamic scheduling and placement of hardware tasks [6].

The FPGA space has been modeled differently in the previous works. For example, in [5], the FPGA space was divided into slots that could accommodate only specific types of dynamic reconfigurable logics. In [7], the FPGA space was divided into slots of several fixed sizes and the placer selected the most suitably sized block for a task at hand, thus resulting in a smaller fragmentation. In [6], the FPGA space is considered as either a 1-dimensional or 2-dimensional area that can configured during scheduling and placement, for which two methods were proposed, namely horizon and stuffing.

Because our goal is to perform scheduling and placement of hardware tasks in an operating system, we focus on dynamic scheduling and placement methods. After a thorough survey we found that the 1-dimensional stuffing method [6] approximately meets our needs; however there are some issues such as significant fragmentation and schedule length so we decided to improve on this method such that we can decrease the resulting fragmentation and reduce the total execution time when hardware tasks are dynamically scheduled and placed in a reconfigurable SoC.

3 FPGA and Task Modeling

The FPGA configurable space is considered to be a set of columns, where a column spans the height of a chip and the set of columns spread across the width of the chip. The basic unit of configuration in this model is a column, which itself is a set of CLBs. This model fits the current technology of partial dynamically reconfigurable Xilinx Virtex II Pro FPGA chips. In this model, the reconfiguration is a 1-dimensional problem.

The hardware to be configured on an FPGA is modeled as a set of hardware tasks, where each task t has a set of attributes including arrival time $A(t)$, execution time $E(t)$, deadline $D(t)$, and area $C(t)$ (in terms of the number of FPGA columns required). These numbers can be obtained by synthesizing a hardware function using a synthesis tool such as Synplify or XST.

Given a set of hardware tasks and an FPGA space, our target problem is to schedule and place the tasks in the FPGA space such that the task attributes are all satisfied and

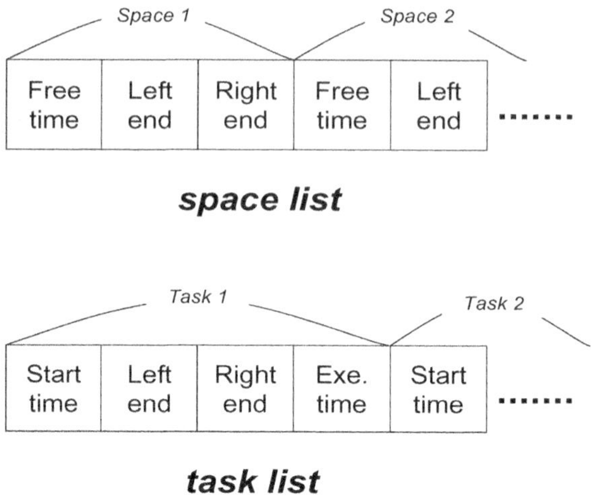

Fig. 3. Data structures used for recording placement and scheduling information

always obtained when we divide the task set considering only their SUR values. The results are described in Section 6 and Table 2.

5.2 Recording Placement Information

During placement, two lists are maintained, namely a *space list* for recording the free spaces and a *task list* for recording the task locations in FPGA after placement. For every free space in the space list we record three data including release time, the leftmost and the rightmost columns of this free space in FPGA. When the placer places a task into FPGA, the task list will store four information about the task, namely (1) the starting execution time of the task, (2) the leftmost column occupied by the task, (3) the rightmost column occupied by the task, and (4) the execution time of the task. The space list supplies information for the placer to find a fit free space for tasks, and the task list allows the placer to detect whether there is any conflict among the tasks. Figure 3 illustrates the two data structures. How to find a fit space and how to detect placement conflicts will be discussed in Section 5.3.

5.3 Placement Method

In the proposed classified stuffing method, placement of hardware tasks in FPGA space is performed as described in the following steps.

1. *Select a task:* The placer chooses a highest priority task from the ready queue according to our scheduling policy as described in Section 4. The task is classified into either high or low SUR as described in Section 5.1.
2. *Find a fit space:* Based on the width of a task, the placer will find a best fit free space from the space list. The best fit space is the earliest released of all free spaces which have enough columns of CLBs for the task. If there are more than one space

released at the same time, the leftmost space will be selected for placing a high SUR task, while the rightmost space will be selected for a low SUR task.

3. *Decide placement location in a free space:* At the second step, the placer found a best fit free space for a task, but this space maybe wider than that required by the task. In this case, according to the task type we determine which columns of CLBs of the best fit space will be used. A *high SUR* task will be placed from the leftmost column and a *low SUR* task will be placed from the rightmost column.
4. *Checking conflict:* At this step we already know where a task is to be placed, but we need to check if there is any conflict between the newly placed task and an existing already placed task. If a conflict exists, we must choose another fit space for the new task by going back to Step (2).
5. *Modify space list:* After a task is placed into a best fit space, not only the information of this fit space need to be modified, but also some other free spaces in the space list may be affected and thus need to be updated.

6 Experiment Results

To evaluate the advantages of the classified stuffing method compared with the original stuffing technique [6], we experimented with 150 sets of randomly generated hardware tasks, one-third of the sets had 50 tasks in each set, one-third had 200 tasks in each set, and one-third had 500 tasks in each set. The input task sets were also characterized by different *set ratios*, where the set ratio of a task set is defined as $|S_{>1}| : |S_{\leq 1}|$, where $S_{>1} = \{t \mid SUR(t) > 1\}$, $S_{\leq 1} = \{t \mid SUR(t) \leq 1\}$ so as to find out the kind of task sets for which our classified stuffing works better than stuffing. We experimented with three sets of tasks with set ratios 4:1, 1:1, and 1:4. The experiments were conducted on a P4 1.6 GHz PC with 512 MB RAM.

In the two-dimensional area of FPGA space versus execution time as illustrated in Fig. 2 each unit of placement is a *column-cycle*, where the space unit is a column and the time unit is a cycle. Table 1 shows the results of applying our method and the stuffing method to the same set of tasks, where the total column-cycles is the amount of column-cycles used by all tasks, the total fragmentation is the number of column-cycle not utilized, the total time is the total number of cycles for executing all tasks, the average fragmentation is the quotient of total fragmentation by total time, and the number of rejected tasks is the number of tasks whose deadlines could not be satisfied. For each task set, the data in Table 1 are the overall averages of the results obtained from experimenting with 50 different sets of randomly generated tasks.

From Table 1, we can observe that for both the methods and for all the sets of tasks the set ratio of 1:4 results in a shorter schedule and more compact placement as evidenced by the smaller fragmentation, which means that it is desirable to have hardware tasks synthesized into tasks with low SUR. The intuition here is that a greater number of high SUR tasks would require wider FPGA spaces resulting in larger fragmentation and thus longer schedules.

From Table 1, we can observe that for all the cases our method performs better than stuffing in terms of both lesser amount of fragmentation and lesser number of cycles. The total fragmentation is reduced by 5.5% to 23.3% and the total execution time is

Table 1. Experimental Results and Comparison

Task Set (S)			**Original Stuffing**				**Classified Stuffing (reduction)**				**S&P Time** (ms)
$\|S\|$	SR	TC	TF	TT	AF	TR	TF	TT	AF	TR	
50	4:1	1,711	505	105	4.8	3	477 (−5.5%)	104 (−1%)	4.6 (−4.2%)	3	3
	1:1	1,707	405	100	4	5	380 (−6.2%)	99 (−1%)	3.8 (−5%)	4	2
	1:4	1,550	418	93	4.5	2	392 (−6.2%)	92 (−1%)	4.3 (−4.4%)	2	2
200	4:1	6,780	1,237	381	3.25	3	1,119 (−9.5%)	376 (−1.3%)	2.97 (−8.6%)	3	5
	1:1	6,478	887	350	2.53	1	760 (−14.3%)	344 (−1.7%)	2.21 (−12.6%)	1	11
	1:4	6,133	823	330	2.49	0	739 (−10.2%)	326 (−1.2%)	2.27 (−8.8%)	0	12
500	4:1	17,145	2,246	922	2.43	5	2,007 (−10.6%)	911 (−1.2%)	2.20 (−9.5%)	5	47
	1:1	16,080	1,619	842	1.92	9	1,242 (−23.3%)	825 (−2.0%)	1.50 (−21.9%)	9	77
	1:4	15,077	1,341	782	1.71	5	1,185 (−11.6%)	775 (−0.9%)	1.53 (−10.5%)	5	98

SR: set ratio, TC: total column-cycles, TF: total fragmentation, TT: total time, AF: average fragmentation (TF/TT), TR: #tasks rejected, S&P: Scheduling and Placement

reduced by 0.9% to 2.0%. The reduction becomes more prominent in the case with set ratio 1:1 because there is an increased interference between the placements of the low SUR tasks and the high SUR tasks resulting in a larger fragmentation and longer schedules in the original stuffing method. These kind of interferences are diminished in classified stuffing. Comparing the task sets with different cardinalities, namely 50, 200, and 500, one can observe in Fig. 4 that the larger the task set is the better is the performance of our method. This shows that our method scales better than stuffing to more complex reconfigurable hardware systems.

As far as the performance of the scheduler and placer is concerned, the time taken by the classified stuffing method and the original stuffing method are almost the same. Thus, we have only one column for the S&P Time in milliseconds in Table 1. This is because the added classification technique does not also expend any significant amount of time, while it does improve the FPGA space utilization and total task execution time.

To support our choice of task classification using SUR value (see Section 5.1) and not considering the number of tasks of each type, we performed several experiments by using different classification ratios (CR) for a task set. The results are tabulated in Table 2, where we can observe that the best results are usually obtained when the classification

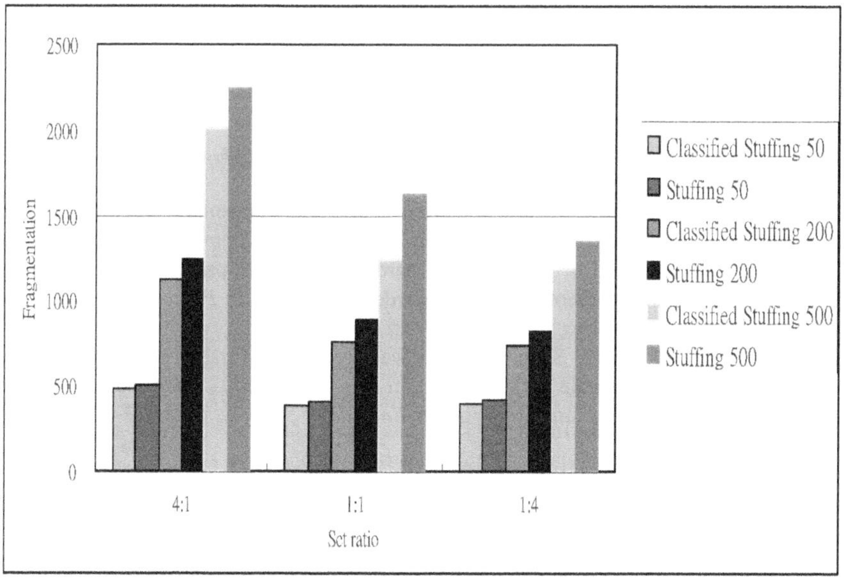

Fig. 4. Classified Stuffing vs. Original Stuffing

Table 2. Finding the Best Classification Ratio

Set Ratio	Scheduling Results	Classification Ratio		
		4:1	1:1	1:4
4:1	Total Fragmentation	**638**	667	667
	Total Time	**191**	192	192
1:1	Total Fragmentation	456	**435**	471
	Total Time	173	**171**	173
1:4	Total Fragmentation	458	438	**432**
	Ttotal Time	166	165	**165**

ratio is the same as the set ratio, that is, the threshold for classification can depend only on the SUR values.

7 Conclusions

A classified stuffing technique was proposed in this work showing significant benefits in both a shorter schedule and a more compact placement, but with little overhead. This was demonstrated through a large number of task sets. The current method focuses only on hardware scheduling. In the future, we will investigate hardware-software coscheduling.

case of the addition of new appliances; it is difficult to implement modules for TCP/IP communication.

To solve these issues, RFID (Radio Frequency IDentification) can be applied to the home network. RFID is an automatic identification technology that replaces traditional barcode technology. It reads and writes information without touching target objects using wireless communication technology. The barcode technology is developed and the price of a barcode is cheap, but they can be identified in close range without any obstruction between a scanner and a barcode because of the use of infrared rays. Moreover, it takes too long to identify a target; several of them cannot be identified at once. The amount of information stored is limited and the security is weak. RFID tags can be identified though there may be an obstruction between reader and tag because RFID uses radio frequency instead of infrared rays, and the tags can be identified at a maximum distance of 30 meters. Furthermore, several targets can be identified at the same time and many more kinds of information can be securely stored and communicated according to the change of time and conditions [2].

Various appliances can be incorporated into a home network because home networking is performed using radio frequency without assigning IP to each appliance if the RFID is applied to the home network. Moreover, a home network system need not be modified much when new appliances are added to the home network. More efficient home networking will be implemented because it is easy to implement and apply the RFID-based home network system.

Therefore, an intelligent agent for efficiently managing the RFID-based home network is stated here. The efficiency of home life at home will be maximized through the home network which has an intelligent agent that learns by itself.

2 Related Works

2.1 Home Network

A home network is a set of components that connects and integrates several appliances which perform calculation, management, monitoring and communication in order to process, manage, transmit and store information in a house. The home network is composed of association of equipments more than two which have the capability to share data and communicate. The structure of a home network is composed of a home gateway which connects the inside network with the outside network, middleware which controls the communication network and information devices in the house, and devices which include the functions for home networking. This is implemented through various networking protocol such as Ethernet, telephone lines, power lines and wireless. It also facilitates the sharing of functions and data, and the remote control between home appliances connected with the network. Furthermore, it offers Internet access, audio/video streaming, and home control applications and services [3].

2.2 RFID (Radio Frequency IDentification)

RFID is a means of storing and retrieving data through electromagnetic transmission to an RF compatible integrated circuit, and is now being seen as a radical means of

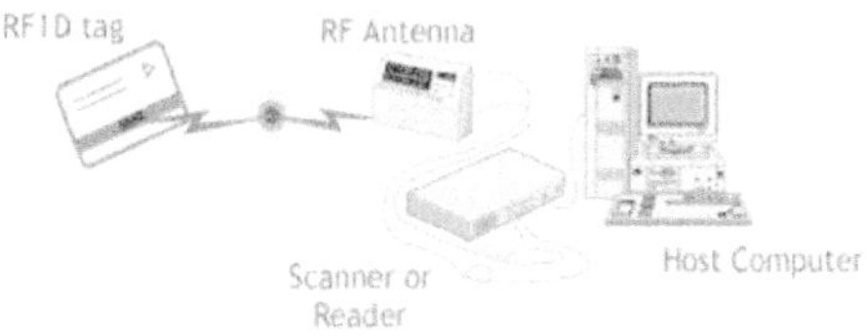

Fig. 1. Components of RFID System

enhancing data handling processes [4]. An RFID system has several basic componentsincluding a number of RFID readers, RFID tags, and the communication between them. The components of RFID system are represented in Figure 1.

The RFID reader can scan data emitted from RFID tags. RFID readers and tags use a defined radio frequency and protocol to transmit and receive data [5].

RFID tags are classified into three sub-classes, namely passive, semi-passive, and active. Passive RFID tags do not require batteries for operation and are, therefore, inherently robust, reliable, and low-cost. Their construction is relatively simple. A high performance passive RFID tag consists of a tiny integrated circuit chip, a printed antenna, and an adhesive label substrate for application to items. Active and semipassive tags require batteries for operation and, therefore, provide a greater range and throughput than passive (batteryless) tags. The simple addition of a battery to an RFID tag is a necessary but incomplete feature that classifies it as active [6][7].

2.3 RFID/USN (Ubiquitous Sensor Network)

RFID/USN manages information through the network by detecting real time information of objects which attach RFID. It binds itself to anything with not only its sensory information but also the information of its surroundings such as temperature, humidity, pollution and cracks. The ultimate purpose of the RFID/USN is to implement ubiquitous environments. RFID/USN focuses on the RFID which stores data, and sensing capability will be added to the RFID in the near future. Finally, networking capability will be added to the RFID [8][9].

The use of RFID/USN will increase step by step according to the development of sensor technology. RFID tags will become smaller in size and more intelligent while the price of them will decrease. Accordingly, the use of RFID will be expanded in the fields of logistics, distribution, circumstances, prevention of accidents, management of medical care and management of food. RFID will be developed into a smarter micro network sensor by adding sensing and communication facilities. In the future, the RFID/USN will be evolved into the level that can recognize and manage surroundings by multifunctional tags from the current level that recognizes the fixed code of objects, and will be developed into an intelligent USN which has a communication facility [9].

3 Architecture of RFID-Based Home Network

Home appliances with RFID sensors which are RFID tags with sensing facillity, RFID readers that read data from RFID tags and write data to RFID tags, and a home server which controls the home network are necessary for the construction of a RFID-based home network. Moreover, mobile devices which can communicate with a home server using wireless LAN are needed in order to control the home network while a user is moving. Figure 2 is the structure of this RFID-based home network.

RFID sensors[7] are attached to all appliances in order to sense the state of appliances in the RFID-based home network. RFID sensors periodically assess the state of home appliances and write the state on to RFID tags. RFID readers read the data from RFID tags and transfer the data to the home server. The intelligent agent of the home server collects and analyzes the data from RFID readers, determines the operations of home appliances in order to maintain an optimal environment for the house owner, and controls the home appliances to perform the operations by transferring them through RFID readers. Furthermore, the agent provides the service that the house owner can directly control and monitor the home network.

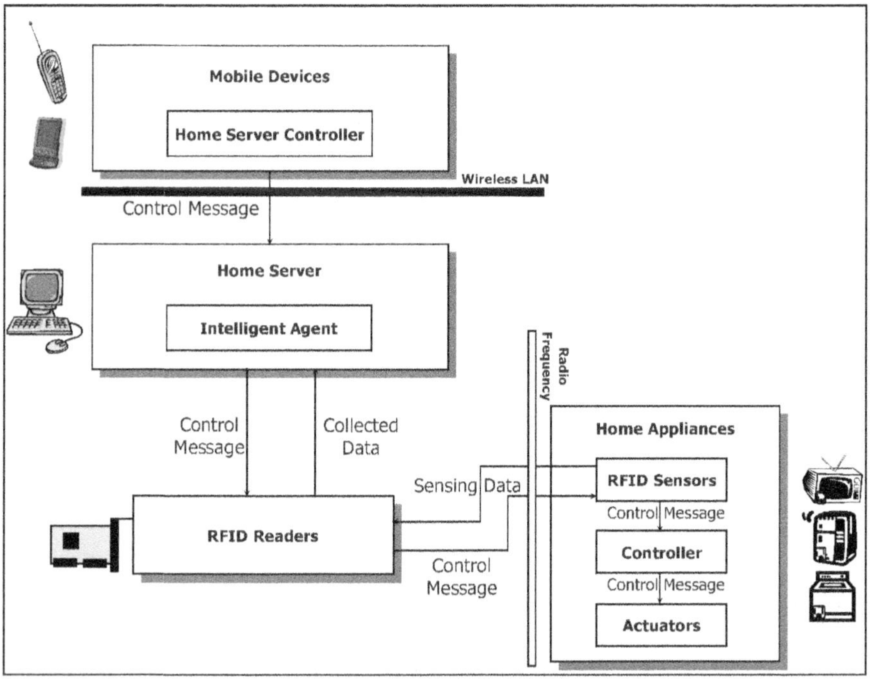

Fig. 2. Architecture of RFID-based Home Network

The following is the process of RFID-based home networking.

① RFID sensors periodically sense the state of home appliances. They sense the current state of appliances, store the state in tags, and transfer the state to RFID readers.
② RFID readers read the state of home appliances from RFID sensors. Not only do RFID readers receive the data transferred from RFID sensors, but also they periodically check the RFID sensors and read data about the state of home appliances.

③ The intelligent agent of the home server collects data from RFID readers, analyzes the data, and determines the operations of home appliances in order to provide an optimal environment to the user of home network.
④ The intelligent agent of the home server sends control messages to the RFID readers after it determines the operations.
⑤ RFID readers transfer the control messages received from the home server to home appliances.
⑥ Home appliances perform operations according to the control messages.

4 Intelligent Agent for RFID-Based Home Networking

An intelligent agent which autonomously controls RFID-based home networking is proposed in this section.

The user of a home network must periodically monitor the environment of his/her home network and manage the home network to maintain an optimal home environment for him/her. This is a labor intensive process on the part of the user. Accordingly, an agent that can autonomously control the home network instead of the user is necessary in order to save the effort and the time of the user. This agent must continuously collect the data from RFID sensors, analyze the collected data, and find out the inclinations of the user based on the analyzed information. Moreover, it must continuously monitor and control the home network to provide an optimal home environment according to the desires of the user.

4.1 Structure

The intelligent agent collects data from RFID sensors, analyzes the data, and controls the home network to maintain the most comfortable home environment based on the data. Figure 3 represents the intelligent agent for RFID-based home networking. This agent consists of six modules: the Agent Manager, the Data Collector, the Execution Controller, the Data Storage, the Data Queue and the User Interface.

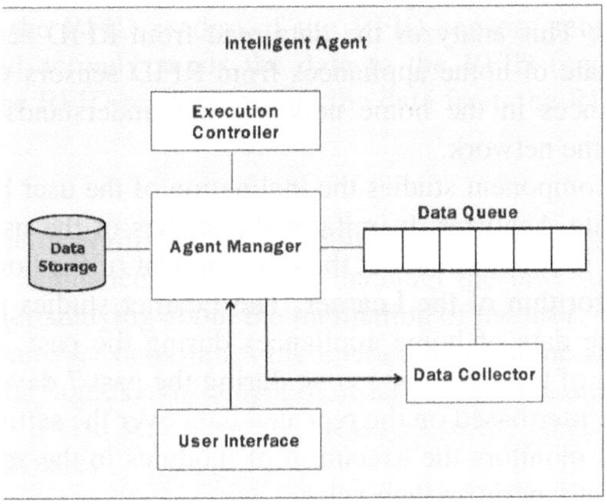

Fig. 3. Intelligent Agent

Data Storage
The information such as the previous operations and the inclination of the user is necessary in order to autonomously maintain the home environments. For this, the storage which stores the information is necessary.

The Data Storage is the database of the agent. Each module of the agent gets the data for operations from the Data Storage, performs its operations and stores the data which must be preserved in the Data Storage according to the result of the operations. The information about the wishes of the user, which is received by analyzing the data of the home network, is stored in the Data Storage and it is updated continuously.

Data Queue
The data which is periodically read from RFID sensors should be temporarily stored in order to analyze the current home environments.

The Data Queue is temporary storage. The data which is read from the RFID sensors is held here for a short time before it is processed. RFID sensors which are attached to home appliances periodically transfer the data to the RFID readers simultaneously and the Data Collector gathers the data which is transferred from several RFID sensors at a time. Therefore, it is necessary to temporarily store the data so that the Execution Controller can analyze the data and perform proper operations.

User Interface
It should be easy and convenient that the user directly controls the home network.

The User Interface is a GUI (Graphical User Interface). The intelligent agent autonomously maintains the optimal home network environment according to the desires of the user, but the user can control the home network using this interface if he or she wants. Moreover, the user can monitor the home network using this interface.

4.2 Collaborations

The modules of the intelligent agent collaborate with each other as figure 5 in order to control the home network. This collaboration shows that the agent autonomously controls the home network. The user can perform these tasks through the User Interface if he or she wants to directly control the home network.

* The Data Collector collects the data that the RFID sensors attached to home appliances such as an indoor thermometer, refrigerator, TV, lighting and water heater, sense the states of the appliances and send to the RFID readers, and stores the collected data in the Data Queue. For example, the Data Collector gathers the data such as the current indoor temperature, the current temperature of refrigerator and the on/off state of the TV, and stores the data in the Data Queue.
* The Agent Manager reads the collected data from the Data Queue, analyzes the data, learns the wishes of the user of the home network and stores the results in Data Storage. For example, the Agent Manager reads the data about the indoor temperature, air conditioner and water heater, and analyzes the data. As a result of the analysis, the Agent Manager may find out that the user of the home network turned on the air conditioner if the indoor temperature was higher than 25°C and turned on the water heater if the indoor temperature was lower than 20°C. The Agent Manager learns that the user prefers indoor temperature between 20°C and 25°C, and stores the result in the Data Storage.

* The Execution Controller determines the operations of home appliances according to the current circumstances based on the desires of the user. For example, the Execution Controller may determine that the air conditioner should be turned on in order to decrease the indoor temperature if the current indoor temperature is higher than 25°C because the user prefers an indoor temperature between 20°C and 25°C.
* The Execution Controller stores the determination in the Data Storage and transfers it to the home appliances through RFID readers to perform the operations. For example, the Execution Controller stores the indoor temperature and the operation of the air conditioner in the Data Storage if it determines that the air conditioner should be turned on, and transfers the information to the RFID sensor attached to the air conditioner. Then the air conditioner is turned on through its controller.

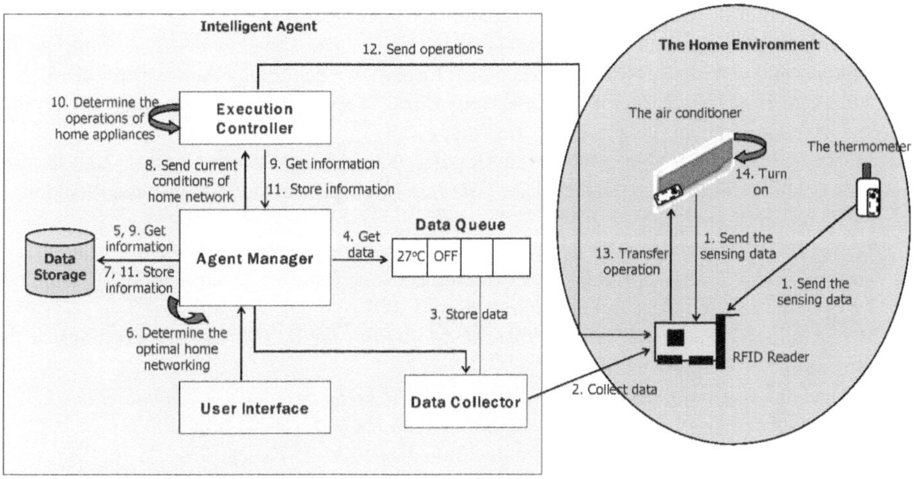

Fig. 5. Collaborations of Modules in the Intelligent Agent

5 Conclusion and Future Work

An intelligent agent for the efficient management of the home network is proposed in this paper. The agent consists of six modules: the Agent Manager, the Data Collector, the Execution Controller, the Data Storage, the Data Queue and the User Interface.

The Agent Manager manages the tasks of the modules in the agent, and the Data Collector collects the data from the home appliances through the RFID readers. The Execution Controller determines the operations of the home appliances according to the conditions of the home network and transfers them to the home appliances through the RFID readers. Moreover, the Data Storage keeps the data which is necessary for the operations of the agent, and the Data Queue temporarily stores the data which is collected from the home appliances. Lastly, the User Interface provides the graphical user interface that the user of the home network can directly control and monitor the home network.

The proposed intelligent agent autonomously learns the circumstances of the home network by analyzing the data about the states of home appliances, and provides the best suited environment for the user. Therefore, the user can live in the most comfortable home environment without effort if he or she performs home networking through the agent.

The proposed intelligent agent will be developed in the near future. Furthermore, a mobile intelligent agent which can control home network that home appliances communicate with each other through RFID will be studied.

References

[1] Changhwan Kim, *The Technical Trend of Wireless Home Networking*, Electronics Information Center of Korea Electronics Technology Institute, 2004.

[2] Junghwan Kim, Cheonkyo Park and Yonggyun Kim, *The Development Direction and Introduction Guideline of RFID*, Institute of Information Technology Assessment, 2004.

[3] Yuncheol Lee, *Recent Technical Trend and Market View of Home Networking*, Electronics and Telecommunications Research Institute, 2003.

[4] Mario Chiesa, Ryan Genz, Franziska Heubler, Kim Mingo, Chris Noessel, Natasha Sopieva, Dave Slocombe, Jason Tester, *RFID*, http://people.interaction-ivrea.it/c.noessel/RFID/research.html, 2002.

[5] Lionel M. Ni, Yunhao Liu, Yiu Cho Lau and Abhishek P. Patil, *LANDMARC: Indoor Location Sensing Using Active RFID*, Proceedings of the First IEEE International Conference on Pervasive Computing and Communications, 2003.

[6] Bridgelall, R., *Bluetooth/802.11 Protocol Adaptation for RFID Tags*, Proceedings of the 4th European Wireless Conference, 2002.

[7] Bridgelall, R., *Enabling Mobile Commerce through Pervasive Communications with Ubiquitous RF Tags*, 2003 Wireless Communications and Networking, 2003.

[8] Ministry of Information and Communication Republic of Korea, *The Basic Plan of U-Sensor Network Construction*, 2004.

[9] Seunghwa Yu, *The Propulsive Direction of RFID/USN Standardization*, The Journal of TTA, No. 94, 2004, pp12-18.

An Intelligent Adaptation System Based on a Self- growing Engine

Jehwan Oh, Seunghwa Lee, and Eunseok Lee

School of Information and Communication Engineering, Sungkyunkwan University,
300 Chunchun jangahn Suwon, 440-746, Korea
{hide7674, jbmania, eslee}@selab.skku.ac.kr

Abstract. In this paper, a self-growing engine based adaptation system, which automatically decides the more efficiency plan about the assigning of jobs, in a mobile, grid computing environment, is proposed. Recently, research relating to grid computing has become an important issue, achieving certain goals by sharing the idle resources of computing devices, and overcoming various constraints of the mobile computing environment. In this domain, most existing research assigns work only by considering the status of resources. Hence the situation of assigning work to a peer having relatively low work efficiency, is possible. The proposed system considers various contexts and selects the most suitable peer. In addition, the system stores the history of the work result, and if the same request occurs in the future, a peer is selected by analyzing the history. In this paper, a prototype used to evaluate the proposed system is implemented, and the effectiveness of the system is confirmed through two experiments.

1 Introduction

In modern society, the handheld device is quickly becoming widespread, its usage and explosive growth can be attributed to the rapid development of wireless network technologies. The computing power of these handheld devices is continually increasing, relative to the growth of associated technologies. However, handheld devices have limited capacity because of a potable feature. For this reason, applications for handheld devices to some extent, are limited, and developers must create applications offering limited services. The expectations of users are increasing, demanding the same the quality of service as the desktop computer. Grid computing technologies, creating distributed processing, operating over a number of low capacity computers, can perform large amounts of work, which is difficult to process in an individual computing device. This technology overcomes the various constraints of handheld devices, and creates large scale applications over a wireless environment.

In grid computing, the allocation of work to the various devices is a significant problem. Most existing research adopts a method of allocating the work only by considering the resource status of the participating peers. Therefore, problems could arise of assigning work to peers, which have relatively low work efficiency. For instance, the processing time of a peer which has the byte code for work, even if the peer has insufficient resources, may still be faster than the processing time of a peer which has sufficient resources, but does not have the byte code.

L.T. Yang et al. (Eds.): EUC 2005, LNCS 3824, pp. 509 – 517, 2005.

To cope with this problem, the proposed system selects the most suitable peer through considering current variable context (resource usage pattern, available resource, network bandwidth, existence of the byte code), therefore more efficient distribution of work is made possible. In addition, the proposed system monitors the processing results for work and stores these values in the history DB. Then, the system computes the average values for each factor and retrieves the more significant context factor. The system assigns the weight value to the selected factor, selects the peer with the most similar context values, and average values among the current participating peers, assigning the work to the selected peer. Next, the results better than average values are stored in the history DB. The system has self learning feature, selecting the more suitable host according to the time passed.

In this paper, a prototype is implemented. In order to evaluate the proposed system, the effectiveness of the system is confirmed through two experiments.

The paper is organized as follows: Section 2 introduces related work. Section 3 describes the comprehensive structure and the behavior process of the proposed system. In Section 4, details of the operational process and algorithm are presented. System evaluation through the implementation of a prototype is described in Section 5. Finally, Section 6 concludes the paper and identifies future work.

2 Related Work

Research overcoming the various constraints has been studied in various laboratories. Firstly, research relating to adaptation, which is adjusting the quality of service, and parameters of the application or system components, has been actively processed [1][2][3][4]. However, this method focuses on the quality of service offered in the past.

Grid computing is becoming an important issue, achieving various goals by sharing idle resources of diverse computing devices. The system can perform large amounts of work, which is difficult to process for individual computing devices. Representative studies include Globus [7] and Condor [8]. However, these studies focus on the wired environment and therefore are not suitable for the mobile environment. Studies dealing with the problems of the mobile environment include the following; Xiaohui Gu *et al.* [6] proposes the Adaptive offloading System, performing distributed processing in a surrogate computer, having relatively rich memory to overcome the limited memory available in mobile devices. Another study, Junseok Hwang *et al.*[10]proposes middleware based on a mobile proxy structure that can execute jobs submitted to mobile devices, in-effect making a grid consisting of mobile devices. However, these systems only consider the available resources of each peer when allocating the jobs. Thus, the possibility of work being assigned to a peer with relatively low work efficiency, exists.

In this paper, an intelligent system is proposed, this system is based on resource usage patterns, existence of the byte code, as well as available resources, and has a self learning feature.

In the subsequent section, the proposed system applying these concepts, is described in detail.

3 Proposed System

3.1 System Framework

This paper proposes the intelligent adaptation system, which continually improves the method of allocating jobs, by using a self growing engine, in order to efficiently allocate jobs. As presented in Fig. 1, the central server monitors/stores the context information of peers. If peer A requests services from the server, then the server selects the peers which can perform the requested services according to various computation processing, allocating the jobs to selected peers. In addition, the system stores the history of the work result, and if the identical request is issued in the future, it selects the most suitable peer by analyzing the history.

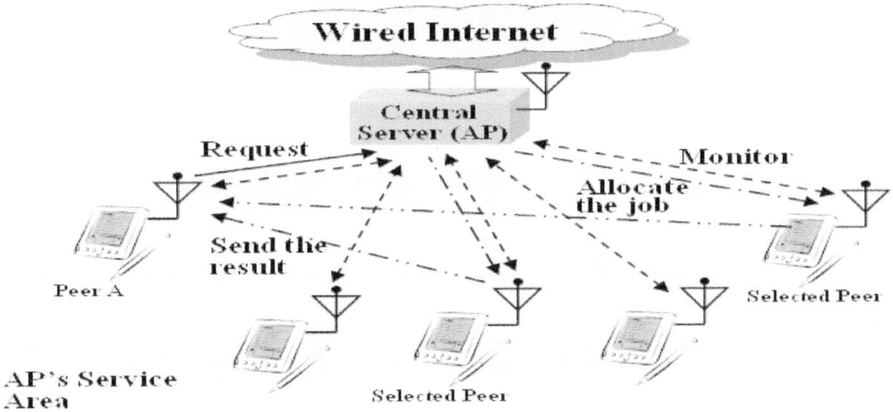

Fig. 1. Overall Architecture of Proposed System

3.2 System Components

As presented in Fig.2 the component of the proposed system is composed of two parts; the Client Module (CM), which is embedded in each peer, and the Server Module (SM), which is embedded in the central server. The SM is located at or close to a wireless network access point. The role of each principal component is as follows.

- *Context Observer (CO):* gathers the variety context information including resource usage pattern and transmits this information to the *SM*
- *Task Division Agent (TDA):* divides the self-executing jobs , entrusted depending on gathered context
- *Integration Agent (IA)*: integrates the received job results from the external agent, and delivers the integrated results to the application
- *Task Executor (TE)*: executes the jobs required from an external peer
- *Communicator (client)*: performs the interaction with the *SM* or peers
- *Communicator (sever)*: performs the interaction with the *CM* in each peer

- *Analysis Agent (AA):* selects the job history DB corresponding to the requested job from the client from the selected job history DB, and computes the average value of a client's condition values when a client performs the each job. In addition, the *AA* stores the context information received from each client, in the Client Information DB. The AA then analyzes the results of the executed job by the selected peer, and updates the job history DB with the result.
- *Decision Agent (DA):* decides peers to be allocated based on various computations and on the peer's condition analyzed by the *AA*
- *Client Information DB*: The location where various context information (resource usage pattern, available resource, network bandwidth, existence of the byte code) of each participating peer is stored. This information is periodically updated.
- *Job history DB*: The location where the executed result each service is stored.

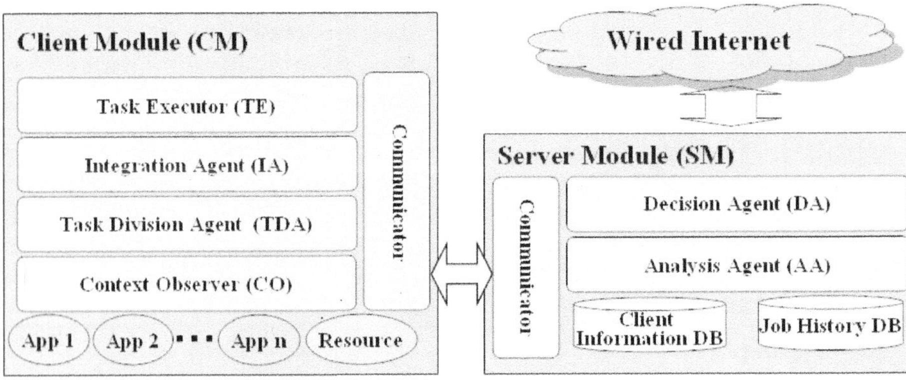

Fig. 2. Components of the Proposed System

3.3 Overall System Behavior

A sequence diagram corresponding to the overall system behavior is presented in Fig.3.

Firstly, when a user connects to the server, the CO continually gathers the current resource status including the resource usage pattern, and transmits this information to the SM. Then, the AA receives this information, and computes the score for this context, storing this score value in the Client Information DB.

Next, when a user executes the application, the TDA decides the jobs to be executed at the current resource status. The jobs, which cannot be executed, are entrusted to the AA via a communicator. The AA retrieves the suitable condition of the peer to execute the Jobs in the Job History DB. The DA finds the peer based-on the retrieved condition of peer AA in Client Information DB. The selected peer is allocated to the jobs. The TE of the selected peer performs the jobs, and then transmits the executed results to the CM requesting the jobs. The IA of the CM receives and integrates the results. Finally, the IA transmits the integrated result to the application.

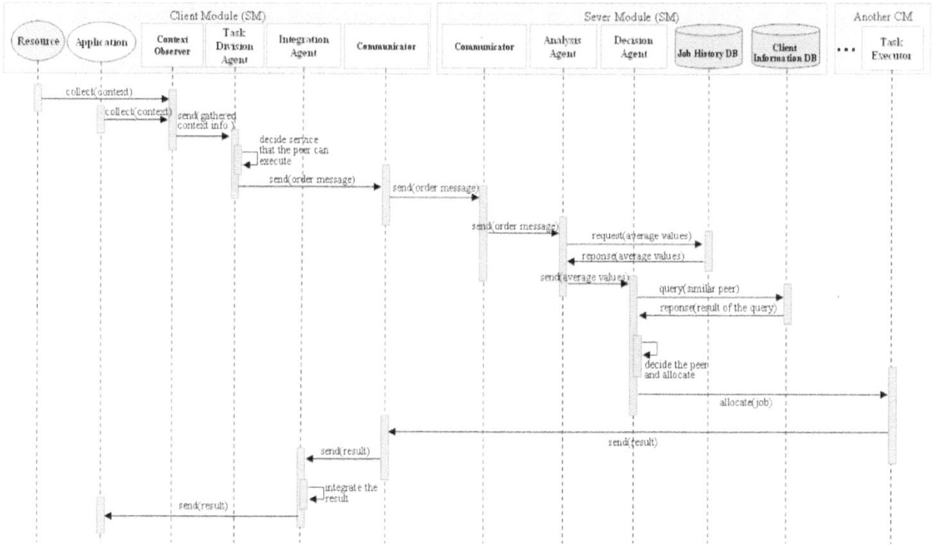

Fig. 3. Sequence Diagram of Overall System Behavior

3.4 Selection Phase of the Peer Via Computation

In the case of the server allocating the requested jobs from the client only by considering the resource status of each participating peer, the case of assigning work to a peer which has a relatively low work efficiency, could exist. For instance, the processing time of a peer which has the byte code for the work may have insufficient resources, but achieves results faster than the processing time of a peer having sufficient resources, but does not have the byte code. To cope with these problems, the proposed system selects the most suitable peer through considering more relevant current context as follows:

- The current available (idle) resources of each participating peers such as CPU, RAM, Battery.
- The network bandwidth of each participating peer
- The changing probability of resources computed via the resource usage pattern analysis of each participating peer
- The existence of the byte code, which will be the completed job

This information is collected in the CM, and periodically stored in the Client Information DB. Then each factor is computed to a relative score using the formulas presented in Table 1.

The SM can obtain the final score of each device using a formula as follows. Then, the SM selects the device, which obtained the highest final score, allocating the jobs to the selected device. The each formula is differently created to become range of values from 0.01 to 1.00.

$$CPU_{level} \cdot w_1 + RAM_{level} \cdot w_2 + \cdots + probability \cdot w_n = Final\,Score \quad (1)$$

Table 1. The Sample Formulas to Compute the Each Factor

Context type	Formula	Example	Score
Idle resource	$\frac{CPU_{availableRate} \times CPU_{clock}}{10000} = CPU_{level}$	$1 - \frac{20 \times 400}{10000} = 0.2$	2
	$\frac{RAM_{freeSpace}}{RAM_{size}} = RAM_{level}$	$\frac{20}{64} = 0.312$	4
	:	:	:
The Changing Probability of Resource	$\frac{(x_1 - m)^2 + (x_2 - m)^2 + \cdots + (x_n - m)^2}{n}$	$1 - \frac{3.26}{3} = 0.92$	10
:	:	:	:

```
(REQUEST
   :sender(agent-identifier :name CM1@HIDE:1099/)
   :receiver (set(agent-identifier :name SM@selab:1099/))
   :context "(action translator)and
            (action image_compression)
      ...
)
```

```
(INFORM
   :sender(agent-identifier :name CM1@HIDE:1099/)
   :receiver (set(agent-identifier :name SM@selab:1099/))
   :context "(service_name(translator)),(entrusted_device(tester76)),
            (execution_time(3.5)),
      ...
)
```

Fig. 4. Example of ACL message, which is requesting the jobs from the CM to the SM, informing the completion of work from the CM to the SM

3.5 Learning Phase Via Self Growing Engine

The selecting phase of the specific peer is described via computation, in the previous section, when the CM requests the jobs from the SM. In this section, the self learning of the most suitable peer using the history for the job result, is introduced.

When the peer requests a job, the AA retrieves the average value of the performed results in the Job History DB. The AA transmits the retrieving result to the DA. The DA assigns the weight to the element having the highest value among the average values, and finds the peer, which is similar to this value in the Client Information DB. If a similar peer exists, the SM allocates the jobs to the similar peer. However, if a similar peer does not exist, the DA selects the most suitable peer via computation, described in the previous section, and the selected peer is allocated the jobs. The TE of the selected CM performs the jobs, then transmits the executed results to the CM requesting the jobs. The CM receiving the result informs the time for executing work and the condition of the device performing the jobs to the AA. The AA analyzes the received information from the CM. If the processing time is less than the average time, the AA stores this information in the job history DB. The AA re-computes the average value in the job history DB.

Table 2 presents sample result data for the translator service in the Job history DB. The average values mean that the condition is the suitable condition of the peer executing the translator service.

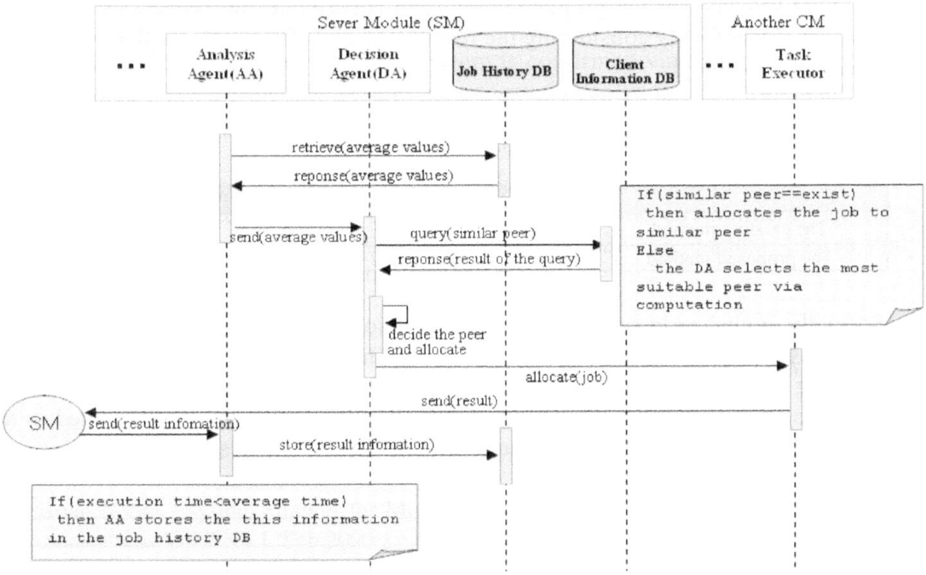

Fig. 5. Sequence Diagram of Learning Phase

Table 2. Sample of the Result Data for the Translator Service in the Job history DB

Device name	Condition	Execution time	Date
Tester 34	7, 5, 4, 1, 4, 8	3.23	20050704
Tester 21	4, 4, 5, 2, 3, 4	3.74	20050621
Tester 28	3, 9, 4, 1, 4, 7	3.59	20050520
:	:	:	:
Average value	**4.7, 7.3, 6.1, 1.4, 7.2, 3.4**	**3.82**	

4 System Evaluation

Each prototype module for the system evaluation was implemented mainly using Embedded Visual C++. In this experiment, the CM and SM are both implemented on the desktop PC, connected by wired Internet. The CM, is tested using a PDA simulator offered by the Embedded Visual Studio. The executed application is 'Remote Video Medical Treatment' for the E-healthcare scenario, studied in the laboratory. The divided jobs are 'Translator', 'Image Converter', and 'Video Converter' respectively.

Dynamically Selecting Distribution Strategies for Web Documents According to Access Pattern*

Wenyu Qu[1], Di Wu[2], Keqiu Li[3], and Hong Shen[1]

[1] Graduate School of Information Science,
Japan Advanced Institute of Science and Technology,
1-1, Asahidai, Nomi, Ishikawa, 923-1292, Japan
[2] Department of Computer Science and Engineering,
Dalian University of Technology,
No 2, Linggong Road, Ganjingzi District, Dalian, 116024, China
[3] College of Computer Science and Technology,
Dalian Maritime University,
No 1, Linghai Road, Dalian, 116026, China
keqiu_01@163.com

Abstract. Web caching and replication are efficient techniques for reducing web traffic, user access latency, and server load. In this paper we present a group-based method for dynamically selecting distribution strategies for web documents according to access patterns. The documents are divided into groups according to access patterns and the documents in each group are assigned to the same distribution strategy. Our group-based model combines performance metrics with the different weights assigned to each of them. We use both trace data and statistical data to simulate our methods. The experimental results show that our group-based method for document distribution strategy selection can improve several performance metrics, while keeping others almost the same.

Keywords: Web caching and replication, distribution strategy, cache replacement algorithm, simulation, trace data, autonomous system (AS).

1 Introduction

In recent years, the effective distribution and maintenance of stored information has become a major concern for Internet users, as the Internet becomes increasingly congested and popular web sites suffer from overloaded conditions caused by large numbers of simultaneous accesses. When users retrieve web documents from the Internet, they often experience considerable latency.

Web caching and replication are two important approaches for enhancing the efficient delivery of web contents, reducing latencies experienced by users. A user's request for a document is directed to a nearby copy, not to the original server, thus reducing access time, average server load, and overall network traffic. Caching [4] was originally applied to distributed file systems. Although

* The preliminary version of this paper appeared in [8]. Corresponding author: K. Li.

L.T. Yang et al. (Eds.): EUC 2005, LNCS 3824, pp. 518–527, 2005.

it has been well studied, its application on the Internet gave rise to new problems, such as where to place a cache, how to make sure that cached contents are valid, how to solve replacement problems, how to handle dynamic web documents, etc. Replication was commonly applied to distributed file systems to increase availability and fault tolerance [9]. Both techniques have complementary roles in the web environment. Caching attempts to store the most commonly accessed objects as close to the clients as possible, while replication distributes a site's contents across multiple replica servers. Caching directly targets minimizing download delays, by assuming that retrieving the required object from the cache incurs less latency than getting it from the web server. Replication, on the other hand, accounts for improved end-to-end responsiveness by allowing clients to perform downloads from their closest replica server.

Although web caching and replication can enhance the delivery efficiency of web contents and reduce response time, they also bring some problems, such as maintaining consistency of documents, propagating content updates to replica servers and caches, and so on. There are many ways to distribute copies of a web document across multiple servers. One has to decide how many copies are needed, where and when to create them, and how to keep them consistent. A good distribution strategy would be an algorithm that makes these decisions. We argue that there is no distribution strategy that is optimal for all performance metrics; in most cases, we have to pay the cost of making some performance metrics worse if we hope to make one or more of the others better. In this paper we present a group-based method for dynamically selecting distribution strategies for web documents according to access patterns. We divide the documents into groups according to access patterns and assign the same distribution strategy to the documents in each group. Further, we present a group-based model that combines performance metrics with the different weights assigned to each of them. Therefore, our method can generate a family of strategy arrangements that can be adapted to different network characteristics. To realize our method, we use a system model [8] in which documents can be placed on multiple Internet hosts . Clients are grouped based on the autonomous systems (ASs) that host them. ASs are used to achieve efficient world-wide routing of IP Packets [3]. In this model, each AS groups a set of clients that are relatively close to each other in a network-topological sense. In this paper, we consider a more general system model, in which an intermediate server is configured either as a replica server, or a cache, or neither. Finally, we use both trace data and statistical data to simulate our methods. The experimental results show that our group-based method for document distribution strategy selection can outperform the global strategy and improve several performance metrics compared to the document-based method, while keeping the others almost the same.

The rest of the paper is organized as follows. Section 2 focuses on our group-based method for dynamically selecting distribution strategies for web documents according to access patterns. The simulation experiments are described in Section 3. Finally, we conclude our paper in Section 4.

2 Selection of Document Distribution Strategy

In this section, we first briefly outline the distribution strategies used in this paper, and then we present a group-based method for dynamically selecting distribution strategies for web documents according to access patterns.

2.1 Distribution Strategies

We considered the following document distribution strategies.

1. No Replication (*NoRepl*): This is a basic strategy that does not use any replication at all. All clients connect to the primary server directly.
2. Verification (CV): When a cache hit occurs, the cache systematically checks the copy's consistency by sending an If-Modified-Since request to the primary server before sending the document to the client. After the primary server revalidates the request, the intermediate decides how to get the document for the client.
3. Limited verification (CLV): When a copy is created, it is given a time-to-live (TTL) that is proportional to the time elapsed since its last modification. Before the expiration of the TTL, the cache manages requests without any consistency checks and sends the copies directly to the client. After the TTL expires, the copies are removed from the cache. In our experiments, we used the following formula to determine the TTL. $\alpha = 0.2$ is the default in the Squid cache [3].

$$T_r = (1 + \alpha)T_c - T_l \tag{1}$$

where T_r is the expiration time, T_c is the cached time, and T_l is the last modified time. α is a parameter which can be selected by the user.
4. Delayed verification (CDV): This policy is almost identical to the CLV strategy, in that a copy is created, it is also given a TTL. However, when the TTL expires, the copies are not removed from the cache immediately; the cache sends an If-Modified-Since request to the primary server before sending the copies to the client. After the primary server revalidates the request, the intermediate decides how to fetch the document for the client.

Ideally, we would have as many replica servers as ASs, so every client could fetch the needed document from the replica server; this, in turn, would produce good results on some performance metrics such as hit ratio and byte hit ratio. However, on the other hand, it also would make other performance metrics, such as consumed bandwidth and server load, worse.
5. $SU50$ (Server Update): The primary server maintains copies at the 50 most relevant intermediate servers.
6. $SU50 + CLV$: The primary server maintains copies at the 50 most relevant intermediate servers; the other intermediate servers follow the CLV strategy.

2.2 A Group-Based Method for Document Distribution Selection

First we introduce a method to group the documents into P groups according to their access patterns. The main factors that influence the access patterns are web resource and user behavior. According to [7], we group the documents according to the value of v_d, which is defined as follows:

$$v_d = (c_d + f_d/u_d)s_d \tag{2}$$

where c_d denotes the cost of fetching document d from the server, f_d denotes the access frequency of document d, u_d denotes the update frequency of document d, and s_d denotes the size of document d. We can see that when P is equal to the number of the documents, i.e., when there is only one document in each group, then our method is the same as the document-based method in [11]. Therefore, from this point of view the method proposed in [11] can be viewed as a special case of our method. For the case of $P = 1$, our method can be considered a global strategy method, since all the documents are assigned to the same strategy.

Now we present our group-based model considering the total effect of the performance metrics from a general point of view, e.g. we define the total function for each performance metric according to its characteristics. The existing method [11] defines the total function for each performance metric by summing the performance metrics of each document. We argue that this method does not always work well for some performance metrics such as total hit ratio.

Let $S = \{s_j, j = 1, 2, \cdots, |S|\}$ be the set of distribution strategies, $G = \{G_j, j = 1, 2, \cdots, |G|\}$ be the set of groups, $M = \{m_j, j = 1, 2, \cdots, |M|\}$ be the set of performance metrics such as total turnaround time, hit ratio, total consumed bandwidth, etc. A pair arrangement $(strategy, group)$ means that a strategy is assigned to the documents in a group. We denote the set of all the possible arrangements as A. We can define a function f_k for each metric m_k on a pair $a \in A$ by $R_{ka} = \sum_{j=1}^{|G|} r_{kaj} = \sum_{j=1}^{|G|} f_k(a, G_j)$, where R_{ka} is the aggregated performance result in metric m_k and r_{kaj} is the performance result in metric m_k for G_j .

Let $w = \{w_1, w_2, \cdots, w_{|M|}\}$ be the weight vector which satisfies:

$$\sum_{k=1}^{M} w_k = 1, w_k \geq 0, k = 1, 2, \cdots, |M| \tag{3}$$

We can get the following general model $R_a^* = \min_k w_k R_{ka}$. We refer to R_a^* as the total cost function for different weight vector w for an arrangement a .

Since there are a total of $|S|^{|G|}$ different arrangements, it is not computationally feasible to achieve the optimal arrangements by the brute-force assignment method. The following result shows that it requires at most$|G||S|$ computations to obtain an optimal strategy arrangement for the documents in each group.

$$R_a^* = \min_{a \in A} \sum_k w_k R_{ka} = \min_{a \in A} \sum_{k=1}^{|M|} w_k (\sum_{j=1}^{|G|} r_{kaj}) = \min_{a \in A} \sum_{k=1}^{|M|} \sum_{j=1}^{|G|} w_k r_{kaj}$$

$$= \min_{a \in A} \sum_{j=1}^{|G|} \sum_{k=1}^{|M|} w_k r_{kaj} \geq \min_{a \in A} \sum_{j=1}^{|G|} (\min_j \sum_{k=1}^{|M|} w_k R_{kaj})$$

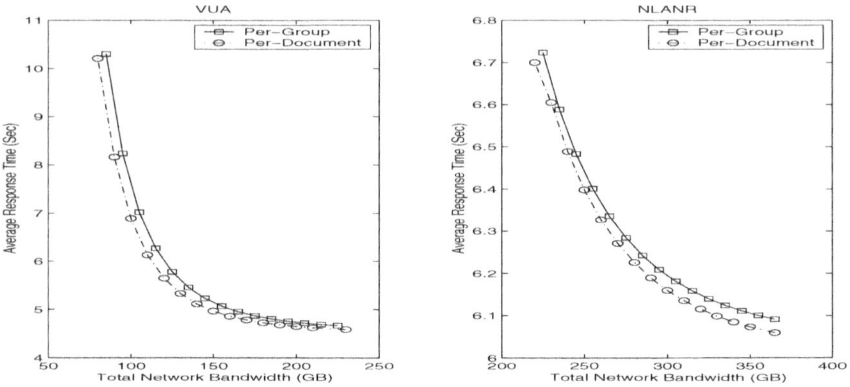

Fig. 1. Different Arrangements

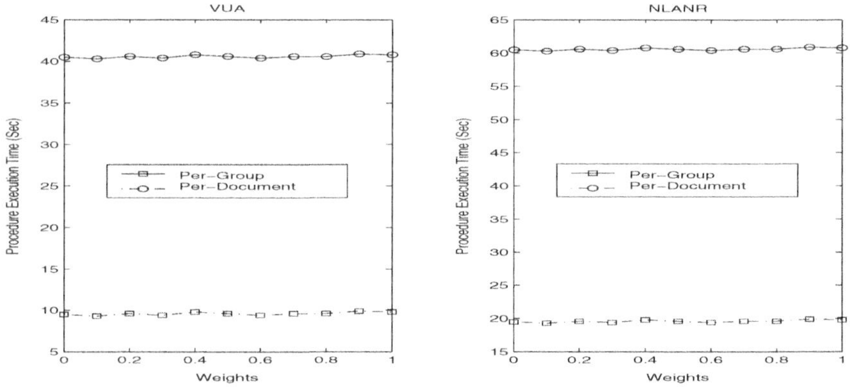

Fig. 2. Procedure Execution Time

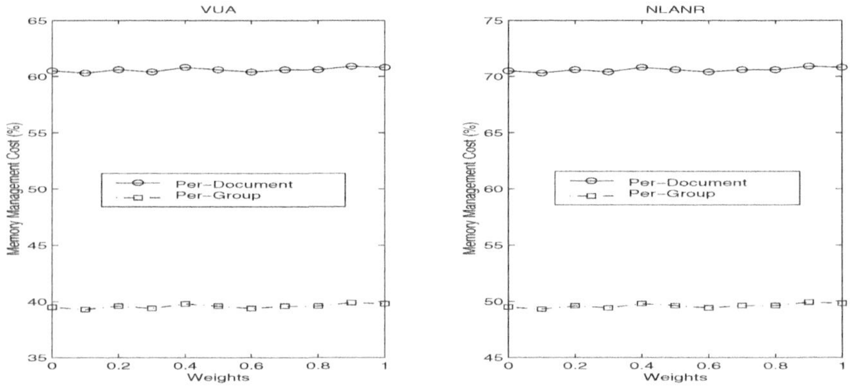

Fig. 3. Memory Management Cost

3.2 Simulation with Statistical Data

In this section we use statistical data to simulate our methods. The parameters shown in Table 3 are chosen from the open literature and are considered to be reasonable [1, 2, 5, 6]. We have conducted experiments for many topologies

Table 3. Parameters Used in Simulation

Parameter	Value
Number of Nodes	200
Number of Web Objects	5000
Number of Requests	500000
Number of Updates	10000
Web Object Size Distribution	Pareto Distribution $p(x) = \frac{ab^a}{a-1}$ $(a = 1.1, b = 8596)$
Web Object Access Frequency	Zipf-Like Distribution $\frac{1}{i^\alpha}$ $(i = 0.7)$
Delay of Links	Exponential Distribution $p(x) = \theta^{-1}e^{-x/\theta}$ $(\theta = 0.06\ Sec)$
Average Request Rate Per Node	$U(1, 9)$ requests per second

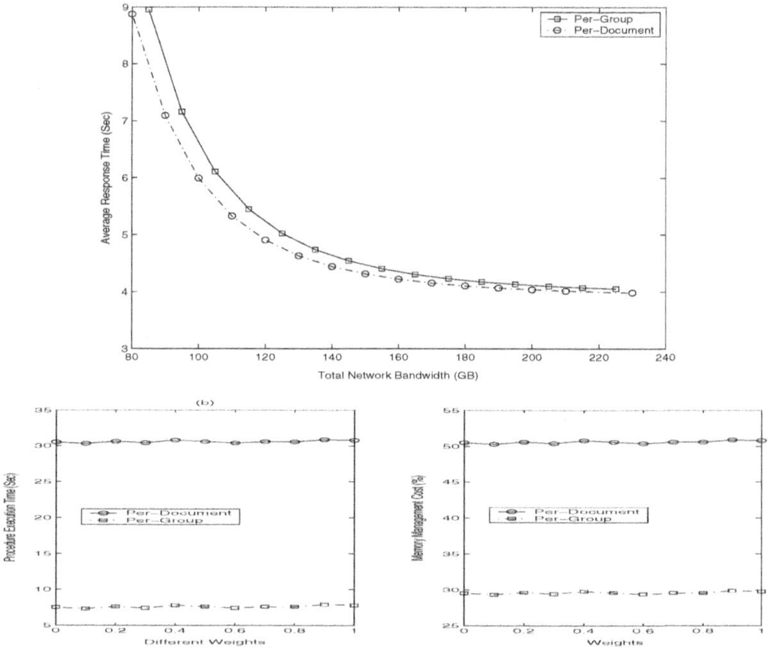

Fig. 4. Performance Results for Per-Group Strategy

with different parameters and the performance of our results was found to be insensitive to topology changes. Here, we list only the experimental results for one topology, due to space limitations.

From Figure 4 we can see that the results of our method approximate those of the existing method when we group the documents into 89 groups. However, our method can improve both the procedure execution time and the memory management cost.

4 Concluding Remarks

Since web caching and replication are efficient ways to reduce web traffic and latency for users, more and more researchers have been paying a lot of attention to this topic. In this paper, we presented a method for dynamically selecting web replication strategies according to the access patterns. We also used both web trace and statistical data to simulate our method. However, we can see that there will be performance problems when more strategies are considered. In the future, this work should be extended to the replication of other types of objects, since we considered only static objects in this paper. The application of our method to dynamical web documents also should be studied. Such studies should lead to a more general solution to web caching and replication problems.

References

1. Aggarwal, C., Wolf, J. L. and Yu, P. S. (1999) *Caching on the World Wide Web.* IEEE Transaction on Knowledge and Data Engineering, 35, 94-107.
2. Barford, P. and Crovella, M. (1998) *Generating representative web workloads for network and server performance evaluation.* Proc. of ACM SIGMETRICS'98, Madison, WI, June, pp. 151-160.
3. Bates, T., Gerich, E., Joncheray, L., Jouanigot, J. M., Karrenberg, D., Terpstra, M. and Yu, J. (1995) *Representation of IP routing policies in a routing registry.* Technical Report, Zvon-RFC 1786, May.
4. Bestavros, A. (1997) *WWW traffic reduction and load balancing through server-based caching.* IEEE Concurrency: Special Issue on Parallel and Distributed Technology, 15, 56-67.
5. Breslau, L., Cao, P., Fan, L., Phillips, G. and Shenker, S. (1999) *Web caching and zipf-like distributions: evidence and implications.* Proc. of IEEE INFOCOM'99, March, pp. 126-134.
6. Calvert, K. L., Doar, M. B. and Zegura, E. W. (1997) *Modelling internet topology.* IEEE Comm. Magazine, 35, 160-163.
7. Krishnamurthy, B. and Rexford, J. (2001) *Web Protocols And Practice.* Addison-Wesley, Boston.
8. Li, K. and Shen, H. (2004) *Dynamically Selecting Distribution Strategies for Web Documents According to Access Pattern,* Proc. of the Fifth International Conference on Parallel and Distributed Computing, Applications and Technologies (PDCAT 04), pp. 554-557.

9. Loukopoulos, T., Ahmad, I. and Papadias, D. (2002) *An overview of data replication on the Internet.* Proc. of the International Symposium on Parallel Architectures, Algorithms and Networks (ISPAN'02), Makati City, Metro Manila, Philippines, 22-24 May, pp, 31-37.
10. Pierre, G. and Makpangou, M. (1998) *CSaperlipopette!: a distributed web caching systems evaluation tool.* Proc. of 1998 Middleware Conference, The Lake District, England, 15-18 September, pp. 389-405.
11. Pierre, G. and Steen, M. (2002) *Dynamically selecting optimal distribution strategies for web documents.* IEEE Transactions on Computers, 51, 637-651.

to make online commerce a more human, personal and friendly experience that appears to mimic the traditional shopping experience for shoppers.

3 The e-Salesman System

This section contains an overview of the e-SS, including its architecture, high-level models, technology, rules, and features [11][12]. There are many qualities and traits that form a good sales person. A good and intelligent sales person should possess an intelligent aura and a likeable persona. This impression creates a welcoming and sincere environment to customers. He or she should be able to communicate using a common language so as to be clearly understood by customers and should possess ample knowledge about products, knowledge about clients, and strategic knowledge. The sales person should know how to sell the right product, to communicate with buyers, to recommend products, and to negotiate with customers.

E-Salesman

The eSS is designed to be an intelligent sales platform that employs all of the intelligent application areas in e-commerce. Unlike existing work, our goal is to develop an intelligent customer representative with human-like conversational capabilities, reasoning, knowledge, and persona. The platform will be based on knowledge driven model with knowledge-based reasoning and architecture. It can be authored to provide information services, as well as sales and business knowledge driven services. The purpose is to make e-commerce as natural, as effortless, and as intelligent as traditional shopping experiences.

The eSS has a set of requirements that makes it useful in its areas of application and must have a few basic qualities to achieve the expected results. The eSS has a *persona*. One of the main features that influence how users perceive intelligence is the interface. The use of animated characters and human persona has proven to be successful. The different expressions of a persona are shown in .Fig.1. The eSS must have *natural language support*; the conversation that a customer has with a salesman should be as seamless and effortless as an online chat or a phone call with an actual human representative. The eSS must possess *product knowledge* and be able to use and query that knowledge on the customer's request. The eSS must also be equipped with *sales knowledge*. It must be aware of any special offers, promotions, and over-stocked inventory and pricing, and should be able to use this information to make a successful sale. The eSS servicing a customer in a session must remember the customer, his or her needs, his or her stated queries and all other customer information throughout the session. The eSS needs *persistence* to keep track of the customer's navigation, choices, needs and purchases all throughout the customer's visit.

Fig. 1. Persona with Different Expression

System Architecture

The overall architecture for this system is a three-tier web-based system that includes the clients, a web server and application server and the database server. Fig. 2 shows the system architecture.

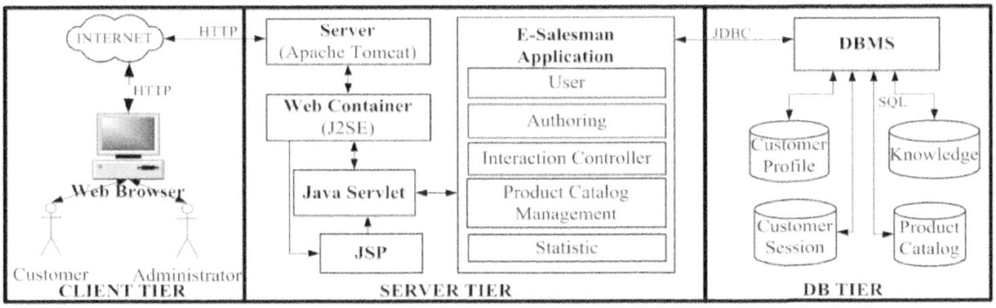

Fig. 2. Overall Architecture

Design for the Authoring Tool

Fig. 3 shows the authoring module design consists of a collection of components that allow the user to access the authoring services provided by the eSS. It consists of the knowledge data access component supporting the display servlet and the author controller component. The knowledge data controls access to the models, nodes, templates, tokens, and expressions that allows the access, author and management of the components. User can access and author model elements or node elements. Model elements include general properties and information of a model whereas node elements consist of general properties, seller properties, buyer properties, node condition, and URL. Buyer properties may also include one or multiple token values. The eSS's authoring tool is a subsystem that is adaptable and can be used with existing e-commerce websites. Our application was implemented with JAVA, JSP, Servlets, HTML, JavaScript, JDBC, and SQL. The web-server used was Jakarta Tomcat.

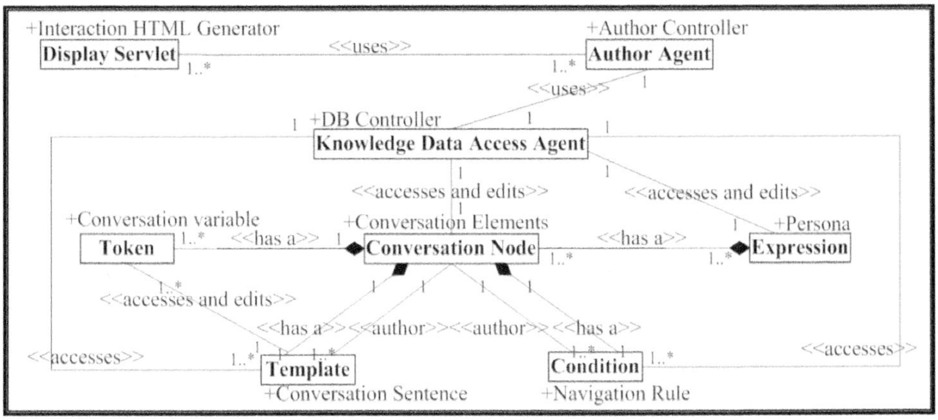

Fig. 3. Authoring Tool Design

4 The Authoring Solution

The eSS includes a comprehensive solution for the interaction between the system and the users and an intricate authoring solution for customization support for web-stores. In order to magnify the details of the authoring subsystem solution, we need to first proceed to give some details of the interaction of the eSS.

4.1 The Underlying Interaction Solution

The interaction structure of the eSS is an intelligent condition-based system. The interaction-processing piece includes the intelligent agent and the interaction controller. The interaction controller receives selected conversation template, with or without token values, from the customer through the user interface and dispatches it to the intelligent agent. The intelligent agent takes the information and dynamically accesses the knowledge repository for the condition that corresponds with the customer's selection. The new information will then be displayed by the user interface after receiving them from the interaction controller.

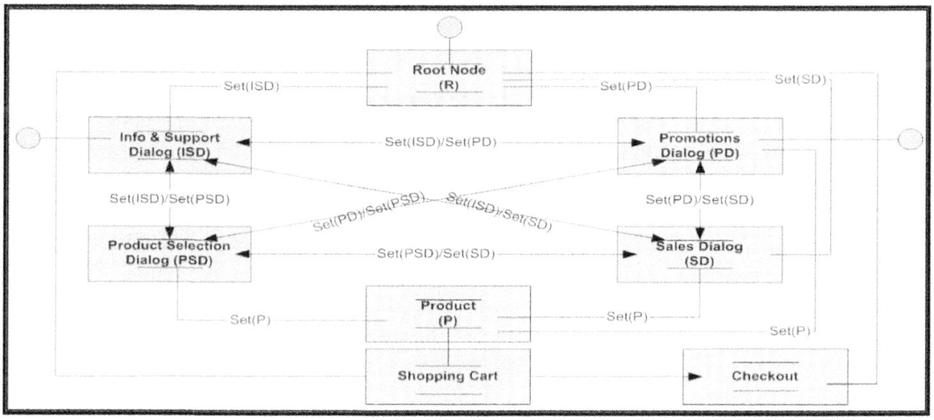

Fig. 4. Context-based Interaction Model

A conversational model is a graph M = (N, L), where N is a set of conversational nodes and L is a set of directed links. A single node, Ni = (CT, P, U, E, C), is a single conversation element that is an utterance from the salesman and customer. A link is a transfer of interaction from one node to another. A node consists of a set of conversational texts called templates, CT, a notice, P, a URL, U, a persona expression, E and a condition, C. A single template, CTi = (S, T, T), consists of a template text, S, a role, R and a set of tokens, T. A single token, Ti, is a variable in the template text that can take a value during the customer-salesman conversation. Examples of tokens are "make" or "model" or "manufacturer" or "price". A token, Ti = (m, f, y), consists of a token name m, a list filename f, which is a locator of the list of possible values, and a type y, which describes the nature of the token. The values that a token may take at any given point are dynamic data generated from a source. Every node has a condition, C

(1). The condition is a test case which returns a true or false value when executed. This value determines whether that particular conversation node is to be traversed during the conversation. The condition utilizes a number of variables that can be tested - the identity of the parent node, the values of tokens previously determined, and the conversation template picked by the customer in the parent node.

Fig. 4 presents a context-based interaction model for the eSS interaction. The model illustrates major conversation subjects for the interaction between the eSS and a shopper. These subjects can be classified into the following four major categories: sales-oriented dialog, support and information oriented dialog, promotion oriented dialog and product selection oriented dialog. The links between two subjects represents a transfer of conversation from one subject to another. From the figure, conversation may start from the root node, promotions dialog or support and information dialog. Conversation may transfer from one subject to another depending on the shopper or the eSS.

4.2 The eSS Authoring Solution

Fig. 5 shows the authoring processing component that includes the authoring agent and the data controller. The data controller controls receiving data from the user interfaces and handing it to the authoring agent. The authoring agent takes the information and appropriately processes it as creation or editing of node, token, or expression. The user interfaces are customized by the different elements that may be authored. The administrator, as the user, can author node, tokens and expressions through the respective interfaces. One of the main objectives of creating the authoring tool is to make the tool straightforward to author the elements; the different user interfaces make it simple for the user to author the different elements. The authoring processing component is designed with detailed rules that build and change the growth of the entire interaction repository. There are many different nodes that make up the entire sales conversation. The features of a node can be that of inquiry, informative, critical, or supplementary.

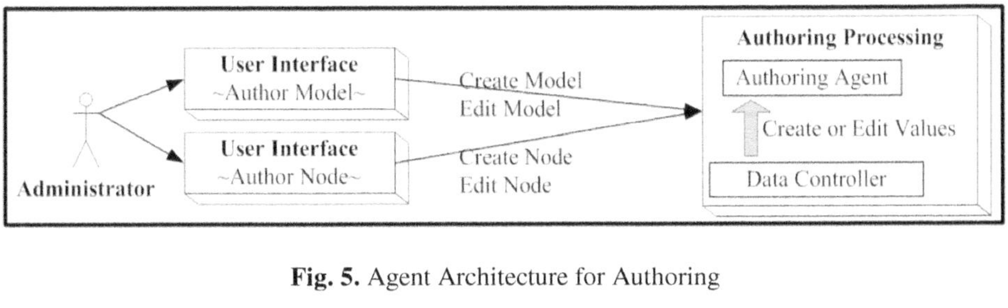

Fig. 5. Agent Architecture for Authoring

The Authoring Module

The authoring module is a detailed ensemble of helpful and user-friendly interfaces, complex rules for managing the collection of nodes and links that form a part of the entire sales-oriented conversation, and intricate algorithms for performing the intelligence of the authoring system. The authoring tool is designed to be rich in usability; methodical with accepting valid information and clever with the ability to

quent GUI after loading an existing car dealership model. Fig 7(a) shows how to create a new model. In the Model Management GUI in Fig 7(b), the window is separated into two important sections; the Model Panel and the Node Properties Panel. These two panels allow the author to manage all the nodes in a tree view and also the information within a single node. Users can author or manage the conversational nodes and links in the Model panel. This panel gives a visual representation of the conversations nodes in a tree view. This visual feature is an organized way to help the author manage the entire conversation nodes.

The Node Properties panel allows the authoring of the content within a single node. This figure shows how a user can author general node properties. Users can author name, description, URL, notice, "goto" node and eSS's expressions for a node. Fig 7(c) and Fig 7(d) show how to author and manage the eSS and the buyer conversations by editing the seller's or the buyer's template. The author can also create or edit tokens within the buyer's template. Fig 7(e) illustrates the GUI when a new token is authored. The condition needed to traverse to a node is authored within the Node Properties panels. Fig 7(f) shows how tokens are linked to token files using Boolean expressions.

Interaction Example

As a test example for our eSS, we chose the online car sales industry. We specialize in selling new Toyota models. The website is like any other Toyota dealership website with numerous links, pictures, and advertisements But with an addition of a friendly salesperson face with a talk button that customers can talk with. On clicking the talk button, the customer is taken to the salesperson page which is a five-panel layout page shown in Fig 8. All interaction with the salesperson takes place on this page. The salesperson page consists of five panels: *the URL panel, the persona panel, the salesperson interaction panel, the customer interaction panel, and the notice panel.*

Fig. 8. Homepage

6 Conclusion and Future Work

In this paper, we propose an intelligent eSS solution to current e-commerce systems. We planned, designed, and implemented the eSS as an entity with an intelligent interaction engine. This eSS possesses persona, natural-language support, and intelligence for smart interaction with users. This system is a cost effective solution for companies wishing to enhance their customers' shopping experience. In addition, we extended our project with a complete design and implementation of a web-based authoring tool to provide data to the interaction component. This authorable component makes the eSS customizable to meet different industries' needs. Future work and research will include support for different clients, for marketing and sales intelligence, for intelligent advertisements, for intelligent negotiations and recommendations, and for voice and video enhancements.

References

1. Ryszard Kowalczyk, Mihaela Ulieru, and Rainer Unland, "Integrating Mobile and Intelligent Agents in Advanced e-Commerce: A Survey", Agent Technologies, Infrastructures, Tools, and Applications for E-Services, 2002.
2. Sanwar Ali, Monsurur Rahman, and Kustim Wibowo. Indiana University of Pennsylvania. "Artificial Intelligence and E-Commerce", *First Annual ABIT Conference*, Pittsburg, Pennsylvania, May 3-5, 2001.
3. Ronald R. Yager and Iona College, "Targeted E-Commerce Marketing Using Fuzzy Intelligent Agents", *2000 IEEE Intelligent Systems.*
4. A. Burns and G. Madey. "Development of a web-based Intelligent Agent for The Fashion Selection and Purchasing Process via Electronic Commerce", *Proceeding from Americas Conference on Information Systems*, 1998, pp. 140-141
5. Aberdeen Group Inc., "Interactive Customer Care: Enriching the Self-Service Experience with Automated Agents. An Executive White Paper", November 2000.
6. C. C. Hayes, "Agents in a nutshell- a very brief introduction", *Knowledge and Data Engineering, IEEE Transactions*, Vol. 11, No: 1, pp: 127 -132, 1999.
7. Toyoaki Nishida, "Social Intelligence Design for the Web", IEEE Computer, 2002.
8. Y. Takeuchi and Y. Katagiri, "ATR MI&C Res. Labs., Kyoto. Social character design for animated agents", *Proceedings of RO-MAN '99, 8th IEEE International Workshop,* Pisa, Italy. September 27-29, pp: 53-58, 1999.
9. José A. Macías and Pablo Castells, "An Authoring Tool for Building Adaptive Learning Guidance Systems on the Web", *Proceedings of the 6th International Computer Science Conference on Active Media Technology*, p.268-278, December 18-20, 2001
10. T. Murray, "Authoring Intelligent Tutoring Systems: An analysis of the state of the art", *International Journal of Artificial Intelligence in Education*, Vol. 10, pp. 89-129, 1999.
11. Magdalene Ting, Vishal Seth, and Jerry Gao, Ph.D., "The e-Salesman System", *CEC 2004 Proceedings - IEEE Conference on E-Commerce Technology*, p.353-357, July 6-9, 2004
12. William Korbe, Valerie Stanton, and Jerry Gao, "iES: An Intelligent Electronic Sales Platform", Proceedings *of International Conference on E-Commerce Research (ICECR2003).* Dallas Texas, Oct. 23-26, 2003.

Agent-Community-Based P2P Semantic Web Information Retrieval System Architecture

Haibo Yu[1], Tsunenori Mine[2], and Makoto Amamiya[2]

Department of Intelligent Systems, {Graduate School[1], Faculty[2]} of Information Science and Electrical Engineering, Kyushu University
6-1 Kasuga-koen, Kasuga, Fukuoka 816-8580, Japan
{yu, mine, amamiya}@al.is.kyushu-u.ac.jp

Abstract. In this paper, we propose a conceptual architecture for a personal semantic Web information retrieval system. It incorporates semantic Web, Web service, P2P and multi-agent technologies to enable not only precise location of Web resources but also the automatic or semi-automatic integration of Web resources delivered through Web contents and Web services. In this architecture, the semantic issues concerning the whole lifecycle of information retrieval were considered consistently and the integration of Web contents and Web services is enabled seamlessly.

1 Introduction

1.1 Motivation

With ever-increasing information overload, Web information retrieval systems are facing new challenges for helping people not only locating relevant information precisely but also accessing and aggregating a variety of information from different resources automatically.

Currently, new technologies for enabling precise and automatic machine processing such as semantic Web and Web services are emerging and have attracted more and more attentions from academia and industry in recent years.

The semantic Web is an extension of the current Web in which information is given well-defined meaning, better enabling computers and people to work in cooperation [4]. Currently, there are a lot of researches such as [10] [9] [24] trying to apply semantic Web technologies to Web information retrieval systems, but they all address only problems concerning certain phases or certain aspects of the total complex issues involved. There isn't any research addressing the semantic issues from the whole life cycle of information retrieval and architecture point of view. However, for the reasons we show below, we argue that it is important to clarify the requirements of a Web information retrieval system architecture to apply semantic web technology to it. First, we need to ensure the semantics are not lost sight of during the whole life cycle of information retrieval, including publishing, querying, accessing, processing, storing and reusing. Hence the interfaces involved in the whole life cycle of information retrieval tasks need to be re-considered. Second, efficient searching for high quality results is based on

L.T. Yang et al. (Eds.): EUC 2005, LNCS 3824, pp. 538–549, 2005.

pertinent matching between well-defined resources and user queries, where the matching reflects user preferences. Therefore the description of Web site capability and the way of submitting queries incorporating user preferences should consistently be considered from an architectural point of view.

Web service mechanisms provide a good solution for application interoperability between heterogeneous environments. It will provide a new way for accessing Web information and play a vital role in Web information retrieval activities in the future. However, the conventional "Web contents" resources target at human consumption but new "Web services" resources target at machine consumption. Thus they have been managed separately for publishing, discovering, accessing, and processing until now. On the other hand, in the semantic Web, contents are given well-defined meaning, and they are becoming such data that can be understood and processed by machine as well. As both Web contents and Web services will be consumed by machines, this introduces the possibility and necessity of managing them together in a personal Web information retrieval system.

In this paper, we propose a conceptual architecture for a personal semantic Web information retrieval system. It incorporates semantic Web, Web services, peer-to-peer and multi-agent technologies to enable not only precise location of Web resources but also the automatic or semi-automatic integration of hybrid semantic information delivered through Web contents and Web services.

1.2 Approach

The conceptual architecture of our semantic Web information retrieval system is constructed based on the following four main ideas.

First, "using peer-to-peer computing architecture with emphasis on efficient method for reducing communication load." As a centralized system has the bottle neck of accessing and its maintenance cost is expensive, scalable and decentralized P2P systems are receiving more and more attention especially in the research and product development for the open and dynamic Web environment. However, due to the decentralization, the performance comes to be a significant concern when a large number of messages are propagated in the network and large amounts of information are being transferred among many peers [14]. Hence, an efficient mechanism for reducing communication load with least loosing of precision and recall is very important in a P2P information retrieval system. We propose our Agent-Community-based Peer-to-Peer information retrieval method called ACP2P method [15]. On the other hand, as we noticed that generally users retrieve and re-use certain amount of information repeatedly for a high percentage, it is essential to store frequently used information locally for the user with an efficient retrieval mechanism. We enable users refining and storing retrieved Web information in their local environment and manage them with semantic Web technology for the later re-use. As the user interested information is limited resource and the storing and retrieving mechanism can be adjusted to the user-specific way, the access time to the most frequently used information will be decreased significantly than searching in the vast open Web. As the

Web resources based on user preferences. Therefore a brief general information description of the Web site is defined at the top level. The GID gives an explicit overview of the Web site capabilities, and can be used as the initial filter for judging congruence with user preferences.

Second, we give the Web content capability description (WCD) and there is a link from GID to WCD for using semantic Web contents. The WCD is the metadata of Web contents and is composed of knowledge bases of all domains involved. We use OWL [13] to describe domain ontologies and the metadata will be described in RDF [12].

Third, we give Web service capability description (WSD) and there is a link from GID to WSD for facilitating the further matching and use of Web services. In order to semantically describe the capabilities and support the concrete realization of services, we express the service capability description in two layers: "semantic Web service description (SWSD)" and "concrete Web service description (CWSD)." This hierarchical capability-describing mechanism enables semantic and non-semantic Web service capability-describing and matchmaking for different levels. we use WSDL [7] for the concrete Web service description and OWL-S [6] to express the semantic Web service description.

For the details of our Web site capability description mechanism, one can refer to document [27].

2.2 "Myportal"

"Myportal" is a "one stop" that links the user to all the information s/he needs. It resites on the user's own desktop which is also a Web server itself and is designed to satisfy user's personal information requirements and to be mastered freely by the user her/himself. It provides both semantic browser and semantic search engine functionalities, and these functions manage not only local user information but also the other Web sites as conventional browser. The information

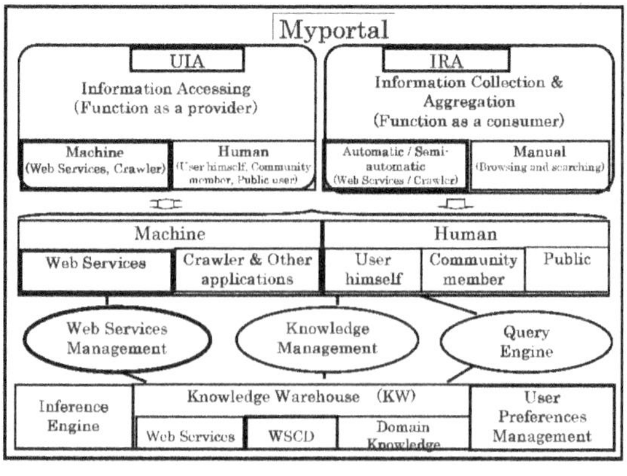

Fig. 3. Structure of "Myportal"

can be shared by others with proper authority. The structure of "Myportal" is shown in figure 3.

"Myportal" is composed of three types of main functional components: core component, consumer component and provider component.

The core component provides basic support for semantic technologies and information management. It consists of "Knowledge Warehouse (KW)," "Knowledge Management," "Query Engine (QE)" and "Inference Engine (IE)." As a consumer, it will bring together a variety of necessary information from different resources automatically or semi-automatically for the user. It is assigned agents to fulfill the information retrieval tasks through the communication with provider agents. As a provider, the contents and services of "Myportal" can be consumed by humans as well as machines. The human can be the user or other permitted persons, and the machine can be local or remote. A unified interface for browsing, searching and facilitating Web contents and services will be provided. We described "Myportal" in a little more detail in document [26].

2.3 Mediator

The communication between consumer and providers is based on an Agent-Community-based Peer-to-Peer information retrieval method called ACP2P method, which uses agent communities to manage and look up information related to a user query.

In order to retrieve information relevant to a user query, an agent uses two histories: a query/retrieved document history (Q/RDH for short) and a query/sender agent history (Q/SAH for short). Making use of the Q/SAH is expected to have a collaborative filtering effect, which gradually creates virtual agent communities, where agents with the same interests stay together. We have demonstrated through several experiments that the method reduced communication loads much more than other methods which do not employ Q/SAH to look up a target agent, and was useful for creating a "give and take" effect, i.e., as an agent receives more queries, it acquires more links to new knowledge[16].

The ACP2P method employs three types of agents: user interface (UI) agent, information retrieval (IR) agent and history management (HM) agent. A set of three agents (UI agent, IR agent, HM agent) is assigned to each user.

The UI agent receives requirements from the user, factors in missing or inherent information based on user preferences, breaks and transforms the requirements into formal queries and sends them to the IR agent.

When receiving a query from a UI agent, an IR agent asks an HM agent to look up target agents with its history or asks a portal agent to do it using a query multicasting technique. When receiving a query from other IR agents, an IR agent looks up the information relevant to the query from its original content and retrieved content files, sends an answer to the query-sender IR agent, and also sends a pair of the query and the address of the query-sender IR agent to an HM agent so that it can update Q/SAH.

The returned answer is either a pair of a 'Yes' message and retrieved information or a 'No' message indicating that there is no relevant information. When

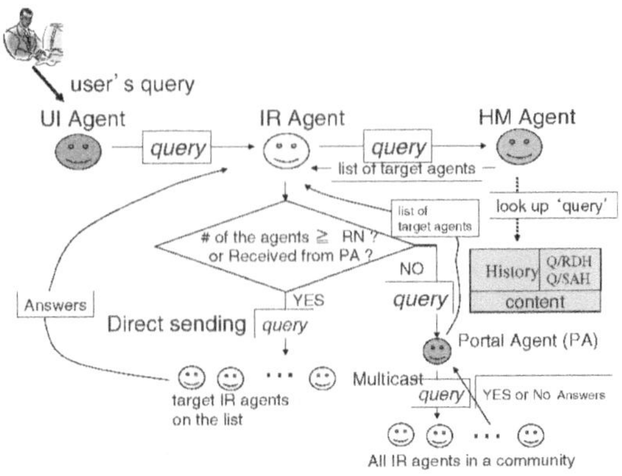

Fig. 4. Actions for Sending a Query

receiving answers with a 'Yes' message from other IR agents, the IR agent sends them to a UI agent, and sends them with a pair of a query and the addresses of answer sender IR agents to an HM agent.

The ACP2P method is implemented with Multi-Agent Kodama (Kyushu university Open & Distributed Autonomous Multi-Agent) [28]. Kodama comprises hierarchical structured agent communities based on a portal-agent model. A portal agent is the representative of all member agents in a community and allows the community to be treated as one normal agent outside the community. A portal agent has its role limited in a community, and the portal agent itself may be managed by another higher-level portal agent. A portal agent manages all member agents in its community and can multicast a message to them. Any member agent in a community can ask the portal agent to multicast its message. Fig.5 shows the agent community structure which the ACP2P method is based on.

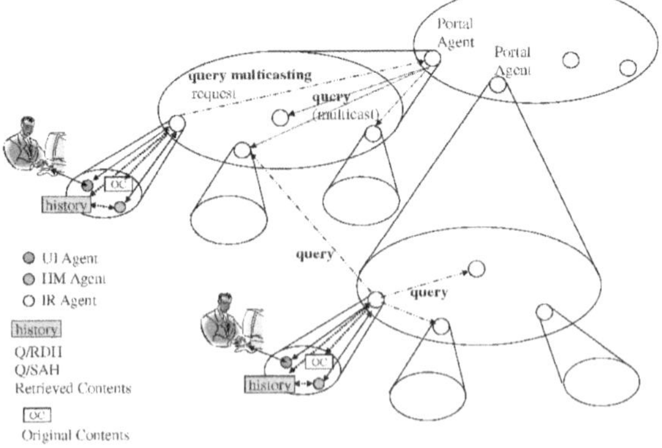

Fig. 5. Agents and their Community Structure

The query language and protocol communicated between IR agents need to be defined. Since the semantic Web information is commonly based on RDF which is a recommendation of W3C, a standard interface for querying and accessing RDF data is ideal for the interoperability between heterogeneous semantic Web information environments. The W3C RDF Data Accessing Working Group (DAWG) has published their working drafts of RDF Query Language SPARQL [19] and SPARQL protocol that are expected to be standards in this field. Although our architecture is designed for any reasonable communication interfaces, we are currently planning to use SPARQL RDF query language and SPARQL protocol as our semantic communication interfaces between providers and consumers.

3 Process Flow of Information Retrieval

The total process flow of the P2P Web information retrieval system can be illustrated as shown in figure 6.

At the beginning, the consumer (the user) will edit his profile and preferences, and providers will describe their capabilities using WSCD which we described in section 2.1. When the user wants to search for the information, a search interface need to be provided. Although various kinds of user interface, such as natural language, template-style or formal equation, can be considered, taking user convenience and reality in account, we provide a template-style search interface, enabling users to input or select their preferences as well as query items from

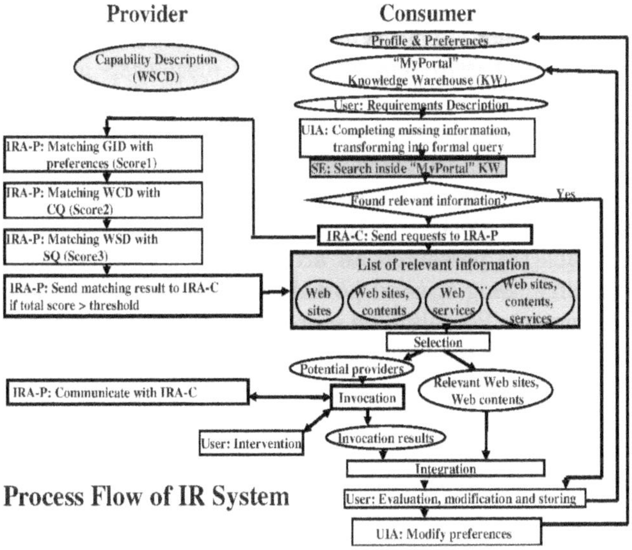

Fig. 6. Process Flow

semantic Web users. In the architecture, the semantic issues and the integration of Web contents and Web services are considered for the whole lifecycle of information retrieval. Our "Myportal" aims at constructing a fully personalized user's local Web portal, which is adapted to user preferences and satisfies all the requirements of a user's local and Web information usage. We use the ACP2P method for the communication between consumer and providers, which uses agent communities to manage and look up information related to a user's query in order to reduce communication loads in a P2P computing architecture.

In the future, we will realize a prototype of an agent community based P2P personal semantic Web information retrieval system, and evaluate the effectiveness of our proposed architecture based on it. Further experiments for the ACP2P method on semantic Web data retrieval need to be done to see its effectiveness.

References

1. KA2 Portal. http://ka2portal.aifb.uni-karlsruhe.de/.
2. Kazaa v3.0. http://www.kazaa.com/.
3. M. Bawa, G. S. Manku, and P. Raghavan. Sets: search enhanced by topic segmentation. In *Proceedings of the 26th annual international ACM SIGIR conference on Research and development in informaion retrieval*, pages 306 – 313, 2003.
4. T. Berners-Lee, J. Hendler, and O. Lassila. The Semantic Web. *Scientific American*, May, 2001.
5. D. Brickley and L. Miller. FOAF Vocabulary Specification. Sept., 2004.
6. David Martin et al. OWL-S 1.1 Release, November, 2004. http://www.daml.org/services/owl-s/1.1/.
7. Erik Christensen et al. Web Services Description Language (WSDL) 1.1, March 15, 2001. http://www.w3.org/TR/wsdl.
8. Gnutella. http://gnutella.wego.com/, 2000.
9. R. Guha, R. McCool, and E. Miller. Semantic Search. In *Proceedings of WWW2003*, pages 700–709, 2003.
10. D. Huynh, D. Karger, and D. Quan. Haystack: A Platform for Creating, Organizing and Visualizing Information Using RDF. In *Proceedings of the International Workshop on the Semantic Web (at WWW2002)*, 2002.
11. J. Lu and J. Callan. Content-based retrieval in hybrid peer-to-peer networks. In *Proceedings of the twelfth international conference on Information and knowledge management*, pages 199–206, 2003.
12. F. Manola and E. Miller. RDF Primer, February 10, 2004. http://www.w3.org/TR/rdf-primer/.
13. D. L. McGuinness and F. van Harmelen. OWL Web Ontology Language Overview, February 10, 2004. http://www.w3.org/TR/2004/REC-owl-features-20040210/.
14. D. S. Milojicic, V. Kalogeraki, R. Lukose, K. Nagaraja, J. Pruyne, B. Richard, S. Rollins, and Z. Xu. Peer-to-Peer Computing. Technical report, HP, 2002. http://www.cs.wpi.edu/ claypool/courses/4513-B03/papers/p2p/p2p-tutorial.pdf.
15. T. Mine, D. Matsuno, A. Kogo, and M. Amamiya. Acp2p : Agent community based peer-to-peer information retrieval. In *Proc. of Third Int. Workshop on Agents and Peer-to-Peer Computing (AP2PC 2004)*, pages 50–61, 7 2004.

16. T. Mine, D. Matsuno, A. Kogo, and M. Amamiya. Design and implementation of agent community based peer-to-peer information retrieval method. In *Proc. of Eighth Int. Workshop CIA-2004 on Cooperative Information Agents (CIA 2004), LNAI 3191*, pages 31–46, 9 2004.
17. M. Nottingham. The Atom Syndication Format 0.3 (pre-draft), December, 2003. http://www.mnot.net/drafts/draft-nottingham-atom-format-02.html.
18. F. Pinto, C. Baptista, and N. Ryan. Using Semantic Searching for Web Portal Interoperability. In *International Workshop on Information Integration on the Web - Technologies and Applications, April 9-11, Rio de Janeiro - Brazil*, April 2001.
19. E. Prud'hommeaux and A. Seaborne. SPARQL Query Language for RDF, April 19, 2005. http://www.w3.org/TR/rdf-sparql-query/.
20. S. Ratnasamy, P. Francis, M. Handley, R. Karp, and S. Shenker. A scalable content-addressable network. In *SIGCOMM*, pages 161–172, 2001.
21. RSS-DEV Working Group. RDF Site Summary (RSS)1.0, 2000-12-06. http://web.resource.org/rss/1.0/.
22. L. Sauermann. The Gnowsys Semantic Desktop for Information Integration. In *IOA Workshop of the VM2005 Conference*, 2005.
23. I. Stoica, R. Morris, D. Karger, M. F. Kaashoek, and H. Balakrishnan. Chord: A scalable peer-to-peer lookup service for internet applications. In *Proceedings of the 2001 conference on applications, technologies, architectures, and protocols for computer communications*, pages 149–160, 2001.
24. N. Stojanovie, A. Maedche, S. Staab, R. Studer, and Y. Sure. SEAL – a framework for developing SEmantic PortALs. In *Proceedings of the International Conference on Knowledge Capture*, pages 155–162, 2001.
25. C. Tang, Z. Xu, and S. Dwarkadas. Peer-to-peer information retrieval using self-organizing semantic overlay networks. In *SIGCOMM*, 2003.
26. H. Yu, T. Mine, and M. Amamiya. Towards a Semantic MyPortal. In *The 3rd International Semantic Web Conference (ISWC 2004) Poster Abstracts*, pages 95–96, 2004.
27. H. Yu, T. Mine, and M. Amamiya. Towards Automatic Discovery of Web Portals -Semantic Description of Web Portal Capabilities-. In *Semantic Web Services and Web Process Composition: First International Workshop, SWSWPC 2004, LNCS 3387/2005*, pages 124–136, 2005.
28. G. Zhong, S. Amamiya, K. Takahashi, T. Mine, and M. Amamiya. The Design and Implementation of KODAMA System. *IEICE Transactions on Information and Systems*, E85-D(4):637–646, April, 2002.

A Scalable and Reliable Multiple Home Regions Based Location Service in Mobile Ad Hoc Networks

Guojun Wang[1], Yingjun Lin[1], and Minyi Guo[2]

[1] School of Information Science and Engineering, Central South University, Changsha, P.R. China, 410083
[2] School of Computer Science and Engineering, University of Aizu, Aizu-Wakamatsu City, Fukushima 965-8580, Japan
csgjwang@mail.csu.edu.cn, linhandsome@126.com, minyi@u-aizu.ac.jp

Abstract. Compared with topology-based routing, location-based routing scales much better in large-scale mobile ad hoc networks. Location-based routing protocols assume that a location service is available to provide location information of each node in the network. Many location service protocols have been proposed in the literature. However, either they do not scale well in large-scale network environment, or they are not reliable if the network is highly dynamic. We propose a multiple home regions based location service protocol in large-scale mobile ad hoc networks. Theoretical analysis shows that the proposed protocol outperforms existing protocols in terms of both scalability and reliability.

Keywords: Mobile ad hoc networks, location service, location-based routing, scalability, reliability

1 Introduction

In recent years the widespread usage of wireless communication and handheld devices has stimulated research on self-organizing networks. Mobile Ad hoc NETworks (MANETs) are self-organizing, rapidly deployable and dynamically reconfigurable networks, which are formed by mobile nodes with no pre-existing and fixed infrastructure. Usually, these mobile nodes function as both hosts and routers at the same time. Two mobile nodes communicate directly if they are within the radio transmission range of each other; otherwise, they reach each other via a multi-hop route. Some typical applications in MANETs include communication in battlefield and disaster relief scenarios, video conferencing and multi-party gaming in conference room or classroom settings.

To route packets is one of the fundamental tasks in MANETs, but it is very challenging because of the highly dynamic topology of the network triggered by node mobility. There are two different approaches to route packets in such a network environment, namely, topology-based routing and location-based routing [1]. Topology-based routing protocols use the information about the communication links that are available in the network to perform packet forwarding. Due to node mobility, topology-based routing protocols can not scale well in large-scale MANETs. In

L.T. Yang et al. (Eds.): EUC 2005, LNCS 3824, pp. 550 – 559, 2005.

location-based routing, however, each node determines its own location information through the use of Global Positioning System (GPS) or some other type of positioning service. A location service, also known as mobility tracking or mobility management, is used by the sender of a packet to determine the location of the destination and to encapsulate it in the header of the packet. The routing decision at each forwarding node is then based on the locations of both the forwarding node's neighbors and the destination node. In this way, the location-based routing does not need to maintain routing tables as topology-based routing does. Therefore, location-based routing can scale quite well in large-scale MANETs [2] [3]. One of the main challenges of a location-based routing protocol is how to get the location information of a packet's destination when needed. Most of these protocols have a location service responsible for accomplishing this task. When a node does not know the location of its correspondent node, it requests the location information from a location service. Generally speaking, each node determines its own location information through the use of GPS or other techniques for finding relative coordinates based on signal strengths [4]. Since it is not necessary to maintain explicit routes in such protocols, location-based routing can scale well in large-scale MANETs even if the network is highly dynamic. This is a major advantage in MANETs where the topological change may occur frequently due to node mobility.

The rest of this paper is organized as follows. Section 2 introduces some related works. Section 3 presents our location service, which is used to update, maintain and query the location information of mobile nodes. Section 4 analyzes the scalability and reliability of the proposed protocol. Finally, we conclude this paper in Section 5.

2 Related Works

Location service is essential for designing location-based routing protocols in large-scale MANETs. Many location service protocols for MANETs have been proposed in the literature as follows.

Distance Routing Effect Algorithm for Mobility (DREAM) [5] is highly reliable and it provides localized information. The search of location of a destination requires only a simple local lookup. However, as the location information is periodically flooded into the whole network, the communication complexity is very large. DREAM thus has poor scalability and is inappropriate for large-scale MANETs.

Quorum-based approach is proposed in [6]. The key merit is the distribution of responsibility among quorums. But the quorum system has a major drawback in that it depends on a non-location-based routing protocol to maintain the integrity of the databases of the entire quorum, the implementation complexity of which is very high in MANETs. In particular, this drawback may greatly reduce the scalability.

To solve the scalability problem, the home-region based location service is proposed. In such a scheme, nodes within some geographical areas maintain the location information of other nodes which have made that area as their home region.

Similar to the Mobile-IP scheme [7], home-agent based location service (HALS) is proposed in [8]. This scheme eliminates the quorum system's major drawback. However, such a scheme is also not perfect due to the following reasons. (1) Since nodes can be hashed to any arbitrarily distant region, it may result in increased communication

1. Function *f* can evenly map the node ID into every region in the whole network, i.e., the probability of being a home region is the same for every region in the network.
2. Function *f* can be used in MANETs with various shapes and different coverage sizes, i.e., the function still works even when the network shape and size change.

3.3 Location Information Update

After a node moving out of the current region, it first gets its home regions by k functions ($f_i(ID), 0 \leq i \leq k-1$), then the location update message (including node ID and current region ID) is sent to the centers of these k home regions separately. We assume to use some routing strategy based on geographic location information such as MFR protocol [13] to forward such a message. If the node which received the update message is not in the destination home region, it will forward the message; otherwise, it will broadcast the message to the rest of nodes within the destination home region. Finally, each node has a copy of its current location information stored in all the nodes of the k home regions. Take node D in Figure 1 as an example, after moving from region 23 to region 29, it will send an update message including its node ID and region 29's region ID to region 8, region 17 and region 26, respectively.

3.4 Maintenance of the Location Information

When a node moves into a new region, the node sends a message to its neighbors requesting location information registered in this region. Any neighbor which has such location information generates a reply message to the node, and then the node uses the reply message to maintain its new location information for the new region.

3.5 Querying the Location Information

A source node computes home region IDs of a destination node and sends a query message for the destination node's location. The proposed MHRLS protocol provides two kinds of queries for the location information:

1. The source node queries all home regions of the destination node, and we call such a scheme Query-All. More specifically, the source node sends one copy of the query message to the center of each home region. The first node receiving the message in the home region sends a reply message (including ID of the region where the destination node currently locates). To prevent the source node from receiving k reply messages, the source node will simply discard the following reply messages associated with the same query message after receiving the first one. This scheme is easy to realize and has high reliability, but the communication overhead is relatively high.
2. The source node queries the nearest one of the k home regions of the destination node, which is called the Query-Nearest scheme, and sets a timeout at the same time. The first node receiving the query message in the destination region sends a reply message. If the source node does not receive any reply message after the timeout period, it will send a query message to the nearest one out of the rest k-1 home regions of the destination node. This process continues until the source node

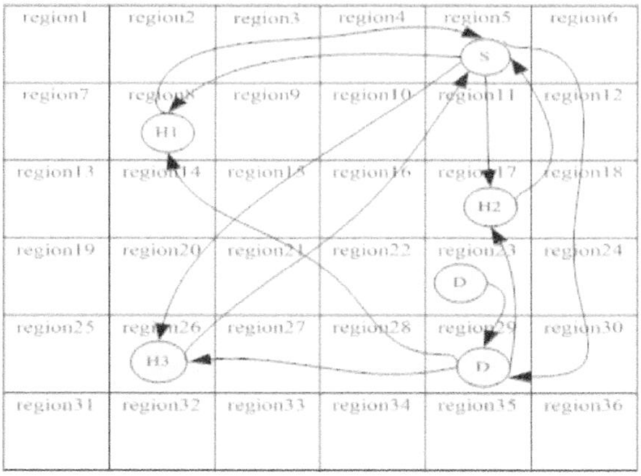

Fig. 1. Location Service of MHRLS

receives a reply message. This scheme uses less query/reply messages compared with the Query-All scheme, and it is highly efficient if all the home regions are not empty and all the home regions are reachable from any node in the network at any time. However, if these conditions do not hold, the query efficiency may be degraded, and the reliability may be reduced too.

4 Performance Analysis

In this section, we analyze the proposed MHRLS protocol in comparison with existing location service protocols in terms of scalability and reliability.

4.1 Scalability Analysis

We do the scalability analysis of our MHRLS protocol similar to the SLURP protocol in [9]. We define the scalability of a location service protocol as the cost to successfully update, maintain and query the location information. The total cost of a location service scheme can be divided into three parts: location update cost, location maintenance cost and location querying cost. In the following formulae, N stands for the number of mobile nodes in the network, and v stands for the moving speed of the mobile nodes. We derive all the formulae according to those in [9].

The location update cost of MHRLS c_u is:

$$c_u \propto kv\sqrt{N} \; ; \tag{1}$$

The location maintenance cost of MHRLS c_m is:

$$c_m \propto vN \; ; \tag{2}$$

The location querying cost of MHRLS c_q is:

$$c_q \propto k\sqrt{N} \text{ (When the Query-All scheme is adopted);} \tag{3}$$

$$c_q \propto \sqrt{N} \text{ (When the Query-Nearest scheme is adopted);} \quad (4)$$

The total cost in the Query-All scheme c is:

$$c \propto (Nkv\sqrt{N} + vN + kN\sqrt{N}) \propto kvN^{3/2}; \quad (5)$$

The total cost in the Query-Nearest scheme is:

$$c \propto (kvN\sqrt{N} + vN + N\sqrt{N}) \propto kvN^{3/2}. \quad (6)$$

Thus, the total cost of MHRLS is: $c \propto kvN^{3/2}$. (7)

Table 1. Scalability Comparison between MHRLS and SLURP

	SLURP	MHRLS
location update cost	$c_u \propto v\sqrt{N}$	$c_u \propto kv\sqrt{N}$
location maintenance cost	$c_m \propto vN$	$c_m \propto vN$
location querying cost	$c_1 \propto \sqrt{N}$	$c_1 \propto k\sqrt{N}$ □the Query-All scheme□
		$c_1 \propto \sqrt{N}$ □the Query-Nearest scheme□
total cost	$c \propto vN^{3/2}$	$c \propto kvN^{3/2}$

Although Table 1 shows that the total cost of the MHRLS protocol is higher than that of the SLURP protocol, both of them scale at the same level when k is small. In fact, the scalability of the SLURP protocol is not as well as that shown in Table 1 because the scalability analysis of the SLURP protocol in [9] takes no account of the possible cost for maintaining location information when some region has no nodes within. Thus, we conclude that MHRLS has comparable scalability with SLURP.

4.2 Reliability Analysis

In this subsection, we compare the reliability of the proposed protocol to existing protocols in two different situations. In this paper, we define the reliability of a location service protocol as the probability to successfully update, maintain and query the location information in a certain situation.

4.2.1 Uniform Distribution of Empty Regions

Firstly, we assume that empty regions are of uniform distribution, i.e., the probability for each region in the network to be empty is the same. And we assume that the probability of any region to be empty is equal to p, which is very small. In the HALS protocol, since location information of each node is kept in a single region which is set to be the node's home region, the reliability of the protocol is equal to 1.0-p; In the SLURP protocol, since a copy of location information of each node is kept in 9 adjacent regions, the reliability of the protocol is 1.0-p^9; In the proposed MHRLS protocol, since a copy of location information of each node is kept in k uniformly distributed regions, the reliability of the protocol is equal to 1.0-p^k, which is close to 1.0 if k is relatively large and p is very small. Therefore, the MHRLS protocol is more reliable than the HALS protocol in such situation. In addition, compared with SLURP, the MHRLS protocol achieves higher reliability if k is larger than 9; even if k is smaller than 9 (but not too small), reliability of the MHRLS protocol can be still very high even though it will be only a little lower than the SLURP protocol does. The analysis results on the reliability of the HALS, SLURP, and MHRLS protocols in the case of uniform distribution of empty regions are given in Table 2.

4.2.2 Non-uniform Distribution of Empty Regions

In this subsection, we consider that multiple adjacent regions become empty at the same time, for example, the 9 adjacent regions in the SLURP protocol are empty. In case of uniform distribution, such a case may not occur, or occurs very rarely. That is, such a case stands for an extreme case of non-uniform distribution of empty regions. This will probably happen when group mobility is of great importance, and thus a relatively large area may become empty. For example, a bombing in the battlefield may damage the region where it occurs, and it may also affect all its neighboring regions of the damaged region. Here we consider the probability that 9 adjacent regions are empty at the same time is equal to P. In this case, reliability of the HALS protocol is equal to 1.0-P, so is the SLURP protocol. However, in the same situation, the reliability of our proposed MHRLS protocol is equal to 1.0-P^k. That is because the k home regions of each node are evenly distributed in our protocol, and they have little probability that several of them happen to locate in the same 9 adjacent regions. Then we conclude that the MHRLS protocol is more reliable than both the HALS protocol and the SLURP protocol. The analysis results on the reliability of the HALS, SLURP, and MHRLS protocols in the case of non-uniform distribution of empty regions are also given in Table 2.

Table 2. Reliability Comparison with HALS and SLURP

	HALS	SLURP	MHRLS
Uniform Distribution of Empty Regions	1.0-p	1.0-p^9	1.0-p^k
Non-Uniform Distribution of Empty Regions	1.0-P	1.0-P	1.0-P^k

4.2.3 Numerical Results

According to Table 2, numerical results about the reliability of the HALS, SLURP and MHRLS protocols are given in Figure 2 and Figure 3 for uniform and non-uniform distributions of empty regions, respectively. In both figures, R stands for the reliability in Table 2, which is a function of the protocol being investigated and the probability for a given region to be empty. For the sake of presentation, we use the value of $-\lg(1.0-R)$ as Y. So the bigger the value of Y, the higher the R is. Therefore, in both Figure 2 and Figure 3, the X-axis essentially stands for the probability for a given region to be empty, and the Y-axis essentially stands for the reliability of the protocol being investigated.

Global State Detection Based on Peer-to-Peer Interactions

Punit Chandra and Ajay D. Kshemkalyani

Computer Science Department, Univ. of Illinois at Chicago,
Chicago, IL 60607, USA
{pchandra, ajayk}@cs.uic.edu

Abstract. This paper presents an algorithm for global state detection based on peer-to-peer interactions. The interactions in distributed systems can be analyzed in terms of the peer-to-peer pairwise interactions of intervals between processes. This paper examines the problem: "If a global state of interest to an application is specified in terms of the pairwise interaction types between each pair of peer processes, how can such a global state be detected?" Devising an efficient algorithm is a challenge because of the overhead of having to track the intervals at different processes. We devise a distributed on-line algorithm to efficiently manage the distributed data structures and solve this problem. We prove the correctness of the algorithm and analyze its complexity.

1 Introduction

The pairwise interaction between processes is an important way of information exchange even in pervasive systems and large distributed systems such as peer-to-peer networks [12, 13] that do collaborative computing. We observe that the pairwise interactions of processes form a *basic building block* for information exchange. This paper advances the state-of-the-art in analyzing this building block by integrating it into the analysis of the dynamics of (i) global information exchange, and (ii) the resulting global states of a distributed system [5]. The study of global states and their observations, first elegantly formalized by Chandy and Lamport [5], is a fundamental problem in distributed computing [5, 9].

Many applications in a distributed peer-to-peer system inherently identify local durations or *intervals* at processes during which certain application-specific local predicates defined on local variables are true in a system execution [1]. Hence, we require a way to *specify* how durations at different processes are related to one another, and also a way to *detect* whether the specified relationships hold in an execution. The formalism and axiom system formulated in [7] identified a complete *orthogonal* set $\Re$ of 40 causality-based fine-grained temporal interactions (or relationships) between a pair of intervals to *specify* how durations at two peer processes are related to one another. The following problem **DOOR** for the Detection of Orthogonal Relations was formulated and addressed in [1]. *"Given a relation $r_{i,j}$ from $\Re$ for each pair of processes i and j, devise*

L.T. Yang et al. (Eds.): EUC 2005, LNCS 3824, pp. 560–571, 2005.

Table 1. Space, message and time complexities. Note: M = maximum queue length at P_0, the central server. $p \geq M$, as all the intervals may not be sent to P_0.

Centralized algorithm	Average time complexity at P_0	Total number of messages	Space at P_0 (= total message space)	Average space at P_i, $i \in [1, n]$
Fine_Rel [3, 4]	$O(n^2 M)$ or $O(n[min(4m, np)])$	$O(min(4m, np))$	$O(min[(4n-2)np, 10nm])$	$O(n)$
Distributed Algorithms	**Average time complexity/proc.**	**Total number of messages**	**Total average message space**	**Total space**
Algorithm [1]	$O(min(np, 4mn))$	$O(n \cdot min(np, 4mn))$	$O(n^2 \cdot min(np, 4mn))$	$O(min(2np(2n-1), 10n^2m))$
this algorithm	$O(min(np, 4mn))$	$O(min(np, 4mn))$	$O(n^2 \cdot min(np, 4mn))$	$O(min(2np(2n-1), 10n^2m))$

a distributed on-line algorithm to identify the intervals, if they exist, one from each process, such that each relation $r_{i,j}$ is satisfied by the (i, j) process pair."

A solution satisfying the set of relations $\{r_{i,j}(\forall i, j)\}$ identifies a global state of the system [5]. Thus, the problem can be viewed as one of detecting a global state that satisfies the specified interval-based conditions per pair of peers.

Devising an efficient on-line algorithm to solve problem DOOR is a challenge because of the overhead of having to track the intervals at different processes. A distributed on-line algorithm to solve this problem was outlined in [1] without any formal discussion, without any analysis of its theoretical basis, and without any correctness proofs. A centralized but on-line algorithm was given in [3, 4]. In this paper, we devise a more efficient distributed on-line algorithm to solve this problem, and then prove its correctness. The algorithm uses $O(\min(np, 4mn))$ number of messages, where n is the number of processes, m is the maximum number of messages sent by any process, and p is the maximum number of intervals at any process. The total space complexity across all the processes is $\min(4n^2p - 2np, 10n^2m)$, and the average time complexity at a process is $O(\min(np, 4mn))$. The performance of the centralized algorithm [3, 4] and the algorithm in [1] are compared with the performance of the algorithm in this paper, in Table 1. The proposed algorithm uses an order of magnitude $O(n)$ messages fewer than the earlier algorithm [1], although that comes at the cost of somewhat larger messages.

2 System Model and Preliminaries

We assume an asynchronous distributed peer-to-peer system in which n processes communicate solely by reliable message passing over logical FIFO channels. $(E, \prec)$, where $\prec$ is an irreflexive partial ordering representing the causality or the "happens before" relation [10] on the event set E, is used as the model for a distributed system execution. E is partitioned into local executions at each process. Each E_i is a linearly ordered set of events executed by process P_i. We use N to denote the set of all processes.

We assume vector clocks [6, 11]. The durations of interest at each process can be the durations during which some local predicate of interest is true. Such a

Table 2. Dependent relations for interactions between intervals are given in the first two columns [7]. Tests for the relations are given in the third column.

Relation r	Expression for $r(X, Y)$	Test for $r(X, Y)$
R1	$\forall x \in X \forall y \in Y, x \prec y$	$V_y^-[x] > V_x^+[x]$
R2	$\forall x \in X \exists y \in Y, x \prec y$	$V_y^+[x] > V_x^+[x]$
R3	$\exists x \in X \forall y \in Y, x \prec y$	$V_y^-[x] > V_x^-[x]$
R4	$\exists x \in X \exists y \in Y, x \prec y$	$V_y^+[x] > V_x^-[x]$
S1	$\exists x \in X \forall y \in Y, x \not\preceq y \bigwedge y \not\preceq x$	$\exists x^0 \in X$: $V_y^-[y] \not\leq V_x^{x^0}[y] \wedge V_x^{x^0}[x] \not\leq V_y^+[x]$
S2	$\exists x_1, x_2 \in X \exists y \in Y, x_1 \prec y \prec x_2$	$\exists y^0 \in Y : V_x^+[y] \not< V_y^{y^0}[y] \wedge V_y^{y^0}[x] \not< V_x^-[x]$

Table 3. The 40 orthogonal relations in $\Re$ [7]. The upper part gives the 29 relations assuming dense time. The lower part gives 11 additional relations for nondense time.

Interaction Type	Relation $r(X, Y)$						Relation $r(Y, X)$					
	R1	R2	R3	R4	S1	S2	R1	R2	R3	R4	S1	S2
$IA(= IQ^{-1})$	1	1	1	1	0	0	0	0	0	0	0	0
$IB(= IR^{-1})$	0	1	1	1	0	0	0	0	0	0	0	0
$IC(= IV^{-1})$	0	0	1	1	1	0	0	0	0	0	0	0
$ID(= IX^{-1})$	0	0	1	1	1	1	0	1	0	1	0	0
$ID'(= IU^{-1})$	0	0	1	1	0	1	0	1	0	1	0	1
$IE(= IW^{-1})$	0	0	1	1	1	1	0	0	0	1	0	0
$IE'(= IT^{-1})$	0	0	1	1	0	1	0	0	0	1	0	1
$IF(= IS^{-1})$	0	1	1	1	0	1	0	0	0	1	0	1
$IG(= IG^{-1})$	0	0	0	0	1	0	0	0	0	0	1	0
$IH(= IK^{-1})$	0	0	0	1	1	0	0	0	0	0	1	0
$II(= IJ^{-1})$	0	1	0	1	0	0	0	0	0	0	1	0
$IL(= IO^{-1})$	0	0	0	1	1	1	0	1	0	1	0	0
$IL'(= IP^{-1})$	0	0	0	1	0	1	0	1	0	1	0	1
$IM(= IM^{-1})$	0	0	0	1	1	0	0	0	0	1	1	0
$IN(= IM'^{-1})$	0	0	0	1	1	1	0	0	0	1	0	0
$IN'(= IN'^{-1})$	0	0	0	1	0	1	0	0	0	1	0	1
$ID''(= (IUX)^{-1})$	0	0	1	1	0	1	0	1	0	1	0	0
$IE''(= (ITW)^{-1})$	0	0	1	1	0	1	0	0	0	1	0	0
$IL''(= (IOP)^{-1})$	0	0	0	1	0	1	0	1	0	1	0	0
$IM''(= (IMN)^{-1})$	0	0	0	1	0	0	0	0	0	1	1	0
$IN''(= (IMN')^{-1})$	0	0	0	1	0	1	0	0	0	1	0	0
$IMN''(= (IMN'')^{-1})$	0	0	0	1	0	0	0	0	0	1	0	0

duration, also termed as an *interval*, at process P_i is identified by the corresponding events within E_i. Each interval can be viewed as defining an event of higher granularity at that process [8], as far as the local predicate is concerned. Such higher-level events, one from each process, can be used to identify a global state. Intervals are denoted using X and Y. An interval X at P_i is denoted by X_i.

It was shown in [7] that there are 29 or 40 causality-based mutually orthogonal ways in which any two durations can be related to each other, depending on whether dense or nondense time is assumed. These orthogonal interaction types were identified by using the six relations given in the first two columns of Table 2. Relations R1 (strong precedence), R2 (partially strong precedence), R3 (partially weak precedence), R4 (weak precedence) define *causality conditions*. S1 and S2 define *coupling conditions*. The set of 40 relations is denoted as $\Re$.

Given a set of orthogonal relations, one between each pair of processes, that need to be detected, each of the 29 (40) possible independent relations in the dense (nondense) model of time can be tested for using the bit-patterns for the dependent relations, as given in Table 3 [7]. The tests for the relations $R1 - R4$, $S1$, and $S2$ using vector timestamps are given in the third column of Table 2. V_i^- and V_i^+ denote the vector timestamp at process P_i at the start and at the end of an interval, respectively. V_i^x denotes the vector timestamp of event x_i at process P_i. When the process is not specified explicitly, we assume that interval X occurs at P_i and interval Y occurs at P_j. For any two intervals X and X' that occur at the same process, if $R1(X, X')$, then we say that X is a *predecessor* of X' and X' is a *successor* of X.

Our goal is to efficiently apply the tests in Table 2 in a distributed manner across all the processes. Each process P_i, $1 \leq i \leq n$, maintains information about the timestamps of the start and end of its local intervals, and certain other local information, in a local queue Q_i. The n processes collectively run some distributed algorithm to process the information in the local queues and solve problem **DOOR**. In order for distributed algorithms to process the queued intervals efficiently, we first give some results about when two given intervals may potentially satisfy a given interaction type we want to detect.

3 Conditions for Satisfying Given Interaction Types

The discussion in this section is based on [1, 3, 4] which gave other (less efficient) solutions to solve problem DOOR.

Definition 1. Prohibition function $\mathcal{H} : \Re \to 2^{\Re}$ *is defined as* $\mathcal{H}(r_{i,j}) = \{R \in \Re \mid if\ R(X,Y)\ is\ true\ then\ r_{i,j}(X,Y')\ is\ false\ for\ all\ Y'\ that\ succeed\ Y\}$.

Definition 2. *The "allows" relation* $\rightsquigarrow$ *is a relation on* $\Re \times \Re$ *such that* $R' \rightsquigarrow R''$ *if the following holds. If* $R'(X,Y)$ *is true then* $R''(X,Y')$ *can be true for some* Y' *that succeeds* Y.

Lemma 1. *If* $R \in \mathcal{H}(r_{i,j})$ *then* $R \not\rightsquigarrow r_{i,j}$ *else if* $R \notin \mathcal{H}(r_{i,j})$ *then* $R \rightsquigarrow r_{i,j}$.

Proof. If $R \in \mathcal{H}(r_{i,j})$, using Definition 1, it can be inferred that $r_{i,j}$ is false for all Y' that succeed Y. This does not satisfy Definition 2. Hence $R \not\rightsquigarrow r_{i,j}$. If $R \notin \mathcal{H}(r_{i,j})$, it follows that $r_{i,j}$ can be true for some Y' that succeeds Y. This satisfies Definition 2 and hence $R \rightsquigarrow r_{i,j}$. □

Table 4 gives $\mathcal{H}(r_{i,j})$ for each of the 40 interaction types in $\Re$.

Theorem 1. *For* $R', R'' \in \Re$ *and* $R' \neq R''$, *if* $R' \rightsquigarrow R''$ *then* $R'^{-1} \not\rightsquigarrow R''^{-1}$.

Lemma 2. *If the relationship* $R(X,Y)$ *between intervals* X *and* Y *(belonging to process* P_i *and* P_j*, resp.) is contained in the set* $\mathcal{H}(r_{i,j})$*, and* $r_{i,j} \neq R$*, then interval* X *can be removed from the queue* Q_i.

Proof: From the definition of $\mathcal{H}(r_{i,j})$, we get that $r_{i,j}(X,Y')$ cannot exist, where Y' is any successor interval of Y. Further, $r_{i,j} \neq R$. So we have that X can never be a part of a solution and can be deleted from the queue. □

type T = **token**
  log: array [1..n] of *Log*;
//Contains the *Log*s of the intervals (at the queue heads) which may be in soln.
  C: array [1..n] of boolean;
//$C[i]$ is true if and only if $Log[i]$ at the head of Q_i can be a part of soln.
end

(1) Initial state for process P_i
(1a) Q_i has a dummy interval

(2) Initial state for the token
(2a) $\forall i : T.C[i] = false$
(2b) T does not contain any *Log*
(2c) A randomly elected process P_i holds the token

(3) On receiving token T at P_i
(3a) **while** $(T.C[i] = false)$
(3b) Delete head of the queue Q_i
(3c) **if** (Q_i is empty) **then** wait until Q_i is non-empty
(3d) $T.C[i] = true$
(3e) X = head of Q_i
(3f) **for** $j = 1$ to n
(3g) **if** $(T.C[j] = true)$ **then**
(3h) $Y = T.log[j]$
(3i) Determine $R(X,Y)$ using the tests given in Fig. 3 and Table 2
(3j) **if** $(r_{i,j} \neq R(X,Y))$ and $(R(X,Y) \in \mathcal{H}(r_{i,j}))$ **then** $T.C[i] = false$
(3k) **if** $(r_{j,i} \neq R(Y,X))$ and $(R(Y,X) \in \mathcal{H}(r_{j,i}))$ **then**
(3l) $T.C[j] = false$
(3m) $T.log[j] = \perp$
(3n) $T.log[i] = Log_i$
(3o) **if** $(\forall k : T.C[k] = true)$ **then**
(3p) solution found. T has the solution *Log*s.
(3q) **else**
(3r) $k = i + 1$
(3s) **while** $(T.C[k] \neq false)$
(3t) $k = (k+1)\ mod\ n$
(3u) Send T to P_k

Fig. 4. Distributed algorithm to solve problem DOOR

queue Q_i. $T.C[i] = true$ implies that the interval at the head of queue Q_i may be a part of the final solution and the corresponding log Log_i is stored in the token. If $T.C[i] = false$ then the interval at the head of queue Q_i is not a part of the solution, its corresponding log is not contained in the token, and the interval can be deleted. The algorithm is given in Figure 4. The process (P_i) receives a token only if $T.C[i] = false$, which means the interval at the head of queue Q_i is not a part of the solution and hence is deleted. The next interval X on the queue Q_i is then compared with each other interval Y whose log Log_j is contained in $T.log[j]$ (in which case $T.C[j] = true$, lines 3e-3i). According to Lemma 3, the comparison between intervals X and Y can result in three cases. (1) $r_{i,j}$ is satisfied. (2) $r_{i,j}$ is not satisfied and interval X can be removed from the queue Q_i. (3) $r_{i,j}$ is not satisfied and interval Y can be removed from the queue Q_j. In the third case, the log Log_j corresponding to interval Y is deleted and $T.C[j]$ is set to false (lines 3l-3m). In the second case, $T.C[i]$ is set to false (line 3j) so that in the next iteration of the **while** loop, the interval X is deleted (lines 3a-3b). Note that both cases (2) and (3) can be true as a result of a comparison. The above process is repeated until the interval at the head of the queue Q_i satisfies the required relationships with each of the interval Logs remaining in the token (T). The process (P_i) then adds the log Log_i corresponding to the interval at the head of queue Q_i to the token $T.Log[i]$ and sets $T.C[i]$ equal to true. A solution is detected when $T.C[k]$ is true for all indices k (lines 3n-3p), and is given by all the n log entries of all the processes, $T.Log[1, \ldots, n]$. If the above condition (line 3o) is not satisfied then the token is sent to some process P_j whose log Log_j is not contained in the token $T.Log[j]$ (in which case $T.C[j] = false$, lines 3r-3u). Note that the wait in (line 3c) can be made non-blocking by restructuring the code using an interrupt-based approach.

5 Correctness Proof

Lemma 4. *After P_i executes the loop in lines (3f-3m), if $T.C[i] = true$ then the relationship $r_{i,j}$ is satisfied for interval X_i at the head of queue Q_i and each interval Y_j at the head of queue Q_j satisfying $T.C[j] = true$.*

Proof: The body of the loop (lines 3j-l) implements Lemma 2 by testing for $R(X_i, Y_j) \in \mathcal{H}(r_{i,j})$ and $R(Y_j, X_i) \in \mathcal{H}(r_{j,i})$, when R is not equal to $r_{i,j}$. If $r_{i,j}$ is not satisfied between interval X and interval Y then by Lemma 3, X or Y is deleted, i.e., (line 3j) or (lines 3k, 3l) is executed and hence $T.C[i]$ or $T.C[j]$ is set to false. This implies if both $T.C[i]$ and $T.C[j]$ are true then the relationship $r_{i,j}(X, Y)$ is true.

It remains to show that for all j for which $T.C[j]$ is true when the loop in (3f-3m) completes, Y_j which is in $T.Log[j]$ is the same as $head(Q_j)$. This follows by observing that (i) $T.Log[j]$ was the same as $head(Q_j)$ when the token last visited and left P_j, and (ii) $head(Q_j)$ is deleted only when $T.C[j]$ is false and hence the token visits P_j. □

Theorem 2. *When a solution $\mathcal{I}$ is detected by the algorithm in Figure 4, the solution is correct, i.e., for each $i, j \in N$ and $I_i, I_j \in \mathcal{I}$, the intervals $I_i = head(Q_i)$ and $I_j = head(Q_j)$ are such that $r_{i,j}(I_i, I_j)$.*

Proof: It is sufficient to prove that for the solution detected, which happens at the time $T.C[k] = true$ for all k (lines 3o,p), (i) $r_{i,j}(I_i, I_j)$ is satisfied for all pairs (i, j), and (ii) none of the queues is empty. To prove (i) and (ii), note that at this time, the token must have visited each process at least once because only the token-holder P_i can set $T.C[i]$ to true. Consider the latest time t_i when process P_i was last visited by the token (and $T.C[i]$ was set to true and $T.Log[i]$ was set to

$head(Q_i)$). Since t_i until the solution is detected, $T.C[i]$ remains true, otherwise the token would revisit P_i again (lines 3s-u) – leading to a contradiction. Linearly order the process indices in array $Visit[1, \ldots, n]$ according to the increasing order of the times of the last visit of the token. Then for k from 2 to n, we have that when the token was at $P_{Visit[k]}$, the intervals corresponding to $T.Log[k]$ and $T.Log[m]$, for all $1 \leq m < k$, were tested successfully for relation $r_{k,m}$ and $T.C[k]$ and $T.C[m]$ were true after this test. This shows that the intervals from every pair of processes got tested, and by Lemma 4, that $r_{k,m}(X_k, Y_m)$ was satisfied for $X_k = head(Q_k)$ and $Y_m = head(Q_m)$ at the time of comparison.

As shown above, since t_k until the solution is detected, $T.C[k]$ remains true and the token does not revisit P_k. Hence, from t_k until the solution is detected, none of the intervals tested at t_k using $T.Log$ got dequeued from their respective queues and $r_{k,m}(X_k, Y_m)$ continues to be satisfied for $X_k = head(Q_k)$ and $Y_m = head(Q_m)$ when the solution is detected. □

Let $\mathcal{I}(h)$ denote the set of intervals at the head of each queue, that are compared during the processing triggered by hop h of the token. Each $\mathcal{I}(h)$ identifies a system state (not necessarily consistent). Observe that for any $\mathcal{I}(h)$ and $\mathcal{I}(h+1)$ and any P_i, interval $I_i(h+1)$ in $\mathcal{I}(h+1)$ is equal to or an immediate successor of interval $I_i(h)$ in $\mathcal{I}(h)$. We thus say that all the $\mathcal{I}$ are linearly ordered, and $\mathcal{I}(h)$ *precedes* $\mathcal{I}(h')$, for all $h' > h$. Let $\mathcal{I}(S)$ denote the set of intervals that form the *first* solution, assuming it exists. Let $\mathcal{I}(b)$ denote the first value of $\mathcal{I}(h)$ that contains one (or more) of the intervals belonging to $\mathcal{I}(S)$. Let $\mathcal{I}(init)$ denote the initial set of intervals. Clearly, $\mathcal{I}(init)$ precedes $\mathcal{I}(b)$ which precedes $\mathcal{I}(S)$.

Lemma 5. *In any hop h of the token, no interval $X_i \in \mathcal{I}(S)$ gets deleted.*

Proof: This can be shown by considering two possibilities.

1. An interval X_i in $\mathcal{I}(S)$ get compared with some interval Y_j that is also in $\mathcal{I}(S)$. In this case, both conditions are false in lines 3j and 3k as $r_{i,j}(X_i, Y_j)$ is satisfied, and *this comparison* does not cause either of the intervals to be deleted from $T.Log[]$. Also, $T.C[i]$ and $T.C[j]$ remain true.
2. An interval X_i gets compared with some $Y_j \in \mathcal{I}(h) \setminus \mathcal{I}(S)$. Observe that Y_j is a predecessor of the interval Y_j' at P_j such that $Y_j' \in \mathcal{I}(S)$ and thus $r_{i,j}(X_i, Y_j')$ holds. We have that $R(X_i, Y_j) \neq r_{i,j}$. We now show that Y_j gets deleted and X_i does not get deleted.
   - Applying Theorem 1, we have $R(X_i, Y_j) \rightsquigarrow r_{i,j}(X_i, Y_j')$ which implies $R^{-1} \not\rightsquigarrow r_{j,i}$. From Lemma 1, we conclude that $R^{-1} \in \mathcal{H}(r_{j,i})$. There are two cases to consider. (a) The token is at P_i. By Lemma 2 which is implemented in lines 3k-m, the comparison results in Y_j being deleted from $T.Log$ and subsequently from Q_j (line 3b when the token reaches P_j). (b) The token is at P_j. By Lemma 2 which is implemented in lines 3j and 3a-3e, the comparison results in Y_j being deleted from Q_j.
   - As $R \rightsquigarrow r_{i,j}$ therefore from Lemma 1, we conclude that $R \notin \mathcal{H}(r_{i,j})$. By Lemma 2 which is implemented in lines 3j and 3k-m (depending on whether P_i or P_j has the token), this comparison does not result in X_i being deleted. □

Lemma 6. *In any hop h of the token, at least one interval $Y_j \in \mathcal{I}(h) \setminus \mathcal{I}(S)$ gets deleted.*

Proof: Line 3b deletes interval $(head(Q_i))$ when the token arrives at P_i. □

Theorem 3. *If a solution $\mathcal{I}$ exists, i.e., for each $i, j \in N$, the intervals I_i, I_j belonging to $\mathcal{I}$ are such that $r_{i,j}(I_i, I_j)$, then the solution is detected by the algorithm in Figure 4.*

Proof: From state $\mathcal{I}(init)$ in which $T.Log$ was initialized to contain no log, onwards until state $\mathcal{I}(b)$, Lemma 6 is true. Hence, in each hop of the token, the interval at the head of the queue of some process must get replaced by the immediate successor interval at that process. This guarantees progress and that state $\mathcal{I}(b)$ is reached.

From state $\mathcal{I}(b)$ onwards until state $\mathcal{I}(S)$, both Lemmas 5 and 6 apply. Lemma 6 guarantees progress (some interval not belonging to $\mathcal{I}(S)$ gets replaced by its immediate successor interval at every hop). Lemma 5 guarantees that no interval belonging to the solution set of $\mathcal{I}(S)$ gets deleted. Once $T.Log$ contains all the intervals of $\mathcal{I}(S)$ and hence $T.C[k]$ is true for all k, the solution is detected. □

Thus, Theorems 2 and 3 show that the algorithm detects a solution if and only if it exists.

6 Complexity Analysis

The complexity analysis sketched below and summarized in Table 1 is in terms of two parameters – the maximum number of messages sent per process (m) and the maximum number of intervals per process (p). Details are given in [2].

Space complexity at P_1 to P_n:

1. In terms of m: It is necessary to store Log for four intervals for every message – two for the send event and two for the receive event. Refer [2, 3, 4] for the reasoning. As there are a total of nm number of messages exchanged between all processes, a total of $4nm$ interval Logs are stored across all the queues, though not necessarily at the same time.
   - The *total space overhead* across all processes is $2.mn.n + 4mn.2n = 10mn^2$. The term $2.mn.n$ arises because for each of the mn messages sent, each of the other n processes eventually (due to transitive propagation of $Interval\ Clock$) may need to insert a $Event\_Interval$ tuple (size 2) in its Log. This can generate $2.mn.n$ overhead in Logs across the n processes. The term $4mn.2n$ arises because the vector timestamp at the start and at the end of each interval is also stored in each Log. It now follows that the average number of Logs per process is $4m$ and the average space overhead per process is $10mn$. Also note that the average size of a Log is $O(n)$.

Nonintrusive Snapshots Using Thin Slices

Ajay D. Kshemkalyani and Bin Wu

Computer Science Department, Univ. of Illinois at Chicago,
Chicago, IL 60607, USA
{ajayk, bwu}@cs.uic.edu

Abstract. This paper gives an efficient algorithm for recording consistent snapshots of an asynchronous distributed system execution. The nonintrusive algorithm requires $6(n-1)$ control messages, where n is the number of processes. The algorithm has the following properties. (P1) The application messages do not require any changes, not even the use of timestamps. (P2) The application program requires no changes, and in particular, no inhibition is required. (P3) Any process can initiate the snapshot. (P4) The algorithm does not use the message history. A simple and elegant three-phase strategy of uncoordinated observation of local states is used to give a consistent distributed snapshot. Two versions of the algorithm are presented. The first version records consistent process states without requiring FIFO channels. The second version records process states and channel states consistently but requires FIFO channels. The algorithm also gives an efficient way to detect any stable property, which was an unsolved problem under assumptions (P1)-(P4).

1 Problem Definition

A distributed system is modeled as a directed graph (N, L), where N is the set of processes and L is the set of links connecting the processes. Let $n = |N|$ and $l = |L|$. A distributed snapshot represents a consistent global state of the system. Recording distributed snapshots of an execution is a fundamental problem in asynchronous message-passing systems. Since the seminal algorithm of Chandy and Lamport [3] which is a non-inhibitory algorithm that requires FIFO channels and $2l$ messages to record a snapshot, plus additional messages to assemble the snapshot, several algorithms have been proposed. A survey is given in [8].

This paper gives an efficient nonintrusive non-inhibitory algorithm for recording consistent snapshots of an asynchronous distributed system execution. The algorithm requires $6(n-1)$ control messages and has the following properties.

P1. The application messages require no changes, not even timestamps.
P2. The application program requires no changes, implying no inhibition.
P3. Any process can initiate the snapshot.
P4. The algorithm does not require the log of the message history.

These properties are important for ubiquitous and pervasive computing. A simple and elegant three-phase strategy of uncoordinated observation of local

L.T. Yang et al. (Eds.): EUC 2005, LNCS 3824, pp. 572–583, 2005.

Table 1. Comparison of global snapshot algorithms. The acronym p.b. denotes that control information is piggybacked on the application messages.

Algorithm	Channels required	Non-inhib-itory	Application messages unmodified	Number of control messages	Snapshot collection not needed	Message history not used
Chandy-Lamport [3]	FIFO	Y	Y	$O(n^2)$	N	Y
Spezialetti-Kearns [16]	FIFO	Y	Y	$O(n^2)$	N	Y
Venkatesan [17]	FIFO	Y	Y	$O(n^2)$	N	Y
Helary [5] (wave sync.)	FIFO	N	Y	$O(n^2)$	N	Y
Helary [5] (wave sync.)	non-FIFO	N	Y	$O(n^2)$	N	Y
Lai-Yang [10]	non-FIFO	Y	N (p.b.)	$O(n^2)$	N	N
LRV [12]	non-FIFO	Y	N (p.b.)	$O(n^2)$	N	N
Mattern [14]	non-FIFO	Y	N (p.b.)	$O(n)$	N	Y
Acharya-Badrinath [1]	CO	Y	Y	$2n$	Y	Y
Alagar-Venkatesan [2]	CO	Y	Y	$3n$	Y	Y
Proposed snapshot	FIFO	Y	Y	$6n$	Y	Y
Proposed snapshot (w/o channel states)	non-FIFO	Y	Y	$6n$	Y	Y

states gives a consistent distributed snapshot. Two versions of the algorithm are presented: the first version records consistent process states without requiring FIFO channels and without using any form of message send/receive or event counters, whereas the second version records process states and channel states consistently but requires FIFO channels. Critchlow and Taylor have shown that for a system with non-FIFO channels, a snapshot algorithm must either use piggybacking or use inhibition [4]. Hence, the second version of the algorithm cannot be improved upon to also record channel states while retaining the properties of no inhibition and no piggybacking while using non-FIFO channels.

Table 1 compares the proposed algorithms with the existing algorithms. Besides serving as a general-purpose snapshot algorithm, the proposed algorithm can detect *any* arbitrary stable predicate [3], which was an unsolved problem under the assumptions P1-P4. While many specialized algorithms are tailored to specific stable properties, such as deadlock, termination, and garbage, the following algorithms detect general stable predicates.

- The Marzullo-Sabel algorithm [13] can detect only *locally stable* predicates.
- The Schiper-Sandoz algorithm [15] can detect only *strong stable* predicates.
- Kshemkalyani-Singhal's two-phase algorithm [9], based on Ho-Ramamoorthy's algorithm [6], showed how to correctly detect deadlocks. A general method to detect stable properties was then outlined [9]. In essence, if a property does not change between the two serial phases of uncoordinated observations, the property must hold at some instant between the two phases. If it is stable, it must hold henceforth. While locally stable predicates can be detected satisfying assumptions (P1)-(P4) and without assuming FIFO channels, details of detecting arbitrary stable predicates are not given.

Neither Marzullo and Sabel [13] nor Schiper and Sandoz [15] showed any relationship between the classes of strong stable and locally stable properties. These existing algorithms can only detect some subclass of stable predicates, and do not satisfy (P1)-(P4). The proposed algorithm can detect *any* stable predicate.

Summary of Main Contributions:

1. The snapshot algorithms we propose for FIFO channels and for non-FIFO channels are linear in the number of messages, and satisfy (P1)-(P4).
2. The non-FIFO version of our snapshot algorithm can be used to detect locally stable predicates, under assumptions (P1)-(P4).
3. The FIFO version of our snapshot algorithm can be used to detect *any* stable predicate, under assumptions (P1) to (P4).

System Model:
An asynchronous execution in a distributed system is modeled as $(E, \prec)$, where $\prec$ is the causality relation [11] on the set of events E in the execution. $E = \bigcup_{i \in N} E_i$, where E_i is the totally ordered chain of event at process P_i. An event executed by P_i is denoted e_i. A *cut* C is a subset of E such that the events of a cut are downward-closed within each E_i. A *consistent cut* is a downward-closed subset of E. The system state after the events in a cut is a global state; if the cut is consistent, the corresponding system state is termed a *consistent global state*. An *execution slice* is defined as the difference of two cuts $D \setminus C$, where $C \subseteq D$. The slice is also referred to as a *suffix* of C with respect to D. When D is not explicitly specified, its default value is the execution E.

The execution history at a process P_i is a sequence of alternating states and local events, $\langle s_i^0, e_i^1, s_i^1, e_i^2, s_i^2, e_i^3, s_i^3, \ldots \rangle$. Events and messages of the snapshot algorithm form a superimposed control execution. Among the application events and messages, those that are relevant to the predicate of interest are the *relevant* events and messages, respectively. We assume that all events, variables, and messages recorded or logged are the relevant ones.

2 The Three-Phase Uncoordinated Snapshot Algorithm

The proposed algorithm is inspired by the two-phase deadlock detection algorithm [9]. The main idea of our algorithm is as follows. The algorithm takes three serial uncoordinated 'snapshots' that may be inconsistent. A consistent global state that lies between the first and the second inconsistent 'snapshots' is computed with the help of the third 'snapshot' and some local processing.

Any process can initiate the algorithm which consists of three phases that are serially executed. The algorithm involves some local processing by the initiator. Each phase involves the initiator sending a request to each other process, and then the processes replying to the initiator. The initiator can communicate directly to/from the various processes, or a *wave algorithm* [5] can be used in conjunction with a superimposed topology such as a ring or a tree. The snapshot algorithm is independent of this detail.

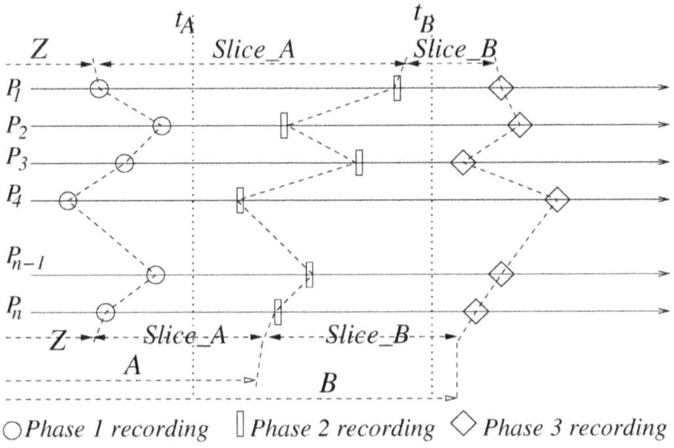

Fig. 1. Three-phase uncoordinated recording of a global snapshot. The initiator could be any of the processes.

Phase I: The initiator requests the processes to begin recording an execution slice. The global state from which processes begin recording is denoted Z, and is represented by the array $Z[1 \ldots n]$ at the initiator. The local states recorded in Z are not coordinated and may be inconsistent.

Phase II: The initiator then collects the slice of each process execution since the time each process began recording its slice and reported its local state in Phase I, until the time each process chooses to reply to the Phase II request. The local slice of each process that is reported to the initiator is stored by the initiator in array $Slice\_A[1 \ldots n]$. Each process begins to record the next slice, denoted *Slice_B*, after replying to the Phase II request.

Phase III: The initiator then collects the slice of each process execution since the time each process reported its local state in Phase II, until the time each process chooses to reply to the Phase III request. The local slice of each process that is reported to the initiator is stored by the initiator in array $Slice\_B[1 \ldots n]$. Based on *Slice_A* and *Slice_B*, the initiator computes a consistent global state.

Slice_B is used in two different ways, depending on whether channel states are to be recorded.

- If channel states are not to be recorded and the channels are non-FIFO, *Slice_B* is used to identify a consistent state within *Slice_A* by helping to eliminate states in *Slice_A* that are inconsistent.
- If channel states are also to be recorded and FIFO channels are assumed, then *Slice_B* is also useful to capture the channel states. In this case, the recording within *Slice_B* completes at each process when the messages sent by other processes to that process in (and before) *Slice_A* have been received. This condition is detectable using the control information distributively sent to the initiator in the Phase II reply messages and then conveyed on the Phase III request received from the initiator.

(variables at an initiator)
array of states: $Z[1 \ldots n]$; // Phase 1 recordings
array of sequence of events: $Slice\_A[1 \ldots n]$; // Phase 2 recordings
array of sequence of events: $Slice\_B[1 \ldots n]$; // Phase 3 recordings
array of int: $Global\_Sent[1 \ldots n, 1 \ldots n]$; //$Global\_Sent[i, j] \equiv$ # msgs, P_i to P_j
array of int: $Global\_Received[1 \ldots n, 1 \ldots n]$;
//$Global\_Received[i, j] \equiv$ # messages received by P_i from P_j
(variables at each process)
array of local events: *Slice_Log*; // log of local events
array of int: $Sent[1 \ldots n]$; // $Sent[k] \equiv$ # messages sent to P_k
array of int: $Received[1 \ldots n]$; // $Received[k] \equiv$ # messages received from P_k
array of int: $Must\_Receive[1 \ldots n]$;
// $Must\_Receive[k] \equiv$ # messages to be recd. from P_k before Phase III report

(1) Process P_{init} initiates the algorithm, where $1 \leq init \leq n$.
(1a) **send** *Request(Phase_1_Report)* to all P_j;
(1b) **await** *Report(Phase_1_Report)* from all processes;
(1c) $(\forall j)\ Z[j] \longleftarrow$ *Phase_1_Report.State* received from P_j;
(1d) $(\forall j)\ Global\_Received[j][1 \ldots n] \longleftarrow Phase\_1\_Report.Received[1 \ldots n]$;
(1e) **send** *Request(Phase_2_Report)* to all P_j;
(1f) **await** *Report(Phase_2_Report)* from all processes;
(1g) $(\forall j)\ Slice\_A[j] \longleftarrow$ *Phase_2_Report.Slice_Log* received from P_j;
(1h) $(\forall j)\ Global\_Sent[j][1 \ldots n] \longleftarrow Phase\_2\_Report.Sent[1 \ldots n]$ from P_j;
(1i) **send** to all P_j, *Request(Phase_3_Report)* + $Global\_Sent[1 \ldots n][j]$ piggybacked;
(1j) **await** *Report(Phase_3_Report)* from all processes;
(1k) $(\forall j)\ Slice\_B[j] \longleftarrow$ Phase 3 report received from P_j;
(1l) $S \longleftarrow Compute\_Consistent\_Snapshot(Slice\_A, Slice\_B)$;
(1m) *Compute_In-transit_Messages*(S).

(2) Process P_j executes the following, where $1 \leq j \leq n$.
(2a) On receiving *Request(Phase_1_Report)* from P_{init},
(2b) **send** local state and $Received[1 \ldots n]$ in *Report(Phase_1_Report)* to P_{init};
(2c) Begin recording log of events in *Slice_Log*;
(2d) On receiving *Request(Phase_2_Report)* from P_{init},
(2e) **send** *Slice_Log* and $Sent[1 \ldots n]$ in *Report(Phase_2_Report)* to P_{init};
(2f) Reset *Slice_Log*;
(2g) On receiving *Request(Phase_3_Report)* and $Must\_Receive[1 \ldots n]$ from P_{init},
(2h) Await until, $(\forall k)$, $Received[k] \geq Must\_Receive[k]$;
(2i) **send** *Slice_Log* in *Report(Phase_3_Report)* to P_{init};
(2j) Stop recording events in *Slice_Log*.

Fig. 3. Three-phase algorithm to record a global snapshot. Underlined code is executed if channel states are needed in a FIFO system.

After *Slice_A* and *Slice_B* have been collected at the end of the three phases, the initiator invokes procedure *Compute_Consistent_Snapshot* in Figure 4 to compute a consistent cut S from *Slice_A* and *Slice_B*. This cut S satisfies $S(t_{A\_start}) \subseteq S \subseteq S_{max} \subseteq A \subseteq S(t_{A\_end})$ and is computed by iteratively re-

(3) Process P_{init} executes *Compute_Consistent_Snapshot(Slice_A, Slice_B)*.
array of int: S_{max}, S, T, U, V;
array of array of int: $Slice\_A\_events[1 \ldots i \ldots n][1 \ldots a_i]$;
array of array of int: $Slice\_B\_events[1 \ldots i \ldots n][1 \ldots b_i]$;
// Alternate representation of slices

(3a) **for** $i = 1$ **to** n **do**
(3b) **if** $Slice\_A[i][x+1]$ is the 1st receive in *Slice_A[i]* of a msg. sent in *Slice_B* **then**
(3c) $S_{max}[i] \longleftarrow x$
(3d) **else** $S_{max}[i] \longleftarrow a_i$;
(3e) $S, T, U \longleftarrow S_{max}$;
(3f) **for** $i = 1$ **to** n **do**
(3g) $V[i] \longleftarrow a_i$;
(3h) **repeat**
(3i) **for** $i = 1$ **to** n **do**
(3j) **for** $y = T[i] + 1$ **to** $V[i]$ **do**
(3k) **if** message($Slice\_A\_events[i][y], Slice\_A\_events[j][z]$) **then**
(3l) $U[j] \longleftarrow \min(U[j], z-1)$; // modify U to make it consistent
(3m) **if** $T = U (= S)$ **then return**(S);
(3n) $S \longleftarrow \min(T, U)$; // $S \equiv$ current upper bound on consistent state
(3o) $V \longleftarrow \max(T, U)$; //current upper bound on source of inconsistency
(3p) $T, U \longleftarrow S$;
(3q) **forever**.

(4) Process P_{init} executes *Compute_In-transit_Messages(S)*.
(4a) $(\forall i \forall j)$ $transit(S[i], S[j]) \longleftarrow \emptyset$;
(4b) $(\forall i)$ compute $Global\_Sent[i, 1 \ldots n]$ for $S[i]$ using *Slice_A*, $Global\_Sent[i, 1 \ldots n]$;
(4c) **for** $j = 1$ **to** n **do**
(4d) **for** each successive event e_j^x in $Slice\_A[j][1 \ldots a_j]$ and $Slice\_B[j][1 \ldots b_j]$ **do**
(4e) **if** a message M was received from i (at this event with seq. # x) **then**
(4f) $Global\_Received[j, i]++$;
(4g) **if** $Global\_Sent[i, j] \geq Global\_Received[j, i]$ **and** $x > S[j]$ **then**
(4h) $transit(S[i], S[j]) \longleftarrow transit(S[i], S[j]) \cup \{M\}$.

Fig. 4. Finding a consistent state iteratively, and computing in-transit messages. Underlined code is executed if channel states are needed in a FIFO system.

moving the minimum slice suffix from S_{max} to get a consistent global state. For convenience, this procedure represents each of the two slices as an array $[1 \ldots n]$ of an array of integers. For example, $Slice\_A\_events[1 \ldots i \ldots n][1 \ldots a_i]$, where $Slice\_A\_events[i][j]$ denotes the jth event at process P_i, represents *Slice_A*.

In Figure 4, lines (3a)-(3d) identify S_{max}. Line (3e) initializes the integer vector variables S, T, and U to S_{max}. These vectors denote global states but the integer values denoting sequence numbers of the states in the slice have significance local to the initiator only. For example, $S[i]$ was assigned by P_i relative to the start of the slice and represents the sequence number of a local state of P_i in the slice. Lines (3f-3g) initialize the vector variable V to the state at the end of *Slice_A*, namely, the state A. S is always set to the current known upper bound of the consistent global state that is sought. Vector V denotes the state that is the best known upper bound on the global state such that messages sent in the slice $V \setminus S$ may cause S to be inconsistent. Vectors T and U are working variables used to update S and V.

The main loop (3h)-(3q) updates S and V iteratively. In lines (3i)-(3l), U is used to track the prefix of the current S such that there are no inconsistencies caused by messages sent in $V \setminus S$. A message at the sender is matched with the same message at the receiver by comparing their hashes or checksums (line (3k)). If the message sent at $Slice\_A\_events[i][y]$ is received at $Slice\_A\_events[j][z]$, then $U[j]$ is updated to the minimum of its current value and $z - 1$ (line (3l)). An inconsistency, if any, is thus eliminated by removing the minimum suffix from the execution slice for the receiver P_j. However, messages sent in the slice $S \setminus U$ may still cause U to be inconsistent; this needs to be tested in the next iteration. Lines (3n)-(3p) initialize the values of S, T, U, and V for the next iteration. The procedure finishes when the loop (3i)-(3l) does not find any inconsistencies in the current value of S in line (3m).

2.2 Consistent State and Channel Recording Under FIFO Channels

This section presents an enhanced algorithm that also records channel states if channels are FIFO. Figure 3 gives the code for the three-phase processing. Underlined pseudo-code and data structures are also executed by this version of the algorithm. Procedure *Compute_Consistent_Snapshot* in Figure 4 computes a consistent cut from *Slice_A* and *Slice_B*, and is common to both versions of the algorithm.

Procedure *Compute_In_Transit_Messages* is used to compute the channel states. This procedure requires the data structures $Z[1 \ldots n]$ and integer arrays $Global\_Sent[1 \ldots n, 1 \ldots n]$ and $Global\_Received[1 \ldots n, 1 \ldots n]$ at the initiator during the processing of the algorithm. Integer vectors $Received[1 \ldots n]$, $Sent[1 \ldots n]$, and $Must\_Receive[1 \ldots n]$ must also be maintained at each node. $Sent[j]$ and $Received[j]$ track the count of the number of messages sent to and received from process P_j, respectively. The main idea is simple. The state of channel $\langle P_i, P_j \rangle$ in a global state containing local states $S[i]$ and $S[j]$ at the processes, denoted as $transit(S[i], S[j])$, is simply those messages sent by P_i till state $S[i]$ that are not received until state $S[j]$ at P_j. One important difference from the previous version is that sequence numbers used to count events at a process are not local to a slice, but local to the entire execution of that process. This is to capture in-transit messages for channel states. Such messages could have been sent before *Slice_A* and need to be detected. To compute the channel state while satisfying conditions (P1) – (P4) and specifically that no sequence numbers can be tagged on messages, three issues need to be addressed.

1. Messages sent by P_i to P_j before state $S[i]$ must have reached P_j by the end of *Slice_B*.
   This is ensured by using the local *Sent* vector at each process and the *Global_Sent* array at the initiator. In the Phase II recording reported to

the initiator, the *Sent* vectors reported (line (2e)) are used to populate *Global_Sent* (line (1h)). The Phase III request sent to each process contains the piggybacked information about how many messages have been sent to that process by other processes (line (1i)). A process postpones its Phase III recording of the end of *Slice_B* until all these number of messages, remembered in array *Must_Receive*, have been delivered locally (line (2h)).

2. The set of messages sent by P_i to P_j up to the snapshot state $S[i]$, denoted here as $\mathcal{X}$, should be identifiable. There are two parts to this.
   - This set contains all the messages received by P_j from P_i with sequence numbers less than the value of $Sent[j]$ at $S[i]$. This value of $Sent[j]$ at $S[i]$ is computed (line (4b)) using *Global_Sent*, constructed from the Phase II report, and working backwards using the log *Slice_A*, also reported in Phase II. The resulting message count (i.e., the value of $Sent[j]$ at $S[i]$) is stored in-situ in the data structure $Global\_Sent[i, j]$ as it is updated.
   - The messages received by P_j are enumerated as per the sequence numbers assigned by P_i, in lines (4d)-(4e). The enumeration of the sequence numbers is done in lines (4c)-(4f) using *Global_Received*, reported in Phase I to the initiator (line (1d)), and working forwards using the log *Slice_A* reported in Phase II and the log *Slice_B* reported in Phase III. The enumeration is done in-situ in $Global\_Received[j, i]$.

   If $Global\_Received[j, i] \leq Global\_Sent[i, j]$ for a message, then that message belongs to $\mathcal{X}$.
3. The set of messages received by P_j from P_i after the snapshot state $S[j]$, denoted here as $\mathcal{Y}$, should be identifiable.

   These are the messages received from P_i at P_j in states numbered x such that $x > S[j]$.

From (2) and (3) above, $transit(S[i], S[j]) = \mathcal{X} \cap \mathcal{Y}$, is expressible as $\{M$ $recd\ by\ P_j\ at\ event\ x \mid Global\_Received[j, i] \leq Global\_Sent[i, j] \bigwedge x > S[j]\}$. Unlike the algorithm in Section 2.1, *Slice_Log*, *Slice_A*, *Slice_B* record messages for send and receive events if the contents of in-transit messages are required. The pseudo-code data structures do not reflect this for simplicity.

3 Complexity

The complexity analysis assumes a flat tree topology with the initiator as the root. A similar analysis can be conducted for the ring and more general tree topologies. Table 2 summarizes the complexity results. Note that the slices *Slice_A* and *Slice_B* are both *thin* slices, and their expected size is the same. Hence, the complexity is expressed in terms of *Slice_A* only. The expected width of *Slice_A* is the execution log that occurs in $\hat{rtt}_{max}$, the expected round-trip time between the two furthest nodes in the network. Let $max(owt_A)$ denote the maximum time for a message sent in *Slice_A* to reach its destination. The expected width of *Slice_B* is $max(rtt_{max}, owt_A)$ which is also $\hat{rtt}_{max}$.

Load Balanced Allocation of Multiple Tasks in a Distributed Computing System

Biplab Kumer Sarker[1], Anil Kumar Tripathi[2], Deo Prakash Vidyarthi[3], Laurence Tianruo Yang[4], and Kuniaki Uehara[5]

[1] Faculty of Computer Science, University of New Brunswick, Fredericton, Canada
sarker@unb.ca
[2] Institute of Technology, Banaras Hindu University, Varanasi, India
anilkt@bhu.ac.in
[3] Jawaharal Nehru University, New Delhi, India
dpv@mail.jnu.ac.in
[4] Department of Computer Science, St. Francis Xavier University, Canada
lyang@stfx.ca
[5] Graduate School of Science and Technology, Kobe University, Japan
uehara@kobe-u.ac.jp

Abstract. A Distributed Computing Systems (DCS) calls for proper partitioning of tasks into modules and allocating them to various nodes so as to enable parallel execution of their modules by individual different processors of the system. A number of algorithms have been proposed for allocation of tasks in a Distributed Computing System. Most of the models proposed in literature consider modules of a single task for static allocation, for the purpose of allocation onto a DCS. Moreover, they did not consider the architectural capability of the processing nodes and the way of connectivity among them. This work considers allocation of disjoint multiple tasks with their corresponding modules and proposes a parallel algorithm for a realistic situation wherein multiple disjoint tasks with their modules compete for execution on an arbitrarily connected DCS based on well-known A* technique. The proposed algorithm also considers a load balanced allocation for the purpose. The paper justifies the effectiveness of the algorithm with the experimental results by comparing with previously reported works.

1 Introduction

In a distributed computing systems, processing nodes networked together, participate in various computational tasks to achieve minimum turn around time of the submitted tasks. The problem becomes more complex when the communicating modules in a task itself are assigned to different processing nodes to achieve the goal. Therefore, the inter module communication cost(IMC) needs to be minimized to obtain the minimum turn around time. On the other hand, the capacity of computational load for each processing node is needed to be considered for the whole system to maximize its throughput. This problem has been studied as task allocation or mapping problem in the literatures [2-6, 8-11]. Since

L.T. Yang et al. (Eds.): EUC 2005, LNCS 3824, pp. 584–596, 2005.

the problem is NP-hard [2, 9] and thus many heuristic solutions are possible for this problem.

Most of the algorithms for Task Allocation (TA) problem proposed by the scientists and researchers [2, 6] so far, do make one or more assumptions. These consider a single task partitioned into corresponding modules for the execution and the repercussion of a single task allocation on a DCS. Whereas in reality, a DCS receives number of tasks from time to time for the execution. Factually, a DCS facilitates concurrent execution of modules belonging to various unrelated tasks [7, 12, 13]. The modules of any particular task, having IMC, do cooperatively execute and do not depend on the modules of the other tasks. This leads to the situation wherein, a processing node may be assigned modules belonging to different tasks. It is to mention that the real issue of task allocation must not ignore the possibility of multiple modules assignment of various tasks to the processing nodes in a dynamic fashion [7].

Considering these view and furthermore, taking into account the architectural capability of the processing nodes and the optimality of the solution guaranteed by A* based TA [2], in this paper we present a parallel algorithm for load balanced allocation in a DCS.

The paper is organized as follows. The next section discusses the load parameter for multiple tasks which is used in our case as a cost function to minimize turnaround time. This is the basis of effectiveness of the allocation. In section 3, the A* algorithm for task allocation is proposed. Three examples are also illustrated in this section. In the next section, the comparative observations with the existing algorithms are presented. Section 5 also justifies the effectiveness and scalability of our algorithm. Finally, the work is concluded indicating the future directions.

1.1 Assumptions

As the task allocation problem remains to be NP-hard, various heuristic solutions are proposed with one or more assumptions [2]. This work also makes certain assumptions that are as follows.

1. The processing nodes in the DCS are heterogeneous. The tasks are disjoint and have no inter-task communication. Only the modules within a task have interdependencies and communication requirements.
2. Execution and communication matrices for the task graphs are assumed to be given. These matrices are different for every task and calculated in units of time. While partitioning the task into modules, we assume that the memory requirements of the modules are also calculated.
3. The assumption of the availability of interconnection graph accommodates nonregular type of interconnection networks.

Here, in this paper, the word 'processor' and 'processing node', 'assignment' and 'allocation' have been used to refer the same.

2 Load

The tasks submitted into a DCS are partitioned into suitable modules and then these modules are to be allocated to the processing nodes. Each task can be represented by a Task Graph $(TG) = (V_t, E_t)$, where (1) V_t is a set of vertices, each of which represents a module of the task $m_1, m_2, ..., m_n$ and (2) $E_t \subseteq V_t \times V_t$ is a set of edges each of which represents the Inter Module Communication (IMC) between the two modules at the end of the edge. We can also represent the network of processors $p_1, p_2, ..., p_n$ in a DCS as a Processor Graph $PG = (V_p, E_p)$; where vertices represent the processors and the edges represent the communication links between processors (see Fig.2). The goal of TA is to allocate the Task Graphs (TG) to a network of processors in a DCS (i.e. to PG) to achieve the minimum turn-around time of tasks [2].

A processor's load comprises of all the execution and communication costs associated with its assigned modules of the task [6]. The time required by the heaviest-loaded processor will determine the entire tasks' completion time. So, the TA problem must find a mapping of the set of m modules of l tasks to n processors so as to minimize tasks completion time. Our goal is to allocate the modules in such a way that does not cause any processing node to be overloaded because an overloaded node may affect adversely in the turn around time of the tasks in a heterogeneous DCS.

The load in a processing node p is calculated as follows

$$\sum_{l=1}^{k}\sum_{i=1}^{mi} X_{ilp}.M_{ilp} + \sum_{\substack{q=1\\q\neq p}}^{n}\sum_{l=1}^{k}\sum_{i=1}^{mi}\sum_{\substack{j=1\\j\neq i}}^{m}(C_{ijl} + CC_{pq}).M_{ilp}.M_{jlq} \qquad (1)$$

where, $CC_{pq} = C_{fi}.L^{i}_{pq}$

X_{ilp} = execution cost of ith module of task l on processing node p
C_{ijl} = Inter-Module Communication(IMC)Cost between i^{th} and j^{th} module of task l
M_{ilp} = assignment matrix of ith module of lth task on processing node p

$$M_{ilp} = \begin{cases} 1 & \text{if module } m_i \text{ of task } l \text{ is assigned to processor } p \\ 0 & \text{otherwise} \end{cases}$$

M_{jlq} = assignment matrix of jth module of lth task on any other processing node q

$$M_{jlq} = \begin{cases} 1 & \text{if module } m_j \text{ of task } l \text{ is assigned to processor } q \\ 0 & \text{otherwise} \end{cases}$$

L^{i}_{pq}= connection matrix of two processors p and q, describing the links (direct/ single indirect/ double indirect etc.) of connection paths among the processing nodes in Processor Graph (PG).

C_{fi}= coefficient matrix which has n entries describing the IPC (Inter Processor Communication) costs for the links of connection paths among the processing nodes. For example, C_{f1}=5 (for direct connection between the processors), C_{f2}=10 (for processors which are indirectly connected by one link), C_{f3}= 20 (for processors which are indirectly connected by two links) etc.

The first part of the above equation 1 is the total execution cost of the modules of all the tasks allocated on a processing node p. The second part is the communication overhead on p with the modules of the tasks allocated on the other processing node such as q in the DCS. The ith entry of the coefficient matrix C_{fi} corresponds to communication between two processors via i links. If processors p and q are not directly connected, we find L^2, multiply it by C_{f2}, (2nd field of C_f), and check whether this comes out to be non-zero; if it does, we replace L^1 in calculation with L^2; if not, we find out $L^3$and multiply it with C_{f3} and check whether the product comes out to be non-zero. We continue like this until we find a non-zero value and then replace L^i in calculation with this (it is to be mentioned that we shall find a non-zero value within n multiplications, where n is the no. of processing nodes).

2.1 Global Table(GT)

To allocate the modules optimally so that no processor becomes overloaded, the load on each of the n processing nodes needs to be computed. By finding the processing node with heaviest load, the optimal assignment out of all possible assignments will allot the minimum load to the heaviest loaded processor. Thus it is necessary to consider realistic view that only a finite number of modules can be allocated to a processor depending on the architectural capability of the processing nodes in a DCS. Consequently, earlier algorithms [2, 5, 6] have continued to assume that all the modules will be eventually allocated no matter how large the memory requirements are, and/or how many modules a processor can accommodate and what is the current status of the system due to the existing allocation. These algorithms do not consider the requirement of allocation of modules of multiple tasks. In the proposed algorithm, we have shed off these unrealistic assumptions and make use of a data structure STATUS associated with every processor, which has two fields showing: the maximum number of modules that can be allocated to the processor and the memory capacity of the processor.

Whenever a module is chosen for allocation onto a processing node, the STATUS is checked and it is ascertained whether the processor can accommodate the module at hand. If not, another processor is chosen if available. The consequence might be that a certain module is not allocated at all. This data structure is implemented by constructing a Global table (GT) to maintain the track of maximum number of modules that can be allocated to a processing node depending upon its memory capacity. This is a dynamic table, which keeps the information of the remaining memory of nodes and the number of modules can be allocated on the nodes. Whenever a new task arrives, this GT is to be consulted and to

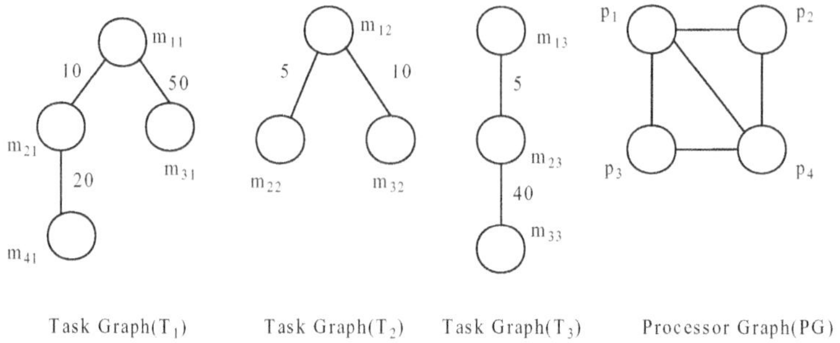

Fig. 1. Example of task graphs T_1, T_2 and T_3 with their modules and a DCS as processor graph

Table 2. The final status of the GT using A* for case 1

P_{node}	M_{mod}	M_{cap}	Mod_{assign}	R_{mod}	R_{mem}
p_1	4	10	$m_{21}m_{41}m_{22}$	1	1
p_2	3	8	$m_{12}m_{32}m_{23}$	0	2
p_3	4	9	$m_{13}m_{33}$	2	2
p_4	5	12	$m_{11}m_{31}$	3	5

unit. For example, the communication cost between m_{11} (the first module of task T_1) with m_{21} (the second module of task T_1) is 10 unit. The adjacency matrix L^i_{pq} of processing nodes are assumed to be given which represents how the processing nodes are connected among each other. For example, the processing nodes p_2 and p_3 are not directly connected, so $L^1_{p2p3} = 0$. But they are connected with at least one indirect link (through p_1 or p_4). So, $L^2_{p2p3} = 1$.

The Results for case 1

Total cost (communication and execution) at all the processing nodes is 500 units. Time required by the algorithm was 0.06 seconds. Note that the results are conducted in a single processor machine.

Case 2

The algorithm is implemented with other two cases. In case 2, a DCS consists of five tasks partitioned with their corresponding modules $T_1(m_{11}, m_{21}, m_{31}, m_{41}, m_{51}), T_2(m_{12}, m_{22}, m_{32}, m_{42}), T_3(m_{13}, m_{23}, m_{33}, m_{43}), T_4$ $(m_{14}, m_{24}, m_{34}, m_{44}, m_{54}, m_{64}, m_{74}), T_5(m_{15}, m_{25}, m_{35}, m_{45}, m_{55}, m_{65}, m_{75}, m_{85})$ and a set of five processing nodes $(p_1, p_2, p_3, p_4, p_5)$ interconnected in some fashion (Fig. 2).

The Results using case 2

Total cost at all the processing nodes is 1585 unit. Time required by the algorithm was 0.17 seconds.

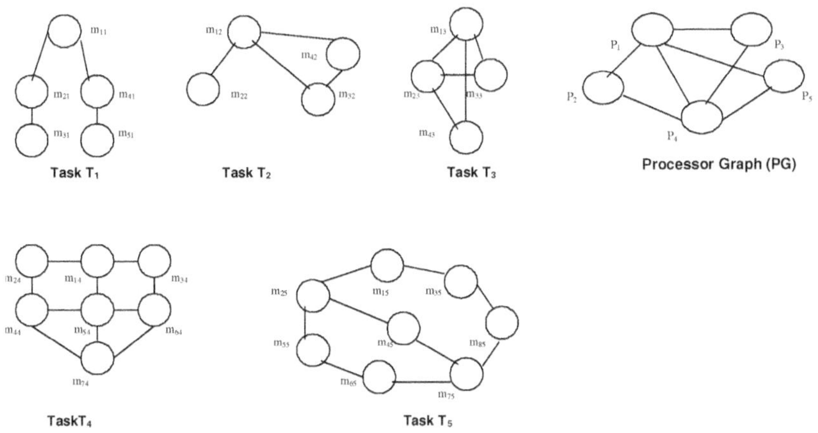

Fig. 2. Example of task graphs T_1, T_2, T_3, T_4 and T_5 with their modules and a DCS as processor graph

Table 3. The final status of the GT using A* for case 2

P_{node}	M_{mod}	M_{cap}	Mod_{assign}	R_{mod}	R_{mem}
p_1	10	50	$m_{21}m_{51}m_{12}m_{42}$ $m_{33}m_{43}m_{14}m_{34}$ $m_{64}m_{74}$	0	19
p_2	9	40	$m_{41}m_{22}m_{13}m_{24}$ $m_{25}m_{85}$	3	21
p_3	7	35	$m_{32}m_{23}m_{44}$ $m_{45}m_{65}$	2	21
p_4	6	30	$m_{11}m_{31}m_{54}m_{15}$	2	14
p_5	4	10	$m_{35}m_{55}m_{75}$	1	2

Case 3

A set of 8(eight) tasks with their corresponding modules $T_1(m_{11}, m_{21}, m_{31}, m_{41})$, $T_2(m_{12}, m_{22}, m_{32}, m_{42}, m_{52})$, $T_3(m_{13}, m_{23}, m_{33}, m_{43}, m_{53}, m_{63})$, T_4 $(m_{14}, m_{24}, m_{34}, m_{44})$, $T_5(m_{15}, m_{25}, m_{35}, m_{45}, m_{55})$, $T_6(m_{16}, m_{26}, m_{36}, m_{46}, m_{56}, m_{66})$, $T_7(m_{17}, m_{27}, m_{37}, m_{47})$, $T_8(m_{18}, m_{28}, m_{38}, m_{48}, m_{58})$ and a set of 6(six) processors $(p_1, p_2, p_3, p_4, p_5, p_6)$ have been considered. Due to space limitation, here, we present only the final status of allocation using GT.

Table 4. The final status of the GT using A* for case 3

P_{node}	M_{mod}	M_{cap}	Mod_{assign}	R_{mod}	R_{mem}
p_1	10	50	$m_{21}m_{51}m_{12}m_{42}$ $m_{33}m_{43}m_{14}m_{34}$ $m_{64}m_{74}$	0	19
p_2	9	40	$m_{41}m_{22}m_{13}m_{24}$ $m_{25}m_{85}$	3	21
p_3	7	35	$m_{32}m_{23}m_{44}m_{45}$ m_{65}	2	21
p_4	6	30	$m_{11}m_{31}m_{54}m_{15}$	2	14
p_5	4	10	$m_{35}m_{55}m_{75}$	1	2

The Results using case 3
Total cost at all the processing nodes is 1380 unit. Time required by the algorithm was 0.19 seconds.

5 Comparative Observations

The TA algorithms that consider only modules of one task do not consider the limitation of memory and the number of modules that can be assigned to a particular processor. This is so because these algorithms are not meant for assignment of modules belonging to the multiple disjoint tasks. Such a single task assignment problem is easier to solve because of this reason.

Table 5. The final status of the GT using EA* for case 1

P_{node}	M_{mod}	M_{cap}	Mod_{assign}	R_{mod}	R_{mem}
p_1	4	10	$m_{21}m_{41}m_{22}m_{32}m_{23}m_{33}$	-2	1
p_2	3	8	$m_{12}m_{13}$	1	2
p_3	4	9		4	2
p_4	5	12	$m_{11}m_{31}$	3	5

However, we can execute the Single Task Allocation (STA) algorithms [2, 5, 6] multiple time ones for each task using the GT data structure to record the status of allocation and the system as done in our proposed algorithm (sec. 4). Now we compare the status of allocation and the execution time requirements of the method used in EA* and our proposed allocation algorithm. The STA based on A* [2] referred to as EA* in the subsequent discussion has been executed multiple times and the run times have been obtained. So, in the experiment, we have executed the tasks one by one for the cases 1, 2 and 3 without considering the processor connectivity (how the processor are connected i.e. with direct connection/indirect connection etc., because it is not possible to do so in EA*) for the EA* as described in the algorithm of [2]. In the work [6], another modified version of EA* is proposed but still it was developed for single task allocation with their modules by using the same idea of [2]. In [5], an algorithm has been presented to reduce the search space using the idea of [2, 6]. Therefore, here we

Table 6. The final status of the GT using EA* for case 2

P_{node}	M_{mod}	M_{cap}	Mod_{assign}	R_{mod}	R_{mem}
p_1	10	50	$m_{21}m_{51}m_{12}m_{42}$ $m_{23}m_{43}m_{14}m_{34}$ $m_{25}m_{85}m_{74}$	-1	19
p_2	9	40	$m_{41}m_{22}m_{13}$ $m_{24}m_{55}$	4	21
p_3	7	35	$m_{32}m_{33}m_{44}$ $m_{45}m_{65}$	2	21
p_4	6	30	$m_{11}m_{31}m_{54}$	2	14
p_5	4	10	$m_{15}m_{65}m_{75}$	1	2

Table 7. The final status of the GT using EA* for case 3

P_{node}	M_{mod}	M_{cap}	Mod_{assign}	R_{mod}	R_{mem}
p_1	10	70	$m_{11}m_{21}m_{41}m_{52}m_{13}m_{33}m_{63}m_{14}m_{34}m_{44}m_{15}$ $m_{55}m_{16}m_{46}m_{66}m_{17}m_{47}m_{18}m_{44}m_{18}m_{58}$	-10	35
p_2	8	50	$m_{31}m_{23}m_{24}m_{35}$ $m_{26}m_{27}m_{38}$	1	23
p_3	6	40	$m_{53}m_{36}m_{37}m_{38}$	2	20
p_4	7	35	$m_{43}m_{25}m_{45}m_{56}$	3	16
p_5	6	40	m_{32}	2	22
p_6	6	33	$m_{12}m_{22}m_{42}$	3	8

present the comparative results with the algorithm proposed in [2], as all the other STA algorithms are basically based on this.

If we look at the results shown in the Tables 5, 6 and 7 for allocation of tasks using EA* for the cases 1, 2 and 3, respectively, it is observed that balanced load allocation can not be achieved. In all the cases, presented in the tables, some processing nodes are overloaded (indicated by '-' sign) according to the Vth column of the GT considering their existing architectural capabilities. Thus, it is justified that the EA*, in the form, as reported in [2, 5, 6], can not be used for the allocation of multiple tasks. Here, A* is used to refer our A* based algorithm proposed in section 4. Furthermore, since we did not get good results using EA* in terms of allocation, hence we did not present here the running time and the total cost required by EA*.

5.1 Experimental Results

It is observed from results using A* in section 4 that the time taken by our algorithm is not very effective considering the small number of tasks and their corresponding modules. But the fact is that the experiments were conducted in a single machine to make comparisons with the earlier algorithms.

Therefore, to investigate the effectiveness and the scalability of our proposed algorithm we further experimented with large number of task graphs with corresponding modules. For simulation purpose we use Sun Fire 12K, 8 processors based Distributed Multiprocessor systems and Message Passing Interface (MPI) as programming environment. In the Fig. 3, 4 and 5, the x-axis represents the no. of tasks and y-axis represents the execution time in seconds. It is observed from the figures that for an amount of large number of tasks, our parallel algorithm performs better (Fig. 5) than the other two (Fig. 3 and 4) with respect to the execution time with an increasing number of processors. In Fig. 3, the 'pink' colored line represents the execution time for 60(approx.) tasks using 8 processing nodes and it is greater than the time required by all other processors. Fig. 4 represents the time required by our algorithm while number of tasks is equal to 100. Here also the 'pink' colored line indicates the number the running time taken by 8 processing nodes and it is still greater than the time required by the other processing nodes. Fig. 5 shows the time required while there is a

4. A.K. Tripathi, B.K. Sarker, N. Kumar and D.P. Vidyarthi, "A GA Based Multiple Task Allocation Considering Load", *International Journal of High Speed Computing*, vol. 11, no. 4, pp. 203-214, 2000.
5. M. Kafil and I. Ahmed , "Optimal Task Assignment in Heterogeneous Distributed Computing System", *IEEE Concurrency*, vol. 6, no. 3, pp. 42-51, 1998.
6. Ramakrishnan, H.Chao, and L.A.Dunning, "A Close Look at Task Assignment in Distributed Systems", *Proceedings of IEEE Infocom-91*, pp. 806-812, 1991.
7. D.P.Vidyarthi, A.K.Tripathi and B.K.Sarker, "Allocation Aspects in Distributed Computing System", *IETE Technical Review*, vol. 18, no. 6, pp. 279-285, 2001.
8. P.Y.R.Richard Ma, E.Y.S.Lee and J. Tsuchiya, "A Task Allocation Model for Distributed Computing Systems", *IEEE Transactions on Computers*, vol. C-31, no. 1, pp. 41-47, 1982.
9. S.H.Bokhari, "On the Mapping Problem", *IEEE Transactions on Computers*, vol. C-30, pp. 207-214, March, 1981.
10. Pradeep K. Sinha, Distributed Operating System, IEEE Press, Prentice Hall of India Ltd., 1998.
11. A.S.Tanenbaum, Distributed Operating Systems, Prentice-Hall, Englewood Cliffs, 1995.
12. A.K.Tripathi, B.K.Sarker, N.Kumar and D.P.Vidyarthi, "Multiple Task Allocation with Load Considerations", *International Journal of Information and Computing Science (IJICS)*, vol.3, no.1, pp. 36-44, 2000.
13. D.P.Vidyarthi, A.K.Tripathi and B.K.Sarker, "Multiple Task Management in Distributed Computing System", *Journal of the CSI*, vol. 31, no. 1, pp. 19-25, 2001.

Table 7. The final status of the GT using EA* for case 3

P_{node}	M_{mod}	M_{cap}	Mod_{assign}	R_{mod}	R_{mem}
p_1	10	70	$m_{11}m_{21}m_{41}m_{52}m_{13}m_{33}m_{63}m_{14}m_{34}m_{44}m_{15}$ $m_{55}m_{16}m_{46}m_{66}m_{17}m_{47}m_{18}m_{44}m_{18}m_{58}$	-10	35
p_2	8	50	$m_{31}m_{23}m_{24}m_{35}$ $m_{26}m_{27}m_{38}$	1	23
p_3	6	40	$m_{53}m_{36}m_{37}m_{38}$	2	20
p_4	7	35	$m_{43}m_{25}m_{45}m_{56}$	3	16
p_5	6	40	m_{32}	2	22
p_6	6	33	$m_{12}m_{22}m_{42}$	3	8

present the comparative results with the algorithm proposed in [2], as all the other STA algorithms are basically based on this.

If we look at the results shown in the Tables 5, 6 and 7 for allocation of tasks using EA* for the cases 1, 2 and 3, respectively, it is observed that balanced load allocation can not be achieved. In all the cases, presented in the tables, some processing nodes are overloaded (indicated by '-' sign) according to the Vth column of the GT considering their existing architectural capabilities. Thus, it is justified that the EA*, in the form, as reported in [2, 5, 6], can not be used for the allocation of multiple tasks. Here, A* is used to refer our A* based algorithm proposed in section 4. Furthermore, since we did not get good results using EA* in terms of allocation, hence we did not present here the running time and the total cost required by EA*.

5.1 Experimental Results

It is observed from results using A* in section 4 that the time taken by our algorithm is not very effective considering the small number of tasks and their corresponding modules. But the fact is that the experiments were conducted in a single machine to make comparisons with the earlier algorithms.

Therefore, to investigate the effectiveness and the scalability of our proposed algorithm we further experimented with large number of task graphs with corresponding modules. For simulation purpose we use Sun Fire 12K, 8 processors based Distributed Multiprocessor systems and Message Passing Interface (MPI) as programming environment. In the Fig. 3, 4 and 5, the x-axis represents the no. of tasks and y-axis represents the execution time in seconds. It is observed from the figures that for an amount of large number of tasks, our parallel algorithm performs better (Fig. 5) than the other two (Fig. 3 and 4) with respect to the execution time with an increasing number of processors. In Fig. 3, the 'pink' colored line represents the execution time for 60(approx.) tasks using 8 processing nodes and it is greater than the time required by all other processors. Fig. 4 represents the time required by our algorithm while number of tasks is equal to 100. Here also the 'pink' colored line indicates the number the running time taken by 8 processing nodes and it is still greater than the time required by the other processing nodes. Fig. 5 shows the time required while there is a

4. A.K. Tripathi, B.K. Sarker, N. Kumar and D.P. Vidyarthi, "A GA Based Multiple Task Allocation Considering Load", *International Journal of High Speed Computing*, vol. 11, no. 4, pp. 203-214, 2000.
5. M. Kafil and I. Ahmed , "Optimal Task Assignment in Heterogeneous Distributed Computing System", *IEEE Concurrency*, vol. 6, no. 3, pp. 42-51, 1998.
6. Ramakrishnan, H.Chao, and L.A.Dunning, "A Close Look at Task Assignment in Distributed Systems", *Proceedings of IEEE Infocom-91*, pp. 806-812, 1991.
7. D.P.Vidyarthi, A.K.Tripathi and B.K.Sarker, "Allocation Aspects in Distributed Computing System", *IETE Technical Review*, vol. 18, no. 6, pp. 279-285, 2001.
8. P.Y.R.Richard Ma, E.Y.S.Lee and J. Tsuchiya, "A Task Allocation Model for Distributed Computing Systems", *IEEE Transactions on Computers*, vol. C-31, no. 1, pp. 41-47, 1982.
9. S.H.Bokhari, "On the Mapping Problem", *IEEE Transactions on Computers*, vol. C-30, pp. 207-214, March, 1981.
10. Pradeep K. Sinha, Distributed Operating System, IEEE Press, Prentice Hall of India Ltd., 1998.
11. A.S.Tanenbaum, Distributed Operating Systems, Prentice-Hall, Englewood Cliffs, 1995.
12. A.K.Tripathi, B.K.Sarker, N.Kumar and D.P.Vidyarthi, "Multiple Task Allocation with Load Considerations", *International Journal of Information and Computing Science (IJICS)*, vol.3, no.1, pp. 36-44, 2000.
13. D.P.Vidyarthi, A.K.Tripathi and B.K.Sarker, "Multiple Task Management in Distributed Computing System", *Journal of the CSI*, vol. 31, no. 1, pp. 19-25, 2001.

ETRI-QM: Reward Oriented Query Model for Wireless Sensor Networks

Jie Yang, Lei Shu, Xiaoling Wu, Jinsung Cho, Sungyoung Lee, and Sangman Han

Department of Computer Engineering,
Kyung Hee University, Korea
{yangjie, sl8132, xiaoling, sylee, i30000}@oslab.khu.ac.kr
chojs@khu.ac.kr

Abstract. Since sensors have a limited power supply, energy-efficient processing of queries over the network is an important issue. As data filtering is an important approach to reduce energy consumption, interest is used to be a constraint to filter uninterested data when users query data from sensor networks. Within these interested data, some of them are more important because they may have more valuable information than that of the others. We use 'Reward' to denote the importance level of data. Among the interested data, we hope to query the most important data first. In this paper, we propose a novel query model ETRI-QM and a new algorithm ETRI-PF (packet filter) dynamically combines the four constraints: Energy, Time, Reward and Interest. Based on our simulation results, we find out that our ETRI-QM together with ETRI-PF algorithm can improve the quality of the information queried and also reduce the energy consumption. [1]

1 Introduction

Wireless sensor networks are envisioned to consist of large numbers of devices, each capable of some limited computation, communication and sensing, operating in an unattended mode. One unifying view is to treat them as distributed databases. The simplest mechanism to obtain information from this kind of database is to use queries for data within the network. However, most of these devices are battery operated, which highly constrains their life-span, and it is often not possible to replace the power source of thousands of sensors. So how to query with the limited energy resources on the nodes is a key challenge in these unattended networks.

Researchers have noted the benefits of a query processor-like interface to sensor networks and the need for sensitivity to limited power and computational resources [1, 3, 6, 7, 9,]. Prior systems, however, tend to view query processing in sensor networks simply as a power-constrained version of traditional query processing: given some set of data, they strive to process that data as energy-efficiently as possible. Typical strategies include minimizing expensive communication by applying aggregation and filtering operations inside the sensor network.

---

[1] Dr. Sungyoung Lee is the corresponding author.

L.T. Yang et al. (Eds.): EUC 2005, LNCS 3824, pp. 597 – 608, 2005.

In our paper, we present a novel query model (ETRI-QM) to query the data with more important information among the interested data. By using this query model, we can dynamically combine these four constraints (Energy, Time, Reward, and Interest) to provide diverse query versions for different applications. Within our query model, each packet has four parameters: (1) energy consumption of the packet; (2) processing time of the packet; (3) important level of the packet; and (4) interest level of the packet. By using this ETRI-QM, we can achieve the following contributions: (1) Using *interest constraint* as the threshold to filter the uninterested incoming packets to reduce the energy consumption; (2) Using *reward constraint* to choose the high quality information and minimize the queried packet number to minimize the energy consumption but still satisfy the minimum information requirement.

The remainder of the paper is structured as follows. In the next section, we describe the related work. We introduce our query/event service APIs to illustrate the design of ETRI-QM in Section 3. The main principle of our ETRI-QM is in Section 4. In the simulation, we examine the performance of our query model and compare with the other different query plans (Section 5). Finally the paper is concluded in Section 6.

2 Related Work

In [8], the authors present a sensor information networking architecture called SINA, which facilitates querying, monitoring, and tasking of sensor networks. To support querying within sensor networks, they design a data structure kept inside the sensor nodes based on the spreadsheet paradigm. In the spreadsheet paradigm, each sensor node maintains a logical datasheet containing a set of cells. By defining the semantic of a cell to specifying scope of the query, the information can be organized and accessed according to specific application needs, and also the number of the packets need to be sent can be reduced, thus the energy consumption will be reduced. However, there exist a tradeoff between the energy cost to run SINA on each sensor node and the energy reduced by using SINA.

In [2], our work also has some similarities to techniques proposed, the authors introduced a new real-time communication architecture (RAP) and also a new packet scheduling policy called velocity monotonic scheduling (VMS). VMS assigns the priority of a packet based on its requested velocity. This work differs from our work in two aspects: one is that the cost-model is different in the two scenarios–in RAP is primarily reducing the end-to-end deadline miss radio while we are minimizing energy consumption and maximizing the querying quality; the second one is that RAP intends to maximize the number of packets meeting their end-to-end deadlines without considering their value (reward, importance level), and in our model, we take reward an important constraint to deal with the queries.

Samuel et al discussed the design of an acquisitional query processor (ACQP) for data collection in sensor network in [10]. They provide a query processor-like interface to sensor networks and use acquisitional techniques to reduce power consumption. Their query languages for ACQP focus on issues related to when and how often samples are acquired. To choose a query plan that will yield the lowest overall power consumption, the query is divided into three steps: creation of query, dissemination of query and execution of query. Optimizations are made at each step.

Our ETRI-QM combines four constraints (**energy, time, interest** and **reward**) to maximize the querying quality with minimum energy consumption. In papers [4, 5]. Cosmin Rusu, *et al.* first time consider **Energy**, **Time**, and **Reward** these three constraints simultaneously while Reward denotes the important level of tasks. They believe that among a set of tasks of real time applications, some of them are more valuable than the others. So instead of processing several unimportant tasks just consuming less energy, it is more meaningful to process one valuable task consuming more energy. In our query model, we use **reward** to denote the importance level of data, so that we can transmit the data with more valuable information first. By considering the four constraints simultaneously, we make out our target that is to query the most valuable (**reward**) packets from the **interested** area to be transmitted while meeting **time** and **energy** constraints.

3 ETRI-QM

Applications may submit queries or register for events through a set of query/event service APIs. The APIs provides a high-level abstraction to applications by hiding the specific location and status of each individual node. These APIs allow applications to specify the timing constraints as well as other constraints of queries.

ETRI-QM provides the following query/event service APIs.

Query {attribute_list, interested_area, system_value, timing_constraints, querier_loc}

Issue a query for a list of attributes in an interested area with the maximum system value (reward). Attributes refer to the data collected by different types of sensors, such as temperature sensors, humidity sensors, wind sensors, rain sensors etc. Interested area specifies the scope of the query, the area from which data is needed by the users. System value is defined as the sum of selected packets' reward. Timing_constraints can be period, deadline and so on. If a period is specified for a command, query results will be sent from the interested area to the issuer of query periodically. The querier_loc is the location of the base station that sends out the query.

Imagine a heterogeneous network consisting of many different types of sensors: temperature sensors, humidity sensors, wind sensors, rain sensors etc. monitoring the chemical found in the vicinity of a volcano. Suppose the volcano has just broken out, and we want to know which five chemicals found have the highest particle concentration. Obviously, sensors near the volcano will have more valuable data, which means that the importance levels of these data are much higher than those of the data collected by the further sensors. Thus, here we can consider reward to be the distance between sensors and the volcano.

Consider another example: lots of sensors are deployed in some area with different densities. For the EventFound case, take noise into account, the data collected by sensors having higher densities will be more reliable. So, here the reward is changed to be the density of the sensors around the interested area in the network.

There is one more example to make you clearly understand the concept of "reward". In the case of real-time communication for wireless sensor network, meeting the end-to-end deadline seems to be the most importance issue, so that we can consider arriving time to be the reward value. Reward is defined to be the importance

selected packets' *value ratio* $V_{x,y}$ to meet the system_value defined in the query/event service APIs. Therefore, the problem is to

$$\text{Maximize} \sum_{x\in A, y\in P} V_{x,y} \leq \text{system\_value} \quad (1)$$

$$\text{Subject to} \sum_{x\in A, y\in P} E_{x,y} \leq E_{\max} \quad (2)$$

$$\sum_{y\in P} T_{x,y} \leq D \quad (3)$$

$$IT_{\min} \leq I_{x,y} \leq IT_{\max} \quad (4)$$

$$x \in \mathrm{A} \quad (5)$$

$$\mathrm{A} \subseteq \{A_1, A_2 \ldots A_M\} \quad (6)$$

$$y \in P_x \quad (7)$$

$$P_x \subseteq \{1, 2 \ldots \mathrm{N}\} \quad (8)$$

Since $\mathrm{P} = P_1 \cup P_2 \cup \ldots \cup P_M$, we can have the following equation as:

$$\sum_{x\in A, y\in P} V_{x,y} = \sum_{A_1, y\in P_1} V_{A_1,y} + \sum_{A_2, y\in P_2} V_{A_2,y} + \ldots + \sum_{A_M, y\in P_M} V_{A_M,y} \quad (9)$$

From equation (9), we can find that the real problem of ETRI-PF is to find out the minimum subset of $P_x \subseteq \{1, 2 \ldots \mathrm{N}\}$ to maximize the *system value* to system_value from each interested area A_x. Thus, the problem is changed to

$$\text{Maximize} \sum_{A_x, y\in P_x} V_{x,y} \leq \text{system\_value} \quad (10)$$

$$\text{Subject to} \quad E_{x,y} \leq RE \quad (11)$$

$$\sum_{y\in P} T_{x,y} \leq D \quad (12)$$

$$IT_{\min} \leq I_{x,y} \leq IT_{\max} \quad (13)$$

$$x \in \mathrm{A} \quad (14)$$

$$\mathrm{A} \subseteq \{A_1, A_2 \ldots A_M\} \quad (15)$$

$$y \in P_x \quad (16)$$

$$P_x \subseteq \{1, 2 \ldots \mathrm{N}\} \quad (17)$$

Inequality (11) guarantees that the *time constraint* is satisfied. Inequality (12) guarantees that only the interested packets are accepted, and inequality (13) guarantees that the energy budget is not exceeded. In order to solve the problem that is presented by (10)-(17), we give the following steps for our ETRI-PF algorithm.

4.2 Steps of ETRI-PF

Before sending the real data of a packet to cluster head, sensor node can send its packet's parameters to the cluster head by including them in a small packet, which just consumes very limited energy. We give a name to this kind of small packet as *Parameter Packet (PP)*. There is a physical buffer that exists inside cluster head to store these *PPs*. After receiving these *parameter packets*, cluster head can decide which packet to be accepted and which packet should be discarded based on these sent parameters. In terms of this Two Tiers Buffer model, basically, we can define our ETRI-PF algorithm into the following steps:

Step 1: Initialization. After receiving PP $\subseteq \{PP_1, PP_2, \ldots, PP_N\}$, we assume that tables exist inside the cluster head for storing parameters of every packet i ($i \in$ PP): *energy consumption* $E_{x,y}$, *processing time* $T_{x,y}$, *reward value* $R_{x,y}$, and *interest value* $I_{x,y}$. For each PP_i, there are energy consumption for checking CE_i and a period of time for checking CT_i. We also use two structure arrays, *considered(i)* and *selected(i)* of size N, to store the information for all received *PPs*. Initially, we start with an empty schedule (*selected(i).status = false*) and no *PP* is considered (*considered(i).status = false*). The set of selected *PPs* (initially empty) is defined as S = {*(i)* | *selected(i).status = true*}. After selecting the *PPs*, cluster head accepts packets that are corresponded to these selected *PPs*. Therefore, packet's parameters can be expressed as *considered(i).*$E_{x,y}$, *considered(i).*$T_{x,y}$, *considered(i).*$R_{x,y}$, *considered(i).*$I_{x,y}$, *selected(i).*$E_{x,y}$, *selected(i).*$T_{x,y}$, *selected(i).*$R_{x,y}$, and *selected(i).*$I_{x,y}$. We define five variables: 1) *checking energy* ($\sum_{i \in PP} CE_i$) is used to store the total energy consumption for checked *PPs*; 2) *checking time* ($\sum_{i \in PP} CT_i$) is used to store the total processing time for checked *PPs*; 3) *processing energy* ($\sum_{i \in PP}$ *selected(i).*$E_{x,y}$) is used to store the total energy consumption for processed packets; and 4) *processing time* ($\sum_{i \in PP}$ *selected(i).*$T_{x,y}$) is used to store the total processing time for processed packets. 5) *system value summation* ($\sum_{i \in PP}$ *selected(i).*$R_{x,y}$) is used to store the total value for packets to be processed in STB. These five variables are all initialized to zero.

Step 2: In FTB, we filter and accept packets based on the ETRI constraints. A packet that can be accepted should satisfy all the following criteria:

- ❑ This packet's *PP* is not considered before (*considered (i).status = false*).
- ❑ The current schedule is feasible (*checking time + processing time*) $\leq D$.
- ❑ By accepting this packet to current schedule, the energy budget is not exceeded (*checking energy + processing energy + considered(i).*$E_{x,y} \leq E_{max}$).
- ❑ This packet is intentionally queried by end user ($IT_{min} \leq$ *considered(i).*$I_{x,y} \leq IT_{max}$).
- ❑ Among all the *PPs* that satisfy the above criteria, select the one that has the largest *considered(i).*$V_{x,y}$ = *considered(i).*$R_{x,y}$ / *considered(i).*$E_{x,y}$.
- ❑ By accepting this packet to current schedule, the summation of the system value is just up to the system_value defined in the query/event service APIs. ($\sum_{i \in PP}$ *selected(i).*$V_{x,y} \leq$ *system_value*)

After choosing the *PP*, cluster head can send Acknowledge back to accept new packet. In addition, for those packets which end user is not interested in, their corresponded sensor nodes will discard them. In this case, we refuse and discard the unnecessary data; consequently, we can reduce the energy consumption by reducing the data transmitting and receiving.

Step 3: In STB, we transmit accepted packets to base station by using Velocity Monotonic Scheduling:

As the algorithm that has been presented in [2], which assigns the priority of a packet based on its requested velocity. VMS minimizes the deadline miss ratios of sensor networks by giving higher priority to packets with higher requested velocities, which also reflects the local urgency. VMS embodies with both the timing constraint and location constraint.

Another aspect: Replace or drop a packet in the STB. A new packet is always accepted if possible. When receiving new *PP* from sensor node, if the STB is full, we can replace or drop a packet based on the following criteria:

- ❑ This packet's *PP* is selected (*selected(i).status = true*).
- ❑ Among all selected packet's *PPs*, find out the one that has the smallest $selected(i).V_{x,y} = selected(i).R_{x,y} / selected(i).E_{x,y}$.
- ❑ If this found one is not the new packet that is going to be accepted, we use this new packet to replace this found one, otherwise, we drop this new packet.

The flowchart and source code of ETRI-PF principles are showed in figure 2 and 3.

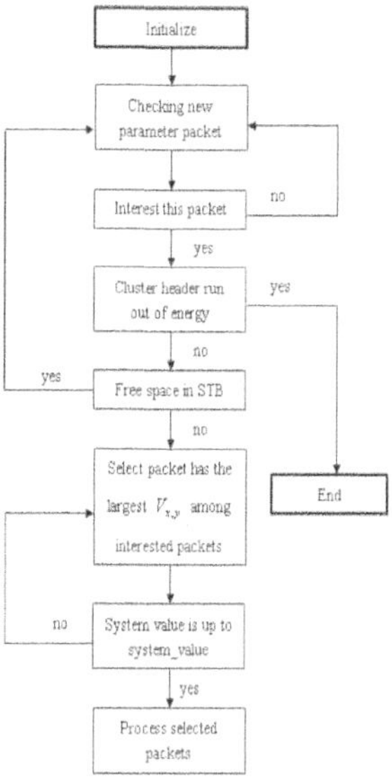

Fig. 2. Flowchart of ETRI-PF

```
Step1  initialize: selected[i].status = false; considered[i].status = false;
       ∀i ∈{1,2,···,N}; checking_energy = 0; checking_time = 0;
       processing_energy = 0; processing_time = 0;
Step2  if(considered[i].interest_value >= interest_threshold) then
           considered[i].status = true;
           if(cluster header buff has free space) then
               receive_pp();
           else
               if(current_pp.ratio > min(pp.ratio in buff)) then
                   receive current_pp; discard min(pp.ratio in buff);
               else
                   discard current_pp;
               end if
           end if
       end if
       calculate_checking_time();
       calculate_checking_energy();
       for i to buff_size
           if(checking_time + processing_time > deadline) then
               stop_working();
           else
               if(total_ratio < system_value) then
                   if(checking_energy + processing_energy <= total_energy)
                       selected[i].status = true;
                   else
                       change selected[i] with
                       max(selected[i].processing_energy in select);
                   end if
               end if
           end if
       next
Step3  for i to buff_size
           if(selected[i].status = true) then
               receive_packet(); process_packet();
               calculate_processing_time(); calculate_processing_energy();
           end if
       Next
Step4  End
```

Fig. 3. Pseudo code of ETRI-PF

5 Simulation Results

A sensor network can be modeled as a graph, where each vertex represents a sensor node and each edge represents the edge between two nodes when they are within each other's communication range. This network tracks the values of certain variables like temperature, humidity, etc. Application users submit their requests as queries and the sensor network transmits the requested data to the application.

For the simulation work, we randomly deploy eleven different sensor nodes. And we randomly initialize these sensor nodes with: the total energy of sensor nodes (scope: from 111 to 888), the buffer size of sensor nodes (scope: from 6 to 9). Ten of these eleven sensor nodes are chosen to be the packet generators which randomly create these ten different packets and send to the remaining one. The remaining one works as the cluster head. For this cluster head, we design five parameters: the *total energy = 666*, the *buffer size = 6*, the *deadline = 5*, the *system_value = 10* and the *interest threshold = 5*. The meaning of threshold is that we just accept the packets when their interest value are larger than 5. Packets from those areas are what the end users are interested in.

In addition, we design ten different packets that are randomly initialized with the following four parameters: energy consumption (scope: from 3 to 10), processing time (scope: from 3 to 10), reward value (scope: from 3 to 10) and interest value (scope: from 3 to 10).

These ten sensor nodes are organized into three groups based on their created packets' interest values. The packets that have the interest values belong to {8, 9, 10} are considered as group A, the packets that have the interest values belong to {6, 7} are considered as group B, and the packet that have interest values belong to {3, 4, 5} are considered as group C. Suppose the cluster head just accepts the packets from area A and B, moreover, within these interested packets it accepts the packet that has the largest $V_{x,y} = R_{x,y} / E_{x,y}$ first. And we also design that this cluster head works in the STB by using the *Velocity Monotonic Scheduling.*

In terms of energy consumption, we mainly consider the following two parts that have strong relationship with our proposed ETRI-PF, which are *processing energy* $\{E_{(Returning\ ACK)} + E_{(Receiving\ packet)} + E_{(Processing)} + E_{(Broadcasting\ event)} + E_{(Listening)} + E_{(Accepting\ ACK)} + E_{(Sending\ packet)}\}$ and *checking energy* $\{E_{(Accepting\ event)} + E_{(Deciding)}\}$. The checking energy is designed to be 0.3, which is 10% of the minimum packet consumption 3; also the checking time is designed to be 0.3, which is 10% of the minimum processing time 3. Besides ETRI-PF, we provide two different existing packet scheduling algorithms to run on the cluster head for comparison as follows:

1) Compared Algorithm one (CA 1):
   a) In FTB: No *interest constraint* and no *reward constraint*
   b) In STB: Minimizing the packet deadline miss ratio (*Velocity Monotonic Scheduling*)

The cluster head doesn't set any threshold to reduce the incoming packets, but just simply receives packets and relays them. Once it gets a packet, it will process this packet based on the *Velocity* determined by *time constraint* and *location constraint.*

2) Compared Algorithm two (CA 2):
   a) In FTB: Consider *interest constraint*, but no *reward constraint*
   b) In STB: Minimizing the packet deadline miss radio (*Velocity Monotonic Scheduling*)

The cluster head always accepts the packet that has the interest value larger than the interest threshold. Once it gets a packet, it will process this packet based on the *Velocity* determined by *time constraint* and *location constraint.*

We used the following metrics to capture the performance of our routing approach and to compare it with other algorithms:

1) *total processing energy* of cluster head, 2) *energy utilization* of cluster head (*energy utilization = processing energy / (checking energy + processing energy)*), 3) *discarded packets ratio* in sensor nodes (*discarded packets number / total created packets number* by sensor nodes), 4) *total time consumption* of cluster head (*checking time + processing time*), 5) *average interest value* per packet, 6) *average reward value* per packet. The simulation results and comparisons are showed as the following figures.

packets based on each packet's content. Therefore, as a challenge issue to be solved in the future, we are going to explore the appropriate measure methods to evaluate the interest level and important level of different packets.

Acknowledgement

This work was supported by grant No. R01-2005-000-10267-0 from Korea Science and Engineering Foundation in Ministry of Science and Technology.

References

1. C. Intanagonwiwat, R. Govindan, and D. Estrin. Directed diffusion: A scalable and robust communication paradigm for sensor networks. In *MobiCOM*, Boston, MA, August 2000.
2. C. Lu, B. M. Blum, T. F. Abdelzaher, J. A. Stankovic, and T. He, RAP: A Real-Time Communication Architecture for Large-Scale Wireless Sensor Networks, In IEEE RTAS 2002.
3. S. Madden and M. J. Franklin. Fjording the stream: An architechture for queries over streaming sensor data. In *ICDE*, 2002.
4. C. Rusu, R. Melhem, D. Mosse, "Maximizing Rewards for Real-Time Applications with Energy Constraints", ACM TECS, vol 2, no 4, 2003.
5. C. Rusu, R. Melhem, D. Mosse, "Multi-version Scheduling in Rechargeable Energy-aware Real-time Systems", to appear in Journal of Embedded Computing, 2004.
6. S. Madden, M. J. Franklin, J. M. Hellerstein, and W. Hong. TAG: A Tiny AGgregation Service for Ad-Hoc Sensor Networks. In *OSDI (to appear)*, 2002.
7. P.Bonnet, J.Gehrke, and P.Seshadri. Towards sensor database systems. In *Conference on Mobile Data Management*, January 2001.
8. Chien-Chung Shen, Chavalit Srisathapornphat, and Chaiporn Jaikaeo. Sensor information networking architecture and applications. IEEE Personal Communications, 8(4):52-59, August 2001.
9. O. Wolfson, A. P. Sistla, B. Xu, J. Zhou, and S. Chamberlain. DOMINO: Databases fOr MovINg Objects tracking. In *ACM SIGMOD*, Philadelphia, PA, June 1999.
10. Samuel R. Madden, Michael J. Franklin, Joseph M. Hellerstein, and Wei Hong. The Design of an Acquisitional Query Processor for Sensor Networks. SIGMOD, June 2003, San Diego, CA

Performance of Signal Loss Maps for Wireless Ad Hoc Networks

Henry Larkin, Zheng da Wu, and Warren Toomey

Faculty of IT, Bond University, Australia
{hlarkin, zwu, wtoomey}@staff.bond.edu.au

Abstract. Wireless ad hoc networks face many challenges in routing, power management, and basic connectivity. Existing research has looked into using predicted node movement as a means to improve connectivity. While past research has focused on assuming wireless signals propagate in clear free loss space, our previous research has focused on using signal loss maps to improve predictions. This paper presents novel testing of signal loss maps in relation to the accuracy used for prediction purposes. Through analysis of test cases and results from a custom built simulator the performance is effectively measured.

Keywords: Signal loss maps, predicting signal loss, signal strength maps.

1 Introduction

In any wireless networking environment where nodes are utilizing predicted location information in order to improve routing, the ability to predict the communication strength from one location to another becomes vital. A prediction of the wireless connectivity between two nodes cannot accurately rely on location information alone. The majority of today's wireless networking environments feature many obstructions which reflect and block wireless signals. This rules out assuming all signals between two physical locations will travel with a clear line-of-sight approach, such as is relied on in [1]. In addition to needing knowledge about nodes' physical locations, the predicted propagation of signals over physical areas is required. Wireless transmission capabilities in an unknown or known environment are difficult to predict with accuracy [2]. Not only do different locations have different communication capabilities, but environmental conditions may change those capabilities over time. Foreign nodes operating on the same channel, radio-frequency interference, environmental noise and even landscape may change radically over time. This will affect any recorded or estimated measurements of signal loss.

To overcome these challenges, our previous work designed a signal loss map solution [3]. Signal loss maps represent the logical signal propagation topology over a physical area. They describe how signals are likely to propagate in various directions over various distances. Due to the constantly changing nature of the wireless environment, a perfect signal loss map is not possible to create with current technologies. However, various estimates may be developed to provide, with appropriate safety margins, predictions on whether two nodes at two locations will have connectivity in the future.

L.T. Yang et al. (Eds.): EUC 2005, LNCS 3824, pp. 609 – 618, 2005.

This signal loss map, dubbed the Communication Map (CM), is tailored to be built in real time using only wireless ad hoc nodes. The map is created using signal strength information provided with each packet as it is received from any node. To provide a physical reference system, some form of location-providing device is required for each node. In this research, a system such as GPS [4] is assumed to be available to provide the coordinates of each node. From these two external sources the CM is constructed.

The CM is made up of cells, defined areas which are square in shape and represent an average signal loss modifier. The signal loss modifier is a value which represents how a signal's loss increases over distance, relative to free space loss. This approach of using cells describes to users of the CM the same information that vendors of wireless cards use to describe range and signal strength capabilities. Vendors of wireless cards often include the maximum range and signal strength of their product in a variety of general scenarios, for example outdoors, home environment, cluttered office, etc. In a similar fashion, the CM of this research generates such scenarios in real time, and delineates where on a map such areas exist.

The general formula for calculating free space loss, S_{loss} (db), in ideal circumstances of wireless signals [5] is:

$$S_{loss} = 32.4 + 20Log_{10}F + 20Log_{10}D \quad (1)$$

where F is the frequency (MHz), and D is the distance (km) between the two nodes.

The free space loss formula may only be used *once* for the entire signal. To have an effect on the overall loss of a signal, each line *segment's* distance (how much a signal travels within a cell) will need to be adjusted by some modifier which represents a cell's effect on signal loss. To overcome this problem, the concept of *logical distance* is introduced. Any signal received or predicted using our CM is based on a *logical distance*. The *logical distance* that a signal travels is the distance it would need to physically travel in order to produce the same amount of loss, thus allowing the above formula to be used, given multiple signal modifiers.

Each cell represents the average signal loss of signals passing through that cell. The value stored for each cell is the modifier that a signal applies to the *physical distance* of a signal as it passes through that cell, which when multiplied together with the physical distance creates a *logical distance*. The minimum modifier value is 1.0, in other words a *logical distance* is identical to the *physical distance*, and thus represents perfect free-space loss. The modifier of each cell is used to extend the distance of a signal to the distance it would need to travel in perfect free space to achieve the same loss.

For an example of this process, consider Fig. 1 below. A signal will travel from Node A to Node B over the given CM. The direct line between the two nodes is formed, and a list of cells over which the signal will pass is created. Each of these cells multiply their modifier by the *physical distance* that the signal travels through their cell. The resulting *logical distance* can be used to find the signal loss, which can consequentially determine whether two nodes are predicted to be neighbours. This formula thus uses the modifier of each cell to *extend* the distance of a signal to the distance it would need to travel in perfect free space to achieve the same loss.

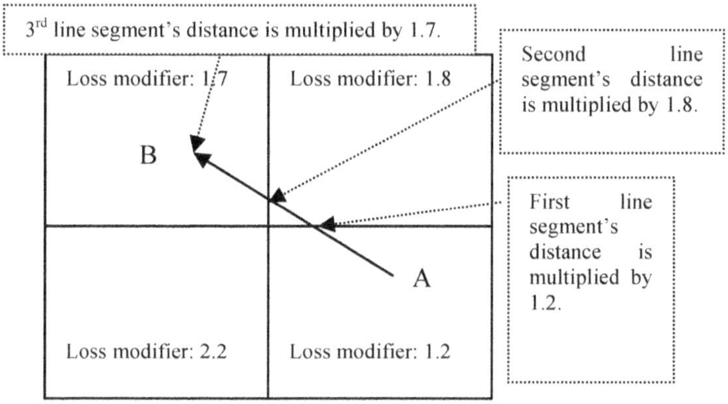

Fig. 1. Signal divided over multiple cells

2 Test Architecture

Existing simulators [6][7][8][9] already exist for basic network simulation. While many of these simulators are extensible, none specifically address the issues of wireless signal mapping and signal loss map testing. Because of this, a custom simulator was created. The simulator was created in response to fulfil the need for an appropriate testing bed for wireless ad hoc protocols that relied specifically on the needs of testing signal loss maps.

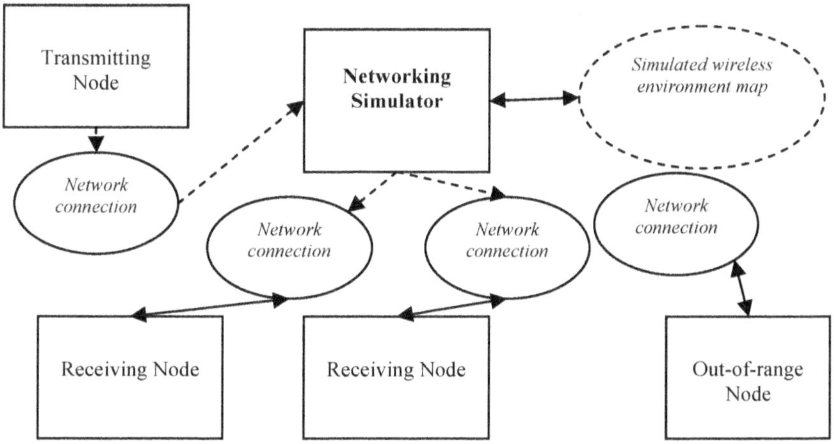

Fig. 2. Example Packet Broadcast

The simulator routes packets between nodes based on a simulated wireless environment map, which details user-created scenarios of how signals will propagate over real-world simulated objects. As each packet is successfully transmitted or lost (based on signal propagation), the simulator records what each node's CM predicted

of each scenario from Node A's viewpoint. Fig. 6 shows how the CM algorithm represented the signal loss surrounding nodes A, B, and F by utilising the smaller cell size of subdividing the DCS as a boundary representation itself. Fig. 7 shows the typical 100m DCS with boundaries, with Fig. 8 and Fig. 9 reducing the DCS to 50m and 25m respectively. The smaller DCS with boundaries hinders the boundary development, as boundaries are more difficult to develop than cells. Fig. 6 without boundaries shows that even with 8 nodes the CM does not perfectly represent even the shape of the simulated building, let alone the accurate signal loss. Without a thorough grid of cells there will be varying quantities of signals mapped over various cells, simply from node positioning and node movement. A perfectly accurate CM is impossible to develop using current technology. With the smaller DCS on the boundary examples, there become too many objects where signals can be mapped. As signals being mapped are averaged over all objects along the assumed signal's path, the greater number of objects requires a greater quantity of node movement to further correlate signal loss to more accurately-placed objects.

To further see the effects of implementing boundaries more scenarios are needed. The same experiments were run on Scenario 5 and Scenario 6, both of which also have high boundary use yet simple simulated environments that have a better chance

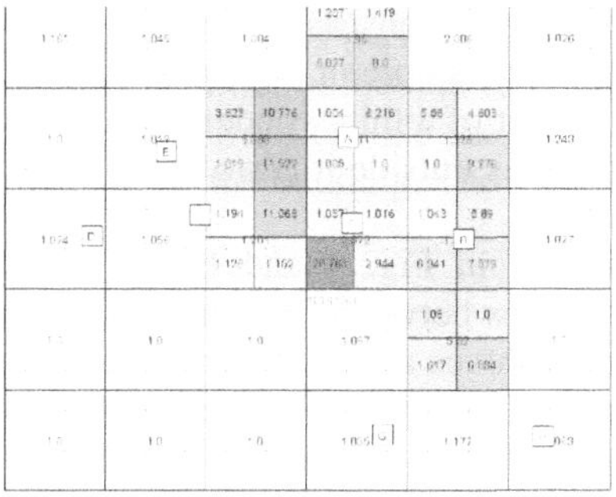

Fig. 6. Scenario 4: 25m DCS without Boundaries

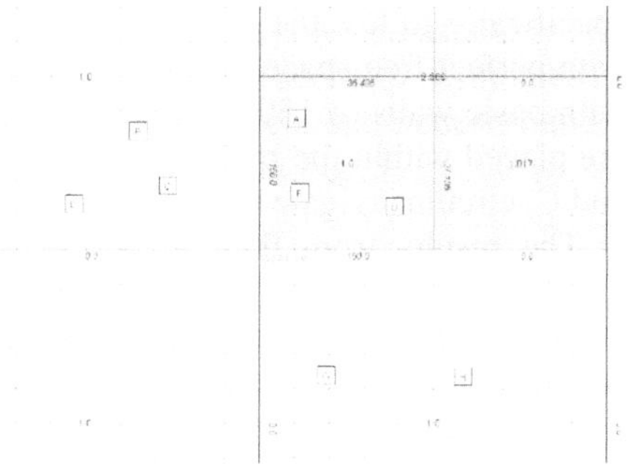

Fig. 7. Scenario 4: 100m DCS with Boundaries

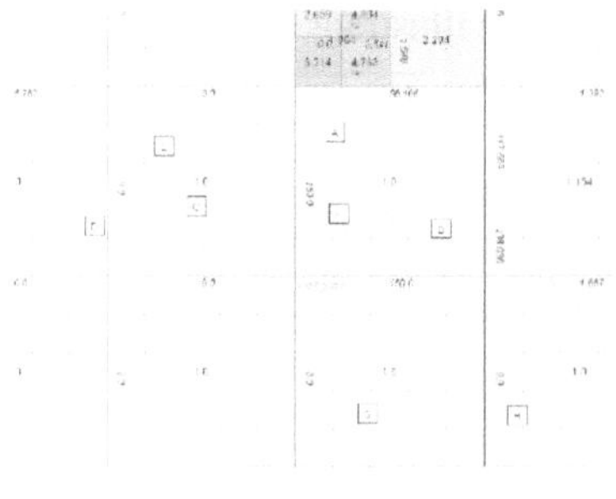

Fig. 8. Scenario 4: 50m DCS with Boundaries

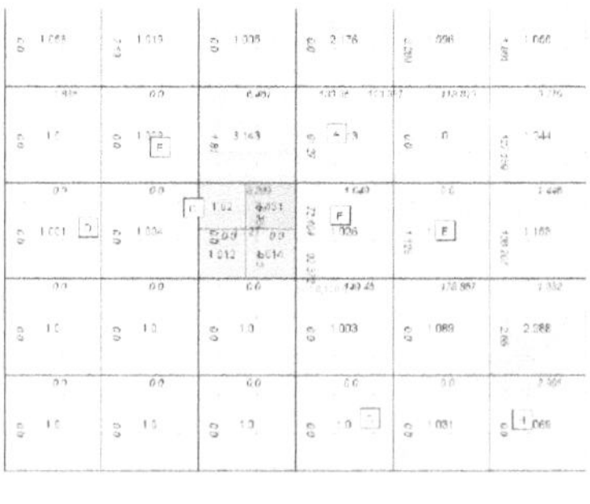

Fig. 9. Scenario 4: 25m DCS with Boundaries

of being mapped. Results are shown in Fig. 10 and Fig. 11. These experiments indicate that overall the varying DCS settings and the implementation of boundaries make little difference to the overall accuracy.

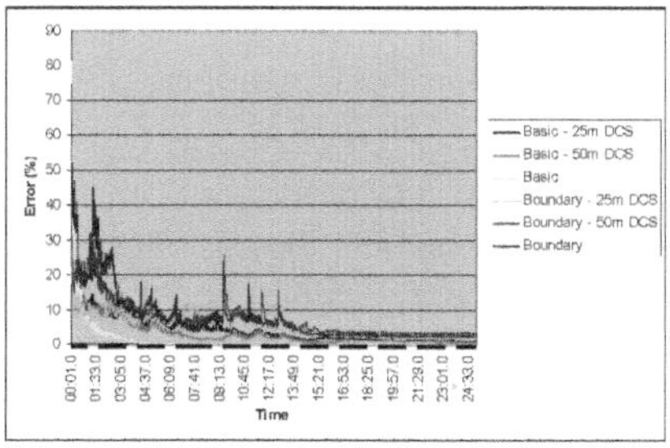

Fig. 10. Scenario 5 Results

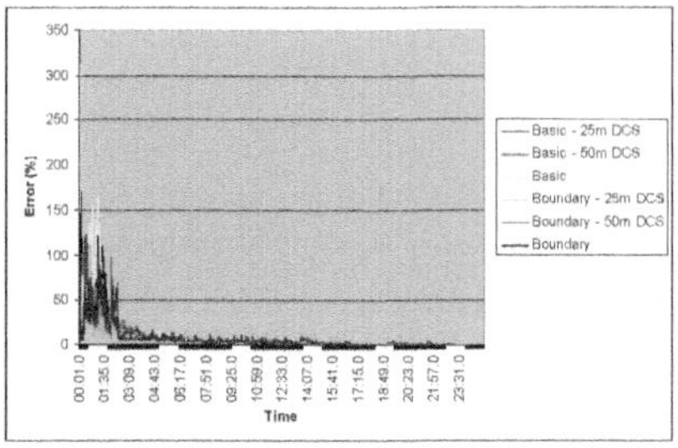

Fig. 11. Scenario 6 Results

The experiments were then run on Scenario 7, which is based on a real street. Despite the number of simulated objects and boundaries, all settings produced similar results (refer to Fig. 12 and Fig. 13). The CMs at the end of the simulations of a 25m DCS without boundaries and a 100m DCS with boundaries experiment are shown in Fig. 14 and Fig. 15 for interest. The favourable results in these experiments can be

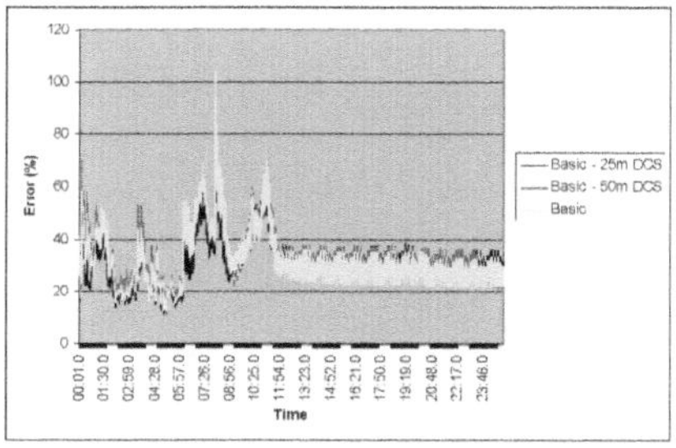

Fig. 12. Scenario 7 without Boundaries

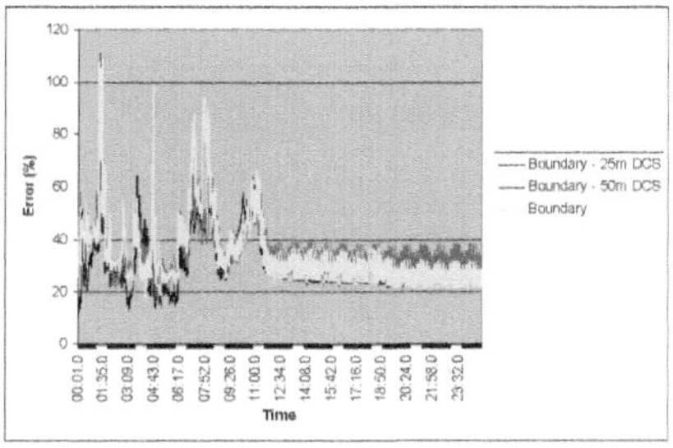

Fig. 13. Scenario 7 with Boundaries

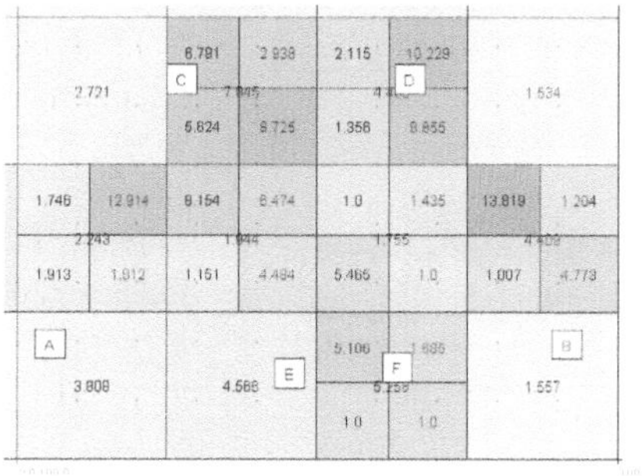

Fig. 14. 25m DCS CM without Boundaries

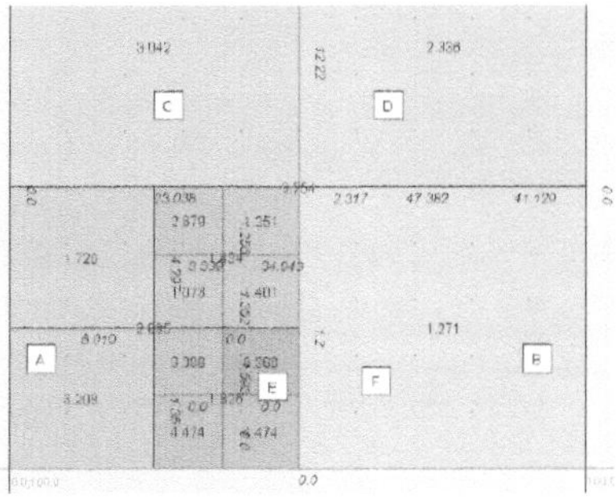

Fig. 15. 100m DCS CM with Boundaries

attributed to the low amount of node movement, where only three nodes are moving in relatively fixed movement patterns. A perfect CM is not required to produce favourable results, only a CM which adequately represents the signal loss as it has and will be used in the future.

4.2 Number of Nodes

Another area of interest was to determine if the number of nodes had an effect of the accuracy of the CM. Fig. 16 and Fig. 17 graph all setting samples over Scenario 1 and Scenario 2 respectively. These are the two main scenarios where the basic layout would allow the number of nodes to play an influential role without new areas being discovered by the increased number of nodes. Scenarios 3 and 4 were included (Fig. 18 and Fig. 19) were tested also, though these examples focus mainly on boundary testing.

The results in these experiments were surprisingly different than anticipated. In theory, the number of nodes would have favourably increased the accuracy of the CM. However, in almost all scenarios tested, an increase in the number of nodes had an adverse effect on accuracy. In Fig. 16, using both 4 and 5 nodes resulted in very similar results, with 5 nodes performing slightly better, as would be expected. Using 6 nodes, however, almost doubled the overall average error.

In Scenario 2 (Fig. 17), 8 moving nodes generate a more accurate map than 6 moving nodes, but only within the first 10 minutes of the experiment. Towards the end of the simulation the average error increases, and unfortunately stabilises this way due to the lack of future node movement. This is simply a case of a new area of signal

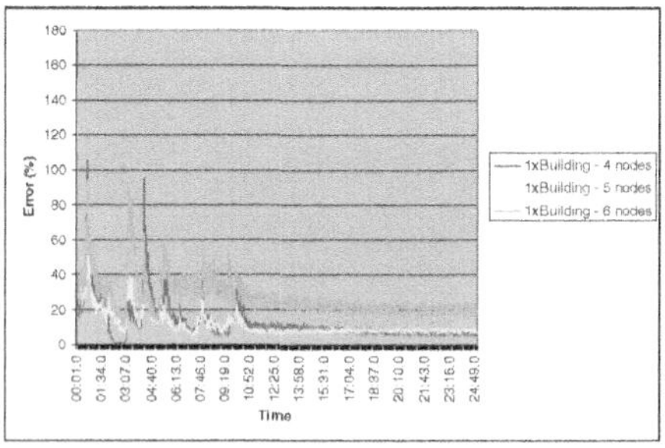

Fig. 16. Scenario 1

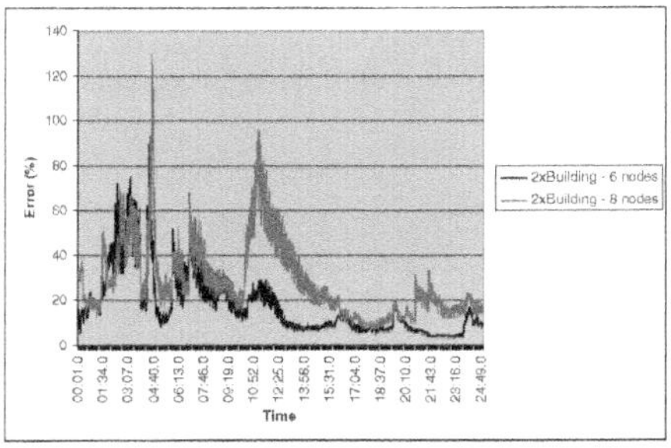

Fig. 17. Scenario 2

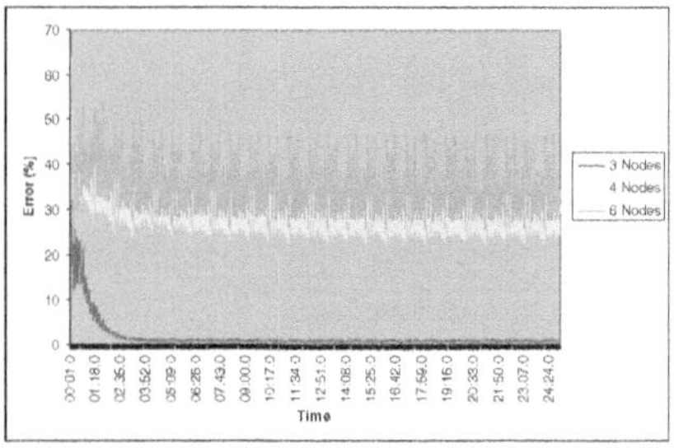

Fig. 18. Scenario 3

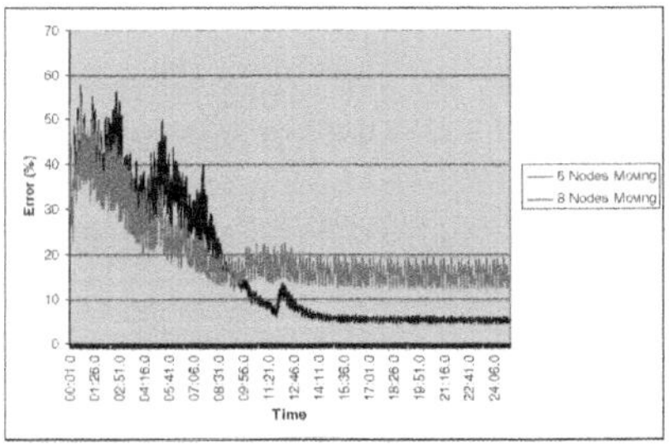

Fig. 19. Scenario 4

loss being discovered, where a lack of node movement fails to accurately identify that loss. In Scenario 3 (Fig. 18), the best performance is surprisingly from using only 3 nodes. While the actual CM built using only 3 nodes is far from being an accurate representation of the simulated signal loss, it provides enough detail given the information the nodes have accumulated.

Both in theory and in the experiments performed, a greater number of nodes has a greater chance of producing a more accurate CM. However, actual prediction accuracy depends largely on how the CM is used by nodes during the scenarios. Nodes which remain in the same approximate area both further improve the accuracy of that area and benefit from the effects. Nodes which use the CM in untested areas are less likely to obtain ideal results. Due to the vast nature of exact node movement and positioning, various experiments will achieve various results. Overall, however, a more accurate CM is created given a greater number of nodes.

4.3 MCSD and MCMD

The Minimum Cell Subdivide Difference (MCSD) and Minimum Cell Merge Difference (MCMD) values have also been considered. These values govern when cells are able to subdivide (split into 4 equal parts) and merge back together when the level of detail required by the CM changes over time. By default, all scenarios use a MCSD of 3.0 and a MCMD of 2.0. This means that if the average modifier within a cell varies by more than 3.0 then the cell will subdivide to allow for a greater level of detail to be mapped. If the average modifier between 4 adjacent nodes falls to less than 2.0, then the cells are merged back together again. These settings have been modified in two groups of settings; the first uses a MCSD of 2.0 and a MCMD of 1.0, and the second uses a MCSD of 1.0 and a MCMD of 0.0. These are all compared with basic settings in Fig. 20 below.

The results from these experiments show that lowering the MCSD and MCMD values increases accuracy. The reasoning behind this is that lower MCSD and MCMD

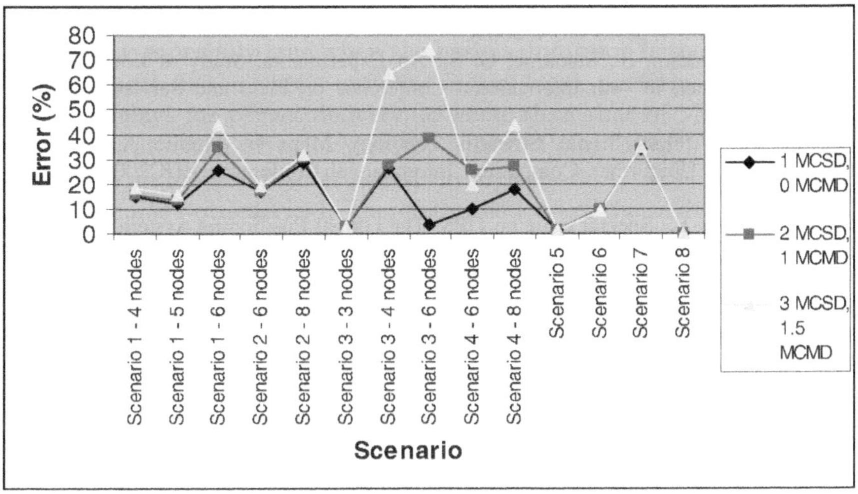

Fig. 20. MCSD and MCMD Performance

management scheme called AHMIPv6. In Section 3, we propose the analytic mobility model based on the random walk. Section 4 formulates the location update cost and the packet delivery cost using the analytic model. Section 5 shows the evaluation of the proposed system's performance and analysis of the results. Finally, our conclusions are presented in Section 6.

2 Adaptive Mobility Management Scheme

This section describes the location update and packet delivery procedure. In our proposal, each MN has a value of m and T_m. While m is the number of subnet crossings within the MAP domain, T_m is the threshold value which decides whether the MN sends a BU message to the CN with the LCoA or the RCoA. Whenever an MN enters a new MAP domain, it sets the value of m to zero. T_m can be adjusted based on the user's mobility pattern and current traffic load.

The procedures for a location update are as follows:

- If an MN moves to a different MAP domain, then:

1) the MN obtains two CoAs: an LCoA and an RCoA.
2) Then, it registers with its MAP and HA by sending a BU message, and it sets the value of m to zero.

- Otherwise, if an MN moves within the same MAP domain, then:

1) the MN gets a new LCoA.
2) The MN registers with its MAP by sending a BU message.

After registration with the MAP, the MN compares the value of m with T_m.
Case 1. If the value of m is less than T_m, then:

3-1) the MN sends a $BU_{[HoA,LCoA]}$[1] message to the CN.

Case 2. Otherwise, if the value of m is greater than or equal to T_m, then:

3-2) the MN sends a $BU_{[HoA,RCoA]}$[2] message to the CN. After the sending of the $BU_{[HoA,RCoA]}$ message, the MN does not send any other BU messages to the CN before it moves out of the MAP domain.

As a result, the MN performs registration with the CNs using an RCoA or an LCoA, depending on its mobility pattern. In our proposal, the packet delivery procedure is exactly the same to that in MIPv6 or HMIPv6.

[1] BU with the binding between the MN's Home Address (HoA) and LCoA.
[2] BU with the binding between the MN's Home Address (HoA) and RCoA.

3 Analytic Mobility Model

Inspired by the initial idea in [1,2], we will describe a two-dimensional random walk model for mesh planes. Our model is similar to [1] and considers a regular MAP domain/subnet overlay structure. In this model, the subnets are grouped into several n-layer MAP domains. Every MAP domain covers $N = 4n^2 - 4n + 1$ subnets.

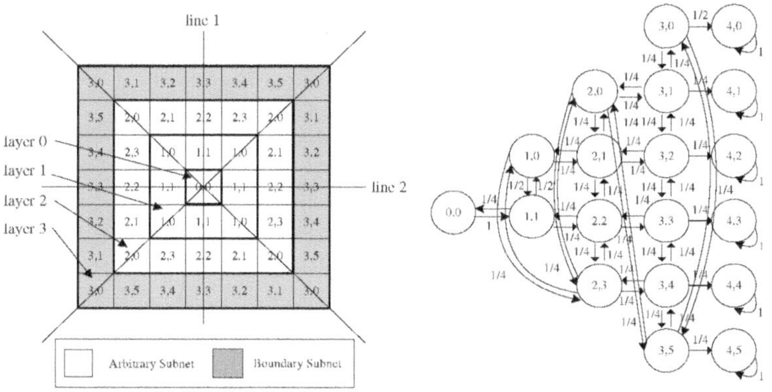

Fig. 1. Type Assignments of the mesh 4-layer MAP domain and the State Diagram

As shown in Fig. 1 (where n = 4), the subnet at the center of a MAP domain is called *layer 0*. An n-layer MAP domain consists of a subnet from layer 0 to layer $n-1$. Based on this domain/subnet structure, we derive the number of subnet crossings before an MN crosses a MAP domain boundary. According to the equal moving probability assumption (i.e., with a probability of 1/n), the subnets in a MAP domain are classified into several subnet types, based on the type classification algorithm in [2]. A subnet type is of the form $< x, y >$, where x indicates that the subnet is in layer x and y represents the $y+1$st type in layer x. Based on the type classification and the concept of absorbing states, the state diagram of the random walk for an n-layer MAP domain is shown in Fig. 1. In this state diagram, state (x, y) represents that the MN is in one of the MAP domains of type $< x, y >$, where the scope of x and y is

$$0 \leq x \leq n, \quad \begin{cases} 0 \leq y \leq 2x - 1 & , if \quad x \geq 1 \\ y = 0 & , if \quad x = 0. \end{cases} \tag{1}$$

State (n, y) represents that the MN moves out of the MAP domain from state $(n-1, y)$, where $0 \leq y \leq 2n-3$. For $x = n$ and $0 \leq y \leq 2n-3$, the states (n, y) are absorbing, and the others are transient. For $n > 1$, the total number $S(n)$ of states for the n-layer MAP domain random walk is $n^2 + n - 1$. The transition matrix of this random walk is an $S(n) \times S(n)$ matrix $P = (p_{(x,y)(x',y')})$. Therefore, $P = (p_{(x,y)(x',y')})$ can be defined as the one-stop transition probability from state (x, y) to state (x', y') (i.e., which represents the probability that the MN moves from a $< x, y >$ subnet to a $< x', y' >$ subnet in one step). We use the Chapman-Kolmogorov equation to compute $p^{(r)}_{(x,y)(x',y')}$, which is the probability that the random walk moves from state (x, y) to state (x', y') with exact r steps. We define $p_{r,(x,y)(n,j)}$ as the probability that an MN initially resides at a $< x, y >$ subnet, moves into a $< n-1, j >$ subnet at the $r-1$ step, and then moves out of the MAP domain at the r step as follows:

$$p_{r,(x,y)(n,y)} = \begin{cases} p_{(x,y)(n,y)} & , for \quad r = 1 \\ p^{(r)}_{(x,y)(n,y)} - p^{(r-1)}_{(x,y)(n,y)} & , for \quad r > 1. \end{cases} \tag{2}$$

4 Signaling Cost Functions

To investigate the performance of MIPv6, HMIPv6 and AHMIPv6, the total signaling costs given to the HA, CN, and MAP to handle mobility of the MNs are analyzed. We assume that the performance metric is the total signaling cost. It consists of the location update cost and packet delivery cost.

4.1 Mobile IPv6

Location Update Cost in MIPv6. We define the costs and parameters used for the performance evaluation of the location update as follows:

- U_{HA} : The location update cost of a BU for the HA
- U_{CN} : The location update cost of a BU for the CN
- U_{MAP} : The location update cost of a BU for the MAP
- u_{hn} : The transmission cost of a BU between the HA and the MN
- u_{cn} : The transmission cost of a BU between the CN and the MN
- u_{mn} : The transmission cost of a BU between the MAP and the MN
- a_h : The processing cost of a location update at the HA
- a_m : The processing cost of a location update at the MAP
- l_{hn} : The average distance between the HA and the MN
- l_{cn} : The average distance between the CN and the MN
- l_{hm} : The average distance between the HA and the MAP
- l_{mn} : The average distance between the MAP and the MN
- δ_U : The proportionality constant for a location update.

According to the signaling message flows for the BU, each cost of location update can be calculated as follows:

$$U_{HA} = a_h + 2u_{hn}, \quad U_{CN} = u_{cn}, \quad U_{MAP} = a_m + 2u_{mn} \tag{3}$$

For simplicity, we assume that the transmission cost is proportional to the distance, in terms of the number of hops between the source and destination mobility agents, such as the HA, MAP, CN and MN. Using the proportional constant δ_U, each cost of location update can be rewritten as follows:

$$U_{HA} = a_h + 2l_{hn} \cdot \delta_U, \quad U_{CN} = l_{nc} \cdot \delta_U, \quad U_{MAP} = a_m + 2l_{mn} \cdot \delta_U \tag{4}$$

We derive the number of subnet crossings and location updates between the beginning of one session and the beginning of the next session before an MN leaves the first MAP domain. Similar to [1], we define the additional costs and parameters used for the performance evaluation of the location update as follows.

- r : The number of the MN's subnet crossings
- d : The number of subnet crossings before an MN leaves the first MAP domain
- t_d : The time interval between the beginning of one session and the beginning of the next session
- $r(t_d)$: The number of the MN's subnet crossings during t_d
- l : The number of subnet crossings before an MN leaves the first MAP domain during t_d
- N : The total number of subnets within a MAP domain
- $1/\lambda_m$: The expected value for the subnet residence time
- $1/\lambda_d$: The expected value for the t_d distribution
- σ : The number of the CNs that have a binding cache for the MN

We assume that an MN is in any subnet of a MAP domain with equal probability. This implies that the MN is in subnet $< 0, 0 >$ with a probability of $1/N$ and is in a subnet of type $< x, y >$ with a probability of $4/N$, where $N = 4n^2 - 4n + 1$ is the number of subnets covered by an n-layer MAP domain. From (2), we derive d as the number of subnet crossings before an MN leaves the first MAP domain as follows:

$$d = \frac{1}{N}\left(\sum_{k=1}^{\infty} k \cdot \sum_{j=0}^{2n-3} p_{k,(0,0)(n,j)}\right) + \frac{4}{N}\left(\sum_{k=1}^{\infty} k \cdot \sum_{x=0}^{n-1} \sum_{y=0}^{2x-1} \sum_{j=0}^{2n-3} p_{k,(x,y)(n,j)}\right) \tag{5}$$

We denote $\alpha(r)$ as the probability that an MN will leave the MAP domain at the rth step provided that the MN is initially in an arbitrary subnet of the MAP domain as follows:

$$\alpha(r) = \frac{1}{N}\left(\sum_{j=0}^{2n-3} p_{r,(0,0)(n,j)}\right) + \frac{4}{N}\left(\sum_{x=1}^{n-1} \sum_{y=0}^{2x-1} \sum_{j=0}^{2n-3} p_{r,(x,y)(n,j)}\right) \tag{6}$$

Note that the above derivations are based on the equal moving probability assumption, thus, we derive the number of subnet updates between the beginning of one session and the beginning of the next session. Fig. 2 shows the timing diagram of the activities for an MN. Assume that the previous session of the MN begins at time t_0, and the next session begins at time t_1. Let $t_d = t_1 - t_0$, which has a general distribution with a density function of $f_d(t_d)$, and expect a value of $1/\lambda_d$, and Laplace Transform

$$f_d^*(s) = \int_{t_d=0}^{\infty} e^{-st_d} f_d(t_d) dt_d \tag{7}$$

We denote $r(t_d)$ as the number of location updates for the MAP during the period t_d. Since an MN needs to register with the MAP whenever it moves in

In HMIPv6, an MN sends a BU message to the MAP whenever it moves within the MAP domain after the registration with the HA. From (4) and (11), we can get the total location update cost before an MN leaves the first MAP domain during t_d in HMIPv6 as follows:

$$U^{'} = U_{HA} + \sigma \cdot U_{CN} + U_{MAP} \sum_{j=0}^{l} (j \cdot Pr[r(t_d) = j] \cdot \alpha(j)) \tag{15}$$

In HMIPv6, all packets destined for the MN are forwarded by the HA and the MAP using the encapsulation and decapsulation process. In a similar manner to HMIPv6, we define a proportionality constant of δ_m. The δ_m is a packet delivery processing constant for the lookup time of a binding cache at the MAP. From (12), we can get the total packet delivery cost during t_d in HMIPv6 as follows:

$$F^{'} = \lambda_\alpha \Big((l_{ch} + l_{hm} + l_{mn}) + (E(S) - 1)(l_{cm} + l_{mn}) \Big) \delta_D + \lambda_\alpha(\delta_h + E(S)\delta_m) \tag{16}$$

Based on the above analysis, we get the total signaling cost function in HMIPv6 from (15) and (16) as follows:

$$C_{HMIP}(\lambda_m, \lambda_d, \lambda_\alpha) = U^{'} + F^{'} \tag{17}$$

4.3 Adaptive Hierarchical Mobile IPv6

The optimal value of T_m is defined as the value of l that minimizes the cost function derived in Section 4.1 and 4.2. To get the value of T_m, we define the cost difference function between MIPv6 and HMIPv6 as follows:

$$\Delta(l, \lambda_m, \lambda_d, \lambda_\alpha) = C_{MIP} - C_{HMIP} \tag{18}$$

Given Δ, the algorithm to find the optimal value of l is defined as follows:

$$T_m(\lambda_m, \lambda_d, \lambda_\alpha) = \begin{cases} 0 & , if\ \Delta(l, \lambda_m, \lambda_d, \lambda_\alpha) > 0 \\ maximum(l : \Delta(l, \lambda_m, \lambda_d, \lambda_\alpha) \leq 0) & , otherwise \end{cases} \tag{19}$$

The optimal value of T_m is a designed value. It is computed before the communications based on the average packet arrival rate λ_α, average mobility rate λ_m, and average λ_d. In the AHMIPv6, an MN sends the BU message to the CN with either an LCoA or an RCoA. If the number of subnet crossings, m, is less than T_m, the MN sends the BU message to the CN with an LCoA after the registration with the HA and MAP. Otherwise, the MN sends a BU message to the CN with an RCoA. From (11),(15) and (19), we can get the total location update cost before an MN leaves the first MAP domain during t_d in the AHMIPv6 as follows:

$$U^{''} = \begin{cases} U_{HA} + (U_{MAP} + \sigma \cdot U_{CN}) \sum_{j=0}^{T_m} (j \cdot Pr[r(t_d) = j]\alpha(j)), & if\ T_m < j \\ U_{HA} + U_{MAP} \sum_{j=0}^{l} (j \cdot Pr[r(t_d) = j]\alpha(j)) + \sigma \cdot U_{CN} & \\ \times \sum_{j=0}^{T_m} (j \cdot Pr[r(t_d) = j]\alpha(j)) & , if\ T_m \geq j \end{cases} \tag{20}$$

In the AHMIPv6, when a CN sends a packet to the MN, the packets are directly forwarded to the MN using an LCoA, if m is less than T_m. Otherwise, the packets are indirectly forwarded to the MN via the MAP using the RCoA. From (12) and (16), therefore, we can get the total packet delivery cost during t_d in AHMIPv6 as follows:

$$F^{''} = \begin{cases} F, & if \;\; T_m < j \\ F^{'}, & if \;\; T_m \geq j \end{cases} \tag{21}$$

Based on the above analysis, we get the total signaling cost function in AHMIPv6 from (20) and (21) as follows:

$$C_{AHMIP}(\lambda_m, \lambda_d, \lambda_\alpha) = U^{''} + F^{''} \tag{22}$$

5 Numerical Results

In this section, we will demonstrate some numerical results. Table 1 shows some of the parameters used in our performance analysis that are discussed in [1]. For simplicity, we assume that the distance between the mobility agents is fixed and has the same number of hops (i.e., $l_{ch} = l_{cm} = l_{hm} = l_{mn} = l_{cn} = 10$).

Table 1. Performance Analysis Parameters

Parameter	Value	Parameter	Value	Parameter	Value	Parameter	Value
N	49	L	28	α	1.5	κ	1-10
λ_α	0.01-10	λ_i	0.01-10	λ_m	0.01-10	λ_d	0.01-10
a_m	20	a_h	30	δ_m	10	δ_D	0.2
δ_U	15	δ_h	15	n	1-10	σ	1-10

Fig. 3 (a) and (b) show the effect of the mobility rate λ_m on the total signaling cost for $\lambda_\alpha = 1$ and $\lambda_d = 0.01$. As shown in Fig. 3 (a) and (b), the total signaling cost increases as the mobility rate λ_m increases. We can see that the performance of the AHMIPv6, on the whole, results in the lowest total signaling cost, compared with MIPv6 and HMIPv6. These results are expected because the AHMIPv6 scheme tries to reduce the signaling loads at the MAP for the small value of λ_m in the same way as MIPv6. For the large value of λ_m, the AHMIPv6 scheme tries to reduce the location update costs by sending a BU message to the CN with an RCoA in the same way as HMIPv6.

Fig. 3 (c) and (d) show the effect of the packet arrival rate λ_α on the total signaling cost for $\lambda_m = 1$ and $\lambda_d = 0.01$. As shown in Fig. 3 (c) and (d), the total signaling cost increases as the packet arrival rate λ_α increases. We can see that the performance of the AHMIPv6, on the whole, results in the lowest total signaling cost compared with MIPv6 and HMIPv6. From the above analysis of the

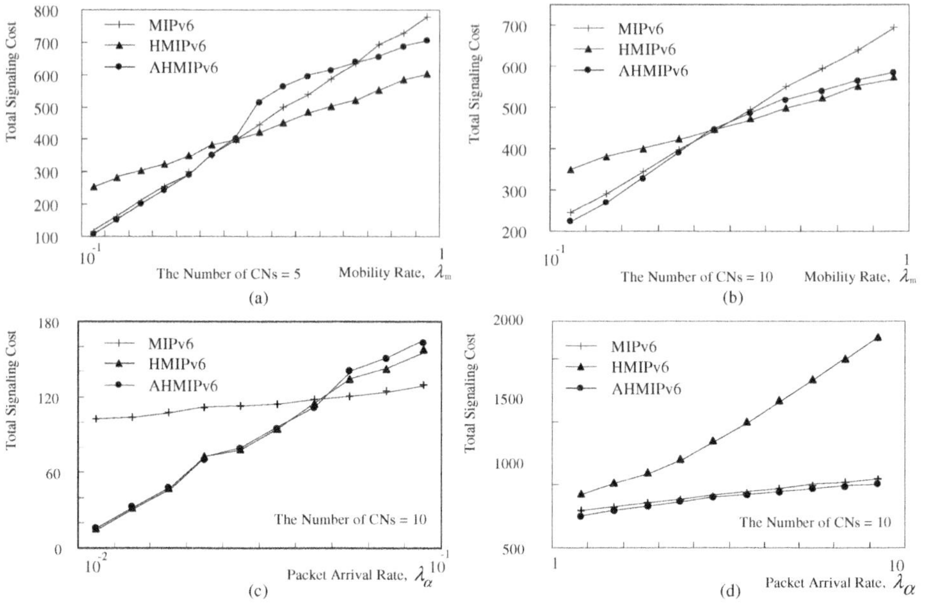

Fig. 3. Effects of Mobility Rate and λ_α on the Total Signaling Cost

results, the AHMIPv6 scheme has a considerable performance advantages over MIPv6 and HMIPv6. So, we conclude that the AHMIPv6 achieves significant performance improvements by using the MN's selection to send a BU message to the CN, either with an LCoA or an RCoA.

6 Conclusions

In this paper, we proposed an adaptive mobility management scheme for minimizing signaling costs in HMIPv6 networks. In our proposal, location registration with the HA and MAP is exactly the same as that in HMIPv6. However, the MN sends a BU message to the CN with either an LCoA or an RCoA, based on the geographical locality properties of the MN's movements. The cost analysis presented in this paper shows that the AHMIPv6 scheme achieves significant performance improvements by using the MN's selection to send a BU message to the CN, either with an LCoA or an RCoA.

References

1. Yi-Bing Lin, Shun-Ren Yang, "A Mobility Management Strategy for GPRS," *IEEE Transactions on Wireless Communications*, vol. 2 ,pp. 1178 - 1188, November 2003.
2. Akyildiz. I.F, Yi-Bing Lin, Wei-Ru Lai, Rong-Jaye Chen, "A New Random Walk Model for PCS Networks," *IEEE Journal on Selected Areas in Communications*, vol. 18, pp1254 - 1260, July 2000.

A Novel Tag Identification Algorithm for RFID System Using UHF

Ho-Seung Choi and Jae-Hyun Kim

School of Electrical and Computer Engineering, Ajou University,
San 5 Woncheon-Dong, Youngtong-Gu, Suwon 442-749, Korea
{lastjoin, jkim}@ajou.ac.kr

Abstract. An anti-collision algorithm is very important in the RFID system, because it decides tag identification time and tag identification accuracy. We propose improved anti-collision algorithms for RFID system using UHF. In the proposed algorithms, if the reader memorizes the Bin slot information, it can reduce the repetition of the unnecessary PingID command and the time to identify tags. If we also use ScrollAllID command in the proposed algorithm, the reader knows the sequence of collided ID bits. Using this sequence, we can reduce the repetition of PingID command and tag identification time. We analyze the performance of the proposed anti-collision algorithms and compare the performance of the proposed algorithms with that of the conventional algorithm. We also validate analytic results using simulation. According to the analysis, for the random tag ID, comparing the proposed algorithms with the conventional algorithm, the performance of the proposed algorithms is about 130% higher when the number of the tags is 200. For the sequential tag ID, the performance of the conventional algorithm decreases. On the contrary, the performance of the proposed algorithm using ScrollAllID command is about 16% higher than the case of using random tag ID.

1 Introduction

The RFID(Radio Frequency Identification) system is a simple form of ubiquitous sensor networks that are used to identify physical objects [1]. The RFID system identifies the unique tags' ID or detailed information saved in them attached to objects. Passive RFID systems generally consist of three components - a reader, passive tags, and a controller. A reader interrogates tags for their ID or detailed information through RF communication link, and contains internal storage, processing power, and so on. Tags get the processing power through RF communication link from the reader and use this energy to power any on-tag computations and to communicate to the reader. A reader in RFID system broadcasts the request message to the tags. Upon receiving the message, all the tags send the response back to the reader. If only one tag responds, the reader receives just one response. However, if two or more tags respond, their responses will collide on the RF communication channel, and thus cannot be received by the reader. The problem is referred to as the "Tag-collision". An effective system must avoid this collision by using anti-collision algorithm be-

L.T. Yang et al. (Eds.): EUC 2005, LNCS 3824, pp. 629 – 638, 2005.

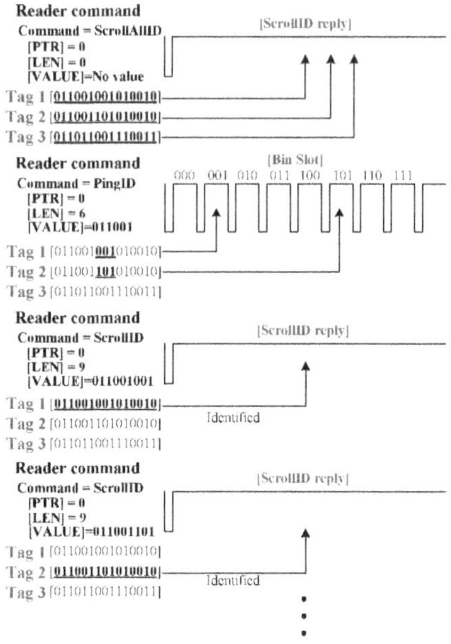

Fig. 3. An example of the proposed algorithm using ScrollAllID command

command and tag identification time. The procedure is as follows. First of all, the reader transmits ScrollAllID command to the tags. All the tags which are in active state send all of their ID bits to the reader. The reader knows the sequence of collided ID bits. So, the reader sets the [PTR] field to the position of second collided bit - 1 and transmits PingID command to the tags. Then, the tags whose first collided bit is '0' reply reader's PingID command, and the reader repeats transmission of PingID command until only one tag reply in one Bin slot. The reader transmits ScrollID command and identifies that tag. After the reader identifies the tag, the reader performs the next procedure using Bin slot information until all the tags are identified. The reader can reduce unnecessary repetition of PingID command. Fig. 3 shows an example of the tag identification procedure of the proposed anti-collision algorithm using ScrollAllID command.

4 Performance Analysis

In this section, we compare the performance of the conventional anti-collision algorithm with that of the proposed anti-collision algorithm for EPC CLASS 1 UHF Tag. For performance matrix, we consider the number of repetition of PingID command and the time to identify the tags.

4.1 The Conventional Anti-collision Algorithm for EPC CLASS 1 UHF Tag

We assume that tag ID is random, the number of total tags is m, and the number of Bin slot is r. Let q_n be the probability that there is no tag reply from Bin 0 to Bin n-1.

q_n is then $[(r\text{-}n)/r)]^m$. The probability that there is no reply in Bin n out of $r\text{-}n$ slots is $[(r\text{-}1\text{-}n)/(r\text{-}n)]^m$, and the probability that there is only one reply in Bin n out of $r\text{-}n$ slots is $[m/(r\text{-}n)]\times[(r\text{-}1\text{-}n)/(r\text{-}n)]^{m\text{-}1}$. The probability that there are two or more tag replies in Bin n out of $r\text{-}n$ slots, q_{rn}, can be derived in

$$q_{rn}=\left[1-\left(\frac{r-1-n}{r-n}\right)^m-m\left(\frac{r-1-n}{r-n}\right)^{m-1}\cdot\frac{1}{r-n}\right]. \tag{1}$$

Let p_{1n} be the probability that there is no tag reply from Bin 0 to Bin n-1 and there are two or more tag replies in Bin n when the reader transmits first PingID command to the tags. Then, p_{1n} is calculated by

$$p_{1n}=\left(\frac{r-n}{r}\right)^m\left[1-\left(\frac{r-1-n}{r-n}\right)^m-m\left(\frac{r-1-n}{r-n}\right)^{m-1}\cdot\frac{1}{r-n}\right] \tag{2}$$

where r is 8 and $0\le n\le 7$ (n is an integer). Let p_1 be the probability that the reader retransmits PingID command in the first state. p_1 is then derived in

$$p_1=\sum_{n=0}^{7}p_{1n}\,. \tag{3}$$

We define that p_{2n} is the probability that there is no tag reply from Bin 0 to Bin n-1 and there are two or more tags' replies in Bin n when the reader transmits second PingID command to the tags. Since the number of Bin slot is r, we can approximate the number of tags in the second state by m/r. Then, m can be substituted by m/r in the second state. p_{2n} is expressed as

$$p_{2n}=\left(\frac{r-n}{r}\right)^{\frac{m}{r}}\left[1-\left(\frac{r-1-n}{r-n}\right)^{\frac{m}{r}}-\frac{m}{r}\left(\frac{r-1-n}{r-n}\right)^{\frac{m}{r}-1}\cdot\frac{1}{r-n}\right]. \tag{4}$$

The probability p_2 that the reader re-transmits PingID command in the second state is derived in

$$p_2=\sum_{n=0}^{7}p_{2n}\,. \tag{5}$$

Using same method, we can also approximate the number of tags in the k-th state by $m/r^{k\text{-}1}$. The probability p_k that the reader re-transmits PingID command in the k-th state is

$$p_k=\sum_{n=0}^{7}p_{kn}=\sum_{n=0}^{7}\left(\frac{r-n}{r}\right)^{\frac{m}{r^{k-1}}}\left[1-\left(\frac{r-1-n}{r-n}\right)^{\frac{m}{r^{k-1}}}-\frac{m}{r^{k-1}}\left(\frac{r-1-n}{r-n}\right)^{\frac{m}{r^{k-1}}-1}\cdot\frac{1}{r-n}\right]. \tag{6}$$

Therefore, for the first identified tag, the number of repetition of PingID command, I_1, can be calculated by

$$I_1 = 1 + \sum_{k=0}^{\infty}\sum_{n=0}^{7}\left(\frac{r-n}{r}\right)^{\frac{m}{r^k}}\left[1-\left(\frac{r-1-n}{r-n}\right)^{\frac{m}{r^k}} - \frac{m}{r^k}\left(\frac{r-1-n}{r-n}\right)^{\frac{m}{r^k}-1}\cdot\frac{1}{r-n}\right], \quad \frac{m}{r^k} > 1 . \tag{7}$$

After the reader identifies a tag, the number of remaining tags is m-1. The reader repeats the same procedure to identify second tag. Using (7), the number of repetition of total PingID command until the reader identifies all the tags, I_{total}, is given by

$$I_{total} = m + \sum_{L=2}^{m}\sum_{k=0}^{\infty}\sum_{n=0}^{7}\left(\frac{r-n}{r}\right)^{\frac{L}{r^k}}\left[1-\left(\frac{r-1-n}{r-n}\right)^{\frac{L}{r^k}} - \frac{L}{r^k}\left(\frac{r-1-n}{r-n}\right)^{\frac{L}{r^k}-1}\cdot\frac{1}{r-n}\right], \quad \frac{m}{r^k} > 1 . \tag{8}$$

The reader repeats the transmission of ScrollID command m times to identify m tags. The total time to identify m tags is composed of ScrollID command transmission time, PingID command transmission time, tag response time, transmission delay of the reader, and transmission delay of the tag. We assume that the size of the packet from reader to tag is RL_C and the data rate of the reader is DR_{reader}. Then, command packet transmission time from reader to tag to identify m tags, t_{reader}, is derived in

$$t_{reader} = \frac{RL\_C(I_{total} + m)}{DR_{reader}} \tag{9}$$

where RL_C is 147 bits and DR_{reader} is 70,180 bps [12].

Assuming that the size of the tag response packet for PingID command is TL_P, the size of the tag response packet for ScrollID command is TL_S, and the data rate of the tag is DR_{tag}. Then, the response time of the tag to identify m tags, t_{tag}, is

$$t_{tag} = \frac{TL\_P \times I_{total} + TL\_S \times m}{DR_{tag}} \tag{10}$$

where TL_P is 8 bits, TL_S is 120 bits, and DR_{tag} is 140,350 bps [12].

To find the total delay to identify m tags, t_{delay} , we define that transmission delay of the reader is DE_{reader} and transmission delay of the tag is DE_{tag} , and t_{delay} is

$$t_{delay} = (I_{total} + m)(DE_{reader} + DE_{tag}) \tag{11}$$

where DE_{reader} is 17.81μs and DE_{tag} is 57μs [12]. Finally, we find the total time to identify m tags t_{total} in

$$t_{total} = t_{reader} + t_{tag} + t_{delay} . \tag{12}$$

4.2 The Proposed Anti-collision Algorithms

Using the same assumption in the section 4.1, the number of total tags is m, and the number of Bin slot is r. Tag ID is also random. Let p_{col} be the probability that there are two or more tag's replies in one Bin slot when the reader transmits the first PingID command to the tags. Then, p_{col} can be calculated as follows

$$p_{col} = \left[1 - \left(\frac{r-1}{r}\right)^m - m\left(\frac{r-1}{r}\right)^{m-1} \cdot \frac{1}{r}\right]. \quad (13)$$

Because the number of Bin slot is r, the number of repetition of PingID command in the first state, I_1, is given by

$$I_1 = r \times \left[1 - \left(\frac{r-1}{r}\right)^m - m\left(\frac{r-1}{r}\right)^{m-1} \cdot \frac{1}{r}\right]. \quad (14)$$

In the case of the proposed algorithm, the reader can memorize Bin slot information so that the number of repetition of PingID command in the k-th state, I_k, (k=1,2,3, ...) is

$$I_k = r^k \times \left[1 - \left(\frac{r-1}{r}\right)^{\frac{m}{k-1}} - \frac{m}{r^{k-1}}\left(\frac{r-1}{r}\right)^{\frac{m}{k-1}-1} \cdot \frac{1}{r}\right]. \quad (15)$$

Finally, the number of repetition of total PingID command until the reader identifies all the tags, I_{total}, can be represented as

$$I_{total} = \sum_{k=0}^{\infty} I_k = I_0 + \sum_{k=1}^{\infty} r^k \times \left[1 - \left(\frac{r-1}{r}\right)^{\frac{m}{r^{k-1}}} - \frac{m}{r^{k-1}}\left(\frac{r-1}{r}\right)^{\frac{m}{r^{k-1}}-1} \cdot \frac{1}{r}\right], \quad \frac{m}{r^{k-1}} > 1. \quad (16)$$

I_0 is the number of the first transmission of PingID command and the value of I_0 is 1.

In the proposed algorithms, we can calculate total time to identify m tags, t_{total}, by (12). In the case of using ScrollAllID command, we can calculate total time to identify m tags, t_{total}, as same as in (12) with substituting m by m+1.

5 Analytic and Simulation Results

In this section, we mathematically compare the performance of the proposed algorithm with that of the conventional anti-collision algorithm for EPC CLASS 1 UHF Tag and validate analytic results using simulation. Tag's ID is 96 bits and the portion of the ID to identify the tags is 36 bits. To maximize the reliability of simulation, we apply the real packet size, packet transmission delay, and date rate [12].

Fig. 4 shows the number of PingID command for the number of used tags in the conventional anti- collision algorithm for EPC CLASS 1 UHF Tag, the proposed algo- rithm not using ScrollAllID command, and the proposed algorithm using ScrollAllID command for random tag ID. Lines and symbols represent analytic and simulation results, respectively. In Fig. 4, we observe the small difference between analytic and simulation results in the conventional algorithm. In the analytic result, we do not consider the addictive number of PingID command in the condition of $m / r^k \leq 1$. That is why there is a small difference between analytic and simulation results. In Fig. 4, the number of PingID command of the proposed algorithms is less than that of the conventional algorithm.

4. H. Vogt, "Efficient Object Identification with Passive RFID tags," International Conference on Pervasive Computing, pp.98-113, Zürich, 2002.
5. C. S. Kim, K. L. Park, H. C. Kim and S. D. Kim, "An Efficient Stochastic Anti-collision Algorithm using Bit-Slot Mechanism," PDPTA04, 2004.
6. S. R. Lee, S. D. Joo, C. W. Lee, "High-Speed Access Technology of Tag Identification Using Advanced Framed Slotted ALOHA in an RFID System," Journal of IEEK, Vol. 41-TC, NO.9, Sep., 2004, pp. 29-37.
7. ISO/IEC 18000-6:2003(E), Part 6: *Parameters for air interface communications at 860-960 MHz*, Nov. 26, 2003.
8. J. L. Massey, "Collision resolution algorithms and random-access communications," Univ. California, Los Angeles, Tech. Rep. UCLAENG -8016, Apr. 1980.
9. K. Finkenzeller, RFID Handbook: *Radio-Frequency Identification Fundamentals and applications*. John Wiley & Sons Ltd, 1999.
10. H. S. Choi, J. R. Cha and J. H. Kim, "Fast Wireless Anti-collision Algorithm in Ubiquitous ID System ," in *Proc. IEEE VTC 2004*, L.A., USA, Sep. 26-29, 2004.
11. H. S. Choi, J. R. Cha and J. H. Kim, "Improved Bit-by-bit Binary Tree Algorithm in Ubiquitous ID System," in *Proc. IEEE PCM 2004*, Tokyo, Japan, Nov. 29-Dec. 3, 2004, pp. 696-703.
12. EPCglobal, *EPC™ Tag Data Standards Version 1.1 Rev.1.24*, Apr. 2004.

Coverage-Aware Sensor Engagement in Dense Sensor Networks*

Jun Lu, Lichun Bao, and Tatsuya Suda

Bren School of Information and Computer Sciences,
University of California, Irvine, CA 92697
{lujun, lbao, suda}@ics.uci.edu

Abstract. The critical issue in sensor networks is the search of balance between the limited battery supply and the expected longevity of network operations. Similar goals exist in providing a certain degree of sensing coverage and maintaining a desirable number of sensors to communicate under the energy constraint. We propose a novel sensor network protocol, called Coverage-Aware Sensor Engagement (CASE) for coverage maintenance. Different from others, CASE schedules active/inactive sensing states of a sensor according to the sensor's contribution to the network sensing coverage. The contribution is quantitatively measured by a metric called coverage merit. By utilizing sensors with large coverage merit, CASE reduces the number of the active sensors required to maintain the level of coverage. Simulation results show that CASE considerably improves the energy efficiency and reduces the computation and communication costs to maintain the required coverage degree in a dense sensor network.

1 Introduction

Wireless sensor networks are networks of a large number of small wireless devices, which collaborate to monitor environments and report sensing data via wireless channels. Wireless sensor networks have emerged rapidly in a variety of applications. For instance, thermal sensors are being deployed to monitor temperature in a forest, and to report the temperature information back to data collection nodes for further analysis. In another instance, a large number of seismic sensors are employed to monitor animal activities in a wild field. The seismic sensors, when triggered by the vibrations caused by animal movements, can record the vibration signals and report them to data collection nodes. Information about animal activities, like their moving tracks and velocities, can be acquired through analyzing the collected signals.

Wireless sensors are very limited in their processing, computing and communication capabilities as well as the storage and power supply. The typical Crossbow MICA mote MPR300CB [XBOW1] has a low-speed 4MHz processor equipped with only 128KB

* This work was supported by the National Science Foundation through grants ANI-0083074 and ANI-9903427, by DARPA through Grant MDA972-99-1-0007, by AFOSR through Grant MURI F49620-00-1-0330, and by grants from the University of California MICRO Program, Hitachi, Hitachi America, Novell, Nippon Telegraph and Telephone Corporation (NTT), NTT Docomo, Fujitsu, and NS-Solutions.

L.T. Yang et al. (Eds.): EUC 2005, LNCS 3824, pp. 639–650, 2005.

flash, 4KB SRAM and 4KB EEPROM. It has a maximal data rate of 40kbps and a transmission range of about 100 feet, powered by two AA batteries. Therefore, a wireless sensor network is usually deployed with high density. Dense deployment not only helps to improve a sensor network's reliability, but also extends its longevity. In practice, large-scale wireless sensor networks are usually deployed randomly.

Given such a randomly and densely deployed wireless sensor network, it is desirable to have sensors autonomously schedule their duty cycles while satisfying the degree of sensing coverage required by the application. The problem is called coverage maintenance.

Coverage maintenance problem in sensor networks has drawn intense research attention recently. Tian *et al.* [TG1] presented a node-scheduling algorithm to turn off redundant sensors if their sensing areas are already covered by their neighbors. Randomized as well as coordinated sleep algorithms were proposed in [HL1] to maintain network coverage using low duty-cycle sensors. The randomized algorithm enables each sensor to independently sleep under a certain probability. The coordinated sleep algorithm allows each sensor to enter sleep state if its sensing area is fully contained by the union set of its neighbors. A K-coverage maintenance algorithm was proposed in [HT1] so that each location of the sensing area is covered by at least K sensors. A sensor decides whether it is redundant only by checking the coverage state of its sensing perimeter. In [GWL1], the redundancy of the sensing coverage of wireless sensor networks is analyzed, and the relation between the number of neighbors and the coverage redundancy is studied. Abrams *et al.* studied a variant of the NP-hard SET K-COVER problem in [AGP1], partitioning the sensors into K covers such that as many areas are monitored as frequently as possible. Yan *et al.* proposed an adaptable energy-efficient sensing coverage protocol, in which each sensor broadcasts a random time reference point, and decides its duty schedule based on neighbors' time reference points [YHS1].

We propose a new coverage maintenance scheme called Coverage-Aware Sensor Engagement (CASE). CASE is based on a probabilistic sensing model, which is more practical than the disk sensing model assumed by many others. Rather than fixing the sensing range of a sensor as the disk sensing model, the probabilistic sensing model defines the sensing ability as the probability to detect an event happening at a location. To the best of our knowledge, this work is the first to address the K-coverage problem under the probabilistic sensing model. In fact, the disk sensing model is a special case of the probabilistic sensing model, and CASE works for the disk sensing model as well. In CASE, each sensor is initially inactive in sensing, but checks to see whether it is necessary to turn on its sensing unit according to its contribution (which we called coverage merit) to meet the required degree of sensing coverage. Before actually turning on itself, each sensor waits for a back-off period decided by its coverage merit. Sensors with larger coverage merit have shorter back-off period. In this way, sensors turn on themselves (if necessary) in the decreasing order of their coverage merit. By utilizing sensors with large coverage merit, CASE can reduce the active sensor density needed to maintain the required coverage degree.

The rest of this paper is organized as follows. The differences of our work from the others are examined in Section 2. Section 3 describes the assumptions of CASE.

Section 4 specifies CASE in more details. Simulation results are presented in Section 5 for performance evaluations. Section 6 concludes the paper.

2 Prior Works

In the scheduling algorithm proposed by [TG1], every sensor is active at the beginning. A sensor is eligible to turn off if its sensing area is covered by the union of the sponsored sectors by its neighbors. A sensor eligible to turn off broadcasts a `TURNOFF` beacon to inform neighbors. Every other sensor receiving such a beacon re-evaluates its eligibility to turn off. If not eligible, the sensor cancels the timer and stays active. [YHS1] presented an elegant approach to dynamically schedule sensors in order to guarantee a certain degree of coverage. Each sensor generates a random reference time and exchanges the reference time with its neighbors. Each sensor can setup its working schedule by examining the reference time of its neighbors.

There are several major differences between the proposed algorithm and the algorithms proposed in [TG1] and [YHS1]. First, we differentiate sensors according to their coverage merit, which decreases the active sensor density to provide the coverage degree required by the application. Second, while both of the existing schemes assume the disk sensing model, CASE solves the K-coverage problem under the probabilistic sensing model. Treating the disk sensing model as a special case of the probabilistic model, CASE also works for the disk sensing model. Third, unlike [TG1], CASE sets sensor initial state as inactive. Following the scheduling procedure, each sensor tries to turn on to provide the required coverage degree. This feature is favorable for dense deployment in that the communication and computation overhead is reduced due to less sensor state changes.

The scheme proposed by [TG1] does not work for the probabilistic sensing model. In order to compare CASE with the scheme proposed in [TG1], we modified the eligibility rule of [TG1] to accommodate the probabilistic sensing model. We refer the scheme proposed in [TG1] as *the sponsored sector scheduling scheme* or *Tian-Sector* and the scheme with the modified eligibility rule as *the grid point scheduling scheme* or *Tian-Grid*. Section 5.1 explains in details about the differences between Tian-Grid and Tian-Sector. The validation of the working schedule setup algorithm in [YHS1] is tightly coupled with the assumption of the disk sensing model, which prevents it from being ported to the probabilistic sensing model. Therefore, in the simulation evaluation, we only compare CASE with Tian-Grid and Tian-Sector.

3 Assumptions

We assume that sensors are static, and that each sensor knows its location as well as its neighbors'. Such assumptions are conveniently taken by other works [HT1] [TG1] [YHS1] and are supported by the existing research [ACZ1] [BHE1] [BP1] [PCB1]. The location information can be absolute or relative to neighbors. We also assume that sensors can synchronize their timers [DH1] [EGE1].

We assume that the sensing ability model of sensors is available before deployment through calibration process. A sensor detects an event based on its measurement, and

Afterward, each sensor sets a back-off timer T to announce its active state. The back-off timer T is determined according to its coverage merit using Eq. (6).

$$T = \xi \cdot (CM_{max} - CM_j) + \epsilon \tag{6}$$

where ξ is a configurable system parameter, and ϵ is a small positive random number. ξ determines the convergence latency of the wakeup phase in CASE. Small value of ξ means fast convergence but may increase the chance of collisions among neighboring sensors. The choice of an appropriate value for ξ is out of the scope of this paper, and will be part of our future work. ϵ is used to prevent the potential collision between two neighboring sensors with the same coverage merit.

According to Eq. (6), sensors with larger coverage merit have shorter back-off period. When a sensor times out, the sensor changes to active state, and broadcasts a `TURNON` message to its neighbors within its transmission range, which is approximated by $2 \cdot SR$. When a sensor receives a `TURNON` message before the timer expires, it recalculates its coverage merit, and adjusts its back-off timer accordingly.

According to Eq. (2), (3) and (4), the sensor's coverage merit is reduced when a new neighbor is turned into active state, thus the back-off timer is always delayed. Once all the locations within the sensing range of a sensor are K-covered, the sensor's coverage merit becomes 0. The sensor cancels its back-off timer and stays inactive.

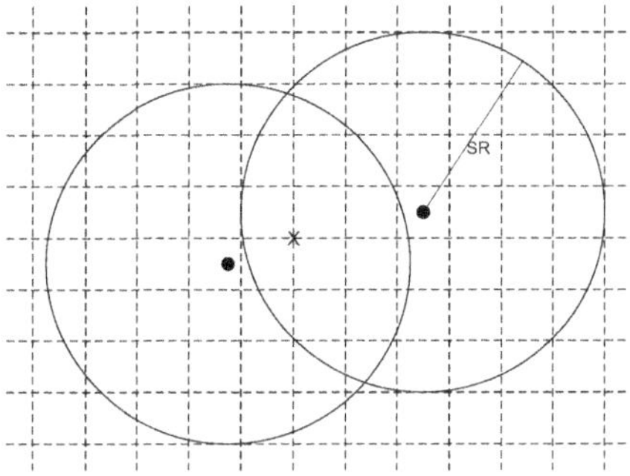

Fig. 1. Grid Point X in the Target Area

The wakeup phase ends at $\xi \cdot CM_{max}$. After the wakeup phase, there may be redundant active sensors. This is because that the coverage of the sensors turning on later may overlap with the sensing area of the active sensors. In the optimization phase, we use a similar random back-off algorithm as [TG1] to turn off redundant sensors. Accordingly, each redundant sensor sets a random timer, and re-checks its eligibility to turn off when received `TURNOFF` messages from other sensors. If the sensor realizes that it is not eligible to turn off, it cancels its timer and stays active. Otherwise, it broadcasts a `TURNOFF` message and turns off upon timeout.

In order to simplify the computation, we cover the target area by a virtual square grid (Fig. 1) and sensors only consider the grid points within the SR when calculating coverage merit (this technique is also used by Yan *et. al* [YHS1]). The coverage merit is approximated by the summation of the coverage merit on the grid points within the SR, *i.e.*, P_i in Eq. (4) is a grid point.

5 Simulation Evaluations

5.1 Experiment Setup

We carried out experiments under two sensing models — the probabilistic sensing model and the disk sensing model, both over a square deployment area of $100 \times 100m^2$.

In Eq. (6), parameters are chosen as $\xi = 0.1$ and $\epsilon = 0.01$. If not otherwise specified, the deployment density is set to 0.08 sensors/m^2, and the network is designed to provide the coverage degree of 1.0.

The probabilistic sensing models depend on the sensor capabilities and environments. Although CASE shall work with any realistic sensing model, for simplicity, we assume a virtual probabilistic sensing model for the sensors, two examples of which are shown below,

$$S_j(P_i) = f(D_{ij}) = \frac{1}{1 + \alpha D_{ij} + \beta D_{ij}^2 + \cdots + \gamma D_{ij}^k}$$

$$S_j(P_i) = f(D_{ij}) = \frac{1}{\chi^{D_{ij}}}$$

where D_{ij} is the distance between sensor j and location P_i; α, β, γ and χ ($\chi > 1$) are system parameters reflecting the physical characteristics of sensor j and deployment environments.

Specifically, we assume the following virtual probabilistic sensing model in the simulations:

$$f(D_{ij}) = \frac{1}{(1 + \alpha D_{ij})^\beta} \tag{7}$$

where α is set to 0.1 and β is set to 3 or 4. Assuming that detection probability lower than 4% is negligible, two SRs, *i.e.*,15 and 20 meters, are simulated. For the disk sensing model, the SR is set to 15 meters.

As we explained in Section 2, under the probabilistic model, CASE is compared with the modified Tian-Sector based on virtual grids, which we call Tian-Grid. Like CASE, Tian-Grid checks the expected number of monitoring sensors at each grid point within its sensing range. A sensor is eligible to turn off if the expected number of monitoring sensors of each grid point within its sensing range is at least K. Also, different from Tian-Sector, which only examines the sectors sponsored by neighbors within SR, Tian-Grid considers all the neighbors within $2 \cdot SR$. In the disk sensing model, we compare CASE with both Tian-Grid and Tian-Sector because Tian-Grid natively works for the disk sensing model.

5.2 Result Analysis

The simulation results show the performance of CASE in terms of active sensor density, communication overhead and computation overhead. The communication overhead is

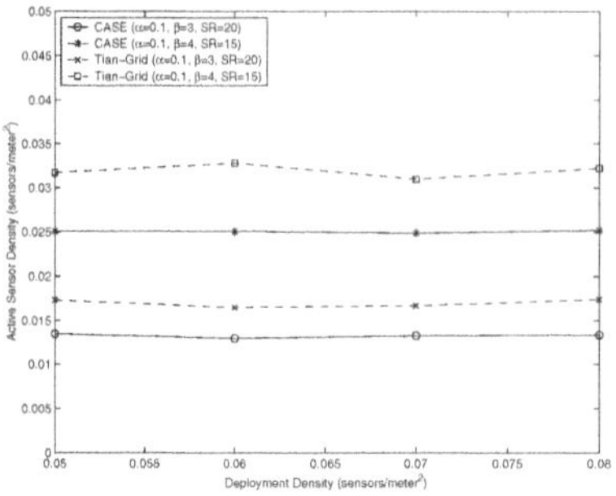

(a) Active Sensor Density

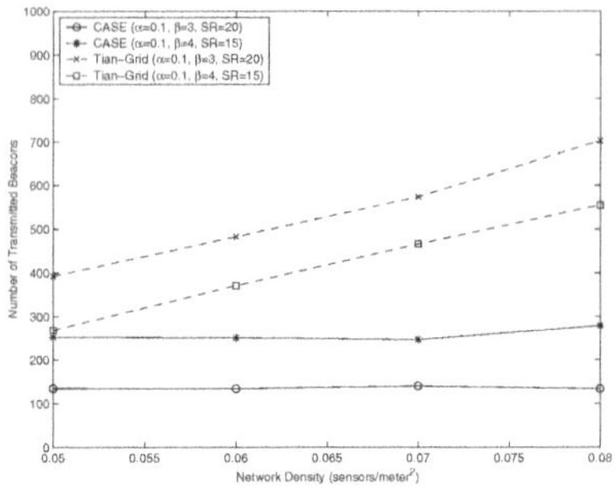

(b) Transmitted Beacons

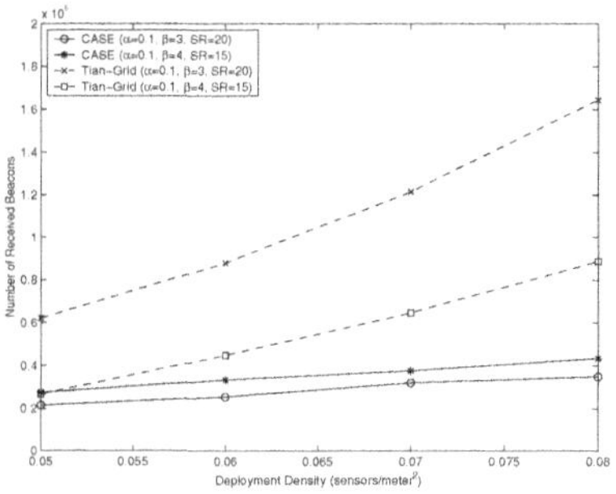

(c) Received Beacons

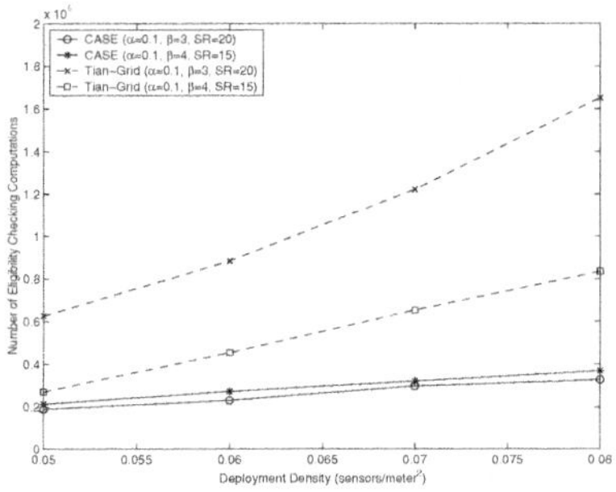

(d) Computation Overhead

Fig. 2. Various Deployment Densities

computed as the number of beacons sent and received for the TURNON messages in the wakeup phase and the TURNOFF messages in the optimization phase in CASE. Because the eligibility checking is the most costly computation operation, the computation overhead is calculated as the times of checking the eligibility of a sensor to be in active state, which is determined by coverage merit.

We analyze the results in the probabilistic sensing model and the disk sensing model, separately.

Probabilistic sensing model. In section 4.3, we have proposed to compute the coverage merit based on virtual grids. For comparison purposes, we simulate the modified Tian-Sector protocol, which we refer as *Tian-Grid* in the figures, and collect corresponding statistics.

The results under various deployment densities are shown in Fig. 2. Results for different required coverage degrees are shown in Fig. 3.

Fig. 2(a) indicates that both CASE and Tian-Grid provide stable active sensor density. However, CASE results lower active sensor density than Tian-Grid under different deployment densities because CASE activates sensors with large coverage merit, therefore allowing less active sensors in order to provide the same degree of coverage. For instance, when the sensor network has the deployment density of 0.05 sensors/m^2 and sensors have the SR of $20 meters$, CASE provides 1.0-coverage with the active sensor density of only 0.0137 sensors/m^2, whereas Tian-Grid requires 0.0175 sensors/m^2.

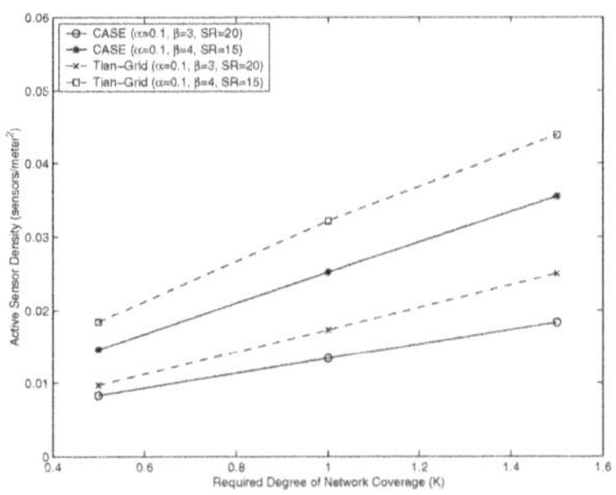

(a) Active Sensor Density

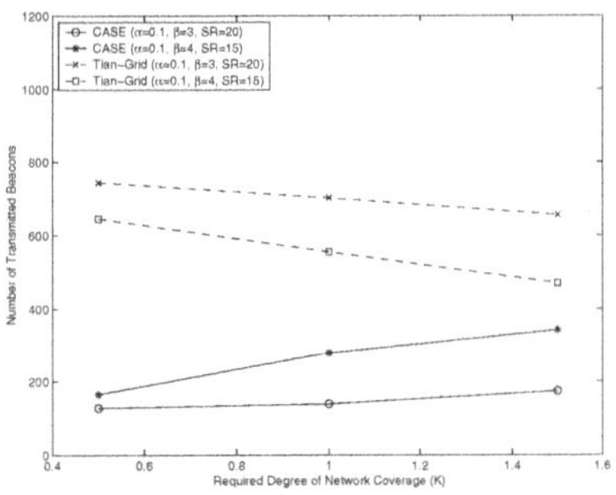

(b) Transmitted Beacons

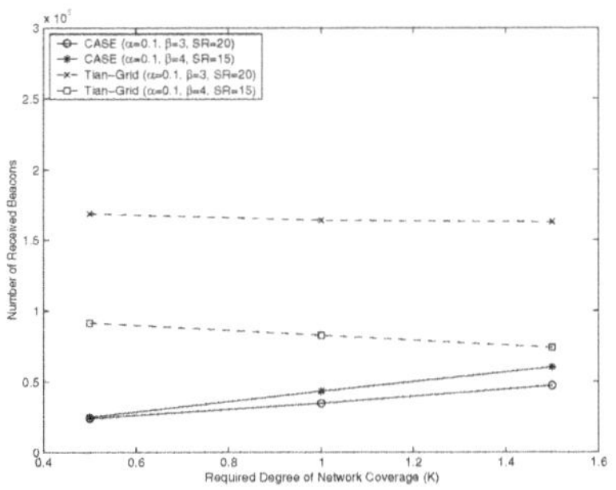

(c) Received Beacons

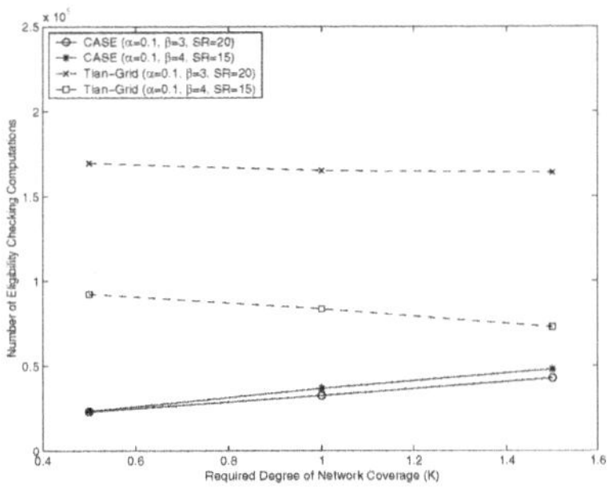

(d) Computation Overhead

Fig. 3. Various Required Coverage Degrees (K)

Fig. 2(b) shows that CASE uses less beacons than Tian-Grid. This is due to the fact that sensors are gradually switched on from inactive state to active state in CASE, whereas Tian-Grid has all sensors initially in active state and turn off redundant sensors, which translates into different amount of beacons transmitted in order to inform state changes. If the network deployment is dense enough, the number of redundant sensors is much larger than the number of active sensors needed to provide the required coverage degree. Thus CASE involves less state changes than Tian-Grid.

Furthermore, we observe that the number of transmitted beacons in CASE changes little along with the increase of deployment density. In contrast, Tian-Grid suffers when the deployment density increases in Fig. 2(b). This is because the active sensor density is almost stable along with the deployment densities in CASE, whereas in Tian-Grid, most beacons are the `TURNOFF` messages sent by redundant sensors. When the deployment density increases, more redundant sensors need to turn off with more beacons.

Similar to Fig. 2(b), Fig. 2(c) shows that CASE has less received beacons than Tian-Grid, and that the number of beacons received in both schemes increases with the deployment density because of the broadcast nature of the wireless channel. However, the increasing rate of received beacons in CASE is less than that in Tian-Grid because the increase of the received beacons in CASE is mainly caused by the increase of sensor density. In Tian-Grid, however, the increase is caused by the increase of both the number of the transmitted beacons and sensor density. Because the eligibility checking

[BHE1] Bulusu, N., Heidemann, J., Estrin, D.: GPS-less Low Cost Outdoor Localization For Very Small Devices. IEEE Personal Communications, 2000.

[BP1] Bahl, P., Padmanabhan, V.: RADAR: An In-Building RF-based User Location and Tracking System. Proceedings INFOCOM, 2000.

[DH1] Dai, H., Han, R.: TSync: A Lightweight Bidirectional Time Synchronization Service for Wireless Sensor Networks. Mobile Computing and Communications Review, 2004.

[EGE1] Elson, J., Girod, L., Estrin, D.: Fine-Grained Network Time Synchronization using Reference Broadcasts. Proceedings OSDI, 2002.

[GWL1] Gao, Y., Wu, K., Li, F.: Analysis on the Redundancy of Wireless Sensor Networks. Proceedings WSNA, 2003.

[HL1] Hsin, C., Liu, M.: Network Coverage Using Low Duty-Cycled Sensors: Random and Coordinated Sleep Algorithms. Proceedings IPSN, 2004.

[HT1] Huang, C., Tseng, Y.: The Coverage Problem in a Wireless Sensor Network. Proceedings WSNA, 2003.

[MKQP1] Meguerdichian, S., Koushanfar, F., Qu, G., Potkonjak, M.: Exposure In Wireless Ad-Hoc Sensor Networks. Proceedings MOBICOM, 2001.

[PCB1] Priyantha, N.B., Chakraborty, A., Balakrishnan, H.: The Cricket Location-Support System. Proceedings MOBICOM, 2000.

[ROB1] Robosoft Advanced Robotics Solutions: http://www.robosoft.fr/SHEET/02Local/1001LAUN/LAUN.html. Last visited on 09/07/2005.

[TG1] Tian, D., Georganas, N.D.: A Coverage-Preserving Node Scheduling Scheme for Large Wireless Sensor Networks. Proceedings WSNA, 2002.

[XBOW1] XBOW Inc.: http://www.xbow.com/Support/Support_pdf_files/MPR-MIB_Series_Users_Manual.pdf. MPR/MIB User's Manual, Last visited on 06/30/2005.

[YHS1] Yan, T., He, T., Stankovic, J.A.: Differentiated Surveillance for Sensor Networks. Proceedings SenSys, 2003.

[YZLZ1] Ye, F., Zhong, G., Lu, S., Zhang, L.: Energy Efficient Robust Sensing Coverage in Large Sensor Networks. UCLA Technical Report, 2002.

A Cross-Layer Approach to Heterogeneous Interoperability in Wireless Mesh Networks

Shih-Hao Shen[1], Jen-Wen Ding[2], and Yueh-Min Huang[1]

[1] Department of Engineering Science National Cheng Kung University, Tainan 701, Taiwan, ROC
{n9892110, huang}@{ccmail, mail}.ncku.edu.tw
[2] Department of Information Management, National Kaohsiung University of Applied Sciences, Kaohsiung 807, Taiwan, ROC
jwding@cc.kuas.edu.tw

Abstract. Routing in a wireless mesh network is a heterogeneous interoperability problem. First, it is possible that some users may disable the relaying functions of their mobile devices in order to save the computing power and battery charge. This will results in heterogeneous relaying capabilities. Second, due to the absence of standard layer-3 ad-hoc routing protocols, various devices may employ different layer-3 routing protocols, making routing difficult. A trivial solution to the above two problem is to flood packets through the un-routable regions to reach the destination region. However, flooding is a brute force approach and will make a broadcast storm, resulting in low throughput of the whole network. In this paper, we propose a cross-layer approach to solve the above problem. Our analysis results show that the proposed cross-layer approach can efficiently provide interoperability without causing broadcast storm.

1 Introduction

There has been a big interest in commercial wireless mesh networks in the recent past. Wireless mesh networks [1] and [2] are ad hoc wireless networks formed to provide an alternate communication infrastructure for mobile and fixed users, in addition to cellular networks. Compared to traditional infrastructure-based networks, wireless mesh networks can be easily deployed and the topology can be easily and rapidly changed via self-organization. Hence wireless mesh networks provide the most economical data transfer capability with support for user mobility [8] and [9]. Many wireless mesh networks have been installed around the world. For example, Nortel networks wireless mesh network solution has been adopted in Taipei city to offer highly scalable, cost-effective last-mile communication to end users [12]. Figure 1 shows the architecture of a wireless mesh network.

Heterogeneous interoperability in a commercial wireless mesh network is an important design issue necessary to be addressed for two reasons. First, since relaying

L.T. Yang et al. (Eds.): EUC 2005, LNCS 3824, pp. 651 – 662, 2005.

takes up nodes' resources such as computing power and battery charge, some users may disable the forwarding functions of their mobile devices, and by doing so we cannot ensure a fully connected network even with high node density. Research has developed numerous layer-3 routing protocols for ad hoc wireless networks [5], [7], [10] and [11]. Though these protocols find efficient routing path for mobile nodes with minimum control overhead, most of them assume homogeneity of mobile nodes, i.e., all nodes support the full functions of a certain layer 3 routing protocol. This, however, is not the case in a commercial wireless mesh network, where some nodes may disable the relaying functions. In practice, the mobile nodes are classified into two types, the ones enabling the relaying functions and the ones disabling the relaying functions. The second reason is that due to the absence of standard layer-3 routing protocols, various devices may employ different layer-3 routing protocols.

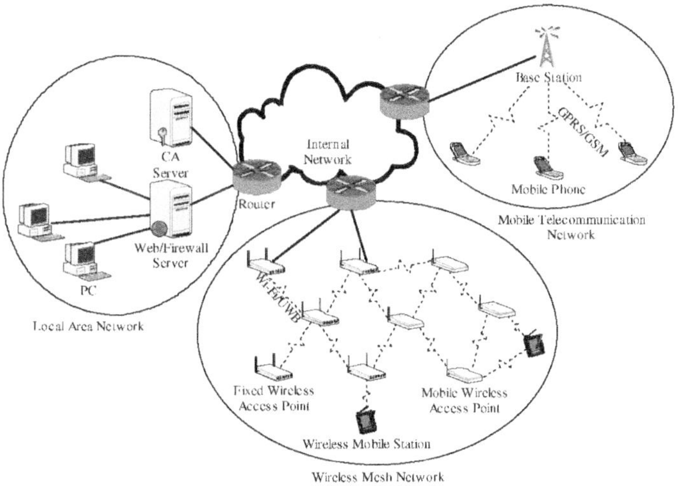

Fig. 1. Architecture of wireless mesh network [8]

Because of the two reasons mentioned above, the whole wireless mesh network can thus be partitioned into many small geographically separated regions belonging to one of the two types. In this paper, the nodes disabling the forwarding function are referred to as un-routable nodes. The nodes using different layer-3 routing protocols are also un-routable nodes for each other. The regions consisting of un-routable nodes are referred to as un-routable regions. It is noted that a region cannot communicate with its un-routable neighbor regions via layer-3 routing.

There are three type of approaches to solving the problem of un-routable regions, (1) the dual stack approach, (2) the naive layer-2 broadcast approach and (3) the cross-layer approach. The dual stack approach employs devices that support more than two protocols and act as a bridge to transform protocols. However, this approach is costly and impractical because of the limited computing power of most mobile devices.

The naive layer-2 broadcast approach floods packets through the un-routable regions to reach the destination region. However, flooding is a brute force approach because it implicates the inability to acquire the whole regional topology of un-routable area. For example, node *d* is a source and node *k* is the destination as shown in Figure 2a. The optimal solution is path *d-c-e-h-k*. Both of the two are routable nodes but separated apart from un-routable regions. Thus, source node (*d*) has no choice but to flood frames. The flooding approach results too many meaningless messages at the MAC layer. As figure 2b illustrated flooding is a very inefficient scheme.

In this paper, we propose a cross-layer approach which consists of a slightly modified version of a common layer-2 protocol, DFWMAC, and a light-weight layer-3 protocol that can cooperate with various layer-3 routing protocols so as to allow the packets to be forwarded without causing a layer-2 broadcast storm. We organize the paper as follows: Section 2 describing related work and providing preliminaries, Section 3 detailing our proposed cross-layer protocol, Section 4 presenting the simulation results, and finally, Section 5 concluding.

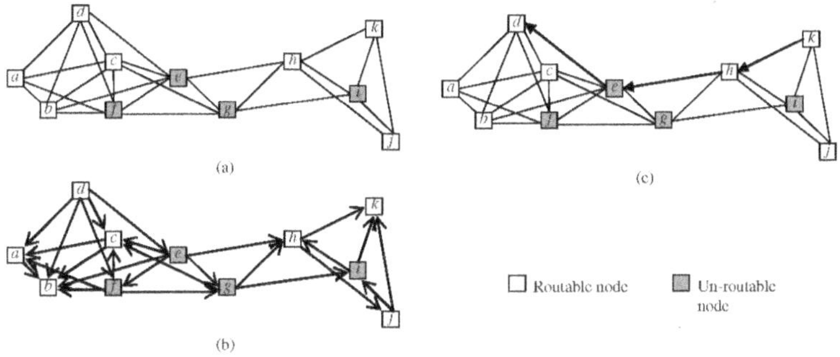

Fig. 2. Using flooding scheme to go through un-routable regions from node *d* to *k*. (a) Connection diagram. (b) Node *d* broadcasting a *search* command. (c) Node *k* responding to a *connect* command.

2 Preliminaries

In this paper, we assume that users have a common MAC layer protocol. In the recent past, numerous MAC protocols have been proposed for ad hoc wireless networks, such as MARCH[13], D-PRMA[4] and DPS[6]. Some of them can even provide guaranteed QoS delivery, such as D-PRMA, DPS. For the sake of compatibility, the proposed cross-layer approach adopts and slightly modifies DFWMAC (Distributed Foundation Wireless Medium Access Control) [3] as its MAC protocol, the DLC (distributed link conjunction) protocol. DFWMAC is the MAC protocol used in IEEE 802.11 recommended standard for wireless ad-hoc and infrastructure LANs. In this section, we briefly review the main operations of DFWMAC that are relevant to our proposed scheme.

frame. A node receiving link discovery frame but not receiving the corresponding link confirmation frame will delete the cache information after the previously set timer is matured. The MAC layer protocol is presented in table 1.

Figure 5 shows a simple example of node *a* communicating to node *b*. Nodes *a*, *b* and *c* are routable nodes. Node *1* and *2* are un-routable nodes. Nodes *a* and *b* communicate via layer-3 routing protocol. Nodes *b* and *c* communicate by DLC. Figure 5a shows how link discovery frame is broadcasted and how intermediate un-routable nodes cache the information carried in the link discovery frame. Figure 5b shows how link confirmation frame is unicasted to the sender node via the reverse path and how intermediate un-routable nodes cache the information carried in the link discovery frame.

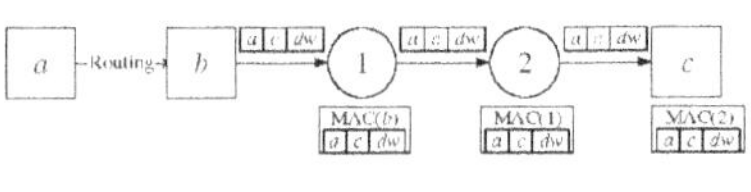

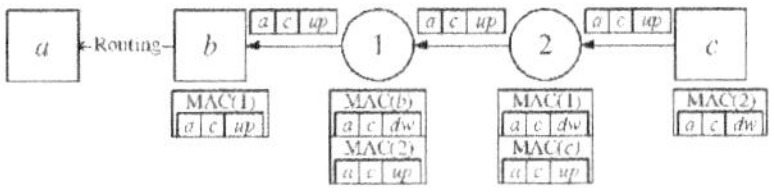

Fig. 5. Example of a caching frame to reserve paths

3.2 GEER Routing Protocol

In the recent past, numerous routing protocols have been proposed for ad hoc wireless networks, such as DSDV[10], WRP[7], DSR[5] and AODV[11]. As mentioned earlier, these protocols cannot solve the interoperability problem. We consider a scenario where heterogeneous nodes are un-routable for each other because some of them may disable the forwarding functions or because they may employ different routing protocols, as shown in Figure 2a. The network is therefore partitioned into many small geographically separated regions. In a routable region, a packet can be directly sent any other node in the same region using a common layer-3 routing protocol, such as DSR or AODV. However, when a packet is sent to a destination that is in an un-routable region, a special design will be required.

Our proposed cross-layer approach employs DLC with very limited broadcast to pass packets through an un-routable region. However, two problems may arise if only DLC is used. First, the layer-2 link discovery frame of DLC may result in a routing cycle. Second, when a packet must travel through several routable and un-routable regions, in order to efficiently relay packets in a routable region without flooding, each region must perform smart relaying. The two problems are illustrated in Figure 6. To cope with the two problems, the proposed cross-layer approach uses a light-weight layer-3 routing protocol, Group Entry and Exit Register (GEER), that can cooperate with existing routing protocols for ad hoc wireless networks, such as DSR and AODV.

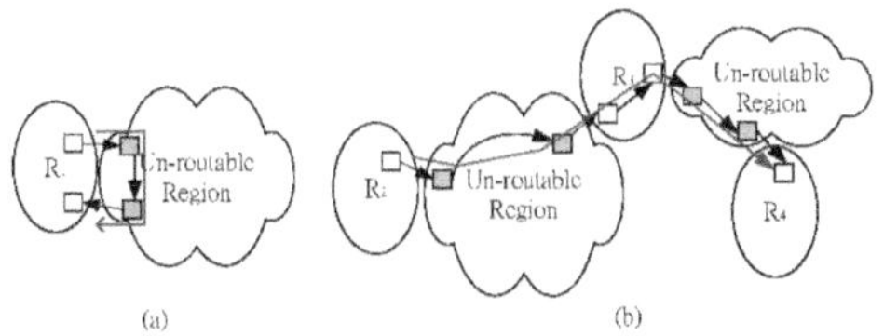

Fig. 6. Effect of routing on wireless mesh network interoperability: (a) Routing cycle. (b) Multi-regions forwarding.

In GEER protocol, three types of nodes are introduced. To prevent routing cycle and to help crossing multi-regions routing we need a node to record the entry and exit of link discovery frame of DLC. The special node is termed *GEER node*. GEER is elected from a group of nodes. To concatenate different routable regions via DLC, the nodes, termed *dam nodes*, sit between a routable and an un-routable region must perform the relaying function. A special un-routable node whose routable neighbors are in the same routable region is referred to as *surrounded node*.

The algorithm is to determine whether the node is GEER by searching a maximum degree node in a region. It is easier when routing protocol is pre-active. Dam nodes and

Table 2. DAM algorithm

```
DAM Algorithm: (Working between layer-2 and layer-3)
Signature:
Input:                                         Output:
  receive(packet_j)_{j,i}, j∈Homo-Network        Send(packet_i)_{i,k}, k∈ Homo-Network
State:
Broadcast storm avoidance set A:=∅
Tasks:
Precondition:
  For every n ∈ H_i, determine adapting to a dam node
  Nodes of homo-group H_i elect a GEER_i.
Effect:
  Periodically deletes timeout element of A.
  ∀Destination j ∈ H_i, send(packet_i)_{i,j}
  ∀Destination k ∉ H_i, send(Send (packet_i)_{i,k})_{i,GEERi}

Transitions:
send(packet_i)_{i,k}
  Effect:
    send(packet_i)_{i,k}

receive(packet_s)_{j,i}, s is source node
Effect:
  if packet_s == GEERtoDam then
    DLC.send()
   if packet_s ∈ cmd then
     For every d∈D_i
       send(GEERtoDam(packet_s∪{IP_GEERi}))_{i,d}
     A:=A∪{ packet_s +t}, t is a timestamp
   else
     Run original routing protocol
  else s∉ H_i
   if packet_s ∈ cmd then
    if i is distination then
     send(GEERtoDam(rep_packet_i) )_{i,j}
    else i is not distination
     For every d∈D_i
       send(GEERtoDam(packet_s∪{IP_GEERi}))_{i,d}
     A:=A∪{ packet_s +t}, t is a timestamp
   else packet_s ∉ cmd
    send(GEERtoDam(rep_packet_i) )_{i,j}
```

surrounded nodes are determined as follows table 2. Every node (routable or un-routable) stores the MAC address of adjacent un-routable nodes. The GEER of a routable region keeps a GURID (Group Un-routable Identifier) table, which records the MAC and IP addresses of each routable node in the region and the MAC addresses of these nodes' adjacent un-routable nodes. If a routable node wants to detect if an adjacent un-routable node is a surrounded un-routable node, it sends a query with the MAC address of the un-routable node to GEER. If the query of GURID table shows that the un-routable node is adjacent to all routable nodes, then it is a surrounded node. A routable node can query the GEER to determine if it is a dam node by sending the MAC addresses of its adjacent nodes. If not all adjacent nodes are surrounded nodes, this routable node is a dam node. As shown in Figure 7, nodes *h*, *k*, and *j* are routable nodes and nodes *e*, *g* and *i* are un-routable nodes. Node *i* is a surrounded un-routable node because all node *i*'s adjacent MAC addresses appear in the GURID. Nodes *h* is a dam node because it is adjacent to out-region nodes *e* and *g*.

Table 3. GEER algorithm

***GEER* Algorithm: (Working on layer-3)**

Signature:

Input:
  $receive(packet_j)_{j,i}$, $j \in$ *Homo-Network*

Output:
  $Send(packet_i)_{i,k}$, $k \in$ *Homo-Network*

State:

Broadcast storm avoidance set $A := \varnothing$

Command set cmd={"Send", "GEERtoDam"}

Tasks:

Precondition:
  For every n $\in H_i$, *determine adapting to a dam node*
  Nodes of homo-group H_i *elect a* $GEER_i$.

Effect:
  Periodically deletes timeout element of A.
  $\forall$*Destination* $j \in H_i$, $send(packet_i)_{i,j}$
  $\forall$*Destination* $k \notin H_i$, $send(Send\ (packet_i)_{i,k})_{i,GEERi}$

Transitions:

$send(packet_i)_{i,k}$
  Effect:
    $send(packet_i)_{i,k}$

$receive(packet_s)_{j,i}$, s is source node
  Effect:
    if $s \in H_i$ *then*
      if $packet_s \in cmd$ *then*
        For every $d \in D_i$
          $send(GEERtoDam(packet_s \cup \{IP_{GEERi}\}))_{i,d}$
        $A := A \cup \{packet_s + t\}$, *t is a timestamp*
      else
        Run original routing protocol
    else $s \notin H_i$
      if $packet_s \in cmd$ *then*
        if i is distination then
          $send(GEERtoDam(rep\_packet_i))_{i,j}$
      else i is not distination
        For every $d \in D_i$
          $send(GEERtoDam(packet_s \cup \{IP_{GEERi}\}))_{i,d}$
      $A := A \cup \{(packet_s, t)\}$, *t is a timestamp*

We then discuss the concept of GEER routing algorithm shown in Table 3. GEER is a centralized control in each routable region. Every packet sent out and sent in the region needs to register to GEER. By storing and comparing packets to see if it is repeatedly received, GEER can avoid a routing cycle mentioned earlier. If a destination node does not exist in the region, GEER forwards packets to its dam nodes to go through un-routable regions to the destination node. As shown in Figure 7, consider a simplified example that node *d* needs to communicate to node *k*. Initially, node *d* sends a *GEER routing query* to *c*. Because node *k* does not exist in *c*'s region, such as *c* multicasts the query to its dam nodes *c* and *d* to go through un-routable region. In the first path, a routing cycle *c-e-d* occurs. When *d* receives a frame with piggyback, it obtains the destination identifier and queries it by GEER *c*. The GEER finds it is a redundant query packet and then returns the command of "discard" to *d*. In the second path, *c-e-h-k*, when receiving a frame with piggyback, *k* obtains the destination identifier and queries it by GEER *e*.

It is noted that the proposed cross-layer scheme can cooperate with other nodes not supporting GEER and therefore maintains interoperability in wireless mesh network as Figure 7 shown. There is at least one node that supports GEER, however. Otherwise, there might be some independent regions that impede routing.

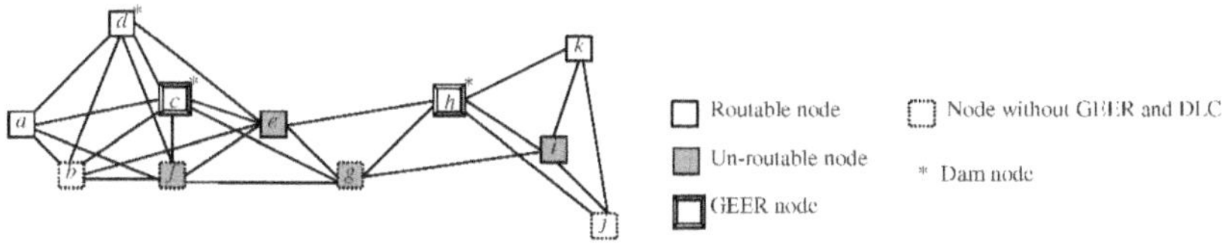

Fig. 7. A GEER operating snapshot in figure 2, where partial network lacks GEER and DLC operation

4 Performance Evaluation

In order to verify the cross-layer protocol, we conduct a series of simulations using the Distribution Wireless Mesh Network Simulator developed by ourselves. We first investigate how heterogeneous nodes will be distributed over an area. We perform a set of simulations for heterogeneous node distribution, which ranges from 50 to 450 nodes (with increase of 50) spreading randomly in a network area of 1500×1500 meter^2. We

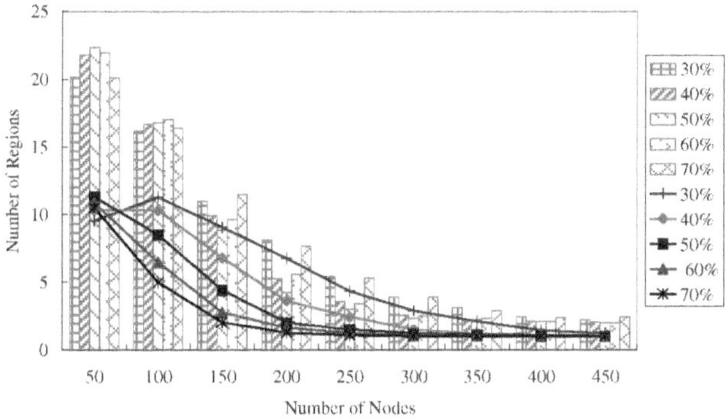

Fig. 8. Heterogeneous case – when the density of routable nodes are 30%, 40%, 50%, 60% and 70%: Average number of routable regions (frequency polygon) and average number of total regions (histogram)

use random distribution on two-dimension space. To take into account the fact that mobility may affect linking topology, we assume that renew process happens prior to rush hour everyday. We simulate different density of routable nodes' from the snapshots as renew and ignore mobility.

11. Perkins, C. E. and Royer, E. M.: Ad-Hoc On-Demand Distance Vector Routing. In Proc. 2nd IEEE Wksp. Mobile Comp. Sys. and Apps., 2 (1999) 90–100
12. Toh, C. K., Vassiliou, V., Guichal, G. and Shih, C. H.: MARCH: A medium Access Control Protocol for Multi-Hop Wireless Ad Hoc Networks. Proc. of IEEE MILCOM'00, Vol. 1, 10 (2000) 512-516

Reliable Time Synchronization Protocol for Wireless Sensor Networks

Soyoung Hwang and Yunju Baek

Department of Computer Science and Engineering,
Pusan National University, Busan 609-735, South Korea
{youngox, yunju}@pnu.edu

Abstract. Sensor network applications need synchronized time to the highest degree such as object tracking, consistent state updates, duplicate detection, and temporal order delivery. In addition to these domain-specific requirements, sensor network applications often rely on synchronization as typical distributed system do: for secure cryptographic schemes, coordination of future action, ordering logged events during system debugging, and so forth. This paper proposes a Reliable Time Synchronization Protocol (RTSP) for wireless sensor networks. In the proposed method, synchronization error is decreased by creating hierarchical tree with lower depth and reliability is improved by maintaining and updating information of candidate parent nodes. The RTSP reduces recovery time and communication overheads comparing to TPSN (Timing-sync Protocol for Sensor Networks) when there are topology changes owing to moving of nodes, running out of energy and physical crashes. Simulation results show that RTSP has about 10% better performance than TPSN in synchronization accuracy and the number of message in the RTSP is 10%~35% lower than that in the TPSN when nodes are failed in the network. In case of different transmission range of nodes, the communication overhead in the RTSP is reduced up to 50% than that in the TPSN at the maximum.

1 Introduction

Recent advances in sensors, MEMS (Micro-Electro-Mechanical Systems), low power and highly integrated digital electronics and low power RF technology have allowed the construction of low-cost small sensors nodes. Such sensor nodes are generally equipped with computation and wireless communication capabilities that can form distributed wireless sensor network systems. The sensing circuitry of sensor nodes measures ambient conditions related to the environment and transforms them into an electric signal. Processing such a signal reveals some properties about objects located and/or events happening in the vicinity of the sensor. The sensor node sends such collected data, usually via radio transmitter, to a command center (sink) either directly or through a data concentration center (a gateway). A natural architecture for such collaborative distributed sensor nodes is a network with wireless links that can be formed among the sensor

L.T. Yang et al. (Eds.): EUC 2005, LNCS 3824, pp. 663–672, 2005.

nodes in an ad hoc manner [1,2]. The most important characteristic of these sensor networks is the crucial need for energy efficiency. To facilitate easy deployment without an infrastructure, many nodes will necessarily be untethered, having only finite energy reserves from a battery [3]. These sensor networks can be used for various application areas such as health, military, home network, managing inventory, monitoring disaster areas and so on.

The main technology in wireless sensor networks includes hardware platforms and OS, low-energy consumption network protocols, time synchronization, localization, middleware, security, and applications. Especially, distributed wireless sensor networks make particularly extensive use of synchronized time: for example, to integrate a time-series of proximity detection into a velocity estimate; to measure the time-of-flight of sound for localizing its source; to distribute a beamforming array; or to suppress redundant messages by recognizing that they describe duplicate detections of the same event by different sensors. In addition to these domain-specific requirements, sensor network applications often rely on synchronization as typical distributed system do: for secure cryptographic schemes, coordination of future action, ordering logged events during system debugging, and so forth [4,5]. Since the characteristic of sensor nodes with limited computation and energy, traditional time synchronization protocols in distributed systems can not be applied to the sensor networks directly. So existing synchronization methods are revised or new approaches are proposed to synchronize the sensor networks.

In this paper we propose reliable time synchronization protocol for wireless sensor networks. It constructs hierarchical topology in the first phase, and performs pair-wise synchronization in the second phase. In the proposed method, synchronization error is decreased by creating hierarchical tree with lower depth and reliability is improved by maintaining and updating information of candidate parent nodes. The RTSP reduces recovery time and costs - communication overhead - comparing to TPSN [6] when there are topology changes owing to moving of nodes, running out of energy and physical crashes.

The rest of this paper is organized as follows. Section 2 discusses motivation and related research in the area. In section 3, we describe proposed time synchronization protocol for wireless sensor networks. Section 4 includes the performance evaluation of the proposed method. Finally, we conclude this paper in section 5.

2 Motivation and Related Work

Since the characteristic of sensor nodes with limited computation and energy, traditional time synchronization protocols in distributed systems can not be applied to the sensor networks directly. So existing synchronization methods are revised or new approaches are proposed to synchronize the sensor networks. In the first stage of research on time synchronization in sensor networks, most approaches are based on the synchronization model such as event ordering or relative clock. These methods do not synchronize the sensor node clocks but generate a right chronology of events or maintains relative clock of nodes. From a viewpoint of network topology, synchronization coverage is limited in a single broadcast domain; however, typical wireless sensor networks operate in areas larger than the broadcast range of a single node, so network-wide time synchronization is needed essentially. Besides, adjusting the local clock has better efficiency than maintaining relative clock since it requires more memory capacity and communication overheads. TPSN and FTSP are the representative ones which meet these requirements [7].

TPSN works in two phases: level discovery and synchronization. The aim of the first phase is to create a hierarchical topology in the network, where each node is assigned a level. Only one node is assigned level 0, the root node. In the second phase, a node of level i synchronizes to a node of level i-1. At the end of the synchronization phase, all nodes are synchronized to the root node, and network-wide synchronization achieved [6].

The goal of the FTSP is to achieve a network wide synchronization of the local clocks of the participating nodes. The assumptions in FTSP are that each node has a local clock exhibiting the typical timing errors of crystals and can communicate over an unreliable but error corrected wireless link to its neighbors. The FTSP synchronizes the time of a sender to possibly multiple receivers utilizing a single radio message time-stamped at both the sender and the receiver sides. It compensates for the relevant error sources by utilizing the concepts of MAC layer time-stamping and skew compensation with linear regression [8].

FTSP achieves robustness against node and link failures by utilizing periodic flooding of synchronization message and implicit dynamic topology update. On the other hand, TPSN does not handle dynamic topology changes; however, FTSP can not be applied generally since the synchronization accuracy in FTSP is seriously affected by the analyzed source of delays and uncertainties which are varied according to changes of the systems. The synchronization accuracy of network-wide multi-hop synchronization is a function of the construction and depth of the tree. The synchronization error is propagated hop by hop. Therefore new approaches are required to reduce the synchronization error and to manage dynamic topology changes.

3 Reliable Time Synchronization Protocol

In the following we present our scheme called *Reliable Time Synchronization Protocol* (RTSP) for wireless sensor networks. As mentioned before, the synchronization accuracy is a function of the construction and depth of the tree in network-wide multi-hop time synchronization. So it is necessary that every node is assigned a level with the shortest path from the root node to reduce synchronization error. Besides, sensor nodes can fail easily such as nodes may move, may run out of energy and may be destroyed physically. Hence a scheme is needed to manage nodes failure for synchronization accuracy and energy efficiency. We designed the protocol considering these issues.

Step 4: When a node can not communicate with its parent, it selects another parent in the candidate list, updates own level - if it is needed - and performs step 3. The level of its child nodes will be updated when they execute synchronization. If the candidate list is empty, it performs step 4 of the topology setup phase ahead. Candidate list can be updated periodically by listening to communications of neighbors.

When the root node fails, a node which has the lowest ID in the next level takes over it. The synchronization accuracy may be improved by utilizing the concepts of MAC layer time-stamping as in the TPSN, and the random back-off mechanism can be adapted to avoid the collision of wireless links.

4 Performance Evaluation

In order to evaluate the performance of the proposed method, we established a simulation model in the NESLsim based on the PARSEC platform. PARSEC (PARallel Simulation Environment for Complex systems) is a C-based discrete-event simulation language. It adopts the process interaction approach to discrete-event simulation [10]. In NESLsim, a sensor network is modeled as a collection of sensor nodes, a channel, and a supervising entity to create the nodes [11].

4.1 Simulation Model

N nodes are deployed in a uniformly random fashion over a sensor terrain of size 100x100. Each node has a transmission range of 28. The number of nodes, N, is varied from 100 to 300 with each increase of 50. All other parameters are arranged with the same value in the TPSN simulation. The setup includes a CSMA MAC. The radio speed is 19.2kb/s, similar to the UC Berkeley MICA Motes, and every packet has a fixed size of 128bits. A node is chosen randomly to act as the root node. The granularity of the node clocks, which is the minimum accuracy attainable, is 10s. The clock model used in simulations has been derived from the characteristics of the oscillators used in sensor nodes. The frequency drift is varied randomly with time, within the specified range, to model the temporal variations in temperature. All sensor node clocks drift independently of each other. There is an initial random offset uniformly distributed over 2 seconds among the sensor node clocks to capture the initial spatial temperature variations and the difference in the boot up times [12].

4.2 Simulation Results

All results are averaged over hundred simulation runs. The performance is compared to TPSN. The depth of a tree means the length of the path from the root node to a node with the highest level number. The synchronization error is defined as the difference between the clocks of the sensor nodes and the root node.

Figure 2 shows average depth of the tree per nodes. The synchronization accuracy of multi-hop synchronization is a function of the construction and depth of the tree. So the lower depth of tree has the better synchronization accuracy. Usually RTSP has 1~2 lower depth than TPSN.

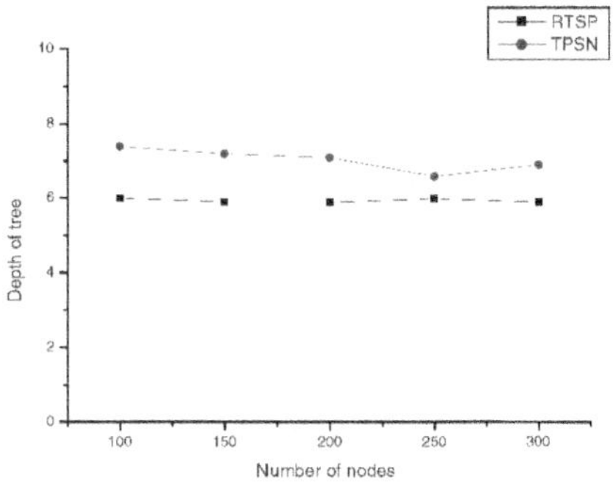

Fig. 2. Depth of tree

In figure 3, the number of messages processed during the simulation and the synchronization accuracy are presented when there is no failure of nodes. In the almost same number of messages, the RTSP has better performance in synchronization accuracy. This is the effect of the tree depth.

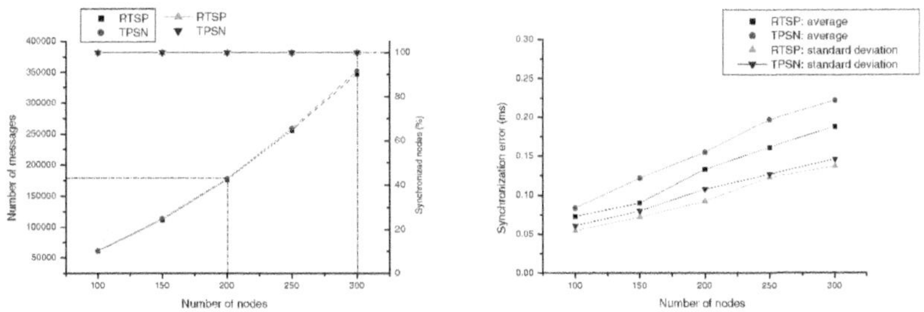

(a) Number of messages (b) Synchronization error

Fig. 3. Without failure of nodes

Figure 4 and figure 5 show the number of messages processed during the simulation, synchronized proportion of nodes and synchronization accuracy when there are 10% and 30% failure of nodes respectively. In sensor networks, sensor nodes can fail easily such as nodes may move, may run out of energy and may be destroyed physically. And this failure of nodes leads to topology changes. In the simulation, node failure means that there are topology changes. In a similar proportion of synchronized nodes to the entire nodes, RTSP reduces the number

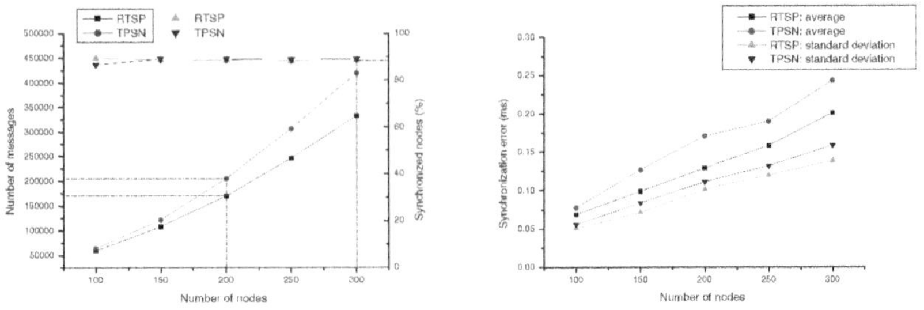

(a) Number of messages (b) Synchronization error

Fig. 4. 10% failure of nodes

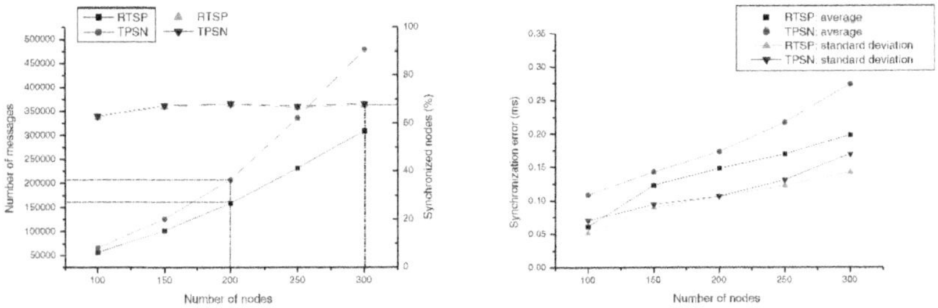

(a) Number of messages (b) Synchronization error

Fig. 5. 30% failure of nodes

of messages and shows better performance in synchronization accuracy. In wireless sensor networks, communication is one of the dominant factors in energy efficiency. Therefore communication overheads must be reduced to save energy. The RTSP reduces the number of messages and improves the synchronization accuracy by handing dynamic topology changes through the candidate parent list.

As can be seen in the results, the performance of RTSP gets better than TPSN as the failure rate (topology changes) is increased. At 10% failure out of 300 nodes, the number of messages in the RTSP is 20% lower than that in the TPSN. At 30% failure out of 300 nodes, the number of messages in the RTSP is decreased by 35% comparing to that in the TPSN.

Additionally, we varied transmission range of nodes. Except transmission range, all other parameters are arranged with the same value as described in the section 4.1 Simulation Model. Each node has different transmission range from 20 to 40. Figure 6 depicts the number of messages processed during the simulation, synchronized proportion of nodes and synchronization accuracy when there is 30% failure of nodes in different transmission range. In case of different transmission range, the number of messages in the RTSP is 25%~50% lower than that in the TPSN when there are topology changes.

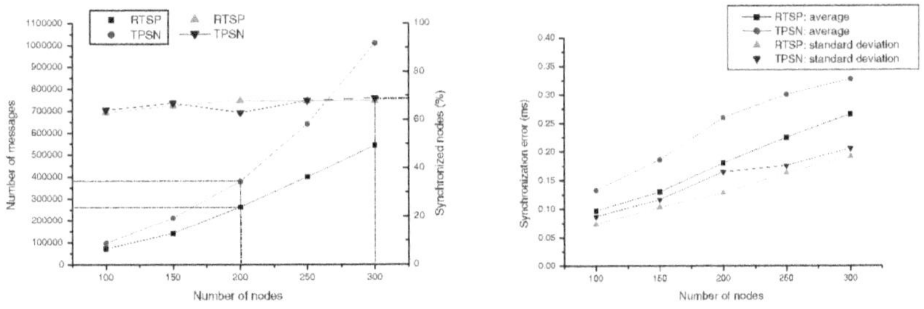

(a) Number of messages (b) Synchronization error

Fig. 6. 30% failure of nodes in different transmission range

5 Conclusions

As in any distributed computer system, time synchronization is a critical issue in sensor networks. Time synchronization is a prerequisite for sensor network applications such as object tracking, consistent state updates, duplicate detection, and temporal order delivery. In addition to these domain-specific requirements, sensor network applications often rely on synchronization as typical distributed system do: for secure cryptographic schemes, coordination of future action, ordering logged events during system debugging, and so forth. But traditional time synchronization methods in distributed systems can not be applied to the sensor networks directly because of the characteristic of sensor networks with limited computation and energy.

In this paper we proposed reliable time synchronization protocol for wireless sensor networks. It constructs hierarchical topology in the first phase, and performs pair-wise synchronization and handling topology changes in the second phase. In the proposed method, synchronization error is decreased by creating hierarchical tree with lower depth and reliability is improved by maintaining and updating information of candidate parent nodes. The RTSP reduces recovery time and costs - communication overheads - comparing to TPSN when there are changes of topology. In order to evaluate the performance of the proposed method, we established a simulation model in the NESLsim based on the PARSEC platform. Simulation results shows that RTSP has about 10% better performance than TPSN in synchronization accuracy. And the number of message in the RTSP is 10%~35% lower than that in the TPSN when there are topology changes. In case of different transmission range of nodes, the communication overhead in the RTSP is reduced up to 50% than that in the TPSN at the maximum.

Acknowledgment. This work was supported by the Regional Research Centers Program (Research Center for Logistics Information Technology), granted by the Korean Ministry of Education and Human Resources Development.

homing, and other issues. These issues are examined in the extended network mobility support part. In particular, the basic support protocol has a serious problem called dog-leg problem; that is, all traffic to or from the MNN of the nested mobile network passes through the HAs (Home Agents) of all preceding mobile networks. To solve this problem, various methodologies have been proposed [5], [6], [7]. However, these ideas are still inefficient for real time data transmission and they remain as the optimal route because they are based on bi-directional tunneling between the root-MR and HA of the nested mobile network. Furthermore, direct message exchange between the MNNs within the same root-MR, which is called intra-domain communication, is not supported and the root-MR can experience a very heavy load because it must maintain full paths for all nested MRs. If there are frequent movements of mobile networks, and intra-domain communication is large, these methodologies are very inefficient. Thus, most previous methods have limitations with regard to signaling overhead, concentrated traffic and load in the root-MR, and packet-header overhead due to multiple encapsulations.

Accordingly, this paper proposes a new route optimization methodology for the efficient support of network mobility based on unidirectional tunneling between the HA of a nested mobile network and the root-MR, and the use of a tree-based intra-domain routing mechanism. The use of unidirectional tunneling facilitates more optimized route construction. When using tree-based routing for intra-domain communication and binding procedures, a hierarchical mobile network routing is more efficient and faster than previous tunneling mechanism for signaling and data transmission.

2 Previous Works

The IETF NEMO working group has defined a basic protocol operation to support the network mobility of a mobile network based on Mobile IPv6. There have already been several Internet drafts related to the goals and requirements, terminology, and basic support protocol for network mobility. Network mobility is essentially defined as Nemo basic support and Nemo extended support, where the purpose of Nemo basic support is to preserve session continuity in a mobile network, while Nemo extended support provides more optimal routing for a nested mobile network [4]. The goal of the Nemo basic support protocol is to support network mobility and backward compatibility by extending Mobile IPv6. As such, its definition of the MR extends the MN of Mobile IPv6, where the MR performs internal routing and external data transmission for an MNN, which moves with the MR. Data transmission between the MNN and the CN is performed using bi-directional tunneling between the HA and the MR. All traffic passes through the HA, and IPSec is used for secure signaling between the MR and the HA [4].

In a mobile network on a visited link, a bi-directional tunnel is created between the HA and the MR for data transmission. Thus, data transmission by a mobile network is achieved using the MR, which is the egress interface of the mobile network. In other words, since only the MR is involved in the acquisition of a CoA in a mobile network handover, an MNN behind the MR can maintain its home network address. For the construction of a bi-directional tunnel, the basic support protocol extends the binding

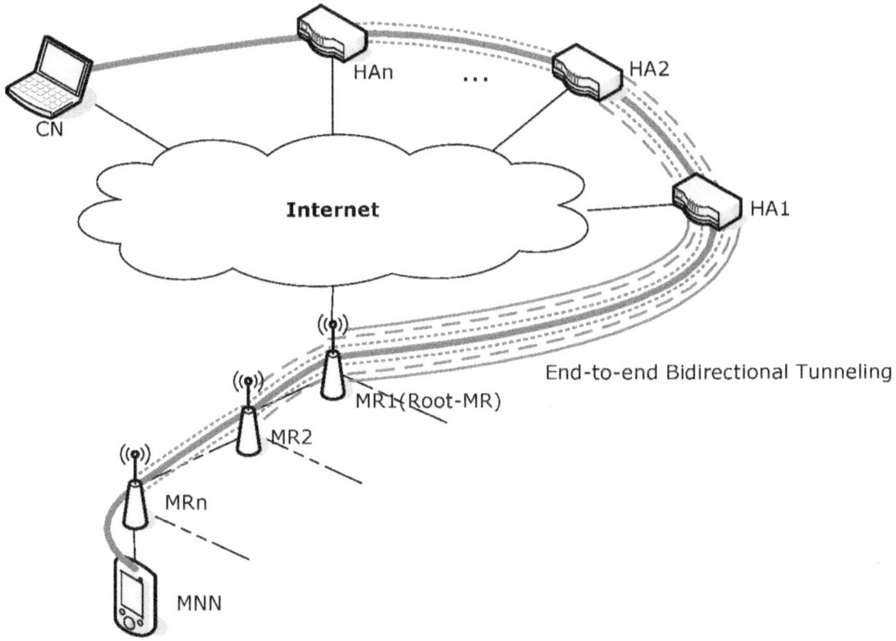

Fig. 1. Dog-leg problem in Nemo basic support protocol

message of Mobile IPv6. The extended BU(Binding Update) message contains a network prefix instead of a home address, and the egress interface address of the MR as the CoA. Thus, by using these extensions, network mobility can be supported without changing the addresses of the MNNs in the mobile network.

The Nemo basic support protocol defines the minimal procedures and extensions required to support network mobility, as such it does not cover route optimization, multi-homing, and so on. Although these issues are being investigated under Nemo extended support, the work has not yet been completed. In the basic support protocol, the tunnel of a nested mobile network is constructed through all preceding mobile network tunnels, and all the traffic of the nested mobile network passes through the HAs of all preceding mobile networks, thereby causing a serious problem called the 'dog-leg problem'. Fig. 1 shows an example of the dog-leg problem in the basic support protocol.

Recently, a lot of research has focused on solving the dog-leg problem, including route optimization of the basic support protocol [5], [7], [9]. Several previous studies on route optimization have used bi-directional tunneling between the HA of the nested mobile network and the root-MR, where two bi-directional tunnels are made between the HA of the nested mobile network and the root-MR, and between the root-MR and the MR of the nested mobile network. By using direct tunneling between the HA of the nested mobile network and the root-MR, the dog-leg problem is solved. Yet, an extended RA(Router Advertisement) message that includes an address of the root-MR egress interface is required to discover and notify the root-MR address to the nested MRs.

Most of previous works in route optimization have used bidirectional tunneling. The methods using bidirectional tunneling has some drawbacks for real-time data transmission. Since these methods have more complex signaling than the basic support protocol. Because if the root-MR moves along with the nested mobile network, the nested mobile network must re-establish the tunnel since the root-MR address was changed. In addition, these methods do not support intra-domain communication, because all traffic passes through either the HA of the nested mobile network or at least the root-MR. The root-MR must maintain full paths for the MRs of all nested mobile networks. If there are frequent movements of mobile networks, these methods become very inefficient due to the large signaling overhead, large data transmission delay, traffic concentration in the root-MR, and packet header overhead resulting from multiple encapsulations. Therefore, a new route optimization methodology is needed to support efficient signaling and optimized routes.

3 Hierarchical Mobile Network Routing Scheme

3.1 Basic Operation of HMNR

To solve the problems as stated above, this paper proposes a HMNR(Hierarchical Mobile Network Routing) scheme consisting of intra-Nemo routing and extra-Nemo tunneling, where tree-based routing is used for intra-domain data transmission and signaling, while unidirectional tunneling is used for data transmission to or from the external network. Fig. 2 shows the operation of the HMNR scheme for route optimization. As shown in Fig. 2, an MNN behind the MR cannot receive data from the CN directly since a mobile network uses the network prefix of the home network. However, data from an MNN can be directly transmitted to the CN using a normal routing scheme. In other words, although a tunnel is required for data transmission from the HA to the MR, the other tunnel from the MR to the HA does not need to be established to optimize the route. As a result, the MNN can communicate with the CN using only a unidirectional tunnel from the HA to the MR. Similarly, route optimization for a nested mobile network can be achieved using unidirectional tunneling from the HA of the nested mobile network to the root-MR by binding the network prefix to the CoA of the root-MR. Only the root-MR can perform decapsulation of the packets from the CN.

The direct tunneling between the HA of the nested mobile network and the root-MR requires the additional handover procedure because the binding address of the mobile network needs to be changed for the root-MR movement along with the nested mobile network. Thus, the handovers are divided into three cases: inter-Nemo, intra-Nemo and root-MR handover. In the vehicular environments, the root-MR handover frequently occurs and it accompanies with the mass signaling for all nested mobile networks, and the root-MR suffers from the large processing load, bottleneck and the service discontinuity.

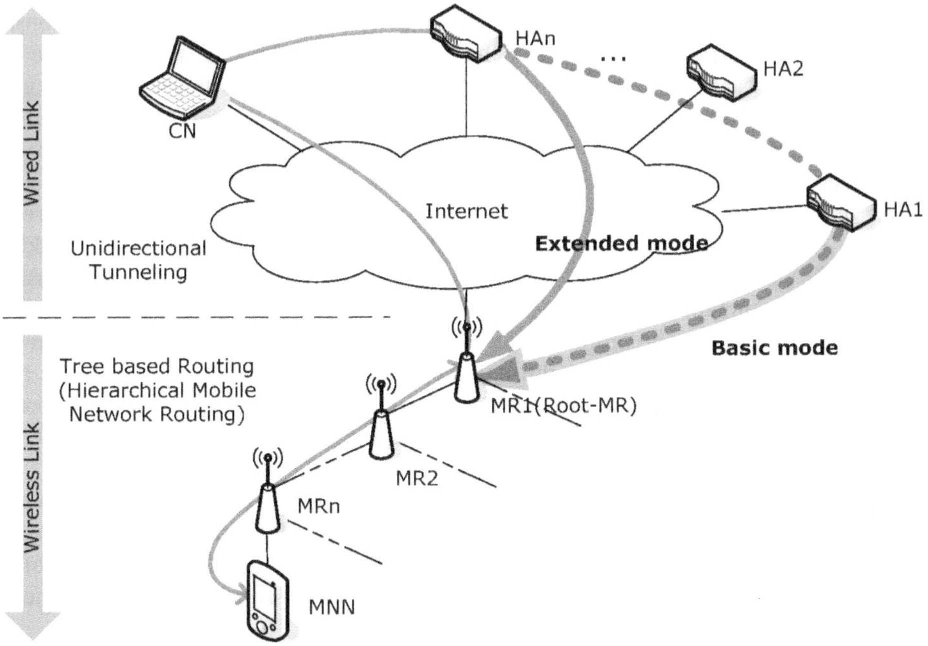

Fig. 2. HMNR Scheme for Route Optimization

To satisfy the requirements, this paper proposes the HMNR scheme with two operating modes for the signaling efficiency and route optimization respectively: the basic mode and the extended mode. In the extended mode, the route optimization is performed by using the direct tunneling from the HA to the root-MR. On the other hands, the MR in the basic mode binds its network prefix to the HoA of the root-MR, thus the data from the CN to the MNN passes through both HAs of the MNN and of the root-MR. By using this mechanism, the MR is independent of the root-MR handover. Moreover, the route is more optimal than the one of the basic support protocol with same signaling complexity because the HMNR scheme has only two intermediate HAs regardless of the nested level of the mobile network. Each operating mode is dynamically switched by sending the BU message including the HoA or CoA of the root-MR for the binding address. Thus the MR decides the basic mode for the vehicular environment with low data traffic, and it can switch into the extended modes if the data traffic or inter-Nemo handover is increased.

3.2 Routing and Handover Procedures

Mobile networks are composed of a tree topology from the root-MR to the MRs of each nested mobile network, where only the root-MR has an egress interface for transmitting data to or from the external network. Thus, a new routing mechanism based on a tree topology is needed where the root-MR is the root of the tree and the nested MRs are the tree nodes. In a tree-based routing scheme, each MR contains a

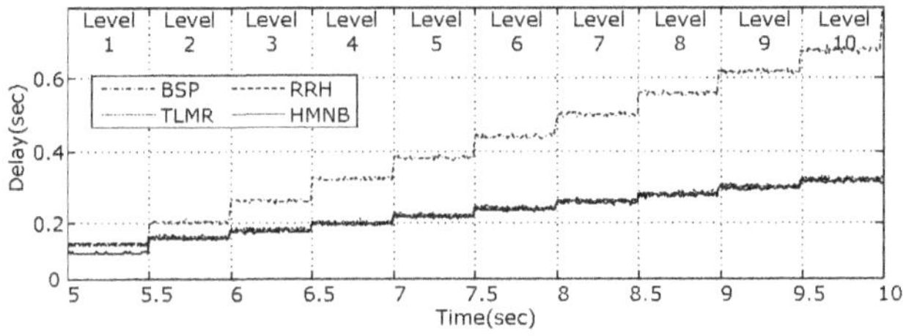

(a) Inter-domain Data Transmission Time vs. MR Level

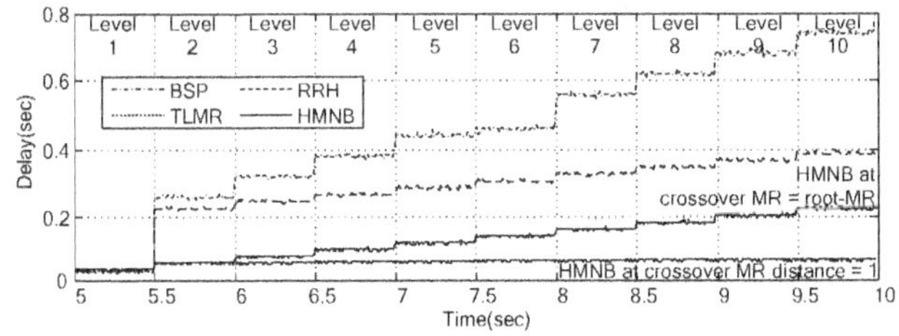

(b) Intra-domain Data Transmission Time vs. MR Level

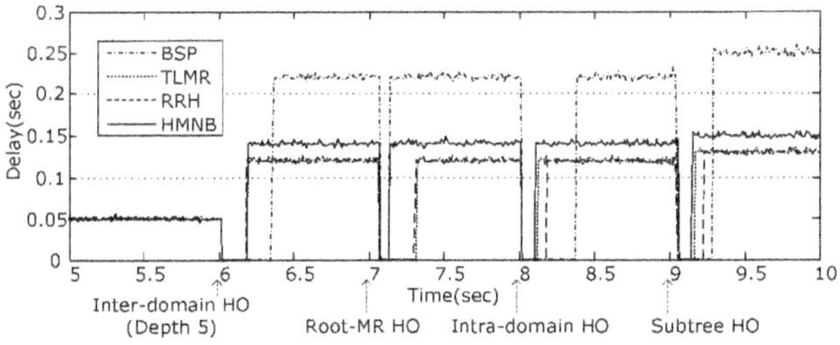

(c) Data Transmission Time for CBR HO Scenario

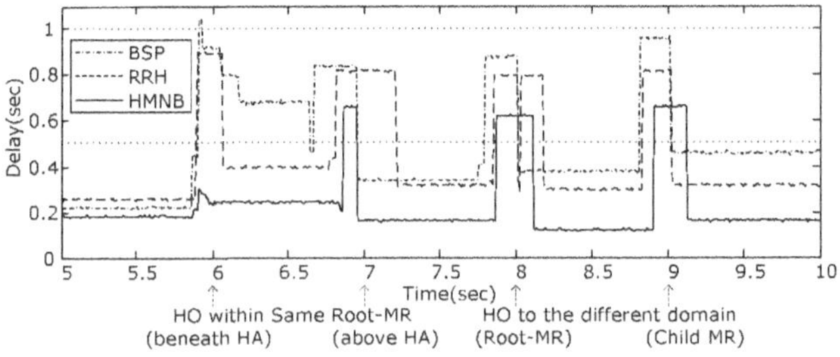

(d) Data Transmission Time for Mobile HA

Fig. 4. The performance analysis of the HMNB scheme

Fig. 4 (a) and (b) show the performance results of the inter-domain and intra-domain data transmission times for the TCP traffic, in accordance with the increase of the depth of the destination MR. In the inter-domain communication environment, the data transmission delays for the route optimization methods i.e. TLMR, RRH and

HMNB schemes were smaller than those of the BSP. In the intra-domain communication environment, the data transmission delays in the RRH scheme are larger than the HMNB scheme because the traffic always passes through the HA. Moreover, the intra-domain communication times of the HMNB scheme show that the delays become smaller than other schemes, if the crossover MR is located below the root-MR. Fig. 4 (c) shows the data transmission delays and the service discontinuity times for the CBR(100 KBps) traffic with the various handover scenarios. In the case of the CBR handover scenario, the delays of the HMNB scheme are larger than those of the RRH and TLMR schemes because it uses two intermediate HAs. The service discontinuity time of HMNB scheme is, however, the smallest in the root-MR handover scenario. At the time of the root-MR handover, the HMNB and BSP schemes can accomplish the handover procedure with just the root-MR, so the discontinuity times of these schemes are the smallest. In the case of the BSP scheme, the nested depth of the MR is deeper, so the service discontinuity time becomes larger than other handover scenarios. Thus, the TLMR and RRH schemes may thus not be suitable for a vehicular environment where the root-MR mobility is usually very high. Fig. 4 (d) shows the performance results of the data transmission times for the mobile-HA scenario, according to the various handover cases. The TLMR scheme does not define any method that supports the mobile-HA. The HMNB scheme has the smallest delay time because the mobile-HA can forward the received binding message to its own HA, so that the traffic does not pass through any additional HAs. In conclusion, the HMNB scheme has minimal signaling complexity and supports an efficient route optimization mechanism for the nested mobile network.

5 Conclusion

In the current study, we have investigated the limitations of current and previous approaches to network mobility management. We have then proposed a new approach for the efficient route optimization in a mobile network, which is called a hierarchical mobile network routing scheme. The proposed scheme uses tree-based routing for intra-domain data transmission and signaling, and unidirectional tunneling for data transmission to or from the external network. It can provide a more optimized solution for route construction and faster signaling, and can also provide intra-domain handover and communication. In addition to these advantages, it can also support micro-mobility without any additional extension.

In summary, the proposed hierarchical mobile network routing eliminates many problems in route optimization such as large signaling delay and the lack of intra-domain communication which are drawbacks of most previous approaches to the mobility management of network groups. We have compared the characteristics of a hierarchical mobile network routing scheme with the NEMO basic support protocol and previous route optimization methods. A hierarchical mobile network routing scheme can be adopted in various mobile environments to efficiently support network mobility such as WPAN, ubiquitous computing, and VNE.

References

1. Hong-Yon Lach, Christophe Janneteau, and Alexandru Petrescu, "Network Mobility in Beyond-3G Systems", IEEE Communication Magazine, July 2003
2. Thierry Ernst, "Network Mobility Support Goals and Requirements", Internet-Draft, IETF, May 2003
3. Thierry Ernst, and Hong-Yon Lach, "Network Mobility Support Terminology", Internet-Draft, IETF, May 2003
4. Vijay Devarapalli, Ryuji Wakikawa, Alexandru Petrescu, and Pascal Thubert, "NEMO Basic Support Protocol", Internet-Draft, IETF, December 2003
5. P. Thubert, M. Molteni, and C. Ng, "Taxonomy of Route Optimization models in the Nemo Context", Internet-Draft, IETF, June 2003
6. H.S. Kang, K.C. Kim, S.Y. Han, K.J. Lee and J.S. Park, "Route Optimization for Mobile Network by Using Bi-directional Between HA and TLMR", Internet-Draft, IETF, June 2003
7. H. Ohnishi, K. Sakitani, and Y. Takagi, "HMIP based Route Optimization method in a mobile network", Internet-Draft, IETF, October 2003
8. Campbell, A.T., Gomez, J., Sanghyo Kim, Chieh-Yih Wan, Turanyi, Z.R., and Valko, A.G., "Comparison of IP micromobility protocols", IEEE Wireless Communications, Volume 9, Issue 1, February 2002
9. Hyunsik Kang, Keecheon Kim, Sunyoung Han, Kyeong-Jin Lee and Jung-Soo Park, "Route Optimization for Mobile Network by Using Bi-directional Between Home Agent and Top Level Mobile Router", Internet-Draft, IETF, June 2003

QoS Routing with Link Stability in Mobile Ad Hoc Networks*

Jui-Ming Chen, Shih-Pang Ho, Yen-Cheng Lin, and Li-Der Chou

Department of Computer Science and Information Engineering,
National Central University,
No.300, Jhongda Rd, Jhongli City, Taoyuan County 32001, Taiwan(R.O.C)
Tel: +886-3-422-7151 ext 57968, Fax: +886-3-422-2681
cld@csie.ncu.edu.tw

Abstract. In this paper, in accordance with requirements of different users and supplying effective usage of limited network resources, we propose a stable QoS routing mechanism to determine a guaranteed route suited for mobile ad hoc wireless networks. The manner exploits the received signal strength (RSS) techniques to estimate the distance and the signal change of the velocity to evaluate the breakaway. To ensure the QoS it chooses a steady path from the source to the destination and tries to reserve the bandwidth. Ultimately, it is clear to find that the performance never decrease even the growth of the overhead and the movement of users via the simulated by ns-2.

1 Introduction

Mobile Ad Hoc Wireless Networks (MANET), also called the Ad hoc network, is lots of moving nodes (mobile hosts) communicating with their adjacent mobile node by radio wave. Every node can contact each other without existence infrastructural network. In the Ad hoc network, it differs from cellular wireless networks that need base stations to deliver and receive the packets. Each node plays the role as a router. When one of them wants to deliver packets to destination out of its coverage, intermediate nodes will forward this packet to the next node till the destination node receive it.

In traditional cellular wireless networks, generally we need to establish base stations in advance. Fixed nodes far and near connect to the backbone and become a wireless network environment. In this network the customer who wants to communicate with another must locate in the base station coverage. If user moved out of base station's service scope, he can't take the communication. Consequently, we need to establish enough base stations to achieve the objective. Ad hoc networks do not demand fixed

* This research was supported in part by National Science Council of the Republic of China under the grant NSC 93-2219-E-008-002, and by Computer and Communications Research Labs, Industrial Technology Research Institute under the grant T1-94081-12.

L.T. Yang et al. (Eds.): EUC 2005, LNCS 3824, pp. 683 – 692, 2005.

B. The Guarantee Index of Quality of Service

In QoS routing protocol, there are many parameters of QoS guarantee [12][13], such as residual bandwidth, residual buffer space, packet loss probability, delay time and delay jitter, etc. In this paper, we refer to the proposal of Z. Wang [13], only take account of bandwidth to evaluate the efficiency of QoS service. In this paper, we support bandwidth guarantee for QoS type traffic, and we can use some dynamic adaptive technologies to keep the Quality of service.

$$BW_r(s,d) = \min(BW_r(s,x),\dots,BW_r(w,d)) \tag{2}$$

3 Proposal of QoS Routing Policy

A. The Prediction Method of Stable Path

In Ad hoc network, we can calculate the variation of signal strength from neighbor link $l_{i,j}$ and predict the broken time with regular beacon signal. In Fig. 1, the signal strength of node j at time $t\text{-}\Delta t$, t, is $S_{i,j}(t\text{-}\Delta t)$, $S_{i,j}(t)$.Then we use equation 1, and we will derive the answer:

$$\because r_{i,j}(t) = R_t\sqrt{\frac{S_t}{S_{i,j}(t)}},\ r_{i,j}(t-\Delta t) = R_t\sqrt{\frac{S_t}{S_{i,j}(t-\Delta t)}}$$

$$\therefore v_{i,j}(t) = \frac{r_{i,j}(t) - r_{i,j}(t-\Delta t)}{\Delta t} = \frac{\sqrt{S_t}}{\Delta t}R_t\sqrt{\frac{1}{S_{i,j}(t)} - \frac{1}{S_{i,j}(t-\Delta t)}} \tag{3}$$

In Fig. 2, we can detect the same variation rate of signal strength. They have same variation rate but their moving ability are not equal in practice. We define the average variation rate of velocity at t time $Avg(v_{i,j}(t-\Delta t))$. We divided the average variation rate of velocity into four cases:case1 indicate node j approach node i, case2 is that node j go away from node i, case3 is that node j start to approach node i, case4 shows node j leave out the range of node I, as in TABLE 1. So we can define a relation equation:

$$Avg(v_{i,j}(t)) = \begin{cases} \dfrac{Avg(v_{i,j}(t-\Delta t)) + v_{i,j}(t)}{2}, & \text{Case 1 \& 4} \\ v_{i,j}(t), & \text{Case 2 \& 3} \end{cases} \tag{4}$$

$$T_{i,j}^{predict} = \begin{cases} \left\lfloor \dfrac{R_t - r_{i,j}(t)}{v_{i,j}(t)} \right\rfloor, & \text{if } avg(v_{i,j}(t)) > 0 \\ T_s, & \text{if } avg(v_{i,j}(t)) = 0 \\ \left\lfloor \dfrac{R_t + r_{i,j}(t)}{v_{i,j}(t)} \right\rfloor, & \text{if } avg(v_{i,j}(t)) < 0 \end{cases} \tag{5}$$

Using equation 4, we can derive the relation equation 5 of $T_{i,j}^{predict}$. Using equation 5, we can calculate the predictive lifetime of path, equation 6.

$$Path_{s,d}^{predict}(k) = \min\left(T_{s,l}^{predict}, \cdots, T_{w,d}^{predict}\right) \tag{6}$$

Table 1. $Avg(V_{i,j}(t-\Delta t))$ and $V_{i,j}(t)$

Case	$Avg(v_{i,j}(t-\Delta t))$	$v_{i,j}(t)$	Status
1	-	-	Keep approahing
2	-	+	Start leaving
3	+	-	Start approaching
4	+	+	Keep leaving

B. The Method of Stable Path and QoS Routing

The method we propose that each node have to maintain two tables, one is Signal Affinity Table (SAT), the other is Zone Route Table (ZRT). Each node will broadcast a routing information packet periodically with a time period T_{beacon}, when a node receives the packet from its neighbor nodes then it records it in its SAT. We can use equation 2.

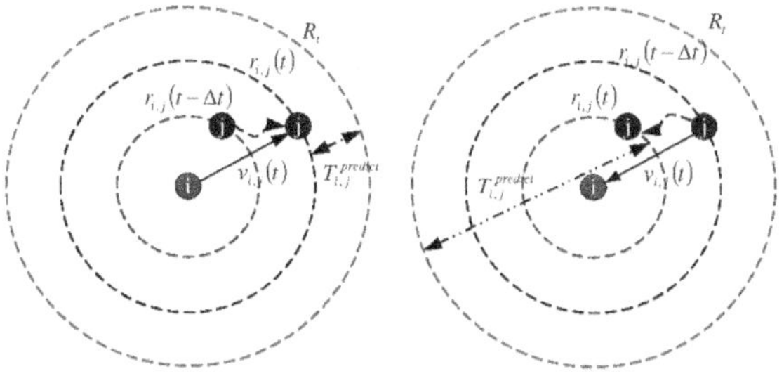

Fig. 1. In the condition of uniform motion, the signal strength of node j per t times

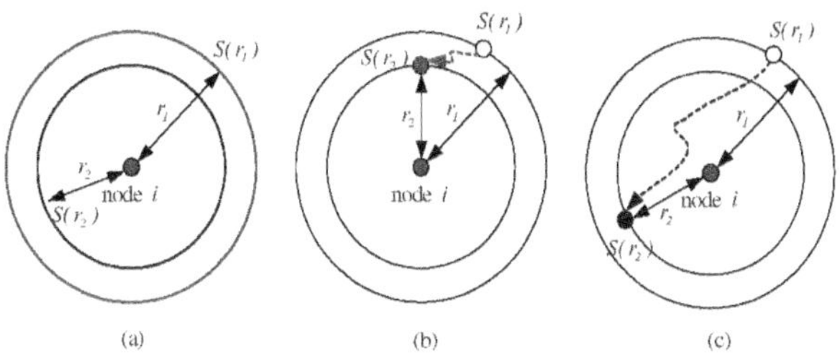

Fig. 2. Different conditions but have the same variation rate of signal strength

Possession of the *BW* and the prediction of invalidity time of path is $Path_{s,d}^{predict}(x)$.ZRT will record the information of hops, next node, sequence number, bandwidth, and signal affinity for prediction time.

When a source node wants to transmit the data to destination, it will find its ZRP first. If the destination did not exist in its table, it will broadcast the request to the far node in its table. The node receive the request packet, they will repeat the step before the destination in they ZRT. When the destination receives the route request packet, it will wait a back-off time; then select the path which has the longest predictive time; then we use this path to transmit the data. Show as equation 7.

$$RPath_{s,d} = \max\{Path_{s,d}(k)\} \tag{7}$$

If has more than one longest path exist, we select the path which has the least number of the hops. When the predictive time of path is equal or less than 1 sec, we will pre-route before the path is failure.If the load of network is heavy, the efficiency of DSDV is better than DSR; otherwise DSR is better than DSDV [14]. In this paper, we attempt to find a QoS routing path using DSR. The destination received the request packet, he will find the path which available bandwidth conformed to the request and it has the longest predictive longest life time. If no path conforms to the request, the destination will decide one with longest predictive time and randomly drop some best effort traffic to reserve the bandwidth whole path.

4 Performance Evaluation

A. Simulation Environment

The *ns-2* [15] simulator was used in the simulation study, as well as can be exploited for academic research. In the simulation, the environment parameters of the system was refer to the reference [14], Inter-Frame Space (IFS) is 10 μs , Short IFS (SIFS) is 10 μs , PCF IFS is 30 μs , DCF IFS is 110 μs , every time slot is 20 μs . If a packet stays in the queue buffer over 20 ns and was not sent yet, it will be dropped. Contention Window, *CW*, CW_{min}=32 and CW_{max}=1024. The maximum size of interface queue is 64, all nodes communicate with identical, half-duplex wireless radio that are modeled available IEEE 802.11-based of 2Mbps and a nominal transmission radius of 250 meters. T_{beacon} = 1 ms. The mobility model referred to [2].Our simulation modeled a network of 50 mobile hosts placed randomly using uniform distribution within 1000 meter multiplied by 300 meter area. The minimum and the maximum velocity set zero and 20 m/s, respectively, while each time user velocity is determined previously, and such velocity maintains 100 s, T_s.

In our simulation model, the transmission ratio uses CBR traffic sources between the communications of nodes, as well as data packets are 64 or 1024 bytes long. The velocities of transmission are a packet per second, four packets per second and eight packets per second. The user arrival procedure is Poisson distribution, as well as the average arrival rate is λ. That $\mu = T_d^{-1}$ and user calling duration is exponential distribution. The average duration T_d is 180s.Their are 1000 calling-requests during the simulation.

B. Simulation Results

Fig. 3 shows the influence of transmission success rate and control overhead by the speed of nodes. Because our proposal possesses the ability of prediction invalidity time of path, we can handle it effectively. Fig. 4 shows the influence of transmission success rate, control overhead and control packet ratio by the arrival time 1/λ (seconds per call), and vice versa the arrival rate defines λ.

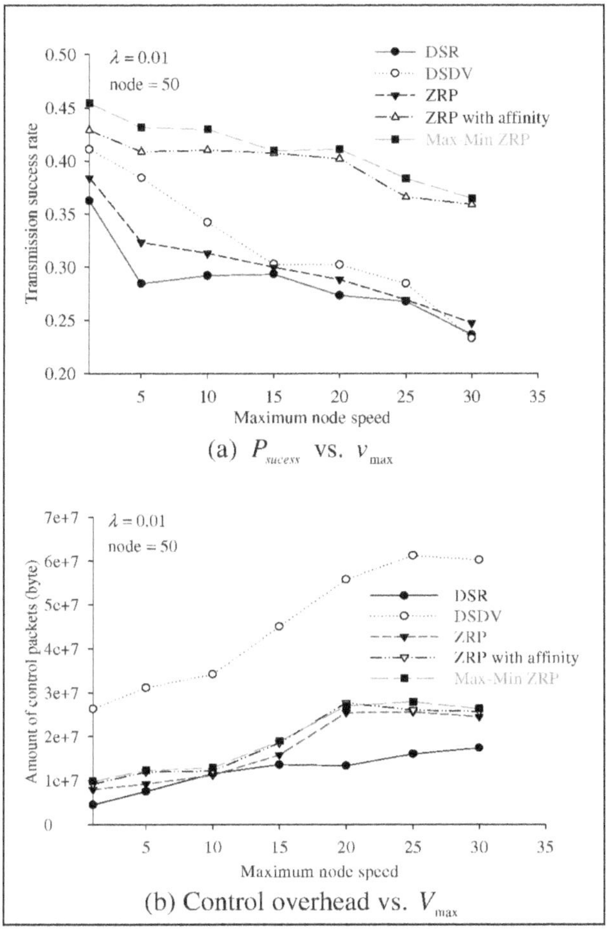

Fig. 3. v_{max} vs. throughput and overhead

[4] J. -H. Ryu, Y. -W. Kim and D. -H. Cho, "A New Routing Scheme Based on the Terminal Mobility in Mobile Ad-Hoc Networks," *Proceedings of 1999 IEEE 50th Vehicular Technology Conference (VTC'99)*, Amsterdam, Netherlands, vol. 2, pp. 1253-1257, Sept. 1999.
[5] K. Paul, S. Bandyopadhyay, A. Mukherjee and D. Saha, "Communication-Aware Mobile Hosts in Ad-hoc Wireless Network," *Proceedings of 1999 IEEE International Conference on Personal Wireless Communication (ICPWC'99)*, Jaipur, India, pp. 83-87, Feb. 1999.
[6] S. Chen and K. Nahrstedt, "Distributed Quality-of-Service Routing in Ad Hoc Networks," *IEEE Journal on Selected Areas in Communications*, vol. 17, no. 8, pp. 1488-1505, August 1999.
[7] V. Vishnumurthy, T. Sandeep, B. S. Manoj and C. S. R. Murthy, "A novel out-of-band signaling mechanism for real-times support in tactical ad hoc wireless network," Real-Time and Embedded Technology and Application Symposium, 2004, Proceedings of RTAS 2004, 10th IEEE, pp. 55-63, May 2004.
[8] D.B. Johnson and D.A. Matlz, "Dynamic Source Routing in Ad Hoc Wireless Networks," Mobile Computing, Kluwer Academic Publishers, vol. 353, pp. 153-181, 1996.
[9] B. S. Manoj and C. Siva Ram Murthy, "Realy-time Traffic Support for Ad Hoc Wireless Networks," Proceedings of IEEE ICON 2002, p. 335-340, August 2002.
[10] T. Bheemarjuna Reddy, I. Karthigeyan, B. S. Manoj, and C. Siva Ram Murthy, "Quality of Service Provisioning in Ad Hoc Wireless Networks: A survey of Issues and Solution," Technical Report, Department of Computer Science and Engineering, Indian Institue of Technology, Mardras, India, July 2003.
[11] W. C. Lynch, K. Rahardja, S. Gehring, "An Analysis of Noise Aggregation from Multiple Distributed RF Emitters," *Interval Research Corporation*, Dec. 1998.
[12] S. Chakrabarti and A. Mishra, "QoS Issues in Ad Hoc Wireless Networks," *IEEE Communications Magazine*, vol. 39, no. 2, pp. 142-148, Feb. 2001.
[13] Z. Wang and J. Crowcroft, "Quality-of-Service Routing for Supporting Multimedia Applications," *IEEE Journal on Selected Areas in Communications,* vol. 14, no. 7, pp. 1228-1234, Sept. 1996.
[14] S. R. Das, C. E. Perkins and E. M. Royer, "Performance Comparison of Two On demand Routing Protocols for Ad Hoc Networks," *IEEE INFOCOM'2000*, Tel Aviv, Israel, vol. 1, pp. 3-12, March 2000.
[15] The Network Simulator – ns-2, http://www.isi.edu/nsnam/ns/.

Efficient Cooperative Caching Schemes for Data Access in Mobile Ad Hoc Networks

Cheng-Ru Young[1,2], Ge-Ming Chiu[1], and Fu-Lan Wu[3]

[1] Department of Computer Science and Information Engineer,
National Taiwan University of Science and Technology
{chiu, D8815005}@mail.ntust.edu.tw
[2] Department of Electronic Engineering, Chin Min College of Technology and Commerce
chengru@ms.chinmin.edu.tw
[3] BenQ Corp. Taipei, Taiwan
fulan@totoro.ee.ntust.edu.tw

Abstract. We study cooperative caching technique for supporting data access in ad hoc networks. Two protocols that are based on the notion of zone are proposed. The IXP protocol is push-based in the sense that a mobile node would broadcast an index message to the nodes in its zone to advertise a caching event. A data requester can fetch a needed item from a nearby node if it knows that it has cached the data. The second protocol, called DPIP, is explicitly pull-based with implicit index pushing property. A data requester may broadcast a special request message to the nodes in its zone asking them to help satisfy its demand. However, this is done only if its own caching information does not result in a successful fetch. Performance study shows that the proposed protocols can significantly improve system performance when compared to existing caching schemes.

1 Introduction

Recent advances in wireless communication technology have greatly increased the functionality of mobile information services and have made many mobile computing applications a rlity. It provides users with ability to access information and services through wireless connections that can be retained while the users are moving. A number of novel mobile information services, such as mobile shopping aids in a large shopping mall and financial information distribution to users via mobile phones and palmtop computers, have alreaeady been implemented.

While many infrastructure-based wireless networks have been deployed to support wireless communication for mobile hosts, they suffer from such drawbacks as the need for installing base stations and the potential bottleneck of the base stations. The ad-hoc-based network structure (or MANET) alleviates this problem by allowing mobile nodes to form a dynamic and temporary network without any pre-existing infrastructure. This can be highly useful in some environments. For example, in a large shopping mall there may be an info-station that stores the prices of all goods for que-

L.T. Yang et al. (Eds.): EUC 2005, LNCS 3824, pp. 693 – 702, 2005.

rying. Due to limited radio range, an info-station itself can only cover a limited geographical area. If shoppers' mobile devices are able to form an ad hoc network, they can have access to the price list even if they are beyond the radio range of the info-station. In such an environment, when a request for a price is forwarded toward the info-station, it is likely that one of the nodes along the path has already cached the requested item. This node can send the data back to the requester so that the access time, the channel bandwidth, and the battery power can be saved.

In light of the above example, we see that caching of data offers significant benefits for applications in ad hoc networks. Cooperative caching, which allows sharing and coordination of cached data among multiple nodes, has been widely used to improve web performance in wired networks [9, 22, 25]. These protocols usually assume fixed network topology and often require high computation and communication overheads. However, in an ad hoc network, the network topology changes frequently, and mobile nodes typically have resource (battery, CPU, and wireless bandwidth) constraints, thus cannot afford high computation or communication overheads. Moreover, ad hoc networks are based on wireless communications that are unreliable in nature. Being able to access data from nearby nodes is important from performance point of view. Hence, there exists a need for new techniques that may be applied to ad hoc networks.

In this paper, we design and evaluate cooperative caching techniques for supporting data access in ad hoc networks. Two protocols that are based on the notion of zone are proposed. In the protocols in-zone broadcasts of small-sized messages are exploited to assist the locating of required data items. The first protocol, called *IXP*, is push-based in the sense that a mobile node broadcasts an index message to the nodes in its zone to advertise a caching event. A data requester can fetch a needed item from a nearby node if it knows the node has cached the item. Otherwise, it issues a request to the data center to ask for it. Any nodes along the path can redirect the request to a nearby node, instead of faraway data center, if it knows the node has cached the item. The second protocol, called *DPIP*, is explicitly pull-based with implicit index pushing property. A data requester may broadcast a special request message to the nodes in its zone asking them to help satisfy its demand. However, this is done only if its own caching information does not result in a successful fetch. *DPIP* allows a wider scope of local caching cooperation without incurring extra communication overhead. In particular, unlike previous techniques [5, 6, 7], *DPIP* exploits the implicit index pushing property in locating data items existing in nearby nodes. In addition, the proposed protocols achieve a greater level of caching cooperation through employing an appropriate cache replacement mechanism. Simulation results show that the proposed protocols may improve system performance in terms of the request success ratio and the data access time.

2 Related Works

To facilitate data access in ad hoc networks, some data replication schemes [11, 12, 13, 24] and caching schemes [18, 23, 26] have been proposed in the literature. Data replication addresses the issue of allocating replicas of data objects to mobile hosts to meet access demands. These techniques normally require a priori knowledge of the operation environment and are vulnerable to node mobility.

Unlike data replication schemes, caching schemes do not rely on distributing data objects beforehand to facilitate data access. In the conventional caching scheme, referred to as *SimpleCache* [26], a data requester always caches the received data. If subsequent requests for the cached data arrive before the cache expires, the node may use the cached copy to serve the requests. In case of a cache miss, it has to get the data from the data center. Getting data from faraway data center will increase the response times for the requests. Recently, a cooperative caching strategy, called *CoCa*, was proposed in [5, 6]. In *CoCa*, mobile hosts share their cache contents with each other to reduce both the number of server requests and the number of access misses. In addition, a group-based cooperative caching scheme, called *GroCoCa*, has been presented in [7], in which a centralized incremental clustering algorithm is adopted by taking node mobility and data access pattern into consideration. *GroCoCa* improves system performance at the cost of extra power consumption. In the *7DS* architecture [19], users cache data and share with their neighbors when experiencing intermittent connectivity to the Internet. However, the above researches focus on the single-hop environment rather than the multi-hop ad hoc networks addressed in this work.

In ad hoc networks, finding the location of a cached copy of a data item is the core of a cooperative caching mechanism. In [17], when an object is requested, the protocol relies on flooding to find the nearest node that has maintained a copy of the object. Using flooding may potentially reduce the response time since the request can be served by a nearby node, instead of the data center faraway. However, flooding can be problematic for network communication. To reduce the overhead, flooding is limited to nodes within k hops from the requester in [17], where k is the number of hops from the requester to the data center. The overhead is still excessive especially when k is large or the network density is high. In [18], flooding is limited by imposing a threshold on route existence probability. Based on the definition of route stability, as a query packet is forwarded by hopping, its route existence probability becomes smaller. By loading the threshold of route probability into the header of a request packet beforehand, the range of cache querying can be limited. However, choosing appropriate threshold for route existence probability is challenging.

Hence options other than flooding are desirable for finding a needed data item in mobile ad hoc networks. In [23], a cooperative caching scheme has been proposed to reduce the communication and energy costs associated with fetching a web object. When a terminal M wants to get a web data W that was not cached locally, M requests W through the base station only if the base station is in the zone of M. Otherwise, M will broadcast a request message for W in its zone. If W is not cached by any of the mobile nodes in the zone, a peer-to-peer communication scheme is realized with the mobile nodes that are known to share interests with M and are at a distance that is less than the one between M and the nearest base station. The communication is based the notion of terminal profile. However, if the data correlation between mobile terminals is small, the effect of terminal profile will be lost. In [26], two caching schemes, called *CacheData* and *CachePath*, had been presented. With *CacheData*, intermediate nodes may cache data to serve future requests. In *CachePath*, a mobile node may cache the path to a nearby data requester while forwarding the data and use the path information to redirect future requests to the nearby caching site. A hybrid protocol *HybridCache* was also proposed, which improves the performance by taking advantages of *CacheData* and *CachePath* methods while avoiding their weakness. In *HybridCache*, when a mobile

their *IV[x].cachednode* entries with *M*, increase *IV[x].count* by one and decrease *IV[y].count* by one. The last two operations, i.e. updating *IV[].count* entries, need to be performed by a buddy node only if the corresponding data items are cached by the node. Furthermore, if a buddy has recorded *M* in its *IV[y].cachednode*, it needs to set the entry to NULL because *y* is no longer cached by *M*.

(b) Cache Replacement

If a node *M* accesses a data item when its cache space is full, some cached item must be removed to make room for the new one. In *IXP*, we use *IV[].count* entry for cache replacement. Recall that this entry indicates the number of *M's* buddies that have cached a data item since *M* cached the same item. *IXP* replaces the data item that has the maximum *IV[].count* among all cached ones. Replacing such a data item tends to induce less impact on *M*'s buddies because there are less buddies relying on *M* for fetching the data item when the associated count becomes bigger. In addition, *M* and its buddies tend to have greater chance in finding the replaced data item in their neighborhood than in finding the other cached items. Moreover, doing so can limit caching duplicates. This may also explain why *M* needs to set the *IV[x].count* to 0 when it first caches a data item *x*. At this time, all of *M's* buddies are supposed to have their *IV[x].cachednode* entries point to *M*, hence we do not want to have *x* replaced too soon. Notice that once a data item *x* is chosen for replacement, the values of *IV[x].count* maintained by *M*'s buddies will also be decremented, implying less chance for these buddies to have *x* replaced. This can alleviate the problem of concurrently replacing the same item by all the nodes in the neighborhood.

3.3 *Data Pull/Index Push (DPIP)* Protocol

IXP is essentially push-based in the sense that a caching node "pushes" the caching information to its buddies. Each node has a view of the caching status in its zone only. However, due to mobility of the nodes and some limitations of mobile devices such as transient disconnection, the caching status reflected by *IV* may be obsolete or not up-to-date. For example, suppose that, according to node *M's IV*, none of *M's* buddies caches *x*. If a new node that has cached *x* moves into *M's* zone now, this caching information cannot be captured by *M's IV* with *IXP*. In the following, we propose a more sophisticated protocol called *Data Pull/Index Push* (*DPIP*) to deal with this problem.

Similar to *IXP*, each node maintains the *IV* vector. When a node *M* wants to access a data item *x* that is not cached by itself, it first examines the entry *IV[x].cachednode* to see if some buddy node in the zone has cached *x*. If such buddy node exists, *M* sends a request message to the node asking for a copy of *x* in the same way as *IXP*. However, unlike *IXP*, if *IV[x].cachednode* entry is NULL, *M* broadcasts a special request message *srg* to all of its buddies. The *srg* message carries the ids of the requested data item, *x*, and the data item that will be replaced if the cache space is already full. Upon receiving the *srg* message a buddy node will reply to *M* if either of the following conditions is met: (1) it has cached *x*, (2) it knows some of its buddies has cached *x* (as per its *IV*). To reduce the number of reply messages, only peripheral nodes, i.e. the nodes at the perimeter of *M's* zone, are required to reply under the second condition, but any node for which the first condition is met should reply. In contrast with *IXP*, *DPIP* increases the chance for the data requester *M* to obtain a copy of *x* from nodes in its vicinity. This can be argued as follows. In addition to the fact that *M* can fetch a copy of *x* from its buddies if the first condition is met, it may possibly obtain caching status of the nodes that are beyond its zone but within the zones of its buddies as specified by the second condition. Consequently, the scope of local cooperation is essentially extended by a factor of two, in terms of radius, at the data requester site. In addition, the in-zone broadcast, which initiates the "data pulling" operation, allows *DPIP* to use the latest caching information. From above description, we see that in-zone broadcast of the *srg* message implicitly advertises the fact that the requester node will cache a copy of the requested data item, and it will soon be able to help others in satisfying their demands for the item. In other words, *srg* messages serve two functions: data pulling and index pushing (in implicit manner). Note that when a *srg* message is broadcast, a timer is started. If no reply is received from *M's* buddies before the timer goes off, *M* sends a request message toward the data center. *IV* vectors are updated in the same way as *IXP* at both the requester site and its buddies. However, the update of *IV* is done by the buddies at the time when they receive either a broadcast *srg* message or a direct (unicast) request message from the requester site. Cache replacement is performed in the same way as *IXP*.

4 Simulation Study

In this section we present simulation results for the proposed protocols and compare them to *HybridCache*.

4.1 Simulation Configuration

We have developed a simulation model based on the ns-2 simulator [27] with CMU wireless extension. The simulated network consists of 50 nodes spread randomly in an area of 1500mx320m, similar to the model used in [26]. One node is designated as the data center, and it is fixed at the upper left-hand corner of the area throughout the simulation. For ease of implementation, we use the DSDV [21] as the underlying routing protocol. It is assumed that the wireless transmission range of the nodes is 250 meters and the channel capacity is 2Mbps. A node moves according to the random waypoint model [2], in which each node selects a random destination in the specified area and moves toward the destination with a speed selected randomly from the range (1m/s, 10 m/s). After the node reaches its destination, it pauses for a period of time and then repeats the movement pattern. The pause time is used to represent node mobility. The default pause time is 300 seconds.

The data center contains 3000 data items. Data updates are not considered in the model. Data requests are served on FCFS basis at all nodes. The size of each data item is 1000 bytes, other messages such as request messages and index messages are all assumed to be 20-byte long. Each node generates a sequence of read-only requests. The inter-arrival times of data requests follows exponential distribution with mean 20 seconds. The data items are accessed uniformly. We consider a data request failed if the requested data item is not returned within a given amount of time. This is employed to account for packet loss in the unreliable wireless network. In addition, a data request that takes an excessive amount of response time is, in most cases, abandoned by the client.

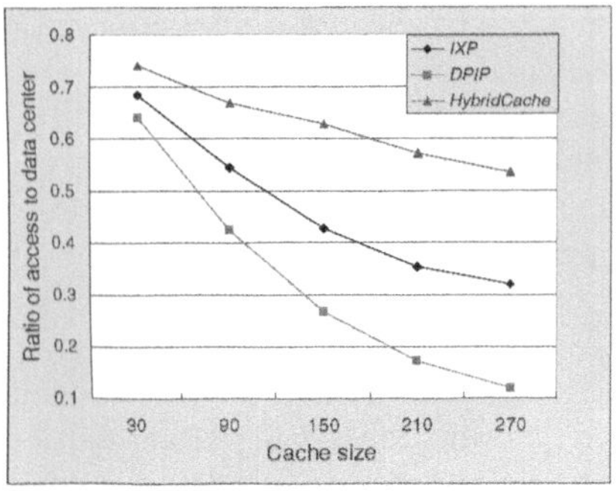

Fig. 1. Request failure ratio vs. cache size

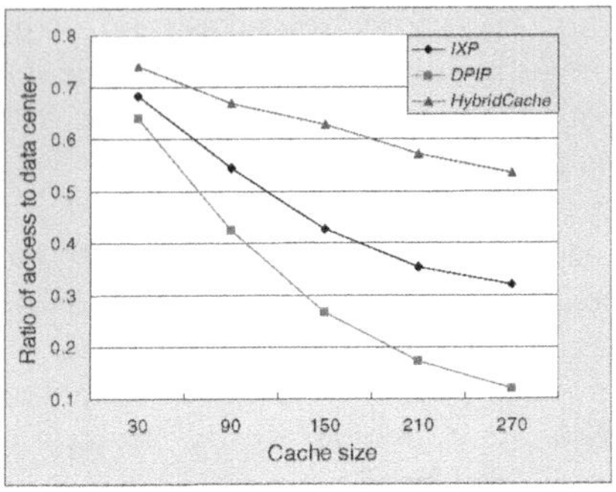

Fig. 2. Ratio of access to data center vs. cache size

To capture the performance of the protocols several metrics are examined in the simulation. The first principal metric is the request failure ratio which gives the ratio of data requests that fail to receive the requested data items. The second metric we measure is the average data access time for a successful data request. The other metric of interest is the ratio of data requests that are served by the data center. Reducing such ratio mitigates the workload of the data center, and better load balance results.

As we are interested in the steady state of the system we allow the simulated network to warm up for 1000 seconds. The simulation results are collected for 4000 seconds. In our simulations the radius of a zone is set to one hop for both *IXP* and *DPIP* protocols.

4.2 Simulation Results

Figure 1 illustrates the request failure ratios for *IXP*, *DPIP* and *HybridCache* with cache size varying from 30 to 270 items. In this simulation the pause time is set to 300 seconds. Apparently, both *IXP* and *DPIP* outperform *HybridCache* by significant margins. In addition, traffic congestion near the data center may cause request failures as well. Note that our schemes, *DPIP* in particular, demonstrate more evident improvement, in comparison with *HybridCache*, as the cache size increases. This result indicates that our protocols offer great capability for exploiting localized cooperative caching.

Figure 2 shows the ratios of the requests messages that are eventually addressed to the data center. Reducing the chances of having data requests satisfied by the data center is essential to the efficiency of the cooperative caching techniques. *DPIP* is least likely to lead the requests to be sent to the data center, followed by *IXP* and then *HybridCache*. A smaller such ratio implies, to some extent, better load balance among the data center and the nodes that have cached the requested data items. Again, *DPIP* is most sensitive to the cache size with respect to this metric.

In Figure 3 we illustrate the average access times of the successful data requests for the same setting as used in Figure 1. Since the access times do not consider the failed data requests, a straightforward comparison of the three protocols using this figure may not be appropriate. From Figure 3 we see that *DPIP* does not offer advantages in terms of the average access time when the cache size is very small. This is mainly due to the fact

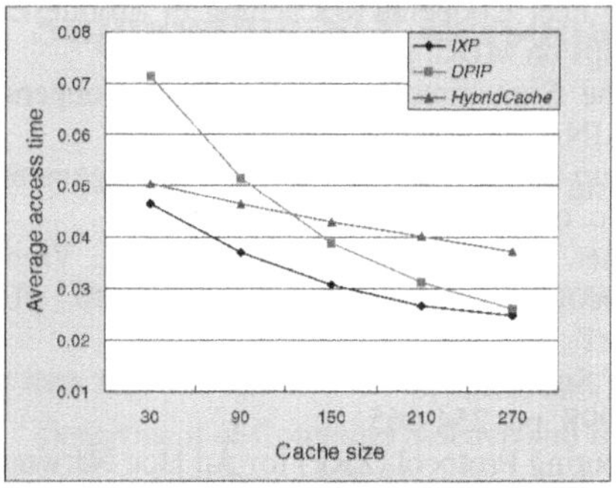

Fig. 3. Average data access time vs. cache size

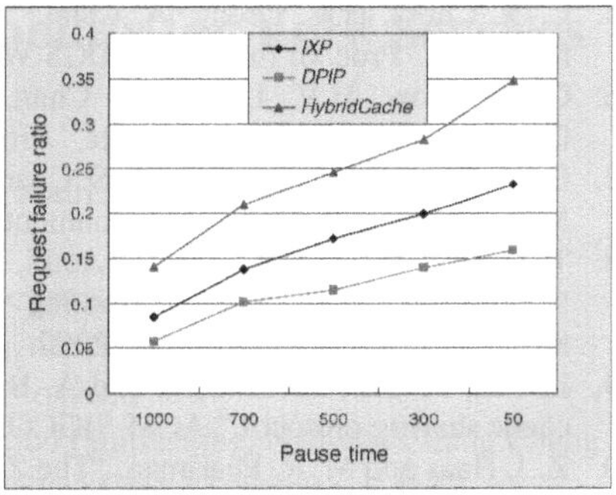

Fig. 4. Request failure ratio vs. pause time

that *srg* broadcasts in *DPIP* are not effective enough to compensate for the timeout intervals experienced by the data requesters when no cache hit among their buddies results. In this situation, both *IXP* and *HybridCache.*

To evaluate the effect of node mobility on the performance of the protocols we have performed simulation with different pause times. The result is shown in Figure 4, in which the request failure ratios are plotted against the pause times. Note that as the pause time decreases the node mobility becomes higher. All three protocols are affected when node mobility increases. *DPIP* is least sensitive to node mobility because it provides a comparatively wide scope of caching cooperation for neighboring mobile nodes. *HybridCache* is the most sensitive with respect to the metric.

5 Conclusion

In this paper, we have presented two zone-based cooperative caching protocols for MANETs. Both protocols demonstrate sensitivity with respect to the cache size. This indicates their capability for exploiting localized cooperative caching. Owing to this observation the benefits of the proposed protocols should be evident for MANETs of large scale.

References

1. R. Beraldi, R. Baldoni, "A Caching Scheme for Routing in Mobile Ad Hoc Networks and Its Application to ZRP," IEEE Transactions on Computers, Vol. 52, Issue 8, August 2003, pp. 1051-1062.
2. J. Broch, D. Maltz, D. Johnson, Y. Hu, and J. Jetcheva, "A Performance Comparison of Multi-Hop Wiress Ad Hoc Network Routing Protocols," ACM MobiCom, October 1998, pp. 85-97.
3. G. Cao, L. Yin, C. R. Das. "Cooperative Cache-Based Data Access in Ad Hoc Networks," Computer, vol. 37, Issue 2, Feb 2004, pp. 32-39.
4. C. C. Chiang, H.K. Wu, W. Liu, and M. Gerla, "Routing in Clustered Multihop Mobile Wireless Networks with Fading Channel," Proc. of IEEE Singapore International Conference on Networks, 103 Singapore, April 1997, pp. 197-211.

The UAs are addressed by SIP-URLs that are similar to the email address form, for example, sip:TPwang@sip.pu.edu.tw or tel: TPwang@sip.pu.edu.tw.

Redirect Servers receive requests and push routing information for requests back in responses to the client. Registrars are special User Agent Servers that handle "REGISTER" requests. SIP users/devices use "REGISTER" requests to dynamically register their current locations. After registration, the SIP user/device can be contacted even when they move.

Typically, UAs will send a "REGISTER" message to a specific registrar server. If username in the "REGISTER" message is authorized, it can receive a final response (200 OK) and the registrar server can store user information to the location database, as shown in Fig. 1.

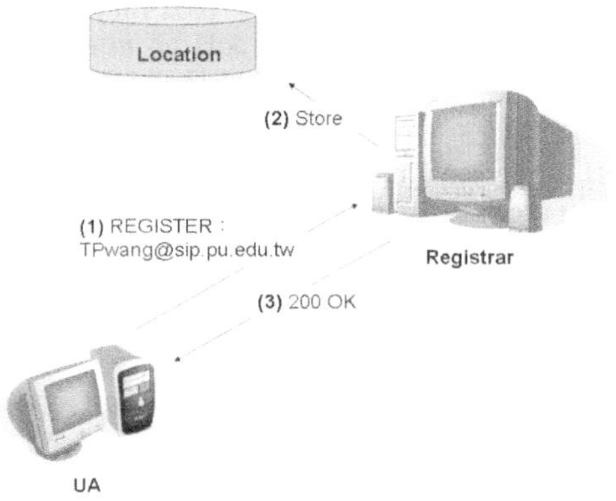

Fig. 1. Registration Scenario

Proxy Servers are elements that route requests to the user agent server and responses to the user agent client. A proxy server can operate in either a stateless proxy or a stateful proxy. A stateless proxy server just simply forwards incoming requests to another server or client, without dealing with any reliability. It forwards every request downstream to a single element determined by making a routing decision based on the request and simply forwards every response it receives upstream. In contrast, a stateful proxy maintains information (specifically, transaction state) about every received request and any responses produced by the request message that it sent.

A stateful proxy can be a *forking proxy* [4] that can route request to multiple destinations. Using forking is useful when proxy servers do not know the exact final destination. Proxy servers can either try a set of destination in pure parallel search, sequential search or other hybrid algorithms.

Practically, we can implement registrar, proxy, redirect server in the same machine, which is called "***Call Server***".

A successful SIP call invitation mush consists of two messages, an INVITE and followed by an ACK [7] [8]. The INVITE request asks the callee to join a particular conference or to establish a two party conversation. The request message's body may include some description of the session using Session Description Protocol (SDP). SDP contains distinction address, codec, connection ports and other information. After the callee agrees and answers to join this call, the caller confirms that it has received a "200 OK" response by sending an ACK message. A success response must indicate which media type the callee wishes to receive and may indicate the media callee is going to send. Finally, the media stream will be established by using Real Time Protocol (RTP) and Real Time Control Protocol (RTCP) to transport digital audio or video.

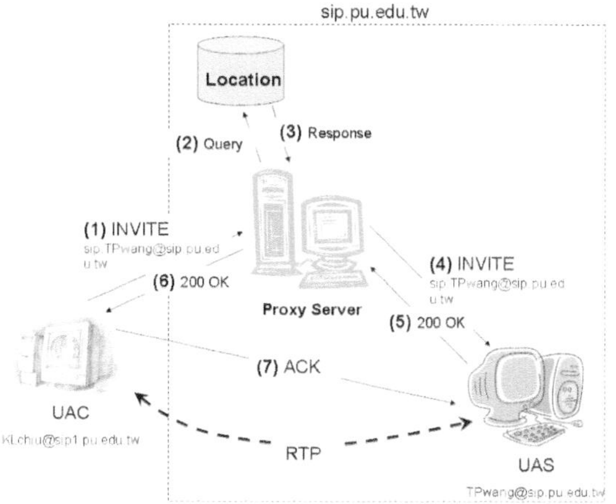

Fig. 2. Session Set-up

Consider an example of the session setup in which an INVITE message is sent from KLchiu@sip1.pu.edu.tw to TPwang@sip.pu.edu.tw, as shown in Fig. 2. Typically, all requests will be sent to a predefined local proxy server. Then the local proxy server would check the registrar's database in order to look up whether the callee is on-line or not. If the callee is found, the proxy server would forward the INVITE message to appropriate UAS. When TPwang answers the call, UAS would send a "200 OK" message to UAC via the proxy server. Finally, this call will be established using RTP protocol.

2 Single and Multiple Registration

In general, most of inter-communication platforms accept their user to register only place at the same time, for instance, MSN messenger and skype. This architecture is referred to as ***single registration (SR)***. The SR architecture does not support personal mobility inherently because the registration cannot be transparent to the user. In other word, it cannot address a single user location at different terminals using the same logical address. This way will be very inhumanity, because we cannot always ask users to sit in front of the computer or hand-carrying terminals. Meanwhile, the proxy server must accept to authorize shorter legal service time in order to alleviate the phenomenon that users have left the terminal. In RFC-3261, the value called Expire is defined to solve this problem. The default value could be 1,800 or 3,600 seconds.

In order to solve the drawback, a good solution is let all terminals of the user can register into registrar server at the same time. This method is called ***multiple registration (MR)***. Fig. 3 demonstrates an example of the contact information stored in the iptel SER's registrar [9] for multiple registration.

username	contact	cseq
0944021400	sip:0944021400@140.128.19.178:5060	130
0944021405	sip:0944021405@140.128.10.167:5060	2120
0944021400	sip:0944021400@140.128.10.99:5060	31302

Fig. 3. iptel SER's registrar for multiple registrations

Using multiple registration, the forking proxy [10] can search several destinations of the callee. Typically, there are two algorithms to search the current location of the callee: sequential search and pure parallel search. The sequential search will use First In First Service (FIFS) to determine the processing order. In worst case, this method has an important and critical shortcoming that calls setup will fail. That is, when user is near device registered recently. Therefore, a timeout mechanism will be necessary to continue searching the next possible location. In contrast, the forking proxy searches all destinations in parallel. However, the pure parallel search consumes more network resource.

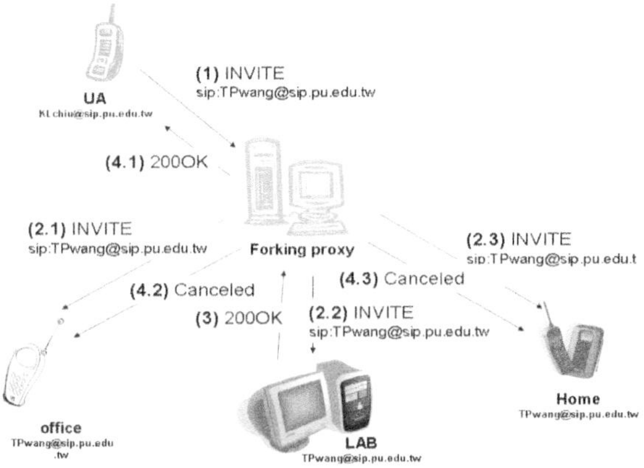

Fig. 4. Pure Parallel Search

Consider an example of the pure parallel search. Suppose that TPwang may move between three locations: LAB, office, and home as shown in Fig. 4. When KLchiu wants to make a phone call to TPwang, the forking proxy will fork three INVITE messages to all of TPwang's possible terminals at the same time if they are on-line. In this example, we assume that TPwang is at laboratory and he answers this call in the

LAB. Therefore, the session will be established from KLchiu's UA to TPwang's UA at laboratory. Finally, other INVITEs will be cancelled using CANCEL method.

3 Pipelined Search Algorithm

In this section, we propose a pipelined search scheme for multiple registration. Pipelined search is a hybrid method which combines sequential search and pure parallel search. It can compromise call setup delay and search cost at the same time. This algorithm defines a "d" parameter value which is used to delay the time of issuing the next request according to network status and user's behaviors. In most situations, d-value ranges from several hundred millions to several seconds. And, we use q-value for priority. It is possible to generate the q-values by analyzing the user's mobility behaviors. We also define "Group" for those sent together. Group members will have the same or similar q-value. The group concept is shown in Fig. 5.

We can get a priority list by calculating q-values and regulating the size of d-values to determine the way of search. When d-value is large, pipelined search is similar to the

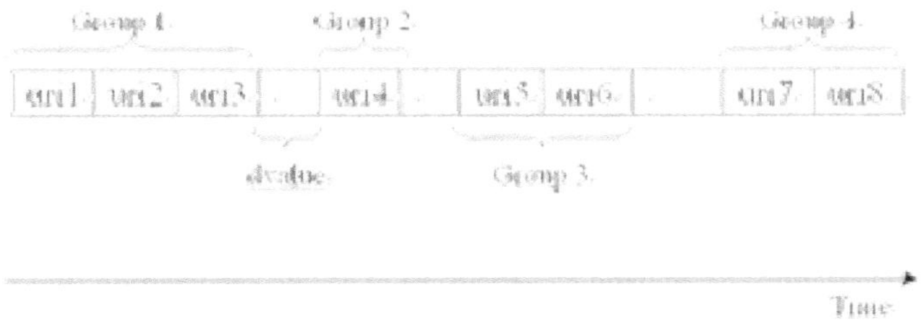

Fig. 5. The group concept

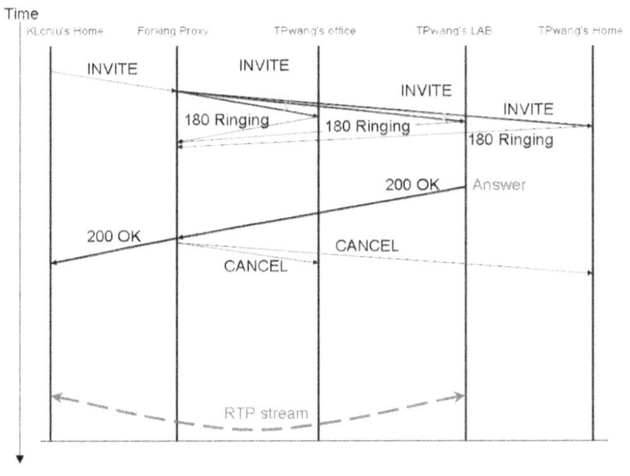

Fig. 6. Timing diagram for parallel search

As we mentioned above, the cost of registration will tend to be ignorable in the long term. Therefore, the total cost of multiple registration (Cost_M) is equal to the paging cost. From Equation (1), the total cost is

$$\begin{aligned} Cost\_M &= \lambda * [4N + 4] + 0 \\ &= 4N\lambda + 4\lambda \end{aligned} \tag{3}$$

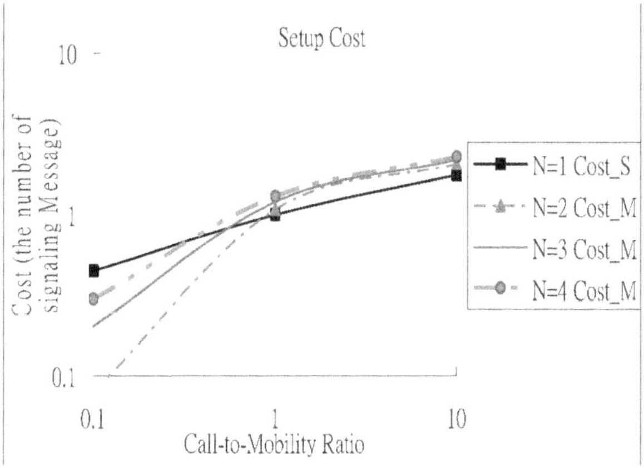

Fig. 8. The impact of CMR to call setup cost

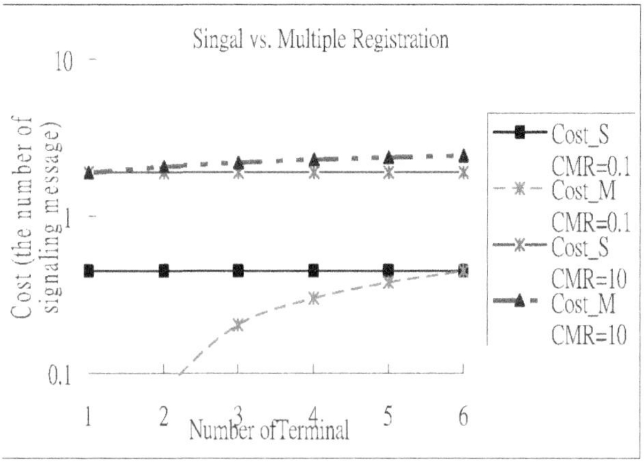

Fig. 9. The impact of n to call setup cost

In equation (3), we assume that "ACK" message will pass through the proxy server for stateful processing.

The results derived from equations (2) and (3), are shown in Fig. 8 and Fig. 9. In order to demonstrate the major difference, we perform nature logarithm treatment to the total cost. Fig. 8 shows the impact of CMR on the total call setup cost. Note that the call setup cost increases as CMR increases. Fig. 9 shows the impact of the number of terminal to the total call setup cost. Single registration accepts only one terminal registering to the registrar at the same time. Consequently, its setup cost is always the same. It is obvious that the costs for single and multiple registrations have only little difference when the user has only two terminals. However, single registration must issues "REGISTER" request message. Therefore, its cost is higher than that of multiple registration.

4.2 Impact of Locality on Pipeline Search

After comparing MR with SR, we further discuss the impact of locality behavior on pipelined search in multiple registration based environment. Performance metrics include the mean call-setup delay and the mean number of message sent to setup a call. In addition, we consider two mobility patterns: uniform and locality distributions. Uniform distribution means the user appears uniformly in all possible locations. In contrast, locality distribution means that the user may appear in a few locations with higher probability.
Prior to deriving the results, we list the used notation as follows.

RT：Response time
d：dvalue
Pi：Probability value
N：The number of terminals
t：The time of successful setting up a call

We first derive the mean delay time (t) for setting up a call.

- **Uniform distribution**

Since the user may appear uniformly in all possible locations, the probability of the user in each location is the same. Therefore, the mean delay for call setup is

$$E(t) = \sum_{i=1}^{N} [RT + (i-1) * d] * p_i$$
$$\because p_n = p_1 = p_2 = \ldots = \frac{1}{N} \qquad (4)$$
$$\therefore E(t) = RT + \frac{N-1}{2} * d$$

- **Locality distribution**

Without loss of generality, we assume that the probability (pBiB) of the user in location i is twice the probability in location i+1 (pBi+BB1B) for all possible i in locality distribution. Consequently, we can easily derive the probability pBiBB.B and the mean call setup delay as follows.

$$C = 1 + 2 + 4 + 8 + \ldots + 2^{N} = 2^{n} - 1$$

$$p_i = \frac{2^{N-i}}{2^{N} - 1} \qquad 1 <= i <= N$$

$$E(t) = \sum_{i=1}^{N} [RT + (i-1) * d] * p_i \tag{5}$$

$$= RT + \frac{d}{2^{N} - 1} * \sum_{i=1}^{N-1} i * 2^{N-i-1}$$

In Fig. 10, we assume the value of RT is 3. The values in the pure parallel search are not changed. Because pure parallel search always sends to all destinations at the same time, it produces no extra delay. And, the curve with uniform distribution will grow up linearly according to the number of group. In contrast, the curve with locality distribution will lead to a fix value when N approaches 10. Note that the difference between different d values is very small.

In Fig. 11, we define the value of M as RT divided by d and N is equal to 10. The result from this figure is very close to that of pure parallel search when M is more and

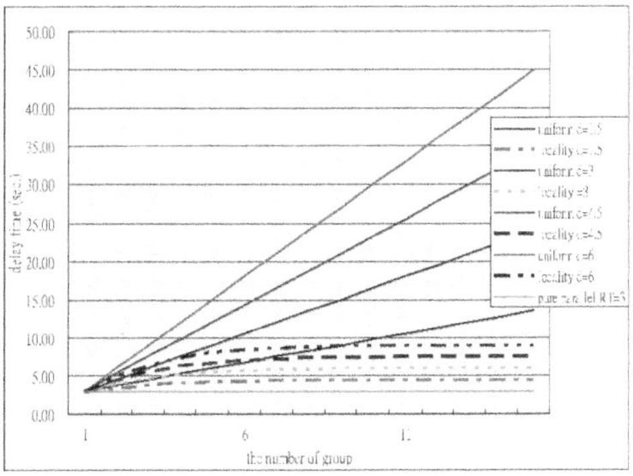

Fig. 10. The Delay Time for Invitation Call

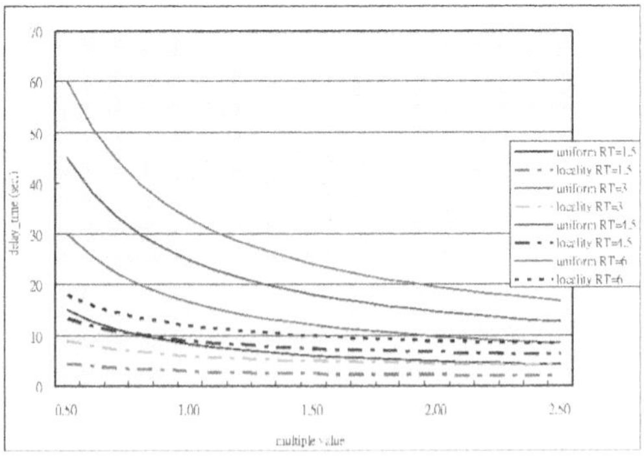

Fig. 11. The Impact of the M to Call Setup

more larger (i.e., RT is more than d) and the delay time will be reduced. In any cases, the one with locality distribution outperforms the one with uniform distribution.

In the following, we derive the mean number of messages sent for call setup. Let n denote the number of messages sent for setting up a call.

- **Uniform distribution**

$$\begin{aligned} E(n) &= \sum_{i=1}^{N} p_i * [(i-1) + \left\lceil \frac{RT}{d} \right\rceil \\ &= \frac{N+1}{2} - 1 + \left\lceil \frac{RT}{d} \right\rceil \end{aligned} \tag{6}$$

- **Locality distribution**

$$\begin{aligned} E(n) &= \sum_{i=1}^{N} p_i * [(i-1) + \left\lceil \frac{RT}{d} \right\rceil \\ &= \frac{1}{2^N - 1} \sum i * (2^{N-i}) - 1 + \left\lceil \frac{RT}{d} \right\rceil \end{aligned} \tag{7}$$

In Fig. 11, the locality distribution approaches to a fixed value when N is near to 10. Regardless of the paging cost (means sent messages) with uniform or locality distribution, pipeline search performs better than pure parallel search.

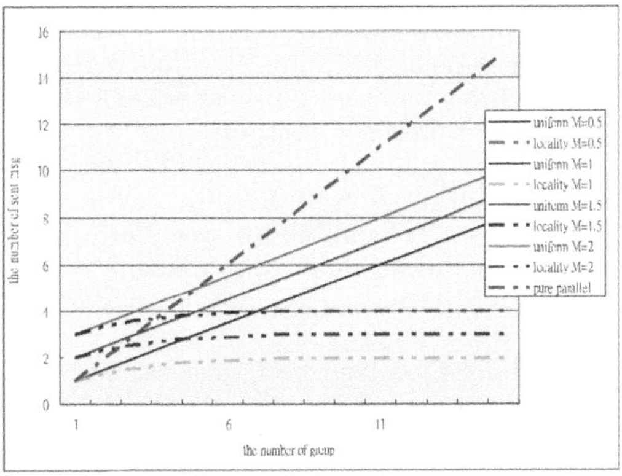

Fig. 12. Impact of the number of group

According to the above results, we observe that the one with locality distribution is very stable when N approaches to 10. It is strongly recommended that the system should provide multiple registration service for the users with locality behavior. In other hand, RT is very difficult to control in different network environment. Network manager can refer to our results (in figures 11 and 12) to adjust the d-value.

5 Conclusions

In this paper, we compare the performance of single registration and multiple registration. The single registration scheme is suitable for users with high call to mobility ratio. In contrast, multiple registration is suitable for users with low call to mobility ratio. Moreover, sequential search suffers from long setup delay, while pure parallel search consumes more resource to paging the user location. A compromise solution we propose is pipelined search. In pipeline search, if we can get a good algorithm for deriving d-value and q-value, the pipelined search would reduce wasted resource and improve system performance.

Acknowledgement

This work was supported in part by NSC under Grants NSC93-2219-E-126-001, NSC 93-2213-E-126-002, and NSC 94-2213-E-126-006, Taiwan, R.O.C.

Reference

1. ITU-T Recommendation H.323, "Packet-based multimedia communication systems", 1998.
2. B. Vlaovic, Z. Brezocnik, "Packet based telephony", EUROCON'2001, Trends in Communications, International Conference on., Vol. 1 , pp. 210 – 213, vol.14-7, July 2001
3. SIP Tutorial, at http://www.iptel.org/sip/ (last visit 2 September 2004)
4. J. Rosenberg, H. Schulzrinne, G. Camarillo, A. Johnston, J. Peterson, R. Sparks, M. Handley, E. Schooler, "SIP: Session Initiation Protocol", RFC 3261, June 2002
5. K. Daniel Wong, Ashutosh Dutta, Jim Burns, Ravi Jain, Kenneth Young "A multilayered mobility management scheme for auto-configured wireless IP networks", IEEE Wireless Communications, Vol. 10, pp.62-69, Oct. 2003
6. H. Schulzrinne, E. Wedlund, "Application layer mobility using SIP",Mobile Computing and Communications Review, Volume 4, Number 3
7. E. Wedlund, H. Schulzrinne, "Mobility support using SIP", 2ndACM/IEEE International Conference on Wireless and Mobile Multimedia, Seattle, Washington, Aug. 1999
8. M. Handley, V. Jacobson "SDP: Session Description Protocol", RFC2327, April 1998
9. http://www.iptel.org/
10. Henry Sinnreich, Alan B. Johnston, "Internet Communications Using SIP", John Wiley & Sons, Inc., New York, NY, USA
11. Jin-Woo Jung, Hyun-Kook Kahng, Ranganathan Mudumbai, Doug Montgomery, "Performance Evaluation of Two Layered Mobility Management using Mobile IP and Session Initiation Protocol", at http://w3.antd.nist.gov/pubs/sip-mip-jwjung-globecom 2003.pdf
12. Peng Sun, Sam Y. Sung, Zhao Li, "Performance Evaluation and Analysis of Protocols for IP Mobility Support: A Quantitative Study", http://www.iscs.nus.edu.sg/~ssung/publications / 1011.pdf

Scalable Spatial Query Processing for Location-Aware Mobile Services

KwangJin Park[1], MoonBae Song[1], Ki-Sik Kong[1], Chong-Sun Hwang[1], Kwang-Sik Chung[2], and SoonYoung Jung[3]

[1] Dept. of Computer Science and Engineering, Korea University, 5-1, Anam-dong, Seongbuk-Ku, Seoul 136-701, Korea
{kjpark, mbsong, kskong, hwang}@disys.korea.ac.kr
[2] Dept. of Computer Science and Engineering, Korea National Open University
kchung0825@knou.ac.kr
[3] Dept. of Computer Science Education, Korea University
jsy@comedu.korea.ac.kr

Abstract. Location-aware mobile services(LAMSs) are characterized by a large number of objects and a large number of queries. Moreover, with a large candidate data set, answering LAMSs via scanning through the whole data set becomes extremely expensive. In broadcast-based services, any number of clients can monitor the broadcast channel and retrieve the data as it arrives through the broadcast channel. Thus, a wireless broadcast system capable of answering LAMSs queries is considered a promising solution because it can serve a virtually unlimited number of users within its coverage. Furthermore, if the data is properly organized to cater to the needs of the clients, such a scheme makes effective use of the low wireless bandwidth, and is ideal for achieving maximal scalability. In this paper, we address the issues of supporting spatial queries of location-aware data via wireless data broadcast. A linear data broadcast based on their location is proposed to answer spatial queries on air. Comprehensive experimentation shows that the proposed scheme is highly scalable and is more efficient in terms of both tuning time and access latency in comparison to other techniques.

1 Introduction

Data dissemination is the delivery of data from the server to a larger set of clients. This is characterized by an inherent asymmetry in the communications. Any number of clients can monitor the broadcast channel and retrieve the data as it arrives on the broadcast channel. If the data is properly organized to cater to the needs of the clients, such a scheme makes effective use of the low wireless bandwidth and is ideal for achieving maximal scalability. Two key requirements for data access in wireless environments are **the conservation of power** and **the minimization of the client waiting time**.

With a large candidates data set, answering LAMSs via scanning through the whole data set becomes extremely expensive. Thus, index structures and related

L.T. Yang et al. (Eds.): EUC 2005, LNCS 3824, pp. 715–724, 2005.

search algorithms have been proposed to provide efficient processing of LAMSs queries. Air indexing is one of techniques used to address this issue, and which operates by interleaving indexing information among the broadcast data items. By first accessing the broadcast index, the mobile client is able to predict the arrival time of the desired data. Thus, it can stay in the power save mode most of time, and tune into the broadcast channel only when the requested data arrives [2][3]. Air indexing techniques can be evaluated in terms of the following two factors: First, *Access Time(AT)*: The average time elapsed from the moment a client issues a query to the moment when the required data item is received by the client. Second, *Tuning Time(TT)*: The amount of time spent by a client listening to the channel. Then, the *Access Time* consists of two separate components, namely: *Probe Wait*: The average duration for getting to the next index segment. *Bcast Wait*: The average duration from the moment the index segment is encountered to the moment when the required data item is downloaded.

There are several indexing techniques which have been developed, such as the distributed indexing approach [3], the signature approach [4], and the hybrid approach [5]. In a recent paper [8], we proposed the concept of data sorting for broadcasting called BBS(Broadcast based Location Dependent Data Delivery Scheme). A preliminary simulation-based results showed that BBS is significantly reduce the AT. In this paper, we attempt to reduce both the TT and AT in the wireless mobile computing environment. After pointing out the limitations of the existing indexing schemes, we present various schemes that can overcome these problems. To the best of our knowledge, this is the first work in which NN query processing without on index segment is proposed and this technique provides the best access time. In this paper, we assume a geometric location model, i.e., a location is specified as a two-dimensional coordinate and the broadcasted data objects are static, such as restaurants, hospitals, and hotels. The mobile clients can identify their locations using systems such as the Global Positioning System(GPS).

The remainder of the paper is organized as follows: Section 2 provides background information. Section 3 describes the proposed algorithms. A performance evaluation is presented in section 4. Finally, section 5 concludes this paper.

2 Background

With the advent of high speed wireless networks and portable devices, data requests based on the location of mobile clients have increased in number. However, there are several challenges to be met in the development of LAMSs [1], such as the constraints associated with the mobile environment and the difficulty of taking the user's movement into account. Hence, various techniques have been proposed to overcome these difficulties.

2.1 Hilbert-Curve

In [9], a linear index structure is proposed based on the Hilbert curve, in order to enable the linear broadcasting of objects in a multi-dimensional space. The

Hilbert curve needs to allocate a sufficient number of bits to represent the index values, in order to guarantee that each of the points in the original space has a distinct value. If k is the number of bits used for a coordinate in the i-th dimension of the targeted m-dimensional space and n is the number of bits assigned to represent the coordinates, then a total of $\sum_{i=1}^{m} k$ bits need to be allocated to represent the coordinates and the expected time for the conversion is $O(n^2)$. Besides, to perform k-NN query processing using the Hilbert curve, more than two broadcast periods are needed.

2.2 Wireless Data Broadcast

The use of broadcasting methods that properly interleave index information and data on the broadcast channel can significantly improve not only the energy efficiency, but also the AT. Let N be the number of data objects and C be the download time for the required records. There are two parameters that need to be optimized in the one dimensional space of the AT and the TT [2][3]:

- Optimal Latency: The best AT is obtained when no index is broadcast along with the data. In this case, the size of the entire Bcast is minimized, and the average AT is $\frac{N}{2} + C$. However, in this case, the worst value of the average TT is obtained, since it is equal to $\frac{N}{2} + C$.
- Optimal Tune: This parameter allows the best TT to be obtained, while simultaneously increasing the AT. The server broadcasts the index at the beginning of each broadcast. In this case, the average TT is $1 + l + C$, where l is the number of levels in the multileveled index tree. In this case, the probe wait is equal to $\frac{N+index}{2}$ and the Bcast wait is equal to $\frac{N+index}{2} + C$. Since the Latency is the sum of the Probe Wait and the Bcast Wait, the average AT is equal to $(\frac{N+index}{2})\times 2+C= N$ + index + C.

3 Proposed Algorithms

In this section, we first introduce the broadcast-based LDIS scheme(BBS) [8]. Then, we describe algorithm for selective tuning, namely Exponential Sequence Scheme(ESS).

3.1 Sequential Data Broadcast

In a recent paper [8], we have proposed the concept of data sorting for broadcasting called BBS(Broadcast-based Location Dependent Data Delivery Scheme). In the BBS method, the server periodically broadcasts the IDs and coordinates of the data objects, without an index segment, to the clients, and these broadcasted data objects are sorted sequentially, according to the location of the data objects, before being sent to the clients. The BBS provides the fastest access time, since no index is broadcasted along with the data and thus, the size of the entire broadcast cycle is minimized. A preliminary simulation-based results showed that BBS is significantly reduce the AT.

A simple sequential broadcast can be generated by linearizing the two dimensional coordinates in two different ways: i.e., horizontal broadcasting(HB) or vertical broadcasting(VB). In HB, the server broadcasts the LDD(location dependent data) in horizontal order, that is, from the leftmost coordinate to the rightmost coordinate. On the other hand, in VB, the server broadcasts the LDD in vertical order, that is, from the bottom coordinate to the top coordinate. In this paper, we assume that the server broadcasts the data objects using HB.

Notations

- O_i: broadcast data object, where $O_i \in S$
- O_{candi}: candidate for the nearest data object
- O_c: current broadcast data object (initially O_c regarded as NN), where $O_c \in S$
- q: a query point
- O_{ps}: one of the data items broadcast before O_i in the current broadcast cycle, where $O_{ps} \in S$
- O_f: the client's first tuned data item in the broadcast channel
- Data_first: the server's first broadcast data item in the current broadcast cycle.
- Flag A: if the dist(x-coordinate of O_{ps}, x-coordinate of q) is larger than dist(O_c, q), then set to 1 (initially set to 0). This flag guarantees that the client dose not miss the NN in the current broadcast channel.
- Flag B: if the dist((x-coordinate of O_c),(x-coordinate of q))$<$ dist(O_{candi}, q)), then set to 1(initially set to 0).

There are two cases in which the clients tune to the broadcast channel.

Case 1: the client could not identify the NN in the current broadcast cycle, since it was not able to determine whether or not the desired data item was broadcasted before it tuned to the broadcast channel(see Fig 1).

Lemma 1: While Flag A=0 and $O_f \neq$ Data_first, the client could not identify the NN in the current broadcast cycle.

Proof: Let the client begin to tune at time T_i. At T_i, O_c=O_i and O_{candi} is O_i(see Fig 1). At T_{i+1}, O_c=O_{i+1} and O_{candi} is O_i, since dist(O_i, q)$<$dist(O_{i+1}, q). At T_{i+2}, O_c=O_{i+2} and O_{candi} is O_{i+2}, since dist(O_{i+2}, q)$<$ dist(O_i, q) and dist(O_{i+2}, q)$<$ dist(O_{i+1}, q). At T_{i+3}, O_c=O_{i+3} and O_{candi} is O_{i+2}, since dist(O_{i+2}, q)$<$ dist(O_{i+3}, q). Then, the client stops tuning to the broadcast channel, since dist(O_{i+2}, q)$<$dist(x-coordinate of O_{i+3}, x-coordinate of q). However, the client could not guarantee O_{i+2} as the NN, since it missed the O_{i-n}, such as O_{i-1} data item, and one of them could also be O_{candi}. Thus, if Flag A=0 and Flag B=1, then the client stops tuning to the broadcast channel and switches to doze mode, until the Data_first of the next period arrives. □

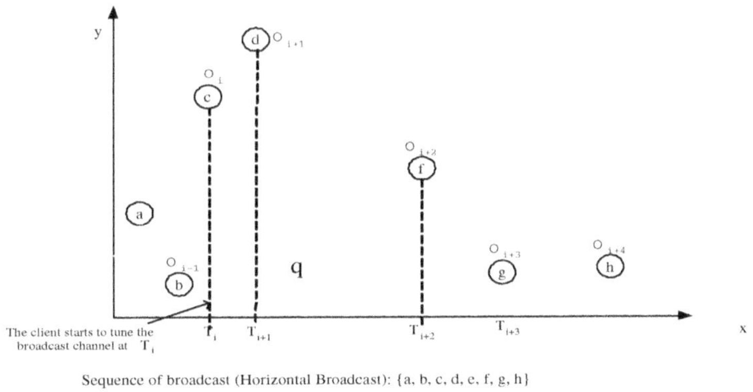

Fig. 1. The client could not identify the NN in the current broadcast cycle

Case 2: the client is able to identify the NN from the current broadcast cycle, since it is sure that the desired data item is going to appear in the current broadcast cycle(see Fig 2).

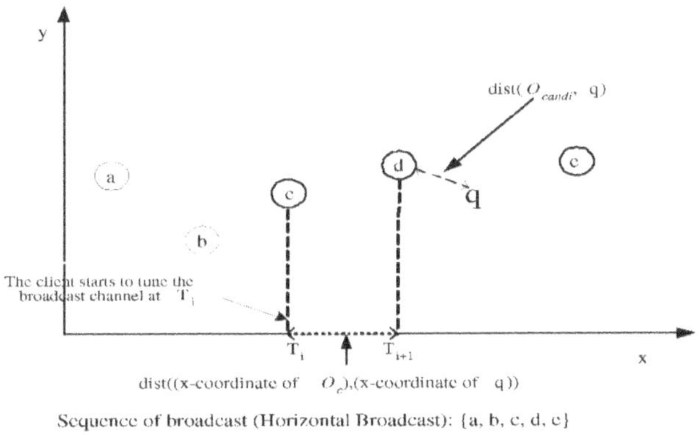

Fig. 2. The client is able to identify the NN in the current broadcast cycle

Lemma 2: If Flag A is set to 1, then the client can identify the NN from the current broadcast cycle.

Proof: Let O_c be data item 'c' in Fig 2. After the client receives data item 'd', Flag A is set to 1, which means that data item 'c' and the data items before 'c', such as 'a' and 'b', are not candidates for the NN, since the distances from the x-coordinates of 'a', 'b', and 'c' to the x-coordinate of q are longer than dist(d, q). Consequently, we can conclude that the client does not miss the NN and can find it from the current broadcast channel. □

```
          then O_c = O_candi
       else O_p = O_candi
    while dist((x-coordinate of O_c),(x-coordinate of q)) < dist(O_candi, q))
O_candi = NN
return NN
```

4 Performance Evaluations

In this section, we evaluate the performance with various kinds of parameter settings.

4.1 Energy Consumption Model

Let $\mathcal{E}$ denotes the amount of energy consumption and the "ec" denotes the energy coefficient which means the active-to-doze ratio, $\frac{\mathcal{E}_{ACTIVE}}{\mathcal{E}_{DOZE}}$.

In this paper, the average energy consumption can be measured by the amount of unit energy in a given time. In order to choose reasonable coefficients, we should have some reference values. Then, the energy coefficients($\widehat{ec}$) can estimated. In our experiment, parameters ec is fixed with 48.61.

4.2 Experimental Evaluation

This section presents the numerical results with the various environmental variables. We assume that the broadcast data objects are static, such as restaurants, hospitals and hotels. In this paper, two datasets are used in the experiments. The first data set, $\mathcal{D}1$, contains data objects randomly distributed in a square Euclidian space, while the second data set, $\mathcal{D}2$, contains the data objects of hospitals in the Southern California area, and is extracted from the data set available at [7].

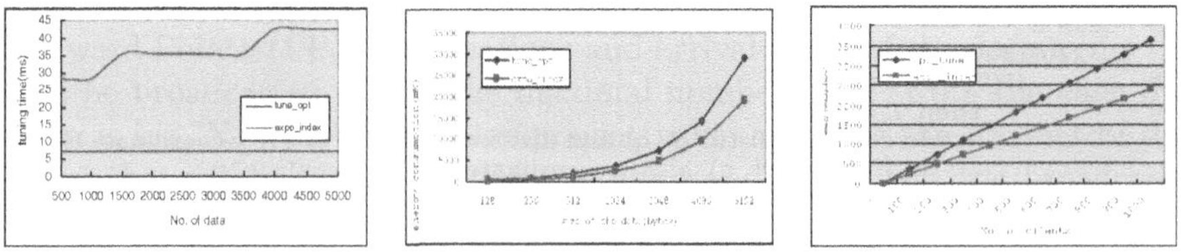

(a) (b) (c)

Fig. 4. Tuning time and energy consumption

4.3 Tuning Time and Energy Consumption

Fig 4(a) shows the tuning time as the number of data items increases. As shown in this figure, tune_opt outperforms the other schemes, since the average tuning time of tune_opt is $1 + l + C$ [3]. Fig 4(b) shows the energy consumption as the size of the data items is increased from 128 bytes to 8192 bytes in $\mathcal{D}1$. As shown in this figure, in this case, the proposed schemes outperform tune_opt, since tune_opt minimizes the tuning time but not the access time, while the proposed schemes reduce the tuning time and AT at the same time. In other words, when we estimate the energy consumption, it is necessary to consider not only the active time, but also the doze time, even if the doze time is considerably smaller than the active time(i.e., we assume a ratio of $\frac{1}{48.61}$). Fig 4(c) shows the energy consumptions as the number of clients is increased in $\mathcal{D}1$. Figs 5(a) and 5(b) show the energy consumptions as the size of the data items and the number of clients are increased in $\mathcal{D}2$, respectively.

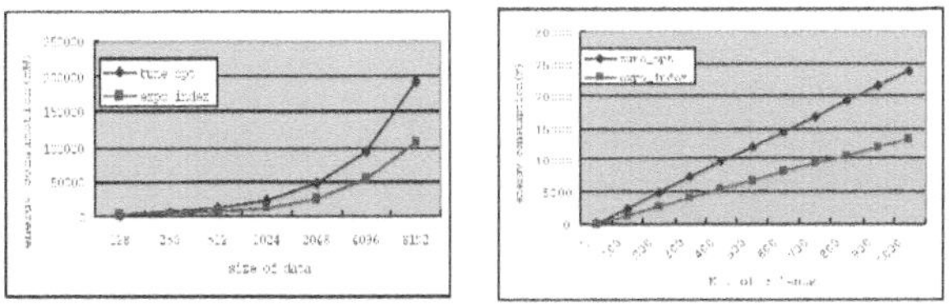

(a) (b)

Fig. 5. Energy consumption in $\mathcal{D}2$

4.4 Access Time

In this section, we evaluate the AT. Fig. 6(a) shows the AT as the size of the data $\mathcal{D}1$. Finally, Fig. 6(b) shows the AT as the items increase in size of the data items increase in $\mathcal{D}2$. Since the clients do not need to wait and tune into the broadcast channel to receive an index segment, if they have already identified the desired objects, the BBS scheme shows increasingly lower latency compared to the other scheme.

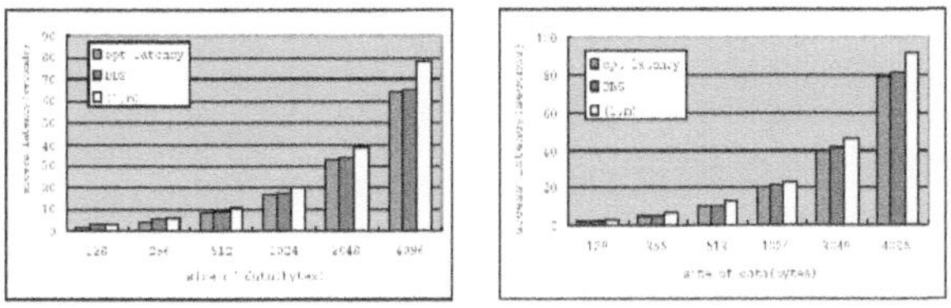

(a) (b)

Fig. 6. Access time in $\mathcal{D}1$ and $\mathcal{D}2$

5 Conclusion

We explored the different broadcasting and tuning methods which can be used for NN query processing. For the purpose of broadcasting in LAMSs, we present the BBS method, and for the purpose of selective tuning with the BBS method, we present the ESS method. The BBS method attempts to reduce the AT, and the ESS method attempts to conserve battery power. The experimental results show that the proposed ESS scheme significantly reduces not only the AT, but also the energy consumption, since the client does not always have to wait for the index segment.

References

1. D. L. Lee, J. Xu, and B. Zheng, "Data Management in Location-Dependent Information Services," *IEEE Pervasive Computing*, 1(3), 2002.
2. T. Imielinski, S. Viswanathan, and B.R.Badrinath, "Energy efficient indexing on air," *Proc. of SIGMOD*, 1994.
3. T. Imielinski, S. Viswanathan, and B.R.Badrinath, "Data on Air: Organization and Access," *IEEE Trans. Knowledge and Data Eng*, 9(3), 1997.
4. W. C. Lee and D. L. Lee, "Using signature techniques for information filtering in wireless and mobile environments," *Distributed and Parallel Databases*, 4(3), 1996.
5. Q. L. Hu, W.-C. Lee, and D. L. Lee, "A hybrid index technique for power efficient data broadcast," *Distributed and Parallel Databases*, 9(2), 2001.
6. B. Zheng, J. Xu, and D. L. Lee, "Cache Invalidation and Replacement Strategies for Location-Dependent Data in Mobile Environments," *IEEE Trans. Comp.*, 51(10), 2002.
7. Spatial Datasets, `http://dias.cti.gr/ ytheod/research/datasets/spatial.html`.
8. K. Park, M. Song, and C.-S. Hwang, "An Efficient Data Dissemination Schemes for Location Dependent Information Services," In *Proc. of ICDCIT*, 2004. Lecture Notes Computer Science.
9. B. Zheng, W.-C. Lee, D. L. Lee, "Search Continuous Nearest Neighbor on Air," In *Proc. The First International Conference on Mobile and Ubiquitous Systems: Networking and Services*, Boston, Massachusetts, August 2004.
10. M.-S. Chen, P. S. Yu, and K. L. Wu, "Optimizing index allocation for sequential data broadcasting in wireless mobile computing," *IEEE Trans. on Knowledge and Data Engineering (TKDE)*, 2003.
11. N. Roussopoulos, S. Kelley, and F. Vincent. "Nearest neighbor queries," *Proc. of SIGMOD*, 1995.

Exploiting Mobility as Context for Energy-Efficient Location-Aware Computing

MoonBae Song, KwangJin Park, and Ki-Sik Kong

Dept. of Computer Science and Engineering, Korea University,
5-1, Anam-dong, Seongbuk-Ku, Seoul 136-701, Korea
{mbsong, kjpark, kskong}@disys.korea.ac.kr

Abstract. The "mobility" has two important aspects: i) how to support mobility and ii) how to exploit mobility. This paper considers the latter, while many existing works only consider the former. This work is trying to prove that system performance will be greatly improved by understanding a user's movement. In this paper, we propose a novel location update protocol, called SLUP which minimizes the energy consumption of a mobile client by exploiting a syntactic information of the user's movement. This concept is called *mobility-awareness*. Moreover, there are three variations of the proposed protocol in terms of choosing optimal state: SLUP/BS, SLUP/UITR, and SLUP/IUT$\langle T_{iut} \rangle$. Experimental results show that the proposed protocol outperforms the well-known protocols such as dead-reckoning and distance-based protocol, that the SLUP/IUT$\langle T_{iut} \rangle$ approach can achieve difference performance tradeoffs between energy efficiency and location imprecision by fine-tuning its algorithmic parameter T_{iut}.

1 Introduction

Definition in *Wikipedia* says that "context includes the circumstances and conditions which *surround* an event". Analyzing contextual information of human behavior from low-level sensor data is the most critical issue in context-aware computing.

Recently, the evolution of mobile computing, location sensing, and wireless networking has created a new class of computing: *location-aware computing* (LAC) [3]. A location-aware system is one that knows where each user is located and can use the location-specific information anywhere and anytime. LAC can be viewed as a kind of context-aware computing based on a context of the very "location". While location is only one small part of a user's state, location is a easily-detected and commercially-useful context. In LAC environments, the mobility of a mobile client (MC) is emerging in many forms and applications such as database, network and so on. MCs can dynamically change their locations over time. A central problem in LAC is the determination of physical location and the transmission of the location information to a server.

Another major issue in LAC is energy efficiency because of a large population of portable, battery-powered devices. Although the improvement of other

L.T. Yang et al. (Eds.): EUC 2005, LNCS 3824, pp. 725–734, 2005.

3.2 Initial Experiment and Mobility-Awareness

Firstly, we introduce a new criterion to compare the efficiency of update protocols using a simple formula by measuring the update cost and the imprecision cost for a certain amount of time. This criterion is called $\mathcal{UITR}$ (*update-and-imprecision to time ratio*). $C_{\mathcal{UITR}}(\Delta, w_u, w_\epsilon) = \frac{\sum_{k=1}^{\Delta}(w_u u_k + w_\epsilon \frac{\epsilon_k}{\delta})}{\Delta}$. The $C_{\mathcal{UITR}}$ model can be interpreted as an integration of location update cost and imprecision cost, and an indirect approach to measure energy consumption by setting $w_u \gg w_\epsilon$. Based on this cost model, we can identify the behavioral difference of existing location update policies. Fig. 2 shows the comparison of distance-based approach and dead-reckoning in terms of $C_{\mathcal{UITR}}$ model. In this comparison, the movement of whole objects is random-walk or linear mobility patterns by turns with a fixed time interval 200. For random-walk, the distance-based approach outperforms the dead-reckoning in which the frequent update of motion vector may cause the increased location imprecision and the resulting increased update cost as well. For linear movement, in contrast, the dead-reckoning approach performs very well. But, the performance of the distance-based approach extremely degraded, since average movement distance per unit time highly increased.

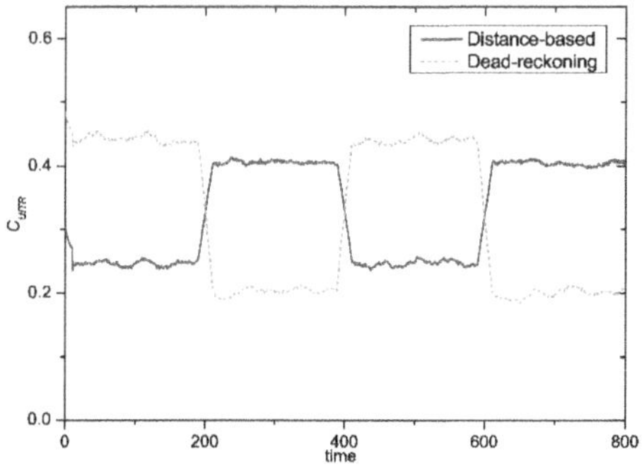

Fig. 2. An example variations of $C_{\mathcal{UITR}}(5, 1, 0.1)$ for two distance-triggered approaches ($\delta = 1.0$)

This initial experiment shows that the *mobility-awareness* is the key to reducing the number of location update messages. Exhibiting complementarity with respect to mobility patterns, different – *mutually complement* – update policies can be applied to the aforementioned states: pause (P), linear (L), and random (R). As shown in Fig. 2, a trajectory can be interpreted differently depending on various location update protocols. These interpretations are highly depends on their assumed mobility patterns. The tightness between the performance of location update protocols and their assumed mobility patterns is depicted in the figure. The efficient operations of location update protocols can be achieved by understanding user's movements. Eventually, an MC should be aware of its own mobility. This is what we called *mobility-awareness.*

Based on the initial experiment, therefore, we attempt to classify the movement pattern into a set of small movement components in the viewpoint of location update policy. This serves as a foundation of mobility-awareness. Consequently, the movement pattern is classified into *pause*, *linear movement*, and *random movement*. This classification is ambiguous/relative and may cause a different result from the different location uncertainty. In this paper, we only consider the performance viewpoint of location update policy. In other words, the syntactic information[2] of current movement state is indirectly recognized by comparing the performance of each location update policy. The concept of *mobility-awareness* is, therefore, a process of inferring the syntactic characteristics of a movement pattern relying on the performance of location update policy.

4 The Proposed Protocol

4.1 Protocol Description

After power-up, each moving object makes transitions through various states depending on its mobility patterns, and updates its location information in location databases using the current update policy (Fig. 3(a)). Because of having more than one update policy, the proposed protocol is called state-based location update protocol (SLUP). The proposed SLUP protocol is represented by a finite set of update policy called *update policy list* $\mathcal{UPL} = \{\mu_1, \mu_2, \ldots, \mu_N\}$ and the optimal update policy index *opt*. Each update policy μ a 6-tuple $(\hat{l}, f, C, UWin, IWin, \delta)$ consisting of the estimated location $\hat{l}$ by f, a location estimation function f, the cost function C, the update window $UWin$, the imprecision window $IWin$, and a predefined location uncertainty δ. The object should examine the $\mathcal{UITR}$ value of all update policies in order to determine an optimal policy over the whole set of update policies. For this purpose, each moving object performs not only the current *opt* update policy but also the others by the pseudo-update procedure which is a self-initiated update procedure within MC's local memory (see Fig. 3(b)). Then the optimal update policy with the minimum $\mathcal{UITR}$ can be decided without any difficulty. The additional cost, a few memory and a small number of operations, is acceptable owing to its reflective effectiveness in the number of update messages and the development of hardware technology.

The behavior of a moving object is modeled as a state-transition diagram. Exploiting temporal locality of mobility patterns, the update policy phase is decomposed into small fraction of *update state* such as P, L, and R. Each update state consists of an update policy that is how the location information of an object is reflected in the location databases, the state-transition function determining the next states of the object, and information related to the state.

From the starting state R, location update is performed with state transition through P, L, and R. If the optimal state is P, then the SLUP protocol will be in time-triggered manner in period $\hat{T}$ and be in the doze mode in the remainder of time. Otherwise, it will performs a distance-triggered manner with distance threshold δ. If the *opt* state is stale[3], then call *chooseOptimalState*() to choose a

[2] In our work, the syntactic information is one of three movement states $\{\mathsf{P}, \mathsf{L}, \mathsf{R}\}$. Similar to our work, Patterson et al. [6] presented a method to learning how a person uses different kinds of transportation in the community. In this work, the mode of transportation is represented as one of three different values $\{\mathsf{BUS}, \mathsf{FOOT}, \mathsf{CAR}\}$.

[3] A state is called *stale* (or inconsistent) if the location information of a state has more location imprecision than a predefined uncertainty δ.

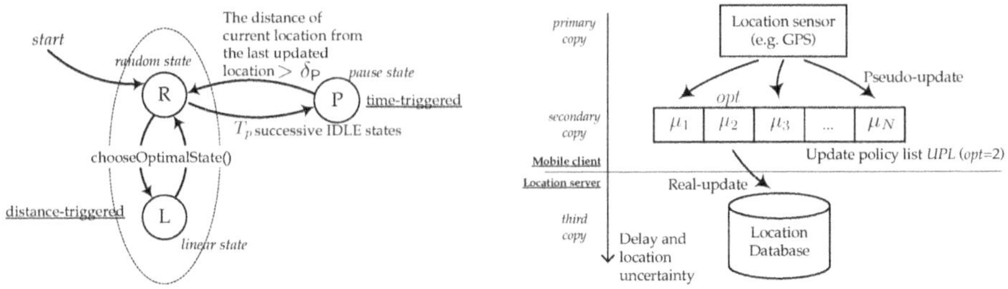

(a) The state transition diagram (b) The flow of location update

Fig. 3. The Proposed Protocol

new (predicted) optimal state and transmit location update message. Otherwise, check the current *opt* is R and still remains for a certain amount of time T_p, then state station to the state P is performed.

Under the pause mode, the moving object is perhaps located at his/her home, office, or meeting room for a long time. It is quite reasonable to consider a location update policy for stationary state as well as moving state. This insight has been tried in the location management of PCS, called *Stop-or-Move* mobility model [9]. We can assume that an object is in a stationary state if the moving object remains still its location for a certain amount of time T_p. The proposed approach performs location updates and makes transitions through different energy states depending on user's movement. These energy states are DOZE, IDLE, and TRANSMIT. In Fig. 4, behavioral differences of each device in terms of various energy states is presented.

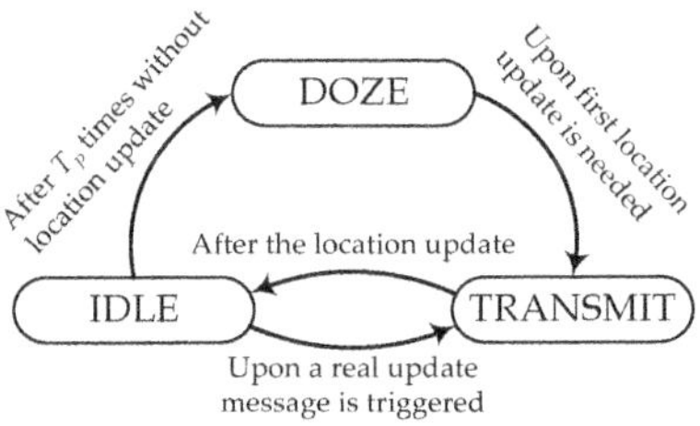

Fig. 4. Energy state transition

4.2 Variations: Choosing the Optimal State

The performance of proposed scheme is greatly dependent on determining the optimal state. When an location update message is sent, a MC should determine whether the location update needs a state transition or not. In order to determine the next *opt* state, *chooseOptimalState*() is called. And there are several variations on the subject.

In Fig. 5, we show three variations. Firstly, one of most simplest approach is "blind switching" (SLUP/BS) in which state transition is required to be done for every location update. With the location update message m_1 in Fig. 5, state transition from L to R is performed concurrently and unconditionally. This is simple, but it is more likely to make a false state transition. The second variation is called SLUP/UITR in which a state with lower $\mathcal{UITR}$ cost among states L and R is selected. In Fig. 5, assuming that the state R is more optimal one than the

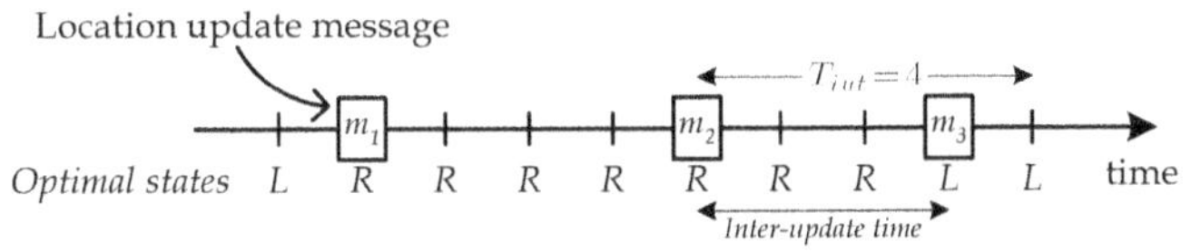

Fig. 5. State Transition Problem: To make or not to make the state transition?

state L, a state transition is not required to issuing the message m_2. The third approach considers not a single location update, but a time interval between two consecutive location updates. Let "inter-update time" be a time interval between two consecutive location updates. A state transition will be delayed until the time interval is smaller than a predefined threshold T_{iut}. In Fig. 5, state transition is made with the message m_3, because the time interval between m_2 and m_3 is smaller than $T_{iut}(4)$. This approach is called SLUP/IUT$\langle T_{iut}\rangle$. Obviously, its performance highly depends on T_{iut}. Consequently, the variants of SLUP protocol are choices on the diversity in the degree of laziness for state transition. Such a "laziness" to the location update is very helpful to the energy efficiency.

5 Performance Evaluation

5.1 Simulation Model and Workload Generation

We evaluate the performance of three traditional approach, and four proposed approaches with variation. The traditional approaches include distance-based and dead-reckoning. The proposed approaches include SLUP/BS, SLUP/UITR, and SLUP/IUT$\langle T_{iut}\rangle$ with different T_{iut} (2,5).

Since the real datasets in spatio-temporal database are very hard to achieve, the method of synthesizing data has widely been used in various area. In this experiment, we adopt the Gauss-Markov mobility model [11]. Specifically, the speed and direction at the n-th instance is calculated based upon the value of speed and direction at the $(n-1)$-th instance and a random variable using the following equations: $s_n = \alpha s_{n-1} + (1-\alpha)\bar{s} + \sqrt{1-\alpha^2} s_{x_{n-1}}$ and $d_n = \alpha d_{n-1} + (1-\alpha)\bar{d} + \sqrt{1-\alpha^2} d_{x_{n-1}}$, where s_n and d_n are new speed and direction of mobile node at time interval n; $0 \le \alpha \le 1$, is the tuning parameter used to vary the randomness; and $s_{x_{n-1}}$ and $d_{x_{n-1}}$ are random variables from a Gaussian distribution. By setting $\alpha = 0$ we get a very random motion, while $\alpha = 1$ gives a completely linear motion. Intermediate levels of randomness are obtained by varying the value of α between 0 and 1. In our experiment, mean speed $\bar{s}$ is 1, mean direction $\bar{d}$ is randomly selected from $[0, 2\pi]$, and α is 0.9.

In order to generate more realistic movements, we also consider stationary state, called pause (P). In conjunction with Gauss-Markov model (denoted as G), these are constructed as a form of Markov chain (see Fig. 6(b)). Then, for the

In Fig. 8, we examine the impact on the temporal locality τ of user movement. Due to fixed $\rho = 1$, the transition matrix with higher τ is likely to have more stationary or linear movements than the opposite one. The dead-reckoning approach, therefore, will be outperform distance-based approach for a higher τ.

6 Conclusions

Context-awareness has motivated various research topics. As a branch of the concept, this work is trying to prove that system performance will greatly improved by understanding the user's movement which is called *mobility-awareness* in the paper. On the basis of our experiment, we argue that the proposed concept, *mobility-awareness*, is the key to reducing the energy consumption of mobile clients. This paper also presents a novel location update protocol, called SLUP which minimizes the energy consumption of a mobile client by exploiting a syntactic information of the user's movement. Moreover, there are three variations of proposed protocol in terms of choosing optimal state: SLUP/BS, SLUP/UITR, and SLUP/IUT$\langle T_{iut} \rangle$.

References

1. A. Bhattacharya and S. K. Das. "LeZi-update: An information-theoretic framework for personal mobility tracking in PCS networks," *Wireless Networks*, 8, 2002.
2. A. Bar-Noy, I. Kessler, and M. Sidi. "Mobile Users: To Update or Not To Update?," *Wireless Networks*, 1(2), 1995.
3. Computer Science and Telecommunications Board (CSTB), National Research Council. *IT Roadmap to a Geospatial Future*, The National Academies Press, 2003.
4. T. Imielinski, S. Viswanathan, and B.R. Badrinath. "Data on Air: Organization and Access", *IEEE Trans. on Knowledge and Data Engineering*, 9(3), 1997.
5. O. Kasten, Energy consumption. Available at `http://www.inf.ethz.ch/~kasten/research/bathtub/energy_consumption.html`.
6. Donald J. Patterson, Lin Liao, Dieter Fox, and Henry A. Kautz. "Inferring High-Level Behavior from Low-Level Sensors", *Proc. of Ubicomp* 2003.
7. MoonBae Song, JeHyok Ryu, SangKeun Lee, and Chong-Sun Hwang. "Considering Mobility Patterns in Moving Objects Database," *Proc. of ICPP*, October 2003.
8. O. Wolfson, A. P. Sistla, S. Chamberlain, and Y. Yesha. "Updating and Querying Databases that Track Mobile Units," *Distributed and Parallel Databases*, 7(3), 1999.
9. Y.-C. Tseng, et al. "A Stop-or-Move mobility model for PCS networks and its location-tracking strategies," *Computer Communications*, 26:1288–1301, 2003.
10. Matthias Grossglauser, "Mobility in Ad Hoc Networks: Friend or Foe?", *Self-organized Wireless Communication Systems*, I&C Research Day 2004.
11. B. Liang and Z.J. Haas, "Predictive distance-based mobility management for PCS networks", In *Proc. of INFOCOM*, 1999.

Mobile User Data Mining: Mining Relationship Patterns

John Goh and David Taniar

School of Business Systems,
Monash University, Clayton Vic 3800 Australia
{Jen.Goh, David.Taniar}@infotech.monash.edu.au

Abstract. Mobile user data mining focuses on finding useful and interesting knowledge out from raw data collected from mobile users. Frequency pattern and location dependent mobile user data mining are among the algorithm used in this field. Parallel pattern, our previous proposed method, extracts how a group of mobile users makes similar decisions, such as by moving towards the similar direction, or by viewing similar contents at the same time. Parallel pattern is triggered group behaviour of mobile users. This paper reports our refinement work on parallel pattern which incorporated *refinement of the relationships among parallel patterns, or relationship pattern*, which shows how 'similarities of decisions' are related to each other. Effects found are such as conditional relationship, where one parallel pattern has to happen before the next one occurs. Other effects includes associative, sequential and loop pattern effects. Our performance evaluation reports how relationship pattern performs in real life dataset and synthetic dataset and discusses some potential implementation issues.

1 Introduction

With the penetrate rate [1] of mobile technologies into the consumer market industry, many consumers are using mobile equipments in different situations in their life. Since mobile users usually carries mobile equipments most of the time, and the mobile equipment stays in touch with the mobile network access point at all times, source data that encompasses the behaviour of mobile users could be captured. Capturing this large amount of source data helps producing quality knowledge [11, 13, 15].

Mobile user data mining [11-15, 24] is a domain of data mining which emphasizes on developing methods into finding useful and interesting patterns from source data generated by mobile users. Data mining [3, 4] has been studied in many domains such as time series environment [5, 16-18], web based environment [6, 9, 10], geographical based environment [7, 8, 21, 22, 25] and location dependent environment [12, 20, 22, 23]. Enhancements in the area of data mining in general are also being developed, such as security enhancements [27] and efficiency in rules generation enhancements [26, 28, 29].

Mobile user data mining [12, 15, 22, 24] focuses extensively on mobile users and the mobile equipment that they carry. Parallel pattern [13, 15] is our previously

L.T. Yang et al. (Eds.): EUC 2005, LNCS 3824, pp. 735 – 744, 2005.

proposed method designed to find out similarities of decisions made by mobile users. In a mobile environment, there is a pattern that exists whereby similarities of decisions are taken among mobile users within a short period of time. The objective of this paper is to overcome the shortcomings of the previous proposed parallel pattern that only shows only one way relationship of similar change of states. In the interest of space, details on mobile user data mining is not provided.

2 Background

Parallel pattern [13, 15] finds out similarities of decision such as physical movements, or access to contents from the web, among mobile users. The word parallel in the parallel pattern reflects the event that happens at the same direction at the same time, such as two separation events from mobile user 1 and mobile user 2 to go from a fashion shop to a grocery shop within a specified period of time. The pattern in the word parallel pattern reflects the component to find out the pattern trend. If there is a pattern, 1) it is more likely to have reasons behind it 2) the pattern is likely to be repeated in the future. Therefore the study of parallel pattern provides a framework for understanding of mobile environment.

Definition 1 (General): The general definition of events, time, locations and mobile users in the mobile environment is as follows.
Let $E = \{e_1, e_2, \ldots, e_n\}$ be the set of events.
Let $T = \{t_1, t_2, \ldots, t_n\}$ be the set of time.
Let $L = \{l_1, l_2, \ldots, l_n\}$ be the set of location or theme.
Let $M = \{m_1, m_2, \ldots, m_n\}$ be the set of mobile users.

Definition 2 (Event): The mobile environment is a space over a time series where mobile users move freely as they wish and intends. Each event is recorded with the time and the mobile user identification and their movement from and movement to in a single event.

$$\sum_{time=0}^{time=n} [\sum_{m=0}^{m=\max} visits(from, to)]$$

Definition 3 (Window): The window is a specified timeframe, from *time_start* to *time_end* where events within this window are treated as occurred within the same window. Two events happening in two different window is considered as remote to each other such that: $E\{M, L(from, to), T]$, where $T > time\_start$ and $T < time\_end$.

Definition 4 (Parallel Pattern): The parallel pattern is a trend evidenced by a higher than threshold volume of similar parallel activities occurring within the same window period of time such that: Parallel Pattern = $E(from, to)$, where $T > time\_start$ and $T <$ *time_end* and $\forall E\ (from, to) : E_x(from, to) = E_y(from, to)$.

There are two types of parallel pattern [13, 15], namely *physical parallel pattern* and *logical parallel pattern*. The principle behind both is the same but the application environments among them are different. Physical parallel pattern looks at the physical location that mobile user travels, which are identified by means of geographical coordinates. Logical parallel pattern, on the other hand, looks at how the current logical state of the mobile user. This can be described as such that mobile user being currently in a shopping centre, even when some are in a shopping centre in the north of the city, and some are in a shopping centre in the south of the city. Logical parallel pattern treats them the same.

3 Proposed Method: Relationship Among Parallel Patterns

Relationship parallel pattern is our proposed method, which examines the relationships among parallel patterns – relationship patterns. There are four kinds of relationships among parallel patterns in a static node. These four relationships are namely *conditional*, *associative*, and *sequential* and *loop* relationship among parallel patterns.

3.1 Conditional Relationship

Definition 5 (Conditional Relationship): Let *P* be a list of parallel patterns found from a mobile user data mining episode. Let *C* be the condition for which two parallel patterns exists. Let $P = \{p_1, p_2, p_3, \ldots, p_n\}$. Let $C = \{c_1, c_2, c_3, \ldots, c_n\}$, where P is a list of parallel patterns, and C is a list of conditions. Let C_{ref} to be the reference condition which determines the existence of the relationship. Conditional relationship for two parallel patterns p_x, p_y is such that: C_n (p_1, p_2). Where $C_n = C_{ref.}$ Consider there is a conditional parallel pattern, *P*1 being Parallel Pattern 1 and *P*2 being Parallel Pattern 2, {If *P*1 = True Then *P*2} in the sample which consists of {*P*1, *P*2, *P*3, *P*4}. *P*1 must occur first before any *P*2 occurrence can occur. Once *P*2 have occurred, and if *P*1 occur after *P*2, then the statement no longer holds true. On the other hand, *P*2 must not occur before *P*1 have occurred. Finally, the statement must satisfy the confidence requirement, that is, must be sufficient frequent enough within the window sample in order to be qualified as a conditional parallel pattern.

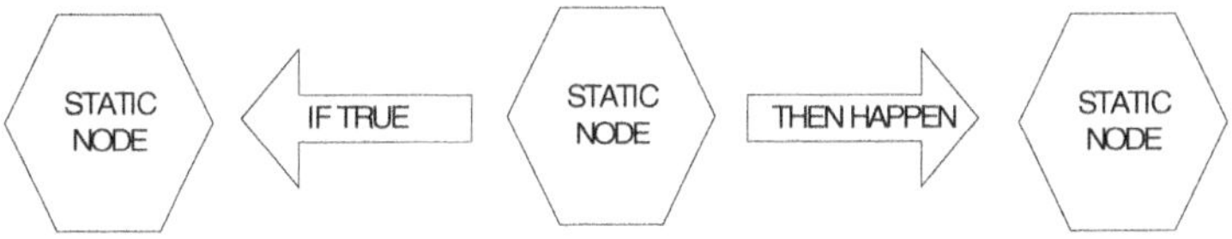

Fig. 1. Conditional Relationship among Parallel Patterns

Figure 1 shows the diagrammatic representation of conditional parallel pattern. Each arrow represents a parallel pattern found from previous data mining exercise, and all parallel patterns were drawn from within a static node in the centre. In the diagram, the left arrow shows a *TRUE* sign and the right arrow shows a *THEN HAPPEN* signs. It represents a conditional relationship in between these two parallel

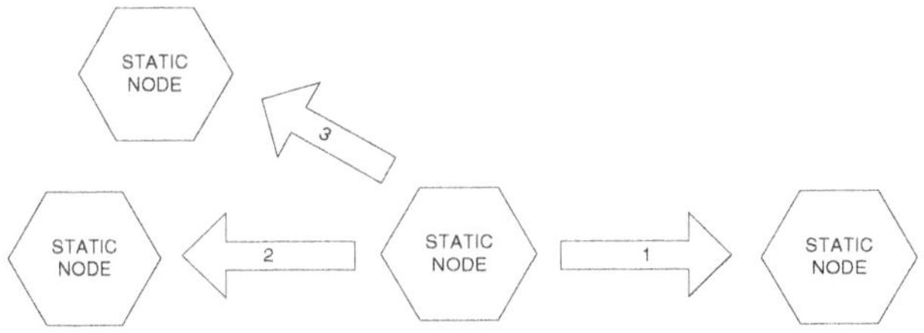

Fig. 5. Sequential Parallel Pattern

show the confidence of the sequence being a sequential parallel pattern. If the condition are satisfied, that is the sequence occurs frequent enough to be considered high confidence, then the sequence will be accepted as a sequential parallel pattern.

```
Boolean Sequential Parallel Pattern (Parallel Pattern List) {
    For I = 0 to formSequence(Parallel Pattern List) Do
        Boolean Result = False;
        SQ = currentSequence();
        If countOccurence(SQ) > sequence_threshold) Then
            If (last(SQ) = nextFirst(SQ) - 1) Then Result = False;
            Result = True;
        Else Result = False;
    Return Result;
}
```

Fig. 6. Sequential Parallel Pattern

3.4 Loop Relationship

Definition 8 (Loop Relationship): Consider the sequential parallel pattern of $\{p_1, p_2, p_3, p_4, p_5\}$. It qualifies as a loop parallel pattern when p_1 occurs after p_5 have occurred and p_1, p_2, p_3, p_4 and p_5 follows a sequence relationship, that is, one occurs after the previous.

Let S be a list of sequence. S_{ref} is the reference sequence in which it has occurred frequently to be considered a sequential relationship pattern. Loop Relationship = $time1(S_{ref}) \rightarrow time2(S_{ref})$ By finding the circular relationships among parallel patterns, it can be said that each circular relationship refers to a phenomenon. A phenomenon is something reoccurs at various frequencies, but the whole cycle do repeats itself. Of course, the window size must be large enough to accommodate the possible loop size of the circular flow. Furthermore, there must exist for a few repetition of the circular relationship in order to suggest a high confidence of the statement.

Figure 7 shows the diagrammatic representation of loop parallel pattern. It can be seen that there are two sets of parallel pattern that occurs over the same period amount of time, namely time series {1, 3, 5, 7} and {2, 4, 6, 8}. Figure 8 shows the algorithm to find the loop characteristics among the parallel patterns. The loop characteristic is an extension of multiple reoccurrence of sequential parallel pattern without any break. If a loop parallel pattern is found, it shows that there is a highly significant

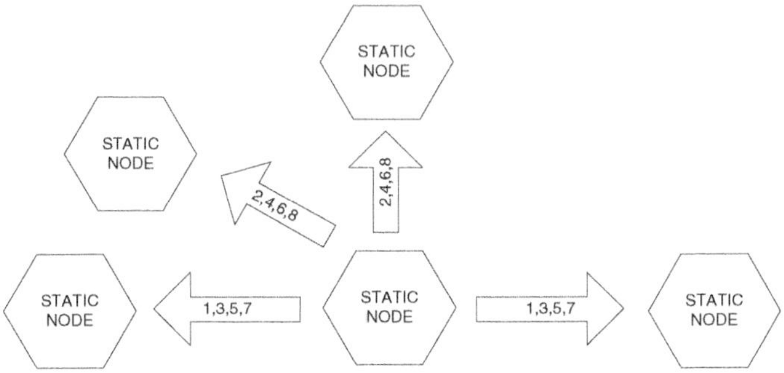

Fig. 7. Loop Parallel Pattern

```
Boolean Loop Parallel Pattern (Parallel Pattern List) {
    For I = 0 to formSequence(Parallel Pattern List) Do {
        Boolean Result = False;
        SQ = currentSequence();
        If countOccurence(SQ) > sequence_threshold) Then {
            If (last(SQ) = nextFirst(SQ) - 1) Then Result = True;
            Else Result = False;
        Else Result = False;
    Return Result;
}
```

Fig. 8. Loop Parallel Pattern

reoccurrence of patterns, in which during random events are highly unlikely. However, this algorithm is written to preserve the need in case this actually occurs so that it could be detected.

4 Performance Evaluation

Performance evaluation is performed under an IBM PC Pentium IV 384MB memory environment. Dataset used are *R*, *R3* and *R5* derived from dataset generator, with random seed derived from generation of integers with repetition but fixed within a specified range. The objective is to examine the relationship among the window size

Variable	Description
window	Size of window used to perform data mining.
frequency	Frequency of occurrence for a certain pattern.

Dataset	Description
R	Fully random dataset.
R3	Sequence repeated after 3 units of time interval.
R5	Sequence repeated after 5 units of time interval.

Fig. 9. Description for R, R3 and R5 Datasets

towards the responsiveness of finding relationships among parallel pattern. Therefore, data for *window size* 10 is towards *time* 10, *window size* 20 is towards *time* 20, *window size* 30 is towards *time* 30. Random source data are sourced from *random.org* [19]. The randomness is sourced from atmospheric noise and fed into the seed for random number generator.

Figure 9 shows the description of variables involved in the performance evaluation and description of individual dataset used for performance evaluation, namely {*R*, *R*3 and *R*5}. Due to lack of real life dataset, performance evaluation is conducted using synthetic dataset. These synthetic dataset are obtained from a random number generator with the seed being replaced via atmospheric noise. *R*, also known as *Random* or *R*1 is a truly random dataset, and it sets as a baseline of a data where no pattern can be found as the whole dataset is random. *R*3 and *R*5 are repeated dataset, where *R*3 have a repeat every 3 units of time interval and *R*5 have a repeat every 5 units of interval. The reason for doing so is to create some form of artificial patterns, so that the algorithms can extract the patterns out.

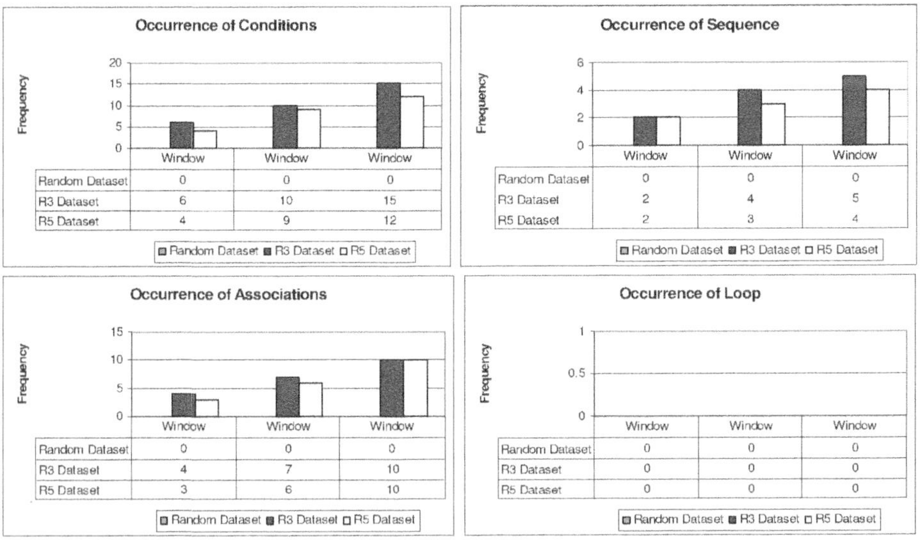

Fig. 10. Performance Result using R, R3 and R5 Datasets

Figure 10 shows the performance result for the 4 different mining algorithms under the 3 different dataset configuration under 3 different window sizes. For conditional relationship pattern, it was observed that during the course of testing Dataset *R*3 always returns higher result than Dataset *R*5. For sequential relationship pattern, it was observed that the trend of graph is growing gradually, and this is caused by increasing window size in the x axis. *R*3 is always higher than *R*5 because there are more complete repetitions in *R*3 than *R*5 dataset. For associative relationship pattern, it was observed that the reading is growing up because window size is increasing in the x axis. *R*3 and *R*5 happen to be equal number of reading because of coincidence. For loop relationship pattern, it was observed that no loop parallel pattern is found, due to its rare occurrence.

5 Conclusion and Future Work

This paper reports our work on finding relationships among parallel pattern - relationship pattern. *Conditional relationship* represents a movement patterns happening one after another such as if users move from *A* to *B*, then it is likely that users will move from *C* to *D* as well. *Sequence relationship* represents a movement patterns happening in sequence such as if users move from *A* to *B*, then it is likely for users to move from *C* to *D*, and the it is likely that users will move from *E* to *F* after this. *Association relationship* represents movement patterns happening at the same time such as users will move from *A* to *B* or *C* to *D* at the same time. *Loop relationship* represents patterns that repeat itself once finished and it is a sequential relationship where the last occurrence of pattern connects back to the first occurrence of pattern, such as users will move to *A* to *B*, then *C* to *D*, then *E* to *F*, and then pattern of users moving from *A* to *B* will occur again.

It represents a progress towards a higher level of mobile user data mining from the previously found patterns in the lower level. With higher level of knowledge being found, higher level knowledge represents knowledge that are rich and simplified as higher level knowledge is extracted based on the summary of previously found knowledge. It has been concluded that the ability for the proposed method being able to find knowledge at a higher level, it is recommended for mobile user data mining. Our future work for this research area is to extend the concept of high level quality knowledge mining over other areas such as *frequency pattern* [11], *group pattern* [24], *association rules* [3], and *sequential patterns* [4].

References

1. Statistics for Telecom Services for2004. http://www.ida.gov.sg/idaweb/media/infopage.jsp?infopagecategory=factsheet:factfigure&versionid=1&infopageid=I2703 Accessed: 20 June 2004
2. University of California (Irvine) Library - Knowledge Discovery in Database Archive. http://kdd.ics.uci.edu/ Accessed: 1st Dec 2004
3. R. Agrawal and R. Srikant. Fast Algorithms for Mining Association Rules. In Proc. *20th International Conference on Very Large Data Bases*, pp. 487-499, 1994.
4. R. Agrawal and R. Srikant. Mining Sequential Patterns. In Proc. *11th International Conference on Data Engineering*, pp. 3-14, 1995.
5. S. Y. Chen, X. Liu, Data mining from 1994 to 2004: an application-oriented review, *Int Journal of Business Intelligence and Data Mining*, vol. 1, no. 1, pp. 4-21, 2005.
6. V. Christophides, G. Karvounarakis, and D. Plexousakis. Optimizing Taxanomic Semantic Web Queries using Labeling Schemes. *Journal of Web Semantics*, **1**(2):207-228, 2003.
7. I. Claude, J.-L. Daire, and G. Sebag. Fetal Brain MRI: Segmentation and Biometric Analysis of the Posterior Fossa. *IEEE Transactions on Biomedical Engineering*, **51**(4):617-626, 2004.
8. D. E. Cooper, P. Ezhilchelvan, and I. Mitrani. High Coverage Broadcasting for Mobile Ad Hoc Networks. *Lecture Notes in Computer Science,* vol. 3042, pp. 100-111, 2004.
9. D. L. Lee, M. Zhu, H. Hu, When location-based services meet databases, *Mobile Information Systems*, vol. 1, no. 2, pp. 81-90., 2005.
10. M. Eirinaki and M. Vazirgaiannis. Web Mining for Web Personalization. *ACM Transactions on Internet Technology*, vol. 3, no. 1, pp. 1-27, 2003.

we have designed and implemented asymmetry-aware link quality services, including *the neighborhood link quality service (NLQS)* and *the link relay service (LRS)*, to provide the timeliness link quality information of neighbors and build a relay framework to alleviate effects of the link asymmetry on the TinyOS platform [7]. We leverage the Window Mean Exponentially Weighted Moving Average Estimator (WMEWMA) [3,8] to estimate the packet reception rate (PRR) between neighbors. Our proposed link quality services are able to identify more outbound neighbors and provide timeliness link quality information of inbound and outbound neighbors. Both of these services are crucial for the design of link quality aware routing protocols. Our services also provide a relay framework to forward packets across unidirectional links, which have more positive contributions to localized coordination between neighbors. To demonstrate our proposed link quality services, we design and implement two example applications, building *the shortest hops routing tree (SHRT)* and *the best path reliability routing tree (BRRT)*. To evaluate our proposed link quality services, we have conducted both static analysis and simulation using the TOSSIM simulator [9]. We found that the performance of two example applications was improved substantially.

The rest of the paper is organized as follows. The design and implementation of the link quality services are presented in Section 2. SHRT and BRRT are described in Section 3. In Section 4, performance evaluation results are discussed. Related work and concluding remarks are listed in Section 5 and 6 respectively.

2 Asymmetry-Aware Link Quality Services

We consider the topology of a WSN as a weighted directed graph (G). All motes in the topology are vertexes of the graph and all vertexes belong to the vertex set, called $V(G)$. In this paper, we also call the vertex of a graph as node. All links in the topology are edges of the graph and all edges belong to the edge set, called $E(G)$. We use $e(u, v)$ to represent the edge from Node u to Node v, and assign the estimated PRR of the link as $weight$ of the edge. Figure 1(a) is an example topology. In this topology, every node has some inbound neighbors and outbound neighbors. In a WSN, a node can identify inbound neighbors only when it receives some packets from them. To identify outbound neighbors, the node should get acknowledgement from them. For example, Node 8 and Node 1 can receive packets from each other, then one of them will identify its counterpart as inbound and outbound neighbor. However, the link quality, in term of PRR, from Node 8 to Node 1 is different from that from Node 1 to Node 8, and the PRR will vary with time. Due to the asymmetric links, node can not identify all of its outbound neighbors. For example, Node 22 can identify Node 8 as its inbound neighbor. But Node 8 can not directly identify Node 22 as its outbound neighbor. Nevertheless, if Node 9 can relay the acknowledgement for Node 22, so that Node 8 will identify Node 22 as its outbound neighbors. In some situations, one step relay is not enough to identify all outbound neighbors. For example, if Node 24 will identify Node 9 as its outbound neighbor, both Node 23 and Node 52 should relay the acknowledgement from Node 9 to Node 24. The more steps the acknowledgement is relayed, the more the outbound neighbors will be identified. Next, we give a formal definition of *theoretical outbound neighbors*, *No Relay outbound neighbors*, *One-Step Relay outbound neighbors*, and *Two-Step Relay outbound neighbors*.

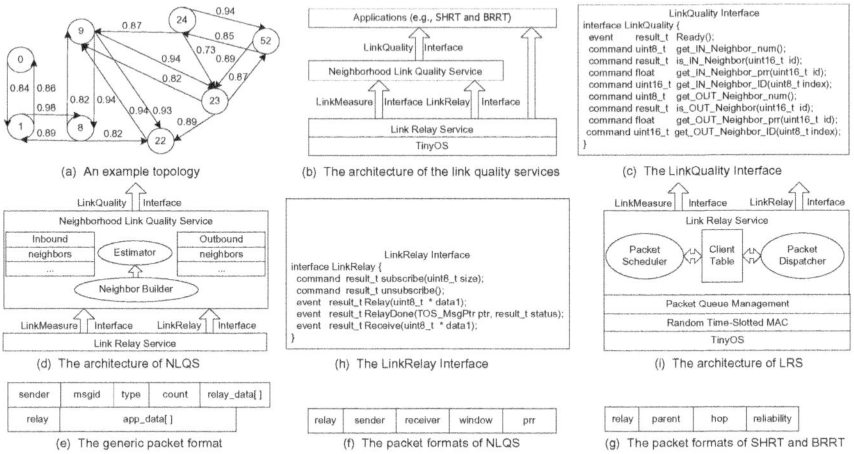

Fig. 1. The figures of the link quality services

Definition 1. *Theoretical outbound neighbors of node v (N(v)):* $\{u|\forall u \in V(G) \wedge e(v,u) \in E(G)\}$

Definition 2. *No Relay outbound neighbors of node v (N0(v)):* $\{u|\forall u \in V(G) \wedge e(v,u) \in E(G) \wedge e(u,v) \in E(G)\}$

Definition 3. *One-Step Relay outbound neighbors of node v (N1(v)):* $\{u|(u \in N0(v)) \vee (\forall u \in V(G) \wedge e(v,u) \in E(G) \wedge \exists m \in V(G) \wedge e(u,m), e(m,v) \in E(G))\}$

Definition 4. *Two-Step Relay outbound neighbors of node v (N2(v)):* $\{u|(u \in N1(v)) \vee (\forall u \in V(G) \wedge e(v,u) \in E(G) \wedge \exists m,n \in V(G) \wedge e(u,m), e(m,n), e(n,v) \in E(G))\}$

Continuing with the above example, $N(24)$ includes Node 9, Node 23 and Node 52; $N0(24)$ only includes Node 52; $N1(24)$ includes Node 23 and Node 52; $N2(24)$ includes Node 9, Node 23, and Node 52. From these definitions and the above example, we know that we might find a relay path to relay packets across unidirectional links. If there is a path, there will be opportunity to relay packets across unidirectional links. If there is only one node in the middle of the path, we call this path *One-Relay path*. If there are two nodes in the middle of the path, we call this path *Two-Relay path* and so on. In next section, we will describe the link quality services, which can build inbound and outbound neighbors with timelessness link quality information and relay packets across unidirectional links.

2.1 System Overview

Next, we describe the design and implementation the link quality services, including NLQS and LRS, on the TinyOS platform. In NLQS, we measure and estimate the link quality using link quality estimator, build the inbound and outbound neighbors tables, and provide the *LinkQuality* interface for applications to query the timeliness link quality information of neighbors. In LRS, we propose a link relay protocol, implement a link relay framework, and provide the *LinkRelay* interface for applications to relay packets across unidirectional links. Furthermore, NLQS uses the *LinkRelay* interface to relay the estimated PRR of the inbound neighbors back to them. Figure 1(b) shows the architecture of the link quality services. Due to space limitation, we provide the high level view only, interested readers please refer the technical report version of this paper [10].

2.2 Neighborhood Link Quality Service

NLQS provides the *LinkQuality* interface. Figure 1(c) lists the interface, which consists of one event and eight commands, complying with the TinyOS and nesC language [7]. When the service is ready, it will signal the *Ready* event to notify the availability of the service. Even the service is ready for use, NLQS will continue measure and estimate the timeliness link quality between neighbors and update inbound and outbound neighbors tables. Applications can call those commands to query the link quality information. The link quality information includes that how many inbound and outbound neighbors are identified, what are their node ID, what are the estimated PRR from inbound neighbors and to outbound neighbors.

To provides this service, we need to measure and estimate the link quality between neighbors and build the inbound and outbound neighbors tables with the estimated PRR. To do this, every node will periodically broadcast some packets, which contain node ID and packet ID. Other nodes overhear the channel for the broadcast packets to measure and estimate the link quality from their inbound neighbors. Every node only measures and estimates PRR of the link from its inbound neighbors. We leverage WMEWMA to estimate PRR based on current and history measured results. WMEWMA uses a time window to observe the received packets and it adjusts the estimation result using latest average value of the measured PRR. When nodes have estimated PRR for their inbound neighbors, they will send the estimated results back to those inbound neighbors. When their inbound neighbors get the estimated results from their outbound neighbors, they can identify those outbound neighbors and build the outbound neighbors table with the estimated results. As we have discussed before, due to the link asymmetry, nodes may not directly receive packets from their outbound neighbors. They will get the estimated PRR to their outbound neighbors from LRS (Section 2.3).

Figure 1(d) shows the architecture of NLQS, which consists of four components: the inbound neighbor table, the outbound neighbor table, the neighbor builder, and the link quality estimator. The neighbor builder builds the inbound neighbor table using the PRR estimated by the link quality estimator and builds the outbound neighbor table using the PRR getting from LRS.

2.3 Link Relay Service

LRS is a general service to relay packets across unidirectional links and it is an additional layer between TinyOS and applications. Every node provided LRS will collaborate with each other to forward relay packets. In LRS, we propose a link relay protocol for inter-node communication, and design a relay framework and provide an interface for applications to relay packets.

Figure 1(e) illustrates a generic packet format used by LRS for inter-node communication. The *type* field indicates the type of the relay data. In LRS, every *type* of the relay data is associated with one application and LRS uses the value of the *type* field to dispatch the relay data to the associated application. The *relay_data* field contains the relay data, which will be forwarded to the application. Usually the first field of the relay data is the *relay* field and the value of this field indicates how many relay steps this relay data can be relayed. The value of the *relay* field will be decreased by one for every relay step until it reaches zero. If every node initializes the *relay* field as one, then the relay packet will be relayed once. We call this *One-Step Relay* algorithm. If every node initializes it as two, then the relay packet will be relayed twice. And we call this *Two-Step Relay* algorithm and so on. The more the packets are relayed, the more neighbors will receive the packets and the more opportunities exist to bypass unidirectional links. Applications will store its data in the *app_data* field. Figure 1(f) is the packet format used in NLQS to relay the estimated PRR to inbound neighbors (Section 2.2). Figure 1(g) is the packet format used in SHRT and BRRT (Section 3).

Figure 1(h) lists the *LinkRelay* interface. This interface is a parameterized interface, which can support 256 applications concurrently. As we have discussed that every application will be associated with an unique ID. This ID will be store in the *type* field of the relay packet. This mechanism is similar to the active message on TinyOS platform. When an application will use LRS to relay packet, it first call the *subscribe* command. When a relay packet arrives this node, the associated application will get the *Receive* event from LRS. At this time, the application can make decision about how to process this incoming relay data. When the radio channel is available to send data, LRS will signal a *Relay* event to get the relay data from applications. At this time, the application can make decision about which relay data will be relayed and how many steps the relay data will be relayed. If the application is not interested in the LRS events any more, it can call the *unsubscribe* command to unsubscribe these events. In LRS, we follow the basic idea in system design to separate mechanism and policy . We design and implement the link relay mechanism and provide this interface for applications to make policy decisions.

Figure 1(i) shows the architecture of LRS. The packet dispatcher dispatches the relay data to applications. The packet scheduler schedules applications to forward relay data. The packet queue management manages packets received from the TinyOS platform and created by applications. The random time-slotted MAC is designed to avoid collisions of simultaneous packets transmissions between neighbors.

3 Example Applications

To demonstrate and evaluate our link quality services, we design and implement two example applications on the TinyOS platform: *the shortest hops routing tree* (SHRT) and *the best path reliability routing tree* (BRRT). In SHRT, every node has a routing path with shortest hops to the sink node. In BRRT, every node has a routing path with best reliability to the sink node. We define the path reliability for every node as follows: $Reliability_A = \prod_A^S PRR$, where the $Reliability_A$ is the path reliability for node A. The PRR is the packet reception rate of the links along the routing path from Node A to the sink node S. For example, in Figure 1(a), Node 0 is the sink node and the path reliability of Node 9 is $0.72 = (0.94 * 0.89 * 0.86)$.

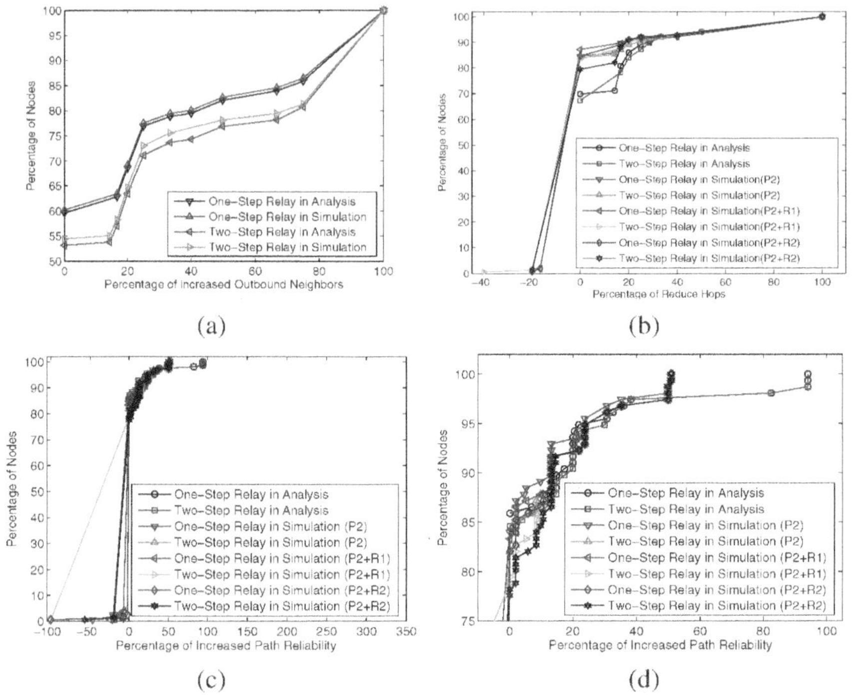

Fig. 2. Evaluation results: (a) The CDF of the percentage of increased outbound neighbors using link quality services, (b) The CDF of the percentage of reduced hops in SHRT, (c) The CDF of the improved path reliability in BRRT, and (d) Zooming of the CDF of the improved path reliability in BRRT

Step Relay algorithm is the worst one of all algorithms. Also we note that there are a lot of nodes improve the path reliability than the number in SHRT. Nearly every neighbor of a node in BRRT has different path reliability while most neighbors of a node in SHRT have same hops to the sink nodes. Therefore, nodes in BRRT have more opportunities to change their parents than they do in SHRT.

Energy Consumption in SHRT and BRRT. Figure 3 (a) shows the CDF of more packets sent by the *One-Step Relay* and *Two-Step Relay* algorithms than *No Relay* in SHRT. In this figure, the x-axis stands for more packets send by every node and the y-axis reports the CDF. From this figure, we can see that all algorithms have little difference in terms of the number of extra packets sent. For the *One-Step Relay* and *Two-Step Relay* algorithms, about 90% of nodes do not send more packets and about 10% of nodes send less packets. Figure 3(b) shows the CDF of more packets received by the *One-Step Relay* and *Two-Step Relay* algorithms than *No Relay* one. In this figure, the x-axis stands for more packets received by every node and the y-axis reports the CDF. From this figure, we can see the following results. The *P2+R2 Policy* of *Two-Step Relay* receives more packets than others. The *P2+R1 Policy* of *Two-Step Relay* is the second worst. The *P2 Policy* of *One-Step Relay* and the *P2 Policy* of *Two-Step Relay* follow the similar pattern and they receive less packets than other algorithms. Except the *P2+R2*

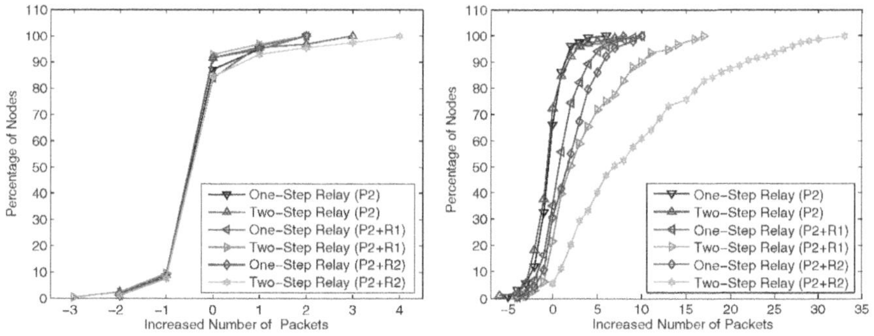

(a) (b)

Fig. 3. (a) The CDF of more packets sent in SHRT, (f) The CDF of more packets received in SHRT

Policy of *Two-Step Relay*, most algorithms have nearly 20% of nodes which receive less packets than the *No Relay* algorithm. The CDF of more packets sent and received by the *One-Step Relay* and *Two-Step Relay* algorithms than *No Relay* one in BRRT have similar results with SHRT [10].

The results in this section show that there is a tradeoff between the energy consumption and the benefits brought by LRS. We argue that it is the application's decision to turn on/off LRS. For example, if the path reliability or path length is more important than the energy, e.g., event notification, then it should choose LRS. However, for monitoring-based applications it's better to turn off this service.

5 Related Work and Discussions

Our work is inspired by a variety of previous work, including *link layer characterization*, *link quality estimation*, and *existing solutions to link irregularity*.

Link layer characterization. Ganesan *et al.* find long links, backward links, asymmetric links, stragglers and clustering in large scale of WSN [1]. Zhao *et al.* measure the spatial and temporal characteristics of packet delivery and find the gray area in which there are significant variabilities in packet delivery performance and the no-determining relationship between signal strength and packet delivery [4]. Zhou *et al.* show that radio irregularity is a common phenomenon, which arises from multiple factors, such as variance in RF sending power, and different path losses depending on the direction of radio signal propagation [5]. All of these research work shows us the reality of the link quality in WSN, which make us have a deeper understanding of the wireless communication in WSN. We are the first to provide a set of APIs for link quality services.

Link quality estimation. Woo *et al.* show that WMEWMA is a very effective estimator, in term of stability and agility [8]. Cerpa *et al.* present a statistical model of lossy links in WSN [11]. Zhou *et al.* establish the Radio Irregularity Model (RIM) for simulation [5]. Zuniga *et al.* intend to identify the causes of the transitional region, and a quantification of their influence [6]. Different from these previous work, we focus on the asymmetry-aware link quality services that alleviate the effect of asymmetric links in the link quality measurement and estimation process, which is neglected in previous research.

Existing solutions to link irregularity. Woo *et al.* study reliable and cost-based routing protocol techniques [3]. Seada *et al.* present energy-efficient forwarding strategies for geographic routing in lossy WSN [2]. Ramasubramanian *et al.* provide a bidirectional abstraction of the unidirectional network to routing protocols in *ad hoc networks* [12]. They results also show that reception based forwarding strategies are more efficient than purely distance-based strategies in the lossy link. We step further to distinguish inbound and outbound neighbors to make good use of them for high level routing service, and to provide a set of link quality interfaces. We also provide LRS for relaying packets across unidirectional links.

6 Conclusions

In this paper, we design and implement two asymmetry-aware link quality services. The performance of the services is evaluated in the context of two example applications, SHRT and BRRT. The detail simulation results using TOSSIM show that the performance of the applications can be improved substantially using proposed services.

References

1. Ganesan, D., Krishnamachari, B., Woo, A., Culler, D., Estrin, D., Wicker, S.: Complex behavior at scale: An experimental study of low-power wireless sensor networks. Technical Report UCLA/CSD-TR-02-0013, University of California, Los Angeles (2002)
2. Seada, K., Zuniga, M., Helmy, A., Krishnamachari, B.: Energy-efficient forwarding strategies for geographic routing in lossy wireless sensor networks. In: Proceedings of SenSys '04. (2004)
3. Woo, A., Tong, T., Culler, D.: Taming the underlying challenges of reliable multihop routing in sensor networks. In: Proceedings of SenSys '03. (2003)
4. Zhao, J., Govindan, R.: Understanding packet delivery performance in dense wireless sensor networks. In: Proceedings of SenSys '03. (2003)
5. Zhou, G., He, T., Krishnamurthy, S., Stankovic, J.A.: Impact of radio irregularity on wireless sensor networks. In: Proceedings of MobiSys '04. (2004)
6. Zuniga, M., Krishnamachari, B.: Analyzing the transitional region in low power wireless links. In: Proceedings of SECON '04. (2004)
7. Levis, P., et al.: The emergence of networking abstractions and techniques in tinyos. In: Proceedings of NSDI '04. (2004)
8. Woo, A., Culler, D.: Evaluation of efficient link reliability estimators for low-power wireless networks. Technical Report UCB/CSD-03-1270, University of California, Berkeley (2003)
9. Levis, P., Lee, N., Welsh, M., Culler, D.: Tossim: Accurate and scalable simulation of entire tinyos applications. In: Proceedings of SenSys '03. (2003)
10. Du, J., Shi, W., Sha, K.: Asymmetry-aware link quality services in wireless sensor networks. Technical Report MIST-TR-2005-006, Wayne State University (2005)
11. Cerpa, A., Wong, J., Kuang, L., Potkonjak, M., Estrin, D.: Statistical model of lossy links in wireless sensor networks. Technical Report CENS Technical Report, University of California, Los Angeles (2004)
12. V. Ramasubramanian, R.C., Mosse, D.: Providing a bidirectional abstraction for unidirectional ad hoc networks. In: Proceedings of INFOCOM '02. (2002)

Incorporating Global Index with Data Placement Scheme for Multi Channels Mobile Broadcast Environment

Agustinus Borgy Waluyo[1], Bala Srinivasan[1], David Taniar[2], and Wenny Rahayu[3]

[1] Caulfield School of Information Technology, Monash University, Australia
{Agustinus.Borgy.Waluyo, Bala.Srinivasan}@infotech.monash.edu.au
[2] Clayton School of Information Technology, Monash University, Australia
David.Taniar@infotech.monash.edu.au
[3] Department of Computer Science and Computer Engineering, Latrobe University, Australia
w.rahayu@latrobe.edu.au

Abstract. A scalable information delivery services like data broadcasting scheme is definitely of great interest especially to deal with the exponential increase of mobile users. In this paper, we present Global Indexing with data placement scheme for multi broadcast channels environment, which aims to minimize query access time, tuning time and power consumption. This scheme considers index and data allocation over separate broadcast channel. Moreover, it concerns with single and multiple data items request. A simulation model is developed to analyze the performance of the proposed scheme. We compare the proposed scheme with conventional scheme. It is found that the proposed scheme provides substantially better performances in every aspect of evaluation.

1 Introduction

In recent years, the use of wireless technology has been growing at an unbelievable rate. Most people are now able to connect to the network using portable size wireless computers powered by batteries (e.g. PDAs) and to conduct their business activities anywhere and anytime. These portable computers communicate with a central stationary server via wireless channel, and this paradigm is known as mobile computing [2,7].

Mobile computing environment is facing inherent limitations particularly power, storage and bandwidth capacity. With power capacity, the life expectancy of a battery (e.g. nickel-cadmium, lithium ion) was estimated to increase time of effective use by only another 15% [8]. Thus, efficient use of energy is definitely one of the main issues. Having considered the limitations of mobile environment, it is very much of benefit to incorporate a scalable and energy efficient mechanism for retrieving database information. Data dissemination (or also called broadcast mechanism) is considered the most appropriate strategy to deliver such services. Wireless broadcasting has been applied for decades in radio and television industry and it is very effective to cope with a massive number of clients. Two factors need to be

L.T. Yang et al. (Eds.): EUC 2005, LNCS 3824, pp. 755 – 764, 2005.

others. On the other hand, a broadcast program is without replication if all data items are broadcast with equal frequencies or uniform frequencies. A broadcast program without replication is also called a flat broadcast program. This paper relates to the later broadcast program and leaves the replication broadcast program for future work. Moreover, our proposed placement scheme is designed under assumption that the queries have equal access frequencies.

3.2 Global Indexing Model

Global Indexing model is designed based on *B*+ tree structure [12]. Global index consists of non-leaf nodes, and leaf node. Leaf node is the bottom most index, where each key point to actual data items.

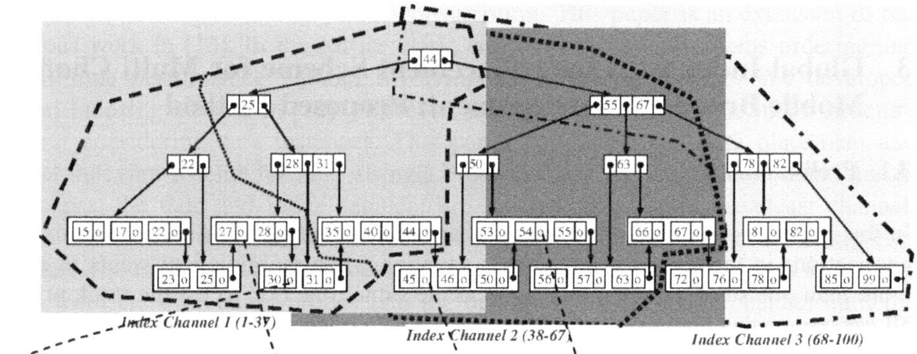

Data Channel 1			
30	Argentina	MerVal	903.680
72	Brazil	Bovespa	18,796.91
44	Canada	S&P TSX Composite	8,191.61
67	Chile	IPSA	1,412.79
53	Mexico	IPC	9,821.000
99	United States	S&P 500	1,098.70
55	Australia	All Ordinaries	3,366.800
78	China	Shanghai Composite	1,562.688
63	Hong Kong	Hang Seng	11,276.86
66	India	BSE 30	5,069.87

Data Channel 2			
25	Indonesia	Jakarta Composite	722.709
28	Japan	Nikkei 225	10,849.63
17	Malaysia	KLSE Composite	793.97
81	New Zealand	NZSE 50	2,564.730
85	Pakistan	Karachi 100	5,454.69
22	Philippines	PSE Composite	1,521.61
23	Singapore	Straits Times	1,754.96
27	South Korea	Seoul Composite	768.46
31	Sri Lanka	All Share	1,321.19
35	Thailand	SET	609.72

Data Channel 3			
46	Taiwan	Taiwan Weighted	5,777.32
50	Austria	ATX	1,798.41
54	Belgium	BEL-20	2,391.09
57	Czech Republic	PX50	750.80
76	Denmark	KFX	252.53
82	France	CAC 40	3,603.26
15	Germany	DAX	3,803.10
56	Italy	MIBTel	20,513.000
40	Netherlands	AEX General	327.39
45	Norway	OSE All Share	327.39

Fig. 2. Global Index Model

When being broadcast, each physical pointer to the neighbouring leaf node as well as actual data item are replaced by a time value, which indicates when the leaf node or data item will be broadcast. Global index scheme is partitioned into a number of channels and each channel has some degree of replication. Each index channel has a different part of the entire index structure, and the overall structure of the entire index is still preserved. As such, Global indexing scheme has the same behaviour as single channel system. Global index is exhibited in Figure 2. Further details on Global Index model can be found in [12]. Query processing in this scheme can be described as follows:

- Mobile client tunes in one of the index channel (i.e. can be of any index channel).
- Mobile client follow the index pointer to the right index key. The pointer may lead to another index channel that contains the relevant index. While waiting for the index to arrive, mobile clients can switch to doze mode.
- Mobile client tunes back on at the index segment that has the right index key, which point to the data channel that contains the desired data item. It indicates a time value of the data to arrive in the data channel.
- Mobile client tunes into the relevant data channel, and switch back to doze mode while waiting for the data item to come.
- Mobile client switches back to active mode just before the desired data item arrives, and retrieves the required items.

3.3 Data Placement Scheme

Let us denote $D = \{d_1, d_2 \ldots d_m\}$, which is a set of data items to be broadcast in the server, and Q as a set of queries $\{Q_1, Q_2, \ldots, Q_n\}$. In this case, we assume the data item has an equal size and the order of the retrieval can be arbitrary, which means if any of the required data by Q_i arrives in the channel, it will be retrieved first. Each query, Q_i, accesses a number of data items j, where $j \subset D$. The broadcast channel is indicated by C, and the length of the broadcast cycle in a channel is given by BC. We denote the broadcast schedule as $S = \{d_x, d_y, \ldots d_z\}$. Similarly, the broadcast program for each channel is defined by SC.

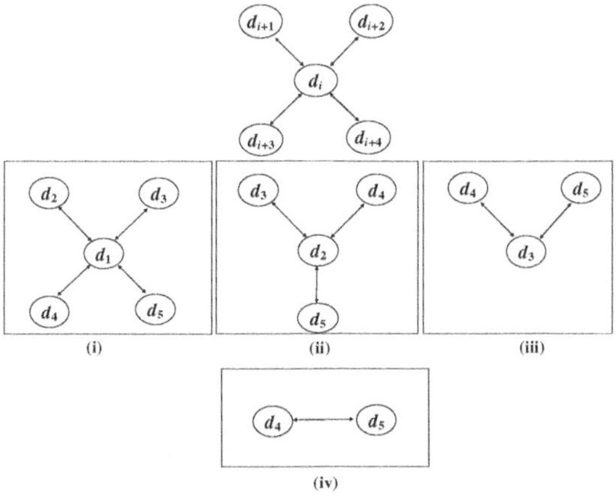

Fig. 3. The architecture of the proposed method

The mechanism of our proposed scheme is divided into three stages.

- *Firstly*, we calculate the access frequency of each data item given by Q. Subsequently, the data items will be sorted in decreasing order of value of access frequency. The result will be temporarily stored in *ST1*, and incorporated into the final broadcast order S after the second stage is finalized. The algorithm of this stage is given in Figure 4 (a).

- *Secondly*, the relationship between one data item and the other will be analyzed. The access frequency of each data item in relation with other data item will be assessed from given *Q*. This stage is required to allocate the related data items close to each other. Thus, the number of calculation required for this purpose will be $\frac{m\times(m-1)}{2}$, *m* is the total number of data items in *D*. Figure 4 illustrates this stage. It shows that each data item to be broadcast will be analyzed for its relationship with other data item based on *Q*. The calculation is done in sequence basis. *i* in Figure 3 reads the data item number. This process iterates until each data item has been counted. A single process includes two ways relationship of the data. Figure 3 also depicts an example when there is 5 number of data items to be broadcast.
  Each data item will be counted for its relationship with the next sequence of the data item from given *Q*. The double point arrows indicate two ways relationship of the two data. In this case, $D = \{d_1, d_2, d_3, d_4, d_5\}$, we count the frequency of the two data items, which appear at the same time in a query. Started from d_1, which is counted towards the relation with the next sequences of the data item that is d_2, d_3, d_4, d_5. This process continues sequentially until *m*-1 data item. After all data item has been analysed, they are sorted in non-increasing order based on the access frequency with other data item, and stored in *ST2*. Each allocation will involve two data items. If there is a duplication of data item within *ST2*, then data item with the highest *ST2* value are kept and the rests are removed. Figure 4 (b) shows the algorithm of the second stage.

- The *final stage* is to combine *ST1* and *ST2* forming a single broadcast order *S*. We start with allocating the data item in *ST2* into *S* also in non-increasing order. This process continues until just one access frequency left to be processed. Subsequently, we take the result from the *ST1*, analyse it against *S*, the data item in *ST1* that has existed in *S* will be discarded. The left over data item is put into *S* with non-increasing order as well. The broadcast order is then allocated over multiple channels. Assuming the required number of data items for each channel is known, which is indicated by *BC*. Once the *BC* is reached, the subsequent data items will be broadcast in another channel. We can employ our previous work in [11] to determine the optimum number of data items in broadcast channel. The algorithm of this mechanism is given in Figure 4 (c).

Having known the broadcast order enable us to determine the sequence of data items that minimize the average access time. The next issue to consider is to specify the broadcast program. The broadcast program indicates the schedule of the first item in *S* at the broadcast cycle, and the sequential items follow the order that has been generated. To achieve the most effective broadcast program, one must note the statistical patterns of users start listening or probing into the channel. In this paper, we assume the pattern follows the behavior of Gaussian distribution. We allocate the broadcast order *SC* and *SIC* into the program, where the first item in each *SC* and *SIC* is placed at point 2/3 in the broadcast program. The point is chosen to minimize the chance of clients missing the data of interest and have to wait for the subsequent

Algorithm 1. Broadcast Ordering Algorithm – Stage 1

Input: An array of data items (D), queries (Q_i) with their related data items (j_i), and the total number of data items to be broadcast (m).
Output: An array of broadcast program ($ST1$)
Procedure:
1. Initialise $i = 1$, $T = 0$
2. **Do while** i: m
3. **For** $n = 1$ to Q_{max}
4. Count the frequency of d_i in Q_n
5. Store and cumulate the result in temporary variable T
6. **If** Q_{max} then
7. $ST1_{(i)} = T$
8. Clear T
9. **End if**
10. **Next** n
11. increment i
12. **Loop**
13. Check the largest value in $ST1$
14. Ordered the value $ST1$ such that $ST1\ (1) \geq ST1\ (2) \geq \ldots \geq ST1\ (m)$
15. **End Procedure**

(a) First Stage Algorithm

Algorithm 2. Broadcast Ordering Algorithm – Stage 2

Input: An array of data items (D), queries (Q_i) with their related data items (j_i), and the total number of data items (m).
Output: Array of broadcast program ($ST2$).
Procedure:
1. Initialise i = 1, $T = 0$
2. **Do while** $i < m$
3. **For** $k = (i + 1)$ to m
4. **For** $n = 1$ to Q_{max}
5. Count the frequency of d_i retrieved at the same time
6. with d_k in Q_n
7. Store and cumulate the result in temporary variable T
8. **If** Q_{max} then
9. $TDarray\ (d_i, d_k) = T$
10. Clear T
11. **End if**
12. **Next** n
13. **Next** k
14. increment i
15. **Loop**
16. Check the largest value in $TDarray$
17. Ordered the value in $TDarray$ from the largest to the smallest value such that $TDarray\ (1) \geq TDarray\ (2) \geq \ldots \geq TDarray\ (\max)$
18. The coordinate value for each $TDarray$ determine the data item
19. Place the coordinate value for each $TDarray$ to $ST2$ with the non-increasing order Check for any duplicate data item within $TDarray$. Data item can only appear one for each cycle. Thus, in case there is any duplication, data item with the highest $TDarray$ value are kept and the rests are removed.
20. **End Procedure**

(b) Second Stage Algorithm

Algorithm 3. Broadcast Ordering Algorithm – Stage 3

Input: Two arrays of Broadcast schedule ($ST1$ *and* $ST2$), optimum length of broadcast cycle in a channel (BC)
Output: An array of Final Broadcast program (S), two dimensional array of broadcast program for each channel (SC)
Procedure:
1. **For** $i = 1$ to $ST2_{(max)}$
2. Move $ST2_{(i)}$ to S
3. **Next** i
4. **For** $i = 1$ to $ST1_{(max)}$
5. Check if $ST1_{(i)}$ exists in S
6. **If** $ST1_{(i)} \subset S$ then
7. skip
8. **Else**
9. Move $ST1_{(i)}$ to S_{max+1}
10. **End if**
11. **Next** i
12. Let channel number = x
13. Initialise $x = 1$, $i = 1$, $j = 1$, $k = 1$
14. **Do While** i : $S_{(max)}$
15. **If** k : BC
16. $SC(x, j) = S(i)$
17. increment j
18. **Else**
19. **if** $k > BC$ then
20. $k = 1$; $j = 1$
21. $x = x + 1$
22. **End if**
23. **End** if
24. increment i
25. increment k
26. **Loop**
27. **End Procedure**

(c) Third Stage Algorithm

Fig. 4. Broadcast Ordering algorithms

cycle. With this way, majority of requests are served within a single broadcast cycle. Although this means about 50% of requests have to wait for a short time period but the overall performance will be better since only a fraction of requests need to wait for the next cycle. The broadcast program can then be generated at a regular interval.

4 Performance Evaluation

In this section, we analyze the performance of our proposed method in two cases. In the *first* case, we compare the proposed method against conventional ordering scheme. In this conventional scheme, the data items are ordered and broadcasted based on the access frequency without considering the relationship with other data items. The first case concerns with the access time performance. The *second* case relates to determining the tuning time of Global index and non-global index. In this last case, we also calculate the average power consumption of mobile clients for listening to the channel.

Table 1. Parameters of Concern

Parameters	Value
Size of each data Item	2KB
Bandwidth	64Kbps
Query Patterns/Profiles	10
Number of Dependent Items in Query	1-4
Number of Broadcast Channel	3
Number of Broadcast Data Items	30 and 45
Number of Request	30
Global Index	
Node Pointer Size	5 bytes
Data Pointer Size	5 bytes
Indexed Attribute Size	4 bytes
Index Arrival Rate	4 index nodes per sec

In this evaluation, we use the same data and indexing scenario as illustrated in Figure 2. The index structure is broadcasted following a breadth-first order. To analyse the schemes, we develop a simulation model. The simulation is carried out using two software packages namely Visual Basic 6.0 and *Planimate* or animated planning platforms [10]. The prototype of our system has been reported in [14]. The simulation environment is set to apply exponential distribution for data and index inter-arrival rate given an average value. In the query profile, we consider request that return one and up to four numbers of items. The parameters of concern are given in Table 1. The channel bandwidth is set to 64Kbps which follows the EDGE standard.

4.1 Access Time

Case 1: This case compares the proposed method with a conventional data ordering method as presented in [9].

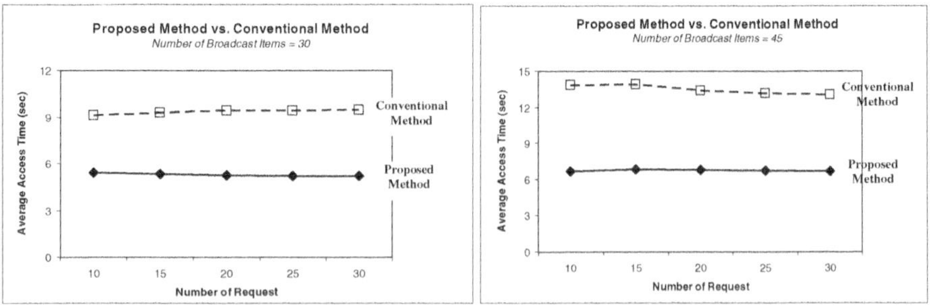

(a) Proposed Method vs. Conventional Method: 30 broadcast items

(b) Proposed Method vs. Conventional Method: 45 broadcast items

Fig. 5. Proposed Method vs. Conventional Method

The conventional ordering scheme relates to the basic ordering scheme that allocates the data items in the channel according to the access frequency in a non-decreasing order and the entire index structure is broadcast within an index channel. Two analyses are also considered, which involve 30 and 45 number of broadcast items. In Figure 5, we can see clearly that the proposed method provides a better access than the conventional method with about one and half times lower access time. A similar trend occurs when the number of broadcast items increased (refer to Figure 5 (b). It is shown, that the increase of broadcast items severely affects the conventional method. In the contrary, the access time of our proposed scheme with Global Index rises just a few seconds or can be considered as minor increase. Consequently, the gap between our proposed method and conventional method is getting larger.

4.2 Tuning Time

Case 2: This case relates to comparing the tuning time of our Global index with non-global index scheme. Non-global index refers as a conventional index broadcasting method, which utilizes a single broadcast channel to broadcast the index structure. Tuning time defines the amount of time clients must listen to the channel to retrieve the desired data instances. The analysis involves 30 numbers of broadcast items. As exhibited in Figure 6 (a), the tuning time of mobile clients accessing our Global index is far less than the non-global index scheme. More importantly, the result also indicates that clients spend much less power consumptions during query operation with Global indexing scheme.

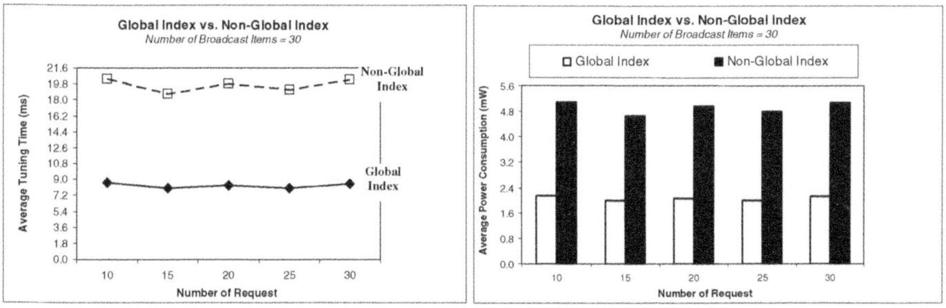

Fig. 6. Tuning time and Power Consumption: Global vs. Non-Global Index

According to Imielinski et al [3] a device with Hobbit chip (AT&T) requires about 250mW power consumption during active mode, and 50μW during power saving mode. Thus, we can see that the duration of clients' listening and not listening to the channel has affected the power consumption. We measure the power consumption of mobile clients based on the duration of active mode and power saving mode that has been obtained from the simulations. The calculation is determined from the following formula:

Power Consumption = (250 x *Time during active mode*) + (0.05 x *Time during power saving mode).* As depicted in Figure 6 (b), the power consumption of clients accessing the Global index is substantially less than non-global index. With little power consumptions, client can reserve battery power more efficiently, which is very much desirable considering the lack of resources in mobile devices.

5 Conclusions and Future Work

In this paper, we have presented Global indexing with data placement scheme for multi broadcast channel environment. We have developed a simulation model to analyze the performance of our proposed scheme. We compare the proposed scheme with conventional scheme. The analysis includes access time, tuning time and power consumption. It is found that the proposed scheme provides substantially better performances in every aspect of evaluation.

For future work, we will incorporate a certain degree of data replication in the broadcast program. We will investigate the most effective degree of the replication as well as the structure and scheduling of the broadcast program.

References

1. Adya A., Bahl P., Qiu L., "Analyzing the Browse Patterns of Mobile Clients" In *Proc. of the 1st ACM SIGCOMM Workshop on Internet Measurement*, pp.189-194, 2001.
2. Barbara D., "Mobile Computing and Databases-A Survey", *IEEE TKDE*, **11**(1):108-117, 1999.
3. Imielinski T., Viswanathan S. and Badrinath B. R., "Data on Air: Organisation and Access", *IEEE TKDE*, **9**(3): 353-371, 1997.
4. Imielinski T., Viswanathan S. and Badrinath B. R., "Energy Efficient Indexing on Air", In *Proc. of the ACM Sigmod Conference*, pp.25-36, 1994.
5. Lee K. C. K., Leong H. V. and Si A., "Semantic Data Access in an Asymmetric Mobile Environment", In *Proc .of the 3rd Mobile Data Management*, pp.94-101, 2002.
6. Leong H. V. and Si A., "Data Broadcasting Strategies Over Multiple Unreliable Wireless Channels", In *Proc. of the 4th CIKM*, pp.96-104, 1995.
7. Myers B.A. and Beigl M., "Handheld Computing", *IEEE Computer Magazine*, **36**(9):27-29, 2003.
8. Paulson L.D.,"Will Fuel Cells Replace Batteries in Mobile Devices?" *IEEE Computer Magazine*, **36**(11):10-12, 2003.
9. Prabhakara K., Hua K.A, and Jiang N., "Multi-Level Multi-Channel Air Cache Designs for Broadcasting in a Mobile Environment", In *Proc. of the ICDE*, pp. 167-176, 2000.
10. Seeley D. et al, *Planimate^{tm}-Animated Planning Platforms*, InterDynamics Pty Ltd, 1997.
11. Waluyo, A.B., Srinivasan B., Taniar D., "Optimal Broadcast Channel for Data Dissemination in Mobile Database Environment", In *Proc. of the 5th APPT*, pp. 655-664, 2003a.
12. Waluyo, A.B., Srinivasan B., Taniar D., "Global Index for Multi Channels Data Dissemination in Mobile Databases", In *Proc.of the 18th ISCIS*, pp.210-217, 2003b.
13. Waluyo, A.B., Srinivasan, B., and Taniar, D., "Allocation of Data Items for Multi Channel Data Broadcasting in a Mobile Computing Environment ", In *Proc. of the 1st EUC*, pp. 409 – 418, 2004.
14. Waluyo, A.B., Goh, G., Srinivasan, B., and Taniar, D., "On-Building Data Broadcast System in a Wireless Environment, *International Journal of Business Data Communications and Networking*, **1**(4), 14-36, 2005.

An Adaptive Mobile Application Development Framework

Ming-Chun Cheng and Shyan-Ming Yuan

Department of Computer and Information Science, National Chiao Tung University,
1001 Ta Hsueh Rd, Hsinchu 300, Taiwan
{native, smyuan}@cis.nctu.edu.tw

Abstract. Although wireless networks and mobile devices become popular these days, the diversity of mobile devices and unsteadiness of wireless networks still cause software development much trouble. Thus, when developing a mobile application, developers are forced to expose to these problems and to be familiar with these technologies and therefore it will spend a lot of time to write a mobile application. Furthermore, a mobile application often needs to be ported to different platform (for example from Java to .NET) which is also burdensome. In order to overcome these problems, the author proposes an adaptive framework to help developers build mobile application effortlessly and rapidly. The mobile application developed on this framework can run in different devices and operating system, so developers does not need to worry about portability. As a result, a mobile application developed on this framework can enjoy the benefit of "write once, run everywhere, and access any services."

1 Introduction

In the past decade, the computing environment has changed tremendously. The bandwidth of wired network increases from 100M to Giga bps, and wireless networks become more and more popular. People often talk about mobile or pervasive computing, because mobile handheld devices get much more powerful and cheaper.

Accordingly, much ink has been spent on pervasive computing. In fact, it is not really so close to us. Owing to the size and battery consumption, processing powers of handheld devices are still insufficient to replace desktop computers do. In addition, the diversity of the computing environments is also a big trouble. Developers have to consider the differences among them and portability is an important issue. Thus, there are still considerable dilemmas needed to be overcome.

In order to solve the problems, the concept of virtual home environment (VHE) has been proposed by 3GPP. Although a large number of studies have been made on how to achieve VHE, such as MExE, OSA and USAT, little is known about providing an adaptive mobile application development framework by leveraging thin-client computing concept [1][2][3]. X window [17][20] and web technologies [4][5][6][7][8][9] are classic samples of thin-client computing. Nevertheless, the previous lacks support for handheld devices and the later lacks better interactions with end-users.

L.T. Yang et al. (Eds.): EUC 2005, LNCS 3824, pp. 765 – 774, 2005.

The aim of this paper is to design and implement a mobile application development framework capable of supporting heterogeneous environments, and the system is called ART. The main idea is to divide an application into two parts, UI and logic, in development time and run time. This idea makes development easier and adaptation possible. Hence, in this framework, the same application could be written once and used everywhere and developers have not to consider portability.

The rest of this paper is organized as following. In the next chapter, system architecture is introduced. Next, adaptation mechanisms are presented in chapter 3 and the workflow of the development process is illustrated in chapter 4. Finally, chapter 5 shows conclusions and future works.

2 System Architecture

First of all, we have to explain the scenario how end-users put our system to use. End-users might own not only desktop computers but also several mobile devices, such as WAP phone, Java-enabled handset, Smart phone, PDA and so on. When outdoors, they probably need some resources or continuing some programs on their desktops and might wish to control appliances, i.e. TV, air conditioner and light, through their mobile devices also. According to the previous scenario, the authors leverage a 3-tiers architecture to fit these requirements. It includes front-tier, middle-tier and backend-tier; it is represented diagrammatically in Fig.1.

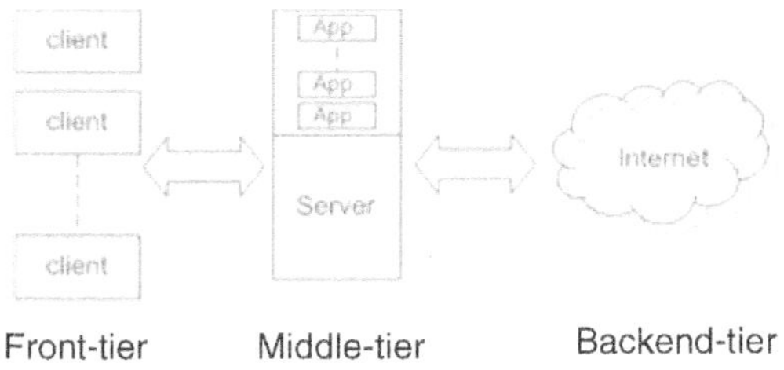

Fig. 1. The 3-tiers architecture

In this architecture, end-users use their own mobile devices or desktops in front-tier to access resources provided by applications run in middle-tier. In addition, the applications might access third-party services, e.g. X10, UPnP and web services [21], in backend-tier by calling some system services provided by server.

According the 3-tier architecture, ART system is designed as a client-server model, shown in Fig.2, and participates in the two tiers of the architecture, front-tier and middle-tier. Client run in front-tier is responsible for user interface as well as server run in middle-tier is responsible for logic computing. They communicate with each other by using asynchronous message delivery mechanism (the top part of the Fig.2) or other existent protocols (the bottom part of the Fig. 2), for example HTTP. In other words, this model could be viewed as a thin-client computing with adaptive capability. This section will present individual parts first and then introduce how they cooperate with each others. In order to simplify terminologies, in ART system, the server is called ARTServer, the client is called ARTClient, and the application is called ARTApp.

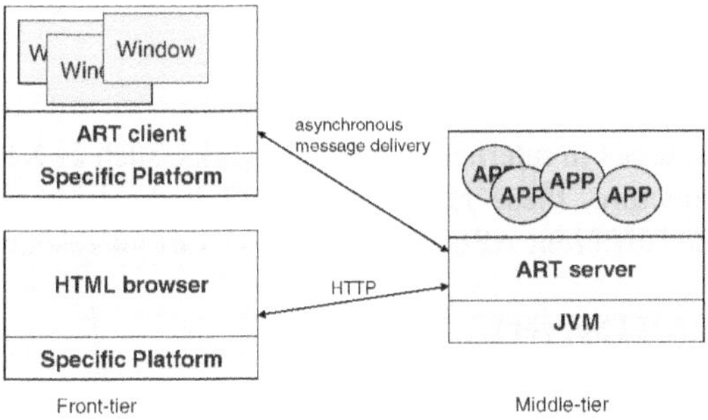

Fig. 2. The client-server model in ART system

2.1 Asynchronous Message Delivery Mechanism

Since wireless networks are not stable enough, the authors designed an asynchronous message delivery mechanism for transmission between ARTServer and ARTClient. This mechanism decouples the ARTApp and low-level network protocols, so it can help ARTServer to handle the situation of disconnection and prevents ARTApp from accessing network directly. Besides, this mechanism provides the communication capability among ARTApps also and it supports one-to-one, one-to-many and many-to-many modes. The four main components in this mechanism are ARTMesg, Queue, Message Dispatcher and Daemon Thread. ARTMesg is a message which carries some information about source, destination, command, request and user etc. For example, when user presses a button in client-side or ARTApp orders the client-side to create a new UI widget, the corresponding ARTMesg will be generated and then routed to correct place. Moreover, Queue is a data structure capable of storing and aggregating the ARTMesg. Finally, Message Dispatcher and Daemon Thread are both working threads which route or forward the ARTMesgs put in the Queue. The details will be described in section 2.4.

2.2 ARTApp

The applications which comply with ART Programming Framework run on ARTServer are called ARTApp and they might provide different services for ARTClient, e.g. search engine, appliance controller, or games. In development time, an ARTApp is separated into two parts, UI and logic, to cut down the development time. ART system leverages XUL to describe the user interface and exploits Java Language to write the logic part. The details about how to write an ARTApp is presented in Chapter 4.

In Runtime, every ARTApp owns an independent runtime space but they could communicate with others through asynchronous message delivery mechanism

2.4.3 Application Runtime Layer

An ARTServer can serve many different ARTClients at the same time, and each ARTClient can also have many ARTApps run on the server at the same time. Application Manager (AppMngr) is responsible for loading, resuming and stopping ARTApps. Before starting an ARTApp, AppMngr will check if any instance of the ARTApp already exists in the memory. If it does, AppMngr will then check what running mode of the ARTApp is and decide to create a new instance or bind the client to the existent one.

2.5 Front-Tier (ARTClient)

The front-tier part of ART system is called ARTClient which is responsible for presentation. It provides user interface to receive orders from end-users and displays results from middle-tier. In ART system, end-users can use many kinds of devices in front-tier and ART system could automatically tailor results to fit diverse environments. In these days, ART system can support four popular kinds of devices, including J2ME MIDP [12][13][14], .NET CF, WAP and HTML browser. Because of diversity of these devices, authors divide these devices into two categories, agent-based and browser-based, and use different mechanisms to design and implement them.

An ARTClient can access many ARTApp simultaneously, so ART system provides a facility, shown in Fig. 5, like Task Manager within Microsoft Windows XP. It helps end-users to select what ARTApp to start, stop or switch to.

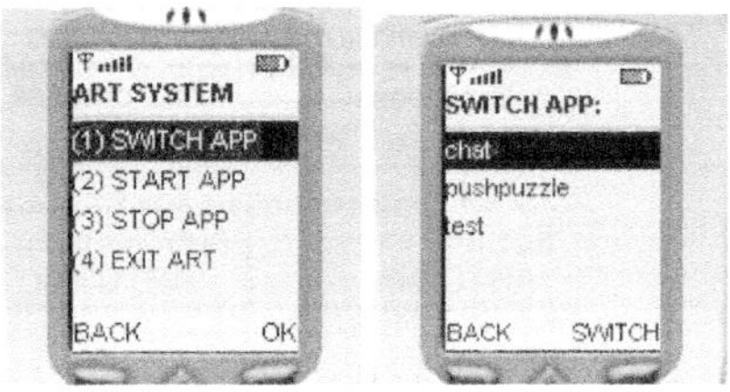

Fig. 5. The screenshot of the task manager within ART system

2.5.1 Agent-Based Client

An agent-based client is defined as a device capable of executing author-developed ARTClient on it. According the definition, it has to provide some programming environments for programmers to develop some programs; nowadays, the most popular programming environments of handheld devices are J2ME MIDP and .NET CF. In order to support both them, two different agent-based clients are implemented and they are all compliant with "ART agent-based client specification".

2.5.2 Browser-Based Client

A browser-based client is defined as a device which is browser enabled. In other words, end-user could use these existent browsers to access many sorts of services in internet. Currently, almost mobile devices are browser enabled. Moreover, owing to adaptive transport layer, ART system can be accessed by these clients.

3 Adaptation Mechanisms

In ART system, adaptation is applied in two positions, network protocols and UI, and both two are implemented in Adaptive Transport Layer. This chapter will introduce how adaptation mechanisms work.

3.1 Network Protocols

Because of diversity of mobile devices, the networks capabilities are not the same. Some devices support TCP connection but some devices might support only HTTP. In order to hide the detailed from mobile application developers, the ARTServer exploits a loosely couple design and the adaptive transport layer is proposed. The layer defines the unified transport interface and the implementation which complies with it could be plugged into ART system easily. At the moment, ART system supports TCP, UDP and HTTP.

3.2 User Interface

In ART system, ARTApp doesn't know what kind of client it servers and it only handles and generates ARTMesgs no matter the type of client. Hence, in order to serve browser-based clients, ART system needs a mechanism to translate ARTMesgs to other formats, such as WML or HTML, and this mechanism is implemented in adaptive transport layer also.

In the section 2.4.1, the CommMngr is introduced and one mission of it is to create a user process for a client. When a client sends login request to ARTServer, CommMngr will analyze CC/PP [11] profile provided by the client. If the client is browser-based, a translator component is within the user process and it is combined with many convert functions and a layout manager.

Every convert function has different capability to translate a XUL [10] widget to the corresponding widget of other formats. Table 1 is a widget mapping among XUL, MIDP and WML.

Table 1. The mapping table among XUL, MIDP and WML

XUL	MIDP	WML
<window>	Form	<wml>+<card>
<canvas>	Canvas	<wml>+<card>+4 direction button+<img src="">
<listbox>	ChoiceGroup	<select>
<button>	Buttom	<a href>
<textbox>	TextField	<input>

The layout manager is similar to WinMngr within agent-based ARTClient but it is capable of arranging the positions of the widgets. Another functionality of layout manager is to call convert functions to translate XUL widgets to specific formats. When serving a browser-based client, ARTMesg does not send to client directly instead of being handled by the layout manager.

4 Programming Framework

This chapter shows how to write an ARTApp. An ARTApp is combined with two different parts, UI and logic, and these two parts could be developed simultaneously by different developers. The development workflow is showed in Fig. 6.

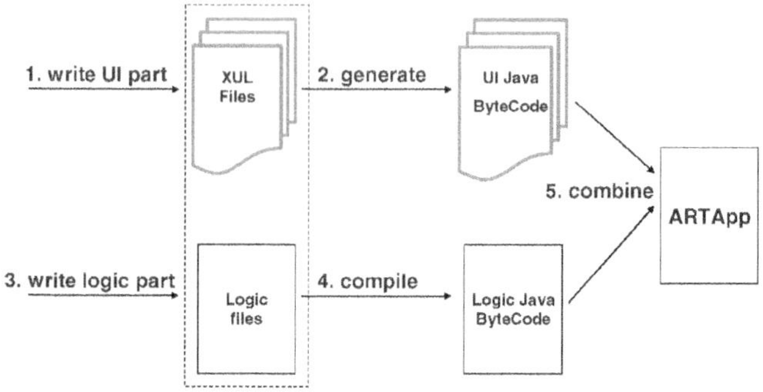

Fig. 6. The application developers have to writes two kinds of files within the dashed box

4.1 Write User Interface Part

In ART system, developers have to use XUL to describe the user interface. Fig. 7 shows a sample; left is a XUL file and right is the presentation result.

When finishing the XUL files, developers use code generator provided by ART system to generate some Java Bytecode and these codes can be used by logic part.

```
<?xml version="1.0"?>
<window id="Example">
        <listbox id="CHOICE" label="Choose one">
                <listitem id="1" label="1"/>
                <listitem id="2" label="2"/>
        </listbox>

        <textbox id="INPUT" label="Input Here"/>
```

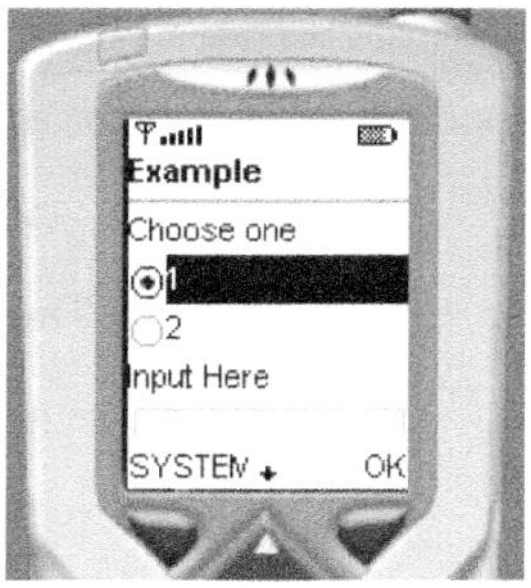

Fig. 7. A sample XUL file and the presentation result

4.2 Write Logic Part

In ART system, Java language is used to write logic part and developers who are familiar with Java have not to learn anything. The only requirement is that the main class of application has to extend the ARTApp class. Fig. 8 shows an example.

```
public class Main extends ARTApp{
    Example window=null;
    public void startApp(){
                //get the reference of the window named "Example"

            window=Example.getInstance();

            //create a listener
            class Listener implements ArtButtonListener{
                    public Listener(){}
                    public void actionPerform(){
                            //change the text of the button named "BUTTON"
                            window.BUTTON.setText("Hello");
                    }
            }

            //register a listener to the button named "BUTTON"
            window.BUTTON.setArtButtonListener(new Listener());
            //bring the window named "Example" to foreground
            window.show();
    }
    public void stopApp(){}
```

Fig. 8. A logic codes written by Java language

5 Conclusions and Future Works

So far, we have described our system, ART system, and how it achieves the objectives mentioned in chapter 1. The key point of design is separating GUI from the application body. Developers write UI descriptions in XUL instead of writing them in program bodies. Then ART will generate the UI objects automatically according to XUL documents. Users can launch numerous applications via a small-size client on mobile devices and ART system will automatically tailor the result to fit different clients.

In the future, the authors hope the agent-based clients could be more powerful. The idea is that ART system can send some scripts to ARTClient and some logics could be run in client-side. This method makes the ART system more flexible and more efficient.

Another issue is how to integrate the services in backend-tier. Currently, the authors are designing a unified interface capable of accessing Jini, UPnP and X10 by a unified method.

References

1. Krikke, J., "Thin clients get second chance in emerging markets", Pervasive Computing, IEEE, Volume 3, Issue 4, Oct-Dec 2004, pp. 6-10
2. Richardson, T., Stafford-Fraser, Q., Wood, K.R., Hopper, A., "Virtual network computing", Internet Computing, IEEE, Volume 2, Issue 1, Jan.-Feb. 1998, pp. 33-38

[18]. Such uncontrollable situations prevent saving the patient in time and waste the social and medical resources [12], [19]. In contrast to a conventional emergency rescue where the EMT person lacks expertise and is unfamiliar with the patient's health history, the EMT person can call doctors at the hospital to obtain treatment suggestions [20]. However, the information from the distance ambulance is insufficient to help doctors make an accurate diagnosis and recommend the appropriate treatment. This uncertainty and lack of instant diagnosis can seriously jeopardize the patient's life [3], [21], [22]

This study proposes a Context-Aware emergeNcy rEmedy system (CANE) to achieve efficient ambulance dispatching and real-time multimedia symptom delivery for emergency rescues. CANE is also a mobile telemedicine system supplying a platform by which the hospital physicians can communicate with the EMT person on the ambulance and give appropriate treatment suggestions to save the patient on the way to the hospital. CANE uses GIS/GPS technologies to achieve the location-base services, which could help the rescue center to dispatch ambulances appropriately for all emergencies [23].

The rest of this study is structured as follows. Section 2 describes the infrastructure and system components of the proposed CANE system. Section 3 describes implementation and the usage of the CANE system. Conclusions are finally drawn in Section 4.

2 System Architecture Design

This section describes the system architecture and components of the CANE system, and the procedure of dispatching ambulances among the patients, the hospital and the rescue center.

2.1 CANE System Architecture

CANE is a three-tier architecture composed of (i) the Front Emergency Point (FEP), (ii) the Emergency Control Center (ECC) and (iii) the Emergency Medical Service Hospital (EMSH). Figure 1 depicts the proposed system architecture. Each subsystem in CANE is described as follows.

1. Front Emergency Point (FEP) subsystem: The FEP subsystem in each ambulance helps the EMT staff to complete emergency operations. The GIS/GPS function of the FEP subsystem helps the ambulance driver find the exact location of the patient and hospital in time. Based on the FEP subsystem, the EMT can send the real-time data about the symptoms, pictures and videos and audios of the patient to the hospital. The doctor at the hospital diagnoses the patient from a distance and gives appropriate treatment suggestions to the EMT staff. To promote the mobility capability of the ambulance and emergency person, Tablet PC and PDA combining mobile communication network, e.g., GPRS, are applied in the FEP subsystem. Because the GPRS bandwidth is limited and critical, the related GIS information is built into the FEP database to reduce the bandwidth consumed.

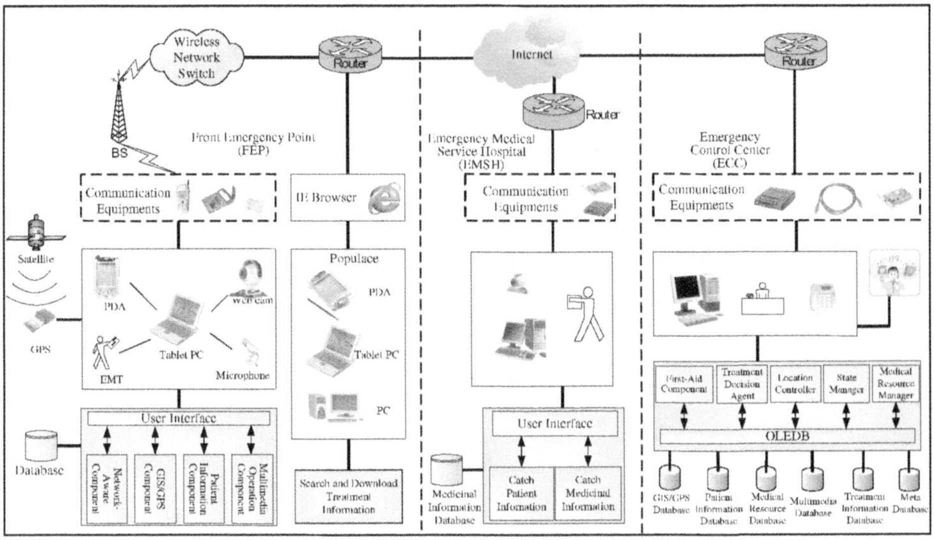

Fig. 1. The CANE system architecture

2. Emergency Control Center (ECC) subsystem: The ECC subsystem coordinates the communications between the FEP and EMSH subsystems. The ECC subsystem constantly collects the information of hospitals' medical resources and ambulances' locations. The context-aware capability of the ECC subsystem can efficiently dispatch ambulances to victims and then to the appropriate hospital, which provides sufficient medical resources and spaces. Based on the proposed dispatching procedure, the ECC subsystem filters the calls for the same incident to prevent multiple ambulances from being dispatched to the same emergency.
3. Emergency Medical Service Hospital (EMSH) subsystem: The EMSH subsystem established in each hospital constantly receives the information of patients' conditions and ambulances' locations. The distance information gives the hospital a head start in assessing the patient and preparing appropriate treatment to ensure successful emergency rescue.

CANE system combines the wire and mobile communication networks to let emergency staff and doctors communicate with each other and help treat the patient. Figure 2 shows the CANE system dispatching process. The operation steps are described as follows.

1. Step 1: ECC subsystem constantly collects the resources of hospitals and the locations/states of ambulances using the messages Inf_A(state, location) and Inf_H(resource).
2. Step 2: When ECC subsystem receives an emergency call and the patient needs an ambulance to carry him to a hospital, the ECC subsystem determines an appropriate ambulance and tells the ambulance to go to the patient's location.
3. Step3: When the EMT staff member in the ambulance receives the message Msg_A(patient information) from the FEP subsystem, he responds by accepting or rejecting the rescue mission to the ECC subsystem via the message ACK_ A (accept, state).

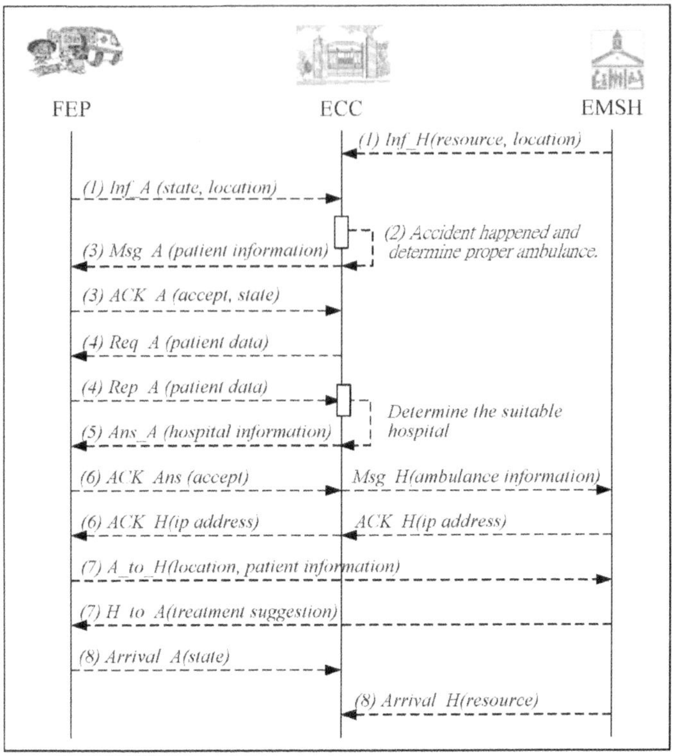

Fig. 2. CANE dispatching process

4. Step 4: The ECC subsystem asks the FEP subsystem to transmit the information of the patient. Therefore, when the ambulance arrives at the accident location, the EMT person transmits the symptoms, including the patient's pictures/videos, from the web cam on a handheld device, to the ECC subsystem.
5. Step 5: The ECC subsystem determines the appropriate hospital according to information received from the FEP subsystem, and directs the ambulance driver.
6. Step 6: When ambulance drivers request to go to the emergency hospital, the ECC subsystem informs the selected hospital and gives the doctors information of the patient. Then, the ECC subsystem establishes a communication channel between the FEP subsystem and the EMSH subsystem, and the EMT staff and doctors can then talk with each other.
7. Step 7: When the communication channel is established between the FEP subsystem and EMSH subsystem, an EMT staff member transmits the patient's symptoms, including pictures, videos and EKG, to doctors at the hospital. Physicians can then immediately diagnose and give appropriate treatment suggestions. Thus, the hospital staff can assess the patient and prepare treatment before the patient arrives.
8. Step 8: When the ambulance arrives at the selected hospital (EMSH subsystem), the FEP subsystem transmits the message Arrival_A(state) to announce that the

first-aid mission is accomplished. The ambulance is thus available to provide assistance on another emergency. The EMSH subsystem also transmits the message Arrival_H(resource) to update the medical resource database in the ECC subsystem. After the appropriate calculation and update, the ECC subsystem can determine an appropriate EMSH subsystem for the next emergency rescue.

2.2 Functionality of CANE System

This sub-section describes the designed functions of the CANE system in detail.

1. Front Emergency Point (FEP) subsystem: FEP provides four main functions, (i) location-aware operations for ambulances, (ii) patient information delivery, (iii) multimedia symptom capability and (iv) network-aware operations. The corresponding system components achieving the four functions are described as follows.
   - The GIS/GPS component provides the location-aware operations for ambulances. This GIS/GPS component obtains the location information from the embedded GPS device. The real-time location information helps the ambulance driver to find the right route quickly.
   - The Patients Information component records the patient information. When the ambulance is on its way to the emergency hospital, the EMT person records the patient information, e.g., personnel information, EKG and blood pressure, and then transmits the collected information to physicians via the mobile network. The information enables hospital staff to start assessing the patient and preparing treatment.
   - The Multimedia Operation component enables symptoms to be depicted using multimedia. The text/voice-based information is usually insufficient to help doctors to perform correct diagnosis and treatment suggestions from a distance. Multimedia symptom information, including pictures and videos of the patient's symptoms, provides doctors with comprehensive information, allowing them to make correct and quick diagnosis and treatment suggestions for the EMT person, and the more preparing time for the doctors themselves, and may make the difference between life and death.
   - The Network-Aware component detects the network connection status. This component ensures stable communication, especially given the large volume requirement of multimedia information and the limited mobile network bandwidth.
2. Emergency Control Center (ECC) subsystem: The ECC subsystem is composed of (i) the First-Aid Information Component, (ii) the Treatment Decision Agent, (iii) the Location Controller, (iv) the Medical Resource Manager and (v) the State Manager.
   - First-Aid Information Component: If the FEP person requires the first-aid information, the FEP person transmits the patient's symptoms to the ECC subsystem. The First-Aid Information Component responds with the first-aid operations to the EMT person. The multimedia database supplies the multimedia

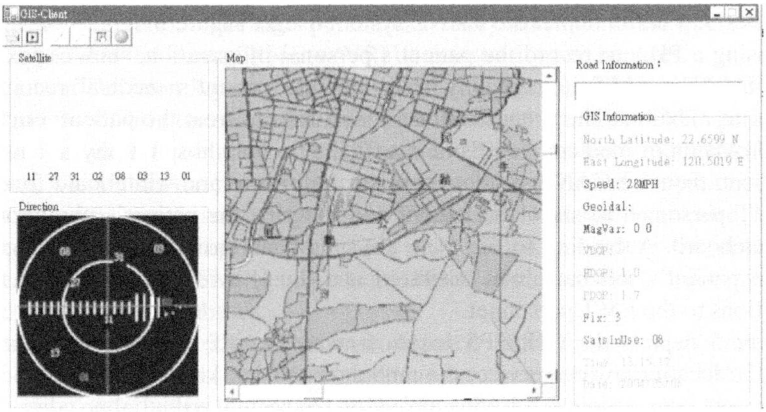

Fig. 5. The GIS on the ambulance

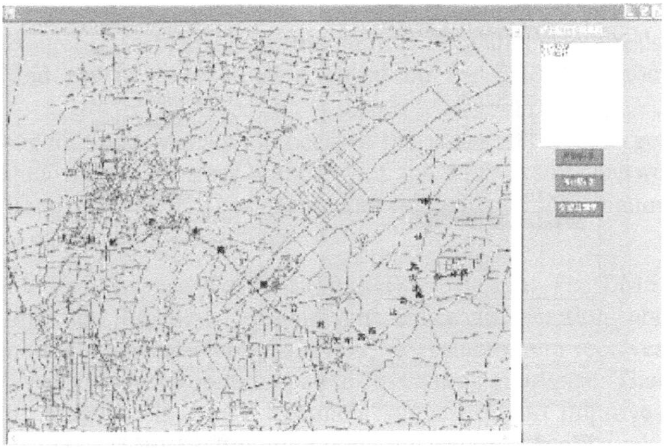

Fig. 6. The ambulance's locations at the Emergency Control Center

signal strength of satellites and the longitude and latitude of current location. When an accident occurs, the staff of the ambulance dispatch center can determine the appropriate ambulance to go to the accident using the functions depicted in Fig. 6. From the functions, the people can understand where the ambulances are and whether they have emergency tasks.

4 Conclusions

The rapidly increasing application of handheld devices and the deployment of mobile communication environment are accelerating the development of pervasive telemedicine services. The proposed CANE system tries to compensate the limitations of conventional emergency medical services, by which the EMT personnel merely inform doctors about patient's symptoms by telephone. CANE improves the efficiency of the emergency remedy using advanced pervasive multimedia techniques. Physicians can make accurate diagnoses and recommend appropriate treatment suggestion to the EMT staff based on the context-aware information, including the real-time multimedia data about the patient's symptoms. The context-aware information helps physicians to diagnose illnesses and gives the hospital staff a head start in assessing the patient and preparing suitable treatment. Real-time pervasive access to the patient is one of the improvement factors in extending lives and lengthening the rescue time. To achieve practical usage in the near future, the researchers are cooperating with a local teaching hospital to refine and verify the effectiveness and value of the CANE system.

Many counties make much of emergency and use a diverse array of information technologies to assist emergency person to complete emergency tasks. However, many emergency staffs think that this approach increases their loads by adding extra equipment in emergency. Moreover, emergency care combining the state-of-art Information technology is required immediately before telemedicine becomes legal in Taiwan.

Acknowledgement

The authors would like to thank the National Science Council of the Republic of China, Taiwan for financially supporting this research under Contract No. NSC 94-2218-E-020 -001.

References

1. Arshad, U., Mascolo, C., and Mellor, M.: Exploiting mobile computing in health-care. Proceeding of the Third International Workshop on Smart Appliance, Vol. 1. (2003) 151-155
2. Miguel, M., Marcela, R., Jesus, F., Ana, I.M., and Victor, M.G.: Context-aware mobile communication in hospitals, Vol. 36. No. 9. IEEE Computer (2003) 38-46
3. Pattichis, S., Kyriacou, E., Voskarides, S., Pattichis, M.S., Lstepanian, R., and Schizas, C.N.: Wireless telemedicine systems: an overview, Vol. 44. No. 2. IEEE Antennas and Propagation Magazine (2002) 143-153
4. Satyanarayanan, M.: Pervasive computing: vision and challenges, Vol. 8. No.4. IEEE Personal Communications (2001) 10-17
5. Baker, B.: East meets west to cure healthcare ills using information technology. Proceedings of The Digital Hospital Medical Information Systems. (2004) 117-128
6. Choudhri, Kagal, L., Joshi, A., Finin, T., and Yesha, Y.: PatientService: electronic patient record redaction and delivery in pervasive environments. Proceedings of 5th International Workshop on Enterprise Networking and Computing in Healthcare Industry. (2003) 41-47
7. Znati, T.: On the challenges and opportunities of pervasive and ubiquitous computing in health care. Third IEEE International Conference on Pervasive Computing and Communications (PerCom 2005). (2005) 396-396
8. Basharat, Catbas, N., and Mubarak, S.: A framework for intelligent sensor network with video camera for structural health monitoring of bridges. Third IEEE International Conference on Pervasive Computing and Communications Workshops (PerCom 2005). (2005) 385-389

9. Perry, M., Dowdall, A., Lines, L., and Hone, K.: Multimodal and ubiquitous computing systems: supporting independent-living older users, Vol. 8. No. 3. IEEE Transactions on Information Technology in Biomedicine (2004) 258-270
10. Abowd, G.D., Mynatt, E.G., and Rodden, T.: The human experience, Vol. 1. No. 1. IEEE Pervasive Computing (2002) 48-57
11. Anand R., Roy H.C., and Anupama M.: ConChat: A context-aware chat program, Vol. 1. No. 3. IEEE Pervasive Computing (2002) 51-57
12. Paolo, Antonio, C., and Cersare, S.: The ubiquitous provisioning of internet services to portable devices, Vol. 1. No. 3. IEEE Pervasive Computing (2002) 81-87
13. Miyamoto, M., Mako, M., Kimura, M., and Kanno, T.: Great eqrthquakes and medical information systems, Vol. 6. Journal of American Medical Informatics Association (JSMIA) (1999) 252-258
14. Delp, S.L., Loan, P., Basdogan, C., Rosen, J.M.: Surgical simulation: An emerging technology for training in emergency medicine, Vol. 6. No. 2. Journal of Virtual Environments in Medicine (1997) 11-29
15. Moore S.K.: Extending healthcare's reach, Vol. 39. No. 1. IEEE Spectrum (2002) 66–71
16. Razzak, J.A. and Kellermann, A.L.: Emergency medical care in developing countries: is it worthwhile, Vol. 80. No. 11. Bulletin of the World Health Organization (2002) 900-905
17. Derekenaris, G., Garofalakis, J., Makris, C., Prentzas, J., Sioutas, S., and Tsakalidis, A.: An information system for the effective management of ambulances. Proceedings of 13th IEEE Symposium on Computer-Based Medical Systems (CBMS'00) (2000) 269-274
18. Helal, S., Winkler, B., Lee, C., Kaddoura, Y., Ran, L., Giraldo, C., Kuchibhotla, S., and Mann, W.: Enabling location-aware pervasive computing applications for the elderly. Proceedings of the First IEEE International Conference on Pervasive Computing and Communications (PerCom 2003) (2003) 531-536
19. Schepps, J. and Rosen, A.: Microwave industry outlook – wireless communications in healthcare, Vol. 50. No. 3. IEEE Transactions on Microwave Theory and Techniques (2002) 1044-1045
20. Lakshmi Narasimhan, V., Irfan, M., and Yefremov, M.: MedNet: a pervasive patient information network with decision support. Proceedings of 6th International Workshop on Enterprise Networking and Computing in Healthcare Industry. (2004) 96-101
21. Varshney, U.: Pervasive healthcare, Vol. 36. No. 12. IEEE Computer (2003) 138-140
22. Mynatt, D., Melenhorst, A.S., Fisk, A.D., and Rogers, W.A.: Aware technologies for aging in place: understanding user needs and attitudes, Vol. 3. No. 2. IEEE Pervasive Computing (2004) 36-41
23. Jakob: Hospitals of the future: ubiquitous computing support for medical work in hospitals. Proceeding of the 2nd International Workshop on Ubiquitous Computing for Pervasive Healthcare Applications (UbiHealth 2003) (2003) 171-175.

Design and Implementation of Interactive Contents Authoring Tool for MPEG-4

Hsu-Yang Kung, Che-I Wu, and Jiun-Ju Wei

Department of Management Information Systems,
National Pingtung University of Science and Technology, Pingtung, Taiwan
{kung, joey, m9156021}@mail.npust.edu.tw

Abstract. This paper proposed and implemented a QoS-Aware MPEG-4 authoring tool with provision of content interaction control, which is named the Q4AT system. Q4AT provides friendly user interface in a WYSWYG manner for users to create their favorite MPEG-4 scenes. The characteristics of Q4AT are as follows. (i) The description of a scene is based on the standard BIFS language. (ii) The creation of the object description is based on the syntactic description language (SDL). (iii) All descriptions are VRML-based. A VRML-based system is compatible to different browsers and operation systems. Therefore, the author could simplify the steps of creating an MPEG-4 scene. (iv) Q4AT supports the functions of the quality of service by the proposed object priority differentiation control. Using Q4AT, authors are transparent to the MPEG-4 processing layers and are capable of concentrating on the editing function usage of the Q4AT. Q4AT makes it possible to easily create a complicated MPEG-4 scene and reduce the difficulty of MPEG-4 media creation and presentation.

1 Introduction

MPEG-4 is a compression standard developed by ISO/IEC MPEG (Moving Picture Experts Group) and is totally different from MPEG-1/2. MPEG-4 standard improves the efficiency of media compression and tries to provide the applications integrating multimedia, communications, and computers [1]. The fundamental infrastructure of MPEG-4 is object-oriented and media operations (presentations) described in an MPEG-4 scene [2], [3]. An MPEG-4 scene combines the object descriptions of natural and synthetic media objects, e.g., the text, image, 3D, audio, and video objects, which can be manipulated by interaction operations [4], [5], [6]. To achieve a user-oriented MPEG-4 scene presentation, a user friendly MPEG-4 authoring tool is urgently required [7], [8]. Using a well-design authoring tool, a film maker could dynamically change the structure of an MPEG-4 scene to achieve the desired presentation contents [9], [10].

In the paper, we proposed and implemented a QoS-Aware MPEG-4 authoring tool with provision of content interaction control (Q4AT). Q4AT is developed using VC++, OpenGL, and VRML languages. *Q4AT* uses the standard BIFS language and the syntactic description language (SDL) to create the descriptions of a scene and the

L.T. Yang et al. (Eds.): EUC 2005, LNCS 3824, pp. 785 – 794, 2005.

2.1.2 OpenGL Device

OpenGL Device translates and displays all editing actions of a scene author. Figure 4 illustrates the display result after editing media object using OpenGL Device. An author can change the coordination and view points of objects. When the properties of objects are changed, OpenGL Device re-displays the modified object at the same time.

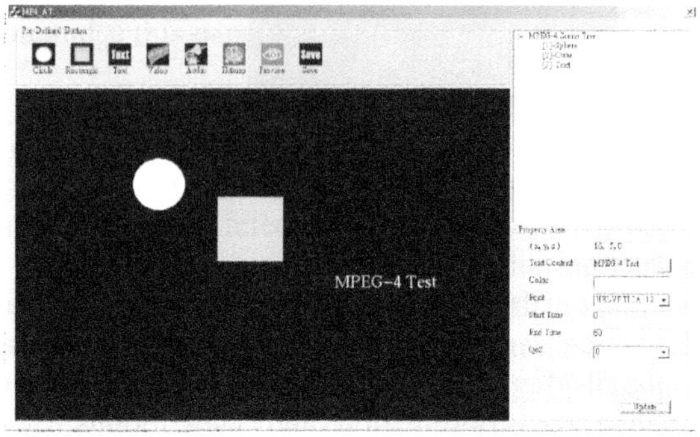

Fig. 4. A display example using OpenGL Device

2.1.3 Property Area

Property Area provides different objects of an MPEG-4 scene with the assignment of object attributes. Different objects may have same properties, e.g., color assignment, spatial/temporal values, and QoS priority, and also have heterogeneous properties, e.g., text font, encoding types of audio/video files, and sphere radius. The Property Area displays the designed object properties and gives the author the limitation of authority for editing different kind of media objects. OpenGL Device directly renders the modification of objects. Figure 5-(a) and -(b) illustrates a dialog example of using Property Area for specifying the attributes of a sphere object and a text object, respectively. In Property Area, some fields for specifying an object are changeable and some files are not. An author can modify the attribute files of a sphere object, including innerRadius, outerRadius, insides, rings, color and QoS.

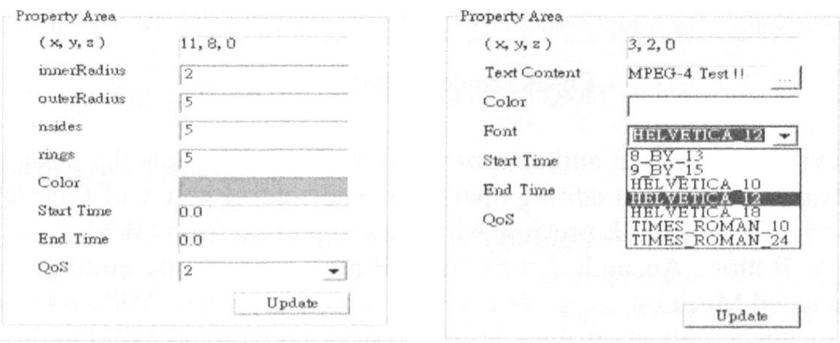

(a) (b)

Fig. 5. The dialog windows of Property Area for (a) sphere object and (b) text object

2.1.4 Preview Window

Scene Tree Structure Area displays the tree structure of an MPEG-4 scene, which illustrates the detailed information about media objects, including the object id, the object name, the object type, and the temporal/spatial relationship between other media objects. Figure 6 depicts the functions of Scene Tree Structure Area and is described as follow.

(i). As an author uses Pre-define Button to add a medium object on OpenGL Device, Scene Tree Structure Area creates the corresponding tree node. A node of the scene tree contains the object information, e.g., object ID and object type.

(ii). When an author clicks a node of Scene Tree Structure Are, Property Area displays its properties to set attribute values of the node, i.e., the medium object.

(iii). An author can drag a node of scene tree to change the relationship between other nodes. To ensure the attribute consistence between tree nodes, Q4AT automatically monitors the legality of scene objects to prevent some violation situations.

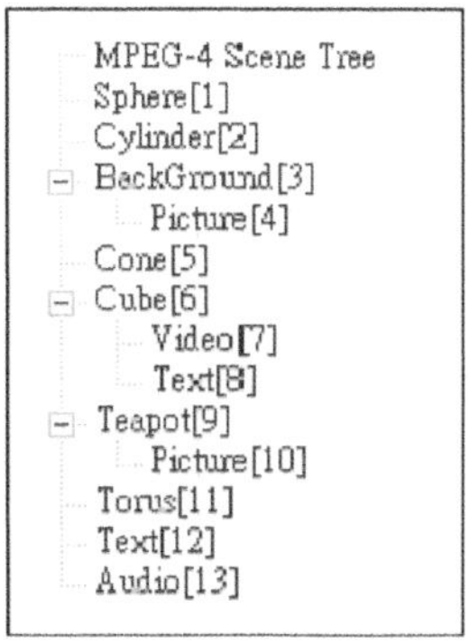

Fig. 6. An illustration example of Scene Tree Structure Area

2.1.5 Preview Window

Preview Window is a pop-up window for scene authors to preview the results of scene realization. Preview Window was manipulated via VRML. Using VRML, the problem that OpenGL Device can't integrate with the video objects is solved. Furthermore, VRML supports the capability of content interaction. A scene author is capable of dynamically and conveniently adjusting the status of a scene in a WYSWYG manner.

2.2 Q4AT Function Component

The Q4AT Function component is responsible for executing and realizing the authoring actions. All authoring actions can be considered as the transmission of action messages between Q4AT Function component and the author i.e., Editing Board component. The Q4AT Function is mainly composed of the Authoring Action Collector, Object Property Controller, BIFS File Translator, VRML Translator, and MP4 File Generator, which provide an author with a transparent environment to easily create a desired MPEG-4 presentation. We describe the main control modules as follows.

(i). Authoring Action Collector gathers the editing actions of a scene author and sends editing actions to Q4AT Manager. Q4AT Manager distributes actions messages to the related Editors to manipulate media object.
(ii). Object Property Controller gets action messages, including the adding, deleting, properties modification, refreshing actions, from the Q4AT Manager. Then, Object Property Controller transmits the gathering messages to OpenGL Device and BIFS File Translator for the displaying and translation of a scene.
(iii). BIFS File Translator detects changes of object properties and keeps up the latest properties prepared for VRML Translator and MP4 File Generator. The main purpose of BIFS File Translator is to create the scene description and object description of MPEG-4 standard, and then generates the BIFS file.
(iv). VRML Translator gets the BIFS file from BIFS File Translator and translates the BIFS file into the formats of VRML syntax used for Preview Window.
(v). The main function of MP4 File Generator is to build the standard MPEG-4 file (.mp4). MP4 File Generator gathers all media files of the corresponding media objects and packs the media files with scene/object description into a standard MPEG-4 file.

3 Usage of Q4AT

The steps of realizing an MPEG-4 scene are to add media objects into a scene, to modify the properties of objects, to preview the authoring results, and to finally save the editing results. Figure 7 illustrates an example of editing an MPEG-4 scene using Q4AT. Figure 7-(a) shows the authoring results of adding two objects into OpenGL Device. A scene author uses mouse to easily drag media objects in a scene and to change their spatial attributes or viewpoint. An author uses Scene Tree Structure Area to add a corresponding node at the same time. There are two ways to modify the properties of a medium object. (i) An author can use the mouse to click the object in OpenGL Device. Or, (ii) an author clicks the node of Scene Tree Structure Area to modify the properties of the node. These two actions will trigger the Object Property Area to display corresponding properties of nodes, and then scene author modifies the changeable attributes in Object Property Area and change the attribute values directly. Note that not all properties in Object Property Area are modifiable, for example, the spatial value of a medium object is unchangeable. Figure 7-(b) depicts the color dialog for modifying the colors of an object. Figure 7-(c) shows the timeline dialog for editing the start/end time of a medium object. OpenGL Device displays all modifications in real-time for the scene author.

Due to the critical limitation of integrating video objects by using OpenGL, Q4AT uses a 2-D rectangle to express a video object and provides VRML Preview Window to solve the problem of OpenGL. Furthermore, the designed interaction functions are useful and convenient for scene authors to adjust the deployment of scene objects by using VRML. Figure 79-(d) shows the display example of a video object in OpenGL Device. Figure 7-(e) illustrates the preview result of using VRML Preview Window to preview the deployment of scene objects.

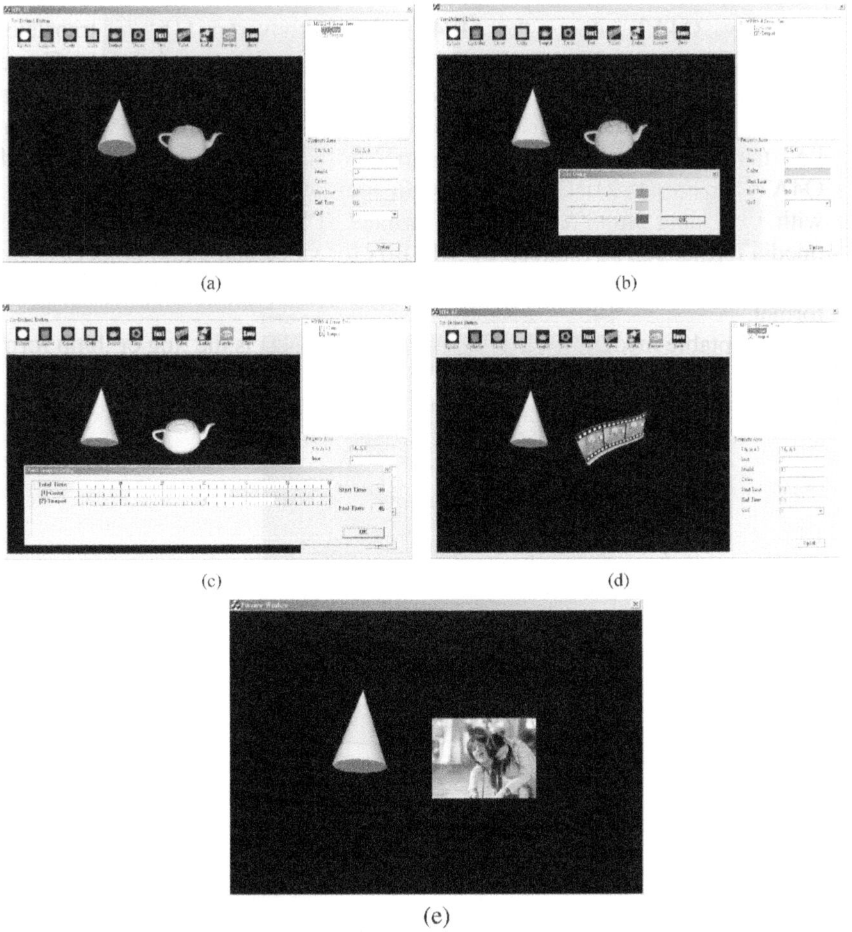

Fig. 7. (a) Adding two media objects. (b) A Color dialog. (c) A TimeLine dialog. (d) Adding video object into a scene. (e) Using VRML Window to preview.

After authoring the MPEG-4 scene, the BIFS File Translator of Q4AT translates the designed scene tree into the scene.bt file, which contains the standard BIFS commands with text format. Q4AT adopts the MP4Box encoder [13] to interpret the BIFS commands in the scene.bt file and then encode the BIFS commands into the scene.mp4 file. The scene.mp4 file is just the scene and object description file with binary format. The related media content files are pointed in the scene.mp4. Figure 8 depicts the processing procedure of generating a recognized .mp4 file and the processing steps are as follows.

(i). The acceptable medium format for the video objects is the .media format. Firstly, Q4AT adopts the DivxEnc converter [14] to translate the original medium file with .avi format into the intermediate file with .m4v format.

provided in the *Q4AT* system. To achieve a smooth MPEG-4 presentation, the *Q4AT* system designs Object Property Area to specify the temporal/spatial relations of the media objects. The main goal of *Q4AT* is to provide powerful functionality for authors, who don't need have the complicated MPEG-4 knowledge, are capable of creating a standard MPEG-4 file.

Acknowledgement

The authors would like to thank the National Science Council of the Republic of China, Taiwan for financially supporting this research under Contract No. NSC-93-2219-E-020-002.

Reference

1. ISO/IEC 14496-1: 1999 Information technology -- Coding of audio-visual objects -- Part 1: Systems (1999)
2. Eleftheriadis, A.: MPEG-4 systems: architecting object-based audio-visual content. IEEE Second Workshop on Multimedia Signal Processing (1998) 535-540
3. Herpel, C.: Elementary stream management in MPEG-4, Vol. 9, Issue 2. IEEE Transactions on Circuits and Systems for Video Technology (1999) 315-324
4. Viljoen, D. W., Calit,z A. P., Cowley, N. L. O.: A 2-D MPEG-4 multimedia authoring tool. Proceedings of the 2nd international conference on Computer graphics, virtual Reality, visualization and interaction (2003) 151-160
5. Kim, K. Y., Hong, J. W., Park, C. M., and Jung, H. K.: The architecture of MPEG-4 based IPMP authoring system. Proceedings of IEEE International Conference on Multimedia and Expo (ICME '04) Vol. 1. (2004) 447 - 450
6. Liu, D. R., Shieh, M. J., Lee, Y. C., and Chen, W. C.: On the Design and Implementation of an MPEG-4 Scene Editor. Digest of Technical Papers of International Conference on Consumer Electronics (2000) 120-121
7. Bulterman, D. C. A. and Hardman, L.: Structured multimedia authoring, Vol. 1. Issue 1. ACM Transactions on Multimedia Computing, Communications, and Applications (TOMCCAP) (2005) 89-109
8. Pourmohammadi-Fallah, Y., Asrar-Haghighi, K., and Alnuweiri, H. M.: Streaming multimedia over the Internet, Vol. 23. Issue 1. IEEE Potentials (2004) 34-37
9. Daras, P., Kompatsiaris, I., Raptis, T., and Strintzis, M. G.: An MPEG-4 tool for composing 3D scenes, Vol. 11. Issue 2. IEEE Multimedia (2004) 58-97
10. Drumm, H. and Kuhhirt, U.: The shadow tool - new visual cues for MPEG-4 authors. Proceeding of 2004 IEEE International Symposium on Consumer Electronics (2004) 77 - 82
11. Kim, K., Lee, I., and Ki, M.: Interactive contents authoring system based on XMT and BIFS. Proceedings of the tenth ACM international conference on Multimedia (2002) 275-278
12. Zhigen, X., Yan, Y., and Chen, J. X.: OpenGL programming in Java, Vol. 7. Issue 1. Computing in Science and Engineering (2005) 51 - 55
13. MP4box, http://www.aziendeassociate.it/cd/gpac/dev/MP4Box.7z
14. DivxEnc, http://www.greatis.com/security/download.htm
15. MP4Creator60, http://www.esato.com/archive/t.php/t-63404
16. Osmo4, http://www.comelec.enst.fr/osmo4/
17. M4Play, http://www.alphaworks.ibm.com/tech/tk4mpeg4
18. MAXPEG, http://www.digimax.com.tw/MPEG4/

A Programmable Context Interface to Build a Context Infrastructure for Worldwide Smart Applications

Kyung-Lang Park, Chang-Soon Kim, Chang-Duk Kang, and Shin-Dug Kim

Super Computing Lab, Department of Computer Science,
Yonsei University, 120-749, 134 Shinchon-Dong,
Seodaemoon-Gu, Seoul, Korea
{lanx, flsoon, niceguy, sdkim}@yonsei.ac.kr
http://supercom.yonsei.ac.kr

Abstract. Context-awareness is one of the most important technologies for the ubiquitous computing. To embed such a technology into applications, first of all, a well-defined architectural framework is required to support applications to obtain necessary contexts. Several studies have been proposed, but most of them overlooked one fundamental feature that contexts are subjective things and context-awareness is subjective behavior. Thus, providing pre-defined, pre-programmed operators which generate contexts by combining a couple of sensed data is very impractical. Instead, in this paper, we provide a well-defined programmable interface to applications, so that they can obtain and use contexts according to their own ideas. To evaluate our architecture and context interface, we implement all components comprising of the context infrastructure and perform several experiments. The results show the proposed method provides a flexible and expressive interface, but does not countervail the performance.

1 Introduction

Ubiquitous computing [11] is being considered as a next generation computing paradigm these days. Computer-based technologies will be embedded into our casual life ubiquitously, so that we can use a variety of smart services anytime and anywhere. One of the most important technologies of the ubiquitous computing is context-awareness. If a service perceives our situational contexts, it will operate much smarter without any artificial intelligence stuff.

The most fundamental idea is to insert various sensors into an application. Then, the application can be aware of our situation by analyzing sensed data. However, such a sensor-driven approach gives developers pain because the developers have to know about all the sensors in detail. They have to spend more time on sensors than the core logics of applications. Several approaches have been proposed to overcome the problem. They attempted to separate context handling modules from applications and provided convenient toolkits and frameworks to develop sensor-driven smart applications much easier [1, 2, 7, 15, 16]. However, they are not sufficient enough to support the development of enormous context-aware applications. Nowadays, thus, an approach to establish a context infrastructure for innumerable context-aware applica-

L.T. Yang et al. (Eds.): EUC 2005, LNCS 3824, pp. 795 – 804, 2005.

tions is on the rise. When a context infrastructure is constructed, we can share a lot of sensors, information sources, and processing components. Consequently, we will design smart applications without any difficulty [8].

Some studies are based on the infrastructure approach [4, 12, 13]. They assume a worldwide model and consider various and enormous context-aware applications which use shared sensors in the world. Although they addressed some infrastructure issues such as scaling up, information dissemination, and unified sensor abstraction, they overlooked one important feature that contexts are subjective things rather than objective. To generate a context, several sensed data have to be aggregated. However, the problem is that the developers of the context infrastructure and developers of applications are different. Even though a well-defined component in the context infrastructure aggregates sensed data and generates contexts with a novel algorithm, they cannot be accepted to some applications. Thus, it is required to support applications by specifying their ideas to generate and use contexts.

In this paper, we propose an architecture for the context infrastructure and describe how applications obtain and use contexts subjectively. Our context interface provides a context description language (CDL) for applications to specify their requests. Thus, based on the CDL given by the application, the infrastructure discovers proper sensors, aggregates sensed data, generates contexts, and sends them to the applications. To evaluate our architecture and context interface, we implemented all components comprising of the context infrastructure and did several experiments. Experimental results show that the proposed method provides a flexible and expressive interface, but does not countervail the performance. Rest of the paper is organized as follows: In Section 2, we introduce several related work. Section 3 describes our context infrastructure and Section 4 explains the programmable context interface which is the core of our infrastructure. Section 5 provides several experimental results to evaluate our research. Finally, we conclude in Section 6.

2 Related Work

There are several studies to support development of context-aware applications. The Context Toolkit [1] is a pioneering work of this area. It suggested a well-defined conceptual framework that supports context-aware applications and provided several software components which aggregate and manage sensed data. Thus, developers can make context-aware applications rapidly by using the Context Toolkit. Since the advent of the Context Toolkit, a number of researches have been appearing. [2, 5, 7, 9, 15, 16].

Those are very convenient to develop a few number of applications in a domain, but not sufficient to support a large number of applications in multiple domains. Hong's article pointed out such a problem and introduced an infrastructure approach to develop a large number of context-aware applications [8]. There are several projects based on the infrastructure approach. Chen et al. proposed Solar, an infrastructure for context-aware applications [4]. Solar generates contexts by using an operator graph, where an operator is a self-contained data-processing component. A higher-level operator can be made by composing existing operators. Because Solar considered a large-scale context fusion network, it addressed several infrastructure issues, scalability and addressing. Contextor Infrastructure [6] took up the similar fashion. It suggested contextors as a building block of the infrastructure, where a contextor is a component which can provide contextual information. Either a sensor or a processing unit like an operator of Solar can be a contextor. They suggested applications retrieved contexts by composing several contextors. SCINet (Strathclyde Context Infrastructure) [13] and NEXUS [12] designed local context servers and extended it to be used for global areas by composing network of servers. SCINet comprises of CSs (Context Server) which maintains a central store of contexts and provides the access point for the applications. When a CS receives a query from an application, a query resolver in the CS generates a path to make the required context. In NEXUS, they defined an AHSS (Aware Home Spatial Service), a kind of context server, which is suitable for mid-size home environments and bridged AHSSs by using a query interface named AWQL. Semantic Space [17] and Gaia's context infrastructure [3] are also aimed to construct an infrastructure for context-aware applications. Semantic Space used context wrappers as a building block of the infrastructure. It also leveraged technologies from the Semantic Web. It provides RDF-based query language to combine sensors and existing semantic web information. Gaia project also assumed that there would be a lot of context providers and defined how context providers generate contexts.

Our work has the same perspective with above researches which are based on the infrastructure approach, but we do not agree with them in terms of context fusion and context inference in the infrastructure. We do not allow any kind of data composition predefined in the infrastructure. Instead, we provide more flexible and programmable interface to applications, so that they can obtain and use subjective contexts.

3 Architecture for a Context Infrastructure

Most of all, a well-defined architecture is required to build a context infrastructure for worldwide smart applications. In infrastructure approach, sensors are not for a specific application. Thus, we should define a bottleneck protocol to glue sensors onto an application. Figure 1 shows our architecture for the context infrastructure. We divide the bottleneck protocol into two layers. One is *abstraction layer* and the other is *collective layer*. The abstraction layer hides complexity of the actual sensors by wrapping them with a single software interface and publishes sensors to the outside. Typically, sensors use different I/O interfaces and express sensed data by using different data models and formats. Thus, it is quite difficult for an application to understand several kinds of I/O interfaces, data models, and formats. When sensors are abstracted, upper-layer components can access to the sensors through a single interface without deep knowledge of each sensor.

Our virtual sensor is based on Web services. It is based on fully open and standard protocols and does not depend on the physical communication method. A virtual

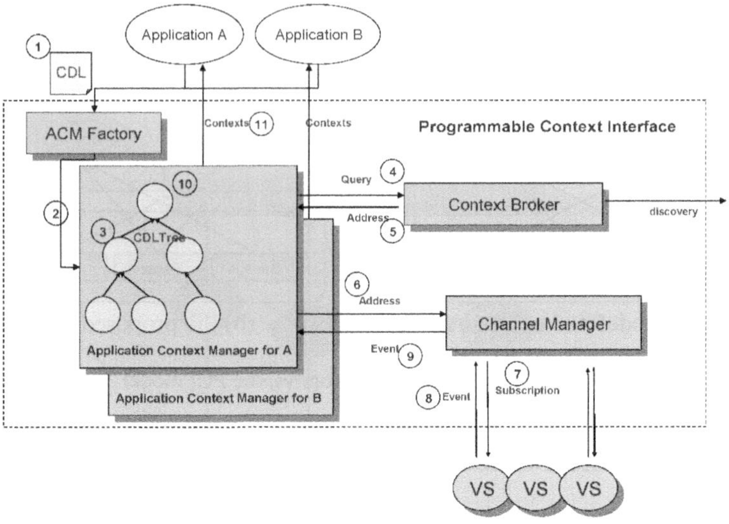

Fig. 3. Operation flow of the Programmable Context Interface

```
<?xml version="1.0" encoding="UTF-8"?>
<cdl:Definitions xmlns:cdl="http://supercom.yonsei.ac.kr/2005/03/cdl090" name="Park Presence">
 <cdl:SensorList>
  <cdl:Sensor type="constant" name="S_ONE">
    <cdl:Query num="1">
            <cdl:Tuple>
              <cdl:Location/>Z1</cdl:Location>
              <cdl:attribute ontologyRef="http://supercom.../2005/03/ont/test/Pressure">Pressure</cdl:Attribute>
            <cdl:Tuple>
    </cdl:Query>
    <cdl:Parents num="1">
      <cdl:Parent name="OP_ONE"/>
    </cdl:Parents>
  </cdl:Sensor>
  <cdl:Sensor type="subscription" name="S_TWO">
    <cdl:Address>
      <cdl:URI>http://121.141.10.199/WS/Sensors/ID_Sensor.wsdl</URI>
      <cdl:Parameter/>
     </cdl:Address>
    <cdl:Parents num="1">
      <cdl:Parent name="OP_ONE"/>
    </cdl:Parents>
  </cdl:Sensor>
 </cdl:SensorList>
 <cdl:OperatorList>
   <cdl:Operator name="OP_ONE">
    <cdl:Inputs num="3">
            <cdl:Input name="S_ONE" driver="true"/>
            <cdl:Input name="S_TWO"/>
    </cdl:Inputs>
    <cdl:Operation type="mapping">
            <cdl:Mapping>
                      <cdl:Condition>
                      <cdl:Cmd>$S_ONE.value > 1 </cdl:Cmd>
                      <cdl:Cmd>$S_TWO value == Park</cdl:Cmd>
                      <cdl:Tuple>
                                <cdl:Entity>Park</cdl:Entity>
                                <cdl:Location>Z1</cdl:Location>
                                <cdl:Time type="new">
                                <cdl:Attribute>Presence</cdl:Attribute>
                                <cdl:Value>true</cdl:Value>
                      </cdl:Tuple>
                      </cdl:Condition>
                      <cdl:Condition>
                      <cdl:Tuple>
                                <cdl:Entity>Park</cdl:Entity>
                                <cdl:Location>Z1</cdl:Location>
                                <cdl:Time type="new">
                                <cdl:Attribute>Presence</cdl:Attribute>
                                <cdl:Value>false</cdl:Value>
                      </cdl:Tuple>
                      </cdl:Condition>
            </cdl:Mapping>
     </cdl:Operation>
    </cdl:Operator>
   </cdl:OperatorList>
   <cdl:RequestList>
            <cdl:Request type="operator" name="OP_ONE"/>
   </cdl:RequestList>
</cdl:Definitions>/
```

Fig. 4. An example of the CDL. It represents a kind of person presence sensor.

can be categorized into two types, i.e., subscription and constant. The constant means that the sensor retrieves sensed data only once, but the subscription means that the sensor retrieves data continuously. A sensor can be specified by either <cdl:query> or <cdl:address>. When the application already knows the sensor, <cdl:address> is used. If the application does not know about the sensor, <cdl:query> has to be used to discover a group of proper sensors. The query is based on the context tuple we defined. The query element is sent to the context broker (CB) and the CB transforms the query element into an address element. In this example, we specified two sensors. One is specified by a query element. The other is specified by an address element.

<cdl:operatorList> specifies operators. An operator is a kind of processing module. It receives data from sensors or other operators and processes the data with own operation. It can be defined by <cdl:inputs> and <cdl:operation>. The <cdl:inputs> specifies sensors and operators that have to send data to the operator. Only input elements marked as the driver can trigger the operation. The operation in an operator is specified by the <cdl:operation>. Current version of the CDL supports five types of operations. Those are mapping, selection, integration, calculation, and manual. Finally, <cdl:Request> is used to mark sensors or operations whose output would be sent to the application. When all nodes marked as request finish their operation, the ACM makes a result by combining events generated from requested nodes and sends it to the application.

5 Evaluation

In this section, we evaluate the proposed context infrastructure based on the programmable context interface. The main difference between previous approaches and our approach is that we do not use pre-defined operations. Instead, we provide an interface to applications to program operations that they need to obtain necessary contexts. Thus, we have to show that our operations can be performed in the same way as the pre-defined and pre-programmed operations.

In our approach, an ACM should construct a CDL tree on the fly. If there is heavy overhead to construct a tree, it cannot be used even though it provides a very flexible and convenient interface. This is because contexts are time-sensitive information. Following experimental results show the construction of a CDL tree does not take much time although there are a number of nodes specified in a CDL. They also show that overall response time of the PCI is as fast as other systems which use predefined, pre-programmed model.

5.1 Experimental Results

All components comprising of the context infrastructure are implemented by using Java SDK 1.5 and WSDP (Web Services Development Package) on Window XP machines. ACMs, the CB, the CM are located in the same machine, and each sensor and application are placed in different machines. A machine with the PCI components is Pentium IV 1.33GHz with 1GB main memory. All machines are connected by local area networks. We firstly make a CDL which consists of two sensors and one operator, and measure the time at several points to see the basic timing diagram. Figure 5 shows the result of the experiment. It takes about 400ms from an application submitted a CDL to the application received the result. Specifically, such a time delay is quite feasible because valid time period of a sensed data is generally a couple of seconds. The time from application launched to the time the ACM received the CDL stands for the communication time between two machines. It is not related to the PCI and depends on the network status. From the time to the CDL tree constructed stands for the tree construction time. It is very important to evaluate the ACM. Thus, we will show other experimental results about the construction time. The next one is the time to discover sensors. It depends on the ability of the CB. The next is the time to subscribe to the sensors. It is very simple operation and depends on the network status rather than the ability of the CM. The time from all events arrived to the result stands for the processing time. It is also very important. The operator generated in the ACM interprets the operation specified in the CDL on the fly. Thus, it takes much more time compared to the pre-programmed operations. Finally, the time for the application to receive the result is also a kind of communication time between the PCI host and the application.

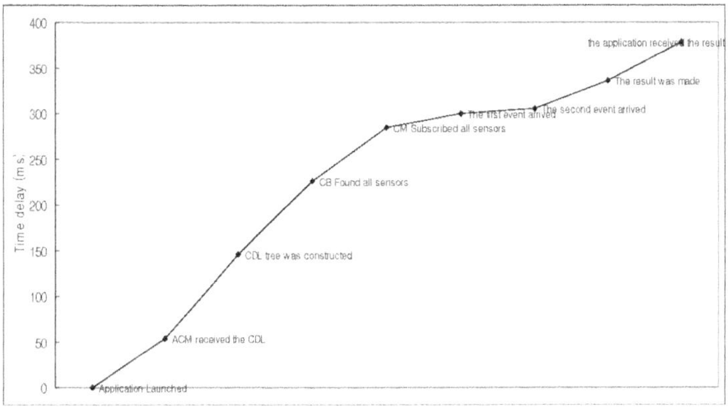

Fig. 5. The timing diagram when an application submits a CDL consisting of two sensors and one operation

The most important point in this time diagram is the construction time, because our approach generates operation trees in running time, which may not exist in other approaches. To measure the construction time, we perform additional experiments. We measure only construction time with changing the number of nodes. Figure 6 shows the result of these experiments. When the number of nodes is two, it takes only 97ms. It takes more time as the number of nodes increases. When the number of nodes becomes more than one hundred, the construction time will be less than one second. However, one CDL include about 10 to 20 sensors typically. It takes only 120ms, so that it does not cause any heavy overhead to the application.

Finally, four context-aware applications are designed by using several context acquisition models. The first model is pre-programmed and pre-defined model. In this model, operators are already developed and published, and applications already know about the operators. Probably, the programmer of operators and the programmer of applications should be same. The Context Toolkit uses this approach. The next one is pre-programmed and not-defined model. Several useful operators are provided by some participants, but the application should discover the operators. A lot of approaches based on the infrastructure such as Solar and GAIA use this model. Our PCI model is not-programmed and not-defined model. There is no pre-programmed

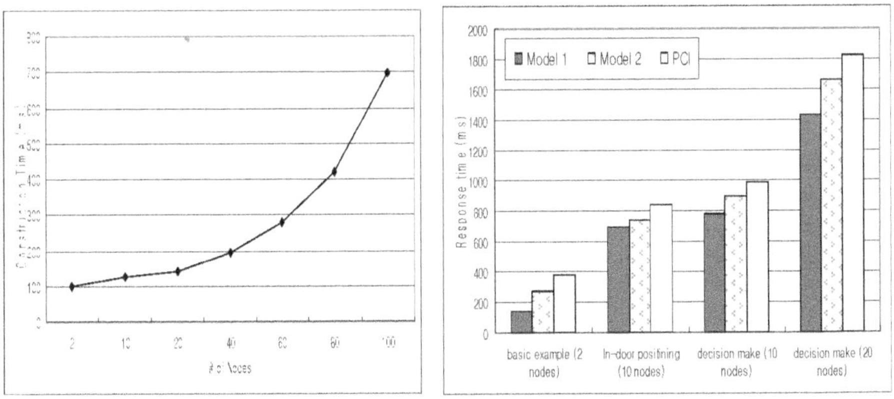

Fig. 6. CDL tree construction time as changing the number of nodes (left). Response time compared to other models (right).

operator. Instead, applications have to generate subjective operators by submitting CDLs. We compare the response time of three models. Definitely, the first model shows the best performance as shown in Figure 6. It is because there is no additional overhead in the model such as construction time and discovery time. The second model only has discovery time as overhead. However, there is no huge difference between three models in terms of the performance. Simply, it means that the construction time and discovery time occupy a small portion of the response time. But, the PCI model provides more convenient and flexible interfaces than other models. Thus, it is more feasible approach to support a number of context-aware applications.

6 Conclusion

In this paper, we have presented an architecture for supporting context-aware applications based on the infrastructure approach. The contribution of this paper is that we suggest a method that applications obtain and use contexts subjectively. When an infrastructure provides predefined and pre-programmed operators to extract contexts by using sensed data, it cannot be used for many applications. It is more efficient to provide a programmable interface to applications to specify their requests for contexts. Experimental results show that it provides feasible response time compared to other context acquisition models.

References

1. A. K. Dey, D. Salber, and G. D. Abowd,: A Conceptual Framework and a Toolkit for Supporting the Rapid Prototyping of Context-Aware Applications, Human Computing Interaction. Vol. 16. (2001) 97-166
2. A. Schemidt, U. Karlsruhe, K. V. Laerhoven,: How to build Smart Applications, IEEE Personal Communications. (2001)

tion, a packet delay may introduce by the signal hand-out or the difference of bandwidth transportation in wireless/fixed networks.

For delay sensitive applications, a dominating portion of packet losses might be likely due to delay constraint. A late packet that arrives after a delay threshold determined by playback time is treated as a lost packet. A tight delay threshold not only degrades the quality of playback but also reduces the effective bandwidth because a large fraction of delivered packets are dropped. In fact, delay and loss are normally not independent of each other. In order to reduce the loss impact, a number of applications utilize an adaptive smoothing technique in which buffers are adopted to reduce the quality damage caused by loss packets. However, a large buffer will introduce excessive end-to-end delay and deteriorate the multimedia quality in interactive real-time applications. Therefore, a tradeoff is required between increased packet loss and buffer delay to achieve satisfactory results for playout buffer algorithms.

In the past, the works on the degradation of the voice quality consider the effect of packet loss, but not that of packet delay. Within literature on predicting delays, the use of Pareto distribution in [1] is of computing the distribution parameters and rebuilding the new distribution to predict the next packet delay, and the use of neural network models to learn traffic behaviors [2]. The use of Pareto distribution or a neural network model requires relatively high complexity or a long learning period. Therefore, we consider the smoothers [3]-[9] which employ statistical network parameters related with the voice characteristic, i.e. loss, delay and talk-spurt that have significant influence to the voice quality. They detect delay spike in traffic and quickly calculate the required buffer size to keep the quality as good as possible.

The E-model is a computational model, standardized by ITU-T in G.107, G.109 and G.113 which uses the various transmission parameters to predict the subjective quality of packetized voice. Unfortunately, the E-model is complex to analyze in the optimization process. An alternative study is to apply a simplified E-model, first proposed by R. Cole and J. Rosenbluth [10], based upon observed transport measurements in the VoIP gateways and the transport paths. Authors indicated the simplified E-model method requires more pattern cases for traces to enhance the validation. Atzori and Lobina [11], and L. Sun and E. Ifeachor [12] proposed to utilize a simplified E-model that considers the loss and delay together to set a dijitter time, which is the optimal playout delay derived by a dynamic programming-based solution. However, the usability and the accuracy of a simplified E-model will be limited by non-typical traffic patterns.

For perceptual-based buffer optimization schemes for VoIP, voice quality is evaluated as a key metric since it represents user's perceived QoS. However, it requires an efficient and accurate objective way to optimize perceived voice quality. To consider the well-defined delay and loss impairments of the E-model, we employ a complete E-model for the quality optimization to obtain optimal perceived voice quality.

In a packet switching network, without a resynchronization scheme, a playback clock with a minor frequency error will eventually cause a buffer overflow or an underflow at the receiving end. The overflow packets are usually discarded due to the finite buffer size and the real-time requirement. This discontinuity caused by discarded packets might create an unpleasant effect to the playback quality because the lost packets could be the important part of the signals. This effect is more serious for audio signals than video signals because human ears are more sensitive to the continuity of sounds than human eyes.

The contributions of this paper are three-fold: (i) A new method optimizing voice quality for VoIP is easily applied to codecs which were well-defined in the ITU-T E-model. (ii) Different from the other optimal smoothers, our optimal smoother has the lowest complexity with $O(n)$. (iii) A feasible scheme is introduced to solve the buffer re-synchronization problem.

2 Related Work

The Spike Detection (SD) algorithm has been studied by many researchers [3]-[9]. A delay spike is defined as a sudden and significant increase of network delay in a short period often less than one round-trip. This algorithm adjusts the smoothing size, i.e. playback delay, at the beginning of each talk-spurt. The results of this algorithm are therefore compared to the results obtained herein.

The SD Algorithm in [3] estimates the playout time p_i of the first packet in a talk-spurt from the mean network delay d_i and the variance v_i for packet i as

$$p_i = t_i + d_i + \gamma v_i \tag{1}$$

where t_i represents the time at which packet i is generated at the sending host and γ is a constant factor used to set the playout time to be "far enough" beyond the delay estimate such that only a small fraction of the arriving packets could be lost due to late arrival . The value of $\gamma = 4$ is used in simulations [3]. The estimates are re-computed each time a packet arrives, but only applied when a new talk-spurt is initiated.

The mean network delay d_i and variance v_i are calculated based on a linear recursive filter characterized by the factors α and β.

$$\begin{cases} \mathit{If}\ n_i > d_{i-1} \Rightarrow \begin{cases} d_i = \beta d_{i-1} + (1-\beta) n_i \\ v_i = \beta v_{i-1} + (1-\beta)\left| d_{i-1} - n_i \right| \end{cases} & (\mathit{SPIKE\_MODE}) \\ \mathit{If}\ n_i \le d_{i-1} \Rightarrow \begin{cases} d_i = \alpha d_{i-1} + (1-\alpha) n_i \\ v_i = \alpha v_{i-1} + (1-\alpha)\left| d_{i-1} - n_i \right| \end{cases} \end{cases} \tag{2}$$

where n_i is the total "delay" introduced by the network [3] and typical values of α and β are 0.998002 and 0.75 [1], respectively.

The decision to select α and β is based on the current delay condition. The condition $n_i > d_{i-1}$ represents network congestion (*SPIKE_MODE*) and the weight β is used to emphasize the current network delay. On the other hand, $n_i \le d_{i-1}$ represents network traffic is stable, and α is used to emphasize the long-term average.

In estimating the delay and variance, the SD Algorithm utilizes only two values, α and β, which are simple but may not be adequate, particularly when the traffic is unstable. For example, an under-estimated problem is when a network becomes spiked, but the delay n_i is just below the d_{i-1}, the SD Algorithm will evaluate the network to be stable and will not enter the *SIPKE_MODE.*

3 Adaptive Smoother with Optimal Delay-Loss Trade Off

The proposed optimal smoother is derived using the E-model to trade off the delay and loss. This method involves, first, building the traffic delay model and the loss model. Second, the delay and loss impairments of the E-model are calculated according to the delay and the loss models. Third, the E-model rank R is maximized and thus the delay and loss optimized solution is obtained.

3.1 E-Model Description

In the E-model, a rating factor *R* represents voice quality and considers relevant transmission parameters for the considered connection. It is defined in [13] as:

$$R = Ro - Is - Id - Ie\_eff + A \tag{3}$$

Ro denotes the basic signal-to-noise ratio, which is derived from the sum of different noise sources which contain circuit noise and room noise, send and receive loudness ratings. *Is* denotes the sum of all impairments associated with the voice signal, which is derived from the incorrect loudness level, non-optimum sidetone and quantizing distortion. Id represents the impairments due to delay of voice signals, that is the sum of Talker Echo delay (*Idte*), Listener Echo delay (*Idle*) and end-to-end delay (*Idd*). Ie_eff denotes the equipment impairments, depending on the low bit rate codecs (*Ie, Bpl*) and packet loss (*Ppl*) levels. Finally, the advantage factor *A* is no relation to all other transmission parameters. The use of factor *A* in a specific application is left to the designer's decision.

3.2 The Delay and Loss Models in E-Model

For perceived buffer design, it is critical to understand the delay distribution modeling as it is directly related to buffer loss. The characteristics of packet transmission delay over Internet can be represented by statistical models which follow Exponential distribution for Internet packets (for an UDP traffic) has been shown to consistent with an Exponential distribution [14]. In order to derive an online loss model, the packet end-to-end delay is assumed as an exponential distribution with parameter $1/\mu$ at the receiving end for low complexity and easy implementation. The CDF of the delay distribution $F(t)$ can also be represented by [15]

$$F(t)=1-e^{\mu^{-1}t} \tag{4}$$

and the PDF of the delay distribution $f(t)$ is

$$f(t)=\frac{dF(t)}{dt}=\mu^{-1}e^{-\mu^{-1}t} \tag{5}$$

where μ is defined as the inverse of the average mean delay.

In a real-time application, a packet loss that is solely caused by extra delay can be derived from the delay model $f(t)$. The value of t_b represents the smoothing time for a smoother. When a packet delay exceeds t_b, a packet loss will occur. The loss function $l(t_b)$ can be derived as

$$l(t_b) = \int_{t_b}^{\infty} f(t)dt = \left(-e^{-\lambda t}\right)\Big|_{t_b}^{\infty} = -e^{-\infty} + e^{-\mu^{-1}t_b} = e^{-\mu^{-1}t_b} \quad (6)$$

3.3 Optimization on E-Model

The delay and loss factors over transmission have greater impacts to the voice quality than the environments or equipments. To simplify the optimization complexity, and investigate on delay and loss impairments, we make three assumptions in a communication connection as the following: (i). The circuit noise, room noise and terminate signals will not change. (*Ro* and *Is* are fixed). (ii). An echo delay in the Sender/Receiver will not change. (Idte and Idle are fixed). (iii). A codec will not change (*Ie* is fixed). In [13], *R* is rewritten as Eq. (7)

$$R = (Ro - Is - Idte - Idle + A) - Idd - Ie\_eff \quad (7)$$

where *Idd* is approximated by

$$Idd = 25\left\{\left(1 + X^6\right)^{1/6} - 3\left(1 + \left[\frac{X}{3}\right]^6\right)^{1/6} + 2\right\},\ X = \frac{ln\left(\frac{t}{100}\right)}{ln(2)}, \quad (8)$$

when $T_a > 100$ ms and *Idd* =0 when $T_a \le 100$,

and

$$Ie\_eff = Ie + (95 - Ie)\cdot\frac{Ppl}{Ppl + Bpl} \quad (9)$$

Factors *Ie* and *Bpl* are defined in [16] and T_a is one-way absolute delay for echo-free connections.

Due to the three assumptions above, the optimization process can be concentrated on the parameters of *Idd* and *Ie_eff*. Eq. (7) is derived to yield Eq. (10)

$$R = Constant - 25\left\{\left(1 + X^6\right)^{1/6} - 3\left(1 + \left[\frac{X}{3}\right]^6\right)^{1/6} + 2\right\} - (95 - Ie)\cdot\frac{Ppl}{Ppl + Bpl}, \quad (10)$$

when $t > 100$ ms

activated; otherwise it stays in Smooth-state for smoothing. In the Play-State the packet is fetched from the buffer and played out. In fetching process, when it encounters three consecutive S packets, implying that the talk-spurt can be ended, the buffer re-synchronization procedure then switches to the Skip-state. In the Skip-state, if "A" is fetched from buffer, it means the new talk-spurt has begun, and then it skips remained silent packets in the buffer, and switches to the Smooth-state to smooth the next talk-spurt. Otherwise, if "S" is fetched from buffer, it implies current talk-spurt is not ended and will be decoded to play out at the same state.

With the above four-state machine, the smoother can smooth the packets at the beginning of the talkspurt to avoid buffer underflow in the Smooth-state and skip the silent packets at the end of the talkspurt to prevent the overflow in the Skip-state.

4.2 Effectiveness of Re-synchronization

To demonstrate the effectiveness of re-synchronization machine for buffer overflow, we analyze the clock inconsistence constraint as the following. C_s and C_r represent the sender clock (frame/sec) and the receiver clock, respectively, and M_a and M_s denote the mean active packets and mean silent packets in a talkspurt, respectively. The buffer overflow caused by the clock inconsistence (difference) will occur when C_s is larger than C_r condition. $C_s - C_r$, the difference value by subtracting the receiver clock from the sender clock, represents the positive clock drift between the sender and the receiver. Therefore, $(C_s - C_r) * ((M_a + M_s) * frame\_time)$ represents the mean extra buffer size caused by the positive clock drift for a mean talkspurt time. In order to distinguish the consecutive talkspurts, at lease k silent packets are utilized. Therefore, the smoother has $M_s - k$ silent packets to be skipped and resynchronizes with the following talkspurt. When the re-synchronization machine satisfies

$$(C_s - C_r) * ((M_a + M_s) * frame\_time) \le (M_s - k), \qquad (12)$$

the buffer overflow caused by the positive clock drift will not occur.

5 Simulation

5.1 Simulation Configuration

A set of simulation experiments are performed to evaluate the effectiveness of the proposed adaptive smoothing scheme. The OPNET simulation tools are adopted to trace the voice traffic transported between two different LANs for a VoIP environment. Ninety personal computers with G.729 traffics are deployed in each LAN. The duration and frequency of the connection time of the personal computers follow Exponential distributions. Ten five-minute simulations were run to probe the backbone network delay patterns, which were used to trace the adaptive smoothers and compare the effects of the original with the adapted voice quality latter.

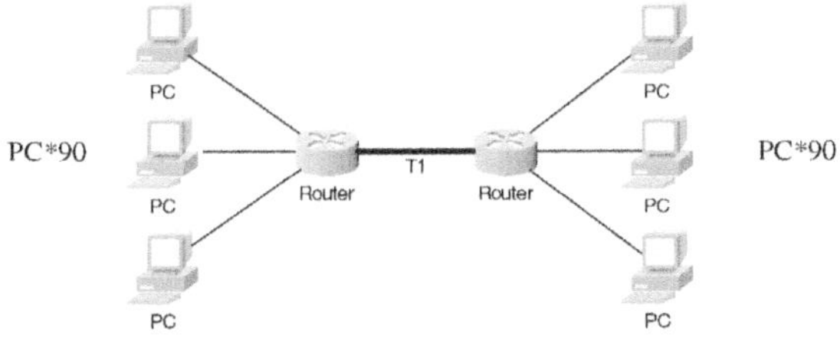

Fig. 2. The simulation environment of VoIP

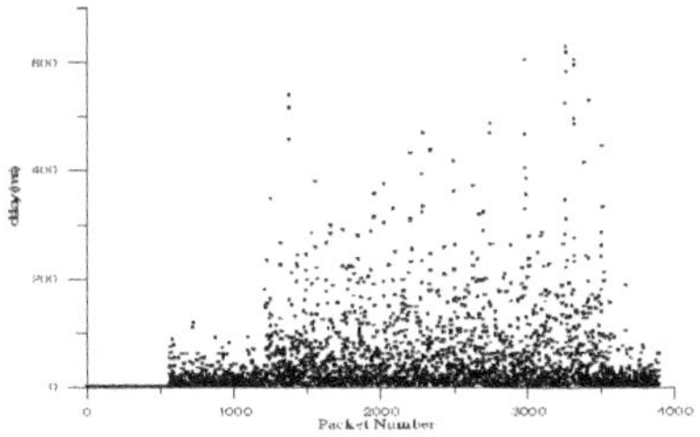

(a) The delay of traffic

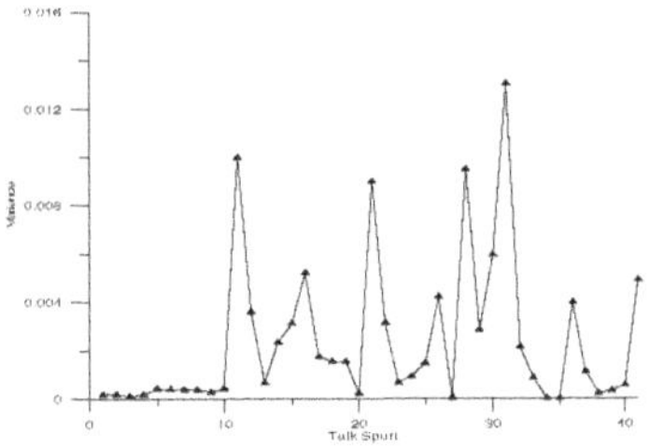

(b) The variance of traffic

Fig. 3. VoIP traffic pattern

Fig. 2 shows the typical network topology in which a T1 (1.544 Mbps) backbone connects two LANs, and 100 Mbps lines are connected within each LAN. The propagation delay of all links is assumed to be a constant value and will be ignored (the derivative value will be zero) in the optimization process. The buffer size of the bottlenecked router is assumed to be infinite since the performance comparison of adaptive smoothers will be affected by overdue packet loss (over the deadline) and not affected by the packet loss in router buffer. The network end-to-end delay of a G.729 packet with data frame size (10 bytes) and RTP/UDP/IP headers (40 bytes) is measured for ten five-minute simulations by employing the OPNET simulation network. Figure 3(a) and 4(b) list one of the end-to-end traffic delay patterns and the corresponding delay variances for VoIP traffic observed at a given receiver.

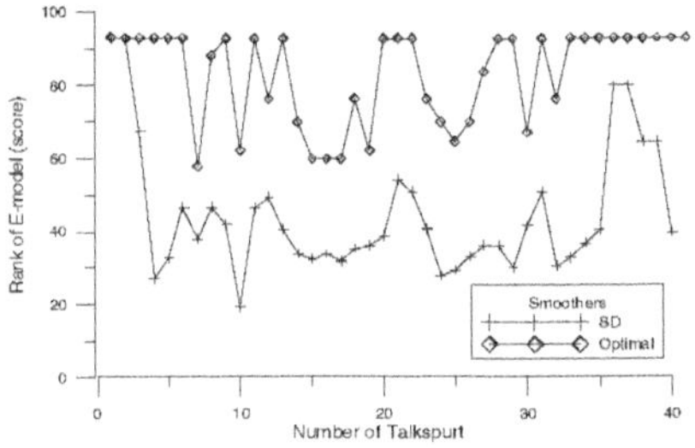

Fig. 4. The quality scores of smoothers

5.2 Voice Quality in Smoothers

The test sequence is sampled at 8 kHz, 23.44 seconds long, and includes English and Mandarin sentences spoken by male and female. Fig. 4 shows the E-model score *R* of the voice quality. It shows that the optimal method has the significant improvement in the voice quality over SD smoother, because our proposed optimal smoother truly optimizes with the delay and loss impairments in a transmission planning of the E-model.

5.3 Re-synchronization Effectiveness for the Positive Clock Drift

A listening evaluation experiment was performed to analyze the required proper number of silent packets to segment the consecutive talk-spurts well. It was found in our experiments that at least three silent packets (e.q. 10 ms per packet in G.729) are required to separate talkspurts.

We analyze the G.729 voice sources used in our experiments and find the percentage of the mean active and mean silent segment length in a talkspurt are 0.51 and 0.49 respectively, and the maximum talkspurt length is 257 packets. p =3 is adopted to segment the consecutive talkspurt. From the Eq. (12), we can calculate the effective clock drift between the sender and the receiver $C_s - C_r$ should be less than or equal to $(257 * 0.49 - 3)\big/\left((257) * 10 * 10^{-3}\right) = 47.8$ (frame/sec). Normally, the clock drift will not be over 47.8 (frame/sec) when a sender of G.729 transmits 100 (frame/sec) to the networks. Consequently, the smoother can avoid the buffer overflow well in our case.

6 Conclusion

This article proposes an adaptive smoothing algorithm that utilizes the complete E-model to optimize the smoothing size to obtain the best voice quality. The buffer re-synchronization algorithm is also proposed to prevent buffer overflow by skipping some silent packets of the tail of talk-spurts. It can efficiently solve the mismatch between the capture and the playback clocks. Numerical results have shown that our proposed method can get significant improvements in the voice quality which balances the target delay and loss.

References

[1] Brazauskas V., Serfling R.: Robust and efficient estimation of the tail index of a one-parameter pareto distribution. North American Actuarial Journal available at http://www.utdallas.edu/~serfling. (2000)

[2] Tien P. L., Yuang M. C.: Intelligent voice smoother for silence-suppressed voice over internet. IEEE JSAC, Vol. 17, No. 1. (1999) 29-41

[3] Ramjee R., Kurise J., Towsley D., Schulzrinne H.: Adaptive playout mechanisms for packetized audio applications in wide-area networks. Proc. IEEE INFOCOM. (1994) 680-686

[4] Jeske D. R., Matragi W., Samadi B.: Adaptive play-out algorithms for voice packets. Proc. IEEE Conf. on Commun., Vol. 3. (2001) 775-779
[5] Pinto J., Christensen K. J.: An algorithm for playout of packet voice based on adaptive adjustment of talkspurt silence periods. Proc. IEEE Conf. on Local Computer Networks. (1999) 224-231
[6] Liang Y. J., Farber N., Girod B.,: Adaptive playout scheduling using time-scale modification in packet voice communications. Proc. IEEE Conf. on Acoustics, Speech, and Signal Processing, Vol. 3. (2001) 1445-1448
[7] Kansal A., Karandikar A.: Adaptive delay estimation for low jitter audio over Internet. IEEE GLOBECOM, Vol. 4. (2001) 2591-2595
[8] Anandakumar A. K., McCree A., Paksoy E.: An adaptive voice playout method for VOP applications. IEEE GLOBECOM, Vol. 3. (2001) 1637-1640
[9] DeLeon P., Sreenan C. J.: An Adaptive predictor for media playout buffering. Proc. IEEE Conf. on Acoustics, Speech, and Signal Processing, Vol. 6. (1999) 3097-3100
[10] Cole R., Rosenbluth J.: Voice over IP performance monitoring, Journal on Computer Commun. Review, Vol. 31. (2001)
[11] Atzori L., Lobina M.: Speech playout buffering based on a simplified version of the ITU-T E-model. IEEE Signal Processing Letters, Vol. 11 , Iss 3. (2004) 382-385
[12] Sun L., Ifeachor E.: New models for perceived voice quality prediction and their applications in playout buffer optimization for VoIP networks. Proc. ICC. (2004)
[13] ITU-T Recommendation G.107,: The E-model, a Computational Model for use in Transmission Planning. (2003)
[14] Bolot J. C.: Characterizing end-to-end packet delay and loss in the internet. Journal of High-Speed Networks, Vol. 2. (1993) 305-323.
[15] Fujimoto K., Ata S., Murata M.: Statistical Analysis of Packet Delays in the Internet and its Application to Playout Control for Streaming Applications. IEICE Trans. Commun., Vol. E84-B, No. 6. (2001) 1504-1512
[16] ITU-T SG12 D.106: Estimates of Ie and Bpl for a range of Codecs. (2003)

to provide video acceleration and off-load the CPU from computation intensive tasks. While the encoder and decoder support only MPEG4-SVIP, the PrP and PP can be used for generic video pre and post processing such as scaling, resizing, and color space conversions.

The features of eMMA support private DMA between CMOS sensor interface module and pre-processor as data input and image scaling function. The eMMA encoder supports MPEG-4 and H.263, full conformance to ISO/IEC 14496-2 Visual Simple Profiles Levels 0 to 3, real-time encoding images of sizes from 32x32 up to CIF at 30 fps and camera stabilization. The eMMA decoder supports MPEG-4 and H.263, full conformance to ISO/IEC 14496-2 Visual Simple Profiles Levels 0 to 3, real-time encoding images of sizes from 32x32 up to CIF at 30 fps and camera stabilization. Post-processor receives the input data of YUV 4:2:0(IYUV, YV12) from system memory and does image resizing with upscaling ranging from 1:1 to 1:4 and downscaling ranging from 1:1 to 2:1 in fractional steps. This ratios provide scaling between QCIF, CIF, QVGA(320x240,240x320).

The Liquid Crystal Display Controller is embedded in the i.MX21 chipset. The Liquid Crystal Display Controller (LCDC) provides display data for external gray-scale or color LCD panels. The LCDC is capable of supporting black-and-white, gray-scale, passive-matrix color (passive color or CSTN), and active-matrix color (active color or TFT) LCD panels.

Camera module in the wearable personal station is controlled by CMOS sensor interface(CSI) characterized by CSI architecture, operation principles, and programming model. The CSI enables the i.MX21 to connect directly to external CMOS image sensors. CMOS image sensors are separated into two classes, dumb and smart. Dumb sensors are those that support only traditional sensor timing (Vertical SYNC and Horizontal SYNC) and output only Bayer and statistics data, while smart sensors support CCIR656 video decoder formats and perform additional processing of the image (for example, image compression, image pre-filtering, and various data output formats).

3.3 Multimedia Card/Secure Digital Host Controller

The MultiMediaCard (MMC) is a universal low cost data storage and communication media that is designed to cover a wide area of applications as electronic toys, organizers, PDAs and smart phones and so on. The MMC communication is based on an advanced 7 pin serial bus designed to operate in a low voltage range, at medium speed.

The Secure Digital Card (SD) is an evolution of MMC with an additional 2 pins as the same form factor and is specifically designed to meet the security, capacity, performance, and environment requirements inherent in newly emerging audio and video consumer electronic devices. An SD card can be categorized as SD Memory or SD I/O card, commonly known as SDIO. The SDIO card provides high-speed data I/O with low-power consumption for mobile electronic devices.

The Multimedia Card/Secure Digital Host module (MMC/SD) integrates MMC support with SD memory and I/O functions. We also mainly used MMC/SD as storage device. We newly made MMC/SD device driver for its use.

3.4 The Battery and an Outward Appearance

We have to get ultra slim battery for our wrist worn device. We need pocketing and free-stacking technology. This battery is lithium-ion rechargeable batteries tested as high temperature storage test (90 °C, 4hr), humidity test (60 °C, 90% RH, 1week), thermal shock test(-40 °C/60 °C, 10 cycles), safety test such as hot-box test (150 °C, 10min), nail penetration test, short circuit test, overcharge test (3C continuous overcharge) and long period storage test(25°C, 60°C, 80°C)

The outward appearance of our WPS hardware is as follows.

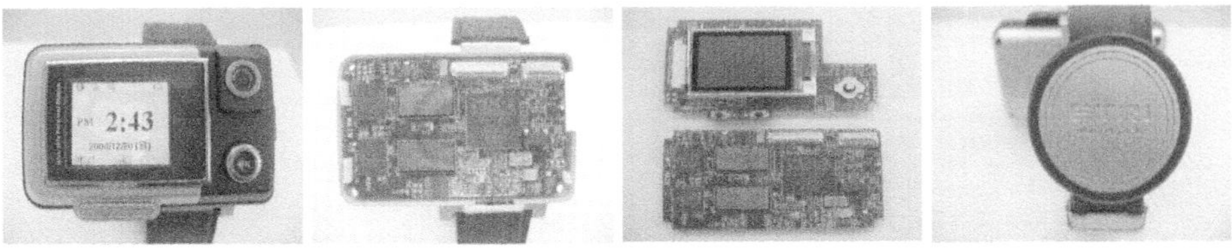

Fig. 2. Front Side, Front Inside, The PCBs, The Battery

4 System Software Specification

4.1 Operating System

We adopted linux operating system for free because open source. We patch linux-2.4.20 with mx2bsp patch. For building operating system, we needed to build a cross-development environment, including cross compilers, assemblers, and binary utilities that would let us generate code for the ARM architecture on our general purpose personal computer. Although there were many resources on the internet to help in this process, it took some time to get everything set up right. We found relevant pieces of source code and patches on the internet. We wrote some of the basic device drivers and modified the memory maps for our hardware configurations. In addition, we wrote some device drivers not supported directly. We used busybox and its init profile on jffs2 filesystem/mtd. We wrote newly mtd device driver for building jffs2 filesystem. We used NOR flash, 512 bytes erase block. We builded and used MMC/SD in evaluation phase. We mainly used MMC/SD, USB memory stick as the secondary memory device for transferring its applications and data. We adopted embedded Qt 2.3.7 as graphical user interface. We made WPS window manager based on embedded Qt 2.3.7. We also implement advanced power management.

4.2 Device Drivers

The CMOS camera is supported by CSI device driver. It supports for 352x288 or 640x480 pixel array, 30 frame/sec, CIF, QCIF, QQCIF or VGA, QVGA, enabling sub-sampling, still image capture.

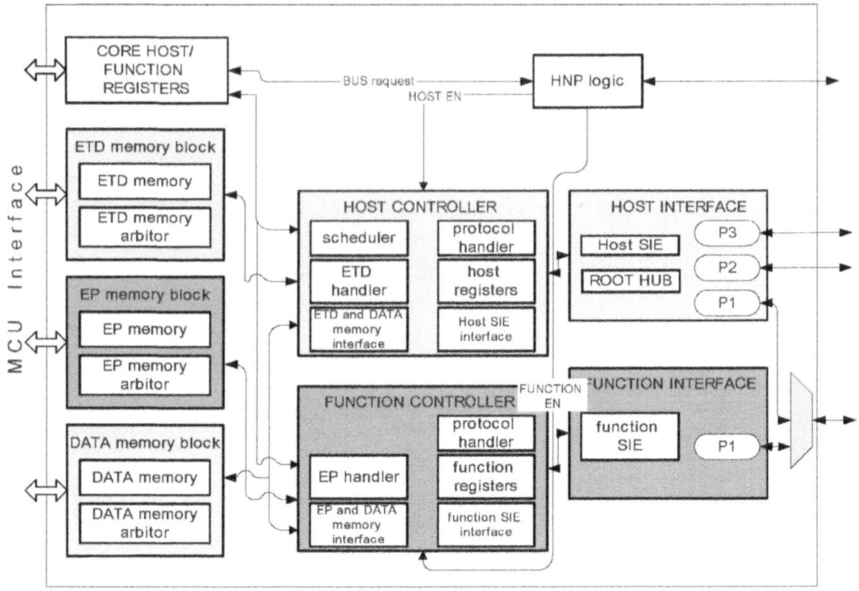

Fig. 3. The USB OTG Block Diagram

LCD driver supports 1.7 inch, 128x128 resolution TFT-LCD. We adopted 26K TFT-LCD and used frame buffer display. We wote MTD device driver newly for jffs2 filesystem. The flash device is interleaved by 2 and supports MTD. We used the flash chip 28F256 of intel.

The APM supports normal mode, doze mode and sleep mode with system software. The normal mode means the main processor and all devices are power on state. The doze mode means the main processor is power off state and all devices are power on state. The sleep mode means the main processor and all devices are power off state. This APM supports frequency scaling, not voltage scaling. The WPS consumes 113 mA in the normal mode, 85 mA in the doze mode, 35 mA in the sleep mode. We are trying to use frequency scaling for power scaling. The button is a simple device driver using interrupt service. We configure and make WM8731 device driver for supporting the sound.

Many of these portable devices would benefit from being able to communicate to each other over the USB interface, yet certain aspects of USB make this difficult to achieve. Specially, USB communication can only take place between a host and a peripheral. So OTG supplement to the USB is needed. The USB OTG block diagram is shown in Fig. 3[1]. We implement USBOTG device driver on the above blocks.

4.3 Making USB Wireless

USB continues to evolve as new technologies and products come to market. USB has already many application interfaces and support versatile device interfaces. It's already the de facto interconnect for PCs, and has proliferated into consumer electronics(CE) and mobile devices as well. Like this, USB has built on many killer applications, many CE devices, many interfaces.

The growing use of wireless technology in PC, CE and mobile communications products, along with the convergence of product functionalities, calls for a common wireless interconnections. If our devices is unwired, it solves the tangle of wires. We want to use Legacy USB functionalities, portabilities, multimedia capabilities with wireless interconnection.

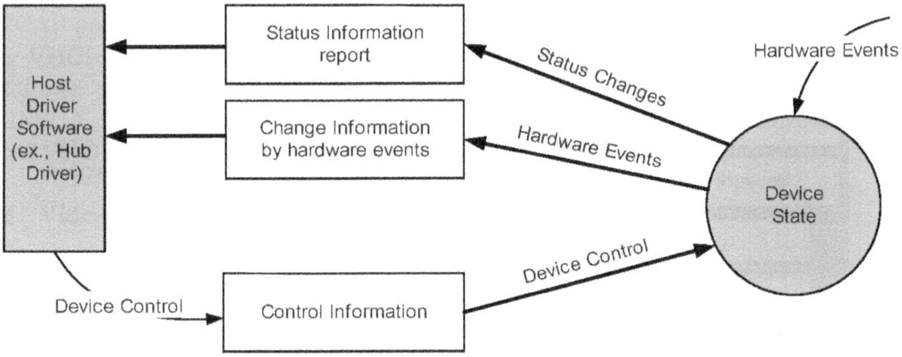

Fig. 4. Relationship of Status, Status Change, and Control Information to Device States

Making USB HUB Wireless. We will make the hub function of USB cordless, so it will connect host with devices without wires. The USB root hub is special device to be able to connect to another devices. We will make USB hub and USB host interface device wireless. There are many status report registers and events in hub. These are implemented by software modules and functions in the device driver level. And the memory uses and several data structures of USB host are also implemented by software modules and functions in the device driver level.

A hub is a standardized type of USB device. A hub is the only USB device that provides connection points for additional USB devices. The root hub is the hub that is an embedded part of every host controller. From an end user perspective, a hub provides the sockets that are used to plug in other USB devices. For making hub wireless, it needs to know the architecture requirements for the USB hub. It contains a description of the three principal sub-blocks: the hub repeater, the hub controller, and the transaction translator. There are major aspects of USB functionality that hubs must support: connectivity behavior, power management, device connect/disconnect detection, bus fault detection and recovery, high-speed, full-speed, and low-speed device support.

In case making USB wireless, it must support the above functionalities. Moreover, It needs the data structure and the resources for host functionalities, e.g. ETD, data memory.

Fig. 4 shows how status, status change, and control information relate to device states[2]. Hub or port status change bits can be set because of hardware or software events. When set, these bits remain set until cleared. While a change bit is set, the hub

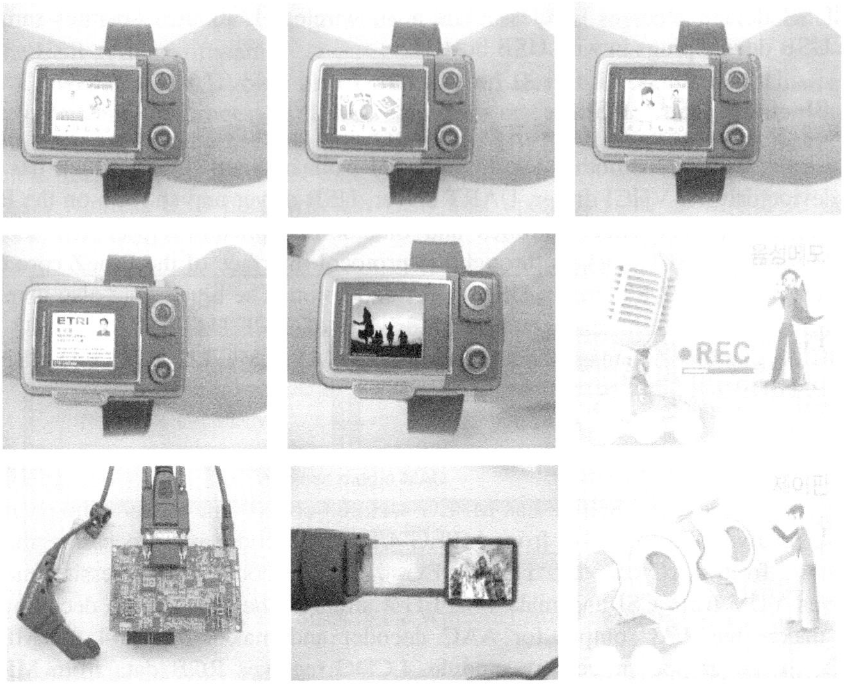

Fig. 6. MP3 Player, Digital Camera, Videophone, Namecard Transfer, MPEG-4 Player, Voice Recoder, Eval B'd with HMD, HMD output and Control Panel

Mounted Display, VGA). For these applications, we provide several intuitive menu screen displays for graphic user interface as shown in Fig. 6

6 Conclusions

Personal computer(PC) has been evolved from desktop to portable PC such as tablet PC and PDA. Technology innovation on semiconductor have made it possible to package a reasonably powerful processor and memory subsystem with advanced input/output devices. Wearable computing becomes more and more feasible and receives growing attention throughout industry and the consumer marketplaces.

Our hardware technology enough to support many software applications and minimize its size. Our developing issue is a wearable personal station as a wearable personal platform with advanced I/O devices in the ubiquitous world. This wearable personal station will interoperate with the ubiquitous objects using network and I/O device.

Our work has convinced us that a lot of functionality can be packaged into small devices. We combine high-function miniature hardware with a robust operating system and well designed applications with intuitive user interfaces and so the wearable personal station forms the basis of personal station platform for the ubiquitous world.

References

1. Freescale,: i.MX21 application processor specification.
2. USB Implementers Forum, inc.,: On-The-Go Supplement to the USB 2.0 Specification.
3. BlueZ, http://www.bluez.org.
4. Chandra Narayanaswami, M. T. Raghunath,: Application design for a smart watch with a high resolution display, Fourth International Symposium on Wearable Computers, Oct 18-21, (2000)

Perception of Wearable Computers for Everyday Life by the General Public: Impact of Culture and Gender on Technology

Sébastien Duval and Hiromichi Hashizume

NII, Hitotsubashi 2-1-2, Chiyoda-ku, Tokyo 101-8430, Japan
duval@grad.nii.ac.jp, has@nii.ac.jp

Abstract. This paper examines the perception of wearable computers for everyday life by the general public, in order to foster the adoption of this technology. We present a social study that focuses on sensors, actuators, autonomy, uses, and privacy. Carried out in 2005, it considers gender and cultural disparities in two dissimilar groups: French (115 males, 59 females) and Japanese (61 males, 54 females) citizens. Acknowledging that exposition to wearables can alter perception about them, we designed a garment-shaped prototype to check our results, estimate shifts of perception, and define guidelines for equipment and services. We describe our prototype, and future experiments dealing with face-to-face contacts, community awareness, and relaxing environments.

1 Introduction

Current trends show that our environment is continuously being filled with new electronic systems. Although the technologies have matured, it remains unclear whether people will accept them willingfully and how we can facilitate their adoption. Wearables, for example, have been developped but their use remains marginal. To understand this situation and provide hints for related technologies, it is critical to examine social factors.

So far, research in wearable computing focused on experts and on technical aspects. We consider here the general public, its perception of wearables, needs, and requests. Because of the diversity of possible wearables, we cannot take people to laboratories and generalize their feedback. Therefore, we decided to begin with questionnaires. We oriented them on cyberclothes [4]: garments possessing special features that can be used as social markers or tools, and possess some autonomy. This was appropriate for laymen because garments are a natural part of their life, and because enhanced clothes are easy to imagine. Results were gathered in 2005, mainly in France and Japan, which allowed the identification of cultural convergences and divergences.

Studies on mobile phones show that perception of a device can vary after acquisition [11]. Although our questionnaire provides an *a-priori* perception of wearables, it provides limited hints for design, and does not reveal all pitfalls.

L.T. Yang et al. (Eds.): EUC 2005, LNCS 3824, pp. 826–835, 2005.

As a consequence, we decided to also carry out experiments with prototypes focusing on problematic aspects revealed by the questionnaire. Feedback enabled us to check initial results, and define guidelines. This hybrid approach, combining the width of scope covered by questionnaires and the depth reached with experiments, favors reliable results.

Our paper is organized as follows. We present related works in section 2 then discuss our social study. In section 4 we describe the concept of cyberclothes. In section 5 we introduce our prototype, and planned experiments. In section 6 we discuss results and propose guidelines. Finally we conclude with future works.

2 Related Works

Diverse wearables were developed, providing functions of desktop computers (e.g. email, calendar, notes), or novel features such as help for navigation in urban spaces, recognition of persons encountered, and display of physiological data. These computers looked like boxes, accessories, or even garments. Digital accessories include jewelry [10], gloves that react to their wearer's stress [12], and badges displaying messages [2] [6]. Enhanced garments were mainly designed for experts [9] [13] [14]; *France Telecom*'s tee-shirt, which displays graphics, is a rare example of model dedicated to the general public.

The evaluation of several prototypes has led to the definition of metrics and guidelines for the design of wearables regarding comfort [1] [7] [8] and social interactions [14]. However, there are few studies on the perception and adoption of wearable computers. In 2001, a user study was planned to evaluate usability and acceptance of digital jewelry [10] but has not been carried out yet [1]. Studies of other devices, such as mobile phones, are of little use because their characteristics are so different: wearables can have any number and type of sensors, actuators, and can be used for a wide range of services.

3 Social Study About Perception of Wearables

The goal was to gather surface information about the general public's perception regarding wearable computers. Because people are not familiar with wearables, we focused on enhanced garments that respondents could easily imagine for uses in everyday life. This choice reduced the time required to answer questionnaires, and avoided confusion. We considered clear families of items (hardware, intelligence, information, uses), and everyday life situations. Therefore the questionnaire provides hints for wearables in general, and to a certain extent for other ubiquitous systems.

Our results reveal a significant effect of gender and culture on the perception of cyberclothes. Analyses show common interests (comfort, safety) and concerns (display of emotions) between the French and the Japanese. However they also indicate important divergences (e.g. system autonomy).

[1] E-mail exchanges with Christopher S. Campbell, IBM Almaden Research Center, 02-May-2005.

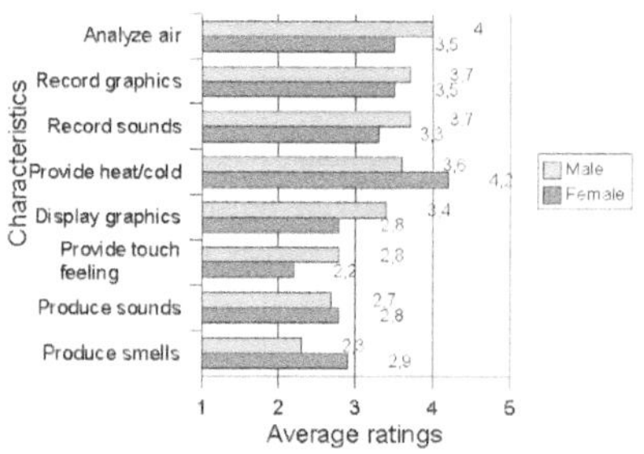

Fig. 5. Acceptance of perceptual sensing and stimulation (Japan)

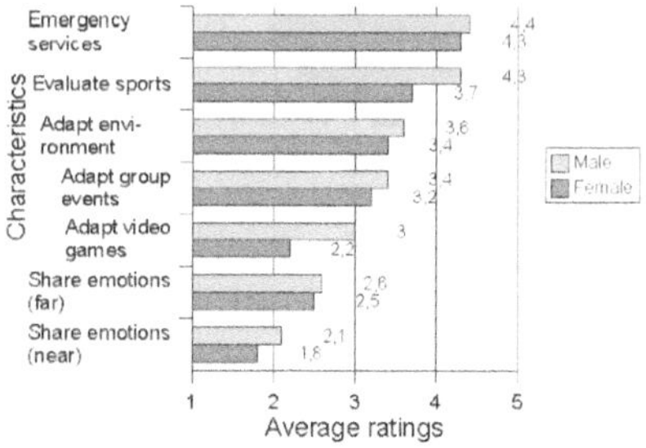

Fig. 6. Acceptance of physiological monitoring (Japan)

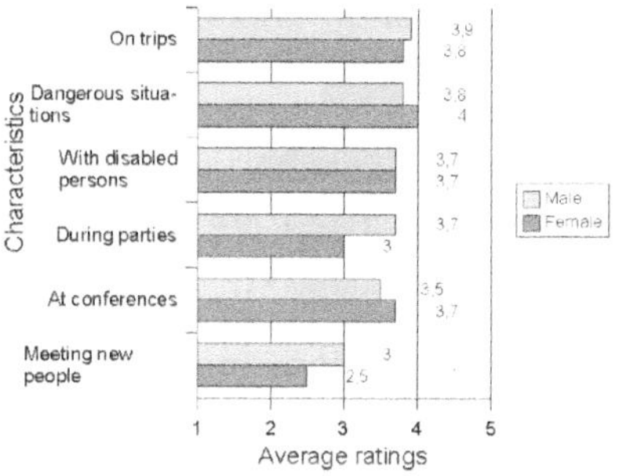

Fig. 7. Interest in usages (Japan)

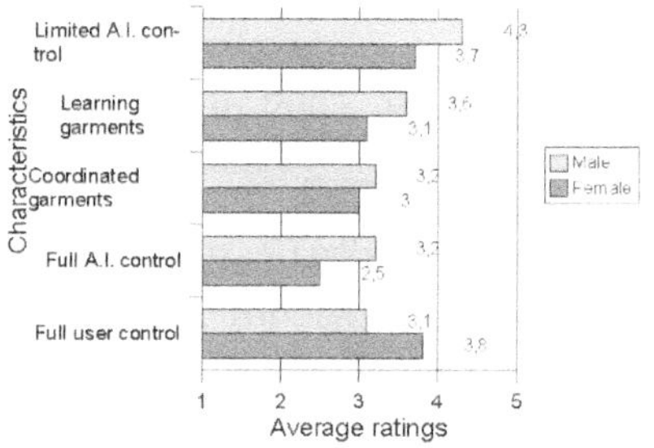

Fig. 8. Wishes for autonomy (Japan)

adapt their temperature to the environment, analyze the air, or record graphics. Males also consider acceptable to record sounds and display graphics on clothes; they reject the production of smells while females reject the generation of touch feelings. Figure 6 indicates a high acceptance (3.7-4.3) of physiological monitoring for emergencies and sports. Males are interested in the adaptation of their environment to fit their needs (3.6). However, there is an opposite trend for the disclosure of emotions (1.8-2.6). Females highly reject (2.2) physiological monitoring to adapt video games, while males remain neutral (3.0).

Attractive usages. Figure 7 shows that participants are attracted by proposed uses, except to meet new people (2.5-3.0). There is a gender effect for *meeting new people* and *parties*; female reject them strongly. Respondents reject the provision of data to surrounding people (2.5) but not for ongoing tasks (2.7-3.4).

Autonomy of the garments. As shown on figure 8, women reject full control of enhanced garments by artificial agents (2.4). Partial or full user control appears more attractive, women preferring full control (3.8), and male limited A.I. control (4.3). These aspects indicate a strong gender effect. The capacity to learn from wearers' reactions is attractive to males (3.6). Results for coordinating actions are not significant.

4 Wearables for the General Public: A Humane Philosophy

Focus on technics limited the development of wearables dedicated to the general public. With *cyberclothes*, we hope to replace human beings at the locus of attention. Creating this concept clarifies our goals, provides an alternative for the design and adoption of wearables on a wide-scale.

We define cyberclothes —in a nutshell— as garments that have special features improving a person's well-being, awareness, and sociability. This definition takes its roots in Maslow's hierarchy of human needs, usually represented as a pyramid, displaying the most fundamental needs at the bottom. Its five main levels are physiological, safety, belonging, esteem, and self-actualization needs. Based on this theory, a wearable that fulfills a person's needs should sustain in priority physiological needs, safety needs, and belonging needs.

Physiological needs include food, water, air, and sleep. Safety needs include physical and psychological security (e.g. health, comfort, absence of danger, good familial situation). Belonging needs are related to relationships with people at large, in clubs, at the office, etc. Informal interviews we carried out in France and Japan indicate an interest for wearables that can monitor the evolution of the body condition: calories absorbed and used, sleep duration, etc. The study presented previously also indicates an interest for wearables that increase comfort and safety. These results indicate that the orientations chosen for cyberclothes are pertinent.

Cyberclothes improve a person's well-being, which encompasses physiological and safety needs. This can be achieved with garments that monitor physiology and contact emergency services, provide guidance, adapt to the environment or adapt the environment to the user (temperature, light). They can also maintain peace of mind by conveying comforting news (kids, lover).

Cyberclothes improve a person's awareness, which help take good decisions and feel secure. Using sensors and Internet, cyberclothes can provide information about the user herself (movements, biosignals), other people (availability of coworkers), or the environment (pollution level).

Cyberclothes improve a person's sociability, sustaining mainly belonging needs. With actuators, garments can become a medium of communication. For example garment could change their shape, modify graphics on their surface, produce smells, process speech, compare profiles of wearers, etc. Uses include easing communication with deaf persons and finding people with similar interests.

5 Experiments Proposed to Check Our First Findings

To complement our social study, we also experiment with prototypes. Our applications deal with *face-to-face contacts*, *community awareness*, and *relaxing environments.* We chose these to investigate privacy, relations with the environment, and full control by artificial agents, as well as the apparent rejection of emotion sharing and support for first contacts.

5.1 Prototype to Investigate Belonging and Safety Needs

We developed a prototype (figure 9) consisting of a jacket that processes data, accesses wireless networks, displays graphics, renders sounds, and acquires biosignals (skin conductivity, heartbeats). The two displays were placed to support conversations, and inform passersby about the wearer. The biosignals equipment aims at identifying the body condition, stress, calm, and intense emotions.

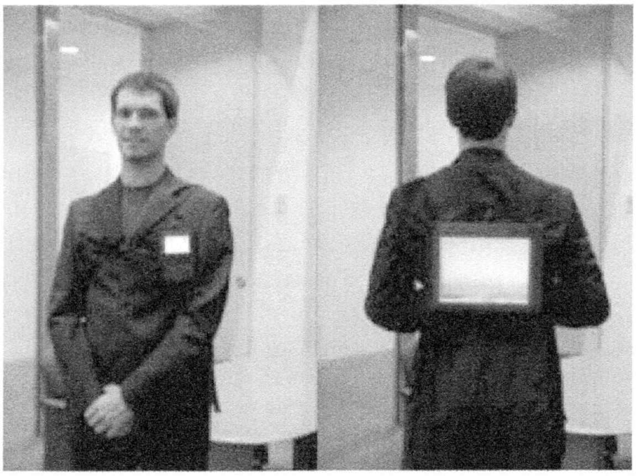

Fig. 9. Support for social events

5.2 Experiments: Contacts, Awareness, and Relaxation

Face-to-face contacts. Using JAVA and XML, we developed a system in which prototypes dynamically generate and display personalized slideshows of photos corresponding to common interests of surrounding wearers. Based on [5], we plan to check the interest of the service, evaluate controls for the system, and investigate private displays to inform wearers about their displays.

Community awareness. Belonging to a community implies keeping in touch and strengthening links with other members, which can be difficult due to temporal or spatial constraints. Our prototype can convey information and represent it with a *night sky* metaphor: it displays a sky where each star represent a community member, colors and intensities representing feelings (based on biosignals or manual choices). We are particularly interested in reactions of users regarding privacy and disclosure of emotions.

Relaxing environments. To improve people's life, we propose to use garments to generate healing, relaxing environments. We still have to develop this system, but we plan to use biosignals as input, to control music, light, and scents around the wearer. This should help us both evaluate environments and generate relaxing ones.

6 Results and Guidelines

The results of our social study in France and Japan show common interests and concerns regarding cyberclothes, in two dissimilar cultures. Using these as a basis, we established guidelines to design wearables. Besides, the creation of our prototype and preparation of experiments raised social and technical issues.

6.1 Results: Cultural Convergences and Divergences

French and Japanese people show similar perceptions of wearable computers concerning the hardware and services. However, there are important differences about the control of the system, especially concerning the amount of artificial intelligence considered acceptable.

Wearables related to comfort and safety are perceived very positively; several respondents even proposed additional applications related to health: sleep monitoring, stress feedback, and support for diets. The French and Japanese give high ratings (3.5-4.2) to garments that analyze the air (e.g. pollution) and adapt their temperature to the environment. In addition, physiological monitoring is considered positively (3.4-4.4) to adapt the environment to users' needs, evaluate sportive performances, and inform emergency services. Finally, respondents had **interest in wearables for situations involving safety and fundamental communication abilities**: on trips (3.5-3.9), to communicate with disabled persons (3.6-3.9), or in potentially dangerous situations (3.8-4.1). There is little variation here between males and females.

However, the **perception of wearables for standard social uses is negative**, and results highlight a gender effect. French and Japanese respondents strongly reject the use of physiological monitoring to reveal emotions to distant or surrounding people (1.4-2.7). Comments indicate that respondents did not want to disclose their emotions because they considered it as private information, and potential harmful, especially if revealed in real-time. Besides both consider that support for meeting new people is not interesting (2.3-2.6). Females have significantly more negative views than males on these issues. In addition, respondents reject the ability to provide data about individuals present at a gathering (1.8-2.6). Finally, French people also reject the possibility to get information about the group as a whole whereas Japanese keep a neutral stance on this issue.

Cultural differences are most visible when considering the control of wearables. The preferred choice for the Japanese would be to use limited artificial intelligence (3.7-4.3) whereas French people prefer full user-control (3.5-3.9). In both cultures, full control by an artificial agent is seen very negatively by women (1.9-2.5); males have a more open attitude but it remains negative in France (2.4) and neutral in Japan (3.2). As highlighted during interviews,

Videoconference System by Using Dynamic Adaptive Architecture for Self-adaptation

Chulho Jung, Sanghee Lee, and Eunseok Lee

School of Information and Communication Engineering Sungkyunkwan University,
300 Chunchun Jangahn Suwon, 400-746, Korea
{jesus98, neomine}@selab.skku.ac.kr
eslee@ece.skku.ac.kr

Abstract. According to the improvements in wireless Internet technology, multimedia applications create new challenges, which must be solved. Internet-based videoconferencing systems have many variable factors, such as changes in the system operating environment or operating status of the hardware, according to the operator using the system. In this paper, we propose the Videoconferencing System, with multi-agents, for efficient videoconferencing, which is able to adapt itself to these various factors. This videoconferencing system has a dynamic architecture which is able to change the own architecture in runtime.

1 Introduction

The improvements in wireless internet technology, create new challenges which must be solved. Internet based applications are facing various factors which affect Quality of Service, the dynamically changing network environment, diverse range of user devices and preferences. Multimedia applications, especially applications in end-to-end wireless networks, need to seriously consider the dynamic network environment and system resources. Internet videoconferencing systems are no exception to this rule, and need various structures and languages for their interoperation with various network systems and operating environments, which have resulted in the development of many new technologies [1], such as Self-Adaptive software. The Self-Adaptive software [1] uses technology that is able to understand, monitor and correct changes by program itself; therefore, it should already have data relating to the program needs, the know how to enable evaluation of these data and to the ability to respond to any changes. This Self-Adaptive software technology helps clients adapt to the videoconferencing environment. For this reason, Self-Adaptive software research has been applied to many Videoconferencing Systems. [2][6]

In this paper, we propose a videoconferencing system in which the clients are able to adapt to the operator's processing capability and network bandwidth. Also, our system includes specific functions that allow it to adapt to various network situations, operating systems (O.S.'s) and devices. Moreover, the system helps a client communicates with the other clients with a different operating platform. However, it is difficult for a mobile device to adapt itself to the videoconferencing environment, as the adaptation mechanism is optimized for a Desktop PC. Thus, we have designed dy-

L.T. Yang et al. (Eds.): EUC 2005, LNCS 3824, pp. 836 – 845, 2005.

namic adaptive architecture that changes the adaptation architecture of the devices according to the circumstances. For this, we have designed and implemented a system with an Architecture Manager, which decides and manages the client's architecture according to the particular environment.

Section 2 contains a summary of related works, in section 3 we describe the proposed system and section 4 discusses the implementation and evaluation of such software. Section 5 is a presentation of our conclusions.

2 Related Works

2.1 Dynamic Software Architecture

2.1.1 C2 – A Component- and Message-Based Architectural Style for GUI Software [7]

C2, which was developed at UCI(University of California - Irvine), is an architecture used to support application software development, which uses a component and message based format. A C2 system is composed of a hierarchy of concurrent components interlinked by connectors – message-routing devices – such that each component within the hierarchy can only be aware of those components "above", and completely unaware of components residing at the same level or "beneath". [7] During runtime, C2 can add, delete or rearrange components, and has been optimized for flexible components.

2.1.2 Weave – Using Weaves for Software Construction and Analysis [8]

Weaves, made by The Aerospace Corporation, are networks of concurrently executing tool fragments that communicate by passing objects, and have a dynamic, object-flow-centric architecture, designed for applications that are characterized by continuous or intermittent voluminous data flows and real-time deadlines.

Weaves embrace a set of architectural principles, known as the laws of blind communication: [8]

- No component in a network is able to recognize the sources of its input objects or the destinations of its output objects;
- No network component is able to recognize the semantics of the connectors that delivered its input objects or transmitted its output objects; and
- No network component is able to recognize the loss of a connection.

Weaves support component manipulation of a like form, emphasize the dynamic distribution, modification and rearrangement of connectors, and has been optimized for flexible connectors.

2.2 Video Conferencing System

2.2.1 JQOS – A QoS-Based Internet Videoconferencing System [2]

The JQOS system was developed at MCR Laboratory, Ottawa Univ. Canada, an is based on QoS; therefore, a QoS adaptation function is included in the Video Conferencing System.

It's functions are as follows:

- First, for the End-User, the Active QoS Self-Adaptive function is now based on the network transportation capability.
- Second, for the Receiver, the smart processing of the requirements from the receiver, and the measurement for proper adaptation of the current system QoS.
- Third, for the Receiver, an expression function of the receiver's interests relating to the transporting stream is required for the QoS adaptation.

The JQOS system limits the Self-Adaptive element to stream the quality of the user, as mentioned above. This system also uses RTPR (Real-time Transport Protocol Report) as a control method, from the RTP (Real-time Transport Protocol) of JMF[4], so the Self-Adaptive function in the JQOS system is only weak.

3 The Proposed System

3.1 Architecture-Based and Model-Based Adaptation

Our self-adaptive videoconferencing system is an "Architecture based approach to Self-Adaptive software"[3]. In this paper, our proposed system is reflected in the above self-adaptive software process. Also, we developed the Videoconferencing system, which is operated by activity, as follows in Fig.1.

For the adaptation to a dynamic environment, all environment information, such as the system components and theirs interactive environmental information, and the available resources and operating environments, are captured and modeled with respect to several multi-aspects. The term "multi-aspect" refers to four main aspects - an architectural aspect, a behavioral aspect, a resource aspect and an environment aspect. Each aspect is defined as follow:

The architectural aspect is used to describe configurative entities, such as the software architecture, its configurative elements, each element's operation or role, and the relationship of each element. Each element is represented by a node, referred to as a "Component", with the relationship of each component represented by arcs, which are referred to as 'connectors'. The behavioral aspect defines the 'Interactive' operation end events between components.

The resource aspect defines the general system environmental entities that execute the necessary videoconferencing system. The target of a system for modeling the resource aspect is classified into two categories, the static and dynamic contexts. The static contexts are elements that have less dynamic changing characteristics, such as the type of user device, OS, executing software and Player information. The dynamic contexts are dynamic changeable elements, such as the current CPU and memory usage, state of camera and audio devices, network bandwidth and user preference. The Environment aspect defines the external environmental element that is mutually applied or affected by the surroundings of the videoconferencing system.

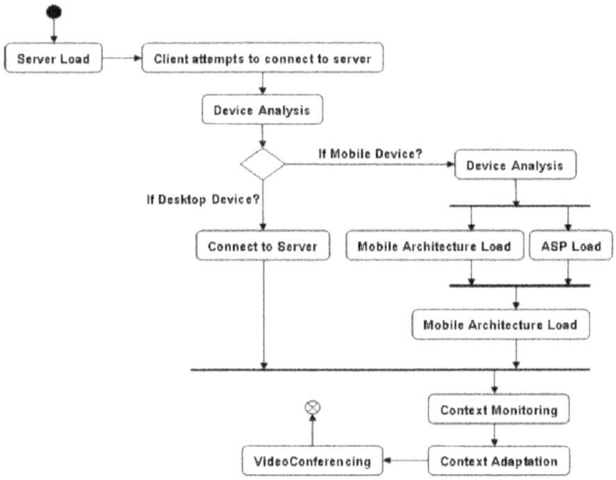

Fig. 1. Activity diagram of Our Videoconferencing System

These four aspects of modeling are graphically and texturally represented using the GME (Generic Modeling Environment) Tool. To adapt for executing system, Modeled elements must be transmitted to be realized by software, so we applied CC/PP technology to recognize system. Fig.2 shows the CC/PP format for recognize system.

```
<?xml version="1.0"?>
 <rdf:RDF xmlns:rdf="http://www.w3.org/1999/02/22-rdf-syntax-ns#"
  xmlns:prf="http://www.testProfile.com/profiles/ccppschema-20030226#">
      <rdf:Description rdf:ID="MyProfile">
            <prf:component>
                  <rdf:Description rdf:ID="HardwarePlatform">
                        <prf:ScreenSize>84x30</prf:ScreenSize>
                        <prf:Type>PDA</prf:Type>
                        <prf:CPU>PPC</prf:CPU>
                        <prf:Memory>16MB</prf:Memory>
                  </rdf:Description>
            </prf:component>
      </rdf:Description>
   </rdf:RDF>
```

Fig. 2. CC/PP format for recognize system

3.2 Overall Architecture

Our general approach for supporting the Dynamic Adaptation Architecture consists of several parts: the *Server, Client, Mobile-Client and Adaptation Proxy Server*. Fig.3. show the overall architecture.

The detailed architecture and algorithm of each part can be described as follows:

a) Server

The server is a manager, which manages the session, Adaptive Proxy Server and context, and consists of 1) Context DB, 2) Adaptive Proxy Server Manager (APSM), 3) Session Manager, 4) Context Manager and 5) Device Analyzer. The server is loaded into Desktop Pc.

The *Transporter* obtains video and audio information from the system, and communicates this contents to the other clients using the Communication Method. *Communication Method* is a transmission code that is received from the communication target. The *Receiver* receives video and audio information from other clients.

c) Mobile Client

The Mobile Client is a client with an architecture for mobile users that have insufficient resources for a contents adaptation. The Mobile Client's architecture is decided by the Architecture Manager, which then organizes the Mobile Client's architecture. The Mobile Client is loaded into PDA or smart phone having video camera.

A Mobile Client has less functionality then a Client because the contents adaptation function is too heavy for a Mobile Client. Therefore, to support a Mobile Client's contents, adaptation is performed by an Adaptation Proxy Server.

d) Adaptation Proxy Server

The Adaptation Proxy Server is a proxy server, which performs contents adaptation in the place of a Mobile Client, which consists of 1) Context DB, 2) Context Agent, 3) Monitoring Agent, 4) Adaptation Agent and 5) Connection Manager. The APS is loaded Desktop Pc. If a Mobile Client connects to an APS through the Connection Manager, the Monitoring Agent gathers the context and session information of the connected Mobile Client, which are then stored to the Context DB. When a client is connecting to an APS, the Context Agent updates the Context DB in the Server. The Context Agent also obtains each client's Communication Methods using the session information of the Server. The Context Agent also sends the session information, context and Communication Method to the Adaptation Agent. The Adaptation Agent decides the appropriate Communication Method for contents adapted communication. The Adaptation Agent then composes the Communication Method for the Communication Agent of the Mobile Client and the Mobile Client then communicates with each client using this Communication Method.

In this paper, we have designed a reconfigurable architecture for a Mobile Client using the dynamic link in JAVA and Weaves Style. Weaves, made by The Aerospace Corporation, are networks of concurrently executing tool fragments that communicate by passing objects, and have a dynamic, object-flow-centric architecture designed for applications that are characterized by continuous or intermittent voluminous data floes and real-time deadlines. We have already addressed Weaves [8] in section 2. Fig.4 shows the concept of dynamic component composition.

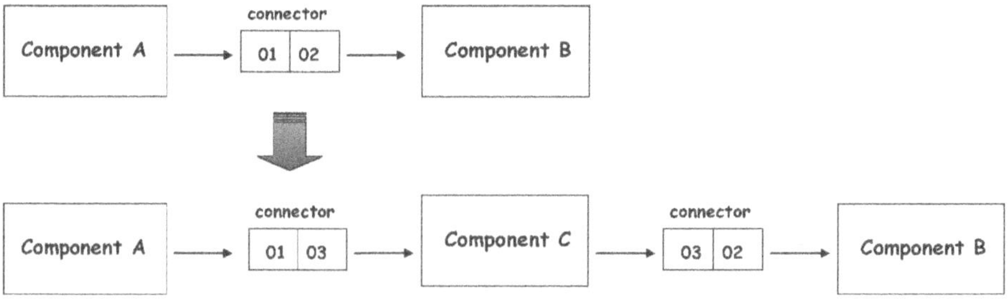

Fig. 4. The concept of Dynamic Component Composition

4 Implementation and Evaluation

The system proposed in this paper has been implemented based on JAVA SDK in Windows, Linux and Solaris environments. The main code for transmission of the picture information is made using JMF [4], for which the user needs a capturing device to obtain the picture information.

Fig. 5. Screen shot of our system

This system is implemented on a component basis, consisting of adjustable components, where each component is associated with an appropriate algorithm for adaptation to the user's operating environment as well as that of the overall network. This is the basic characteristic of self-adaptive software, which has been implemented using the Fractal [5] library for our proposed system.

Evaluation: According to the location of adaptation, an adaptation system is separated into the client-side, server-side and proxy server-side adaptation systems. [11] First, the client side adaptation system monitors and adapts the environment on its own side [12, 13], which could prevent the exposure of personnel information to the outside, and could also be suitable for performing reconfiguration of a control device configuration or to modify its functionality. Second, the server-side adaptive system monitors each client and performs contents adaptation, involving adaptive modules on their side. [14] Third, the proxy adaptation system has adaptive modules installed, which sets the proxy server between a client and server [15, 16], which can take advantage of being able to adapt, by the addition of the proxy server, without modification to the server or client components. In this paper, the difference between a general videoconferencing system and our proposed system, using the self-adaptive concept, has been evaluated, and the quantitative differences between the use of three adaptation mechanism - Server side, Client side and Proxy Server side adaptation - based approaches and a Dynamic adaptive architecture based approach. In Fig.11, the horizontal axis represents the adaptation time, and the vertical axis the number of clients.

In Fig.6, the use of the three adaptation mechanisms required more time than that with the Dynamic Adaptive Architecture. Evaluation environment is following.

Server : HP net Server. Os. Windows 2003 Server CPU 3.0G, RAM 1024Mb
Proxy Server : Os. Windows XP Pro, CPU 3.0G G RAM 1024Mb
Client : Os. Windows XP Pro, CPU. 2.4G RAM 512Mb

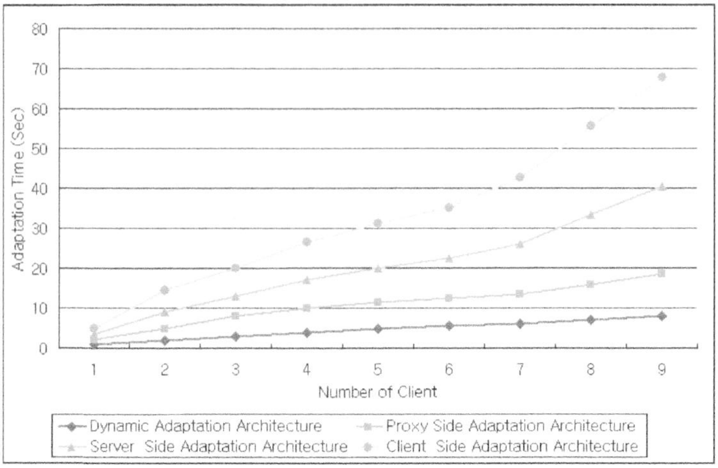

Fig. 6. Comparison of the adaptation and dynamic adaptation architectures when a mobile client is connecting. The use of dynamic adaptation architecture is more effective than those of the three adaptation mechanisms – Server side, Client side and Proxy Server side adaptation.

An almost mobile device has less resources for adaptation; therefore, a mobile device requires a proxy. However, if mobile devices have sufficient resources, they work more efficiently than if the client performs the adaptation themselves. In view of these facts, the use of Dynamic adaptive architecture is more effective. If the number of clients per APS is optimized, our system will spend less time on adaptation.

5 Conclusion and Future Works

In this paper, architecture based self-adaptive videoconferencing system, with dynamic adaptive architecture, has been proposed for internet based videoconferencing. Our system was able to adapt to the user's environment, requests and network environment. The users of our videoconferencing system are able to utilize a system that is optimized for their environment and network surroundings. Also, this system can apply as a self-configuring and self-healing system, because it is able to cope with new problems by the addition of new components. It also includes monitoring techniques that can deal with problems while the program is running.

In future work, this architecture will be applied to various multimedia systems and additional factors, which affect QoS, will be considered. In addition, the reconfiguration of software architecture will be focused on, and applied to adaptive multimedia systems.

References

1. R. Laddaga.: Active Software. Lecture Notes in Computer Science, Vol. 1936. Springer-Verlag, Oxford UK(2000)11–26.
2. Wenbiao Zhu, etc. al..: JQOS: a QoS-based Internet videoconferencing system using the Java media framework (JMF). IEEE ECE 2001. Vol. 1, 13-16. Canada (2001)625 - 630